CONTRACT AND RELATED OBLIGATION:

THEORY, DOCTRINE, AND PRACTICE

Fifth Edition

By

Robert S. Summers
*McRoberts Research Professor of Law,
Cornell Law School*

Robert A. Hillman
Edwin H. Woodruff Professor of Law, Cornell Law School

AMERICAN CASEBOOK SERIES®

WEST

Mat # 40348219

American Casebook Series and West Group are trademarks registered in the U.S. Patent and Trademark Office.

COPYRIGHT © 1987, 1992, 1997 WEST PUBLISHING CO.
© West, a Thomson business, 2001
© 2006 Thomson/West
     610 Opperman Drive
     P.O. Box 64526
     St. Paul, MN 55164–0526
     1–800–328–9352

ISBN–13: 978–0–314–15983–0
ISBN–10: 0–314–15983–5

 TEXT IS PRINTED ON 10% POST CONSUMER RECYCLED PAPER

1st Reprint — 2009

*IN MEMORY OF OUR FATHERS
WHO ALWAYS FULLY PERFORMED*

*Herman D. Hillman
(1911–1977)
Orson William Summers
(1909–1975)*

*

Preface to Fifth Edition

As with the Fourth Edition, this edition primarily updates important developments and supplements some excerpts, notes, and problems. For example, we have new cases or materials on the nature of a bargain, electronic standard forms, parol evidence, interpretation, incomplete contracts, mistake, and novation. Notwithstanding the new material, the book's structure and purposes remain as described in the preface to the first edition.

We have kept materials on current and amended Article 2 in this edition, although the focus is on the former in light of the lack of state adoptions of the latter. Amended Article 2 nonetheless serves as an excellent vehicle for observing and analyzing possible developments in the evolution of sales law.

We hope you enjoy these materials.

ROBERT A. HILLMAN
Myron Taylor Hall
Ithaca, N.Y.

ROBERT S. SUMMERS
Myron Taylor Hall
Ithaca, N.Y.

August, 2006

*

Preface to Fourth Edition

Primarily, the fourth edition updates the materials to include major recent developments in the law of contracts as we begin the 21st century. One new development involves electronic contracting over the Internet and through electronic mail. We have included new cases, excerpts, and notes on electronic contracting and related topics.

Another area of increased importance concerns the relationship between tort and contract, including the modern law of misrepresentation and recent "trends" concerning bad faith breach as a tort, especially in the employment area. We have supplemented and revised our existing materials in these areas too. We also include provisions of the new Restatement (Third) of Torts concerning developments in strict-tort liability.

A third recent development is the revision of Article 2 of the Uniform Commercial Code on the sale of goods. As this edition goes to press, the National Conference of Commissioners on Uniform State Laws and the American Law Institute are scheduled to review the final draft in Spring 2001. We continue to include ample materials on existing Article 2, but we have supplemented them with draft revisions where these involve substantial proposed changes in existing law. For example, Section 2-207, dealing with the "battle of the forms," has been thoroughly revised and we include materials on these changes. We also include new developments concerning the problem of "terms in the box," also called "rolling contracts," where a buyer purchases an item only to have new terms appear on or in the container.

We have also updated and supplemented many of our notes, added some new cases to substitute for others that have worn thin, and included new secondary sources that contribute to the themes of our book and that have appeared since the third edition. We have also revised the order of the sections in a few of the chapters in minor ways.

Notwithstanding these revisions, the book remains essentially the same in structure and purpose. For those interested in reading more about our goals in these materials, please see the preface to the first edition. The co-editors (on view at page 949) believe this fourth edition is an improvement and we hope you find it stimulating and rewarding.

> ROBERT A. HILLMAN
> Myron Taylor Hall
> Ithaca, N.Y.
>
> ROBERT S. SUMMERS
> Myron Taylor Hall
> Ithaca, N.Y.

October, 2000

*

Preface to Third Edition

In this third edition, we continue to emphasize contract doctrine, contract theory, and problems of contract practice of general educational value. We include twenty-four new cases and omit several others. This edition includes additional passages on contract theory as well. These and other theoretical writings in the book invite students to think beyond the nuts and bolts, yet are neither too lengthy nor, in our experience, too difficult for the first-year student.

The third edition also contains new materials on the various roles of the practitioner of contract law. We thus add to what we believe is already a rich and distinctive assortment of actual contracts, opinion letters, portions of briefs, and comments from lawyers that require students to consider concrete problems of contract planning, drafting, counseling, negotiating, as well as litigating.

We also update our explanatory notes, add new problems, and include more photographs and cartoons! These materials reinforce our view that the study of contract law can be enjoyable as well as stimulating.

The co-editors (on view at page 967) certainly enjoy teaching these materials. Measured on this scale, too, we believe that the third edition is an improvement.

ROBERT A. HILLMAN
Myron Taylor Hall
Ithaca, N.Y.

ROBERT S. SUMMERS
Myron Taylor Hall
Ithaca, N.Y.

November, 1996

*

Preface to Second Edition

There is no sharp break between this second edition and the first. Our goals and philosophy remain the same. (See the Preface to the First Edition.) We have mainly sought to improve upon the implementation of our earlier goals and philosophy, and to update the materials. This edition is slightly shorter than the first.

We have expanded or revamped the sections dealing with the statute of frauds, interpretation, agreements to agree, and the battle of the forms. Many other sections have been revised in less ambitious ways. We have added further materials from the archives of practitioners. As in the first edition, these include extracts from briefs, opinion letters, and draft agreements. We have also added twenty-three new cases, most relatively recent. To make way for these cases, we have omitted some cases past their prime. In addition, we include fresh contributions from scholars and some new and revised problems throughout the book.

We hope that the first edition has been a successful teaching tool for a wide variety of teachers. We believe the second edition is an improvement.

ROBERT A. HILLMAN
Myron Taylor Hall
Ithaca, N.Y.

ROBERT S. SUMMERS
Goodhart Lodge
Cambridge, England

February, 1992

*

Preface to First Edition

Goals. Five primary goals have guided the design and content of this book. We have sought to provide materials that will enable students to:

—understand the leading rules and principles governing contract and related obligation, including the substantive reasons behind these rules and principles;

—develop substantially the basic lawyer skills required to plan, draft, interpret, counsel, litigate, and negotiate in this field;

—understand and deploy general theories of the nature, functions, and limits of contract and related law;

—develop the general analytical and critical abilities and attitudes (including a keen regard for facts) that typify the good lawyer;

—learn not only the deficiencies of, but also some of what is best about, American contract law, including its intellectual richness and what it teaches us about ourselves and our society.

Our Philosophy of Instruction. We believe in the case method, and in extensive dialectical exchange between teacher and student, and between student and student. Accordingly, this is predominantly a case book. The book also provides a framework, and numerous opportunities, for concentrated dialogue on the justificatory reasoning, authoritative and substantive, to be found in the opinions. (See Appendix A: "Judicial Reasons".)

We have generally chosen not to impose our own personal pedagogical grid on the cases and other materials, so that, except in the first chapter, we pose very few questions of our own. In each chapter, we have inserted several problems devoted to planning, drafting, and other roles of lawyers.

Criteria Affecting Selection of Materials. We have selected cases with an eye to the usual factors: the richness of the facts (including their potential for hypothetical variation), the quality of the opinion, the doctrinal, transactional, or relational significance, the depiction of lawyer performances, historical or social import, and more. Occasionally, we have included a case partly for cultural reasons. Various statutes appear here, including many sections from Article Two of the Uniform Commercial Code. The book includes additional materials on the sale of goods, for the teacher who chooses (or is required) to cover this subject.

We also include extracts from the two Restatements of Contracts. For students who acquire too much of a taste for the ready-made formulas of a restatement, and thus tend to think of the common law case merely as something to be "boiled down" into a sentence or phrase, we also offer Appendix C: "The Restatement Idea—Some Skepticism".

The book includes some sample documents drawn from the world of practice. These consist of actual contracts, opinion and other letters, portions of briefs, and some comments from lawyers who litigated a few of the cases in the book.

Role of Text. We have seldom relied on text to convey knowledge of law. More often, we have used text to introduce the subject of each chapter, to treat lawyers' roles, to convey a sense of structure within an area, and to provide background material to facilitate discussion.

Organization. The organization of our book furthers our primary goals. In Part One, called "Foundations of Contract and Related Obligation," we include three chapters. The first opens with an actual agreement and stresses the function of contracts as social exchange devices frequently planned and drafted by lawyers, but which the parties normally perform without any involvement of lawyers, let alone courts. The second chapter systematically presents the major general theories of obligation operative in contract and related areas. (Of course, remedies inevitably enter here, too.) The emergence and development of one general theory of obligation—promissory estoppel—is treated historically. Some of the major forms of interplay between contract and tort are also considered. The third chapter treats the general law of remedies as it applies to each theory of obligation.

Together, Chapters One, Two, and Three introduce most of the basic themes of the book. Although we follow many of the ideas of the late Professor Fuller, we emphasize that the reality of contract obligations resides more in their voluntary observance and in the force of the normative reasoning the obligations generate, than in the predicted efficacy of remedies for their breach.

Parts Two through Four are organized to reflect the main chronological stages of contractual activity: agreement, performance, and cessation. In Part Two, "The Agreement Process," we stress contract planning, the law governing the formation of agreements, the private administration of agreements (with and without the aid of lawyers), and the theories on which agreements are policed. Part Three, "The Performance Process," deals mainly with the parol evidence rule, the interpretation of agreements, the general obligation of good faith, the law of conditions, and breach and the permissible responses thereto. Part Four, "The Cessation Process," presents the grounds of rightful cessation and any remedies available thereafter. Here we offer systematic treatment of the complex interplay between such grounds of cessation as mistake, impracticability, and frustration on the one hand, and general theories of obligation and remedies on the other. (See especially Chapter Nine.)

Part Five is devoted to the rights and duties of third parties.

Hours. The book is designed for a six semester hour course, but the book can, of course, readily suit other hour allocations.

Some Words of Justification. There are already some outstanding teaching books in this field. Why add to them? Here we undertake briefly to explain ourselves, and perhaps we may be forgiven if we sometimes overstate a bit.

(1) We include much material designed to acquaint students with the entire range of lawyer roles in contractual matters, and to foster the development of sophistication and skill required in most of these roles. We stress the lawyer's planning role. Our effort here is reflected in a variety of forms, including various planning problems and some materials gathered from practitioners who handled recent cases included in the book.

(2) We focus on privately-made law in the form of agreements and customary norms. For example, as already noted, we begin with detailed consideration of an actual agreement. We emphasize that lawyers not only create and apply state-made law but create and apply the terms of private agreements as well. We stress, too, that judges frequently invoke the terms of privately created law as authoritative reasons for judicial decisions.

(3) We draw on the writings of Atiyah, Corbin, Dawson, Eisenberg, Farnsworth, Fried, Fuller, Gilmore, Llewellyn, Macneil, Posner, and others, all of whom have contributed significantly to the enrichment of contract theory. In addition, we add some theorizing of our own. For example, we introduce the concept of a multi-dimensional general theory of obligation in Chapter One, explore and compare a variety of such theories in Chapter Two, and regularly return to these theories in later chapters.

(4) We believe that today there is far less dialectical teaching in the first year of law school than was true only twenty years ago. In our view, the students are the main losers in this development. Gradual and cumulative changes in the nature of published teaching materials help explain this decline. The smaller proportion of principal cases, the heavy editing of those cases, the inclusion of numerous summaries and notes after each principal case, the extensive use of general textual notes on the law aimed at covering ground, the frequent resort to extracts from black-letter Restatements, the use of numerous lengthy excerpts from articles, and the infrequent sequences of principal cases on a single topic, all illustrate what we perceive to be an unfortunate trend. We have tried to prepare a book that will maximize analysis, criticism, and dialogue, both in and out of the classroom.

(5) In our view, contract teaching materials should not present all valid law as something essentially laid down or acted upon by officials, nor present formal legal reasoning and substantive moral reasoning as sharply distinct. Contrary to these positivist views, contract and related law comprise a complex intermixture of private agreement (tacit as well as express), custom, case law, statute, regulatory law, *and* substantive reasoning—moral, political, economic, and other. We show from the beginning that substantive reasoning is far from "extra-legal" in nature. It is intrinsic to law, and no sharp line can be drawn here between the legal and the non-legal.

(6) This is not just a book about contract and related law. We also seek to develop a number of other more general perspectives and insights, including the power of general theory; the strengths and limits of a common law system; the recent rise of statutory and regulatory law, and the problems that this poses for lawyers and private parties; the differences between formalistic and instrumentalist legal method; the interactions of substantive right and judicial remedy in private law fields; the inevitable overlap among fields of private law; the subtlety and pervasiveness of the obligation of good faith; the interactions

of law and fact; the social uses and limits of private ordering; the multi-faceted character of contract as a social institution; and the decline of freedom of contract.

Conventions. Bracketed material in cases and excerpts are ours, as are lettered footnotes. Other footnotes by judges in opinions or by authors in excerpts have been renumbered. We omitted some footnotes from these materials without indication.

R.A.H.
R.S.S.

February, 1987

General Acknowledgments
to Fifth Edition

We gratefully acknowledge our indebtedness to the following authors and publishers who gave us permission to reprint excerpts from copyrighted articles: Albany Law Review, for excerpts from Note, Risk of Loss and Distribution of Insurance Proceeds Under Real Estate Contracts in New York, 28 Alb.L.Rev. 253 (1964); American Bar Association Journal, for excerpts from Williston, Restatement of Contracts is Published by the American Law Institute, 18 A.B.A.J. 775 (1932)—Reprinted with permission from the *ABA Journal,* The Lawyer's Magazine; American Bar Association, for excerpt from Winn & Pullen, Despatches from the Front: Recent Skirmishes Along the Frontier of Electronic Contracting, 55 Bus.Law. 455 (1999), reprinted with permission; The American Law Institute, for excerpts from 1970 Proceedings of the American Law Institute, 47 A.L.I.Proc. 489–91 (1970)—Copyright © 1970 by The American Law Institute, reprinted with the permission of The American Law Institute; The American Law Institute and Professor Stewart Macaulay, for excerpts from Macaulay, The Use and Non-Use of Contract in the Manufacturing Industry, 9 Practical Lawyer, Nov. 1963—Copyright © 1963 by The American Law Institute, reprinted with the permission of *The Practical Lawyer.* Subscription rates $25 a year; $5.00 a single issue (this article appeared in 9 *The Practical Lawyer*); Annual Survey of American Law and Professor Charles L. Knapp, for excerpts from Knapp, Judgment Call: Theoretical Approaches to Contract Decisionmaking, 1988 Ann.Surv.Am.L. 307, 333, 336; Boston University Law Review and the Trustee of the Literary Estate of John P. Dawson, for excerpts from Dawson, Judicial Revision of Frustrated Contracts: Germany, 63 B.U.L. Rev. 1039 (1983); Boston University Law Review and the Trustee of the Literary Estate of John P. Dawson, for excerpts from Dawson, Judicial Revision of Frustrated Contracts: The United States, 64 B.U.L.Rev. 1 (1984); Boston University Law Review and the Trustee of the Literary Estate of John P. Dawson, for excerpts from Dawson, Restitution Without Enrichment, 61 B.U.L.Rev. 563 (1981); Boston University Law Review and Professor Mark Pettit, Jr., for excerpts from Pettit, Modern Unilateral Contracts, 63 B.U.L.Rev. 551 (1983); California Law Review and Professor Andrew Kull, for excerpts from Kull, Rationalizing Restitution, © 1995 by California Law Review Inc., reprinted from California Law Review, Vol. 83 No. 5; California Law Review, for excerpts from Whittier, The Restatement of Contracts and Mutual Assent, 17 Cal.L.Rev. 441 (1929)—1929 by 17 California Law Review, reprinted by permission; Columbia Law Review and Professor E. Allan Farnsworth, for excerpts from Farnsworth, Disputes Over Omission in Contracts, 68 Colum.L.Rev. 860 (1968) —Copyright © 1968 by the Directors of the Columbia Law Review Association, Inc. All rights reserved (this article originally appeared at 68 Colum.L.Rev. 860 (1968)), reprinted by permission; Columbia Law Review, for excerpts from Fuller, Consideration and Form, 41 Colum.L.Rev. 799 (1941); Columbia Law Review and Professor James Gordley, for excerpts from Gordley, European Codes and American Restatements: Some Difficulties, 81 Colum.L.Rev. 140 (1981)—Copyright © 1981 by the Directors of the Columbia Law Review Association, Inc. All rights reserved. Reprinted by permission; Columbia Law Review, for excerpts from Kessler, Contracts of Adhesion—Some Thoughts About Freedom of Contract, 43 Colum.L.Rev. 629 (1943); Columbia Law Review, for excerpts from Patterson, Constructive Conditions in Contracts, 42 Colum.L.Rev. 903 (1942); Columbia Law Review and Professor Joseph M. Perillo, for excerpts from Perillo, Restitution in a Contractual Context, 73 Colum. L.Rev. 1208 (1973)—Copyright © 1973 by the Directors of the Columbia Law Review Association, Inc. All rights reserved (this article originally appeared at 73 Colum.L.Rev. 1208 (1973)), reprinted by permission; Columbia Law Review and Professor Joseph M. Perillo, for excerpts from Perillo, Restitution in the Second Restatement of Contracts, 81 Colum.L.Rev. 37 (1981)—Copyright © 1981 by the Directors of the Columbia Law Review Association, Inc. All rights reserved (this article originally appeared at 81 Colum.L.Rev. 37 (1981)), reprinted by permission; Columbia Law Review and Professor William F. Young, for excerpts from Young, Half Measures, 81 Colum.L.Rev. 19 (1981)—Copyright © 1981 by the Directors of the Columbia Law Review Association, Inc. All rights reserved (this article originally appeared at 81 Colum.L.Rev. 19 (1981)), reprinted by permission; Cornell Law Review, Fred B. Rothman & Co., for excerpts from Hillman, An Analysis of the Cessation of Contractual Relations, 68 Cornell L.Rev. 617 (1983); Cornell Law Review, Fred B. Rothman & Co., for excerpts from Hillman, Contract Modification Under the Restatement (Second) of Contracts, 67 Cornell L.Rev. 680 (1982); Cornell Law Review, Fred B. Rothman & Co., for excerpts from Hillman, Debunking Some Myths About Unconscionability: A New Framework for U.C.C. Section 2–302, 67 Cornell L.Rev. 1 (1982); Cornell Law Review, Fred B. Rothman & Co. and Professor Robert Hudec, for excerpts from Hudec, Restating the "Reliance Interest," 67 Cornell L.Rev. 704 (1982); Cornell Law Review, Fred B. Rothman & Co., for excerpts from Summers, The General Duty of Good Faith—Its Recognition and Conceptualization, 67 Cornell L.Rev. 810 (1982); Cornell Law Review, Fred B. Rothman & Co. and Professor James J. White, for excerpts from White, Eight Cases and Section 251, 67 Cornell L.Rev. 841 (1982); Duke Law Journal and Professor John Weistart, for excerpts from Weistart, Requirements and Output Contracts: Quantity Variations Under the UCC, 1973 Duke L.J. 599; Fordham Law Review and Professor John D. Calamari, for excerpts from Calamari, Duty to Read—A Changing Concept, 43 Fordham L.Rev. 341 (1974); Professor Patricia B. Fry for excerpts from Fry, X Marks the Spot: New Technologies Compel New Concepts for Commercial Law, 26 Loy.L.A.L.Rev. 607 (1993); Harvard Law Review Association and Professor Patrick Atiyah, for excerpts from Atiyah, Book Review: C. Fried, Contract as Promise, 95 Harv.L.Rev. 509 (1981); Harvard Law Review Association and Professor David A. Charny, for excerpts from Charny, Nonlegal Sanctions in Commercial Relationships, 104 Harv.L.Rev. 373 (1990); Harvard Law Review Association and Professor Melvin Eisenberg, for excerpts from Eisenberg, The Bargain Principle and Its Limits, 95 Harv.L.Rev. 741 (1982); Harvard Law Review Association, for excerpts from Holmes, The Path of the Law, 10 Harv. L.Rev. 457 (1897); Harvard Law Review Association, for excerpts from Kessler & Fine, *Culpa in Contrahendo,* Bargaining in Good Faith, and Freedom of Contract: A Comparative Study, 77 Harv.L.Rev. 401 (1964); Harvard Law Review Association, for excerpts from Llewellyn, Book Review: O. Prausnitz, The Standardization of Commercial Contracts in English and Continental Law, 52 Harv.L.Rev. 700 (1939); Harvard Law Review Association, for excerpts from Seavey, Reliance Upon Gratuitous Promises or Other Conduct, 64 Harv.L.Rev. 913 (1957); Harvard Law Review Association and Professor W. David Slawson, for excerpts from Slawson, Standard Form Contracts and Democratic Control of Lawmaking Power, 84 Harv.L.Rev. 529 (1971); Harvard Law Review Association and Professor Anthony J. Waters, for excerpts from Waters, The Property in the Promise: A Study of the Third Party Beneficiary Rule, 98 Harv.L.Rev. 1109 (1985); Indiana Law Journal and Fred B. Rothman & Co., for excerpts from Calamari & Perillo, A Plea for a Uniform Parol Evidence Rule and Principles of Contract Interpretation, 42 Indiana Law Journal 333 (1967); Journal of Law & Commerce and Professor Richard Speidel, for excerpts from Speidel, The New Spirit of Contract, 2 J.L. & Com. 193 (1982)— Copyright © *The Journal of Law & Commerce,* University of Pittsburgh, 1982, reprinted with permission from 2 J.L. & Com. 193 (1982); Journal of Legal Education and Professor Walter E. Oberer, for excerpts from Oberer, On Law, Lawyering and Law Professing: The Golden Sand, 39 J.Leg.Educ. 203 (1989); Journal of Legal Studies and Professor Anthony Kronman, for excerpts from Kronman, Mistake, Disclosure, Information and the Law of Contracts, 7 J. of Legal Stud. 1 (1978); Journal of Legal Studies, The University of Chicago Press and Judge Richard Posner, for excerpts from Posner & Rosenfield, Impossibility and Related Doctrines in Contract Law: An Economic Analysis, 6 Journal of Legal Studies 83 (1977); Michigan Law Review, for excerpts from Hillman, Online Boilerplate: Would Mandatory Website Disclosure of E-Standard Terms Backfire?, 104 Mich.L. Rev. 837 (2006); New York University Law Review, for excerpts from Pound, Discretion, Dispensation and Mitigation: The Problem of the Individual Special Case, 35 N.Y.U.L.Rev. 925 (1960); North Carolina Law Review Association, for excerpts from Dalzell, Duress by Economic Pressure I, 20 N.C.L.Rev. 237 (1942)—Reprinted with permission from 20 N.C.L.Rev. (1942), Copyright © 1942 by the North Carolina Law Review Association; Northern Kentucky Law Review and Professor Richard Speidel, for excerpts from Speidel, The Borderland of Contract, 10 N.Ky.L.Rev. 164 (1983); Northwestern University Law Review, for excerpts from Childres & Garamella, The Law of Restitution and the Reliance Interest in Contract, 64 Nw.U.L.Rev. 433 (1969)—Reprinted by special permission of Northwestern University, School of Law, 64 Nw.U.L.Rev. 433 (1969); Northwestern University Law Review, for excerpts from Havighurst, The Restatement of the Law of Contracts, 27 Ill.L.Rev. 910 (1933)—Reprinted by special permission of Northwestern University, School of Law, 27 Ill.L.Rev. 910 (1933); Ohio State Law Journal, for excerpts from Dunbar, Drafting the Liquidated Damages Clause—When and How, 20 Ohio State L.J. 221 (1959); Pennsylvania Bar Association and David W. Maxey, for excerpts from Maxey, Fundamentals of Draftsmanship—A Guide for the Apprentice in Preparing Agreements, 51 Pa.Bar Ass'n Quarterly 47 (1980); Saint Louis Law Journal and Professor Donald King, for excerpts from King, The Tort of Unconscionability: A New Tort for New Times, 23 St. Louis L.J. 97 (1979); Southern California Law Review and Professor Ian Macneil, for excerpts from Macneil, A Primer of Contract Planning, 48 S.Cal.L. Rev. 627 (1975); Stanford Law Review and Professor Melvin Eisenberg, for excerpts from Eisenberg, The Responsive Model of Contract Law, 36 Stan.L.Rev. 1107 (1984); Stanford Law Review and Professor Lawrence Friedman, for excerpts from Friedman, Legal Rules and the Process of Social Change, 19 Stan.L.Rev. 786 (1967); Tulane Law Review, for excerpts from Dawson, Economic Duress and the Fair Exchange in French and German Law, 11 Tulane L.Rev. 345 (1937); Tulane Law Review and Professor Robert Riegert, for excerpts from Riegert, The West German Civil Code: Its Origin and Its Contract Provisions, 45 Tulane L.Rev. 48 (1970); UCLA Law Review and Fred B. Rothman & Co., for excerpts from Note, Attorney Malpractice in California: The Liability of a Lawyer Who Drafts an Imprecise Contract or Will, 24 U.C.L.A. L.Rev. 422 (1976); UCLA Law Review, Fred B. Rothman & Co., and Professor Arthur Rosett, for excerpts from Rosett, Contract Performance: Promises, Conditions and the Obligation to Communicate, 22 U.C.L.A.L.Rev. 1083 (1975); University of Chicago Law Review and Professor Melvin Eisenberg, for excerpts from Eisenberg, Donative Promises, 47 U.Chicago L.Rev. 1 (1979); University of Chicago Law Review, for excerpts from Lieberman & Henry, Lessons from Alternative Dispute Resolution, 53 U.Chi.L.Rev. 424 (1996); University of Chicago Law Review, for excerpts from Schultz, The Firm Offer Puzzle: A Study of Business Practice in the Construction Industry, 19 U.Chi. L.Rev. 237 (1952); Virginia Law Review Association, for excerpts from Cavers, Legal Education and Lawyer-Made Law, 54 Va.L.Rev. 177 (1952); Virginia Law Review Association, Fred B. Rothman & Co. and Professor Stanley Henderson, for excerpts from Henderson, Promises Grounded in the Past: The Idea of Unjust Enrichment and the Law of Contracts, 57 Va.L.Rev. 1115 (1971); Virginia Law Review Association & Fred B. Rothman & Co., for excerpts from Summers, "Good Faith" in General Contract Law and the Sales Provisions of the Uniform Commercial Code, 54 Va.L.Rev. 195 (1968); Wisconsin Law Review and Professor Russell J. Weintraub, for excerpts from Weintraub, A Survey of Contract Practice and Policy, 1992 Wis.L.Rev. 1, reprinted by permission of the Wisconsin Law Review; Wisconsin Law Review and Professor William Whitford, for excerpts from Whitford, Ian Macneil's Contribution to Contracts Scholarship, 1985 Wis.L.Rev. 545; The Yale Law Journal Company and William S. Hein Company, for excerpts from Ben-Shahar & Bernstein, The Secrecy Interest in Contract Law, 109 Yale L.J. 1885 (2000)—Reprinted by permission of the Yale Journal Company and William S. Hein Company from the Yale Law Journal, Vol. 109, pages 1885–1925; The Yale Law Journal Co. and Fred B. Rothman & Co., for excerpts from Clark, The Restatement of the Law of Contracts, 42 Yale L.J. 643 (1933)—Reprinted by permission of The Yale Law Journal Company and Fred B. Rothman & Co. from *The Yale Law Journal,* Vol. 42, p. 643; The Yale Law Journal Co. and Fred B. Rothman & Co., for excerpts from Comment, Apportioning Loss After Discharge of a Burdensome Contract: A Statutory Solution, 69 Yale L.J. 1054 (1960)—Reprinted by permission of The Yale Law Journal Company and Fred B. Rothman & Co. from *The Yale Law Journal,* Vol. 69, pp. 1054, 1056–1057; The Yale Law Journal Co. and Fred B. Rothman & Co., for excerpts from Corbin, Conditions in the Law of Contract, 28 Yale L.J. 739 (1919)—Reprinted by permission of The Yale Law Journal Company and Fred B. Rothman & Co. from *The Yale Law Journal,* Vol. 28, pp. 739, 743, 745–746; The Yale Law Journal Co. and Fred B. Rothman & Co., for excerpts from Corbin, Offer and Acceptance, and Some of the Resulting Legal Relations, 26 Yale L.J. 169 (1917)—Reprinted by permission of The Yale Law Journal Company and Fred B. Rothman & Co. from *The Yale Law Journal,* Vol. 26, pp. 169, 199–200; The Yale Law Journal Co., Fred B. Rothman & Co., and Marjorie Fuller, for excerpts from Fuller & Perdue, The Reliance Interest in Contract Damages, 46 Yale L.J. 52 (1963)—Reprinted by permission of The Yale Law Journal Company and

Fred B. Rothman & Co. from *The Yale Law Journal*, Vol. 46, pp. 52, 53–57, 60–62, 75–80; The Yale Law Journal Co., Fred B. Rothman & Co. and Professor Paul Gewirtz, for excerpts from Gewirtz, Commentary on Karl N. Llewellyn, What Price Contract?—An Essay in Perspective, 100 Yale L.J. 1508 (1991)—Reprinted by permission of The Yale Law Journal Company and Fred B. Rothman & Co. from *The Yale Law Journal*, Vol. 100, pp. 1508, 1508–10; The Yale Law Journal Co., Fred B. Rothman & Co., and Professor Stanley Henderson, for excerpts from Henderson, Promissory Estoppel and Traditional Contract Doctrine, 78 Yale L.J. 343 (1969)—Reprinted by permission of The Yale Law Journal Company and Fred B. Rothman & Co. from *The Yale Law Journal*, Vol. 78, pp. 343, 358–360; The Yale Law Journal Co. and Fred B. Rothman & Co., for excerpts from Llewellyn, Our Case-Law of Contract: Offer and Acceptance II, 48 Yale L.J. 779 (1939) —Reprinted by permission of The Yale Law Journal Company and Fred B. Rothman & Co. from *The Yale Law Journal*, Vol. 48, pp. 779, 803–04; and The Yale Law Journal Co. and Fred B. Rothman & Co., for excerpts from Wormser, The True Conception of Unilateral Contracts, 26 Yale L.J. 136 (1916).

We also gratefully acknowledge our indebtedness to the following authors and publishers who gave us permission to reprint excerpts from copyrighted books: The American Law Institute, for excerpts from Explanatory Notes in Restatement (First) of Contracts, copyright © 1928 by The American Law Institute, reprinted with the permission of The American Law Institute; The American Law Institute, for excerpts from Restatement (First) of Contracts, copyright © 1932 by The American Law Institute, reprinted with the permission of The American Law Institute; The American Law Institute, for excerpts from Restatement (Second) of Contracts, copyright © 1981 by The American Law Institute, reprinted with the permission of The American Law Institute; The American Law Institute, for excerpts from Restatement (Second) of Torts, copyright © 1965 by The American Law Institute, reprinted with the permission of The American Law Institute; The American Law Institute and the National Conference of Commissioners on Uniform State Laws, for excerpts from Uniform Commercial Code, copyright © 1990 by The American Law Institute and the National Conference of Commissioners on Uniform State Laws. Reprinted with the permission of the Permanent Editorial Board for the Uniform Commercial Code; Aspen Law & Business and Professor E. Allan Farnsworth, for excerpts from Farnsworth, Contracts (3d ed. 1999); Professor Louis M. Brown, for excerpts from Planning by Lawyers; Carolina Academic Press, for excerpts from Stiviglia, Writing Contracts (1996); Harvard University Press and Professor Charles Fried, for excerpts from Fried, Contract as Promise (1981); The Lawyers Cooperative Publishing Co., for excerpts from Williston & Jaeger, A Treatise on the Law of Contracts (3d ed. 1957); The Lawyers Cooperative Publishing Co., for excerpts from Williston & Thompson, A Treatise on the Law of Contracts (rev'd ed. 1936); Little Brown & Co. and Judge Richard Posner, for excerpts from Posner, Economic Analysis of Law (2d ed. 1977); J.C.B. Mohr (Paul Siebeck), for excerpts from Arthur von Mehren, Contracts in General, International Encyclopedia of Comparative Law VII; Northwestern University Press, for excerpts from Fuller, The Law in Quest of Itself (1940); Oceana Publications, Inc. and Professor Rudolf Schlesinger, for excerpts from Schlesinger, Formation of Contracts (R. Schlesinger ed., 1968); Ohio State University, for excerpts from Gilmore, The Death of Contract—Excerpts from THE DEATH

OF CONTRACT, by Grant Gilmore, copyright © 1974 by the Ohio State University Press, reprinted by permission; Professor George Palmer, for excerpts from Palmer, Mistake and Unjust Enrichment (1962); University of Chicago Law School and Professor William Twining, for excerpts from Twining, The Karl Llewellyn Papers (1968); Warren, Gorham & Lamont and Professors Robert A. Hillman, Julian McDonnell and Steve Nickles, for excerpts from Hillman, McDonnell & Nickles, Common Law and Equity Under the UCC (1985); West Publishing Company and Professor Dan B. Dobbs, for excerpts from Dobbs, Remedies (1973); West Publishing Company and Professors Harry Edwards and James J. White for excerpts from The Lawyer as Negotiator (1977); West Publishing Company, for excerpts from 19 Leopold, Beyer, Park, West's Legal Forms (2d ed. 1986); West Publishing Company, for excerpts from Prosser & Keeton on Torts (5th ed. 1984); West Group and Professors James J. White and Robert S. Summers for excerpts from Uniform Commercial Code (5th ed. 2000); Yale University Law School, for excerpts from 1 Corbin on Contracts (1963), 3 Corbin on Contracts (1960), and 3A Corbin on Contracts (1960); Yale University Press and Professors Ian Ayres and Gregory Klass for excerpts from Ayres & Klass, Insincere Promises (2005); and Yale University Press and the Trustee of the Literary Estate of John P. Dawson, for excerpts from Dawson, Gifts and Promises (1980).

The authors also wish to thank the following practitioners for permitting us to use materials from their files: Mr. John A. Coppeler of Flynn, Py & Krause, Sandusky, Ohio; Mr. David B. Cotner of Datsopoulos, MacDonald & Lind, Missoula, Montana; Mr. Michael S. Danian, Attorney at Law, Wauke-gan, Illinois; Mr. James E. Dixon, Attorney at Law, Dixon, Illinois; Mr. Lawrence C. Force of Force & Baldwin, Adrian, Michigan; Mr. Stephen J. Hajduch, Attorney at Law, Milwaukee, Wisconsin; Mr. Edward A. Monsky of Fine & Wyatt, Scranton, Pennsylvania; Mr. Donald L. Steerman of the Shinn law firm, Lamar, Colorado; Mr. Charles T. Rubin of Kroll & Tract, New York, New York; Mr. John B. Waldron of Courey, Schwinn, Kodadek & McRoberts, P.A., Minneapolis, Minnesota; and Mr. Timothy W. Woods of Jones, Obenchain, Ford, Pankow, Lewis & Woods, South Bend, Indiana.

We also wish to thank: Harvard Art Collection for photographs of Professors John Dawson and Lon L. Fuller, courtesy of Art & Visual Materials, Special Collections Department, Harvard Law School Library; University of Miami School of Law for a photograph of Professor Soia Mentschikoff, and Yale University Archives, Yale University Library for a photograph of Professor Arthur Corbin.

Personal Acknowledgments
to Fifth Edition

Professors Hillman and Summers thank Cornell Law School students Jared Grauer, Jonathan Grossberg, Nathaniel Holland, Kenneth Hwang, Yousef Ibrahimi, Amanda Klopf, Michael Prehogan, and Conray Tseng for excellent research and production assistance.

We are also grateful to Dean Stewart Schwab for institutional support and Professor Claire Germain, Law Librarian, for library assistance.

As always, Betsy Hillman and Dorothy Summers offered their unwavering support.

*

Personal Acknowledgments
to Fourth Edition

Professors Hillman and Summers thank Cornell Law School students Matthew A. Peterson, James E. Sampson, Robert L. Schultz, Lisa A. Shrayer, and Milena Sterio for excellent research assistance. Robert L. Schultz helped oversee production of the fourth edition and we thank him for that too. Karen Wilson helped prepare the manuscript for publication.

We thank Dean Lee Teitelbaum for institutional support and Professor Claire Germain, Law Librarian, for library assistance.

We also thank Betsy Hillman and Dorothy Summers for their steadfast support.

*

Personal Acknowledgments
to Third Edition

Professors Summers and Hillman thank Cornell Law School students Hera Arsen, John Bueker, Gillian Crenshaw, Donald Kochan, Anita Lee, Laura McClellan, Aaron Pichel, and Carol Timm for excellent research assistance. Jessica Hillman (Cornell B.A. 1996) patiently proofread much of the manuscript. We also thank Karen Wilson for helping to prepare the manuscript for publication.

We thank Cornell Law School Dean Russell Osgood for institutional aid. Professor Claire Germain, John Hasko, and the Cornell Law School Library staff provided helpful library assistance.

We also thank Betsy Hillman and Dorothy Summers for their unwavering support.

*

Personal Acknowledgments
to Second Edition

———————

Professors Summers and Hillman thank Stephen Wade Angus '93, Wendy Boucher '93, Keith Dobbins '92, Johnathan Mansfield '93, Brian Moran '93, Pamela Moreau '91, Lisa Murphy '93, Steven Nadel '92, Matthew Oppenheim '93, and Elizabeth Anne Summers '91, for excellent research assistance. We also are indebted to Karen Wilson, who prepared the manuscript for the printer.

We also thank Cornell Law School Dean Russell Osgood for institutional and other support and Professors Dan Coenen, University of Georgia School of Law, Alfred Meyer, Valparaiso University School of Law, Douglas Newell, Lewis and Clark Northwestern School of Law, and James J. White, University of Michigan Law School, for their extended suggestions.

As always we are grateful to Dorothy Summers and Betsy Hillman for their continued support and encouragement.

*

Personal Acknowledgments
to First Edition

The editors wish to record their indebtedness and gratitude to the following Cornell Law School students for help on this book: Julianne Cloutier '88, Charles Eberhardt '87, Stuart Harris '86, John Held '87, Lucile McConnell '87, Andrew McGaan '86, Kathryn Moore '88, Candace Ridgway '87, Robin Rowland '85, Sanford Shatz '86, Jonathan Wood '86, and Jennifer Zimmerman '88. Professor Hillman also wishes to thank George Boerger '88, University of Michigan.

The editors are also indebted to and wish to thank their colleague Kevin M. Clermont for helpful thoughts with respect to the title of the book, Dr. Geoffrey Marshall of The Queens College, Oxford (and Andrew D. White Professor-at-Large, Cornell University) for the two original poems that appear in the book (after Hadley v. Baxendale at page 231 and Krell v. Henry at page 959), and Elizabeth Anne Summers who performed numerous helpful chores on the manuscript.

The editors also wish to thank Dean Peter Martin of the Cornell Law School for research support and Professor Jane Hammond and the Cornell Law School Library staff for many forms of assistance.

Both Professors Summers and Hillman are most grateful to Anna Tileston who assisted in the preparation of this manuscript in countless ways and whose help was invaluable. The authors are also grateful to Karen Wilson for her assistance in the preparation of the manuscript at an early stage.

Both editors also wish to acknowledge their indebtedness to editors of existing casebooks that have set such a high standard in this field. The late Grant Gilmore once remarked that "most casebooks are not much more than cannibalizations of the other casebooks in the field."* We are certain that we have risen above this, but we are nonetheless conscious of having learned a good deal from existing books, including J. Dawson, W. Harvey, S. Henderson, Cases and Comment on Contracts (4th ed. 1982); E. Farnsworth and W. Young, Cases and Materials on Contracts (3d ed. 1980); L. Fuller and M. Eisenberg, Basic Contract Law (4th ed. 1981); F. Kessler and G. Gilmore, Contracts—Cases and Materials (2d ed. 1970); I. Macneil, Contracts—Exchange Transactions and Relations (2d ed. 1978); A. Mueller, A. Rosett, and G. Lopez, Contract Law and Its Application (3d ed. 1984); E. Murphy and R. Speidel, Studies in Contract Law (3d ed. 1984); and D. Vernon, Contracts: Theory and Practice (1980).

The authors also thank Dorothy Summers and Betsy Hillman, for many forms of support and encouragement.

* Gilmore, Friedrich Kessler, 84 Yale L.J. 672, 679 (1974).

*

Summary of Contents

PART FIVE.   RIGHTS AND DUTIES OF THIRD PARTIES

Appendices

Table of Contents

PART TWO.   THE AGREEMENT PROCESS

PART FIVE.   RIGHTS AND DUTIES OF THIRD PARTIES

*

Table of Cases

The principal cases are in bold type. Cases cited or discussed in the text are roman type. References are to pages. Cases cited in principal cases and within other quoted materials are not included.

*

CONTRACT AND RELATED OBLIGATION:

THEORY, DOCTRINE, AND PRACTICE

Fifth Edition

*

Part One

FOUNDATIONS OF CONTRACT AND RELATED OBLIGATION

Chapter One

INTRODUCTION

Chapter Two

GENERAL THEORIES OF OBLIGATION

Chapter Three

REMEDIES

Chapter One

INTRODUCTION

*Suppose contracts freely made and
effectively sanctioned and the most
elaborate social organization
becomes possible.*

SIDGWICK

This book is about the theory, doctrine, and practice of contract and
related law. We will study several general theories of legal obligation and
several types of law. We define a theory of obligation as a recognized general
basis for imposing legal duties. The predominant theory of obligation we will
study is that legal duties arise from a valid agreement with consideration—a
"contract." Nevertheless, legal duties arise pursuant to other general theories
of obligation as well. For example, we will study the theory called "promissory
estoppel" that duties arise from a party's justified reliance on a promise.
Thus, although we most often concentrate here on contract in the sense of
"agreement with consideration," our subject is much broader.

Among the types of law to be studied here are judge-made common law,
statutes adopted by legislatures, and regulations made by administrators.
Officials make all of these types of law. But most of the law in this field is not
made by officials. It is made by private parties (with or without the aid of
lawyers), and consists of the terms of their agreements, express and implied.
Moreover, officials have relatively little to do with the administration of most
such agreements. Instead, the parties themselves administer them in countless situations that never come before courts at all. For example, even when
you agree to mow your neighbor's lawn for $10, perform the services and are
paid, you and your neighbor have made and administered private contract
law.

Although this book consists largely of reported cases in which judges
follow or create what is called "common law," few of these cases would have
arisen if the parties had not made agreements (or had not claimed to have
done so). And in most of these cases, the express or implied terms of the
parties' agreement generate strong reasons for deciding in favor of one party,
reasons which judges often adopt either as the sole or as a partial basis for
their decisions. Even when judges do not decide on the basis of such reasons,
they frequently invoke principles and policies that facilitate and implement
private agreements.

Moreover, when a private agreement conflicts with the common law, the
former generally prevails. Private parties usually have the right to adopt
terms that displace or override common law rules that would otherwise
govern. However, we will also study some important rules of the common law

that judges may invoke to invalidate or police the terms of private agreements.

In addition to the terms of agreements and the common law, we will study some statutory law. We will focus on various sections of Article 2 of the Uniform Commercial Code governing the sale of goods.[a] Parties can also displace or override most of the rules of Article 2 by agreement. Article 2 is designed primarily to facilitate and implement the terms of private sales agreements. Thus, Article 2 includes many provisions for filling gaps in private agreements that would otherwise be invalid because too indefinite or incomplete. But Article 2 also includes some exceptional sections that displace or override contrary terms in private agreements. In addition, in various specialized fields of contract, studied in upper level law courses, such as consumer protection, insurance, employee collective bargaining, automobile dealer franchising, storage, and transportation, numerous regulatory statutes apply. Many of the provisions of such regulatory statutes cannot be superseded by private agreement.

What roles do lawyers perform when they practice in this field? Their practice consists mainly of activities outside of the courtroom such as fact-finding, planning, drafting, interpreting, counseling, and negotiating. Accordingly, a major focus of this book is on the lawyer's work outside of court.

Notwithstanding our emphasis on the primacy of the parties' agreement as a source of governing law, and notwithstanding our focus on the skills of lawyers outside the courtroom, for many reasons this book includes lots of appellate judicial opinions. Within the American law school, the basic course on contract law is a wonderful vehicle for developing the analytical and critical faculties that mark the good lawyer. Without these skills, a lawyer cannot effectively find facts, plan, draft, interpret, counsel, negotiate, or litigate. Knowledge of the relevant principles of the common law and of common law method are likewise essential prerequisites to effective practice in this field. The intensive study of appellate cases is indispensable to the acquisition of these faculties and forms of knowledge. In addition, cases are vital sources of authentic knowledge about the social institution of contract as it actually functions in our society.

SECTION ONE: CONTRACT AND RELATED OBLIGATION

An important professor of our subject, Karl N. Llewellyn, once stressed that "[i]n the normal modern case the first measure of the parties' rights is the contract."[b] Two other distinguished scholars and teachers, David F. Cavers and Lon L. Fuller, stressed the special law-making role of lawyers in these terms:

a. The National Conference of Commissioners on Uniform State Laws (NCCUSL) and the American Law Institute (ALI) combined forces to draft the Code. Pennsylvania, in 1953, became the first state to enact it. After some editorial revision, many other states adopted it in the 1960's and 1970's. Today the Code is law in all states except Louisiana (where parts of it are in force). The Code is divided into eleven articles. Insofar as we study the Code in this course, we will focus almost entirely on Article 2, which deals with the sale of goods. On the history of the Code project, see J. White and R. Summers, Handbook of the Law Under the Uniform Commercial Code 1–7 (5th ed. 2000).

b. K. Llewellyn, Cases And Materials On Sales xiv (1930).

CAVERS, LEGAL EDUCATION AND LAWYER MADE LAW

54 W.Va.L.Rev. 177, 178–80 (1952).

Let me call your attention to one of those commonplaces which we tend to ignore, perhaps because they are so obvious.

It is a fact that a great deal of law under which all of us live and work in these United States is written, not by Congress and the state legislatures or by the courts and the administrative agencies, but by American lawyers, sitting in their offices, striving to carry out the lawful wishes of their clients.

Now the laws that the lawyer writes are not called statutes, regulations, and ordinances, or judgments, decrees, and orders. We have labels for them such as contracts, deeds, mortgages, indentures, leases, wills, trusts, settlements, charters, by-laws, and scores of other terms, but, if these instruments have been drawn and executed in accordance with law, they are just as effective a means of creating or transferring rights and duties, powers and privileges, as the most solemn enactments of a legislature.

If your client disregards a duty imposed by statute, he may have to pay a sum of money called a fine; if he disregards a duty imposed by a deed or a contract, he may have to pay a sum of money called damages. The people who start the machinery of justice turning to extract that sum in either case may be different, but the effect on his pocketbook may be very much the same.

* * *

In carrying out his work as law-maker, the lawyer is at once the architect and the builder of human relationships. He draws on his legal learning for knowledge of the legal tools and materials he can use and their capacity to bear loads and withstand stresses. At the same time, he draws on his knowledge of human nature and of business practice to gauge the workability of the arrangements he is considering. In addition, he employs his skill in analyzing problems and in using language effectively to make sure that the documents embodying the arrangements he has designed cover all significant contingencies and, at the same time, do not create other risks by ambiguities of plan or language.

FULLER, PROFESSIONAL RESPONSIBILITY[c]

44 A.B.A.J. 1159, 1161–62 (1958).

In our society the great bulk of human relations are set, not by government decree, but by the voluntary action of the affected parties. * * * Successful voluntary collaboration usually requires for its guidance something equivalent to a formal charter, defining the terms of collaboration, anticipating and forfending against possible disputes, and generally providing a framework for the parties' future dealings. In our society the natural architect of

---

c. Lon L. Fuller (1902–1978) was probably the leading American contract theorist of the twentieth century. He was also a major figure in the fields of jurisprudence and legal philosophy. He taught at Oregon, Illinois, Duke, and Harvard. His article, The Reliance Interest in Contract Damages, 46 Yale L.J. 52 (1936), is one of the two or three most influential articles in the history of the subject. Another important article is Fuller, Consideration and Form, 41 Colum. L. Rev. 799 (1941). For a systematic introductory treatment of Fuller's work, see R. Summers, Lon L. Fuller (1984). A photograph of Fuller appears at page 41.

this framework is the lawyer. * * * [Here] the lawyer functions, not as an expert in the rules of an existing government, but as one who brings into existence a government for the regulation of the parties' own relation. * * * The fruits of [the lawyer's] skill enter in large measure into the drafting of ordinary legal documents, though this fact is obscured by the mistaken notion that the lawyer's only concern in such cases is with possible future litigation, it being forgotten that an important part of his task is to design a framework of collaboration that will function in such a way that litigation will not arise.

A.   THE NONCOMMERCIAL SPECIALLY DRAFTED AGREEMENT

Many thousands of noncommercial specially drafted agreements are made every day in the United States. The episode set forth below is based on actual facts.

FACTS

In the fall of 1962, Virgil White (a police officer) and his wife, Gwynneth, wished to buy a residence in Oak Creek, Wisconsin, located next to a home owned by Paul and Ruth Benkowski, Jr. The water supply for the residence the Whites wished to purchase came through pipes from a well on the Benkowskis' property, and the control valves for that water system were located inside the Benkowskis' residence. Mr. White concluded it would be too costly to drill a well on the residence he wished to buy. He talked with the Benkowskis and they agreed to supply water to the Whites through the pipes from their well. Accordingly, the Whites went ahead with their purchase. Afterwards, the Whites proposed that the Benkowskis enter a formal agreement for the supply of water to the Whites' residence. Mr. Benkowski agreed but, instead of consulting a lawyer, he had a friend, Joe Artz, a real estate agent, draft an agreement. As part of the overall arrangement, the Whites paid $400 to the Benkowskis to enable them to buy the new pump and larger tank required to serve both premises. The actual agreement drafted by the real estate agent is set forth below:

AGREEMENT AS TO SUPPLY OF WATER

This agreement, made this 28 day of November, 1962, between Paul Benkowski Jr., and Ruth Benkowski, his wife (first parties), and Virgil A. White and Gwynneth A. White, his wife (second parties),

WITNESSETH

WHEREAS, first parties are the owners of the following described real estate situated in the City of Oak Creek, Milwaukee County, Wisconsin, to-wit:

[legal description of real estate omitted]

AND, WHEREAS, second parties are the owners of the following described real estate situated in the City of Oak Creek, Milwaukee County, Wisconsin, to-wit:

[legal description of real estate omitted]

*This agreement shall become null and void whenever water is supplied by any municipal system or if the existing well should go dry or become inadequate to supply said 2 homes or if second parties would drill their own well.

AND, WHEREAS, there is now situated on the above real estate of first parties, one certain water well operated by an electric submersible system motor,

AND, WHEREAS, the parties hereto desire that the source of water from the well upon parties of the first part's property be supplied unto the parties of the second part's home through the system of piping now there existing, it is hereby mutually agreed:

1.   That first parties will furnish water for the use of the occupants of the house located on the lands of the second parties for a period of ten (10) years from November, _____ 1962.

2.   That the second parties will pay for said water supply service the sum of Three ($3.00) Dollars per month, commencing with 1 December, 1962, payable on the first day of each and every month, in advance, and that in addition, second parties shall contribute to first parties, one-half (½) of the cost of any repairs or maintenance expense to said water system; also including replacements of motor, tank or accessories; (* above)

3.   It is further hereby agreed between the parties hereto that at the end of the ten year period referred to in Paragraph One above, parties of the second part shall have the option to renew this agreement.

This agreement shall be binding upon and shall extend unto the respective grantees, successors, heirs, executors, administrators and assigns of each of the respective parties hereto.

IN WITNESS WHEREOF, the parties hereto have hereunto set their hands and seals of the day and year first above written.

WITNESSES TO FOUR SIGNATURES:

Ron Allen   Paul Benkowski Jr. (SEAL)
                   Paul Benkowski Jr.

James J. White   Ruth Benkowski (SEAL)
                   Ruth Benkowski

                   Virgil A. White (SEAL)
                   Virgil A. White

                   Gwynneth A. White (SEAL)
                   Gwynneth A. White

Comments and Questions

1.   Assuming the above agreement meets all the requirements of a valid contract, is it law? Theorists of jurisprudence have sought to define "law." According to the "positivist" tradition in jurisprudence, law is defined essentially as something laid down by officials in power. For example, John Austin (1790–

1859), a leading English positivist whose influence is still widespread, defined positive law as the 'general commands of a sovereign legislature backed by sanctions.' J. Austin, I Lectures on Jurisprudence 180–185, 225–26 (4th ed. Campbell 1873). If this definition is applied strictly, did the Whites and Benkowskis make law here? Nevertheless, if their agreement gave rise to "legal obligations," and if a court would provide a remedy for breach of their agreement, is it not appropriate to call their agreement law?

2.   Consider the importance for the Whites and Benkowskis of legal recognition of their agreement. For one thing, the agreement provided for an exchange. What are the basic elements of the White–Benkowski exchange? Why does exchange occur? Consider this view: "[I]t is precisely the disparity in the value attached to the objects exchanged that results in their being exchanged. People buy and sell only because they appraise the things they give up less than those received." L. Von Mises, Human Action: A Treatise on Economics 204 (3d ed. 1963). Apply this analysis to both sides of the White–Benkowski exchange.

Another value of a legally valid agreement is that it allocates risks. What risks are allocated to the Whites? To the Benkowskis?

3.   Consider the special importance to society of legal recognition of agreements. Such recognition is one way a society expresses its regard for freedom. Through agreements, individuals such as the Whites and the Benkowskis can, within the limits of their own resources, organize important elements of their own lives, and thereby experience self-determination. This is a value to the parties themselves, as well. Of course, we must bear in mind that freedom of contract and self-governance are less meaningful to persons who have relatively little bargaining power.

Society also benefits from the legal recognition of private agreement because private exchange usually provides a more efficient allocation and distribution of resources than a system of governmental allocation and distribution. The French economist, Frederic Bastiat, once cited this example:

> On entering Paris, which I had come to visit, I said to myself—Here are a million of human beings who would all die in a short time if provisions of every kind ceased to flow towards this great metropolis. Imagination is baffled when it tries to appreciate the vast multiplicity of commodities which must enter to-morrow through the barriers in order to preserve the inhabitants from falling a prey to the convulsions of famine, rebellion and pillage. And yet all sleep at this moment, and their peaceful slumbers are not disturbed for a single instant by the prospect of such a frightful catastrophe. On the other hand, eighty departments have been labouring to-day, without concern, without any mutual understanding, for the provisioning of Paris. How does each succeeding day bring what is wanted, nothing more, nothing less, to so gigantic a market? What, then, is the ingenious and secret power which governs the astonishing regularity of movements so complicated, a regularity in which everybody has implicit faith, although happiness and life itself are at stake? That power is an *absolute principle,* the principle of freedom in transactions.

F.   Bastiat, Economic Sophisms 104–05 (1922).

4.   Why did the Whites and Benkowskis rely on Joe Artz, a real estate broker, to draft their agreement? Some lawyers have complained that such activity by real estate agents is a source of unnecessary litigation. Of course, not everyone can afford a lawyer. And even though a person can afford a lawyer, there

may be additional reasons why he or she might not wish to retain one. For example, Rollie Massimino, formerly head coach of Villanova's basketball team, is reported to have said in response to why he turned down a coaching job with the New Jersey Nets: "The Nets were very professional in all their dealings. We had some 20 telephone conversations and about five face-to-face meetings. Everything was agreed on verbally and then the lawyers took over with their legalese and there were snags. * * * " Ithaca Journal, June 26, 1985, § 2, at 16 Col. 3 & 4.

————

If the Whites and the Benkowskis had retained lawyers, their roles would likely have included: ascertaining the facts, determining the parties' goals, evaluating alternative possible means to achieve those goals, anticipating possible problems and conflicts of interests between the parties, identifying any legal issues, researching and applying applicable law, planning and drafting a proposed agreement, negotiating with the other side concerning problems and conflicts, revising the proposed agreement accordingly, and securing a final signed agreement. Before preparing a draft of the agreement, the lawyers would have had conferences with their clients. Let us assume that the Whites and their lawyer had such a conference pursuant to a letter such as the one set out below:

Virgil & Gwynneth White 3837 East Garden Place Oak Creek, Wisconsin

Dear Mr. & Mrs. White:

You have asked me to draft an agreement with Paul and Ruth Benkowski to supply you with water from their well through existing pipes connected to your new home. You have told me that you have already agreed to a monthly service charge of $3.00 to be paid in advance on the first day of each month, that you have agreed to pay $400 for a new pump and an additional tank, and that you have agreed to pay one-half of the cost of additional repairs, maintenance or replacement expenses. The agreement is to last for ten years with an option to renew, but will terminate when water is supplied by a municipal system, or the Benkowskis' well goes dry or is inadequate to supply the two homes, or if you drill your own well.

Before I draft the agreement there are certain additional issues that we should clear up with the Benkowskis. Concerning the duration of the agreement, if you exercise the renewal option is the renewal period for ten years? May you renew the agreement more than once? You certainly should have that right since you do not want to be without a water supply after one renewal period. Are you *required* to be connected to the municipal system if it becomes available or may you continue to receive water from the Benkowskis' well (it may be cheaper from the Benkowskis)? When does the Benkowskis' well "become inadequate" to supply both homes? For example, will merely one or a few periods of low water pressure be sufficient? We need to discuss this further with the Benkowskis and see if we can nail down some agreement on precisely when the well "becomes inadequate."

Concerning the price to you of the water service, does the $3.00 per month charge continue under all circumstances during the period of the agreement? For example, suppose the value of water in this general area increases dramatically because of a drought or pollution or the like? We need to include a provision specifically indicating that such events do not trigger a right of the Benkowskis to raise the price (or to get out of the agreement). In addition, you agree to pay one-half of repairs, maintenance and replacement costs to the system. We should make it clear that only such repairs, maintenance and replacement costs that are necessary to continue the supply of water to both homes are included, not repairs, etc. that are solely beneficial to the Benkowskis.

You have not reached an agreement concerning water quality. We should seek to include a provision in which the Benkowskis warrant the quality of the water they will supply to you. Quality should be tied to Milwaukee County Health Department regulations.

Are there to be any limits on your usage of water? I assume that the Benkowskis' attorney (if they retain one) will raise this issue. If the issue is not raised, we need to decide whether to raise it ourselves by seeking a provision specifically ensuring that you can use all of the water you desire. Offering such a provision may prod the Benkowskis into seeking a price scheme based on the amount of water usage. I assume that we can agree on a mutually agreeable scale. If we remain silent on this issue, I can foresee disagreements about water usage later on, so perhaps we should consider the issue now.

Finally, while I know you people are on good terms now, unfortunately we lawyers have seen too many deals go sour. So it is appropriate to think of remedies that you desire if the Benkowskis break their agreement, for example, by turning off the water on you. We should try to get an agreement as to how much the Benkowskis will have to pay you for each hour that the water is purposefully turned off to discourage such behavior, should your relationship with the Benkowskis not remain cordial. Such an amount must necessarily reflect the damages to you or it will not be legally enforceable.

We need to have a meeting first on these matters, and then later with the Benkowskis. Of course we will need to compromise on many of them, but the important thing is to have your agreement clearly deal with these issues so as to avoid trouble in the future.

Sincerely yours,
Jean L. Smith

Comments and Questions

1. Does it appear that Joe Artz, the real estate broker who drafted the White–Benkowski agreement, satisfactorily ascertained the facts, determined the parties' goals, and anticipated problems prior to planning and drafting the agreement? Identify what you consider to be the biggest deficiency in the agreement from the Whites' point of view. In thinking about this, consider Jean Smith's letter.

2. Assume that after Jean Smith wrote the foregoing letter, she had conferences with the Whites and, after further fact finding, planned and drafted a proposed agreement. Assume the agreement included the following clause:

The Benkowskis promise that the water they are to supply under this agreement shall be potable according to the standard of water potability incorporated in the regulations of the Milwaukee County Health Department applicable to residential use. The Benkowskis warrant that the water in their well, as presently chlorinated by them, now complies with the foregoing standard. If the water falls below the foregoing standard, the Whites shall have no duty to pay for water affected and shall have all other legal remedies.

Does the agreement drafted by Joe Artz deal with this problem? In light of the clause above and Jean Smith's letter, in what ways does it appear that Jean Smith could have done a better overall job for the Whites than Joe Artz? How might this be explained? An obvious factor is that Jean Smith has had formal education and training. But is there rather more to it than this? What are the attributes of a lawyer?

3. It is one thing to plan and draft a proposed agreement for a client and quite another to secure the assent of the other party. Thus the lawyer may be called upon to negotiate. What is the most opportune time to negotiate for a clause such as that in question 2 above—at the stage of initial agreement or later, after a breakdown? Why?

4. It appears that Joe Artz purported here to act for both sides. Would it have been appropriate for Jean Smith to have done this? Consider the following provision.

MODEL RULES OF PROFESSIONAL CONDUCT
Rule 1.7 (1998).

CONFLICT OF INTEREST: GENERAL RULE

(a) A lawyer shall not represent a client if the representation of that client will be directly adverse to another client, unless:

(1) the lawyer reasonably believes the representation will not adversely affect the relationship with the other client; and

(2) each client consents after consultation.

(b) A lawyer shall not represent a client if the representation of that client may be materially limited by the lawyer's responsibilities to another client or to a third person, or by the lawyer's own interests, unless:

(1) the lawyer reasonably believes the representation will not be adversely affected; and

(2) the client consents after consultation. When representation of multiple clients in a single matter is undertaken, the consultation shall include explanation of the implications of the common representation and the advantages and risks involved.

THE RELATIONSHIP BREAKS DOWN

As we know, Joe Artz, the real-estate broker, wrote no such letter as the above, and conducted no fact-finding conferences or negotiations. Instead, he simply drafted the agreement set forth at pages 5 and 6 (copying partly from a standard form), and the parties signed it on November 28, 1962. The Benkowskis eventually claimed that the Whites were using "too much" water! Beginning on March 5, 1964, on several occasions the Benkowskis turned off the Whites' water supply. The Whites were very much distressed. Let us now assume that the Whites retained Jean Smith as their lawyer, and that she contacted the Benkowskis by means of the following letter:

July 7, 1964

Mr. & Mrs. Paul Benkowski, Jr. 3835 East Garden Place Oak Creek, Wisconsin

Dear Mr. & Mrs. Benkowski:

My clients, Mr. and Mrs. Virgil White, have informed me of difficulties they are having with you over their water supply. They have shown me their agreement with you which assures them an adequate supply of water for the life of the agreement. Would you or your lawyer get in touch with me at your earliest convenience?

Sincerely yours,

Jean L. Smith
Attorney-at-Law

Assume that the Benkowskis also saw a lawyer, Mr. Joel Westin, and that Mr. Westin began to negotiate with Jean Smith over the foregoing matters.

Comments and Questions

1.   Private agreements are usually performed without dispute. Why? What are the possible explanations for the breakdown here? Would a breakdown have been as likely if lawyers had planned and drafted the agreement?

2.   How strong is the Whites' negotiating position? In particular, do you agree with Jean Smith's interpretation of the agreement as set forth in her letter, namely that the language of the agreement "assures" the Whites of an "adequate supply of water for the life of the agreement"? What arguments might be made, pro and con, as to the proper interpretation of the agreement in this regard? Interpretation is itself a complex and significant lawyer skill. (We study it systematically in Chapter Six.)

3.   What do you think would be the usual result of efforts between lawyers to negotiate the settlement of such a dispute? A voluntary settlement with, perhaps, the Whites agreeing to pay $1.00 a month more for water and agreeing not to use more than a given number of gallons per day? A lawsuit in which the dispute is ultimately resolved by a judge or jury in a court of law? Actually, we need not speculate at all. Only a tiny fraction of disputes arising under written agreements is ultimately resolved by court decision. How might this be explained? Here are some possibilities. Try to think of others.

(a) Parties prefer (or are compelled by circumstances) to order their own affairs.

(b) Many written agreements are carefully planned and drafted. As a result, they ultimately serve as effective bases for private settlement without resort to courts.

(c) Lawyers expert in the conduct of negotiations are readily available, and they regularly achieve settlements.

"Look, I'm not saying it's going to be today. But someday—someday—you guys will be happy that you've taken along a lawyer."

Drawing by Ziegler; © 1986 The New Yorker Magazine, Inc.

THE LAWSUIT

In the actual episode, possibly in part because the parties had not asked lawyers to prepare their agreement, the unusual happened. The relationship between the Whites and the Benkowskis not only broke down, but the parties were unable to resolve their differences through negotiation. As a result, the Whites sued the Benkowskis, seeking through a pleading called a complaint: (1) a sum of money as compensatory damages for the losses they sustained, and (2) a sum of money as "punitive" damages.[d]

The principal "legal papers" filed in this case prior to trial are set forth below:

STATE OF WISCONSIN: CIRCUIT COURT: MILWAUKEE COUNTY CIVIL DIVISION

VIRGIL A. WHITE and GWYNNETH A. WHITE, his wife, Plaintiffs, vs. PAUL BENKOWSKI, JR. and RUTH BENKOWSKI, his wife, Defendants.	COMPLAINT Case No. 324–264

---

d. The Whites also initially sought a court order (a temporary restraining order) directing the Benkowskis to perform their contract to supply water without interruption, a preliminary form of the remedy called "specific performance," to be studied in Chapter 3. The Whites sought this remedy through a document called an "order to show cause," but abandoned their request when they decided to change residences.

NOW come the above named plaintiffs, VIRGIL A. WHITE and GWYN-NETH A. WHITE, his wife, by their attorney, JEAN L. SMITH, and as for a cause of action against the above named defendants, PAUL BENKOWSKI, JR. and RUTH BENKOWSKI, his wife, and allege * * * as follows: to-wit:

1. That the plaintiffs, VIRGIL A. WHITE and GWYNNETH A. WHITE, his wife * * * reside at 3837 East Garden Place.

2. That the defendants, PAUL BENKOWSKI, JR. and RUTH BEN-KOWSKI, his wife * * * reside at 3835 East Garden Place.

3. That on or about the 28th day of November, 1962, the plaintiffs and defendants entered into an agreement entitled "AGREEMENT AS TO SUP-PLY OF WATER", said agreement constituting a valid contract. * * *

4. That said agreement provided, among other things, that the defendants would furnish water for use of the plaintiffs, their respective grantees, successors, heirs, executors, administrators and assignees for a period of ten (10) years commencing on the 28th day of November 1962, providing further that the plaintiffs have an option to renew said agreement at the end of the ten year period; said agreement being further conditioned on the payment of the sum of Three ($3.00) Dollars per month to the defendants, said sum to be payable on the first day of each and every month, and further to pay one-half (½) of the cost of repairs and maintenance expenses to said water system.

5. That the plaintiffs duly performed all the conditions and covenants of the said agreement on their part to be performed * * * and that the defendants have failed to live up to the conditions and covenants of said agreement and still refuse to do so.

6. That the defendants have, on many occasions violated the conditions and covenants of said agreement by turning off the water supply to the home of the plaintiffs and as instances of such violations when the water was completely shut off, cite the following:

March 5,	1964 —	From	7:10 P.M.	to	7:25 P.M.
March 9,	1964 —	"	3:40 P.M.	to	4:00 P.M.
March 11,	1964 —	"	6:00 P.M.	to	6:15 P.M.
April 14,	1964 —	"	9:30 P.M.	to	10:55 P.M.
June 10,	1964 —	"	6:20 P.M.	to	7:03 P.M.
July 1,	1964 —	"	5:30 P.M.	to	9:40 P.M.
July 6,	1964 —	"	2:00 P.M.	to	4:00 P.M.
July 6,	1964 —	"	4:05 P.M.	to	5:15 P.M.
July 6,	1964 —	"	8:50 P.M.	to	9:20 P.M.

7. That further the defendants on several occasions turned the water off partially, allowing only a trickle of water to be obtained by the plaintiffs on their premises. * * *

8. That such action on the part of the defendants has caused great inconvenience to the plaintiffs, creating an unhealthy and unsanitary condition on the plaintiffs' premises; such condition being damaging to the health

and safety of the plaintiffs and their family and causing them great mental anguish and consequently suffered compensatory and punitive damages in the sum of Five thousand ($5,000.00) Dollars.

WHEREFORE, plaintiffs demand judgment against the defendants for compensatory and punitive damages in the sum of Five thousand ($5,000.00) Dollars, plus the costs and disbursements of this action and for such other and further relief as the Court may deem just and equitable.

Jean L. Smith

Attorney for the Plaintiffs
September 4, 1964

Comments and Questions

1.   Does the foregoing pleading cite legal authorities? Set forth evidence in proof of facts? Allege facts which, if proved or admitted, constitute a valid claim in law?

2.   Assume that the foregoing pleading alleges facts which, if proved, would constitute a valid claim for breach of contract. Reread the complaint and see if you can isolate and formulate the various elements of such a claim.

3.   What preparation was necessary before Jean Smith drafted this complaint?

STATE OF WISCONSIN: CIRCUIT COURT: MILWAUKEE COUNTY CIVIL DIVISION

VIRGIL A. WHITE and	)
GWYNNETH A. WHITE, his wife,	) MOTION TO DISMISS FOR
Plaintiffs,	) FAILURE TO STATE A CLAIM
vs.	) Case No. 324–264
PAUL BENKOWSKI, JR. and	)
RUTH BENKOWSKI, his wife,	)
Defendants.	)

Defendants, by Joel Westin, their attorney, move the Court for an order dismissing that portion of Plaintiffs' complaint in the above entitled action demanding punitive damages, on the ground that such relief cannot be awarded in a contract action.

Joel Westin

Attorney for Defendants
September 20, 1964

———

Assume the trial judge set October 9, 1964 as the date for a hearing on the above motion to dismiss (also sometimes called a demurrer). Consider whether this motion raises a question of fact or only a question of law. On October 9, after hearing argument from both lawyers, the judge denied the defendants' motion. (We see later that the judge was in error.) The Benkowskis then served their answer.

STATE OF WISCONSIN: CIRCUIT COURT: MILWAUKEE COUNTY CIVIL DIVISION

VIRGIL A. WHITE and	)	
GWYNNETH A. WHITE, his wife,	)	
Plaintiffs,	)	ANSWER
vs.	)	Case No. 324–264
PAUL BENKOWSKI, JR. and	)	
RUTH BENKOWSKI, his wife,	)	
Defendants.	)	

Now come the above named defendants by Joel Westin, their attorney, and as for an answer to the plaintiffs' complaint, admit, deny, allege and show to the court as follows:

[In paragraphs 1–3 of this answer, the defendants admitted the allegations of paragraphs 1–4 of the plaintiffs' complaint.]

4. Answering Paragraph 5 of the plaintiffs' complaint, the defendants admit that the plaintiffs have paid the monthly service charge of $3.00 provided for in said agreement although some of these payments have been made late; the defendants deny that the plaintiffs have paid any sums towards the cost of repair and maintenance of the water system because there have been no such costs; * * * the defendants' [sic] admit that the plaintiffs have performed one of the express conditions and covenants of said agreement on their part to be performed, namely, the payment of the monthly charge of $3.00 but deny that the plaintiffs have performed any other express conditions and covenants of said agreement. * * *

5. Answering Paragraph 6 of the plaintiffs' complaint, the defendants deny that they have * * * turned off the water supply to the home of the plaintiffs and in particular the defendants deny that they turned off the water supply to the home of the plaintiffs on the occasions cited in Paragraph 6 of the plaintiffs' complaint.

6. Answering Paragraph 7 of the plaintiffs' complaint, the defendants deny that on any occasion they turned off the water supply to the plaintiffs' home partially. * * *

7. Answering Paragraph 8 of the plaintiffs' complaint, the defendants deny that any action on their part has caused any inconvenience to the plaintiffs and has created an unhealthy and unsanitary condition on the plaintiffs' premises, that they have damaged the health and safety of the plaintiffs and their family in any way, that they have caused them any mental anguish and that the plaintiffs have, consequently, suffered compensatory and punitive damages to the sum of $5000.00 or in any other amount. * * *

And as and for an affirmative defense, the defendants allege:

1. that said agreement provides that it shall become null and void whenever the existing well shall go dry or become inadequate to supply said homes, and

2. that the existing well has become inadequate. * * *

WHEREFORE, the defendants demand judgment as follows:

1. Dismissing the plaintiffs' complaint upon its merits.

2. Terminating the said agreement between the parties hereto.

3. For the costs and disbursements of this action.

Joel Westin

Attorney for defendants
October 28, 1964

Note
Responses to a Complaint

Upon examining the preceding motion and pleadings filed by counsel for the Benkowskis, you can see that a defendant may make various responses to a complaint. A defendant may assume the facts alleged and assert that the plaintiff still has no valid claim in light of applicable law. (See the motion to dismiss, above.) Or a defendant may simply admit the facts alleged, or deny them, or state that the defendant does not have information sufficient to form a belief as to the truth of the facts. A defendant may also set forth "new matter"—make new allegations that would, if proved, afford a defense. This response is called an "affirmative defense." For example, the Benkowskis' affirmative defense was that the well had become inadequate. A defendant may also assert a counterclaim. For example, the Benkowskis might claim that the Whites failed to pay their water bills and owed the Benkowskis the amount of the unpaid bills. Knowledge of the foregoing possible responses to a complaint will help you grasp the procedural posture of many of the cases to be studied in the rest of this book.

THE TRIAL

After the foregoing papers were filed, the Whites moved to another residence. Further attempts at a negotiated settlement were made, but without success. Thus a trial of the factual issues in dispute became necessary. Make a list of these issues by rereading the above complaint and answer. A jury trial was held on September 26–27, 1966.

At trial, Virgil White testified that Paul Benkowski told him that the water was shut off to remind the Whites that they were using too much water and that the Benkowskis wished to terminate the water agreement because the well was not adequate for the two families. Virgil White also testified that he asked his wife to keep a record of the times the water was turned off. The Whites both testified about an odor on one occasion and inconveniences caused by the water interruptions, including the necessity of taking their children to a neighbor's home to be bathed.

Virgil and Gwynneth White also testified about the relationship of the families just prior to and during the period of water interruptions. Gwynneth testified that the relationship of the families was good until about September of 1963, when the Whites' daughter picked an apple in the Benkowskis' yard. Ruth Benkowski then called the daughter an "S.O.B." Gwynneth told Ruth that "she didn't like this." Later Ruth called Gwynneth "a redheaded bitch." Virgil White stated that Paul Benkowski lodged a complaint with Virgil's superior that Virgil had tried to run over Paul's child. The district attorney's investigation absolved Virgil. Paul Benkowski also complained to the police chief that Virgil took too long for lunch at home from time to time, and had wild parties at home. Virgil was again absolved of any wrongdoing.

Paul Benkowski, in his testimony, denied that there were "hard feelings" between the families. He testified that "most of the difficulty" with the water supply was because of a blown fuse or because sand got into the pump and nozzle, thereby "reducing the water to a trickle." Ruth Benkowski testified that she concluded that the Whites used an excessive amount of water "because dirty water was drawn into the system and the pump was going on and off and we were drawing sand and dirty water." The Benkowskis therefore felt the system was inadequate to supply the two families. Ruth stated that the Benkowskis never had an expert come out to test the amount of water that was in the well.

At the close of the trial on September 27, 1966, the trial judge requested counsel for both parties to submit proposed instructions to the jury. Thereafter, he instructed the jury on the law applicable to the facts of this case as follows:

EXCERPTS FROM JUDGE HOLR'S INSTRUCTIONS TO THE JURY, SEPTEMBER 27, 1966

Now, as counsel have indicated, there are two questions. The first one reads: "Did the defendants maliciously, vindictively or wantonly shut off the water supply of the plaintiffs for the purpose of harassing the plaintiffs?"[e]

If you answer the first question "Yes", then answer this second set of questions: "(a) What compensatory damages did the plaintiffs suffer? (b) What punitive damages should be assessed?"

Now, in an action for a breach of contract the plaintiff is entitled to such damages as shall have been sustained by him which resulted naturally and directly from the breach if you find that the defendants did in fact breach the contract. Such damages include pecuniary loss and inconvenience suffered as a natural result of the breach and are called compensatory damages. In this case the plaintiffs have proved no pecuniary damages which you or the Court could compute. In a situation where there has been a breach of contract which you find to have damaged the plaintiff but for which the plaintiffs have proven no actual damages, the plaintiffs may recover nominal damages.

By nominal damages is meant trivial—a trivial sum of money.

Now, the second part of the second question refers to punitive damages. Punitive damages cannot be awarded for a mere breach of a contract alone. The mere fact that the breach has distressed the parties against whom the contract was breached is not sufficient to award punitive damages. However,

---

e. The parties had agreed that for purposes of the trial, the Whites' theory of recovery was that the Benkowskis maliciously, vindictively, and wantonly broke the contract by turning off the water.

if you find from the evidence that the defendants acted maliciously, vindictively or wantonly for the purpose of harassing the plaintiffs by shutting off the water, you may, if you see fit, but you're not obliged to do so, award, in addition to the nominal damages, such sum as you think proper under the circumstances as punitive damages by way of an example or punishment in order to deter the defendants and others from offending in a like manner in the future. You may also consider the seriousness of the wrong committed in reaching your answer.

Punitive damages are never a matter of right, but when allowable may be awarded or withheld in the discretion of the jury. Punitive damages may not be awarded unless the acts of the defendants in question were done maliciously, vindictively or wantonly as I will define those terms to you. Even if you find malice, vindictiveness or wantonness, you may award or withhold punitive damages as you see fit.

Now, by malice is meant ill will, bad intent or malevolence towards the plaintiff.

Vindictively means revengeful or desire to see another person suffer.

By wanton we mean a reckless or intentional disregard of the consequences to others.

If you award punitive damages you may consider the defendants' wealth so far as it appears from the evidence because such damages, to accomplish their purpose, may be proportionate in some general way to the defendants' ability to respond.

———

Assume that after giving the above instructions, Judge Holr requested the jury to remain seated while he retired to his chambers to hear possible objections from counsel to the instructions given. The Whites' attorney, Jean Smith, objected to the judge's instruction that no compensatory damages could be recovered. The judge overruled this objection and Smith took exception. The Benkowskis' attorney, Joel Westin, objected to the judge's instruction that punitive damages could be awarded and moved to strike the question pertaining to punitive damages on the "special verdict"[f] form to be submitted by the judge to the jury. The judge reserved his ruling on this objection and motion. Thereafter, he returned to the courtroom and asked the jury to retire and deliberate on the evidence in light of his instructions on the law, and to return its answers on the special verdict form. The form, and the answers the jury returned, appear below:

STATE OF WISCONSIN: CIRCUIT COURT: MILWAUKEE COUNTY CIVIL DIVISION

VIRGIL A. WHITE and   )
GWYNNETH A. WHITE, his wife,)
                Plaintiffs,)

f. In a special verdict, the jury reports to the judge specific factual findings, while in a general verdict the jury finds generally in favor of one of the parties.

```
                vs.              )   Case No. 324–264
PAUL BENKOWSKI, JR. and          )
RUTH BENKOWSKI, his wife,        )
              Defendants.        )
```

SPECIAL VERDICT

QUESTION 1:   Did the defendants maliciously, vindictively or wantonly shut off the water supply of the plaintiffs for the purpose of harassing the plaintiffs?

ANSWER: Yes _____

                      Dissenting
                      Jurors: _____

                      _____

QUESTION 2:   If you answered Question 1 "Yes", then answer this question:

(a) What compensatory damages, if any, did the plaintiffs suffer?[g]

ANSWER: Ten Dollars _____

                      Dissenting
                      Jurors: _____

                      _____

(b) What punitive damages should be assessed?

ANSWER: $2,000.00 _____

               Dissenting
               Jurors: _____

               _____
               Edwin West
               Foreman or Forelady

Dated at Milwaukee, Wisconsin, this 28 day of September, 1966.

———

      Some weeks after the verdict was returned, a post-trial proceeding was held in which counsel for the parties were given an opportunity to make motions requesting the trial judge to correct claimed errors that might have occurred during the proceedings. On December 17, 1966, the trial judge rendered his decision on these motions:

---

    g. The judge submitted this special verdict form allowing for compensatory damages, but apparently expected the jury to award only nominal damages pursuant to his instructions.

STATE OF WISCONSIN: CIRCUIT COURT: MILWAUKEE COUNTY CIVIL DIVISION

VIRGIL A. WHITE and⠀⠀⠀⠀⠀⠀)
GWYNNETH A. WHITE, his wife,⠀)
⠀⠀⠀⠀⠀⠀⠀⠀Plaintiffs,⠀)
⠀⠀⠀⠀⠀vs.⠀⠀⠀⠀⠀⠀⠀)⠀⠀Case No. 324–264
PAUL BENKOWSKI, JR. and⠀⠀⠀)
RUTH BENKOWSKI, his wife,⠀⠀)
⠀⠀⠀⠀⠀⠀⠀Defendants.⠀)

DECISION—MOTIONS AFTER VERDICT

* * * The defendants now move for a new trial for the reason that the Court erred in submitting the issue of punitive damages to the jury, that the verdict is contrary to the evidence and the law, that the damages awarded are excessive, and not in the interest of justice. In the alternative the defendants move to strike the answer as to punitive damages. The plaintiffs move the judgment upon the verdict. [The Court discussed the facts]

* * *

Upon this record counsel were advised that the Court would and did instruct the jury that no pecuniary loss had been proven, but that if the jury found that there was a breach of contract which damaged the plaintiff the plaintiff could recover nominal damages which was defined as a trivial sum.

* * *

This Court's research and analysis of the Wisconsin decision leads it to the conclusion that a claim for punitive damages must be supported by a showing of actual injury which justifies an award of something more than nominal compensatory damages.

* * *

The Court concludes that the rule in Wisconsin is to the effect that punitive damages are not allowable where there can be a finding of only nominal damages from the evidence. Thus the court should not have instructed the jury that it could find punitive damages.

Because the jury's findings of a deliberate breach is supported by the evidence and the plaintiffs conceded that they had proven only nominal damages there is no need for a new trial. The Court grants the defendants' motion to strike from the verdict the question and answer concerning punitive damages.

The defendants also challenge the jury's answer of $10.00 for compensatory damages. This finding was contrary to the Court's instruction and cannot be sustained upon the evidence. The Court considers this situation to be one within the authority of Campbell v. Sutliff (1927), 193 Wis. 370 which authorizes the Court to reduce damages without a new trial. Therefore it is ordered that the answer to that part of the verdict be reduced to nominal damages in the amount of $1.00.

Plaintiff is entitled to judgment for $1.00 together with costs and disbursements.

Marvin C. Holr, Circuit Judge

————

After the trial court entered judgment for $1.00 in damages against the Benkowskis, the Whites appealed to the Wisconsin Supreme Court. Their lawyer filed a formal notice of appeal and thereafter prepared and filed several copies of a brief and a transcript of the trial record with the Wisconsin Supreme Court. In preparing the brief, Jean Smith reviewed a copy of the trial transcript and studied applicable law to identify rulings made by the trial judge that might be legally erroneous and prejudicial. The major function of the appellant's brief is to demonstrate that, in light of applicable law, the trial judge did prejudicially err and that a new trial or some other appropriate relief is required. Once the parties have completed their briefs, a time is set for oral argument. Following the oral argument, the judges deliberate, decide the case, and hand down a written opinion (in most cases).

Bear in mind this general observation while studying the Wisconsin Supreme Court's opinion:

> Now a case never reaches a court of review until it has first been through a tribunal of trial—else there would be nothing to review. But the cases, so called, in your casebooks are almost exclusively chosen from courts of review. To understand them, therefore, you must get at what has gone on before they got there. * * * [A] court of review has as its business of review to listen to complaints that a lower court has done some job improperly, i.e. as the phrase goes, has been in error, has made some ruling not in accord with the rules of law, correctly understood. (K. Llewellyn, The Bramble Bush 26 (1930).)

WHITE v. BENKOWSKI
Supreme Court of Wisconsin, 1967.
37 Wis.2d 285, 155 N.W.2d 74.

This case involves a neighborhood squabble between two adjacent property owners.

Prior to November 28, 1962, Virgil and Gwynneth White, the plaintiffs, were desirous of purchasing a home in Oak Creek. Unfortunately, the particular home that the Whites were interested in was without a water supply. Despite this fact, the Whites purchased the home.

The adjacent home was owned and occupied by Paul and Ruth Benkowski, the defendants. The Benkowskis had a well in their yard which had piping that connected with the Whites' home.

On November 28, 1962, the Whites and Benkowskis entered into a written agreement wherein the Benkowskis promised to supply water to the White home for ten years or until an earlier date when either water was supplied by the municipality, the well became inadequate, or the Whites drilled their own well. The Whites promised to pay $3 a month for the water and one-half the cost of any future repairs or maintenance that the Benkowski well might require. As part of the transaction, but not included in the written agreement, the Whites gave the Benkowskis $400 which was used to purchase and install a new pump and an additional tank that would increase the capacity of the well.

Initially, the relationship between the new neighbors was friendly. With the passing of time, however, their relationship deteriorated and the neighbors actually became hostile. In 1964, the water supply, which was controlled by the Benkowskis, was intermittently shut off. Mrs. White kept a record of the dates and durations that her water supply was not operative. Her record showed that the water was shut off on the following occasions:

(1) March 5, 1964, from 7:10 p.m. to 7:25 p.m.

(2) March 9, 1964, from 3:40 p.m. to 4:00 p.m.

(3) March 11, 1964, from 6:00 p.m. to 6:15 p.m.

(4) June 10, 1964, from 6:20 p.m. to 7:03 p.m.

The record also discloses that the water was shut off completely or partially for varying lengths of time on July 1, 6, 7, and 17, 1964.

Mr. Benkowski claimed that the water was shut off either to allow accumulated sand in the pipes to settle or to remind the Whites that their use of the water was excessive. Mr. White claimed that the Benkowskis breached their contract by shutting off the water.

Following the date which the water was last shut off * * * the Whites commenced an action to recover compensatory and punitive damages for an alleged violation of the agreement to supply water. A jury trial was held. Apparently it was agreed by counsel that for purposes of the trial "plaintiffs' case was based upon an alleged deliberate violation of the contract consisting of turning off the water at the times specified in the plaintiffs' complaint." * * *

[The court then set forth the special verdict submitted to the jury.]

Before the case was submitted to the jury, the defendants moved to strike the verdict's punitive-damage question. The court reserved its ruling on the motion. The jury returned a verdict which found the Benkowskis maliciously shut off the Whites' water supply for harassment purposes. Compensatory damages were set at $10 and punitive damages at $2,000. On motions after verdict, the court reduced the compensatory award to $1 and granted defendants' motion to strike the punitive-damage question and answer.

Judgment for plaintiffs of $1 was entered and they appeal. * * *

WILKIE, J. Two issues are raised on this appeal.

1. Was the trial court correct in reducing the award of compensatory damages from $10 to $1?

2. Are punitive damages available in actions for breach of contract?

REDUCTION OF JURY AWARD

The evidence of damage adduced during the trial here was that the water supply had been shut off during several short periods. Three incidents of inconvenience resulting from these shut-offs were detailed by the plaintiffs. Mrs. White testified that the lack of water in the bathroom on one occasion caused an odor and that on two other occasions she was forced to take her children to a neighbor's home to bathe them. Based on this evidence, the court instructed the jury that: [The court set forth the portion of the jury charge at pages 17–18 indicating that the Whites could recover only nominal damages for their harm suffered from the breach.]

* * * In the trial court's decisions on motions after verdict it states that the court so instructed the jury because, based on the fact that the plaintiffs paid for services they did not receive, their loss in proportion to the contract rate was approximately 25 cents. This rationale indicates that the court disregarded or overlooked Mrs. White's testimony of inconvenience. In viewing the evidence most favorable to the plaintiffs, there was some injury. The plaintiffs are not required to ascertain their damages with mathematical precision, but rather the trier of fact must set damages at a reasonable amount. Notwithstanding this instruction, the jury set the plaintiffs' damages at $10. The court was in error in reducing that amount to $1.

The jury finding of $10 in actual damages, though small, takes it out of the mere nominal status. The award is predicated on an actual injury. This was not the situation present in Sunderman v. Warnken.[1] Sunderman was a wrongful-entry action by a tenant against his landlord. No actual injury could be shown by the mere fact that the landlord entered the tenant's apartment, therefore damages were nominal and no punitory award could be made. Here there was credible evidence which showed inconvenience and thus actual injury, and the jury's finding as to compensatory damages should be reinstated.

PUNITIVE DAMAGES

"If a man shall steal an ox, or a sheep, and kill it, or sell it; he shall restore five oxen for an ox, and four sheep for a sheep."[2]

Over one hundred years ago this court held that, under proper circumstances, a plaintiff was entitled to recover exemplary or punitive damages.[3]

Kink v. Coombs[4] is the most recent case in this state which deals with the practice of permitting punitive damages. In *Kink* the court relied on Fuchs v. Kupper[5] and reaffirmed its adherence to the rule of punitive damages.

In Wisconsin compensatory damages are given to make whole the damage or injury suffered by the injured party. On the other hand, punitive damages are given

" * * * on the basis of punishment to the injured party not because he has been injured, which injury has been compensated with compensatory damages, but to punish the wrongdoer for this malice and to deter others from like conduct."[6]

Thus we reach the question of whether the plaintiffs are entitled to punitive damages for a breach of the water agreement.

---

1. (1947), 251 Wis. 471, 29 N.W.2d 496.

2. Exodus 22:1.

3. McWilliams v. Bragg (1854), 3 Wis. 377 (424).

4. (1965), 28 Wis.2d 65, 135 N.W.2d 789.

5. (1963), 22 Wis.2d 107, 125 N.W.2d 360.

6. Malco, Inc. v. Midwest Aluminum Sales (1961), 14 Wis.2d 57, 66, 109 N.W.2d 516, 521.

The overwhelming weight of the authority supports the proposition that punitive damages are not recoverable in actions for breach of contract. In Chitty on Contracts, the author states that the right to receive punitive damages for breach of contract is now confined to the single case of damages for breach of a promise to marry.

Simpson states:

> "Although damages in excess of compensation for loss are in some instances permitted in tort actions by way of punishment * * * in contract actions the damages recoverable are limited to compensation for pecuniary loss sustained by the breach."[7]

Corbin states that as a general rule punitive damages are not recoverable for breach of contract.[8]

* * *

Persuasive authority from other jurisdictions supports the proposition (without exception) that punitive damages are not available in breach of contract actions. This is true even if the breach, as in the instant case, is wilful.

Although it is well recognized that breach of a contractual duty may be a tort, in such situations the contract creates the relation out of which grows the duty to use care in the performance of a responsibility prescribed by the contract. Not so here. No tort was pleaded or proved.

Reversed in part by reinstating the jury verdict [$10] relating to compensatory damages and otherwise affirmed. Costs to appellants.

Comments and Questions

1. You should consider at least the following questions about each appellate opinion you study in this book (and some instructors will want you to prepare written "briefs" dealing with all such matters).

    a. What were the essential facts of the case (as set forth in the appellate opinion)?

    b. What was the procedural posture of the case on appeal? For example, was the appeal from a ruling on demurrer? From a ruling on the admissibility of evidence? From an instruction to the jury? From a post-trial ruling? And so on.

    c. What substantive legal issue (or issues) did the case present?

    d. How did the court rule on the issue (or issues)?

    e. What were the court's reasons for the decision? Did the court rely on previous cases or other legal authority? Did the court offer substantive reasons (moral, economic, social, institutional etc.)?[h] Other reasons?

    f. Is the decision sound? The reasoning?

2. An influential professor of law, John Henry Wigmore, once wrote that "[w]e must be students of reasons as well as of rules." The point is important. For

---

7. Simpson, Contracts, (2d ed. Hornbook series), p. 394, sec. 195.

8. 5 Corbin, Contracts, p. 438, sec. 1077.

h. See Appendix A.

example: (1) a court's reasons frequently clarify the decision; (2) a court decision, as an exercise of state power, must be justified, which depends on the availability of supporting reasons; (3) stated reasons commonly influence future cases.

3. As a matter of policy, should the Benkowskis have been liable for punitive damages? As we saw in White v. Benkowski, Wisconsin generally does not permit their recovery for breach of contract. This is a very common rule in the United States and has many explanations that you will study later. See page 277. (For now, consider one explanation: unlike wrongs such as torts and violations of the criminal law, contract breaches do not cause indignation so there is little reason to punish a contract breaker.)

Notwithstanding the general rule, punitive damages may be available for an "independent tort" associated with a breach of contract, such as a deliberate misrepresentation at the time of contracting. The Benkowskis did not engage in any such misrepresentation. Another *possible* independent tort, however, is malicious breach of contract, recognized in some jurisdictions. Note that the jury found that the Benkowskis acted "maliciously, vindictively or wantonly * * * for purposes of harassing the plaintiffs." Moreover, compensatory damages here were so low ($10) that they could not effectively deter a breach. Given these factors, should the court have held that there was an "independent tort"? What principles and policies favor denial of punitive damages even for malicious breach of contract?

Even if Wisconsin recognized the independent tort cause of action for punitive damages, the Whites would have had to give the Benkowskis appropriate advance notice of this claim. Would it be sufficient that the Whites asked for punitive damages in their formal complaint and that the parties at trial stipulated that the case was being tried on the theory of "deliberate violation"?

4. Could the Whites' attorney, Jean Smith, have done a better job of conducting the litigation? What seems to have been her most serious mistake?

5. Was the Whites' decision to pursue legal remedies a sound decision? What else could they have done? Should Jean Smith have advised the Whites not to sue because of the probability of a small recovery?

6. We return now to our opening theme: Could this litigation have been avoided by better planning and drafting? Suppose the agreement had provided a careful definition of when the Benkowskis were entitled to cease supplying water? Would this have helped to avoid litigation? Suppose the Whites had consulted Jean Smith before they purchased their home and she had prepared a well-drawn agreement (from the Whites' point of view), but the Benkowskis had refused to sign it. Would Jean Smith necessarily have failed to serve her clients? What if, as a result of Jean Smith's advice, the Whites did not enter a contract with the Benkowskis at all?

Note
The General Theory of Obligation in White v. Benkowski

According to the Supreme Court of Wisconsin, the Benkowskis owed a legal duty to the Whites to provide water. We saw that the primary source of this duty was the agreement between the parties. Without the agreement, the Benkowskis' duty would not have arisen. (Nor would the lawsuit.) The agreement was not the sole source of the Benkowskis' legal duty, however. The legal system determines which agreements give rise to legal duties. Most of the law giving legal effect to agreements is common law made by courts. The common law recognizes several *general theories of obligation.* As we have said, a theory of obligation is a recognized general basis for imposing legal duties. The predominant theory in contract and related law, invoked by the Whites against the Benkowskis, is that legal duties arise from a valid agreement with consideration (a contract). We study the concept of valid agreement in Chapters Four and Five. We study consideration in Chapter Two, along with other general theories of obligation.

For now, we will offer *preliminary* definitions of "agreement" and "consideration." Professor Arthur L. Corbin, an important scholar of our subject,[i] once defined an agreement as follows: "To say that there is an agreement generally means that two or more persons have expressed themselves in harmony." 1 Corbin on Contracts 20 (1963). Professor Corbin refused, however, to define consideration, and denied that our law recognizes a unitary concept of consideration. Other authorities, however, have been willing to define consideration as a "bargained for exchange." We will later see that this definition, and the above definition of agreement, are useful points of departure, but require much elaboration and some modification.

B. OTHER BASIC TYPES OF AGREEMENTS

In addition to noncommercial specially drafted agreements of the type studied in White v. Benkowski, there are other basic types of agreements. Of course, commercial parties also enter specially drafted agreements. In addition, both commercial and non-commercial parties also enter standard form agreements, oral agreements, and informal agreements. Examples of the latter include ordering a meal at a restaurant for a price or buying a coat off the rack. We will see throughout this book that the lawyer's planning and drafting role, if any, varies with the type of agreement involved. For now, consider these introductory materials on standard form agreements:

SLAWSON, STANDARD FORM CONTRACTS AND DEMOCRATIC CONTROL OF LAW MAKING POWER

84 Harv.L.Rev. 529, 530, 532 (1971).

Standard form contracts probably account for more than ninety-nine percent of all the contracts now made. Most persons have difficulty remembering the last time they contracted other than by standard form; except for casual oral agreements, they probably never have. But if they are active, they contract by standard form several times a day. Parking lot and theater tickets, package receipts, department store charge slips, and gas station credit card purchase slips are all standard form contracts.

Moreover, standard forms have come to dominate more than just routine transactions. For individuals, if not quite yet for corporations, form contracts are in common use for even such important matters as insurance, leases, deeds, mortgages, automobile purchases, and all of the various forms of consumer credit. The contracting still imagined by courts and law teachers as

---

i. Arthur L. Corbin (1874–1967) taught contract law at Yale Law School from 1903 to 1943. His treatise, Corbin on Contracts, is per-   haps the most respected of all legal treatises. A photograph of Professor Corbin appears at page 761.

typical, in which both parties participate in choosing the language of their entire agreement, is no longer of much more than historical importance.

* * *

The predominance of standard forms is the best evidence of their necessity. They are characteristic of a mass production society and an integral part of it. They provide information and enforce order. A typical automobile insurance policy, for example, informs the policyholder how to conduct himself should he become involved in an accident or other kind of occurrence from which liability of the kind covered may arise. It enforces all or a part of such conduct by the sanction of denying insurance protection unless it is performed. These services are essential, and if they are to be provided at reasonable cost, they must be standardized and mass-produced like other goods and services in an industrial economy. The need for order could, in theory, be fully satisfied by officially drafted rules—by laws in the traditional sense. One of the beliefs by which our society is organized, however, is that at least some lawmaking is better accomplished in a decentralized manner. We therefore prefer that the economy be controlled privately to a large extent, and private control today means control largely by standard form.

* * *

* * * The extreme specialization of function of modern life requires that we contract with each other too frequently to take the time to reach even a mildly complicated agreement every time we do, and the complexity of modern life and modern law combine to demand that even minor agreements usually be complicated.

———

In some settings in which form agreements are used, one of the parties is virtually certain not to consult a lawyer and not to bargain with the other party over terms. Can you imagine bringing a lawyer along with you to Sears when you buy a new video recorder for your home? In today's world, Sears has the power to dictate the terms of its sale of the recorder to you. You must accept its terms or not buy the recorder from Sears. (Of course, the power of buyers in the aggregate will affect some of Sears' decisions.) Later, in Chapter Five, we will see that the law may intercede on behalf of the consumer in such "contracts of adhesion," but at the stage when the consumer purchases the item there is usually no role for a lawyer acting on behalf of the consumer to help draft and negotiate the agreement. Of course, lawyers for Sears will draft its forms.

Form agreements are also common in commercial transactions. Examples are purchase orders and sales confirmations. In addition to drafting such forms, lawyers may be asked to review them to help clients decide whether to sign. Even a consumer may ask a lawyer for such advice if the transaction is important enough.

When a lawyer chooses to use a standard form, he or she may still alter it in some way. This is often done in real estate transactions, for example. Consider these general thoughts on when a lawyer should utilize a standard form in a particular transaction:

MACNEIL, A PRIMER OF CONTRACT PLANNING
48 S.Cal.L.Rev. 627, 653–56 (1975).

A lawyer must also be aware of the nature and optimal use of standardized forms in planning the performance relationship. Forms are but one aspect of the standardization of the specification of performance relationships, a phenomenon always resulting from techniques of mass production of goods and services. * * *

* * *

* * * The lawyer is justified in using an *unaltered* form only when he knows from prior experience or otherwise that the proposed relationship will be identical to the one for which the form was designed, and that the form is still well designed for its purpose. * * * [Emphasis supplied.]

Advantages of forms in legal framework planning itself are obvious: they are convenient and efficient. There is, however, vast variation in the quality of forms. Moreover, using any form can be dangerous. First, the legal framework contained in the form simply may not fit the relationship being planned. In addition, however good the form may be as far as it goes, it may not constitute complete legal framework planning. Finally, a form may have become outdated because of changes in the law.

Every lawyer has to decide for himself on numerous occasions the extent to which he will utilize a form. Few will or should always rise to Dickerson's suggestion that:

> the danger that the form will lull him into a false sense of accomplishment is so great that in other than the most routine situations he is wise to use it mainly as a cross check.[j]

But the lawyer failing to follow Dickerson's next dictum is no lawyer, simply a hack: "He must not forget that he has been engaged to exercise his professional judgment, not to serve as a mere retrieval system."

C. A BRIEF INTRODUCTION TO RELATIONAL EXCHANGE

Planning the White–Benkowski agreement entailed special challenges. Unlike buying a coat off the rack (sometimes called a discrete exchange largely because there is relatively little interaction between the parties), the White–Benkowski exchange was relational in nature in that it occurred through time in a process of continuous interaction between the parties.

The differences between discrete and relational exchanges are important for the lawyer planning an agreement. The more "relational" an exchange, that is, the more it is projected into the future, the more likely the parties and their lawyers will be unable in advance to define performance obligations with precision or to allocate risks optimally. One result is that the parties and their lawyers may have to rely on norms to govern their relation other than those arising from the original agreement. These norms may call for cooperation and compromise, if the parties are to achieve the fruits of their agreement.[k]

---

j. Dickerson, Fundamentals of Legal Drafting 19, 53 (1965).

k. The pioneering scholarship on relational exchange is by Professor Ian R. Macneil of

SECTION TWO: MAJOR SOCIAL RESOURCES THAT FACILITATE AGREEMENTS AND THEIR PERFORMANCE

The making and performance of agreements flourish in our society. Consider how many agreements you are a party to at this moment. Presumably you have one with your law school and one with your landlord. What others?

The reasons why agreements are so widespread in our society are complex. One explanation is that specialization of labor, which results because of its efficiency, creates the need for exchange behavior. As individuals specialize, they become less self-sufficient and more dependent on others' goods and services, which they then must secure through agreements.

K. LLEWELLYN, CONTRACT: INSTITUTIONAL ASPECTS
Encyclopedia of Social Science 330–31 (1931).

Bargain is * * * the social and legal machinery appropriate to arranging affairs in any specialized economy which relies on exchange rather than tradition (the manor) or authority (the army) for apportionment of productive energy and of product. Contract in the strict sense is the specifically legal machinery appropriate when such an economy moves into the phase of credit dealings, i.e. of future dealings in general—in which aspect the mutual reliance of two dealers on their respective promises comes of course into major importance. This machinery of contract applies in general to the market for land, goods, services, credit or any combination of these. * * *

———

We now introduce in subsections A and B below a number of major resources of society deployed directly and indirectly to facilitate agreements and to secure the benefits that may come from them.

A. RESOURCES NOT PRIMARY OBJECTS OF STUDY IN THIS BOOK, BUT OF IMPORTANCE TO ITS THEMES

Our society invests enormous resources in ways that directly or indirectly facilitate the making and performance of agreements. Some of these, while very important, are not the focus of this book. For example, we expend vast legal resources every day to keep order and social peace. The criminal law, for example, is deployed in part to this end. If our society were not tolerably well-ordered, the making and performance of agreements could not flourish.

At least of equal importance, our society provides a system of public education. As a result, people have much greater capacity to plan and manage their lives. Among other things, they are better able to realize personal goals

Northwestern University Law School (formerly of Cornell and Virginia). See, e.g., Macneil, The New Social Contract (1980); Macneil, "Contracts: Adjustment of Long-Term Economic Relations Under Classical, Neoclassical, and Relational Contract Law," 72 Nw.U.L.Rev. 854 (1978).

through agreements. Our educational system also fosters technological and other advances that vastly expand the range of human choice and thus the fruits of agreements.

Our society also deploys resources to help people obtain jobs and to help business entities succeed. As a result, more people have the means to enter agreements. Examples range from the use of a central banking system to provide credit and stimulate investment to a social security system that helps people meet the basic needs of life.

Through governmental activity, society also facilitates the daily functioning of communications networks and transportation systems. These networks and systems today extend the reach of markets far beyond what they once were.

Our legal system also invests resources to prevent private parties and governmental bodies from erecting unjustified barriers to the making and performance of agreements. For example, we have constitutional and other laws forbidding one state from imposing tariffs against goods from another state. In this and other ways our legal system nurtures and protects national markets in which private parties from different states may contract freely. Our system has also adopted antitrust and other regulatory laws prohibiting various forms of anti-competitive behavior that reduce the range and variety of choice. (Of course, not all such laws work well toward these ends.)

The legal system also provides for the creation and operation of various kinds of business organizations and other entities capable of entering and performing agreements. These include: unions, corporations, trade associations, partnerships, and so on.

A great many additional laws facilitate exchange through agreements. These laws include rules providing for a uniform monetary system, establishing a uniform system of weights and measures, imposing regulatory obligations of disclosure, setting standards of product quality, protecting against third party interference with contractual rights, and recognizing property interests in the fruits of exchange—in goods bought, in houses purchased, in wages and salaries earned, and so on.

B. RESOURCES TO BE STUDIED IN THIS BOOK

We now turn to the main types of resources to be studied closely in this course. All these resources are deployed directly or indirectly to facilitate agreements and the realization of benefits from them.

A Legal Profession With Generalists and Specialists in Contract and Related Law. As indicated in the case of White v. Benkowski, our system recognizes and facilitates the availability of specially trained personnel—lawyers—who can, in various ways, help parties realize their goals through agreements. We have now identified most of the diverse roles of the lawyer in the practice of contract and related law. Throughout this book we will study these roles, and will develop standards for evaluating the performance of the lawyer.

Valid Agreements Between Individuals and Various Entities. This book opened with the White–Benkowski agreement, and we will encounter a number of other more or less complete agreements in the course of our study. Such agreements are the main source of legal duties that parties incur in this field. When such agreements are drafted by third parties, they are usually drafted by lawyers. The requirements of a valid legal agreement are studied in Chapters Four and Five.

Law Recognizing and Structuring General Theories of Legal Obligation. As we have noted, the predominant theory of legal obligation studied in this book is agreement with consideration. The Whites invoked this theory as the basis for their legal claim against the Benkowskis for compensatory damages. We will study this and other theories of obligation in Chapter Two.

Law Defining the Boundaries of Freedom to Enter Agreements. Various forms of law define limitations on the freedom of parties to enter agreements. In White v. Benkowski, the parties did not include any language in their agreement that ran afoul of legal limitations on their freedom. But there are several such limitations. Suppose, for example, that the Whites and the Benkowskis had agreed that if the Benkowskis turned off the Whites' water, the Whites would be entitled to exact a private "fine" of $100 for each such occasion? This would not have been upheld in court. We will study this particular limitation in Section Six of Chapter Three, and others in later chapters. Upper-level law courses consider numerous other limitations.

Law Policing the Consummation and Content of Agreements. A major function of our law is to police the consummation and content of agreements. We will study several policing doctrines, mainly in Chapter Five. One such doctrine is that a contract or a clause of a contract may be unenforceable because "unconscionable." One authoritative version of this doctrine appears in section 2–302(1) of the Uniform Commercial Code:

> If the court as a matter of law finds the contract or any clause of the contract to have been unconscionable at the time it was made the court may refuse to enforce the contract, or it may enforce the remainder of the contract without the unconscionable clause, or it may so limit the application of any unconscionable clause as to avoid any unconscionable result.

Can you think of a clause the Whites and Benkowskis might have included that would have been unconscionable? We will see that this general body of law overlaps with the law defining the freedom to enter agreements.

Law Determining the Content of Duties to Perform Agreements. As we saw in White v. Benkowski, agreements are often incomplete or unclear. For example, what is the meaning of "become inadequate" in the clause providing for termination of the agreement if the well "should * * * become inadequate to supply said 2 homes"? In such situations, various forms of general law—law not explicitly embodied in the agreement—may be applied to determine the duties imposed by the agreement. This general law includes rules of interpretation, rules governing the sequence of performance, rules filling gaps in agreements, rules governing the admissibility of evidence of terms not included in written agreements, rules structuring the effect of custom, rules of good faith, and more. These are the subject of Chapters Six and Seven.

Rules and techniques of interpretation facilitate drafting, counseling, and negotiating, and guide the courts in the event of a lawsuit. For example, suppose water agreements such as the Whites' and Benkowskis' were common in Oak Creek, Wisconsin, and that in Oak Creek, the phrase "inadequate water supply" had taken on special meaning (e.g., muddy water more than once a week). Courts often rely on such evidence under the rubric of "custom and usage." When this is so, the parties' lawyers can use such language in the agreement and can tell their clients with some confidence how the language will be interpreted in court. If a dispute arises as to the meaning of the language, the parties can be expected to settle their differences without litigation.

Law Governing Breach, Repudiation, and Permissible Responses. Whether action or inaction constitutes a breach or repudiation depends largely on the content of the parties' agreement. For example, the agreement between the Whites and the Benkowskis might have provided that the Whites would be in breach for failing to pay $400 for a new pump by a particular date. The agreement might also have set forth the Benkowskis' appropriate responses to any such breach. On the other hand, the agreement might fail to define breach or to set forth responses or both. Here, legal rules fill the gaps. See Chapter Seven.

Law Governing the Maturation and Excuse of Contract Duties. For various reasons, one party may not become obligated to perform duties under an agreement. For example, the duty to perform may not "mature" under the very language of the agreement. Assume the Benkowskis agreed to deliver water only after the Whites performed their promise to provide $400 for a new pump. Must the Benkowskis deliver any water if the Whites breach by failing to pay the $400? This breach would constitute a failure of an express condition and would excuse the Benkowskis from delivering any water. A change in circumstances following the consummation of an agreement also may excuse a party from performance. For example, an unanticipated drought might greatly reduce the water supply from the Benkowskis' well, and thereby excuse the Benkowskis from performance. These matters are studied in Chapters Seven, Eight, and Nine.

Law Governing the Rights and Duties of Third Parties. Contract and related law governs not only the rights and duties of immediate parties, but also the rights and duties of more remote parties, such as those who "buy" a contract right and those who are benefited by a contract performance. For example, this area of the law determines whether a purchaser of the Whites' home could enforce the Benkowskis' obligation to supply water to the home. We study third-party rights and duties in Chapters Ten and Eleven.

Law Defining and Providing Remedies. Much general law in this field deals with the availability of judicial remedies. We caught a glimpse of some of this law "in action" in the case of White v. Benkowski, including law on both compensatory and punitive damages. We will now introduce two basic questions which we will study intensively in Chapters Two and Three: (1) What judicial remedies are available in this field? (2) What is the relationship between these remedies and the general theories of obligation operative here?

SECTION THREE: GENERAL THEORIES OF OBLIGATION AND REMEDIES— AN INTRODUCTION

A. THEORIES OF OBLIGATION

In general, judges and lawyers do not recognize legal duties merely in an *ad hoc* fashion from case to case. Rather, they decide on the existence of such duties largely in accord with the requirements of a general theory of obligation. We introduced this concept earlier and defined it as a recognized general basis for imposing legal duties. Recall that the applicable general theory of obligation in White v. Benkowski was agreement with consideration.

Although the rights and duties of the Whites and Benkowskis arose from an agreement with consideration—an enforceable contract—and although this is the predominant theory of obligation in this field, you should not pose issues of obligation and remedy in an all-or-nothing fashion: either there is an enforceable contract and hence a remedy available for its breach, or there is no enforceable contract and hence no duties and no remedies of any kind. To pose such issues in this way is to invoke what Professor Fuller called the "contract-no contract" dichotomy, a highly misleading mode of analysis. In truth, there are the following general theories of obligation, all of which will be studied in some detail in Chapter Two:

1. Obligation arising from an agreement with consideration (and any required writing)

2. Obligation arising from justified reliance on a promise—"promissory estoppel"

3. Obligation arising from unjust enrichment

4. Obligation arising from promises for benefit received

5. Obligation arising from tort

6. Obligation arising solely from "form"

7. Obligation arising from a statutory warranty

We now briefly introduce the reliance and unjust enrichment theories merely to demonstrate the range and variety of potentially operative theories in this field. The facts of White v. Benkowski illustrate these theories. Suppose the water-supply agreement required the Whites to buy a pump for $400 to be installed on the Benkowskis' premises and, after purchase but prior to installation, the Benkowskis repudiated the agreement. Suppose further that the Whites resold the pump for $350. In this example, the Whites reasonably relied on the Benkowskis' promise to supply water and sustained a loss. If, for some reason, the agreement was not enforceable (let us assume, for example, that it was too indefinite), the Whites could not recover the $50 loss on the theory that the Benkowskis breached a valid agreement with consideration. Nevertheless, in most states they could recover on the independent theory of justified reliance—"promissory estoppel."

Another theory affords relief for unjust enrichment in contract and related contexts. Suppose the Benkowskis actually installed the $400 pump on their premises and put it to use, but thereafter they repudiated their deal with the Whites. Assume again that the agreement was too indefinite to be enforced. Here the Benkowskis would still be enriched at the Whites' expense and, pursuant to a widely accepted general theory of obligation, the Whites would be entitled to recover the value of the benefit conferred to prevent unjust enrichment of the Benkowskis.

Sometimes more than one theory of obligation will be applicable to the same set of facts. Even so, each theory may have independent significance.

B. REMEDIES

A theory of obligation includes various dimensions in addition to the requirements for a prima facie duty to arise under the theory. One of the most important dimensions specifies remedies for breach of a duty arising under a theory. Monetary remedies include: (1) lost expectancy damages designed to put the plaintiff in the monetary position he or she would have been in if the agreement or promise had been performed; (2) reliance damages designed to put the plaintiff in the monetary position he or she would have been in if the agreement or promise had not been made; and (3) a sum equivalent to the value of any benefit the plaintiff conferred on the defendant, thereby restoring this value to the plaintiff. Beyond these, there are other possibilities, as we will see. Indeed, even though the requirements of a theory of obligation are met, an aggrieved plaintiff may recover no more than nominal damages.

Basic remedial possibilities and their relationships to theories of obligation are explored further in the problem and case that follow.

Problem 1–1

Sam Grainseller was a grain dealer in Omaha where there is a well-organized grain market. Grainbuyer Inc. was a milling company in a town 20 miles away. On January 10, Sam agreed in writing to sell 1000 bushels of Orfed bearded white wheat to Grainbuyer for $3.55 per bushel, delivery September 1 at Sam's grain elevator in Omaha. On September 1, Grainbuyer sent trucks to Sam's elevator at a cost of $500, but when they arrived the drivers were told that Sam would not deliver, having "sold out." On September 2, after a careful survey of possibilities, Grainbuyer bought 1000 bushels of the same type of wheat from another seller near Sam at $5.55 a bushel, and again incurred $500 shipping costs. Grainbuyer Inc. wants to know its rights and remedies against Sam.

This deal is governed by the Uniform Commercial Code.[1] Article 2 of the Code, entitled "Sales," by its terms applies to "transactions in goods." U.C.C. § 2–102. "Goods" include "all things * * * which are movable at the time of identification to the contract for sale * * *." U.C.C. § 2–105(1). While the "transactions in goods" language is broader than mere sales and presumably includes leases and

---

1. Most of Articles 1 and 2 of the Code (the latter dealing with the sale of goods) were drafted by Professor Karl N. Llewellyn (1893–1962). He was a professor of law at Columbia University, Yale University and the University of Chicago, and was one of this country's leading legal scholars and a major theorist of jurisprudence. He was chief draftsman of the Uni- form Commercial Code and author of many articles and books, including The Bramble Bush (1930) (a set of lectures for beginning law students), and The Common Law Tradition— Deciding Appeals (1960). A fine biography is W. Twining, Karl Llewellyn and The Realist Movement (1972). A photograph appears at page 559.

bailments of goods, many sections of Article 2 refer specifically to sales. For example, note the definition of goods in section 2–105(1), above. This curious approach to the scope of Article 2 produces some confusion. In this problem, however, is there any question as to whether Article 2 applies? Article 1 of the Code, entitled "General Provisions," also is relevant whenever another Article applies to a problem. Among the various Code sections applicable here is section 1–106, set forth below. Under it, what damages would Grainbuyer receive for Sam's breach? Is this appropriate? On what theory of obligation would this remedy be based?

U.C.C. § 1–106. Remedies to be Liberally Administered

(1) The remedies provided by this Act shall be liberally administered to the end that the aggrieved party may be put in as good a position as if the other party had fully performed but neither consequential or special nor penal damages may be had except as specifically provided in this Act or by other rule of law.

SULLIVAN v. O'CONNOR

Supreme Judicial Court of Massachusetts, 1973.
363 Mass. 579, 296 N.E.2d 183.

KAPLAN, JUSTICE.

The plaintiff patient secured a jury verdict of $13,500 against the defendant surgeon for breach of contract in respect to an operation upon the plaintiff's nose. The substituted consolidated bill of exceptions presents questions about the correctness of the judge's instructions on the issue of damages.

The declaration was in two counts. In the first count, the plaintiff alleged that she, as patient, entered into a contract with the defendant, a surgeon, wherein the defendant promised to perform plastic surgery on her nose and thereby to enhance her beauty and improve her appearance; that he performed the surgery but failed to achieve the promised result; rather the result of the surgery was to disfigure and deform her nose, to cause her pain in body and mind, and to subject her to other damage and expense. The second count, based on the same transaction, was in the conventional form for malpractice, charging that the defendant had been guilty of negligence in performing the surgery. Answering, the defendant entered a general denial.

On the plaintiff's demand, the case was tried by jury. At the close of the evidence, the judge put to the jury, as special questions, the issues of liability under the two counts, and instructed them accordingly. The jury returned a verdict for the plaintiff on the contract count, and for the defendant on the negligence count. The judge then instructed the jury on the issue of damages.

As background to the instructions and the parties' exceptions, we mention certain facts as the jury could find them. The plaintiff was a professional entertainer, and this was known to the defendant. The agreement was as alleged in the declaration. More particularly, judging from exhibits, the plaintiff's nose had been straight, but long and prominent; the defendant undertook by two operations to reduce its prominence and somewhat to shorten it, thus making it more pleasing in relation to the plaintiff's other features. Actually the plaintiff was obliged to undergo three operations, and her appearance was worsened. Her nose now had a concave line to about the midpoint, at which it became bulbous; viewed frontally, the nose from bridge to midpoint was flattened and broadened, and the two sides of the tip had lost symmetry. This configuration evidently could not be improved by further surgery. The plaintiff did not demonstrate, however, that her change of appearance had resulted in loss of employment. Payments by the plaintiff covering the defendant's fee and hospital expenses were stipulated at $622.65.

The judge instructed the jury, first, that the plaintiff was entitled to recover her out-of-pocket expenses incident to the operations. Second, she could recover the damages flowing directly, naturally, proximately, and foreseeably from the defendant's breach of promise. These would comprehend damages for any disfigurement of the plaintiff's nose—that is, any change of appearance for the worse—including the effects of the consciousness of such disfigurement on the plaintiff's mind, and in this connection the jury should consider the nature of the plaintiff's profession. Also consequent upon the defendant's breach, and compensable, were the pain and suffering involved in the third operation, but not in the first two. As there was no proof that any loss of earnings by the plaintiff resulted from the breach, that element should not enter into the calculation of damages.

By his exceptions the defendant contends that the judge erred in allowing the jury to take into account anything but the plaintiff's out-of-pocket expenses (presumably at the stipulated amount). The defendant excepted to the judge's refusal of his request for a general charge to that effect, and, more specifically, to the judge's refusal of a charge that the plaintiff could not recover for pain and suffering connected with the third operation or for impairment of the plaintiff's appearance and associated mental distress.

The plaintiff on her part excepted to the judge's refusal of a request to charge that the plaintiff could recover the difference in value between the nose as promised and the nose as it appeared after the operations. However, the plaintiff in her brief expressly waives this exception and others made by her in case this court overrules the defendant's exceptions; thus she would be content to hold the jury's verdict in her favor.

We conclude that the defendant's exceptions should be overruled.

It has been suggested on occasion that agreements between patients and physicians by which the physician undertakes to effect a cure or to bring about a given result should be declared unenforceable on grounds of public policy. See Guilmet v. Campbell, 385 Mich. 57, 76, 188 N.W.2d 601 (dissenting opinion). But there are many decisions recognizing and enforcing such contracts, see annotation, 43 A.L.R.3d 1221, 1225, 1229–1233, and the law of Massachusetts has treated them as valid, although we have had no decision meeting head on the contention that they should be denied legal sanction. Small v. Howard, 128 Mass. 131; Gabrunas v. Miniter, 289 Mass. 20, 193 N.E. 551; Forman v. Wolfson, 327 Mass. 341, 98 N.E.2d 615. These causes of action are, however, considered a little suspect, and thus we find courts straining sometimes to read the pleadings as sounding only in tort for negligence, and not in contract for breach of promise, despite sedulous efforts by the pleaders to pursue the latter theory. See Gault v. Sideman, 42 Ill.App.2d 96, 191 N.E.2d 436 * * *.

It is not hard to see why the courts should be unenthusiastic or skeptical about the contract theory. Considering the uncertainties of medical science and the variations in the physical and psychological conditions of individual patients, doctors can seldom in good faith promise specific results. Therefore it is unlikely that physicians of even average integrity will in fact make such promises. Statements of opinion by the physician with some optimistic coloring are a different thing, and may indeed have therapeutic value. But patients may transform such statements into firm promises in their own minds, especially when they have been disappointed in the event, and testify in that sense to sympathetic juries.[1] If actions for breach of promise can be readily maintained, doctors, so it is said, will be frightened into practising "defensive medicine." On the other hand, if these actions were outlawed, leaving only the possibility of suits for malpractice, there is fear that the public might be exposed to the enticements of charlatans, and confidence in the profession might ultimately be shaken. See Miller, The Contractual Liability of Physicians and Surgeons, 1953 Wash.L.Q. 413, 416–423. The law has taken the middle of the road position of allowing actions based on alleged contract, but insisting on clear proof. Instructions to the jury may well stress this requirement and point to tests of truth, such as the complexity or difficulty of an operation as bearing on the probability that a given result was promised. See annotation, 43 A.L.R.3d 1225, 1225–1227.

If an action on the basis of contract is allowed, we have next the question of the measure of damages to be applied where liability is found. Some cases have taken the simple view that the promise by the physician is to be treated like an ordinary commercial promise, and accordingly that the successful plaintiff is entitled to a standard measure of recovery for breach of contract— "compensatory" ("expectancy") damages, an amount intended to put the plaintiff in the position he would be in if the contract had been performed, or, presumably, at the plaintiff's election, "restitution" damages, an amount corresponding to any benefit conferred by the plaintiff upon the defendant in the performance of the contract disrupted by the defendant's breach. See Restatement: Contracts § 329 and comment a, §§ 347, 384(1). Thus in Hawkins v. McGee, 84 N.H. 114, 146 A. 641, the defendant doctor was taken to have promised the plaintiff to convert his damaged hand by means of an operation into a good or perfect hand, but the doctor so operated as to damage the hand still further. The court, following the usual expectancy formula, would have asked the jury to estimate and award to the plaintiff the difference between the value of a good or perfect hand, as promised, and the value of the hand after the operation. (The same formula would apply, although the dollar result would be less, if the operation had neither worsened nor improved the condition of the hand.) If the plaintiff had not yet paid the doctor his fee, that amount would be deducted from the recovery. There could be no recovery for the pain and suffering of the operation, since that detriment would have been incurred even if the operation had been successful; one can say that this detriment was not "caused" by the breach. But where the plaintiff by reason of the operation was put to more pain than he

hand example

---

1. Judicial skepticism about whether a promise was in fact made derives also from the possibility that the truth has been tortured to give the plaintiff the advantage of the longer period of limitations sometimes available for actions on contract as distinguished from those in tort or for malpractice. See Lillich, The Malpractice Statute of Limitations in New York and Other Jurisdictions, 47 Cornell L.Q. 339; annotation, 80 A.L.R.2d 368.

would have had to endure, had the doctor performed as promised, he should be compensated for that difference as a proper part of his expectancy recovery. It may be noted that on an alternative count for malpractice the plaintiff in the *Hawkins* case had been nonsuited; but on ordinary principles this could not affect the contract claim, for it is hardly a defence to a breach of contract that the promisor acted innocently and without negligence. The New Hampshire court further refined the *Hawkins* analysis in McQuaid v. Michou, 85 N.H. 299, 157 A. 881, all in the direction of treating the patient-physician cases on the ordinary footing of expectancy. * * *

Other cases, including a number in New York, without distinctly repudiating the *Hawkins* type of analysis, have indicated that a different and generally more lenient measure of damages is to be applied in patient-physician actions based on breach of alleged special agreements to effect a cure, attain a stated result, or employ a given medical method. This measure is expressed in somewhat variant ways, but the substance is that the plaintiff is to recover any expenditures made by him and for other detriment (usually not specifically described in the opinions) following proximately and foreseeably upon the defendant's failure to carry out his promise. Robins v. Finestone, 308 N.Y. 543, 546, 127 N.E.2d 330. * * * This, be it noted, is not a "restitution" measure, for it is not limited to restoration of the benefit conferred on the defendant (the fee paid) but includes other expenditures, for example, amounts paid for medicine and nurses; so also it would seem according to its logic to take in damages for any worsening of the plaintiff's condition due to the breach. Nor is it an "expectancy" measure, for it does not appear to contemplate recovery of the whole difference in value between the condition as promised and the condition actually resulting from the treatment. Rather the tendency of the formulation is to put the plaintiff back in the position he occupied just before the parties entered upon the agreement, to compensate him for the detriments he suffered in reliance upon the agreement. This kind of intermediate pattern of recovery for breach of contract is discussed in the suggestive article by Fuller and Perdue, The Reliance Interest in Contract Damages, 46 Yale L.J. 52, 373, where the authors show that, although not attaining the currency of the standard measures, a "reliance" measure has for special reasons been applied by the courts in a variety of settings, including noncommercial settings. See 46 Yale L.J. at 396–401.[2]

For breach of the patient-physician agreements under consideration, a recovery limited to restitution seems plainly too meager, if the agreements are to be enforced at all. On the other hand, an expectancy recovery may well be excessive. The factors, already mentioned, which have made the cause of action somewhat suspect, also suggest moderation as to the breadth of the recovery that should be permitted. Where, as in the case at bar and in a number of the reported cases, the doctor has been absolved of negligence by the trier, an expectancy measure may be thought harsh. We should recall here that the fee paid by the patient to the doctor for the alleged promise would usually be quite disproportionate to the putative expectancy recovery. To

2. Some of the exceptional situations mentioned where reliance may be preferred to expectancy are those in which the latter measure would be hard to apply or would impose too great a burden; performance was interfered with by external circumstances; the contract was indefinite. See 46 Yale L.J. at 373–386; 394–396.

attempt, moreover, to put a value on the condition that would or might have resulted, had the treatment succeeded as promised, may sometimes put an exceptional strain on the imagination of the fact finder. As a general consideration, Fuller and Perdue argue that the reasons for granting damages for broken promises to the extent of the expectancy are at their strongest when the promises are made in a business context, when they have to do with the production or distribution of goods or the allocation of functions in the market place; they become weaker as the context shifts from a commercial to a noncommercial field. 46 Yale L.J. at 60–63.

There is much to be said, then, for applying a reliance measure to the present facts, and we have only to add that our cases are not unreceptive to the use of that formula in special situations. We have, however, had no previous occasion to apply it to patient-physician cases.[3]

The question of recovery on a reliance basis for pain and suffering or mental distress requires further attention. We find expressions in the decisions that pain and suffering (or the like) are simply not compensable in actions for breach of contract. The defendant seemingly espouses this proposition in the present case. True, if the buyer under a contract for the purchase of a lot of merchandise, in suing for the seller's breach, should claim damages for mental anguish caused by his disappointment in the transaction, he would not succeed; he would be told, perhaps, that the asserted psychological injury was not fairly foreseeable by the defendant as a probable consequence of the breach of such a business contract. See Restatement: Contracts, § 341, and comment a. But there is no general rule barring such items of damage in actions for breach of contract. It is all a question of the subject matter and background of the contract, and when the contract calls for an operation on the person of the plaintiff, psychological as well as physical injury may be expected to figure somewhere in the recovery, depending on the particular circumstances. The point is explained in Stewart v. Rudner, 349 Mich. 459, 469, 84 N.W.2d 816. Cf. Frewen v. Page, 238 Mass. 499, 131 N.E. 475; McClean v. University Club, 327 Mass. 68, 97 N.E.2d 174. Again, it is said in a few of the New York cases, concerned with the classification of actions for statute of limitations purposes, that the absence of allegations demanding

---

3. In Mt. Pleasant Stable Co. v. Steinberg, 238 Mass. 567, 131 N.E. 295, the plaintiff company agreed to supply teams of horses at agreed rates as required from day to day by the defendant for his business. To prepare itself to fulfill the contract and in reliance on it, the plaintiff bought two "Cliest" horses at a certain price. When the defendant repudiated the contract, the plaintiff sold the horses at a loss and in its action for breach claimed the loss as an element of damages. The court properly held that the plaintiff was not entitled to this item as it was also claiming (and recovering) its lost profits (expectancy) on the contract as a whole. Cf. Noble v. Ames Mfg. Co., 112 Mass. 492. (The loss on sale of the horses is analogous to the pain and suffering for which the patient would be disallowed a recovery in Hawkins v. McGee, 84 N.H. 114, 146 A. 641, because he was claiming and recovering expectancy damages.) The court in the *Mt. Pleasant* case referred, however, to Pond v. Harris, 113

Mass. 114, as a contrasting situation where the expectancy could not be fairly determined. There the defendant had wrongfully revoked an agreement to arbitrate a dispute with the plaintiff (this was before such agreements were made specifically enforceable). In an action for the breach, the plaintiff was held entitled to recover for his preparations for the arbitration which had been rendered useless and a waste, including the plaintiff's time and trouble and his expenditures for counsel and witnesses. The context apparently was commercial but reliance elements were held compensable when there was no fair way of estimating an expectancy. See, generally, annotation, 17 A.L.R.2d 1300. A noncommercial example is Smith v. Sherman, 4 Cush. 408, 413–414, suggesting that a conventional recovery for breach of promise of marriage included a recompense for various efforts and expenditures by the plaintiff preparatory to the promised wedding. * * *

recovery for pain and suffering is characteristic of a contract claim by a patient against a physician, that such allegations rather belong in a claim for malpractice. See Robins v. Finestone, 308 N.Y. 543, 547, 127 N.E.2d 330; Budoff v. Kessler, 2 A.D.2d 760, 153 N.Y.S.2d 654. These remarks seem unduly sweeping. Suffering or distress resulting from the breach going beyond that which was envisaged by the treatment as agreed, should be compensable on the same ground as the worsening of the patient's condition because of the breach. Indeed it can be argued that the very suffering or distress "contracted for"—that which would have been incurred if the treatment achieved the promised result—should also be compensable on the theory underlying the New York cases. For that suffering is "wasted" if the treatment fails. Otherwise stated, compensation for this waste is arguably required in order to complete the restoration of the status quo ante.[4]

In the light of the foregoing discussion, all the defendant's exceptions fail: the plaintiff was not confined to the recovery of her out-of-pocket expenditures; she was entitled to recover also for the worsening of her condition,[5] and for the pain and suffering and mental distress involved in the third operation. These items were compensable on either an expectancy or a reliance view. We might have been required to elect between the two views if the pain and suffering connected with the first two operations contemplated by the agreement, or the whole difference in value between the present and the promised conditions, were being claimed as elements of damage. But the plaintiff waives her possible claim to the former element, and to so much of the latter as represents the difference in value between the promised condition and the condition before the operations.

Plaintiff's exceptions waived.[m]

Defendant's exceptions overruled.

———

4. Recovery on a reliance basis for breach of the physician's promise tends to equate with the usual recovery for malpractice, since the latter also looks in general to restoration of the condition before the injury. But this is not paradoxical, especially when it is noted that the origins of contract lie in tort. See Farnsworth, The Past of Promise: An Historical Introduction to Contract, 69 Col.L.Rev. 576, 594–596. * * *

It would, however, be a mistake to think in terms of strict "formulas." For example, a jurisdiction which would apply a reliance measure to the present facts might impose a more severe damage sanction for the wilful use by the physician of a method of operation that he undertook not to employ.

5. That condition involves a mental element and appraisal of it properly called for consideration of the fact that the plaintiff was an entertainer. Cf. McQuaid v. Michou, 85 N.H. 299, 303–304, 157 A. 881 (discussion of continuing condition resulting from physician's breach).

m. For a discussion of the different types of reasons set forth by Justice Kaplan, see Appendix A of this book.

Dec. 8, 1938

Professor Karl N. Llewellyn
School of Law
Columbia University
New York City

Dear Karl:

* * * To me it seems clear that no analysis of contract law can be realistic or adequate which does not recognize that there exists a hierarchy of contract interests, which may be sloganized by saying that they extend from restitution through the reliance interest to the expectation interest, with a number of little midstations, disturbing to elegantia juris, along the way. * * * I feel, incidentally, that your failure to employ this approach is attributable in part to your preoccupation with businessmen's business agreements, especially sales. * * * I consider the contribution made in my article on the reliance interest to lie, not in calling attention to the reliance interest itself, but in an analysis which breaks down the contract-no contract dichotomy, and substitutes an ascending scale of enforceability. * * *

Sincerely yours,
Lon L. Fuller[n]

LON L. FULLER

n. Harvard Law School Library, Lon L. Fuller Papers.

Note
More on the "Contract-no Contract" Dichotomy

Professor Fuller's letter indicates that leading professors of law such as Karl Llewellyn may have been fooled by the contract-no contract dichotomy. Not surprisingly, the dichotomy is very challenging for students too. Professor Fuller's "hierarchy of contract interests" should become much clearer to you as you study Chapter 2.

The dichotomy also misleadingly suggests that lost expectancy damages are (and should be) automatically available for breach of an enforceable contract. Consistent with this interpretation, instead of varying in force depending on the context, a theory of obligation either applies or it does not with nothing in between. A natural corollary of such a view is an all-or-nothing approach to remedies rather than a variable approach in accord with Fuller's analysis in his letter to Llewellyn and in Sullivan v. O'Connor. The latter case nicely exposes the fallacy of "on-off" thinking in relation to the theory of agreement with consideration. In Sullivan, the award of lost expectancy damages would have imposed extensive liability on the defendant. In the court's view, such an award would therefore require the strongest rationales. But as the court pointed out, the context suggested that Sullivan may not have received a "firm promise" at all. Moreover, the consideration paid by Sullivan was disproportionate to the putative expectancy recovery. Further, the value of the promised result was very difficult to measure. Not every valid agreement with consideration, when broken, will justify the award of full lost expectancy damages.

The contract-no contract dichotomy is misleading in still other ways. We explore this general subject in later chapters.

*

Chapter Two

GENERAL THEORIES
OF OBLIGATION

*The most important general feature
of law is that certain kinds of
human conduct are no longer
optional, but in some sense
obligatory.*

H.L.A. HART

SECTION ONE: THEORIES OF OBLIGATION AND THEIR RELEVANCE TO THE LAWYER'S ROLE

In this chapter, we study in depth various theories of obligation operative in contractual and related affairs, including agreement with consideration, promissory estoppel, and unjust enrichment. The number of such theories is not fixed and occasionally new theories emerge. Moreover, the dimensions of existing theories may change. Further, even the most developed theory of obligation may not alone resolve all the legal issues that arise in a case. Thus, a court may decide a case soundly even though the outcome cannot be justified solely on the basis of an existing theory of obligation. For example, in Sullivan v. O'Connor in Chapter One, the court decided the issues partly on the basis of a general theory and partly on the basis of considerations peculiar to the circumstances.

Nevertheless, general theories of obligation predominate in this field. The lawyer must understand these theories and deploy them effectively as a planner, drafter, counselor, negotiator, and litigator. The primacy of basic theory is hardly exceptional. As Justice Oliver Wendell Holmes, Jr. once remarked, "[t]heory is the most important part * * * of the law, as the architect is the most important man who takes part in the building of a house."[a]

When the requirements of a general theory of obligation are satisfied, primary duties and correlative rights arise. For example, when the Benkowskis and the Whites entered into a valid agreement with consideration, the

---

a. Holmes, The Path of the Law, 10 Harv. L.Rev. 457, 477 (1897). Oliver Wendell Holmes, Jr. (1841–1935) practiced law, taught law briefly at Harvard, served as a justice of the Supreme Judicial Court of Massachusetts for twenty years, and served for thirty years as a Justice of the Supreme Court of the United States. His writings have had great influence. All students of the law should read something by and about him. Perhaps the most readable biography is C. Bowen, Yankee from Olympus (1943). Holmes's book, The Common Law (1881), is a landmark that includes three important chapters on contract. The late Justice Felix Frankfurter said of this book that it "is a classic in the sense that its stock of ideas has been absorbed and become part of common juristic thought. * * *" F. Frankfurter, Of Law and Men 167 (1956).

Benkowskis incurred a primary duty to provide household water to the Whites and the Whites acquired a correlative right to that water. A primary duty is a duty to perform, and it must be differentiated from a remedial duty—a duty to pay damages, for example, in the event of breach.

Because of the undoubted importance of a remedy for the breach of a primary duty, and because a general theory of obligation serves as a premise for such a remedy, one common view among judges, lawyers, and theorists of contract is that the significance of theories, and of the primary duties that arise under them, may be measured *solely* in terms of the remedies available for breach of those duties. Even Justice Holmes took this narrow view:

> [I]n the law of contract * * * so called primary * * * duties are invested with a mystic significance. * * * [But] the duty to keep a contract at common law means a prediction that you must pay damages if you do not keep it,—and nothing else. If you commit a tort, you are liable to pay a compensatory sum. If you commit a contract, you are liable to pay a compensatory sum unless the promised event comes to pass, and that is all the difference.[b]

Of course, the "cash value" of the breach of a primary duty *is* important to business people and others. It must also be conceded that remedial considerations may distinctively influence judges when they decide whether and how far a theory of obligation applies to a particular case. (Again, see Sullivan v. O'Connor.) It follows that the lawyer practicing in this field must be remedies-minded.

But the significance of general theories of obligation and of the primary duties arising under them cannot be measured solely in terms of the remedies available for breach. For example, the parties want their agreement to be a source of *legal* duties not only so that a remedy will be available in the event of breach, but also, and more importantly, so that those duties have what theorists call *normative* significance.[c] The normative significance of legal duties arising under a valid agreement can take a variety of forms. Legal duties serve for the parties as sources of *justifying reasons* to perform the required actions. Partly because the parties attach such normative significance to the duties and rights they create, disputes in contractual and related affairs arise less frequently. And when a dispute does arise, one or both of the parties (sometimes with the aid of lawyers) will cite duties under the agreement as bases for *claims of right,* which may help resolve the dispute. Even when the deal breaks down, the duties that arose under the agreement may still function as *grounds for criticizing* the parties' actions, and this, in turn, may lead to a settlement without resort to court action. Moreover, the agreement serves as a source of *standards for evaluating* a court's decision and justifications, when the court resolves a dispute in light of the agreement.

b. Holmes, The Path of the Law, 10 Harv. L.Rev. 457, 462 (1897).

c. See H.L.A. Hart, The Concept of Law, chs. IV and V (1961). Professor Hart is the first Anglo–American legal theorist to clarify and stress the normative character of private law duties. He is one of the two or three most influential English speaking legal theorists of the twentieth century. After study at Oxford and preparation for the bar, he practiced for nine years at the Chancery bar (1931–1939). He was at the British War Office during World War II and then returned to Oxford, where he became professor of jurisprudence in 1952. Hart is an innovative adherent of the positivist tradition. For a fine general treatment and a bibliography, see D. Neil MacCormick, H.L.A. Hart (Stanford, 1981).

In the foregoing ways, then, the parties will ordinarily view the duties (and rights) arising under a theory of obligation (here, agreement with consideration) from an internal *normative* vantage-point, rather than merely from the external *predictive* point of view (as per *Holmes*) in which "the duty to keep a contract * * * [merely] means a prediction that you must pay damages if you do not keep it." Viewed normatively, a valid agreement is far more than a mere basis for predicting the availability of judicial remedies for its breach.[d]

In the materials that follow in this chapter, we concentrate mainly on two basic dimensions of general theories of obligation of major interest to the lawyer. The first consists of the substantive requirements, defined by law, for the prima facie applicability of each theory. For example, what are the requirements of a valid agreement with consideration? The second consists of the general justifying rationale (or rationales) supporting each theory. We will see that theories vary not only in their basic requirements for applicability, but also in their justifying rationales. We stress these rationales here for they often influence judicial decisions on whether a theory applies.

In later chapters, we will see that theories of obligation have still other dimensions. For example, although the basic requirements of a theory are satisfied so that a prima facie duty arises, the party obligated may assert a defense such as the "unconscionability" of a term, or a "material breach" by the other party.

SECTION TWO: OBLIGATION ARISING FROM AN AGREEMENT WITH CONSIDERATION—THE LEADING THEORY

In this section, we concentrate on the "bargain" concept of consideration. Consideration is one of the basic requirements of the leading theory of obligation in contractual and related affairs. We also touch on aspects of the second basic requirement of this theory, a valid "agreement," but we postpone systematic study of this requirement until Chapter Four.

We open with cases on the concept of consideration as bargained-for exchange. This concept has deep historical roots, including roots in ancient common-law pleading and procedure. We explore these early roots in Appendix B.

HARDESTY v. SMITH
Supreme Court of Indiana, 1851.
3 Ind. 39.

[One Isham sold the rights to an invention, allegedly improving a lamp, to the defendant, Smith. Smith paid for the rights by signing some promissory notes. The notes were assigned to the plaintiff, Hardesty, who sought to collect on them. Smith alleged an affirmative defense that the supposed improvement in the lamp was worthless.]

PERKINS, J.

d. A few contemporary economic analysts of law deny that legally valid contractual duties have any normative significance. We will return to this question at page 345.

[T]he plaintiff demurred generally. The Court * * * overruled [the demurrer] * * * and the defendant had final judgment in his favor.

* * *

* * * [T]he Court erred in not sustaining the demurrer. * * * The simple fact that the improvement in the lamp was of no utility, is not sufficient to bar a suit on these notes. Parties of sufficient mental capacity for the management of their own business, have a right to make their own bargains. The owner of a thing has the right to fix the price at which he will part with it, and a buyer's own judgment ought to be his best guide as to what he should give to obtain it. The consideration agreed upon may indefinitely exceed the value of the thing for which it is promised, and still the bargain stand. The doing of an act by one at the request of another, which may be a detriment or inconvenience, however slight, to the party doing it, or may be a benefit, however slight, to the party at whose request it is performed, is a legal consideration for a promise by such requesting party. So the parting with a right, which one possesses, to another, at his request, may constitute a good consideration. And where one person examines an invention to the use of which another has the exclusive right, and, upon his own judgment, uninfluenced by fraud, or warranty, or mistake of facts, agrees to give a certain sum for the conveyance of that right to him, such conveyance forms a valid consideration for such agreement. The judgment of the purchaser is the best arbiter of whether the thing is of any value, and how great, to him. The chance he may acquire of gain, the power he may obtain of preventing any other person from attempting to introduce the use of the invention in competition with some rival one such purchaser may, at the time, own the right to, or some other motive, may induce him willingly to pay a sum of money, in such case, for that which, in the end, may prove valueless in itself. On the other hand, as we have already said, loss, or trouble, or inconvenience, or expense, on the part of the grantor, or seller, without any profit to the buyer, is a good consideration. So the simple parting with a right which is one's own, and which he has a right to fix a price upon, must be a good consideration for a promise to pay that price. In such cases, the purchaser *gets a something* * * *.

* * * When a party gets all the consideration he honestly contracted for, he cannot say he gets no consideration, or that it has failed. If this doctrine be not correct, then it is not true that parties are at liberty to make their own contracts. And if, where an article is fairly sold and purchased, for a stipulated consideration, a Court or jury may annul the bargain if they come to the conclusion the article sold was of no value, then they should be permitted, in every case, where they may conclude the article is worth something, to determine whether it is worth as much as has been promised for it, and, if it is not, to reduce the amount to be paid to that point; thus doing away with all special contracts. * * *

Per Curiam.—The judgment is reversed with costs. Cause remanded.

DOUGHERTY v. SALT

New York Court of Appeals, 1919.
227 N.Y. 200, 125 N.E. 94.

Appeal from Supreme Court, Appellate Division, Second Department.

Action by Charles Napoleon Dougherty, an infant, by Susan M. Teves, his guardian, against Emma L. Salt, as executrix of the last will and testament of Helena M. Dougherty, deceased. From a judgment of the second department of the Appellate Division of the Supreme Court (184 App.Div. 910, 170 N.Y.Supp. 1076), reversing a judgment of the Trial Term, which set aside a verdict of the jury in favor of plaintiff and dismissed the complaint, and reinstating the verdict and directing judgment thereon, the defendant appeals. Judgment of Appellate Division reversed, and judgment of Trial Term modified by granting a new trial. Affirmed.

CARDOZO, J.[e] The plaintiff, a boy of eight years, received from his aunt, the defendant's testatrix, a promissory note for $3,000, payable at her death or before. Use was made of a printed form, which contains the words "value received." How the note came to be given was explained by the boy's guardian, who was a witness for his ward. The aunt was visiting her nephew.

> "When she saw Charley coming in, she said, 'Isn't he a nice boy?' I answered her, Yes; that he is getting along very nice, and getting along nice in school; and I showed where he had progressed in school, having good reports, and so forth, and she told me that she was going to take care of that child; that she loved him very much. I said, 'I know you do, Tillie, but your taking care of the child will be done probably like your brother and sister done, take it out in talk.' She said, 'I don't intend to take it out in talk; I would like to take care of him now.' I said, 'Well, that is up to you.' She said, 'Why can't I make out a note to him?' I said, 'You can, if you wish to.' She said, 'Would that be right?' And I said, 'I do not know, but I guess it would; I do not know why it would not.' And she said, 'Well, will you make out a note for me?' I said, 'Yes, if you wish me to,' and she said, 'Well, I wish you would.' "

A blank was then produced, filled out, and signed. The aunt handed the note to her nephew, with these words:

> "You have always done for me, and I have signed this note for you. Now, do not lose it. Some day it will be valuable."

The trial judge submitted to the jury the question whether there was any consideration for the promised payment. Afterwards, he set aside the verdict in favor of the plaintiff, and dismissed the complaint. The Appellate Division, by a divided court, reversed the judgment of dismissal, and reinstated the verdict on the ground that the note was sufficient evidence of consideration.

We reach a different conclusion. The inference of consideration to be drawn from the form of the note has been so overcome and rebutted as to

e. Benjamin N. Cardozo (1870–1938) was a judge of the New York Court of Appeals from 1914 until 1932 (Chief Judge the last six years). In 1932, President Hoover appointed Cardozo to the United States Supreme Court to replace the retiring Oliver Wendell Holmes, Jr. A highly literate judge, Cardozo also wrote a number of books. The best known is The Nature of the Judicial Process (1921).

leave no question for a jury. This is not a case where witnesses, summoned by the defendant and friendly to the defendant's cause, supply the testimony in disproof of value. Strickland v. Henry, 175 N.Y. 372, 67 N.E. 611. This is a case where the testimony in disproof of value comes from the plaintiff's own witness, speaking at the plaintiff's instance. The transaction thus revealed admits of one interpretation, and one only. The note was the voluntary and unenforcible promise of an executory gift. Harris v. Clark, 3 N.Y. 93, 51 Am.Dec. 352; Holmes v. Roper, 141 N.Y. 64, 66, 36 N.E. 180. This child of eight was not a creditor, nor dealt with as one. The aunt was not paying a debt. She was conferring a bounty. Fink v. Cox, 18 Johns. 145, 9 Am.Dec. 191. The promise was neither offered nor accepted with any other purpose. "Nothing is consideration that is not regarded as such by both parties." (Philpot v. Gruninger, 14 Wall. 570, 577 * * *).

A note so given is not made for "value received," however its maker may have labeled it. The formula of the printed blank becomes, in the light of the conceded facts, a mere erroneous conclusion, which cannot overcome the inconsistent conclusion of the law. * * * The plaintiff through his own witness, has explained the genesis of the promise, and consideration has been disproved. Neg.Instr.Law, § 54 (Consol. Laws, c. 38).

We hold, therefore, that the verdict of the jury was contrary to law, and that the trial judge was right in setting it aside.

[The court then ordered a new trial based on a New York procedural rule.]

* * *

The judgment of the Appellate Division should be reversed, and the judgment of the Trial Term modified by granting a new trial, and, as modified, affirmed, with costs in all courts to abide the event.

Judgment accordingly.

STONESTREET v. SOUTHERN OIL CO., 226 N.C. 261, 263, 37 S.E.2d 676, 677 (1946). "[W]hen one receives a naked promise and such promise is not kept, he is no worse off than he was before the promise was made. He gave nothing for it, loses nothing by it, and upon its breach he suffers no recoverable damage."

Problem 2–1

Suppose you had been counsel to the guardian of Charles Napoleon Dougherty and had been asked to draft an agreement with consideration obligating Helena M. Dougherty to pay the sum promised. Draft the agreement.

RESTATEMENT (FIRST) OF CONTRACTS § 75 (1932).

Definition of Consideration.

(1) Consideration for a promise is

    (a) an act other than a promise, or

    (b) a forbearance, or

(c) the creation, modification or destruction of a legal relation, or

(d) a return promise,

bargained for and given in exchange for the promise.

(2) Consideration may be given to the promisor or to some other person. It may be given by the promisee or by some other person.

WILLISTON,[f] RESTATEMENT OF CONTRACTS IS PUBLISHED BY THE AMERICAN LAW INSTITUTE
18 A.B.A.J. 775, 776–77 (1932).

The rules to be derived from a multitude of decisions are sometimes clear and sometimes open to dispute; but in any event the sources from which the rules are to be sought become more and more bulky as time passes. Inconsistencies, uncertainties and complexities are the sure accompaniments of bulk, as well as increased expenditure of time in seeking applicable rules. The difficulty has not become overwhelming as yet, but surely must become so. One need only multiply the annual production of law reports by a number of years, say fifty to one hundred, small in the history of a country, to realize what search in an accumulated mass of decisions may mean.

* * * The situation is sufficiently serious now to make it evident that the prodigious material from which our law must be sought should be summarized as effectively and as soon as possible.

* * *

* * * Statutes, however, are not likely at present, or in the immediate future, to afford an adequate solution to the problem presented by the bulk and diversity of decisions. And so far as a solution is ultimately approximated in that way the solution will be aided and more satisfactorily carried out if a preliminary attempt is made, as it is in the Restatement, to frame rules in statutory form, the correctness of which can be tested by the courts when there is not the rigidity that statutes necessarily have.

* * *

It was the essence of the plan that it should be a cooperative effort in which each statement should receive the careful thought of the body of experts, and later receive the approval of the Council and of the whole body of the Institute. Every sentence of the Restatement of Contracts has been prepared and considered in this way. * * * It seemed that the Restatement would be more likely to achieve an authority of its own that would to some extent, at least, free courts from part of the troublesome weighing of cases and arguments if exact rules were clearly stated without argument. Those who have prepared the Restatement have had arguments among themselves— hundreds of them. They believe it better to give the net results of their

---

f. Samuel Williston (1861–1963) was a Professor of Law at Harvard Law School. He was one of the two foremost scholars of American contract law in this century, and was Reporter of the Restatement (First) of Contracts. He authored an influential multi-volume treatise, Williston on Contracts, and drafted a number of influential statutes, including the Uniform Sales Act. He also wrote an autobiography, Life and Law (1940).

arguments than to present the arguments themselves with supporting authorities.

L. FULLER, INTRODUCTION TO THE JURISPRUDENCE OF INTERESTS
xx (M. Schoch trans. 2d ed. 1948).

[T]he Restatements represent a * * * systematic statement of legal principles. The law they expound is not exactly a purposeless law, but it is a law intentionally abstracted from its purposes in the process of exposition, on the theory that this divorce is conducive to certainty in application.[g]

FULLER, AMERICAN LEGAL PHILOSOPHY AT MIDCENTURY
6 J. Legal Ed. 457, 470 (1954).

The essential meaning of a legal rule lies in a purpose, or more commonly, in a congeries of purposes.

K. LLEWELLYN, THE BRAMBLE BUSH
157–58 (1951 ed.).

[T]he rule follows where its reason leads; where the reason stops, there stops the rule.

FULLER, CONSIDERATION AND FORM
41 Colum.L.Rev. 799, 799–802, 806–07, 810–11, 812–15 (1941).

What is attempted in this article is an inquiry into the rationale of legal formalities, and an examination of the common-law doctrine of consideration in terms of its underlying policies. * * *

That consideration may have both a "formal" and a "substantive" aspect is apparent when we reflect on the reasons which have been advanced why promises without consideration are not enforced. It has been said that consideration is "for the sake of evidence" and is intended to remove the hazards of mistaken or perjured testimony which would attend the enforcement of promises for which nothing is given in exchange. Again, it is said that enforcement is denied gratuitous promises because such promises are often made impulsively and without proper deliberation. In both these cases the objection relates, not to the content and effect of the promise, but to the manner in which it is made. Objections of this sort * * * touch the form rather than the content of the agreement. * * * On the other hand, it has been said that the enforcement of gratuitous promises is not an object of sufficient importance to our social and economic order to justify the expenditure of the time and energy necessary to accomplish it. Here the objection is one of "substance" since it touches the significance of the promise made and not merely the circumstances surrounding the making of it.

g. For discussion of the idea of a "restatement," and also of legal method and reasoning, see Appendix C.

The task proposed in this article is that of disentangling the "formal" and "substantive" elements in the doctrine of consideration. * * *[T]he policies underlying the doctrine are generally left unexamined in the decisions and doctrinal discussions * * *.

I.   The Functions Performed by Legal Formalities

§ 2. *The Evidentiary Function.*—The most obvious function of a legal formality is, to use Austin's words, that of providing "evidence of the existence and purport of the contract, in case of controversy." The need for evidentiary security may be satisfied in a variety of ways: by requiring a writing, or attestation, or the certification of a notary. * * *

§ 3. *The Cautionary Function.*—A formality may also perform a cautionary or deterrent function by acting as a check against inconsiderate action. The seal in its original form fulfilled this purpose remarkably well. The affixing and impressing of a wax wafer—symbol in the popular mind of legalism and weightiness—was an excellent device for inducing the circumspective frame of mind appropriate in one pledging his future. To a less extent any requirement of a writing, of course, serves the same purpose, as do requirements of attestation, notarization, etc.

§ 4. *The Channeling Function.*—Though most discussions of the purposes served by formalities go no further than the analysis just presented, this analysis stops short of recognizing one of the most important functions of form. * * * In seeking to understand [the] channeling function of form, perhaps the most useful analogy is that of language * * *. One who wishes to communicate his thoughts to others must force the raw materials of meaning into defined and recognizable channels; he must reduce the fleeting entities of wordless thought to the patterns of conventional speech. One planning to enter a legal transaction faces a similar problem. His mind first conceives an economic or sentimental objective, or * * * set of overlapping objectives. He must then, with or without the aid of a lawyer, cast about for the legal transaction (written memorandum, sealed contract, lease, conveyance of the fee, etc.) which will most nearly accomplish these objectives.

* * *

II.   The Substantive Bases of Contract Liability

§ 7. *Private Autonomy.*—Among the basic conceptions of contract law the most pervasive and indispensable is the principle of private autonomy. This principle simply means that the law views private individuals as possessing a power to effect, within certain limits, changes in their legal relations. The man who conveys property to another is exercising this power; so is the man who enters a contract. When a court enforces a promise it is merely arming with legal sanction a rule or *lex* previously established by the party himself. This power of the individual to effect changes in his legal relations with others is comparable to the power of a legislature. * * *

* * *

* * * Though occasional philosophers may seem to dispute the proposition, most of us are willing to concede that some kind of regulation of men's relations among themselves is necessary. It is this general desideratum which underlies the principle of private autonomy. Whenever we can reinforce this

general need for regulation by a showing that in the particular case private agreement is the best or the only available method of regulation, then in such a case "the principle of private autonomy" may properly be referred to as a "substantive" basis of contract liability.

§ 9. *Reliance.*—A second substantive basis of contract liability lies in a recognition that the breach of a promise may work an injury to one who has changed his position in reliance on the expectation that the promise would be fulfilled. * * *

* * *

§ 10. *Unjust Enrichment.*—In return for B's promise to give him a bicycle, A pays B five dollars; B breaks his promise. We may regard this as a case where the injustice resulting from breach of a promise relied on by the promisee is aggravated. The injustice is aggravated because not only has A lost five dollars but B has gained five dollars unjustly. If, following Aristotle, we conceive of justice as being concerned with maintaining a proper proportion of goods among members of society, we may reduce the relations involved to mathematical terms. Suppose A and B have each initially ten units of goods. The relation between them is then one of equivalence, 10:10. A loses five of his units in reliance on a promise by B which B breaks. The resulting relation is 5:10. If, however, A paid these five units over to B, the resulting relation would be 5:15. This comparison shows why unjust enrichment resulting from breach of contract presents a more urgent case for judicial intervention than does mere loss through reliance not resulting in unjust enrichment.

* * *

§ 12. *The Relation of Form to the Substantive Bases of Contract Liability.*—Form has an obvious relationship to the principle of private autonomy. Where men make laws for themselves it is desirable that they should do so under conditions guaranteeing the desiderata described in our analysis of the functions of form. Furthermore, the greater the assurance that these desiderata are satisfied, the larger the scope we may be willing to ascribe to private autonomy. * * *

* * *

III. The Policies, "Formal" and "Substantive," Underlying the Common–Law Requirement of Consideration

§ 13. *Reasons for Refusing to Enforce the Gratuitous and Unrelied-on Promise.*—A promises to give B $100; B has in no way changed his position in reliance on this promise, and he has neither given nor promised anything in return for it. In such a situation enforcement of the promise is denied both in the common law and in the civil law. We give as our reason, "lack of consideration"; the civilians point to a failure to comply with statutory formalities. In neither case, of course, does the reason assigned explain the policies which justify excluding this promise from enforcement. An explanation in terms of underlying policies can, however, be worked out on the basis of the analysis just completed.

Looking at the case from the standpoint of the substantive bases of contractual liability we observe, first of all, that there is here neither reliance nor unjust enrichment. Furthermore, gratuities such as this one do not present an especially pressing case for the application of the principle of private autonomy, particularly if we bear in mind the substantive deterrents to judicial intervention. While an exchange of goods is a transaction which conduces to the production of wealth and the division of labor, a gift is, in Bufnoir's words, a "sterile transmission." If on "substantive" grounds the balance already inclines away from judicial intervention, the case against enforcement becomes stronger when we draw into account the desiderata underlying the use of formalities. That there is in the instant case a lack of evidentiary and cautionary safeguards is obvious. As to the channeling function of form, we may observe that the promise is made in a field where intention is not naturally canalized. There is nothing here to effect a neat division between tentative and exploratory expressions of intention, on the one hand, and legally effective transactions, on the other. In contrast to the situation of the immediate gift of a chattel (where title will pass by the manual tradition), there is here no "natural formality" on which the courts might seize as a test of enforceability.

§ 14. *The Contractual Archetype—the Half–Completed Exchange.*—A delivers a horse to B in return for B's promise to pay him ten dollars; B defaults on his promise, and A sues for the agreed price. In this case are united all the factors we have previously analyzed as tending in the direction of enforcement of a promise. On the substantive side, there is reliance by A and unjust enrichment of B. The transaction involves an exchange of economic values, and falls therefore in a field appropriately left to private autonomy in an economy where no other provision is made for the circulation of goods and the division of labor, or where (as perhaps in primitive society) an expanding economy makes the existing provision for those ends seem inadequate. On the side of form, the delivery and acceptance of the horse involve a kind of natural formality, which satisfies the evidentiary, cautionary, and channeling purposes of legal formalities.

KREITNER, THE GIFT BEYOND THE GRAVE: REVISITING THE QUESTION OF CONSIDERATION
101 Colum. L. Rev. 1876, 1937; 1941–42 (2001).

When looking for the underlying justification for the doctrine, the purpose served by consideration could be viewed in a number of ways: The most influential way was as a test of when it is useful for the legal system to intervene in disputes, raising the question of whether the interaction between the parties is "productive" and therefore worthy of the effort of enforcement. The critique of this view is primarily that it relies on a false intuition that gratuitous promises are unproductive, whereas in fact there is nothing to support such an intuition and much to refute it.

* * *

[Professor Melvin] Eisenberg revisits his first attempt to justify the donative promise principle * * *. If at first Eisenberg favored nonenforcement of donative promises for essentially negative reasons (i.e., that the legal system was not well equipped to deal with the problems they raised, especially questions of proof and deliberativeness), his recent discussion proposes a positive, if counterintuitive, explanation: Our social world is richer, according to Eisenberg, when donative promises remain outside the scope of legal intervention. He writes:

> The world of gift is a world of our better selves, in which affective values like love, friendship, affection, gratitude, and comradeship are the prime motivating forces. These values are too important to be enforced by law and would be undermined if the enforcement of simple, affective donative promises were to be mandated by the law. It is just because these values are usually missing from the more impoverished world of contract that the law must play a central role in that world.

Eisenberg reaches this conclusion by presenting the world of contract as one driven by alienated and impersonal values, reducible for the most part to commodities and prices. The world of gift, on the other hand, characterized by affective considerations, should be protected from commodification. The counterintuitive aspect of Eisenberg's position is that he sets out to protect the world of gift, arguing that such protection must come not by direct enforcement of its values, but rather through nonenforcement of transactions in the gift world, which can then remain pure of the alienated forces of legal intervention.

Problem 2–2

Fuller offers what he calls "substantive reasons" and "reasons of form" that may provide supporting justifications for the *content* of Restatement (First) of Contracts section 75. He thus fleshes out the bare bones of the section, drafted by Professor Williston, who thought such "exact rules" should be "clearly stated" *without* supporting reasons. (Do you agree with Williston?) Fuller also undertakes to fill gaps in many judicial opinions. According to him, "the policies underlying the doctrine [of consideration] are generally left unexamined in the decisions." Were these policies in fact left unexamined in the first two decisions in this chapter? In light of Fuller's reasons of substance and reasons of form, were these two cases correctly decided? What of the cases that immediately follow?

MAUGHS v. PORTER

Virginia Supreme Court of Appeals, 1931.
157 Va. 415, 161 S.E. 242.

PRENTIS, C.J.

The record discloses that to the plaintiff's notice of motion for $461 the defendant filed a general demurrer, which was sustained. To that judgment plaintiff has been allowed a writ of error.

The motion is based upon these facts: The defendant inserted this advertisement in the "Daily Progress," a newspaper published in Charlottesville, Va.:

"New Model Ford Free

"At the auction fifty (50) beautiful residence lots Fry's Spring, Thursday, October 13, 1:30 on time. Every white person over sixteen (16) years of age has an equal chance at the New Ford regardless of buying or bidding. Come to the auction of Oak Lawns."

Responding to that advertisement, the plaintiff, a white person over sixteen years of age, attended the sale, and received from the defendant a slip of paper upon which, by direction of the auctioneer, she placed her name, and deposited it in a box held by the auctioneer. Upon the drawing of the slip from the box, she was adjudged the winner of the automobile. In response to the auctioneer's demand, she paid him $3 for his services in drawing the lucky number.

The defendant placed an order for the car with the Albemarle Motor Company, but refused to pay for it when it was ready for delivery, and has also refused the demand of the plaintiff that he pay her the value of the car, alleged to be $461.

The defendant demurred to the notice of motion, alleging two grounds, thus stated: (1) That the matters alleged in the plaintiff's notice of motion fail to show a sufficient consideration for defendant's promise, and that defendant's promise is nudum pactum, and hence unenforceable; (2) that, in so far as there was any consideration for defendant's promise, the scheme alleged in the notice of motion is a lottery or raffle, and any contract which might otherwise arise therefrom is illegal and unenforceable.

The questions then are: (1) Whether the alleged offer to make the gift can be enforced as supported by a sufficient consideration; and, if it should be determined that there was such a consideration as would otherwise support the gift, then (2) whether the transaction constitutes a lottery, which is prohibited by Constitution, § 60, and by statute, Code, §§ 4693, 4694.

First. In Spooner v. Hilbish, 92 Va. 341, 23 S.E. 751, 753, we find this clear statement by Riely, J.: "A gift is a contract without a consideration, and, to be valid, must be executed. A valid gift is therefore a contract executed. It is to be executed by the actual delivery by the donor to the donee, or to some one for him, of the thing given, or by the delivery of the means of obtaining the subject of the gift, without further act of the donor to enable the donee to reduce it to his own possession. 'The intention to give must be accompanied by a delivery, and the delivery must be made with an intention to give.' Otherwise there is only an intention or promise to give, which, being gratuitous, would be a mere nullity. Delivery of possession of the thing given, or of the means of obtaining it so as to make the disposal of it irrevocable, is indispensable to a valid gift." * * *

* * *

Clearly then the plaintiff, under the facts shown here, cannot recover, unless defendant is bound by a promise which is supported by a consideration sufficient to support the action.

It is often quite difficult to determine in such cases whether or not there is such a consideration.

1 Williston on Contracts, § 112, p. 232, thus illustrates the difficulty: "If a benevolent man says to a tramp: 'If you go around the corner to the clothing shop there, you may purchase an overcoat on my credit,' no reasonable person would understand that the short walk was requested as the consideration for the promise, but that in the event of the tramp going to the shop the promisor would make him a gift. Yet the walk to the shop is in its nature capable of being consideration. It is a legal detriment to the tramp to make the walk,

and the only reason why the walk is not consideration is because on a reasonable construction it must be held that the walk was not requested as the price of the promise, but was merely a condition of a gratuitous promise. It is often difficult to determine whether words of condition in a promise indicate a request for consideration or state a mere condition in a gratuitous promise. An aid, though not a conclusive test in determining which construction of the promise is more reasonable is an inquiry whether the happening of the condition will be a benefit to the promisor. If so, it is a fair inference that the happening was requested as a consideration. On the other hand, if, as in the case of the tramp stated above, the happening of the condition will be not only of no benefit to the promisor but is obviously merely for the purpose of enabling the promisee to receive a gift, the happening of the event on which the promise is conditional, though brought about by the promisee in reliance on the promise, will not properly be construed as consideration. In case of doubt where the promisee has incurred a detriment on the faith of the promise, courts will naturally be loath to regard the promise as a mere gratuity and the detriment incurred as merely a condition. But in some cases it is so clear that a conditional gift was intended that even though the promisee has incurred detriment, the promise has been held unenforceable."

Under the first ground of demurrer in this case it is contended for the defendant that this was not a promise for a consideration, but on the contrary, was a mere condition of the proposed gift.

We conclude, however, that there was sufficient consideration to support the gift and but for the other question involved this would determine the case. The object of the defendant unquestionably was to attract persons to the auction sale with the hope of deriving benefit from the crowd so augmented. Even though persons attracted by the advertisement of the free automobile might attend only because hoping to draw the automobile, and with the determination not to bid for any of the lots, some of these even might nevertheless be induced to bid after reaching the place of sale. So we conclude that the attendance of the plaintiff at the sale was a sufficient consideration for the promise to give an automobile, which could be enforced if otherwise legal.

[The court went on to hold that defendant's promise was unenforceable as a lottery.]

Affirmed.

HAMER v. SIDWAY

Court of Appeals of New York, 1891.
124 N.Y. 538, 27 N.E. 256.

Appeal from an order of the general term of the supreme court in the fourth judicial department, reversing a judgment entered on the decision of the court at special term in the county clerk's office of Chemung county on the 1st day of October, 1889. The plaintiff presented a claim to the executor of William E. Story, Sr., for $5,000 and interest from the 6th day of February, 1875. She acquired it through several mesne assignments from William E. Story, 2d. The claim being rejected by the executor, this action was brought. It appears that William E. Story, Sr., was the uncle of William E. Story, 2d;

that at the celebration of the golden wedding of Samuel Story and wife, father and mother of William E. Story, Sr., on the 20th day of March, 1869, in the presence of the family and invited guests, he promised his nephew that if he would refrain from drinking, using tobacco, swearing, and playing cards or billiards for money until he became 21 years of age, he would pay him the sum of $5,000. The nephew assented thereto, and fully performed the conditions inducing the promise. When the nephew arrived at the age of 21 years, and on the 31st day of January, 1875, he wrote to his uncle, informing him that he had performed his part of the agreement, and had thereby become entitled to the sum of $5,000. The uncle received the letter, and a few days later, and on the 6th day of February, he wrote and mailed to his nephew the following letter: "Buffalo, Feb. 6, 1875. W.E. Story, Jr.—Dear Nephew: Your letter of the 31st ult. came to hand all right, saying that you had lived up to the promise made to me several years ago. I have no doubt but you have, for which you shall have five thousand dollars, as I promised you. I had the money in the bank the day you was twenty-one years old that I intend for you, and you shall have the money certain. Now, Willie, I do not intend to interfere with this money in any way till I think you are capable of taking care of it, and the sooner that time comes the better it will please me. I would hate very much to have you start out in some adventure that you thought all right and lose this money in one year. The first five thousand dollars that I got together cost me a heap of hard work. You would hardly believe me when I tell you that to obtain this I shoved a jack-plane many a day, butchered three or four years, then came to this city, and, after three months' perseverance, I obtained a situation in a grocery store. I opened this store early, closed late, slept in the fourth story of the building in a room 30 by 40 feet, and not a human being in the building but myself. All this I done to live as cheap as I could to save something. I don't want you to take up with this kind of fare. * * * Willie, you are twenty-one, and you have many a thing to learn yet. This money you have earned much easier than I did, besides acquiring good habits at the same time, and you are quite welcome to the money. Hope you will make good use of it. I was ten long years getting this together after I was your age. * * * Truly yours, W.E. STORY. P.S. You can consider this money on interest." The nephew received the letter, and thereafter consented that the money should remain with his uncle in accordance with the terms and conditions of the letter. The uncle died on the 29th day of January, 1887, without having paid over to his nephew any portion of the said $5,000 and interest. * * *

PARKER, J. * * * The defendant contends that the contract was without consideration to support it, and therefore invalid. He asserts that the promisee, by refraining from the use of liquor and tobacco, was not harmed, but benefited; that that which he did was best for him to do, independently of his uncle's promise,—and insists that it follows that, unless the promisor was benefited, the contract was without consideration,—a contention which, if well founded, would seem to leave open for controversy in many cases whether that which the promisee did or omitted to do was in fact of such benefit to him as to leave no consideration to support the enforcement of the promisor's agreement. Such a rule could not be tolerated, and is without foundation in the law. The exchequer chamber in 1875 defined "consideration" as follows: "A valuable consideration, in the sense of the law, may consist either in some right, interest, profit, or benefit accruing to the one party, or some forbearance, detriment, loss, or responsibility given, suffered, or undertaken by the other." Courts "will not ask whether the thing which forms the consideration does in fact benefit the promisee or a third party, or is of any substantial value to any one. It is enough that something is promised, done, forborne, or suffered by the party to whom the promise is made as consideration for the promise made to him." Anson, Cont. 63. "In general a waiver of any legal right at the request of another party is a sufficient consideration for a promise." Pars.Cont. *444. "Any damage, or suspension, or forbearance of a right will be sufficient to sustain a promise." 2 Kent, Comm. (12th Ed.) *465. Pollock in his work on Contracts, (page 166,) after citing the definition given by the exchequer chamber, already quoted, says: "The second branch of this judicial description is really the most important one. 'Consideration' means not so much that one party is profiting as that the other abandons some legal right in the present, or limits his legal freedom of action in the future, as an inducement for the promise of the first." Now, applying this rule to the facts before us, the promisee used tobacco, occasionally drank liquor, and he had a legal right to do so. That right he abandoned for a period of years upon the strength of the promise of the testator that for such forbearance he would give him $5,000. We need not speculate on the effort which may have been required to give up the use of those stimulants. It is sufficient that he restricted his lawful freedom of action within certain prescribed limits upon the faith of his uncle's agreement, and now, having fully performed the conditions imposed, it is of no moment whether such performance actually proved a benefit to the promisor, and the court will not inquire into it; but, were it a proper subject of inquiry, we see nothing in this record that would permit a determination that the uncle was not benefited in a legal sense. Few cases have been found which may be said to be precisely in point, but such as have been, support the position we have taken. * * *

The order appealed from should be reversed, and the judgment of the special term affirmed, with costs payable out of the estate. All concur.

RESTATEMENT (SECOND) OF CONTRACTS § 81.
Consideration as Motive or Inducing Cause

(1) The fact that what is bargained for does not of itself induce the making of a promise does not prevent it from being consideration for the promise.

(2) The fact that a promise does not of itself induce a performance or return promise does not prevent the performance or return promise from being consideration for the promise.[h]

Comment:

a. *"Bargained for."* Consideration requires that a performance or return promise be "bargained for" in exchange for a promise; this means that the promisor must manifest an intention to induce the performance or return promise and to be induced by it, and that the promisee must manifest an

---

h. Does this section of the second Restatement also consist solely of bare bones in need of Fullerian flesh? Do Comments a and b provide some flesh?

intention to induce the making of the promise and to be induced by it. * * * In most commercial bargains the consideration is the object of the promisor's desire and that desire is a material motive or cause inducing the making of the promise, and the reciprocal desire of the promisee for the making of the promise similarly induces the furnishing of the consideration.

b. *Immateriality of motive or cause.* This Section makes explicit a limitation on the requirement that consideration be bargained for. Even in the typical commercial bargain, the promisor may have more than one motive, and the person furnishing the consideration need not inquire into the promisor's motives. Unless both parties know that the purported consideration is mere pretense, it is immaterial that the promisor's desire for the consideration is incidental to other objectives and even that the other party knows this to be so. * * * Subsection (2) states a similar rule with respect to the motives of the promisee.

ALLEGHENY COLLEGE v. NATIONAL CHAUTAUQUA COUNTY BANK OF JAMESTOWN, 246 N.Y. 369, 373, 159 N.E. 173, 174 (1927).

Cardozo, C.J.

"A classic form of statement identifies consideration with detriment to the promisee sustained by virtue of the promise. (Hamer v. Sidway * * *.) So compendious a formula is little more than a half truth. There is need of many a supplementary gloss before the outline can be so filled in as to depict the classic doctrine. 'The promise and the consideration must purport to be the motive each for the other, in whole or at least in part. It is not enough that the promise induces the detriment or that the detriment induces the promise if the other half is wanting.' * * * If A promises B to make him a gift, consideration may be lacking, though B has renounced other opportunities for betterment in the faith that the promise will be kept."

G. GILMORE, THE DEATH OF CONTRACT
111 n. 34 (1974).

Hamer v. Sidway * * * illustrates * * * that the New York Court of Appeals (unlike most American courts) * * * rejected the so-called bargain theory of consideration.

BAEHR v. PENN–O–TEX OIL CORP.
Supreme Court of Minnesota, 1960.
258 Minn. 533, 104 N.W.2d 661.

Loevinger, Justice.

This is an action for rents which defendant is claimed to owe plaintiff because of possession and contract.

Plaintiff leased certain gasoline filling stations to one Kemp, doing business as Webb Oil Company, under written leases. Kemp was purchasing the business known as Webb Oil Company and certain related property from defendant. On account of these transactions and purchases of petroleum products, Kemp was heavily indebted to defendant. Kemp became unable to meet payments due to defendant and on December 10, 1955, gave defendant an assignment of accounts receivable and to become receivable, including those involving the plaintiff's filling stations. Thereafter, during the period involved here, defendant collected rents paid by the operators of the filling stations, received other payments made to Webb Oil Company, paid some of its debts at Kemp's direction out of these sums, and installed its agent in the office to run the business.

Plaintiff was in Florida when he received a letter dated December 28, 1955, from Kemp, stating that defendant had all of Kemp's assets tied up. A short time after this, plaintiff called defendant's agent to ask about payment of the filling station rents. Plaintiff was told "that Mr. Kemp's affairs were in a very mixed up form but that he would get them straightened out and mail me [plaintiff] my checks for the rent." Hearing nothing further, plaintiff wrote a letter to defendant asking what he had to do to get his rent checks and adding: "Or will I have to give it to an attorney to sue." [Ed. note: Whom was the plaintiff threatening to sue, and why?]

Defendant replied by letter stating it was attempting to assist Kemp in keeping the business going, "but in no way are operating or taken possession." The letter denied knowledge of or responsibility for any rent due plaintiff. A week or 10 days after receiving this letter, plaintiff again called defendant and asked for his rent. Defendant's agent then said to plaintiff, "they [the company] were interested and that they would see that I [plaintiff] got my rent, and would take care of it, and they would work it out with the head office. * * * He said he would take it up with them and they would assure me my rent."

The rent was not paid, and in April or May 1956 plaintiff returned to Minneapolis from Florida. Soon after this plaintiff consulted a lawyer, and "shortly thereafter, as rapidly as the lawyer could get moving, a suit was started." On June 2, 1956, plaintiff sent defendant a letter advising that he was reentering and taking possession under the leases of the filling stations and because of failure to receive rent. On July 10, 1956, this suit was started for rents due on the filling stations for the period December 1, 1955, through June 2, 1956, upon the grounds that defendant was in possession of the stations and had contracted to pay the rent during this period.

The case was fully tried on all issues in the district court. At the conclusion of plaintiff's evidence, the court ruled that the evidence was conclusive that defendant neither took possession of the filling stations nor an assignment of Kemp's leases. Defendant then presented evidence on the issue of a contract to pay the rents, and this issue was submitted to the jury under proper instructions. The amount that would be due under such a contract was agreed upon; and the jury returned a verdict for plaintiff in that amount. Thereafter, the district court granted defendant's motion for judgment notwithstanding the verdict; and ordered a new trial in the event of reversal. Plaintiff appealed.

[The court first affirmed the trial court's ruling that defendant did not take possession of the stations or an assignment of the leases.]

The issue whether there was a contract by defendant to pay plaintiff is more doubtful. Unfortunately, contract, like most of the basic terms constituting the intellectual tools of law, is conventionally defined in a circular fashion.

By the most common definition, a contract is a promise or set of promises for the breach of which the law gives a remedy or the performance of which the law recognizes as a duty. This amounts to saying that a contract is a legally enforceable promise. But a promise is legally enforceable only if it is a contract. Thus nothing less than the whole body of applicable precedents suffices to define the term "contract."

Although the definition of contract does not help much in determining what expressions shall be held to impose legal obligations, it does direct attention to a promise as the starting point of inquiry. Both in popular and legal usage, a promise is an assurance, in whatever form of expression given, that a thing will or will not be done. While we must take care to distinguish between statements meant to express merely present intention and those meant to give an assurance as to a future event, this involves no more than the common difficulty of seeking precise meaning in the usually imprecise, and often careless, expressions of ordinary colloquy.

If we accept plaintiff's version of the statements made by defendant's agent, as we are required to do by the verdict, there was an unequivocal assurance given that the rents would be paid. This cannot be anything but a promise.

However, the fact that a promise was given does not necessarily mean that a contract was made. It is clear that not every promise is legally enforceable. Much of the vast body of law in the field of contracts is concerned with determining which promises should be legally enforced. On the one hand, in a civilized community men must be able to assume that those with whom they deal will carry out their undertakings according to reasonable expectations. On the other hand, it is neither practical nor reasonable to expect full performance of every assurance given, whether it be thoughtless, casual and gratuitous, or deliberately and seriously made.

The test that has been developed by the common law for determining the enforceability of promises is the doctrine of consideration. This is a crude and not altogether successful attempt to generalize the conditions under which promises will be legally enforced. Consideration requires that a contractual promise be the product of a bargain. However, in this usage, "bargain" does not mean an exchange of things of equivalent, or any, value. It means a negotiation resulting in the voluntary assumption of an obligation by one party upon condition of an act or forbearance by the other. Consideration thus insures that the promise enforced as a contract is not accidental, casual, or gratuitous, but has been uttered intentionally as the result of some deliberation, manifested by reciprocal bargaining or negotiation. In this view, the requirement of consideration is no mere technicality, historical anachronism, or arbitrary formality. It is an attempt to be as reasonable as we can in deciding which promises constitute contracts. Although the doctrine has been criticized, no satisfactory substitute has been suggested. It is noteworthy that the civil law has a corresponding doctrine of "causa" which, to the eye of a common-law lawyer, is not much different than consideration.

Consideration, as essential evidence of the parties' intent to create a legal obligation, must be something adopted and regarded by the parties as such. Thus, the same thing may be consideration or not, as it is dealt with by the parties. In substance, a contractual promise must be of the logical form: "If

* * * (consideration is given) * * * then I promise that * * *." Of course, the substance may be expressed in any form of words, but essentially this is the logical structure of those promises enforced by the law as contracts.

Applying these principles to the present case, it appears that although defendant's agent made a promise to plaintiff, it was not in such circumstances that a contract was created. Plaintiff correctly states that an agreement of forbearance to sue may be sufficient consideration for a contract. Plaintiff further contends that his failure to institute suit immediately upon learning of Kemp's assignment to defendant permits an inference of an agreement to forbear from suit in consideration for defendant's assurance of payment of rents to plaintiff. This court has held that circumstantial evidence may support the inference of such an agreement to forbear. However, such an inference must rest upon something more than the mere failure to institute immediate suit. The difficulty with plaintiff's case is that there is no more than this.

Plaintiff's conversation with defendant's agent was about the middle of February 1956 while plaintiff was in Florida. Plaintiff returned to Minneapolis, which was his residence as well as the jurisdiction where defendant was found, about the latter part of April or the first of May 1956. Soon after this he consulted a lawyer, and suit was started "as rapidly as the lawyer could get moving." There is nothing in the evidence to suggest that plaintiff deferred initiating legal action any longer than suited his own personal convenience. There is nothing in the evidence to suggest that defendant sought any forbearance by plaintiff or thought that it was securing such action; nor is there any evidence that plaintiff's delay from the middle of February until April or May in undertaking legal action was related to defendant's promises. There is no evidence that either of the parties took defendant's assurances seriously or acted upon them in any way. There was, therefore, no consideration, and the promises did not amount to a contract. Since the district court was correct in ordering judgment entered for the defendant, notwithstanding the verdict, on this ground, it is unnecessary to consider other points relating to enforceability of the alleged contract.

Affirmed.

NEUHOFF v. MARVIN LUMBER AND CEDAR CO.

United States Court of Appeals, First Circuit, 2004.
370 F.3d 197.

TORRUELLA, CIRCUIT JUDGE

The Neuhoffs allege that Marvin breached an oral contract to provide replacement windows for free. The oral contract was allegedly made in March 1998 when [Marvin's agent] informed the Neuhoffs that their decaying [Marvin] windows would be replaced once Marvin's production problems were fixed and the windows reached a more advanced stage of decay. * * *

[T]he Neuhoffs' breach of contract claim fails because Marvin's alleged promise to repair lacked consideration. * * *

The Neuhoffs allege three types of consideration: (1) forbearance of their legal claims, (2) the time and labor expended assisting Marvin in connection with Marvin's promise to replace the defective windows, and (3) the benefit Marvin received to their reputation by agreeing to replace the windows.

It is well-settled that "abandonment of a claim believed to be well founded . . . is the surrender of a thing of value and is a sufficient consideration for a contract." * * * The claim need not be "of such character in law or fact or both as finally to commend itself to the judgment of the tribunal of last resort," rather it need only be "well founded and made in good faith and not frivolous, vexatious or unlawful." *Id.* (internal quotations and citations omitted). But, "[m]ere forbearance to sue [on] a claim, without any promise either in express terms or by fair implication from all of the circumstances, does not form sufficient consideration. * * *" *Merrimac Chem. Co. v. Moore,* 279 Mass. 147, 181 N.E. 219, 222 (1932). It is undisputed that the Neuhoffs never expressed their willingness to forbear suit before or after the promise to replace the defective windows was made. Nonetheless, the Neuhoffs argue that their willingness to forbear suit could be implied. An "agreement to forbear to sue may be implied when the circumstances are such as to lead to the reasonable conclusion that the * * * thing of value was given to induce the [other party] to forbear." *Id.* The record shows that the alleged promise to replace all of the windows was not given to induce the Neuhoffs to relinquish a claim against Marvin. Thus, the Neuhoffs' claims of forbearance is not sufficient for consideration since such forbearance was neither express nor could be found by fair implication from all the circumstances.

[The court went on to hold that the record did not support Neuhoffs' claims that they assisted Marvin or that Marvin wanted to improve its reputation. Further, as to the latter, the court held that "not every benefit is consideration. * * * We cannot conclude, based on the record, that a hypothetical and tangential benefit to Marvin's reputation is sufficient consideration to make Marvin's statement a binding contract."]

SPRINGSTEAD v. NEES

Supreme Court of New York, Appellate Division, 1908.
125 App.Div. 230, 109 N.Y.S. 148.

Action by Anna Springstead and others against George Nees and another. Judgment for defendants, and plaintiffs appeal. Affirmed.

JENKS, J. This action was tried by stipulation as a common-law action before the court without a jury. The parties are all of the surviving children of Nees, deceased, who died intestate, leaving them his sole heirs at law. Nees died, the owner and seised of realty called the "Sackett Street Property" and the owner of realty, called the "Atlantic Avenue Property," which he held by deed to him as trustee for his children, Sophia and George. Shortly after Nees' death all of the parties, an attorney at law, and friends met in Nees' house. Nees' strong box was opened, and when the deed to the Atlantic avenue property was found therein the attorney handed it to Sophia, saying: "This is yours." The evidence for the plaintiffs is that they, or some of them, were surprised to learn that this deed was to their father in trust for two of the children; for theretofore they had believed that he was the owner and seised in fee. They expressed their surprise, and there were murmurings. Thereupon Sophia spoke up, saying, "We will give you our share in the Sackett street property if you don't bother us about the Atlantic avenue property," and George assented. The Sackett street property was sold thereafter. This action is brought by the other three children against Sophia and George, upon that alleged promise of Sophia and George, to recover their proportionate share of the proceeds of that sale. Sophia and George testified that no such promise ever was made. The learned court gave judgment for the defendants, dismissing the complaint, with costs.

After finding the preliminary facts, which were not disputed, the court found that the defendants, after the death of their father, were seised in fee simple of the Atlantic avenue property and held indefeasible title thereto; that the plaintiffs had no color of right in the Atlantic avenue property, and did not at any time threaten or attempt to assert any claim of right hostile to the defendants in that property; that there was no compromise, either wholly or partly executed, between the parties, affecting rights which the plaintiffs might have in that property; that the plaintiffs had given up no rights in that property, nor had they changed their position therein; and that a promise (referring to which I have heretofore described as shown by the testimony for the plaintiffs) made by the defendants to the plaintiffs that, if the plaintiffs "would not 'molest,' or 'bother,' or 'make a fuss' about, the defendants' rights on the Atlantic avenue property, the defendants would give the plaintiffs their share in the Sackett street property, if made, would have been without consideration." The plaintiffs appeal.

The record sustains the facts found. Assuming that such promise was made, I am of opinion that there was no consideration shown. * * *

The consideration for the promise cannot be found in the fact that there was a compromise of a disputed claim, for there is no evidence thereof. It must rest, then, upon the forbearance to exercise a legal right. Forbearance to assert either a legal or an equitable claim is sufficient consideration, as we have seen. * * * It seems unnecessary to consider the conflict over the question whether forbearance as to a claim without foundation can constitute good consideration. See 1 Parsons on Contracts (8th Ed.) p. 441, note, discussing the various authorities. It seems to be the rule with us that it is not essential that the claim should be valid; but it is enough if it could be regarded as doubtful or colorable. But if the claim be not even doubtful, or colorable, or plausible, in that there is no reason for an honest belief that it has some foundation in law or in equity, then forbearance applied to it is not good consideration. * * *

* * *

In the case at bar the court, as I have said, found properly that the plaintiffs had no color of right in the Atlantic avenue property; nor did they at any time threaten or attempt to assert any claim. The evidence of the plaintiffs is that, when they were surprised to find that the deed to the Atlantic avenue property was in trust for but two of their number, thereupon and without any further reason, save that they expressed surprise and were dissatisfied, the defendants made the promise in question. The promise was not even in response to any suggestion of any possible claim then or thereafter against the deed, or despite it, or of any action adverse to it. There was no suggestion, then or at any time thereafter, made that the deed was invalid for any reason, or of any ground upon which it was open to attack. Indeed, I can discover no reason upon the evidence how any of the parties could seriously suppose that even a doubtful or a colorable claim could be asserted then or thereafter. It does not appear that anything was ever done, then or thereafter, in consequence of the alleged promise, or that the rights of the parties were in any way thereby changed or affected.

I think that the judgment must be affirmed, with costs. All concur, except HOOKER, J., who dissents.

HOOKER, J. (dissenting). The circumstances surrounding the opening of the strong box after decedent's death and the finding there of a deed running to the defendants, and the conversation then between the children, seem to me such as to present a situation where there was at least color of a valid claim by the plaintiffs, by reason of their heirship, to the Atlantic avenue property. One of these circumstances is that the strong box where the deed was found belonged to the decedent, and it might well be doubted whether there had ever been a delivery of the deed before the grantor's death, which was necessary to pass title. If such claim was open to be urged, there was consideration for the promise.

The judgment should be reversed.

1 CORBIN ON CONTRACTS
§ 140 at 596–600 (1963).

Forbearance to bring a suit, or to proceed with one already brought, or to press a claim in any other way, is not a sufficient consideration if the forbearance is with knowledge that the claim is ill founded and void. This is on grounds of public policy, not because the forbearance is not beneficial to the promisor or detrimental to the promisee. * * * The reason for this is that, if [such forbearance] * * * were recognized as sufficient, ill-founded claims would be infinitely increased in number and the offense that is known as blackmail would become a profitable racket.

* * *

In a good many court opinions, it is stated that forbearance to press a claim (or a promise to forebear) is not sufficient consideration unless the claim was doubtful, that is, unless the claimant had some reasonable ground for belief in the justice of the claim. All agree that the claim must be made in good faith. No doubt the absence of any reasonable ground for belief in its validity is some evidence that the claim was not made in good faith; but it would not be conclusive evidence. Many courts are satisfied if the claimant had an honest belief in his claim, without regard to whether he had any reasonable basis for it. As a practical matter, the difference between the two stated doctrines may not be great.

Note
Promise for Promise as Consideration

In Baehr v. Penn–O–Tex Oil Corp., Justice Loevinger points out that a bargained-for *promise* is a sufficient consideration for a promise. See also Restatement (Second) of Contracts § 71(1); Restatement (First) of Contracts § 75(1)(d). Thus, one of Baehr's approaches to recovery was based on his alleged promise to forbear from suing in exchange for defendant's promise to pay the rents. See also Neuhoff v. Marvin Lumber and Cedar Co. Similarly, in Springstead v. Nees, a bargained for *promise* by the other children not to "bother" George and Sophie about the Atlantic Avenue property would have been sufficient consideration for the promise of George and Sophie to give up their share of the Sackett Street property (assuming the other children had a colorable claim in the Atlantic Avenue property).

Because a bargained-for promise may constitute consideration, a party may become obligated to perform even though the other has not relied on the agreement. Thus, if Arnold promises to sell his car to Kate for $400, delivery next Saturday, and Kate promises to pay the $400, Arnold is legally bound to perform even if he attempts to recant five minutes after the deal is made and before any change of position by Kate. The same applies, of course, to a promissory exchange involving millions of dollars between corporate titans. Why such a rule? Would the following rule be superior? A party is always free, upon giving appropriate advanced notice, to back out of a wholly executory exchange except when the other party has reasonably relied in some way. Consider the material below.

FULLER, CONSIDERATION AND FORM
41 Colum.L.Rev. 799, 816–17 (1941).

§ 15. *The Wholly Executory Exchange.*—B promises to build a house for A, and A, in return, promises to pay B $5,000 on the completion of the house. B defaults on his promise, and A, without having had occasion to pay anything on the contract, sues B for damages. Judicial intervention in this kind of case apparently began in England toward the end of the sixteenth century. This development we describe by saying that after *Strangborough v. Warner*[i] and related cases the bilateral contract as such became for the first time enforceable. It is now generally assumed that so far as consideration is concerned the executory bilateral contract is on a complete parity with the situation where the plaintiff has already paid the price of the defendant's promised performance. Yet if we examine the executory bilateral contract in terms of the policies underlying consideration, it will become apparent that this assumption is unjustified, and that Lord Holt in reality overshot the mark in his assertion that "where the doing a thing will be a good consideration, a promise to do that thing will be so too."

Where a bilateral contract remains wholly executory the arguments for judicial intervention have been considerably diminished in comparison with the situation of the half-completed exchange. There is here no unjust enrichment. Reliance may or may not exist, but in any event will not be so tangible and direct as where it consists in the rendition of the price of the defendant's performance. On the side of form, we have lost the natural formality involved in the turning over of property or the rendition and acceptance of services. There remains simply the fact that the transaction is an exchange and not a gift. This fact alone does offer some guaranty so far as the cautionary and channeling functions of form are concerned, though, except as the Statute of Frauds interposes to supply the deficiency, evidentiary safeguards are largely lacking. This lessening of the factors arguing for enforcement not only helps to explain why liability in this situation was late in developing, but also

i. 74 Eng.Rep. 686 (K.B.1589).

explains why even today the executory bilateral contract cannot be put on complete parity with the situation of the half-completed exchange.

In the situation of the half-completed exchange, the element of exchange is only one factor tending toward enforcement. Since that element is there reinforced by reliance, unjust enrichment, and the natural formality involved in the surrender and acceptance of a tangible benefit, it is unnecessary to analyze the concept of exchange closely, and it may properly be left vague. In the executory bilateral contract, on the other hand, the element of exchange stands largely alone as a basis of liability and its definition becomes crucial. Various definitions are possible. We may define exchange vaguely as a transaction from which each participant derives a benefit, or, more restrictively, as a transaction in which the motives of the parties are primarily economic rather than sentimental. Following Adam Smith, we may say that it is a transaction which, directly or indirectly, conduces to the division of labor. Or we may take Demogue's notion that the most important characteristic of exchange is that it is a situation in which the interests of the transacting parties are opposed, so that the social utility of the contract is guaranteed in some degree by the fact that it emerges as a compromise of those conflicting interests. The problem of choosing among these varying conceptions may seem remote and unimportant, yet it underlies some of the most familiar problems of contract law. For example, suppose a nephew promises his uncle that he will not smoke until he is twenty-one, and the uncle promises him $5,000 as a reward if he will keep his promise. Where the nephew sues after having earned the reward by following the prescribed line of conduct recovery has been permitted. But would such an agreement be enforced as an executory bilateral contract? Could the uncle, for example, sue the nephew for smoking a cigarette? In answering this question it is at once apparent that we are faced with the necessity of defining the particular kind of exchange which is essential to the enforcement of a bilateral contract.

VON MEHREN, CONTRACTS IN GENERAL

7 Int'l Ency. of Comp. L. 20 (ch. 1) (1982).

But if contracts are not enforceable, in nonsimultaneous exchanges one party runs the risk that the other will not render his performance in due course. Hence, the enforceability of contract can also be viewed as a response to the sequential character of much economic activity. Indeed,

> "the absence of legally enforceable rights would, among other consequences, bias investment toward economic activities where the interval in which the contemplated economic activity could be completed was short, and this would reduce the efficiency of resource use."[j]

In the absence of enforceable contract rights, many sequential transactions would presumably still be carried on. But the party who performed first would seek to protect himself against the possibility of nonperformance by the other party; the resulting

> "system would not be very efficient. Apart from the costs involved in maintaining credit bureaus and administering security deposits (especial-

---

j. R. Posner, Economic Analysis of Law § 4.1 at 66 (1977).

ly in a world where the return of the deposit could not be legally compelled), self-protection would not always work."[k]

There are thus strong economic arguments to support the enforceability of contracts.

FULLER & PERDUE, THE RELIANCE INTEREST IN CONTRACT DAMAGES

46 Yale L.J. 52, 61–62 (1936).

It may be said that there is not only a policy in favor of preventing and undoing the harms resulting from reliance, but also a policy in favor of promoting and facilitating reliance on business agreements. * * * Agreements can accomplish little, either for their makers or for society, unless they are made the basis for action. When business agreements are not only made but are also acted on, the division of labor is facilitated, goods find their way to the places where they are most needed, and economic activity is generally stimulated. These advantages would be threatened by any rule which limited legal protection to the reliance interest. Such a rule would in practice tend to discourage reliance. The difficulties in proving reliance and subjecting it to pecuniary measurement are such that the business man knowing, or sensing, that these obstacles stood in the way of judicial relief would hesitate to rely on a promise in any case where the legal sanction was of significance to him. To encourage reliance we must therefore dispense with its proof. For this reason it has been found wise to make recovery on a promise independent of reliance, both in the sense that in some cases the promise is enforced though not relied on (as in the bilateral business agreement) and in the sense that recovery is not limited to the detriment incurred in reliance.

DE LOS SANTOS v. GREAT WESTERN SUGAR COMPANY

Supreme Court of Nebraska, 1984.
217 Neb. 282, 348 N.W.2d 842.

CAMBRIDGE, DISTRICT JUDGE.

This is an appeal by the plaintiff of a summary judgment entered by the trial court in favor of the defendant in an action for breach of contract.

* * *

This appeal centers around the following provision contained in the "Hauling Contract" executed by the plaintiff and the defendant in October 1980:

The Contractor [i.e., plaintiff] shall transport in the Contractor's trucks *such tonnage of beets as may be loaded by the Company* [i.e., defendant] from piles at the beet receiving stations of the Company, and unload said beets at such factory or factories as may be designated by the Company. The term of this contract shall be from October 1, 1980, until February 15, 1981.

k. *Id.* at 67.

(Emphasis supplied.) The plaintiff, as an independent contractor, was obligated under the "Hauling Contract" to furnish certain insurance, suitable trucks and equipment, and all necessary labor, maintenance, fuel, and licenses required for his operations thereunder, and the compensation which he was to receive for his services was based solely upon the amount of beets which he transported, the rate per ton varying with the length of the haul.

It is undisputed that upon executing the hauling contract the plaintiff knew that the defendant had executed identical such contracts with other independent truckers who would also be hauling the defendant's beets and that the plaintiff would therefore transport on his trucks only "such tonnage of beets as may be loaded by" the defendant upon the plaintiff's trucks, not all of the beets "as may be loaded by" the defendant from piles at the defendant's beet receiving stations. The plaintiff had been transporting beets under the contract for approximately 2 months when, in early December 1980, the defendant informed the plaintiff that his services would no longer be needed. The plaintiff does not claim that he was entitled to transport all of the beets, but he does contend that he was entitled to continue to haul until all of the beets had been transported to the factory, that the defendant did not allow him to do so, and that the defendant thereby wrongfully terminated the hauling contract, causing the plaintiff loss of profits, forced sale of his trucks at a loss, and other damages to be proved on trial. In his petition the plaintiff predicated his action against the defendant upon the hauling contract. The defendant in its amended answer thereto alleged, among other defenses not relevant to the disposition of this appeal, that the defendant was not obligated under the contract to allow the plaintiff to haul any particular amount of tonnage and that its determination that it would no longer require the plaintiff's services was a determination which was within the defendant's discretion under the terms of the contract. * * * The plaintiff was paid in full for all beets which were in fact hauled by him, and there is no issue in this case in that regard.

Considering the words contained therein together with the aforesaid undisputed facts known to both the plaintiff and the defendant when they executed the hauling contract, it is clear that neither the plaintiff nor the defendant intended to or did, either in fact or law, promise to transport a specific quantity of beets or promise to transport beets during a specific period of time. The term of the contract set forth therein, i.e., October 1, 1980, until February 15, 1981, did not constitute a promise, but merely established the period of time during which the promises which were contained in the contract would be in effect. Although the plaintiff made a number of promises in the hauling contract, all centered around the plaintiff's promise to transport beets as loaded by the defendant on the plaintiff's trucks during the period of October 1, 1980, through February 15, 1981, the defendant made no promises at all other than the promise to pay for the transportation of those beets which were in fact loaded by the defendant onto the trucks of the plaintiff during that period. An agreement which depends upon the wish, will, or pleasure of one of the parties is unenforceable. See 56 C.J.S. *Master and Servant* § 6 (1948). In *Garsick v. Dehner,* 145 Neb. 73, 79, 15 N.W.2d 235, 238 (1944), this court stated:

> Speaking generally, mutuality of obligation is an essential element of every enforceable agreement. However, "Mutuality of contract consists in

the obligation on each party to do, or to permit something to be done, in consideration of the act or promise of the other. * * * Mutuality is absent when one only of the contracting parties is bound to perform, and the rights of the parties exist at the option of one only."

Where a promisor agrees to purchase services from the promisee on a per unit basis, but the agreement specifies no quantity and the parties did not intend that the promisor should take all of his needs from the promisee, there is no enforceable agreement, and the promisor is not obligated to accept any services from the promisee and may terminate the relationship at any time without liability other than to pay for the services accepted. The fact that the promisor has accepted services from the promisee in the past under such an agreement does not furnish the consideration necessary to require the promisor to accept such services in the future under the agreement. Nor does the specification in such an agreement of the period of time during which it will be operative impose an obligation that is not already present under the agreement. *Waco Fire & C. Ins. Co. v. Plant,* 150 Ga.App. 888, 259 S.E.2d 95 (1979). * * * Applying the foregoing to this case, it is apparent that the right of the defendant to control the amount of beets loaded onto the plaintiff's trucks was in effect a right to terminate the contract at any time, and this rendered the contract as to its unexecuted portions void for want of mutuality. In the absence of a specification of quantity, the defendant had no obligation to use any of the plaintiff's services, and the defendant's decision to cease using those services after a certain point is not actionable.

* * *

AFFIRMED.

WOOD v. LUCY, LADY DUFF–GORDON

Court of Appeals of New York, 1917.
222 N.Y. 88, 118 N.E. 214.

CARDOZO, J. The defendant styles herself "a creator of fashions." Her favor helps a sale. Manufacturers of dresses, millinery, and like articles are glad to pay for a certificate of her approval. The things which she designs, fabrics, parasols, and what not, have a new value in the public mind when issued in her name. She employed the plaintiff to help her to turn this vogue into money. He was to have the exclusive right, subject always to her approval, to place her indorsements on the designs of others. He was also to have the exclusive right to place her own designs on sale, or to license others to market them. In return she was to have one-half of "all profits and revenues" derived from any contracts he might make. The exclusive right was to last at least one year from April 1, 1915, and thereafter from year to year unless terminated by notice of 90 days. The plaintiff says that he kept the contract on his part, and that the defendant broke it. She placed her indorsement on fabrics, dresses, and millinery without his knowledge, and withheld the profits. He sues her for the damages, and the case comes here on demurrer.

The agreement of employment is signed by both parties. It has a wealth of recitals. The defendant insists, however, that it lacks the elements of a contract. She says that the plaintiff does not bind himself to anything. It is true that he does not promise in so many words that he will use reasonable efforts to place the defendant's indorsements and market her designs. We think, however, that such a promise is fairly to be implied. The law has outgrown its primitive stage of formalism when the precise word was the sovereign talisman, and every slip was fatal. It takes a broader view today. A promise may be lacking, and yet the whole writing may be "instinct with an obligation," imperfectly expressed (Scott, J., in McCall Co. v. Wright, 133 App.Div. 62, 117 N.Y.Supp. 775; Moran v. Standard Oil Co., 211 N.Y. 187, 198, 105 N.E. 217). If that is so, there is a contract.

The implication of a promise here finds support in many circumstances. The defendant gave an exclusive privilege. She was to have no right for at least a year to place her own indorsements or market her own designs except through the agency of the plaintiff. The acceptance of the exclusive agency was an assumption of its duties. * * * We are not to suppose that one party was to be placed at the mercy of the other. * * *

Many other terms of the agreement point the same way. We are told at the outset by way of recital that:

> "The said Otis F. Wood possesses a business organization adapted to the placing of such indorsements as the said Lucy, Lady Duff–Gordon, has approved."

The implication is that the plaintiff's business organization will be used for the purpose for which it is adapted. But the terms of the defendant's compensation are even more significant. Her sole compensation for the grant of an exclusive agency is to be one-half of all the profits resulting from the plaintiff's efforts. Unless he gave his efforts, she could never get anything. Without an implied promise, the transaction cannot have such business "efficacy, as both parties must have intended that at all events it should have." Bowen, L.J., in the Moorcock, 14 P.D. 64, 68. But the contract does not stop there. The plaintiff goes on to promise that he will account monthly for all moneys received by him, and that he will take out all such patents and copyrights and trade-marks as may in his judgment be necessary to protect the rights and articles affected by the agreement. It is true, of course, as the Appellate Division has said, that if he was under no duty to try to market designs or to place certificates of indorsement, his promise to account for profits or take out copyrights would be valueless. But in determining the intention of the parties the promise has a value. It helps to enforce the conclusion that the plaintiff had some duties. His promise to pay the defendant one-half of the profits and revenues resulting from the exclusive agency and to render accounts monthly was a promise to use reasonable efforts to bring profits and revenues into existence. For this conclusion the authorities are ample. * * *

The judgment of the Appellate Division should be reversed, and the order of the Special Term affirmed, with costs in the Appellate Division and in this court.

CUDDEBACK, MCLAUGHLIN, and ANDREWS, JJ., concur. HISCOCK, C.J., and CHASE and CRANE, JJ., dissent.

UNIFORM COMMERCIAL CODE § 1–203.
Obligation of Good Faith

Every contract or duty within this Act imposes an obligation of good faith in its performance or enforcement.

UNIFORM COMMERCIAL CODE § 2–306(2).

A lawful agreement by either the seller or the buyer for exclusive dealing in the kind of goods concerned imposes unless otherwise agreed an obligation by the seller to use best efforts to supply the goods and by the buyer to use best efforts to promote their sale.

Problem 2–3

1. Assume that U.C.C. sections 1–203 and 2–306(2) applied to the Wood and De Los Santos cases. Would they change the results? On the meaning of good faith, see the Summers excerpt, set forth at page 744.

2. Assume you were counsel for Wood in Wood v. Lucy, Lady Duff–Gordon, and he had asked you at the outset to set up the arrangement so it would "without doubt be legal without having to go to court." What wording would you have included? What approach in De Los Santos to ensure the enforceability of the "hauling contract"?

H.G. WOOD, A TREATISE ON THE LAW OF MASTER AND SERVANT

§ 134 (1877).

With us the rule is inflexible that a general or indefinite hiring is *prima facie* a hiring at will, and if the servant seeks to make it out a yearly hiring, the burden is upon him to establish it by proof. A hiring at so much a day, week, month, or year, or no time being specified, is an indefinite hiring, and no presumption attaches that it was for a day even, but only at the rate fixed for whatever time the party may serve.

WEINER v. McGRAW–HILL, INC.

Court of Appeals of New York, 1982.
57 N.Y.2d 458, 457 N.Y.S.2d 193, 443 N.E.2d 441.

FUCHSBERG, JUDGE.

In a matter raising an issue of wide concern to employers and employees, we must decide whether, in the circumstances of this case, the plaintiff, though not engaged for a fixed term of employment, pleaded a good cause of action for breach of contract against his employer * * *.

The operative facts deserve emphasis. Taken most favorably to the plaintiff, as they must in the context of an appeal [from an order dismissing the complaint] they show that, in 1969, the plaintiff, Walton Lewis Weiner, a young man who four years earlier had entered upon a career in book publishing with another employer, Prentice–Hall, was invited to engage in discussions looking towards his joining the staff of the defendant, McGraw–Hill, Inc. In the course of these talks, McGraw's representative, aware of Weiner's position with Prentice–Hall, assured his prospect that, since his company's firm policy was not to terminate employees without "just cause", employment by it would, among other things, bring him the advantage of job security. Concomitantly, the application Weiner thereafter signed and submitted, on a printed McGraw form, specified that his employment would be subject to the provisions of McGraw's "handbook on personnel policies and procedures". This reference as relevant here, represented that "[t]he company will resort to dismissal for just and sufficient cause only, and only after all practical steps toward rehabilitation or salvage of the employee have been taken and failed. However, if the welfare of the company indicates that dismissal is necessary, then that decision is arrived at and is carried out forthrightly" (Handbook, § 8.20, par. [8]).

Statement from handbook

These undertakings were important to Weiner, who alleges not only that he placed "good faith reliance" on them in leaving his existing employer, but in the process forfeited all his accrued fringe benefits and a salary increase proffered by Prentice–Hall to induce him to remain in its employ.

π alleges "good faith reliance" also gave up $ to leave

Following written approval, affixed at the foot of the application form by two members of the defendant's staff, one the interviewer and the other a supervisor, McGraw engaged Weiner's services. For the next eight years, so far as escalation in rank (to director of promotion services) and periodic raises in his level of compensation would seem to indicate, Weiner had every reason to believe he had, if anything, more than met the reasonable requirements of his new post. Other offers of employment he routinely rejected. Nevertheless, in February, 1977, he suddenly found himself discharged for "lack of application".

fact

There ensued this litigation, by which, in a complaint speaking broadly in the language of breach of contract, the plaintiff seeks damages for his wrongful termination. To support its * * * motion to dismiss, defendant's argument was, and is, that there existed no contract of employment under which McGraw–Hill's evaluation of Weiner's job performance could be challenged in a court of law. In its view, the form signed by the parties was just an application for employment and nothing more. Defendant further contends that its oral promise of job security was in no way binding on it.

π files complaint

Δ's motion to dism

Δ's argum

* * *

[The trial court upheld the complaint, but the Appellate Division reversed and granted the motion to dismiss on the basis that Weiner's employment was at will.]

For the reasons which follow, we believe the plaintiff stated a cause of action.

Procedural posture

opin. Ct of Appeals * * *

Turning now to substance, it is * * * clear that the fact that plaintiff was free to quit his employment at will, standing by itself, was not entitled to conclusory effect. Such a position proceeds on the oversimplified premise that, since the plaintiff was not bound to stay on, the agreement for his employment lacked "mutuality", thus leaving the defendant free to terminate at its pleasure. But this would lead to the not uncommon analytical error of engaging in a search for "mutuality", which is not always essential to a binding contract, rather than of seeking to determine the presence of consideration, which is a fundamental requisite. For, while coextensive promises

Mutuality not essential. Considera. YES.

may constitute consideration for each other, "mutuality", in the sense of requiring such reciprocity, is not necessary when a promisor receives other valid consideration * * *.

* * *

Apt * * * in the circumstances before us now is the following comment by Corbin: "[I]f the employer made a promise, either express or implied, not only to pay for the service but also that the employment should continue for a period of time that is either definite or capable of being determined, that employment is not terminable by him 'at will' after the employee has begun or rendered some of the requested service or has given any other consideration * * * This is true even though the employee has made no return promise and has retained the power and legal privilege of terminating the employment 'at will'. The employer's promise is supported by the service that has been begun or rendered or by the other executed consideration" (1A Corbin, Contracts, § 152, p. 14). So understood, an agreement on the part of an employer not to dismiss an employee except for "good and sufficient cause only" and, if such cause was given, until the prescribed procedures to rehabilitate had failed, does not create an ineluctable employment at will.

These propositions in mind, we find * * * sufficient evidence of a contract and a breach to sustain a cause of action. First, plaintiff was induced to leave Prentice–Hall with the assurance that McGraw–Hill would not discharge him without cause. Second, this assurance was incorporated into the employment application. Third, plaintiff rejected other offers of employment in reliance on the assurance. Fourth, appellant alleged that, on several occasions when he had recommended that certain of his subordinates be dismissed, he was instructed by his supervisors to proceed in strict compliance with the handbook and policy manuals because employees could be discharged only for just cause. He also claims that he was told that, if he did not proceed in accordance with the strict procedures set forth in the handbook, McGraw–Hill would be liable for legal action. In our view, these factors combine to present a question for trial: Was defendant bound to a promise not to discharge plaintiff without just and sufficient cause and an opportunity for rehabilitation? * * *

* * *

Consequently, the order of the Appellate Division should be reversed and the order of Special Term reinstated.

[JUDGE WACHTLER'S dissent is omitted.]

BLADES, EMPLOYMENT AT WILL VS. INDIVIDUAL FREEDOM: ON LIMITING THE ABUSIVE EXERCISE OF EMPLOYER POWER

67 Colum. L. Rev. 1404, 1419 (1967).

[T]here is a multitude of cases in which even contracts for permanent employment, that is, for indefinite terms, have been held unenforceable on the ground that they lack mutuality of obligation. But these cases demonstrate that mutuality is a high-sounding phrase of little use as an analytical tool. If the employee in addition to his services has given other "good" consideration, such as foregoing a claim against the employer or giving up a business to accept the employment, the agreement will be enforced on behalf of the employee even though he is free to quit at any time. Thus it seems clear that mutuality of obligation is not an inexorable requirement and that lack of mutuality is simply, as many courts have come to recognize, an imperfect way of referring to the real obstacle to enforcing any kind of contractual limitation on the employer's right of discharge—lack of consideration.

Inevitable

MATTEI v. HOPPER

Supreme Court of California, 1958.
51 Cal.2d 119, 330 P.2d 625.

SPENCE, JUSTICE.

Plaintiff brought this action for damages after defendant allegedly breached a contract by failing to convey her real property in accordance with the terms of a deposit receipt which the parties had executed. After a trial without a jury, the court concluded that the agreement was "illusory" and lacking in "mutuality." From the judgment accordingly entered in favor of defendant, plaintiff appeals.

Plaintiff was a real estate developer. He was planning to construct a shopping center on a tract adjacent to defendant's land. For several months, a real estate agent attempted to negotiate a sale of defendant's property under terms agreeable to both parties. After several of plaintiff's proposals had been rejected by defendant because of the inadequacy of the price offered, defendant submitted an offer. Plaintiff accepted on the same day.

fact

The parties' written agreement was evidenced on a form supplied by the real estate agent, commonly known as a deposit receipt. Under its terms, plaintiff was required to deposit $1,000 of the total purchase price of $57,500 with the real estate agent, and was given 120 days to "examine the title and consummate the purchase." At the expiration of that period, the balance of the price was "due and payable upon tender of a good and sufficient deed of the property sold." The concluding paragraph of the deposit receipt provided: "Subject to Coldwell Banker & Company obtaining leases satisfactory to the purchaser." This clause and the 120–day period were desired by plaintiff as a means for arranging satisfactory leases of the shopping center buildings prior to the time he was finally committed to pay the balance of the purchase price and to take title to defendant's property.

Plaintiff took the first step in complying with the agreement by turning over the $1,000 deposit to the real estate agent. While he was in the process of securing the leases and before the 120 days had elapsed, defendant's attorney notified plaintiff that defendant would not sell her land under the terms contained in the deposit receipt. Thereafter, defendant was informed that satisfactory leases had been obtained and that plaintiff had offered to pay the balance of the purchase price. Defendant failed to tender the deed as provided in the deposit receipt.

fact

Initially, defendant's thesis that the deposit receipt constituted no more than an offer by her, which could only be accepted by plaintiff notifying her that all of the desired leases had been obtained and were satisfactory to him, must be rejected. Nowhere does the agreement mention the necessity of any such notice. Nor does the provision making the agreement "subject to" plaintiff's securing "satisfactory" leases necessarily constitute a condition to the existence of a contract. Rather, the whole purchase receipt and this particular clause must be read as merely making plaintiff's performance dependent on the obtaining of "satisfactory" leases. Thus a contract arose, and plaintiff was given the power and privilege to terminate it in the event he did not obtain such leases. (See 3 Corbin, Contracts (1951), § 647, pp. 581–585.) This accords with the general view that deposit receipts are binding and enforceable contracts. (Cal.Practice Hand Book, Legal Aspects of Real Estate Transactions (1956), p. 63.)

However, the inclusion of this clause, specifying that leases "satisfactory" to plaintiff must be secured before he would be bound to perform, raises the basic question whether the consideration supporting the contract was thereby vitiated. When the parties attempt, as here, to make a contract where promises are exchanged as the consideration, the promises must be mutual in obligation. In other words, for the contract to bind either party, both must have assumed some legal obligations. Without this mutuality of obligation, the agreement lacks consideration and no enforceable contract has been created. Shortell v. Evans–Ferguson Corp., 98 Cal.App. 650, 660–662, 277 P. 519; 1 Corbin, Contracts (1950), § 152, pp. 496–502. Or, if one of the promisees leaves a party free to perform or to withdraw from the agreement at his own unrestricted pleasure, the promise is deemed illusory and it provides no consideration. See J.C. Millett Co. v. Park & Tilford Distillers Corp., D.C.N.D.Cal., 123 F.Supp. 484, 493. Whether these problems are couched in terms of mutuality of obligation or the illusory nature of a promise, the underlying issue is the same—consideration. Ibid.

While contracts making the duty of performance of one of the parties conditional upon his satisfaction would seem to give him wide latitude in avoiding any obligation and thus present serious consideration problems, such "satisfaction" clauses have been given effect. They have been divided into two primary categories and have been accorded different treatment on that basis. First, in those contracts where the condition calls for satisfaction as to commercial value or quality, operative fitness, or mechanical utility, dissatisfaction cannot be claimed arbitrarily, unreasonably, or capriciously (Collins v. Vickter Manor, Inc., 47 Cal.2d 875, 882–883, 306 P.2d 783), and the standard of a reasonable person is used in determining whether satisfaction has been received. * * * However, it would seem that the factors involved in determining whether a lease is satisfactory to the lessor are too numerous and varied to permit the application of a reasonable man standard as envisioned by this line of cases. Illustrative of some of the factors which would have to be considered in this case are the duration of the leases, their provisions for renewal options, if any, their covenants and restrictions, the amounts of the rentals, the financial responsibility of the lessees, and the character of the lessees' businesses.

This multiplicity of factors which must be considered in evaluating a lease shows that this case more appropriately falls within the second line of authorities dealing with "satisfaction" clauses, being those involving fancy, taste, or judgment. Where the question is one of judgment, the promisor's determination that he is not satisfied, when made in good faith, has been held to be a defense to an action on the contract. Tiffany v. Pacific Sewer Pipe Co.,

180 Cal. 700, 702–705, 182 P. 428, 6 A.L.R. 1493 * * *. Although these *Holding* decisions do not expressly discuss the issues of mutuality of obligation or illusory promises, they necessarily imply that the promisor's duty to exercise his judgment in good faith is an adequate consideration to support the contract. None of these cases voided the contracts on the ground that they were illusory or lacking in mutuality of obligation. * * *

Moreover, the secondary authorities are in accord with the California cases on the general principles governing "satisfaction" contracts. * * * (3 Corbin, Contracts (1951), §§ 644, 645, pp. 560–572.) "A promise conditional upon the promisor's satisfaction is not illusory since it means more than that validity of the performance is to depend on the arbitrary choice of the promisor. His expression of dissatisfaction is not conclusive. That may show only that he has become dissatisfied with the contract; he must be dissatisfied with the performance, as a performance of the contract, and his dissatisfaction must be genuine." * * *

2 Satisf clause

* * *

We conclude that the contract here was neither illusory nor lacking in mutuality of obligation because the parties inserted a provision in their contract making plaintiff's performance dependent on his satisfaction with the leases to be obtained by him.

Judgment

The judgment is reversed.

Problem 2–4

On January 10, Seller agrees to deliver 12 jet engines to Buyer on February 1. Payment is due on delivery of the engines. The agreement also provides that "Seller may terminate this agreement on 24 hours notice." Valid contract? Suppose on January 11, Seller notifies Buyer that Seller "will not perform"? Suppose on February 1, Seller failed to deliver without having given notice?

Professors Ben Shahar and White report that automaker Ford's contract with its suppliers states that "[t]he buyer may terminate the Purchase Order, in whole or in part, at any time and for any or no reason, upon Written Notice to the Supplier." They observe that this provision "come[s] close to rendering the contract[] illusory. Still, the requirement of a written notice in Ford's contract * * * may constitute the necessary restriction to render these contracts enforceable." Omri Ben–Shahar & James J. White, Boilerplate and Economic Power In Auto Manufacturing Contracts, 104 Mich. L. Rev. 953, 958 n. 20 (2006).

Note
The Preexisting Duty Doctrine

The "preexisting duty" doctrine is the subject of much discussion among contract scholars. In his treatise, Professor Corbin stated:

> Most acts and forebearances, or promises of future performance, are a sufficient consideration for a promise if they are bargained for by the maker of that promise and are given in exchange for it. One of the most important exceptions consists of those performances that are required of the performer, exactly as rendered by him, by a pre-existing legal duty. The same is true of a promise to render such a performance. The very frequently stated rule is that

neither the performance of duty nor the promise to render a performance already required by duty is a sufficient consideration for a return promise.

There has been a growing doubt as to the soundness of this doctrine.[1]

example

Suppose Ajax Construction Company agrees to construct a drive-in theatre for Brown's Cinema for $60,000. The contract provides that Ajax will clear the site and provide all of the fill necessary for the job. After Ajax begins performance, it discovers that the amount of fill needed will be greater than it contemplated. The cost of additional fill will be over $5,000. Ajax therefore seeks and receives Brown's promise to pay an additional $5,000 for the completed work. According to standard doctrine, Ajax gave no consideration for Brown's promise to pay the additional $5000 because Ajax had a preexisting duty to provide all of the fill necessary for $60,000. Thus, under the preexisting duty rule, Brown's promise to pay the extra $5000 would be unenforceable.

Assume, however, that the parties had freely and fairly agreed to their contract modification. For example, suppose Brown's believed rightly that it had received too good a deal, but Brown's later refuses to pay the $5,000. Predictably, many courts decline to apply the preexisting duty rule to such a case. Conversely, assume that Brown's was the victim of unfair pressure. For example, knowing that Brown's could not find another contractor, Ajax refuses to perform without a price increase even though it would not suffer higher costs in providing the fill. Here, courts usually "apply" the preexisting duty rule. Because the rule is thus principally a policing doctrine, we consider it more fully in Chapter 5.

HAIGH v. BROOKS, 113 Eng.Rep. 119 (Q.B.1839), *aff'd*, 113 Eng.Rep. 124 (Ex.1840). [Brooks allegedly gave Haigh an objectively valuable guarantee. In return Haigh surrendered a piece of paper Brooks had earlier given Haigh, which Brooks apparently assumed rendered him legally liable to Haigh, but which may have had no objective legal effect. The court held that giving up this piece of paper (however objectively worthless it may have been) would be consideration.]

1 CORBIN ON CONTRACTS
§ 127 at 543, 546–47 (1963).

Parting with a document, the contents of which can in fact render no service, has been held to be a sufficient consideration for a promise to pay a large sum of money. Services or property are sufficient consideration for a promise to pay much more money than anyone else would pay for them. * * *

* * *

The rule that market equivalence of consideration is * * * to be left solely to the free bargaining process of the parties, leads in extreme cases to seeming absurdities. When the consideration is only a "peppercorn" or a "tomtit" or a worthless piece of paper, the requirement of a consideration appeared to Holmes to be as much of a mere formality as is a seal. In such extreme cases, a tendency may be observed to refuse to apply the rule; but it is a tendency that has not been carried very far. Such cases can sometimes be explained on the ground that the court feels that there was no bargain in fact and that the stated consideration was a mere pretense.

1. 1A Corbin on Contracts § 171 at 105 (1963).

Problem 2–5

Compare the following two provisions of the Restatement (Second) of Contracts:

§ 79. Adequacy of Consideration * * *

If the requirement of consideration is met, there is no additional requirement of * * * equivalence in the values exchanged. * * *

§ 208. Unconscionable Contract or Term

If a contract or term thereof is unconscionable at the time the contract is made a court may refuse to enforce the contract, or may enforce the remainder of the contract without the unconscionable term, or may so limit the application of any unconscionable term as to avoid any unconscionable result.

How might such provisions be reconciled? If the owner of a car worth $10,000, offers to trade it for a worthless wrist watch, will the law uphold the deal? Does the imbalance in such an exchange suggest that something else is wrong with the deal?

Comments and Questions

1. It is sometimes suggested that the only function of the consideration doctrine today is to identify gift promises and isolate them for nonenforcement. What other functions does the doctrine perform, according to Professor Fuller? According to other materials in this chapter?

2. Another basic legal requirement that must be met before a prima facie duty arises under an agreement with consideration is that the parties made a valid agreement. Although this Chapter includes materials on this requirement, it is studied systematically in Chapters Four and Five. In some types of cases a writing is also required under the statute of frauds. We encounter cases involving the statute of frauds in the next several sections, and return to it again in Section Nine of this chapter.

3. Specialized branches of law dealing with specific types of exchanges may modify or add to the *general* requirements of an agreement with consideration. For example, some statutes require large type and plain English in certain agreements with consumers. See, for example, New York General Obligations Law § 5–702, set forth at page 611.

SECTION THREE: OBLIGATION ARISING FROM JUSTIFIED RELIANCE— PROMISSORY ESTOPPEL

PAPINIAN (CIRCA 200 A.D.) IN JUSTINIAN, DIGEST

50.17.75 (circa 534).

"Nemo potest mutare consilium suum in alterius iniuriam" [No one may change his mind to the injury of another.]

S. PUFENDORF, DE JURE NATURAE ET GENTIUM

Book III, ch. v., sec. 11 (1688).

[I]f a man has suffered any damage from the non-fulfilment of a promise (suppose a man has trusted another's word, and has in some way or other neglected to look to his own necessities), the promisor is bound by natural law to make good the matter; and from this it is right to conclude that a promise can be exacted, and a person must perform it, lest another suffer loss thereby.

MacCORMICK, VOLUNTARY OBLIGATIONS AND NORMATIVE POWERS

46 Proceedings Aristotelian Society Supp. vol. 59, 68 (1972).

[I]f one person acts in a potentially detrimental way in reliance upon beliefs about another's future conduct, and if the latter person has by some act of his intentionally or knowingly induced the former to rely upon him, then the latter has an obligation not to act in a manner which will disappoint the other's reliance.

ATIYAH, CONTRACTS, PROMISES AND THE LAW OF OBLIGATIONS

94 L.Q.Rev. 193, 202–03 (1978).

Is it not manifest that a person who has actually worsened his position by reliance on a promise has a more powerful case for redress than one who has not acted in reliance on the promise at all? A person who has not relied on a promise (nor paid for it) may suffer a disappointment of his expectations, but he does not actually suffer a pecuniary loss. The disappointment of an expectation may of course be treated as a species of loss by definition, as indeed, the law generally does treat it, if the expectation derives from Contract. But no definitional jugglery can actually equate the position of the party who suffers a diminution of his assets in reliance on a promise, and a person who suffers no such diminution.

KIRKSEY v. KIRKSEY

Supreme Court of Alabama, 1845.
8 Ala. 131.

Assumpsit by the defendant, against the plaintiff in error. The question is presented in this Court, upon a case agreed, which shows the following facts:

The plaintiff was the wife of defendant's brother, but had for some time been a widow, and had several children. In 1840, the plaintiff resided on public land, under a contract of lease, she had held over, and was comfortably settled, and would have attempted to secure the land she lived on. The defendant resided in Talladega County, some sixty or seventy miles off. On the 10th October, 1840, he wrote to her the following letter:

"Dear Sister Antillico,—Much to my mortification, I heard that brother Henry was dead, and one of his children. I know that your situation is one of grief and difficulty. You had a bad chance before, but a great deal worse now. I should like to come and see you, but cannot with convenience at present. * * * I do not know whether you have a preference on the place you live on or not. If you had, I would advise you to obtain your preference, and sell the land and quit the country, as I understand it is very unhealthy, and I know society is very bad. If you will come down and see me, I will let you have a place to raise your family, and I have more open land than I can tend; and on account of your situation, and that of your family, I feel like I want you and the children to do well.''

Within a month or two after the receipt of this letter, the plaintiff abandoned her possession, without disposing of it, and removed with her family, to the residence of the defendant, who put her in comfortable houses, and gave her land to cultivate for two years, at the end of which time he notified her to remove, and put her in a house, not comfortable, in the woods, which he afterwards required her to leave.

A verdict being found for the plaintiff, for $200, the above facts were agreed, and if they will sustain the action, the judgment is to be affirmed, otherwise it is to be reversed.

* * *

ORMOND, J. The inclination of my mind is that the loss and inconvenience which the plaintiff sustained in breaking up and moving to the defendant's, a distance of sixty miles, is a sufficient consideration to support the promise to furnish her with a house, and land to cultivate, until she could raise her family. My brothers, however, think that the promise on the part of the defendant was a mere gratuity, and that an action will not lie for its breach. The judgment of the court below must therefore be reversed, pursuant to the agreement of the parties.

RYERSS v. TRUSTEES OF PRESBYTERIAN CONGREGATION OF BLOSSBURG

Supreme Court of Pennsylvania, 1859.
33 Pa. 114.

WOODWARD, J.

* * *

The other assignments of error relate to the charge of the court.

Where a party encourages a congregation, in the manner and to the extent Ryerss did, to go on and build a church in a specified locality, promising a subscription or gift of $100, and recognising and repeating that promise under such circumstances as are detailed in the evidence—and they go on, within a reasonable time, and build a church in substantial conformity with the understanding and intention of the promisor, it is in vaine for him afterwards to deny the contract, its consideration, or its obligatory force.

The contract was evidenced by his repeated declarations and admissions—the consideration was in the labour, trouble, and expense to which he subjected the party promised, as well as in the benefit he expected * * * would accrue from the enterprise, to property wherein he was interested, in *unusual b/c promise is repeated. There was reliance on the promise.*

Holding:

the neighbourhood. If he did not mean it should be a denominational church, he should have stipulated for a free church. If he did not like the plan on which it was built, he should have prescribed a better, or urged his objection before other people expended their money on the faith of his promise.

There are no grounds of defence against a promise so well proved, and which is so abundantly supported by a consideration both good and valuable.

Issue:

Judgment:

The court [was] right in instructing the jury, that if they believed the evidence of the contract, the defendant was liable.

Was there consideration in his promise to give $100?

The judgment is affirmed.

H. MAINE, ANCIENT LAW
30 (10th ed. 1993).

I employ the expression "Legal Fiction" to signify any assumption which conceals, or affects to conceal, the fact that a rule of law has undergone alteration, its letter remaining unchanged, its operation being modified.

π filed suit
Δ moved to dismiss

SEAVEY v. DRAKE
Supreme Court of New Hampshire, 1882.
62 N.H. 393.

π   *Δ*

Bill in Equity, for specific performance of a parol agreement of land. At the hearing the plaintiff offered to prove that he was the only child of Shadrach Seavey, the defendants' testate, who died in 1880. In January, 1860, the testator, owning a tract of land, and wishing to assist the plaintiff, went upon the land with him and gave him a portion of it, which the plaintiff then accepted and took possession of. The plaintiff had a note against his father upon which there was due about $200, which he then or subsequently gave up to him. Subsequently his father gave him an additional strip of land adjoining the other tract. Ever since the gifts, the plaintiff has occupied and still occupies the land, and has paid all taxes upon it. He has expended $3,000 in the erection of a dwelling-house, barn, and stable, and in other improvements upon the premises. Some of the lumber for the house was given him by his father, who helped him to do some of the labor upon the house.

fact

fact

The defendants moved to dismiss the bill because no cause for equitable relief was stated, and because the parol contract, which is sought to be enforced, was without consideration, and is executory. The bill alleges a gift of the land to the plaintiff and a promise to give him a deed of it. The defendants also demurred, and answered denying the material allegations of the bill.

* * *

If the bill can be sustained on proof of these facts, or if not on these facts, but would be with the additional proof of a consideration for the promise, there is to be a further hearing, the plaintiff having leave to amend his bill. If on proof of these facts, either with or without proof of consideration, the bill cannot be sustained, it is to be dismissed.

SMITH, J. The bill alleges a promise by the defendants' testator to give the plaintiff a deed. The plaintiff offered to prove that the deceased gave him the land, and that he thereupon entered into possession and made valuable improvements. We assume that the plaintiff in his offer meant that he was induced by the gift of land to enter into possession and make large expenditures in permanent improvement upon it. The evidence offered is admissible. Specific performance of a parol contract to convey land is decreed in favor of the vendee who has performed his part of the contract, when a failure or refusal to convey would operate as a fraud upon him. * * * The statute of frauds (G.L., c. 220, s. 14) provides that "No action shall be maintained upon a contract for sale of land, unless the agreement upon which it is brought, or some memorandum thereof, is in writing, and signed by the party to be charged, or by some person by him thereto authorized in writing." Equity, however, lends its aid, when there has been part performance, to remove the bar of the statute, upon the ground that it is a fraud for the vendor to insist upon the absence of a written instrument, when he has permitted the contract to be partly executed.

It is not material in this case to know whether the promissory note given up by the plaintiff was or was not intended as payment or part payment for the land, for equity protects a parol gift of land equally with a parol agreement to sell it, if accompanied by possession, and the donee has made valuable improvements upon the property induced by the promise to give it. * * * There is no important distinction in this respect between a promise to give and a promise to sell. The expenditure in money or labor in the improvement of the land induced by the donor's promise to give the land to the party making the expenditure, constitutes, in equity, a consideration for the promise and the promise will be enforced.

Case discharged.

COMMONWEALTH v. SCITUATE SAVINGS BANK, 137 Mass. 301, 302 (1884) (Holmes, J.). "It would cut up the doctrine of consideration by the roots, if a promisee could make a gratuitous promise binding by subsequently acting in reliance on it." [Do you agree?]

Note
Differences Between Equity and Law

Seavey v. Drake begins with the statement "Bill in Equity, for specific performance of a parol agreement of land." It ends with a reference to what "constitutes, in equity, a consideration." The case appears here for its historic role in the emergence of a new theory of obligation in promissory contexts—the reliance theory (a theory that eventually came to be called "promissory estoppel"). That the case arose "in equity" rather than "at law" is relevant to this development. Among other things, courts of equity were generally less rigid than courts of law. To understand the reference in the opinion to "equity," you need further background.

In England during the middle ages a legal system emerged in which there were courts of law and a court of equity. Judges sitting in courts of law applied what was called the common law, which consisted primarily of judge-made law. The court of equity evolved partly because of the rigidity and inflexibility of substantive common law rules. Although the court of equity (presided over by the Chancellor or his deputies) usually followed the common law, that court also evolved some distinctively equitable doctrines that modified the common law. These doctrines included such equitable defenses as fraud, mistake, estoppel, unclean hands, laches, and unconscionability—all defenses that might be interposed in a contract case.

The English court of equity also arose because it met distinct remedial needs. For example, courts of law in contract actions would ordinarily grant only money damages for breach of contract. The court of equity, on the other hand, would grant "specific relief"—a decree directing the defendant to do or refrain from specific action. For example, the court of equity might order the defendant to perform a contract (a remedy called specific performance), or not to commit a tort (a remedy called an injunction). Ordinarily, the court of equity would require the party seeking relief to show that the remedy available in a court of law (usually a claim for money damages) would be inadequate. Only then would the court of equity grant specific relief. For example, a plaintiff in a contract action would have to show that money damages would be difficult to measure or that the goods promised were unique.

Courts of law and the court of equity also differed in rules of pleading and procedure. One of the most important differences was the absence of a jury in the equity court; the judge sat both as fact finder and as applier of substantive doctrines. The forms of pretrial discovery available in equity were also more elaborate. Certain other differences were largely formal. For example, the plaintiff at law would commence a case with a declaration, or later, a complaint. In equity, the claimant would file a bill. A legal proceeding at law was called an action, but a proceeding in equity was called a suit.

In addition, decrees (orders) of the court of equity were enforced largely by contempt proceedings, whereas judgments of a court of law were enforced by writs of execution empowering a sheriff to take property of the defendant, sell it, and pay off the judgment. Contempt proceedings are explained in Chapter 3 at pages 341–342.

Most of the distinctions between law and equity were transported to America in colonial times. Today in England and in nearly all states in this country, courts of law and courts of equity have merged into one court—a trial court of general jurisdiction with power to grant all remedies formerly granted by the two separate courts, and with power to apply all applicable substantive law, whether it originated as common law or as equitable doctrine. This merger took place in England from the 1840's through the 1870's largely through legislation. A similar merger movement took root in the United States about the same time, and separate courts of law and of equity are to be found today only in a very few states. In an important respect, the merger can never be complete in the United States because of constitutional guarantees of a jury trial in cases "at common law" (a topic you will study in the course on civil procedure). Partly for this reason, many states still maintain separate dockets for law actions and for equity suits even under modern unified court systems.

Because the plaintiff sought an equitable remedy, the trial judge in Seavey v. Drake (decided in 1882) was sitting as a court of equity. (What was that remedy?) The plaintiff also urged the judge to apply two distinctively equitable doctrines of substantive law in deciding the case. These doctrines modified the effect of rules that would have been applied if the case were before a court of law. Reread Seavey v. Drake and identify these two equitable doctrines. In this casebook, and in many of your other courses, you will encounter further cases that "arose in equity."

J. POMEROY'S EQUITY JURISPRUDENCE

264, 272–73 (1886).

[T]he following are the essential elements which must enter into and form part of an equitable estoppel in all of its phases and applications. * * * (1) There must be conduct—acts, language, or silence—amounting to a representation or concealment of material facts. (2) These facts must be known to the party estopped at the time of his said conduct, or at least, the circumstances must be such that knowledge of them is necessarily imputed to him. (3) The truth concerning these facts must be unknown to the other party claiming the benefit of the estoppel, at the time when such conduct was done, and at the time when it was acted upon by him. (4) The conduct must be done with the intention, or at least with the expectation, that it will be acted upon by the other party; or under such circumstances that it is both natural and probable that it will be so acted upon. * * * (5) The conduct must be relied upon by the other party, and thus relying he must be led to act upon it. (6) He must in fact act upon it in such a manner as to change his position for the worse; in other words, he must so act that he would suffer a loss if he were compelled to surrender or forego or alter what he has done by reason of the first party being permitted to repudiate his conduct and to assert rights inconsistent with it. * * *

* * *

* * * The conduct creating the estoppel must be something which amounts either to a representation or a concealment of the existence of facts. * * * The facts represented or concealed must, in general, be either existing or past, or at least represented to be so. A statement concerning future facts would either be a mere expression of opinion, or would constitute a contract and be governed by rules applicable to contracts.

RICKETTS v. SCOTHORN, 57 Neb. 51, 77 N.W. 365 (1898). [Katie Scothorn was a bookkeeper. Her grandfather said to her while she was at work: "I have fixed out something that you have not got to work any more. None of my grandchildren work and you don't have to." Katie's grandfather then gave her a promissory note for $2,000 and Katie immediately quit her job. More than a year later she took another job. Her grandfather died without paying the note. Judgment for Katie against her grandfather's executor was upheld. The court reasoned that the grandfather's executor was estopped to deny there was consideration for the promissory note.] "Having intentionally influenced the plaintiff to alter her position for the worse on the faith of the note being paid when due, it would be grossly inequitable to permit the maker, or his executor, to resist payment on the ground that the promise was given without consideration. The petition charges the elements of an equitable estoppel, and the evidence conclusively establishes them."

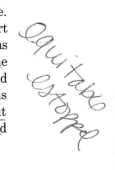

Tc for π
aff. by AD
△ appeals

SIEGEL v. SPEAR & CO.

Court of Appeals of New York, 1923.
234 N.Y. 479, 138 N.E. 414.

Action by William Siegel against Spear & Co. A determination of the Appellate Term affirming a judgment in favor of plaintiff was affirmed by the Appellate Division (195 App.Div. 845, 187 N.Y.S. 284), and defendant appeals by permission. Affirmed.

CRANE, J. The plaintiff commenced this action in the City Court of the city of New York, to recover his loss sustained by failure of the defendant to insure his household furniture stored in its storehouse. The action is based upon an alleged agreement to insure made with defendant's credit man. So far the plaintiff has been successful, the Appellate Division, however, certifying that in its opinion there is a question of law involved which should be reviewed by this court.

In August of 1917 and January of 1918 the plaintiff purchased of the defendant certain household furniture for the sum of $909.25 and took it to his apartment in New York City. He gave back to the defendant two chattel mortgages, which provided for monthly payments of the purchase price, and also that the furniture should not be removed from the plaintiff's residence without the written consent of the mortgagee.

By May of 1918 the plaintiff had paid in all $295. In that month, desiring to move from the city for the summer months and give up his apartment, the plaintiff went to the defendant's place of business in New York City to see about storing his furniture until his return. It was arranged with the defendant's credit man, McGrath, that the plaintiff should send his furniture by his own truck to the defendant's storehouse, and that defendant would keep it for him free of charge. It is claimed that McGrath at the time of making these arrangements also promised and agreed to insure the furniture for the plaintiff's benefit. The furniture had not been insured by the plaintiff at any time. The conversation is given by Mr. Siegel as follows:

"At that time he said, 'You had better transfer your insurance policy over to our warehouse.' I said: 'I haven't any insurance. I never thought of taking it out, as I never had time to take it out.' But I said: 'Before the furniture comes down I will have my insurance man, who insures my life, have the furniture insured and transferred over to your place.' He said: 'That won't be necessary to get that from him; I will do it for you; it will be a good deal cheaper; I handle lots of insurance; when you get the next bill—you can send a check for that with the next installment.' "

The furniture was sent to the defendant's storehouse about the 15th of May, and about the 15th of the following June was destroyed by fire. No insurance had been placed upon it.

Upon these facts the plaintiff has recovered the amount of his loss. The defendant raises at least two objections to this result. It claims, first, that there was no consideration for the alleged agreement made with McGrath to insure the furniture, and, second, that McGrath had no authority to make any such contract even if he did.

We are inclined to think that if the contract were made—and we must assume it was, as there is evidence to sustain the findings of the jury to this effect—there was in the nature of the case a consideration sufficient to sustain the promise. It is, of course, a fact that the defendant undertook to store the plaintiff's property without any compensation. The fact that it had a chattel mortgage upon the property did not affect its relationship as a bailee without pay. Under these circumstances it was not liable for the destruction of the goods by fire unless due to its gross neglect. * * * There is no such element in this case.

But if, in connection with taking the goods, McGrath also voluntarily undertook to procure insurance for the plaintiff's benefit, the promise was part of the whole transaction and was linked up with the gratuitous bailment. The bailee, if such a contract were within McGrath's agency, was then under as much of an obligation to procure insurance as he was to take care of the goods.

When McGrath stated that he would insure the furniture it was still in the plaintiff's possession. It was after his statements and promises that the plaintiff sent the furniture to the storehouse. The defendant or McGrath entered upon the execution of the trust. It is in this particular that this case differs from Thorne v. Deas, 4 Johns. 84, 99, so much relied upon by the defendant. In that case A. and B. were joint owners of a vessel. A. voluntarily undertook to get the vessel insured but neglected to do so. The vessel having been lost at sea, it was held that no action would lie against A. for the nonperformance of his promise, although B. had relied upon that promise to his loss. It was said that there was no consideration for the promise. In that case there was the mere naked promise of A. that he would insure the vessel. B. parted with nothing to A. He gave up possession of none of his property to A., nor of any interest in his vessel. The case would have been decided differently, no doubt, if he had. As Chancellor Kent said in referring to the earlier cases:

B didn't do anything to enforce the promise

"There was no dispute or doubt but that an action upon the case lay for a misfeasance, in the breach of a trust undertaken voluntarily."

* * *

In the case of Rutgers v. Lucet, 2 Johns.Cas. 92, 95, the law on this point was stated to be as follows:

"A mere agreement to undertake a trust, in futuro, without compensation, it is true, is not obligatory; but when once undertaken, and the trust actually entered upon, the bailee is bound to perform it, according to the terms of his agreement. The confidence placed in him, and his undertaking to execute the trust, raise a sufficient consideration; a contrary doctrine would tend to injure and deceive his employer, who might be unwilling to consent to the bailment on any other terms."

In Hammond v. Hussey, 51 N.H. 40, 50 (12 Am.Rep. 41), the court, quoting Professor Parsons, says:

"If a person makes a gratuitous promise, and then enters upon the performance of it, he is held to a full execution of all he has undertaken."

Where one had gratuitously undertaken to carry the money of a bailor to a certain place and deliver it to another, and, after receiving the money, the bailee gave it to a neighbor who undertook to make delivery and lost it, it was held that the bailee had violated his trust in handling the money, that he was guilty of gross negligence in not fulfilling the terms of the bailment. Colyar v. Taylor, 41 Tenn. (1 Cold.) 372 * * *.

From this aspect of the case we think there was a consideration for the agreement to insure. This renders it unnecessary to determine whether the plaintiff, in refraining from insuring through his own agent at the suggestion of McGrath, surrendered any right which would furnish a consideration for McGrath's promise.

I find that Thorne v. Deas, supra, has been seldom cited upon this question of consideration, and whether or not we would feel bound to follow it to-day must be left open until the question comes properly before us.

As to McGrath's authority to act in this matter, we do not find the point raised by any sufficient exception.

For the reasons here stated, the judgment must be affirmed, with costs.

SEAVEY, RELIANCE UPON GRATUITOUS PROMISES OR OTHER CONDUCT

64 Harv.L.Rev. 913, 925–28 (1951).

This brings us, at last, to the Thorne v. Deas situation, where there has been a failure to perform a gratuitous promise which, it is assumed, was made in good faith. * * *

[A] way of dealing with it is to use tort principles. * * * Estoppel is basically a tort doctrine. * * * The wrong is not primarily in depriving the plaintiff of the promised reward but in causing the plaintiff to change position to his detriment. * * *

* * *

* * * [T]he judges are not even yet sure of themselves in the application of the general tort principle that one is responsible for harm caused by unprivileged conduct which he had reason to know would harm another. The application of this principle to the special field of promises and representations might perhaps be expressed as follows:

> Where a person represents by word or act that he has done or will do something upon the performance of which he should realize that others will rely, he is liable for expected harm caused by the reliance of others and his failure of performance, if his representation was negligently or intentionally false, or if without excuse he fails to perform.

Problem 2–6

Fred and Martha Shippers owned a farm and buildings that were insured by the Prudential Insurance Company. The farmhouse burned to the ground. Fred asked Jones, Prudential's agent, if Jones would file the claim required under the policy and Jones replied, "yes." Fred then said, "I leave it up to you." Jones failed to file the claim. When Prudential refused to pay on the policy, Fred brought an action against Jones. Jones asserts that his promise to file the claim was not supported by consideration and that, at most, he was a gratuitous agent, who is not liable for his failure to perform his promise, i.e. not liable for nonfeasance.

You are the judge in the case of Shippers v. Jones. Consider first Jones's defense. What cases that we have studied, if any, would Jones cite in support? Can Fred Shippers satisfactorily distinguish the above cases? What cases will Fred cite, and in support of what theories of obligation? Can these be distinguished? Decide the appeal.

RESTATEMENT (FIRST) OF CONTRACTS § 90 (1932).

Promise Reasonably Inducing Definite and Substantial Action

A promise which the promisor should reasonably expect to induce action or forebearance of a definite and substantial character on the part of the promisee and which does induce such action or forebearance is binding if injustice can be avoided only by enforcement of the promise.

EXPLANATORY NOTES IN RESTATEMENT (FIRST) OF CONTRACTS

245–50 (Special Limited Ed. 1928).[m]

SECTION 90

As this Section states a broader rule than has often been laid down, a somewhat full discussion of it seems appropriate.

* * *

Specific performance lies on a gratuitous promise to convey land if the promisee has been given possession or has both been given possession and made improvements. * * *

* * *

Charitable subscriptions are generally enforced in the United States at least after action in reliance upon them has been taken.

* * *

Promises to others than to charities have been upheld on similar grounds. Sometimes this is done with the frank admission that estoppel rather than consideration is the basis of recovery. * * * Compare with these cases the contrary decision of Kirksey v. Kirksey (1845), 8 Ala. 131. * * * The injustice of the result is manifest.

* * *

Gratuitous undertakings of bailees and sometimes of other persons have been enforced when relied upon. * * * Frequently these cases can be supported on the ground of tort but not always. A striking recent case is Siegel v. Spear, [1923], 234 N.Y. 479, 138 N.E. 414.

* * *

m. The following is Professor Williston's testimony before the American Law Institute. He was Chief Reporter of the Restatement (First) of Contracts.

A large body of cases ordinarily classified under the heading of "Waiver" in reality involve nothing but promises held binding on the promisor. * * * The law is clear that in any case where a party to a contract agrees to give up a possible future defence or forgo the advantage of a condition of an existing contract provided for his benefit, the promise is binding if the promisee relying thereon changes his position.

* * *

If the law is to be simplified and clarified, it can be done only by coordinating the decisions under general rules not by stating empirically a succession of specific cases without any binding thread of principle. In fact there is a binding thread in all the classes of cases which have been enumerated, namely, the justifiable reliance of the promisee. * * *

It is not to be denied that there are numerous cases in which this element is held not sufficient to make a gratuitous promise binding. Therefore, Section 90 does not assert a sweeping rule that in every case action in reliance is sufficient support for a promise. In the first place it is only where the action induced is definite and substantial that any legal consequences follow from the gratuitous promise. In the second place such an action should reasonably have been expected by the promisor. Under these words it will not be enough that some action of the promisee, even of substantial character, has been induced by the promise. The promise of one thousand dollars for the purchase of a motor car may be binding under the Section if the promisee induced thereby has purchased the car. A promise of a thousand dollars generally without specification of the purpose will not bind the promisor even though induced by the promise a contract is made for the purchase of a car.

Finally, the words are added at the end of the Section for greater caution: "If injustice can be avoided only by enforcement of the promise." With these qualifications it is believed that the provisions of Section 90 do not go beyond existing law, in many jurisdictions at least, and that the Section is a useful co-ordination of the classes of cases enumerated above.

Note
The Emergence of a New Theory of Obligation

When the American Law Institute adopted section 90 of the Restatement (First) of Contracts in 1931[n], it recognized a new theory of obligation called "promissory estoppel." Be sure you can identify the main requisites of this theory. Consider, too, how Kirksey v. Kirksey and Thorne v. Deas would have been decided under it. Can you differentiate Section 90 from the theory of agreement with consideration? If you can, you will see that the theory of Section 90 has independent significance—it can generate a duty in some circumstances in which the theory of agreement with consideration would not. At the same time, the theory of agreement with consideration also has independent significance—it can generate a duty in some circumstances in which the theory of promissory estoppel would not.

Observe that Ryerss v. Trustees, Seavey v. Drake, Ricketts v. Scothorn, and Siegel v. Spear & Co. were all decided in favor of the relying party. Nevertheless, a

n. See the materials at pages 48–50.

new *theory of obligation* was not explicitly recognized in those cases. Can you explain?

The explicit recognition of a new theory of obligation in the law is a rare development, and one of great potential significance. Theory tends to dominate practice. Consider, for example, how a court would have decided Problem 2–6 if the court in Siegel v. Spear & Co. had articulated the theory of section 90.

S. WILLISTON AND G. THOMPSON, 1 A TREATISE ON THE LAW OF CONTRACTS

§ 139 at 494 (1936).

Estoppel as a substitute for consideration. It is generally true that one who has led another to act in reasonable reliance on his representations of fact cannot afterwards in litigation between the two deny the truth of the representations, and some courts have sought to apply this principle to the formation of contracts, where, relying on a gratuitous promise, the promisee has suffered detriment.

NOTE, CONTRACTS, PROMISSORY ESTOPPEL

20 Va.L.Rev. 214, 218–219 (1933).

The prime objection to the recognition of promissory estoppel lies in the upheaval which would be caused in the law of contract, especially with regard to the rules of consideration, consequent upon its application. The fear that general adoption of the doctrine would tend to abolish consideration in contract cases is almost universal. * * * The doctrine definitely lies outside of contract law; * * * the question of what limits would be applied to it, once adopted, seems potent; the certainty which seems requisite in a great basic branch of law like that of contract, would seem doomed to demolition * * *. On the other hand, we must consider the plight into which the courts have forced themselves by their general refusal to acknowledge the applicability of promissory estoppel. In the main they have resorted to contract law, and by indulging in fictions and unfortunate analogies have jammed, stretched, and distorted "rules" of consideration * * * where consideration has no real application according to its established conception. * * *

1A CORBIN ON CONTRACTS

§ 200 at 221 (1963).

A limitation on the reliance doctrine * * * may be stated as follows: If a promisor offers his promise as part of a bargain for and in consideration of a specified equivalent, the promisee can not make the promise binding by acting in reliance upon it in a manner that constitutes no part of that specified equivalent. * * *

WHEELER v. WHITE

Supreme Court of Texas, 1965.
398 S.W.2d 93.

SMITH, JUSTICE.

This is a suit for damages brought by petitioner, Ellis D. Wheeler, against respondent, S.E. White. Wheeler alleged that White had breached a contract[1] to secure a loan or furnish the money to finance the construction of improvements upon land owned by Wheeler. Wheeler further pleaded, in the alternative, that if the contract itself was not sufficiently definite, then nevertheless White was estopped from asserting such insufficiency. White filed special exceptions to all of Wheeler's Third Amended Original Petition. The special exceptions asserted that the pleaded contract did not contain essential ele-

---

1. Contract between Ellis D. Wheeler, Party of the First Part, and S.E. White, Party of the Second Part:

"That said Party of the First Part is the owner of Lots Nine (9), Ten (10), and Eleven (11) (excepting the South one hundred ten (110') feet of Lot Nine (9), all of Block Number Seven (7), of BRINKMAN ADDITION to the City of Port Arthur, Jefferson County, Texas. Said Party of the First Part hereby employs Party of the Second Part for the purpose of securing a loan to finance the construction of improvements upon said property; said improvements to face on the Port Arthur–Orange Highway one hundred forty feet (140') and extend back a depth of eighty feet (80'); said building to be constructed according to plans and specifications heretofore agreed on by the parties hereto. The loan to be made by, or obtained by, Party of the Second Part for the Party of the First Part, and to be in the sum of SEVENTY THOUSAND AND 00/100 ($70,-000.00) DOLLARS and to be payable in monthly installments over a term of fifteen (15) years and bear interest at a rate of not more than six (6%) per cent per annum.

"Said loan is to be obtained on or before six (6) months from date of this contract, either from funds provided by Party of the Second Part or from third persons whom Party of the Second Part may negotiate with to provide such funds. In either event Party of the First Part agrees to sign all necessary papers required of Lendor to create proper liens.

"Party of the First Part agrees to pay to Party of the Second Part the sum of FIVE THOUSAND AND 00/100 ($5,000.00) DOLLARS for his services in making or securing said loan for Party of the First Part. Said FIVE THOUSAND AND 00/100 ($5,000.00) DOLLARS shall be due and payable to Party of the Second Part as soon as the SEVENTY THOUSAND AND 00/100 ($70,000.00) DOLLARS loan is made available for construction of said premises; and should party of the First Part fail and refuse to pay said FIVE THOUSAND DOLLARS ($5,000.00) when due, Party of the

Second Part shall have the right to enforce payment by filing suit in a Court of competent jurisdiction, and Party of the First Part hereby specifically agrees to pay ten (10%) per cent additional on said sum as Attorney Fees and all costs of Court in connection with said suit.

"This agreement voids and takes precedence over previous agreements by and between Ellis D. Wheeler and S.E. White, concerning the hereinabove described property.

"Party of the First Part agrees that when said loan has been obtained that he will proceed with all reasonable haste and diligence in having the improvements for which said loan is obtained constructed, and to execute all necessary agreements, liens, etc., that may be required in the process of, and consummating said loan. In the event that Party of the Second Part obtains said loan but Party of the First Part does not use the financing thus obtained by Party of the Second Part for any reason, then Party of the First Part will pay to Party of the Second Part the sum of FIVE THOUSAND AND 00/100 ($5,000.00) DOLLARS for his services in obtaining said loan.

"In addition to the above, Party of the First Part agrees to allow Party of the Second Part six (6) months exclusive right to secure reliable tenants to occupy seventy (70') feet frontage in the Commercial Building which he contemplates building, said seventy (70') feet fronting on the Port Arthur–Orange Highway; said rentals to be not less than ONE AND 60/100 ($1.60) DOLLARS per square foot per year. Should Party of the Second Part secure tenants to the remaining seventy (70') feet frontage before tenants are secured by Party of the First Part, or others, then Party of the Second Part may secure tenants for the remaining portion of said building. Party of the First Part agrees to pay Party of the Second Part, in addition to the payment of said FIVE THOUSAND AND 00/100 ($5,000.00) DOLLARS as above specified, a five (5%) per cent commission on all rentals paid by tenants obtained by Party of the Second Part; said five (5%) per cent commission to be paid for the life of the lease granted to said tenants."

ments to its enforceability in that it failed to provide the amount of monthly installments, the amount of interest due upon the obligation, how such interest would be computed, when such interest would be paid, and that the alternative plea of estoppel was, as a matter of law, insufficient to establish any ground of recovery. All special exceptions were sustained, and upon Wheeler's declination to amend his pleadings, the trial court entered its judgment dismissing the case and ordered that Wheeler take nothing from White by reason of his suit. The Court of Civil Appeals has affirmed the judgment of the trial court. 385 S.W.2d 619. We have concluded that the trial court did not err in sustaining the special exceptions directed at the sufficiency of the contract itself, but that Wheeler's pleadings on the theory of estoppel state a cause of action. Accordingly, we reverse the judgments of the trial court and the Court of Civil Appeals and remand the cause for trial.

Since the trial court sustained White's special exceptions to Wheeler's petition, we necessarily must assume that all the alleged material facts are true. Wheeler alleged that as the owner of a three-lot tract of land in Port Arthur, Texas, he desired to construct a commercial building or shopping center thereon. He and White entered into an agreement, embodied in the written contract involved here, whereby White was to obtain the necessary loan for Wheeler from a third party or provide it himself on or before six months from the date of the contract. The loan as described in the contract, was to be " * * * in the sum of SEVENTY THOUSAND AND 00/100 ($70,000.00) DOLLARS and to be payable in monthly installments over a term of fifteen (15) years and bear interest at a rate of not more than six (6%) per cent per annum." Additionally, under the contract White was to be paid $5,000.00 for obtaining the loan and a five per cent commission on all rentals received from any tenants procured by White for the building. Wheeler alleged that he has been ready and willing to comply with his part of the agreement at all times since the contract was made.

After the contract had been signed by both parties, White assured Wheeler that the money would be available and urged him to proceed with the necessary task of demolishing the buildings presently on the site so as to make way for construction of the new building. The buildings on the site had a reasonable value of $58,500.00 and a rental value of $400.00 per month. By way of reassurance, White stressed the fact that in the event the money was unobtainable elsewhere, he would make the loan himself. Pursuant to such promises Wheeler proceeded to raze the old building and otherwise prepare the land for the new structure; thereafter, he was told by White that there would be no loan. After White's refusal to perform, Wheeler made reasonable efforts to obtain the loan himself but was unsuccessful. In the pleadings[2]

---

2. "Pleading further plaintiff shows the Court that if for any reason said contract is not sufficiently specific and definite, then nevertheless defendant is estopped to so claim and to set up any insufficiency because of the defendant's act in entering into said contract and exhorting plaintiff to clear the premises to make ready for the construction and defendant's representations after the date of said contract to proceed with the demolition of said buildings and clearing the site and that the money would be forthcoming and that defendant would obtain said loan and if for any reason said money could not be obtained elsewhere then said defendant would himself loan the money and plaintiff in reliance on said contract and said exhortations and said representations, both in said contract and given verbally by the defendant after the date of said contract defendant is estopped to claim any deficiency of said contract."

Wheeler pleaded the necessary elements of inducement and reliance which entitle him to recover if he can prove the facts alleged.

Where a promisee acts to his detriment in reasonable reliance upon an otherwise unenforceable promise, courts in other jurisdictions have recognized that the disappointed party may have a substantial and compelling claim for relief. The Restatement, Contracts, § 90, says:

> "A promise which the promisor should reasonably expect to induce action or forbearance of a definite and substantial character on the part of the promisee and which does induce such action or forbearance is binding if injustice can be avoided only by enforcement of the promise."

According to Dean Hildebrand's Texas Annotation to the Restatement, Texas follows Section 90, supra. * * *

The binding thread which runs through the cases applying promissory estoppel is the existence of promises designedly made to influence the conduct of the promisee, tacitly encouraging the conduct, which conduct, although not necessarily constituting any actual performance of the contract itself, is something that must be done by the promisee before he could begin to perform, and was a fact known to the promissor. As to the argument that no new cause of action may be created by such a promise regardless of its established applicability as a defense, it has been answered that where one party has by his words or conduct made to the other a promise or assurance which was intended to affect the legal relations between them and to be acted on accordingly, then, once the other party has taken him at his word and acted on it, the party who gave the promise cannot afterward be allowed to revert to the previous relationship as if no such promise had been made. This does not create a contract where none existed before, but only prevents a party from insisting upon his strict legal rights when it would be unjust to allow him to enforce them. See 1 Williston, Contracts, §§ 139–40 (Rev. ed. 1936); and 48 A.L.R.2d 1069 (1956).

The function of the doctrine of promissory estoppel is, under our view, defensive in that it estops a promisor from denying the enforceability of the promise. It was said in the case of Dickerson v. Colgrove, 100 U.S. 578, 580, 25 L.Ed. 618, that:

> "The vital principle is that he who by his language or conduct leads another to do what he would not otherwise have done, shall not subject such person to loss or injury by disappointing the expectations upon which he acted. Such a change of position is sternly forbidden * * *. This remedy is always so applied as to promote the ends of justice."

* * * Under this theory, losses of expected profits will not be allowed even if expected profits are provable with certainty. The rule thus announced should be followed in the present case. We agree with the reasoning announced in those jurisdictions that, in cases such as we have before us, where there is actually no contract the promissory estoppel theory may be invoked, thereby supplying a remedy which will enable the injured party to be compensated for his foreseeable, definite and substantial reliance. Where the promisee has failed to bind the promisor to a legally sufficient contract, but where the promisee has acted in reliance upon a promise to his detriment, the promisee is to be allowed to recover no more than reliance damages measured

by the detriment sustained. Since the promisee in such cases is partially responsible for his failure to bind the promisor to a legally sufficient contract, it is reasonable to conclude that all that is required to achieve justice is to put the promisee in the position he would have been in had he not acted in reliance upon the promise. * * *

The judgments of the trial court and the Court of Civil Appeals are both reversed and judgment is here entered remanding the cause to the trial court for trial on its merits in accordance with this opinion.

GREENHILL, JUSTICE (concurring).

The Court of Civil Appeals denied a recovery of damages here because the contract, it felt, was too indefinite in its provisions under Bryant v. Clark, 163 Tex. 596, 358 S.W.2d 614 (1962). The holding in Bryant v. Clark was that the contract was not sufficiently definite to be specifically enforceable. The contract here in question, viewed in context, is different in some respects from that in the Bryant case; and I would not extend Bryant v. Clark. See the criticism of that case in 5A Corbin, Contracts 283 (1964).

But assuming that the contract here, under Bryant v. Clark, is not definite enough to be specifically enforced, it is sufficiently definite to support an action for damages. Restatement, Contracts § 370, comment b.

There are Texas cases in which damages have been denied after a holding that the contract was not specifically enforceable. In each of these cases, however, the contracts were held to be within the Statute of Frauds and not enforceable for that reason in a suit for damages. 1 Williston, Contracts § 16 (Rev. ed. 1936). The contract here in question is not within the Statute of Frauds and will support an action for damages.

While I agree with the judgment entered by the Court, it seems to me that the above is a sounder ground upon which to rest our decision.

HOFFMAN v. RED OWL STORES

Supreme Court of Wisconsin, 1965.
26 Wis.2d 683, 133 N.W.2d 267.

Action by Joseph Hoffman (hereinafter "Hoffman") and wife, plaintiffs, against defendants Red Owl Stores, Inc. (hereinafter "Red Owl") and Edward Lukowitz.

The complaint alleged that Lukowitz, as agent for Red Owl, represented to and agreed with plaintiffs that Red Owl would build a store building in Chilton and stock it with merchandise for Hoffman to operate in return for which plaintiffs were to put up and invest a total sum of $18,000; that in reliance upon the above mentioned agreement and representations plaintiffs sold their bakery building and business and their grocery store and business; also in reliance on the agreement and representations Hoffman purchased the building site in Chilton and rented a residence for himself and his family in Chilton; plaintiffs' actions in reliance on the representations and agreement disrupted their personal and business life; plaintiffs lost substantial amounts of income and expended large sums of money as expenses. Plaintiffs demanded recovery of damages for the breach of defendants' representations and agreements.

The action was tried to a court and jury. The facts hereafter stated are taken from the evidence adduced at the trial. Where there was a conflict in the evidence the version favorable to plaintiffs has been accepted since the verdict rendered was in favor of plaintiffs.

Hoffman assisted by his wife operated a bakery at Wautoma from 1956 until sale of the building late in 1961. The building was owned in joint tenancy by him and his wife. Red Owl is a Minnesota corporation having its home office at Hopkins, Minnesota. It owns and operates a number of grocery supermarket stores and also extends franchises to agency stores which are owned by individuals, partnerships and corporations. Lukowitz resides at Green Bay and since September, 1960, has been divisional manager for Red Owl in a territory comprising Upper Michigan and most of Wisconsin in charge of 84 stores. Prior to September, 1960, he was district manager having charge of approximately 20 stores.

In November, 1959, Hoffman was desirous of expanding his operations by establishing a grocery store and contacted a Red Owl representative by the name of Jansen, now deceased. Numerous conversations were had in 1960 with the idea of establishing a Red Owl franchise store in Wautoma. In September, 1960, Lukowitz succeeded Jansen as Red Owl's representative in the negotiations. Hoffman mentioned that $18,000 was all the capital he had available to invest and he was repeatedly assured that this would be sufficient to set him up in business as a Red Owl store. About Christmastime, 1960, Hoffman thought it would be a good idea if he bought a small grocery store in Wautoma and operated it in order that he gain experience in the grocery business prior to operating a Red Owl store in some larger community. On February 6, 1961, on the advice of Lukowitz and Sykes, who had succeeded Lukowitz as Red Owl's district manager, Hoffman bought the inventory and fixtures of a small grocery store in Wautoma and leased the building in which it was operated.

After three months of operating this Wautoma store, the Red Owl representatives came in and took inventory and checked the operations and found the store was operating at a profit. Lukowitz advised Hoffman to sell the store to his manager, and assured him that Red Owl would find a larger store for him elsewhere. Acting on this advice and assurance, Hoffman sold the fixtures and inventory to his manager on June 6, 1961. Hoffman was reluctant to sell at that time because it meant losing the summer tourist business, but he sold on the assurance that he would be operating in a new location by fall and that he must sell this store if he wanted a bigger one. Before selling, Hoffman told the Red Owl representatives that he had $18,000 for "getting set up in business" and they assured him that there would be no problems in establishing him in a bigger operation. The makeup of the $18,000 was not discussed; it was understood plaintiff's father-in-law would furnish part of it. By June, 1961, the towns for the new grocery store had been narrowed down to two, Kewaunee and Chilton. In Kewaunee, Red Owl had an option on a building site. In Chilton, Red Owl had nothing under option, but it did select a site to which plaintiff obtained an option at Red Owl's suggestion. The option stipulated a purchase price of $6,000 with $1,000 to be paid on election to purchase and the balance to be paid within 30 days. On Lukowitz's assurance that everything was all set plaintiff paid $1,000 down on the lot on September 15th.

On September 27, 1961, plaintiff met at Chilton with Lukowitz and Mr. Reymund and Mr. Carlson from the home office who prepared a projected financial statement. Part of the funds plaintiffs were to supply as their investment in the venture were to be obtained by sale of their Wautoma bakery building.

On the basis of this meeting Lukowitz assured Hoffman: " * * * [E]verything is ready to go. Get your money together and we are set." Shortly after this meeting Lukowitz told plaintiffs that they would have to sell their bakery business and bakery building, and that their retaining this property was the only "hitch" in the entire plan. On November 6, 1961, plaintiffs sold their bakery building for $10,000. Hoffman was to retain the bakery equipment as he contemplated using it to operate a bakery in connection with his Red Owl store. After sale of the bakery Hoffman obtained employment on the night shift at an Appleton bakery.

The record contains different exhibits which were prepared in September and October, some of which were projections of the fiscal operation of the business and others were proposed building and floor plans. Red Owl was to procure some third party to buy the Chilton lot from Hoffman, construct the building, and then lease it to Hoffman. No final plans were ever made, nor were bids let or a construction contract entered. Some time prior to November 20, 1961, certain of the terms of the lease under which the building was to be rented by Hoffman were understood between him and Lukowitz. The lease was to be for 10 years with a rental approximating $550 a month calculated on the basis of 1 percent per month on the building cost, plus 6 percent of the land cost divided on a monthly basis. At the end of the 10–year term he was to have an option to renew the lease for an additional 10–year period or to buy the property at cost on an instalment basis. There was no discussion as to what the instalments would be or with respect to repairs and maintenance.

On November 22nd or 23rd, Lukowitz and plaintiffs met in Minneapolis with Red Owl's credit manager to confer on Hoffman's financial standing and on financing the agency. Another projected financial statement was there drawn up entitled, "Proposed Financing For An Agency Store." This showed Hoffman contributing $24,100 of cash capital of which only $4,600 was to be cash possessed by plaintiffs. Eight thousand was to be procured as a loan from a Chilton bank secured by a mortgage on the bakery fixtures, $7,500 was to be obtained on a 5 percent loan from the father-in-law, and $4,000 was to be obtained by sale of the lot to the lessor at a profit.

A week or two after the Minneapolis meeting Lukowitz showed Hoffman a telegram from the home office to the effect that if plaintiff could get another $2,000 for promotional purposes the deal could go through for $26,000. Hoffman stated he would have to find out if he could get another $2,000. He met with his father-in-law, who agreed to put $13,000 into the business provided he could come into the business as a partner. Lukowitz told Hoffman the partnership arrangement "sounds fine" and that Hoffman should not go into the partnership arrangement with the "front office." On January 16, 1962, the Red Owl credit manager teletyped Lukowitz that the father-in-law would have to sign an agreement that the $13,000 was either a gift or a loan subordinate to all general creditors and that he would prepare the agreement. On January 31, 1962, Lukowitz teletyped the home office that the father-in-law would sign one or other of the agreements. However, Hoffman testified that it was not until the final meeting some time between January 26th and February 2nd, 1962, that he was told that his father-in-law was expected to sign an agreement that the $13,000 he was advancing was to be an outright gift. No mention was then made by the Red Owl representatives of the alternative of the father-in-law signing a subordination agreement. At this meeting the Red Owl agents presented Hoffman with the following projected financial statement:

"Capital required in operation:

"Cash		$ 5,000.00
"Merchandise		20,000.00
"Bakery		18,000.00
"Fixtures		17,500.00
"Promotional Funds		1,500.00
	"TOTAL:	$62,000.00

"Source of funds:

"Red Owl 7–day terms		$ 5,000.00
"Red Owl Fixture contract (Term 5 years)		14,000.00
"Bank loans (Term 9 years) Union State Bank of Chilton (Secured by Bakery Equipment)		8,000.00
"Other loans (Term No-pay) No interest Father-in-law (Secured by None)		13,000.00
(Secured by Mortgage on Wautoma Bakery Bldg.)		2,000.00
"Resale of land		6,000.00
"Equity Capital:	$ 5,000.00–Cash	
"Amount owner has to invest:	17,500.00–Bakery Equip.	
		22,500.00
	"TOTAL:	$70,500.00"

Hoffman interpreted the above statement to require of plaintiffs a total of $34,000 cash made up of $13,000 gift from his father-in-law, $2,000 on mortgage, $8,000 on Chilton bank loan, $5,000 in cash from plaintiff, and $6,000 on the resale of the Chilton lot. Red Owl claims $18,000 is the total of the unborrowed or unencumbered cash, that is, $13,000 from the father-in-law and $5,000 cash from Hoffman himself. Hoffman informed Red Owl he could not go along with this proposal, and particularly objected to the requirement that his father-in-law sign an agreement that his $13,000 advancement was an absolute gift. This terminated the negotiations between the parties.

The case was submitted to the jury on a special verdict with the first two questions answered by the court. This verdict, as returned by the jury, was as follows:

"Question No. 1: Did the Red Owl Stores, Inc. and Joseph Hoffman on or about mid-May of 1961 initiate negotiations looking to the establishment of Joseph Hoffman as a franchise operator of a Red Owl Store in Chilton? Answer: Yes. (Answered by the Court.)

"Question No. 2: Did the parties mutually agree on all of the details of the proposal so as to reach a final agreement thereon? Answer: No. (Answered by the Court.)

"Question No. 3: Did the Red Owl Stores, Inc., in the course of said negotiations, make representations to Joseph Hoffman that if he fulfilled certain conditions that they would establish him as a franchise operator of a Red Owl Store in Chilton? Answer: Yes.

"Question No. 4: If you have answered Question No. 3 'Yes,' then answer this question: Did Joseph Hoffman rely on said representations and was he induced to act thereon? Answer: Yes.

"Question No. 5: If you have answered Question No. 4 'Yes,' then answer this question: Ought Joseph Hoffman, in the exercise of ordinary care, to have relied on said representations? Answer: Yes.

"Question No. 6: If you have answered Question No. 3 'Yes' then answer this question: Did Joseph Hoffman fulfill all the conditions he was required to fulfill by the terms of the negotiations between the parties up to January 26, 1962? Answer: Yes.

"Question No. 7: What sum of money will reasonably compensate the plaintiffs for such damages as they sustained by reason of:

"(a) The sale of the Wautoma store fixtures and inventory?

"Answer: $16,735.00.

"(b) The sale of the bakery building?

"Answer: $2,000.00.

"(c) Taking up the option on the Chilton lot?

"Answer: $1,000.00.

"(d) Expenses of moving his family to Neenah?

"Answer: $140.00.

"(e) House rental in Chilton?

"Answer: $125.00."

Plaintiffs moved for judgment on the verdict while defendants moved to change the answers to Questions 3, 4, 5, and 6 from "Yes" to "No", and in the alternative for relief from the answers to the subdivisions of Question 7 or a new trial. On March 31, 1964, the circuit court entered the following order:

"IT IS ORDERED in accordance with said decision on motions after verdict hereby incorporated herein by reference:

"1. That the answer of the jury to Question No. 7(a) be and the same is hereby vacated and set aside and that a new trial be had on the sole issue of the damages for loss, if any, on the sale of the Wautoma store, fixtures and inventory.

"2. That all other portions of the verdict of the jury be and hereby are approved and confirmed and all after-verdict motions of the parties inconsistent with this order are hereby denied."

Defendants have appealed from this order and plaintiffs have cross-appealed from paragraph 1, thereof.

* * *

CURRIE, CHIEF JUSTICE.

The instant appeal and cross-appeal present these questions:

Issues

(1) Whether this court should recognize causes of action grounded on promissory estoppel as exemplified by sec. 90 of Restatement, 1 Contracts?

(2) Do the facts in this case make out a cause of action for promissory estoppel?

(3) Are the jury's findings with respect to damages sustained by the evidence?

Recognition of a Cause of Action Grounded on Promissory Estoppel.

* * *

* * * Not only did the trial court frame the special verdict on the theory of sec. 90 of Restatement, 1 Contracts, but no other possible theory has been presented to or discovered by this court which would permit plaintiffs to recover. Of other remedies considered that of an action for fraud and deceit seemed to be the most comparable. An action at law for fraud, however, cannot be predicated on unfulfilled promises unless the promisor possessed the present intent not to perform. Suskey v. Davidoff (1958), 2 Wis.2d 503, 507, 87 N.W.2d 306, and cases cited. Here, there is no evidence that would support a finding that Lukowitz made any of the promises, upon which plaintiffs' complaint is predicated, in bad faith with any present intent that they would not be fulfilled by Red Owl.

Many courts of other jurisdictions have seen fit over the years to adopt the principle of promissory estoppel, and the tendency in that direction continues. * * *

* * *

Because we deem the doctrine of promissory estoppel, as stated in sec. 90 of Restatement, 1 Contracts, is one which supplies a needed tool which courts may employ in a proper case to prevent injustice, we endorse and adopt it.

Applicability of Doctrine to Facts of this Case.

The record here discloses a number of promises and assurances given to Hoffman by Lukowitz in behalf of Red Owl upon which plaintiffs relied and acted upon to their detriment.

Foremost were the promises that for the sum of $18,000 Red Owl would establish Hoffman in a store. After Hoffman had sold his grocery store and paid the $1,000 on the Chilton lot, the $18,000 figure was changed to $24,100. Then in November, 1961, Hoffman was assured that if the $24,100 figure were increased by $2,000 the deal would go through. Hoffman was induced to sell his grocery store fixtures and inventory in June, 1961, on the promise that he would be in his new store by fall. In November, plaintiffs sold their bakery building on the urging of defendants and on the assurance that this was the last step necessary to have the deal with Red Owl go through.

We determine that there was ample evidence to sustain the answers of the jury to the questions of the verdict with respect to the promissory representations made by Red Owl, Hoffman's reliance thereon in the exercise of ordinary care, and his fulfillment of the conditions required of him by the terms of the negotiations had with Red Owl.

There remains for consideration the question of law raised by defendants that agreement was never reached on essential factors necessary to establish a contract between Hoffman and Red Owl. Among these were the size, cost, design, and layout of the store building; and the terms of the lease with respect to rent, maintenance, renewal, and purchase options. This poses the question of whether the promise necessary to sustain a cause of action for promissory estoppel must embrace all essential details of a proposed transaction between promisor and promisee so as to be the equivalent of an offer that would result in a binding contract between the parties if the promisee were to accept the same.

Originally the doctrine of promissory estoppel was invoked as a substitute for consideration rendering a gratuitous promise enforceable as a contract. See Williston, Contracts (1st ed.), p. 307, sec. 139. In other words, the acts of reliance by the promisee to his detriment provided a substitute for consideration. If promissory estoppel were to be limited to only those situations where the promise giving rise to the cause of action must be so definite with respect to all details that a contract would result were the promise supported by consideration, then the defendants' instant promises to Hoffman would not meet this test. However, sec. 90 of Restatement, 1 Contracts, does not impose the requirement that the promise giving rise to the cause of action must be so comprehensive in scope as to meet the requirements of an offer that would ripen into a contract if accepted by the promisee. Rather the conditions imposed are:

(1) Was the promise one which the promisor should reasonably expect to induce action or forbearance of a definite and substantial character on the part of the promisee?

(2) Did the promise induce such action or forbearance?

(3) Can injustice be avoided only by enforcement of the promise?

We deem it would be a mistake to regard an action grounded on promissory estoppel as the equivalent of a breach of contract action. As Dean Boyer points out, it is desirable that fluidity in the application of the concept be maintained. 98 University of Pennsylvania Law Review (1950), 459, at page 497. While the first two of the above listed three requirements of promissory estoppel present issues of fact which ordinarily will be resolved by a jury, the third requirement, that the remedy can only be invoked where necessary to avoid injustice, is one that involves a policy decision by the court. Such a policy decision necessarily embraces an element of discretion.

We conclude that injustice would result here if plaintiffs were not granted some relief because of the failure of defendants to keep their promises which induced plaintiffs to act to their detriment.

HENDERSON, PROMISSORY ESTOPPEL AND TRADITIONAL CONTRACT DOCTRINE

78 Yale L.J. 343, 358–60 (1969).

Because the doctrine of promissory estoppel imposes liability without regard to expressed intention, its use in pre-agreement negotiations is bound to alter the traditional scheme of offer and acceptance. This is particularly so where, after lengthy and expensive negotiations, no agreement is in fact reached. * * *

* * * The parties in *Hoffman* dealt with each other with the intent of effecting a business exchange without reaching agreement on a contract. In fact, the failure to reach agreement upon essential terms prevented defendant's promises from achieving even the level of an operative offer. * * *

* * * The key to the court's opinion is its apparent belief that the conventional use of promissory estoppel as a "substitute for consideration" in connection with gratuitous promises is now obsolete and that section 90 should serve as a distinct basis of liability without regard to * * * bargain, contract, or consideration. * * *

* * * [T]he use of the doctrine in pre-agreement bargaining is inconsistent with a line of authority * * * [that] maintains that pre-agreement discussions and negotiations can at most constitute an agreement to agree, which is not generally enforceable. * * * With respect to the allocation of the risks of reliance inherent in business negotiations, it would appear that the practical differences between a clearly expressed offer and a promise which contemplates the settling of other matters ought to be taken into account. The original judgment that Section 90 was not to apply to bargains was undoubtedly influenced by doubts about the reasonableness, in bargain situations, of reliance that takes unbargained-for forms. Those same doubts are relevant to the negotiation stages of bargain.

ELVIN ASSOCIATES v. FRANKLIN, 735 F.Supp. 1177 (S.D.N.Y.1990). [A Broadway musical producer, Springer, sought to hire Aretha Franklin for the title role in a musical about Mahalia Jackson. Franklin "expressed her strong interest" and the parties negotiated for several months, working out most details but never executing a final agreement. During negotiations, Springer incurred substantial expenses making arrangements for the production based on Franklin's assurances that the producer's "final proposal" was acceptable and that she would perform. Springer also learned that Franklin had recently canceled several obligations because of a newly developed fear of flying. Franklin never appeared for rehearsals and Springer sued.]

WHITMAN KNAPP, DISTRICT JUDGE.

The central issue pertaining to plaintiff's claim for breach of contract is whether or not the parties to that proposed contract * * * evinced an intent not to be formally bound before execution of a written, integrated contract. Language inserted in a draft of the agreement referring to its validity upon execution has generally been found to be strong (though not conclusive) evidence of intent *not* to be bound prior to execution. * * * Although we based our tentative findings largely on the fact that all of the incidental terms had been worked out by the final draft, and that the understanding was that Franklin would sign the agreement when she came to New York, there remains the obstacle of the preamble that Kramer, [Springer's lawyer], drafted and that remained in every draft, namely: "This letter, when countersigned by you, shall constitute our understanding until a more formal agreement is prepared." After reviewing the above cited authorities and the post-trial submissions, we are constrained to find that such language indicates that [Franklin] was not to be contractually bound to Springer until the draft agreement was executed. * * * The cause of action for breach of contract must therefore be dismissed. * * *

That, however, does not end the case. As above noted, plaintiff has asserted, in the alternative, a right to recover on a theory of promissory estoppel. * * *

It is difficult to imagine a more fitting case for applying the doctrine. * * * We find that Franklin had unequivocally and intentionally committed herself to appear in the production long before the day on which it was intended that the finalized agreement with her corporation would be signed.

First, it is clear from the testimony of all of the witnesses that Franklin was enthusiastic about appearing in the production and that at all times during the relevant period gave it the highest professional priority. She early on stated to Springer: "This is what I am doing." Combined with her oral agreement, through her agents, to the basic financial terms of her engagement, her continued expression of this enthusiasm to Springer more than amply afforded Springer a reasonable basis for beginning to make the various arrangements and expenditures necessary to bring the production to fruition.

Second, Franklin could not possibly have assumed that Springer could have performed his obligations to her—which, among other things, included arranging a complicated schedule of performances to commence shortly after her arrival in New York—without committing himself to and actually spending considerable sums prior to her affixing her signature to the contract on the date of such arrival. Throughout the time that he was making those commitments and advancing the necessary sums, she accepted his performance without any disclaimer of her prior promises to him. Indeed, she actively participated in many aspects of the necessary arrangements.

Third, Franklin's expression to Springer of her fear of flying did not, as she has contended, make her promise conditional or coat it with a patina of ambiguity that should have alerted Springer to suspend his efforts to mount the production. Although Franklin rejected Springer's offer to make alternative ground transportation arrangements, her primary reason for doing so was that she was determined to overcome her fear of flying, and it was reasonable for Springer to rely on her reassurances that she would be able to fly. Moreover, it was also entirely reasonable for him to assume that if she could not overcome her fear she would travel to New York by other means, even if it meant spreading the trip over several days. In short, Franklin's fear of flying provides no basis whatsoever for avoiding liability for failing to fulfill her promise, reiterated on several occasions, to appear in "Mahalia." If she could not bring herself to fly, she should have traveled by way of ground transportation. It has not been established that she was otherwise unable to come to New York to meet her obligations.

We conclude that under the circumstances as we have outlined them it would be unconscionable not to compensate Springer for the losses he incurred through his entirely justified reliance on Franklin's oral promises. A determination of the exact amount to be awarded has been reserved for a later trial on damages.

Note
Another Pop Star's Experience With Promissory Estoppel

Before his death, Elvis Presley (the "King") promised his fiancé's mother, Jo Laverne Alden, that he would, among other things, pay off the mortgage on her home. In reliance on this promise, Alden filed for divorce from her husband and, in a proposed property settlement, agreed to release her husband from further liability on the mortgage. After the King's untimely death, his estate refused to pay off the mortgage. Subsequently, the divorce court dismissed Alden's divorce action for lack of prosecution but, after she refiled, the divorce court granted Alden a divorce and approved the initial property settlement. Was the King's estate liable to Alden on the ground of promissory estoppel, as Alden claimed? The court hearing that claim held that the King's estate was not liable because Alden had pursued the divorce settlement, including her husband's release on the mortgage, in her second divorce action. By this time, Alden had been notified that the King's estate would not pay off the mortgage. Therefore Alden had not detrimentally relied on the King's promise. Alden v. Presley, 637 S.W.2d 862 (Sup. Ct. Tenn. 1982).

LOCAL 1330, UNITED STEEL WORKERS v. UNITED STATES STEEL CORP.
United States Court of Appeals, Sixth Circuit, 1980.
631 F.2d 1264.

EDWARDS, CHIEF JUDGE.

This appeal represents a cry for help from steelworkers and townspeople in the City of Youngstown, Ohio who are distressed by the prospective impact upon their lives and their city of the closing of two large steel mills. These two mills were built and have been operated by the United States Steel Corporation since the turn of the century. The Ohio Works began producing in 1901; the McDonald Works in 1918. The District Court which heard this cause of action found that as of the notice of closing, the two plants employed 3,500 employees.

The leading plaintiffs are two labor organizations, locals 1330 and 1307 of the United Steel Workers of America. This union has had a collective bargaining contract with the United States Steel Corporation for many years. These local unions represent production and maintenance employees at the Ohio and McDonald Works respectively.

In the background of this litigation is the obsolescence of the two plants concerned, occasioned both by the age of the facilities and machinery involved and by the changes in technology and marketing in steelmaking in the years intervening since the early nineteen hundreds.

For all of the years United States Steel has been operating in Youngstown, it has been a dominant factor in the lives of its thousands of employees and their families, and in the life of the city itself. The contemplated abrupt departure of United States Steel from Youngstown will, of course, have direct impact on 3,500 workers and their families. It will doubtless mean a devastating blow to them, to the business community and to the City of Youngstown itself. While we cannot read the future of Youngstown from this record, what the record does indicate clearly is that we deal with an economic tragedy of major proportion to Youngstown and Ohio's Mahoning Valley. As the District Judge who heard this case put the matter:

> Everything that has happened in the Mahoning Valley has been happening for many years because of steel. Schools have been built, roads have been built. Expansion that has taken place is because of steel. And to accommodate that industry, lives and destinies of the inhabitants of that community were based and planned on the basis of that institution: Steel.

In the face of this tragedy, the steel worker local unions, the Congressman from this district, and the Attorney General of Ohio have sued United States Steel Corporation, asking the federal courts to order the United States Steel Corporation to keep the two plants at issue in operation. * * *

Defendant United States Steel Corporation answered plaintiffs complaints, claiming that the plants were unprofitable and could not be made otherwise due to obsolescence and change in technology, markets, and transportation. The company also asserts an absolute right to make a business decision to discharge its former employees and abandon Youngstown. It states that there is no law in either the State of Ohio or the United States of America which provides either legal or equitable remedy for plaintiffs.

The District Judge, after originally restraining the corporation from ceasing operations as it had announced it would, and after advancing the case for prompt hearing, entered a formal opinion holding that the plants had become unprofitable and denying all relief. We believe the dispositive paragraphs of a lengthy opinion entered by the District Judge are the following:

> This Court has spent many hours searching for a way to cut to the heart of the economic reality—that obsolescence and market forces demand the close of the Mahoning Valley plants, and yet the lives of 3500 workers and their families and the supporting Youngstown community cannot be dismissed as inconsequential. United States Steel should not be permitted to leave the Youngstown area devastated after drawing from the lifeblood of the community for so many years.

> Unfortunately, the mechanism to reach this ideal settlement, to recognize this new property right, is not now in existence in the code of laws of our nation.

* * *

This Court is mindful of the efforts taken by the workers to increase productivity, and has applauded these efforts in the preceding paragraphs. In view of the fact, however, that this Court has found that no contract or enforceable promise was entered into by the company and that, additionally, there is clear evidence to support the company's decision that the plants were not profitable, the various acts of forebearance taken by the plaintiffs do not give them the basis for relief against defendant.

Plaintiffs-appellants claim that certain of the District Judge's findings of fact are clearly erroneous [and] that he has misconstrued federal and state contract law. * * *

* * *

The primary issue in this case is a claim on the part of the steel worker plaintiffs that United States Steel made proposals to the plaintiffs and/or the membership of the plaintiffs to the general effect that if the workers at the two steel plants concerned put forth their best efforts in terms of productivity and thereby rendered the two plants "profitable," the plants would then not be closed. It is clear that this claimed contract does not rest upon any formal written document, either authorized or signed by the parties to this lawsuit.

* * *

Thus, appellants' contract claim depends essentially upon oral statements and newspaper releases concerning the efforts of the company to secure increased productivity by enlisting the help of the workers of the plant and upon the employee responses thereto. The representations as set forth in the steelworkers' complaint include many oral statements made over the "hot-line" employed by management in the plants[1] to advise U.S. Steel employees of company policy. They began in the Fall of 1977 in the midst of much public speculation that the Ohio and McDonald works at Youngstown were to be closed. In general they follow the very first statement made by William Ashton, then superintendent of Youngstown works of U.S. Steel, on September 1, 1977, which said:

> In response to many rumors, I want to tell you that there are no immediate plans to permanently shut down either the Ohio Works or McDonald Mills.

> However, steps will have to be taken to improve these plants' profitability. These steps, which have been and are currently under study, will require the suspension and consolidation of some operations in the months ahead.

> Ohio Works and McDonald Mills are faced with very serious profit problems caused by a combination of heavy imports of foreign steel, higher energy costs, higher taxes and, of course, environmental expenditures.

> The continued operation of these plants is absolutely dependent upon their being profit-makers.

> In the months ahead, we will be calling for the full support of each and every one of you. Your cooperation and assistance is absolutely necessary if our facilities are to continue to operate.

Many similar statements were made by the company and were responded to by the employees. As 1977 and 1978 went by, there began to be statements

---

1. Telephones were placed strategically in these plants so that employees could hear pre-   recorded management policy statements.

over similar facilities and sometimes by company press releases indicating improvement in productivity at the two Youngstown facilities. Some of these included reference to "a complete turnaround" and reference to the Youngstown plants as "profitable" and once again viable.

* * *

As we read this lengthy record, and as the District Judge read it, it does not contain any factual dispute over the allegations as to company statements or the responsive actions of steelworkers in relation thereto. It is beyond argument that the local management of U.S. Steel's Youngstown plants engaged in a major campaign to enlist employee participation in an all-out effort to make these two plants profitable in order to prevent their being closed. It is equally obvious that the employees responded wholeheartedly.

The District Judge, however, rejected the promissory estoppel contract theory on three grounds. The first ground was that none of the statements made by officers and employees of the company constituted a definite promise to continue operation of the plants if they did become profitable. The second ground was that the statements relied upon by plaintiffs were made by employees and public relations officers of the company and not by company officers. The third ground was a finding of fact that "The condition precedent of the alleged contract and promise—profitability of the Youngstown facilities—was never fulfilled, and the actions in contract and for detrimental reliance cannot be found for plaintiffs."

The District Judge's fundamental disposition of plaintiffs-appellants' contract claims is stated in this finding of fact:

> [T]here is clear evidence to support the company's decision that the plants were not profitable, the various acts of forebearance taken by the plaintiffs do not give them the basis for relief against defendant.

Our examination of this record offers no ground for our holding that this finding of fact is "clearly erroneous." See Fed.R.Civ.P. 52(a).

* * *

We believe that this record demonstrates without significant dispute that the profitability issue in the case depends in large part upon definition. The plaintiffs wish to employ the direct costs of operating the two plants, compared to the total selling price of their products. The difference, they contend, is "profit." This formula would eliminate such charges as corporate purchasing and sales expense allocable to the Youngstown plants, and allocable corporate management expenses including, but not limited to marketing, engineering, auditing, accounting, advertising. Obviously, any multiplant corporation could quickly go bankrupt if such a definition of profit was employed generally and over any period of time.

Plaintiffs-appellants point out, however, that this version of Youngstown profitability was employed by the Youngstown management in setting a goal for its employees and in statements which described achieving that goal. The standard of Restatement (Second) of Contracts 90, upon which plaintiffs-appellants rely, however, is one of reasonable expectability of the "promise" detrimentally relied upon. The District Judge did not find, nor can we, that reliance upon a promise to keep these plants open on the basis of coverage of plant fixed costs was within reasonable expectability. We cannot hold that the District Judge erred legally or was "clearly erroneous" in his fact finding when he held that the "promise" to keep the plants open had to be read in the context of normal corporate profit accounting and that profitability had not been achieved.

[After affirming the district judge's dismissal of the promissory estoppel claim, the court considered and rejected plaintiffs' theory that their long-term relationship with U.S. Steel established a "property right" in the plaintiffs. The court found no authority for such a theory and stated that only the legislature could deal with the problem. The court remanded the case for further proceedings, however, on the basis of an antitrust claim that U.S. Steel refused to sell the two mills to the plaintiffs, thereby eliminating a potential competitor.]

29 U.S.C. § 2102 (1994).

Notice required before plant closings and mass layoffs

(a) Notice to employees, State dislocated worker units, and local governments

An employer shall not order a plant closing or mass layoff until the end of a 60–day period after the employer serves written notice of such an order—

(1) to each representative of the affected employees as of the time of the notice or, if there is no such representative at that time, to each affected employee; * * *

(b) Reduction of notification period

(1) An employer may order the shutdown of a single site of employment before the conclusion of the 60–day period if as of the time that notice would have been required the employer was actively seeking capital or business which, if obtained, would have enabled the employer to avoid or postpone the shutdown and the employer reasonably and in good faith believed that giving the notice required would have precluded the employer from obtaining the needed capital or business.

(2)(A) An employer may order a plant closing or mass layoff before the conclusion of the 60–day period if the closing or mass layoff is caused by business circumstances that were not reasonably foreseeable as of the time that notice would have been required.

(B) No notice under this chapter shall be required if the plant closing or mass layoff is due to any form of natural disaster, such as a flood, earthquake, or the drought currently ravaging the farmlands of the United States.

(3) An employer relying on this subsection shall give as much notice as is practicable and at that time shall give a brief statement of the basis for reducing the notification period.

METZGER AND PHILLIPS, THE EMERGENCE OF PROMISSORY ESTOPPEL AS AN INDEPENDENT THEORY OF RECOVERY

35 Rutgers L.Rev. 472, 550 (1983).

* * * Promisors desirous of limiting estoppel-based liability are, however, not without devices for achieving a measure of protection. Tactics like employing a conditional or indefinite promise, attaching a termination date to the promise, or revoking and promptly communicating this to the promisee can affect the foreseeability and reasonableness of reliance and thus defeat a promissory estoppel claim. * * *

Note
Promissory Estoppel in the Restatement (Second) of Contracts

The Restatement (Second) of Contracts, published in 1981, includes a new version of section 90. It provides:

Promise Reasonably Inducing Action or Forbearance

(1) A promise which the promisor should reasonably expect to induce action or forbearance on the part of the promisee or a third person which does induce such action or forbearance is binding if injustice can be avoided only by enforcement of the promise. The remedy granted for breach may be limited as justice requires.

(2) A charitable subscription or a marriage settlement is binding under Subsection (1) without proof that the promise induced action or forbearance.

In the above text, one finds at least four changes in the wording of old section 90. Can you identify them? Do they all expand or do some of them restrict the scope of the theory?[o]

KNAPP, RELIANCE IN THE REVISED RESTATEMENT: THE PROLIFERATION OF PROMISSORY ESTOPPEL

81 Colum. L. Rev. 52, 53 (1981).

[T]he principle of section 90 * * * has become perhaps the most radical and expansive development of this century in the law of promissory liability. * * *

HILLMAN, QUESTIONING THE "NEW CONSENSUS" ON PROMISSORY ESTOPPEL: AN EMPIRICAL AND THEORETICAL STUDY

98 Colum. L. Rev. 580, 580–81, 590, 596 (1998).

The purpose of this Article is to present evidence of a fundamental misunderstanding of how courts apply the theory of obligation called promissory estoppel. Contrary to the accepted wisdom, the data and analysis presented here (1) demonstrate that the theory seldom leads to victory in reported decisions, (2) underscore the immense importance of reliance as a substantive

o. Among other sections of the new restatement that apply section 90 are section 87 (on option contracts) and section 139 (on the statute of frauds). We study both later.

element of the theory, and (3) suggest the willingness of courts to grant reliance damages to successful litigants.

The first point, the lack of success of the theory in the courts, contradicts theorists who predicted that promissory estoppel would "swallow up" the bargain theory of contract and become the dominant promissory theory of obligation. Although some writers have questioned the prediction, this Article is the first comprehensive empirical study that demonstrates promissory estoppel's limited role.

* * *

I decided to examine all of the reported decisions in the United States in which a promissory estoppel claim succeeded or failed or in which promissory estoppel was discussed from July 1, 1994 through June 30, 1996. * * * [T]he data demonstrate the remarkable lack of success of promissory estoppel claims in the reported decisions.

* * *

* * * [T]he most accurate measure of success and failure may be gained by comparing success and failure rates on the merits. * * * [O]nly 9.70% of promissory estoppel claims that reached a decision on the merits of the claim were successful.

* * *

The lingering question is, of course, why is promissory estoppel not faring well in the courts? * * * One possible explanation for the low win rate is that parties miscomprehended the nature of promissory estoppel. Although the theory of promissory estoppel still receives wide publicity as a principal basis for promise enforcement, the rhetoric may no longer reflect the reality of judicial attitudes toward the theory. Parties in the mid–1990s simply may not have comprehended a judicial souring on the theory, which is consistent with courts' recent reluctance to intervene in the contracting process on other grounds. Such parties might therefore fail to settle what they should have predicted as likely wins for defendants (but did not).

Another possible explanation for the low win rate is that claimants are bringing weak promissory estoppel claims and not making an effort to settle them. Claimants may bring promissory estoppel claims only as subsidiary theories tacked on to a contract or other claim, sometimes even as an afterthought. The abstract call for "justice" in the second Restatement's definition of promissory estoppel may add to the allure of "throwing in" the claim. Evidence supporting this explanation comes from examining the tenuous nature of many of the claims in the multitude of cases in which promissory estoppel failed.

Problem 2–7

The ABA Journal eReport reported that in the summer of 2005 an associate in a major New York City law firm, whom we shall call Ira, sued the firm for $100 million for breaking a promise to "put him up for partnership." Ira claimed that his evaluations from the firm were excellent, that a partner told him he had "a great future" with the firm, and that several partners promised to "put him up for consideration in a year." Further, they assured Ira that the partnership process was a "rubber stamp, so long as his name was put up." Finally, Ira explained that, at the time of these assurances, the partners thought they might lose certain clients if Ira left the firm. Ira sent an e-mail to the managing partner and other partners outlining his understanding about his candidacy for partnership based on the above facts, which the partnership confirmed. According to Ira, the law firm then reneged on considering him for partnership. The law firm denied these allegations and stated it would "vigorously defend the case."

Assume the facts alleged by Ira are correct. Does he have a claim based on agreement with consideration? Based on promissory estoppel?

SECTION FOUR: OBLIGATION ARISING FROM UNJUST ENRICHMENT

POMPONIUS (CIRCA 150 A.D.) IN JUSTINIAN, DIGEST

50.17.206 (circa 534).

Lure naturae aequum est neminem cum alterius detrimento et iniuria fieri locupletiorem. [For this by nature is equitable, that no one be made richer through another's loss.]

MOSES v. MacFERLAN, 97 Eng.Rep. 676 (K.B.1760) (MANSFIELD, J.). "If the defendant be under an obligation, from the ties of natural justice, to refund, the law implies a debt, and gives this action, founded in the equity of the plaintiff's case. * * *

This kind of action, to recover back money, which ought not in justice be kept, is very beneficial. * * * "

FIBROSA SPOLKA AKCYJNA v. FAIRBAIRN LAWSON COMBE BARBOUR, LTD., A.C. 32 at 62, [1943] 2 All E.R. 122 (LORD WRIGHT.). "Lord Mansfield does not say that the law implies a promise. The law implies a debt or obligation which is a very different thing. In fact, he denies that there is a contract; the obligation is as efficacious as if it were upon a contract. The obligation is a creation of law, just as much as an obligation in tort."

RESTATEMENT OF RESTITUTION § 1 (1937).

Unjust Enrichment

A person who has been unjustly enriched at the expense of another is required to make restitution to the other.

G. PALMER, LAW OF RESTITUTION

§ 1.1 at 1–2 (1978).

It has been traditional to regard tort and contract as the two principal sources of civil liability at common law. * * * There is another category. * * * [T]his is liability based in unjust enrichment. In particularized form this has been a part of our law from an early time, but it has been slow to emerge as a general theory. In present American law, however, the idea of unjust enrichment has been generally accepted and widely applied.

Restitution based upon unjust enrichment cuts across many branches of the law, including contract, tort, and fiduciary relationship, but it also occupies much territory that is its sole preserve.

BLOOMGARDEN v. COYER

United States Court of Appeals, District of Columbia Circuit, 1973.
479 F.2d 201.

SPOTTSWOOD W. ROBINSON, III, CIRCUIT JUDGE:

This appeal follows appellant Bloomgarden's unsuccessful effort in the District Court to recover a $1 million finder's fee. The fee was sought for services leading to the inauguration of an enterprise to extensively develop certain property on the Georgetown waterfront in Washington. The principals in the enterprise are appellees Coyer and Guy, individual real estate developers, and appellee Georgetown–Inland Corporation (Georgetown–Inland), one of five companies organized, with Coyer and Guy as two of the stockholders in each, to effectuate the project. At the center of the controversy is Bloomgarden's assertion that it was he who brought the organizers together in this mutually beneficial venture and who, by the same token, should be rewarded for that contribution.

It is fully conceded that Bloomgarden introduced Coyer and Guy to those with whom they were later to join forces. There was, however, no express agreement, written or oral, pertaining to the part Bloomgarden played or calling for compensation therefor from any of the appellees. Bloomgarden's quest for a finder's fee proceeded on the theory that he was entitled to remuneration by virtue of a contract which should either be factually implied from prevalent custom and usage or recognized as a legal consequence of the transaction when viewed in light of the surrounding circumstances.

After the close of the pleadings and some amount of discovery, Bloomgarden moved for partial summary judgment on the issue of liability and appellees for summary judgment on the entire case. The District Court denied Bloomgarden's motion and granted appellees', in each instance on two separate grounds. The court held that because Bloomgarden did not hold the license required of real estate and business-chance brokers in the District of Columbia he was precluded from charging for what he did. The court further held that Bloomgarden had no enforceable claim for recompense because it appeared without dispute that at the time he introduced the parties he did not expect to be personally compensated for so doing. Without reaching the first ground relied on by the District Court, we affirm for reasons underlying the second.

Bloomgarden's suit traces its origin to a series of events commencing in the fall of 1969 and extending into the spring of 1970. Throughout this period he was serving as president of Socio–Dynamics Industries, Inc. (SDI), a consulting and research firm in the field of urban and environmental affairs. Nearly half of SDI's capital stock was owned by David Carley, president of Public Facilities Associates, Inc. (PFA), which was engaged in the development of public and private housing and the redevelopment of urban areas.[1]

---

1. In February, 1970, PFA became a subsidiary of Inland Steel Company (Inland Steel), and in April its name was changed to Inland Steel Development Corporation (ISDC).

Carley had requested Bloomgarden to remain alert to any potentially fruitful investment opportunities for PFA in the Washington area.

At the time, Coyer and Guy held contracts or options on several parcels of real estate on the Georgetown waterfront. Bloomgarden met Coyer in the summer of 1969 while arranging to lease office space in a building in which Coyer had an interest. At one of their meetings, Coyer revealed to Bloomgarden the details of a plan for the assembly and development of a sizeable segment of the waterfront into a multipurpose business complex. Coyer explained that he and Guy lacked the financial resources needed to carry the project through, and Bloomgarden offered to put him in touch with Carley.

Bloomgarden promptly apprised Carley of Coyer's project and set up a meeting between them and others for January 26, 1970. Ideas were then exchanged but no suggestion was made by Bloomgarden to Carley or Coyer that he expected to be paid for bringing them together. By Bloomgarden's arrangement the group attended another meeting, on February 19 in Chicago, with representatives of subsidiaries of Inland Steel Company (Inland Steel). Again the plan was discussed and again Bloomgarden gave no indication that he anticipated a fee for introducing Coyer and Guy to Carley and his Inland associates. On the contrary, during a ride to the airport on the day after the Chicago meeting, Guy inquired of Bloomgarden as to what he hoped to get out of the project, and Bloomgarden responded merely that possibly SDI, his company, might garner some work in implementing the plan.[2] Aside from furnishing three of the principals—Coyer, Guy and Carley—with information about the others, Bloomgarden had no further role in the transaction.

An agreement in principle was reached between Coyer, Guy and the Inland Steel group in early April, 1970. This was formalized by a contract in June and a shareholders' agreement executed in August. Five corporations, among them Georgetown–Inland, were organized to handle the project. It was not until the end of March, 1970, however, that Bloomgarden asserted any monetary claim on behalf of SDI for bringing about the initial contact, and it was not until May that he asked for compensation for himself.[3] After each of these demands was rejected, Bloomgarden, on September 14, wrote to Coyer, again claiming a fee for sparking the business opportunity culminating in the Georgetown project. That likewise failing, Bloomgarden commenced his suit on October 1.

* * *

2. The conversation, as portrayed by Bloomgarden on deposition, was:

Q. You had discussed the [SDI] role in this project in February with Mr. Coyer, had you not?

A. Yes, I had in the cab coming from the Palmer House to the airport * * * Bill Guy said to me at some point and not in any context—I don't even know what we were discussing—he surprised me with the question, "Hank, if this project goes through, what do you expect out of it?" And I really wasn't prepared for the question because I had not thought it through in detail and I really didn't know in detail what I expected out of it. I expected something out of it and something substantial. I said, "Well, for one thing we have some capability in the environmental field and Chuck Coyer mentioned a possibility of a closed energy system here," and I said "We might be involved in that kind of thing." That was about the whole conversation. We did not at that point discuss a finder's fee or anything else.

3. The change from a company to a personal claim resulted from SDI's ultimate decision not to participate in the Georgetown waterfront project. * * *

In the case at bar, the District Court, relying on Bloomgarden's own deposition, as was its prerogative in evaluating the summary-judgment motions made by the parties, concluded that Bloomgarden did not contemplate personal remuneration for his services, and that in consequence he lacked an indispensable prerequisite to recovery on either an implied-in-fact contract or a quasi-contract. Like the District Court, we are unable to perceive any factual basis upon which it could be asserted that, at the time he introduced the parties, Bloomgarden looked forward to any finder's fee for himself, as distinguished from a fee and future business for his company. His silence on the matter at the January meeting in Washington and again at the February meeting in Chicago, followed by his statements on the day after the Chicago meeting and later in his deposition, indicated unequivocally that at most the gain he then anticipated was work and compensation for SDI, of which he was president. Bloomgarden summed it up when in his deposition he said:

> It was always my intention that [SDI] should benefit, not myself personally, from putting Inland and Coyer together. [SDI] should have the credit; that [SDI] should get work assignments and that a finder's fee should be paid to [SDI]. It wasn't until I was told that I could not bring suit in the name of [SDI] and was urged to see if I wanted to sue Coyer as an individual that I began to recognize that I was in a very, very difficult spot.[4]

In addition, the pleadings and depositions reveal that it was not until after Bloomgarden had done his service for the parties that they were put on notice that he had in mind a finder's fee, either for his company or for himself. Both Coyer and Guy avowed in their depositions that they thought Bloomgarden was acting either for SDI or Carley when in January he made the introductions. Their understanding in that regard was buttressed in February by Bloomgarden during the ride to the Chicago airport when, asked pointedly as to his expectations, he omitted reference to individual recompense and replied simply that he had in view the possibility that his company would receive work assignments flowing from the Georgetown project if it materialized. Moreover, Bloomgarden admitted in his deposition that not until the end of March—long after completion of the services for which remuneration was demanded—did he suggest compensation for SDI, his company, and not until May did he indicate that he anticipated personal compensation.

* * * Our careful examination of the record leads us to concur with the District Court that appellees bore their burden as to the nonexistence of any genuine factual issue, and that Bloomgarden offered nothing substantial to bar their request for summary judgment. It remains for us to determine whether the principles of substantive law governing recovery on contracts implied in fact and quasi-contracts were correctly applied.

Despite the marked dissimilarity of contracts implied in fact to quasi-contracts, their separate characteristics have been blurred by courts and commentators over the years. For any satisfactory understanding of Bloom-

---

4. The events referred to in the last sentence of the quoted material occurred when SDI decided not to take part in the Georgetown project, and that decision was not made until long after the parties had been brought together. See note 3, *supra.* Thus, by Bloom-garden's own statement—which harmonizes with all else in the record—his expectation was at most a benefit for his company, rather than for himself, at the time he introduced the parties.

garden's twofold legal approach, it is important to keep the two concepts clear and distinct. An implied-in-fact contract is a true contract, containing all necessary elements of a binding agreement; it differs from other contracts only in that it has not been committed to writing or stated orally in express terms, but rather is inferred from the conduct of the parties in the milieu in which they dealt. A quasi-contract, on the other hand, is not a contract at all, but a duty thrust under certain conditions upon one party to requite another in order to avoid the former's unjust enrichment. The principles governing the two remedies differ, though in particular cases they may dictate the same result.

It is well settled that, in order to establish an implied-in-fact contract to pay for services, the party seeking payment must show (1) that the services were carried out under such circumstances as to give the recipient reason to understand (a) that they were performed for him and not for some other person, and (b) that they were not rendered gratuitously, but with the expectation of compensation from the recipient; and (2) that the services were beneficial to the recipient.

Particularly where commission-type fees are sought in business-opportunity transactions, such a contract will not be implied unless the recipient knows or has reasonable grounds to believe that the beneficial acts were performed in anticipation of remuneration therefor. The reasons underlying these requirements are evident. Activities beneficial to a party frequently proceed on behalf of another. Often they are engaged in without thought of remuneration. Not uncommonly, and irrespective of motivation, they are not really helpful to the recipient. An agreement to pay for services defies implication where the recipient not unreasonably fails to realize that the services were rendered for him in contemplation of quid pro quo for value conferred. And the point in time at which the elements essential to implication must concur is the time at which the services are rendered.[5]

We may assume on the record before us that Bloomgarden's introductions were valuable to appellees, or that at least there was a genuine issue as to whether they were. Yet, for Bloomgarden to recover on the basis of a contract implied in fact, he would have to show additionally that he looked forward to personal payment for his services, and that the circumstances under which he introduced Coyer and Guy to Carley were such as would reasonably have put them on notice that he had that in mind. From aught that appears from the record, Bloomgarden could not have met these standards at a trial.

* * *

* * * The record establishes without controversy that Bloomgarden introduced appellees on the chance that a coalition to develop the Georgetown waterfront would eventually produce business for SDI, his company, and that appellees reasonably understood that his activities were directed solely to that

---

5. That is because an implied-in-fact contract to compensate for services arises, if at all, at the time the services are rendered, and only if the then-existing circumstances enable implication of a contract to come into being. These precepts are elemental, and so much is implicit in the decisions holding that services performed without expectation of remunera-tion or simply in expectation of a non-monetary business advantage do not warrant implication of a contract to pay. In all of these cases there was at some point a change of heart, and an effort in the suit to recover cash compensation not contemplated when the acts were performed. * * *

Holding on implied contract

end. The record further establishes that even if Bloomgarden then entertained the notion of charging a finder's fee, appellees were not alerted to that possibility until long after his activities had ended. On these uncontradicted bases we find ample legal support for the District Court's conclusion that Bloomgarden failed to show an implied-in-fact contract supporting his claim.

We turn finally to examine the sufficiency of Bloomgarden's quasi-contract theory as a basis for recovery of the finder's fee which he sought. At the outset, we again call attention to the need for conceptual clarity. The quasi-contract, as we have said, is not really a contract, but a legal obligation closely akin to a duty to make restitution. There is, of course, no need to resort to it when the evidence sustains the existence of a true contract, either express or implied in fact. For the purpose of preventing unjust enrichment, however, a quasi-contract—an obligation to pay money to another—will be recognized in appropriate circumstances, even though no intention of the parties to bind themselves contractually can be discerned. And where, as here, the essential facts are not in dispute, the question whether a quasi-contract should be erected is one of law, and as such is a proper subject for summary disposition.

what to prove for quasi-contract

Generally, in order to recover on a quasi-contractual claim, the plaintiff must show that the defendant was unjustly enriched at the plaintiff's expense, and that the circumstances were such that in good conscience the defendant should make restitution. Because quasi-contractual obligations rest upon equitable considerations, they do not arise when it would not be unfair for the recipient to keep the benefit without having to pay for it. Thus, to make out his case, it is not enough for the plaintiff to prove merely that he has conferred an advantage upon the defendant, but he must demonstrate that retention of the benefit without compensating the one who conferred it is unjustified. What must be resolved here is whether Bloomgarden made such a showing or evinced his capability of possibly doing so at trial.

△ *must show*

issue

By their very nature, the equitable principles of quasi-contracts are more difficult to apply where the court must determine whether services rendered by one person to another are to go unrewarded than where it must make that determination with respect to money or property unjustly retained. But since there is no general responsibility in quasi-contract law to pay for services *irrespective* of the circumstances in which they are carried out, a number of factual criteria have been utilized by courts to ascertain whether in a given case the defendant has undeservedly profited by the plaintiff's efforts. Thus, in situations involving personal services, it has been variously stated (1) that a duty to pay will not be recognized where it is clear that the benefit was conferred gratuitously or officiously, (2) or that the question of payment was left to the unfettered discretion of the recipient. (3) Nor is compensation mandated where the services were rendered simply in order to gain a business advantage. And the courts have reached the same conclusion where the plaintiff did not contemplate a personal fee, or the defendant could not reasonably have supposed that he did. * * * Nor, we add, can an uncommunicated expectation of remuneration serve the plaintiff's purpose where the defendant had no cause to believe that such was the fact.

w/out consideration

test

Holding

Thus we come full circle to the identical considerations which were dispositive of Bloomgarden's claim for recovery on an implied-in-fact contract.

There simply was no basis on which a jury could rationally find that when he brought the parties together[6] he entertained any thought of a finder's fee for himself, or that those with whom he dealt held the payment of such a fee in prospect. These circumstances defeat Bloomgarden's quasi-contract claim as well. On what emerges clearly and undisputably from the record, we find that the District Court was fully warranted in holding that, as a matter of law, Bloomgarden was not entitled to recover on either a contract implied-in-fact or a quasi-contract, and its action in so doing is accordingly

Holding

Judgment

Affirmed.

SPARKS v. GUSTAFSON

Supreme Court of Alaska, 1988.
750 P.2d 338.

MATTHEWS, JUSTICE.

Robert J. Sparks, Jr., executor of his father's estate (Estate), appeals from a superior court decision ordering the Estate to pay $65,706.07 to the plaintiff, Ernie Gustafson, in compensation for management services that Gustafson rendered to the Estate and for maintaining and improving Estate property. The central issue presented here is whether it is unjust to allow the Estate to retain these benefits without paying for them. In particular, Sparks argues that Gustafson gave his services to the Estate gratuitously, without the Estate's knowledge or consent.

Issue

FACTS AND PROCEEDINGS

The decedent, Robert Sparks, Sr., and the plaintiff, Ernie Gustafson, were personal friends and business associates for many years. In 1980 Sparks purchased a one-half interest in the Nome Center Building. Gustafson managed the building for Sparks without charge until Sparks died on March 1, 1981. Thereafter Gustafson continued to manage the building and collect rents on behalf of Sparks, Sr.'s estate, with the knowledge and approval of the executor, Robert Sparks, Jr. Gustafson did not request any compensation for his services.

Under Gustafson's management, Nome Center operated at a loss. The Estate deposited $10,000 in a Nome Center account to cover operating expenses, but the amount was not sufficient to meet the necessary costs of insurance, mortgage payments, utility bills, and repairs. Gustafson often paid Nome Center expenses out of his own pocket. Maintenance and remodeling work were performed by Gustafson, using in part his own funds. Although he mailed monthly reports of the Nome Center's income and expenses, these reports did not include all of his own expenditures.

In February, 1982, the Estate signed a document entitled "purchase agreement" which indicated that Gustafson had purchased the building from

---

6. As in the instance of an implied-in-fact contract, the circumstances allegedly creating a quasi-contractual obligation to pay for services must have existed when the services were performed. No unfairness results from a denial of compensation to the claimant who had no expectation of personal remuneration at the time of performance. On the contrary, it would be unjust to impose a liability for payment on the party who accepts the services without any warning, from the surrounding circumstances or otherwise, that they were rendered for a price.

the Estate, and would assume the deed of trust as soon as the purchase details could be worked out. However, no purchase details were ever agreed upon. The Estate sold the building to a third party in February, 1983, and Gustafson ceased to manage the property at that time.

On July 14, 1983, Gustafson and his business corporation, Nome Business Venture, Inc., filed suit against the Estate and the executor in Nome, claiming that the defendants breached an oral agreement to sell the Nome Center Building to Gustafson. Plaintiffs subsequently filed an amended complaint which further alleged that Gustafson was entitled to recover for funds and services that he expended on the building under a statutory or equitable lien theory. Defendants filed an answer and counterclaimed for an accounting of all monies collected and expended on the building.

At trial the superior court found that Gustafson had no enforceable lien. The court also concluded that it would be inequitable to allow the Estate to retain the benefits that Gustafson had conferred upon Nome Center at his own expense. The court ordered the Estate to pay Gustafson $65,706.07 in compensation for the services and improvements that he conferred upon the Estate during his two years of managing the Nome Center Building. This appeal followed.

* * *

Unjust enrichment exists where the defendant has received a benefit from the plaintiff and it would be inequitable for defendant to retain the benefit without compensating plaintiff for its value. * * * Sparks claims that plaintiffs failed to prove either element of unjust enrichment: first, that the Estate received any benefit from plaintiffs, and second, that if a benefit was received then its retention would be unjust.

A person confers a benefit upon another if he gives the other some interest in money, land or possessions; performs services beneficial to or at the request of the other; satisfies a debt of the other; or in any way adds to the other's advantage. *Restatement of the Law of Restitution* § 1, comment b (1937). In this case Gustafson made substantial repairs and improvements to the Nome Center, provided management services that kept Nome Center operating, and paid debts incurred by Nome Center, all arguably on the Estate's behalf. There is no question that Gustafson conferred a benefit upon the Estate.

Even where a person has conferred a benefit upon another, however, he is entitled to compensation only if it would be just and equitable to require compensation under the circumstances. *Restatement of the Law of Restitution* § 1, comment c (1937). Courts will allow the defendant to retain a benefit without compensating plaintiff in several situations, one of which is relevant to the case at hand: where the benefit was given gratuitously without expectation of payment. * * * Appellants argue that this situation is present in the case before us.

This court has not yet addressed the circumstances which give rise to a finding of gratuitous intent. A good discussion of this issue in the context of a decedent's estate can be found in *Kershaw v. Tracy Collins Bank & Trust Co.,* 561 P.2d 683 (Utah 1977). In that case the decedent's best friend provided a variety of services to the decedent's widow, including chauffeuring, buying *test*

groceries, running errands, and performing minor repair work. *Id.* at 684. The court looked at the extent of the services provided to the widow, the closeness of the relationship between the parties, and the fact that the plaintiff never sought compensation until after the widow died. The court found that the widow had not been unjustly enriched, since plaintiff's services were not necessary for the widow's existence and were of the sort which could reasonably be expected from a long time friend. *Id.* at 687.

cites ex where it is a gratuitous intent

In this case there was a similarly close relationship between the plaintiff and the decedent. It appears that Gustafson managed the Nome Center Building for the decedent without requesting compensation, in recognition of many long years of friendship and business association together. At trial, the executor testified that he thought Gustafson would continue to manage the building for two years after Sparks' death out of the goodness of his heart, without expectation of payment. Gustafson never requested compensation for his services during his tenure as the Nome Center manager for the Estate. The closeness of the parties' relationship and Gustafson's failure to request compensation in a timely manner suggest that Gustafson offered his services to the Estate gratuitously.

∆'s argument

However, the services that Gustafson performed for the Estate were not the sort which one would ordinarily expect to receive from a friend as a mere gratuity. Gustafson spent approximately five hours a day for two years collecting rents for Nome Center, soliciting new tenants, making repairs and improvements, paying utility, insurance and mortgage bills out of his own pocket when rental income fell short of expenses, and performing other general maintenance and management services for the Estate. These are the types of extensive business services for which one would ordinarily expect to be paid. We therefore agree with the trial court that Gustafson's services were not offered gratuitously.

Courts Holding Reasoning

* * *

The judgment of the superior court is AFFIRMED.

benefit by intermeddler volunteer

D. DOBBS, REMEDIES
298–99 (1973).

The Gift Principle and the Choice Principle

When one person confers a benefit upon another not required by contract or legal duty, the recipient of the benefit is often unjustly enriched and required to make restitution of the benefit or its value. But this is not always so. He is not unjustly enriched, and therefore not required to make restitution, where the benefit was conferred by a volunteer or intermeddler.

principle

(1)

This general rule involves two entirely distinct principles. The first principle is that one who has conferred a benefit upon another with an intention to make a gift, has no equitable claim for relief against the recipient of the benefit in the absence of fraud, mistake, duress or undue influence. In such a case the recipient of the benefit is enriched, but not unjustly, since there is no injustice in retaining a completed gift. This principle holds no matter what form the gift might take. Gratuitously rendered services are within this principle, for example, as are any other benefits.

[handwritten margin note: Princip #2 painter ex]

The second principle is that one who confers a benefit upon another without affording that other the opportunity to reject the benefit, has no equitable claim for relief against the recipient of the benefit in the absence of some special policy that would outweigh the right of free choice in the benefited party. For instance, a house painter cannot paint an owner's home in his absence and then recover for the benefit conferred, even though the house needed paint and is much increased in value. In such a case the recipient of the benefit is enriched, and perhaps unjustly, but such enrichment is preferable to payment of the intermeddler, who should not thus be encouraged to invade another's freedom of choice about his own affairs. There are, as would be expected, situations in which this policy is outweighed by other considerations, * * * but the basic principle is solidly established.

The terminology in which these principles are carried forward in the cases has not been well standardized. Very often it has been obscure at best and entirely misleading at worst. Courts often refer to free choice principle in terms of intermeddlers, and the whole idea that one may not foist a benefit upon another against his will, or deprive him of choice in the matter, is often expressed eliptically by saying simply that the party who conferred the benefit is an intermeddler. Sometimes this same idea is expressed by saying the party who conferred the benefit is a volunteer.

At other times the term "volunteer" is used to refer to the gift principle, and this is the label frequently applied to one who has intended to make a gift. Since the term "volunteer" is used both in cases that involve the gift principle and in cases that involve the choice principle, some care must be exercised in analyzing opinions to determine which is involved.

[handwritten margin note: family is usually a gift]

BROWN v. BROWN, 524 A.2d 1184 (D.C.App.1987). "Substantial policy considerations ... underlie the presumption that services rendered between siblings are gratuitous. We believe that, as a matter of common human experience, such services are usually performed out of a sense of family responsibility, not pursuant to a contractual agreement with the legitimate expectation of payment."

GAY v. MOONEY

Supreme Court of New Jersey, 1901.
67 N.J.L. 27, 50 A. 596, aff'd per curiam, 67 N.J.L. 687, 52 A. 1131.

Action by Michael Gay against Hugh Mooney, administrator of Hugh Mooney, deceased. Judgment for plaintiff, and defendant brings error. Affirmed.

* * *

DIXON, J. The defendant's intestate was the uncle of the plaintiff's wife, and for several years before his death resided in the plaintiff's family. In the present suit the plaintiff sought to recover compensation for the board and lodging furnished to the deceased.

In order to rebut a presumption that the service was rendered and received as a gratuity, the plaintiff put in evidence tending to show an understanding between himself and the deceased that the latter would devise

[handwritten: ✱ Proof was good to enforce $ not land b/c of Statute of Frauds. ?]

a certain dwelling house to the plaintiff's children in return for what he should receive as a member of the family. For such a purpose this evidence was plainly legitimate. It came within the rule laid down in Disbrow v. Durand, 54 N.J. Law, 343, 24 Atl. 545, 33 Am.St.Rep. 678, that in cases like the present a reasonable and proper expectation that there would be compensation must, and hence may, be shown. The bargain thus exhibited is not one on which an action at law could be maintained, because it related to land, and was not susceptible of such proof as the statute of frauds requires; but when, in pursuance of a bargain for this reason unenforceable, services have been rendered, the legal remedy is by an action on the quantum meruit for the value of the services. McElroy v. Ludlum, 32 N.J.Eq. 828. As was said in Stone v. Todd, 49 N.J.Law, 274, 281, 8 Atl. 300, the intended devise was but the method of paying an admitted obligation, and, if payment in that manner be not made, the creditor is entitled to recover the value of the services.

Although the bargain between the plaintiff and the intestate contemplated payment to be made to the plaintiff's children, and not directly to himself, yet, as that bargain did not take the form of an actionable contract, it falls out of view as a ground of legal remedy, and appears only to give color to the conduct of the parties in furnishing and accepting the service rendered. It affords the means of determining that the service was not a gift, but a sale, and out of that determination the law deduces a right in him who sold the service to be paid its value by him who bought it. These principles sufficiently answer the important exceptions taken at the trial and all the exceptions mentioned in the brief of counsel. The other exceptions, therefore, need not be noticed.

The judgment of the Middlesex pleas is affirmed.

PERILLO, RESTITUTION IN A CONTRACTUAL CONTEXT

73 Colum.L.Rev. 1208, 1215–16 (1973).

We are attuned by custom and long usage to think in terms of a contract action for damages as an action on the contract and therefore based upon agreement. We are also attuned by custom and long usage to think in terms of an action for restitution, even in a contract setting, as an action which is not based on contract. * * * By way of illustration, let us assume the plaintiff performed services under an oral contract which provided for a two year term of employment. An action for damages would require the setting out of the contract in the declaration and would be met by a plea of the Statute of Frauds. Plaintiff, therefore, to avoid the plea would bring an action in general assumpsit for the reasonable value of his services. Such an action required a two act scenario. First, it is pretended that the contract made by the parties never existed. It is either ignored or retroactively avoided. Then the plaintiff must state that he had rendered work, labor and services at the request of the defendant and that the defendant had promised to pay him "so much money as he therefore reasonably deserved to have." The promise is not the contractual promise but a fictional promise. How, then, could one assert that the action was on the unenforceable contract? The answer is to be found not in the pleadings but in the actual trial of the action, where one will find constant reference to the oral contract itself. How does one prove the request for services? By introducing evidence of the oral contract. What if the defendant wishes to show that, although plaintiff has rendered services, plaintiff has breached the oral contract and therefore should not recover? May he raise this defense based upon the terms of the contract? Indeed he may. May the rate of compensation stated in the contract be put into evidence to establish the reasonable value of the services? Yes, say the vast majority of cases. At every step and turn questions of fact and questions of law are definitively or partially resolved by reference to the [unenforceable] contract.

KEARNS v. ANDREE

Supreme Court of Errors of Connecticut, 1928.
107 Conn. 181, 139 A. 695.

Action by John T. Kearns against Joseph W. Andree to recover damages for alleged breach of contract by the defendant to purchase real estate from the plaintiff, brought to the court of common pleas for Hartford county, and tried to the court. Judgment for the plaintiff for $167, and appeal by the defendant. Error, and new trial ordered.

* * *

MALTBIE, J. The plaintiff was the owner of a lot of land at the corner of Prospect and Edwards streets in the town of East Hartford, on which stood a dwelling house then in the process of construction, but practically finished. In the rear of the land upon which this house stood, he owned other land upon which another house was located. He and the defendant entered into an oral contract, whereby, as it is stated in the finding, "the defendant agreed to purchase the house and lot at the corner of Prospect and Edwards streets at a price of $8,500; it being agreed the defendant should assume a first mortgage of $4,500, a bank mortgage, and pay $4,000 in cash." This mortgage was not then in existence, but the plaintiff promised to obtain it; there being no agreement, however, as to the identity of the mortgagee or as to its terms.

The defendant thereafter became dissatisfied with his purchase, but finally agreed to stand by the bargain, if certain alterations were made in the house, if it was finished in a certain way, and if certain trees standing upon the lot were cut down. The plaintiff proceeded to make the changes and finish the house as desired by the defendant, and to cut down the trees, and he also secured a bank mortgage upon the premises in the sum of $4,500. The defendant, however, refused to complete the purchase. The way in which the house had been finished at the defendant's request made the premises less salable, but the plaintiff finally secured a purchaser for the price of $8,250, after, to meet this purchaser's desires, he had repainted the house a different color and repapered certain rooms. The plaintiff brings this action to recover for the expenses to which he was put in order to finish the house to meet the defendant's wishes, and thereafter, to adapt it to the desires of the purchaser, and also to recover the difference between the price agreed to be paid by the defendant and that for which the house was finally sold.

The trial court reached the conclusion that the acts of the plaintiff in finishing the house were sufficient to take the case out of the statute of frauds, but that the agreement between the plaintiff and defendant was too indefinite to be enforceable, because the land sold was not sufficiently identified, and because the agreement as to the mortgage to be secured and assumed by the defendant did not specify either the identity of the mortgagee or the terms it was to contain, and it gave judgment for the plaintiff to recover the value of the trees cut and the cost of repainting and repapering to meet the desires of the ultimate purchaser.

If the trial court was right in its conclusion that the agreement was too indefinite to be enforced, it becomes of no moment whether the acts done by the plaintiff were sufficient part performance to take the case out of the statute of frauds. The finding, particularly when read in the light of the memorandum of decision made a part of it, does not present the situation with reference to the land and houses owned by the plaintiff in such a way as to afford any satisfactory basis for a review of its conclusion that the premises sold were not sufficiently described so as to make the agreement definite enough to be enforceable. But its conclusion as to the indefiniteness of the provision concerning the mortgage which the plaintiff was to secure is clearly sound. * * *

* * *

The case is then one where the plaintiff seeks to recover the expense and loss which he has incurred in reliance upon the performance by the defendant of an agreement unenforceable because too indefinite in its terms. That in such a case recovery may often be had admits of no doubt. * * * But the work done and the expenditures made by the plaintiff to adapt it to meet the wishes of the defendant in the instant case have been of no benefit to the latter, and his main contention is that the basis of a recovery in such cases is the benefit conferred. Several decisions might be cited in which it has been so held. No doubt there are cases where, to support a recovery, it must appear that benefit has accrued to the defendant. For instance, such is the rule where a vendee of real estate has made improvements upon the land in reliance upon an oral agreement of sale and upon his own initiative, but the vendor refuses thereafter to carry out the agreement (Wainwright v. Talcott, 60 Conn. 43, 52, 22 A. 484) so, where one, in the honest belief that he is the absolute owner of property, makes improvements thereon, he is entitled to an allowance of their fair value in a suit to foreclose a mortgage on the premises (Ensign v. Batterson, 68 Conn. 298, 307, 36 A. 51). Within the same category fall, perhaps, those actions wherein a plaintiff who has substantially but not fully performed a contract is yet in certain circumstances permitted to recover for the work he has done. * * *

But there are other cases wherein a plaintiff, who cannot bring an action upon a special contract for some reason other than his own fault, is permitted a recovery for the reasonable value of the services which he has performed, without regard to the extent of the benefit conferred upon the other party to the contract. Examples are those where the defendant has himself prevented full performance of the contract * * * or where there has been a rescission of the contract during the course of performance * * * or where a building which is in the course of construction under a contract is destroyed by fire * * * or where one has agreed to perform personal services for another during the latter's life upon a promise of compensation by will, and dies before that other * * * or where services have been performed by one who has been promised compensation by will or by an heir, who has been promised that no will would be made * * *.

The rationale of these decisions is best seen in the latter class of cases, where a special promise to make compensation by will is unenforceable by reason of the statute of frauds. In such a case the services have been performed at the request of him for whom they were done, and in the expectation that compensation would be made for them, to his knowledge, and with his acquiescence. In the absence of any special contract, the law would in such a situation imply an agreement that reasonable compensation should be made. The basis of that implication is that the services have been requested and have been performed by the plaintiff in the known expectation that he would receive compensation, and neither the extent nor the presence of benefit to the defendant from their performance is of controlling significance. * * * If there were a valid and subsisting special contract, that would control; but where, though an attempt has been made to bring about such a contract, it has proved unavailing, the attempted contract is ordinarily of no consequence save as it shows the expectation of the parties that compensation for the services was to be made. It therefore leaves unimpaired the legal implication arising out of the rendition of the services upon request and in the known expectation of receiving compensation therefor. The measure of recovery is the reasonable value of the services performed, and not the amount of benefit which actually accrued from them to him for whom they were performed. * * *

The same principles apply where the parties have attempted to make a contract which is void because its terms are too indefinite, but where one party has, in good faith, and believing that a valid contract existed, performed part of the services which he had promised in reliance upon it. He has performed those services at the request of the other party to the contract, and in the expectation, known to the other, that he would be compensated therefor. Here is a sufficient basis for an implication in law that reasonable compensation would be made. The attempted special contract being void, there is nothing to overcome that implication. Vickery v. Ritchie, 202 Mass. 247, 88 N.E. 835, 26 L.R.A. (N.S.) 810. The situation is therefore one recognized by the law as falling within the underlying principle of implied contracts, which, in the various situations we have noted, and no doubt others, places a legal obligation upon one to do that which in equity and good conscience he ought to do. Fischer v. Kennedy, 106 Conn. 484, 492, 138 A. 503.

The sums allowed to the plaintiff for the repapering and repainting, which was done after the defendant refused to purchase, do not fall within the principles applicable to the case; to allow them in this action would be, in effect, to permit a recovery upon an unenforceable contract, which may not be done. But, if the work done on the property to adapt it to the desires of the defendant was done under the terms of an oral agreement for the sale of the premises, in good faith, and in the honest belief that the agreement was sufficiently definite to be enforced, the plaintiff is entitled to recover reasonable compensation therefor. In fixing the amount of that compensation, however, a proper deduction must be made for any benefit that has accrued to the plaintiff himself by reason of the work he did upon the premises at the defendant's request.

There is error, the judgment is set aside, and a new trial ordered.

All concur.

DAWSON, RESTITUTION WITHOUT ENRICHMENT[p]
61 Boston U.L.Rev. 563, 582–83 (1981).

[T]he promisor whose substantial breach derailed the exchange must restore whatever was given or done in response to and in conformity with its terms and it will not matter in the slightest degree whether this had brought profit or advantage to him. This proposition is reaffirmed in settings that differ widely. Most often tested in litigation have been the successful claims of architects and other designers for the market value of their services in preparing plans that were never used. In some instances the plans had been completed but other services were due that had not been rendered. In others the owner who had asked for and agreed to pay for the preparation of plans then abandoned his project and instructed the architect to desist at a time when the plans were incomplete and entirely unusable for any purpose. Or where a broker was employed under an unenforceable contract to advertise and sell the employer's produce (in this instance, asparagus), his recovery by way of restitution was the reasonable value of the services rendered with no deduction because a decline in market demand made it necessary to sell the produce at a loss. Still less productive is the alteration of real estate so as to add nothing to and perhaps subtract from its value. For example, an owner of land agrees, in one of the provisions in an unenforceable contract to sell it, that he will alter a building on the land to adapt it to the purchaser's special tastes. The seller can recover the reasonable value of the labor and materials expended even if the purchaser then refuses to complete the sale, so that no advantage can accrue to him or anyone else, since the changes reduce the sale value of the house and much of the work has to be done over.

KULL, RATIONALIZING RESTITUTION
83 Cal.L.Rev. 1191, 1200 (1995).

Rules that govern nonconsensual transfers account for the bulk of restitution law and certainly reflect the mainstream of restitution doctrine. Dawson's search for instances of restitution without enrichment led him to focus on a narrow group of cases, those that unwind incomplete consensual exchanges, in which the law's observed response is far more easily described as imposing a liability in contract. The short answer to most of Dawson's examples of restitution without enrichment is therefore that they are not restitution at all. Each is an example, rather, of surreptitious contract enforcement.

ANDERCO, INC. v. BUILDEX DESIGN, INC.
United States District Court, District of Columbia, 1982.
538 F.Supp. 1139.

MEMORANDUM

GESELL, DISTRICT JUDGE.

In this civil action tried to the Court, Anderco, Inc. (hereinafter "A"), sues Buildex Design, Inc. (hereinafter "B"), alleging breach of contract and,

p. John P. Dawson (1902–1985) was one of the leading private law scholars of the Western world. He wrote several major monographs, including Gifts and Promises (1980), and Unjust Enrichment, A Comparative Analysis (1951). His numerous articles on unjust enrichment and contract cast much light. His casebook on contracts (with W. Harvey and S. Henderson) is widely used. A photograph appears at page 975.

in the alternative, seeking quasi-contractual recovery to prevent B's unjust enrichment. B counterclaims for damages allegedly caused by A's breach of contract. For the reasons expressed in these findings of fact and conclusions of law, neither party is entitled to any recovery.

A is an established firm specializing in a form of foundation work known as grouting, which consists of pressurized injection of a cement-based mixture into the soil underlying a building for the purpose of arresting subsidence and in some cases actually raising foundation walls. In the summer of 1980, B, a small construction firm, entered into a contract with the Brazilian Embassy to stabilize and partially reconstruct a building in the District of Columbia known as the Brazilian Annex. The Annex was a relatively old building constructed in large part on filled ground. The structure had sunk on all four sides with the result that the floors bowed in the middle. B's task, among other things, was to stabilize the structure to prevent further sinking and to raise certain parts of the foundation, particularly the northeast corner, in order partially to alleviate the unevenness of the floors. This lawsuit arises from B's decision to ask A to perform this aspect of the job using A's grouting technique in lieu of alternative methods available.

During early August, 1980, Davis, a vice-president of A, and Downey, B's president, discussed the project in a number of conferences and telephone calls. On August 15, 1980, Davis submitted a written proposal to which was annexed a standard set of conditions. This proposal, to the extent here material, made no guarantee that efforts either to stabilize or lift the building would be successful, made no commitment as to time of completion of the job, and contemplated that the work would be billed at a per diem rate without any stated limitation on the total price of the job. After further conversations with Davis—the precise contents of which are hotly disputed—Downey sent Davis a telegram on August 25 indicating that A's proposal was accepted subject to "verbally agreed changes" and that a signed revision would follow. The next day Downey prepared and signed an edited version of A's written proposal to be mailed to Davis. The purport of the revision was to indicate that A was committed to stabilize the building and to lift the northeast corner by at least one and one-half inches and that the job would be undertaken in approximately ten days with a maximum payment of $20,000. A never received this document nor inquired why it had not been received as promised.

Both parties proceeded on the assumption that they had come to some type of agreement and work on the site commenced August 28. Although A was eventually able to stabilize the perimeter of the building it was unable despite protracted effort to achieve the desired rise in the northeast corner of the building.[1] As the work proceeded A reported in writing daily to B and B

---

1. The reasons why the grouting technique was unsuccessful in achieving the desired result were vigorously disputed at trial but are immaterial to the Court's resolution of this case. There is no claim A used improper methods or materials.

therefore had full knowledge that A was proceeding without marked success. At the end of 11 days of work A billed B at the per diem rate in A's proposal and this work was paid for in the total amount of $9,936.75. B at no time indicated to A that it should stop working. Downey constantly reiterated, however, that B only had $20,000 to pay for the work. A never consented to a $20,000 cap and urged B to seek an adjustment in the contract price from the Brazilian Embassy which B consistently refused to do. After approximately 25 days of continuous work A concluded that it would not be possible to lift the building one and one-half inches and, requiring the equipment for another job, informed B that it was terminating work.

A contends it is entitled to payment under an alleged contract with B at the per diem rate indicated in the August 15 proposal for the full 25 days for which a total of $14,111.34 would be owing. It claims to have fulfilled its obligation to attempt to stabilize the building and to lift the northeast corner, that the total contract price was never limited to $20,000, and that it was not obligated to complete the work in ten days. B presents a radically different version of the contract. It contends that A is barred from any recovery because it failed to follow through on its commitment to lift the corner of the building and to complete the work within ten days and, in any event, A's claim exceeds the contract amount. B's counterclaim alleging that A's failure to complete the work within ten days and to raise the northeast corner caused it extra expense is consistent with this position.

A's Contention of Contract

B's Contention of Contract

Holding

The Court concludes that neither side has established their version of the contract. Indeed, no contract was ever formed since the parties never came to a meeting of the minds as to its essential terms. Accordingly, both A's claim for recovery in contract and B's counterclaim for alleged breach of contract must fail.

The outlines of an agreement are contained in A's written proposal of August 15, 1982, and B's telegram of August 25 accepting the proposal subject to "verbally agreed changes." However, the testimony offered at trial clearly demonstrates that the parties had significantly different understandings of what Downey and Davis "verbally agreed" to in conversations between August 15 and August 25. The testimony of the two principals so lacks precision that it is impossible for the Court to determine the precise nature of the conversations. Davis, acting on behalf of A, believed that the parties' only oral modification of the written proposal was that A would receive payment for its services pursuant to a somewhat different timetable than indicated in the written proposal. This understanding is corroborated by the fact that Davis, upon receiving B's confirmatory telegram, sent a copy of the telegram to A's president and indicated in the margin that the "verbally agreed changes" referred to in the telegram related only to the payment schedule. Downey, on the other hand, believed that as a result of his conversations with Davis A made the following specific guarantees: that the soil would be stabilized under the building on all sides, that the northeast corner of the building would be raised one and one-half to two inches, that the work could be completed for less than $20,000, and that the work would be completed in approximately ten days. Downey's view of the parties' verbal understanding also has some documentary support in the record. Downey's edited version of A's written proposal, which was apparently mailed to but never received by A, contains in substance all of the specific changes [B] claims were orally agreed to between Downey and Davis.

The bona fides of each party's version of the contract is underscored by their conduct in the course of actual performance. After work had been proceeding for more than ten days, Downey called Davis to inquire as to why the work had not been completed within that period and to reiterate that a total of only $20,000 had been allocated to pay for the work. [Davis], for his part, steadfastly refused to acknowledge the $20,000 cap, insisting that B could and should request the Brazilian government to increase the contract price. Also, on September 15, A sent its first invoice to B, indicating that payment was being sought under "our Proposed Contract dated August 15, 1980." These actions clearly demonstrate that although both parties proceeded initially under the belief that they had a contract, their understanding as to the terms of that contract diverged in several key respects.

Reasoning

→ In order to form a contract it is necessary that the parties manifest their agreement or mutual assent to its essential terms. * * * It is evident that in this instance there was no mutuality of assent. Moreover, there is no evidence tending to show that either party ignored the only reasonable interpretation of the words used or that either knew or had reason to know the intention or understanding of the other. *See* 1 Corbin on Contracts § 104 at 464 (1963). Under these circumstances A's written proposal of August 15, B's telegram of August 26, and the parties' intervening conversations do not make a contract.

Reasoning

→ Sometimes the course of the parties' performance will permit the Court to recognize an implied contract, *see Bloomgarden v. Coyer,* 479 F.2d 201, 208 (D.C.Cir.1973), or supply the missing terms of an indefinite contract, *see* 1 Corbin on Contracts § 101 (1963). But though a contract may be inferred from various facts and circumstances it must conform with all the elements of a binding agreement, 479 F.2d at 208, including the requirement of mutuality of assent, *see Martens v. Metzgar,* 524 P.2d 666, 672 (Alaska 1974); 1 Williston on Contracts § 3 at 11 (3d ed. 1957). Certain disputed elements of the parties' understanding can arguably be resolved based on the parties' conduct. For example, B's failure to terminate A after ten days of work might be interpreted as a tacit acknowledgement that the contract did not have a specific time limitation. Also, B's payment of A's invoice of September 15 could be taken as evidencing an agreement as to the per diem rate as well as the fact that A was not limited to ten days' work. Nevertheless, the record demonstrates that at least up until the time A abandoned the job the parties either had a mutual misunderstanding concerning or were actively disputing both the total contract price and the nature of the performance that had been promised. These facts demonstrate an absence of mutual assent and therefore a contract may not be found by implication.

Alternative pleading

In the absence of either an express or implied contract, A seeks recovery on its quasi-contractual claim on the theory "that the defendant was unjustly enriched at the plaintiff's expense, and that the circumstances were such that in good conscience the defendant should make restitution." *Bloomgarden v. Coyer,* 479 F.2d 201, 211 (D.C.Cir.1973); *see also* 1 Corbin on Contracts § 19 (1963). The primary elements of the work were to stabilize the soil around the perimeter of the building and to raise the northeast corner by one and one-half to two inches. It is conceded that A succeeded in stabilizing the soil and this was of benefit to B in carrying out its contract with the Brazilian Embassy. There is a substantial difference of opinion as to whether A succeeded in raising the building and, if so, how much. [A] acknowledges, however, that it failed to raise the level of the northeast corner a full one and one-half inches. Moreover, in weighing the conflicting testimony as to whether or not there was any movement the Court finds more credible the testimony *Reasoning* offered on behalf of B, especially in view of the fact that the critical measurement relied on by A had to be taken using different benchmarks than were established at the beginning of the job. [Thus the Court concludes that B received no benefit as a result of A's strenuous efforts to raise the northeast corner.] *Holding on Alternative*

Based on the present record it is impossible for the Court to determine whether the $9,936.75 already received by A in partial payment for the work performed represents either more or less than the value of A's successful efforts to stabilize the foundation. Plaintiff has presented no proof as to how *Reasoning* the $20,000—whether that amount is viewed as a cap or a mere estimate— was to be allocated among the various aspects of the job. Nor is there any evidence in the record of the reasonable value of A's partial performance ← based on any other standard. The appropriate result therefore is for the Court to leave the parties where it finds them.

Both the complaint and the counterclaim will be dismissed. An appropriate Order is filed herewith. *Judgment*

POSNER v. SEDER

Supreme Judicial Court of Massachusetts, 1903.
184 Mass. 331, 68 N.E. 335.

CONTRACT, against manufacturers of clothing, by a foreman and cutter for his services, according to an account annexed. * * *

[After a trial, the judge found for the plaintiff; and the defendants alleged exceptions.]

* * *

HAMMOND, J. Under the contract the defendants were to employ the plaintiff for one year, and pay him for his services $17 a week, "the same to be paid at the end of each and every week." The plaintiff was to report at the shop for duty at 6:30 a.m., and remain there on duty until 6 p.m., with the exception of the hour between noon and 1 p.m., and was "also, without extra pay, to work overtime at said shop * * * not more than two hours in one day and not more than two months in the aggregate for the year." The defendants broke the contract by the discharge of the plaintiff. In such a case the innocent party may either sue on the contract for damages for the breach, or, if he so elects, he may regard the action of the defendants as indicating a purpose on their part to repudiate the contract, may accept the repudiation, and recover upon a quantum meruit the value of his services as if the special contract had not existed. Brown v. Woodbury, 183 Mass. 279, 67 N.E. 327. In this case the plaintiff has sued upon a quantum meruit for the value of only a part of the services, namely, for those rendered in the extra hours named in the contract.

The plaintiff contends that the $17 which he received each week was payment for only the time between 6:30 a.m. and 6 p.m., and not for the extra time; and that, therefore, he may, upon breach of the contract, appropriate the weekly sum to the payment of the services during the regular hours, and recover on quantum meruit for the extra time. The defendants, on the contrary, contend that the $17 was a payment for the services of the week, whatever they were, and therefore that the plaintiff has been fully paid, and so cannot recover.

Neither view seems to us correct. The contract was to continue a year. The weekly hours of labor were variable, and it is fair to assume that there would be a weekly variation in the value of the services. The contract is to be taken as a whole. On the one hand, the defendants could not hold the plaintiff to the work during the extra hours in any week for the sum of $17 except in connection with the other part of the contract, namely, that they were to pay him $17 in other weeks when there was no extra time; nor, on the other hand, could the plaintiff hold the defendants to the payment of $17 for a week in which he did not work extra time, except in connection with the other part of the contract, namely, that in any week in which he did work extra time he should receive only $17. The true construction of the contract is that it was a hiring for a year, payments to be made by weekly installments, without reference to * * * the amount of work done. Since the payments were made during the existence of the contract, they cannot be considered as having no reference to the other parts of the contract.

If the plaintiff desires to proceed upon the theory that the contract has been repudiated, his proper course is to proceed upon quantum meruit for the value of all his services, less what he has received. If he has been paid what they are worth, he can recover nothing; if he has not, he may recover the balance due him. But it is plain that the sum due him is not necessarily the fair price for the extra hours in addition to the sum of $17 per week which he has received. He cannot appropriate the $17 to the payment of the ordinary week's work, and sue only for the balance, because, for the reasons above stated, that is not in accordance with the contract under which the payment was made. Upon quantum meruit the question is, what are his whole services fairly worth, and is there anything due him. Manifestly, under a contract like this, that may be an entirely different sum from the market value of the services during the extra hours. * * *

* * * It is not necessary that the plaintiff, before bringing his action, should return what he has received. It is necessary only that the amount received should be credited upon his claim. Brown v. Woodbury, supra.

Exceptions sustained.

KELLEY v. HANCE

Supreme Court of Errors of Connecticut, 1928.
108 Conn. 186, 142 A. 683.

BANKS, J. In September, 1926, the plaintiff and defendant entered into a contract in which the former agreed to excavate to the proper level and construct a concrete sidewalk and curb in front of the latter's property for the agreed price of $420, being at the rate of $3 per running foot for 140 feet. The plaintiff agreed to start the work within a week and to complete it before cold weather set in. The plaintiff did not start work until December 4, 1926. He removed a strip of earth along the frontage of defendant's premises to a width of 12 feet and a depth of 8 [inches] and then left the premises and has not since done anything further toward the completion of his contract. On March 2, 1927, the defendant notified the plaintiff that he canceled the contract. The reasonable value of the work done by the plaintiff was $158.60. Judgment was rendered in favor of the plaintiff for $133.68 which amount imports an award of nominal damages of $25 to the defendant upon his counterclaim for the value of the earth removed by the plaintiff.

The trial court reached the conclusion that the defendant was justified in canceling the contract because of the failure of the plaintiff to perform, but that the latter was entitled to recover the reasonable value of the benefits accruing to the defendant from the work done by the plaintiff.

While the plaintiff's contract was for the construction of a sidewalk and curb at a unit price per running foot, no section of the walk and curb was completed, and it is not claimed that plaintiff could recover upon the theory of a performance of a divisible portion of the contract; nor was he entitled to recover upon the theory of a substantial performance. This was in the nature of a construction contract as to which class of contracts the rule is liberally applied permitting a recovery where a contractor has deviated slightly from the terms of the contract, not willfully, but in good faith, and there has been a substantial performance of the contract of which the other party has received the benefit. Pinches v. Swedish Lutheran Church, 55 Conn. 183, 10 A. 264; Daly v. New Haven Hotel Co., 91 Conn. 280, 99 A. 853. Here, however, not only is there no finding of substantial performance, but it appears from the finding that no portion of the sidewalk and curb was actually constructed by the plaintiff, who, after making an excavation along the front of defendant's premises, left the work and has not done anything since toward its completion. The court has found that the reasonable worth of the work done by the plaintiff was $158.60, slightly more than a third of the contract price, and that the defendant has benefited to that extent from the plaintiff's work. The case, therefore, is one where a contractor has without justification abandoned his contract before completion, but seeks to recover from the defendant the reasonable worth to the latter of the work done prior to the abandonment.

Though a contractor has failed of performance for reasons which would not excuse a breach, and where there has not been even substantial performance, the breach being merely negligent, many of the more recent decisions have held that he could recover the value of his work, less the damages caused by his default. 3 Williston on Contracts, § 1475, and cases cited. Such recovery is allowed, not upon the original contract, for that has been breached, but in quasi contract upon the theory that, if such recovery were not allowed, the other party would be unjustly enriched at the expense of the contractor. 6 Page on Contracts, § 3262. Some cases have gone so far as to allow an employee who has performed part of his employment to recover reasonable compensation, though his failure to render further performance was due to his willful abandonment of his contract. 3 Williston on Contracts, § 1477. By the weight of authority, however, there can ordinarily be no recovery where the contractor has willfully abandoned his contract without justification. * * *

While the mere fact that part performance has been beneficial to the defendant will not entitle the plaintiff to recover where he has abandoned performance without justification, the defendant may nevertheless make himself liable by his voluntary acceptance of the benefits under circumstances sufficient to raise an implied promise to pay for them notwithstanding the nonperformance of the contract. Where one retains goods received in part performance of a contract, a promise to pay for them is ordinarily implied since he has the option either to pay for or return them. Where, however, work has been done upon one's land, the benefit cannot well be returned and an acceptance of the benefit cannot be implied from the mere retention of possession of the land. In such cases, therefore, the better rule would seem to be that, except where there has been an actual acceptance of the work prior to its abandonment by the plaintiff, mere inaction on the part of the defendant will not be treated as an acceptance of the work from which a promise to pay for it may be implied. * * *

We have held that recovery can be had for partial performance which has been beneficial only when the benefit has been appropriated by the defendant under circumstances sufficient to raise an implied promise to pay for the reasonable value of what has been received. Jones v. Marlborough, 70 Conn. 583, 589, 40 A. 460; Jones & Hotchkiss Co. v. Davenport, 74 Conn. 418, 420, 50 A. 1028.

The finding discloses an abandonment of his contract by the plaintiff after the excavation was made, but before any portion of the sidewalk and curb had been constructed. No justification for this abandonment appears and the plaintiff cannot therefore recover the reasonable value of the work done, unless there has been such an acceptance of it by the defendant as to raise an implied promise on his part to pay for it. No acceptance of the work by the defendant prior to the breach is found and no promise to pay for the benefit received can be implied from the mere fact that he has received a benefit which from the nature of the case he could not avoid receiving and was powerless to return. It follows that the court erred in its conclusion that the plaintiff was entitled to recover the reasonable value of the work done by him in the partial performance of his contract.

In the absence of any evidence of the market value of the dirt which it is found was wrongfully disposed of by the plaintiff, the defendant cannot justly complain of the award to him of nominal damages.

There is error, the judgment is reversed, and the city court of Meriden is directed to enter its judgment in favor of the defendant for nominal damages upon his counterclaim.

All concur.

BRITTON v. TURNER

Supreme Court of Judicature of New Hampshire, 1834.
6 N.H. 481.

Assumpsit, for work and labor, performed by the plaintiff, in the service of the defendant, from March 9, 1831, to December 27, 1831.

The declaration contained the common counts, and among them a count in *quantum meruit*, for the labor, averring it to be worth $100. At the trial in the C. C. Pleas, the plaintiff proved the performance of the labor as set forth in the declaration.

The defense was that it was performed under a special contract; that the plaintiff agreed to work one year, from some time in March, 1831, to March, 1832, and that the defendant was to pay him for said year's labor the sum of $120; and the defendant offered evidence tending to show that such was the contract under which the work was done.

Evidence was also offered to show that the plaintiff left the defendant's service without his consent, and it was contended by the defendant that the plaintiff had no good cause for not continuing in his employment.

There was no evidence offered of any damage arising from the plaintiff's departure, farther than was to be inferred from his nonfulfilment of the entire contract.

The court instructed the jury that, if they were satisfied from the evidence that the labor was performed under a contract to labor a year, for the sum of $120, and if they were satisfied that the plaintiff labored only the time specified in the declaration, and then left the defendant's service, against his consent, and without any good cause, yet the plaintiff was entitled to recover, under his *quantum meruit* count, as much as the labor he performed was reasonably worth, and under this direction the jury gave a verdict for the plaintiff for the sum of $95.

The defendant excepted to the instructions thus given to the jury.

* * *

PARKER, J., delivered the opinion of the court.

* * *

It is clear * * * that [plaintiff] is not entitled to recover upon the contract itself, because the service, which was to entitle him to the sum agreed upon, has never been performed.

But the question arises, can the plaintiff, under these circumstances, recover a reasonable sum for the service he has actually performed, under the count in *quantum meruit?* Upon this, and questions of a similar nature, the decisions to be found in the books are not easily reconciled.

It has been held, upon contracts of this kind for labor to be performed at a specified price, that the party who voluntarily fails to fulfil the contract by performing the whole labor contracted for, is not entitled to recover anything for the labor actually performed, however much he may have done towards the performance, and this has been considered the settled rule of law upon this subject. * * *

That such rule in its operation may be very unequal, not to say unjust, is apparent. A party who contracts to perform certain specified labor, and who breaks his contract in the first instance, without any attempt to perform it, can only be made liable to pay the damages which the other party has sustained by reason of such non-performance, which in many instances may be trifling—whereas a party who in good faith has entered upon the performance of his contract, and nearly completed it, and then abandoned the further performance, although the other party has had the full benefit of all that has been done, and has perhaps sustained no actual damage—is in fact subjected to a loss of all which has been performed, in the nature of damages for the nonfulfilment of the remainder, upon the technical rule, that the contract must be fully performed in order to [sustain] a recovery of any part of the compensation.

By the operation of this rule, then, the party who attempts performance may be placed in a much worse situation than he who wholly disregards his contract, and the other party may receive much more, by the breach of the contract, than the injury which he has sustained by such breach, and more than he could be entitled to were he seeking to recover damages by an action.

The case before us presents an illustration. Had the plaintiff in this case never entered upon the performance of his contract, the damage could not probably have been greater than some small expense and trouble incurred in procuring another to do the labor which he had contracted to perform. But having entered upon the performance, and labored nine and a half months, the value of which labor to the defendant as found by the jury is $95, if the defendant can succeed in this defense, he in fact receives nearly five-sixths of the value of a whole year's labor, by reason of the breach of contract by the plaintiff, a sum not only utterly disproportionate to any probable, not to say possible damage which could have resulted from the neglect of the plaintiff to continue the remaining two and [a] half months, but altogether beyond any damage which could have been recovered by the defendant, had the plaintiff done nothing towards the fulfilment of his contract.

* * *

It is said that in those cases where the plaintiff has been permitted to recover there was an acceptance of what had been done. The answer is that where the contract is to labor from day to day, for a certain period, the party for whom the labor is done in truth stipulates to receive it from day to day, as it is performed, and although the other may not eventually do all he has contracted to do, there has been, necessarily, an acceptance of what has been done in pursuance of the contract, and the party must have understood when he made the contract that there was to be such acceptance.

If, then, the party stipulates in the outset to receive part performance from time to time, with a knowledge that the whole may not be completed, we see no reason why he should not equally be holden to pay for the amount of value received, as where he afterwards takes the benefit of what has been done, with a knowledge that the whole which was contracted for has not been performed. In neither case has the contract been performed. In neither can an action be sustained on the original contract. In both the party has assented to receive what is done. The only difference is that in the one case the assent is prior, with a knowledge that all may not be performed; in the other it is subsequent, with a knowledge that the whole has not been accomplished.

* * *

* * * [W]e think the technical reasoning, that the performance of the whole labor is a condition precedent, and the right to recover anything dependent upon it; that the contract being entire there can be no apportionment—and that there being an express contract no other can be implied, even upon the subsequent performance of service—is not properly applicable to this

species of contract, where a beneficial service has been actually performed; for we have abundant reason to believe, that the general understanding of the community is that the hired laborer shall be entitled to compensation for the service actually performed, though he do not continue the entire term contracted for, and such contracts must be presumed to be made with reference to that understanding, unless an express stipulation shows the contrary.

* * *

It is easy, if parties so choose, to provide by an express agreement that nothing shall be earned, if the laborer leaves his employer without having performed the whole service contemplated, and then there can be no pretense for a recovery if he voluntarily deserts the service before the expiration of the time.

The amount, however, for which the employer ought to be charged, where the laborer abandons his contract, is only the reasonable worth, or the amount of advantage he receives upon the whole transaction (*Wadleigh v. Sutton*, 6 N.H. 15), and, in estimating the value of the labor, the contract price for the service cannot be exceeded. * * *

If a person makes a contract fairly, he is entitled to have it fully performed, and if this is not done, he is entitled to damages. He may maintain a suit to recover the amount of damage sustained by the non-performance. The benefit and advantage which the party takes by the labor, therefore, is the amount of value which he receives, if any, after deducting the amount of damage; and if he elects to put this in defense he is entitled so to do, and the implied promise which the law will raise, in such case, is to pay such amount of the stipulated price for the whole labor, as remains after deducting what it would cost to procure a completion of the residue of the service and also any damage which has been sustained by reason of the nonfulfilment of the contract. If in such case it be found that the damages are equal to or greater than the amount of the labor performed, so that the employer, having a right to the full performance of the contract, has not upon the whole case received a beneficial service, the plaintiff cannot recover.

This rule, by binding the employer to pay the value of the service he actually receives, and the laborer to answer in damages where he does not complete the entire contract, will leave no temptation to the former to drive the laborer from his service, near the close of his term, by ill treatment, in order to escape from payment; nor to the latter to desert his service before the stipulated time, without a sufficient reason. * * *

* * *

Applying the principles thus laid down, to this case, the plaintiff is entitled to judgment on the verdict. The defendant sets up a mere breach of the contract in defense of the action, but this cannot avail him. He does not appear to have offered evidence to show that he was damnified by such breach, or to have asked that a deduction should be made upon that account. The direction to the jury was therefore correct, that the plaintiff was entitled to recover as much as the labor performed was reasonably worth, and the jury appear to have allowed a *pro rata* compensation, for the time which the plaintiff labored in the defendant's service.

As the defendant has not claimed or had any adjustment of damages, for the breach of the contract, in this action, if he has actually sustained damage he is still entitled to a suit to recover the amount.

* * *

Judgment on the verdict.

Problem 2–8

Frank Stein is negotiating with Ken's Drugs, Inc. concerning a one-year appointment with Ken's as a chemist. Ken tells you that the first four months of a new chemist's time is mostly in training and that Ken's receives little benefit during this time. Ken therefore asks you to draft a provision in the proposed employment contract ensuring that Frank will receive no compensation unless he completes at least six months work. Draft the provision. Consider N.Y. Labor Law § 191(d) (McKinney Supp. 2000):

1. Clerical and other worker.—A clerical and other worker shall be paid the wages earned in accordance with the agreed terms of employment, but not less frequently than semi-monthly, on regular pay days designated in advance by the employer.

2. No employee shall be required as a condition of employment to accept wages at periods other than as provided in this section.

3. If employment is terminated, the employer shall pay the wages not later than the regular pay day for the pay period during which the termination occurred, as established in accordance with the provisions of this section. If requested by the employee, such wages shall be paid by mail.

DE LEON v. ALDRETE, 398 S.W.2d 160 (Tex.Civ.App.1965). [Plaintiff Aldrete defaulted after having paid installments of $1,070 out of a total due of $1,500 for the purchase of a tract of land from the De Leons. Aldrete was not in possession of the land. The De Leons thereupon sold the land to another for $1,300. Plaintiff sought the return of the $1,070. The trial court found for plaintiff. On appeal, the court deducted $200 from the $1,070 and affirmed.]

CADENA, JUSTICE.

* * *

What is generally described as the majority rule in this country is that a defaulting purchaser cannot recover any money paid by him under the contract to the vendor even though, as a result of the purchaser's breach, the vendor has abandoned all idea of further performance and retains the money, not for application on the purchase price, but as forfeited. Anno.: 31 A.L.R.2d 8, 11–12 (1953).[q]

* * *

* * * Dogmatic application of the majority rule leads to indefensibly absurd results. Under that rule of forfeiture the amount of the forfeiture will

---

q. In New York, defaulting purchasers of real estate cannot recover their down payments, at least if they are in the neighborhood of 10%. In Maxton Builders, Inc. v. Lo Galbo, 68 N.Y.2d 373, 509 N.Y.S.2d 507, 502 N.E.2d 184 (1986), the court reasoned that down payments of about 10% roughly equal the amount of damages to the seller.

always and necessarily depend simply on the stage to which the purchaser's performance has progressed, with complete disregard of the amount of damages suffered by the vendor. * * *

* * *

In the case before us, plaintiff had paid in excess of 70% of the purchase price. The damages which defendants suffered as a result of plaintiff's breach are definite and ascertainable from the evidence by resort to simple mathematical calculation. Had plaintiff fully performed, defendants would have received $1,500.00 for their land. Because of such breach, they received only $1,300.00. Plaintiff makes no contention that this was not a fair price. Clearly, in order to prevent defendants from suffering as a result of plaintiff's default, it is only necessary to allow them to retain, from the amount paid by plaintiff, the sum of $200.00. To allow them to retain the $1,070.00 paid by plaintiff, after they had received $1,300.00 as a result of their termination of the contract and sale of the land to a third party, would result in a situation where defendants would be unjustly enriched in the amount of $870.00. This result can be justified only if we are prepared to hold that plaintiff must be punished for his breach. Punitive damages are alien to the law of contract. The fundamental principle of our law concerning the liability of one who breaches his contract is the principle of compensation. This principle contemplates that the liability to respond in compensatory, as distinguished from punitive, damages will afford sufficient protection to the innocent party, and this is the only interest, absent extraordinary circumstances which are not present here, which the social welfare demands should be the subject of judicial solicitude. * * *

Note
Variant Terminology: Unjust Enrichment, Restitution, Quasi–Contract, Quantum Meruit, Common Counts

Confucius is supposed to have said:

Now, if names of things are not properly defined, words will not correspond to facts. When words do not correspond to facts, it is impossible to perfect anything. Where it is impossible to perfect anything, the arts and institutions of civilization cannot flourish. When the arts and institutions of civilization cannot flourish, law and justice do not attain their ends; and when law and justice do not attain their ends, the people will be at a loss to know what to do. (Confucius, The Analects, xiii, 3.)

In our study of unjust enrichment in Section Four, we have encountered much variant terminology. We now offer some clarifying remarks with the caveat that, as to some terms, usage is by no means uniform. The term "unjust enrichment" is ordinarily used as the name of a legally recognized general theory of obligation. The core idea of this theory is that a person who has been unjustly enriched at the claimant's expense incurs a duty to satisfy the claim asserted to the extent of the enrichment (absent a defense). Another name sometimes used for this theory of obligation is "restitution." But restitution is more frequently employed to designate any *remedy*, whether at law or in equity, that redresses unjust enrichment. In addition, restitution may refer to one kind of remedy for breach of contract, as where an aggrieved plaintiff simply seeks to recover money paid to the breaching party. See Chapter Three. In Bloomgarden v. Coyer, at page

112, we saw that courts also refer to the unjust enrichment theory of obligation as "quasi-contract."

Still another phrase sometimes used to designate the theory of unjust enrichment is "contract implied in law." You should distinguish between contract implied in fact and contract implied in law. A contract implied in fact is one kind of enforceable agreement with consideration—one in which the facts of agreement and consideration are based on implication and inference rather than on explicit assent as in an express contract. Consider again Bloomgarden v. Coyer (page 112 and Anderco, Inc. v. Buildex Design, Inc. (page 125). But something rather different is meant by a contract implied in law, for this expression ordinarily refers to obligations arising under the theory of unjust enrichment.

The general theory of obligation known as unjust enrichment is applicable in many diverse contexts, promissory and non-promissory. In Section Four, we have seen the relevance of unjust enrichment theory to contract and related areas. But the theory may be invoked in other fields, too. For example, if A uses B's goods for one month, thinking that they belong to A, and then returns them after learning the facts, B is entitled under unjust enrichment theory to the reasonable rental value of the goods for the month involved.

In several cases in this section we also encountered the expression "quantum meruit." This Latin phrase means, literally, "as much as he deserved." It originally designated a simplified form of pleading used to bring an action at law to obtain payment for services rendered. This form of pleading was called a "common count" in general assumpsit. There were two related common counts that should be noted, a count called "quantum valebant" (for goods sold and delivered) and a count for "money had and received." Each of these counts included not only an allegation of "services rendered" or the equivalent, but also an allegation of a promise to pay for such (which did not have to be proved).

The common count of quantum meruit is often used today in pleadings, but in modern usage it does not alone reveal the theory of obligation on which the asserted claim ultimately rests. A count in quantum meruit may be based on (1) an express contract (agreement with consideration), or (2) an implied-in-fact contract (agreement with consideration), or (3) on an obligation arising from unjust enrichment (as for example, in Gay v. Mooney, page 120).

WATTS v. WATTS

Supreme Court of Wisconsin, 1987.
137 Wis.2d 506, 405 N.W.2d 303.

SHIRLEY S. ABRAHAMSON, JUSTICE.

* * *

The case involves a dispute between Sue Ann Evans Watts, the plaintiff, and James Watts, the defendant, over their respective interests in property accumulated during their nonmarital cohabitation relationship which spanned 12 years and produced two children. The case presents an issue of first impression and comes to this court at the pleading stage of the case, before trial and before the facts have been determined.

The plaintiff asked the circuit court to order an accounting of the defendant's personal and business assets accumulated between June 1969 through December 1981 (the duration of the parties' cohabitation) and to determine plaintiff's share of this property. The circuit court's dismissal of *Issue* plaintiff's amended complaint [for failure to state a claim] is the subject of this appeal. * * *

* * *

The plaintiff commenced this action in 1982. The plaintiff's amended complaint alleges the following facts, which for purposes of this appeal must be accepted as true. The plaintiff and the defendant met in 1967, when she was 19 years old, was living with her parents and was working full time as a nurse's aide in preparation for a nursing career. Shortly after the parties met, the defendant persuaded the plaintiff to move into an apartment paid for by him and to quit her job. According to the amended complaint, the defendant "indicated" to the plaintiff that he would provide for her.

Early in 1969, the parties began living together in a "marriage-like" relationship, holding themselves out to the public as husband and wife. The plaintiff assumed the defendant's surname as her own. Subsequently, she gave birth to two children who were also given the defendant's surname. The parties filed joint income tax returns and maintained joint bank accounts asserting that they were husband and wife. The defendant insured the plaintiff as his wife on his medical insurance policy. He also took out a life insurance policy on her as his wife, naming himself as the beneficiary. The parties purchased real and personal property as husband and wife. The plaintiff executed documents and obligated herself on promissory notes to lending institutions as the defendant's wife.

During their relationship, the plaintiff contributed childcare and home-making services, including cleaning, cooking, laundering, shopping, running errands, and maintaining the grounds surrounding the parties' home. Additionally, the plaintiff contributed personal property to the relationship which she owned at the beginning of the relationship or acquired through gifts or purchases during the relationship. She served as hostess for the defendant for social and business-related events. The amended complaint further asserts that periodically, between 1969 and 1975, the plaintiff cooked and cleaned for the defendant and his employees while his business, a landscaping service, was building and landscaping a golf course.

From 1973 to 1976, the plaintiff worked 20–25 hours per week at the defendant's office, performing duties as a receptionist, typist, and assistant bookkeeper. From 1976 to 1981, the plaintiff worked 40–60 hours per week at a business she started with the defendant's sister-in-law, then continued and managed the business herself after the dissolution of that partnership. The plaintiff further alleges that in 1981 the defendant made their relationship so intolerable that she was forced to move from their home and their relationship was irretrievably broken. Subsequently, the defendant barred the plaintiff from returning to her business.

The plaintiff alleges that during the parties' relationship, and because of her domestic and business contributions, the business and personal wealth of the couple increased. Furthermore, the plaintiff alleges that she never received any compensation for these contributions to the relationship and that the defendant indicated to the plaintiff both orally and through his conduct that he considered her to be his wife and that she would share equally in the increased wealth.

The plaintiff asserts that since the breakdown of the relationship the defendant has refused to share equally with her the wealth accumulated through their joint efforts or to compensate her in any way for her contributions to the relationship.

* * *

The plaintiff's third legal theory on which her claim rests is that she and the defendant had a contract to share equally the property accumulated during their relationship. The essence of the complaint is that the parties had a contract, either an express or implied in fact contract, which the defendant breached.

The plaintiff has alleged that she quit her job and abandoned her career training upon the defendant's promise to take care of her. A change in one party's circumstances in performance of the agreement may imply an agreement between the parties. * * * In addition, the plaintiff alleges that she performed housekeeping, childbearing, childrearing, and other services related to the maintenance of the parties' home, in addition to various services for the defendant's business and her own business, for which she received no compensation. Courts have recognized that money, property, or services (including housekeeping or childrearing) may constitute adequate consideration independent of the parties' sexual relationship to support an agreement to share or transfer property. * * *

According to the plaintiff's complaint, the parties cohabited for more than twelve years, held joint bank accounts, made joint purchases, filed joint income tax returns, and were listed as husband and wife on other legal documents. Courts have held that such a relationship and "joint acts of a financial nature can give rise to an inference that the parties intended to share equally." Beal v. Beal, 282 Or. 115, 122, 577 P.2d 507, 510 (1978). The joint ownership of property and the filing of joint income tax returns strongly implies that the parties intended their relationship to be in the nature of a joint enterprise, financially as well as personally. * * *

* * * [W]e conclude that the plaintiff in this case has pleaded the facts necessary to state a claim for damages resulting from the defendant's breach of an express or an implied in fact contract to share with the plaintiff the property accumulated through the efforts of both parties during their relationship. Once again, we do not judge the merits of the plaintiff's claim; we merely hold that she be given her day in court to prove her claim.

The plaintiff's fourth theory of recovery involves unjust enrichment. Essentially, she alleges that the defendant accepted and retained the benefit of services she provided knowing that she expected to share equally in the wealth accumulated during their relationship. She argues that it is unfair for the defendant to retain all the assets they accumulated under these circumstances and that a constructive trust should be imposed on the property as a result of the defendant's unjust enrichment. In his brief, the defendant does not attack specifically either the legal theory or the factual allegations made by the plaintiff.

Unlike claims for breach of an express or implied in fact contract, a claim of unjust enrichment does not arise out of an agreement entered into by the parties. Rather, an action for recovery based upon unjust enrichment is grounded on the moral principle that one who has received a benefit has a duty to make restitution where retaining such a benefit would be unjust. Puttkammer v. Minth, 83 Wis.2d 686, 689, 266 N.W.2d 361, 363 (1978).

Because no express or implied in fact agreement exists between the parties, recovery based upon unjust enrichment is sometimes referred to as "quasi contract," or contract "implied in law" rather than "implied in fact." Quasi contracts are obligations created by law to prevent injustice. * * *

In Wisconsin, an action for unjust enrichment, or quasi contract, is based upon proof of three elements: (1) a benefit conferred on the defendant by the plaintiff, (2) appreciation or knowledge by the defendant of the benefit, and (3) acceptance or retention of the benefit by the defendant under circumstances making it inequitable for the defendant to retain the benefit. Puttkammer, supra, 83 Wis.2d at 689, 266 N.W.2d 361; Wis.J.I.Civil No. 3028 (1981).

The plaintiff has cited no cases directly supporting actions in unjust enrichment by unmarried cohabitants, and the defendant provides no authority against it. This court has previously extended such relief to a party to a cohabitation in Estate of Fox, 178 Wis. 369, 190 N.W. 90, 31 A.L.R. 420 (1922). In Fox, the plaintiff was a woman who had believed in good faith that she was married to the decedent, when in fact she was not. The court found that the decedent "husband" had "by fraudulent representations induced the plaintiff to enter into the illicit relationship." Fox, supra, 178 Wis. at 372, 190 N.W. 90. Under those circumstances, the court reasoned that it was "just and logical" to infer "from the nature of the transaction" that "the supposed husband [can be] held to have assumed to pay [for services rendered by his 'spouse'] because in point of law and equity it is just that he should pay." Id.

In Fox, the court expressly refused to consider whether the same result would necessarily follow in other circumstances. Thus, Fox does not supply explicit support for the plaintiff's position here where she does not claim that she thought the parties were actually married.

The Steffes case, [95 Wis.2d 490, 290 N.W.2d 697 (1980)] however, does provide additional support for the plaintiff's position. Although Steffes involved a claim for recovery in contract by an unmarried cohabitant for the value of services she performed for the decedent, the same equitable principles that governed that case would appear to apply in a case where the plaintiff is seeking recovery based upon unjust enrichment. In Steffes, the court cited with approval a statement by the trial judge that "[t]he question I have in mind is why should the estate be enriched when that man was just as much a part of the illicit relationship as she was and not let her have her fair dues. I don't understand that law that would interpret unjust enrichment that way and deprive one and let the other benefit and do it on the basis that there was an illicit relationship but not equally held against the both...." Steffes, supra, 95 Wis.2d at 508, 290 N.W.2d 697.

* * *

[Holding] * * * Many courts have held, and we now so hold, that unmarried cohabitants may raise claims based upon unjust enrichment following the termination of their relationships where one of the parties attempts to retain an unreasonable amount of the property acquired through the efforts of both.

In this case, the plaintiff alleges that she contributed both property and services to the parties' relationship. She claims that because of these contributions the parties' assets increased, but that she was never compensated for her contributions. She further alleges that the defendant, knowing that the plaintiff expected to share in the property accumulated, "accepted the services rendered to him by the plaintiff" and that it would be unfair under the circumstances to allow him to retain everything while she receives nothing. We conclude that the facts alleged are sufficient to state a claim for recovery based upon unjust enrichment. *[12(b)(6) was incorrect]*

[Judgment] The judgment of the circuit court is reversed and the cause remanded.

Note
Regulation of Private Relations

Watts v. Watts involved a nonmarital relationship, but suppose the parties were married. Could the parties have contracted for compensation for Sue Ann Evans Watts? For all of her contributions? Some private relations, such as marriage, are heavily regulated by the state, which supplies most of the rules that govern the marriage, including in many states a prohibition against compensation for certain contributions of a spouse. For example, "courts have refused to enforce such agreements between spouses as: payment by one spouse to another for domestic, child care, or other services in the home; planned termination of the marriage after a given period of time; alteration of statutory duties of support; and provision in advance for the eventuality of divorce." Shultz, Contractual Ordering of Marriage: A New Model for State Policy, 70 Calif. L. Rev. 204, 231 (1982). (However, spouses are entitled to share in the accumulated property of the marital estate. In addition, many states allow spouses to make certain agreements, such as those concerning property rights and post-separation support.)

Several theorists have argued for greater freedom of contract even within a marriage. They assert the diminished importance of communal and religious standards governing marriage, the greater tolerance of diversity in the form of relationships, and the increasing need and desire for partners to make their own arrangements. Moreover, "[t]he contracting process * * * helps the parties articulate and clarify their goals and expectations. It stimulates straightforward, open communication * * *." L. Weitzman, The Marriage Contract 232 (1981).

The April 6, 2006 New York Times reported that pre-nuptial agreements are now "all but routine in some circles as a way for the rich to protect their assets from the ravages of divorce court." Further, post-nuptial agreements, "although a novelty" are gaining in popularity and "are often requested by wives who leave the work force to raise children. Many of them are corporate lawyers or investment bankers who 'want to compensate for the loss they'll be taking.' "

G. GILMORE, THE DEATH OF CONTRACT
87–88 (1974).

Speaking descriptively, we might say that what is happening is that "contract" is being reabsorbed into the mainstream of "tort." * * * We have had more than one occasion to notice the insistence of the classical theorists on the sharp differentiation between contract and tort—the [early] refusal to admit any liability in "contract" until the formal requisites of offer, acceptance and consideration had been satisfied, the dogma that only "bargained-for" detriment or benefit could count as consideration, and notably, the limitations on damage recovery. Classical contract theory might well be described as an attempt to stake out an enclave within the general domain of tort. The dykes which were set up to protect the enclave have, it is clear enough, been crumbling at a progressively rapid rate. With the growth of the ideas of quasi-contract and unjust enrichment, classical consideration theory was breached on the benefit side. With the growth of the promissory estoppel idea, it was breached on the detriment side. We are fast approaching the point where, to prevent unjust enrichment, any benefit received by a defendant must be paid for unless it was clearly meant as a gift; where any detriment, reasonably incurred by a plaintiff in reliance on the defendant's assurances must be recompensed. When that point is reached, there is really no longer any viable distinction between liability in contract and liability in tort.

J. DAWSON, GIFTS AND PROMISES
2–4 (1980).

Some of the critics [of the consideration doctrine] condemn it altogether and demand that it be abolished. One of the most ardent of the abolitionists, however, was able recently to report some good news: that bargain consideration, produced only a century ago by that odd couple, Christopher Columbus Langdell and Oliver Wendell Holmes, has recently and quietly expired. No active surgery was needed, it seems, merely a denial of life support. For this coincided with the Death of Contract when Contract was consumed by the law of Tort, an event that was celebrated at a festive funeral not quite ten years ago.

To me it has seemed that the account of both deaths was exaggerated. In these essays the premise will be that bargain consideration has been and will remain for a long time to come a central feature of our law of contract, central in the sense that it provides a strong affirmative reason for enforcing promises, the reason that is by a wide margin the most often used, though it is not the only one. The reason is persuasive: the promisor receives or is assured that he will receive the kind of advantage that he in fact desires and has expressly promised to pay for. * * * Actually, this is not the issue on which battle is joined. Even the most embittered critics of bargain consideration do not really object to the enforcement of bargains. The objection has been to its transformation into a formula of denial, a formula that would deny legal effect to most promises for which there is nothing given or received in exchange.

In our own law of course the negation is not complete. Some promises are enforced for other reasons.

SECTION FIVE: OBLIGATION ARISING FROM PROMISES FOR BENEFIT RECEIVED

MILLS v. WYMAN

Supreme Judicial Court of Massachusetts, 1825.
20 Mass. (3 Pick.) 207.

[handwritten margin note: father of son]

This was an action of assumpsit brought to recover a compensation for the board, nursing, etc. of Levi Wyman, son of the defendant, from the 5th to the 20th of February, 1821. The plaintiff then lived at Hartford, in Connecticut; the defendant, at Shrewsbury, in this county. Levi Wyman, at the time when the services were rendered, was about 25 years of age, and had long ceased to be a member of his father's family. He was on his return from a voyage at sea, and being suddenly taken sick at Hartford, and being poor and in distress, was relieved by the plaintiff in the manner and to the extent above stated. On the 24th of February, after all the expenses had been incurred, the defendant wrote a letter to the plaintiff, promising to pay him such expenses. There was no consideration for this promise, except what grew out of the relation which subsisted between Levi Wyman and the defendant, and Howe, J., before whom the cause was tried in the court of common pleas, thinking this not sufficient to support the action, directed a nonsuit. To this direction the plaintiff filed exceptions.

[handwritten margin note: TC filed nonsuit]

* * *

PARKER, C.J. General rules of law established for the protection and security of honest and fair-minded men, who may inconsiderately make promises without any equivalent, will sometimes screen men of a different character from engagements which they are bound in *foro conscientiae* to perform. This is a defect inherent in all human systems of legislation. The rule that a mere verbal promise, without any consideration, cannot be enforced by action, is universal in its application, and cannot be departed from to suit particular cases in which a refusal to perform such a promise may be disgraceful.

The promise declared on in this case appears to have been made without any legal consideration. The kindness and services towards the sick son of the defendant were not bestowed at his request. The son was in no respect under the care of the defendant. He was twenty-five years old, and had long left his father's family. On his return from a foreign country, he fell sick among strangers, and the plaintiff acted the part of the good Samaritan, giving him shelter and comfort until he died. The defendant, his father, on being informed of this event, influenced by a transient feeling of gratitude, promised in writing to pay the plaintiff for the expenses he had incurred. But he has determined to break this promise, and is willing to have his case appear on record as a strong example of a particular injustice sometimes necessarily resulting from the operation of general rules.

It is said a moral obligation is a sufficient consideration to support an express promise; and some authorities lay down the rule thus broadly; but upon examination of the cases we are satisfied that the universality of the rule cannot be supported, and that there must have been [some preexisting obligation, which has become inoperative by positive law, to form a basis for an effective promise. The cases of debts barred by the statute of limitations, of debts incurred by infants, of debts of bankrupts, are generally put for illustration of the rule. Express promises founded on such preexisting equitable obligations may be enforced; there is a good consideration for them; they merely remove an impediment created by law to the recovery of debts honestly due, but which public policy protects the debtors from being compelled to pay. In all these cases there was originally a *quid pro quo;* and according to the principles of natural justice the party receiving ought to pay; but the legislature has said he shall not be coerced; then comes the promise to pay the debt that is barred, the promise of the man to pay the debt of the infant, of the discharged bankrupt to restore to his creditor what by the law he had lost. In all these cases there is a moral obligation founded upon an antecedent valuable consideration. These promises therefore have a sound legal basis. They are not promises to pay something for nothing; not naked pacts; but the voluntary revival or creation of obligation which before existed in natural law, but which had been dispensed with, not for the benefit of the party obliged solely, but principally for the public convenience. If moral obligation, in its fullest sense, is a good substratum for an express promise, it is not easy to perceive why it is not equally good to support an implied promise. What a man ought to do, generally he ought to be made to do, whether he promise or refuse. But the law of society has left most of such obligations to the *interior* forum, as the tribunal of conscience has been aptly called. Is there not a moral obligation upon every son who has become affluent by means of the education and advantages bestowed upon him by his father, to relieve that father from pecuniary embarrassment, to promote his comfort and happiness, and even to share with him his riches, if thereby he will be made happy? And yet such a son may, with impunity, leave such a father in any degree of penury above that which will expose the community in which he dwells, to the danger of being obliged to preserve him from absolute want. Is not a wealthy father under strong moral obligation to advance the interest of an obedient, well disposed son, to furnish him with the means of acquiring and maintaining a becoming rank in life, to rescue him from the horrors of debt incurred by misfortune? Yet the law will uphold him in any degree of parsimony, short of that which would reduce his son to the necessity of seeking public charity.

Without doubt there are great interests of society which justify withholding the coercive arm of the law from these duties of imperfect obligation, as they are called; imperfect, not because they are less binding upon the conscience than those which are called perfect, but because the wisdom of the social law does not impose sanctions upon them.

A deliberate promise, in writing, made freely and without any mistake, one which may lead the party to whom it is made into contracts and expenses, cannot be broken without a violation of moral duty. But if there was nothing paid or promised for it, the law, perhaps wisely, leaves the execution of it to the conscience of him who makes it. It is only when the party making the promise gains something, or he to whom it is made loses something, that the law gives the promise validity. And in the case of the promise of the adult to pay the debt of the infant, of the debtor discharged by the statute of limitations or bankruptcy, the principle is preserved by looking back to the

cases the law inter-venes

origin of the transaction, where an equivalent is to be found. An exact equivalent is not required by the law; for there being a consideration, the parties are left to estimate its value: though here the courts of equity will step in to relieve from gross inadequacy between the consideration and the promise.

These principles are deduced from the general current of decided cases upon the subject as well as from the known maxims of the common law. The general position, that moral obligation is a sufficient consideration for an express promise, is to be limited in its application, to cases where at some time or other a good or valuable consideration has existed.

A legal obligation is always a sufficient consideration to support either an express or an implied promise; such as an infant's debt for necessaries, or a father's promise to pay for the support and education of his minor children. But when the child shall have attained to manhood, and shall have become his own agent in the world's business, the debts he incurs, whatever may be their nature, create no obligation upon the father; and it seems to follow, that his promise founded upon such a debt has no legally binding force.

Rule

* * *

For the foregoing reasons we are all of opinion that the nonsuit directed by the court of common pleas was right, and that judgment be entered thereon for costs for the defendant.

Note
Mills v. Wyman: Additional Facts

Relying on court records of Mills v. Wyman, Professor Watson has reported that caring for Levi Wyman was no lark. See Watson, In the Tribunal of Conscience: Mills v. Wyman Reconsidered, 71 Tulane L. Rev. 1749 (1997). Levi, "in a dergan'd state * * * leaped out of a chamber window" and required two guards for his safety. Id. at 1755 (quoting court records). However, apparently Levi did not die from his illness: "All available evidence suggests that Levi in fact recovered and eventually settled in Springfield, Massachusetts." Id. at 1756. Why the court believed Levi died remains a mystery: "Perhaps a stray suggestion of counsel at oral argument influenced the court; only the plaintiff's attorneys appeared in person." Id. at 1757–58.

Perhaps most interesting, defendant Wyman's letter to Mills, which the court interpreted as a promise to pay for Levi's *previous* care, may only have pertained to care in the future. The letter stated:

Dear Sir

I received a line from you relating to my Son Levi's sickness and requesting me to come up and see him, but as the going is very bad I cannot come up at the present, but I wish you to take all possible care of him and if you cannot have him at your house I wish you to remove him to some convenient place and if he cannot satisfy you for it I will.

I want that you should write me again immediately how he does and greatly oblige your most obedient servant.

Seth Wyman
Shrewbury Feb 24th

Id. at 1760–61.

RESTATEMENT (SECOND) OF CONTRACTS § 82(1).

A promise to pay all or part of an antecedent contractual or quasi-contractual indebtedness owed by the promisor is binding if the indebtedness is still enforceable or would be except for the effect of a statute of limitations.

WEBB v. McGOWIN

Court of Appeals of Alabama, 1935.
27 Ala.App. 82, 168 So. 196.

Action by Joe Webb against N. Floyd McGowin and Joseph F. McGowin, as executors of the estate of J. Greeley McGowin, deceased. From a judgment of nonsuit, plaintiff appeals.

BRICKEN, PRESIDING JUDGE.

This action is in assumpsit. The complaint as originally filed was amended. The demurrers to the complaint as amended were sustained, and because of this adverse ruling by the court the plaintiff took a non-suit, and the assignment of errors on this appeal are predicated upon said action or ruling of the court.

A fair statement of the case presenting the questions for decision is set out in appellant's brief, which we adopt.

"On the 3d day of August, 1925, appellant while in the employ of the W.T. Smith Lumber Company, a corporation, and acting within the scope of his employment, was engaged in clearing the upper floor of mill No. 2 of the company. While so engaged he was in the act of dropping a pine block from the upper floor of the mill to the ground below; this being the usual and ordinary way of clearing the floor, and it being the duty of the plaintiff in the course of his employment to so drop it. The block weighed about 75 pounds.

"As appellant was in the act of dropping the block to the ground below, he was on the edge of the upper floor of the mill. As he started to turn the block loose so that it would drop to the ground, he saw J. Greeley McGowin, testator of the defendants, on the ground below and directly under where the block would have fallen had appellant turned it loose. Had he turned it loose it would have struck McGowin with such force as to have caused him serious bodily harm or death. Appellant could have remained safely on the upper floor of the mill by turning the block loose and allowing it to drop, but had he done this, the block would have fallen on McGowin and caused him serious injuries or death. The only safe and reasonable way to prevent this was for appellant to hold to the block and divert its direction in falling from the place where McGowin was standing and the only safe way to divert it so as to prevent its coming into contact with McGowin was for appellant to fall with it to the ground below. Appellant did this, and by holding to the block and falling with it to the ground below, he diverted the course of its fall in such way that McGowin was not injured. In thus preventing the injuries to McGowin appellant himself received serious bodily injuries, resulting in his right leg being broken, the heel of his right foot torn off and his right arm broken. He was badly crippled for life and rendered unable to do physical or mental labor.

"On September 1, 1925, in consideration of appellant having prevented him from sustaining death or serious bodily harm and in consideration of the injuries appellant had received, McGowin agreed with him to care for and maintain him for the remainder of appellant's life at the rate of $15 every two weeks from the time he sustained his injuries to and during the remainder of appellant's life; it being agreed that McGowin would pay this sum to appellant for his maintenance. Under the agreement McGowin paid or caused to be paid to appellant the sum so agreed on up until McGowin's death on January 1, 1934. After his death the payments were continued to and including January 27, 1934, at which time they were discontinued. Thereupon plaintiff brought suit to recover the unpaid installments accruing up to the time of the bringing of the suit.

"The material averments of the different counts of the original complaint and the amended complaint are predicated upon the foregoing statement of facts."

In other words, the complaint as amended averred in substance: (1) That on August 3, 1925, appellant saved J. Greeley McGowin, appellee's testator, from death or grievous bodily harm; (2) that in doing so appellant sustained bodily injury crippling him for life; (3) that in consideration of the services rendered and the injuries received by appellant, McGowin agreed to care for him the remainder of appellant's life, the amount to be paid being $15 every two weeks; (4) that McGowin complied with this agreement until he died on January 1, 1934, and the payments were kept up to January 27, 1934, after which they were discontinued.

The action was for the unpaid installments accruing after January 27, 1934, to the time of the suit.

The principal grounds of demurrer to the original and amended complaint are: (1) It states no cause of action; (2) its averments show the contract was without consideration; (3) it fails to allege that McGowin had, at or before the services were rendered, agreed to pay appellant for them; (4) the contract declared on is void under the statute of frauds.

The averments of the complaint show that appellant saved McGowin from death or grievous bodily harm. This was a material benefit to him of infinitely more value than any financial aid he could have received. Receiving this benefit, McGowin became morally bound to compensate appellant for the services rendered. Recognizing his moral obligation, he expressly agreed to pay appellant as alleged in the complaint and complied with this agreement up to the time of his death; a period of more than 8 years.

Had McGowin been accidentally poisoned and a physician, without his knowledge or request, had administered an antidote, thus saving his life, a subsequent promise by McGowin to pay the physician would have been valid. Likewise, McGowin's agreement as disclosed by the complaint to compensate appellant for saving him from death or grievous bodily injury is valid and enforceable.

Where the promisee cares for, improves, and preserves the property of the promisor, though done without his request, it is sufficient consideration for the promisor's subsequent agreement to pay for the service, because of the material benefit received. * * *

In Boothe v. Fitzpatrick, 36 Vt. 681, the court held that a promise by defendant to pay for the past keeping of a bull which had escaped from defendant's premises and been cared for by plaintiff was valid, although there was no previous request, because the subsequent promise obviated that objection; it being equivalent to a previous request. On the same principle, had the promisee saved the promisor's life or his body from grievous harm, his subsequent promise to pay for the services rendered would have been valid. Such service would have been far more material than caring for his bull. Any holding that saving a man from death or grievous bodily harm is not a material benefit sufficient to uphold a subsequent promise to pay for the service, necessarily rests on the assumption that saving life and preservation of the body from harm have only a sentimental value. The converse of this is true. Life and preservation of the body have material, pecuniary values, measurable in dollars and cents. Because of this, physicians practice their profession charging for services rendered in saving life and curing the body of its ills, and surgeons perform operations. The same is true as to the law of negligence, authorizing the assessment of damages in personal injury cases based upon the extent of the injuries, earnings, and life expectancies of those injured.

In the business of life insurance, the value of a man's life is measured in dollars and cents according to his expectancy, the soundness of his body, and his ability to pay premiums. The same is true as to health and accident insurance.

It follows that if, as alleged in the complaint, appellant saved J. Greeley McGowin from death or grievous bodily harm, and McGowin subsequently agreed to pay him for the service rendered, it became a valid and enforceable contract.

It is well settled that a moral obligation is a sufficient consideration to support a subsequent promise to pay where the promisor has received a material benefit, although there was no original duty or liability resting on the promisor. * * *

The case at bar is clearly distinguishable from that class of cases where the consideration is a mere moral obligation or conscientious duty unconnected with receipt by promisor of benefits of a material or pecuniary nature. * * * Here the promisor received a material benefit constituting a valid consideration for his promise.

Some authorities hold that, for a moral obligation to support a subsequent promise to pay, there must have existed a prior legal or equitable obligation, which for some reason had become unenforceable, but for which the promisor was still morally bound. This rule, however, is subject to qualification in those cases where the promisor, having received a material benefit from the promisee, is morally bound to compensate him for the services rendered and in consideration of this obligation promises to pay. In such cases the subsequent promise to pay is an affirmation or ratification of the services rendered carrying with it the presumption that a previous request for the service was made. * * *

Under the decisions above cited, McGowin's express promise to pay appellant for the services rendered was an affirmance or ratification of what appellant had done raising the presumption that the services had been rendered at McGowin's request.

The averments of the complaint show that in saving McGowin from death or grievous bodily harm, appellant was crippled for life. This was part of the consideration of the contract declared on. McGowin was benefited. Appellant was injured. Benefit to the promisor or injury to the promisee is a sufficient legal consideration for the promisor's agreement to pay. * * *

Under the averments of the complaint the services rendered by appellant were not gratuitous. The agreement of McGowin to pay and the acceptance of payment by appellant conclusively shows the contrary.

The contract declared on was not void under the statute of frauds * * *. The demurrer on this ground was not well taken. * * *

From what has been said, we are of the opinion that the court, below erred in the ruling complained of; that is to say, in sustaining the demurrer, and for this error the case is reversed and remanded.

Reversed and remanded.

SAMFORD, JUDGE (concurring).

The questions involved in this case are not free from doubt, and perhaps the strict letter of the rule, as stated by judges, though not always in accord, would bar a recovery by plaintiff, but following the principle announced by Chief Justice Marshall in Hoffman v. Porter, Fed.Cas. No. 6,577, 2 Brock. 156, 159, where he says, "I do not think that law ought to be separated from justice, where it is at most doubtful," I concur in the conclusions reached by the court.

HARRINGTON v. TAYLOR

Supreme Court of North Carolina, 1945.
225 N.C. 690, 36 S.E.2d 227.

PER CURIAM.

The plaintiff in this case sought to recover of the defendant upon a promise made by him under the following peculiar circumstances:

The defendant had assaulted his wife, who took refuge in plaintiff's house. The next day the defendant gained access to the house and began another assault upon his wife. The defendant's wife knocked him down with an axe, and was on the point of cutting his head open or decapitating him while he was laying on the floor, and the plaintiff intervened, caught the axe as it was descending, and the blow intended for defendant fell upon her hand, mutilating it badly, but saving defendant's life.

Subsequently, defendant orally promised to pay the plaintiff her damages; but, after paying a small sum, failed to pay anything more. So, substantially, states the complaint.

The defendant demurred to the complaint as not stating a cause of action, and the demurrer was sustained. Plaintiff appealed.

The question presented is whether there was a consideration recognized *Issue* by our law as sufficient to support the promise. The Court is of the opinion that, however much the defendant should be impelled by common gratitude to alleviate the plaintiff's misfortune, a humanitarian act of this kind, voluntarily performed, is not such consideration as would entitle her to recover at law. *Holding*

The judgment sustaining the demurrer is *Judgment*

Affirmed.

OBERER, ON LAW, LAWYERING AND LAW PROFESSING: THE GOLDEN SAND

39 J. Legal Educ. 203, 203–05 (1989).

Proposition 1: In all of time there have never been two cases *exactly* alike.

This is the premise for sophisticated lawyering, but it is a rare law student who comprehends it, and an unrare practitioner who does not.

Why is this proposition so seminally profound? Because it articulates the truth that *your* case has never before been decided, that the cases more or less like it that have been decided are, at most, relevant. And you will never know what really moved those other courts to decision in those seemingly like cases. Not even by reading their opinions a dozen times. Indeed, the very rereading may mislead: You will never get all the facts in the record, much less those without. When a judge sits down to write an opinion in a case already, at least tentatively, decided, the judge becomes an advocate in support of that decision, and the ardency of the advocacy may vary inversely with the certitude of the propriety of the decision. This has obvious implications for the adequacy of the factual abstraction from the record found in the opinion.

* * *

Proposition 2: If a case belongs in court, it belongs in court because the legal doctrines do not decide it.

Easy cases are resoluble in lawyers' offices by the application of legal doctrines to provable facts. In such cases, the lawyer tells the client "no" or "yes." Hard cases, by contrast, are hard because the legal doctrines working for the potential plaintiff encounter, head on, the counterdoctrines working for the potential defendant. Where these doctrines meet is in an area of "murk" in which legal and/or factual line drawing must be done; the case is "hard" because reasonable minds may disagree as to the drawing of those lines. In such cases, the lines are not drawn by the "law." They are drawn by human beings called "judges," sometimes aided by other human beings called "jurors."

These human beings decide the case on the totality of the relevant evidence and law, bringing to bear in their search for "justice" ("sense," "fairness") the totality of their life experiences. The case is not (should not be) decided mechanistically on the basis of some doctrinal technicality, even though, in explaining the decision after the fact, that human being, the judge—obeisant to the shortness of life and the longness of the docket—may make it seem so in the written opinion.

In these hard cases, the ones that belong in court, legal doctrine is not irrelevant. There is not, accordingly, any cynicism in my dealing with it. Indeed, the opposite is true; it is the ultimate idealism to declare that justice between and among human beings is the product of the application of human judgment to the totality of the evidence and the arguments rallied in this particular, never before decided, case.

* * *

Legal doctrine is, of course, highly relevant in deciding even the hard cases, despite the fact that it does not, itself, decide them. The reason lies in the next proposition.

Proposition 3: Tools, not rules.

Every legal doctrine exists for the sake of achieving justice, a sensible result in the context of a particular kind of problem—i.e., a particular fact pattern. And since facts permute infinitely, even in relatively narrow spectrums, the applicability of a particular legal doctrine waxes or wanes with factual change. The "bull's-eye" of the doctrine's *raison d'être* lies at one end of the pertinent factual spectrum; the *raison d'être* attenuates with movement toward the other end of that spectrum.

Moreover, legal doctrines may coexist in their applicability to a given set of facts and impinge upon one another's territory. A thorough understanding of the rationale of each doctrine is therefore of the essence in applying it. And since its ultimate rationale is to achieve justice, its force waxes or wanes with factual permutation. It operates as a "rule" only in the easy, bull's-eye cases; in the hard cases, it is at most a "tool."

Accordingly, legal doctrines do not decide the cases that belong in court; they do, however, establish the "toolery" for seeking justice in the particular case. They represent, that is, relevant concerns, time-tested approaches for determining what facts are relevant, why they are relevant, the degree of strength of the relevance. In short, they provide time-tested *issues* for structuring a case—guides for lawyers to present the case and for judges to decide it. The doctrines thus provide the tools for winnowing through the totality of facts, for evaluating the relevance, for determining a just result, and finally, for the judge to rationalize that result in an opinion that brings the law determined to be relevant to bear upon the facts determined to be relevant.

EDSON v. POPPE

South Dakota Supreme Court, 1910.
24 S.D. 466, 124 N.W. 441.

Action by George F. Edson against William Poppe. Judgment for plaintiff, and defendant appeals. Affirmed.

* * *

McCoy, J. The plaintiff recovered judgment upon the verdict of a jury in the circuit court. The case was tried upon the following complaint: That the defendant at all the times hereinafter named was the owner of the following described premises situated in Turner county, S.D., to wit (describing the land); that at all the times herein named George Poppe was in possession of said premises as the tenant of defendant; that during the year 1904 this plaintiff, at the instance and request of said George Poppe, drilled and dug upon said premises a well 250 feet deep, and obtained water in said well, and placed casing therein; that the reasonable value of the digging and casing of said well was and is the sum of $250; that said well was and is a valuable improvement upon the said premises, and greatly adds to the value thereof, and has been used by the occupants of said premises since the said digging thereof, with the knowledge and consent of defendant; that on or about the 5th day of August, 1905, the defendant, at the said premises, after having examined the said well, and in consideration of the said well to him, and of the improvement it made upon said premises, expressly ratified the acts of his said tenant in having said well drilled, and then and there promised and agreed to pay plaintiff the reasonable value of the digging and casing of the said well as aforesaid; that defendant has since refused, and still refuses, to pay plaintiff anything for said well. Wherefore, etc. To the said complaint defendant made the following answer: Denies generally and specifically each and every allegation in said complaint, except such as is hereinafter specifically admitted. Defendant admits that he is the owner of the said premises as stated in the complaint. At the opening of the trial, and upon the offer of testimony on the part of plaintiff, defendant objected to the introduction of any evidence, for the reason that the complaint did not state a cause of action, in that the consideration alleged in the contract is a past consideration, and no consideration for any promise, if any was made, and no consideration for the promise alleged. The objection was overruled, and defendant excepted. This ruling of the trial court is assigned and now urged as error, but we are of the opinion that the ruling of the learned trial court was correct.

It seems to be the general rule that past services are not a sufficient consideration for a promise to pay therefor, made at a subsequent time, and after such services have been fully rendered and completed; but in some courts a modified doctrine of moral obligation is adopted, and it is held that a moral obligation, founded on previous benefits received by the promisor at the hands of the promisee, will support a promise by him. * * *

The authorities are not so clear as to the sufficiency of past services, rendered without previous request, to support an express promise; but, when proper distinctions are made, the cases as a whole seem to warrant the statement that such a promise is supported by a sufficient consideration if the services were beneficial, and were not intended to be gratuitous. * * * In Drake v. Bell, 26 Misc.Rep. 237, 55 N.Y.Supp. 945, a mechanic, under contract to repair a vacant house, by mistake repaired the house next door, which belonged to the defendant. The repairing was a benefit to the latter, and he agreed to pay a certain amount therefor. It was held that the promise rested upon sufficient consideration. Gaynor, J., says: "The rule seems to be that a subsequent promise, founded on a former enforceable obligation, or on value previously had from the promisee, is binding." * * * In Boothe v. Fitzpatrick, 36 Vt. 681, it is held that if the consideration, even without request, moves directly from the plaintiff to the defendant, and inures directly to the defendant's benefit, the promise is binding though made upon a past consideration. In this case the court held that a promise by defendant to pay for the past keeping of a bull, which had escaped from defendant's premises and been cared for by plaintiff, was valid, although there was no previous request, but that the subsequent promise obviated that objection; it being equivalent to a previous request. The allegation of the complaint here is that the digging and casing of the well in question inured directly to the defendant's benefit, and that, after he had seen and examined the same, he expressly promised and agreed to pay plaintiff the reasonable value thereof. It also appears that said well was made under such circumstances as could not be deemed gratuitous on the part of plaintiff, or an act of voluntary courtesy to defendant. We are therefore of the opinion that under the circumstances alleged, the subsequent promise of defendant to pay plaintiff the reasonable value for digging and casing said well was binding, and supported by sufficient consideration. We are also of the opinion that the instructions based on this complaint, and in particular as to the validity of the subsequent promise of defendant, properly submitted the issues to the jury.

* * *

Finding no error in the record, the judgment of the circuit court is affirmed.

HENDERSON, PROMISES GROUNDED IN THE PAST: THE IDEA OF UNJUST ENRICHMENT AND THE LAW OF CONTRACTS

57 Va.L.Rev. 1115, 1115, 1159–62 (1971).

[T]he promise supported solely by an earlier receipt of benefit has come to occupy a curious and uncertain position. * * *

* * * [R]ecognition of the promise for benefit received has come slowly in our law largely because of the very policy reasons responsible for singling out gifts for special treatment. Because a price is not presently asked for a promise anchored in the past, the general assumption has been that the promisor is vulnerable to dangers similar to those that threaten donors of gift promises. As a result, policies designed to protect the interests of the makers of unexecuted gifts have been transferred to the moral obligation promisor. The vehicle for implementation of those policies is, of course, consideration doctrine. The question * * * is whether the natural formalities and substantive basis of the promise for benefit received dictate a classification that rejects the policies thought to require a denial of enforcement of gift promises.

Certainly it is settled beyond recall that unjust enrichment, viewed independently or as reinforcement of bargain, itself constitutes a substantive ground for the enforcement of promises. Moreover, one is hard pressed to resist the proposition that the impressiveness of the ground is enhanced when the enrichment factor is coupled with a promissory confession that it has created in the recipient a sense of moral obligation. * * *

Consideration doctrine declares many promises unenforceable because the maker's deliberations are thought to be inadequate to impress upon him the seriousness of the transaction. * * * [C]oncern about ill-considered promise making is largely misplaced. Given the usual sequence in which events unfold—i.e., a performance on one side, resulting in an often identifiable gain in the hands of the other party, followed by the other's promissory response— the transaction itself involves natural safeguards equivalent to those of form or present exchange. The time lag between performance and promise affords an opportunity for deliberation and the exercise of caution, as well as an evaluation of "price," not present in most conventional bargains. * * *

* * *

Looking to other functions of formalities, it is clear that the issue of promissory liability raised by the doctrines of moral obligation and past consideration is much involved with the problem of evidentiary security. * * * Since many claims arising out of the past are supported only by oral assurances, and by their nature must depend on notions of moral obligation and past consideration, there is cause to believe that much of the accumulated hostility to those doctrines stem from a general assumption against stale or delayed claims lacking readily demonstrated merit.

Note
The Concept of Moral Obligation

The concept of moral obligation (or moral consideration) plays a role in most of the cases in this section. The courts using this concept seldom attempt to define it or otherwise subject it to careful analysis. But in Park Falls State Bank v. Fordyce, 206 Wis. 628, 238 N.W. 516 (1931), the Supreme Court of Wisconsin offered these remarks:

> It is true that there are numerous cases holding that a mere moral consideration will not support a promise to pay. But it is equally true that there are numerous cases holding a moral consideration sufficient where the promisor originally received from the promisee something of value sufficient to arouse a moral, as distinguished from a legal obligation. One, ought, in morals, to make return for things of value not intended as a gift that he has accepted, and he ought, in morals to do what he knowingly and advisedly gave one acting for his benefit and to his own hurt to understand he would do.

Do you agree? Consider whether the foregoing analysis of the concept of moral obligation applies to the cases in this section in which the plaintiff prevailed. Consider also the following remarks of Lon L. Fuller:

> When we say the defendant was morally obligated to do the thing he promised, we in effect assert the existence of a substantive ground for enforcing the promise. * * * The court's conviction that the promisor ought to do the thing, plus the promisor's own admission of his obligation, may tilt the scales in favor of enforcement where neither standing alone would be sufficient. If it be argued that moral consideration threatens certainty, the solution would seem to lie, not in rejecting the doctrine, but in taming it by continuing the process of judicial exclusion and inclusion already begun in cases involving infant's contracts, barred debts, and discharged bankrupts.

Fuller, Consideration and Form, 41 Colum.L.Rev. 799, 821–22 (1941).

RESTATEMENT (SECOND) OF CONTRACTS § 86.
Promise for Benefit Received

(1) A promise made in recognition of a benefit previously received by the promisor from the promisee is binding to the extent necessary to prevent injustice.

(2) A promise is not binding under Subsection (1)

(a) if the promisee conferred the benefit as a gift or for other reasons the promisor has not been unjustly enriched; or

(b) to the extent that its value is disproportionate to the benefit.

Comment:

a. "Past consideration"; "moral obligation." Enforcement of promises to pay for benefit received has sometimes been said to rest on "past consideration" or on the "moral obligation" of the promisor, and there are statutes in such terms in a few states. Those terms are not used here: "past consideration" is inconsistent with the meaning of consideration stated in § 71, and there seems to be no consensus as to what constitutes a "moral obligation." The mere fact of promise has been thought to create a moral obligation, but it is clear that not all promises are enforced. Nor are moral obligations based solely on gratitude or sentiment sufficient of themselves to support a subsequent promise.

* * *

b. Rationale. Although in general a person who has been unjustly enriched at the expense of another is required to make restitution, restitution is denied in many cases in order to protect persons who have had benefits thrust upon them. See Restatement of Restitution §§ 1, 2, 112. In other cases restitution is denied by virtue of rules designed to guard against false claims, stale claims, claims already litigated, and the like. In many such cases a subsequent promise to make restitution removes the reason for the denial of relief, and the policy against unjust enrichment then prevails. Compare Restatement, Second, Agency § 462 on ratification of the acts of a person who officiously purports to act as an agent. Enforcement of the subsequent promise sometimes makes it unnecessary to decide a difficult question as to the limits on quasi-contractual relief.

* * * [T]he broader principle [of Section 86] * * * may not be applied if there is doubt whether the objections to restitution are fully met by the subsequent promise. Facts such as the definite and substantial character of the benefit received, formality in the making of the promise, part performance of the promise, reliance on the promise or the probability of such reliance may be relevant to show that no imposition results from enforcement.

* * *

e. Benefit conferred as a gift. In the absence of mistake or the like, there is no element of unjust enrichment in the receipt of a gift, and the rule of this Section has no application to a promise to pay for a past gift. Similarly, when a debt is discharged by a binding agreement, the transaction is closed even though full payment is not made. But marginal cases arise in which both parties understand that what is in form a gift is intended to be reimbursed indirectly, or in which a subsequent promise to pay is expressly contemplated. * * * Enforcement of the subsequent promise is proper in some such cases.

SECTION SIX: OBLIGATION ARISING FROM TORT

W. PROSSER AND W. KEETON ON TORTS
3, 6 (5th ed. 1984).

Included under the head of torts are miscellaneous civil wrongs, ranging from simple, direct interferences with the person, such as assault, battery and false imprisonment, or with property, as in the case of trespass or conversion, up through various forms of negligence, to disturbances of intangible interests, such as those in good reputation, or commercial or social advantage. * * *

* * *

* * * So far as there is one central idea [in tort law], it would seem that it is that liability must be based upon conduct which is socially unreasonable. The common thread woven into all torts is the idea of unreasonable interference with the interests of others.

BUSCH v. INTERBOROUGH RAPID TRANSIT CO., 187 N.Y. 388, 80 N.E. 197 (1907). "The dividing line between breaches of contract and torts is often dim and uncertain. There is no definition of either class of defaults which is universally accurate or acceptable. In a general way, a tort is distinguished from a breach of contract in that the latter arises under an agreement of the parties; whereas, the tort ordinarily is a violation of a duty fixed by law, independent of contract or the will of the parties, although it may sometimes have relation to obligations growing out of or coincident with a contract, and frequently the same facts will sustain either class of action."

SPEIDEL, THE BORDERLAND OF CONTRACT
10 N.Ky.L.Rev. 164, 168–71 (1983).

Doctrinal Differences Between Contract and Tort

Despite continuing disputes over historical cause and effect, important doctrinal differences between Contract and Tort emerged from the 19th Century and are still imprinted on American law. They can be grouped around three headings: (1) The nature of the conduct causing the loss; (2) the interest protected against loss; and (3) the scope of the available remedy. Consider the following contrasts.

(A) *Conduct.*

In Contract, the actionable conduct is a failure without justification to perform an enforceable promise. A must make and break a promise, but B is not required to prove that the breach was negligent or intentional or otherwise "wrongful." To this extent, Contract is a law of strict rather than fault based liability. The concept of breach also covers a defective promised performance (misfeasance) and a failure to perform as promised (nonfeasance). In Tort, liability is usually imposed for affirmative conduct that causes loss. Unless there are special circumstances, the failure to act is not a tort. In addition, not all conduct which causes loss is actionable. The conduct must be intentional or negligent or, perhaps, that which creates unreasonable danger to others. In short, fault and motive play a greater role in Tort than in Contract. But in both, liability is imposed in a selective process by the courts: not all broken promises are contracts and not all conduct which causes loss is a tort.

(B) *Duty and Interest Protected.*

In Contract, A's duties extend to persons to whom or for whose benefit the enforceable promise is made. The content of those duties is determined by agreement, occasionally supplemented by the court. Thus, through agreement with A, B can limit both the scope and content of contract duties. Within this framework, B's protected interest is limited by the reasonable expectations created by that enforceable promise, no more or no less. Contract law is concerned about what B invested or what opportunities were foregone in reliance on the promise and the gains prevented if A fails to perform as promised. These are the interests protected by Contract. In Tort, A's duty extends to those persons within a legally defined zone of risk created by his actionable conduct. The content of those duties, i.e., what must A do to avoid harming B, is imposed by operation of law. Within this framework, B's interests which are protected against A's conduct include his person, property and some existing "relationships". In short, Tort protects B's existing state of affairs—his person, property and relationships—from A's wrongful conduct. To this extent, the functions and protected interests in Contract and Tort complement each other. Tort law protects the existing entitlements or interests of the individual from unauthorized intrusion and Contract law permits the owners of those entitlements to shape or reallocate them through bargain and exchange.

(C) *Remedies.*

In Contract, the primary remedial objective has been to protect B's reasonable expectations by giving him the value of A's promised performance—to put B in the position that he would have been in if A had fully performed. This is normally accomplished by the award of damages rather than specific performance. B's unreimbursed reliance on the promise may also be compensated. Contract remedies usually redress economic losses caused by breach, but these are limited by special policies; e.g., B cannot recover losses caused by the breach that were not reasonably foreseeable at the time of contracting and must make reasonable efforts to avoid the consequences of the breach. Mental anguish caused by a breach is rarely recoverable and punitive damages will not be awarded for breach of contract, even though that action is deliberate. In Tort, the primary remedial objective is to restore B to the position occupied before the tort and, where appropriate, to enjoin future tortious conduct. Thus, if A causes damage to B's protected interests, justice requires that A restore or correct the loss through compensation. The compensation is usually limited to damage to person and property, although gains prevented may be recovered when A's intentional and wrongful conduct interferes with B's economic opportunities. In contrast with Contract, mental anguish is a frequent element of Tort damages and punitive damages are awarded when A's tortious conduct is particularly outrageous. Finally, if A owes a duty to B and an intentional tort causes some loss, A will be liable for all of the losses caused even though not foreseeable at the time of the tort.

MAULDIN v. SHEFFER

Court of Appeals of Georgia, 1966.
113 Ga.App. 874, 150 S.E.2d 150.

FRANKUM, JUDGE.

L. Miles Sheffer, doing business as L. Miles Sheffer & Associates, sued John G. Mauldin, doing business as Coastal Engineering Company, for damages. The original petition did not clearly set forth a cause of action, either ex contractu or ex delicto [tort] but after the defendant had demurred thereto and the petition had been once amended, and the defendant had orally moved to dismiss the petition as amended, the plaintiff filed a redrafted petition in which he set forth the following material facts. Plaintiff was a licensed architect engaged in the practice of his profession. He entered into an oral contract with the defendant, a registered professional mechanical engineer actively engaged in such profession under the terms of which defendant agreed to provide plaintiff with certain engineering designs, plans, drawings and specifications to be drawn, written and produced by defendant who was to serve as consulting engineer for plaintiff's architectural work and projects. Pursuant thereto the defendant did, in June, 1961, undertake to furnish plaintiff with certain engineering designs, plans, drawings, specifications and engineering data for the plaintiff's use in the design and construction of additions to five specified school buildings. In consideration for such services plaintiff agreed to pay defendant $200 per week, and plaintiff did pay to the defendant such sums. Defendant did, in his professional engineering capacity, produce certain designs, drawings, plans, specifications, engineering data, and revisions thereof which he furnished to plaintiff in December, 1961, and in January, April, and May of 1962, all with respect to the aforesaid additions to school buildings. Said plans were incorporated by plaintiff in his overall architectural plans and delivered by plaintiff to the various school boards by whom plaintiff had been employed. Said designs, plans, specifications and engineering data and revisions prepared by the defendant and delivered to plaintiff were in numerous respects erroneous, incorrect and contrary to generally accepted engineering standards, in that they were contrary to and in violation of the fundamental laws of physics and were contrary to and in violation of the promulgated policies, regulations and standards of the Georgia State School Building Authority, the Georgia Department of Education, and the county boards of education by whom plaintiff was employed. The errors in the defendant's work concerned the plumbing, heating and electrical designs of the said projects, a detailed list of said errors being attached as Exhibit A and by reference incorporated in the petition. Plaintiff used defendant's work in his designs and delivered the same to his clients for approval and acceptance, and thereafter, the various projects were advertised for construction bids, but before the contract was let the State School Building Authority recalled the bids and returned the plans to the plaintiff for correction of the engineering errors of defendant. Defendant prepared revisions of his designs which were duly resubmitted by plaintiff, and the same procedure resulted in a rejection of the plans by the State School Building Authority on two subsequent occasions, each revision of defendant being rejected as being unsatisfactory for the various reasons set forth in the petition and the exhibit attached thereto. As the result of the rejection of the plans as aforesaid, plaintiff's clients and the State School Building Authority made certain charges against the plaintiff for expenses incurred in advertising and readvertising the projects for bids, and it was necessary ultimately for plaintiff to employ other engineering personnel to completely redesign, re-engineer, redraw and rewrite the designs, plans, specifications and data which defendant had been employed by plaintiff to prepare, and plaintiff incurred in so doing, specified expenses which are set forth in the petition in detail. Plaintiff also incurred other specified losses and expenses, including the loss of a contract to perform architectural services on certain other school building projects planned by one of the plaintiff's clients who, as a result of the engineering errors and mistakes perpetrated by the defendant, refused to permit plaintiff to serve as architect on said projects, although having previously contracted with plaintiff to so serve. All of plaintiff's special damages alleged to have proximately resulted from the defendant's negligence are set forth in the petition in detail.

* * *

Paragraphs 38 and 39 of the petition are as follows: "38. That the defendant, in the preparation of said designs, drawings, specifications, plans and data did willfully and intentionally utilize designs, drawings, specifications, plans and data from other building projects and other engineering projects on which defendant had worked in the past, which were not suited or in any way reasonabl[y] intended to be suited or adapted to the plaintiff's architectural plans for said five school building projects; that the defendant did frivolously utilize said other and non-related plans, drawings, specifications, designs and data with full knowledge that the same were not usable or adaptable to the plaintiff's architectural plans and the said conduct of the defendant was willful and wanton and was in deliberate disregard of his ethical, moral and legal duties as an engineer registered under the laws of Georgia and was in deliberate and willful disregard of his duty to plaintiff to perform said engineering work in a skilled, conscientious and diligent manner according to his ability and was in willful, deliberate and intentional disregard of his duty to use reasonable and ordinary care in the performance of his engineering duties. 39. That the defendant, in thus frivolously, willfully, deliberately and intentionally failing to exercise ordinary care and reasonable care in the performance of his duties as an engineer in the preparation of said plans, designs, drawings, specifications and data for the plaintiff, did perpetrate an act of aggravated tortious conduct within the meaning and scope of Section 105–2002 of the Code of Georgia and plaintiff taxes punitive and exemplary damages against defendant in the sum of Five Hundred Thousand ($500,000.00) Dollars to deter the defendant from repeating such wrongdoing and sued the defendant for said punitive damages." In paragraph 40 plaintiff alleged that all of his injury and damage was directly and proximately caused by the negligence of the defendant in enumerated particulars therein set out. Exhibit A, referred to in the petition, listed 151 errors alleged to have been committed by the defendant in the preparation of the engineering plans and specifications for the plaintiff. To the redrafted petition the defendant filed general and special demurrers. The trial court overruled the grounds of general demurrer. This judgment is enumerated as error in this appeal.

While it does not appear from the record, counsel for the appellant in their brief before this court state, in effect, that counsel for the plaintiff declared in open court that it was their intention to proceed in tort rather than ex contractu. Counsel for the appellee do not deny this statement or in any way directly refer to it in their brief, but from the tenor of their argument it is apparent that their contention was and is that the petition as finally amended set forth a cause of action ex delicto. We will accordingly treat the case as being one where such an election has been made and will consider the issue of whether or not the petition as finally amended is sufficient to set forth a cause of action ex delicto. * * *

Generally, a mere breach of a valid contract amounting to no more than a failure to perform in accordance with its terms does not constitute a tort or authorize the aggrieved party to elect whether he will proceed ex contractu or ex delicto. * * * Accordingly, under the foregoing authorities, if there is no liability except that arising out of a breach of the express terms of the contract, the action must be in contract, and an action in tort cannot be maintained. Of course, as was said in City & c. Ry. Co. of Savannah v. Brauss, 70 Ga. 368, 377, in referring to those situations where from the nature of the breach or the duty violated an election may be made by the aggrieved party "private duties may arise from statute, or flow from relations created by contract, express or implied. The violation of any such specific duty, accompanied with damage, gives a right of action." * * * Thus, if a contract imposes a legal duty upon a party thereto, which duty exists apart from the specific obligation of the contract, the neglect of that duty is a tort founded upon a contract. * * * In such a case the liability arises out of the breach of duty incident to and created by the contract, but is only dependent upon the contract to the extent necessary to raise the duty * * *. So, it is well settled * * * that in some cases the plaintiff may have an election to sue for a breach of contract or for damages in tort. Code § 105–105. * * * From the foregoing authorities it can be seen that it is not in every case where a contract has been breached that a right accrues to the opposite party to make an election. * * *

The rule which affords an election to sue ex delicto or ex contractu in cases involving a breach of a duty implied by reason of a contractual relation has been applied to contractual relations between principal and agent, bailor and bailee, attorney and client, physician and patient, carrier and passenger or shipper, master and servant, and possibly other well recognized relations. * * * As may be seen from a mere casual perusal of the cases * * * the formulation of a definitive rule workable upon application to all cases is most difficult, and the Georgia authorities, numerous as they may be, leave room for considerable doubt as to the proper application of the rule in particular cases. However, one clear distinction seems to have been made which is indicative of the scope and application of the rule, and that is the distinction between nonfeasance or the mere failure to perform the contract at all, and misfeasance or the negligent performance of the contract. * * * As to the former of these the cases have fairly consistently held that it affords no basis for an action ex delicto, even though the failure to perform may have been characterized as negligent * * * while in the latter a cause of action ex delicto may be had. * * * Though some may contend that in cases of misfeasance there is always a right to make such an election, no case expressly so holding has been found and such a holding being patently unnecessary to a decision of the question now before us, we are unwilling to go that far. There may be exceptions to the rule even in misfeasance cases. It is sufficient to say that the opposite appears to be more nearly the true rule, that is, that it is *only* in such cases that the right to elect between a tort action and a contract action exists.

From the authorities to which we have referred and from others which we have examined, the rule may be fairly deduced that in order to maintain an action ex delicto because of a breach of duty growing out of a contractual relation the breach must be shown to have been a breach of a duty imposed by law and not merely the breach of a duty imposed by the contract itself. * * * This is consistent with the definition of a tort set forth in Code § 105–101. "Duty imposed by law" as used in this context means, of course, either a duty imposed by a valid statutory enactment of the legislature or a duty imposed by a recognized common law principle declared in the reported decisions of the appellate courts of the State or jurisdiction involved. The question in this case then resolves itself to whether the petition sufficiently alleges the violation of such a "duty imposed by law."

The law imposes upon persons of professional standing performing medical, architectural, engineering, and those performing other and like skilled services, pursuant to their contracts made with their clients, an obligation to exercise a reasonable degree of care, skill and ability, such as is ordinarily exercised under similar conditions and like circumstances by persons employed in the same or similar professions. * * * This is a duty apart from any express contractual obligation. Therefore, persons of this class performing services pursuant to their contracts with their clients have been held to be liable in tort for their negligence in failing to exercise the required degree of skill, and thus to be liable to a suit ex delicto under the doctrine applicable to the second category above referred to. * * * In a proper case the question of whether the defendant exercised the required degree of skill is, like any other question of fact, to be decided by a jury. * * * We think then that it is clear that the petition in this case does allege the violation of a duty imposed by law under the principles which we have set forth above. Clearly, if the defendant undertook to perform the contract for the plaintiff in the manner alleged, a jury would be authorized to find that he had failed to exercise that reasonable degree of care, skill and ability such as is ordinarily exercised under the same or similar conditions and under like circumstances by engineers generally in practicing their professions. The petition stated a cause of action ex delicto as against the general demurrer interposed, and the trial court did not err in overruling the general demurrer.

Judgment affirmed.

W. PROSSER AND W. KEETON ON TORTS

660–661, 656–657, 664–666 (5th ed. 1984).

[T]he American courts have extended the tort liability for misfeasance to virtually every type of contract where defective performance may injure the promisee. An attorney or an abstractor examining a title, a physician treating a patient, a surveyor, an agent collecting a note or lending money or settling a claim, or a liability insurer defending a suit, all have been held liable in tort for their negligence. The same is true of contractors employed to build a structure, to transport people or goods, to install a windmill or a lightning rod, or to shoot an oil well, or a beauty shop giving a permanent wave, of suppliers of chattels, and of many others. The principle which seems to have emerged from the decisions in the United States is that there will be liability in tort for misperformance of a contract whenever there would be liability for gratuitous performance without the contract—which is to say, whenever such misperformance involves a foreseeable, unreasonable risk of harm to the interests of the plaintiff.

* * *

Where on the facts either an action in contract or one in tort is open to the plaintiff, his choice may have important consequences. Some considerations may lead the plaintiff to prefer action on the contract. A contract may lead to strict liability for failure to perform, as in the case of a physician's undertaking to cure his patient, where the tort action would require proof of negligence or some other wrongful conduct. A shorter statute of limitations may bar the tort action, or it may not survive the death of one of the parties. Some immunities, such as those of municipal corporations or charities may prevent recovery in tort, but not in contract. The damages recoverable on the contract may sometimes be greater, to the extent that they give the plaintiff the benefit of the bargain made, rather than compensation for a loss. A contract claim may be assignable where a tort claim is not, or an inferior court may have jurisdiction over it, or the venue may offer more latitude, or the contract suit may open the way to remedies such as attachment or summary judgment, or be available as a set-off or counterclaim, where the other remedy would not. Finally, the plaintiff may, by his own conduct so far, have accepted and affirmed the contract as to be bound by it, to the exclusion of tort remedies he might otherwise have had.

Generally speaking, the tort remedy is likely to be more advantageous to the injured party in the greater number of cases, if only because it will so often permit the recovery of greater damages. Under the rule of Hadley v. Baxendale, the damages recoverable for breach of contract are limited to those within the contemplation of the defendant at the time the contract was made, and in some jurisdictions, at least, to those for which the defendant has tacitly agreed to assume responsibility. They may be further limited by the contract itself, where a tort action might avoid the limitation. In contract actions, other than those for breach of promise to marry, punitive damages are not allowed, and there can ordinarily be no recovery for mental suffering. In the tort action the only limitations are those of "proximate cause," and the policy which denies recovery to certain types of interests themselves.

The tort action may offer other advantages. It may permit recovery for wrongful death, for which a contract action normally will not lie. It may be open where the contract fails for lack of proof, for uncertainty, for illegality, for want of consideration, or because of the statute of frauds or the parol evidence rule. It may sometimes avoid some defenses, such as infancy or a discharge in bankruptcy; and it may avoid some counterclaims. It may avoid the necessity of joining several defendants, or permit successive actions for multiple breaches of a single contract, or the application of a favorable rule under the conflict of laws.

* * *

* * * It has often been assumed that as between the parties of a contract or bargaining transaction, tort as well as contract obligations can be disclaimed if this is clearly and unmistakably done so that the intent of both parties is clearly manifested. But to accept this is simply to approve the notion that the manifested intent of the parties, as ascertained through appropriate rules of construction, controls the obligations of the parties. But since tort obligations are based on policy considerations apart from manifested intent, the extent to which such obligations can be impaired by contract depends a great deal on the relationship between the parties, the nature of the bargaining transaction, and the type of loss for which liability is disclaimed. This is especially true as regards disclaimers by those who make and sell products.

* * *

* * * The position of the consumer in the market place may be such as to justify certain obligations on those who supply goods and render service apart from promises made and intentions manifested. No doubt there are some consumer transactions where courts or legislatures do conclude that certain obligations cannot be disclaimed and when freedom of contract is restricted and regulated. But if this be so and if freedom to negotiate is restricted in such a way that even without a defect in the negotiation process there is liability notwithstanding a disclaimer, the liability would appear to be tortious in nature and ought to be regarded as such.

HARGRAVE v. OKI NURSERY, INC.

United States Court of Appeals, Second Circuit, 1980.
636 F.2d 897.

NICKERSON, DISTRICT JUDGE:

Plaintiffs appeal from an order of the United States District Court for the Eastern District of New York dismissing the complaint against defendant Oki Nursery, Inc. for lack of personal jurisdiction.

Plaintiff Long Island Vineyards, Inc., is a New York corporation of which plaintiff Hargrave is president. Plaintiffs operate a vineyard in Suffolk County, New York, and make wine from the grapes they produce. Oki is a California corporation with its main office in Sacramento and grows and sells nursery stocks including wine grape vines. The complaint, brought in the Supreme Court of the State of New York, Suffolk County, asserts six claims against Oki. The first alleges that during 1973 and 1974 Oki represented to plaintiffs that vines purchased from Oki would be healthy, free of disease, and suitable for wine production, that plaintiffs relied on the representations and in May 1974 purchased vines from Oki, that the representations were knowingly false, and that the vines sold to plaintiffs were diseased and incapable of bearing fruit of adequate quality or quantity for plaintiffs' commercial wine production.

The other five claims allege substantially the same facts and assert, respectively, breach of contract, breach of express warranty, breach of implied warranty of merchantability, breach of warranty of fitness for a particular purpose, and negligent performance of the contract.

Asserting diversity of citizenship, Oki removed the action to the District Court and moved to dismiss for lack of personal jurisdiction. The court granted the motion. In this case New York State law determines whether personal jurisdiction over Oki was obtained. Rule 4(e) of the Federal Rules of Civil Procedure. Section 302(a)(3), of the New York Civil Practice Law and Rules recites, in pertinent part, "(a)s to a cause of action arising from any of the acts enumerated in this section, a court may exercise personal jurisdiction over any nondomiciliary, . . . who in person or through an agent: . . . commits a tortious act without the state causing injury to person or property within the state, . . . if he . . . expects or should reasonably expect the act to have consequences in the state and derives substantial revenue from interstate or international commerce."

Plaintiffs say that Oki's false representations constituted fraudulent and tortious acts committed in California and causing injury in New York and that Oki should reasonably have expected its fraudulent representations to have New York consequences, and derived substantial revenue from interstate commerce. Oki does not dispute that it could reasonably have expected its representations to have consequences in New York or that it derives substantial revenue from interstate commerce. Oki argues, however, that no "tortious act" has been alleged in the complaint since plaintiffs, by applying the fraud label, may not convert a claim for breach of a contractual representation into a tort claim * * *.

The law of torts and the law of contracts are said to protect different interests. Albemarle Theatre Inc. v. Bayberry Realty Corp., 27 A.D.2d 172, 277 N.Y.S.2d 505 (1st Dept.1967). A plaintiff may recover in contract because the defendant has made an agreement, and the law thinks it desirable that he be held to that agreement. Tort liability is imposed on the basis of some social policy that disapproves the infliction of a specific kind of harm irrespective of any agreement. Id. Specifically the law of fraud seeks to protect against injury those who rely to their detriment on the deliberately dishonest statements of another.

Thus, it does not follow that because acts constitute a breach of contract they cannot also give rise to liability in tort. Where the conduct alleged breaches a legal duty which exists "independent of contractual relations between the parties" a plaintiff may sue in tort. Channel Master Corporation v. Aluminum Limited Sales, Inc., 4 N.Y.2d 403, 408, 176 N.Y.S.2d 259, 263, 151 N.E.2d 833, 836 (1958). If the only interest at stake is that of holding the defendant to a promise, the courts have said that the plaintiff may not transmogrify the contract claim into one for tort. * * * But if in addition there is an interest in protecting the plaintiff from other kinds of harm, the plaintiff may recover in tort whether or not he has a valid claim for breach of contract.

In the present case the complaint sets forth all the elements of an action in tort for fraudulent representations, namely, "representation of a material existing fact, falsity, scienter, deception and injury." Channel Master Corporation v. Aluminum Limited Sales, Inc., 4 N.Y.2d at 407, 176 N.Y.S.2d 259, 151 N.E.2d 833, and see cases cited. Oki is alleged to have knowingly misrepresented the material existing fact that the vines were healthy. Plaintiffs assert they relied on the misrepresentations, paid for the vines, and sustained injury because they were in fact diseased. These allegations state a claim for fraud, and if Oki indeed made the fraudulent representations it "is subject to liability in tort whether the agreement is enforcible or not." Id. at 408, 176 N.Y.S.2d 259, 151 N.E.2d 833.

* * *

The court need not consider plaintiffs' other contentions.

The order is reversed.

[Eds. Note: Section Three of Chapter Five of this book continues the investigation of the doctrine of misrepresentation.]

Note
Additional Elaboration of Oki Nursery's Argument

Oki Nursery made the following argument in its brief to the Court of Appeals for the Second Circuit:

> * * * [E]ven a cursory review of the complaint reveals [that] the acts constituting the alleged breach of contract and warranties are the same acts which form the basis for the fraud and negligent causes of action and, as such, do not give rise to a tort action.

> The true basis of HARGRAVE'S claim against Oki is set forth in paragraph 22 (A. 26a) of the verified complaint, as follows:

>> "On or about December, 1973, plaintiffs and Oki entered into an agreement whereby plaintiffs were to purchase from Oki approximately 12,000 grapevines FOB Sacramento, California, for the sum of approximately $7,839.00 plus freight. Said vines were to be free from all disease and infection, suitable for commercial wine production and to be delivered within a reasonable time."

> It is clear that the contract entered into between HARGRAVE and Oki provided that the vines were to be free of disease and infection and suitable for commercial wine production. The contract unquestionably fully occupied all of the rights and responsibilities between the parties and specifically encompassed the acts upon which the fraud and negligent causes of action are predicated. The breach of warranty causes of action are nothing more than a restatement of the contractual breaches allegedly committed by Oki.

Under these circumstances, the alleged breach of contract and warranties cannot form the basis for the fraud and negligence claims.

I. AYRES & G. KLASS, INSINCERE PROMISES
4, 6, 7, 9 (2005).

An oft-forgotten corner of the law, the doctrine of promissory fraud, provides an entry into the idea that promises can say things. The doctrine recognizes that a promisor, by the very act of promising, typically communicates that she intends to perform her promise. That representation concerns an existing fact—as Lord Bowen put it in an early promissory fraud case, "[T]he state of a man's mind is as much a fact as the state of his digestion."

By saying something about the promisor's present intent, the act of promising creates the opportunity to lie. If a court finds that a defendant-promisor did not intend *ab initio* (at the time of promising) to perform her promise, it can subject her to both compensatory and punitive damages under the doctrine of promissory fraud or even sentence her to prison under the corresponding crime of false promise.

* * *

While a fair amount of intellectual energy has been expended on doctrines like mistake and impossibility, contract theorists have, in recent years, had very little to say about promissory fraud. Similarly, promissory fraud receives relatively little attention in the typical first-year contracts (or torts) textbooks and is almost never taught in first-year torts or contracts courses.

* * *

Yet in many jurisdictions, claims of promissory fraud are more common than invocations of either the mistake or the impossibility doctrines. * * * And the empirical prevalence of promissory fraud is hardly surprising. Alleging promissory fraud is one of the few ways that an aggrieved promisee can seek punitive damages for breach of contract. It is also one of the few ways to enforce promises that would otherwise be unenforceable because of the statute of frauds or the parol evidence rule. Promissory fraud is an important cog in the apparatus of contract law * * *.

* * *

If a promisee's entitlement to performance were truly protected by fully compensatory damages, then at the time of promising he would not care whether the promisor intended to perform, for he would expect to be made whole in the case of nonperformance. The primary reason why promisees care about promisor initial intent—and the reason why the law correctly protects the promisee's entitlement to truthful representations of that intent—is that breach-of-contract damages in the United States typically do not compensate for litigation costs, for speculative damages, and for emotional and other non-pecuniary damages, and that they don't compensate at all if the promisor is judgment proof. And, of course, there is always the chance that a meritorious breach-of-contract claim won't prevail in court. * * *

* * *

In order for a court properly to conclude that a promisor made a material promissory misrepresentation for which she should be held liable, it must make three key inferences: first, it must decide what the promisor said with her promise, explicitly or implicitly; second, it must ascertain whether, at the time of promising, that representation was true; and third, it must determine whether the promisor made the promissory misrepresentation in question recklessly or knowingly, that is, with the scienter necessary for punitive sanctions.

FOLEY v. INTERACTIVE DATA CORP., 47 Cal.3d 654, 254 Cal.Rptr. 211, 765 P.2d 373 (1988). [Foley alleged that Interactive Data fired him because he informed his supervisor that the person hired to succeed the supervisor was under investigation by the FBI for embezzlement in a previous job. One of Foley's causes of action was based on "tortious breach of the implied covenant of good faith and fair dealing." Foley argued that the court "should recognize tort remedies for such a breach in the context of employment termination." Noting that the obligation of good faith performance is a "contract term" and that most courts have excluded tort remedies for breach of the obligation, the court dismissed Foley's cause of action. The court distinguished breach of employment contracts from breach of insurance contracts where courts have allowed tort remedies for bad faith breach. In insurance cases, the court reasoned, the insured "seeks protection against calamity" instead of "commercial advantage" and the insurance company supplies a service of a "quasi-public nature." Moreover the "the relationship of the insurer and insured is inherently unbalanced." The court was "not convinced" that employment contracts merit the same treatment.] "[A] breach in the employment context does not place the employee in the same economic dilemma that an insured faces when an insurer in bad faith refuses to pay a claim to accept a settlement offer within policy limits. When an insurer takes such actions, the insured cannot turn to the marketplace to find another insurance company willing to pay for the loss already incurred. The wrongfully terminated employee, on the other hand, can (and must, in order to mitigate damages * * *) make reasonable efforts to seek alternative employment. Moreover, the role of the employer differs from that of the 'quasi-public' insurance company with whom individuals contract specifically in order to obtain protection from potential specified economic harm. The employer does not similarly 'sell' protection to its employees; it is not providing a public service."

VANLENTE v. UNIVERSITY OF WYOMING RESEARCH CORP., 975 P.2d 594 (Wyoming, 1999). [VanLente, an employee-at-will, worked successfully for nine years as Human Resources Manager for the University of Wyoming's Western Research Institute. He claimed the institute's termination of his employment constituted a bad-faith tort because he failed to cooperate in retaliating against another employee who had submitted a complaint under the Equal Employment Opportunity Act. The Wyoming Supreme Court affirmed a summary judgment against VanLente in part because VanLente failed to demonstrate any genuine issues of fact with respect to his claim of a "special relationship between him and the Institute."]

THOMAS, JUSTICE

* * * [A] breach of the implied covenant of good faith and fair dealing will be the premise for a tort action if a "special relationship of trust and reliance is demonstrated * * *." The situations are rare in which such a special relationship exists when employment is at-will. Up to this time, no case has been presented to this Court in which the facts demonstrate the existence of the requisite special relationship.

* * * In Wilder [v. Cody Country Chamber of Commerce, 868 P.2d 211 (Wyo. 1994)], we held that mere longevity of service does not suffice to create the special relationship leading to the tort remedy. * * * Garcia v. UniWyo Federal Credit Union, 920 P.2d 642, 646 (Wyo.1996), added another factor to the concept of the special relationship. There we ruled that usually such a special relationship can be found only in a "long term employment relation-

ship coupled with a discharge calculated to avoid employer responsibilities to the employee * * *." Id. at 646. * * *

* * * The only point that VanLente presented in his Response in Opposition to Motion for Summary Judgment was that he had a special relationship of trust and confidence that justified the invocation of the tort remedy. VanLente contends that the relationship was one of "trust and reciprocal confidence with regard to extremely sensitive human resource policy and employment matters * * *." The relationship articulated by VanLente is simply one that is inherent in the duties of a human resources manager. It, therefore, was no more than one of the functions with which he was tasked, and did not arise from any special relationship as we have defined it. Longevity, coupled with performance of job duties, is not sufficient to structure the special relationship required by Wilder. Further, the record does not disclose any effort on the part of VanLente to demonstrate that the termination was driven by some motive to deprive him of the potential benefits. In light of this record, the district court correctly entered summary judgment in favor of the Institute * * * on the alleged tort remedy of breach of the implied covenant of good faith and fair dealing.

RESTATEMENT (SECOND) OF TORTS § 402A.

Special Liability of Seller of Product for Physical Harm to User or Consumer

(1) One who sells any product in a defective condition unreasonably dangerous to the user or consumer or to his property is subject to liability for physical harm thereby caused to the ultimate user or consumer, or to his property, if

(a) the seller is engaged in the business of selling such a product, and

(b) it is expected to and does reach the user or consumer without substantial change in the condition in which it is sold.

(2) The rule stated in Subsection (1) applies although

(a) the seller has exercised all possible care in the preparation and sale of his product, and

(b) the user or consumer has not brought the product from or entered into any contractual relation with the seller.

Caveat:

The Institute expresses no opinion as to whether the rules stated in this Section may not apply

(1) to harm to persons other than users or consumers;

(2) to the seller of a product expected to be processed or otherwise substantially changed before it reaches the user or consumer; or

(3) to the seller of a component part of a product to be assembled.

Comment:

* * *

m. * * * The consumer's cause of action does not depend upon the validity of his contract with the person from whom he acquires the product, and it is not affected by any disclaimer or other agreement, whether it be between the seller and his immediate buyer, or attached to and accompanying the product into the consumer's hands.

RESTATEMENT (THIRD) OF TORTS §§ 1 & 2.

1. Liability of Commercial Seller or Distributor for Harm Caused by Defective Products

One engaged in the business of selling or otherwise distributing products who sells or distributes a defective product is subject to liability for harm to persons or property caused by the defect.

Comment:

a. History. This Section states a general rule of tort liability applicable to commercial sellers and other distributors of products generally. * * * The liability established in this Section draws on both warranty law and tort law. Historically, the focus of products liability law was on manufacturing defects. A manufacturing defect is a physical departure from a product's intended design. See § 2(a). Typically, manufacturing defects occur in only a small percentage of units in a product line. Courts early began imposing liability without fault on product sellers for harm caused by such defects, holding a seller liable for harm caused by manufacturing defects even though all possible care had been exercised by the seller in the preparation and distribution of the product. In doing so, courts relied on the concept of warranty, in connection with which fault has never been a prerequisite to liability.

* * * In the early 1960s, American courts began to recognize that a commercial seller of any product having a manufacturing defect should be liable in tort for harm caused by the defect regardless of the plaintiff's ability to maintain a traditional negligence or warranty action. Liability attached even if the manufacturer's quality control in producing the defective product was reasonable. A plaintiff was not required to be in direct privity with the defendant seller to bring an action. Strict liability in tort for defectively manufactured products merges the concept of implied warranty, in which negligence is not required, with the tort concept of negligence, in which contractual privity is not required. See § 2(a).

Questions of design defects and defects based on inadequate instructions or warnings arise when the specific product unit conforms to the intended design but the intended design itself, or its sale without adequate instructions or warnings, renders the product not reasonably safe. If these forms of defect are found to exist, then every unit in the same product line is potentially defective. * * * A number of restrictive rules made recovery for such defects, especially design defects, difficult to obtain. As these rules eroded, courts sought to impose liability without fault for design defects and defects due to inadequate instructions or warnings under the general principles of § 402A of the Restatement, Second, of Torts. However, it soon became evident that § 402A, created to deal with liability for manufacturing defects, could not appropriately be applied to cases of design defects or defects based on inadequate instructions or warnings. A product unit that fails to meet the manufacturer's design specifications thereby fails to perform its intended function and is, almost by definition, defective. However, when the product unit meets the manufacturer's own design specifications, it is necessary to go outside those specifications to determine whether the product is defective.

Sections 2(b) and 2(c) recognize that the rule developed for manufacturing defects is inappropriate for the resolution of claims of defective design and defects based on inadequate instructions or warnings. These latter categories of cases require determinations that the product could have reasonably been made safer by a better design or instruction or warning. Sections 2(b) and 2(c) rely on a reasonableness test traditionally used in determining whether an actor has been negligent. * * * Nevertheless, many courts insist on speaking of liability based on the standards described in §§ 2(b) and 2(c) as being "strict."

* * *

"[S]trict products liability" is a term of art that reflects the judgment that products liability is a discrete area of tort law which borrows from both negligence and warranty. It is not fully congruent with classical tort or contract law. Rather than perpetuating confusion spawned by existing doctrinal categories, §§ 1 and 2 define the liability for each form of defect in terms directly addressing the various kinds of defects. As long as these functional criteria are met, courts may utilize the terminology of negligence, strict liability, or the implied warranty of merchantability, or simply define liability in the terms set forth in the black letter.

2.   Categories of Product Defect

A product is defective when, at the time of sale or distribution, it contains a manufacturing defect, is defective in design, or is defective because of inadequate instructions or warnings. A product:

(a) contains a manufacturing defect when the product departs from its intended design even though all possible care was exercised in the preparation and marketing of the product;

(b) is defective in design when the foreseeable risks of harm posed by the product could have been reduced or avoided by the adoption of a reasonable alternative design by the seller or other distributor, or a predecessor in the commercial chain of distribution, and the omission of the alternative design renders the product not reasonably safe;

(c) is defective because of inadequate instructions or warnings when the foreseeable risks of harm posed by the product could have been reduced or avoided by the provision of reasonable instructions or warnings by the seller or other distributor, or a predecessor in the commercial chain of distribution, and the omission of the instructions or warnings renders the product not reasonably safe.

Note
Major Types of Relations Between Contract and Tort Theory

Sometimes tort principles foster or even shape an emerging theory of obligation "in contract." Similarly, contract ideas may shape tort theories of liability or affect their applicability. For example, the law may permit a party to contract away rights he or she might otherwise have in tort.

A tort theory and a contract theory may overlap, so that both theories are available in the same action. See, e.g., Mauldin v. Sheffer (page 159) and Sullivan

v. O'Connor (page 35). Far more often, only one theory will be available in a given situation.

A tort theory may emerge and largely displace a contract theory. The emergence of strict liability of product manufacturers is an example. See Restatement (Second) of Torts, § 402A, above. Or, a tort theory may supplement a contract theory, as where punitive damages are allowed in a contract case on the theory that the breach of contract also involved an "independent" tort. See White v. Benkowski (Chapter One). The foregoing are only some of the relations between contract and tort.

SECTION SEVEN: OBLIGATION ARISING SOLELY FROM FORM

The least prominent theory of obligation in contract and related areas is based on a promise made in accordance with a legally prescribed formality. Such a formality may take the form of a promise "under seal" or a written promise of some type.

In the English common law a promise made under seal was binding in an action at law even without consideration. What was a "seal"? According to Comment a to section 96 of the Restatement (Second) of Contracts,

> Originally a seal often consisted of wax bearing the imprint of an individualized signet ring, and in the seventeenth century Lord Coke said that wax without impression was not a seal. But in the United States the courts have not required either wax or impression. Impressions directly on the paper were recognized early and are still common for notarial and corporate seals, and gummed wafers have been widely used. In the absence of statute decisions have divided on the effectiveness of the written or printed word "seal," the printed initials "L.S." (locus sigilli, meaning place of the seal), a scrawl made with a pen (often called a "scroll") and a recital of sealing.

As Comment a intimates, at one time in this country a promise under seal also gave rise to a binding obligation. Today, many state statutes specifically provide that a mere donative promise under seal has no binding effect. Other states recognize the seal, but only as presumptive evidence of consideration. (The presumption, of course, can be rebutted by contrary evidence, but in some circumstances, such as when the promisor has died, this may be difficult.) In still other states, there is no statute or other law dealing with the seal, but in the vast majority of these states the defense of lack of consideration is probably available to a donative promisor.

In a few states a binding obligation arises in certain circumstances if a promise is made in writing. For example, the New York General Obligations Law, sections 5–1103 to 5–1115 and section 15–303, provide that certain agreements and promises are enforceable if in writing and signed (for example, agreements involving securities and agreements assigning rights), although without consideration. See also Miss.Code Ann. § 75–19–3. In some states, a promise in writing is merely presumptive evidence of consideration.

It has not infrequently been lamented that the demise of the seal in our system and the general failure to recognize a formal substitute means that we have no generally available device for making donative promises binding.

Some scholars point to continental models and recommend their adoption here. For example, the German Civil Code recognizes certain formally notarized donative promises as binding (section 518 BGB), but provides that the promisor may be excused from liability if he was improvident in making the promise or later suffers adversity (section 519 BGB), or if the donee is guilty of "gross" ingratitude (section 530 BGB). Consider these reflections by a leading contracts scholar:

EISENBERG, DONATIVE PROMISES
47 U.Chi.L.Rev. 1, 13–18 (1979).

[F]ormalities certainly address the problems of deliberative intent and evidentiary security. Form alone, however, cannot meet the problems of improvidence and ingratitude. * * *

* * * [O]ur legal system could not appropriately follow the lead of the civil law by making donative promises enforceable on the basis of their form * * * unless we are also prepared to [have] a body of rules dealing with the problems of improvidence and ingratitude. Certainly such an enterprise is possible. It may be questioned, however, whether the game would be worth the candle. * * * Perhaps the civil-law style of adjudication is suited to wrestling with these kinds of inquiries, but they have held little appeal for common-law courts, which have traditionally been oriented toward inquiry into acts rather than into personal characteristics.

* * *

Of course, the result of the common-law regime is that some promises that should be kept—those made with the requisite intention and excused by neither improvidence nor ingratitude—are not enforced, just as some completed gifts that should be returned are permitted to be kept. In contrast, a regime like that of the civil law appears more closely tailored to the morality of donation. The question is whether the social and economic gains of recognizing a formality that will make donative promises enforceable are worth the social and economic costs. The answer seems to be that—except perhaps for categories recognized as involving some special social utility, such as formal promises to charitable institutions—the advantages and disadvantages of an enforcement regime are in rough balance. If the common-law rules cannot be defended as preferable, the arguments for change cannot be regarded as compelling.

Problem 2–9

Can you reconcile the following sections of the Restatement (Second) of Contracts?

§ 71   Requirement of Exchange

(1) To constitute consideration, a performance or a return promise must be bargained for. * * *

§ 87   Option Contract

(1) An offer is binding as an option contract if it

(a) is in writing and signed by the offeror, recites a purported consideration for the making of the offer, and proposes an exchange on fair terms within a reasonable time. * * *

SECTION EIGHT: OBLIGATION ARISING FROM A STATUTORY WARRANTY

Our law widely recognizes the idea that sellers, lessors, or others make "warranties" or promises concerning the quality of their performance. For example, in many states the seller or lessor of a residence may make a "warranty of habitability." In addition, the seller of goods may warrant that they are fit for the ordinary purposes for which such goods are used. Lessors of goods and providers of services may also make warranties of quality. Some warranties, usually called "express warranties," arise solely from the parties' agreement. Others arise from a combination of agreement and common law or statute. The most pervasive example of the latter involves warranties arising under Article 2 of the Uniform Commercial Code, the sales article. Here we merely introduce warranty theory. Most law schools also treat this subject extensively in the upper level commercial law course.

KEITH v. BUCHANAN

California Court of Appeals, 1985.
173 Cal.App.3d 13, 220 Cal.Rptr. 392.

OCHOA, ASSOCIATE JUSTICE.

This breach of warranty case is before this court after the trial court granted defendants' motion for judgment at the close of plaintiff's case during the trial proceedings. We hold that an express warranty under section 2313 of the California Uniform Commercial Code was created in this matter, and that actual reliance on the seller's factual representation need not be shown by the buyer. The representation is presumed to be part of the basis of the bargain, and the burden is on the seller to prove that the representation was not a consideration inducing the bargain. We affirm all other aspects of the trial court's judgment but reverse in regard to its finding that no express warranty was created and remand for further proceedings consistent with this opinion.

STATEMENT OF FACTS

Plaintiff, Brian Keith, purchased a sailboat from defendants in November 1978 for a total purchase price of $75,610. Even though plaintiff belonged to the Waikiki Yacht Club, had attended a sailing school, had joined the Coast Guard Auxiliary, and had sailed on many yachts in order to ascertain his preferences, he had not previously owned a yacht. He attended a boat show in Long Beach during October 1978 and looked at a number of boats, speaking to sales representatives and obtaining advertising literature. In the literature, the sailboat which is the subject of this action, called an "Island Trader 41," was described as a seaworthy vessel. In one sales brochure, this vessel is described as "a picture of sure-footed seaworthiness." In another, it is called "a carefully well-equipped, and very seaworthy live-aboard vessel." Plaintiff testified he relied on representations in the sales brochures in regard to the purchase. Plaintiff and a sales representative also discussed plaintiff's desire for a boat which was ocean-going and would cruise long distances.

Plaintiff asked his friend, Buddy Ebsen, who was involved in a boat building enterprise, to inspect the boat. Mr. Ebsen and one of his associates, both of whom had extensive experience with sailboats, observed the boat and advised plaintiff that the vessel would suit his stated needs. A deposit was paid on the boat, a purchase contract was entered into, and optional accessories for the boat were ordered. After delivery of the vessel, a dispute arose in regard to its seaworthiness.

Plaintiff filed the instant lawsuit alleging causes of action in breach of express warranty and breach of implied warranty. The trial court granted defendants' Code of Civil Procedure section 631.8 motion for judgment at the close of plaintiff's case. The court found that no express warranty was established by the evidence because none of the defendants had undertaken in writing to preserve or maintain the utility or performance of the vessel, nor to provide compensation for any failure in utility or performance. It found that the written statements produced at trial were opinions or commendations of the vessel. The court further found that no implied warranty of fitness was created because the plaintiff did not rely on the skill and judgment of defendants to select and furnish a suitable vessel, but had rather relied on his own experts in selecting the vessel.

I. EXPRESS WARRANTY

California Uniform Commercial Code section 2313[1] provides, inter alia, that express warranties are created by (1) any affirmation of fact or promise made by the seller to the buyer which relates to the goods and becomes part of the basis of the bargain, and (2) any description of the goods which is made part of the basis of the bargain. Formal words such as "warranty" or "guarantee" are not required to make a warranty, but the seller's affirmation of the value of the goods or an expression of opinion or commendation of the goods does not create an express warranty.

In addition, the Song–Beverly Consumer Warranty Act (Civ.Code, § 1790 et seq.) establishes broad statutory control over warranties in consumer sales where consumer goods are used or bought for use primarily for personal, family, or household purposes. Provisions of the Civil Code relating to warranties do not affect the rights and obligations of parties under the Commercial Code, except that where conflicts exist between the code provisions, the rights guaranteed to buyers of consumer goods under the provisions of the Consumer Warranty Act prevail. (Civ.Code, § 1790.3.)

The Act defines an express warranty, in pertinent part, as "[a] written statement arising out of a sale to the consumer of a consumer good pursuant to which the manufacturer, distributor, or retailer undertakes to preserve or

---

1. Section 2313: "Express Warranties by Affirmation, Promise, Description, Sample. (1) Express warranties by the seller are created as follows:

"(a) Any affirmation of fact or promise made by the seller to the buyer which relates to the goods and becomes part of the basis of the bargain creates an express warranty that the goods shall conform to the affirmation or promise.

"(b) Any description of the goods which is made part of the basis of the bargain creates an express warranty that the goods shall conform to the description.

"(c) Any sample or model which is made part of the basis of the bargain creates an express warranty that the whole of the goods shall conform to the sample or model.

"(2) It is not necessary to the creation of an express warranty that the seller use formal words such as 'warrant' or 'guarantee' or that he have a specific intention to make a warranty, but an affirmation merely of the value of the goods or a statement purporting to be merely the seller's opinion or commendation of the goods does not create a warranty."

maintain the utility or performance of the consumer good or provide compensation if there is a failure in utility or performance. * * * " (Civ.Code, § 1791.2, subd. (a)(1).) Again, formal words are not required in order to create an express warranty, but statements of value, opinion, or commendation do not create a warranty.

The trial court appropriately found that there was no written undertaking to preserve or maintain the utility or performance of a consumer good or to provide compensation if there was a failure in utility or performance at the time the purchase contract for the sailboat was made. No claim, therefore, is cognizable that an express warranty existed in this action pursuant to the provisions of the Song–Beverly Consumer Warranty Act. However, at the time of argument on the motion for judgment, plaintiff's counsel had argued claims based on express warranty under the provisions of *both* the Civil Code and the Commercial Code, and no analysis was undertaken in regard to express warranty under the provisions of the California Uniform Commercial Code.

California Uniform Commercial Code section 2313, regarding express warranties, was enacted in 1963 and consists of the official text of Uniform Commercial Code section 2–313 without change. In deciding whether a statement made by a seller constitutes an express warranty under this provision, the court must deal with three fundamental issues. First, the court must determine whether the seller's statement constitutes an "affirmation of fact or promise" or "description of the goods" under California Uniform Commercial Code section 2313, subdivision (1)(a) or (b) or whether it is rather "merely the seller's opinion or commendation of the goods" under section 2313, subdivision (2). Second, assuming the court finds the language used susceptible to creation of a warranty, it must then be determined whether the statement was "part of the basis of the bargain." Third, the court must determine whether the warranty was breached. (See *Sessa v. Riegle* (E.D.Pa. 1977) 427 F.Supp. 760, 765.)

A warranty relates to the title, character, quality, identity, or condition of the goods. The purpose of the law of warranty is to determine what it is that the seller has in essence agreed to sell. (*A.A. Baxter Corp. v. Colt Industries, Inc.* (1970) 10 Cal.App.3d 144, 153, 88 Cal.Rptr. 842.) "Express warranties are chisels in the hands of buyers and sellers. With these tools, the parties to a sale sculpt a monument representing the goods. Having selected a stone, the buyer and seller may leave it almost bare, allowing considerable play in the qualities that fit its contours. Or the parties may chisel away inexactitudes until a well-defined shape emerges. The seller is bound to deliver, and the buyer to accept, goods that match the sculpted form. [Fn. omitted.]" (*Special Project: Article Two Warranties in Commercial Transactions, Express Warranties—Section 2–313* (1978–79) 64 Cornell L.Rev. 30 (hereafter cited as *Warranties in Commercial Transactions*) at pp. 43–44.)

A. *Affirmation of fact, promise or description versus statement of opinion, commendation or value.*

"The determination as to whether a particular statement is an expression of opinion or an affirmation of fact is often difficult, and frequently is dependent upon the facts and circumstances existing at the time the statement is made." (*Willson v. Municipal Bond Co.* (1936) 7 Cal.2d 144, 150, 59 P.2d 974.) Recent decisions have evidenced a trend toward narrowing the scope of representations which are considered opinion, sometimes referred to as "puffing" or "sales talk," resulting in an expansion of the liability that flows from broad statements of manufacturers or retailers as to the quality of their products. Courts have liberally construed affirmations of quality made by sellers in favor of injured consumers. (*Hauter v. Zogarts* (1975) 14 Cal.3d 104, 112, 120 Cal.Rptr. 681, 534 P.2d 377; see also 55 Cal.Jur.3d, Sales, § 74, p. 580.) It has even been suggested "that in an age of consumerism all seller's statements, except the most blatant sales pitch, may give rise to an express warranty." (1 Alderman and Dole, A Transactional Guide to the Uniform Commercial Code (2d ed.1983) p. 89.)

Courts in other states have struggled in efforts to create a formula for distinguishing between affirmations of fact, promises, or descriptions of goods on the one hand, and value, opinion, or commendation statements on the other. The code comment indicates that the basic question is: "What statements of the seller have in the circumstances and in objective judgment become part of the basis of the bargain?" The commentators indicated that the language of subsection (2) of the code section was included because "common experience discloses that some statements or predictions cannot fairly be viewed as entering into the bargain." (See U.Com.Code com. 8 to Cal.U.Com.Code, § 2313, West's Ann.Com.Code (1964) p. 250.)

Statements made by a seller during the course of negotiation over a contract are presumptively affirmations of fact unless it can be demonstrated that the buyer could only have reasonably considered the statement as a statement of the seller's opinion. Commentators have noted several factors which tend to indicate an opinion statement. These are (1) a lack of specificity in the statement made, (2) a statement that is made in an equivocal manner, or (3) a statement which reveals that the goods are experimental in nature. (See *Warranties in Commercial Transactions, supra,* at pp. 61–65.)

It is clear that statements made by a manufacturer or retailer in an advertising brochure which is disseminated to the consuming public in order to induce sales can create express warranties. * * * In the instant case, the vessel purchased was described in sales brochures as "a picture of sure-footed seaworthiness" and "a carefully well-equipped and very seaworthy vessel." The seller's representative was aware that appellant was looking for a vessel sufficient for long distance ocean-going cruises. The statements in the brochure are specific and unequivocal in asserting that the vessel is seaworthy. Nothing in the negotiation indicates that the vessel is experimental in nature. In fact, one sales brochure assures prospective buyers that production of the vessel was commenced "after years of careful testing." The representations regarding seaworthiness made in sales brochures regarding the Island Trader 41 were affirmations of fact relating to the quality or condition of the vessel.

B.   *"Part of the basis of the bargain" test.*

Under former provisions of law, a purchaser was required to prove that he or she acted in reliance upon representations made by the seller. (*Grinnell v. Charles Pfizer & Co.* (1969) 274 Cal.App.2d 424, 440, 79 Cal.Rptr. 369.) California Uniform Commercial Code section 2313 indicates only that the seller's statements must become "part of the basis of the bargain." According to official comment 3 to this Uniform Commercial Code provision, "no particular reliance ... need be shown in order to weave [the seller's affirmations of fact] into the fabric of the agreement. Rather, any fact which is to take such affirmations, once made, out of the agreement requires clear affirmative proof." (See U.Com.Code com. 3 to Cal.U.Com.Code, § 2313, West's Ann.Com.Code (1964) p. 249.)

The California Supreme Court, in discussing the continued viability of the reliance factor, noted that commentators have disagreed in regard to the impact of this development. Some have indicated that it shifts the burden of proving non-reliance to the seller, and others have indicated that the code eliminates the concept of reliance altogether. (*Hauter v. Zogarts, supra,* 14 Cal.3d at pp. 115–116, 120 Cal.Rptr. 681, 534 P.2d 377.) The court did not resolve this issue, but noted that decisions of other states prior to that time had "ignored the significance of the new standard and have held that consumer reliance still is a vital ingredient for recovery based on express warranty." (*Id.,* at p. 116, fn. 13, 120 Cal.Rptr. 681, 534 P.2d 377; see also *Fogo v. Cutter Laboratories, Inc.* (1977) 68 Cal.App.3d 744, 760, 137 Cal.Rptr. 417.)

The shift in language clearly changes the degree to which it must be shown that the seller's representation affected the buyer's decision to enter into the agreement. A buyer need not show that he would not have entered into the agreement absent the warranty or even that it was a dominant factor inducing the agreement. A warranty statement is deemed to be part of the basis of the bargain and to have been relied upon as one of the inducements for the purchase of the product. In other words, the buyer's demonstration of reliance on an express warranty is "not a prerequisite for breach of warranty, as long as the express warranty involved became part of the bargain. See White & Summers, Uniform Commercial Code (2d ed. 1980) § 9–4. If, however, the resulting bargain does not rest at all on the representations of the seller, those representations cannot be considered as becoming any part of the 'basis of the bargain.' * * * " (*Allied Fidelity Ins. Co. v. Pico* (Nev.S.Ct.1983) 656 P.2d 849, 850.)

The official Uniform Commercial Code comment in regard to section 2–313 "indicates that in actual practice affirmations of fact made by the seller about the goods during a bargain are regarded as part of the description of those goods; hence no particular reliance on such statements need be shown in order to weave them into the fabric of the agreement." (*Young & Cooper, Inc. v. Vestring* (1974) 214 Kan. 311, 521 P.2d 281, 291; *Brunner v. Jensen* (1974) 215 Kan. 416, 524 P.2d 1175, 1185.) It is clear from the new language of this code section that the concept of reliance has been purposefully abandoned. * * *

The change of the language in section 2313 of the California Uniform Commercial Code modifies both the degree of reliance and the burden of proof in express warranties under the code. The representation need only be part of the basis of the bargain, or merely a factor or consideration inducing the buyer to enter into the bargain. A warranty statement made by a seller is presumptively part of the basis of the bargain, and the burden is on the seller to prove that the resulting bargain does not rest at all on the representation.

The buyer's actual knowledge of the true condition of the goods prior to the making of the contract may make it plain that the seller's statement was not relied upon as one of the inducements for the purchase, but the burden is on the seller to demonstrate such knowledge on the part of the buyer. Where the buyer inspects the goods before purchase, he may be deemed to have waived the seller's express warranties. But, an examination or inspection by the buyer of the goods does not necessarily discharge the seller from an express warranty if the defect was not actually discovered and waived. * * *

Appellant's inspection of the boat by his own experts does not constitute a waiver of the express warranty of seaworthiness. Prior to the making of the contract, appellant had experienced boat builders observe the boat, but there was no testing of the vessel in the water.[2] Such a warranty (seaworthiness) necessarily relates to the time when the vessel has been put to sea (*Werner v. Montana* (1977) 117 N.H. 721, 378 A.2d 1130, 1134–35) and has been shown to be reasonably fit and adequate in materials, construction, and equipment for its intended purposes. * * *

In this case, appellant was aware of the representations regarding seaworthiness by the seller prior to contracting. He also had expressed to the seller's representative his desire for a long distance ocean-going vessel. Although he had other experts inspect the vessel, the inspection was limited and would not have indicated whether or not the vessel was seaworthy. It is clear that the seller has not overcome the presumption that the representations regarding seaworthiness were part of the basis of this bargain.

II. IMPLIED WARRANTY

Appellant also claimed breach of the implied warranty of fitness for a particular purpose[3] in regard to the sale of the subject vessel. An implied warranty of fitness for a particular purpose arises when a "seller at the time of contracting has reason to know any particular purpose for which the goods are required and that the buyer is relying on the seller's skill or judgment to select or furnish suitable goods," which are fit for such purpose. (Cal.U.Com. Code, § 2315.) The Consumer Warranty Act makes such an implied warranty applicable to retailers, distributors, and manufacturers. (Civ.Code, §§ 1791.1, 1792.1, 1792.2, subd. (a).) An implied warranty of fitness for a particular purpose arises only where (1) the purchaser at the time of contracting intends to use the goods for a particular purpose, (2) the seller at the time of contracting has reason to know of this particular purpose, (3) the buyer relies on the seller's skill or judgment to select or furnish goods suitable for the particular purpose, and (4) the seller at the time of contracting has reason to know that the buyer is relying on such skill and judgment. (*Metowski v. Traid Corp.* (1972) 28 Cal.App.3d 332, 341, 104 Cal.Rptr. 599.)

---

2. Evidence was presented of examination or inspection of the boat after the making of the contract of sale and prior to delivery and acceptance of the vessel. Such an inspection would be irrelevant to any issue of express warranty. Although it deals with implied warranties as opposed to express warranties, the Uniform Commercial Code comment 8 to section 2–316 (Cal.U.Com.Code, § 2316) is instructive: "Under paragraph (b) of subdivision (3) warranties may be excluded or modified by the circumstances where the buyer examines the goods or a sample or model of them *before*

entering into the contract. 'Examination' as used in this paragraph is not synonymous with inspection before acceptance or at any other time after the contract has been made. It goes rather to the nature of the responsibility assumed by the seller at the time of the making of the contract." (See U.Com.Code com. 8 to Cal. U.Com.Code, § 2316, West's Ann.Com.Code (1964) p. 308, emphasis added.)

3. No claim of breach of implied warranty of merchantability has been presented in this action.

The reliance elements are important to the consideration of whether an implied warranty of fitness for a particular purpose exists. "If the seller had no reason to know that he was being relied upon, his conduct in providing goods cannot fairly be deemed a tacit representation of their suitability for a particular purpose. And if the buyer did not in fact rely, then the principal justification for imposing a fitness warranty disappears." (See *Warranties in Commercial Transactions, supra,* at p. 89.) The major question in determining the existence of an implied warranty of fitness for a particular purpose is the reliance by the buyer upon the skill and judgment of the seller to select an article suitable for his needs. * * *

The trial court found that the plaintiff did not rely on the skill and judgment of the defendants to select a suitable vessel, but that he rather relied on his own experts. "Our sole task is to determine 'whether the evidence, viewed in the light most favorable to [respondent], sustains [these] findings.' [Citations.] Moreover, 'in examining the sufficiency of the evidence to support a questioned finding an appellate court must accept as true all evidence tending to establish the correctness of the finding as made, taking into account, as well, all inferences which might reasonably have been thought by the trial court to lead to the same conclusion.' [Citations.] If appellate scrutiny reveals that substantial evidence supports the trial court's findings and conclusions, the judgment must be affirmed." (*Board of Education v. Jack M.* (1977) 19 Cal.3d 691, 697, 139 Cal.Rptr. 700, 566 P.2d 602.)

A review of the record reveals ample evidence to support the trial court's finding. Appellant had extensive experience with sailboats at the time of the subject purchase, even though he had not previously owned such a vessel. He had developed precise specifications in regard to the type of boat he wanted to purchase. He looked at a number of different vessels, reviewed their advertising literature, and focused on the Island Trader 41 as the object of his intended purchase. He also had friends look at the boat before making the final decision to purchase. The trial court's finding that the buyer did not rely on the skill or judgment of the seller in the selection of the vessel in question is supported by substantial evidence.

The trial court's judgment that no express warranty existed in this matter is reversed. The trial court's judgment is affirmed in all other respects. Since considerable contradictory evidence was elicited at trial relating to the asserted breach of warranty of seaworthiness of the subject vessel, and since the trial court made no finding in regard to that issue, the matter is remanded to the trial court for further proceedings consistent with this opinion. Each party is to bear his own costs on appeal.

WEBSTER v. BLUE SHIP TEA ROOM

Supreme Judicial Court of Massachusetts, 1964.
347 Mass. 421, 198 N.E.2d 309.

REARDON, JUSTICE.

This is a case which by its nature evokes earnest study not only of the law but also of the culinary traditions of the Commonwealth which bear so heavily upon its outcome. It is an action to recover damages for personal injuries sustained by reason of a breach of implied warranty of food served by the defendant in its restaurant. An auditor, whose findings of fact were not to be final, found for the plaintiff. On a retrial in the Superior Court before a judge and jury, in which the plaintiff testified, the jury returned a verdict for her. The defendant is here on exceptions to the refusal of the judge (1) to strike certain portions of the auditor's report, (2) to direct a verdict for the defendant, and (3) to allow the defendant's motion for the entry of a verdict in its favor under leave reserved.

The jury could have found the following facts: On Saturday, April 25, 1959, about 1 P.M., the plaintiff, accompanied by her sister and her aunt, entered the Blue Ship Tea Room operated by the defendant. The group was seated at a table and supplied with menus.

This restaurant, which the plaintiff characterized as "quaint," was located in Boston "on the third floor of an old building on T Wharf which overlooks the ocean."

The plaintiff, who had been born and brought up in New England (a fact of some consequence), ordered clam chowder and crabmeat salad. Within a few minutes she received tidings to the effect that "there was no more clam chowder," whereupon she ordered a cup of fish chowder. Presently, there was set before her "a small bowl of fish chowder." She had previously enjoyed a breakfast about 9 A.M. which had given her no difficulty. "The fish chowder contained haddock, potatoes, milk, water and seasoning. The chowder was milky in color and not clear. The haddock and potatoes were in chunks" (also a fact of consequence). "She agitated it a little with the spoon and observed that it was a fairly full bowl * * *. It was hot when she got it, but she did not tip it with her spoon because it was hot * * * but stirred it in an up and under motion. She denied that she did this because she was looking for something, but it was rather because she wanted an even distribution of fish and potatoes." "She started to eat it, alternating between the chowder and crackers which were on the table with * * * [some] rolls. She ate about 3 or 4 spoonfuls then stopped. She looked at the spoonfuls as she was eating. She saw equal parts of liquid, potato and fish as she spooned it into her mouth. She did not see anything unusual about it. After 3 or 4 spoonfuls she was aware that something had lodged in her throat because she couldn't swallow and couldn't clear her throat by gulping and she could feel it." This misadventure led to two esophagoscopies at the Massachusetts General Hospital, in the second of which, on April 27, 1959, a fish bone was found and removed. The sequence of events produced injury to the plaintiff which was not insubstantial.

We must decide whether a fish bone lurking in a fish chowder, about the ingredients of which there is no other complaint, constitutes a breach of implied warranty under applicable provisions of the Uniform Commercial Code,[1] the annotations to which are not helpful on this point. As the judge put

---

1. "(1) Unless excluded or modified by section 2–316, a warranty that the goods shall be merchantable is implied in a contract for their sale if the seller is a merchant with respect to goods of that kind. Under this section the serving for value of food or drink to be consumed either on the premises or elsewhere is a sale. (2) Goods to be merchantable must at least be such as * * * (c) are fit for the ordinary purposes for which such goods are used * * *." G.L. c. 106, § 2–314.

"* * * (3)(b) [W]hen the buyer before entering into the contract has examined the goods or the sample or model as fully as he desired or has refused to examine the goods there is no implied warranty with regard to defects which

it in his charge, "Was the fish chowder fit to be eaten and wholesome? * * * [N]obody is claiming that the fish itself wasn't wholesome. * * * But the bone of contention here—I don't mean that for a pun—but was this fish bone a foreign substance that made the fish chowder unwholesome or not fit to be eaten?"

The plaintiff has vigorously reminded us of the high standards imposed by this court where the sale of food is involved (see Flynn v. First Natl. Stores Inc., 296 Mass. 521, 523, 6 N.E.2d 814) and has made reference to cases involving stones in beans (Friend v. Childs Dining Hall Co., 231 Mass. 65, 120 N.E. 407, 5 A.L.R. 1100), trichinae in pork (Holt v. Mann, 294 Mass. 21, 22, 200 N.E. 403), and to certain other cases, here and elsewhere, serving to bolster her contention of breach of warranty.

The defendant asserts that here was a native New Englander eating fish chowder in a "quaint" Boston dining place where she had been before; that "[f]ish chowder, as it is served and enjoyed by New Englanders, is a hearty dish, originally designed to satisfy the appetites of our seamen and fisher-men"; that "[t]his court knows well that we are not talking of some insipid broth as is customarily served to convalescents." We are asked to rule in such fashion that no chef is forced "to reduce the pieces of fish in the chowder to miniscule size in an effort to ascertain if they contained any pieces of bone." "In so ruling," we are told (in the defendant's brief), "the court will not only uphold its reputation for legal knowledge and acumen, but will, as loyal sons of Massachusetts, save our world-renowned fish chowder from degenerating into an insipid broth containing the mere essence of its former stature as a culinary masterpiece." Notwithstanding these passionate entreaties we are bound to examine with detachment the nature of fish chowder and what might happen to it under varying interpretations of the Uniform Commercial Code.

Chowder is an ancient dish preexisting even "the appetites of our seamen and fishermen." It was perhaps the common ancestor of the "more refined cream soups, purees, and bisques." Berolzheimer, The American Woman's Cook Book (Publisher's Guild Inc., New York, 1941) p. 176. The word "chowder" comes from the French "chaudière," meaning a "cauldron" or "pot." "In the fishing villages of Brittany * * * 'faire la chaudière' means to supply a cauldron in which is cooked a mess of fish and biscuit with some savoury condiments, a hodge-podge contributed by the fishermen themselves, each of whom in return receives his share of the prepared dish. The Breton fishermen probably carried the custom to Newfoundland, long famous for its chowder, whence it has spread to Nova Scotia, New Brunswick, and New England." A New English Dictionary (MacMillan and Co., 1893) p. 386. Our literature over the years abounds in references not only to the delights of chowder but also to its manufacture. A namesake of the plaintiff, Daniel Webster, had a recipe for fish chowder which has survived into a number of modern cookbooks and in which the removal of fish bones is not mentioned at all. One old time recipe recited in the New English Dictionary study defines chowder as "A dish made of fresh fish (esp. cod) or clams, stewed with slices

an examination ought in the circumstances to have revealed to him * * *." G.L. c. 106, § 2–316.

of pork or bacon, onions, and biscuit. 'Cider and champagne are sometimes added.' " Hawthorne, in The House of the Seven Gables (Allyn and Bacon, Boston, 1957) p. 8, speaks of "[a] codfish of sixty pounds, caught in the bay, [which] had been dissolved into the rich liquid of a chowder." A chowder variant, cod "Muddle," was made in Plymouth in the 1890s by taking "a three or four pound codfish, head added. Season with salt and pepper and boil in just enough water to keep from burning. When cooked, add milk and piece of butter." The recitation of these ancient formulae suffices to indicate that in the construction of chowders in these parts in other years, worries about fish bones played no role whatsoever. This broad outlook on chowders has persisted in more modern cookbooks. "The chowder of today is much the same as the old chowder * * *." The American Woman's Cook Book, supra, p. 176. The all embracing Fannie Farmer states in a portion of her recipe, fish chowder is made with a "fish skinned, but head and tail left on. Cut off head and tail and remove fish from backbone. Cut fish in 2–inch pieces and set aside. Put head, tail, and backbone broken in pieces, in stewpan; add 2 cups cold water and bring slowly to boiling point * * *." The liquor thus produced from the bones is added to the balance of the chowder. Farmer, The Boston Cooking School Cook Book (Little Brown Co., 1937) p. 166.

Thus, we consider a dish which for many long years, if well made, has been made generally as outlined above. It is not too much to say that a person sitting down in New England to consume a good New England fish chowder embarks on a gustatory adventure which may entail the removal of some fish bones from his bowl as he proceeds. We are not inclined to tamper with age old recipes by any amendment reflecting the plaintiff's view of the effect of the Uniform Commercial Code upon them. We are aware of the heavy body of case law involving foreign substances in food, but we sense a strong distinction between them and those relative to unwholesomeness of the food itself, e.g., tainted mackerel (Smith v. Gerrish, 256 Mass. 183, 152 N.E. 318), and a fish bone in a fish chowder. Certain Massachusetts cooks might cavil at the ingredients contained in the chowder in this case in that it lacked the heartening lift of salt pork. In any event, we consider that the joys of life in New England include the ready availability of fresh fish chowder. We should be prepared to cope with the hazards of fish bones, the occasional presence of which in chowders is, it seems to us, to be anticipated, and which, in the light of a hallowed tradition, do not impair their fitness or merchantability. While we are bouyed up in this conclusion by Shapiro v. Hotel Statler Corp., 132 F.Supp. 891 (S.D.Cal.), in which the bone which afflicted the plaintiff appeared in "Hot Barquette of Seafood Mornay," we know that the United States District Court of Southern California, situated as are we upon a coast, might be expected to share our views. We are most impressed, however, by Allen v. Grafton, 170 Ohio St. 249, 164 N.E.2d 167, where in Ohio, the Midwest, in a case where the plaintiff was injured by a piece of oyster shell in an order of fried oysters, Mr. Justice Taft (now Chief Justice) in a majority opinion held that "the possible presence of a piece of oyster shell in or attached to an oyster is so well known to anyone who eats oysters that we can say as a matter of law that one who eats oysters can reasonably anticipate and guard against eating such a piece of shell * * *." (P. 259 of 170 Ohio St., p. 174 of 164 N.E.2d.)

Thus, while we sympathize with the plaintiff who has suffered a peculiarly New England injury, the order must be

Exceptions sustained.

Judgment for the defendant.

J. WHITE & R. SUMMERS, UNIFORM COMMERCIAL CODE
342–43 (5th ed. 2000).

[O]ne should understand how a warranty lawsuit looks to a plaintiff's lawyer and how it differs from a suit against an "insurer" on the one hand and an allegedly negligent defendant on the other. If an insurance company insures against the loss of an arm, all the claimant need do to recover is show the bloody stump. If the same claimant wishes to recover in warranty from the seller of the offending chain saw, he has a much tougher case to prove. Proof of injury—the loss of his arm—is just the beginning. First, he must prove that the defendant made a warranty, express or implied, under 2–313, 2–314, or 2–315. Second, he must prove that the goods did not comply with the warranty, that is, that they were defective at the time of the sale. Third, he must prove that his injury was caused, proximately and in fact, by the defective nature of the goods (and not, for example, by his careless use of the saw). Fourth, he must prove his damages. Finally, the warranty plaintiff must fight off all sorts of affirmative defenses such as disclaimers, statute of limitations, privity, lack of notice, and assumption of the risk.

Although the warranty plaintiff need not prove negligence, warranty liability has much more in common with negligence liability than it does with a life, collision, or health insurer's liability. The two causes of action pose common problems for the plaintiff's lawyer. In both the lawyer must prove cause in fact and proximate causation on the part of a specific defendant. And too much should not be made of the fact that in a negligence suit the plaintiff must also prove that the defendant was negligent. Professor Whitford has suggested that the *res ipsa loquitur* doctrine will often carry the plaintiff to the jury and that the jury will find defendant negligent even absent explicit proof of negligence.

Finally, one should distinguish between warranty (particularly express warranty) and fraud or misrepresentation. Typically, only a naughty seller is guilty of misrepresentation or fraud, but a seller can be Simon pure and yet break an express warranty. The former cases usually require at least that the defendant be negligent in making its representation and in some cases that it intentionally state a mistruth. There is no such requirement of evil doing on the part of a warranty defendant. A seller can fully believe that the representations he makes are accurate and yet find himself liable for the breach of an express warranty.

CONVENTION ON CONTRACTS FOR THE INTERNATIONAL SALE OF GOODS.
Article 35

(1) The seller must deliver goods which are of the quantity, quality and description required by the contract and which are contained or packaged in the manner required by the contract.

(2) Except where the parties have agreed otherwise, the goods do not conform with the contract unless they:

(a) Are fit for the purposes for which goods of the same description would ordinarily be used;

(b) Are fit for any particular purpose expressly or impliedly made known to the seller at the time of the conclusion of the contract, except where the circumstances show that the buyer did not rely, or that it was unreasonable for him to rely, on the seller's skill and judgment;

(c) Possess the qualities of goods which the seller has held out to the buyer as a sample or model;

(d) Are contained or packaged in the manner usual for such goods or, where there is no such manner, in a manner adequate to preserve and protect the goods.

(3) The seller is not liable under subparagraphs (a) to (d) of the preceding paragraph for any lack of conformity of the goods if at the time of the conclusion of the contract the buyer knew or could not have been unaware of such lack of conformity.

SECTION NINE: THE STATUTE OF FRAUDS

Unlike other sections of this chapter, this section does not present a distinct general theory of obligation. Instead, it concerns a formal requirement for the enforceability of certain agreements with consideration, namely the requirement of a writing. We have already encountered the statute of frauds in cases such as Gay v. Mooney and Kearns v. Andree (pages 120 and 122). We now pause for a more concentrated analysis. The subject is vast. (Corbin devotes an entire volume of his treatise to it.) Here we mainly explore the basic nature of statute of frauds problems and introduce relevant methodology. But first, a brief historical sketch:

> In 1671, in Old Marston, Oxfordshire, England, defendant Egbert was sued by plaintiff John over an alleged oral promise by Egbert to sell to John a fighting [rooster] named Fiste. John's friend, Harold, claimed he overheard the "deal" and by that dubious means John won, though in fact there apparently was no deal. In 1671 courts did not allow parties to a lawsuit to testify so Egbert could not testify to rebut Harold's story. Compounding the problem was the fact that courts then could not throw out jury verdicts manifestly contrary to the evidence. So, in response to the plight of the Egberts of the world and to the recurring mischief of the Johns, as well as to combat possible "Fraude and perjurie" by the Harolds, Parliament passed in 1677 a "Statute of Frauds" which required [among other things] that certain contracts for the sale of goods be in writing to be enforceable.

Thomson Printing Machinery Co. v. B.F. Goodrich Co., 714 F.2d 744, 746 (7th Cir.1983), quoting J. White and R. Summers, The Uniform Commercial Code 50 (2d ed. 1980).

Sections (4) and (17) of the English Statute of Frauds provided as follows:

§ 4. * * * [N]o action shall be brought (1) whereby to charge any executor or administrator upon any special promise, to answer damages out of his own estate; (2) or whereby to charge the defendant upon any special promise to answer for the debt, default or miscarriages of another person; (3) or to charge any person upon any agreement made upon consideration of marriage; (4) or upon any contract or sale of lands, tenements or hereditaments, or any interest in or concerning them; (5) or upon any agreement that is not to be performed within the space of one year from the making thereof; (6) unless the agreement upon which such action shall be brought, or some memorandum or note thereof, shall be in writing, and signed by the party to be charged therewith, or some other person thereunto by him lawfully authorized.

§ 17. * * * [N]o contract for the sale of any goods, wares and merchandises, for the price of ten pounds sterling or upwards, shall be allowed to be good, except the buyer shall accept part of the goods sold, and actually receive the same, or give something in earnest to bind the bargain, or in part of payment, or that some note or memorandum in writing of the said bargain be made and signed by the parties to be charged by such contract, or their agents thereunto lawfully authorized.

Although the above statute is no longer in force, some important writing requirements still exist under English law, including for the creation or transfer of certain interests in land and for contracts of suretyship. Observe, too, that the original English Statute of Frauds was far from complete in coverage. For example, it omitted construction contracts and insurance contracts.

Courts have treated the statute of frauds in the United States differently. Almost all states copied or adopted some version of the *general* English Statute of Frauds, set forth above. These state versions, with occasional modification, extensive judicial gloss, and even some judicial revision, are in force today. In addition to the general statute of frauds, one or more *special* statutes imposing additional writing requirements, such as for real estate brokerage agreements and certain contracts to make a will, are also in force in virtually all American jurisdictions. The Uniform Commercial Code embodies several special writing requirements, as well as the modern day sale of goods counterpart to old section 17 of the English statute. See U.C.C. § 2–201.

For illustrative purposes, consider Hawaii's version of the general statute of frauds. Although Hawaii is farther away from England than any other American state, Hawaii's statute tracks the English version rather closely.

HAWAII REVISED STATUTES § 656–1

Certain contracts, when actionable. No action shall be brought and maintained in any of the following cases:

(1) To charge a personal representative, upon any special promise to answer for damages out of the personal representative's own estate:

(2) To charge any person upon any special promise to answer for the debt, default, or misdoings of another;

(3) To charge any person, upon an agreement made in consideration of marriage;

(4) Upon any contract for the sale of lands, tenements, or hereditaments, or of any interest in or concerning them;

(5) Upon any agreement that is not to be performed within one year from the making thereof;

(6) To charge any person upon any agreement authorizing or employing an agent or broker to purchase or sell real estate for compensation or commission;

(7) To charge the estate of any deceased person upon any agreement which by its terms is not to be performed during the lifetime of the promisor * * *

unless the promise, contract, or agreement upon which the action is brought, or some memorandum or note thereof, is in writing, and is signed by the party to be charged therewith, or by some person thereunto by the party in writing lawfully authorized.

Compliance with the statute of frauds does not itself prove the existence of a contract. If put to proof, the plaintiff must show all the requirements of an agreement with consideration. Thus, the plaintiff will not prevail merely by satisfying the statute of frauds. Conversely, if the defendant has a statute of frauds defense, i.e., the statute applies, the contract is not in writing and no exception applies, the plaintiff will not recover on the grounds of an agreement with consideration even if the plaintiff proves the contract. But the plaintiff may be able to recover the value of any benefit conferred on a restitution theory. See, e.g., Gay v. Mooney (page 120).

A statute of frauds can pose problems of conscience for the practicing lawyer. With the exception of U.C.C. § 2–201(3)(b), involving the sale of goods, the statute unqualifiedly allows a defendant to admit an oral agreement, yet plead the statute as a bar to recovery by the plaintiff. "In the conflict between conscience and judicially approved practice, what is the lawyer to do? Conscience tells * * * that the practice is wrong, but the literature from insurance companies reminds * * * [the lawyer] of liability for malpractice." Stevens, Ethics and the Statute of Frauds, 37 Cornell L.Q. 355, 356 (1952).

The basic problems arising under a statute of frauds and its case law are these: (1) Does the statute apply; or, in legal jargon, is the case "within the statute?" (2) If the case is within the statute, does a memorandum, note, or other writing satisfy the statute? (3) If the case is within the statute and there is no complying writing, does the statute or the case law recognize an exception? And (4) If the case is within the statute, there is no complying writing, and there is no applicable exception, does any other doctrine mitigate what would otherwise be the effect of non-compliance?

The cases below treat several of the most important statute of frauds issues. The cases also reveal the propensity of courts to treat the statute as a "common law" statute subject to judicial revision.

HOWARD M. SCHOOR ASSOCIATES, INC. v. HOLMDEL HEIGHTS CONSTRUCTION CO.

Supreme Court of New Jersey, 1975.
68 N.J. 95, 343 A.2d 401.

MOUNTAIN, J.

Plaintiffs, two engineering and surveying firms with identical or very similar management and ownership, brought this action to recover amounts due for professional services rendered by them to defendant, Holmdel Heights Construction Company. The latter is in receivership and the suit has proceeded, in effect, solely against defendant, Alan Sugarman. Plaintiffs' claim is that Sugarman, an attorney at law of this state, personally undertook to pay for the services rendered. He defends on the factual ground that he made no promises to do so and upon the legal ground that even had he made such a promise, it would be unenforceable under the Statute of Frauds.

The trial judge, sitting without a jury, resolved both the factual and legal issues in favor of plaintiffs and entered judgment against defendant in the amount of $24,105.30, together with interest. On appeal to the Appellate Division the judgment was reversed, with one judge dissenting. Plaintiffs have appealed to this Court as a matter of right.

Holmdel Heights Construction Company was in the process of developing a tract of land upon which it was constructing homes. Defendant, Sugarman, owned slightly more than 18% of the capital stock of this corporation and at all relevant times acted as its attorney. Plaintiff corporations were engaged to do surveying, engineering and professional planning work in connection with the development. The amount of their fees was not fixed by agreement but there has never been any dispute as to the reasonableness of their charges. Some of the invoices they submitted to the developer were paid, but others were not. The total of these unpaid charges continued to increase and plaintiffs became concerned.

On April 14, 1970 an important conference took place in the office of Mr. Sugarman. In addition to Mr. Sugarman there were also present at this meeting Howard M. Schoor, president of the plaintiff corporations, and Lawrence Schwartz, Esq., their attorney. The question of plaintiff's unpaid bills was a principal subject of discussion. Both Mr. Schoor and Mr. Schwartz testified that at this meeting Mr. Sugarman agreed personally to pay all outstanding bills as well as any charges that might be incurred in the future, if plaintiffs would continue with the work they were doing. The developer, Holmdel Heights Construction Company, was then busily engaged in seeking additional financing. Everyone concedes that in order to secure this financing, it was essential that further engineering work be done at once. Mr. Sugarman drew a check on his trust account for $2,000 and gave it to Mr. Schoor. According to the latter, the delivery of the check was accompanied by a statement made by Mr. Sugarman that this was intended to show his good faith in giving his personal guaranty as to payment of the outstanding and continuing obligation. On redirect examination Mr. Schoor again stated,

At the April 14th meeting Mr. Sugarman very pointedly said that the corporation had no money at this time and was giving me his own money to attempt to satisfy me and have us continue to work on the project.

The testimony of Mr. Schwartz was substantially the same.

Defendant disagreed as to the purport of the conversation. His recollection was that after indicating the corporation's lack of liquidity, he gave Schoor the check for $2,000, indicating that that was the best the corporation could do at that time and that as further funds were received by it, additional payments would be made. At about this period Sugarman seems to have been actively managing many of the corporation's financial affairs; large amounts of corporate funds passed through his trust account.

Schoor and Schwartz left the meeting apparently satisfied, and the needed engineering work went forward. On June 12, 1970, Sugarman wrote a letter to Schoor, enclosing a further check in the sum of $1,000. The letter stated,

> I have enclosed to your order a check in the sum of $1,000.00. The Corporation does not have this money. This is my money being submitted to you in good faith because I promised it to you last week. I certainly hope you don't let us down.

The letter also contained a detailed specification of further engineering work that was needed at once in connection with the proposed new financing. Plaintiffs appear to have done all the work requested, but received no further payment. Shortly thereafter Holmdel Heights Construction Company went into receivership and this suit followed.

The trial judge made the following findings of fact:

   1. At the April 14, 1970 meeting Sugarman led Schoor and Schwartz to believe:

   a. that the corporation was in financial difficulty;

   b. that there was a legitimate prospect of securing further financing;

   c. that such financing could not be obtained without further work by Schoor's companies;

   d. Sugarman knew that if Schoor would not continue, the corporation did not have sufficient funds to secure the essential engineering services from another source;

   e. Sugarman believed that the corporation could solve its difficulties as is evidenced by his July 16, 1970 loan of $5,000;[1]

   f. Sugarman had a substantial financial interest in seeing to it that Holmdel Heights was a success;

   g. to induce Schoor to continue work, Sugarman intentionally led Schoor and Schwartz to believe that he was pledging his personal finances to payment of past and future corporate debt to Schoor's companies;

   h. and that this latter finding is corroborated by the language of Sugarman's letter to Schoor on July 16, 1970.[2]

   1. A loan of $5,000 was in fact later made by Sugarman to Holmdel Heights Construction Company on July 16, 1970.

   2. The date should probably be June 12, 1970.

He further concluded that Sugarman

> * * * made an oral promise to Schoor to pay out of his personal finances, if necessary, past and future debts of Holmdel Heights to Schoor's companies in exchange for Schoor's agreement to continue engineering work for the corporation.

The majority of the Appellate Division neither accepted nor rejected these findings, concluding that even if the defendant made a promise to pay, it was unenforceable under the Statute of Frauds. The dissenting member of that Court accepted the findings of the trial judge and also agreed with his resolution of the legal issue.

We have carefully examined the trial record. It contains ample support for the findings and factual conclusions reached by the trial judge. He was in a position to observe the witnesses, take note of their demeanor and acquire a "feel of the case" that cannot make its way to a reviewing tribunal. Even on the cold record, however, we would be inclined to reach the same result. We find that the promise was made.

This brings us to the legal issue. Defendant contends that his promise—conceding it to have been made, as we have concluded it was—is unenforceable under the Statute of Frauds. The relevant section of that act reads as follows:

> No action shall be brought upon any of the following agreements or promises, unless the agreement or promise, upon which such action shall be brought or some memorandum or note thereof, shall be in writing, and signed by the party to be charged therewith, or by some other person thereunto by him lawfully authorized:

> * * *

> b. A special promise to answer for the debt, default or miscarriage of another person; [N.J.S.A. 25:1–5]

It is conceded by everyone that the promise was not in writing, nor was there any written memorandum or note thereof. Defendant contends that the promise—again assuming it to have been made—obligated him only secondarily to pay the debt owed by Holmdel Heights Construction Company in the event it should default, and that as such it comes squarely within the purview of the statute. Plaintiffs argue that the promise was made largely if not principally for defendant's personal benefit, that it did not create a suretyship relationship but rather was an "original" promise resting upon consideration sought by defendant for his personal ends, and that this being so the promise is not controlled by the statute. This latter argument rests upon what is sometimes referred to as the "leading object or main purpose rule." It has been stated as follows:

> When the leading object of the promise or agreement is to become guarantor or surety to the promisee for a debt for which a third party is and continues to be primarily liable, the agreement, whether made before or after or at the time with the promise of the principal, is within the statute, and not binding unless evidenced by writing. On the other hand, when the leading object of the promisor is to subserve some interest or purpose of his own, notwithstanding the effect is to pay or discharge the debt of another, his

promise is not within the statute. [2 *Corbin on Contracts* § 366, at 273–74 (1950)]

Thus in applying this rule, which we think expresses sound doctrine, it becomes important, and probably decisive, to determine what interest, purpose or object was sought to be advanced by defendant's promise to pay plaintiff's fees. As noted above defendant owned slightly more than 18% of the capital stock of Holmdel Heights Construction Company, for which he had paid $10,000. He was also attorney for the corporation and at the time of trial, January 18, 1973, was still owed $14,000 for legal services. Some part of this, how much we are not specifically told, was already owing to him at the time of the April 14, 1970 conference. Defendant, in the course of his testimony, agreed that had the corporation eventually been successful, the amount he would have received upon his investment, together with reasonably anticipated legal fees, would have been a substantial sum.

On the other hand, defendant was acting as counsel for the development corporation and presumably, in this capacity, was doing all he could to maintain its solvency and to further its best interests. The consideration that was sought and received from plaintiffs took the form of a continuing professional effort on their part to provide the developer with vital materials and data intended to become part of its submission to a finance agency in connection with its application for a substantial loan. Obviously this consideration would be of benefit both to defendant personally, even though indirectly, as well as to the client he served.

Although the leading object or main purpose rule has been widely accepted, neither courts nor commentators have reached agreement as to the analytical method that courts should adopt and follow in determining whether a particular set of facts does or does not come within the scope of the rule. Professor Williston identified eight different tests as having been from time to time applied by various courts. 3 *Williston on Contracts* §§ 467–475 (3d ed. Jaeger 1960).

Recent cases in this state seem to have placed most reliance upon the "original-collateral promise" test and the "credit" test. * * * The former test amounts to little more than a restatement of the rule itself and may be stated thus: where the leading object or main purpose of the promisor is to become surety for another's debt, the promise is a collateral one and within the Statute of Frauds; on the other hand, where the principal purpose is to subserve or promote some interest personal to the promisor, then the promise will be deemed an original one and not controlled by the Statute. In applying this test, as is mentioned below, emphasis is placed upon discovering the *leading* object and the *principal* or *main* purpose of the promisor. A chief reason for this approach is that in most cases the consideration for which the new promise is given will clearly benefit *both* the promisor and the original debtor.

The "credit" test calls upon the court to decide to whom in fact credit was given. While this test is useful, it appears to suffer from two drawbacks. In the first place the inquiry focuses upon the subjective intent and state of mind of the promisee. By the time of trial, either consciously or subconsciously, the promisee will probably have come to the conclusion that he extended credit to that person—generally the promisor—who will be the more readily able to respond in damages. Other evidence in the case may very likely be insufficient to overcome what may too often be essentially a self-serving determination by the promisee. In the second place, it will often if not generally be true that the promisee has in fact relied upon the credit of *both* the promisor and the original debtor.

Ct uses Main purpose Rule

* * *

Restatement leading or main purpose test

The leading object or main purpose rule has been set forth in the *Restatement of Contracts* § 184 (1932) in the following form:

> Where the consideration for a promise that all or part of a previously existing duty of a third person to the promisee shall be satisfied is in fact or apparently desired by the promisor mainly for his own pecuniary or business advantage, rather than in order to benefit the third person, the promise is not within [the Statute of Frauds]. * * * [Emphasis added]

does recognize both

The identical formulation of the rule appears in the *Restatement of Security* § 93 (1941). This statement implicitly recognizes what has been adverted to above, that in many if not most cases the consideration for which the new promise is given will be beneficial *both* to the promisor and to the original debtor. Whether or not the Statute of Frauds will apply is then to depend upon whether this consideration was *mainly* desired for the promisor's benefit or for the benefit of the original debtor. In applying this rule the finder of fact must examine all circumstances bearing upon the transaction, the relationship of the parties to one another and endeavor to discern the intent, purpose and object of the promisor. In undertaking this examination the nature of the consideration will be of great if not paramount importance. To what extent will performance by the promisee benefit the promisor, directly or indirectly?

what ct should look @

* * *

* * * A * * * pertinent example appears in the *Restatement of Contracts,* as an illustration under § 184,

> 2.   D owes C $1000. C is about to levy an attachment on D's factory. S, who is also a creditor of D's, fearing that the attachment will ruin D's business and thereby destroy his own chance of collecting his claim, orally promises C that if C will forbear to take legal proceedings against D for three months, S will pay D's debt if D fails to do so. S's promise is enforceable.

Holding

The interest of defendant, Sugarman, in inducing plaintiffs to undertake the work that they did after the April 14 conference seems obvious. His substantial pecuniary and business interest to be furthered is abundantly clear. On the other hand there is little to support the view that he meant to commit his personal assets to so considerable an extent only to further his client's interest. We have no difficulty in agreeing with the trial court and with the dissenting member of the Appellate Division that the consideration was *mainly* desired for his personal benefit.

Accordingly the judgment of the Appellate Division is reversed and the judgment of the Law Division is hereby reinstated.

For reversal: JUSTICES MOUNTAIN, SULLIVAN, PASHMAN, CLIFFORD and SCHREIBER and JUDGE CONFORD—6.

For affirmance: None.　*Specific performance*

Apellants

JONESBORO INVESTMENT CORP. v. CHERRY

Supreme Court of Arkansas, 1965.
239 Ark. 1035, 396 S.W.2d 284.

This is a suit for <u>specific performance</u> filed by appellants, Jonesboro Investment Corporation and M.G. Spurlock, against appellees, James C. Cherry and his wife, Frances D. Cherry. The plaintiffs, appellants here, allege in the complaint that appellees offered to sell and convey a 2,400 acre plantation and equipment thereon to appellants for the consideration of $900,000; that appellants closed the contract by accepting the offer; that appellees breached the contract by refusing to convey the property. Appellees, Mr. & Mrs. Cherry, the property owners, demurred to the complaint on the ground that it shows on its face that the alleged contract is barred by the statute of frauds. The demurrer was sustained. The statute of frauds may be invoked by demurrer. * * *

(motion to dismiss)
demurred stating Stat. of frau
TC Sustained dismissed complaint as um

The pertinent part of the statute of frauds, Ark.Stat.Ann. § 38–101 (Repl.1962) provides:

> "No action shall be brought * * * to charge any person upon any contract for the sale of lands, tenements, or hereditaments, or any interest in or concerning them * * * unless the agreement, promise or contract, upon which such action shall be brought, or some memorandum or note thereof, shall be made in writing, and signed by the party to be charged therewith, or signed by some other person by him thereunto properly authorized."

To affirm the chancellor's action in sustaining the demurrer, the appellees contended that the statute of frauds is applicable because <u>the property to be sold is not sufficiently described</u>; <u>that the memorandum or note relied on by appellants is not sufficient to take the contract to sell out of the statute of frauds insofar as appellants' alleged right to purchase is concerned</u>; and that <u>the written memorandum is not sufficient because it does not show the terms and conditions of the sale and time for payment.</u>

As contend S of F is applicable (3)

We need to discuss only one of the points involved, and that is the question of whether the alleged contract is barred by the statute of frauds because it does not state the conditions and terms of the sale and the time of payment. At first blush it would appear that there can be no valid objection to the contract on this ground. The sale price is given at $900,000 "to be paid according to the price and terms herein given". The price is stated but not the terms. The listing contract was prepared by filling in spaces on a listing contract form. That part of the contract form designated "terms", to be used in showing encumbrances, the down payment, balance owed and how it was to be paid, was left blank.

"terms" section was left blank

Appellants argue that in a situation of this kind it is presumed the agreement is for the payment of the entire purchase price in cash and cites Kempner v. Gans, 87 Ark. 221, 111 S.W. 1123, 112 S.W. 1087. This case does appear to sustain appellants' view. But there, apparently the court determined that the contract did provide for the terms and conditions of the sale.

This court said: "The price was to be $35,500 payable $10,000 cash and the balance to be arranged to the satisfaction of the owners."

* * *

All of our cases directly in point with the case at bar hold that the terms and conditions of the sale must be stated in the written memorandum in order to take the transaction out of the statute of frauds.

Perrin v. Price, 210 Ark. 535, 196 S.W.2d 766, is in point. There, the memorandum in question provided: "Pocahontas, Arkansas, March 5, 1945. Received from W.F. Perrin, $100.00 payment on town lots, north Pocahontas at a price of $1,500.00, known as the J.W. Price pasture lots. (Signed) Clifford Price, Executor." We said: "We think the memorandum or receipt in question here is totally lacking as to the time within which payment was to be made and the method and conditions of payment."

In Kromray v. Stobaugh, 212 Ark. 377, 206 S.W.2d 171, the court said: "In our recent case of Perrin v. Price, 210 Ark. 535, 196 S.W.2d 766, we had occasion to discuss the essentials required of a memorandum to fulfill the Statute of Frauds. Some of our cases are reviewed therein. It may be true, as counsel state, that we have gone further than most courts, to require that all the essential provisions of the contract be in writing in order to satisfy the Statute of Frauds; but at all events, such is our holding, and to it we adhere."

* * *

The listing contract on which appellants rely was made an exhibit to the complaint. As heretofore pointed out, it does not show the terms and conditions of the sale and the time of payment. The chancellor was, therefore, correct in sustaining the demurrer and dismissing the complaint.

Affirmed.

Note
What Kind of Writing?

What kind of writing satisfies the statute of frauds? The answer depends on the language of the statute and the case law thereunder. But it is possible to generalize. The Restatement of Contracts (Second), section 131 states:

Unless additional requirements are prescribed by the particular statute, a contract within the Statute of Frauds is enforceable if it is evidenced by any writing, signed by or on behalf of the party to be charged, which

(a) reasonably identifies the subject matter of the contract,

(b) is sufficient to indicate that a contract with respect thereto has been made between the parties or offered by the signer to the other party, and

(c) states with reasonable certainty the essential terms of the unperformed promises in the contract.

Several further propositions (with Restatement Second section references) also command wide support either in statutory language or case law:

1. The memorandum may take the form of several writings, provided one of them is signed and the evidence shows that they relate to the same transaction. See section 132.

2. In general, the parties do not have to create the writing specifically to serve as a memorandum of a contract. For example, a letter obliquely referring to the contract may suffice. Even a writing that purports to cancel or repudiate the contract will suffice if the writing is otherwise sufficient. See section 133.

3. The signature need not be handwritten. Any symbol will do if made or adopted with the intent of authenticating the writing as that of the signer. See section 134.

4. The memorandum "may be made or signed at any time before or after the formation of the contract." See section 136.

5. If the original memorandum has been lost or destroyed, its contents may be shown by "an unsigned copy or by oral evidence." See section 137.

6. If the memorandum omits or inaccurately states a term, some case law permits the introduction of oral or written evidence to show the term, but only if the parties did not intend the agreement to be complete on its face. When the omission or inaccuracy is due to mutual mistake or fraud, the memorandum can be reformed, thereby satisfying the statute.

See E.A. Farnsworth, Contracts 400 (3d ed. 1999).

McINTOSH v. MURPHY

Supreme Court of Hawaii, 1970.
52 Hawaii 29, 52 Hawaii 112, 469 P.2d 177.

Levinson, Justice.

This case involves an oral employment contract which allegedly violates the provision of the Statute of Frauds requiring "any agreement that is not to be performed within one year from the making thereof" to be in writing in order to be enforceable. HRS § 656–1(5). In this action the plaintiff-employee Dick McIntosh seeks to recover damages from his employer, George Murphy and Murphy Motors, Ltd., for the breach of an alleged one-year oral employment contract.

While the facts are in sharp conflict, it appears that defendant George Murphy was in southern California during March, 1964 interviewing prospective management personnel for his Chevrolet–Oldsmobile dealerships in Hawaii. He interviewed the plaintiff twice during that time. The position of sales manager for one of the dealerships was fully discussed but no contract was entered into. In April, 1964 the plaintiff received a call from the general manager of Murphy Motors informing him of possible employment within thirty days if he was still available. The plaintiff indicated his continued interest and informed the manager that he would be available. Later in April, the plaintiff sent Murphy a telegram to the effect that he would arrive in Honolulu on Sunday, April 26, 1964. Murphy then telephoned McIntosh on Saturday, April 25, 1964 to notify him that the job of assistant sales manager was open and work would begin on the following Monday, April 27, 1964. At that time McIntosh expressed surprise at the change in job title from sales manager to assistant sales manager but reconfirmed the fact that he was arriving in Honolulu the next day, Sunday. McIntosh arrived on Sunday, April 26, 1964 and began work on the following day, Monday, April 27, 1964.

As a consequence of his decision to work for Murphy, McIntosh moved some of his belongings from the mainland to Hawaii, sold other possessions, leased an apartment in Honolulu and obviously forwent any other employment opportunities. In short, the plaintiff did all those things which were incidental to changing one's residence permanently from Los Angeles to Honolulu, a distance of approximately 2200 miles. McIntosh continued working for Murphy until July 16, 1964, approximately two and one-half months, at which time he was discharged on the grounds that he was unable to close deals with prospective customers and could not train the salesmen.

At the conclusion of the trial, the defense moved for a directed verdict arguing that the oral employment agreement was in violation of the Statute of Frauds, there being no written memorandum or note thereof. The trial court ruled that as a matter of law the contract did not come within the Statute, reasoning that Murphy bargained for acceptance by the actual commencement of performance by McIntosh, so that McIntosh was not bound by a contract until he came to work on Monday, April 27, 1964. Therefore, assuming that the contract was for a year's employment, it was performable within a year exactly to the day and no writing was required for it to be enforceable. Alternatively, the court ruled that if the agreement was made final by the telephone call between the parties on Saturday, April 25, 1964, then that part of the weekend which remained would not be counted in calculating the year, thus taking the contract out of the Statute of Frauds. With commendable candor the trial judge gave as the motivating force for the decision his desire to avoid a mechanical and unjust application of the Statute.[1]

The case went to the jury on the following questions: (1) whether the contract was for a year's duration or was performable on a trial basis, thus making it terminable at the will of either party; (2) whether the plaintiff was discharged for just cause; and (3) if he was not discharged for just cause, what damages were due the plaintiff. The jury returned a verdict for the plaintiff in the sum of $12,103.40. The defendants appeal to this court on four principal grounds, three of which we find to be without merit. The remaining ground of appeal is whether the plaintiff can maintain an action on the alleged oral employment contract in light of the prohibition of the Statute of Frauds making unenforceable an oral contract that is not to be performed within one year.

I. Time of Acceptance of the Employment Agreement

The defendants contend that the trial court erred in refusing to give an instruction to the jury that if the employment agreement was made more than one day before the plaintiff began performance, there could be no recovery by the plaintiff. The reason given was that a contract not to be performed within one year from its making is unenforceable if not in writing.

The defendants are correct in their argument that the time of acceptance of an offer is a question of fact for the jury to decide. But the trial court

1. THE COURT: You make the law look ridiculous, because one day is Sunday and the man does not work on Sunday; the other day is Saturday; he is up in Fresno. He can't work down there. And he is down here Sunday night and shows up for work on Monday. To me that is a contract within a year. I don't want to make the law look ridiculous, Mr. Clause, because it is one day later, one day too much, and that one day is a Sunday, and a non-working day.

alternatively decided that even if the offer was accepted on the Saturday prior to the commencement of performance, the intervening Sunday and part of Saturday would not be counted in computing the year for the purposes of the Statute of Frauds. The judge stated that Sunday was a non-working day and only a fraction of Saturday was left which he would not count. In any event, there is no need to discuss the relative merits of either ruling since we base our decision in this case on the doctrine of equitable estoppel which was properly briefed and argued by both parties before this court, although not presented to the trial court.

II.   ENFORCEMENT BY VIRTUE OF ACTION IN RELIANCE ON THE ORAL CONTRACT

In determining whether a rule of law can be fashioned and applied to a situation where an oral contract admittedly violates a strict interpretation of the Statute of Frauds, it is necessary to review the Statute itself together with its historical and modern functions. The Statute of Frauds, which requires that certain contracts be in writing in order to be legally enforceable, had its inception in the days of Charles II of England. Hawaii's version of the Statute is found in HRS § 656–1 and is substantially the same as the original English Statute of Frauds.

The first English Statute was enacted almost 300 years ago to prevent "many fraudulent practices, which are commonly endeavored to be upheld by perjury and subornation of perjury". 29 Car. 2, c. 3 (1677). Certainly, there were compelling reasons in those days for such a law. At the time of enactment in England, the jury system was quite unreliable, rules of evidence were few, and the complaining party was disqualified as a witness so he could neither testify on direct-examination nor, more importantly, be cross-examined. Summers, The Doctrine of Estoppel and the Statute of Frauds, 79 U.Pa.L.Rev. 440, 441 (1931). The aforementioned structural and evidentiary limitations on our system of justice no longer exist.

Retention of the Statute today has nevertheless been justified on at least three grounds: (1) the Statute still serves an evidentiary function thereby lessening the danger of perjured testimony (the original rationale); (2) the requirement of a writing has a cautionary effect which causes reflection by the parties on the importance of the agreement; and (3) the writing is an easy way to distinguish enforceable contracts from those which are not, thus channelling certain transactions into written form.[2]

In spite of whatever utility the Statute of Frauds may still have, its applicability has been drastically limited by judicial construction over the years in order to mitigate the harshness of a mechanical application.[3] Further-

---

2. Fuller, Consideration and Form, 41 Colum.L.Rev. 799, 800–03 (1941); Note: Statute of Frauds—The Doctrine of Equitable Estoppel and the Statute of Frauds. 66 Mich.L.Rev. 170 (1967).

3. Thus a promise to pay the debt of another has been construed to encompass only promises made to a creditor which do not benefit the promisor (Restatement of Contracts § 184 (1932); 3 Williston, Contracts § 452 (Jaeger ed. 1960)); a promise in consideration of marriage has been interpreted to exclude mutual prom-

ises to marry (Restatement, *supra* § 192; 3 Williston, *supra* § 485); a promise not to be performed within one year means a promise not performable within one year (Restatement, *supra* § 198; 3 Williston, *supra,* § 495); a promise not to be performed within one year may be removed from the Statute of Frauds if one party has fully performed (Restatement, *supra* § 198; 3 Williston, *supra* § 504); and the Statute will not be applied where all promises involved are fully performed (Restatement, *supra* § 219; 3 Williston, *supra* § 528).

courts use
part
perform
or
equitable
estoppel

more, learned writers continue to disparage the Statute regarding it as "a statute for promoting fraud" and a "legal anachronism."[4]

Another method of judicial circumvention of the Statute of Frauds has grown out of the exercise of the equity powers of the courts. Such judicially imposed limitations or exceptions involved the traditional dispensing power of the equity courts to mitigate the "harsh" rule of law. When courts have enforced an oral contract in spite of the Statute, they have utilized the legal labels of "part performance" or "equitable estoppel" in granting relief. Both doctrines are said to be based on the concept of estoppel, which operates to avoid unconscionable injury. * * *

PART
PERFOR

Part performance has long been recognized in Hawaii as an equitable doctrine justifying the enforcement of an oral agreement for the conveyance of an interest in land where there has been substantial reliance by the party seeking to enforce the contract. * * * Other courts have enforced oral contracts (including employment contracts) which failed to satisfy the section of the Statute making unenforceable an agreement not to be performed within a year of its making. This has occurred where the conduct of the parties gave rise to an estoppel to assert the Statute. * * *

It is appropriate for modern courts to cast aside the raiments of conceptualism which cloak the true policies underlying the reasoning behind the many decisions enforcing contracts that violate the Statute of Frauds. There is certainly no need to resort to legal rubrics or meticulous legal formulas when better explanations are available. The policy behind enforcing an oral agreement which violated the Statute of Frauds, as a policy of avoiding unconscionable injury, was well set out by the California Supreme Court. In Monarco v. Lo Greco, 35 Cal.2d 621, 623, 220 P.2d 737, 739 (1950), a case which involved an action to enforce an oral contract for the conveyance of land on the grounds of 20 years performance by the promisee, the court said:

policy
of
state
of
fraud

> The doctrine of estoppel to assert the statute of frauds has been consistently applied by the courts of this state to prevent fraud that would result from refusal to enforce oral contracts in certain circumstances. Such fraud may inhere in the unconscionable injury that would result from denying enforcement of the contract after one party has been induced by the other seriously to change his position in reliance on the contract * * *.

In seeking to frame a workable test which is flexible enough to cover diverse factual situations and also provide some reviewable standards, we find very persuasive section [139] of the Second Restatement of Contracts. That section specifically covers those situations where there has been reliance on an oral contract which falls within the Statute of Frauds. Section [139] states:

TEST
from
Restatem

> (1) A promise which the promisor should reasonably expect to induce action or forbearance on the part of the promisee or a third person and which does induce the action or forbearance is enforceable notwithstanding the Statute of Frauds if injustice can be avoided only by enforcement of the promise. The remedy granted for breach is to be limited as justice requires.

4. Burdick, A Statute for Promoting Fraud, 16 Colum.L.Rev. 273 (1916); Willis, The Statute of Frauds—A Legal Anachronism, 3 Ind. L.J. 427, 528 (1928).

(2) In determining whether injustice can be avoided only by enforcement of the promise, the following circumstances are significant: (a) the availability and adequacy of other remedies, particularly cancellation and restitution; (b) the definite and substantial character of the action or forbearance in relation to the remedy sought; (c) the extent to which the action or forbearance corroborates evidence of the making and terms of the promise, or the making and terms are otherwise established by clear and convincing evidence; (d) the reasonableness of the action or forbearance; (e) the extent to which the action or forbearance was foreseeable by the promisor.

We think that the approach taken in the Restatement is the proper method of giving the trial court the necessary latitude to relieve a party of the hardships of the Statute of Frauds. Other courts have used similar approaches in dealing with oral employment contracts upon which an employee had seriously relied. See Alaska Airlines, Inc. v. Stephenson, 217 F.2d 295 (9th Cir.1954); Seymour v. Oelrichs, 156 Cal. 782, 106 P. 88 (1909). This is to be preferred over having the trial court bend over backwards to take the contract out of the Statute of Frauds. In the present case the trial court admitted just this inclination and forthrightly followed it.

There is no dispute that the action of the plaintiff in moving 2200 miles from Los Angeles to Hawaii was foreseeable by the defendant. In fact, it was required to perform his duties. Injustice can only be avoided by the enforcement of the contract and the granting of money damages. No other remedy is adequate. The plaintiff found himself residing in Hawaii without a job.

It is also clear that a contract of some kind did exist. The plaintiff performed the contract for two and one-half months receiving $3,484.60 for his services. The exact length of the contract, whether terminable at will as urged by the defendant, or for a year from the time when the plaintiff started working, was up to the jury to decide.

In sum, the trial court might have found that enforcement of the contract was warranted by virtue of the plaintiff's reliance on the defendant's promise. Naturally, each case turns on its own facts. Certainly there is considerable discretion for a court to implement the true policy behind the Statute of Frauds, which is to prevent fraud or any other type of unconscionable injury. We therefore affirm the judgment of the trial court on the ground that the plaintiff's reliance was such that injustice could only be avoided by enforcement of the contract.

Affirmed.

ABE, JUSTICE (dissenting).

The majority of the court has affirmed the judgment of the trial court; however, I respectfully dissent.

I.

Whether alleged contract of employment came within the Statute of Frauds:

As acknowledged by this court, the trial judge erred when as a matter of law he ruled that the alleged employment contract did not come within the

Statute of Frauds; however, I cannot agree that this error was not prejudicial as this court intimates.

On this issue, the date that the alleged contract was entered into was all important and the date of acceptance of an offer by the plaintiff was a question of fact for the jury to decide. In other words, it was for the jury to determine when the alleged one-year employment contract was entered into and if the jury had found that the plaintiff had accepted the offer[1] more than one day before plaintiff was to report to work, the contract would have come within the Statute of Frauds and would have been unenforceable. * * *

II.

majority opinion

This court holds that though the alleged one-year employment contract came within the Statute of Frauds, nevertheless the judgment of the trial court is affirmed "on the ground that the plaintiff's reliance was such that injustice could only be avoided by enforcement of the contract."

I believe this court is begging the issue by its holding because to reach that conclusion, this court is ruling that the defendant agreed to hire the plaintiff under a one-year employment contract. The defendant has denied that the plaintiff was hired for a period of one year and has introduced into evidence testimony of witnesses that all hiring by the defendant in the past has been on a trial basis. The defendant also testified that he had hired the plaintiff on a trial basis.

Here on one hand the plaintiff claimed that he had a one-year employment contract; on the other hand, the defendant claimed that the plaintiff had not been hired for one year but on a trial basis for so long as his services were satisfactory. I believe the Statute of Frauds was enacted to avoid the consequences this court is forcing upon the defendant. In my opinion, the legislature enacted the Statute of Frauds to negate claims such as has been made by the plaintiff in this case. But this court holds that because the plaintiff in reliance of the one-year employment contract (alleged to have been entered into by the plaintiff, but denied by the defendant) has changed his position, "injustice could only be avoided by enforcement of the contract." Where is the sense of justice?

Now assuming that the defendant had agreed to hire the plaintiff under a one-year employment contract and the contract came within the Statute of Frauds, I cannot agree, as intimated by this court, that we should circumvent the Statute of Frauds by the exercise of the equity powers of courts. As to statutory law, the sole function of the judiciary is to interpret the statute and the judiciary should not usurp legislative power and enter into the legislative field. A.C. Chock, Ltd. v. Kaneshiro, 51 Haw. 87, 93, 451 P.2d 809 (1969); Miller v. Miller, 41 Ohio Op. 233, 83 N.E.2d 254 (Ct.C.P.1948). Thus, if the Statute of Frauds is too harsh as intimated by this court, and it brings about undue hardship, it is for the legislature to amend or repeal the statute and not for this court to legislate.

UNIFORM COMMERCIAL CODE § 2–201.

Formal Requirements; Statute of Frauds

(1) Except as otherwise provided in this section a contract for the sale of goods for the price of $500 or more is not enforceable by way of action or

---

1. Plaintiff testified that he accepted the offer in California over the telephone.

defense unless there is some writing sufficient to indicate that a contract for sale has been made between the parties and signed by the party against whom enforcement is sought or by his authorized agent or broker. A writing is not insufficient because it omits or incorrectly states a term agreed upon but the contract is not enforceable under this paragraph beyond the quantity of goods shown in such writing.

(2) Between merchants if within a reasonable time a writing in confirmation of the contract and sufficient against the sender is received and the party receiving it has reason to know its contents, it satisfies the requirements of subsection (1) against such party unless written notice of objection to its contents is given within 10 days after it is received.

(3) A contract which does not satisfy the requirements of subsection (1) but which is valid in other respects is enforceable

(a) if the goods are to be specially manufactured for the buyer and are not suitable for sale to others in the ordinary course of the seller's business and the seller, before notice of repudiation is received and under circumstances which reasonably indicate that the goods are for the buyer, has made either a substantial beginning of their manufacture or commitments for their procurement; or

(b) if the party against whom enforcement is sought admits in his pleading, testimony or otherwise in court that a contract for sale was made, but the contract is not enforceable under this provision beyond the quantity of goods admitted; or

(c) with respect to goods for which payment has been made and accepted or which have been received and accepted (Sec. 2–606).

Note
Part Performance and the Statute of Frauds

Reliance in the form of part performance may be sufficient to bar assertion of the statute of frauds as a defense. McNamee Schmetterer Euro RSCG Inc. v. Aegis Group, 93 N.Y.2d 229, 689 N.Y.S.2d 674, 711 N.E.2d 953 (1999). For example, under section 2–201(3)(c) of the Uniform Commercial Code, an oral agreement for the sale of goods is enforceable "with respect to goods for which payment has been made and accepted or which have been received and accepted." Why this approach? Official Comment 1 to Section 2–201 states that "[a]ll that is required is that the writing afford a basis for believing that the offered oral evidence rests on a real transaction." Does part performance, for example, part payment for the goods, provide a reliable substitute for such a writing?

Generally, in an action for damages, part performance of an oral land sale contract does not remove the bar of the statute of frauds. In addition, courts generally hold that a vendee's partial (or sometimes even full) payment of the price in a suit for specific performance does not remove the bar of the statute of frauds. More is required than "something beyond injury adequately compensable in money." Jasmin v. Alberico, 135 Vt. 287, 290, 376 A.2d 32, 33 (1977). For example, if the vendee takes possession with the vendor's assent and makes improvements or pays a portion of the price, the vendee can get specific performance. Review again Seavey v. Drake (page 82). Was there part performance in that case?

An employee's part performance of an employment contract with a duration of more than one year generally does not take the contract out of the statute of frauds. Consider, for example, a football coach who accepts a university's seven-year, seven million dollar contract. After four months on the job, but before the parties sign a written contract, the coach is fired for alleged misbehavior. (This is based on a real event.) The coach cannot enforce the seven-year contract even if the firing was wrongful.

Problem 2–10

1. If the requirement of consideration is satisfied, is it necessary to satisfy any otherwise applicable statute of frauds requirement? Yes,

2. Is the statute of frauds applicable to each of the theories of obligation studied in this chapter? Answer this question with reference to the Hawaii statute, a common version of the statute of frauds. No. Partial perform reliance

FRY, X MARKS THE SPOT: NEW TECHNOLOGIES COMPEL NEW CONCEPTS FOR COMMERCIAL LAW

26 Loy.L.A.L.Rev. 607, 607–609, 611–612, 622 (1993).

Predictions of a paperless society have been around for years—so many years that many of us no longer pay much attention. In spite of all the prophesying, people still write checks, send letters and reduce agreements to paper. Office supply stores and catalogs are filled with pads of standard form purchase orders, invoices, notes and leases, which are ready for the small business to purchase.

While paper has not disappeared—and shows few signs of doing so—some of the prophets' predictions of a paperless society have come and will continue to come to pass. We may not eliminate paper in the foreseeable future, but a constantly increasing stream of transactions are consummated without the use of a single piece of paper. Still more are consummated in reliance on information transmitted electronically, and pieces of paper are generated after the fact only to be placed in overstuffed filing cabinets and forgotten.

Currently, approximately five percent of sales transactions are conducted through the use of standardized computer-to-computer communications. In the paper-based sales transaction familiar to most of us, a clerk inserts information into blanks on standardized paper forms, copies of which are sent to trading partners and relevant intracompany departments, such as shipping and accounting. Not too long ago the paper form would have been mailed to the addressee; today it may be faxed. In other situations, the information may be telephoned and the papers filled out and mailed (or faxed) only after a verbal agreement has been reached. In any of these scenarios, the paper may be stored in a filing cabinet, or the information may be scanned into a computer and stored on disc.

In a firm using computer-to-computer methods, standard forms are completed on the computer screen by clerical workers and then transmitted via modem to the intended recipient. The recipient's computer will receive the data contained in these standardized formats, process it, perhaps signal acceptance of transactions and instruct the appropriate departments to process the order, prepare to receive the goods and so forth.

The entire sales cycle, from bid solicitation, purchase order and acceptance, through shipment and delivery of goods and payment for them, can be effected without the need to produce a single piece of paper. A record of the transaction, from inception through closure, may be stored electronically in a reliable, enduring manner, and the necessary information may be relayed to the appropriate departments through the company's computer network. Using a computer network, the cycle may be completed at a significant savings in processing costs, with a reduction in processing errors by eliminating any need to transcribe information onto new forms, and permitting information to be stored in less physical space for a period at least as long as the life of a piece of paper. Fewer employees are required to process the information for each discrete transaction. The efficiencies that may be achieved in this manner are critical to implementing improved methods of production, such as just-in-time and quick-response production modes.

* * *

The benefits of a memorial of a transaction may now exist without paper; no longer does the absence of paper mean reliance on human memory. Many of the functions formerly served exclusively by paper may be served by relying on information stored on computer discs, tapes and memories. Adapting to these simple facts, both operationally and in terms of understanding the processes involved, takes time and experience.

Parties to electronically based sales transactions believe they have the right to expect one another to perform, deliver and pay for the goods in a timely manner. But for commercial law assumptions of the existence of paper, there is little reason to believe that once the fact of a transaction is established a court would refuse to enforce it. For several years, commentators have suggested various approaches to resolve the difficulties raised by paper requirements, but each of these suggestions has turned ultimately on the reform of commercial law to accommodate electronically based transactions.

* * *

[O]ne of the first targets for reformers has been UCC section 1–201(46) which states: " 'Written' or 'writing' includes printing, typewriting or any other intentional reduction to tangible form." * * *

* * *

One approach to writing requirements is to revise the definition of "written" or "writing" contained in section 1–201(46). The revision might explicitly include certain forms of technology, as was done in the United Nations Convention on Contracts for the International Sale of Goods (CISG). While such an approach furnishes clarity, it may be outdated as soon as new technologies are adopted; the Convention does not incorporate into its definition computer-to-computer communications or electronic storage of data, although both are used increasingly in commerce.

A second method of revision would seek to devise statutory language broad enough to incorporate future technologies as they emerge (in other words, be media neutral). * * *

* * *

A number of words have been suggested, but at the moment "record" is favored as a label for the concept. The dictionary definitions of the word "record" include the idea of "writing" something down, or placing the information in some permanent or durable form. The word also embraces the idea of a number of other media, including phonographs, tapes and compact discs. Thus, the connotations borne by the word "record" suggest the desired media neutrality.

Note
The Statute of Frauds and Electronic Contracting

The 2003 Amendments to Uniform Commercial Code section 2–201 deal with electronic contracting and the statute of frauds. Section 2–201(a) provides that

> [A] contract for the sale of goods for the price of $5000 or more is not enforceable by way of action or defense unless there is some record sufficient to indicate that a contract for sale has been made between the parties and signed by the party against which enforcement is sought or by the party's authorized agent or broker.

Section 2–103(1)(m) defines "record" as "information that is inscribed on a tangible medium or that is stored in an electronic or other medium and is retrievable in perceivable form." Section 2–103(1)(p) defines "sign" as follows: "with present intent to authenticate or adopt a record: (i) to execute or adopt a tangible symbol; or (ii) to attach to or logically associate with the record an electronic sound, symbol, or process." (At the time of publication of this book, no state had enacted these amendments.)

The Electronic Signatures in Global and National Commerce Act, 15 U.S.C. § 7001 (as amended 2006), allows parties to bind themselves to contracts online through electronic signatures. The law governs, among other things, banking, insurance and brokerage contracts made online. For more on this act, see, e.g., Carl, Ciocchetti, Barton & Christensen, Are Online Business Transactions Executed by Electronic Signatures Legally Binding? 2001 Duke LTR 5.

Problem 2–11

Review: Alec had roto-tilled his lawn, readying it for some sorely needed seeding. Unfortunately, he injured his back and was not able to seed the lawn himself. Time was of the essence because it was getting hot. Alec asked his neighbor, Iris, for help. She agreed to help, worked for three days, and completed the job. Nothing was said at the time about payment. Months later, while admiring his lawn, Alec told Iris that it was about time for him to "settle up." He asked her how much he owed her and, after protestations, she replied that $250 would be fine. Later Alec refused to pay anything. Iris consults you about possible causes of action and possible recoveries. Advise! (Before working through this problem, you should reread the introduction and peruse the general contents of this chapter.)

*

Chapter Three

REMEDIES

> *Different measures of recovery*
> *cannot be [explained] without an*
> *inquiry into the reasons which*
> *underlie the enforcement of*
> *promises generally.*
>
> Fuller

SECTION ONE: REMEDIES AND
THE ROLE OF LAWYERS

We have now studied a variety of theories of obligation that serve as general bases for imposing particular legal duties. Typically, the parties honor their duties and no dispute arises. But when a party fails to perform a duty or repudiates a duty not yet due, the general law of remedies becomes relevant. Of course, even in the face of a significant breach, the aggrieved party may not seek a remedy. For example, that party may want to preserve the relationship, hoping to do business with the breacher in the future. But not infrequently, the aggrieved party sees a lawyer, and the lawyer will, among other things, turn to the general law of remedies at an early stage. This body of law incorporates rules dealing with such topics as: the general availability of damages for breach or repudiation; the different measures of damages; unforeseeability and other limits on recoverable damages; restitutionary relief in promissory contexts; the validity of private remedial clauses in agreements; specific performance and other forms of specific relief; and punitive damages.

The general law of remedies is fundamental and important. Indeed, one must study the remedies available for breach of a duty arising under a theory of obligation before that theory can be completely understood. The general law of remedies itself starkly reveals most of the leading policies of contract and related law, and is worthy of special emphasis for this reason.

Lawyers turn to the general law of remedies as planners, drafters, interpreters, counselors, negotiators, and litigators. While much of this law cannot be varied or displaced by the parties' agreement, the parties do enjoy significant freedom to include their own remedial provisions. When planning an agreement, the lawyer must consider the limits on the power of private parties to create their own remedies. The effective lawyer works within such limits to plan and draft remedial provisions that meet the particular needs of the client.

When planning an arrangement or when helping to settle a dispute, the lawyer is frequently called upon to interpret and apply general law governing available remedies, as well as to interpret and apply contract clauses setting forth remedies. The lawyer also commonly negotiates the settlement of disputes against the background of a particular remedy likely to be available if settlement fails. In addition, the lawyer advises the client concerning appropriate conduct after the other party's breach so the client will not pile up losses that will be uncompensated under the general law of remedies. Of course, when preparing for and litigating lawsuits, lawyers must keep their eyes riveted on the specific judicial remedy or remedies available at the end of the line.

Because of the interplay between theories of obligation and remedies (already explored to a limited extent in the first two chapters), it should be no surprise that this chapter, too, is organized mainly around theories of obligation.

SECTION TWO: REMEDIAL THEORY— SOME FUNDAMENTALS

POUND, THE LIMITS OF EFFECTIVE LEGAL ACTION
3 A.B.A.J. 55, 67–68 (1917).

Law secures interests by punishment, by prevention, by specific redress and by substitutional redress; and the wit of man has discovered no further possibilities of judicial action. * * * [I]n the great majority of cases substitutional redress by way of money damages is the only resource, and this has been the staple remedy of the law at all times.

FULLER AND PERDUE, THE RELIANCE INTEREST IN CONTRACT DAMAGES
46 Yale L.J. 52, 53–57 (1936).

The Purposes Pursued in Awarding Contract Damages

It is convenient to distinguish three principal purposes which may be pursued in awarding contract damages. These purposes, and the situations in which they become appropriate, may be stated briefly as follows:

First, the plaintiff has in reliance on the promise of the defendant conferred some value on the defendant. The defendant fails to perform his promise. The court may force the defendant to disgorge the value he received from the plaintiff. The object here may be termed the prevention of gain by the defaulting promisor at the expense of the promisee; more briefly, the prevention of unjust enrichment. The interest protected may be called the *restitution interest.* For our present purposes it is quite immaterial how the suit in such a case be classified, whether as contractual or quasi-contractual, whether as a suit to enforce the contract or as a suit based upon a rescission of the contract. These questions relate to the superstructure of the law, not to the basic policies with which we are concerned.

Secondly, the plaintiff has in reliance on the promise of the defendant changed his position. For example, the buyer under a contract for the sale of land has incurred expense in the investigation of the seller's title, or has neglected the opportunity to enter other contracts. We may award damages to the plaintiff for the purpose of undoing the harm which his reliance on the defendant's promise has caused him. Our object is to put him in as good a position as he was in before the promise was made. The interest protected in this case may be called the *reliance interest.*

Thirdly, without insisting on reliance by the promisee or enrichment of the promisor, we may seek to give the promisee the value of the expectancy which the promise created. We may in a suit for specific performance actually compel the defendant to render the promised performance to the plaintiff, or, in a suit for damages, we may make the defendant pay the money value of this performance. Here our object is to put the plaintiff in as good a position as he would have occupied had the defendant performed his promise. The interest protected in this case we may call the *expectation interest.*

It will be observed that what we have called the *restitution interest* unites two elements: (1) reliance by the promisee, (2) a resultant gain to the promisor. It may for some purposes be necessary to separate these elements. In some cases a defaulting promisor may after his breach be left with an unjust gain which was not taken from the promisee (a third party furnished the consideration), or which was not the result of reliance by the promisee (the promisor violated a promise not to appropriate the promisee's goods). Even in those cases where the promisor's gain results from the promisee's reliance it may happen that damages will be assessed somewhat differently, depending on whether we take the promisor's gain or the promisee's loss as the standard of measurement. Generally, however, in the cases we shall be discussing, gain by the promisor will be accompanied by a corresponding and, so far as its legal measurement is concerned, identical loss to the promisee, so that for our purposes the most workable classification is one which presupposes in the restitution interest a correlation of promisor's gain and promisee's loss. If, as we shall assume, the gain involved in the restitution interest results from and is identical with the plaintiff's loss through reliance, then the restitution interest is merely a special case of the reliance interest; all of the cases coming under the restitution interest will be covered by the reliance interest, and the reliance interest will be broader than the restitution interest only to the extent that it includes cases where the plaintiff has relied on the defendant's promise without enriching the defendant.

It should not be supposed that the distinction here taken between the reliance and expectation interests coincides with that sometimes taken between "losses caused" (damnum emergens) and "gains prevented" (lucrum cessans). In the first place, though reliance ordinarily results in "losses" of an affirmative nature (expenditures of labor and money) it is also true that opportunities for gain may be foregone in reliance on a promise. Hence the reliance interest must be interpreted as at least potentially covering "gains prevented" as well as "losses caused". (Whether "gains prevented" through reliance on a promise are properly compensable in damages is a question not here determined. Obviously, certain scruples concerning "causality" and "foreseeability" are suggested. It is enough for our present purpose to note that there is nothing in the definition of the reliance interest itself which would exclude items of this sort from consideration.) On the other hand, it is not possible to make the expectation interest entirely synonymous with "gains prevented". The disappointment of an expectancy often entails losses of a positive character.

It is obvious that the three "interests" we have distinguished do not present equal claims to judicial intervention. It may be assumed that ordinary standards of justice would regard the need for judicial intervention as decreasing in the order in which we have listed the three interests. The "restitution interest," involving a combination of unjust impoverishment with unjust gain, presents the strongest case for relief. If, following Aristotle, we regard the purpose of justice as the maintenance of an equilibrium of goods among members of society, the restitution interest presents twice as strong a claim to judicial intervention as the reliance interest, since if A not only causes B to lose one unit but appropriates that unit to himself, the resulting discrepancy between A and B is not one unit but two.

On the other hand, the promisee who has actually relied on the promise, even though he may not thereby have enriched the promisor, certainly presents a more pressing case for relief than the promisee who merely demands satisfaction for his disappointment in not getting what was promised him. In passing from compensation for change of position to compensation for loss of expectancy we pass, to use Aristotle's terms again, from the realm of corrective justice to that of distributive justice. The law no longer seeks merely to heal a disturbed status quo, but to bring into being a new situation. It ceases to act defensively or restoratively, and assumes a more active role. With the transition, the justification for legal relief loses its self-evident quality. It is as a matter of fact no easy thing to explain why the normal rule of contract recovery should be that which measures damages by the value of the promised performance.

CHARNY, NONLEGAL SANCTIONS IN COMMERCIAL RELATIONSHIPS

104 Harv.L.Rev. 373, 392–95 (1990).

The nonlegal sanction for breach of a commitment is the sacrifice of something valuable to the breaching party—a value often called the "bond" posted by that party. Three types of bonds are common in commercial transactions. The simplest type of nonlegal sanction is the sacrifice of *a relationship-specific prospective advantage*. The committing party places a particular asset under the control of another party; that party will confiscate or destroy the asset if the promisor breaches. The posting of collateral for a loan provides a familiar, albeit imperfect, example. Other examples include a franchisor's rendering the franchisee's investment worthless by revoking the right to use a trademark and a bank's destroying a small business by cutting off a line of credit or calling a note payable on demand. A particularly important and common form of relationship-specific prospective advantage is the opportunity to deal again with the same transactor—the "repeat deal." The asset posted is the value of future dealings; if one party breaches, the other party will terminate the relationship and refuse to deal with the breacher again, destroying the asset.

A second type of nonlegal sanction is loss of *reputation* among market participants. The promisor develops a reputation for reliability among market participants who are potential transactors. If the promisor improperly breaches his commitments, he damages his reputation and thereby loses valuable opportunities for future trade. Familiar examples of reputational bonds include trademarks in consumer markets and credit ratings for individual and corporate borrowers.

A third type of nonlegal sanction is the sacrifice of *psychic and social goods*. The breaching promisor may suffer loss of opportunities for important or pleasurable associations with others, loss of self-esteem, feelings of guilt, or an unfulfilled desire to think of himself as trustworthy and competent. An unsavory businessperson may be snubbed at the local club or suffer pangs of guilt during the Sunday sermon. Encouraging trust among workers or long-term customers is one function of the "corporate culture" of firms and of the feeling of responsibility to clientele that may develop at schools, banks, or other "quasi-public" institutions.

These three types of nonlegal sanctions operate side-by-side with legal sanctions. Most commercial relationships involve some commitments that are legally enforceable; some commitments that are legally enforceable but are also, or primarily, enforced by nonlegal sanctions; and some commitments that are enforced exclusively by nonlegal sanctions. For example, commitments regarding consumer product quality are legally enforceable under warranty provisions. However, nonlegal sanctions—particularly the manufacturer's reputation in consumer markets—are the major determinant of the manufacturer's adherence to commitments to maintain product quality above minimal standards. The warranty provisions cover only basic features of the goods, and for many products it is too costly for consumers to sue to enforce even these basic commitments.

Indeed, contracts that formally provide for legal sanctions depend upon nonlegal sanctions for their effectiveness whenever the legal sanctions are ineffective in inducing the promisor to perform. Though the contract is legally enforceable as a formal matter, the promisor may be judgment-proof or the promisee may not find it worthwhile to sue if breach occurs. For example, Macaulay's often-cited data that merchants rarely sued when sales contracts were breached suggest that those contracts were primarily enforced through nonlegal sanctions. On this interpretation of the data, the legally enforceable contract formally stated the parties' obligations, but nonlegal pressures—particularly concern with business reputation—actually induced compliance.

SECTION THREE: EXPECTANCY DAMAGES FOR BREACH OF AN AGREEMENT WITH CONSIDERATION—THE RULE, ITS RATIONALES, AND ITS APPLICATION IN VARIOUS CONTEXTS

GROVES v. JOHN WUNDER CO.

Supreme Court of Minnesota, 1939.
205 Minn. 163, 286 N.W. 235.

STONE, JUSTICE.

Action for breach of contract. Plaintiff got judgment for a little over $15,000. Sorely disappointed by that sum, he appeals.

In August, 1927, S.J. Groves & Sons Company, a corporation (hereinafter mentioned simply as Groves), owned a tract of 24 acres of Minneapolis suburban real estate. It was served or easily could be reached by railroad trackage. It is zoned as heavy industrial property. But for lack of development of the neighborhood its principal value thus far may have been in the deposit of sand and gravel which it carried. The Groves company had a plant on the premises for excavating and screening the gravel. Nearby defendant owned and was operating a similar plant.

In August, 1927, Groves and defendant made the involved contract. For the most part it was a lease from Groves, as lessor, to defendant, as lessee; its term seven years. Defendant agreed to remove the sand and gravel and to leave the property "at a uniform grade, substantially the same as the grade now existing at the roadway * * * on said premises, and that in stripping the overburden * * * it will use said overburden for the purpose of maintaining and establishing said grade."

Under the contract defendant got the Groves screening plant. The transfer thereof and the right to remove the sand and gravel made the consideration moving from Groves to defendant, except that defendant incidentally got rid of Groves as a competitor. On defendant's part it paid Groves $105,000. So that from the outset, on Groves' part the contract was executed except for defendant's right to continue using the property for the stated term. (Defendant had a right to renewal which it did not exercise.)

Defendant breached the contract deliberately. It removed from the premises only "the richest and best of the gravel" and wholly failed, according to the findings, "to perform and comply with the terms, conditions, and provisions of said lease * * * with respect to the condition in which the surface of the demised premises was required to be left." Defendant surrendered the premises, not substantially at the grade required by the contract "nor at any uniform grade." Instead, the ground was "broken, rugged, and uneven." Plaintiff sues as assignee and successor in right of Groves.

As the contract was construed below, the finding is that to complete its performance 288,495 cubic yards of overburden would need to be excavated, taken from the premises, and deposited elsewhere. The reasonable cost of doing that was found to be upwards of $60,000. But, if defendant had left the premises at the uniform grade required by the lease, the reasonable value of the property on the determinative date would have been only $12,160. The judgment was for that sum, including interest, thereby nullifying plaintiff's claim that cost of completing the contract rather than difference in value of the land was the measure of damages. The gauge of damage adopted by the decision was the difference between the market value of plaintiff's land in the condition it was when the contract was made and what it would have been if defendant had performed. The one question for us arises upon plaintiff's assertion that he was entitled, not to that difference in value, but to the reasonable cost to him of doing the work called for by the contract which defendant left undone.

1. Defendant's breach of contract was wilful. There was nothing of good faith about it. Hence, that the decision below handsomely rewards bad faith and deliberate breach of contract is obvious. That is not allowable. Here the rule is well settled, and has been since Elliott v. Caldwell, 43 Minn. 357, 45 N.W. 845, 9 L.R.A. 52, that, where the contractor wilfully and fraudulently varies from the terms of a construction contract, he cannot sue thereon and

have the benefit of the equitable doctrine of substantial performance. That is the rule generally. See Annotation, "Wilful or intentional variation by contractor from terms of contract in regard to material or work as affecting measure of damages," 6 A.L.R. 137.

Jacob & Youngs, Inc. v. Kent, 230 N.Y. 239, 243, 244, 129 N.E. 889, 891, 23 A.L.R. 1429, is typical. It was a case of substantial performance of a building contract. (This case is distinctly the opposite.) Mr. Justice Cardozo, in the course of his opinion, stressed the distinguishing features. "Nowhere," he said, "will change be tolerated, however, if it is so dominant or pervasive as in any real or substantial measure to frustrate the purpose of the contract." Again, "the willful transgressor must accept the penalty of his transgression."

2.   In reckoning damages for breach of a building or construction contract, the law aims to give the disappointed promisee, so far as money will do it, what he was promised. 9 Am.Jur. Building and Construction Contracts, § 152. It is so ruled by a long line of decisions in this state, beginning with Carli v. Seymour, Sabin & Co., 26 Minn. 276, 3 N.W. 348, where the contract was for building a road. There was a breach. Plaintiff was held entitled to recover what it would cost to complete the grading as contemplated by the contract. * * *

Never before, so far as our decisions show, has it even been suggested that lack of value in the land furnished to the contractor who had bound himself to improve it any escape from the ordinary consequences of a breach of the contract.

A case presently as interesting as any of our own, is Sassen v. Haegle, 125 Minn. 441, 147 N.W. 445, 446, 52 L.R.A.,N.S., 1176. The defendant, lessee of a farm, had agreed to haul and spread manure. He removed it, but spread it elsewhere than on the leased farm. Plaintiff had a verdict, but a new trial was ordered for error in the charge as to the measure of damages. The point was thus discussed by Mr. Justice Holt [125 Minn. page 443, 147 N.W. page 446, 52 L.R.A.,N.S., 1176]: "But it is also true that the landlord had a perfect right to stipulate as to the disposal of the manure or as to the way in which the farm should be worked, and the tenant cannot evade compliance by showing that the farm became more valuable or fertile by omitting the agreed work or doing other work. Plaintiff's pleading and proof was directed to the reasonable value of performing what defendant agreed but failed to perform. Such reasonable cost or value was the natural and proximate damages. The question is not whether plaintiff made a wise or foolish agreement. He had a right to have it performed as made, and the resulting damage, in case of failure, is the reasonable cost of performance. Whether such performance affects the value of the farm was no concern of defendant."

Even in case of substantial performance in good faith, the resulting defects being remediable, it is error to instruct that the measure of damage is "the difference in value between the house as it was and as it would have been if constructed according to contract." The "correct doctrine" is that the cost of remedying the defect is the "proper" measure of damages. Snider v. Peters Home Building Co., 139 Minn. 413, 414, 416, 167 N.W. 108.

Value of the land (as distinguished from the value of the intended product of the contract, which ordinarily will be equivalent to its reasonable cost) is no proper part of any measure of damages for wilful breach of a building contract. The reason is plain.

The summit from which to reckon damages from trespass to real estate is its actual value at the moment. The owner's only right is to be compensated for the deterioration in value caused by the tort. That is all he has lost.[1] But not so if a contract to improve the same land has been breached by the contractor who refuses to do the work, especially where, as here, he has been paid in advance. The summit from which to reckon damages for that wrong is the hypothetical peak of accomplishment (not value) which would have been reached had the work been done as demanded by the contract.

The owner's right to improve his property is not trammeled by its small value. It is his right to erect thereon structures which will reduce its value. If that be the result, it can be of no aid to any contractor who declines performance. As said long ago in Chamberlain v. Parker, 45 N.Y. 569, 572: "A man may do what he will with his own, * * * and if he chooses to erect a monument to his caprice or folly on his premises, and employs and pays another to do it, it does not lie with a defendant who has been so employed and paid for building it, to say that his own performance would not be beneficial to the plaintiff." To the same effect is Restatement, Contracts, § 346, p. 576, Illustrations of Subsection (1), par. 4.

Suppose a contractor were suing the owner for breach of a grading contract such as this. Would any element of value, or lack of it, in the land have any relevance in reckoning damages? Of course not. The contractor would be compensated for what he had lost, i.e., his profit. Conversely, in such a case as this, the owner is entitled to compensation for what he has lost, that is, the work or structure which he has been promised, for which he has paid, and of which he has been deprived by the contractor's breach.

To diminish damages recoverable against him in proportion as there is presently small value in the land would favor the faithless contractor. It would also ignore and so defeat plaintiff's right to contract and build for the future. To justify such a course would require more of the prophetic vision than judges possess. This factor is important when the subject matter is trackage property in the margin of such an area of population and industry as that of the Twin Cities.

For purposes of measuring damages for breach of construction contracts, those with municipal corporations (see City of St. Paul v. Bielenberg, 164 Minn. 72, 204 N.W. 544) are no exception to the general rule. No sound reason is assigned why they should be. We have seen no case indicating their supposed exceptional character as a factor of decision. If these so-called public contracts were in the suggested special category for measuring damages, a municipal corporation would be dealt with more favorably than the ordinary litigant. But courts cannot be more generous with one class of litigants than with another. Such partiality runs counter to the law's demand for equal treatment of litigants who stand on the same footing both as to right and as to remedy.

---

1. So also in condemnation cases, where the owner loses nothing of promised contractual performance.

[handwritten: difference btw tort + contract]

The genealogy of the error pervading the argument contra is easy to trace. It begins with Seely v. Alden, 61 Pa. 302, 100 Am.Dec. 642, a tort case for pollution of a stream. Resulting depreciation in value of plaintiff's premises, of course, was the measure of damages. About 40 years later, in Bigham v. Wabash–Pittsburg T. Ry., 223 Pa. 106, 72 A. 318, the measure of damages of the earlier tort case was used in one for breach of contract, without comment or explanation to show why. That case was followed in Sweeney v. Lewis Construction Co., 66 Wash. 490, 119 P. 1108, and Sandy Valley & Elkhorn Ry. Co. v. Hughes, 175 Ky. 320, 194 S.W. 344, with no thought given to the anomaly of using in a case in contract a standard ordinarily applicable only in cases of tort. The Washington case, by the way, is sui generis. The contract was to waive damages for the lowering of a street grade. So it adopted as matter of express contract the measure of damages applicable in cases of trespass.

[handwritten margin notes: "of its own kind" / unique]

It is at least interesting to note Morgan v. Gamble, 230 Pa. 165, 79 A. 410, decided two years after the Bigham case. The doctrine of substantial performance is there correctly stated, but plaintiff was denied its benefit because he had deliberately breached his building contract. It was held that: "Where, a building contractor agrees to lay an extra strong lead water pipe, and he substitutes therefor an iron pipe, he will be required to allow to the owners in a suit upon the contract, not the difference [in value] between the iron and lead pipes, but the cost of laying a lead pipe as provided in the agreement."

[handwritten margin note: correct app of substan. perform.]

To show how remote any factors of value were considered, it was also held that: "Where a contractor of a building agrees to construct two gas lines, one for natural gas, and one for artificial gas, he will not be relieved from constructing both lines, because artificial gas was not in use in the town in which the building was being constructed."

The objective of this contract of present importance was the improvement of real estate. That makes irrelevant the rules peculiar to damages to chattels, arising from tort or breach of contract. Crowley v. Burns Boiler & Mfg. Co., 100 Minn. 178, 187, 110 N.W. 969, 973, dealt with a breach of contract for the sale of a steam boiler. The court observed: "If the application of a particular rule for measuring damages to given facts results in more than compensation, it is at once apparent that the wrong rule has been adopted."

That is unquestioned law, but for its correct application there must be ascertainment of the loss for which compensation is to be reckoned. In tort, the thing lost is money value, nothing more. But under a construction contract, the thing lost by a breach such as we have here is a physical structure or accomplishment, a promised and paid for alteration in land. That is the "injury" for which the law gives him compensation. Its only appropriate measure is the cost of performance.

It is suggested that because of little or no value in his land the owner may be unconscionably enriched by such a reckoning. The answer is that there can be no unconscionable enrichment, no advantage upon which the law will frown, when the result is but to give one party to a contract only what the other has promised; particularly where, as here, the delinquent has had full payment for the promised performance.

[handwritten margin note: Reasoning]

3.   It is said by the Restatement, Contracts, § 346, comment b: "Sometimes defects in a completed structure cannot be physically remedied without tearing down and rebuilding, at a cost that would be imprudent and unreasonable. The law does not require damages to be measured by a method requiring such economic waste. If no such waste is involved, the cost of remedying the defect is the amount awarded as compensation for failure to render the promised performance."

The "economic waste" declaimed against by the decisions applying that rule has nothing to do with the value in money of the real estate, or even with the product of the contract. The waste avoided is only that which would come from wrecking a physical structure, completed, or nearly so, under the contract. The cases applying that rule go no further. Illustrative are Bucholz v. Rosenberg, 163 Wis. 312, 156 N.W. 946; Burmeister v. Wolfgram, 175 Wis. 506, 185 N.W. 517. Absent such waste, as it is in this case, the rule of the Restatement, Contracts, § 346, is that "the cost of remedying the defect is the amount awarded as compensation for failure to render the promised performance." That means that defendants here are liable to plaintiff for the reasonable cost of doing what defendants promised to do and have wilfully declined to do.

It follows that there must be a new trial. The initial question will be as to the proper construction of the contract. Thus far the case has been considered from the standpoint of the construction adopted by plaintiff and acquiesced in, very likely for strategic reasons, by defendants. The question has not been argued here, so we intimate no opinion concerning it, but we put the question whether the contract required removal from the premises of any overburden. The requirement in that respect was that the overburden should be used for the purpose of "establishing and maintaining" the grade. A uniform slope and grade were doubtless required. But whether, if it could not be accomplished without removal and deposit elsewhere of large amounts of overburden, the contract required as a condition that the grade everywhere should be as low as the one recited as "now existing at the roadway" is a question for initial consideration below.

The judgment must be reversed with a new trial to follow.

So ordered.

JULIUS J. OLSON, JUSTICE (dissenting).

* * *

There is no case directly in point in this state. * * *

The involved lease provides that the granted premises were to be used by defendant "for the purpose of removing the sand and gravel therefrom." The cash consideration was $105,000, plus defendant's covenant to level and grade the premises to a specified base. There was no segregation or allocation of the cash consideration made applicable to any of the various items going into the deal, and the instrument does not suggest any sum as being representative of the cost of performance by defendant of the leveling and grading process. Nor is there any finding that the contractor "wilfully and fraudulently" violated the terms of its contract. All that can be said is that defendant did nothing except to mine the sand and gravel purchased by it and deemed best suited to its own interest and advantage. No question of partial or substantial performance of its covenant is involved since it did nothing in that behalf. The sole question here is whether the rule adopted by the court respecting recoverable damages is wrong. The essential facts, not questioned, are that "The fair and reasonable value as of the end of the term of said lease, May 1, 1934, of performing the said work necessary to put the premises in the condition in which they were required by the terms of said lease to be left, is the sum of $60,893.28," and that if defendant "had left said premises at a uniform grade as required by said lease, the fair and reasonable value of said premises on May 1, 1934, would have been the sum of $12,160." In that sum, plus interest from May 1, 1934, plaintiff was awarded judgment, $15,053.58. His sole contention before the trial court and here is that upon these findings the court, as a matter of law, should have allowed him the cost of performance, $60,893.28, plus interest since date of the breach, May 1, 1934, amounting to more than $76,000.

Since there is no issue of fact we should limit our inquiry to the single legal problem presented: What amount in money will adequately compensate plaintiff for his loss caused by defendant's failure to render performance?

When the parties entered into this contract each had a right to rely upon the promise of full and complete performance on the part of the other. And by "performance" is meant "such a thorough fulfillment of a duty as puts an end to obligations by leaving nothing more to be done." McGuire v. J. Neils Lumber Co., 97 Minn. 293, 298, 107 N.W. 130, 132. But the "obligation of the contract does not inhere or subsist in the agreement itself proprio vigore, but in the law applicable to the agreement, that is, in the act of the law in binding the promisor to perform his promise. When it is said that one who enters upon an undertaking assumes the legal duties relating to it, what is really meant is that the law imposes the duties on him. A contract is not a law, nor does it make law. It is the agreement plus the law that makes the ordinary contract an enforceable obligation." 12 Am.Jur., Contracts, § 2.

There is here no room for dispute as to contract obligation; therefore it is the duty of the court to enforce its terms "without a leaning in either direction," the parties being "on an equal footing" and as such "were free to do what they chose." Id. § 226.

Another principle, of universal application, is that a party is entitled to have that for which he contracted, or its equivalent. What that equivalent is depends upon the circumstances of each case. If the effect of performance is such that the defective part "may be remedied without the destruction of any substantial part of the benefit which the owner's property has received by reason of the contractor's work, the equivalent to which the owner is entitled is the cost of making the work conform to the contract." 9 Am.Jur., Building and Construction Contracts, § 152. Here, however, defendant did nothing. As such plaintiff "is entitled to be placed, in so far as this can be done by money, in the same position he would have occupied if the contract had been performed." But "his recovery is limited to the loss he has actually suffered by reason of the breach; he is not entitled to be placed in a better position than he would have been in if the contract had not been broken." 15 Am.Jur., Damages, § 43. * * *

* * *

That the subject matter here involved was one within the proper scope of contractual obligation, and its purpose entirely lawful, is obvious. Plaintiff, as owner of the tract upon which the work was to be done, had the undoubted right to insist upon that kind of contract and to its performance. We are not concerned with whether he exercised economic wisdom or displayed lack thereof. Defendant agreed to do the work for what is conceded to have been legally sufficient consideration. It must either perform or pay plaintiff for all damages by him suffered. * * *

* * *

But to be noted, in none of the cited cases was it made to appear that the cost of completion or construction would exceed the value of the property as and when completed. Public contracts are in a separate class, and as to these comment will be made later.

As the rule of damages to be applied in any given case has for its purpose compensation, not punishment, we must be ever mindful that, "If the application of a particular rule for measuring damages to given facts results in more than compensation, it is at once apparent that the wrong rule has been adopted." Crowley v. Burns Boiler & Mfg. Co., 100 Minn. 178, 187, 110 N.W. 969, 973.

We have here then a situation where, concededly, if the contract had been performed, plaintiff would have had property worth, in round numbers, no more than $12,000. If he is to be awarded damages in an amount exceeding $60,000 he will be receiving at least 500 per cent more than his property, properly leveled to grade by actual performance, was intrinsically worth when the breach occurred. To so conclude is to give him something far beyond what the parties had in mind or contracted for. There is no showing made, nor any finding suggested, that this property was unique, specially desirable for a particular or personal use, or of special value as to location or future use different from that of other property surrounding it. Under the circumstances here appearing, it seems clear that what the parties contracted for was to put the property in shape for general sale. And the lease contemplates just that, for by the terms thereof defendant agreed "from time to time, as the sand and gravel are removed from the various lots * * * leased, it will surrender said lots to the lessor" if of no further use to defendant "in connection with the purposes for which this lease is made."

The theory upon which plaintiff relies for application of the cost of performance rule must have for its basis cases where the property or the improvement to be made is unique or personal instead of being of the kind ordinarily governed by market values. His action is one at law for damages, not for specific performance. As there was no affirmative showing of any peculiar fitness of this property to a unique or personal use, the rule to be applied is, I think, the one applied by the court. The cases bearing directly upon this phase so hold. Briefly, the rule here applicable is this: Damages recoverable for breach of a contract to construct is the difference between the market value of the property in the condition it was when delivered to and received by plaintiff and what its market value would have been if defendant had fully complied with its terms. Bigham v. Wabash–Pittsburg T. Ry. Co., 223 Pa. 106, 72 A. 318 * * *.

* * *

The principle for which I contend is not novel in construction contract cases. It is well stated in McCormick, Damages, § 168, pp. 648, 649, as follows: "In whatever way the issue arises, the generally approved standards for measuring the owner's loss from defects in the work are two: First, in cases where the defect is one that can be repaired or cured without undue expense, so as to make the building conform to the agreed plan, then the owner recovers such amount as he has reasonably expended, or will reasonably have to spend, to remedy the defect. Second, if, on the other hand, the defect in material or construction is one that cannot be remedied without an expenditure for reconstruction disproportionate to the end to be attained, or without endangering unduly other parts of the building, then the damages will be measured not by the cost of remedying the defect, but by the difference between the value of the building as it is and what it would have been worth if it had been built in conformity with the contract."

And the same thought was expressed by Mr. Justice Cardozo in Jacob & Youngs, Inc. v. Kent, 230 N.Y. 239, 244, 129 N.E. 889, 891, 23 A.L.R. 1429, 1433, thus: "The owner is entitled to the money which will permit him to complete, unless the cost of completion is grossly and unfairly out of proportion to the good to be attained. When that is true, the measure is the difference in value." To the same effect is 5 Williston, Contracts (Rev. ed.) § 1363, p. 3825. (The supporting cases are found under note 12.) In 1 Restatement, Contracts, § 346 p. 576, Illustrations of Subsection (1), par. 3, reads: "A contracts with B to sink an oil well on A's own land adjacent to the land of B, for development and exploration purposes. Other exploration wells prove that there is no oil in that region; and A breaks his promise to sink the well. B can get judgment for only nominal damages, not the cost of sinking the well."

* * *

If this were a case to recover damages for tortious injury the applicable rule is the difference in the market value and not the cost of restoring the premises to the former condition if such exceeds the diminution in value. Karst v. St. Paul, S. & T.F.R. Co., 23 Minn. 401; Ziebarth v. Nye, 42 Minn. 541, 547, 44 N.W. 1027. In Heath v. Minneapolis, St. P. & S. Ste. M. Ry. Co., 126 Minn. 470, 475, 148 N.W. 311, 312, L.R.A.1916E, 977, it was held that, "The rental value plus the cost of restoration is the true measure of damages, in cases of continuing trespass, when it appears that this is less than the difference between the value of the premises before and immediately after the wrong."

* * *

No one doubts that a party may contract for the doing of anything he may choose to have done (assuming what is to be done is not unlawful) "although the thing to be produced had no marketable value." 45 N.Y. page 572. In 1 Restatement, Contracts, § 346, pp. 576, 577, Illustrations of Subsection (1), par. 4, the same thought is thus stated: "A contracts to construct a monumental fountain in B's yard for $5,000, but abandons the work after the foundation has been laid and $2800 has been paid by B. The contemplated fountain is so ugly that it would decrease the number of possible buyers of the place. The cost of completing the fountain would be $4000. B can get judgment for $1800, the cost of completion less the part of price unpaid." But that is not what plaintiff's predecessor in interest contracted for. Such a provision might well have been made, but the parties did not. They could undoubtedly have provided for liquidated damages for nonperformance (2 Dunnell, Minn.Dig., 2d ed. & Supps., §§ 2536, 2537), or they might have determined in money what the value of performance was considered to be and thereby have contractually provided a measure for failure of performance.

The opinion also suggests that this property lies in an area where the owner might rightly look for future development, being in a so-called industrial zone, and that as such he should be privileged to so hold it. This he may of course do. But let us assume that on May 1, 1934, condemnation to acquire this area had so far progressed as to leave only the question of price (market value) undetermined; that the area had been graded in strict conformity with the contract but that the actual market value of the premises was only $12,160, as found by the court and acquiesced in by plaintiff, what would the measure of his damages be? Obviously, the limit of his recovery could be no more than the then market value of his property. In that sum he has been paid with interest and costs; and he still has the fee title to the premises, something he would not possess if there had been condemnation. In what manner has plaintiff been hurt beyond the damages awarded? As to him "economic waste" is not apparent. Assume that defendant abandoned the entire project without taking a single yard of gravel therefrom but left the premises as they were when the lease was made, could plaintiff recover damages upon the basis here established? The trouble with the prevailing opinion is that here plaintiff's loss is not made the basis for the amount of his recovery but rather what it would cost the defendant. No case has been decided upon that basis until now.

Plaintiff asserts that he knows of no rule "giving a different measure of damages for public contracts and for private contracts in case of nonperformance." It seems to me there is a clear distinction to be drawn with respect to the application of the rule for recoverable damages in case of breach of a public works contract from that applicable to contracts between private parties. The construction of a public building, a sewer, drainage ditch, highway, or other public work, permits of no application of the market value doctrine. There simply is and can be no "market value" as to such. And for this cogent reason there can be but one rule of damages to apply, that of cost of completion of the thing contracted to be done.

* * * I think the judgment should be affirmed.

HOLT, J. I join in the foregoing dissent.

PEEVYHOUSE v. GARLAND COAL & MINING CO., 382 P.2d 109 (Okl. 1962), cert. denied, 375 U.S. 906 (1963). [Willie and Lucille Peevyhouse sued the defendant, Garland Coal & Mining Co., for damages for breach of a five-year lease of a farm containing coal deposits. The lease permitted the defendant to do strip mining on the farm and required it to perform certain restorative and remedial work at the end of the lease period. This work involved the moving of many thousands of cubic yards of dirt at a cost estimated by expert witnesses at about $29,000. Plaintiffs sued for $25,000. The evidence showed that the failure of defendants to do the restorative and remedial work reduced the value of the premises no more than $300. The jury returned a verdict for $5000, which was more than the total value of the farm.]

JACKSON, J.

On appeal, the issue is sharply drawn. Plaintiffs contend that the true measure of damages in this case is what it will cost plaintiffs to obtain performance of the work that was not done because of defendant's default. Defendant argues that the measure of damages is the cost of performance "limited, however, to the total difference in the market value before and after the work was performed".

* * *

It may be observed that Groves v. John Wunder Co. is the only case which has come to our attention in which the cost of performance rule has been followed under circumstances where the cost of performance greatly exceeded the diminution in value resulting from the breach. * * *

* * *

* * * The primary purpose of the lease * * * was merely to accomplish the economical recovery and marketing of coal from the premises, to the profit of all parties. The special provisions of the lease contract pertaining to remedial work were incidental to the main object involved.

* * *

23 O.S.1961 §§ 96 and 97 provide as follows:

"§ 96 * * * Notwithstanding the provisions of this chapter, no person can recover a greater amount in damages for the breach of an obligation, than he would have gained by the full performance thereof on both sides.

* * *

"§ 97 * * * Damages must, in all cases, be reasonable, and where an obligation of any kind appears to create a right to unconscionable and grossly oppressive damages, contrary to substantial justice no more than reasonable damages can be recovered."

Although it is true that the above sections of the statute are applied most often in tort cases, they are by their own terms, and the decisions of this court, also applicable in actions for damages for breach of contract. It would seem that they are peculiarly applicable here where, under the "cost of performance" rule, plaintiffs might recover an amount about nine times the total value of their farm. Such would seem to be "unconscionable and grossly oppressive damages, contrary to substantial justice" within the meaning of the statute. Also, it can hardly be denied that if plaintiffs here are permitted to recover under the "cost of performance" rule, they will receive a greater benefit from the breach than could be gained from full performance, contrary to the provisions of Sec. 96.

* * *

Holding

We * * * hold that where * * * the economic benefit which would result to lessor by full performance of the work is grossly disproportionate to the cost of performance, the damages which lessor may recover are limited to the diminution in value resulting to the premises because of the non-performance.

* * * [T]he rule as stated does not interfere with the property owner's right to "do what he will with his own" * * * or his right, if he chooses, to contract for "improvements" which will actually have the effect of reducing his property's value. Where such result is in fact contemplated by the parties, and is a main or principal purpose of those contracting, it would seem that the measure of damages for breach would ordinarily be the cost of performance.

* * *

Judgment

* * * We are of the opinion that the judgment of the trial court for plaintiffs should be, and it is hereby, modified and reduced to the sum of $300.00, and as so modified it is affirmed.

IRWIN, JUSTICE (dissenting):

* * * Defendant admitted in the trial of the action, that plaintiffs insisted that the * * * [restorative and remedial] provisions be included in the contract and that they would not agree to the coal mining lease unless the above provisions were included.

* * *

* * * [I]n my opinion * * * the proper measure of damages should be the cost of performance. Any other measure of damage would be holding for naught the express provisions of the contract. * * *

EISENBERG, THE RESPONSIVE MODEL
OF CONTRACT LAW
36 Stan.L.Rev. 1107, 1163–64 (1984).

It might be argued that since the plaintiff has paid for completion, anything less than cost-of-completion damages would leave the defendant unjustly enriched. For example, assume that prior to its negotiations with Peevyhouse, Garland Coal had decided it was willing to pay royalties to Peevyhouse of one dollar per ton. When Peevyhouse demanded that Garland would have to restore the land, Garland would presumably have calculated the cost of restoration, prorated over the expected tonnage, and agreed to pay Peevyhouse a royalty of a dollar per ton minus the prorated amount. On completion of the mining, Peevyhouse would then in effect have paid Garland an amount equal to the cost of restoration. Limiting damages to diminished value would confer a windfall on Garland equal to that cost. It can also be implied from this argument that instead of measuring damages by diminished value, the court should grant a decree of specific performance: If the plaintiff really wants completion, he will enforce the decree. If he does not, he will make a settlement that divides the windfall at some level between the amount at which he subjectively values the performance and the contractor's cost of completion.

The problem with this argument and its implication is that in many cases the disparity between cost of completion and diminished market value results in large part from circumstances that were not anticipated when the contract was made. In *Peevyhouse*, for example, Garland's brief suggests that the restoration plan was based on the use of a spoil bank that was to be created by the mining operation. As matters turned out, however, Garland found much less coal than anticipated, the mine was not extended across the entire property, the planned spoil bank was not created, and restoration became much more expensive than originally contemplated. * * * In such [a case], the parties have not factored the cost of completion into the price paid by the plaintiff. Saving that cost would not, therefore, result in a windfall to the defendant, and if the plaintiff has no intent to complete, a decree of specific performance would enable the plaintiff to extract a windfall settlement.

Suppose, however, that the value the plaintiff assigns to the difference between the existing and promised states of the subject matter, although less than the cost of completion, is higher than the market-value differential. In principle, the plaintiff's recovery should be measured by this intermediate figure. (The jury in *Peevyhouse* may have done just that.)

ROCK ISLAND IMPROVEMENT COMPANY v. HELMERICH & PAYNE, INC.

United States Court of Appeals, Tenth Circuit, 1983.
698 F.2d 1075.

LOGAN, CIRCUIT JUDGE.

In this diversity case Helmerich & Payne, Inc. appeals a jury verdict in favor of Rock Island Improvement Company for breach of contract and appeals the trial court's denial of its motions for judgment notwithstanding the verdict and for a new trial or amendment of the judgment.

From 1968 to 1977 Helmerich & Payne leased two tracts of land in Oklahoma from Rock Island for coal mining purposes. These tracts are referred to as the "Rees–Heavener" and "Rees–Petros" mines. The lease contained a reclamation clause that stated: "Upon the abandonment or completion of any mining operation, or part thereof, including but not limited to any strip operation, the surface shall be restored as nearly as possible to its condition prior to said mining operation...." Helmerich & Payne subleased the land to Sam Sexton, Jr., who used stripmining techniques to remove substantial amounts of coal. When the lease period ended, the tracts were left with two strip pits and were not otherwise reclaimed to Rock Island's satisfaction. Rock Island sued Helmerich & Payne for breach of the lease's reclamation provision, seeking damages equal to the amount necessary to reclaim the land. Helmerich & Payne filed a third party complaint against Sexton, who agreed to pay any judgment won by Rock Island. The jury awarded Rock Island $375,000.

* * *

Helmerich & Payne contends that the trial court improperly applied

Oklahoma damages law. In instructing the jury on damages,[1] the trial court relied on Peevyhouse v. Garland Coal & Mining Company, 382 P.2d 109 (Okl.), cert. denied, 375 U.S. 906, 84 S.Ct. 196, 11 L.Ed.2d 145 (1963). In Peevyhouse the Oklahoma Supreme Court examined a coal mining lease requiring the lessee to reclaim any land it stripmined. At issue was whether the proper measure of damages for the lessee's failure to reclaim was the cost of performance ($29,000) or the diminution in the fair market value of the land ($300). The court held that the proper measure of damages was the reasonable cost of reclamation, unless the reclamation requirement was incidental to the lease's main purpose and the cost of reclamation would be grossly disproportionate to the diminution in the land's fair market value. In the latter case, the lessor's damages were limited to the diminution in value. Id. at 114.

In the instant case the trial court submitted the issue of the reclamation clause's importance to the jury. We have held that a trial court must submit this issue to the jury when the parties have introduced extrinsic evidence of their intent, Hitchcock v. Peter Kiewit & Sons Co., 479 F.2d 1257 (10th Cir.1973); otherwise, the trial court should treat interpretation of the contract clause as a matter of law. See Walker v. Telex Corp., 583 P.2d 482, 485 (Okl.1978). Neither Rock Island nor Helmerich & Payne introduced evidence establishing the parties' intent in including the restoration clause. Therefore, the trial court should not have submitted interpretation of the contract to the jury.

Helmerich & Payne asserts the trial court should have held that the lease unambiguously focused upon coal mining as its main purpose and that reclamation was merely an incidental purpose. Furthermore, Helmerich & Payne argues that because the parties stipulated the diminution in value of the land was $6,797, and the evidence presented showed that restoring the land would cost $375,000, the court should have held the cost of reclamation was disproportionate to the diminution in land value. Thus, following Peevyhouse, the proper measure of damages would be diminution in market value, an amount the parties stipulated, and thus not a jury issue. Rock Island's response is that Peevyhouse no longer represents Oklahoma law on damages for breach of mining contracts because of subsequent developments in that state's policy toward reclamation.

At the time the parties in Peevyhouse entered into their lease, Oklahoma had no stated policy concerning land reclamation after mining operations. Thus, in Peevyhouse the court considered only the economic benefits to the parties of a situation the court termed "artificial," "unreasonable," and "unrealistic": that a property owner would agree to pay a great deal for "improvements" that would increase the property's value by only a small

1. The trial court instructed the jury as follows: "The measure of damages is the reasonable cost of performing the contract, or in this case, restoring the land to the same condition it was in before stripmining, unless you find: 1. That the lease provision requiring restoration of Plaintiff's land to the same condition it was in before stripmining was merely incidental to the main purpose of the lease; and 2. That the economic benefit to the Plain-tiff by restoring the land would be grossly disproportionate to the cost of restoring the land. Then, if you so find, the amount of damages to which Plaintiff is entitled is the reduced value of Plaintiff's land, that is, the difference between the present fair market value of the land as it is, and the present fair market value of the land restored to the same condition it was in before the stripmining."

the statute now outweighs Peevyhouse.

amount. The court was concerned that if the landowner did not spend the large amount to reclaim the land, he would receive a windfall by recovering the amount from the lessee. 382 P.2d at 112.

However, after the decision in Peevyhouse but before Rock Island leased the tracts to Helmerich & Payne, Oklahoma enacted the Open Cut Land Reclamation Act. 1967 Okla.Sess.Laws Ch. 186 (current version at Okla.Stat. Ann. tit 45, §§ 721–729). The Act stated in part:

> "It is hereby declared to be the policy of this State to provide, after mining operations are completed, for the reclamation and conservation of land subjected to surface disturbance by open cut mining and thereby to preserve natural resources, to aid in the protection of wildlife and aquatic resources, to establish recreational, home and industrial sites, to protect and perpetuate the taxable value of property, and to protect and promote the health, safety and general welfare of the people of this State."

Id. at § 2 (current version at Okla.Stat.Ann. tit 45, § 722).

The statute declares today, as it did in 1967, that the operator of a strip mine has a duty to reclaim the land and that the state may contract for the work to be done if the operator defaults. The statute makes no exception for cases in which the expenditures for reclamation are disproportionate to the resulting increase in value of the land. To be sure the statute looks to the operator as the party responsible for reclamation, and limits the state's recovery to the amount of the bond it has required.[2] Nevertheless, there are *Reasons for both parties to comply w reclaim provision* many reasons a landowner in Rock Island's position would want a reclamation provision in the lease—to enhance its image in the community, to protect against possible tort liability for conditions on its premises, and to allay any fear that under the recently enacted law it might somehow be held responsible for defaults of the operator. There are reasons a lessee might readily accept such a provision—it already has a duty to reclaim under the state statute.

We are convinced that the Oklahoma Supreme Court would no longer apply the rule it established in Peevyhouse in 1963 if it had the instant dispute before it. Peevyhouse was a 5–4 decision with a strong dissent. More importantly, the public policy of the state has changed, as expressed in its statutes. Although we are bound by decisions of a state supreme court in diversity cases, we need not adhere to a decision if we think it no longer would be followed. *reasoning*

* * *

* * * When the parties negotiated the contract in question, they expressly included a reclamation clause and required the lessee to bear the cost of reclamation. Given the attention focused by Oklahoma on the importance of reclaiming stripmined lands, it is more logical to assume that the parties meant what they said, calculated their costs and benefits under the contract accordingly, and intended the provision to insure proper reclamation of the

---

2. At the time of the Rock Island–Helmerich & Payne contract the maximum bond required was $50 per acre. Today there is no maximum; the bond must cover the estimated reclamation costs. Okla.Stat.Ann. tit. 45, § 728(B).

judgment

land, than it is to assume that they expected the reclamation clause to have no force.[3]

Even though the trial court should not have submitted the issue of the reclamation clause's importance to the jury, we need not reverse. Because we hold that cost of performance is the proper measure of damages, and the jury used this measure in calculating damages, the court's error is harmless.

* * *

AFFIRMED.

RADFORD v. DE FROBERVILLE

Chancery Division, 1977.
[1978] 1 All Eng.Rep. 33.

[Radford was the owner of a house which he had broken up into flats leased to tenants. Next to the house was a large garden and plot where another house could be built. Radford obtained planning permission to build in the plot but sold it to De Froberville for (1) £6,500 and (2) the latter's promise to build a wall to divide the plot sold from the remaining land area owned by Radford. Later, after De Froberville failed to build the wall, Radford sued, claiming as damages the £3,400 cost of building the wall. The failure to build the wall did not diminish the market value of Radford's property. The court granted cost of completion damages.]

OLIVER J:

* * *

It may be that, viewed objectively, it is not to the plaintiff's financial advantage to be supplied with the article or service for which he has stipulated. It may be that another person might say that what the plaintiff has stipulated for will not serve his commercial interest so well as some other scheme or course of action. And that may be quite right. But that, surely, must be for the plaintiff to judge. Pacta sunt servanda. If he contracts for the supply of that which he thinks serves his interests, be they commercial, aesthetic or merely eccentric, then if that which is contracted for is not supplied by the other contracting party I do not see why, in principle, he should not be compensated by being provided with the cost of supplying it through someone else or in a different way, subject to the proviso, of course, that he is seeking compensation for a genuine loss and not merely using a technical breach to secure an uncovenanted profit.

* * *

In the course of the argument, I instanced the case of the man, with a garden by the sea or a river, subject to inundation on rare occasions by freak floods. He sells a part of his garden as part of the sale and stipulates that the purchaser shall erect a flood wall on the property purchased to protect both

---

3. In Peevyhouse the court relied in part on Oklahoma damages statutes requiring that a party receive no more in damages than it would have gained by full performance. See 382 P.2d at 113 (citing Okla.Stat.Ann. tit 23, §§ 96, 97). Helmerich & Payne contends that these statutes limit the amount of its damages. Because the anticipated cost of reclamation may have affected the contract price, these damages statutes do not preclude use of the cost-of-performance measure of damages.

properties. If the purchaser fails to build the wall and the court is satisfied that the plaintiff intends to build on his own land what the defendant has failed to build on his, why should he be limited to the amount by which his land is diminished in value as a saleable asset by the possibility of an occasional flood? He is interested in cultivating his garden, not selling his property.

* * * What the court does is to use its common-sense in measuring, in the case of the individual plaintiff and by reference to *his* particular circumstances, what he has lost by the breach.

* * *

In the instant case, I am entirely satisfied that the plaintiff genuinely wants this work done and that he intends to expend any damages awarded on carrying it out. In my judgment, therefore, the damages ought to be measured by the cost of the work, unless there are some other considerations which point to a different measure.

Problem 3–1

Pervis Ellington and Acme Construction Company entered a contract for the latter to construct an indoor swimming pool at Ellington's home. The contract provided for the pool to have a maximum depth of 9.5 feet. The construction price was $40,000. Acme constructed the pool, meeting all specifications except that the pool as constructed had a maximum depth of 7.5 feet. Ellington refused to make the final payment of $5000. After fruitless discussions with Acme about the problem, Ellington brought a breach of contract action. He seeks $80,000, the cost of demolishing the existing pool and constructing a new one according to the specifications.

You are the judge in the non-jury trial of Ellington v. Acme Construction Company. You have heard the following testimony: Ellington is a former collegiate diver of some renown. Two experts testified that diving is safe in a pool with a depth of 9.5 feet, but that they "would not recommend" diving in a pool with a depth of less than 7.5 feet. Ellington testified that he "felt unsafe" diving into the pool as constructed. Ellington failed to produce any evidence that the shortfall in the depth of the pool diminished its market value. Nor did he testify that he actually intended to arrange for the reconstruction of the pool.

Acme produced testimony of two real estate agents that the pool increased the market value of Ellington's home by $45,000. Acme's president testified that he did not know that Ellington was a diver. He testified that the total cost of constructing the pool was $35,000.

Please decide the case of Ellington v. Acme Construction Company.

RESTATEMENT (SECOND) OF CONTRACTS § 347, COMMENT B.

The first element that must be estimated in attempting to fix a sum that will fairly represent the expectation interest is the loss in the value to the injured party of the other party's performance that is caused by the failure of, or deficiency in, that performance. * * * In principle, this requires a determination of the [value of that performance] * * * to the injured party himself and not [the value] to some hypothetical reasonable person or on some market. * * * [The value of performance] therefore depend[s] on his own particular circumstances or those of his enterprise * * *.

Roof

THORNE v. WHITE

District of Columbia Court of Appeals, 1954.
103 A.2d 579.

QUINN, ASSOCIATE JUDGE.

Appellant, hereinafter referred to as Thorne, contracted to put a new roof on appellee's residence and to make certain repairs in connection therewith for the sum of $225. Pursuant to the contract, Thorne delivered certain materials to the job and began work. Within a few hours the work was discontinued because of inclement weather. Thorne never returned to the job and a few days later had his materials hauled away. White then entered into an agreement with the Koons Roofing Company to have the work completed at a cost of $582.26. This was $357.26 more than the amount of Thorne's contract. He sued Thorne for that difference alleging breach of contract. The court, hearing the case without a jury, ruled in favor of White, and Thorne brings this appeal.

We find no error in the trial court's ruling that Thorne had breached the contract. He testified that he had not completed the work because White had ordered him to discontinue, but White denied ever having made such a statement. Thus, the issue as to the breach of contract was clearly one of fact. There was ample support in the evidence to sustain the court's finding.

The aspect of the case which gives us more concern is the question of damages. White was awarded a judgment for $357.26, which amount represents the difference between the contract price with Thorne and the amount paid to the Koons Company for the completion of the work. This sum would be the correct measure of damages, provided the second contract did not call for additional work not contemplated by nor included in the first one. This is in accord with the general rule that a party damaged by a breach may only recover for losses which are the natural consequence and proximate result of that breach. Damages are awarded for the purpose of compensation and the injured party should not be placed in a better position than he would have been in had no breach occurred. In cases such as the present one the successful plaintiff should only be allowed to recover what it has cost him to complete the same work, over and above the original contract price.

Natural and probable

In the instant case the trial court found that the two roofing contracts were substantially the same and that the damages were therefore the amount by which Koons' contract exceeded Thorne's price. We rule that such a holding was error. Besides the large difference between the two contract prices, the evidence was that Thorne's contract called for a 4–ply roof, while the second contract was for what was in effect a 5–ply roof; that Thorne was merely to put a new roof over the old one, while the Koons Company entirely removed the old roof; and that several additional items were provided for under the second contract not called for in the first. A representative of the Koons Company testified that these additional items added to the cost of their contract. As the evidence clearly shows that White received more from the

New Roof!

Koons Company than he was to receive from Thorne, we think an improper measure of damages was applied.

* * *

Reversed with instructions to grant a new trial on the issue of damages.

MORELLO v. J.H. HOGAN, INC., 1 Conn.App. 150, 468 A.2d 1248 (1984). [A subcontractor contracted to do masonry work for a total price of $44,000. After doing work with a reasonable value of $9,411.87, the subcontractor wrongfully abandoned the job and the prime contractor reasonably spent $54,356.36 to complete the work. The subcontractor sued for $9,411.87 and the prime contractor counterclaimed for the difference between $44,000 and $54,356.36, or $10,356.36. The trial court awarded the prime contractor $944.49, the difference between $9,411.87 and $10,356.56.]

"Viewed through a different prism, the court's judgment violated the basic rule of contract damages that the award should place the injured party in the same position as it would have been had the contract been performed. * * * The defendant was required to spend $54,356.36 to complete the work after the plaintiff left the job. Thus the $54,356.36 already took into account the value of the work performed by the plaintiff. Awarding the plaintiff $9,411.87 on the complaint coupled with the award on the counterclaim limiting the defendant to $10,356.36 gave the plaintiff double credit for his work and left the defendant $9411.87 short of the position in which it would have been placed had the contract been performed.

"There is error, the judgment on the complaint is set aside and the case remanded with direction to render judgment for the defendant on the complaint."

FREUND v. WASHINGTON SQUARE PRESS, 34 N.Y.2d 379, 357 N.Y.S.2d 857, 314 N.E.2d 419 (1974). [Defendant, Washington Square Press, broke its contract to publish Freund's book. The contract obligated the defendant to pay royalties based upon percentages of sales. The Appellate Division affirmed the trial court's award to Freund of the cost of publication. The Appellate Division "analogized to the construction contract situation where the cost of completion may be the proper measure of damages for a builder's failure to complete a house or for use of wrong materials."]

SAMUEL RABIN, JUDGE.

Since the damages which would have compensated plaintiff for anticipated royalties were not proved with the required certainty, we agree with the dissent in the Appellate Division that nominal damages alone are recoverable. (Cf. Manhattan Sav. Inst. v. Gottfried Baking Co., 286 N.Y. 398, 36 N.E.2d 637.) Though these are damages in name only and not at all compensatory, they are nevertheless awarded as a formal vindication of plaintiff's legal right to compensation which has not been given a sufficiently certain monetary valuation. * * *

In our view, the analogy by the majority in the Appellate Division to the construction contract situation was inapposite. In the typical construction contract, the owner agrees to pay money or other consideration to a builder and expects, under the contract, to receive a completed building in return. The value of the promised performance to the owner is the properly constructed building. In this case, unlike the typical construction contract, the value to plaintiff of the promised performance—publication—was a percentage of sales of the books published and not the books themselves. Had the plaintiff contracted for the printing, binding and delivery of a number of hardbound copies of his manuscript, to be sold or disposed of as he wished, then perhaps the construction analogy, and measurement of damages by the cost of replacement or completion, would have some application.

Here, however, the specific value to plaintiff of the promised publication was the royalties he stood to receive from defendant's sales of the published book. Essentially, publication represented what it would have cost the defendant to confer that value upon the plaintiff, and, by its breach, defendant saved that cost. The error by the courts below was in measuring damages not by the value to plaintiff of the promised performance but by the cost of that performance to defendant. Damages are not measured, however, by what the defaulting party saved by the breach, but by the natural and probable consequences of the breach *to the plaintiff.* In this case, the consequence to plaintiff of defendant's failure to publish is that he is prevented from realizing the gains promised by the contract—the royalties. But, as we have stated, the amount of royalties plaintiff would have realized was not ascertained with adequate certainty and, as a consequence, plaintiff may recover nominal damages only.

Accordingly, the order of the Appellate Division should be modified to the extent of reducing the damage award of $10,000 for the cost of publication to six cents, but with costs and disbursements to the plaintiff.

WARNER v. McLAY

Supreme Court of Errors, Connecticut, 1918.
92 Conn. 427, 103 A. 113.

Appeal from City Court of New Haven: JOHN R. BOOTH, JUDGE.

Action by Hubert E. Warner, Jr., against James McLay for breach of contract. There was a verdict and judgment for plaintiff, and defendant appeals. Error, and new trial ordered.

The theory of the plaintiff as shown by his complaint and prayer for relief is that he is entitled to recover damages for expenditures and loss of profits occasioned by the breach of a written building contract. It is apparently here conceded that there was an unjust abrogation of this contract, by the defendant. An important question presented by the appeal is as to the measure of damages. Upon this branch of the case the jury were told that:

"He also claims that he is entitled to 10 per cent profit upon this contract. Of course, in the event of a breach of contract, and the contract was broken, the evidence discloses that, there is no dispute about it. The contract was broken by Mr. McLay's refusal to allow it to proceed, and he does not deny it. Therefore, the contract having been broken, if Mr. Warner was willing and ready to carry out his part of it, but was prevented by Mr. McLay from doing so, he is entitled to any damage he may suffer by reason of the failure of Mr. McLay to allow him to proceed, and he would be entitled to recover any amount of money he was obliged to expend in the securing of materials, but also a reasonable profit upon his contract, which he says is 10 per cent. I haven't the figures. He gave you figures of the different parts of the building showing that there would be a profit."

The jury were also told that:

"Of course, you will be guided by the evidence submitted before you, and there is no conflict of evidence, because the defendant has offered none, so you will then be obliged to take the evidence as submitted by the plaintiff."

RORABACK, J. (after stating the facts as above). * * *

In the present case the plaintiff had the right to recover such sum in damages as he would have realized in profits if the contract had been fully performed. To ascertain this it was necessary to find the cost and expense of the work and materials necessary to complete the contract. This sum, deducted from the contract price, would have given a balance which would be the profit which would have accrued to the plaintiff out of the contract if it had been fulfilled. This the plaintiff had a right to receive in addition to his expenditures for work and labor supplied towards the completion of the contract. Fox v. Harding, 61 Mass. (7 Cush.) 523; United States v. Behan, 110 U.S. 338, 4 Sup.Ct. 81, 28 L.Ed. 168.

The substance of the instruction to the jury upon this branch of the case was that the plaintiff was entitled to recover for his necessary expenditures and also a reasonable profit upon his contract, which might be, as the plaintiff claimed, 10 per cent. It is apparent that these instructions were not sufficient for the proper guidance of the jury upon the question of profits. There was no attempt to make an application of the principles of law which we have just cited. There was no attempt to define profits, nor any instruction given as to how these profits were to be estimated. The remarks of the court upon this point may have been proper as a statement of the plaintiff's claim for damages, but adopting this claim as the proper rule for damages was making these claims the law for the jury, instead of directing their attention to the correct legal principles applicable to such a situation.

* * *

There is error. The judgment is reversed, and a new trial ordered. The other Judges concurred.

Comments and Questions

Why should an aggrieved party recover lost expectancy rather than merely out-of-pocket or other reliance costs? Consider the following views.

FULLER AND PERDUE, THE RELIANCE INTEREST IN CONTRACT DAMAGES
46 Yale L.J. 52, 57, 58, 60–62 (1936).

It is a matter of fact no easy thing to explain why the normal rule of contract recovery should be that which measures damages by the value of the promised performance. Since this "natural rule" throws its shadow across our whole subject it will be necessary to examine the possible reasons for its existence. It may be said parenthetically that the discussion which follows, though directed primarily to the normal measure of recovery where damages are sought, also has relevance to the more general question, why should a promise which has not been relied on ever be enforced at all * * * ?

* * *

A * * * possible explanation for the rule protecting the expectancy may be found in * * * [the principle of private autonomy].ᵃ This theory views the contracting parties as exercising, so to speak, a legislative power, so that the legal enforcement of a contract becomes merely an implementing by the state of a kind of private law already established by the parties. * * *

* * * If a contract represents a kind of private law, it is a law which usually says nothing at all about what shall be done when it is violated. * * * There would, therefore, be no necessary contradiction between * * * [the principle of private autonomy] and a rule which limited damages to the reliance interest.

* * *

* * * [E]ven if our interest were confined to protecting promisees against an out-of-pocket loss, it would still be possible to justify the rule granting the value of the expectancy, both as a cure for, and as a prophylaxis against, losses of this sort.

It is a cure for these losses in the sense that it offers the measure of recovery most likely to reimburse the plaintiff for the (often very numerous and very difficult to prove) individual acts and forbearances which make up his total reliance on the contract. If we take into account "gains prevented" by reliance, that is, losses involved in foregoing the opportunity to enter other contracts, the notion that the rule protecting the expectancy is adopted as the most effective means of compensating for detrimental reliance seems not at all far-fetched. * * *

The rule that the plaintiff must after the defendant's breach take steps to mitigate damages tends to corroborate the suspicion that there lies hidden behind the protection of the expectancy a concern to compensate the plaintiff for the loss of the opportunity to enter other contracts. * * *

* * *

In seeking justification for the rule granting the value of the expectancy there is no need, however, to restrict ourselves by the assumption, hitherto made, that the rule can only be intended to cure or prevent the loss caused by reliance. A justification can be developed from a less negative point of view. It may be said that there is not only a policy in favor of preventing and undoing the harms resulting from reliance, but also a policy in favor of promoting and facilitating reliance on business agreements. As in the case of the stop-light ordinance we are interested not only in preventing collisions but in speeding traffic. Agreements can accomplish little, either for their makers or for

---

a. We have, in accord with Fuller's later writings, inserted "the principle of private au-tonomy" in place of "the will theory of con-tract."

society, unless they are made the basis for action. When business agreements are not only made but are also acted on, the division of labor is facilitated, goods find their way to the places where they are most needed, and economic activity is generally stimulated. These advantages would be threatened by any rule which limited legal protection to the reliance interest. Such a rule would in practice tend to discourage reliance. The difficulties in proving reliance and subjecting it to pecuniary measurement are such that the businessman knowing, or sensing, that these obstacles stood in the way of judicial relief would hesitate to rely on a promise in any case where the legal sanction was of significance to him. To encourage reliance we must therefore dispense with its proof. For this reason it has been found wise to make recovery on a promise independent of reliance, both in the sense that in some cases the promise is enforced though not relied on (as in the bilateral business agreement) and in the sense that recovery is not limited to the detriment incurred in reliance.

VON MEHREN, CONTRACTS IN GENERAL

7 Int'l Ency.Comp.L. 89 (ch. 1) (1982).

A larger question remains for discussion: Do economic considerations provide a basis for choosing, in principle, between the reliance measure * * * and the expectation measure?

Use of the expectation measure rather than the reliance measure means both that a party bears less risk with respect to the ultimate receipt of the promised performance and that a higher price (to cover the increased protection) is paid for that performance. If parties who contract for future performances typically do so in order to increase substantially the likelihood that the performances will ultimately be made, use of the expectation measure is economically rational; in particular, the additional negotiation costs are avoided that such parties would incur to obtain the protection they desire were the reliance measure adopted in principle. Of course, those who desire less protection and a lower price must incur such costs. However, if this group is in a distinct minority, society's interests are served by the use, in principle, of the expectation measure.

There may be a further general reason for, in principle, preferring the expectation to the reliance measure. The latter measure gives no protection against breach until reliance involving a demonstrable economic cost has taken place. In market transactions, any market movement that would make breach attractive to the promisor results at the same time in a reliance loss as the contract deterred the promisee from obtaining performance or the commitment to perform elsewhere. Accordingly, the reliance measure operates in these cases as effectively as the expectation measure to give meaning to the promisor's obligation. This result is another example of the extent to which the reliance and expectation measures come together in market transactions.

On the other hand, in nonmarket transactions—except to the extent that the values of component parts of the performance in question are affected by market movements—nonaction by the party promised a performance does not give rise to a reliance loss on his part. Accordingly, until that party actually incurs expenses in reliance on the other party's promise of future performance, only a "gentlemen's agreement" exists if damages for failure to perform are limited to the reliance interest. Therefore, except to the extent that sociological, commercial, or ethical considerations give binding force to such agreements, where prompt reliance by the promisee will not occur there seems little point in contracting unless the parties can agree upon a penalty clause or upon a measure of damages other than reliance. Furthermore, should the parties in circumstances where prompt reliance is not normal enter into a contract for whose breach damages are to be assessed on the basis of reliance, the promisee might well, in order to put pressure on the promisor to perform, rely in a manner that, judged in terms of economic efficiency, was premature or excessive. The expectation measure seems, therefore, appropriate in principle if the legal order wishes to give effect to wholly executory transactions.

HANDICAPPED CHILDREN'S EDUCATION BD. OF SHEBOYGAN COUNTY v. LUKASZEWSKI

Supreme Court of Wisconsin, 1983.
112 Wis.2d 197, 332 N.W.2d 774.

CALLOW, JUSTICE.

This review arises out of an unpublished decision of the court of appeals which affirmed in part and reversed in part a judgment of the Ozaukee county circuit court, Judge Warren A. Grady.

In January of 1978 the Handicapped Children's Education Board (the Board) hired Elaine Lukaszewski to serve as a speech and language therapist for the spring term. Lukaszewski was assigned to the Lightfoot School in Sheboygan Falls which was approximately 45 miles from her home in Mequon. Rather than move, she commuted to work each day. During the 1978 spring term, the Board offered Lukaszewski a contract to continue in her present position at Lightfoot School for the 1978–79 school year. The contract called for an annual salary of $10,760. Lukaszewski accepted.

In August of 1978, prior to the beginning of the school year, Lukaszewski was offered a position by the Wee Care Day Care Center which was located not far from her home in Mequon. The job paid an annual salary of $13,000. After deciding to accept this offer, Lukaszewski notified Thomas Morrelle, the Board's director of special education, that she intended to resign from her position at the Lightfoot School. Morrelle told her to submit a letter of resignation for consideration by the Board. She did so, and the matter was discussed at a meeting of the Board on August 21, 1978. The Board refused to release Lukaszewski from her contract. On August 24, 1978, the Board's attorney sent a letter to Lukaszewski directing her to return to work. The attorney sent a second letter to the Wee Care Day Care Center stating that the Board would take legal action if the Center interfered with Lukaszewski's performance of her contractual obligations at the Lightfoot School. A copy of this letter was sent to the Department of Public Instruction.

Lukaszewski left the Wee Care Day Care Center and returned to Lightfoot School for the 1978 fall term. She resented the actions of the Board, however, and retained misgivings about her job. On September 8, 1978, she discussed her feeling with Morrelle. After this meeting Lukaszewski felt quite upset about the situation. She called her doctor to make an appointment for that afternoon and subsequently left the school.

Dr. Ashok Chatterjee examined Lukaszewski and found her blood pressure to be high. Lukaszewski asked Dr. Chatterjee to write a letter explaining his medical findings and the advice he had given her. In a letter dated September 11, 1978, Dr. Chatterjee indicated that Lukaszewski had a hypertension problem dating back to 1976. He reported that on the day he examined Lukaszewski she appeared agitated, nervous, and had blood pressure readings up to 180/100. It was his opinion that, although she took hypotensive drugs, her medical condition would not improve unless the situation which caused the problem was removed. He further opined that it would be dangerous for her to drive long distances in her agitated state.

Lukaszewski did not return to work after leaving on September 8, 1978. She submitted a letter of resignation dated September 13, 1978, in which she wrote:

> "I enclose a copy of the doctor's statement concerning my health. On the basis of it, I must resign. I am unwilling to jeopardize my health and I am also unwilling to become involved in an accident. For these reasons, I tender my resignation."

A short time later Lukaszewski reapplied for and obtained employment at the Wee Care Day Care Center.

After Lukaszewski left, the Board immediately began looking for a replacement. Only one qualified person applied for the position. Although this applicant had less of an educational background than Lukaszewski, she had more teaching experience. Under the salary schedule agreed upon by the Board and the teachers' union, this applicant would have to be paid $1,026.64 more per year than Lukaszewski. Having no alternative, the Board hired the applicant at the higher salary.

In December of 1978 the Board initiated an action against Lukaszewski for breach of contract. The Board alleged that, as a result of the breach, it suffered damage in the amount of the additional compensation it was required to pay Lukaszewski's replacement for the 1978–79 school year ($1,026.64). A trial was held before the court. The trial court ruled that Lukaszewski had breached her contract and awarded the Board $1,249.14 in damages ($1,026.64 for breach of contract and $222.50 for costs).

Lukaszewski appealed. The court of appeals affirmed the circuit court's determination that Lukaszewski breached her contract. However, the appellate court reversed the circuit court's damage award, reasoning that, although the Board had to pay more for Lukaszewski's replacement, by its own standards it obtained a proportionately more valuable teacher. Therefore, the court of appeals held that the Board suffered no damage from the breach. We granted the Board's petition for review.

There are two issues presented on this review: (1) whether Lukaszewski breached her employment contract with the Board; and (2) if she did breach her contract, whether the Board suffered recoverable damages therefrom.

* * *

Health and contract

A health danger will not excuse nonperformance of a contractual obligation when the danger is caused by the nonperforming party. *See Jennings v. Lyons,* 39 Wis. at 557–58. Nor will a health condition or danger which was foreseeable when the contract was entered into justify its breach. *Id.* It would be fundamentally unfair to allow a breaching party to escape liability because of a health danger which by his or her own fault has precluded performance.

[The court upheld the trial court's findings that (1) Lukaszewski's medical condition resulted from the "stress condition she had created" by an attempted repudiation of her contract," and (2) that Lukaszewski resigned for reasons other than health. The court therefore affirmed the holdings below that Lukaszewski breached her employment contract.]

As argument

In the instant case it is undisputed that, as a result of the breach, the Board hired a replacement at a salary exceeding what it had agreed to pay Lukaszewski. There is no question that this additional cost ($1,026.64) necessarily flowed from the breach and was within the contemplation of the parties when the contract was made. Lukaszewski argues and the court of appeals held, however, that the Board was not damaged by this expense. The amount a teacher is paid is determined by a salary schedule agreed upon by the teachers' union and the Board. The more education and experience a teacher has the greater her salary will be. Presumably, then, the amount of compensation a teacher receives reflects her value to the Board. Lukaszewski argues that the Board suffered no net loss because, while it had to pay more for the replacement, it received the services of a proportionately more valuable teacher. Accordingly, she maintains that the Board is not entitled to damages because an award would place it in a better position than if the contract had been performed.

what the board expected matters

✕ We disagree. Lukaszewski and the court of appeals improperly focus on the objective value of the services the Board received rather than that for which it had bargained. Damages for breach of contract are measured by the expectations of the parties. The Board expected to receive the services of a speech therapist with Lukaszewski's education and experience at the salary agreed upon. It neither expected nor wanted a more experienced therapist who had to be paid an additional $1,026.64 per year. Lukaszewski's breach forced the Board to hire the replacement and, in turn, to pay a higher salary. Therefore, the Board lost the benefit of its bargain. Any additional value the Board may have received from the replacement's greater experience was imposed upon it and thus cannot be characterized as a benefit. We conclude that the Board suffered damages for the loss of its bargain in the amount of additional compensation it was required to pay Lukaszewski's replacement.

This is not to say that an employer who is injured by an employee's breach of contract is free to hire the most qualified and expensive replacement and then recover the difference between the salary paid and the contract
→ salary. An injured party must take all reasonable steps to mitigate damages. *Kuhlman, Inc. v. G. Heileman Brewing Co.,* 83 Wis.2d 749, 752, 266 N.W.2d 382 (1978). Therefore, the employer must attempt to obtain equivalent services at the lowest possible cost. In the instant case the Board acted reasonably in hiring Lukaszewski's replacement even though she commanded a higher salary. Upon Lukaszewski's breach, the Board immediately took steps to locate a replacement. Only one qualified person applied for the

position. Having no alternative, the Board hired this applicant. Thus the Board properly mitigated its damages by hiring the least expensive, qualified replacement available.

We hold that the Board is entitled to have the benefit of its bargain restored. Therefore, we reverse that portion of the court of appeals' decision which reversed the trial court's damage award.

The decision of the court of appeals is affirmed in part and reversed in part.

[JUSTICE DAY dissented.]

Note
The Concept of "Efficient Breach"—an Introduction and Caveat

The concept of "efficient breach of contract" has recently figured prominently in the contract theory of economists and others who stress the importance of economic analysis of contract law. Most of these theorists argue that the concept of efficient breach provides a further justification for granting lost expectancy damages in contract cases. Although the concept applies in theory to any contract setting, it is perhaps most readily grasped in the sale of goods context. The first excerpt that follows introduces the concept, the second offers a caveat. Consider how the Posner excerpt applies to Handicapped Children's Education Bd. v. Lukaszewski.

R. POSNER, ECONOMIC ANALYSIS OF LAW
89–90 (2d ed. 1977).

[I]n some cases a party would be tempted to breach the contract simply because his profit from breach would exceed his expected profit from completion of the contract. If his profit from breach would also exceed the expected profit to the other party from completion of the contract, and if damages are limited to loss of expected profit, there will be an incentive to commit a breach. There should be. The opportunity cost of completion to the breaching party is the profit that he would make from a breach, and if it is greater than his profit from completion, then completion will involve a loss to him. If that loss is greater than the gain to the other party from completion, breach would be value-maximizing and should be encouraged. And because the victim of the breach is made whole for his loss, he is indifferent; hence encouraging breaches in these circumstances will not deter people from entering into contracts in the future.

An arithmetical illustration may be helpful here. I sign a contract to deliver 100,000 custom-ground widgets at $.10 apiece to A, for use in his boiler factory. After I have delivered 10,000, B comes to me, explains that he desperately needs 25,000 custom-ground widgets at once since otherwise he will be forced to close his pianola factory at great cost, and offers me $.15 apiece for 25,000 widgets. I sell him the widgets and as a result do not complete timely delivery to A, who sustains $1000 in lost profits from my breach. Having obtained an additional profit of $1250 on the sale to B, I am better off even after reimbursing A for his loss. Society is also better off. Since B was willing to pay me $.15 per widget, it must mean that each widget was worth at least $.15 to him. But it was worth only $.14 to A—the $.10 that he paid plus his expected profit of $.04 ($1000 divided by 25,000). Thus the breach resulted in a transfer of the 25,000 widgets from a less to a more valuable use. To be sure, had I refused to sell to B, he could have gone to A and negotiated an assignment of part of A's contract with me to him. But this would have introduced an additional step and so imposed additional transaction costs.

Thus far the emphasis has been on the economic importance of not awarding damages in excess of the lost expectation. It is equally important, however, not to award less than the expectation loss. Suppose A contracts to sell B for $100,000 a machine that is worth $110,000 to B, i.e., that would yield him a profit of $10,000. Before delivery C comes to A and offers him $109,000 for the machine promised B. A would be tempted to breach were he not liable to B for B's loss of expected profit. Given that measure of damages, C will not be able to induce a breach of A's contract with B unless he offers A more than $110,000, thereby indicating that the machine really is worth more to him than to B. The expectation rule thus assures that the machine ends up where it is most valuable.

L. FULLER, THE MORALITY OF LAW

28 (rev. ed. 1969).

Before the principle of marginal utility nothing is sacred; all existing arrangements are subject to being reordered in the interest of increased economic return. The economics of exchange is, in contrast, based on two fixed points: property and contract. While it permits interested calculation to reign everywhere else, such calculation is excluded when the question is fidelity to contract or respect for property. Without a self-sacrificing deference toward these institutions, a regime of exchange would lose its anchorage and no one would occupy a sufficiently stable position to know what he had to offer or what he could count on receiving from another.

Problem 3–2

On January 2, 1984, Edgar Janis entered into a one-year contract of employment at $1500 per month with Addis Corp. The market value of his services was $1200 per month. On January 31, after receiving one month's pay, Janis was wrongfully terminated. Despite a diligent search for a suitable alternative position, Janis remained unemployed until December 1, 1984, when he took a comparable job for comparable pay. You are Janis's lawyer. What will you seek to recover against Addis Corp.?

Problem 3–3

Arvid Anderson contracted at 11:00 a.m. on May 7, 1984 to buy a farm owned by Olaf Norgaard, closing to be July 15, with Anderson to pay a purchase price of $125,000. On the evening of May 7, Anderson changed his mind and telephoned Norgaard to that effect. An average of three appraisals indicated that the fair market value of the farm at all relevant times was about $122,000. Assume that Norgaard tried without success to resell to others for $125,000. Is Norgaard entitled to damages of $3,000? Should Norgaard receive any damages in such a case? Consider these remarks from Karl N. Llewellyn, Our Case–Law of Contract: Offer and Acceptance, II, 48 Yale L.J. 779, 803–04 (1939):

> The case is thus made, in ethics and in policy, for some type of legal remedy when agreement has been expressed, and each party knows of the other's expression, and a bit of time has elapsed. The case remains to be made, in ethics or in policy, for the snapping of the legal trap when the attempted retraction rolls in so quickly that any action taken in reliance becomes questionable, or when the quantity or degree of action taken is patently slight, or even when the retracting side can demonstrate the absence of any such action. Plainly, in such situations, policy becomes more tenuous; and to my mind only resort to formalism can keep ethics from openly acknowledging "moral" obligation to be here often on slippery footing. * * *

> What I think I see here is this: First, and most, a contagion of attitude from deals where there has been no attempt at early retraction, and where it is plain that the deal has been, shall I say, *lived* into, and where men's minds and courts' minds then naturally (though quite without necessity) date the closing as of the easiest time to see and think about: to wit, the time when agreement was expressed. * * * To allow free retraction is uncomfortable and disturbing, both vaguely and demonstrably. It unsettles, and the whole measure of the unsettling is not easy to see in advance. But especially unsettling would free retraction be in regard to * * * the closing of deals for the very purpose of shifting or hedging against the risks of market fluctuation.

COOPER v. CLUTE

Supreme Court of North Carolina, 1917.
174 N.C. 366, 93 S.E. 915.

BROWN, J. There are seven assignments of error by plaintiff. Five of them aver that the court erred in refusing to set aside the verdict upon certain issues, and the sixth avers that the court erroneously refused to set aside the verdict upon all the issues, based upon the ground that it was contrary to the weight of the evidence.

* * *

Seventh assignment avers that the court erred in failing to give judgment for the plaintiff for the difference between 10⅞ cents, the contract price of the cotton, and 11.03 cents, the price which it was admitted the defendant obtained from Sprunt for the sale of the said cotton, and the costs of the action, and in signing the judgment set out in the record. The findings of the jury establish that the defendant entered into a contract with plaintiff to deliver to him at the Hilton compress, near Wilmington, 1,430 bales of cotton not compressed at the price of 10⅞ cents per pound, delivery to be made on February 26, 1916; that plaintiff was ready, able, and willing to take and pay for the cotton according to contract; that defendant failed to deliver the cotton; and that its market value at time and place of delivery was 10⅞ cents per pound.

The measure of damage to be recovered for breach of an executory contract of this character is well settled to be the difference between the contract price and the actual or market value of the property at the time and place of the breach of the contract. Under this rule, if the market value is the same as the contract price when the contract is breached, only nominal damages can be recovered. * * * There are cases where the evidence warrants the allowance of special damages, but we see nothing in this case that takes it out of the general rule. * * *

* * *

Plaintiff contends that the court should have rendered judgment for plaintiff for the difference between 10⅞ cents, the contract price, and 11.03 cents, which plaintiff claims the defendant received from Sprunt for the cotton. The plaintiff tendered no such issue, and there is no finding of fact that defendant received 11.03 for the cotton. But that is immaterial. The written contract shows that the defendant did not sell to plaintiff any particular cotton. Defendant could have performed the contract by purchasing similar cotton on the market and making the delivery.

* * * The evidence is conflicting as to the value of similar cotton at place of delivery on February 26, 1916, but the jury have fixed it at 10⅞, which is the contract price. It therefore follows that the plaintiff has sustained no actual damage.

No error.

π suffered no damages

Problem 3–4

1. Consider how Cooper v. Clute would be decided under the Uniform Commercial Code:

U.C.C. § 1–106. Remedies to be Liberally Administered

(1) The remedies provided by this Act shall be liberally administered to the end that the aggrieved party may be put in as good a position as if the other party had fully performed * * *.

U.C.C. § 2–713. Buyers Damages for Non–Delivery or Repudiation

(1) * * * [T]he measure of damages for non-delivery or repudiation by the seller is the difference between the market price at the time when the buyer learned of the breach and the contract price together with any incidental and consequential damages provided in this Article (Section 2–715), but less expenses saved in consequence of the seller's breach.

(2) Market price is to be determined as of the place for tender or, in cases of rejection after arrival or revocation of acceptance, as of the place of arrival.

K–MV or MV–K +incid/ conseq. –savings

2. Assume that the seller in Cooper v. Clute repudiated the deal before delivery. At this time, the market price was 11⅜ cents per pound and the buyer immediately bought cotton in substitution at this price. What are buyer's damages under U.C.C. § 2–712(1) and (2), set forth below? What if buyer bought at 11⅛ cents per pound and the market price was 11⅜? Does U.C.C. § 2–713 apply?

U.C.C. § 2–712. "Cover"; Buyer's Procurement of Substitute Goods

(1) After a breach within the preceding section the buyer may "cover" by making in good faith and without unreasonable delay any reasonable purchase of or contract to purchase goods in substitution for those due from the seller.

(2) The buyer may recover from the seller as damages the difference between the cost of cover and the contract price together with any incidental

or consequential damages as hereinafter defined (Section 2–715), but less expenses saved in consequence of the seller's breach.

3. Assume that the buyer, not the seller, breached in Cooper v. Clute, and assume that at the time and place for tender the market price was 9 cents per pound. What would the seller recover according to the principle of Cooper v. Clute? According to U.C.C. § 1–106 above? According to U.C.C. § 2–708(1), set forth below?

U.C.C. § 2–708. Seller's Damages for Non–Acceptance or Repudiation

(1) Subject to subsection (2) * * *, the measure of damages for non-acceptance or repudiation by the buyer is the difference between the market price at the time and place for tender and the unpaid contract price together with any incidental damages provided in this Article (Section 2–710), but less expenses saved in consequence of the buyer's breach.

(2) If the measure of damages provided in subsection (1) is inadequate to put the seller in as good a position as performance would have done then the measure of damages is the profit (including reasonable overhead) which the seller would have made from full performance by the buyer, together with any incidental damages provided in this Article (Section 2–710), due allowance for costs reasonably incurred and due credit for payments or proceeds of resale.

4. Again, assume the buyer, not the seller, breached in Cooper v. Clute and assume that at the time and place for tender the market price was 10 cents per pound. The next day, seller resold at 9⅞ cents per pound. What are seller's damages under U.C.C. § 2–706(1), set forth below?

U.C.C. § 2–706. Seller's Resale Including Contract for Resale

(1) Under the conditions stated in Section 2–703 on seller's remedies, the seller may resell the goods concerned or the undelivered balance thereof. Where the resale is made in good faith and in a commercially reasonable manner the seller may recover the difference between the resale price and the contract price together with any incidental damages allowed under the provisions of this Article (Section 2–710), but less expenses saved in consequence of the buyer's breach.

5. Assume in Cooper v. Clute that the seller agreed to sell to buyer first quality seed grain and that the contract price was 15 cents per pound. Seller delivered smutty grain worth 5 cents per pound. On the date of delivery, the market price of first quality seed grain was 17 cents per pound. Buyer accepted and paid the contract price for the grain, fed it to his hogs, and sued seller for breach of warranty. What damages under U.C.C. § 2–714, set forth below?

U.C.C. § 2–714. Buyer's Damages for Breach in Regard to Accepted Goods

(1) Where the buyer has accepted goods and given notification (subsection (3) of Section 2–607) he may recover as damages for any non-conformity of tender the loss resulting in the ordinary course of events from the seller's breach as determined in any manner which is reasonable.

(2) The measure of damages for breach of warranty is the difference at the time and place of acceptance between the value of the goods accepted and the value they would have had if they had been as warranted, unless special circumstances show proximate damages of a different amount.

(3) In a proper case any incidental and consequential damages under the next section may also be recovered.

NERI v. RETAIL MARINE CORP.

Court of Appeals of New York, 1972.
30 N.Y.2d 393, 334 N.Y.S.2d 165, 285 N.E.2d 311.

GIBSON, JUDGE.

The appeal concerns the right of a retail dealer to recover loss of profits and incidental damages upon the buyer's repudiation of a contract governed by the Uniform Commercial Code. This is, indeed, the correct measure of damage in an appropriate case and to this extent the code (§ 2–708, subsection [2]) effected a substantial change from prior law, whereby damages were ordinarily limited to "the difference between the contract price and the market or current price". Upon the record before us, the courts below erred in declining to give effect to the new statute and so the order appealed from must be reversed.

The plaintiffs contracted to purchase from defendant a new boat of a specified model for the price of $12,587.40, against which they made a deposit of $40. They shortly increased the deposit to $4,250 in consideration of the defendant dealer's agreement to arrange with the manufacturer for immediate delivery on the basis of "a firm sale", instead of the delivery within approximately four to six weeks originally specified. Some six days after the date of the contract plaintiffs' lawyer sent to defendant a letter rescinding the sales contract for the reason that plaintiff Neri was about to undergo hospitalization and surgery, in consequence of which, according to the letter, it would be "impossible for Mr. Neri to make any payments". The boat had already been ordered from the manufacturer and was delivered to defendant at or before the time the attorneys' letter was received. Defendant declined to refund plaintiffs' deposit and this action to recover it was commenced. Defendant counterclaimed, alleging plaintiffs' breach of the contract and defendant's resultant damage in the amount of $4,250, for which sum defendant demanded judgment. Upon motion, defendant had summary judgment on the issue of liability tendered by its counterclaim; and Special Term directed an assessment of damages, upon which it would be determined whether plaintiffs were entitled to the return of any portion of their down payment.

Upon the trial so directed, it was shown that the boat ordered and received by defendant in accordance with plaintiffs' contract of purchase was sold some four months later to another buyer for the same price as that negotiated with plaintiffs. From this proof the plaintiffs argue that defendant's loss on its contract was recouped, while defendant argues that but for plaintiffs' default, it would have sold two boats and have earned two profits instead of one. Defendant proved, without contradiction, that its profit on the sale under the contract in suit would have been $2,579 and that during the period the boat remained unsold incidental expenses aggregating $674 for storage, upkeep, finance charges and insurance were incurred. Additionally, defendant proved and sought to recover attorneys' fees of $1,250.

The trial court found "untenable" defendant's claim for loss of profit, inasmuch as the boat was later sold for the same price that plaintiffs had contracted to pay; found, too, that defendant had failed to prove any incidental damages; further found "that the terms of section 2–718, subsection 2(b), of the Uniform Commercial Code are applicable and same make adequate and fair provision to place the sellers in as good a position as performance would have done" and, in accordance with paragraph (b) of subsection (2) thus relied upon, awarded defendant $500 upon its counterclaim and directed that plaintiffs recover the balance of their deposit, amounting to $3,750. The ensuing judgment was affirmed, without opinion, at the Appellate Division, 37 A.D.2d 917, 326 N.Y.S.2d 984, and defendant's appeal to this court was taken by our leave.

The issue is governed in the first instance by section 2–718 of the Uniform Commercial Code which provides, among other things, that the buyer, despite his breach, may have restitution of the amount by which his payment exceeds: (a) reasonable liquidated damages stipulated by the contract or (b) absent such stipulation, 20% of the value of the buyer's total performance or $500, whichever is smaller (§ 2–718, subsection [2], pars. [a], [b]). As above noted, the trial court awarded defendant an offset in the amount of $500 under paragraph (b) and directed restitution to plaintiffs of the balance. Section 2–718, however, establishes, in paragraph (a) of subsection (3), an alternative right of offset in favor of the seller, as follows: "(3) The buyer's right to restitution under subsection (2) is subject to offset to the extent that the seller establishes (a) a right to recover damages under the provisions of this Article other than subsection (1)".[b]

Among "the provisions of this Article other than subsection (1)" are those to be found in section 2–708, which the courts below did not apply. Subsection (1) of that section provides that "the measure of damages for non-acceptance or repudiation by the buyer is the difference between the market price at the time and place for tender and the unpaid contract price together with any incidental damages provided in this Article (Section 2–710), but less expenses saved in consequence of the buyer's breach." However, this provision is made expressly subject to subsection (2), providing: "(2) If the measure of damages provided in subsection (1) is inadequate to put the seller in as good a position as performance would have done then the measure of damages is the profit (including reasonable overhead) which the seller would have made from full performance by the buyer, together with any incidental

---

b. Uniform Commercial Code § 2–718 states in part:

§ **2–718. Liquidation or Limitation of Damages; Deposits**

(1) Damages for breach by either party may be liquidated in the agreement but only at an amount which is reasonable in the light of the anticipated or actual harm caused by the breach, the difficulties of proof of loss, and the inconvenience or nonfeasibility of otherwise obtaining an adequate remedy. A term fixing unreasonably large liquidated damages is void as a penalty.

(2) Where the seller justifiably withholds delivery of goods because of the buyer's breach, the buyer is entitled to restitution of any amount by which the sum of his payments exceeds

(a) the amount to which the seller is entitled by virtue of terms liquidating the seller's damages in accordance with subsection (1), or

(b) in the absence of such terms, twenty per cent of the value of the total performance for which the buyer is obligated under the contract or $500, whichever is smaller.

(3) The buyer's right to restitution under subsection (2) is subject to offset to the extent that the seller establishes

(a) a right to recover damages under the provisions of this Article other than subsection (1), and

(b) the amount or value of any benefits received by the buyer directly or indirectly by reason of the contract.

damages provided in this Article (Section 2–710), due allowance for costs reasonably incurred and due credit for payments or proceeds of resale."

* * *

Prior to the code, the New York cases "applied the 'profit' test, contract price less cost of manufacture, only in cases where the seller [was] a manufacturer or an agent for a manufacturer" (1955 Report of N.Y.Law Rev.Comm., vol. 1, p. 693). Its extension to retail sales was "designed to eliminate the unfair and economically wasteful results arising under the older law when fixed price articles were involved. This section permits the recovery of lost profits in all appropriate cases, which would include all standard priced goods." (Official Comment 2, McKinney's Cons.Laws of N.Y., Book 62½, Part 1, p. 605, under Uniform Commercial Code, § 2–708.) Additionally, and "[i]n all cases the seller may recover incidental damages" (*id.*, Comment 3). The buyer's right to restitution was established at Special Term upon the motion for summary judgment, as was the seller's right to proper offsets, in each case pursuant to section 2–718; and, as the parties concede, the only question before us, following the assessment of damages at Special Term, is that as to the proper measure of damage to be applied. The conclusion is clear from the record—indeed with mathematical certainty—that "the measure of damages provided in subsection (1) is inadequate to put the seller in as good a position as performance would have done" (Uniform Commercial Code, § 2–708, subsection [2]) and hence—again under subsection (2)—that the seller is entitled to its "profit (including reasonable overhead) * * * together with any incidental damages * * *, due allowance for costs reasonably incurred and due credit for payments or proceeds of resale."

It is evident, first, that this retail seller is entitled to its profit and, second, that the last sentence of subsection (2), as hereinbefore quoted, referring to "due credit for payments or proceeds of resale" is inapplicable to this retail sales contract.[1] Closely parallel to the factual situation now before us is that hypothesized by Dean Hawkland as illustrative of the operation of the rules: "Thus, if a private party agrees to sell his automobile to a buyer for $2,000, a breach by the buyer would cause the seller no loss (except incidental damages, i.e., expense of a new sale) if the seller was able to sell the automobile to another buyer for $2000. But the situation is different with dealers having an unlimited supply of standard-priced goods. Thus, if an automobile dealer agrees to sell a car to a buyer at the standard price of $2000, a breach by the buyer injures the dealer, even though he is able to sell the automobile to another for $2000. If the dealer has an inexhaustible supply of cars, the resale to replace the breaching buyer costs the dealer a sale,

---

1. The concluding clause, "due credit for payments or proceeds of resale", is intended to refer to "the privilege of the seller to realize junk value when it is manifestly useless to complete the operation of manufacture" (Supp. No. 1 to the 1952 Official Draft of Text and Comments of the Uniform Commercial Code, as Amended by the Action of the American Law Institute of the National Conference of Commissioners on Uniform Laws [1954], p. 14). The commentators who have considered the language have uniformly concluded that "the reference is to a resale as scrap under * * * Section 2–704" * * *. Another writer, reaching the same conclusion, after detailing the history of the clause, says that " 'proceeds of resale' previously meant the resale value of the goods in finished form; now it means the resale value of the components on hand at the time plaintiff learns of breach" (Harris, Seller's Damages, 18 Stanf.L.Rev. 66, 104). [Eds. note: Revised U.C.C. Article 2 (April 2000), section 2–708(b) omits the language "due credit for payments or proceeds of resale."]

because, had the breaching buyer performed, the dealer would have made two sales instead of one. The buyer's breach, in such a case, depletes the dealer's sales to the extent of one, and the measure of damages should be the dealer's profit on one sale. Section 2–708 recognizes this, and it rejects the rule developed under the Uniform Sales Act by many courts that the profit cannot be recovered in this case." (Hawkland, Sales and Bulk Sales [1958 ed.], pp. 153–154; and see Comment, 31 Fordham L.Rev. 749, 755–756.)

The record which in this case establishes defendant's entitlement to damages in the amount of its prospective profit, at the same time confirms defendant's cognate right to "any incidental damages provided in this Article (Section 2–710)[2] (Uniform Commercial Code, § 2–708, subsection [2]). From the language employed it is too clear to require discussion that the seller's right to recover loss of profits is not exclusive and that he may recoup his "incidental" expenses as well. * * * Although the trial court's denial of incidental damages in the uncontroverted amount of $674 was made in the context of its erroneous conclusion that paragraph (b) of subsection (2) of section 2–718 was applicable and was "adequate * * * to place the sellers in as good a position as performance would have done", the denial seems not to have rested entirely on the court's mistaken application of the law, as there was an explicit finding "that defendant completely failed to show that it suffered any incidental damages." We find no basis for the court's conclusion with respect to a deficiency of proof inasmuch as the proper items of the $674 expenses (being for storage, upkeep, finance charges and insurance for the period between the date performance was due and the time of the resale) were proven without objection and were in no way controverted, impeached or otherwise challenged, at the trial or on appeal. Thus the court's finding of a failure of proof cannot be supported upon the record and, therefore, and contrary to plaintiffs' contention, the affirmance at the Appellate Division was ineffective to save it.

The trial court correctly denied defendant's claim for recovery of attorney's fees incurred by it in this action. Attorney's fees incurred in an action such as this are not in the nature of the protective expenses contemplated by the statute (Uniform Commercial Code, § 1–106, subd. [1]; § 2–710; § 2–708, subsection [2]) and by our reference to "legal expense" in Procter & Gamble Distr. Co. v. Lawrence Amer. Field Warehousing Corp. (16 N.Y.2d 344, 354–355, 266 N.Y.S.2d 785, 792–793, 213 N.E.2d 873, 878–879, *supra*), upon which defendant's reliance is in this respect misplaced.

It follows that plaintiffs are entitled to restitution of the sum of $4,250 paid by them on account of the contract price less an offset to defendant in the amount of $3,253 on account of its lost profit of $2,579 and its incidental damages of $674.

The order of the Appellate Division should be modified, with costs in all courts, in accordance with this opinion, and, as so modified, affirmed.

* * *

Ordered accordingly.

2. "Incidental damages to an aggrieved seller include any commercially reasonable charges, expenses or commissions incurred in stopping delivery, in the transportation, care and custody of goods after the buyer's breach, in connection with return or resale of the goods or otherwise resulting from the breach" (Uniform Commercial Code, § 2–710).

Problem 3–5

In the excerpt that follows, Professor Melvin A. Eisenberg sets forth several justifications supporting the award of expectancy damages. Consider whether these justifications support the award of such damages in his two "merchant to consumer" hypothetical cases that follow the excerpt. Consider, too, what the plaintiff should recover in such cases. (The excerpt and the problems appear in Eisenberg, The Bargain Principle and Its Limits, 95 Harv.L.Rev. 741, 787, 794, 797 (1982).)

"First, fairness normally requires that a promisee should at least be compensated for the cost he incurred in reasonably relying on a bargain promise. * * * [I]n many transaction-types enforcement of an executory contract to its full extent is desirable on the ground that expectation damages are approximately equal to cost, but much easier to measure. I shall call this justification the surrogate-cost theory.

"Second, a contract for forward delivery typically is made with the purpose of enabling the parties to plan their future conduct reliably. Efficiency normally requires that such planning should be facilitated. The award of expectation damages conduces to that end by making breach unprofitable in the normal case. I shall call this justification the planning theory.

"Third, when a contract is made for forward delivery at a fixed price, it is frequently a purpose of the contract to allocate the risk of price changes. Efficiency normally requires effectuating this allocation, and that is just what is done by expectation damages. Risk allocation also implicates considerations of fairness. As Sharp observed:

> [T]his is not only an industrial and credit economy, but also a risk taking, profit making, more or less gambling economy. This may mean not only that harmful reliance, in fluctuating markets, is best remedied by expectation damages, but also that the profits dependent on good guesses about the future are generally to be assured to the person who is willing to gamble on his judgment.

To put this differently, when parties gamble on market movements and the market does in fact move, the contract is in a sense half-completed rather than executory, and the breaching promisor is like a gambler who welshes on his bet. I shall call this justification the risk theory.

* * *

"*Dance Lessons.* E, an electrical engineer, wants to learn to dance. S operates a dancing school. On May 1, E signs a contract with S to take Dancing I, a group class, which begins on July 1. Dancing I meets two hours a week, runs twenty-six weeks and costs $500. E understands all the provisions of the contract and considered the matter in a deliberative frame of mind, but knows nothing about damage rules. On June 15, E changes his mind and repudiates.

"S incurs little or no incremental out-of-pocket costs for group classes, since its instructors work on full-year contracts and it owns its own studios. S's classes usually don't fill to capacity. The capacity of Dancing I is twenty students. On June 15 sixteen students had enrolled. No additional students enrolled thereafter.

* * *

"*Buick Buyer.* T, a high school teacher, wants to buy a new Buick. After shopping around, T decides to buy at Seller's dealership, since Seller's price matches the lowest price available from competing dealers and Seller has a good reputation for servicing. On October 1, T signs a contract to buy from Seller a new Buick, with specified accessories, for $10,000, delivery on December 1. On November 1, before the factory has begun to fill Seller's order for T's car, T repudiates the contract. Seller's factory cost for the Buick ordered by T is $8,500, and Seller can buy as many new Buicks from the factory as it sells."

Note
Lost Expectancy, General Damages, and Consequential Damages

Most of the damage claims asserted by injured parties in the preceding cases and problems were for lost expectancy damages in the form of "general" damages. General damages are losses from a breach that arise "naturally or ordinarily." For example, a purchaser of a defective stove "naturally or ordinarily" suffers damages measured by the difference between the value of what was accepted and what was promised. Often, however, general damages will be insufficient to make the injured party whole. For example, the stove buyer may have needed the stove to make hamburgers at her new restaurant. She may, therefore, also suffer lost profits at the restaurant due to the defective stove. In this context, the claim for lost profits would be called "special" or "consequential" damages because many aggrieved stove purchasers would not suffer such damages. One can see that to award the aggrieved party full lost expectancy, courts often must award both general and consequential damages.

Is the lost profits claim in Neri v. Retail Marine Corp. general or consequential? The lost profits recovery is general in the sense that it substitutes for the seller's right to the contract-market differential. Still, many sellers of boats will not suffer damages as measured by lost profits. What if the seller in Neri was not a lost-volume seller?

While the distinction between general and consequential damages may be blurred in cases such as Neri (the second Restatement of Contracts § 351, Comment b, states that the terms "general" and "special" damages "are often misleading"), the distinction is still important. Typically, consequential damages are subject to greater qualifications and limits than general damages, as we shall see in the next section.

SECTION FOUR: AVAILABILITY OF LOST EXPECTANCY DAMAGES— QUALIFICATIONS AND LIMITS

HADLEY v. BAXENDALE

Court of Exchequer, 1854.
9 Exch. 341.

At the trial before Crompton, J., at the last Gloucester Assizes, it appeared that the plaintiffs carried on an extensive business as millers at Gloucester; and that, on the 11th of May, their mill was stopped by a breakage of the crank shaft by which the mill was worked. The steam-engine was manufactured by Messrs. Joyce & Co., the engineers, at Greenwich, and it became necessary to send the shaft as a pattern for a new one to Greenwich.

The fracture was discovered on the 12th, and on the 13th the plaintiffs sent one of their servants to the office of the defendants, who are the well-known carriers trading under the name of Pickford & Co., for the purpose of having the shaft carried to Greenwich. The plaintiffs' servant told the clerk that the mill was stopped, and that the shaft must be sent immediately; and in answer to the inquiry when the shaft would be taken, the answer was, that if it was sent up by twelve o'clock any day, it would be delivered at Greenwich on the following day. On the following day the shaft was taken by the defendants before noon, for the purpose of being conveyed to Greenwich, and the sum of 2£. 4s. was paid for its carriage for the whole distance; at the same time the defendants' clerk was told that a special entry, if required, should be made to hasten its delivery. The delivery of the shaft at Greenwich was delayed by some neglect; and the consequence was, that the plaintiffs did not receive the new shaft for several days after they would otherwise have done, and the working of their mill was thereby delayed, and they thereby lost the profits they would otherwise have received.

On the part of the defendants, it was objected that these damages were too remote, and that the defendants were not liable with respect to them. The learned Judge left the case generally to the jury, who found a verdict with 25£. damages beyond the amount paid into Court.

Whateley, in last Michaelmas Term, obtained a rule nisi for a new trial, on the ground of misdirection.

* * *

The judgment of the Court was now delivered by ALDERSON, B. We think that there ought to be a new trial in this case; but, in so doing, we deem it to be expedient and necessary to state explicitly the rule which the Judge, at the next trial, ought, in our opinion, to direct the jury to be governed by when they estimate the damages.

It is, indeed, of the last importance that we should do this; for, if the jury are left without any definite rule to guide them, it will, in such cases as these, manifestly lead to the greatest injustice. The Courts have done this on several occasions; and, in Blake v. Midland Railway Company, 18 Q.B. 93, the Court granted a new trial on this very ground, that the rule had not been definitely laid down to the jury by the learned Judge at Nisi Prius.

* * *

Now we think the proper rule in such a case as the present is this:— Where two parties have made a contract which one of them has broken, the damages which the other party ought to receive in respect to such breach of contract should be such as may fairly and reasonably be considered either arising naturally, i.e., according to the usual course of things, from such breach of contract itself,[c] or such as may reasonably be supposed to have been in the contemplation of both parties, at the time they made the contract, as the probable result of the breach of it. Now, if the special circumstances under which the contract was actually made were communicated by the plaintiffs to

---

c. What are the "general" damages for breach of such a contract of carriage? One court answered, much later: "[W]e conclude that [such damages] * * * would be limited to a recovery of the rental value of the shipment for the time of the unreasonable delay." New Orleans & N.E.R. Co. v. J.H. Miner Saw Mfg. Co., 117 Miss. 646, 657, 78 So. 577, 578 (1918).

the defendants, and thus known to both parties, the damages resulting from the breach of such a contract, which they would reasonably contemplate, would be the amount of injury which would ordinarily follow from a breach of contract under these special circumstances so known and communicated. But, on the other hand, if these special circumstances were wholly unknown to the party breaking the contract, he, at the most, could only be supposed to have had in his contemplation the amount of injury which would arise generally, and in the great multitude of cases not affected by any special circumstances, from such a breach of contract. For, had the special circumstances been known, the parties might have specially provided for the breach of contract by special terms as to the damages in that case; and of this advantage it would be very unjust to deprive them.

Now the above principles are those by which we think the jury ought to be guided in estimating the damages arising out of any breach of contract. It is said, that other cases, such as breaches of contract in the non-payment of money, or in the not making a good title to land, are to be treated as exceptions from this, and as governed by a conventional rule. But as, in such cases, both parties must be supposed to be cognisant of that well-known rule, these cases may, we think, be more properly classed under the rule above enunciated as to cases under known special circumstances, because there both parties may reasonably be presumed to contemplate the estimation of the amount of damages according to the conventional rule. Now, in the present case, if we are to apply the principles above laid down, we find that the only circumstances here communicated by the plaintiffs to the defendants at the time the contract was made, were, that the article to be carried was the broken shaft of a mill, and that the plaintiffs were the millers of that mill. But how do these circumstances shew reasonably that the profits of the mill must be stopped by an unreasonable delay in the delivery of the broken shaft by the carrier to the third person? Suppose the plaintiffs had another shaft in their possession put up or putting up at the time, and that they only wished to send back the broken shaft to the engineer who made it; it is clear that this would be quite consistent with the above circumstances, and yet the unreasonable delay in the delivery would have no effect upon the intermediate profits of the mill. Or, again, suppose that, at the time of the delivery to the carrier, the machinery of the mill had been in other respects defective, then, also, the same results would follow.

Here it is true that the shaft was actually sent back to serve as a model for a new one, and that the want of a new one was the only cause of the stoppage of the mill, and that the loss of profits really arose from not sending down the new shaft in proper time, and that this arose from the delay in delivering the broken one to serve as a model. But it is obvious that, in the great multitude of cases of millers sending off broken shafts to third persons by a carrier under ordinary circumstances, such consequences would not, in all probability, have occurred; and these special circumstances were here never communicated by the plaintiffs to the defendants. It follows, therefore, that the loss of profits here cannot reasonably be considered such a consequence of the breach of contract as could have been fairly and reasonably contemplated by both the parties when they made this contract. For such loss would neither have flowed naturally from the breach of this contract in the great multitude of such cases occurring under ordinary circumstances, nor were the special circumstances, which, perhaps, would have made it a reasonable and natural consequence of such breach of contract, communicated to or known by the defendants. The Judge ought, therefore, to have told the jury that, upon the facts then before them, they ought not to take the loss of profits into consideration at all in estimating the damages. There must therefore be a new trial in this case.

Rule absolute.

"Trouble at the Mill"

To Baxendale was told a tale
And urgent words were spoken
We need to send a shaft to mend
Our old crank-shaft is broken.

Defendant swore, for £2–4
In one day he'd transport it
But days went by, with no shaft nigh
(My goodness, who'd have thought it?)

So Hadley's mill stood sadly still
And not a shaft was cranked
So who should pay for this delay
And all the cash unbanked?

Said Baxendale (so runs the tale)
This sorry loss of profit
Is naught to me, because you see
You never told me of it.

So held the court. You can't be caught
For loss you don't foresee
Now Hadley's rule is taught at school
And at each mother's knee.

GEOFFREY MARSHALL
22 SEPTEMBER 1986

Problem 3–6

You represent the miller in *Hadley v. Baxendale*. On May 12, the day the broken shaft was discovered, you are asked to draft a letter to be handed to the carrier that would assure your client of a consequential damages recovery if the carrier delays carriage of the shaft. Draft the letter. Will the carrier agree to it?

SPANG INDUSTRIES, INC. v. AETNA CASUALTY & SURETY CO., 512 F.2d 365 (2d Cir.1975). "In *Hadley v. Baxendale* a miller sought to recover the profits lost from the closing of the mill as a result of a carrier's failure to make timely delivery of a broken crank shaft to an engineering firm where it was to be used as a model for a replacement. A recovery of those profits was disallowed on the ground that it was not reasonably foreseeable that profits would be lost as a result of the breach of the contract of carriage. Lord Justice Asquith pointed out in Victoria Laundry, Ltd. v. Newman Indus., Ltd., that the headnote in Hadley v. Baxendale is misleading in stating that the clerk of the defendant carrier knew that the mill was stopped and that the broken shaft had to be delivered immediately. The *Victoria* court stated that the Court of Exchequer must have rejected this statement and decided to deny the loss of profits from the closing of the mill because the only knowledge possessed by the defendant was that the mill shaft was broken and that the plaintiffs were the millers. Otherwise, 'the court must, one would suppose, have decided the case the other way round * * *.' [1949] 2 K.B. at 537. The misleading headnote, however, was considered to reflect the actual facts by at least two scholarly articles on the famous case. Bauer, Consequential Damages in Contract, 80 U.Penn.L.Rev. 687, 689 (1932); McCormick, Damages for Breach of Contract, 19 Minn.L.Rev. 497, 500 (1935)."

R. POSNER, ECONOMIC ANALYSIS OF LAW

105 (5th ed.1998).

The task for a court asked to interpret a contract to cover a contingency that the parties did not provide for is to imagine how the parties would have provided for the contingency if they had decided to do so. Often there will be clues in the language of the contract. But often there will not be, and then the court may have to engage in economic thinking–may have to decide what the most efficient way of dealing with the contingency is. For this is the best way of deciding how the parties would have provided for it. Each party, it is true, is interested just in his own profit, and not in the joint profit; but the larger the joint profit is, the bigger the "take" of each party is likely to be. So they have a mutual interest in minimizing the cost of performance. The court can make use of this interest to fill out a contract along lines that the parties would have approved at the time of making the contract.

AYRES AND GERTNER, FILLING GAPS IN INCOMPLETE CONTRACTS: AN ECONOMIC THEORY OF DEFAULT RULES

99 Yale L.J. 87, 101–02 (1989).

The holding in *Hadley* operates as a penalty default. The miller could have informed the carrier of the potential consequential damages and contracted for full damage insurance. The *Hadley* default of denying unforeseeable damages may not be consistent with what fully informed parties would have wanted. The miller's consequential damages were real and the carrier may have been the more efficient bearer of this risk. As a general matter, millers may want carriers to compensate them for consequential damages that carriers can prevent at lower cost. The default can instead be understood as a purposeful inducement to the miller as the more informed party to reveal that information to the carrier. Informing the carrier creates value because if the carrier foresees the loss, he will be able to prevent it more efficiently. At the same time, however, revealing the information to the carrier will undoubtedly increase the price of shipping. Nonetheless, so long as transaction costs are not prohibitive, a miller with high consequential damages will gain from revealing this information and contracting for greater insurance from the carrier because the carrier is the least-cost avoider.

ARMSTRONG v. BANGOR MILL SUPPLY CORP.

Maine Supreme Judicial Court, 1929.
128 Me. 75, 145 A. 741.

STURGIS, J. General motion for a new trial in an action for damages resulting from the defendant's failure to repair a crankshaft from the plaintiff's lath mill in a workmanlike manner.

There is evidence to support the plaintiff's claim that in February, 1927, he sent a broken crankshaft from his lath mill at Vanceboro to the defendant's machine shop in Bangor for repairs, and that in making the repairs the defendant's workmen left the shaft out of alignment, necessitating its return from Vanceboro for realignment. The plaintiff's mill was shut down six days with resultant loss of earnings and expenses of maintenance. For these losses and expenses incidental to the crankshaft repairs he has a verdict.

It is an elementary principle that in the defendant's contract to repair the crankshaft the law implies an undertaking on its part to perform the work in a reasonably skillful and workmanlike manner. * * * Upon the facts here in evidence the jury were justified in finding that this undertaking was not fulfilled.

The damages awarded were not excessive. Wages, fuel, board of men and horses, and other fixed operating charges, continued through the shutdown period. The mill, with an established business yielding regular profits, was "impeded in its efficient operation" by the defendant's failure to fulfill the obligations impliedly imposed by its contract. The jury could properly include this element of loss in their award. * * * The damages awarded do not exceed the losses sustained.

Motion overruled.

Note
The Tacit Agreement Test

Although predominant today, Hadley v. Baxendale is not always followed. For example, some courts have permitted a recovery of consequential damages only when the defendant tacitly agreed to assume the risk. In Lamkins v. International Harvester Co., 207 Ark. 637, 182 S.W.2d 203 (1944), a farmer purchased a tractor for over $1400 from a dealer, and told the dealer that he desired lighting equipment worth $20 so that he could work at night. The tractor was delivered without the lighting equipment and the farmer claimed he was therefore unable to plant 25 acres of soybeans. The farmer sought damages of $450. The court stated:

Conceding that * * * appellant communicated notice to the dealer on or before December 4, 1941, that he desired lighting equipment so that he might work at night, there is nothing in the testimony showing circumstances surrounding and connected with the transaction which were calculated to bring home to the dealer knowledge that appellant expected him to assume liability for a crop loss, which might amount to several hundreds of dollars, if he should fail to deliver a $20 lighting accessory. There was, of course, no such express contract on the dealer's part, and the facts and circumstances are not such as to make it reasonable for the trier of facts to believe that the dealer at the time tacitly consented to be bound for more than ordinary damages in case of default on his part.

[handwritten: dealer didn't know about potentially being liable for crop loss]

Although Professor Farnsworth reports that courts have generally "discarded" the tacit agreement test, E. Farnsworth, Contracts 838 (3d ed. 1999), courts understandably balk at imposing inordinate liability when the breaching party receives relatively insignificant consideration, even if the injured party communicated special circumstances to the breaching party. Do you see why?

Problem 3–7

1. How would the Lamkins case in the previous note be decided under the provisions that follow? *[handwritten: for Lamkins]*

UNIFORM COMMERCIAL CODE § 2–715(2)(a).

Consequential damages resulting from the seller's breach include

(a) any loss resulting from general or particular requirements and needs of which the seller at the time of contracting had reason to know and which could not reasonably be prevented by cover or otherwise. * * *

[handwritten: couldn't buy lights anywhere that night!]

Official Comment

* * *

2. Subsection (2) operates to allow the buyer, in an appropriate case, any consequential damages which are the result of the seller's breach. The "tacit agreement" test for the recovery of consequential damages is rejected. * * *

3. In the absence of excuse under the section on merchant's excuse by failure of presupposed conditions, the seller is liable for consequential damages in all cases where he had reason to know of the buyer's general or particular requirements at the time of contracting. * * *

Particular needs of the buyer must generally be made known to the seller while general needs must rarely be made known to charge the seller with knowledge.

RESTATEMENT (SECOND) OF CONTRACTS § 351(3).

A court may limit damages for foreseeable loss by excluding recovery for loss of profits, by allowing recovery only for loss incurred in reliance, or otherwise if it concludes that in the circumstances justice so requires in order to avoid disproportionate compensation.

[handwritten: ex?]

2. Resolve the following case under all relevant code provisions. WS, a wholesaler, contracts to sell screws to RB, a manufacturer, at $10 per carton. RB intends to use the screws in manufacturing widgets. RB changes its plans and contracts to resell the screws to TB for $20 per carton. WS fails to deliver and the market price is $18 on the date of delivery. RB learns of the breach on the date of delivery. RB is unable to buy substitute screws for delivery to TB. RB sues WS. How much can RB recover?

CONVENTION ON CONTRACTS FOR THE INTERNATIONAL SALE OF GOODS.

Article 74

Damages for breach of contract by one party consist of a sum equal to the loss, including loss of profit, suffered by the other party as a consequence of the breach. Such damages may not exceed the loss which the party in breach foresaw or ought to have foreseen at the time of the conclusion of the contract, in the light of the facts and matters of which he then knew or ought to have known, as a possible consequence of the breach of contract.

CLARK v. MARSIGLIA

Supreme Court of New York, 1845.
1 Denio 317, 43 Am.Dec. 670.

Error from the New York common pleas. Marsiglia sued Clark in the court below in assumpsit, for work, labor and materials, in cleaning, repairing and improving sundry paintings belonging to the defendant. The defendant pleaded non assumpsit.

The plaintiff proved that a number of paintings were delivered to him by the defendant to clean and repair, at certain prices for each. They were delivered upon two occasions. As to the first parcel, for the repairing of which the price was seventy-five dollars, no defense was offered. In respect to the other, for which the plaintiff charged one hundred and fifty-six dollars, the defendant gave evidence tending to show that after the plaintiff had commenced work upon them, he desired him not to go on, as he had concluded not to have the work done. The plaintiff, notwithstanding, finished the cleaning and repairing of the pictures, and claimed to recover for doing the whole, and for the materials furnished, insisting that the defendant had no right to countermand the order which he had given. The defendant's counsel requested the court to charge that he had the right to countermand his instructions for the work, and that the plaintiff could not recover for any work done after such countermand.

The court declined to charge as requested, but, on the contrary, instructed the jury that inasmuch as the plaintiff had commenced the work before the order was revoked, he had a right to finish it, and to recover the whole value of his labor and for the materials furnished. The jury found their verdict accordingly, and the defendant's counsel excepted. Judgment was rendered upon the verdict.

* * *

PER CURIAM. * * * The plaintiff was allowed to recover as though there had been no countermand of the order; and in this the court erred. The defendant, by requiring the plaintiff to stop work upon the paintings, violated his contract, and thereby incurred a liability to pay such damages as the plaintiff should sustain. Such damages would include a recompense for the labor done and materials used, and such further sum in damages as might, upon legal principles, be assessed for the breach of the contract: but the plaintiff had no right, by obstinately persisting in the work, to make the penalty upon the defendant greater than it would otherwise have been.

To hold that one who employs another to do a piece of work is bound to suffer it to be done at all events, would sometimes lead to great injustice. A man may hire another to labor for a year, and within the year his situation may be such as to render the work entirely useless to him. The party employed cannot persist in working, though he is entitled to the damages consequent upon his disappointment. So if one hires another to build a house, and subsequent events put it out of his power to pay for it, it is commendable in him to stop the work, and pay for what has been done and the damages sustained by the contractor. He may be under a necessity to change his residence; but upon the rule contended for, he would be obliged to have a house which he did not need and could not use. In all such cases the just claims of the party employed are satisfied when he is fully recompensed for his part performance and indemnified for his loss in respect to the part left unexecuted; and to persist in accumulating a larger demand is not consistent with good faith towards the employer. The judgment must be reversed, and a venire de novo awarded.

Judgment reversed.

Problem 3–8

On January 7, 1986, Seller Co. and Buyer Co. agree that Seller will manufacture standard valves for Buyer for delivery on July 1 at a price of $40,000. On January 30, Buyer repudiates. Seller tells you that (1) its cost of manufacture would have been $27,000, and it can (2) cease manufacturing the valves, (3) reallocate the $15,000 worth of labor allocated to the Buyer Co. contract to less skilled tasks to produce goods worth $10,000, and (4) resell for $8,000 components purchased for this contract for $10,000. Overhead of $2,000 allocated to the contract cannot be saved. What can seller recover under U.C.C. § 2–708(2), set forth at page 239?

Seller wants to know if it can complete manufacture. Assume that Seller tells you that the market for such valves is "firm," and that in July it is "very likely" a buyer could be found for such valves "at $40,000 or above." You advise Seller to complete on the basis of U.C.C. § 2–704(2), which provides:

> Where the goods are unfinished an aggrieved seller may in the exercise of reasonable commercial judgment for the purposes of avoiding loss and of effective realization either complete the manufacture and wholly identify the goods to the contract or cease manufacture and resell for scrap or salvage value or proceed in any other reasonable manner.

On July 1, Seller is able to sell the valves for only $15,000, the market having unexpectedly fallen because of a new technological breakthrough. What, if anything, can Seller recover from Buyer? Would the recovery conflict with the principle of Clark v. Marsiglia?

CONVENTION ON CONTRACTS FOR THE INTERNATIONAL SALE OF GOODS.

Article 77

A party who relies on a breach of contract must take such measures as are reasonable in the circumstances to mitigate the loss, including loss of profit, resulting from the breach. If he fails to take such measures, the party in breach may claim a reduction in the damages in the amount by which the loss should have been mitigated.

SCHIAVI MOBILE HOMES, INC. v. GIRONDA

Supreme Judicial Court of Maine, 1983.
463 A.2d 722.

NICHOLS, JUSTICE.

The principal issue in this appeal involves a retailer's duty to mitigate damages following a customer's breach of a contract for the purchase from the retailer of a mobile home.

On January 23, 1979, the Defendants, Frank Gironda, Jr., and Patricia Gironda, signed a contract with the Plaintiff, Schiavi Mobile Homes, Inc., for the purchase from that corporation of a yellow, two-bedroom mobile home for a total purchase price of $23,028.69. The Defendants paid a $1,000 deposit.

After undergoing difficulties—medical, financial and marital—the Defendants breached the purchase contract. In September 1979, Howard Palmer, an agent of Schiavi, contacted Frank Gironda, Sr., the father of Frank, Jr. Palmer asked if Frank, Jr., was still planning to purchase the mobile home. Frank Gironda, Sr., responded that because of his son's problems and his son's relocation to the West Coast, he did not know what he planned to do. Frank, Sr., then asked Palmer if he could purchase the home so his son would not lose his deposit. He expressed a willingness to mortgage his own home for this purpose. Palmer responded that this would not be necessary.

On November 7, 1979, the Plaintiff sold this mobile home to a third party for $22,000, and then commenced this action in Superior Court, Oxford County, seeking from the Defendants $4,800 in lost profits and interest expense allegedly incurred as a result of the Defendants' breach. Following a jury-waived trial, the Superior Court awarded the Plaintiff judgment in the amount of $759.45.[1] [Defendants appealed, asserting that the plaintiff failed to mitigate damages.]

The determinative issue in this case concerns the retailer's alleged failure to mitigate damages. At trial only one witness, Frank Gironda, Sr., was called. The father testified as to his conversation with Palmer, in which he expressed his willingness to purchase the mobile home. Although admitting that he did not at that time have ready cash sufficient to cover the cost of the home, he testified that he owned a $30,000 house free and clear and had been ready to mortgage it for that purpose. Questioned by the court as to his willingness to purchase the mobile home in place of his son, the witness testified that he told Palmer that he was willing to buy the mobile home if his son could not be found. He said, "That's the way we operate in our family, Your Honor."

The Plaintiff presented no evidence on the issue of mitigation. After argument by counsel, the Superior Court ruled from the bench that the

---

1. This judgment reflected the retention by the Plaintiff of the $1,000 deposit. The Superior Court calculated damages by subtracting the resale price of the home ($22,000) from the contract price ($23,028.69) and then adding in incidental damages for floor-plan interest ac-

cruing from the breach ($731.45). We note that these figures yield a damage amount of $1,760.14, which after subtracting the deposit, should have resulted in a judgment of $760.14. The court also awarded the Plaintiff $500 in interest, costs and attorney's fees.

Plaintiff had not failed to properly mitigate damages, because the offer by the Defendant's father was conditional and vague.[2] In so ruling, the court misapplied the doctrine of mitigation.

It has long been the rule in this state that when a contract is breached, the nonbreaching party has an affirmative duty to take reasonable steps to mitigate his damages. As early as 1830 this Court declared that if a party "has it in his power to take measures, by which his loss may be less aggravated, this will be expected of him." *Miller v. Mariner's Church,* 7 Me. 51, 55 (1830). * * *

* * *

The touchstone of the duty to mitigate is reasonableness. The nonbreaching party need only take reasonable steps to minimize his losses; he is not required to unreasonably expose himself to risk, humiliation or expense.

In the instant case the Superior Court never focused directly on the reasonableness of the Plaintiff's failure to pursue the offer of Frank Gironda, Sr., to purchase the mobile home in the place of his son. Instead the court solely concerned itself with the legal sufficiency of the father's offer. This approach was fraught with error.

First, the father's announced willingness to purchase the mobile home was conditioned only on his son not being found; that is, upon there being a breach of the son's contractual obligation. That was the same contingency from which arose the Plaintiff's duty to mitigate. As soon as that duty to mitigate arose, the Plaintiff had available to it a then unconditional willingness on the father's part to buy the mobile home.

Second, the father asked the Plaintiff if he could purchase the mobile home in place of his son, and at the time he was ready, willing and able to make the purchase. We cannot agree with the Superior Court's conclusion that the father's offer was too vague to have constituted the foundation for a binding contract when accepted by the Plaintiff.

In any event, the duty to mitigate is more than just a duty to accept legally enforceable offers. Upon learning of the Defendants' breach, the Plaintiff was obligated to take reasonable affirmative measures to keep its losses to a minimum. Palmer's conversation with Frank Gironda, Sr., in September, 1979, revealed that he had a party willing to pay the full price of the mobile home. Regardless of whether the father actually made a valid "offer," the retailer had a duty to pursue this opportunity to minimize the effects of the breach. Instead, the Plaintiff waited another two months and then sold the home for $1,028.69 less than Frank Gironda, Sr., was willing to pay.

There is no evidence in the record that the Plaintiff's failure to sell to its customer's father rested on any legitimate ground. Because the Plaintiff did not take reasonable measures to mitigate its damages, we conclude that the Superior Court erred in awarding it damages based on the ultimate reduction

---

2. The court ruled:

I'm going to find for Schiavi on this issue. It is conditional. Even if it weren't, I think this is similar to purchase and sale where you have an actual intent before suing to recover damages. You can't do business on this kind of vague promises and understanding otherwise nobody would know where he stands.

in the selling price of the mobile home. This case must be returned to that court for a recomputation of damages.

* * *

We note * * * that the Plaintiff's failure to sell the home to Frank Gironda, Sr., in September bars recovery of any interest expense incurred after that point in time. * * *

* * *

[Defendants' appeal was granted.]

Problem 3–9

On May 1, 1978, the Illinois Furnace Co. entered into a long-term (6 year) contract with Ohio Valley Coke, Inc. for the purchase of coke at $40 a ton. Assume that on May 20, 1981, Ohio Valley Coke, Inc. repudiated its contract. At this time, other suppliers were offering long-term contracts at between $50 to $53 a ton. This appreciable increase in price was attributable to flooding in the Ohio Valley that had interfered with the mining of coke during three successive years. Illinois Furnace Co. assumed it could always buy on the spot market and declined to enter into a long-term contract when Ohio Valley repudiated. Six months later, unable to buy sufficient quantities of coke on the spot market, Illinois Furnace was forced to close one of its plants for three weeks at a loss in profits of $450,000. Can Illinois Furnace recover this sum from Ohio Valley Coke, Inc.?

1 defense!

PARKER v. TWENTIETH CENTURY–FOX FILM CORP.

Supreme Court of California, 1970.
3 Cal.3d 176, 89 Cal.Rptr. 737, 474 P.2d 689.

BURKE, JUSTICE.

Defendant Twentieth Century–Fox Film Corporation appeals from a summary judgment granting to plaintiff the recovery of agreed compensation under a written contract for her services as an actress in a motion picture. As will appear, we have concluded that the trial court correctly ruled in plaintiff's favor and that the judgment should be affirmed.

Plaintiff [Shirley MacLaine] is well known as an actress, and in the contract between plaintiff and defendant is sometimes referred to as the "Artist." Under the contract, dated August 6, 1965, plaintiff was to play the female lead in defendant's contemplated production of a motion picture entitled "Bloomer Girl." The contract provided that defendant would pay plaintiff a minimum "guaranteed compensation" of $53,571.42 per week for 14 weeks commencing May 23, 1966, for a total of $750,000. Prior to May 1966 defendant decided not to produce the picture and by a letter dated April 4, 1966, it notified plaintiff of that decision and that it would not "comply with our obligations to you under" the written contract.

By the same letter and with the professed purpose "to avoid any damage to you," defendant instead offered to employ plaintiff as the leading actress in another film tentatively entitled "Big Country, Big Man" (hereinafter, "Big Country"). The compensation offered was identical, as were 31 of the 34 numbered provisions or articles of the original contract.[1] Unlike "Bloomer Girl," however, which was to have been a musical production, "Big Country" was a dramatic "western type" movie. "Bloomer Girl" was to have been filmed in California; "Big Country" was to be produced in Australia. Also, certain terms in the proffered contract varied from those of the original.[2] Plaintiff was given one week within which to accept; she did not and the offer lapsed. Plaintiff then commenced this action seeking recovery of the agreed guaranteed compensation.

The complaint sets forth two causes of action. The first is for money due under the contract; the second, based upon the same allegations as the first, is for damages resulting from defendant's breach of contract. Defendant in its answer admits the existence and validity of the contract, that plaintiff complied with all the conditions, covenants and promises and stood ready to complete the performance, and that defendant breached and "anticipatorily repudiated" the contract. It denies, however, that any money is due to plaintiff either under the contract or as a result of its breach, and pleads as an affirmative defense to both causes of action plaintiff's allegedly deliberate failure to mitigate damages, asserting that she unreasonably refused to accept its offer of the leading role in "Big Country."

Plaintiff moved for summary judgment under Code of Civil Procedure section 437c, the motion was granted, and summary judgment for $750,000 plus interest was entered in plaintiff's favor. This appeal by defendant followed.

The familiar rules are that the matter to be determined by the trial court on a motion for summary judgment is whether facts have been presented which give rise to a triable factual issue. The court may not pass upon the

1. Among the identical provisions was the following found in the last paragraph of Article 2 of the original contract: "We [defendant] shall not be obligated to utilize your [plaintiff's] services in or in connection with the Photoplay hereunder, our sole obligation, subject to the terms and conditions of this Agreement, being to pay you the guaranteed compensation herein provided for."

2. Article 29 of the original contract specified that plaintiff approved the director already chosen for "Bloomer Girl" and that in case he failed to act as director plaintiff was to have approval rights of any substitute director. Article 31 provided that plaintiff was to have the right of approval of the "Bloomer Girl" dance director, and Article 32 gave her the right of approval of the screenplay.

Defendant's letter of April 4 to plaintiff, which contained both defendant's notice of breach of the "Bloomer Girl" contract and offer of the lead in "Big Country," eliminated or impaired each of those rights. It read in part as follows: "The terms and conditions of our offer of employment are identical to those set forth in the 'BLOOMER GIRL' Agreement, Articles 1 through 34 and Exhibit A to the Agreement, except as follows:

"1. Article 31 of said Agreement will not be included in any contract of employment regarding 'BIG COUNTRY, BIG MAN' as it is not a musical and it thus will not need a dance director.

"2. In the 'BLOOMER GIRL' agreement, in Articles 29 and 32, you were given certain director and screenplay approvals and you had preapproved certain matters. Since there simply is insufficient time to negotiate with you regarding your choice of director and regarding the screenplay and since you already expressed an interest in performing the role in 'BIG COUNTRY, BIG MAN,' we must exclude from our offer of employment in 'BIG COUNTRY, BIG MAN' any approval rights as are contained in said Articles 29 and 32; however, we shall consult with you respecting the director to be selected to direct the photoplay and will further consult with you with respect to the screenplay and any revisions or changes therein, provided, however, that if we fail to agree * * * the decision of * * * [defendant] with respect to the selection of a director and to revisions and changes in the said screenplay shall be binding upon the parties to said agreement."

issue itself. Summary judgment is proper only if the affidavits or declarations[3] in support of the moving party would be sufficient to sustain a judgment in his favor and his opponent does not by affidavit show facts sufficient to present a triable issue of fact. The affidavits of the moving party are strictly construed, and doubts as to the propriety of summary judgment should be resolved against granting the motion. Such summary procedure is drastic and should be used with caution so that it does not become a substitute for the open trial method of determining facts. The moving party cannot depend upon allegations in his own pleadings to cure deficient affidavits, nor can his adversary rely upon his own pleadings in lieu or in support of affidavits in opposition to a motion; however, a party can rely on his adversary's pleadings to establish facts not contained in his own affidavits. * * * Also, the court may consider facts stipulated to by the parties and facts which are properly the subject of judicial notice. * * *

As stated, defendant's sole defense to this action which resulted from its deliberate breach of contract is that in rejecting defendant's substitute offer of employment plaintiff unreasonably refused to mitigate damages.

The general rule is that the measure of recovery by a wrongfully discharged employee is the amount of salary agreed upon for the period of service, less the amount which the employer affirmatively proves the employee has earned or with reasonable effort might have earned from other employment. * * * However, before projected earnings from other employment opportunities not sought or accepted by the discharged employee can be applied in mitigation, the employer must show that the other employment was comparable, or substantially similar, to that of which the employee has been deprived; the employee's rejection of or failure to seek other available employment of a different or inferior kind may not be resorted to in order to mitigate damages. * * *

In the present case defendant has raised no issue of *reasonableness of efforts* by plaintiff to obtain other employment; the sole issue is whether plaintiff's refusal of defendant's substitute offer of "Big Country" may be used in mitigation. Nor, if the "Big Country" offer was of employment different or inferior when compared with the original "Bloomer Girl" employment, is there an issue as to whether or not plaintiff acted reasonably in refusing the substitute offer. Despite defendant's arguments to the contrary, no case cited or which our research has discovered holds or suggests that reasonableness is an element of a wrongfully discharged employee's option to reject, or fail to seek, different or inferior employment lest the possible earnings therefrom be charged against him in mitigation of damages.[4]

---

3. In this opinion "affidavits" includes "declarations under penalty of perjury." (See Code Civ.Proc., § 2015.5.)

4. Instead, in each case the reasonableness referred to was that of the *efforts* of the employee to obtain other employment that was not different or inferior: his right to reject the latter was declared as an unqualified rule of law. Thus, Gonzales v. Internat. Assn. of Machinists, 213 Cal.App.2d 817, 823–824, 29 Cal. Rptr. 190, 194, holds that the trial court correctly instructed the jury that plaintiff union member, a machinist, was required to make

"such *efforts* as the average [member of his union] desiring employment would make at that particular time and place" (italics added); but, further, that the court *properly rejected* defendant's *offer of proof* of the *availability of other kinds of employment* at the same or higher pay than plaintiff usually received and all outside the jurisdiction of his union, as plaintiff could not be required to accept different employment or a nonunion job.

In Harris v. Nat. Union, etc., Cooks and Stewards, 116 Cal.App.2d 759, 761, 254 P.2d

Applying the foregoing rules to the record in the present case, with all intendments in favor of the party opposing the summary judgment motion— here, defendant—it is clear that the trial court correctly ruled that plaintiff's failure to accept defendant's tendered substitute employment could not be applied in mitigation of damages because the offer of the "Big Country" lead was of employment both different and inferior, and that no factual dispute was presented on that issue. The mere circumstance that "Bloomer Girl" was to be a musical review calling upon plaintiff's talents as a dancer as well as an actress, and was to be produced in the City of Los Angeles, whereas "Big Country" was a straight dramatic role in a "Western Type" story taking place in an opal mine in Australia, demonstrates the difference in kind between the two employments; the female lead as a dramatic actress in a western style motion picture can by no stretch of imagination be considered the equivalent of or substantially similar to the lead in a song-and-dance production.

[margin note: diff. role! song/dance v western]

Additionally, the substitute "Big Country" offer proposed to eliminate or impair the director and screenplay approvals accorded to plaintiff under the original "Bloomer Girl" contract (see fn. 2, *ante*), and thus constituted an offer of inferior employment. No expertise or judicial notice is required in order to hold that the deprivation or infringement of an employee's rights held under an original employment contract converts the available "other employment" relied upon by the employer to mitigate damages, into inferior employment which the employee need not seek or accept. (See Gonzales v. Internat. Assn. of Machinists, *supra*, 213 Cal.App.2d 817, 823–824, 29 Cal. Rptr. 190 * * *.)

[margin note: inferior employm b/c eliminates her say in director]

Statements found in affidavits submitted by defendant in opposition to plaintiff's summary judgment motion, to the effect that the "Big Country" offer was not of employment different from or inferior to that under the "Bloomer Girl" contract, merely repeat the allegations of defendant's answer to the complaint in this action, constitute only conclusionary assertions with respect to undisputed facts, and do not give rise to a triable factual issue so as to defeat the motion for summary judgment. * * *

In view of the determination that defendant failed to present any facts showing the existence of a factual issue with respect to its sole defense— plaintiff's rejection of its substitute employment offer in mitigation of damages—we need not consider plaintiff's further contention that for various reasons, including the provisions of the original contract set forth in footnote 1, *ante,* plaintiff was excused from attempting to mitigate damages.

The judgment is affirmed.

SULLIVAN, ACTING CHIEF JUSTICE (dissenting). *[margin note: → thinks it is a factual issue not to be decided on sum jud.]*

The basic question in this case is whether or not plaintiff acted reasonably in rejecting defendant's offer of alternate employment. The answer depends upon whether that offer (starring in "Big Country, Big Man") was an

---

673, 676, the issues were stated to be, inter alia, whether comparable employment was open to each plaintiff employee, and if so whether each plaintiff made a *reasonable effort* to secure such employment. It was held that the trial court *properly sustained an objection to an offer to prove a custom of accepting a job*

in a lower rank when work in the higher rank was not available, as "The duty of mitigation of damages * * * does not require the plaintiff 'to seek or to accept other employment of a different or inferior kind.' " (p. 764 [5], 254 P.2d p. 676.)

offer of work that was substantially similar to her former employment (starring in "Bloomer Girl") or of work that was of a different or inferior kind. To my mind this is a factual issue which the trial court should not have determined on a motion for summary judgment. The majority have not only repeated this error but have compounded it by applying the rules governing mitigation of damages in the employer-employee context in a misleading fashion. Accordingly, I respectfully dissent.

The familiar rule requiring a plaintiff in a tort or contract action to mitigate damages embodies notions of fairness and socially responsible behavior which are fundamental to our jurisprudence. Most broadly stated, it precludes the recovery of damages which, through the exercise of due diligence, could have been avoided. Thus, in essence, it is a rule requiring reasonable conduct in commercial affairs. This general principle governs the obligations of an employee after his employer has wrongfully repudiated or terminated the employment contract. Rather than permitting the employee simply to remain idle during the balance of the contract period, the law requires him to make a reasonable effort to secure other employment.[1] He is not obliged, however, to seek or accept any and all types of work which may be available. Only work which is in the same field and which is of the same quality need be accepted.[2]

Over the years the courts have employed various phrases to define the type of employment which the employee, upon his wrongful discharge, is under an obligation to accept. Thus in California alone it has been held that he must accept employment which is "substantially similar" * * * "comparable employment" * * * employment "in the same general line of the first employment" * * * "equivalent to his prior position" * * * "employment in a similar capacity" * * * employment which is "not * * * of a different or inferior kind. * * *" * * *

For reasons which are unexplained, the majority cite several of these cases yet select from among the various judicial formulations which contain one particular phrase, "Not of a different or inferior kind," with which to analyze this case. I have discovered no historical or theoretical reason to adopt this phrase, which is simply a negative restatement of the affirmative standards set out in the above cases, as the exclusive standard. Indeed, its emergence is an example of the dubious phenomenon of the law responding not to rational judicial choice or changing social conditions, but to unrecognized changes in the language of opinions or legal treatises. However, the

1. The issue is generally discussed in terms of a duty on the part of the employee to minimize loss. The practice is long-established and there is little reason to change despite Judge Cardozo's observation of its subtle inaccuracy. "The servant is free to accept employment or reject it according to his uncensored pleasure. What is meant by the supposed duty is merely this: That if he unreasonably reject, he will not be heard to say that the loss of wages from then on shall be deemed the jural consequence of the earlier discharge. He has broken the chain of causation, and loss resulting to him thereafter is suffered through his own act." (McClelland v. Climax Hosiery Mills

(1930) 252 N.Y. 347, 359, 169 N.E. 605, 609, concurring opinion.)

2. This qualification of the rule seems to reflect the simple and humane attitude that it is too severe to demand of a person that he attempt to find and perform work for which he has no training or experience. Many of the older cases hold that one need not accept work in an inferior rank or position nor work which is more menial or arduous. This suggests that the rule may have had its origin in the bourgeois fear of resubmergence in lower economic classes.

phrase is a serviceable one and my concern is not with its use as the standard but rather with what I consider its distortion.

distortion

The relevant language excuses acceptance only of employment which is of a *different kind.* * * * It has never been the law that the mere existence of *differences between two jobs in the same field* is sufficient, as a matter of law, to excuse an employee wrongfully discharged from one from accepting the other in order to mitigate damages. Such an approach would effectively eliminate any obligation of an employee to attempt to minimize damage arising from a wrongful discharge. The only alternative job offer an employee would be required to accept would be an offer of his former job by his former employer.

policy

Although the majority appear to hold that there was a difference "in kind" between the employment offered plaintiff in "Bloomer Girl" and that offered in "Big Country" * * * an examination of the opinion makes crystal clear that the majority merely point out differences between the two *films* (an obvious circumstance) and then apodically assert that these constitute a difference in the *kind* of *employment*. [Eds. note: a student pointed out to us that Justice Sullivan meant "apodictically"—pretty impressive, don't you think?] The entire rationale of the majority boils down to this: that the *"mere circumstances"* that "Bloomer Girl" was to be a musical review while "Big Country" was a straight drama "demonstrates the difference in kind" since a female lead in a western is not "the equivalent of or substantially similar to" a lead in a musical. This is merely attempting to prove the proposition by repeating it. It shows that the vehicles for the display of the star's talents are different but it does not prove that her employment as a star in such vehicles is of necessity different *in kind* and either inferior or superior.

films v employment

I believe that the approach taken by the majority (a superficial listing of differences with no attempt to assess their significance) may subvert a valuable legal doctrine.[3] The inquiry in cases such as this should not be whether differences between the two jobs exist (there will always be differences) but whether the differences which are present are substantial enough to constitute differences in the *kind* of employment or, alternatively, whether they render the substitute work employment of an *inferior kind*.

what Sull. wants the rule to be.

It seems to me that *this* inquiry involves, in the instant case at least, factual determinations which are improper on a motion for summary judgment. Resolving whether or not one job is substantially similar to another or whether, on the other hand, it is of a different or inferior kind, will often (as here) require a critical appraisal of the similarities and differences between them in light of the importance of these differences to the employee. This necessitates a weighing of the evidence, and it is precisely this undertaking which is forbidden on summary judgment. (Garlock v. Cole (1962) 199 Cal.App.2d 11, 14, 18 Cal.Rptr. 393.)

This is not to say that summary judgment would never be available in an action by an employee in which the employer raises the defense of failure to

POLICY

3. The values of the doctrine of mitigation of damages in this context are that it minimizes the unnecessary personal and social (e.g., nonproductive use of labor, litigation) costs of contractual failure. If a wrongfully discharged employee can, through his own action and without suffering financial or psychological loss in the process, reduce the damages accruing from the breach of contract, the most sensible policy is to require him to do so. I fear the majority opinion will encourage precisely opposite conduct.

mitigate damages. No case has come to my attention, however, in which summary judgment has been granted on the issue of whether an employee was obliged to accept available alternate employment. Nevertheless, there may well be cases in which the substitute employment is so manifestly of a dissimilar or inferior sort, the declarations of the plaintiff so complete and those of the defendant so conclusionary and inadequate that no factual issues exist for which a trial is required. This, however, is not such a case.

It is not intuitively obvious, to me at least, that the leading female role in a dramatic motion picture is a radically different endeavor from the leading female role in a musical comedy film. Nor is it plain to me that the rather qualified rights of director and screenplay approval contained in the first contract are highly significant matters either in the entertainment industry in general or to this plaintiff in particular. Certainly, none of the declarations introduced by plaintiff in support of her motion shed any light on these issues. Nor do they attempt to explain why she declined the offer of starring in "Big Country, Big Man." Nevertheless, the trial court granted the motion, declaring that these approval rights were "critical" and that their elimination altered "the essential nature of the employment."

The plaintiff's declarations were of no assistance to the trial court in its effort to justify reaching this conclusion on summary judgment. Instead, it was forced to rely on judicial notice of the definitions of "motion picture," "screenplay" and "director" (Evid.Code, § 451, subd. (e)) and then on judicial notice of practices in the film industry which were purportedly of "common knowledge." (Evid.Code, § 451, subd. (f) or § 452, subd. (g).) This use of judicial notice was error. Evidence Code section 451, subdivision (e) was never intended to authorize resort to the dictionary to solve essentially factual questions which do not turn upon conventional linguistic usage. More important, however, the trial court's notice of "facts commonly known" violated Evidence Code section 455, subdivision (a). Before this section was enacted there were no procedural safeguards affording litigants an opportunity to be heard as to the propriety of taking judicial notice of a matter or as to the tenor of the matter to be noticed. Section 455 makes such an opportunity (which may be an element of due process, see Evid.Code, § 455, Law Revision Com. Comment (a)) mandatory and its provisions should be scrupulously adhered to. "Judicial notice can be a valuable tool in the adversary system for the lawyer as well as the court" (Kongsgaard, Judicial Notice (1966) 18 Hastings L.J. 117, 140) and its use is appropriate on motions for summary judgment. Its use in this case, however, to determine on summary judgment issues fundamental to the litigation without complying with statutory requirements of notice and hearing is a highly improper effort to "cut the Gordion knot of involved litigation." (Silver Land & Dev. Co. v. California Land Title Co. (1967) 248 Cal.App.2d 241, 242, 56 Cal.Rptr. 178, 179.)

The majority do not confront the trial court's misuse of judicial notice. They avoid this issue through the expedient of declaring that neither judicial notice nor expert opinion (such as that contained in the declarations in opposition to the motion) is necessary to reach the trial court's conclusion. *Something*, however, clearly *is* needed to support this conclusion. Nevertheless, the majority make no effort to justify the judgment through an examination of the plaintiff's declarations. Ignoring the obvious insufficiency of these declarations, the majority announce that "the deprivation or infringement of an employee's rights held under an original employment contract" changes the alternate employment offered or available into employment of an inferior kind.

I cannot accept the proposition that an offer which eliminates *any* contract right, regardless of its significance, is, as a matter of law, an offer of employment of an inferior kind. Such an absolute rule seems no more sensible than the majority's earlier suggestion that the mere existence of differences between two jobs is sufficient to render them employment of different kinds. Application of such per se rules will severely undermine the principle of mitigation of damages in the employer-employee context.

I remain convinced that the relevant question in such cases is whether or not a particular contract provision is so significant that its omission create employment of an inferior kind. This question is, of course, intimately bound up in what I consider the ultimate issue: whether or not the employee acted reasonably. This will generally involve a factual inquiry to ascertain the importance of the particular contract term and a process of weighing the absence of that term against the countervailing advantages of the alternate employment. In the typical case, this will mean that summary judgment must be withheld.

In the instant case, there was nothing properly before the trial court by which the importance of the approval rights could be ascertained, much less evaluated. Thus, in order to grant the motion for summary judgment, the trial court misused judicial notice. In upholding the summary judgment, the majority here rely upon per se rules which distort the process of determining whether or not an employee is obliged to accept particular employment in mitigation of damages.

I believe that the judgment should be reversed so that the issue of whether or not the offer of the lead role in "Big Country, Big Man" was of employment comparable to that of the lead role in "Bloomer Girl" may be determined at trial.

Rehearing denied; SULLIVAN, J., dissenting.

HILLMAN, KEEPING THE DEAL TOGETHER AFTER MATERIAL BREACH—COMMON LAW MITIGATION RULES, THE UCC, AND THE RESTATEMENT (SECOND) OF CONTRACTS

47 U. of Colo.L.Rev. 553, 559–60 (1976).

Under the rule of avoidable consequences, the injured party must, when reasonable, make substitute agreements with third parties to avoid loss from the breach. The extent to which the injured party must deal with the breaching party to avoid loss is less clear. Many courts are mindful that upon material breach an injured party is entitled to cease performance, treat the contract as ended, and seek damages. These courts, perhaps unwilling to allow the breaching party to "escape" full liability, are reluctant to apply the avoidable consequences rule when the only alternative, or the least damaging alternative for the injured party, is to accept a new offer from the breaching party. These courts have, in effect, taken the fact-finding function away from the jury by deciding that it is *never* reasonable to deal further with the breacher.

Such decisions often view the contract breaker as one who should not be "rewarded" for the breach by "requiring" the injured party to accept the new offer. They focus on the "bad" actions of the contract breaker rather than on making the injured party whole. * * *

Problem 3–10

Alan Turlway calls your law office and tells you that Arlo Electronics has wrongfully fired him from his job as a typewriter salesperson. Alan had a contract for one more year of employment, but Arlo's business was slow. Alan was earning $275 per week. He tells you that he has been offered employment at Teale Electronics as a computer salesperson for $300 per week for one year. Teale Electronics is 20 miles from Alan's home, however, whereas Arlo Electronics is only five miles away, and Alan is reluctant to accept. He asks you whether he should take the job, and what the consequences will be if he does not. Advise Alan. What further information would you seek?

OLDS v. MAPES–REEVES CONSTRUCTION CO.

Supreme Judicial Court of Massachusetts, 1900.
177 Mass. 41, 58 N.E. 478.

KNOWLTON, J. The only question argued in this case relates to the subject of damages. The defendant, as a contractor, had agreed to erect on land of another a large building in Northampton. The plaintiffs, as subcontractors, had agreed with the defendant to furnish and set up all the marble work in the building for $3,000. A controversy afterwards arose between the defendant and the owner of the building, on account of which the defendant ordered the plaintiffs to discontinue the work, and do nothing further under the contract. The defendant, having broken the contract, immediately became liable to the plaintiffs for damages, the measure of which was the difference between the sum which it would cost to complete the work in accordance with the contract, and the sum which the plaintiffs were to receive. * * * This breach which fixed the liability occurred on November 9, 1896, and two days afterwards (on November 11th) this suit was brought. On the same day (whether before or after the commencement of the suit does not appear, and is not material) the plaintiffs made a new contract with the owner of the building, to complete the work called for by their contract with the defendant, and also to do certain other work, for a round sum agreed upon between them. The profits on this last contract, as found by the auditor, were $335.23, and the only question before us is whether the plaintiffs are to allow the amount of these profits in diminution of the damages to which they would otherwise be entitled.

The rule which is applicable to one who is under a contract to render personal services, and who, being discharged without cause before the end of his term, sues for damages, requires him, in estimating the damages, to allow for his services during the unexpired term whatever he is able to obtain for them, or, if damages are assessed before the end of the term, whatever he reasonably can be expected to obtain for them during the time covered by the contract. That is, on the breach of the contract he is left with his personal services as his property, in his own control, and he must allow for them, in the computation, their fair value for such use as he is able reasonably to make of them. In estimating the damages in the present case the auditor found that the actual cost of completing the work after the breach of the contract was $717.27, although, with such allowances as he made for work included in the plaintiffs' contract with the landowner which was not included in their contract with the defendant, he found that the plaintiffs received $1,052.50 for completing the work called for by the original contract. In making this estimate of the cost of completing the work, the auditor charged the plaintiffs with all labor and services which would have entered into it, whether personal to themselves or rendered by agents or employes, just as one under a contract to render personal services, when recovering damages for a broken contract, would be charged with the value of the personal services which remained unused after the breach of the contract. But there is this difference between the case of one who is discharged while under a contract to render personal services and a case like the present: In the former case the person discharged, whose personal services come back to him, is bound to dispose of them in a reasonable way, so as to make the damages to the other party not unreasonably large, while, in a case like the present, one deprived of his contract is under no obligation to enter into new contracts with a view to make profits for the other party. In a contract of the kind before the court, personal services are not necessarily included. The labor or supervision may be personally performed by the contractor, or may be furnished through agents or employees. In either case the value of it is all included, for the benefit of the other party, when the contractor is charged with the whole cost of completing the work, as an amount to be deducted from the contract price in estimating his damages. Since the damages properly are assessable in this way immediately after the breach of the contract, can it make any difference that the contractor afterwards makes a new contract with the owner, which includes the unfinished work? In making this contract the plaintiffs did not include anything which originally belonged to the defendant, in specie, under the original contract. Their agreement was not to render personal services, but only to accomplish a specific result. The plaintiffs were at liberty to leave this work entirely to the care of the hired servants, and to take as many other contracts as they chose elsewhere, and to give their personal time and attention to any occupation that they might choose. The question is whether the profits from the new contract with the landowner were a direct result of the defendant's breach of contract, or whether they came from an independent, intervening cause. It does not appear, and it is not to be assumed, that the plaintiffs were not competent to carry on several contracts at one time, and the making of profits on a new contract does not appear to be because of relief from the obligations of the old one. There is usually plenty of work to be contracted for, and the addition of one more possible job for which contractors may bid does not make the subsequent contract to do the work a direct result of the increase of opportunities for work. The addition of a new piece of work is merely a condition of the subsequent contract to do the work, and not a direct or proximate cause of it. Moreover, the making of such a contract involves many considerations besides the existence of the work to be done. There must be calculations and estimates. In making a contract of this kind there is always a risk of loss, as well as a possibility of gain. To say nothing of the fact that the plaintiffs' new contract included work which was not included in the old one, the cost of which could be fixed only as a matter of estimate, this contract with the landowner was a new undertaking, in which the plaintiffs were under no obligation to engage, and which involved risks that they could assume for themselves alone. If the contract had resulted in a loss to them, they could not have charged the defendant with the loss, to the increase of their damages. As the contract resulted in a gain to them, there is no reason why the defendant should receive this gain in diminution of the damages for which it was liable. There is no privity between the defendant and the plaintiffs, or between the defendant and the landowner, in reference to the new contract. There was an independent arrangement made between the plaintiffs and the landowner, and the only relation which the defendant's breach of the former contract had to it was that it furnished one of the conditions, namely, the work to be done, without which the new contract could not have been made. But the existence of this condition was not the cause of the contract, and the creator of this condition has no title to the fruits of the contract. If another person had taken this contract and made profits on it, as the plaintiffs did, it would hardly have been contended that the plaintiffs' damages were to be diminished on that account; or if the plaintiffs, instead of taking this contract after the breach of the former one, had gone elsewhere, and taken another contract, which afforded them similar profits, there would be no ground for a claim of the defendant to be allowed these profits in diminution of the damages. We are of opinion that the ruling at the trial was erroneous, and that the plaintiffs' damages should have been assessed without reference to their profits obtained under the new contract with the landowner. Exceptions sustained.

EVERGREEN AMUSEMENT CORP. v. MILSTEAD

Court of Appeals of Maryland, 1955.
206 Md. 610, 112 A.2d 901.

HAMMOND, JUDGE.

The Evergreen Amusement Corporation, the appellant, operator of a drive-in movie theater, was held liable by the court, sitting without a jury, to Harold D. Milstead, the appellee, a contractor, for the balance due on a written contract for the clearing and grading of the site of the theater and certain extras, less the cost of completing a part of the work and damages for delay in completion, based on rental value of the theater property during the period of delay and out-of-pocket costs for that time.

The appellant, by counterclaim, sought recovery of lost profits for the period of delay. The court held the amount claimed to have been so lost to be too uncertain and speculative, and refused evidence proffered to support appellant's theory. * * *

* * *

The real reliance of the Evergreen Amusement Corporation is on the slowness of the contractor in completing the work. It says that the resulting delay in the opening of the theater from June first to the middle of August cost it twelve thousand five hundred dollars in profits. It proffered a witness to testify that he had built and operated a majority of the drive-in theaters in the area, that he is in the theater equipment business and familiar with the profits that drive-in theaters make in the area, that a market survey was made in the area before the site of the theater was selected, and that it had shown the need for such a theater in the neighborhood. It was said he would testify as to the reasonably anticipated profits during the months in question by comparing the months in its second year of operation with those in which it could not operate the year before, and would say that the profits would have been the same. His further testimony would be, it was claimed, that weather conditions, the population, and competition were all approximately the same in the year the theater opened and the following year.

We think the court did not err in refusing the proffered evidence. Under the great weight of authority, the general rule clearly is that loss of profit is a definite element of damages in an action for breach of contract or in an action for harming an established business which has been operating for a sufficient length of time to afford a basis of estimation with some degree of certainty as to the probable loss of profits, but that, on the other hand, loss of profits from a business which has not gone into operation may not be recovered because they are merely speculative and incapable of being ascertained with the requisite degree of certainty. Restatement, Contracts, Sec. 331, states the law to be that damages are recoverable for profits prevented by breach of contract "only to the extent that the evidence affords a sufficient basis for estimating their amount in money with reasonable certainty", and that where the evidence does not afford a sufficient basis, "damages may be measured by the rental value of the property." Comment "d" says this: "If the defendant's breach has prevented the plaintiff from carrying on *a well-established business,* the amount of profits thereby prevented is often capable of proof with reasonable certainty. On the basis of its past history, a reasonable prediction can be made as to its future." (Italics supplied.) * * * See also The Requirement of Certainty for Proof of Lost Profits, 64 Harvard Law 317. The article discusses the difficulties of proving with sufficient certainty the profits which were lost, and then says: "These difficulties have given rise to a rule in some states that no new business can recover for its lost profits." While this Court has not laid down a flat rule (and does not hereby do so), nevertheless, no case has permitted recovery of lost profits under comparable circumstances. In Abbott v. Gatch, 13 Md. 314, the claim for loss of profits arose because of delay in completion of a flour mill. The Court held that the mill owner's loss was to be established by fair rental value for the time of the delay resulting from failure to complete it according to contract, that he could not recover estimated profits, because it was dependent, as they were, upon the quality of flour available, the fluctuation of prices of flour, continuance of the mill in running order and other variants. The Court labelled the damages claimed speculative and refused to follow a Vermont case which had allowed them to be shown. The rule laid down in this case has been followed in a number of others. In Winslow Elevator & Machine Co. v. Hoffman, 107 Md. 621, 69 A. 394, 17 L.R.A., N.S., 1130, an elevator was not installed within the specified time and was defective. The owner sought to recover loss of rents because of the refusal of prospective tenants to lease offices and the moving out of others. The Court followed Abbott v. Gatch, supra, and held that the claim for loss of rentals must be denied as too uncertain and remote. * * *

* * *

We think that the case below was tried and decided without reversible error.

Judgment affirmed, with costs.

Note
The New Business Rule Today

The "new business rule" of Evergreen Amusement Corp. is in decline. Some courts find it "grossly unfair" to deny recovery of lost profits where the defendant's breach prevented the plaintiff from establishing the amount of lost profits. See, e.g., Drews Co. v. Ledwith–Wolfe Assoc., Inc., 296 S.C. 207, 371 S.E.2d 532 (1988). Other courts are wary of denying recovery of lost profits to a new business because doing so would encourage parties contracting with such businesses to breach. Vickers v. Wichita State University, 213 Kan. 614, 518 P.2d 512 (1974). Many courts allow for the recovery of a new business's lost profits when there is "a reasonably certain factual basis for computation of probable losses. * * *" Earle M. Jorgensen Co. v. Tesmer Mfg. Co., 10 Ariz.App. 445, 450, 459 P.2d 533, 538 (1969); see also Kenford Company, Inc. v. County of Erie, 108 A.D.2d 132, 141, 489 N.Y.S.2d 939, 946 (1985) (no strict rule against new business recovering lost profits; only a rule of evidence "permitting recovery of lost profits if there is some rational basis on which to calculate such an award"). For cases enforcing the new business rule, see Kinesoft Dev. Corp. v. Softbank Holdings, Inc., 139 F. Supp. 2d 869 (N.D. Ill. 2001); Hunters Intl. Man. Corp. v. Christiana Metals Corp., 561 F.Supp. 614 (E.D.Mich.1982); Doner v. Snapp, 98 Ohio App.3d 597, 649 N.E.2d 42 (1994). For a more thorough discussion of the new business rule today, see Kinesoft Dev. Corp. v. Softbank Holdings, Inc., 139 F. Supp. 2d 869 (N.D. Ill. 2001).

LAKOTA GIRL SCOUT COUNCIL, INC. v. HAVEY FUND–RAISING MANAGEMENT, INC.

United States Court of Appeals, Eighth Circuit, 1975.
519 F.2d 634.

[The Lakota Girl Scout Council's fund-raising venture was impaired when Havey Fund–Raising, hired to assist in the venture, breached its agreement.]

WEBSTER, CIRCUIT JUDGE

The evidence submitted by the Council to prove breach of contract centered upon the failure of Havey Fund–Raising to provide the degree of assistance and supervision promised. Shifting personnel, inadequate consultation and direction, and failure to provide follow-up assistance on collections were the principal derelictions. The campaign was in shambles throughout the period of the drive and fell far short of its goal of $345,000. The drive grossed $88,842.32; the Council paid $24,000 to Havey Fund–Raising, Inc., and incurred $10,000 in additional expenses.

In its complaint, the Council sought to recover for many specific items of damages.[1] The District Court submitted the damage issue to the jury only upon the theory of lost profits: "what the plaintiff would have made if the contract had been performed minus a deduction for savings made possible by the breach." [The jury reached a verdict of $35,000 against Havey, and Havey appealed.]

Appellants contend that there was no liability under Iowa law since the receipts from the drive exceeded the expenses. This argument assumes, however, that the fact of the Council's claimed lost profits was "too uncertain for recovery," since an "expense" approach to damages is recognized as appropriate only when other measures of damages are inappropriate. *See C.C. Hauff Hardware, Inc. v. Long Manufacturing Co.*, 260 Iowa 30, 148 N.W.2d 425, 428 (1967). Our first consideration must therefore be the propriety of an award based upon lost profits under the circumstances of this case.

Under Iowa law, when a contract has been breached, the innocent party is generally entitled to be placed in the position he would have occupied had there been performance. *DeWaay v. Muhr*, 160 N.W.2d 454 (Iowa 1968); *C.C. Hauff Hardware, Inc. v. Long Manufacturing Co.*, *supra*. Lost profits are recoverable under Iowa law, provided: (1) there is proof that some loss occurred, (2) that such loss flowed directly from the agreement breached and was foreseeable, and (3) there is proof of a rational basis from which the amount can be inferred or approximated. * * *

Fact of Loss. At trial, evidence was admitted which tended to show that the capital fund drive, as planned and programmed by Havey Fund–Raising, with a goal of $345,000 was feasible. Indeed, Francis P. Havey himself so testified. Instead, due to the derelictions which constituted the breach, the Council grossed only $88,842.32 in a campaign which cost it at least $34,000. We think the District Judge had a sufficient basis from which to conclude as a matter of law that some damage resulted from the breach and thus properly submitted the question of lost profits to the jury for the purpose of computing damages.

Proximate Cause. While Iowa law does recognize the "new business rule" under which potential profits from an untried enterprise are deemed too speculative to afford a basis for recovery, *see City of Corning v. Iowa–Nebraska Light & Power Co.*, 225 Iowa 1380, 282 N.W. 791 (1938); * * * the campaign in this case differs materially from a general business enterprise. The campaign was a single venture, conducted apart from the general business operations of the Girl Scout Council. It had a specific goal to be achieved within a reasonably clear time frame. It was certainly foreseeable to defendants that a goal reasonably believed by the parties to be capable of achievement would be prejudiced by the failure of Havey Fund–Raising to provide the services contemplated by the agreement, and that such a dimin-

---

1. The Council sought a total of $399,000 from the defendants. Its prayer was broken down as follows:

(a) No Cookie Sale in 1969.......	$ 11,000.
(b) Total payment to defendant ...	24,000.
(c) Extra office expense	10,000.
(d) Deprived of 1969 operating funds......................	8,000.
(e) Deprived of the use of the La-kota Girl Scout Camp	50,000.

(f) Deprived of an effective Campaign Drive for ten years, and secured only $29,000 in cash of a total of $160,000 pledged, as reported in defendant's Final Report, rather than $325,000 to $350,000.................... 269,000.

TOTAL..................... $399,000.

ished return would be the "immediate fruit" of the breach. * * * Of special significance here is the case of *Wachtel v. National Alfalfa Journal Co.,* [190 Iowa 1293, 176 N.W. 801 (Iowa 1920).] Therein the Iowa Supreme Court ruled that the value of a chance to win a specific prize already in existence was not so speculative, contingent or uncertain as to limit a plaintiff's recovery to a minimal amount where defendant had deprived her of that chance by breaching its contract with her.

Collateral issues do not dominate here as they did in *Benshoof v. Reese* [250 Iowa 868, 97 N.W.2d 297 (1959)], where diseased hogs sold by defendant prevented plaintiff from full utilization of his business and full utilization of his business might have resulted in more profits, and *Love v. Ross,* 89 Iowa 400, 56 N.W. 528 (1893), where a stallion's poor breeding performance was to an important degree dependent upon the health and condition of the mares. No evidence was offered in the instant case to cast doubt upon the Council's claim that the campaign failed solely because of Havey Fund–Raising's breach of its agreement with the Council. While evidence of extraordinary conditions, such as a severe economic depression, might have been relevant to show that the claim was remote or speculative, none was offered in this case.

Basis for Computation. Under Iowa law, the jury need not make the computation of damages with mathematical exactness. It is enough if there is proof of a rational basis for computation. * * * Expert testimony was adduced at trial from which a jury might determine how much less the Council netted than it would have received with full performance by Havey Fund–Raising.

Ed Breen, a long-time resident of the area in which the campaign was conducted, who served as the campaign's general chairman, testified that he had previously worked on United Fund campaigns and chaired a Y.M.C.A. drive which netted $850,000 in the area and that the general feeling of the people involved with the campaign was that the goal would be achieved. He added that it was reasonable to expect considerable help from all the Girl Scout families in the area since Girl Scouting was not new to the area and since the camp had been in existence a long time. Breen also stated that there was a general public interest in the development of the camp.

James D. Harrison, a former campaign director and director of sales for Havey Fund–Raising, Inc., who had worked on the Lakota drive, was deposed before trial. In his deposition, which was read to the jury, he stated that in 1967 he had helped direct a Boy Scout campaign in Joliet, Illinois, which had raised over $426,000; that he had been co-director of a drive in Tacoma, Washington, which had raised its goal of about $1.5 million; and that he had directed a Boy Scout drive in Springfield, Illinois, and nine surrounding counties which had raised $18,000 more than its goal of $350,000. He added that he had indirectly participated in other drives. It was Harrison's opinion that the outcome of the campaign would have been much different if it had been handled properly. His testimony was:

> Q. Based upon your experience as a director and an associate director of campaigns, as well as sales director for Havey, and based upon your almost two months as acting director of Lakota Girl Scouts Council Campaign, do you have an opinion as to what amounts of money could have been raised if the director had properly conducted the campaign?

* * *

A. My opinion is if we would have had a director on the scene as we so stated in the original contract, with an associate or co-director in residence at the assigned dates, that we probably would have had the success in Fort Dodge. I feel that way for two reasons. No. 1, the Council itself had conducted a lot of preliminary work in building or readying itself for the campaign as I mentioned earlier. The committee of businessmen that they had there and advisors to work with, the National Council, this type of thing. They had a slide presentation which was good. It was long, but it could have been adapted as I said earlier to our purpose in the campaign. It would have been a hard campaign, not an easy one, and of course I can't—you know, again, this is my opinion, but I feel that with the proper work with the volunteers that were there in the area from the very beginning, and following that campaign time-table which we had set out originally in the contract, if that would have been followed, that there is an excellent chance that they would have achieved their goal, yes. [Evidentiary objection omitted.]

In contesting the computation of damages, appellants challenge the admission of this expert opinion testimony. The admission of an expert's opinion on a particular subject and that expert's qualifications are matters given to the sound discretion of the trial court. An appellate court will not overrule a ruling of one of these points absent an abuse of discretion. As stated by Wigmore:

> [T]he only true criterion is: On *this subject* can a jury from *this person* receive appreciable help? In other words, the test is a relative one, depending on the particular subject and the particular witness with reference to that subject, and is not fixed or limited to any class of persons acting professionally * * *.

VII J. Wigmore, Evidence § 1923, at 21 (1940). * * *

* * *

* * * [W]e note that expert opinion testimony has been deemed competent in at least one other case where a unique promotional venture did not lend itself to any other reasonable basis for computing damages. In *Riley v. General Mills, Inc.,* 226 F.Supp. 780 (E.D.Pa.1964), *rev'd on other grounds,* 346 F.2d 68 (3d Cir.1965), insurance agents brought an action against General Mills, claiming that the abortive termination of a free gift promotional program had cost them profits which would otherwise have been earned. Damages for lost profits were assessed by the district court which held:

> Therefore, *considering the nature of the instant transaction* which was a *unique* promotional venture we find that one reasonable source for computing the damages rests with the opinion testimony of expert witnesses. Where there is no other "reasonably safe basis" for measuring the substantial damages which the plaintiff has suffered by reason of the defendant's breach of his contract, expert testimony may be utilized for the purpose. *Western Show Company Inc. v. Mix,* 315 Pa. 139, 141, 173 A. 183 (1934).

226 F.Supp. at 783. While reversing the district court (on the basis of insurance laws), the Third Circuit expressly approved the trial court's approach to computation of damages. 346 F.2d at 72. We think this approach

was warranted in the instant case. "[A] defendant whose wrongful conduct has rendered difficult the ascertainment of the precise damages suffered by the plaintiff, is not entitled to complain that they cannot be measured with the same exactness and precision as would otherwise be possible. * * * The wrongdoer should bear the risk of uncertainty that his own conduct has created." *Autowest, Inc. v. Peugeot, Inc., supra,* 434 F.2d at 565, *citing Eastman Kodak Co. v. Southern Photo Materials Co.,* 273 U.S. 359, 379, 47 S.Ct. 400, 71 L.Ed. 684 (1927), and *Bigelow v. RKO Radio Pictures, Inc.,* 327 U.S. 251, 264–65, 66 S.Ct. 574, 90 L.Ed. 652 (1946).

As summarized by Professor Corbin:

It is not possible to state the precise degree of approach to certainty required by the recovery of profits as damages for breach of contract. If the mind of the court is certain that profits would have been made if there had been no breach by the defendant, there will be a greater degree of liberality in allowing the jury to bring in a verdict for the plaintiff, even though the amount of profits prevented is scarcely subject to proof at all. In this respect, at least, doubts will generally be resolved in favor of the party who has certainly been injured and against the party committing the breach. The trial court has a large amount of discretion in determining whether to submit the question of profits to the jury; and when it is so submitted, the jury will also have a large amount of discretion in determining the amount of its verdict.

5 Corbin on Contracts § 1022 (1964).

* * *

[Affirmed.]

[The dissent of Judge Bright is omitted.]

BEN–SHAHAR AND BERNSTEIN, THE SECRECY INTEREST IN CONTRACT LAW

109 Yale L. J. 1885, 1886–89 (2000).

* * * When a breach occurs and expectation damages are sought, the expectation measure will often include lost profit. Lost profit is typically calculated on the basis of business information related to the promisee's operations, such as materials and labor costs, inventory size, availability of alternative suppliers, the identity of her downstream contracting partners (customers), and, in the case of newer businesses, her business plan. This and other information revealed during the discovery process may be information that the promisee would prefer to keep private. First, revealing the information might damage her bargaining position in future contract negotiations with this or another transactor and might lead to her having to pay a higher price in future transactions. The promisee's weakened bargaining position arises not only because the promisor will know that, in the event of breach, he will have to pay higher damages, but also, and more importantly, because he will learn the true value of performance to the promisee. Knowing the value of performance to the promisee should enable the promisor to extract a greater share of the bargaining surplus in subsequent transactions. Second, if, at the time a dispute arises, there are other executory contracts between the

transactors, the promisor may be able to use the information he obtains during the pretrial discovery process to engage in profitable holdup under these other contracts. Finally, even if the promisee does not intend to transact with the breaching promisor again, the information revealed during the course of the dispute may be used by other transactors with whom the promisee has ongoing relationships, to engage in holdup, to justify demands for adequate assurances of performance, or to extract additional increments of the bargaining surplus in future negotiations. The revelation of the information may also weaken her bargaining position vis-a-vis banks, unions, insurance companies, and secured creditors, as well as damage her competitive position in a market. More generally, to the extent that the value of a firm is based on the value of the private information it possesses—whether this information takes the form of a customer list or any of a variety of forms of intellectual property—legal rules that require the revelation of this information in order to obtain a remedy for breach of contract or to enforce any other substantive legal right, may be undesirable.

Recognizing that an aggrieved party will often prefer to keep the information necessary to establish the magnitude of expectation damages private suggests that while the traditional literature on remedies has focused on the aggrieved party's interest in being made whole (her "compensatory interest"), there is another, potentially conflicting interest that needs to be taken into account, namely her desire to keep information private (her "secrecy interest"). Although the secrecy interest and the compensatory interest are often in direct conflict, they cannot be reconciled simply by elevating one over the other ex post. When the secrecy interest is sufficiently strong, the cost of revealing the underlying private information may well exceed the aggrieved party's expected recovery at trial. As a consequence, the aggrieved party may not file suit and may therefore receive no compensation. Because the existence of the promisee's secrecy interest will often be known to a promisor who has either breached or is contemplating breach, the secrecy interest may undermine the credibility of the promisee's threat to sue. This in turn suggests that once the effect of the secrecy interest on the aggrieved party's incentive to sue is taken into account, it may be necessary to rethink the wisdom of fully compensatory expectation damages. In contracting contexts in which the secrecy concern is important, the use of a fully compensatory expectation measure in a regime with liberal rules of civil discovery may fail to achieve the widely accepted remedial goal of full ex post compensation. It may also fail to induce efficient breach-or-perform decisions because promisors will realize that promisees with a sufficiently strong secrecy interest may not have a credible threat to sue. In addition, the availability of the expectation measure may, in some contexts, lead a promisor to breach solely in the hope that a promisee will sue and that he will be able to obtain valuable information.

CHRUM v. CHARLES HEATING AND COOLING, INC.

Court of Appeals of Michigan, 1982.
121 Mich.App. 17, 327 N.W.2d 568.

GILLESPIE, JUDGE.

In November 1978, Mr. and Mrs. Chrum (hereinafter plaintiffs) purchased a furnace from the defendant, Charles Heating & Cooling, Inc., which the defendant agreed to, and did, install.

On April 11, 1979, the furnace caused a fire which destroyed the plaintiffs' home and its contents. There were no physical injuries. Mr. and Mrs. Chrum were insured by plaintiff State Farm Fire & Casualty Company, who paid the Chrums $43,782.49 as a result of the loss.

State Farm Fire & Casualty Company commenced an action against Charles Heating & Cooling, Inc. on October 17, 1979, seeking subrogation. On December 10, 1979, Mr. and Mrs. Chrum filed a separate action seeking additional compensation for economic loss, alleging negligence in installation. The complaint alleged that the defendant "carelessly, recklessly and negligently" installed the furnace and:

"9. That as a direct and proximate result of Defendant's negligence and breach of implied warranties, Plaintiffs have suffered loss of their home, household effects and personal belongings. In addition, Plaintiffs have suffered emotional distress, fright, mental anguish and loss of income."

The action brought by the Chrums was consolidated with the action brought by State Farm. Defendant moved for partial summary judgment, pursuant to GCR 1963, 117.2(1), with respect to plaintiffs' emotional distress claim. The trial court denied defendant's motion, stating:

"It would be the Court's opinion that it is more personal to the purchasers than it would be commercial. We're not talking about a contract to pay money. We're talking about a thing—at least in Michigan—which is essential for life—at least in the months of November through March. Without it, we could not live. It therefore becomes noncommercial, and not in any way commercial to the pecuniary interests of the purchasers.

"It is likely that if—most reasonable people, at least, would likely conclude that a furnace is a potentially dangerous item. It can blow up. It can cause fires. I'm sure there's all sorts of other things that can happen as a result of a defective furnace, which not only could cause total destruction of what could be a married couple's property, but it could be their total economic picture—their total marital estate—which, today, normally is a home and all their furniture; and it would be reasonable for this Court to conclude that someone selling a furnace understands the potential and foresees the fact that if there are problems or difficulties with the furnace, they could be totally disruptive to the purchaser's life; and if someone were to lose their home, all their contents, all their personal belongings, that certainly would be likely to cause a great deal of emotional distress, and mental anguish would have to necessarily result."

The remaining claims against defendant were dismissed following a settlement, leaving only the mental distress claim. By order entered August 7, 1981, defendant's application for leave to appeal the trial court's denial of the motion for partial summary judgment was granted.

The law governing damages for mental distress in contract cases was enunciated by the Michigan Supreme Court in the case of *Kewin v. Massachu-*

setts Mutual Life Ins. Co., 409 Mich. 401, 295 N.W.2d 50 (1980), *reh. den.,* 409 Mich. 1116 (1980). In that case, the Supreme Court relied upon the rule of *Hadley v. Baxendale,* 9 Exch. 341, 156 Eng.Rep. 145 (1854), and held that damages recoverable for breach of contract are generally limited to damages arising naturally from the breach or contemplated by the parties at the time the contract is made. Where an action is for a breach of a commercial contract, damages for mental distress are not recoverable.

[margin note: damages to the person]

The Supreme Court in *Kewin* recognized a general exception to the above rule, developed in *Stewart v. Rudner,* 349 Mich. 459, 84 N.W.2d 816 (1957). In *Stewart,* plaintiff sued her doctor for breach of an agreement to deliver her child by Caesarean section, alleging that his breach resulted in the stillbirth of her child. The Court allowed damages for mental distress, holding that where the contract breached is a personal agreement involving matters of "mental concern and solicitude", damages for emotional suffering are recoverable. 349 Mich. at 471, 84 N.W.2d 816. See also *Avery v. Arnold Home, Inc.,* 17 Mich.App. 240, 169 N.W.2d 135 (1969), allowing damages for failure of a nursing home to notify plaintiff of his mother's impending death, and *Allinger v. Kell,* 102 Mich.App. 798, 302 N.W.2d 576 (1981), allowing damages for a funeral director's mutilation of the body of plaintiffs' murdered daughter.
* * *

[margin note: exception in Stewart]

[margin note: examples]

Generally, and as evidenced by the above-cited cases, damages for mental distress are allowed where the injury suffered is to the person. This Court has considered another line of cases, where damages for mental distress in breach of contract actions were sought for injuries to property. Plaintiffs in these cases have been uniformly unsuccessful. See *Jankowski v. Mazzotta,* 7 Mich. App. 483, 152 N.W.2d 49 (1967), where damages for mental distress were sought for defendant's failure to conform a house to specifications; *Caradonna v. Thorious,* 17 Mich.App. 41, 169 N.W.2d 179 (1969), involving damages for mental distress in a dispute over rebuilding a tornado damaged home; *Scott v. Hurd–Corrigan Moving & Storage Co., Inc.,* 103 Mich.App. 322, 302 N.W.2d 867 (1981), *lv. den.* 412 Mich. 881 (1981), where damages for mental distress were sought for a storage company's wrongful sale of plaintiff's household goods.

[margin note: damage to the property]

Still another line of cases denying damages for mental distress in breach of contract cases involve intangible claims such as failure to pay insurance claims and breach of employment contracts. See *Van Marter v. American Fidelity Fire Ins. Co.,* 114 Mich. 171, 318 N.W.2d 679 (1982) * * *.

These illustrative cases demonstrate that the rule of *Stewart* applies where deep, personal human relations are involved. Where property loss is involved, the courts have generally not allowed recovery for mental distress in breach of contract actions. One's property can be lost on a public carrier, in a fire, or as the result of a bailment and, under *Kewin,* damages for mental distress will not be recoverable. Other than the *Stewart* exception, the only grounds upon which damages for mental distress are recoverable in a breach of contract case is where plaintiff alleges tortious conduct, independent of any breach of the commercial contract.

[margin note: Rule in Stewart]

[margin note: tort is another exception]

* * *

In this case, plaintiffs seek to bring their mental distress claim for damages within the purview of the *Stewart* exception. However, the installation of a furnace as well as other home improvements clearly arise by commercial contract and do not involve matters of mental concern and solicitude. The injury suffered by plaintiffs was to property and not person. Neither the *Stewart* exception nor the general rule of *Kewin* authorize damages for mental distress in this case.

We must next examine whether plaintiffs' complaint sufficiently pleads an independent tort, allowing for damages for mental distress under a theory of tort rather than contract.

In *Hart v. Ludwig*, 347 Mich. 559, 564–565, 79 N.W.2d 895 (1956), the Supreme Court held that the unskilled performance of a contract may give rise to an independent tort action and may be a basis for damages for mental distress.

The case of *Daley v. LaCroix*, 384 Mich. 4, 179 N.W.2d 390 (1970), clarifies the law of Michigan governing damages for mental distress in tort actions, as *Kewin* does in contract actions. In that case, the defendant's vehicle ran off the road, shearing a utility pole which snapped a number of high voltage lines. These voltage lines, in turn, tangled with electrical lines leading to the plaintiffs' house, causing an electrical explosion in their home. Plaintiffs sued for mental distress resulting from the accident though no direct physical injury occurred to either of them, except for emotional disturbance and traumatic neurosis.

The Court in *Daley* overturned the rule previously recognized in Michigan which required some impact on the plaintiff before damages for mental distress could be recovered. The Court prospectively laid down the rule as follows:

"We hold that where a definite and objective physical injury is produced as a result of emotional distress proximately caused by defendant's negligent conduct, the plaintiff in a properly pleaded and proved action may recover in damages for such physical consequences to himself notwithstanding the absence of any physical impact upon plaintiff at the time of the mental shock.

"The rule we adopt today is, of course, subject to familiar limitations.

"Generally, defendant's standard of conduct is measured by reactions to be expected of normal persons. Absent specific knowledge of plaintiff's unusual sensitivity, there should be no recovery for hypersensitive mental disturbance where a normal individual would not be affected under the circumstances." 384 Mich. at 12–13, 179 N.W.2d 390.

The complaint in the case before us was designed to fall under the rule of *Stewart*, acknowledged and accepted in *Kewin* as an exception to the rule that damages for mental distress are not allowed in contract cases. This pleading is inadequate to support an independent claim for mental distress in tort. However, under GCR 1963, 117.3, "[e]ach party shall be given opportunity to amend his pleadings as provided by Rule 118 unless the evidence then before the court shows amendment would not be justified".

Reversed and remanded for further proceedings in light of this opinion.

Note
Punitive Damages in Contract Cases

Recall the approach to punitive damages in White v. Benkowski (page 21). In the following excerpt from Thyssen, Inc. v. S.S. Fortune Star, 777 F.2d 57, 63 (2d Cir.1985), Judge Friendly set forth the prevailing view as reflected in the Restatement, and then offered some reasons for this view.

Restatement (Second) of Contracts § 355 (1979) [states]:

> Punitive damages are not recoverable for a breach of contract unless the conduct constituting the breach is also a tort for which punitive damages are recoverable.

See also 11 *Williston on Contracts* § 1340, at 209–11 (W. Jaeger 3d ed. 1968); 5 *Corbin on Contracts* § 1077, at 438–39 (1964); Sullivan, *Punitive Damages in the Law of Contract*, 61 Minn.L.Rev. 207, 207 (1977). This rule applies although the breach is intentional or even when it has been affected with malicious intent. Simpson, *Punitive Damages for Breach of Contract*, 20 Ohio St.L.J. 284, 284 (1959); Farnsworth, *Contracts* § 12.8, at 874 [(2d ed. 1990).] Under Holmes' theory that a contract is simply a set of alternative promises either to perform or to pay damages for nonperformance, Holmes, *The Common Law* 235–36 (M. Howe ed. 1963), the rule would require no other explanation. Nevertheless, a good many have been offered. One is that the law of contracts governs primarily commercial relationships, where the amount required to compensate for loss is easily fixed, in contrast to the law of torts, which compensates for injury to personal interests that are more difficult to value, thus justifying noncompensatory recovery. Sullivan, *supra*, at 222. Another, given by Corbin, *supra* § 1077, at 438, is that breaches of contract do not cause the kind of "resentment or other mental and physical discomfort as do the wrongs called torts and crimes," and no retributive purpose would be served by punitive damages in contract cases. A third explanation, offered by economists, is the notion that breaches of contract that are in fact efficient and wealth-enhancing should be encouraged, and that such "efficient breaches" occur when the breaching party will still profit after compensating the other party for its "expectation interest." The addition of punitive damages to traditional contract remedies would prevent many such beneficial actions from being taken. *See* Farnsworth, *supra*, § 12.3, at 848; *Restatement (Second) of Contracts* ch. 16 reporter's note. In any event the general rule is well established, although certain exceptions have been adopted.

The most common exception, which is specifically incorporated in the general rule in the *Restatement* and comprehends several other exceptions listed below, is where the breach constitutes an independent, wilful tort in addition to being a breach of contract, 5 Corbin, *supra*, § 1077, at 445; Farnsworth, *supra*, § 12.8, at 875–76. Others include breach of a contract to marry, Sullivan, *supra*, at 222–23; Corbin, *supra*, § 1077, at 440–43; failure of a public service company enjoying monopoly or quasi-monopoly power to discharge its obligations to the public, Sullivan, *supra*, at 223–26; Corbin, *supra*, § 1077, at 443–44; breach of a fiduciary duty, Sullivan, *supra*, at 226–29; breach of contract accompanied by fraudulent conduct (where, for example, the defendant conveys to a third party property given as security for the plaintiff's debt when the defendant has promised to reconvey the property to the plaintiff upon repayment of the debt), *id.* at 229–36; and the bad faith refusal by an insurer to settle an insurance claim for which it is liable, *id.* at 844 * * *.

Note
Other Qualifications and Limits
on Lost Expectancy Recovery

There are many additional qualifications and limits on the recovery of lost expectancy damages. Some of the most noteworthy of these are identified below.

Denial of lost expectancy recovery in medical contexts. As we saw in Sullivan v. O'Connor (page 35), a court may deny lost expectancy in a medical context. As Judge Kaplan pointed out, "considering the uncertainties of medical science and the variations in the physical and psychological conditions of individual patients, doctors can seldom in good faith promise specific results."

Denial of recovery for loss of reputation or goodwill. According to some courts, the measure of damages for lost expectancy does not include compensation for loss of reputation or loss of goodwill. Stancil v. Mergenthaler Linotype Co., 589 F.Supp. 78, 84 (D.Hawaii 1984); Quinn v. Straus Broadcasting Group, Inc., 309 F.Supp. 1208 (S.D.N.Y.1970). But in AM/PM Franchise Assoc. v. Atlantic Richfield Co., 526 Pa. 110, 584 A.2d 915 (1990), the court approved, as a general proposition, the award of damages for loss of goodwill. The court defined goodwill as "the reputation that businesses have built over the course of time that is reflected by the return of customers to purchase goods and the attendant profits that accompanies such sales." The court noted that many of the cases denying damages for loss of goodwill "were written in a time * * * where market studies and economic forecasting were unexplored," and that "a significant majority of the cases have allowed for the recovery of lost goodwill in proper circumstances." Finally, the court held that the party claiming damages for loss of goodwill must "provide the trier of fact with a reasonable basis from which to calculate damages."

Denial of lost expectancy to attorneys. Some courts allow wrongfully discharged lawyers only the reasonable value of their services up to the date of discharge. Barwick, Dillian, & Lambert, P.A. v. Ewing, 646 So.2d 776, (Fla.App. 1994); Rosenberg v. Levin, 409 So.2d 1016 (Fla.1982); Hardman v. Snyder, 183 W.Va. 34, 393 S.E.2d 672 (1990).

Denial of attorneys' fees and interest. Typically, the largest, although not the only type of litigation cost, is attorneys' fees. The general rule is that a victorious party cannot recover attorneys' fees from the losing party. D. Dobbs, Remedies 276 (1993). Thus, even though a plaintiff may receive a judgment for expectancy damages, the fees that a party may have to pay may consume a large part of the award. One rationale for the rule often heard is that taxing the losing party for attorney's fees would discourage the poor from litigating possibly meritorious claims.

Courts and legislatures have created some exceptions to the rule against recovery of attorneys' fees. The most important exception is that courts will generally enforce a specific contract clause providing for recovery of attorneys' fees *to the extent the fees are reasonable.* Trustees of the Prince Condominium Trust v. Prosser, 412 Mass. 723, 592 N.E.2d 1301 (1992); Leventhal v. Krinsky, 325 Mass. 336, 90 N.E.2d 545 (1950). A plaintiff also may recover attorneys' fees as reliance damages if the plaintiff wasted the fees due to the defendant's breach. For example, a plaintiff can recover attorneys' fees to pay for a title search if the vendor of land later repudiates the contract of sale. The latter fees, of course, are not a litigation expense.

A few state legislatures authorize the award of attorneys' fees to the prevailing party. Alaska Stat. § 09.60.010 (Supp.1991); Nev.Rev.Stat. § 18.010 (Michie 1986). Some federal statutes also provide for the award of attorneys' fees, usually to induce private enforcement of public policies. One such statute is the Truth in Lending Act, 15 U.S.C.A. § 1640(a) (1982).

Among academic commentators critical of the general rule against the award of attorneys' fees are Ehrenzweig, Reimbursement of Counsel Fees and the Great Society, 54 Cal.L.Rev. 792 (1966); McLaughlin, The Recovery of Attorney's Fees: A New Method of Financing Legal Services, 40 Ford.L.Rev. 761 (1972); Sands, Attorney's Fees as Recoverable Costs, 63 A.B.A.J. 510 (1977).

Now we turn briefly to a further major limitation on the general principle of expectancy recovery. Plaintiffs generally cannot recover pre-judgment interest unless the amount of damages is ascertained or liquidated prior to entry of judgment. Waukesha Concrete Prods. Co., Inc. v. Capitol Indemnity Corp., 127 Wis.2d 332, 379 N.W.2d 333 (1985); D. Dobbs, Remedies 246–48 (1993). For example, if a contractor breaches his agreement to build a structure, the owner, who sues two years later and recovers a judgment against the contractor, receives interest not from the date of breach but only from the date of judgment. (Most states have statutes prescribing the rate of post-judgment interest.) One reason often given for denying pre-judgment interest on unliquidated claims is that it would unfairly penalize the defendant, who could not pay the sum owed and thus end the accrual of interest because he could not determine how much was owed. But is such an approach fair to the plaintiff?

HILLMAN, CONTRACT LORE

27 J. Corp. L. 505, 507–508 (2002).

* * * Whatever the reasons behind the expectancy approach, contracts people continue to report that the goal of expectancy damages is to make injured parties whole. The reality is dramatically different. A large set of remedial rules often limits the recovery of injured parties to well below expectancy. For example, in our legal system, parties usually must pay their own lawyers and can rarely recover prejudgment interest. These impediments, of course, constitute costs of litigation and apply across all areas of the law. More specific to contract law, injured parties cannot recover unforeseeable or difficult-to-prove damages, even though often real and large. In addition, courts typically compute damages objectively, thereby ignoring a party's special circumstances, including emotional distress and sentimental value.

Of course, the failure of expectancy damages to make injured parties whole is not the world's best kept secret, and many theorists have recognized this reality and have discussed reasons for it. One obvious reason is that the expectancy goal runs into institutional counter policies. We do not want to discourage parties from exercising their right to a day in court for fear of having to pay the other party's legal fees. We do not want to license courts to award baseless recoveries, so we require injured parties to prove their damages with some precision.

Another reason is the existence of contradictory substantive policies. For example, we want to avoid discouraging people from making contracts based on a fear (rational or not) of inordinate liability. We also want to encourage promisees to disclose special circumstances, so we deny them consequential damages when the breaching promisor could not reasonably foresee a particular loss and the injured promisee did not disclose its possibility. In addition, contract law's actual remedial goal may be to protect an injured party from reliance losses, which are often more difficult to prove than expectancy damages. Expectancy damages therefore may serve as a surrogate for reliance damages, thereby diminishing concern when the former fails to give the injured party the full value of her promise.

SECTION FIVE: REIMBURSEMENT OF RELIANCE COSTS AS AN ALTERNATIVE REMEDY WHERE THERE IS A BREACH OF AN AGREEMENT WITH CONSIDERATION

NURSE v. BARNS

Kings Bench, 1664.
Raym. Sir T. 77, 83 Eng.Rep. 43.

The plaintiff declares, that the defendant in consideration of [10£] promised to let him enjoy certain iron mills for six months; and it appeared that the iron mills were worth but [20£] per annum, and yet damages were given [in the amount of 500£] by reason of the loss of stock laid in; and *per Curiam* the jury may well find such damages, for they are not bound to give only the [10£] but also all the special damages.

CHICAGO COLISEUM CLUB v. DEMPSEY

Appellate Court of Illinois, 1932.
265 Ill.App. 542.

MR. JUSTICE WILSON delivered the opinion of the court.

Chicago Coliseum Club, a corporation, as plaintiff, brought its action against William Harrison Dempsey, known as Jack Dempsey, to recover damages for breach of a written contract executed March 13, 1926, but bearing date of March 6 of that year.

Plaintiff was incorporated as an Illinois corporation for the promotion of general pleasure and athletic purposes and to conduct boxing, sparring and wrestling matches and exhibitions for prizes or purses. The defendant William Harrison Dempsey was well known in the pugilistic world and, at the time of the making and execution of the contract in question, held the title of world's Champion Heavy Weight Boxer.

Under the terms of the written agreement, the plaintiff was to promote a public boxing exhibition in Chicago, or some suitable place to be selected by the promoter, and had engaged the services of one Harry Wills, another well known boxer and pugilist, to engage in a boxing match with the defendant Dempsey for the championship of the world. By the terms of the agreement Dempsey was to receive $10, receipt of which was acknowledged, and the plaintiff further agreed to pay to Dempsey the sum of $300,000 on the 5th day of August 1926,—$500,000 in cash at least 10 days before the date fixed for the contest, and a sum equal to 50 per cent of the net profits over and above the sum of $2,000,000 in the event the gate receipts should exceed that amount. In addition the defendant was to receive 50 per cent of the net revenue derived from moving picture concessions or royalties received by the plaintiff, and defendant agreed to have his life and health insured in favor of the plaintiff in a manner and at a place to be designated by the plaintiff. Defendant further agreed not to engage in any boxing match after the date of the agreement and prior to the date on which the contest was to be held. * * *

March 6, 1926, the plaintiff entered into an agreement with Harry Wills, in which Wills agreed to engage in a boxing match with the Jack Dempsey named in the agreement hereinbefore referred to. Under this agreement the plaintiff, Chicago Coliseum Club was to deposit $50,000 in escrow in the National City Bank of New York City, New York, to be paid over to Wills on the 10th day prior to the date fixed for the holding of the boxing contest. Further conditions were provided in said contract with Wills, which, however, are not necessary to set out in detail. There is no evidence in the record showing that the $50,000 was deposited nor that it has ever been paid, nor is there any evidence in the record showing the financial standing of the Chicago Coliseum Club, a corporation, plaintiff in this suit. This contract between the plaintiff and Wills appears to have been entered into several days before the contract with Dempsey.

March 8, 1926, the plaintiff entered into a contract with one Andrew C. Weisberg, under which it appears that it was necessary for the plaintiff to have the services of an experienced person skilled in promoting boxing exhibitions and that the said Weisberg was possessed of such qualifications and that it was necessary for the plaintiff to procure his help in the promoting of the exhibition. It appears further from the agreement that it was necessary to incur expenditures in the way of traveling expenses, legal services and other costs in and about the promotion of the boxing match, and Weisberg agreed to investigate, canvass and organize the various hotel associations and other business organizations for the purpose of securing accommodations for spectators and to procure subscriptions and others for the erection of an arena and other necessary expense in order to carry out the enterprise and to promote the boxing match in question. Under these agreements Weisberg was to furnish the funds for such purposes and was to be reimbursed out of the receipts from the sale of tickets for the expenses incurred by him, together with a certain amount for his services.

Both the Wills contract and the Weisberg contract are referred to at some length, inasmuch as claims for damages by plaintiff are predicated upon these two agreements. Under the terms of the contract between the plaintiff and Dempsey and the plaintiff and Wills, the contest was to be held during the month of September, 1926.

July 10, 1926, plaintiff wired Dempsey at Colorado Springs, Colorado, stating that representatives of life and accident insurance companies would call on him for the purpose of examining him for insurance in favor of the Chicago Coliseum Club, in accordance with the terms of his contract, and also requesting the defendant to begin training for the contest not later than

August 1, 1926. In answer to this communication plaintiff received a telegram from Dempsey, as follows:

date of breach

"BM Colorado Springs Colo
B.E. Clements

July 10th 1926

President Chicago Coliseum Club Chgo Entirely too busy training for my coming Tunney match to waste time on insurance representatives stop as you have no contract suggest you stop kidding yourself and me also

Jack Dempsey."

We are unable to conceive upon what theory the defendant could contend that there was no contract, as it appears to be admitted in the proceeding here and bears his signature and the amounts involved are sufficiently large to have created a rather lasting impression on the mind of anyone signing such an agreement. It amounts, however, to a repudiation of the agreement and from that time on Dempsey refused to take any steps to carry out his undertaking. It appears that Dempsey at this time was engaged in preparing himself for a contest with Tunney to be held at Philadelphia, Pennsylvania, sometime in September, and on August 3, 1926, plaintiff, as complainant, filed a bill in the superior court of Marion county, Indiana, asking to have Dempsey restrained and enjoined from engaging in the contest with Tunney, which complainant was informed and believed was to be held on the 16th day of September, and which contest would be in violation of the terms of the agreement entered into between the plaintiff and defendant at Los Angeles, March 13, 1926.

Personal service was had upon the defendant Dempsey in the proceeding in the Indiana court and on August 27, 1926, he entered his general appearance, by his attorneys, and filed his answer in said cause. September 13, 1926, a decree was entered in the superior court of Marion county, finding that the contract was a valid and subsisting contract between the parties, and that the complainant had expended large sums of money in carrying out the terms of the agreement, and entering a decree that Dempsey be perpetually restrained and enjoined from in any way, wise, or manner, training or preparing for or participating in any contracts or engagements in furtherance of any boxing match, prize fight or any exhibition of like nature, and particularly from engaging or entering into any boxing match with one Gene Tunney, or with any person other than the one designated by plaintiff.

It is insisted among other things that the costs incurred by the plaintiff in procuring the injunctional order in Marion county, Indiana, were properly chargeable against Dempsey for his breach of contract and recoverable in this proceeding. Under the evidence in the record in this proceeding there appears to have been a valid subsisting agreement between the plaintiff and Dempsey, in which Dempsey was to perform according to the terms of the agreement and which he refused to do, and the plaintiff, as a matter of law, was entitled at least to nominal damages. For this reason, if for no other, judgment should have been for the plaintiff.

During the proceeding in the circuit court of this county it was sought to introduce evidence for the purpose of showing damages, other than nominal damages, and in view of the fact that the case has to be retried, this court is asked to consider the various items of expense claimed to have been incurred and various offers of proof made to establish damages for breach of the agreement. Under the proof offered, the question of damages naturally divides itself into the four following propositions:

1st. Loss of profits which would have been derived by the plaintiff in the event of the holding of the contest in question;

2nd. Expenses incurred by the plaintiff prior to the signing of the agreement between the plaintiff and Dempsey;

3rd. Expenses incurred in attempting to restrain the defendant from engaging in other contests and to force him into a compliance with the terms of his agreement with the plaintiff; and

4th. Expenses incurred after the signing of the agreement and before the breach of July 10, 1926.

Proposition 1. Plaintiff offered to prove by one Mullins that a boxing exhibition between Dempsey and Wills held in the City of Chicago on September 22, 1926, would bring a gross receipt of $3,000,000, and that the expense incurred would be $1,400,000, leaving a net profit to the promoter of $1,600,000. The court properly sustained an objection to this testimony. The character of the undertaking was such that it would be impossible to produce evidence of a probative character sufficient to establish any amount which could be reasonably ascertainable by reason of the character of the undertaking. The profits from a boxing contest of this character, open to the public, is dependent upon so many different circumstances that they are not susceptible of definite legal determination. The success or failure of such an undertaking depends largely upon the ability of the promoters, the reputation of the contestants and the conditions of the weather at and prior to the holding of the contest, the accessibility of the place, the extent of the publicity, the possibility of other and counter attractions and many other questions which would enter into consideration. Such an entertainment lacks utterly the element of stability which exists in regular organized business. This fact was practically admitted by the plaintiff by the allegation of its bill filed in the Marion county court of Indiana asking for an injunction against Dempsey. Plaintiff in its bill in that proceeding charged, as follows:

"That by virtue of the premises aforesaid, the plaintiff will, unless it secures the injunctive relief herein prayed for, suffer great and irreparable injury and damages, not compensable by any action at law in damages, the damages being incapable of commensuration, and plaintiff, therefore, has no adequate remedy at law."

Compensation for damages for a breach of contract must be established by evidence from which a court or jury are able to ascertain the extent of such damages by the usual rules of evidence and to a reasonable degree of certainty. We are of the opinion that the performance in question is not susceptible of proof sufficient to satisfy the requirements and that the damages, if any, are purely speculative. * * *

Proposition 2: Expenses incurred by the plaintiff prior to the signing of the agreement between the plaintiff and Dempsey.

Rule →

can't recover $50K for Wills b/c it was never paid

The general rule is that in an action for a breach of contract a party can recover only on damages which naturally flow from and are the result of the act complained of. *O'Conner v. Nolan,* 64 Ill.App. 357. The Wills contract was entered into prior to the contract with the defendant and was not made contingent upon the plaintiff's obtaining a similar agreement with the defendant Dempsey. Under the circumstances the plaintiff speculated as to the result of his efforts to procure the Dempsey contract. It may be argued that there had been negotiations pending between plaintiff and Dempsey which clearly indicated an agreement between them, but the agreement in fact was never consummated until sometime later. The action is based upon the written agreement which was entered into in Los Angeles. Any obligations assumed by the plaintiff prior to that time are not chargeable to the defendant. Moreover, an examination of the record discloses that the $50,000 named in the contract with Wills, which was to be payable upon a signing of the agreement, was not and never has been paid. There is no evidence in the record showing that the plaintiff is responsible financially, and, even though there were, we consider that it is not an element of damage which can be recovered for breach of the contract in question.

Proposition 3: Expenses incurred in attempting to restrain the defendant from engaging in other contests and to force him into a compliance with the terms of his agreement with the plaintiff.

can't recover b/c π knew Δ wasn't going to proceed w/ contract

After the repudiation of the agreement by the defendant, plaintiff was advised of defendant's match with Tunney which, from the evidence, it appears, was to take place in Philadelphia in the month of September and was in direct conflict with the terms of the agreement entered into between plaintiff and defendant. Plaintiff's bill, filed in the superior court of Marion county, Indiana, was an effort on the part of the plaintiff to compel defendant to live up to the terms of his agreement. The chancellor in the Indiana court entered his decree, which apparently is in full force and effect, and the defendant in violating the terms of that decree, after personal service, is answerable to that court for a violation of the injunctional order entered in said proceeding. The expenses incurred, however, by the plaintiff in procuring that decree are not collectible in an action for damages in this proceeding; neither are such similar expenses as were incurred in the trips to Colorado and Philadelphia, nor the attorney's fees and other expenses thereby incurred. *Cuyler Realty Co. v. Teneo Co., Inc.,* 188 N.Y.S. 340. The plaintiff having been informed that the defendant intended to proceed no further under his agreement, took such steps at its own financial risk. There was nothing in the agreement regarding attorney's fees and there was nothing in the contract in regard to the services of the defendant from which it would appear that the action for specific performance would lie. After the clear breach of contract by the defendant, the plaintiff proceeded with this character of litigation at its own risk. We are of the opinion that the trial court properly held that this was an element of damages which was not recoverable.

Proposition 4: Expenses incurred after the signing of the agreement and before the breach of July 10, 1926.

After the signing of the agreement plaintiff attempted to show expenses incurred by one Weisberg in and about the furtherance of the project. Weisberg testified that he had taken an active part in promoting sports for a number of years and was in the employ of the Chicago Coliseum Club under a written contract during all of the time that his services were rendered in furtherance of this proposition. This contract was introduced in evidence and bore the date of March 8, 1926. Under its terms Weisberg was to be reimbursed out of the gate receipts and profits derived from the performance. His compensation depended entirely upon the success of the exhibition. Under his agreement with the plaintiff there was nothing to charge the plaintiff unconditionally with the costs and expenses of Weisberg's services. The court properly ruled against the admissibility of the evidence.

We find in the record, however, certain evidence which should have been submitted to the jury on the question of damages sustained by the plaintiff. The contract on which the breach of the action is predicated shows a payment of $10 by the plaintiff to the defendant and the receipt acknowledged. It appears that the stadium located in the South Park District, known as Soldier's Field, was considered as a site for the holding of the contest and plaintiff testified that it paid $300 to an architect for plans in the event the stadium was to be used for the performance. This item of damage might have been made more specific and may not have been the best evidence in the case but, standing alone, it was sufficient to go to the jury. There were certain elements in regard to wages paid assistant secretaries which may be substantiated by evidence showing that they were necessary in furtherance of the undertaking. If these expenses were incurred they are recoverable if in furtherance of the general scheme. The defendant should not be required to answer in damages for salaries paid regular officials of the corporation who were presumed to be receiving such salaries by reason of their position, but special expenses incurred are recoverable. The expenses of Hoffman in going to Colorado for the purpose of having Dempsey take his physical examination for insurance, if before the breach and reasonable, are recoverable. The railroad fares for those who went to Los Angeles for the purpose of procuring the signing of the agreement are not recoverable as they were incurred in a furtherance of the procuring of the contract and not after the agreement was entered into. The services of Shank in looking after railroad facilities and making arrangements with the railroad for publicity and special trains and accommodations were items which should be considered and if it develops that they were incurred in a furtherance of the general plan and properly proven, are items for which the plaintiff should be reimbursed.

The items recoverable are such items of expense as were incurred between the date of the signing of the agreement and the breach of July 10, 1926, by the defendant and such as were incurred as a necessary expense in furtherance of the performance. Proof of such items should be made subject to the usual rules of evidence.

For the reasons stated in this opinion the judgment of the circuit court is reversed and the cause remanded for a new trial.

Judgment reversed and cause remanded.

Note
Subsequent Developments: Dempsey v. Tunney

Perhaps Dempsey should have honored his contract to fight Wills. On September 23, 1926, Dempsey fought Tunney in Philadelphia and lost on points. When asked by his wife why he lost, he responded: "Honey, I guess I forgot to duck." In a rematch a year later, Dempsey knocked Tunney down, but continued to stand over him instead of going to a neutral corner. This delayed the referee's count and allowed Tunney over 14 seconds to recover. Tunney subsequently won the fight. © 1983 Reuters, Ltd.; Reuters North European Service.

ANGLIA TELEVISION LTD. v. REED, 3 All Eng.Rep. 690 (C.A.1971). [Plaintiff Anglia sued Reed for expenditures incurred by Anglia prior to contracting with Reed. Anglia had been preparing to make a film and had spent money to hire a director and other key persons. Reed then agreed to play the lead role. Later, Reed repudiated, and Anglia, unable to find another lead actor, abandoned the film. The Court of Appeal, per Lord Denning, held for Anglia.] "[Plaintiff] * * * can claim also the expenditures incurred *before* the contract, provided that it was such as would reasonably be in the contemplation of the parties as likely to be wasted if the contract was broken. Applying that principle here, it is plain that, when Mr. Reed entered into this contract, he must have known perfectly well that much expenditure had already been incurred * * *. He must have contemplated—or, at any rate, it is reasonable to be imputed to him—that if he broke his contract, all that expenditure would be wasted, whether or not it was incurred before or after the contract. He must pay damages for all the expenditures so wasted * * *."

L. ALBERT & SON v. ARMSTRONG RUBBER CO., 178 F.2d 182 (2d Cir.1949). [Albert agreed to sell Armstrong four machines ("refiners") designed to recondition old rubber. The trial court found that Albert breached the contract by delivering late, that Armstrong failed to prove any damages, and that Armstrong used some of the equipment and was liable in quasi-contract. One of the issues on appeal was whether Armstrong was entitled to recover $3,000, the cost of the foundation that it had built for the refiners.]

L. HAND, CHIEF JUDGE.

Normally a promisee's damages for breach of contract are the value of the promised performance, less his outlay, which includes, not only what he must pay to the promisor, but any expenses necessary to prepare for the performance; and in the case at bar the cost of the foundation was such an expense. The sum which would restore the Buyer to the position it would have been in, had the Seller performed, would therefore be the prospective net earnings of the "Refiners" while they were used (together with any value they might have as scrap after they were discarded), less their price—$25,500—together with $3,000, the cost of installing them. The Buyer did not indeed prove the net earnings of the "Refiners" or their scrap value; but it asserts that it is nonetheless entitled to recover the cost of the foundation upon the theory that what it expended in reliance upon the Seller's performance was a recoverable loss. In cases where the venture would have proved profitable to the promisee, there is no reason why he should not recover his expenses. On the other hand, on those occasions in which the performance would not have covered the promisee's outlay, such a result imposes the risk of the promisee's contract upon the promisor. We cannot agree that the promisor's default in performance should under this guise make him an insurer of the promisee's venture; yet it does not follow that the breach should not throw upon him the duty of showing that the value of the performance would in fact have been less than the promisee's outlay. It is often very hard to learn what the value of the performance would have been; and it is a common expedient, and a just one, in such situations to put the peril of the answer upon that party who by his wrong has made the issue relevant to the rights of the other. On principle therefore the proper solution would seem to be that the promisee may recover his outlay in preparation for the performance, subject to the privilege of the promisor to reduce it by as much as he can show that the promisee would have lost, if the contract had been performed. * * *

Much the fullest discussion of the whole subject is Professor Fuller's in the Yale Law Journal. The situation at bar was among those which he calls cases of "essential reliance," and for which he favors the rule we are adopting. It is one instance of his "very simple formula: We will not in a suit for reimbursement of losses incurred in reliance on a contract knowingly put the plaintiff in a better position than he would have occupied, had the contract been fully performed."

The judgment will therefore be affirmed with the following modifications. * * * The Buyer will be allowed to set off $3,000 against the Seller's recovery with interest from October, 1945, subject to the Seller's privilege to deduct from that amount any sum which upon a further hearing it can prove would have been the Buyer's loss upon the contract, had the "Refiners" been delivered on or before May 1st, 1945.

Judgment modified as above, and affirmed as so modified.

COPPOLA v. KRAUSHAAR, 102 App.Div. 306, 92 N.Y.S. 436 (1905). [Plaintiff alleged that he was engaged to be married, had ordered two gowns for his fiancee from defendant on January 3, 1902, to be delivered on January 18, and had told defendant he was incurring great expense for the wedding to be held on January 19. Plaintiff alleged further that the defendant failed to deliver the gowns on January 18, that as a result the wedding "was broken off" by his fiancee, and that $500 in expenses for "presents, wines, clothes" etc. were expended uselessly. Plaintiff claimed $500 damages. Held, plaintiff could recover $10 allegedly paid on the price of the gowns, but not the $500. The court stated that the latter expenses were "too remote," citing Hadley v. Baxendale, 9 Exch. 341 (1854).]

FULLER AND PERDUE, THE RELIANCE INTEREST IN CONTRACT DAMAGES
46 Yale L.J. 52, 75–80 (1936).

In the contracts upon which suit is brought the value of the expectancy ordinarily exceeds the reliance interest. It is possible, however, that the reliance interest may offer the plaintiff a more generous measure of recovery than the expectation interest. In such cases should the value of the expectancy be regarded as setting a limit on recovery? * * * Is there any basis for this notion that recovery based on reliance should never be allowed to exceed the value of the expectancy?

* * *

To pass on this question it is necessary to inquire what things may bring it about that the reliance interest exceeds the "reasonable value" of the defendant's promised performance. The most obvious possibility is that the plaintiff has entered a losing contract. A manufacturer has undertaken to construct a machine for $1,000 failing to foresee that it will be necessary at a cost of $1,500 to tear down and replace a wall of his plant in order to remove the machine when it is completed. If the manufacturer here should seek to recover the full reliance interest ($1,500 plus the cost of materials and labor on the machine) the obvious objection might seem to be that he is trying to shift the burden of his own improvidence to the other party.

* * *

But does an excess of the reliance over the expectation interest necessarily imply that the plaintiff has entered a losing bargain? In the old case of *Nurse v. Barns* the defendant "in consideration of 10£" promised to give the plaintiff the use of certain premises for a period of six months. Relying on this promise the plaintiff laid in a stock of goods. The defendant then failed to perform his promise. Because his expenditures for goods were thus rendered vain the plaintiff lost £500, which he was permitted to recover from the defendant. Here there was nothing to indicate that the plaintiff entered a losing bargain; on the contrary it was expressly found that the lease was worth just what the plaintiff agreed to pay for it.

It is obvious that we need a distinction between two kinds of reliance. Certain acts of reliance are in a loose sense the "price" of whatever benefits the contract may involve for the plaintiff. This type of reliance we shall call "essential reliance". Under this heading would be included the performance of * * * [the agreed exchange], preparations to perform, * * * and the losses involved in entering the contract itself, as, for instance, in foregoing the opportunity to enter other profitable contracts. As to this kind of reliance ("essential reliance") if we do not limit recovery by the "contract price" we are permitting the plaintiff to shift to the defendant his own contractual losses, when the defendant is guilty of nothing more reprehensible than breach of contract.

In contrast to "essential reliance" is the kind of reliance involved in *Nurse v. Barns,* which we shall call "incidental reliance." The plaintiff's reliance there (laying in a stock of goods) followed naturally, and, we may assume, foreseeably, from the contract. It did not, however, consist of acts necessary to the perfection of the plaintiff's rights on the contract; it cannot be regarded as the "price" of the defendant's performance. To shift the burden of such reliance to the defendant in an amount exceeding "the full contract price" is not to shift to the defendant the plaintiff's contractual losses. In such a case therefore there appears no valid reason to limit the plaintiff's recovery by the expectation interest measured "objectively." If there is to be any limit at all it must be according to some standard more generous than the "contract price."

Should there be any limit on recovery in cases like *Nurse v. Barns?* Suppose it had been shown in that case that the business contemplated by the plaintiff would have been operated at a loss and that this loss would have exceeded the amount which the plaintiff sought to recover as reimbursement for his reliance. If the plaintiff is in such a situation permitted to recover, it is obvious that we are in effect shifting to the defendant the loss which the plaintiff would have incurred in the venture undertaken in reliance on the contract. To prevent this we must limit the plaintiff's recovery by the expectation interest measured "subjectively," that is, with reference to the profit or loss reasonably to be anticipated from the contemplated business. In practice this limitation will be of slight significance since in cases like *Nurse v. Barns* it will seldom be possible to judge with any accuracy what the fate of the venture would have been had it not been interrupted by the defendant's failure to perform his contract.

* * * All of these points are contained by implication in a very simple formula: *We will not in a suit for reimbursement for losses incurred in reliance on a contract knowingly put the plaintiff in a better position than he would have occupied had the contract been fully performed.*

We have spoken so far only of a gross limitation on the plaintiff's recovery. However, the proposition that we will avoid conferring on the plaintiff advantages beyond those which performance of the contract would have involved carries the further corollary that there should be deducted from the plaintiff's recovery any losses he would have suffered had the contract been performed. If a contractor sues for reimbursement for $5,000 spent in partial performance of a contract on which he would have lost $1,000 had he been permitted to complete it, probably most courts would award the plaintiff only $4,000. In cases of incidental reliance the deduction of prospective losses might conceivably be twofold, and embrace both contractual losses (the plaintiff entered a bad bargain with the defendant) and the losses he would have suffered in the dependent venture even if that venture had not been frustrated by the defendant's breach.

AUTOTROL CORP. v. CONTINENTAL WATER SYSTEMS CORP.

United States Court of Appeals, Seventh Circuit, 1990.
918 F.2d 689.

Posner, Circuit Judge.

This is a diversity suit, primarily for breach of contract. The suit was tried to a jury, and the plaintiff, Autotrol Corporation, obtained a judgment of more than $1.5 million. The appeal raises a large number of issues, only a handful of which require discussion. * * *

* * *

The contract, signed in May 1986, established a joint venture between Autotrol's controls division and Continental Water Systems Corporation to create a system for water purification based on a patented new technology, known as "electrodiarese," that Continental owned the exclusive right to exploit. Autotrol was to manufacture the control for the system and Continental the rest and both companies would sell the completed systems—Autotrol the large systems, Continental the small ones. There was an ambiguity, later to prove critical, about the dividing line between large and small.

Before production could begin, there had to be product specifications. These had not been completed when the contract was signed. Anticipating this possibility, the contract provided that when approved by both parties the specifications would be attached to, and thereby made a part of, the contract; and should the parties be "unable, in good faith, to agree upon the contents of the Products Specifications Schedule by June 30, 1986, either party hereto may elect to terminate this Agreement." On June 25 the parties agreed to extend this deadline to July 17. July 17 came and went and the product specifications had not been agreed upon but neither party exercised its right of termination. It was almost a year later, with the product specifications still not having been agreed upon, that Continental declared the contract terminated. That is the alleged breach. * * *

* * *

[Judge Posner held in part that the] jury was entitled to find that the parties had modified the contract to forbid termination on this ground at least until such time as the need to agree on product specifications was urgent and agreement impossible. That deadline had not been reached when the defendants terminated—on a ground, moreover, that had nothing to do with *product* specifications, but rather with the division of the market for the product. * * *

The remaining issues relate to damages. During the year in which the contract was in force, Autotrol incurred $245,000 in out-of-pocket costs of performance. There is no quarrel over the appropriateness of awarding these costs as damages for breach of the contract. But in addition the jury awarded Autotrol more than $700,000 in overhead expenses. If, for example, a salaried engineer spent 25 percent of his time on the project, then 25 percent of his salary and benefits during the period he was working on the project were considered to be damages from the breach. The defendants object, pointing out that it is merely a conjecture that if the contract had never been made in the first place Autotrol would have replaced it with a project that would have covered the engineer's salary and benefits.

Economists distinguish between a firm's fixed and variable costs. The former, as the name implies, are the same whether or not the firm does anything; a good example is the fee that a state charges for a corporate charter. The fee is paid before the firm begins operations and is utterly invariant to the firm's fortunes. It would be an improper item of damages for the breach of a contract because the breach could not have caused the expense to be incurred.

Variable costs are those that vary with the firm's activity—more precisely that are caused by fluctuations in that activity. It is easy to see how the out-of-pocket expenses that Autotrol incurred in the joint venture were variable costs—specifically, variable costs of the joint venture, that is, of the contract. Had it not been for the contract, those expenses would not have been incurred. They are recoverable as damages because the breach deprived Autotrol of the opportunity to recover them by making and selling the water-purification systems envisaged by the contract.

It is more difficult to see how any part of the salary of the engineer in our illustration is a variable cost of the contract. His salary would presumably have been paid, for a time anyway, whether or not he worked on the electrodiarese project or, for that matter, on some substitute project. His salary was an expense but not an expense "caused" even in part by the project and hence, it might seem, was not a loss when the project collapsed because of Continental's breach and Autotrol was as a consequence unable to recoup the money that it had expended on the project.

But this analysis is superficial. * * * If the contract had never been signed, the engineer would have had more time to devote to some other project of Autotrol's. If we assume that the project would have been sufficiently profitable (which does not mean grandly profitable) to cover the salary and benefits of Autotrol's salaried employees who worked on it, it follows that the electrodiarese project turned this expense into a loss by preempting the substitute project that would have enabled the expense to be covered. Autotrol was left at the end of the day—thanks to Continental's breach—with no customer to charge 25 percent of the engineer's salary and benefits to.

It is a question of fact whether, as the example assumes, salary and other overhead items allocated as a bookkeeping matter to a broken contract would in fact have been recovered in a substitute contract. If the victim of the breach of contract is a growing firm—as Autotrol was—it is quite likely that they will be recovered. Growth implies alternative uses for the company's workforce. If not this contract there would have been another, and it would not have been broken—or if it would have been broken, there would have been the same entitlement to damages. But if the firm is declining, then it might well have had to pay its overhead expenses out of its own pocket had this contract not been signed, although before concluding this one would have to consider the possibility that the firm could have economized on those expenses by layoffs and other adjustments.

It might be a useful simplification of the law of damages to have a flat rule that any firm whose business was growing in real (i.e., inflation-adjusted) terms over the period of the contract is entitled to recover the overhead on the contract that was broken; for in all likelihood the firm could have substituted another contract profitable enough to cover that overhead. But this we need not decide; and naturally we are reluctant to speculate about the course of Texas law, let alone try to influence it. It is enough that a reasonable jury could conclude that Autotrol probably would have recouped its overhead expenses on other projects had the contract with Continental never been signed, instead of wasting a year of its employees' time on this barren contract. There was testimony that Autotrol's controls division was consistently overbooked with new projects and that its new projects had a consistent record of profitability—and remember that any project that Autotrol would have substituted for the electrodiarese project, had the latter never existed, need only have been profitable enough to cover the overhead expenses that Autotrol would have incurred in the substitute project, using the inputs that instead it wasted on electrodiarese, in order to justify an award of those overhead expenses to Autotrol as damages.

Of course if this substitute project were the last of Autotrol's promising projects, then the only thing the breach would have done was to accelerate Autotrol's having to swallow its overhead expenses. But this is merely a variant of the declining-firm scenario, one in which the award of overhead expenses will sometimes be inappropriate. Sometimes, perhaps often, but not always. To repeat a previous point, a declining firm may be able to slash its overhead expenses; and if it did not do so because they were necessary to the performance of the contract, and now it is left holding the bag because the contract has been broken, then those expenses are a loss caused by the breach and are recoverable as contract damages.

The question of the proper treatment of overhead expenses arises more frequently in cases in which the plaintiff is seeking not the expenses themselves—they have not been incurred—but the price of a contract that has not yet been fully performed, and the defendant asks that the overhead expenses assigned by the plaintiff on the uncompleted portion of the contract be deducted, on the theory that they were saved by the breach and therefore that their inclusion would exaggerate the plaintiff's loss. The proper analysis of that case is symmetrical with the proper analysis of our case. * * * If the plaintiff can either cut his overhead expenses or recover them in a substitute contract, then he indeed has not lost them as a result of the breach and they should not be figured in his damages. But if he cannot do either of these things—if in other words these really are fixed costs—then the breach gives him no scope to economize and there should be no deduction.

The breach in this case of course occurred *after* the overhead expenses were incurred. This sequence meant that the breach, far from enabling those expenses to be covered in a substitute contract, converted them from a bookkeeping entry into a loss, because it was too late for the plaintiff to make the substitute contract that would have enabled the plaintiff to recover the expenses. If there had been a contract price, therefore, the jury would not have been entitled to subtract the overhead expenses from it in figuring Autotrol's damages. The only thing to be subtracted would be expenses not yet incurred, and therefore saved by the breach. But there was no contract price. Autotrol was not selling something to Continental; they were joint venturers. That made figuring profits difficult and the implicit theory of the damages award is that Autotrol would have had zero profits on the venture, and is thus conservative. The defendants do not deny that Autotrol would have done well enough on the contract to cover the overhead expenses allocated to it, and with that concession Autotrol's case is complete.

The assumption of zero profits is based on the rule of Texas law "that the loss of anticipated profits from a new business is too speculative and conjectural to support a recovery of damages." *Universal Commodities, Inc. v. Weed,* 449 S.W.2d 106, 113 (Tex.Civ.App.1969); see also *Southwest Battery Corp. v. Owen,* 131 Tex. 423, 427, 115 S.W.2d 1097, 1099 (1938). Were it not for that rule Autotrol would not be seeking reliance damages, but instead expectation damages, and the issue of overhead expenses to which we have been devoting such complex attention would be simplified. Autotrol would have presented an estimate of the price at which it would have sold the water-purification systems envisaged by the contract and would have subtracted the costs that it would have incurred to complete the systems after the breach. The difference would be its damages. Suppose that the overhead and other expenses that Autotrol incurred before the breach were $1 million, the costs it would have (but had not yet) incurred to complete the systems after the breach $2 million, and the price it would have obtained for the systems $4 million. Then its damages would be $2 million ($4 million–$2 million), and this would cover the overhead expenses plus an allowance for profit. Since Autotrol was not in fact a new business, and had an established track record on new projects from which a projection could have been made of the likely success of the joint venture with Continental, we are far from certain that the Texas "new business" rule should apply to this case; but that is a matter for the Texas courts to think about; it is not an issue for us.

The defendants place great weight on a passage in *Kansas City Bridge Co. v. Kansas City Structural Steel Co.,* 317 S.W.2d 370, 377 (Mo.1958), from which we quote the gist: "prerequisite to plaintiff's recovery of this general overhead item as part of its damages, some evidence was essential from which the jury reasonably could have found that such general overhead was not only an *expense* but also represented a *loss* to plaintiff * * * [E]ven though a percentage of that fixed overhead was properly allocable to the Leavenworth job during the period of delay, nevertheless any amount so allocated could not represent a *loss* or *damage* to plaintiff unless plaintiff would have, but for the delay, obtained other work (which it did not have or which it did not in fact obtain) sufficient in amount to have absorbed the allocated portion of general overhead." (Italics in original.) We have no quarrel with this; it is our analysis in a nutshell. But since the plaintiff is being asked to prove a counterfactual (what would have happened had the contract in suit *not* been signed in the first place), he should not be subjected to too demanding a burden of proof. The degree of precision that can reasonably be demanded of a litigant, unless you want to doom his case from the outset, depends on the nature of the issue. The most that can fairly be asked of a plaintiff in Autotrol's shoes is to establish a reasonable probability that it would have covered its overhead expenses by means of another contract had the contract in suit never been made. A higher burden would not only be unrealistic but reward people who break their contracts. A lower burden might, as noted earlier, be justified by a desire to simplify litigation to the ultimate benefit of both plaintiffs and defendants.

* * *

Affirmed.

SECTION SIX: VALIDITY OF CLAUSES PROVIDING FOR A SPECIFIC MONETARY REMEDY IN THE EVENT OF BREACH OR REPUDIATION OF AN AGREEMENT WITH CONSIDERATION

H.J. McGRATH CO. v. WISNER

Court of Appeals of Maryland, 1947.
189 Md. 260, 55 A.2d 793.

HENDERSON, JUDGE.

G. Herbert Wisner, a farmer, brought an action at law in the Circuit Court for Baltimore County against the J.H. McGrath Co., a Maryland corporation operating a cannery in that county, to recover under the common counts and under a special count for the sale and delivery of 10.99 tons of tomatoes at an agreed price of $28 per ton, of which a balance of $300 was alleged to be due and unpaid. The defendant filed general issue pleas, and a special plea of set-off, alleging that delivery was made pursuant to a written contract to deliver the whole crop; that the plaintiff delivered only a part thereof; and that under the contract the plaintiff became liable to pay $300 as liquidated damages for the breach. A demurrer to the special plea was sustained. Thereafter, the case was removed to the Superior Court for Baltimore City and tried before the court without a jury. From a verdict and judgment for the plaintiff in the sum of $300, the case comes here on appeal.

It is undisputed that on March 7, 1944, the parties entered into a written contract whereby Wisner agreed to grow tomatoes on six acres of his farm in Baltimore County, and to sell and deliver all the tomatoes grown thereon during the season of 1944 (except those used domestically) to the cannery of the McGrath Company at a price of $28 per ton. Clause 12 of the contract read as follows: "It is understood by Grower that the Company, depending upon the performance of this and numerous similar agreements, has entered into and intends to enter into agreements for the sale of its products, and that if Grower shall fail to deliver to the Company any part or all of the Tomatoes herein contracted for, except as aforesaid, the Company will sustain substantial damages, uncertain in amount, and not readily susceptible of proof under the rules of evidence, and great and irreparable damage to the Company will result from a breach of this agreement on the part of Grower, and Grower hereby covenants and agrees with the Company that in case of such failure on Grower's part Grower shall and will pay to the Company the sum of $300.00 as liquidated damages and not as a penalty, and in such case the Company may deduct and retain the said sum or any part thereof from any moneys due or to become due to Grower under this agreement, but the failure of the Company to do so shall not be construed as a waiver by the Company of such damages. This provision shall not be construed as rendering this agreement an alternative one, or as giving Grower an option to perform this agreement, or to refuse to perform the same and pay the damages as specified."

Wisner testified that he delivered two loads aggregating 10.99 tons of tomatoes to the Company on August 31 and September 1, 1944. The third

[handwritten: only suppose to sell to Heil Kannery]

picking, 2½ loads of about 14 tons, he sold in the Baltimore market at a price of $1 per bushel or $33.33 per ton. He did this because he "got more money for it." The Company learned of his action and entered suit against him. Thereafter, Wisner sold 6 or 7 more loads, about 30 to 35 tons, on the open market at a price of $1.10 per bushel, or $36.63 per ton. He testified that the Company paid him $7.70 on account of the tomatoes he delivered to it, claiming the right to deduct liquidated damages of $300 from the contract price.

Robert W. Mairs, a vice-president of the Company, testified, over objection, that from past experience the Company estimated that it would normally be advantageous to a grower, during the "glut" period when market prices were low, to deliver one-third of his crop under the contract, and sell two-thirds on the open market. Taking into account the average yield per acre and the range of prices in the previous year, the prospective loss to the Company in the event of default was estimated at about $50 per acre. The $300 figure was arrived at in this way. On motion, the trial Judge struck out this testimony. We find no error in this ruling.

Mairs also testified, without contradiction, that the quoted market price of tomatoes, on the dates when Wisner delivered tomatoes to the Company, was 50 cents per bushel, or $16.66 per ton. At the conclusion of the case the Court struck out all the testimony as to the sale of tomatoes on the open market by Wisner, and entered judgment for the plaintiff in the sum of $300, the balance of the contract price.

[handwritten margin: TJ struck out testimony by Wisner + entered judg in his favor.]

The appellant contends that the sole question on this appeal is the correctness of the Court's ruling on demurrer. He maintains that the plea of set-off was proper, in that clause 12 of the contract was for liquidated damages, and not a penalty. We take a different view. *[handwritten: ISSUE]*

* * *

The Maryland cases seem to be in accord with the rule announced in the Restatement, Contracts, § 339: "(I) An agreement, made in advance of breach, fixing the damages therefor, is not enforceable as a contract and does not affect the damages recoverable for the breach, unless (a) the amount so fixed is a reasonable forecast of just compensation for the harm that is caused by the breach, and (b) the harm that is caused by the breach is one that is incapable or very difficult of accurate estimation". Compare Willson v. Baltimore, 83 Md. 203, 34 A. 774, 55 Am.St.Rep. 339. See also Sutherland, Damages, 3d Ed., § 283. In comment b of the Restatement it is said that where a contract "promises the same reparation for the breach of a trivial or comparatively unimportant stipulation as for the breach of the most important one or of the whole contract, it is obvious that the parties have not adhered to the rule of just compensation". * * *

[handwritten margin: Rule reasonable not ascertain]

* * *

In the case at bar the specified damages are in no way proportionate to the possible extent of the prospective breach, nor do we find that the prospective damages for failure to deliver tomatoes having a ready market are incapable or difficult of ascertainment. Under the facts of this case we hold that clause 12 of the contract is a penalty and hence unenforceable.

[handwritten margin: Not proportion and Not difficult to put a # on]

[The court went on to hold that, taking into account the tomatoes delivered to McGrath and the damages caused it by the breach ($275.00), the judgment should have been for the plaintiff Wisner in the amount of $25.00.]

* * *

Judgment reversed and judgment of non pros. entered upon verdict for $25, costs in this Court to be paid by the appellee, costs below by the appellant.

UNIFORM COMMERCIAL CODE § 2–718(1).

Damages for breach by either party may be liquidated in the agreement but only at an amount which is reasonable in the light of the anticipated or actual harm caused by the breach, the difficulties of proof of loss, and the inconvenience or nonfeasibility of otherwise obtaining an adequate remedy. A term fixing unreasonably large liquidated damages is void as a penalty.

REVISED UNIFORM COMMERCIAL CODE § 2–718(a)

Discussion Draft, April 2000

Damages for breach by either party may be liquidated in the agreement but only at an amount that is reasonable in the light of the anticipated or actual harm caused by the breach and, in a consumer contract, in addition the difficulties of proof of loss and the inconvenience or nonfeasibility of otherwise obtaining an adequate remedy. * * *

TRUCK RENT–A–CENTER, INC. v. PURITAN FARMS 2ND, INC.

Court of Appeals of New York, 1977.
41 N.Y.2d 420, 393 N.Y.S.2d 365, 361 N.E.2d 1015.

JASEN, JUDGE.

The principal issue on this appeal is whether a provision in a truck lease agreement which requires the payment of a specified amount of money to the lessor in the event of the lessee's breach is an enforceable liquidated damages clause, or, instead, provides for an unenforceable penalty.

Defendant Puritan Farms 2nd, Inc. (Puritan), was in the business of furnishing milk and milk products to customers through home delivery. In January, 1969, Puritan leased a fleet of 25 new milk delivery trucks from plaintiff Truck Rent–A–Center for a term of seven years commencing January 15, 1970. Under the provisions of a truck lease and service agreement entered into by the parties, the plaintiff was to supply the trucks and make all necessary repairs. Puritan was to pay an agreed upon weekly rental fee. It was understood that the lessor would finance the purchase of the trucks through a bank, paying the prime rate of interest on the date of the loan plus 2%. The rental charges on the trucks were to be adjusted in the event of a fluctuation in the interest rate above or below specified levels. The lessee was granted the right to purchase the trucks, at any time after 12 months following commencement of the lease, by paying to the lessor the amount then due and owing on the bank loan, plus an additional $100 per truck purchased.

Article 16 of the lease agreement provided that if the agreement should terminate prior to expiration of the term of the lease as a result of the lessee's breach, the lessor would be entitled to damages, "liquidated for all purposes", in the amount of all rentals that would have come due from the date of termination to the date of normal expiration of the term less the "re-rental value" of the vehicles, which was set at 50% of the rentals that would have become due. In effect, the lessee would be obligated to pay the lessor, as a consequence of breach, one half of all rentals that would have become due had the agreement run its full course. The agreement recited that, in arriving at the settled amount of damage, "the parties hereto have considered, among other factors, Lessor's substantial initial investment in purchasing or reconditioning for Lessee's service the demised motor vehicles, the uncertainty of Lessor's ability to re-enter the said vehicles, the costs to Lessor during any period the vehicles may remain idle until re-rented, or if sold, the uncertainty of the sales price and its possible attendant loss. The parties have also considered, among other factors, in so liquidating the said damages, Lessor's saving in expenditures for gasoline, oil and other service items."[1]

The bulk of the written agreement was derived from a printed form lease which the parties modified by both filling in blank spaces and typing in alterations. The agreement also contained several typewritten indorsements which also made changes in the provisions of the printed lease. The provision for lessee's purchase of the vehicles for the bank loan balance and $100 per vehicle was contained in one such indorsement. The liquidated damages clause was contained in the body of the printed form.

Puritan tendered plaintiff a security deposit, consisting of four weeks' rent and the lease went into effect. After nearly three years, the lessee sought to terminate the lease agreement. On December 7, 1973, Puritan wrote to the lessor complaining that the lessor had not repaired and maintained the trucks as provided in the lease agreement. Puritan stated that it had "repeatedly notified" plaintiff of these defaults, but plaintiff had not cured them. Puritan, therefore, exercised its right to terminate the agreement "without any penalty and *without purchasing the trucks*". (Emphasis added.) On the date set for termination, December 14, 1973, plaintiff's attorneys replied to Puritan by letter to advise it that plaintiff believed it had fully performed its obligations under the lease and, in the event Puritan adhered to the announced breach, would commence proceedings to obtain the liquidated damages provided for in article 16 of the agreement. Nevertheless, Puritan had its drivers return the

---

1. The text of article 16 of the lease, in pertinent part, reads as follows:

"16. Upon termination of this agreement, * * * Lessor * * * shall be entitled to damages, herein liquidated for all purposes * * * as follows:

"(a) The sum of all rents designated as 'Fixed Rental Charges' which would have become due under the normal operation of this agreement from the date of the said termination * * * including any effective renewal period; less

"(b) The re-rental value of said motor vehicles which is hereby agreed upon as fifty per cent (50%) of the sum of such 'Fixed

Rental Charges' as are set forth in subdivision '(a)' of this article.

"In arriving at said liquidated damages, the parties hereto have considered, among other factors, Lessor's substantial * * * investment in purchasing or reconditioning for Lessee's service the demised motor vehicles, the uncertainty of Lessor's ability to re-enter the said vehicles, the costs to Lessor during any period the vehicles may remain idle until re-rented, or if sold, the uncertainty of the sales price and its possible attendant loss. The parties have also considered, among other factors, in so liquidating the said damages, Lessor's saving in expenditures for gasoline, oil and other service items."

trucks to plaintiff's premises, where the bulk of them have remained ever since. At the time of termination, plaintiff owed $45,134.17 on the outstanding bank loan.

Plaintiff followed through on its promise to commence an action for the payment of the liquidated damages. Defendant counterclaimed for the return of its security deposit. At the nonjury trial, plaintiff contended that it had fully performed its obligations to maintain and repair the trucks. Moreover, it was submitted, Puritan sought to cancel the lease because corporations allied with Puritan had acquired the assets, including delivery trucks, of other dairies and Puritan believed it cheaper to utilize this "shadow fleet". The home milk delivery business was on the decline and plaintiff's president testified that efforts to either re-rent or sell the truck fleet to other dairies had not been successful. Even with modifications in the trucks, such as the removal of the milk racks and a change in the floor of the trucks, it was not possible to lease the trucks to other industries, although a few trucks were subsequently sold. The proceeds of the sales were applied to the reduction of the bank balance. The other trucks remained at plaintiff's premises, partially protected by a fence plaintiff erected to discourage vandals. The defendant countered with proof that plaintiff had not repaired the trucks promptly and satisfactorily.

At the close of the trial, the court found, based on the evidence it found to be credible, that plaintiff had substantially performed its obligations under the lease and that defendant was not justified in terminating the agreement. Further, the court held that the provision for liquidated damages was reasonable and represented a fair estimate of actual damages which would be difficult to ascertain precisely. "The parties, at the time the agreement was entered into, considered many factors affecting damages, namely: the uncertainty of the plaintiff's ability to re-rent the said vehicles; the plaintiff's investment in purchasing and reconditioning the vehicles to suit the defendant's particular purpose; the number of man hours not utilized in the non-service of the vehicles in the event of a breach; the uncertainty of reselling the vehicles in question; the uncertainty of the plaintiff's savings or expenditures for gasoline, oil or other service items, and the amount of fluctuating interest on the bank loan." The court calculated that plaintiff would have been entitled to $177,355.20 in rent for the period remaining in the lease and, in accordance with the liquidated damages provision, awarded plaintiff half that amount, $88,677.60. The resulting judgment was affirmed by the Appellate Division, with two Justices dissenting. (51 A.D.2d 786, 380 N.Y.S.2d 37.)

The primary issue before us is whether the "liquidated damages" provision is enforceable. Liquidated damages constitute the compensation which, the parties have agreed, should be paid in order to satisfy any loss or injury flowing from a breach of their contract. (*Wirth & Hamid Fair Booking v. Wirth*, 265 N.Y. 214, 223, 192 N.E. 297, 301.) In effect, a liquidated damage provision is an estimate, made by the parties at the time they enter into their agreement, of the extent of the injury that would be sustained as a result of breach of the agreement. (5 Williston, Contracts [3d ed.], § 776, p. 668.) Parties to a contract have the right to agree to such clauses, provided that the clause is neither unconscionable nor contrary to public policy. (*Mosler Safe Co. v. Maiden Lane Safe Deposit Co.*, 199 N.Y. 479, 485, 93 N.E. 81, 83.) Provisions for liquidated damage have value in those situations where it would be difficult, if not actually impossible, to calculate the amount of actual damage. In such cases, the contracting parties may agree between themselves as to the amount of damages to be paid upon breach rather than leaving that amount to the calculation of a court or jury. (14 N.Y.Jur., Damages, § 155, pp. 4–5.)

On the other hand, liquidated damage provisions will not be enforced if it is against public policy to do so and public policy is firmly set against the imposition of penalties or forfeitures for which there is no statutory authority. (*City of Rye v. Public Serv. Mut. Ins. Co.*, 34 N.Y.2d 470, 472–473, 358 N.Y.S.2d 391, 392–393, 315 N.E.2d 458, 459.) It is plain that a provision which requires, in the event of contractual breach, the payment of a sum of money grossly disproportionate to the amount of actual damages provides for penalty and is unenforceable. * * * A liquidated damage provision has its basis in the principle of just compensation for loss. (Cf. Restatement, Contracts, § 339, and Comment thereon.) A clause which provides for an amount plainly disproportionate to real damage is not intended to provide fair compensation but to secure performance by the compulsion of the very disproportion. A promisor would be compelled, out of fear of economic devastation, to continue performance and his promisee, in the event of default, would reap a windfall well above actual harm sustained. * * *

The rule is now well established. A contractual provision fixing damages in the event of breach will be sustained if the amount liquidated bears a reasonable proportion to the probable loss and the amount of actual loss is incapable or difficult of precise estimation. * * * If, however, the amount fixed is plainly or grossly disproportionate to the probable loss, the provision calls for a penalty and will not be enforced. * * * In interpreting a provision fixing damages, it is not material whether the parties themselves have chosen to call the provision one for "liquidated damages", as in this case, or have styled it as a penalty. * * * Such an approach would put too much faith in form and too little in substance. Similarly, the agreement should be interpreted as of the date of its making and not as of the date of its breach. * * *

In applying these principles to the case before us, we conclude that the amount stipulated by the parties as damages bears a reasonable relation to the amount of probable actual harm and is not a penalty. Hence, the provision is enforceable and the order of the Appellate Division should be affirmed.

Looking forward from the date of the lease, the parties could reasonably conclude, as they did, that there might not be an actual market for the sale or re-rental of these specialized vehicles in the event of the lessee's breach. To be sure, plaintiff's lost profit could readily be measured by the amount of the weekly rental fee. However, it was permissible for the parties, in advance, to agree that the re-rental or sale value of the vehicles would be 50% of the weekly rental. Since there was uncertainty as to whether the trucks could be re-rented or sold, the parties could reasonably set, as they did, the value of such mitigation at 50% of the amount the lessee was obligated to pay for rental of the trucks. This would take into consideration the fact that, after being used by the lessee, the vehicles would no longer be "shiny, new trucks", but would be used, possibly battered, trucks, whose value would have declined appreciably. The parties also considered the fact that, although plaintiff, in the event of Puritan's breach, might be spared repair and maintenance costs necessitated by Puritan's use of the trucks, plaintiff would have to assume the cost of storing and maintaining trucks idled by Puritan's refusal to use them. Further, it was by no means certain, at the time of the contract, that lessee would peacefully return the trucks to the lessor after lessee had breached the contract.

With particular reference to the dissent at the Appellate Division, it is true that the lessee might have exercised an option to purchase the trucks. However, lessee would not be purchasing 25 "shiny, new trucks" for a mere $2,500. Rather, lessee, after the passage of one year from the commencement of the term, could have purchased trucks that had been used for at least one year for the amount outstanding on the bank loan, in addition to the $2,500. Of course, the purchase price would be greater if the option were exercised early in the term rather than towards the end of the term since plaintiff would be making payments to the bank all the while.[2] More fundamental, the existence of the option clause has absolutely no bearing on the validity of the discrete, liquidated damages provision. The lessee could have elected to purchase the trucks but elected not to do so. In fact, the lessee's letter of termination made a point of the fact that the lessee did not want to purchase the trucks. The reality is that the lessee sought, by its wrongful termination of the lease, to evade all obligations to the plaintiff, whether for rent or for the agreed upon purchase price. Its effort to do so failed. That lessee could have made a better bargain for itself by purchasing the trucks for $48,134.17[3] pursuant to the option, instead of paying $92,341.79 in damages for wrongful breach of the lease is not availing to it now. Although the lessee might now wish, with the benefit of hindsight, that it had purchased the trucks rather than default on its lease obligations, the simple fact is that it did not do so.

We attach no significance to the fact that the liquidated damages clause appears on the preprinted form portion of the agreement. The agreement was fully negotiated and the provisions of the form, in many other respects, were amended. There is no indication of any disparity of bargaining power or of unconscionability. The provision for liquidated damages related reasonably to potential harm that was difficult to estimate and did not constitute a disguised penalty. We also find no merit in the claim of trial error advanced by Puritan.

Accordingly, the order of the Appellate Division should be affirmed, with costs.

Problem 3–11

In a number of cases in the preceding section, losses of the type involved were not recoverable under the general law of damages. Would a properly drafted liquidated damages clause have made recovery possible in any of these cases? For example, would a liquidated damages provision compensating for mental distress damages be enforceable in Chrum v. Charles Heating & Cooling, Inc. (page 273)?

---

2. According to the lease agreement, the amount of plaintiff's bank loan payments were not to vary and interest and amortization were to be constant.

3. This sum represents the $45,634.17 still owed by plaintiff on the bank loan, plus $2,500 ($100 for each of the 25 trucks).

Note
Possible Recovery Under a Liquidated Damages Clause When There Are No Actual Damages

Can a party recover under a liquidated damages clause even though the other party's breach caused no actual damages? There are cases suggesting or holding in the affirmative. An example is Southwest Engineering Co. v. United States, 341 F.2d 998 (8th Cir.1965). There the court stated:

We believe that the cases holding that the situation existing at the time of the contract is controlling in determining the reasonableness of liquidated damages are based upon sound reasoning and represent the weight of authority. Where parties have by their contract agreed upon a liquidated damage provision as a reasonable forecast of just compensation for breach of contract and damages are difficult to estimate accurately, such provision should be enforced. If in the course of subsequent developments, damages prove to be greater than those stipulated, the party entitled to damages is bound by the liquidated damage agreement. It is not unfair to hold the contractor performing the work to such agreement if by reason of later developments damages prove to be less or nonexistent. Each party by entering into such contractual provision took a calculated risk and is bound by reasonable contractual provisions pertaining to liquidated damages.

Do you agree with the court? If the parties assume that the breach will cause some damages when they draft a liquidated damages provision, should the court interpret the clause to deny recovery when there are no damages? See also Guiliano v. Cleo, Inc., 995 S.W.2d 88 (Tenn.1999); California and Hawaiian Sugar Co. v. Sun Ship, Inc., 794 F.2d 1433 (9th Cir.1986).

Not all courts enthusiastically award liquidated damages in the absence of actual damages. For example, in Massman Construction Co. v. City Council of Greenville, 147 F.2d 925 (5th Cir.1945), Massman failed to complete certain bridge construction within the time specified. Nonetheless, the delay caused no damages because, among other things, Massman completed the bridge before the construction of a road to the bridge. The court refused to enforce the liquidated damages clause. To the same effect, see Harty v. Bye, 258 Or. 398, 483 P.2d 458 (1971); Fields Foundation, Ltd. v. Christensen, 103 Wis.2d 465, 309 N.W.2d 125 (App.1981).

Problem 3–12

According to Dunbar, Drafting The Liquidated Damage Clause—When And How, 20 Ohio State L.J. 221, 234–35 (1959):

The draftsman should:

(1) Make sure that the damages stipulated will fall within the range between the upper and lower limits of potential actual damages foreseeable at the time of the making of the contract. Otherwise, the provision is likely to be held to be invalid as prescribing a penalty. *did not*

(2) See to it that the parties actually, seriously negotiate on the question of the amount of measure of the liquidated damages, with full consideration of all foreseeable consequences of breach. Then, for added protection, incorporate in the contract recitals which will show that they have done so. *yes*

(3) If the contemplated breach is of a covenant which requires the party to perform a particular act within a time limit, provide suitable machinery for

reasonable extensions to adjust for delays which may result from actions or derelictions of the other party or of third parties. Especially do so in construction contracts. *Irrelevant*

(4) Make the amount of damages agreed upon vary with extent of the breach, such as duration of the delay or period of default. *didn't do/true*

(5) Incorporate a suitable recital indicating that it was the intention of the parties to provide for liquidated damages; at least, characterize by using the words "liquidated damages." Before some courts, it may help. *yes*

(6) Recite the facts which caused the parties to incorporate the provision in the contract, such as that, for stated reasons, the amount of damages upon the breach will be very difficult to ascertain with precision. *yes*

In H.J. McGrath Co. v. Wisner (page 294), the court held a purported liquidated damages clause invalid as a penalty. If Dunbar's advice had been followed so far as possible, would the clause have been upheld? *yes*

Reasonable not ascertainable

BETTER FOOD MARKETS v. AMERICAN DIST. TELEGRAPH CO.

Supreme Court of California, 1953.
40 Cal.2d 179, 253 P.2d 10.

SHENK, JUSTICE.

This is an action brought on counts alleged in tort and in contract wherein the plaintiff seeks to recover damages resulting from the alleged failure of the defendants to properly transmit burglar alarm signals to their own guards and to the headquarters of the municipal police department. Such failure is alleged to have permitted a burglar to escape with the sum of $35,930 taken from the plaintiff's food market.

* * * On this appeal * * * the plaintiff contends that there is sufficient evidence of the defendant's negligence and breach of contract to sustain a verdict for the plaintiff, and that it was error to grant the motion for a directed verdict.

contract-agree-ment

In June of 1947 the parties entered into a written agreement whereby the defendant was to install and maintain its standard "Central Station Burglar Alarm and Holdup System" in the plaintiff's food market. The contract provided that the defendant "on receipt of a burglar alarm signal from the Subscriber's [plaintiff's] premises, agrees to send to said premises, its representatives to act as agent of and in the interest of the Subscriber * * *. The Subscriber hereby authorizes and directs the Contractor [defendant] to cause the arrest of any person or persons unauthorized to enter his premises and to hold him or them until released by the Subscriber * * *. The Contractor, on receipt of a holdup alarm signal from the Subscriber's premises, agrees to transmit the alarm promptly to headquarters of the public police department."

[On November 16, 1947, plaintiff's market was robbed. Defendant received an alarm signal but did not inform the police or call its own guards for 9 minutes. The court held that there was sufficient evidence to find that the loss was the proximate result of the defendant's delay in responding to the alarm and that it was error to order judgment for defendant on its motion for a directed verdict.]

* * *

There remains the question of the validity of the following provisions of the contract for liquidated damages: "It is agreed by and between the parties that the Contractor is not an insurer, that the payments hereinbefore named are based solely on the value of the service in the maintenance of the system described, that it is impracticable and extremely difficult to fix the actual damages, if any, which may proximately result from a failure to perform such services and in case of failure to perform such services and a resulting loss its liability hereunder shall be limited to and fixed at the sum of fifty dollars as liquidated damages, and not as a penalty, and this liability shall be exclusive."

[handwritten margin note: liquidated damages provision. $50]

It is generally recognized that a valid agreement may be made for the payment of liquidated damages, whereas an agreement for the payment of a penalty is invalid. Under the law generally the parties are allowed to contract for liquidated damages if it is necessary to do so in order that they may know with reasonable certainty the extent of liability for a breach of the agreement. Where the parties exercise their business judgment in providing that it is impracticable and extremely difficult to fix the damages which may result from the defendant's failure to render its service such a provision is not controlling as to the actual difficulty in fixing damages, although it is entitled to some weight. * * *

The statutory law and its interpretation in this state are in accord with the general law. Civil Code section 1670 states that a provision in a contract which provides for the amount of damages to be paid in the event of a breach of the contract is void, except as expressly provided in section 1671 as follows: "The parties to a contract may agree therein upon an amount which shall be presumed to be the amount of damage sustained by a breach thereof, when, from the nature of the case, it would be impracticable or extremely difficult to fix the actual damage." * * *

[handwritten margin note: π says Not difficult to put $ on damage.]

The plaintiff argues that there is no difficulty in the present case in fixing the actual damage and that the amount of money stolen should be the actual damage. Its contention is that the time for the determination of the question of the impracticability and difficulty in fixing the damages is after the loss has occurred. This is not the rule. In determining this question the court should place itself in the position of the parties at the time the contract was made and should consider the nature of the breaches that might occur and any consequences that were reasonably foreseeable. * * *

[handwritten margin note: Ct says]

In the present case there was no finding with respect to the impracticability or extreme difficulty in fixing damages. Where a trial court does find that such a situation did exist but it appears to a reviewing court that from the nature of the possible detriment the damages could have been fixed without difficulty, a judgment based on the finding will be reversed, Stark v. Shemada, supra, 187 Cal. 785, 204 P. 214. The question becomes one of law where the facts are not in dispute and admit of but a single conclusion. Such is the present case. When the uncertainties as to what might have happened if the plaintiff's store were entered is viewed from the position of the contracting parties, it satisfactorily appears that there is no basis whatever for a conclusion that it would have been practicable or reasonably possible for the parties to fix the probable damage. The question, upon the admitted facts, is clearly one of law.

The possibilities of the consequences of a failure of the defendant to perform its obligation under the contract are innumerable. A failure to receive the signals, or to respond to them, or to report them to the plaintiff would be a violation of the agreement. Entrances to the building after working hours might be made by persons having authority as well as by burglars or by persons bent upon mischief. They might or might not cause damage. There might be the theft of a ham, or of a truckload of goods, or the contents of a safe. There might be a breaking in for the purpose of theft and no theft. If money was taken it might be a few dollars or many thousands. Books might be tampered with, or papers abstracted. Damage might be caused in many ways that were not foreseeable. In short, it was extremely difficult to predict the nature and extent of the loss. Furthermore, there was no way of ascertaining what portion of any loss sustained could be attributed to the defendant's failure to perform. The contract specifically provided that the defendant was not an insurer. Therefore, if it should have fully performed on the contract and a loss resulted nevertheless it could in no way be liable. The parties recognized, then, that losses might have resulted which were not causally connected with the defendant's failure of performance. Where there had been a failure of performance and a loss, what part of that loss could be attributed to the failure of performance; or how much of that loss would have resulted had there not been a failure of performance? Under the complexity of the circumstances in this case the parties could not answer this question. There being no reasonable basis upon which to predict the nature and extent of any loss, or how much of that loss the defendant's failure of performance might account for, it is certain that it would have been "impracticable or extremely difficult to fix the actual damage" § 1671, Civ.Code.

The validity of a clause for liquidated damages requires that the parties to the contract "agree therein upon an amount which shall be presumed to be the amount of damage sustained by a breach thereof * * *." Civ.Code § 1671. This amount must represent the result of a reasonable endeavor by the parties to estimate a fair average compensation for any loss that may be sustained. * * * It had been suggested that the greater the difficulty encountered by the parties in estimating the damages which might arise from a breach, the greater should be the range of estimates which the courts should uphold as reasonable. (5 Corbin on Contracts, § 1059, p. 291.) The plaintiff's contention that the agreed amount did not represent an endeavor by the parties to estimate the probable damage is based on evidence that the liquidation clause was part of the printed material in a form contract generally used by the defendant in dealing with subscribers such as the plaintiff, and that the defendant did not investigate the plaintiff's manner of conducting its business or the character and value of its stock. Nevertheless the parties agreed to the liquidation provisions, and there is no evidence that they were not fully aware of circumstances making it desirable that liquidated damages be provided for.

In the present case the impracticability or extreme difficulty in fixing actual damages appeared as a matter of law. In the exercise of their business judgment the parties reasonably agreed that in all cases of breach by the defendant the damages would be fixed at $50 whether in fact the defendant's loss for a given breach was greater or less than that amount. As previously stated the stipulation that the amount was to be paid "as liquidated damages and not as a penalty" while entitled to some weight is not conclusive. Nevertheless, it is clear that the actual loss resulting from a breach could in many cases be less than the amount provided for. It is equally clear that in many other cases the actual loss would exceed that amount. To construe this as a penalty it would have to be said that the amount provided to be paid bore no reasonable relation to the losses the parties thought might be sustained. This may not rightly be stated.

The plaintiff seeks to avoid the effect of the liquidation clause on the ground that it has no application to a tort action. However, the plaintiff makes no claim that a duty was owed to it outside of that created by the contract, and no breach of duty was alleged other than a failure to render the contracted for service. Although an action in tort may sometimes be brought for the negligent breach of a contractual duty, Jones v. Kelly, 208 Cal. 251, 280 P. 942, still the nature of the duty owed and the consequences of its breach must be determined by reference to the contract which created that duty. In the present case the duty created by the contract was one for which liability for a breach thereunder was fixed, and whether the action is brought in tort or in contract the nature of the duty remains the same. The plaintiff cites no authority and none has been discovered to the effect that where the breach of a duty created only by contract is a negligent one the application of a valid clause for liquidated damages may be avoided by bringing an action in tort.

* * *

The order directing a verdict for the defendants involved questions of fact which could have been found in the plaintiff's favor. However, the error warrants only a qualified reversal of the judgment, as the plaintiff's recovery is limited to $50 if he should prevail on a retrial.

The judgment of the trial court is modified to provide as follows: "It is ordered, adjudged and decreed that plaintiff recover from the defendant, American District Telegraph Company, the sum of $50.00 without costs." As so modified the judgment is affirmed. Each party shall bear its own costs on appeal.

* * *

CARTER, JUSTICE.

I dissent.

* * *

It is conceded that defendant failed to perform its duty; that plaintiff's loss resulted therefrom; that plaintiff's loss was the sum of $35,930 which was taken, by a burglar, from plaintiff's food market.

In order to uphold the so-called $50 liquidated damage provision, it was necessary for the majority to find that damages were "impracticable and extremely difficult" to fix at the time the contract was entered into, and further that the $50 provision bore a reasonable relation to any loss which the parties contemplated might be sustained as a result of a breach of the contract.

It is said in the majority opinion that "In determining this question [the losses which might be expected to occur] the court should place itself in the position of the parties at the time the contract was made and should consider the nature of the breaches that might occur and any consequences that were reasonably foreseeable." Placing myself in the position of the parties at the time the contract was entered into, I would say that one way of ascertaining the loss which might occur, was to take an average of the amount of cash left in the safe in the store overnight; an inventory of the average merchandise kept in the store. * * *

[handwritten margin note: what should have been done to reasonably ascertain]

It is also necessary that the amount agreed upon by the parties "represent the result of a reasonable endeavor by the parties to estimate a fair average compensation for any loss that may be sustained. Dyer Bros. Golden West Iron Wks. v. Central Iron Wks., supra, 182 Cal. 588, 189 P. 445; Rice v. Schmid, supra, 18 Cal.2d 382, 386, 115 P.2d 498; Restatement, Contracts, § 339, p. 554." In other words, the amount agreed upon must bear some reasonable relation to the losses which might occur as a result of a breach. In my opinion, the $50 provision bears no reasonable relation to any amount which might have been lost by a failure of the system to operate.

* * *

I would reverse the judgment with directions to the trial court to retry the case and submit the issue of damages to the jury.

RINALDI AND SONS, INC. v. WELLS FARGO ALARM SERVICE, INC., 39 N.Y.2d 191, 197, 383 N.Y.S.2d 256, 259, 347 N.E.2d 618, 620 (1976). A limitation of damages to $50 must be distinguished from a liquidated damages clause, "analytically a different category with different governing rules."

Problem 3–13

Fran Burns and Blanken Construction Company are negotiating for the construction of a house. You are a senior partner in Truman & Budweiser and Blanken is an important client. Blanken's president, Alice Drake, asks the firm to draft a clause that will protect the company from unlimited liability in case it is late in completing the house. You ask your associate, Darlene Brown, to draft the provision. Brown gives you the following proposed provision:

> The Owner will suffer financial loss if the Project is not completed by the above date. The Contractor shall be liable for and shall pay to the Owner, on an actual expense basis as established by receipts, not more than $1,000 for packing and storage of furnishings and $30 per day for temporary accommodation.

Evaluate the provision. What additional language would you include, if any? What changes would you make, if any? Is the provision one for liquidated damages or is it a limitation of consequential damages? Does it matter? (For the rule governing the latter type of clause in the sale of goods setting, see U.C.C. § 2–719(3), which states in part: "Consequential damages may be limited or excluded unless the limitation or exclusion is unconscionable.").

HILLMAN, THE LIMITS OF BEHAVIORAL DECISION THEORY IN LEGAL ANALYSIS: THE CASE OF LIQUIDATED DAMAGES

85 Cornell L. Rev. 717, 718–719, 726–728, 738 (2000).

Based on society's respect for individual freedom, its moral view that people should keep their promises, and its perspective that private exchange best allocates and distributes resources, freedom of contract enjoys a predominant role as a justificatory principle of contract law. Contract law allows parties to agree on contract terms as they choose and, in the absence of demonstrable market failures such as unequal bargaining power or concrete infirmities such as diminished capacity, evaluates the validity of their choices largely based on their objective manifestation of assent. Courts operating within this conceptual framework rarely intercede in parties' agreements to test the adequacy of consideration.

On the other hand, courts readily impinge on freedom of contract when assessing the validity of agreed (also called liquidated) damages clauses. Regardless of the quality of bargaining and the type of parties, if a court determines that an agreed damages provision is a "penalty," the court will refuse to enforce the provision. Why do judges single out liquidated damages provisions for special treatment? * * *

* * *

* * * Courts and commentators offer several explanations related to either the substance of agreed damages provisions, the bargaining process that produced them, or both. None of these explanations seems wholly satisfactory. For example, some analysts explain the modern judicial antipathy for agreed damages provisions as a holdover from the equity court's practice of refusing to enforce penal bonds, in which a party promised to pay a certain sum if that party broke a contract. The equity court believed that contract remedies were designed to compensate the injured party for the loss, not to punish or coerce the breaching party into performing, even when the parties had agreed to the penal bond precisely for those latter purposes.

Modern courts apparently have greeted with open arms the equity court's response to penal bonds. Indeed, courts now seem to have a curiously heightened sensitivity to any agreed damages provision, whether penal or not. Courts have also accepted the equity court's estimation of the coercive and punitive effect of penal bonds without seriously investigating the accuracy and validity of that position. Whether courts should consider an agreed remedy that is incommensurate with actual damages to be punitive and coercive, however, depends on the nature of the bargaining that produced the clause. After all, if the promisee paid a premium for an agreed damages provision that is greater than actual damages and the promisor understood the significance of agreeing to the term, "just compensation" arguably would entail enforcing the provision. In fact, in the context of fair bargaining between business people, courts sometimes find palatable (and enforceable) provisions that amount to penalties, such as "take or pay" contracts in which purchasers of natural gas agree to pay regardless of whether they take the gas.

Modern courts therefore reinforce their antipathy to penalties by finding the bargaining process deficient. For example, courts generalize that parties do not negotiate agreed remedies provisions. Instead, courts believe that promisors share an " 'illusion[ ] of hope' "that nothing will go wrong and consequently fail to bargain adequately over remedial provisions. But even if this is an empirically accurate and otherwise persuasive explanation, why have courts singled out liquidated damages provisions for special treatment on this ground? For example, why do courts fail to police the parties' purported allocation of risk of unanticipated but calamitous circumstances with the same vigor to determine whether the parties were too optimistic that nothing would go wrong?

In addition, courts apparently believe that promisors are peculiarly susceptible to being coerced into agreeing to penalty provisions. Little evidence from actual cases supports this assertion and nothing about the nature of agreed remedies explains why promisees would have more leverage with respect to these clauses than any other clause.

Another alleged deficiency in the bargaining process with respect to agreed remedies is "the limits of cognition" of contracting parties in this context. Professor Eisenberg asserts that although parties can easily understand terms "such as subject matter, quantity, and price," they cannot comprehend "the scenarios of breach" and the "application of a liquidated damages provision" to these scenarios. In addition, parties discount the probability of breach based on a cost-benefit analysis tainted by optimism about performance. For these reasons, parties may fail to focus on liquidated damages provisions when agreeing to a contract, thereby supplying courts with a justification for scrutinizing these provisions more closely.

As with the other explanations for the policing of liquidated damages, the "limits of cognition" approach depends on the speculative assertion that parties' planning and bargaining of liquidated damages provisions are less effective than their planning and bargaining of other provisions. * * *

* * *

* * *[P]erhaps courts should abandon the special tests for agreed damages and simply apply traditional policing doctrines, such as unconscionability and duress. Courts employing this approach would strike an agreed damages provision only if they found it "oppressive" or the product of "unfair surprise." In short, agreed damages provisions probably should be treated like any other contract term.

SECTION SEVEN: MONETARY REMEDIES WHERE THE THEORY OF OBLIGATION IS PROMISSORY ESTOPPEL

Recall that section 90 of the Restatement (First) of Contracts provides:

A promise which the promisor should reasonably expect to induce action or forbearance of a definite and substantial character on the part of the promisee and which does induce such action or forbearance is binding if injustice can be avoided only by enforcement of the promise.

In 1926 at an American Law Institute meeting devoted in part to proposed Section 90, the Reporter, Professor Samuel Williston, put the following hypothetical case: Suppose Johnny says to his uncle: "I want to buy a Buick car." The uncle responds: "I will give you $1000." A member of the ALI, Mr. Frederick Coudert, asked Professor Williston whether, if Johnny thereafter bought the car in reliance on his uncle's promise but paid only $500 for it, Uncle would still be liable for $1000. The exchange below ensued. Consider who is right.

Mr. Williston: "If Johnny had done what he was expected to do, or is acting within the limits of his uncle's expectation, I think the uncle would be liable for $1000; but not otherwise."

Mr. Coudert: "In other words, substantial justice would require that uncle should be penalized in the sum of $500."

Mr. Williston: "Why do you say 'penalized'?"

* * *

Mr. Coudert: "Because substantial justice there would require, it seems to me, that Johnny get his money for his car, but should he get his car and $500 more? * * *"

Mr. Williston: "Either the promise is binding or it is not. If the promise is binding it has to be enforced as it is made. As I said to Mr. Coudert, I could leave this whole thing to the subject of quasi contracts so that the promisee under the circumstances shall never recover on the promise but he shall recover such an amount as will fairly compensate him for any injury incurred; but it seems to me you have to take one leg or the other. You have either to say the promise is binding or you have to go on the theory of restoring the *status quo.*" American Law Institute Proceedings, vol. IV, Appendix 98–99, 103–04 (1926).

RESTATEMENT (SECOND) OF CONTRACTS § 90.
Promise Reasonably Inducing Action or Forbearance

(1) A promise which the promisor should reasonably expect to induce action or forbearance on the part of the promisee or a third person and which does induce such action or forbearance is binding if injustice can be avoided only by enforcement of the promise. The remedy granted for breach may be limited as justice requires.

* * *

Comment:

b. *Character of Reliance Protected.* The principle of this Section is flexible. The promisor is affected only by reliance which he does or should foresee, and enforcement must be necessary to avoid injustice. Satisfaction of the latter requirement may depend on the reasonableness of the promisee's reliance, on its definite and substantial character in relation to the remedy sought, on the formality with which the promise is made, on the extent to which the evidentiary, cautionary, deterrent and channeling functions of form are met by the commercial setting or otherwise, and on the extent to which such other policies as the enforcement of bargains and the prevention of unjust enrichment are relevant. * * *

* * *

d. *Partial Enforcement.* A promise binding under this section is a contract, and full-scale enforcement by normal remedies is often appropriate. But the same factors which bear on whether any relief should be granted also bear on the character and extent of the remedy. In particular, relief may sometimes be limited to restitution or to damages or specific relief measured by the extent of the promisee's reliance rather than by the terms of the promise. * * *

* * *

Reporter's Note.

The principal change from former sec. 90 is the recognition of the possibility of partial enforcement. See Fuller and Perdue, The Reliance Interest in Contract Damages, 46 Yale L.J. 52, 63–65 (1936). * * *

GOODMAN v. DICKER

U.S. Court of Appeals, District of Columbia Circuit, 1948.
169 F.2d 684.

PROCTOR, ASSOCIATE JUSTICE.

This appeal is from a judgment of the District Court in a suit by appellees for breach of contract.

Appellants are local distributors for Emerson Radio and Phonograph Corporation in the District of Columbia. Appellees, with the knowledge and encouragement of appellants, applied for a "dealer franchise" to sell Emerson's products. The trial court found that appellants by their representations and conduct induced appellees to incur expenses in preparing to do business under the franchise, including employment of salesmen and solicitation of orders for radios. Among other things, appellants represented that the application had been accepted; that the franchise would be granted, and that appellees would receive an initial delivery of thirty to forty radios. Yet, no radios were delivered, and notice was finally given that the franchise would not be granted.

The case was tried without a jury. The court held that a contract had not been proven but that appellants were estopped from denying the same by reason of their statements and conduct upon which appellees relied to their detriment. Judgment was entered for $1500, covering cash outlays of $1150 and loss of $350, anticipated profits on sale of thirty radios.

The main contention of appellants is that no liability would have arisen under the dealer franchise had it been granted because, as understood by appellees, it would have been terminable at will and would have imposed no duty upon the manufacturer to sell or appellees to buy any fixed number of radios. From this it is argued that the franchise agreement would not have been enforceable (except as to acts performed thereunder) and cancellation by the manufacturer would have created no liability for expenses incurred by the dealer in preparing to do business. Further, it is argued that as the dealer franchise would have been unenforceable for failure of the manufacturer to supply radios appellants would not be liable to fulfill their assurance that radios would be supplied.

We think these contentions miss the real point of this case. We are not concerned directly with the terms of the franchise. We are dealing with a promise by appellants that a franchise would be granted and radios supplied, on the faith of which appellees with the knowledge and encouragement of appellants incurred expenses in making preparations to do business. Under these circumstances we think that appellants cannot now advance any defense inconsistent with their assurance that the franchise would be granted. Justice and fair dealing require that one who acts to his detriment on the faith of conduct of the kind revealed here should be protected by estopping the party who has brought about the situation from alleging anything in opposition to the natural consequences of his own course of conduct. Dair v. United States, 1872, 16 Wall. 1, 4, 21 L.Ed. 491. In Dickerson v. Colgrove, 100 U.S. 578, 580, 25 L.Ed. 618, the Supreme Court, in speaking of equitable estoppel, said: "The law upon the subject is well settled. The vital principle is that he who by his language or conduct leads another to do what he would not otherwise have done, shall not subject such person to loss or injury by disappointing the expectations upon which he acted. Such a change of position is sternly forbidden. * * * This remedy is always so applied as to promote the ends of justice." * * *

In our opinion the trial court was correct in holding defendants liable for moneys which appellees expended in preparing to do business under the promised dealer franchise. These items aggregated $1150. We think, though, the court erred in adding the item of $350 for loss of profits on radios promised under an initial order. The true measure of damage is the loss sustained by expenditures made in reliance upon the assurance of a dealer franchise. As thus modified, the judgment is

Affirmed.

D & G STOUT, INC. v. BACARDI IMPORTS, INC.

United States Court of Appeals, Seventh Circuit, 1991.
923 F.2d 566.

CUDAHY, CIRCUIT JUDGE.

D & G Stout, Inc., operating at all relevant times under the name General Liquors, Inc. (General), was distributing liquor in the turbulent Indiana liquor market in 1987. When two of its major suppliers jumped ship in early 1987, General faced a critical dilemma: sell out at the best possible price or continue operating on a smaller scale. It began negotiating with another Indiana distributor [National Wine & Spirits] on the terms of a possible sale. Bacardi Imports, Inc. (Bacardi), was still one of General's remaining major suppliers. Knowing that negotiations were ongoing for General's sale, Bacardi promised that General would continue to act as Bacardi's distributor for Northern Indiana. Based on this representation, General turned down the negotiated selling price it was offered. One week later, Bacardi withdrew its account. Realizing it could no longer continue to operate, General went back to the negotiating table, this time settling for an amount $550,000 below the first offer. The question is whether General can recover the price differential from Bacardi on a theory of promissory estoppel. The district court believed that as a matter of law it could not, and entered summary judgment for defendant Bacardi. We disagree, and so we remand for trial.

* * *

* * * On appeal, Bacardi does not argue the facts and is apparently willing to rest on [the district court's] legal analysis. * * * Before us then is the legal question whether the plaintiff has alleged any injury which Indiana's law of promissory estoppel redresses.

* * *

* * * The district judge dismissed the complaint on the ground that Bacardi's alleged promise was not one on which it should reasonably have expected General to rely.

The district court first noted that the relationship between General and Bacardi had always been terminable at will. Because Bacardi's promises that it would continue to use General as its distributor contained no language indicating that they would be good for any specific period, the court reasoned that the relationship remained terminable at will. It then concluded that the promise was not legally enforceable, and thus was not one on which General reasonably might rely. We agree with each of these conclusions but the last. Notwithstanding the continuation of an at-will relationship between Bacardi and General, the promises given between July 9 and July 23 were not without legal effect.

In Indiana, as in many states, an aspiring employee cannot sue for lost wages on an unfulfilled promise of at-will employment. * * * Because the employer could have terminated the employee without cause at any time after the employment began, the promise of a job brings no expectation of any determinable period of employment or corresponding amount of wages. The promise is therefore unenforceable under either a contract or a promissory estoppel theory in an action for lost wages. Nevertheless, lost wages are not the only source of damages flowing from a broken promise of employment, enforceable or not. Indiana courts acknowledge certain damages as recoverable when the employer breaks a promise of employment, even if the employment is to be terminable at will. For example, in *Eby v. York–Division, Borg–Warner,* 455 N.E.2d at 627, a plaintiff who gave up a job and moved from Indiana to Florida on a promise of employment sued for recovery of preparation and moving expenses incurred on the basis of the promise. The Indiana appellate court reversed the lower court's summary judgment for the defendant employer, holding that the plaintiff employee had stated a cause of action for promissory estoppel. The court found that the defendant could have expected the plaintiff and his wife to move in reliance on the promise of employment and therefore might be liable for reneging. * * *

Our review of Indiana law thus leaves us a simple if somewhat crude question: are the damages plaintiff seeks here more like lost future wages or like moving expenses? We can better answer the question if we determine why Indiana draws this distinction. Unlike lost wages, moving expenses represent out-of-pocket losses; they involve a loss of something already possessed. It would be plausible, although not very sophisticated, to distinguish between the loss of something yet to be received and the loss of something already in hand. But this is not precisely where Indiana draws the distinction, nor where we would draw it if it were our choice to make. *Eby* itself involved not only moving expenses, but wages lost at plaintiff's old job during the few days plaintiff was preparing to move. 455 N.E.2d at 625. Those wages were not out-of-pocket losses: plaintiff had no more received those wages than he had received wages from his promised employment.

In fact, the line Indiana draws is between expectation damages and reliance damages. In future wages, the employee has only an expectation of income, the recovery of which promissory estoppel will not support in an at-will employment setting. In wages forgone in order to prepare to move, as in moving expenses themselves, the employee gave up a presently determinate sum for the purpose of relocating. Both moving expenses and forgone wages were the hopeful employee's costs of positioning himself for his new job; moving expenses happen to be out-of-pocket losses, while forgone wages are opportunity costs. Both are reliance costs, not expectancy damages.

Thus, the question has become whether the loss incurred from the price drop was attributable to lost expectations of future profit or resulted from an opportunity forgone in reliance on the promise. At first blush, the injury might seem more like the loss of future wages. Bacardi was a major supplier whose business was extremely valuable to General. While the loss of this "asset" might cause a decline in General's market value as measured by the loss of future income from the sale of Bacardi's products, this loss is not actionable on a promissory estoppel theory. Those damages would presumably be measured by the present value of General's anticipated profit from the sale of Bacardi's products, and Indiana will not grant relief based on promissory estoppel to compensate an aggrieved party for such expectancy damages. Lost future income expected from an at-will relationship, whether from wages or from profits, is not recoverable on a theory of promissory estoppel, and neither is the present value of such losses.

But the fact is that recovery of lost profits is not a question before us. Bacardi's account was never an "asset" that National could acquire by purchasing General. As counsel for the defendant candidly but carefully explained, National never assumed that it would retain the Bacardi account by buying General; in fact, National assumed the opposite. Bacardi's major competitor in the rum distilling business distributed through National, and the two top distillers in a given category of liquor would not choose the same distributor. Both before and after Bacardi decided to withdraw its products, all National wanted from General were its assets other than the Bacardi account. But Bacardi's repudiation of its promise ostensibly affected the price of General's business so drastically because, as everyone in the industry understood, General's option to stay in business independently was destroyed by Bacardi's withdrawal of its account. Thus, through its repudiation, Bacardi destroyed General's negotiating leverage since General no longer had the alternative of continuing as an independent concern. Presumably, after Bacardi's withdrawal General's only alternative to selling to National was to liquidate. Thus, Bacardi's repudiation turned General's discussions with National from negotiations to buy a going concern into a liquidation sale. Instead of bargaining from strength, knowing it could reject a junk-value offer and carry on its business, General was left with one choice: sell at any price.

Under these facts, General had a reliance interest in Bacardi's promise. General was in lively negotiations with National, and it repeatedly informed Bacardi of this fact. A price was agreed upon, and based on that figure, Stout had to decide whether to close his doors or continue operating. General had a business opportunity that all parties knew would be devalued once Bacardi announced its intention to go elsewhere. The extent of that devaluation represents a reliance injury, rather than an injury to General's expectation of future profit. The injury is analogous to the cost of moving expenses incurred as a result of promised employment in *Eby* * * *.

Nor were these promises merely meaningless restatements of an under-stood at-will relationship. With its current business opportunity, General stood at a crossroads. Circumstances foreshadowed a costly demise for the company, but it was able to negotiate an alternative. Far from confirming the obvious, Bacardi wrote its assurances on a clean slate with full knowledge that General was just as likely to reject the offered relationship as embrace it. That this was the situation is indicated most clearly by Bacardi's repeated calls to check on Stout's impending decision. Bacardi reassured Stout of its commitment in full knowledge that he planned to reject National's offer and with the reasonable expectation that an immediate pull out would severely undermine General's asking price. Like the plaintiffs in *Eby* who moved based on the promise of a job, General incurred a cost in rejecting the deal that was non-recoverable once Bacardi's later decision became known.

There may always exist the potential for a quandry in a promissory estoppel action based on a promise of at-will employment. When could Bacardi terminate the relationship with General without fear of liability for reliance costs, once it made the assurances in question? Obviously we do not hold that General and Bacardi had formed a new, permanent employment relationship. How long an employee can rely on the employer's promise is not a matter we can decide here. The issue is one of reasonable reliance, and to the extent that there might be questions, they should be for trial.

We have, of course, reviewed this case in the posture of summary judgment. General's allegations still must be proven at trial. However, under Indiana law, we think that Bacardi's promise was of a sort on which General might rely, with the possibility of damages for breach. * * *

REVERSED AND REMANDED.

[Counsel for Bacardi reports that after a trial on the merits, the court awarded damages to General on the theory of promissory estoppel. Bacardi appealed but the case was settled just before oral argument.]

WALTERS v. MARATHON OIL CO.

United States Court of Appeal, Seventh Circuit, 1981.
642 F.2d 1098.

SPEARS, DISTRICT JUDGE.

This action arose as a result of the Iranian revolution and the uncertainty of oil supplies. Marathon Oil Company, the appellant, is engaged in the business of reselling and distributing petroleum products. The appellee, Dennis E. Walters, contacted appellant in late December, 1978, about the possibility of locating a combination foodstore and service station on a vacant gasoline service station site in Indianapolis. Appellees (husband and wife) purchased the service station in February, 1979, and continued to make improvements upon it, based upon promises made, and the continuing negotiations with representatives from appellant. Paper work apparently proceeded normally, and appellees' proposal was delivered to appellant along with a three-party agreement, signed by appellees and Time Oil Company, the previous supplier to the service station site appellees had purchased. Before appellees' proposal was accepted by appellant, but after it was received at the office, appellant placed a moratorium on the consideration of new applications for dealerships and seller arrangements, and refused to sign the three-party agreement.

After a bench trial, the court found for appellees and against appellant on the theory of promissory estoppel. This finding has not been challenged. The two issues presented for review in this appeal pertain only to the award of damages in the form of lost profits, and the alleged failure of appellees to take reasonable steps to mitigate their damages. We affirm the judgment of the district court.

The appellant first argues that the trial court committed error by ignoring evidence that appellees failed to take reasonable steps to mitigate their damages. The record clearly reflects, however, the appellees contacted Shell Oil Company, Standard Oil of Indiana, and Texaco with respect to becoming a new supplier of their service station, after appellant notified them it would not provide them with gasoline. Appellee, Dennis E. Walters, testified that he had telephoned the president of Time Oil, to seek a supply, but his request was declined. Appellees did not contact appellant, but they could hardly have been expected to do so, considering the treatment appellant had already given them. There are ample facts in the record to support the finding of the trial court that appellees exercised the ordinary care of a person in the same circumstances to mitigate their damages. That finding, under the evidence, was not clearly erroneous. Furthermore, the trial court found that the plaintiffs "had no gasoline market experience and were not familiar with the marketing practices of gasoline companies." Thus, the fact that alternative suppliers may have existed if appellees had asserted legal rights, and complied with Department of Energy regulations, does not alone impose the duty to mitigate damages by searching for additional sources, if appellees lacked the sophistication with which to conduct such a search.

The appellant next argues that the trial court's computation of damages is clearly erroneous and contrary to the law. The trial court found that appellees lost anticipated profits of six cents per gallon for the 370,000 gallons they were entitled to receive under their allocation for the first year's gasoline sales, totalling $22,200.00, and awarded this amount in damages. The appellant insists that since appellees succeeded at trial solely on a promissory estoppel theory, and the district court so found, loss of profits is not a proper measure of damages. It contends that appellees' damages should have been the amount of their expenditures in reliance on the promise, measured by the difference between their expenditures and the present value of the property. Using this measure of damages, appellees would have received no award, for the present value of the real estate and its improvements is slightly more than the amount expended by appellees in reliance upon the promise. As a consequence, the appellant says that because appellees can recoup all they spent in reliance on appellant's promise, they would be in the same position they would have been in had the promise not been made.

However, in reliance upon appellant's promise to supply gasoline supplies to them, appellees purchased the station, and invested their funds and their time. It is unreasonable to assume that they did not anticipate a return of profits from this investment of time and funds, but, in reliance upon appellant's promise, they had foregone the opportunity to make the investment elsewhere. As indicated, the record reflects that had appellant performed according to its promise, appellees would have received the anticipated net profit of $22,200.00. The findings of the trial court in this regard were fully supported by the evidence. For example, it was shown that the [1977/78] base period for this particular station was 375,450 gallons. The appellant's own exhibit reflected the same amount. The testimony of the previous owner showed that the location pumped 620,000 gallons in 1972, and that he pumped 375,450 gallons in 1978. Furthermore, an expert witness testified that the site would pump 360,000 gallons a year. Appellant's own witness testified that all of its dealers received 100% of their base period allocation for the time in question. Thus, the trial court was not clearly erroneous in its finding that appellees would have sold 370,000 gallons of gasoline had appellant's promise been performed.

An equity court possesses some discretionary power to award damages in order to do complete justice. * * * Furthermore, since it is the historic purpose of equity to secure complete justice, the courts are able to adjust the remedies so as to grant the necessary relief, * * * and a district court sitting in equity may even devise a remedy which extends or exceeds the terms of a prior agreement between the parties, if it is necessary to make the injured party whole. *Levitt Corp. v. Levitt,* 593 F.2d 463 (2d Cir.1979).

Since promissory estoppel is an equitable matter, the trial court has broad power in its choice of a remedy, and it is significant that the ancient maxim that "equity will not suffer a wrong to be without a remedy" has long been the law in the State of Indiana. * * *

In this case the promissory estoppel finding of the district court is not challenged. Moreover, it is apparent that the appellees suffered a loss of profits as a direct result of their reliance upon the promise made by appellant, and the amount of the lost profits was ascertained with reasonable certainty.[1] In addition, appellees took reasonable steps to mitigate their damages, and an award of damages based upon lost profits was appropriate in order to do complete justice.

---

1. In *Goodman v. Dicker,* 169 F.2d 684 (D.C.Cir.1948), relied upon by appellant, the court held that the true measure of damages in that equitable estoppel case was the loss in the sum of $1150 sustained by expenditures made in reliance on assurances given to the injured parties, and that the trial court had erred in *adding* the item of $350 for lost profits. No reasons were assigned or authorities cited by the court for the action it took, and there was no suggestion that in an appropriate case loss of profits could not be a true measure of damages. In any event, it is apparent that the award of double damages was rejected and the higher figure of $1150 was chosen in order to do complete justice. In this connection, it is interesting to note that in *National Savings and Trust Company v. Kahn,* 300 F.2d 910 (D.C.Cir.1962), the same circuit commented that "(T)he cost of performance may be the proper measure of damages where plaintiff renders part performance *and it is impossible to estimate the profits he would have received but for defendant's breach.* (Citing authorities). That is not this case." (Emphasis supplied). *See id.* at 914 n. 7.

Under the circumstances, and concluding, as we do, that the findings of the district court are not clearly erroneous, we affirm the judgment which awards damages to appellees based upon lost profits.

AFFIRMED.

GROUSE v. GROUP HEALTH PLAN

Supreme Court of Minnesota, 1981.
306 N.W.2d 114.

OTIS, JUSTICE.

Plaintiff John Grouse appeals from a judgment in favor of Group Health Plan, Inc., in this action for damages resulting from repudiation of an employment offer. The narrow issue raised is whether the trial court erred by concluding that Grouse's complaint fails to state a claim upon which relief can be granted. In our view, the doctrine of promissory estoppel entitles Grouse to recover and we, therefore, reverse and remand for a new trial on the issue of damages.

The facts relevant to this appeal are essentially undisputed. Grouse, a 1974 graduate of the University of Minnesota School of Pharmacy, was employed in 1975 as a retail pharmacist at Richter Drug in Minneapolis. He worked approximately 41 hours per week earning $7 per hour. Grouse desired employment in a hospital or clinical setting, however, because of the work environment and the increased compensation and benefits. In the summer of 1975 he was advised by the Health Sciences Placement office at the University that Group Health was seeking a pharmacist.

Grouse called Group Health and was told to come in and fill out an application. He did so in September and was, at that time, interviewed by Cyrus Elliott, Group Health's Chief Pharmacist. Approximately 2 weeks later Elliott contacted Grouse and asked him to come in for an interview with Donald Shoberg, Group Health's General Manager. Shoberg explained company policies and procedures as well as salary and benefits. Following this meeting Grouse again spoke with Elliott who told him to be patient, that it was necessary to interview recent graduates before making an offer.

On December 4, 1975, Elliott telephoned Grouse at Richter Drug and offered him a position as a pharmacist at Group Health's St. Louis Park Clinic. Grouse accepted but informed Elliott that 2 week's notice to Richter Drug would be necessary. That afternoon Grouse received an offer from a Veteran's Administration Hospital in Virginia which he declined because of Group Health's offer. Elliott called back to confirm that Grouse had resigned.

Sometime in the next few days Elliott mentioned to Shoberg that he had hired, or was thinking of hiring, Grouse. Shoberg told him that company hiring requirements included a favorable written reference, a background check, and approval of the general manager. Elliott contacted two faculty members at the School of Pharmacy who declined to give references. He also contacted an internship employer and several pharmacies where Grouse had done relief work. Their responses were that they had not had enough exposure to Grouse's work to form a judgment as to his capabilities. Elliott did not contact Richter because Grouse's application requested that he not be contacted. Because Elliott was unable to supply a favorable reference for Grouse, Shoberg hired another person to fill the position.

On December 15, 1975 Grouse called Group Health and reported that he was free to begin work. Elliott informed Grouse that someone else had been hired. Grouse complained to the director of Group Health who apologized but took no other action. Grouse experienced difficulty regaining full time employment and suffered wage loss as a result. He commenced this suit to recover damages; the trial judge found that he had not stated an actionable claim.

In our view the principle of contract law applicable here is promissory estoppel. Its effect is to imply a contract in law where none exists in fact. *Del Hayes & Sons, Inc. v. Mitchell*, 304 Minn. 275, 230 N.W.2d 588 (1975). On these facts no contract exists because due to the bilateral power of termination neither party is committed to performance and the promises are, therefore, illusory. The elements of promissory estoppel are stated in *Restatement of Contracts* § 90 (1932):

> A promise which the promisor should reasonably expect to induce action or forbearance * * * on the part of the promisee and which does induce such action or forbearance is binding if injustice can be avoided only by enforcement of the promise.

Group Health knew that to accept its offer Grouse would have to resign his employment at Richter Drug. Grouse promptly gave notice to Richter Drug and informed Group Health that he had done so when specifically asked by Elliott. Under these circumstances it would be unjust not to hold Group Health to its promise.

The parties focus their arguments on whether an employment contract which is terminable at will can give rise to an action for damages if anticipatorily repudiated. * * * Group Health contends that recognition of a cause of action on these facts would result in the anomalous rule that an employee who is told not to report to work the day before he is scheduled to begin has a remedy while an employee who is discharged after the first day does not. We cannot agree since under appropriate circumstances we believe section 90 would apply even after employment has begun.

When a promise is enforced pursuant to section 90 "[t]he remedy granted for breach may be limited as justice requires." Relief may be limited to damages measured by the promisee's reliance.

The conclusion we reach does not imply that an employer will be liable whenever he discharges an employee whose term of employment is at will. What we do hold is that under the facts of this case the appellant had a right to assume he would be given a good faith opportunity to perform his duties to the satisfaction of respondent once he was on the job. He was not only denied that opportunity but resigned the position he already held in reliance on the firm offer which respondent tendered him. Since, as respondent points out, the prospective employment might have been terminated at any time, the measure of damages is not so much what he would have earned from respondent as what he lost in quitting the job he held and in declining at least one other offer of employment elsewhere.

Reversed and remanded for a new trial on the issue of damages.

Problem 3–14

At the end of Alice White's 40 year career as an airplane mechanic, her employer, Federal Aviation, promised White a pension of $200 per week. A few days after retirement, Alice refused an offer of employment for 3 years at $175 per week from American Aviation, a competitor of Federal. After three months of retirement, it became clear that Federal was not going to honor its promise of a pension. Alice comes to your law office and asks you what her rights are against Federal. Please explain. Consider all theories and appropriate remedies.

Note
Reliance Recovery When the Agreement Has Been Disrupted

In Chapter Eight, we will see that a contracting party occasionally may rightfully cease performance because of the occurrence of an unforeseen contingency that makes performance unfairly onerous or impossible or even because of a shared mistaken assumption about the facts existing at the time of contracting. Upon such a rightful cessation, we will see that the Restatement (Second) of Contracts and some modern courts suggest that a party may be entitled to recover reliance expenses. See Chapter Nine, Section Three.

SECTION EIGHT: RESTITUTIONARY RELIEF AND THEORIES OF OBLIGATION

Courts use the term "restitutionary relief" to refer both to monetary remedies and to certain forms of specific relief, such as an order requiring the defendant to return a specific item. In this section, we concentrate on monetary remedies. A monetary remedy is restitutionary in nature insofar as it requires A to pay B the monetary value of any benefit B conferred on A. This language authorizes courts to base the measure of relief on either Restatement (Second) of Contracts, section 371(a) or (b), below. In addition, we will encounter additional measures of restitutionary relief. For example, courts sometimes award B its full outlay in preparing to perform or in performing, even if this measure exceeds A's gain.

In this section, we focus not only on restitutionary remedies but also on theories of obligation that justify the remedies. Sometimes the theory of obligation is unjust enrichment. Sometimes it is breach of an agreement with consideration. Sometimes the theory is quite obscure.

RESTATEMENT (SECOND) OF CONTRACTS § 371.

Measure of Restitution Interest

If a sum of money is awarded to protect a party's restitution interest, it may as justice requires be measured by either

(a) the reasonable value to the other party of what he received in terms of what it would have cost him to obtain it from a person in the claimant's position, or

(b) the extent to which the other party's property has been increased in value or his other interests advanced.

Comment:

a. *Measurement of benefit.* * * * An especially important choice is that between the reasonable value to a party of what he received in terms of what it would have cost him to obtain it from a person in the claimant's position and the addition to the wealth of that party as measured by the extent to which his property has been increased in value or his other interests advanced. In practice, the first measure is usually based on the market price of such a substitute. Under the rule stated in this Section, the court has considerable discretion in making the choice between these two measures of benefit. Under either choice, the court may properly consider the purposes of the recipient of the benefit when he made the contract, even if those purposes were later frustrated or abandoned.

b. *Choice of measure.* * * * [A] party seeking restitution for part performance is commonly allowed the more generous measure of reasonable value, unless that measure is unduly difficult to apply, except when he is in breach.

CRASWELL, AGAINST FULLER AND PERDUE

67 U. Chi. L. Rev. 99, 142 (2000).

* * * [T]here are actually many different remedial measures—some more generous to the promisee, some less so—that could plausibly pass under the name of restitution. If, for example, a builder finishes building half of a house before the homeowner unjustifiably repudiates the contract, and the builder then sues for the reasonable value of the half-completed house, that value could be measured in several different ways. To name just four, the builder might collect (a) any increase in the market value of the home-owner's land resulting from having a half-completed house on it; (b) whatever price the home-owner would have to pay another builder, at current construction rates, to build that half-completed house; (c) half of the price the home-owner originally agreed to pay this builder, for the fully completed house; or even (d) whatever this builder spent to build the first half of the house, taking the builder's actual costs as a rough measure of the house's value. Depending on how favorable the original contract was, and also on what has happened to property values and construction costs since the original contract was signed, any one of these measures could (in a particular case) be larger or smaller than the others. They could also be either larger or smaller than any of the ways in which expectation damages might be measured, and so could exceed or fall short of the builder's expectation interest. As a result, it is highly misleading to speak of "restitution" as though it were a single unified remedy.

Of course, if these excesses and shortfalls were randomly distributed, there would be little reason to comment on them. But * * * there is some evidence that courts are influenced in their choice of measurement by how well or badly the breaching party behaved. For example, if the breach was particularly egregious, the courts may be more inclined to measure the nonbreacher's services in a way that gives him a particularly generous measure of recovery (or to measure the breacher's services in a way that minimizes their value). The egregiousness of the breacher's behavior may also be one factor in deciding whether the breach was "total" or "material," which is the doctrinal prerequisite for the nonbreacher to have the option of figuring his damages in restitution.

A. WHERE A NON–BREACHING PLAINTIFF CONFERRED A BENEFIT AND ELECTS A RESTITUTIONARY RECOVERY

In Posner v. Seder (page 129), we saw that a party injured by the breach of an agreement with consideration may elect to recover the benefit conferred on the breacher under the theory of unjust enrichment, instead of expectancy damages for breach of contract. Here we focus on the problem of measurement of the benefit conferred when an injured party seeks restitution in this context.

UNITED STATES FOR USE OF SUSI CONTRACTING CO. v. ZARA CONTRACTING CO.

United States Court of Appeals, Second Circuit, 1944.

146 F.2d 606.

CLARK, CIRCUIT JUDGE.

Plaintiffs, Susi Contracting Co., Inc., and D'Agostino & Cuccio, Inc., brought this action under the provisions of the Miller Act, 40 U.S.C.A. § 270a et seq., in the name of the United States against Zara Contracting Co., Inc., and American Bonding Company of Baltimore, the surety on its bond, to recover for work performed for and equipment supplied Zara in the performance of its contract with the United States, dated March 4, 1941, for the extension of Tri–Cities Airport, Endicott, New York. On April 2, 1941, Zara entered into a subcontract with plaintiffs, wherein plaintiffs agreed, except for one $100 item, to perform the entire work called for by the main contract with the United States. This work involved the excavation of material and placing, manipulating, rolling, and compacting it as a base and surface course for landing strips or runways. During the course of the excavation plaintiffs encountered unexpected soil conditions, mostly due to the presence of a great deal of clay material, which made progress of their work extremely difficult, caused the breakdown of their tools, and, according to their allegations, generally required the performance of work not called for by the contract. Consequently on several occasions they made demands on Zara for extra money; and eventually the dispute arose which led to mutual claims of breach of contract and, by easy stages, to the opposing claims for monetary solace of this action. At any rate, defendant Zara took over the completion of the contract about July 12, 1941, or two months after plaintiffs had begun work. It also took possession of and for some three months utilized the equipment furnished by plaintiffs at the contract site.

In this action plaintiffs alleged that Zara wrongfully terminated the subcontract, and sought recovery for the reasonable cost and value of the actual work performed, and the fair and reasonable rental value of the equipment for the period of its retention and use. Defendant Zara put in issue the material allegations of the complaint and also filed a counterclaim wherein it alleged that it was compelled to terminate the contract by plaintiffs' refusal to perform it, and demanded damages for its breach against plaintiffs. Defendant American also put in issue the material allegations of the complaint and asserted further that plaintiffs had failed to state a claim against it upon which relief could be granted. The District Court found generally for the plaintiffs, holding that Zara had wrongfully terminated the contract and that there was due them $39,107.10 for work done at the contract rate, $18,600 for increased cost of excavation due to the soil conditions encountered, and $5,157.75 as rental allowance for plaintiffs' equipment, less $43,345.20, the amount advanced by Zara during the course of the work, or a net of $19,519.65, together with interest from the date of the filing of the suit. * * *

* * *

This * * * disposes of Zara's claim for damages and leaves for consideration the amount of recovery due the plaintiffs. In their complaint originally plaintiffs had a second count claiming an accounting of profits; but this they abandoned, and they have made no claim for damages for breach of contract. Their only claim, therefore, is for the value of the work performed and of the rental of equipment retained by Zara on the job. Taking up, first, the value of the work performed, three theories are suggested to justify the additional award made below—in addition to that made at the regular contract rate—of $18,600 for the increased cost of excavating the clay material. The first, apparently most favored by the plaintiffs, is that this excavating (as well as the separate mixing of materials to form the airport runways made necessary by the soil condition) was extra work, not covered by the contract figures, and hence was separately compensable. * * * The second, relied on by the trial court, is that, since the subcontract made the provisions of the main contract determinative and applicable to the subparties, except where otherwise provided, the plaintiffs should have the advantage of the provisions of the main contract under which Zara successfully sought additional compensation against the United States. And the third is that, in view of Zara's default, they may waive the contract entirely and sue in quantum meruit for the reasonable value of the work performed.

Defendants contend, however, that under the terms of the subcontract plaintiffs were not entitled to any allowance for extra costs over and above the contract price, even though entailed in consequence of the misrepresentations as to the subsoil conditions. They rely principally on Article 5 of the subcontract, reprinted in the margin,[1] wherein plaintiffs agreed that no representations as to subsurface conditions have been made, nor have they been induced to enter into the contract in reliance upon the drawings or plans, and they promised to make no claim for damages for unknown conditions. In support of their contention they cite such cases as T.J.W. Corporation v. Board of Higher Education of City of New York, 251 App.Div. 405, 296 N.Y.S. 693, affirmed 276 N.Y. 644, 12 N.E.2d 800, and Niewenhous Co. v. State, 248 App.Div. 658, 288 N.Y.S. 22, affirmed 272 N.Y. 484, 3 N.E.2d 880. But these cases are

---

1. "No representations have been made to the Sub–Contractor as to any sub-surface or latent conditions at the site; nor has the Sub–Contractor been induced to enter into this subcontract in reliance upon any representations shown on the drawings or indicated in the specifications as to any sub-surface or latent conditions at the site. The Sub–Contractor agrees that it will make no claim against the Contractor for damages in the event that, during the progress of the work, the Sub–Contractor encounters sub-surface and/or latent conditions at the site materially differing from those shown on the drawings or indicated in the specifications, or unknown conditions of an unusual nature differing materially from those ordinarily encountered and generally recognized as inhering in work of the character provided for in the plans and specifications."

limited to claims for extra work, where the contract has not been wrongfully terminated by the employer. ~~The situation is quite otherwise where, as here, defendants have breached the agreement.~~ We agree that the definite commitment which the plaintiffs have made in Article 5 is one they must stand by so long as they must rely upon their contract; and hence we find it difficult to see why the first two theories presented above, that particularly pressed by the plaintiffs and that relied on by the trial court, do not conflict directly with this agreement, which seems to contemplate the very situation to which it would then be held inapplicable. No such infirmity attaches to the third theory, however.

For it is an accepted principle of contract law, often applied in the case of construction contracts, ~~that the promisee upon breach has the option to forego any suit on the contract and claim only the reasonable value of his performance.~~ * * * *Restitution*

It also appears to be the general view, save for an occasional case viewed as illogical by the text writers, who are solidly in support of the doctrine. * * *

These authorities make it quite clear that under the better rule the contract price or the unit price per cubic yard of a construction or excavation contract does not limit recovery. * * * This doctrine is particularly applicable to unit prices in construction contracts; as Professor Patterson points out, 31 Col.L.Rev. at page 1303, a plaintiff may well have completed the hardest part of a job for which an average cost had been set. But it seems settled now in New York that with the breach fall all the other parts of the contract. * * * Hence it is clear that plaintiffs are not limited to the contract prices in the situation disclosed here.

As we have noted, the trial court granted recovery for $39,107.10 for the work done at the contract price, together with an additional sum of $18,600 for the extra cost of excavation of the clay, computed as 62,000 cubic yards at the additional expense of 30 cents per cubic yard. * * * As to the monetary amounts, these are based on the cost of the work to Zara, as well as expert testimony for plaintiffs, and are not seriously disputed. Indeed, in fixing the additional allowance at 30 cents per cubic yard, the judge relied particularly on Zara's claim to the United States wherein it stated that its records showed an actual cost to it of the extra work, amounting to 28.7 cents per cubic yard for the excavating, and 2½ cents per cubic yard for placing the excavated material in the runways. Professor Williston points out that the measure of recovery by way of restitution, though often confused with recovery on the contract, should not be measured or limited thereby; but he does point out that the contract may be important evidence of the value of the performance to the defendant, as may also the cost of the labor and materials. 5 Williston on Contracts, Rev.Ed., §§ 1482, 1483, 1485. It is therefore appropriate here, particularly in default of any challenging evidence, to base recovery on proper expenditures in performance * * * and to make use of the contract as fixing the basic price. * * *

It is to be noted that, since it is the defendant who is in default, and plaintiffs' performance here is "part of the very performance" for which the defendant had bargained, "it is to be valued, not by the extent to which the defendant's total wealth has been increased thereby, but by the amount for which such services and materials as constituted the part performance could have been purchased from one in the plaintiff's position at the time they were rendered." Restatement, Contracts, § 347, comment c. * * * It is to be noted that in fact defendant Zara did receive benefits most substantial from plaintiffs' performance. Plaintiffs had actually excavated 211,390 cubic yards, for which Zara's profit, as determined by the spread between the main and the subcontract of 5½ cents per cubic yard as a minimum, with higher amounts for a part, would be around $12,000; it had already collected $17,115.79 from the United States for the additional cost of removing the "cohesive silt," of which most was done by plaintiffs, and it had pending a claim against the United States for $18,840.10 more; and what is perhaps most important, it had received a performance which it needed to make to ensure recovery of these profits and sums from the United States and avoid the danger of being in default, and which it would have had to do itself or purchase in the market. Hence the allowance made by the District Court is justified on the evidence and the law, and we find no error, therefore, in this item of recovery.

* * *

[The Court's discussion of measurement of the retail value of the equipment retained by Zara is omitted.]

The judgment is modified by increasing the allowance for the fair rental value of equipment furnished from $5,157.75 to $7,227.50, and as so modified is affirmed.

HENDERSON, PROMISES GROUNDED IN THE PAST: THE IDEA OF UNJUST ENRICHMENT AND THE LAW OF CONTRACTS

57 Va.L.Rev. 1115, 1150–51, 1153–54, and n. 149 (1971).

[It] is possible to disguise the theories of contract and quasi-contract simply by attaching the label quantum meruit to an action for the recovery of the monetary equivalent of a performance rendered. * * * The decisions leave no room for doubt that the bulk of the work of quantum meruit is in the field of quasi-contractual liabilities [unjust enrichment]. One cannot speak of the law of restitution without confronting the many mysteries of the idea of quantum meruit. It is a restitution which, almost without exception, restores the status quo by awarding a claimant the reasonable market value of his performance, not by forcing the defending party [merely] to disgorge benefit unjustly retained. The contract results arrived at under quantum meruit are undoubtedly explained by the contractual form of statement that characterizes the common count for work and labor done. * * * The essence of the quantum meruit count is an allegation of indebtedness for the labor and services of the plaintiff, "done and bestowed at the request of" the defendant, who, being so indebted, in consideration thereof promised the plaintiff to pay him on request. * * *

* * *

* * * A claim in quantum meruit therefore authorizes a court to alter the parties' basic risk allocation. The necessity for fashioning relief outside the bargain is usually placed on the ground that defendant's conduct has resulted

in the enjoyment of gain which is the product of plaintiff's loss. In plain terms, gain thought to be unjust given the circumstances is an essential factor in the remedial scheme. Yet contract ideas return to shape in many ways the process and product of restitution. By focusing attention on plaintiff's outlay, unjust gain held by one party triggers the impulse to award the other a market equivalent for his efforts.

[handwritten: Quantum meruit]

[handwritten: Lawyer]

OLIVER v. CAMPBELL, 43 Cal.2d 298, 273 P.2d 15 (1954). [Plaintiff Oliver, a lawyer, agreed to represent defendant Campbell in a divorce proceeding for a flat sum of $850, including $100 for costs etc. The trial lasted 29 days, with the trial judge finally indicating an intention to grant a divorce, so that Oliver's services were worth far more than the agreed flat sum. When Oliver's services were essentially complete (according to the appellate court), Campbell discharged Oliver, who had at that point been paid $550. Oliver then sued upon a *quantum meruit* for the reasonable value of his services and the court below found this to be $5,000. Held, reversed.]

[handwritten margin: actually paid $550]
[handwritten margin: $850 flat agreed]
[handwritten margin: $5,000 MV]

"It is well settled that one who is wrongfully discharged and prevented from further performance of his contract may elect as a general rule to treat the contract as rescinded, may sue upon a quantum meruit as if the special contract of employment had never been made and may recover the reasonable value of the services performed even though such reasonable value exceeds the contract price. * * * Under [the] * * * circumstances [of this case] it would appear that in effect, plaintiff had completed the performance of his service and the rule would apply that "[t]he remedy of restitution in money is not available to one who has fully performed his part of a contract, if the only part of the agreed exchange for such performance that has not been rendered by the defendant is a sum of money constituting a liquidated debt * * *."

[handwritten margin: may recover reasonable value of services performed even if it exceeds the original contract price before perform is complete]

B. WHERE A NON–BREACHING PLAINTIFF CONFERRED A BENEFIT BUT HAD A NEGATIVE EXPECTANCY (A "LOSING" CONTRACT)

[handwritten: Restitution is better here ↑]

RESTATEMENT (SECOND) OF CONTRACTS § 373

Comment d.

An injured party who has performed in part will usually prefer to seek damages based on his expectation interest (§ 347) instead of a sum of money based on his restitution interest because such damages include his net profit and will give him a larger recovery. Even if he cannot prove what his net profit would have been, he will ordinarily seek damages based on his reliance interest * * *, since this will compensate him for all of his expenditures, regardless of whether they resulted in a benefit to the party in breach. * * * In the case of a contract on which he would have sustained a loss instead of having made a profit, however, his restitution interest may give him a larger recovery than would damages on either basis. The right of the injured party under a losing contract to a greater amount in restitution than he could have recovered in damages has engendered much controversy. The rules stated in this Section give him that right. He is entitled to such recovery even if the contract price is stated in terms of a rate per unit of work and the recovery exceeds that rate.

[handwritten margin: example]

[handwritten margin: recovery can exceed rate]

CITY OF PHILADELPHIA v. TRIPPLE, 230 Pa. 480, 79 A. 703 (1911). [Contractor Dietrich was hired by the city of Philadelphia to construct the foundations and superstructure for a fire engine house. For the sum of $34,500 to be paid in monthly cash payments as the work progressed, Dietrich engaged subcontractor McMenamy to perform necessary excavation work and to construct the main conduit from the Delaware River to the engine house. The contract provided that the work was to be completed within 125 working days from its date. Difficulties arose in the course of the excavation work resulting in flooding and delays.

Although the period of 125 days specified in the contract had expired, no action was taken by Dietrich in view of the non-completion of the work at that time, and McMenamy continued work under his contract with the knowledge and acquiescence of Dietrich. Subsequently, however, Dietrich became dissatisfied with the rate of progress and requested McMenamy to discontinue further work on the conduit.

McMenamy ceased work and brought suit in "indebitatus assumpsit"[d] to recover the actual cost of his labor and materials. The lower court found that Dietrich had broken the contract and was equitably estopped from asserting the failure to complete within the specified time as a defense, since he had known of and acquiesced in McMenamy's further performance after the lapse of the time period. The referee awarded McMenamy the actual cost of his labor and material. The referee held that a plaintiff may recover from a defaulting defendant the cost of labor and materials less payments made, although such cost exceeds the price fixed in the contract. The court affirmed per curiam. Excerpts from the referee's report follow.]

* * * "Let it be assumed that, in an extreme case, a builder has actually expended in the course of his work a sum in excess of the contract price and has not yet completed performance. If, under such circumstances, the builder finishes his work, the owner, upon paying the contract price, will receive the benefit of a large expenditure actually made, in return for the payment of a smaller sum of money. This result, which may well involve a hardship upon the builder, is made necessary by a proper regard for the contractual rights of the owner. The owner has made a valid contract, and this contract must be protected and enforced, even if the builder suffers.

"Let it further be supposed, however, that the owner, who finds himself in this position of advantage, voluntarily puts an end to his contract rights in the premises. This in legal effect he does if he himself breaks the contract or discharges the builder from his obligation to perform it. The situation which then presents itself is one in which the builder has in good faith expended money in the course of work done for the benefit of the owner, and has, in the absence of contract, an equitable claim to be reimbursed. The owner, on the other hand, has deprived himself of the legal right which would have sufficed to defeat the equity. He accordingly stands defenseless in the presence of the builder's claim.

d. Indebitatus assumpsit is analogous to quantum meruit. However, in indebitatus assumpsit the claim is for a specific sum, whereas in quantum meruit the claim is for reasonable value. See Appendix B.

"Such, it is submitted, is the legal analysis of the situation in which the parties to this action find themselves. It may, of course, be contended that Dietrich did not receive an actual benefit coextensive with McMenamy's expenditure. It is a sufficient answer to this contention to observe that (upon the facts as heretofore found) McMenamy expended the money in good faith and in the course of attempted performance. That is sufficient to give him an equitable claim for reimbursement."

[handwritten: suggests that Contract is a ceiling on recovery]

JOHNSON v. BOVEE, 40 Colo.App. 317, 574 P.2d 513 (1978). [Plaintiff agreed in a written contract to build a house for defendants according to a specified set of plans for $47,176. During the course of construction, plaintiff and defendants orally agreed to many deviations from the original plans, resulting in both additions ("extras") and deletions.

Defendants became dissatisfied with the quality of the construction and stopped making required payments to plaintiff. Plaintiff therefore stopped work on the house and filed suit to foreclose on his mechanics lien. *[handwritten: ?]*

The lower court found that plaintiff had substantially performed his obligations under the contract and that defendants' refusal to make payments constituted a breach. It also found that the house was 90% complete when construction was stopped. Plaintiff was awarded damages calculated as follows:

[handwritten margin note: Ct found ∆s breached by non payment]

Contract Price	$47,176.00
Net Value of Agreed Extras	$ 7,700.78
Payments Made by Defendants	$ – 49,485.18
Cost to Plaintiff had he Completed the House (10% of $47,176)	$ – 4,717.60
Total	$ 674.00

Plaintiff appealed as to damages, arguing that he was entitled to recover in *quantum meruit* for the reasonable value of the services he rendered, which he claimed exceeded the original contract price and agreed extras by $9,000. Held, where the owners breached the contract by refusing to make required payments to builder, builder was entitled to recover the reasonable value of his services, but the contract price constituted a ceiling on his recovery of restitution.] "Courts and commentators are divided over the question of whether restitution should be limited by the contract. * * *

[handwritten margin note: π appealed saying he was entitled to recover quantum meruit]

"We believe using the contract price as a ceiling on restitution is the better-reasoned resolution of this question. Had Johnson fully performed, his recovery would be limited to the contract price, since he would be suing for specific performance of the liquidated debt obligation under the contract. * * * It is illogical to allow him to recover the full cost of his services when, if he completed the house, he would be limited to the contract price plus the agreed upon extras."

CHILDRES & GARAMELLA, THE LAW OF RESTITUTION AND THE RELIANCE INTEREST IN CONTRACT
64 Nw.U.L.Rev. 433, 439–40 (1969).

There is no justification for the position that the terms of the promise do not regulate the recovery of reliance damages in some cases which may be twisted into an "action in *quantum meruit.*" A promise excites expectations and causes reliance, for both of which the law should justly give protection. The crucial question, then, is whether or not the promise which was relied upon, being the *provocateur* of the reliance, will regulate the damages recoverable in event of a breach.

It may be thought undesirable to admit that *quantum meruit* restitution, insofar as it rests not on unjust enrichment but upon abuse of a contracting party's reliance interest, is merely a variant of the contract reliance claim. However, sufficient reason exists for the admission.

By way of example, a firm agrees to manufacture X number of rifles for the government at Y unit price. After the government requires that performance cease, the firm seeks five times Y for each rifle delivered, saying that this was the reasonable value of what it did. The argument is an attempt to entirely upset the parties' original business arrangement. If freedom of contract means freedom to deviate from the standards of reasonable men, fully informed, and enjoying levels of knowledge and intelligence to be expected in the situation, it can have no more fertile field than that of allocating market and other relevant risks in a business transaction. Specifically, the parties' own allocation of the market or other risks should be upset, if at all, by substantive doctrine and not by whether one chooses the label "*quantum meruit*" or "common count" on the one hand, or "reliance damages" on the other.

KULL, RESTITUTION AS A REMEDY FOR BREACH OF CONTRACT

67 S. Cal. L. Rev. 1465, 1482–83 (1994).

* * * If our moral condemnation of promise-breakers were strenuous enough, the social judgment underlying the remedy of restitution for breach might indeed be that any advantage conferred by the contractual exchange upon one who later defaults becomes, ipso facto, unjust enrichment in the defaulter's hands. Yet the explanation seems strained at best. A more straightforward way of putting the same proposition would be to say that courts in some circumstances favor a punitive remedy for breach of contract, and that stripping a defendant of the benefits secured by a contract he has failed to perform has seemed to judges, in some circumstances, to be no more than poetic justice. If promise-breakers are wrongdoers we can, of course, choose to punish them any way we see fit: Forcing them to surrender a favorable bargain may be an appropriate form of punishment, however rarely and haphazardly applied. But the argument at this point involves contract remedies, not unjust enrichment by any useful definition.

Problem 3–15

Ajax Construction Company agreed to construct a restaurant for Hal Evans on his land for $350,000. After Ajax had spent $105,000 in preparation and part performance, only $5,000 of which was salvageable, Hal repudiated the contract because of a lack of funds. The cost of completing construction would have been $255,000. The partial performance increased the value of Hal's land by $100,000. Hal can hire another contractor to complete the work for $270,000. Ajax received no progress payments. Ajax's president, Turlway, has asked you how much the company can recover from Hal Evans. Turlway tells you that he has received a settlement offer of $60,000. Should he accept the offer?

C. WHERE A NON–BREACHING PLAINTIFF CONFERRED A BENEFIT BUT CANNOT PROVE LOST EXPECTANCY

BAUSCH & LOMB, INC. v. BRESSLER

United States Court of Appeals, Second Circuit, 1992.
977 F.2d 720.

WALKER, CIRCUIT JUDGE: *distributor*

This case involves Bausch & Lomb, Inc.'s ("B & L") claims for damages arising from the alleged breach by Sonomed Technology, Inc. ("Sonomed") of a contract whereby B & L agreed to purchase and distribute ophthalmic diagnostic instruments manufactured and supplied by Sonomed. The district court, after a bench trial, entered judgment in favor of B & L in the amount of $555,000 in damages plus interest. On appeal, Sonomed attacks the judgment by challenging: (1) the finding that Sonomed, not B & L, breached the purchase and distribution agreement [and] (2) the damage award to B & L * * *. For reasons that will be discussed, we affirm the district court's * * * determination that Sonomed is liable to B & L for breach of contract. * * * However, we vacate in part the district court's damage award.

Background

* * *

Sonomed develops, manufactures and markets ultrasound devices used for ophthalmologic diagnosis. Sonomed makes two complementary products, the "A–Scan"—which measures distances in the eye—and the "B–Scan"—which provides a two-dimensional image of the eye. B & L is engaged in the optical products business, including the purchase and distribution of ophthalmic devices manufactured by other companies. On December 21, 1984, Sonomed and B & L entered into a sale and distribution agreement (the "1984 Agreement"). Under the terms of the 1984 Agreement, B & L was to become the exclusive world-wide distributor of Sonomed's A–Scan and B–Scan products for a period of three years. In return for the exclusive distributorship rights, B & L paid $500,000 to Sonomed and agreed to make annual minimum *Contract* purchases of Sonomed's products beginning in 1985.

On July 1, 1986, the parties rescinded the 1984 Agreement and entered into a new contract (the "1986 Agreement" or the "Agreement"). Among other things, the 1986 Agreement reduced the size of B & L's exclusive *reduced territory* distributorship to a territory including the United States, Puerto Rico and Canada and extended the expiration date of the distributorship until December 31, 1989, two years beyond the expiration date of the 1984 Agreement. It *+2 yrs* is the 1986 Agreement that is largely at issue in this case. Unless otherwise indicated, the contract provisions we refer to are those of the 1986 Agreement.

* * *

Section 12.07 stated that the $500,000 payment made by B & L to Sonomed in connection with the 1984 Agreement constituted a "prepaid royalty" and that "[i]n the event of any dispute with respect to this Agreement, such payment shall be deemed to be payment for exclusive distribution rights."

* * *

[In 1987, after disputes over Sonomed's violation of the terms of the agreement by selling its products in B & L's territory and over whether Sonomed could supply on time], Sonomed stated that it would no longer accept or fill product orders from B & L and intended to market Sonomed products itself. * * *

* * *

On November 30, 1987, B & L commenced this action, asserting claims for * * * breach of contract against Sonomed. * * *

Following trial, the district court entered judgment for B & L [for $555,000 in damages and interest] on * * * its breach of contract claims * * *. Specifically, the court found two separate breaches by Sonomed. First, the court determined that Sonomed breached the Agreement by selling products in B & L's exclusive territory. This claim was not challenged at trial. Sonomed's agents admitted that Sonomed sold products in B & L's territory.

Second, the district court determined that Sonomed wrongfully terminated the Agreement. * * *

* * *

Discussion

1. *Breach of Contract*

Sonomed accepts the district court's finding that, by selling Sonomed products in B & L's exclusive territory, it breached the Agreement. However, Sonomed challenges the finding that it materially breached the Agreement by wrongfully refusing to perform its contractual duties and terminating the Agreement.

* * *

[W]e affirm the district court's finding that Sonomed, not B & L, is liable for breach of the Agreement * * *.

2. *Damages*

* * * Sonomed challenges the $500,000 damage award to B & L. * * *

a. *The $500,000 Award*

At trial, B & L made claims for lost profits, and sought to prove these alleged damages by pointing to the profits Sonomed realized through its violative sales before and after Sonomed terminated the Agreement. However, B & L offered no evidence tending to prove that it would have made the same sales—or realized the same profits—as Sonomed absent Sonomed's breaches of the Agreement. New York law requires that a plaintiff prove with a reasonable degree of certainty that any claimed loss of profits was caused by the defendant's breach. * * * The district court thus denied these claims as speculative, a determination B & L does not challenge on appeal.

The district court found, as an alternative, non-speculative measure of B & L's loss the $500,000 "prepaid royalty" paid by B & L under the 1984 Agreement in return for the right to purchase and serve as exclusive distributor of Sonomed's products. The court stated that B & L was denied its full rights to exclusive distribution, first, because of Sonomed's sales in B & L's territory while the Agreement was still in force, and, second, because of Sonomed's repudiation of the Agreement. Thus, the district court reasoned, "in fairness and in accordance with the law of contract damages, the defendant Sonomed should return the $500,000."

In granting B & L the $500,000 award, the district court may have been seeking to apply the doctrine of expectation damages. This doctrine gives force to the provisions of a contract by placing the aggrieved party in the same economic position it would have been in had both parties fully performed. * * * If it awarded the $500,000 as expectation damages, we think the district court erred. Although to be sure B & L did not receive the full benefits of the distribution rights it contracted for, it does not follow that B & L would have realized a $500,000 return if the contract had been fully performed. There is simply no evidence connecting this $500,000 to any profit that B & L would have received had Sonomed fully performed the Agreement. Thus, the district court's award cannot be sustained pursuant to an expectation theory of recovery.

The district court suggested that its award of the $500,000 payment might alternatively be appropriate pursuant to the doctrine of reliance damages. Under this doctrine, a plaintiff may recover "his expenses of preparation and of part performance, as well as other foreseeable expenses incurred in reliance upon the contract." J. Calimari & J. Perillo, Contracts § 14–9, at 603 (3d ed. 1987); see also L. Albert & Son v. Armstrong Rubber Co., 178 F.2d 182, 190–91 (2d Cir.1949). However, the alternative reliance "measure of damages rests on the premise that the injured party's reliance interest is no greater than the party's expectation interest." 3 E.A. Farnsworth, Farnsworth on Contracts § 12.16, at 265 (2d ed. 1990). And courts will not "knowingly put the plaintiff [receiving a reliance recovery] in a better position than he would have occupied had the contract been fully performed." Fuller & Perdue, The Reliance Interest in Contract Damages (Pt. 1), 46 Yale L.J. 52, 59 (1936); see L. Albert & Son, 178 F.2d at 191. Thus, a reliance recovery will be offset by the amount of "any loss that the party in breach can prove with reasonable certainty the injured party would have suffered had the contract been fully performed." Restatement (Second) of Contracts § 349 (1979); see Farash v. Sykes Datatronics, Inc., 59 N.Y.2d 500, 504, 465 N.Y.S.2d 917, 919, 452 N.E.2d 1245, 1247 (1983). If the breaching party establishes that the plaintiff's losses upon full performance would have equalled or exceeded its reliance expenditures, the plaintiff will recover nothing under a reliance theory.

The district court did not address the "losing contract" limitation upon awards of reliance damages, and thus, as far as we can tell, did not examine what revenues B & L would have received absent Sonomed's breach. Portions of the district court opinion, in fact, seem to offer support for Sonomed's contention on appeal that the Agreement was a losing contract for B & L, entitling Sonomed to an offset of all or part of the $500,000 payment under a reliance theory. The district court found that during 1987 B & L was having difficulty selling Sonomed products, was engaged in a "massive crash sales operation" and was discounting its prices by as much as 40 percent. We see no justification on this record for an award of the $500,000 as reliance damages.

We believe, however, that B & L may be entitled to a damage award by way of restitution, a remedies doctrine not addressed by the district court. * * * The doctrine of restitution is premised upon the equitable principle that "[a] person who has been unjustly enriched at the expense of another is required to make restitution to the other." Restatement of Restitution § 1 (1937). Upon a demonstration that a defendant is liable for material breach, the plaintiff may recover "the reasonable value of services rendered, goods delivered, or property conveyed less the reasonable value of any counter-performance received by him." Calimari & Perillo, supra, § 15–4, at 651; see United States v. Zara Contracting Co., 146 F.2d 606, 610 (2d Cir.1944); Farash, 59 N.Y.2d at 506, 465 N.Y.S.2d at 920, 452 N.E.2d at 1248. Because the doctrine of restitution looks to the reasonable value of any benefit conferred upon the defendant by the plaintiff, and is not governed by the terms of the parties' agreement, restitution is available even if the plaintiff would have lost money on the contract if it had been fully performed. * * *

Following a restitution theory, B & L would be entitled to recover as much of the $500,000 payment it made to Sonomed as it can show unjustly enriched Sonomed. We reject Sonomed's contention that an award of any portion of the $500,000 payment is precluded by the terms of the Agreement which states that the prepaid royalty "under no circumstances is refundable to B & L". The terms of the Agreement do not control an award of restitution.

However, restitution does not permit B & L to recover the entire $500,000 payment. B & L paid the $500,000 for the right to distribute Sonomed products over the duration of both agreements and it had that right from early 1985 (under the rescinded 1984 Agreement) until Sonomed's termination of the Agreement in 1987. These several years of distribution rights constitute a benefit the value of which must be offset against the $500,000 paid.

In order to determine how much of the $500,000 payment Sonomed must pay to B & L under a restitution theory, the district court must ascribe a value to the distribution right B & L enjoyed for the years preceding the Agreement's termination and then use it as an offset to the $500,000. As set forth above, the reasonable value of the benefit unjustly received, not the contract price, determines the amount of an award in restitution. However, the contract may provide probative evidence of the value of the benefit. See United States v. Western States Mechanical Contractors, Inc., 834 F.2d 1533, 1552 (10th Cir.1987); Constantino v. American S/T Achilles, 580 F.2d 121, 122–23 (4th Cir.1978); Calimari & Perillo, supra, § 15–4, at 652. Indeed, in the absence of a readily available market price, the value that the parties ascribed to a benefit in their contract may be the best valuation measure available to the court. See, e.g., 12 S. Williston & W.H.E. Jaeger, Williston on

Contracts §§ 1480, 1482 (3d ed. 1970) (contract price is important evidence of value of performance to defendant).

It may be that the $500,000 price that B & L agreed to pay and Sonomed agreed to accept for the exclusive right to distribute Sonomed products for an approximately five year period—from the commencement of the 1984 Agreement until the date set for termination of the Agreement—offers the best evidence available of the reasonable value of the right. If the district court on remand determines this to be the case, it would then be appropriate to pro-rate the $500,000 to determine the value of the right actually received and exercised by B & L.

The district court should also take into account the fact that B & L did not receive the exclusive distributorship promised by Sonomed in the Agreement. As set forth above, Sonomed sold its products in various parts of B & L's exclusive territory even before it terminated the Agreement. These violative sales may have diminished the value of the benefit B & L received, although it may be difficult to calculate the amount of the diminution. The profits Sonomed obtained through its violative sales may, however, provide some evidence of the diminished value of the distribution right.

We thus vacate this portion of the district court's award and direct the court on remand to grant a restitutionary award to B & L consistent with this opinion.

* * *

Conclusion

For the reasons set forth above, the judgment of the district court is affirmed in part and vacated in part and remanded for further proceedings consistent with this opinion.

OSTEEN v. JOHNSON

Colorado Court of Appeals, 1970.
473 P.2d 184.

DUFFORD, JUDGE. * * *

This was an action for breach of an oral contract. Trial was to the court, which found that the plaintiffs had paid the sum of $2,500. In exchange, the defendant had agreed to "promote" the plaintiffs' daughter, Linda Osteen, as a singer and composer of country-western music. More specifically, it was found that the defendant had agreed to advertise Linda through various mailings for a period of one year; to arrange and furnish the facilities necessary for Linda to record several songs; to prepare two records from the songs recorded; to press and mail copies of one of the records to disc jockeys throughout the country; and, if the first record met with any success, to press and mail out copies of the second record.

The trial court further found that the defendant did arrange for several recording sessions, at which Linda recorded four songs. A record was prepared of two of the songs, and 1,000 copies of the record were then pressed. Of the pressed records, 340 copies were mailed to disc jockeys, 200 were sent to the plaintiffs, and the remainder were retained by the defendant. Various mailings were made to advertise Linda; flyers were sent to disc jockeys throughout the country; and Linda's professional name was advertised in trade magazines. The record sent out received a favorable review and a high rating in a trade magazine.

Upon such findings the trial court concluded that the defendant had substantially performed the agreement. However, a judgment was entered in favor of the plaintiffs in the sum of $1.00 and costs on the basis that the defendant had wrongfully caused the name of another party to appear on the label of the record as co-author of a song which had been written solely by Linda. The trial court also ordered the defendant to deliver to the plaintiffs certain master tapes and records in the defendant's possession.

1. RIGHT OF RESTITUTION

Although plaintiffs' reasons are not clearly defined, they argue here that the award of damages is inadequate, and that the trial court erred in concluding that the defendant had substantially performed the agreement. However, no evidence was presented during the trial of the matter upon which an award of other than nominal damages could be based. In our opinion, the remedy which plaintiffs proved and upon which they can rely is that of restitution. See 5 A. Corbin, Contracts § 996. This remedy is available where there has been a contract breach of vital importance, variously defined as a substantial breach or a breach which goes to the essence of the contract. See 5 A. Corbin, Contracts § 1104, where the author writes:

> "In the case of a breach by non-performance, * * * the injured party's alternative remedy by way of restitution depends upon the extent of the non-performance by the defendant. The defendant's breach may be nothing but a failure to perform some minor part of his contractual duty. Such a minor non-performance is a breach of contract and an action for damages can be maintained. The injured party, however, can not maintain an action for restitution of what he has given the defendant unless the defendant's non-performance is so material that it is held to go to the 'essence'; it must be such a breach as would discharge the injured party from any further contractual duty on his own part. Such a vital breach by the defendant operates, with respect to the right of restitution, in the same way that a repudiation of the contractual obligation would operate. A minor breach by one party does not discharge the contractual duty of the other party; and the latter being still bound to perform as agreed can not be entitled to the restitution of payments already made by him or to the value of other part performances rendered."

This rule is modified somewhat where the damages which might have been awarded would be difficult or impossible to determine or inadequate. * * *

2. BREACH OF CONTRACT

The essential question here then becomes whether any breach on the part of the defendant is substantial enough to justify the remedy of restitution. Plaintiffs argue that the defendant breached the contract in the following ways: First, the defendant did not promote Linda for a period of one year as agreed; secondly, the defendant wrongfully caused the name of another party to appear on the label as co-author of the song which had been composed solely by Linda; and thirdly, the defendant failed to press and mail out copies of the second record as agreed.

The first argument is not supported by the record. Plaintiffs brought the action within the one-year period for which the contract was to run. There was no evidence that during this period the defendant had not continued to promote Linda through the use of mailings and advertisements. Quite obviously the mere fact that the one-year period had not ended prior to the commencement of the action does not justify the conclusion that the defendant had breached the agreement. Plaintiffs' second argument overlooks the testimony offered on behalf of the defendant that listing the other party as co-author of the song would make it more likely that the record would be played by disc jockeys.

The plaintiffs' third argument does, however, have merit. It is clear from the record and the findings of the trial court that the first record had met with some success. It is also clear that copies of the second record were neither pressed nor mailed out. In our opinion the failure of the defendant to press and mail out copies of the second record after the first had achieved some success constituted a substantial breach of the contract and, therefore, justifies the remedy of restitution. * * * Both parties agree that the essence of their contract was to publicize Linda as a singer of western songs and to make her name and talent known to the public. Defendant admitted and asserted that the primary method of achieving this end was to have records pressed and mailed to disc jockeys. * * *

* * *

3. DETERMINING DAMAGES

It is clear that the defendant did partially perform the contract and, under applicable law, should be allowed compensation for the reasonable value of his services. See 5 A. Corbin, Contracts § 1114, where the author writes:

> "[A]ll courts are in agreement that restitution by the defendant will not be enforced unless the plaintiff returns in some way what he has received as a part performance by the defendant."

It shall, therefore, be the ultimate order of this court that prior to restoring to the plaintiffs the $2,500 paid by them to the defendant further proceedings be held during which the trial court shall determine the reasonable value of the services which the defendant rendered on plaintiffs' behalf.

The judgment is reversed, and this case is remanded with directions that a new trial be held to determine the one issue of the amount to which the plaintiffs are entitled by way of restitution. Such amount shall be the $2,500 paid by plaintiffs to defendant less the reasonable value of the services which the defendant performed on behalf of plaintiffs.

Note
The Importance of Formal Written Contracts

The Osteens paid $500 to Johnson in advance and $2000 at Linda's first rehearsal. The Osteens' brief to the Supreme Court of Colorado reports that at the time the Osteens paid Johnson (also known as "Little Richie Johnson") they requested a written contract. Little Richie told them that "he did not write out contracts and that if his word was not as good as a contract, he didn't even want to make one." (page 4) How should the Osteens have responded?

D. WHERE THE PLAINTIFF HAS CONFERRED A BENEFIT BUT THE CONTRACT IS INVALID, FRUSTRATED, OR OTHERWISE UNENFORCEABLE

Restitutionary relief may be granted to a party whose agreement is unenforceable. For example, suppose B agrees to convey certain land to A, and, in anticipation, A, who is in possession, improves the land. Even if the parties' agreement is unenforceable, e.g., for lack of consideration, for indefiniteness, or for lack of a writing, and even if A cannot recover on the theory of promissory estoppel (assume, for example, that B should not reasonably have expected A to rely on B's promise to convey), A may be able to recover on unjust enrichment grounds. The substantive requirements for recovery were presented in Section Four of Chapter Two. See especially Kearns v. Andree (page 122). The difficulties of measuring A's recovery (market value of improvements, cost to A, increase in the market value of land, or some other measure) are similar to the problems of measuring the benefit in the other contexts presented in this section.

In Chapters Eight and Nine, we will see that restitution is also sometimes available after still other grounds of disruption. Grounds of disruption studied in Chapter Eight include mistake, impossibility, impracticability and frustration. Chapter Nine considers restitutionary and other remedies available for such grounds of disruption.

E. WHERE THE PLAINTIFF HAS MATERIALLY BROKEN THE CONTRACT AFTER CONFERRING A BENEFIT

A plaintiff who has committed an uncured material breach of contract (see Chapter Seven) cannot recover on a contract theory (agreement with consideration). Nevertheless, the plaintiff may have conferred a benefit on the defendant and it may be unjust for the defendant to retain the benefit, in whole or in part. In a proper case, our law permits such a plaintiff to have restitutionary relief premised on the prevention of unjust enrichment. At this point, you may profitably review Britton v. Turner (page 132) and De Leon v. Aldrete (page 136).

Problem 3–16

Assume that A contracts to make repairs to B's building in exchange for a promise by B to pay $10,000 for this work. A expends $8,000 making repairs but inadvertently fails to follow the specifications so that he does not substantially perform and therefore cannot recover his expectancy "in contract." Assume that to correct the defects a large portion of the repairs would have to be redone. Nevertheless, A's work has increased the value of the building by $4,000. B can hire another contractor for $9,000 to complete the work promised by A. B has not yet paid A anything. How much should A recover? $8,000? $4,000? $1,000? Nothing? Does the unjust enrichment theory for imposing liability on B suggest an answer? Comment b to section 374 of the Restatement (Second) Contracts, on restitution in favor of a party in breach, states:

> Since the party seeking restitution is responsible for posing the problem of measurement of benefit, doubts will be resolved against him, and his recovery will not exceed the less generous of the two measures stated in [§ 371], that of the other party's increase in wealth. * * * If no value can be put on this, he cannot recover. * * * Although the contract price is evidence of the benefit, it is not conclusive. However, in no case will the party in breach be allowed to recover more than a ratable portion of the total contract price where such portion can be determined.

Do you agree with the approach of the Restatement?

SECTION NINE: SPECIFIC PERFORMANCE

KITCHEN v. HERRING

Supreme Court of North Carolina, 1851.
42 N.C. 190.

PEARSON, J. In December 1846, the defendant, Herring, executed a contract in writing in these words, "Rec'd. of John L. Kitchen payment in full for a certain tract of land lying on the southwest side of Black River, adjoining the lands of William Haffland and Martial, for which I am to give him a good deed etc." The defendant Pridgen wrote the contract and is a subscribing witness. The plaintiff was put into possession in March 1847. Pridgen united with him; and the other defendant, Musgrove, under a contract with Pridgen, with a large number of hands, commenced cutting down the timber, which constitutes the chief value of the land. Pridgen was the surety of the plaintiff, to a note of $325, given payable at three months for the price of the land. In January, Herring executed a deed for the land to Pridgen, and under this title the plaintiff was turned out of possession.

The prayer of the Bill is for a specific performance, for an account of the profits and for an injunction. After the Bill was filed, an arrangement was made, by which Musgrove continued his operations in getting timber, and agreed to account with the successful party. * * *

* * *

It was * * * insisted, that, as it appears by the plaintiff's own showing, that "the land is chiefly valuable on account of the timber," this case does not come within the principle, on which a specific performance is decreed.

The position is new, and the Counsel admitted, that there was no authority to sustain it, but he contended with earnestness, that it was so fully sustained by "the reason of the thing," as to justify a departure from a well settled rule of this Court, under the maxim, *cessante ratione cessat lex.*

The argument failed wholly to prove, that "the reason of the thing" called for an exception. The principle in regard to land was adopted, not because it was fertile or rich in minerals or *valuable for timber,* but simply because it was land—a favorite and favored subject in England, and every country of Anglo Saxon origin. Our constitution gives to land preeminence over every other species of property; and our law, whether administered in

Courts of law or of equity, gives to it the same preference. Land, whether rich or poor, cannot be taken to pay debts until the personal property is exhausted. Contracts concerning land must be in writing. Land must be sold at the Court House, must be conveyed by deeds duly registered, and other instances "too tedious to mention." The principle is, that land is *assumed* to have a peculiar value, so as to give an equity for a specific performance, without reference to its quality or quantity. * * * [I]n regard to other property, less favored, a specific performance will not be decreed, unless there be peculiar circumstances; for, if with the money, an article of the same description can be bought in market—corn, cotton, etc., the remedy at law is adequate.

There must be a decree for the plaintiff with costs.

Note
Remedial Rights Under a Contract for the Sale of Land

According to the general view today (stated in Kitchen v. Herring), a vendee of land is entitled to specific performance (absent a defense). The theory is that land is inherently unique and thus damages cannot be an adequate remedy. (In addition to specific performance, the vendee can also recover money damages for any delay. Daves v. Potter, 92 Wash.App. 1047 (1998)). There are a few qualifications to the vendee's right to specific performance, however. For example, if, before performance of a contract to sell land, the vendor contracts to convey the same land to a bona fide purchaser, courts generally hold that the first vendee is entitled only to damages and that the subsequent bona fide purchaser has the right to the land, i.e., to specific performance. But the court may impose a "constructive trust" in favor of the first vendee on the vendor's proceeds from the second sale. Thus if the first sale's contract price was $20,000 (which, let us assume, was also the market price on the date of performance), and the vendor sold to the second vendee for $23,000, the first vendee may recover the $3,000. See, e.g., Timko v. Useful Homes Corp., 114 N.J.Eq. 433, 168 A. 824 (1933).

The Supreme Court of Idaho has announced a different rule on the vendee's right to specific performance. That court will grant specific performance only to a vendee who can show some "particular, unique purpose" for which he or she wanted the land. See Watkins v. Paul, 95 Idaho 499, 511 P.2d 781 (1973).

Many courts also grant specific performance for the unpaid purchase price to disappointed vendors of land (through "money decrees"). Jackson v. Schultz, 38 Del.Ch. 332, 151 A.2d 284 (1959). The theory, of course, is not that money is inherently unique. Rather, one theory (now largely discredited) is that "equality is equity"; since the vendee of land is entitled to specific performance, the vendor should have the same right. Another theory is that the value of land is too speculative and the vendor will be unable to prove damages. Note that when a court grants a vendor specific performance in the form of a money decree for the unpaid purchase price, the court may condition enforcement of the decree on the vendor's tender of the deed or the vendor's deposit of the deed with the clerk of the court for delivery to the vendee. In this way, the court may secure "mutuality of performance."

In addition to specific performance, the vendor in most states has a further remedy—an action at law for the unpaid balance of the purchase price. Again, the court can ensure that the vendor tenders a deed before payment by issuing a conditional stay of execution. The modern abolition of differences between law and equity reduces the circumstances in which a vendor might prefer this remedy over a money decree for specific performance. This topic is treated in courses on property.

Suppose the vendor grants possession to the vendee under a land sale contract providing for the vendee to make periodic payments on the price. After making some of the payments, the vendee repudiates the agreement. In many states, the vendor can both retake possession of the land and retain the payments. (But see De Leon v. Aldrete, at page 136.) It should be obvious that this remedy of the vendor may produce harsh results when the payments exceed the rental value. Such remedies are also treated in property courses.

CURTICE BROTHERS CO. v. CATTS

Court of Chancery of New Jersey, 1907.
72 N.J.Eq. 831, 66 A. 935.

Complainant is engaged in the business of canning tomatoes and seeks the specific performance of a contract wherein defendant agreed to sell to complainant the entire product of certain land planted with tomatoes. Defendant contests the power of this court to grant equitable relief.

LEAMING, V.C. The fundamental principles which guide a court of equity in decreeing the specific performance of contracts are essentially the same whether the contracts relate to realty or to personalty. By reason of the fact that damages for the breach of contract for the sale of personalty are, in most cases, easily ascertainable and recoverable at law, courts of equity in such cases withhold equitable relief. Touching contracts for the sale of land, the reverse is the case. But no inherent difference between real estate and personal property controls the exercise of the jurisdiction. Where no adequate remedy at law exists, specific performance of a contract touching the sale of personal property will be decreed with the same freedom as in the case of a contract for the sale of land. Prof. Pomeroy, in referring to the distinction, says: "In applying these principles, taking into account the discretionary nature of the jurisdiction an agreement for the sale of land is prima facie presumed to come within their operation, so as to be subject to specific performance, but a contrary presumption exists in regard to agreements concerning chattels." Pomeroy on Contracts, Specific Performance, § 11.

Judge Story urges that there is no reasonable objection to allowing the party who is injured by the breach of any contract for the sale of chattels to have an election either to take damages at law or to have a specific performance in equity. 2 Story's Eq. Juris. (13th Ed.) § 717a. While it is probable that the development of this branch of equitable remedies is decidedly toward the logical solution suggested by Judge Story, it is entirely clear that his view cannot at this time be freely adopted without violence to what has long been regarded as accepted principles controlling the discretion of a court of equity in this class of cases. The United States Supreme Court has probably most nearly approached the view suggested by Judge Story. In Mechanics' Bank of Alexandria v. Seton, 1 Pet. (U.S.) 229, 305, 7 L.Ed. 152, Mr. Justice Thompson, delivering the opinion of that court, says: "But, notwithstanding this distinction between personal contracts for goods and contracts for lands is to be found laid down in the books, as a general rule; yet there are many cases to be found where specific performance of contracts, relating to personalty, have been enforced in chancery; and courts will only view with greater nicety contracts of this description than such as relate to land." See, also, Barr v. Lapsley, 1 Wheat. (U.S.) 151, 4 L.Ed. 58. In our own state contracts for the sale of chattels have been frequently enforced and the inadequacy of the remedy at law, based on the characteristic features of the contract or peculiar situation and needs of the parties, have been the principal grounds of relief. * * *

I think it clear that the present case falls well within the principles defined by the cases already cited from our own state. Complainants' factory has a capacity of about 1,000,000 cans of tomatoes. The season for packing lasts about six weeks. The preparations made for this six weeks of active work must be carried out in all features to enable the business to succeed. These preparations are primarily based upon the capacity of the plant. Cans and other necessary equipments, including labor, must be provided and secured in advance with reference to the capacity of the plant during the packing period. With this known capacity and an estimated average yield of tomatoes per acre the acreage of land necessary to supply the plant is calculated. To that end, the contract now in question was made, with other like contracts, covering a sufficient acreage to insure the essential pack. It seems immaterial whether the entire acreage is contracted for to insure the full pack, or whether a more limited acreage is contracted for and an estimated available open market depended upon for the balance of the pack. In either case a refusal of the parties who contract to supply a given acreage to comply with their contracts leaves the factory helpless, except to whatever extent an uncertain market may perchance supply the deficiency. The condition which arises from the breach of the contracts is not merely a question of the factory being compelled to pay a higher price for the product. Losses sustained in that manner could, with some degree of accuracy, be estimated. The condition which occasions the irreparable injury by reason of the breaches of the contracts is the inability to procure at any price at the time needed and of the quality needed, the necessary tomatoes to insure the successful operation of the plant. If it should be assumed as a fact that upon the breach of contracts of this nature other tomatoes of like quality and quantity could be procured in the open market without serious interference with the economic arrangements of the plant, a court of equity would hesitate to assume to interfere; but the very existence of such contracts proclaims their necessity to the economic management of the factory. The aspect of the situation bears no resemblance to that of an ordinary contract for the sale of merchandise in the course of an ordinary business. The business and its needs are extraordinary in that the maintenance of all of the conditions prearranged to secure the pack are a necessity to insure the successful operation of the plant. The breach of the contract by one planter differs but in degree from a breach by all.

The objection that to specifically perform the contract personal services are required will not divest the court of its powers to preserve the benefits of the contract. Defendant may be restrained from selling the crop to others, and, if necessary, a receiver can be appointed to harvest the crop.

A decree may be advised pursuant to the prayer of the bill.

By reason of the manner in which the facts on which this opinion is based were stipulated, no costs will be taxed.

UNIFORM COMMERCIAL CODE § 2–716
Buyer's Right to Specific Performance or Replevin

(1) Specific performance may be decreed where the goods are unique or in other proper circumstances.

(2) The decree for specific performance may include such terms and conditions as to payment of the price, damages, or other relief as the court may deem just.

REVISED UNIFORM COMMERCIAL CODE § 2–716
Discussion Draft, April 2000

(a) Specific performance may be decreed where the goods are unique or in other proper circumstances. In a contract other than a consumer contract, specific performance may be decreed if the parties have agreed to that remedy. However, even if the parties agree to specific performance, specific performance may not be decreed if the breaching party's sole remaining contractual obligation is the payment of money.

Note
Enforcement of Specific Performance Decrees

Decrees for specific performance are enforced differently from decrees or judgments for damages. If a defendant against whom a judgment for damages has been entered refuses to pay the judgment, the clerk of the court will issue to the plaintiff a writ of execution, which empowers the sheriff to take custody of property of the defendant, sell it, and apply the proceeds to satisfy the judgment. This process is in accordance with an elaborate scheme of rules, mostly statutory.

What if a defendant against whom a decree of specific performance is entered fails to perform as ordered? Where the performance calls for a ministerial act, such as the execution of a deed, statutes in most states provide either that the decree will *automatically operate* as if the defendant had performed or that an officer of the court, such as a sheriff, will carry out the act required of the defendant (e.g., execution of the deed). Such statutes thus modify the traditional doctrine that a decree of specific performance operates only "in personam" to coerce the defendant personally to perform upon threat of imprisonment or fine for "contempt" of the decree.

Even when the decree calls for the defendant to perform an act that is not ministerial, the court's procedures of enforcement may go beyond coercing the defendant. Thus, the plaintiff may ignore the defendant's failure to perform and ask the court to appoint a "receiver" or other officer of the court to carry out the contract. See, again, the reference to a receiver in Curtice Brothers Co. v. Catts.

In still other cases, the act involved will be neither ministerial nor one that can otherwise be performed satisfactorily by an actor, such as a receiver, substituting for the defendant. What if the defendant refuses to obey such a decree? The plaintiff may then initiate a "show-cause" proceeding in which the defendant must show cause why he or she should not be cited for contempt of the court's decree and subjected to imprisonment or a fine. In such a show-cause proceeding, the defendant may assert various defenses such as that he complied with the decree, or that the decree was too vague, or that he could not comply because of changed circumstances. The risk of non-persuasion in such a proceeding typically rests on the defendant, who sometimes must meet a standard of proof that is somewhat higher than "a preponderance of the evidence," yet is below "beyond a reasonable doubt." If the court finds the defendant to be in contempt of the decree, the court has power to imprison the defendant. The usual theory of such imprisonment is not punitive. Rather, it is to coerce the defendant to comply with the decree. As the United States Supreme Court has said, when such a defendant goes to jail, he "carries the keys to his freedom in his willingness to comply with the court's directive." Uphaus v. Wyman, 360 U.S. 72 (1959). One (of several) important limitations on a court's power to imprison for contempt is the constitutional or statutory prohibition (in most states) against imprisonment for nonpayment of debt.

A second sanction for contempt is a fine. Again, the usual theory of this sanction is not to punish, but rather to coerce compliance or to provide direct reparation to the plaintiff (in which case the amount will be measured by the injury caused by the failure to satisfy the decree). A court may, for example, impose a fine of so many dollars per day, until the defendant complies.

The foregoing uses of imprisonment and fines to bring about compliance with the decree are classic illustrations of the ancient maxim that a decree of specific performance may be enforced "in personam"—against the person of the defendant. The enforcement of decrees is treated in D. Dobbs, Remedies 130–62 (1993).

STEPHAN'S MACHINE & TOOL, INC. v. D & H MACHINERY CONSULTANTS, INC., 65 Ohio App.2d 197, 417 N.E.2d 579 (1979). [Plaintiff bought a machine from defendant, borrowing $96,000 to pay for it. The machine failed to function. Defendant agreed to replace the machine but failed to do so. Plaintiff was unable to raise the money to buy a replacement elsewhere, although such machines were available. Was plaintiff entitled to specific performance of defendant's agreement to replace? Held, yes.] "The inoperable condition of machine no. 1, for which plaintiff borrowed $96,000 from Toledo Trust Company, placed an unsurmountable financial strain on plaintiff, causing a default on plaintiff's note to the bank, followed by a judgment on the renewal note. The financial circumstances of plaintiff were such that [it] is folly to contend that plaintiff could have avoided his business losses by buying a comparable boring machine from a source other than the defendant. Plaintiff, therefore, did suffer irreparable harm and had no adequate remedy at law."

LACLEDE GAS CO. v. AMOCO OIL CO., 522 F.2d 33 (8th Cir.1975). [Laclede and Amoco entered into a long-term written agreement designed to provide central propane gas distribution systems to various residential developments in Jefferson County, Missouri, until such time as natural gas mains were extended into those areas. The agreement contemplated that, as individual developments were planned, the owners or developers would apply to Laclede for central propane gas systems. If Laclede determined that a system was appropriate in a given development, it could request Amoco to supply the propane to that development. Laclede's request was made in the form of a supplemental form letter, as provided in the agreement, and if Amoco decided to supply the propane, it agreed to do so by signing this supplemental form. When Amoco terminated the agreement, Laclede sought specific performance.]

Ross, C.J.

[I]n Missouri, as elsewhere, specific performance may be ordered even though personalty is involved in the "proper circumstances." Mo.Rev.Stat. § 400.2–716(1); Restatement of Contracts, § 361. And a remedy at law adequate to defeat the grant of specific performance "must be as certain, prompt, complete, and efficient to attain the ends of justice as a decree of specific performance." * * *

One of the leading Missouri cases allowing specific performance of a contract relating to personalty because the remedy at law was inadequate is *Boeving v. Vandover,* 240 Mo.App. 117, 218 S.W.2d 175, 178 (1949). In that case the plaintiff sought specific performance of a contract in which the defendant had promised to sell him an automobile. At that time (near the end of World War II) new cars were hard to come by, and the court held that specific performance was a proper remedy since a new car "could not be obtained elsewhere except at considerable expense, trouble or loss, which cannot be estimated in advance."

We are satisfied that Laclede has brought itself within this practical approach taken by the Missouri courts. As Amoco points out, Laclede has propane immediately available to it under other contracts with other suppliers. And the evidence indicates that at the present time propane is readily available on the open market. However, this analysis ignores the fact that the contract involved in this lawsuit is for a long-term supply of propane to these subdivisions. The other two contracts under which Laclede obtains the gas will remain in force only until March 31, 1977, and April 1, 1981, respectively; and there is no assurance that Laclede will be able to receive any propane under them after that time. Also it is unclear as to whether or not Laclede can use the propane obtained under these contracts to supply the Jefferson County subdivisions, since they were originally entered into to provide Laclede with propane with which to "shave" its natural gas supply during peak demand periods.[1] Additionally, there was uncontradicted expert testimony that Laclede probably could not find another supplier of propane willing to enter into a long-term contract such as the Amoco agreement, given the uncertain future of world-wide energy supplies. And, even if Laclede could obtain supplies of propane for the affected developments through its present contracts or newly negotiated ones, it would still face considerable expense and trouble which cannot be estimated in advance in making arrangements for its distribution to the subdivisions.

Specific performance is the proper remedy in this situation, and it should be granted by the district court.

E. FARNSWORTH, CONTRACTS
773 (3d ed. 1999).

The tendency is, however, to liberalize the granting of specific performance and injunction by enlarging the classes of cases in which damages are

---

1. During periods of cold weather, when demand is high, Laclede does not receive enough natural gas to meet all this demand. It, therefore, adds propane to the natural gas it places in its distribution system. This practice is called "peak shaving."

regarded as an inadequate remedy. The contemporary approach is to compare remedies to determine which is more effective in affording suitable protection to the injured party's legally recognized interest, which is usually that party's expectation interest. The concept of adequacy has thus tended to become relative, and the comparison more often leads to granting equitable relief than was historically the case.

Note
Defenses to and Limitations on Availability
of Specific Performance

We have seen that specific performance is available only if the remedy at law is inadequate. In addition, there are numerous other defenses to and limitations on specific performance. We will consider most of the major ones here. Although such a defense or limitation is applicable to bar specific performance, the plaintiff may still usually recover any damages for contract breach.

Courts of equity, from which the remedy of specific performance emerged, were said to be "courts of conscience." Accordingly, those courts evolved a number of defenses to specific performance based on unfairness. The grounds of unfairness (many of which overlap) include sharp practice, unfair advantage taking, non-disclosure, post-contractual unconscionability, inadequacy of consideration, mistake, misrepresentation, duress, undue influence, and the like. Suppose, for example, that F is an old, ill, and illiterate farmer "who moves in a small circle." B is an experienced businessman who is acquainted with a real estate developer, D. B knows that D wishes to buy F's farm in anticipation of a general rise in the market value of real estate likely to occur because a railway is planned for the area, and that D is willing to pay above current market price for the farm. F is unaware of these facts. B offers to buy F's farm at the current market price, and persuades F not to seek advice from others. F agrees to sell to B at this price, which is much below the price D subsequently agrees to pay B for the land. F learns all the facts and refuses to perform. B sues for specific performance and F defends on the ground of unfairness. In a leading case, Wollums v. Horsley, 93 Ky. 582, 20 S.W. 781 (1892), this defense carried the day on facts similar to those posed. See also Chapter Five, infra.

A second defense is sometimes called "lack of mutuality of performance." The essence of this defense is that a court will not grant specific performance to P unless D can be reasonably assured of receiving the return performance for which he has contracted. Suppose D contracts to build custom-made logging equipment for P in accord with detailed specifications, P to pay $5,000 down, $10,000 at the halfway point, and $25,000 on completion. After P has paid $5,000 and D has begun work, D repudiates and P seeks specific performance. D defends on the ground that P's financial position is shaky. The court may grant P a decree of specific performance on condition that P post a bond satisfactory to the court. If P cannot post the bond, specific performance will be denied. The Restatement (Second) of Contracts deals with this defense in section 363.

Still another important defense is based on indefiniteness of the agreement. See Linderkamp v. Hoffman, 562 N.W.2d 734 (N.D.1997). A contract may not be invalid on this ground, yet be too indefinite to serve as the basis for a decree of specific performance. If a contract is too indefinite, the court cannot draft with precision a decree ordering performance of the contract. It would, of course, be unfair to hold a party in contempt for failing to abide by an imprecise decree of specific performance. For example, B contracts to build a "first class theater" on land he is to buy from P, which theater will enhance the value of P's land. P cannot get specific performance of this promise, although he may get damages for B's failure to enhance P's land value. Cf. Bettancourt v. Gilroy Theatre Co., 120 Cal.App.2d 364, 261 P.2d 351 (1953).

A related defense is sometimes called "impracticability of performance," or "difficulty in enforcement or supervision." Some of the flavor of this defense is captured in the following quotation from a case in which specific performance was denied: "It must, I think, be conceded that the items of renovation and construction work are numerous and noticeably diversified. Moreover, by their nature they are such as to render their actual performance and accomplishment provocative of frequent disputes. The difficulty in supervision that would be necessary is obvious." Lester's Home Furnishers, Inc. v. Modern Furniture Co., 1 N.J.Super. 365, 370–71, 61 A.2d 743, 746 (1948).

Courts will not grant specific performance of a contract to provide personal services. Pingley v. Brunson, 272 S.C. 421, 252 S.E.2d 560 (1979) (specific performance of contract to play music at plaintiff's restaurant denied). What reasons might be given to justify this limitation? If, however, the plaintiff can show that a party has agreed to provide "unique" personal services, this party may be enjoined from providing those services to a third person, at least where the contract includes a covenant not to render such services to a third person. Dallas Cowboys Football Club, Inc. v. Harris, 348 S.W.2d 37 (Tex.Civ.App.1961) (injunction prohibiting James B. Harris from playing for Dallas Texans of newly organized American Football League).

In the employer-employee context, the personal services limitation generally operates to preclude granting specific performance to either party. Felch v. Findlay College, 119 Ohio App. 357, 200 N.E.2d 353 (1963) (employer could not be forced to reinstate faculty member even if discharged in breach of contract). However, labor law statutes, cases, and collective bargaining agreements may provide that an employer must grant reinstatement on request after wrongful dismissal. Such agreements may be specifically enforceable. 5A Corbin on Contracts § 1204 at 403–04 (1964). In addition, courts can reinstate an employee when an employer intentionally engages in an "unlawful employment practice" under 42 U.S.C. § 2000e–5(g) (1988).

Suppose the seller of real estate is unable to convey precisely what was promised. For example, suppose an acreage deficiency or an encumbrance on the title. Many courts will grant specific performance to the purchaser with an abatement in the purchase price corresponding to the value of the defect. However, if the deficiency is sufficiently material so that the abatement would be a large portion of the contract price, specific performance may be denied. Ide v. Joe Miller & Co., 703 P.2d 590 (Colo.App.1984).

PRATT FURNITURE CO. v. McBEE

Supreme Court of Hampshire, 1987.
337 H.2d 119.

BODWEIS, J. This case comes to us on appeal from a decision of the trial judge denying specific performance, granting general damages, and striking plaintiff's claims for punitive damages and restitution. We affirm.

Pratt Furniture Co. ("Pratt"), is a large furniture wholesaler with its main office in Burlington, Vermont. On February 10, 1984, George Pratt, President of Pratt, entered a contract with Ivan McBee, a sole proprietor in Weston, Hampshire, whereby McBee was to manufacture and sell to Pratt 90,000 chairs at $10.00 per chair, delivered July 3, 1984, at Burlington. McBee calculated that he would make $2.00 per chair on the contract or $180,000 in total profit.

On March 5, 1984, before McBee had allocated any resources to the Pratt chair order, McBee received an order for 50,000 tables at $32.00 a table from Thompson Table Co. McBee calculated that he could make and deliver the tables for $25.00 each, for a total profit of $350,000. However, McBee would have to break his chair contract with Pratt because McBee's plant could handle only one more order. Although there were several manufacturers of chairs in the area, only McBee could make the type of tables required. Before repudiating his contract with Pratt, McBee talked to his lawyer, Steven Hanks. Hanks told McBee that the damages for breaking the Pratt contract would not exceed the difference between the contract price and the market price on the date when Pratt learned of the repudiation.[1] Hanks also said: "Anytime you can make a better deal, the law lets you do so, but you have to pay off the damages you cause, of course. This is called the doctrine of efficient breach. I learned about it in law school."

McBee then calculated that in the foreseeable future the market price of the chairs he had contracted to make for Pratt would climb to at most $11.00. On that basis, McBee would owe Pratt $90,000 in damages. Deducting these damages from his expected additional $170,000 profit on the Table Co. contract, McBee would end up $80,000 ahead by breaching. McBee then decided not to perform for Pratt and so informed Pratt on March 23, 1984, when the fair market price of the chairs was $11.00. In early April, the market price of the chairs climbed to $15.50.

On April 1, Pratt brought this proceeding in the court below to enjoin McBee from making the tables, for an order of specific performance as to the chairs, and should this be denied, for general damages and restitution of the amount of profit McBee would realize on the deal with Table Co. Pratt also sought punitive damages arising from McBee's deliberate and willful breach. The trial judge denied Pratt's requests for specific relief and, after a hearing on April 10, determined that the fair market price of the chairs on March 23, the date Pratt learned of the repudiation, was in fact $11.00 a chair. Because the contract price was $10.00, the court determined that McBee owed Pratt $90,000 in damages. Accordingly, the trial judge entered judgment for this sum and denied Pratt's claims for other relief.

We affirm. Section 2–716(1) of the Uniform Commercial Code allows specific performance "where the goods are unique or in other proper circumstances." Chairs are not unique. Comment 2 to the section says that "other proper circumstances" refers mainly to "inability to cover." Pratt did not show an inability to cover. Parties have no business tying up the courts with demands for specific relief when they have ready market alternatives as here. The award of $90,000 damages was correct. There is no authority in this

---

1. In some cases the market price might be measured a reasonable time after the buyer learned of the repudiation. See U.C.C. §§ 2–610 and 2–713.

jurisdiction for requiring the willful breacher (here, McBee) to disgorge his ill-gotten gains. Nor has this court ever awarded punitive damages merely for deliberate breach. Judgment affirmed.

POSNIER, J. Concurring. I concur on a different ground from that explicitly articulated by the majority (although what they say, properly construed, really means what I am about to say here).

The result reached here is correct because it appropriately serves the social goal of increased allocative efficiency of scarce resources. Resources are allocated efficiently from one use to another whenever they are used or consumed by those who are willing to pay the most for them in the market place (unless there is a market imperfection such as a monopolistic practice). Society is better off because the resources are moved from a less to a more valuable use—i.e. the resources are used in their most productive manner.

The institution of contract in a free society is the primary (not exclusive) mechanism for the efficient allocation and reallocation of scarce resources. Contract facilitates gains from trade, as judged by the parties themselves. Value is subjective and depends on existing personal preferences of the contracting parties, given their ability and willingness to pay for the resources in question. Thomas Hobbes saw this long ago when he said: "The value of all things contracted for, is measured in the appetite of the Contractors: and therefore the just value, is that which they be contented to give."[2] Modern economists and other sound social theorists concur. For example, Ludwig von Mises, the great Austrian economist, wrote not long ago that "[t]he basis of modern economics is the cognition that it is precisely the disparity in the value attached to the objects exchanged that results in their being exchanged. People buy and sell only because they appraise the things they give up less than those received. Thus the notion of [an objective] measurement of value is vain."[3]

The rules of contract law applied by the trial judge here and affirmed by the majority facilitate allocative efficiency, and it is for this reason that I concur in the result of this appeal. Here the defendant McBee, after contracting with Pratt, had an opportunity to move his resources to an even more highly valued use by making tables instead of chairs. After breaching and paying Pratt's damages, McBee still would come out ahead, and Pratt would not be worse off. Thus, there would be a net social gain. This is precisely the correct result for contract law. As one law professor (now a judge) wrote not long ago: "If damages are limited to [expectancy loss], there will be incentive to commit breach. There should be. * * * The expectation rule thus assures that the [goods] end up where [they are] most valuable."[4] In the present case, contract law carries out its primary function, that of maintaining appropriate incentives for individuals to maximize their own personal self interest, by allowing only lost expectation damages.

It is important to see that contract law encourages efficient breach not only by adopting the lost expectation rule but also by *refusing* to grant other remedies. Thus it generally refuses specific performance. If specific perform-

2. Hobbes, The Leviathan 78 (1651, 1928 ed.).

3. L. Von Mises, Human Action: A Treatise on Economics 204 (3d ed. 1966).

4. R. Posner, Economic Analysis of Law 89–90 (2d ed. 1977). See also, R. Posner, Economic Analysis of Law 107–08 (3d ed. 1986).

ance had been granted here, Pratt would have received the resources, a less valuable use for them (unless, of course, McBee had thereafter successfully bargained with Pratt to "buy out" his right to specific performance, itself an unnecessary and therefore wasteful use of bargaining resources when specific performance could be denied in the first place). In addition, if McBee were forced to turn over his gain on the Table Co. deal to Pratt (the restitution claim) this would deter McBee from maximizing value in some cases and there would be a net social loss.[5] Also, if punitive damages were allowed, this would eat up some or all of McBee's projected gains and so, too, would thus reduce the correct incentives. It is not surprising that the rules of contract here all point in the same direction: that of encouraging efficient breach. The great advantages of efficient breach should be stressed in the law schools. It is unfortunate that courts do not explicitly recognize it. But the acts of courts speak louder than their words.

In sum, I concur. The majority reached the right result. But with respect, there is one serious flaw in the majority opinion. There is too much talk of McBee's breach being "willful" and "deliberate" and his gains "ill-gotten." My colleagues on the bench would do well to go back and read Oliver Wendell Holmes Jr.'s great critique of legal moralism in his essay "The Path of the Law."[6] They would see that Holmes understood the true nature of contract. A contract is utterly amoral. Nowhere is this more clearly revealed than in the law of remedies for breach of contract. As Holmes put it, the law simply and *merely* says to the party to a contract: "perform or pay lost expectancy damages."[7] This is the efficient result and therefore it is right and good and the law is as it should be.

RAWLZ, J., Dissenting. I dissent in part from the decision in this case and also disagree with the concurring opinion. I would not grant specific relief, but I would allow the plaintiff to recover the amount of profit McBee makes on the Table Co. deal. I would, in this type of case, require McBee to disgorge his gain because I think contracting parties should be given further incentives to perform contracts beyond what the grant of mere lost expectancy recovery affords. I fear that contract law may be becoming unduly tolerant of non-performance. It happens often enough that people are simply *unable* to perform. And there is an ever-enlarging list of recognized *legal* excuses for non-performance: unfairness, mistake, failure of presupposed conditions, impracticability, frustration of purpose, etc. Now today we are urged to acknowledge explicitly the so-called doctrine of "efficient breach," on which I will say more later. My own view is that if more people performed their contracts we would all be better off. I note, too, that there is growing scholarly opinion in support of granting restitution in some cases.[8]

Judge Posnier's concurring opinion raises more questions than it answers. First, I do not believe that it is accurate to interpret the law governing contract remedies as signifying an intent to encourage efficient breach. My

---

5. Birmingham, "Breach of Contract, Damage Measures, and Economic Efficiency," 24 Rutgers L.Rev. 273, 284 (1970).

6. Holmes, "The Path of the Law," 10 Harv.L.Rev. 456 (1897).

7. *Id.* at 462.

8. See, e.g., Friedmann, "Restitution of Benefits Obtained Through the Appropriation of Property or the Commission of a Wrong," 80 Colum.L.Rev. 504 (1980). See also Farnsworth, "Your Loss or My Gain? The Dilemma of the Disgorgement Principle in Breach of Contract," 94 Yale L.J. 1339 (1985).

view is that contract law generally favors and even encourages *performance*.[9] In modern contract law, including the new Restatement, there is great and growing emphasis on keeping the deal together, even after a material breach.[10] Moreover, in countless close cases, courts resolve issues of liability and damages (or let juries do so) in a fashion that favors the innocent party over the deliberate breacher.[11] And some contract doctrines, such as the material breach doctrine, explicitly take willfulness into account.[12]

I think Judge Posnier places too much weight on mere consistency. It is true that a whole cluster of contract remedial doctrines might be construed to be *consistent* with recognition of efficient breach: the rule confining recovery to lost expectancy, the general rule against specific performance, the rule allowing the breaching party to keep his ill-gotten gains, the general rule against punitive damages and maybe even the rule against the enforcement of penalty clauses. But consistency is one thing, affirmative supporting justification quite another. The existence of virtually all of these rules of law can be explained on other grounds. For example, the rules confining recovery to lost expectancy, barring punitive damages, and barring the enforcement of penalty clauses make contracting less hazardous, and thus encourage parties to enter into contracts in the first place. The parties know that if they are unable to perform, and their non-performance is not legally excused, they will still be responsible only for making the other party whole.

Further, specific performance may be limited for reasons other than facilitating efficient breach. For example, as a matter of history, specific performance was rarely available because of the view that such an "equitable remedy" should only be awarded when the "legal remedy" of damages was inadequate. In this way, conflicts between the court of equity and the common law courts were minimized. The efficient breach theory ignores this history.

In addition, it is questionable whether the lost expectancy measure of damages generally operates to encourage a contracting party to breach on efficiency grounds. For example, in many cases, lost expectancy includes consequential damages. These damages are often large, and when so, breach will rarely be efficient under the expectancy approach.

It also troubles me that Judge Posnier says judges "really" decide cases on the basis of the efficient breach analysis when, in fact, they do not articulate such a ground. In this very instance, the majority does not cite the efficient breach theory as a ground, although Judge Posnier seems to conclude that this is, in fact, at least one basis of the decision. Surely, if this was a basis

9. Many others read the courts the same way I do. See, e.g., Barton, "The Economic Basis of Damages for Breach of Contract," 1 J.Leg.Stud. 277, 279 (1972) ("Common law courts * * * are concerned that the damages doctrines not encourage default."). And much contract law is quite explicit to this effect. See, e.g., U.C.C. § 1–203, which provides that "Every contract or duty within this Act imposes an obligation of good faith in its performance or enforcement." See also, Marschall, "Wilfulness: A Crucial Factor in Choosing Remedies for Breach of Contract," 24 Ariz.L.Rev. 733 (1982).

10. See, e.g., Restatement (Second) of Contracts §§ 266, 267; Hillman, "Keeping The Deal Together After Material Breach—Common Law Mitigation Rules, The UCC, And The Restatement (Second) of Contracts," 47 U.Colo.L.Rev. 553 (1976).

11. See, e.g., Groves v. John Wunder Co., 205 Minn. 163, 286 N.W. 235 (1939).

12. See especially, Restatement (Second) of Contracts § 205 (and Comments). See also § 241(e); § 261 (and Comment d); § 352 (and Comment a); and § 374 (and Comment b).

for contract remedies, courts would have said so long ago. Yet one only finds a very few cases using the expression, and fewer still relying on it.[13]

Judge Posnier's efficient breach theory also ignores the reality that our law does not allow the parties to recover some damages flowing from breach. For example, in determining the efficiency of a particular breach, Judge Posnier assumes that contract damage rules measure and count all the true losses to the *aggrieved party,* yet we know that these rules explicitly fail to count all losses. Thus contract law restricts the recovery of an aggrieved party's consequential damages, such as lost profits, to those that are foreseeable and sufficiently certain. Also, contract law restricts recovery of certain costs such as attorneys' fees, and restricts recovery of pre-judgment interest. As a result, some parties will not even sue to recover lost expectancy unless the amount involved is significant and the legal requirements for recovery are clearly satisfied. In such cases, the legal system already induces an aggrieved party to swallow noncompensable yet real losses. It may well be that some of these rules should be changed, but that is not the issue I am addressing now.

The efficient breach theory fails to account for all of the *breaching party's* costs, as well. A businessperson's reputation among customers of being fair, dependable, and trustworthy, for example, suffers upon breach, especially willful breach to gain more elsewhere. Of course, the value of lost future business due to lost reputation, largely incalculable, probably itself deters many potential breaches of contract. (Relatedly, the fact that most business people think highly of those who do not break their contracts suggests that the law should not encourage breach, if the law is to reflect commercial reality.)

A rule that encourages breach may ultimately be inefficient also because it will likely lead to litigation over precisely how much the breacher must pay the aggrieved party in order to buy the right to breach. One scholar has pointed out that the efficient breach theory has

> a bias in favor of individual, uncooperative behavior as opposed to behavior requiring the cooperation of the parties. * * * The whole thrust * * * is breach first, talk afterwards * * * [however] talking after a breach may be one of the more expensive forms of conversation to be found, involving, as it so often does, engaging high-priced lawyers, and gambits like starting litigation, engaging in discovery, and even trying and appealing cases.[14]

A party like McBee contemplating "efficient" breach may be confronted with many additional questions, both of law and fact, at a time when definitive answers may be unavailable. For example, it is unclear under the Uniform Commercial Code whether, on these facts, the contract-market differential would be calculated as of the time Pratt learned of the repudiation. It might instead be calculated a reasonable time *after* Pratt learned of

---

13. Nearly all of the opinions invoking efficient breach theory have been written by Judge Richard Posner of the Federal Seventh Circuit. See, e.g., Patton v. Mid–Continent Systems, Inc., 841 F.2d 742 (7th Cir.1988); Northern Indiana Public Service Company v. Carbon County Coal Company, 799 F.2d 265 (7th Cir. 1986); Lake River Corp. v. Carborundum Co.,

769 F.2d 1284 (7th Cir.1985). See also, Friedmann, The Efficient Breach Fallacy, 18 J. Legal Stud. 1 (1989).

14. Macneil, "Efficient Breach of Contract: Circles in the Sky," 68 Virginia L.Rev. 947, 968 (1982).

the repudiation.[15] This time had not even arrived when McBee had to make his decision. Parties like McBee, to cite another example, will be faced with the prospect of uncertain and potentially large consequential damages liability when a decision whether to breach must be made. Such a decision is costly to make, and may still turn out to be in error. Thus a general rule requiring performance may be more efficient overall than a doctrine allowing parties to decide for themselves case by case whether particular breaches would be efficient.

Judge Posnier also apparently assumes that, because Pratt does not bid as high for McBee's resources as Thompson Table Co., this conclusively shows that Table Co.'s use is the highest valued use. But is this necessarily so? Suppose, for example, that Pratt was unable to bid as high as Table Co. because Pratt had already allocated resources irreversibly in reliance on the prospect of performance?[16] Suppose, for example, that after entering the contract with McBee, Pratt cancelled negotiations with other sellers, and made contracts with third parties for transportation, storage, and resale of the chairs. Because of incurring these (not wholly salvageable) costs and commitments, Pratt might not have been able to bid as high as Table Co. for McBee's resources. Thus, it is not necessarily true that Table Co. is the highest valued user. Indeed, if Pratt's deal with McBee had gone through, *Pratt* might even have made enough to pay McBee what McBee would have "lost" in not selling to Table Co. and have had something left over!

For that matter, what does "highest valued use" really mean? Does it mean highest valued *effective* use? Suppose Table Co.'s highest bid was economically irrational in the sense that it was above market price. If, as a result, Table Co. found it could not ultimately resell the tables except at a loss, can it be argued that McBee's breach and sale to Table Co. was not efficient? If so, how are parties like McBee to predict whether a third party is going to be an *effective* user or not?

Efficiency may be an important value. It means that resources will go to those who value them more highly in the sense that they can pay the most for them. But efficiency thus accepts as a given the existing distribution of wealth among individuals. In addition, efficiency conflicts with other values. As I have mentioned, it is important socially and morally for people to keep their word and for the legal system to foster trust and cooperation, not merely individualistic self-advancement.[17]

Finally, I wish to remind the majority again that if, as one professor has put it, "all existing arrangements are subject to being reordered in the interest of increased economic return," our system of exchange "would lose its anchorage and no one would occupy a sufficiently stable position to know

---

15. See U.C.C. §§ 2–610, 2–713, and J. White and R. Summers, The Uniform Commercial Code 240–52 (2d ed. 1980).

16. See Shiro, "Prospecting for Lost Profits in the Uniform Commercial Code: The Buyer's Dilemmas," 52 So.Calif.L.Rev. 1727, 1743 (1979).

17. Legal rules derive some of their significance from the extent to which they serve as standards for the evaluation of behavior that falls under them. Where those rules are themselves salutary, behavior contrary to those rules is rightly the subject of criticism. See H.L.A. Hart, The Concept of Law 88 (1961). I fear that all this talk of "efficient breach" will stifle criticism of breach of contract, and erode the sense that there is generally something objectionable about breaking contracts.

what he had to offer or what he could count on receiving from another."[18] We would not encourage theft (assuming the thief is willing to pay off the owner) in order to get property to its "highest valued user," and the economists have not told us why a party with a contract expectancy should be given any less protection than a property owner. In short, I do not believe they should be treated differently. Do we want a system in which the law positively encourages breach and thus positively discourages reliance? It seems to me this would seriously interfere with planned economic production.

I have other questions, too, but for now I urge only that the majority of this court not adopt this efficient breach idea, even as a secondary supporting justification. And I also hope the law schools are not running off with this idea without thinking more about it. I note with concern that the defendant's lawyer in this case actually seems to have given some advice based on the idea.

SECTION TEN: ALTERNATIVE DISPUTE RESOLUTION: AN INTRODUCTION

LIEBERMAN & HENRY, LESSONS FROM THE ALTERNATIVE DISPUTE RESOLUTION MOVEMENT
53 U.Chi.L.Rev. 424, 424–426 (1986).

The ADR roster includes such well-known processes as arbitration, mediation, conciliation, and, perhaps, negotiation. These processes can be used to settle existing disputes or to prevent disputes from developing. There are also new hybrid devices that borrow from courtroom procedure—including, most prominently, the mini-trial. The roster may also be expanded to include the roles played by certain officials and quasi-officials (such as court appointed masters, special masters, and neutral experts), by private persons retained as neutrals, by ombudsmen, and by private judges. Changes in procedural rules to provide incentives to the parties to settle (for example, further penalizing parties who turn down reasonable settlement offers) and the greater use of partial summary judgment might also be viewed as ADR techniques.

It is easier to point to discrete practices than to discern the entire direction of the new movement. ADR has no generally accepted abstract or theoretical definition. But it does have a fundamental premise: it is worthwhile both to reduce the costs of resolving disputes, however this can be accomplished, and to improve the quality of the final outcome. We offer a working definition of ADR as a starting point for analysis: ADR is a set of practices and techniques that aim (1) to permit legal disputes to be resolved outside the courts for the benefit of all disputants; (2) to reduce the cost of conventional litigation and the delays to which it is ordinarily subject; or (3) to prevent legal disputes that would otherwise likely be brought to the courts.

SHAVELL, ALTERNATIVE DISPUTE RESOLUTION: AN ECONOMIC ANALYSIS
24 J.Leg. Studies 1, 2–3 (1994).

* * * ADR may be adopted because it is to the mutual benefit of the parties to a contract or to those who have some other relationship with each

18. L. Fuller, The Morality of Law 28 (rev. ed. 1969).

other. * * * First, ADR may lower the cost of resolving disputes or risk. Second, ADR may engender superior incentives through greater accuracy of result or other characteristics. Suppose, for instance, that substandard performance of a contract would be correctly assessed by expert arbitrators under ADR but not by courts. Then the parties to the contract might well prefer to adopt ADR because it would induce good performance, thereby raising the willingness of the promisee to pay for the contract. Third, ADR may result in improved incentives to engage in disputes or to refrain from that. For example, it may be that the number of disputes brought under the legal process would be excessive, dissipating substantial resources of the parties without instigating mutually desirable changes in behavior; thus an ADR agreement that would serve to limit the number of disputes would be advantageous.

MENTSCHIKOFF,[e] THE SIGNIFICANCE OF ARBITRATION— A PRELIMINARY INQUIRY

17 Law & Contemp. Probs. 698, 698–704, 707, 710 (1952).

[W]hen the method of settling a dispute shifts from one of compromise to one of decision, we tend to think primarily of the court process and to overlook or discount the importance of the arbitration process or else to dismiss it as another type of compromise machinery. The thesis of this paper is that in so doing we fail to perceive the importance and generative power of the arbitration process.

* * *

The four essential aspects of arbitration are (1) it is resorted to only by agreement of the parties; (2) it is a method not of compromising disputes but of deciding them; (3) the person making the decision has no formal connection with our system of courts; but (4) before the award is known it is agreed to be "final and binding."

Inherent in the consensual character of the arbitration process is the fact that its procedure can be adjusted to fit the particular needs of the particular case or disputants. This * * * does not mean that there are no rules of evidence or of procedure or of presentation. It only means that these may and frequently do vary from those used in our formal legal system.

* * *

* * * [A]lthough there are indeed standards or criteria for decision in arbitration, they are as in matters of procedure and evidence more flexible and more dependent on the requirements of the particular case or particular disputants than we normally find in the formal legal system. Whether those

e. Soia Mentschikoff (1915–1984) was professor of law at the University of Chicago and dean at the University of Miami Law School. She was one of the drafters of the Uniform Commercial Code and served as Associate Chief Reporter of the entire Code project (1944–51). She authored Cases and Materials on Commercial Transactions (1970), and The Theory and Craft of American Law (with I. Stotzky) (1981). Her scholarly interests also included commercial arbitration. A photograph appears at page 357.

arbitration standards are as live to the needs of all-of-us as are our formal legal criteria is, however, open to question.

The fact that the person chosen to make the decision in the arbitration process is not connected with the formal legal system bears an important relation (1) to the type of proof necessary in a proceeding, (2) to the explicit criteria involved in decision, and (3) to the growth and extent of the doctrine of precedent in arbitration.

One obvious illustration of the difference in the proof necessary is the use made of experts. If the arbitrator is himself an expert the concept of "judicial notice" is automatically enlarged to cover the area of his expertness and the proof tends to become limited to the particulars of the dispute before him. This expert quality of the arbitrator may also influence the type of hearing. There is something to be said for showing an expert how a piece of machinery or a particular operation actually runs. There may even sometimes be some justification for using that showing in lieu of testimony and for limiting the hearing to argument. There clearly is no such justification in the case of a non-expert tribunal, be it judge, jury, or arbitrator.

On the question of explicit criteria for decision, the fact that the arbitrator need not be a member of any craft connected with the formal legal institution is of peculiar importance. Who would think of arguing to a lay arbitrator in a commercial case the rules of formal law alone? Obviously he is as much if not more interested, and explicitly so, in the conflict of interest which exists, the practices which are normal, the allocation of risks which parties in the business normally make, and any factor which makes the particular case materially different from the normal.

The question of criteria for decision is intimately linked with the value and use of precedent and of course conditions that use. The doctrine of precedent is not an institution peculiar to our common law. It is in essence a response to the human need in any group for reckonability and predictability of result. Who has not heard a small child say "But one time you let me," and been thereby forced into meticulous and careful distinction (if that is possible) of the prior case? It is strange to me, therefore, to hear the drums beat for arbitration on the ground that it is an "ad hoc" process without precedent value. What is really meant is that formal legal precedent formally used is not the only controlling criterion for decision. But this is no real point of departure from the formal legal system. The decided law itself has never, even in the short wooden period from about 1880 to 1910, been applied as by a slot machine. The felt drive for the just result, even when hidden below the manipulation of prior cases and statutes, has always been present. The trouble has been that too many of the bar have been fooled by their law school educations into believing that rules, especially as built out of the narrow holdings, are necessarily definitive of the outcome of cases and that argument of the policy involved is somehow non-respectable and must be done in an undercover or even underhanded manner. No really successful appellate lawyer has ever labored under this illusion and no court sitting as a bench has ever really believed it. The proponents of "ad hoc" arbitration are only urging that in arbitration the policy factors can be brought out into the open and made the explicit bases for decision, *and that arbitration knows no convention* *against that being done;* and, further, that the error of a prior decision should not control the determination of future cases. * * *

* * *

Let us now examine some of the arguments which are advanced in favor of arbitration and test their validity. It is said to be a speedier process than that of the courts on two counts, one, that there is no like delay in going to trial or hearing and two, that there is no appeal. In most arbitrations, this statement is true. But the law governing arbitration is not such as to make it necessarily true. For example, preliminary to any hearing there may be a legal test of the validity of the agreement to arbitrate and an appeal all the way on that issue; there may be a legal test of whether the issue is arbitrable and appeal all the way upon that one; there may be a legal test on the qualification of the arbitrator or arbitrators and appeal all the way upon that one, as well. Subsequent to hearing and award there may be an appeal for fraud or mistake apparent on the face of the award or, even for error of law apparent on the face of the award or simply for error of law, or for lack of fairness in the procedure. The point to be made in favor of arbitration is that typically such legal testing or appeal is not indulged in by the parties. There are non-legal pressures to accept the process and the award.

* * *

* * * There is a view abroad in the land that lawyers are not necessary to the satisfactory handling of an arbitration, and more significantly, that that is a most desirable thing.

Tied to the feeling of non-necessity of lawyers in arbitration is the proposition that rules of evidence and procedure are not used in arbitration. In analyzing this proposition, it is first necessary to examine the nature of controversy and its resolution. * * * [T]o the extent that rules of procedure or evidence are adapted to the rational process of disputation, they are as much a part of the arbitration process as they are a part of the legal process. The difference lies in their mechanics of application and in the nature of the deflecting factors. The basic question is not whether rules of procedure or evidence are used in arbitration, for they clearly must be; the question is whether the ones used in arbitration are geared to the production of a better, in the sense of more just, result, than those used in the court process.

* * *

In sum, on the procedural side, * * * arbitration is more informal than the legal process, but intrinsically it parallels the horse-sense aspects of the formal legal rules in every phase except that of framing issues. It can be said, therefore, that the arbitration process is more humanly satisfying because of its procedures but that it carries inherent in it the risk of poorer decision because of its poorer issue-framing.

* * *

We can summarize * * * on the level of substantive decision by saying that the flexibility of the selection of an arbitrator, when coupled with the lack of distortion of vision which is encouraged by our formal legal system's legends, can frequently lead to more just decisions, but that in cases which involve the necessity for certainty of future outcome the avowed precedent values of the formal legal system are attractive enough to out-balance considerable in the way of poorer decision, and that when that precedent value is supplied to the arbitration award by the rules or practices of trade associations or exchanges, we run the risk that the "law" thus made is law in which the needs of the total polity have been inadequately considered. The important point for inquiry is the extent to which awards have such precedent values in industries which either maintain or encourage arbitration.

This much can be said. There appears to be much more of good than of evil in the arbitration process, unless it be thought that the ability to resolve disputes without the use of lawyers is an evil outweighing the values of better decisions. But arbitration is only the judicial aspect of a fundamental change in our system of government. There is also the legislative aspect implicit in the actions of trade associations and exchanges and their formulation of their own rules, practices, and customs. I do not believe that the relation which seems to exist between the organization of business and labor into groups and the growth of arbitration is coincidental. I think that self-government of such groups has necessitated a system of dispute resolution among its members and that arbitration has been chosen in preference to the courts, just as trade-rule or custom formulation was chosen in preference to formal legislative action. The implications to our society of this growing group of organizations which in fact control by rule and decision the activities not only of their members but also those with whom their members deal require much detailed study.

SOIA MENTSCHIKOFF

STONE, RUSTIC JUSTICE: COMMUNITY AND COERCION UNDER THE FEDERAL ARBITRATION ACT

77 N.C. L. Rev. 931, 933–936 (1999).

A Gateway 2000 computer arrives in a box together with numerous advertising brochures, instruction manuals, and forms setting out product descriptions, warranties, and other technical information concerning the purchase. One of these forms, entitled "Standard Terms and Conditions," states, "[a]ny dispute or controversy arising out of or relating to this Agreement or its interpretation shall be settled exclusively and finally by arbitration." Arbitration clauses such as this one are often buried in fine print and obscure language so that they are, for all practical purposes, invisible to the average consumer. Even if visible, however, the average consumer has no reason to suspect that the clause is anything but innocuous.

Arbitration is an increasingly common feature of modern life. Once confined to the specialized provinces of international commercial transactions and labor-management relations, arbitration clauses now appear in many day-to-day consumer transactions. Banks frequently include arbitration clauses in their terms for maintaining bank accounts; health maintenance organizations ("HMOs") routinely have provisions requiring that all disputes between the health consumer and the HMO be arbitrated; employment handbooks often state that employees must utilize arbitration to resolve employment-related disputes; many standard residential and commercial lease forms say that all disputes between the tenant and the landlord must be submitted to arbitration; homeowner associations and residential condominiums frequently include arbitration clauses in their charter documents. Before long, routine consumer products, like Gateway Computers, will come with product and warranty information that includes a mandatory arbitration clause.

* * *

In tandem with the expanded use of arbitration in consumer transactions has been an expansion in the scope of arbitration within the legal order. In recent years, the Supreme Court has reinterpreted the Federal Arbitration Act ("FAA"), the statute that defines the boundary between the public legal system and arbitration. The FAA provides that agreements to arbitrate are "valid, irrevocable, and enforceable." Before the 1980s, the FAA was interpreted as applying only to federal question cases or diversity cases involving commerce that were in federal court. Further, the FAA applied only to cases that were in federal court on an independent federal question basis. In the past fifteen years, however, the Supreme Court has expanded the reach of the FAA and has adopted a national policy of promoting the use of arbitration in all relationships that have a contractual element.

This Article describes the expanding scope of arbitration under the FAA and explains the trend in light of the history of the statute. It concludes that the Supreme Court's expansive doctrines, when applied to consumer transactions, contravene the statute's intent and undermine many important due process and substantive rights. In brief, the argument is as follows: The FAA, which made agreements to arbitrate judicially enforceable, was designed to facilitate arbitration between members of trade associations. It was enacted to further a vision of voluntarism, delegation, and self-regulation within the business and commercial communities. Recently, courts have applied the FAA in contexts such as consumer transactions and employment relations that often go far beyond the original understanding of the legislation. By such interpretations of the FAA, courts condone and encourage the use of arbitration to resolve disputes between individuals and entities who, far from sharing in a common normative community, occupy vastly different positions of power vis-vis each other. These expansive interpretations of the FAA facilitate the exercise of invisible private coercion in many facets of contemporary life.

*

Part Two

THE AGREEMENT PROCESS

Chapter Four
AGREEMENTS AND PROMISES
Chapter Five
POLICING AGREEMENTS AND PROMISES

Chapter Four

AGREEMENTS AND PROMISES

*Whereas tradition has [the lawyer]
as a participant in specific
controversies, today he has the
added major role of planner who
seeks not only to avoid controversy
but affirmatively to advance his
client's interests.*

DICKERSON

SECTION ONE: THE AGREEMENT PROCESS AND THE ROLE OF LAWYERS

Lawyers frequently play major roles in the process whereby parties reach and formulate an agreement. They are often asked to advise on the general law applicable to an agreement, to find facts that bear on prospective terms, to ascertain and particularize the goals of the parties, to plan and draft the overall agreement, and to negotiate with the other side. These tasks are the primary subjects of Sections Two and Three.

After considering these lawyer roles, we turn to the requirements of a valid agreement. By considering planning and drafting first, you can develop a planner's perspective from which to view the agreement stage and all that follows in this book.

SECTION TWO: PLANNING AND DRAFTING

Most contract planning and drafting occurs at the agreement stage. We introduced these topics in the White–Benkowski episode in Chapter One. Here we consider the main types of planning, introduce several basic criteria of good planning and drafting, and explore the main tasks lawyers must discharge in the course of planning and drafting an agreement.

A. TWO MAIN TYPES OF PLANNING

MACNEIL, A PRIMER OF CONTRACT PLANNING
48 S.Cal.L.Rev. 627, 639–41 (1975).

Parties enter contracts to achieve particular known goals at the expense of incurring particular known costs. These particular goals and costs may or may not be planned specifically at the time of making a contract. For example, one goes to a doctor for an examination knowing that the doctor's fee will have to be paid, but often not knowing just what the fee will be. Goals and costs of this nature are central to party purposes in making the contract, and planning for them can usefully be called performance planning. A shorthand way of identifying performance planning is to ask: Will what is planned almost certainly have to be carried out if this contract is to go through to a successful conclusion as planned? An affirmative answer identifies performance planning.

Like any other human activity, engaging in contractual behavior involves risks of loss. Sometimes dealing with risks of loss is the central purpose of the contract, as in the case of insurance. Where this is the case, planning for those risks is performance planning. In many circumstances, however, risks of loss exist which are peripheral to the main purposes of the parties in making the contract in the sense that the contract may be carried to a completely successful conclusion without the cost of such loss ever being incurred. Planning for such risks can usefully be distinguished from performance planning and called risk planning. A shorthand way of identifying risk planning is to ask: Is this contract likely to go through to a successful conclusion without what is being planned having to be carried out? An affirmative answer identifies risk planning as that term is used here.

The questions at the end of each of the two preceding paragraphs are not always easy to answer. Just as certainty and uncertainty are part of a single spectrum, so are performance and risk planning. Some risk hovers about even the most certain of human events including the most certain performance planning of contracts, and risk planning *can* often be argued to be central to party purposes.

B. DRAFTING TECHNIQUES

In Chapters Six and Seven we focus on particular issues of contract interpretation that guide the lawyer in drafting an agreement. The following excerpt offers some preliminary guidance on the problem of draftsmanship generally.

MAXEY, FUNDAMENTALS OF DRAFTSMANSHIP—A GUIDE FOR THE APPRENTICE IN PREPARING AGREEMENTS

51 Pa.B.Ass'n.Q. 47, 48–51, 56, 58–62 (1980).

[T]here is a tendency to accept uncritically the product of the past, to give prominence to pure boilerplate, and to lose sight of what the essential and peculiar ingredients of this transaction—this understanding—are.

The test of good draftsmanship is to identify these ingredients and to express them in language that can be read and enforced by others who will not necessarily have been involved in the discussions preceding the agreement and who, as a matter of fact, when the time comes for interpretation, may be at a considerable distance from the negotiating process.

* * *

It is hard to imagine, however, a good lawyer-negotiator who is not a good draftsman, able to come up with a solution in words, for the benefit of his client, right in the middle of the fray while the parties are having at each other. When time is a factor (and it usually is), this lawyer is much in demand: and if the other side is represented by a cloistered draftsman, reluctantly compelled to participate in negotiations, the advantage can be decisive.

The objective of the apprentice is, therefore, to organize language for a purpose, and to do it under pressure, without always having the security of a prior draft or a model form to refer to. As it is largely instinct that comes from experience which we are talking about, no one should expect to qualify as a full-fledged draftsman over night. When that precocious individual does appear on the scene, those of us who are still improving will be around in number to acknowledge the accomplishment.

* * *

THE ENTIRE AGREEMENT

The entire document is the draftsman's concern. It starts with the title centered at the top of the first page, which can be simply "AGREEMENT" or a more specific, ample reference reaching toward substance. Does it matter? It may, marginally. And if it is a large-scale transaction, with numerous documents to be collected and indexed in a binder after closing, some labeling will eventually be necessary.

The caption where the parties are identified for the first time is critical. Who are the parties? Who ought they to be to make the agreement enforceable? What are their correct names? What legal entities are contracting, and correspondingly what formalities of execution and evidence of authority to act should the draftsman be contemplating as he moves toward the end of the document and the signatures on the last page or the acknowledgments before a notary?

* * *

MODEL DOCUMENTS AND STANDARD PROVISIONS

Boilerplate is recognizable as such too late in the game for the apprentice to conclude that it exists at all. Nor is there anything sacred about a printed form or a document whose lineage can be traced to a distinguished draftsman.

Most printed forms are one-sided documents, produced in quantity to meet the needs of the party having the greater bargaining power or the stronger representation in the market place. That was true of the old indenture of apprenticeship, and it remains true today of leases, mortgages, and agreements of sale.

A carefully drawn document that performed well for a client in one transaction does not inevitably fulfill that function for another client in a different transaction. Changes may have been negotiated in provisions where you least expect to find them—default provisions, for example; and by borrowing wholesale, the draftsman faces the potential embarrassment of explaining to his client how eccentric language, which served a definite purpose in the prior document, found its way into this document.

* * *

PUNCTUATION, PARAGRAPHS, AND HEADINGS

The draftsman has a duty to help the reader. It might be called courtesy were it only a question of good manners.

Punctuation, used correctly, promotes meaning and buttresses intent. Sentences which go on forever, without any internal ordering, show a lack of concern for the exercise of reading. Endlessness becomes thoughtlessness—whether so characterized to account for the reader's wavering eye or to describe the content of the draftsman's work.

* * *

Paragraphing, like punctuation, is something of an art form: there can be flexibility depending on the writer and on that writer's own sense of what constitutes the breakpoint between one set of related thoughts and another. For the legal draftsman, however, the standard is more exacting. In a carefully prepared (and conceived) agreement, the reader is pushed more than nudged by the draftsman's paragraphing technique because it is not just a matter of what pleases the eye. A new paragraph in an agreement will usually mean a different obligation, separately labeled and given a new section or paragraph number.

No more than any other writer can the legal draftsman avoid long paragraphs, but he must avoid that density which comes from mixing recital information with covenants or from trying to say everything in the first and only paragraph.

Headings are intended as visual aids. Even in short agreements, they are helpful. In longer agreements, headings are signposts that guide the reader to his destination without having to plow through the whole document. In a long and complicated agreement, headings have their greatest usefulness when first referred to in a table of contents.

But the conscientious draftsman worries about the headings. Just as with the descriptive title for the agreement which attempts to condense in a few words what it has taken pages to write, the heading may imply more (or less) than the provision itself conveys. Gone in the bold language at the beginning of the section or paragraph are the nuances, cross-references, provisos, and exceptions carefully shaped in the text that follows. Such a concern is invariably met by a provision like this one:

The table of contents and the headings to the various sections of this Agreement are inserted only for convenience of reference and are not intended, nor shall they be construed, to modify, define, limit, or expand the intent of the parties as expressed in this Agreement.

* * *

MISCELLANEOUS

The agreement comes to a close with a variety of provisions grouped under the heading of *"Miscellaneous."* In a rush to conclude, the draftsman should not skip over these provisions which are fertile ground for litigation.

Is the agreement meant to reach more than the named parties—"to extend to and bind," as is usually provided, "their respective heirs, executors, administrators, successors, and assigns?" When obligations incurred can be carried out only by the contracting individual, the answer is "no" or at least subject to significant qualification. The standard language itself raises the related issue whether one party may assign its position under the agreement to someone else, and if so, with what control being exercised by the party or parties whose consent is sought in advance or will then have to be obtained.

* * *

As with a lease, does the agreement need a defined term, which may be extended or renewed? Contracts for the delivery of services do typically specify a period of time in which the services will be rendered at the bargained-for compensation. May an agreement be terminated prior to the expiration of the term, and if so, on what grounds, with what notice, and at what cost to the terminating party?

Should the time for performance be specified as of the essence of the agreement? What happens if it isn't? The temptation is to try and require the other side to perform exactly on time while giving your own client greater latitude. Some events are beyond the control of even the most diligent. Should the protection of a force majeure clause be available, and if so, for how long, with what absolute deadline set for performance?

* * *

Finally, there is the mechanical problem of how to collect signatures. The parties may be scattered in different places. Should the agreement allow for counterpart execution? No harm in such a provision or in counterpart signatures, even though, if only for aesthetic reasons, the draftsman may have a marked preference for everyone's signing the same document—to the point of being willing to put up with inconvenience to achieve that result.

STYLE AND DRAFTSMANSHIP

While the legal draftsman is not, by rule, denied the right to be stylish, his aspirations to style must be controlled. If there is style in language used with precision and in a document that has logic to its structure and consistency in its provisions, then the draftsman, when he succeeds, may claim for his product the adornment of style.

Drafting does not provide the opportunity for that innovative use of words sometimes associated with stylish writing, and the beginner should immediately shy away from the idea of elegant variation. A fundamental precept, learned early, is that having said something one way (and, it is hoped, the right way), repeat that formulation in exactly the same terms wherever in the document you mean to say the same thing. To change words solely for the sake of style might suggest a change in substance that was not intended.

The vocabulary of the draftsman need not strike the layman as either unintelligible or antiquated. Jargon should be avoided. Even so, words that we would find well-chosen in an essay, a newspaper article, a letter a lawyer sends to his client, a brief submitted to court, or a court opinion may jar when introduced into a formal agreement. The draftsman is always looking for words that have an established coefficient of value, and his search, not surprisingly, brings him to prefer the old over the new, the heavier over the lighter, the specific over the allusive.

Sadness descends upon the connoisseur when he thinks of the lost forms files of celebrated lawyers of the past. Oh, to browse among the forms of a John G. Johnson, a Charles Evans Hughes, or a John W. Davis! Memoirs and collected papers omit this material—perhaps because the draftsman's identity is meant to be concealed: the legal document is designed to fit the wearer, not flatter the tailor.

But in Lincoln's case we have an exception. Since everything he touched has, according to the calculation of the autograph collector, its premium value, fragments of his draftsmanship have survived. In drafting legal documents, Lincoln adhered to form. (So also, one suspects, did Johnson, Hughes, and Davis.) Lincoln did not try to improve on the deed, mortgage, will, or power of attorney which was used in his day and remains with us now. Still, his instinctive feel for substance comes through in a document like this lease which, as landlord, Lincoln drafted on the eve of his first departure for Washington [to serve in the House of Representatives]:

> It is hereby agreed by and between Abraham Lincoln of the City of Springfield, Illinois, and Cornelius Ludlum of the same place, that the said Lincoln lets to the said Ludlum the dwelling house in which said Lincoln now lives, in said City, together with the lot on which it stands, and the other appurtenances of said lot, for the term of one year, to commence on the first day of November next; for which the said Ludlum agrees to pay said Lincoln the sum of ninety dollars, in quarter yearly payments, to be especially careful to prevent any destruction by fire, to allow said Lincoln, the use of the North-upstairs room, during the term, in which to store his furniture, and to return the premises at the end of the year in as good repair as he may receive them ordinary decay only excepted.

October 23, 1847

A.   Lincoln
C.   Ludlum[1]

What is the hallmark of Lincoln as a supreme stylist? It is economy of language joined to an intensity of purpose fully realized. Certainly that holds good for all that is honored as quintessentially his: the Farewell Address at Springfield, the Gettysburg Address, the Letter to Mrs. Bixby (if he wrote it), and the Second Inaugural. Is it too much, therefore, to contend that, after the Bible and Shakespeare, whose cadences and intonations reverberate in Lincoln's prose, his style reflects the discipline of his training as a draftsman?

Lesser talents are not, of course, to be confused with genius. It will be enough, that the apprentice—which is to say, all of us—recognizes the respect, even veneration, Lincoln had for the written word. "Writing—the art of communicating thoughts to the mind, through the eye—is," he said, "the great invention of the world."[2]

---

1. The Collected Works of Abraham Lincoln 406–07 (Basler ed. 1953).

2. Collected Works, at 360.

C. PLANNING AND DRAFTING FOR PERFORMANCE

P. SIVIGLIA, WRITING CONTRACTS
41 (1996).

* * * [T]wo of the three essential functions that the commercial lawyer performs are (A) to identify the considerations involved in the transaction, and (B) to determine how to deal with those considerations. Often the client negotiates the basic business terms before introducing the matter to the attorney:—for example, in the case of an employment arrangement: compensation and period of employment; in the case of a loan: amount of the loan and drawdown schedule, interest rate, payment terms and collateral; in the case of a license: property subject to the license, territory of use, terms of exclusivity, period, royalty rate and, perhaps, minimum royalties. Many times, though, the client's information on these matters is incomplete and requires further refinement. On other occasions, the client, about to consider an unfamiliar transaction, may come to the attorney for advice on what points he or she should discuss with the other party.

In these circumstances, experience is the attorney's best asset. Checklists are helpful, and even seasoned attorneys will use them; but since all transactions differ, the checklist must not be relied upon to comprehend every aspect of the deal.

D. BENDER, P. BERGMAN & S. PRICE, LAWYERS AS COUNSELORS: A CLIENT–CENTERED APPROACH
95 (1991).

* * * [N]ot every client about to enter into a "deal" wants the best possible price. Business people, perhaps to preserve a long term relationship, save legal fees, or other reasons, often will agree to terms that are less favorable than they might have insisted on. Hence, rather than overlooking entirely a client's desired outcome when it seems obvious, you might at least check out your assumption * * *.

MACNEIL, A PRIMER OF CONTRACT PLANNING
48 S.Cal.L.Rev. 627, 641 n. 31 (1975).

The goal of performance planning must always be the smoothly efficient accomplishment of the aims of the parties. (Since contract planning reflects the lack of identity of interests of the parties, the performance planning goal of one party is the smoothly efficient accomplishment of that party's aims; this may or may not correspond to goals the other party would favor.) Except respecting application of legal knowledge, this often involves many subjects in which the lawyer has little or no expertise. Whole courses and sequences of courses at business, engineering, technical, and many other schools are devoted to the development of understanding of planning and coordinating such expertise. Major portions of the commercial and financial world devote their energies to contract performance planning of this nature. * * *

The tasks may or may not be performed by members of the bar. Shocking though the fact may be to those laying out good time and money to gain entry to the lawyer's profession, lawyers have at best only a partial monopoly on the right to perform many of these tasks. Since, however, the activities described below have so often been handled by lawyers describing them as lawyer's tasks has some basis in reality.

––––––––

1. *Fact Finding*

The lawyer asked to plan the essential duties of performance typically first must engage in fact finding. The lawyer must, at minimum, determine the general objectives of the client and how the client proposes to realize those objectives. Often, when the client is knowledgeable and experienced, the client is a reliable and adequate source of most information required to prepare a first draft of the essential performance duties of each party. Shaffer and Elkins report that "several studies of legal interviewing have found * * * that open-ended interview questions produce the fullest answers * * *." T. Shaffer & J. Elkins, Legal Interviewing and Counseling in a Nutshell 107 (3d ed. 1997). The lawyer also will often have to dig into notes, memoranda, letters, or other writings of the client. The lawyer's investigation may extend into the overall financial position of the client (or the other party) and even into general market conditions. Sometimes the lawyer will have to consult experts.

Problem 4–1

Michael Green is president of Universal Lithographics, Inc. He has come to your office for help. Harold's Printing Company, which prints about 125 magazines monthly for numerous publishers, has done all of its printing by the letterpress method, and now seeks to use offset printing. To that end, Harold's has bought a large offset web press for installation in its plant. A press of this kind requires a daily supply of lithographic plates of the kind your client, Universal, makes. Harold's wants Universal to contract to supply the plates. Universal is now located in a distant city, and would have to rent space from Harold's and buy and set up machinery on Harold's premises in order to supply the plates efficiently. All of this would entail substantial start-up costs for Universal. Harold's has told Universal that Harold's is willing to pay a price that would "cover such costs" and also give Universal "a satisfactory return." Assume that Green has told you that start-up costs would be $35,000 and that Harold's says it would need a minimum of 5000 plates a year (and perhaps as many as 6000 or more). Assume Green has asked you to prepare drafts of proposed contract clauses defining Harold's duties of performance as to quantity, price, and contract duration. (These, of course, would not be the only clauses defining the duty of performance. For example, the parties would also want to include a clause dealing with the quality of the plates.) What additional items of information would you need before you could begin this task? Make a list of the items.

2. *Devising or Selecting An Appropriate Contract "Design"*

A contract must be planned and drafted to achieve the goals of the parties. Towards that end, the lawyer must devise or select an appropriate contract "design." For example, the needs of a buyer of goods may vary over time. Thus a fixed quantity contract may be inappropriate. One way to cope with this quantity problem is by adopting a contract design that ensures some flexibility in the quantity that the buyer must purchase.

Lawyers have accumulated vast experience with a variety of basic contract designs. Such designs are found in form books published for practitioners as well as in general files kept by practitioners in their offices. Often, a large body of law will develop around a contract design. When a basic design is appropriate, it may greatly facilitate the process of defining the performance duties of the parties. For example, one widely used contract design involving the sale of goods is the so-called "requirements contract," a contract in which the seller agrees to supply the buyer's requirements for goods and the buyer agrees to take all of its requirements from the seller. Consider these remarks:

WEISTART, REQUIREMENTS AND OUTPUT CONTRACTS: QUANTITY VARIATIONS UNDER THE UCC

1973 Duke L.J. 599, 609–12, 614–16.

Production Flexibility

A true requirements contract allows the buyer to adjust his intake of materials and supplies to fluctuations in markets in which he sells his products or in the markets from which he secures supplies. As demand for his product decreases, for example, the requirements buyer is both able to reduce his production and to avoid the economic burden of committing capital to unneeded supplies. Similarly, if demand for his product increases, he is able to adjust his production immediately to the extent his supplies are furnished on a requirements basis. Also, if costs for labor and equipment increase to the point of seriously impairing profitability, the buyer can respond by reducing production.

* * *

In short, a requirements contract can serve as a risk-shifting device. By his utilization of this form of agreement, the buyer can shift to the requirements seller some of the risks of the buyer's business. Among the most important of these is the risk that the market in which the buyer sells his product will contract. And the seller who agrees to a fixed-price requirements arrangement also accepts the risk that the market price for his commodity will increase and thus he must forego potential opportunities for more profitable sales to other buyers.

* * *

While the flexibility in production which is assured by a requirements contract may offer a substantial advantage to the buyer, such arrangements must offer some inducement to the seller to accept the risks which the buyer avoids. The nature of the incentive for the seller will ultimately depend upon his perception of the extent of the risk which he confronts. In the situation in which there is considerable uncertainty as to the buyer's requirements, the means which the seller will most likely use is a price adjustment; he can use the fact of his risk-assumption as a basis for bargaining for a selling price above that of the then established market price. While this would seem to be the most typically applicable means for compensating the seller, there are other features of the arrangement which may be attractive. As the rate of the requirements buyer's consumption becomes more predictable, price adjustments are less likely and these other considerations presumably will play a greater role. The seller may anticipate, for example, that the buyer will buy the contract goods in sufficiently large quantities that he is compensated for the risk of a quantity fluctuation. The guaranteed market of the requirements contract will relieve the seller of the burden of pursuing other markets and may yield a substantial reduction in selling expenses. Similarly, a predictable demand will assist the seller in planning for his business and permit the more efficient allocation of resources.

* * * If the market is already occupied by established sellers, a prospective competitor may be unwilling to enter it unless he secures a protected market, such as that provided by a requirements buyer with a stable demand. When the seller has secured such a contract, the decision to commit resources to the development of a market position can be made with an assurance that a demand will exist for the seller's product. In this situation, the seller exchanges the risk of his own lack of competitiveness during the start-up period for what he may perceive as a lesser risk that his prediction of the buyer's demands will prove to be inaccurate.

* * *

Minimization of supply risks. For a particular manufacturer, there may be a substantial risk that the availability of material will be restricted. The cause may be supply limitations which exist irrespective of price, as in the case of scarce natural resources, or which are related to the presence of unpredictably fluctuating cost. By resort to a requirements contract, the purchaser can surmount these supply risks. The buyer is locked into a source of supply and assured that the seller will not market a product of limited availability to other buyers. * * *

* * *

Increased operational efficiency. * * * The buyer under a requirements contract can also increase his operational efficiency and may commit himself to such an arrangement with that objective. He is assured that his supply of materials will be constant, which in turn allows him greater control of his production schedule than would exist if he were forced to secure his supplies through periodic negotiations with suppliers. Variations in the availability of the material, which might otherwise affect the buyer's ability to arrive at an even production schedule, are avoided. In addition, the buyer may substantially enhance the predictability of his cost if he can secure his requirements on a fixed-price basis. By isolating some of his costs in advance of production, he can plan for more efficient allocation of his other resources. * * *

Decreased direct operational cost. While increased operational efficiency will produce cost savings, cost reduction of a more direct sort can be identified as flowing from an open-quantity arrangement. Once a source of supply is secured under an open-quantity contract, the requirements buyer no longer needs to devote time or personnel to searching out suppliers and negotiating materials contracts. Moreover, a buyer who attempts to satisfy uncertain supply needs by fixed-quantity contracts is likely to make purchases in quantities greater than those needed for immediate consumption in order to minimize both transactions costs and the risk of price variations. The resulting expenditures for storage and maintenance of inventory could be more closely controlled by a requirements arrangement in which the level of periodic orders reflects short-term needs.

Problem 4–2

1. Let us return to Universal's problem. Assume that you decide to suggest the "requirements" contract to Universal as one possible contract design that might serve Universal's needs. List one major advantage and one major disadvantage of that design for Universal.

2. Which clause listed below imposing a quantity obligation on Harold's would you favor? Why? What, if anything, would you add? In answering these questions, consider Stacks v. F & S Petroleum Co., below, and the sections of the Uniform Commercial Code cited therein.

    (a) a clause providing that Harold's would decide on the quantity of plates to be purchased;

    (b) a clause setting forth an estimate of Harold's requirements;

    (c) a clause requiring Harold's to buy a stated minimum;

    (d) a clause requiring Harold's to buy a stated minimum and any other requirements above that minimum;

    (e) a clause requiring Harold's to buy its requirements from Universal in good faith;

    (f) a clause requiring Harold's to buy its reasonable requirements from Universal.

STACKS v. F & S PETROLEUM CO.

Court of Appeals of Arkansas, 1982.
6 Ark.App. 327, 641 S.W.2d 726.

[Under a requirements agreement, F & S Petroleum, the appellee, supplied gasoline to Stacks. When Stacks would not pay, F & S brought an action against Stacks for the outstanding balance due. Stacks claimed that he had leased the station and that he was not liable for gasoline purchased by the lessee. The jury returned a verdict against Stacks. The portion of the opinion dealing with the enforceability of a requirements contract is set forth below.]

GLAZE, JUDGE.

* * *

This legal controversy largely centers on the following March 9, 1977, agreement:

March 9, 1977

Mr. John B. Stacks
Route 1
Damascus, Arkansas

Dear Mr. Stacks:

With further reference to our conversations in regard to our supplying you with motor gasoline at your gasoline outlet which is now under construction in Bee Branch, I have listed below the agreed points which we discussed Sunday, February 20, 1977:

1. We agree to furnish you fuel in an amount up to 50,000 gallons per month. We will withhold this amount from our various allotments. The amounts will be subject to allocation adjustment by the Federal Energy Administration.

2. We will be your exclusive supplier upon the following terms:

     a. Costs will be laid-in costs per gallon plus $.01 per gallon.

     b. Gallons will be temperature corrected.

     c. Billing terms will be net 4 days from invoice.

3. If the Federal Energy Administration allocation falls below 96%, terms in "a" will be negotiated and revised upward.

The above is, in substance, the terms upon which we agreed in our meeting. Please sign below after our signature and return the original to me.

> F & S Petroleum Company, Inc.
> /s/ Dee Francy, President
> /s/ John B. Stacks

In brief, appellant contends the foregoing agreement is indefinite [in that] the agreement did not require him to purchase gas—even a minimum order— nor did it specify how long the agreement would last. * * *

This transaction is controlled by Ark.Stat.Ann. § 85–2–306(1) (Add.1961), which provides:

> 85–2–306. Output, requirements and exclusive dealings.—(1) A term which measures the quantity by the output of the seller or the requirements of the buyer means such actual output or requirements as may occur in good faith, except that no quantity unreasonably disproportionate to any stated estimate or in the absence of a stated estimate to any normal or otherwise comparable prior output or requirements may be tendered or demanded.

Both at common law and under the Uniform Commercial Code, a requirements contract is simply an agreement by the buyer to buy his good faith requirements of goods exclusively from the seller. *See Wilsonville Concrete Products v. Todd Building Co.,* 281 Or. 345, 574 P.2d 1112 (1978). Comment 2 to § 85–2–306(1) explicitly rejects the notion that requirements contracts are too indefinite to enforce because such contracts are held to mean the actual good faith requirements of the particular party. Therefore, Professors White and Summers conclude that a party who seeks to invalidate a requirements contract bears a heavy burden. See White and Summers, *Uniform Commercial Code,* § 3–8 (2d ed. 1980). Comment 2 further provides that a requirements contract does not lack mutuality of obligation since the party who will determine quantity is required to operate his plant or conduct his business in good faith and according to commercial standards of fair dealing in the trade so that his requirements will approximate a reasonably foreseeable figure.

In view of the foregoing rules and guidelines, the fact that the parties' March 9 agreement left open the number of gallons to be purchased monthly does not support invalidation of the agreement. The Code imposed on the appellant, as a buyer, the responsibility to conduct his business in good faith and in accordance with commercial standards of fair dealing in the trade so that his requirements would approximate a reasonably foreseeable figure, in this instance, 50,000 gallons per month. Appellee agreed to furnish this amount on the terms specifically contained in the March 9 agreement. Additionally, appellant agreed to purchase gasoline exclusively from appellee. The parties' agreement undoubtedly qualifies as a requirements contract and is enforceable as such. Although the agreement failed to provide for when it would terminate, Ark.Stat.Ann. § 85–2–309(2) states that if a contract provides for successive performances but is indefinite in duration, it is valid for a reasonable time.

* * *

Since we find no error, we affirm.

AFFIRMED.

D. PLANNING AND DRAFTING AGAINST RISKS

The effective lawyer combines legal knowledge, business knowledge, foresight, and imagination to identify possible risks and to prevent them from causing the breakdown of an agreement. In order to assess the nature of such risks and the probability of their occurrence, the lawyer must often seek facts beyond those needed to plan and draft the essential duties of performance. We now identify a number of common types of risks. Should Universal's agreement include clauses dealing with any of the following risks?

Invalidity Risks

Requirements of validity are the lawyer's special province. In the typical case, the lawyer must, at the very least, plan the agreement so that it satisfies all requirements of legal validity, both substantive and formal. Otherwise, the client cannot invoke the theory of agreement with consideration.

We have already studied consideration and the statute of frauds in Chapter Two. Stacks v. F & S Petroleum Co. poses a consideration issue in the context of a requirements contract. In Sections Four through Eleven of this chapter, we study further requirements of validity.

Regulatory Violation Risks

This is another special province of the lawyer. Local ordinances, state and federal statutes, and state and federal agency regulations may bear on the agreement in some way. The lawyer may want to include a clause allocating the risk that arises from a violation of such law. Regulatory laws are numerous and deal with such diverse matters as labor, health and safety, zoning, environmental control, import controls, and so on. An illustrative clause is set forth below:

Neither party shall be liable for any failure to make or accept any one or more deliveries (or portions thereof) arising out of compliance with any law, ordinance, regulation, ruling, order or other governmental action. * * * In the event of the occurrence of any such contingencies and its consequent inability to supply the total demands for goods specified herein, seller may allocate its available supply among any or all purchasers, as well as departments and divisions of seller, upon such basis as seller may deem fair and practical without liability for any failure of performance which may result therefrom.[a]

Risks of Losing Tax Benefits and of Incurring Tax Burdens

Local, state, or federal tax laws may provide benefits to one or both parties to a contract, but only if the contract is planned and drafted to take advantage of those laws. In addition, a carefully drafted clause may allocate a tax burden to the other party instead of to one's client:

ARTICLE 4. Taxes. (a) In addition to the purchase price of the equipment described in Article 1 hereof, Buyer shall pay to Seller upon demand:

(i) the amount of any sales value added or use taxes imposed by any federal, state or local taxing authority within the United States, and the amount of all taxes imposed by any taxing authority without the United States, required to be paid by Seller as a result of any sale, use, delivery, storage or transfer under this Agreement of any of the equipment furnished or delivered hereunder. * * *[b]

Third Party Liability Risks

Contracts are not performed in a vacuum. Performance sometimes causes loss or damage to third parties. When this is a significant risk, indemnity clauses or similar devices should be included to deal with it. An illustrative clause is set forth below:

The buyer agrees to indemnify the seller and save him harmless from any loss which he might sustain by reason of the manufacture of the goods called for by this contract according to the plans and specifications furnished to the seller by the buyer.[c]

"Force Majeure" Risks

A strike may occur. A plant may burn down. Unusually bad weather may occur. An oil embargo may be imposed. Many contracts include clauses that allocate the risk of such occurrences to one party, or provide for insurance or the like:

Seller shall not be liable for delays in delivery or failure to deliver due to circumstances beyond its control, including but not limited to strikes and other labor difficulties, fire or flood or other natural disaster.[d]

Dispute Risks

Disputes frequently arise over the meaning of contract language. Recall White v. Benkowski. In Chapters Six and Seven we treat the major sources of such disputes and also how courts generally resolve them. The lawyer may wish to provide for some mode of dispute resolution, such as arbitration. An illustrative arbitration clause follows:

a. R. Smith and D. Clifford, Jr., North Carolina Practice: Uniform Commercial Code Forms Annotated § 2–615–Form 1 (1968).

b. Smith, Drafting A Major Sales Agreement Under the Code: Drafting—Checklists—Forms, 4 U.C.C.L.J. 109, 126 (1971).

c. 26 C. Everberg, Massachusetts Practice: Uniform Commercial Code Forms Annotated § 2–312–Form 7 (1966).

d. C. Kuenzel, Florida Uniform Commercial Code § 672.2–306 (1967).

ARBITRATION

A. All questions subject to arbitration under this Contract shall be submitted to arbitration at the choice of either party to the dispute.

B. The parties may agree upon one arbitrator. In all other cases there shall be three arbitrators. One arbitrator shall be named by each party to this Contract; each party shall notify the other party and the Engineer of such choice in writing. The third arbitrator shall be chosen by the two arbitrators named by the parties. If the two arbitrators fail to select a third within fifteen days, the third arbitrator shall be chosen by the presiding officer of the bar association nearest to the location of the work. Should the party demanding arbitration fail to name an arbitrator within ten days of his demand, his right to arbitration shall lapse. Should the other party fail to choose an arbitrator within the said ten days, the presiding officer of the bar association nearest to the location of work shall appoint such arbitrator. Should either party refuse or neglect to supply the arbitrators with any papers or information demanded in writing, the arbitrators are empowered by both parties to proceed ex parte.

C. If there be one arbitrator, his decision shall be binding; if there are three, the decision of any two shall be binding. Such decision shall be a condition precedent to any right of legal action, and wherever permitted by law it may be judicially enforced.

Inapposite Remedy Risks

In Chapter Three, we saw that for a variety of reasons remedies for breach of contract may not make the injured party whole. An effective lawyer will be alert to this risk and will plan and draft accordingly. For example, recall that, within limits, the lawyer can draft a personalized set of remedies for the parties called a liquidated damages provision. The lawyer can also draft self-help remedies, such as the right to suspend performance or to retain what the other party has already tendered under the contract.

LOUIS BROWN, PLANNING BY LAWYERS
E–10 (Temporary ed. 1967).

In general, a completed agreement locks the parties into the rights and duties specified in the agreement. If there were opportunity to enlarge the rights and diminish the duties before the agreement is finalized, such opportunity usually vanishes when the agreement is fixed. A right overlooked or not bargained for, may be lost forever. Some examples will help explain the principle and illustrate the sort of thing that can often be accomplished.

1. The right (option) to terminate duties sooner. When a tenant signs a lease, he obligates himself for the agreed period. Unless the lease gives the tenant an "out", the tenant is obligated to make rental payments for the entire term. During the lease term, a tenant who desires to terminate his tenancy may endeavor to negotiate an agreed termination, or breach the lease and subject himself to the landlord's claim. One avenue open to a tenant before he signs the lease is to endeavor to negotiate a provision giving him an option to terminate. After the lease is signed, the opportunity to engage in that negotiation is usually lost.

The advisability of negotiating a termination provision is perhaps best illustrated by the example of the tenant of an apartment or house who dies during the lease term. The tenant's estate continues to be liable at a time when neither the tenant nor his estate has use for the premises. It may be that the best time to obtain legal protection regarding such a contingency (the contingency of death) is at the time the lease is negotiated.

Problem 4–3

While limitations on successful planning and drafting are unavoidable (see Section Three), the goal of the attorney is to eliminate or minimize as many problems as possible at the least cost to the client. Consider the language of the actual agreement set forth below between Paramount Lithographic Plate Service, Inc. and Hughes Printing Company in a situation essentially identical to that of Universal and Harold's. Could you do better?

"This letter is to forulate [sic] the lattest [sic] and only agreement between Paramount Lithographic Plate Service or it's [sic] subsidiary and Hughes Printing Company. Paramount will be referred to as "SUPPLIER" and Hughes Printing will be referred to as "CUSTOMER". It has been agreed that:

"1. The supplier is to make within an 8 hour period offset plates and negatives from crona press conversions, 3M scotchprints or original art work.

"2. The supplier is to provide 3 shifts provided the customer has the work to be turned out. Until such time as 3 shifts are required, supplier agrees that a standby crew for emergency work during night hours will be provided.

"3. Supplier is to be exclusive supplier as long as he can meet customer schedule requirements.

"4. Contract shall run for two years and every two years consecutively unless written notice is given 90 days prior to contract renewal of following years.

"5. Prices will normally be reviewed on a yearly basis except where there had been an unusual increase in the cost of Lithographic supplies.

"6. The prices for all Printing Corporation of America's subsidiaries[e] will be the same except where the conditions set forth in our covering letter are not met or where type of supplies used differ.

This agreement when signed by an officer of our company and an officer of your company shall constitute a contract binding on both parties and shall be the only contract between us."[f]

Note
Negotiation Techniques

The study of the art of negotiation is beyond the scope of these materials. The three propositions set forth below are probably most pertinent to contract negotiations.

e. Hughes was a subsidiary of Printing Corp. of America.

f. Paramount Lithographic Plate Service, Inc. v. Hughes Printing Co., 2 Pa. D. & C.3d 677, 678 n. 2, (1977), *aff'd mem.*, 249 Pa.Super. 625, 377 A.2d 1001 (1977).

H. EDWARDS & J. WHITE, THE LAWYER AS A NEGOTIATOR

112–13 (1977).

[I]t is perhaps useful to state three propositions, truisms really, that hold true for almost every negotiation and that define the negotiator's role to a considerable degree. In every negotiation a principal responsibility of the negotiator is to find his opponent's settling point. In almost every negotiation in which there is at least a moderately well-defined controversy the opponent will have or will develop some point at which he will settle. With a union in a bargaining session this may be the number of cents per hour it must have in order not to strike; for the plaintiff's lawyer, the number of dollars he must receive in settlement in order not to go to trial; for the landlord this is the minimum number of dollars and cents per square foot at which he will lease.

In any negotiation, and particularly in lawsuit settlement negotiation, the opposing negotiators may have widely different views of the same case. Commonly, one will assign a lower value to an opponent's case than the opponent will assign to it. Because of that fact and because one assumes that the opponent regards his case as stronger than it looks from across the table, negotiators frequently assume the opponent's settling point is higher than it really is. One should always keep the possibility in mind—notwithstanding the statements of the opposing negotiator—that his opponent has evaluated his own case as weaker than you evaluate it. If somehow one can determine that settling point, he can settle the case for that amount not for some higher amount which he has placed on the case himself.

The logical corollary to the foregoing principle is that one should not reveal his own settling point. Much of the material that follows on nonverbal communication is designed to assist the negotiator in reading his opponent. Conversely the negotiator should be aware that he is transmitting not only verbal but also nonverbal signals. Particularly if his settling point is some distance from the point at which he is bargaining, one should use care not to reveal that settling point. Presumably in the optimal negotiation, one will determine his opponent's settling point without revealing his own. Doubtless such absolute knowledge on one side coupled with absolute ignorance on the other seldom occurs in practice.

The third truism with respect to most negotiations deals with the negotiator's responsibility to change his opponent's position. In some cases it will be enough simply to know the opponent's settling point and to agree to settle at that point. More commonly it will be the job of the negotiator not only to determine the settling point but also to convince the opponent that his case has a lower value than he has put upon it.

Question

If lawyers for both sides of a negotiation have read and acted on the Edwards & White excerpt advising that "one should not reveal his own settling point," how is it that the negotiation can, nevertheless, lead to agreement?

"Well, I just gave it a quick glance, but everything seems to be in order with this contract."

SECTION THREE: THE LIMITS OF PLANNING

Even the able lawyer who works hard at planning and drafting will not always achieve success. Too many hurdles stand in the way. Indeed, the parties might not even believe in the efficacy of lawyers and the law!

MACAULAY, THE USE AND NON–USE OF CONTRACT IN THE MANUFACTURING INDUSTRY

9 Practical Lawyer, Nov. 1963 at 14, 17–18.

Most businessmen I have talked to have an attitude toward contracts that can be best described as indifferent or even hostile to the whole idea. They remark, "Contracts are a waste of time. We've never had any trouble, because we know our customers and our suppliers. If we needed a contract with a man, we wouldn't deal with him." "Lawyers are overprotective and just get in the way of buying or selling. If business had to be done by lawyers as buyers and sellers, the economy would stop. No one would buy or sell anything; they'd just negotiate forever."

Yet, some businessmen look at things differently: "We've been sued (or our competitor has been sued), and one ought to be careful. There is no need to skate on thin ice legally. We've learned the hard way." "If you get the intent spelled out, you won't have any trouble. People perform commitments they understand. It's worth a little extra time to make sure everyone is talking about the same thing."

* * *

When disputes occur, there is a hesitancy to use legal sanctions or even to refer to the contract. Businessmen try to "work things out without bringing lawyers into it." Contract lawsuits and appellate cases concerning contract problems are relatively rare.

Why Business Can and Does Ignore Contract

Businessmen can deal without contract for obvious reasons. They have little, if any, trouble, even if they run risks of trouble. It is in the interest of everyone to perform agreements. There are personal relationships between buyers and sellers on all levels of the two corporations. Purchasing agents know salesmen, corporate presidents know corporate presidents, and so forth. This creates an incentive to get along in a continuing relationship. Most importantly, the two businesses want to do business in the future. You don't get repeat orders from unsatisfied customers, and one's reputation can influence future business if word gets around. And word does get around.

Using contract, of course, can have a number of disadvantages. If, in planning a business transaction, one is going to mention all the horrible things that can happen, he may scare off the other side so that the deal is lost. If one does set up a contractual relationship, there is some risk that one will get only performance to the letter of the contract most narrowly construed. Conversely, there is also a risk that one will be held to the letter of the contract and lose "flexibility." Using legal sanctions for breach of contract to settle disputes is costly. Usually it ends the business relationship between the parties. Furthermore, I need not tell you that lawsuits and lawyers cost money.

Of course, there is some use of legal sanctions. Typically, this occurs when someone with power thinks the gains from proceeding this way outweigh the costs. Often this is the lawyer's view, but lawyers do not always get to run their clients' affairs in the way lawyers might wish to run them.

———

Time constraints also explain why, in some cases, the conscientious lawyer's efforts at planning and drafting may not be successful. Sometimes clients "must" have an agreement "at the end of today"—or even "yesterday." Similarly, the costs of planning, drafting, and negotiating an agreement may, on some points, simply be too high.

COMMENT, ATTORNEY MALPRACTICE IN CALIFORNIA:
THE LIABILITY OF A LAWYER WHO DRAFTS AN
IMPRECISE CONTRACT OR WILL

24 U.C.L.A.L.Rev. 422, 431–32 (1976).

Substantive Imprecision

Most unintentional uncertainties are substantive in nature and result from the attorney's ignorance of some fact or law pertinent to the instrument he is drafting. Although such ignorance is never desirable, the costs of conducting an investigation thorough enough to eliminate all possible imprecision might be so high compared to the value of any information likely to be uncovered that it would be economically impractical for a draftsman to conduct one. The determination of whether, and to what extent, the desire to eliminate ignorance or the desire to minimize costs should prevail requires the weighing of at least seven different factors: the client's willingness or ability to pay; the cost of conducting an investigation; the probability that an investigation will yield any relevant information that the lawyer does not already know; the importance of the information being sought; the frequency with which the instrument being drafted will be used; the extent to which the lawyer can reasonably rely on his client to know and inform him of the facts that an independent investigation would uncover; and finally, the extent of the lawyer's experience with the particular subject matter involved and with the particular client.

Given these many considerations and the fact that no two instruments are exactly alike, the decision as to how thorough an investigation should be conducted is essentially a matter of the attorney's judgment. If the draftsman decides that some investigation of the facts is warranted, the sources usually available to him include: the client; notes, memoranda, or other writings possessed by the client; textbooks dealing with the subject matter in question; and persons who are specialists in the field. Knowledge of the substantive law can be obtained through standard research techniques, which may include reference to such secondary sources as treatises and law review articles.

––––––

Another set of limits derives from the very limits of language. Words simply may be unavailable in which to express desires with precision. See Chapter Six. In addition, the inability of the human mind to foresee the future, an increasing problem in a rapidly changing technological society, inevitably limits the efficacy of planning. Further aspects of this problem are treated in Chapter Eight.

An agreement also may fail to deal with some matter simply because the parties cannot agree on it. For example, the parties to the Universal–Harold's negotiations discussed in Section Two of this chapter might be unable to agree on a minimum quantity of plates to be purchased by Harold's.

LOUIS BROWN, PLANNING BY LAWYERS

E–9 (Temporary ed. 1967).

Disputes also arise on legal issues. Sometimes—perhaps often—the likelihood of such disputes, if visualized in advance, can be minimized by careful legal work. Words and phrases in documents that are or may be legally ambiguous can often be rephrased. But not always. The parties to a negotiation may be able to agree on ambiguous language, but might not be able to agree on clear language. For example, the parties to a labor negotiation may agree that each employee who has been employed for two years or more shall be entitled to two weeks vacation with pay. The agreement, however, does not define "two years." Such lack of definition can lead to dispute, and it may be that the lawyers (and the parties) realize at the time of negotiation that an ambiguity exists. But the parties may prefer the ambiguous document, allowing the ambiguity to be later resolved by subsequent agreement or proceeding, rather than to endeavor to resolve the ambiguity by negotiation.

Note
Contracts in Russia in the 1990's

In the early to mid 1990's, few laws governing private exchange existed in Russia. Nonetheless, the New York Times reported that the "free market [was] not waiting for a legal system." (New York Times, January 17, 1992, page A1.) Private parties increasingly made contracts to exchange goods and services and the legal system tried to catch up. What kinds of deals take place in the absence of a mature contract-law system? First, parties attempted to account for everything in detail because there were no "default rules" to fill in the gaps in their contracts. Second, the parties tried to ensure that each of them profited from the deal so that there would be no incentive to break the contract. (The parties could not count on help from a court.) Third, the parties sought immediate returns from their deal. They could not plan long term because they could not predict the future law. Fourth, many transactions were performed by both parties at the same time.

SECTION FOUR: THE NATURE OF ASSENT

One element of contract planning mentioned in Section Two involves invalidity risks. The lawyer must plan for the legal enforceability of the agreement. In order to do this, the lawyer must understand the legal requirements of a valid agreement. Of course, this body of law is also a concern of lawyers consulted for the first time after a dispute has arisen. Indeed, as we will see, this body of law has very largely grown out of cases in which lawyers seem to have played little or no role until after the beginning of a dispute.

The law governing the validity of an agreement that you study here, and the law of consideration that you already studied in Chapter Two, specify the principal requirements of an "agreement with consideration." Nevertheless, remember that even if a party's contract claim fails because of the absence of a valid agreement, another theory of obligation may still apply.

EMBRY v. HARGADINE, McKITTRICK DRY GOODS CO.

St. Louis Court of Appeals, Missouri, 1907.
127 Mo.App. 383, 105 S.W. 777.

Action by Charles R. Embry against the Hargadine, McKittrick Dry Goods Company. From a judgment for defendant, plaintiff appeals. Reversed and remanded.

* * *

Goode, J. * * * The appellant was an employé of the respondent company under a written contract to expire December 15, 1903, at a salary of $2,000 per annum. His duties were to attend to the sample department of respondent, of which he was given complete charge. It was his business to select samples for the traveling salesmen of the company, which is a wholesale dry goods concern, to use in selling goods to retail merchants. Appellant contends that on December 23, 1903, he was re-engaged by respondent, through its president, Thos. H. McKittrick, for another year at the same compensation and for the same duties stipulated in his previous written contract. On March 1, 1904, he was discharged, having been notified in February that, on account of the necessity of retrenching expenses, his services and that of some other employés would no longer be required. The respondent company contends that its president never re-employed appellant after the termination of his written contract, and hence that it had a right to discharge him when it chose. The point with which we are concerned requires an epitome of the testimony of appellant and the counter testimony of McKittrick, the president of the company, in reference to the alleged re-employment. Appellant testified: That several times prior to the termination of his written contract on December 15, 1903, he had endeavored to get an understanding with McKittrick for another year, but had been put off from time to time. That on December 23d, eight days after the expiration of said contract, he called on McKittrick, in the latter's office, and said to him that as appellant's written employment had lapsed eight days before, and as there were only a few days between then and the 1st of January in which to seek employment with other firms, if respondent wished to retain his services longer he must have a contract for another year, or he would quit respondent's service then and there. That he had been put off twice before and wanted an understanding or contract at once so that he could go ahead without worry. That McKittrick asked him how he was getting along in his department, and appellant said he was very busy, as they were in the height of the season getting men out—had about 110 salesmen on the line and others in preparation. That McKittrick then said: "Go ahead, you're all right. Get your men out, and don't let that worry you." That appellant took McKittrick at his word and worked until February 15th without any question in his mind. It was on February 15th that he was notified his services would be discontinued on March 1st. McKittrick denied this conversation as related by appellant, and said that, when accosted by the latter on December 23d, he (McKittrick) was working on his books in order to get out a report for a stockholders' meeting, and, when appellant said if he did not get a contract he would leave, that he (McKittrick) said: "Mr. Embry, I am just getting ready for the stockholders' meeting tomorrow. I have no time to take it up now. I have told you before I would not take it up until I had these matters out of the way. You will have to see me at a later time. I said: 'Go back upstairs and get your men out on the road.' I may have asked him one or two other questions relative to the department, I don't remember. The whole conversation did not take more than a minute."

Embry also swore that, when he was notified he would be discharged, he complained to McKittrick about it, as being a violation of their contract, and McKittrick said it was due to the action of the board of directors, and not to any personal action of his, and that others would suffer by what the board had done as well as Embry. Appellant requested an instruction to the jury setting out, in substance, the conversation between him and McKittrick according to his version, and declaring that those facts, if found to be true, constituted a contract between the parties that defendant would pay plaintiff the sum of $2,000 for another year, provided the jury believed from the evidence that plaintiff commenced said work believing he was to have $2,000 for the year's work. This instruction was refused, but the court gave another embodying in substance appellant's version of the conversation, and declaring it made a contract "if you (the jury) find both parties thereby intended and did contract with each other for plaintiff's employment for one year from and including December 23, 1903, at a salary of $2,000 per annum." Embry swore that, on several occasions when he spoke to McKittrick about employment for the ensuing year, he asked for a renewal of his former contract, and that on December 23d, the date of the alleged renewal, he went into Mr. McKittrick's office and told him his contract had expired, and he wanted to renew it for a year, having always worked under year contracts. Neither the refused instruction nor the one given by the court embodied facts quite as strong as appellant's testimony, because neither referred to appellant's alleged statement to McKittrick that unless he was re-employed he would stop work for respondent then and there.

It is assigned for error that the court required the jury, in order to return a verdict for appellant, not only to find the conversation occurred as appellant swore, but that both parties intended by such conversation to contract with each other for plaintiff's employment for the year from December, 1903, at a salary of $2,000. If it appeared from the record that there was a dispute between the parties as to the terms on which appellant wanted re-employment, there might have been sound reason for inserting this clause in the instruction; but no issue was made that they split on terms; the testimony of McKittrick tending to prove only that he refused to enter into a contract with appellant regarding another year's employment until the annual meeting of stockholders was out of the way. Indeed, as to the proposed terms McKittrick agrees with Embry, for the former swore as follows: "Mr. Embry said he wanted to know about the renewal of his contract. Said if he did not have the contract made he would leave." As the two witnesses coincided as to the terms of the proposed re-employment, there was no reason for inserting the above-mentioned clause in the instruction in order that it might be settled by the jury whether or not plaintiff, if employed for one year from December 23, 1903, was to be paid $2,000 a year. Therefore it remains to determine whether or not this part of the instruction was a correct statement of the law in regard to what was necessary to constitute a contract between the parties; that is to say, whether the formation of a contract by what, according to Embry, was said, depended on the intention of both Embry and McKittrick. Or, to put the question more precisely: Did what was said constitute a contract of re-employment on the previous terms irrespective of the intention or purpose of McKittrick?

Judicial opinion and elementary treatises abound in statements of the rule that to constitute a contract there must be a meeting of the minds of the parties, and both must agree to the same thing in the same sense. Generally speaking, this may be true; but it is not literally or universally true. That is to say, the inner intention of parties to a conversation subsequently alleged to create a contract cannot either make a contract of what transpired, or prevent one from arising, if the words used were sufficient to constitute a contract. In so far as their intention is an influential element, it is only such intention as the words or acts of the parties indicate; not one secretly cherished which is inconsistent with those words or acts. * * * In Smith v. Hughes, L.R. 6 Q.B. 597, 607, it was said: "If, whatever a man's real intention may be, he so conducts himself that a reasonable man would believe that he was assenting to the terms proposed by the other party, and that other party upon that belief enters into the contract with him, the man thus conducting himself would be equally bound as if he had intended to agree to the other party's terms." And that doctrine was adopted in Phillip v. Gallant, 62 N.Y. 256. In 9 Cyc. 245, we find the following text: "The law imputes to a person an intention corresponding to the reasonable meaning of his words and acts. It judges his intention by his outward expressions and excludes all questions in regard to his unexpressed intention. If his words or acts, judged by a reasonable standard, manifest an intention to agree in regard to the matter in question, that agreement is established, and it is immaterial what may be the real, but unexpressed, state of his mind on the subject." * * * In view of those authorities, we hold that, though McKittrick may not have intended to employ Embry by what transpired between them according to the latter's testimony, yet if what McKittrick said would have been taken by a reasonable man to be an employment, and Embry so understood it, it constituted a valid contract of employment for the ensuing year.

The next question is whether or not the language used was of that character, namely, was such that Embry, as a reasonable man, might consider he was re-employed for the ensuing year on the previous terms, and act accordingly. We do not say that in every instance it would be for the court to pronounce on this question, because, peradventure, instances might arise in which there would be such an ambiguity in the language relied on to show an assent by the obligor to the proposal of the obligee that it would be for the jury to say whether a reasonable mind would take it to signify acceptance of the proposal. * * * With [this rule] in mind, let us recur to the conversation of December 23d between Embry and McKittrick as related by the former. Embry was demanding a renewal of his contract, saying he had been put off from time to time, and that he had only a few days before the end of the year in which to seek employment from other houses, and that he would quit then and there unless he was re-employed. McKittrick inquired how he was getting along with the department, and Embry said they, i.e., the employés of the department, were very busy getting out salesmen. Whereupon McKittrick said: "Go ahead, you are all right. Get your men out, and do not let that worry you." We think no reasonable man would construe that answer to Embry's demand that he be employed for another year, otherwise than as an assent to the demand, and that Embry had the right to rely on it as an assent. The natural inference is, though we do not find it testified to, that Embry was at work getting samples ready for the salesmen to use during the ensuing season. Now, when he was complaining of the worry and mental distress he was under because of his uncertainty about the future, and his urgent need, either of an immediate contract with respondent, or a refusal by it to make one, leaving him free to seek employment elsewhere, McKittrick must have answered as he did for the purpose of assuring appellant that any apprehension was needless, as appellant's services would be retained by the respondent. The answer was unambiguous, and we rule that if the conversation was according to appellant's version, and he understood he was employed, it constituted in law a valid contract of re-employment, and the court erred in making the formation of a contract depend on a finding that both parties intended to make one. It was only necessary that Embry, as a reasonable man, had a right to and did so understand. * * *

The judgment is reversed, and the cause remanded. All concur.

HOTCHKISS v. NATIONAL CITY BANK OF NEW YORK, 200 Fed. 287, 293 (S.D.N.Y.1911) (Learned Hand, District Judge). "A contract has, strictly speaking, nothing to do with the personal, or individual, intent of the parties. A contract is an obligation attached by the mere force of law to certain acts of the parties, usually words, which ordinarily accompany and represent a known intent. If, however, it were proved by twenty bishops that either party, when he used the words, intended something else than the usual meaning which the law imposes upon them, he would still be held, unless there were some mutual mistake, or something else of the sort."

Problem 4–4

The Kabil Development Corporation negotiated with Inland Helicopters for the latter to provide helicopter services needed by Kabil for a construction job. Munroe, Kabil's vice president, discussed with Inland's agent, Honeycutt, the proposed job, the helicopter equipment, the time required and Inland's rates. Kabil then used the information in preparing its bid for the construction job. At a subsequent meeting, Munroe told Honeycutt that Kabil's bid had been accepted and Honeycutt said that Inland would do the job. After Inland refused to perform Kabil brought an action for contract breach. During the trial the following exchange took place:

Q. Mr. Munroe, going back to the meeting of June 25th, that was where you and Mr. Klovstad and Mr. Honeycutt were all present, after your meeting did you feel at that time in your mind that Kabil Development Corporation was obligated to give the helicopter work to Inland Helicopter?

MR. COULTER: Objection, Your Honor. What he felt in his mind wouldn't be at all probative of whether a contract was or was not formed.

THE COURT: I think he can testify as to what his feelings as to whether or not he was bound. As I understand it, the question was whether or not Kabil Development Company felt that they were bound by the contract.

MR. HAMPTON: That's correct, Your Honor.

MR. COULTER: And it wouldn't make any difference, your honor. I think it is the objective manifestations of the contract that are the only elements that are involved in this case. What is subjective in the mind of an offeror or an offeree and not expressed or communicated does not have probative weight of establishing a contract.

THE COURT: He may answer.

A. Yes, I felt that we were obligated to Inland Helicopter, and equally I felt they were obligated to us.

Was the court correct in permitting Mr. Munroe to answer? In light of the Embry case, evaluate the following argument made by the court: Although the "manifestations of a party's intention, rather than the actual or real intention is controlling," the testimony is admissible because "a factfinder might well believe that what a party thought he was doing would show in fact what he did."

LUCY v. ZEHMER

Supreme Court of Appeals of Virginia, 1954.
196 Va. 493, 84 S.E.2d 516.

BUCHANAN, JUSTICE.

This suit was instituted by W.O. Lucy and J.C. Lucy, complainants, against A.H. Zehmer and Ida S. Zehmer, his wife, defendants, to have specific performance of a contract by which it was alleged the Zehmers had sold to W.O. Lucy a tract of land owned by A.H. Zehmer in Dinwiddie county containing 471.6 acres, more or less, known as the Ferguson farm, for $50,000. * * *

The instrument sought to be enforced was written by A.H. Zehmer on December 20, 1952, in these words: "We hereby agree to sell to W.O. Lucy the Ferguson Farm complete for $50,000.00, title satisfactory to buyer," and signed by the defendants, A.H. Zehmer and Ida S. Zehmer.

The answer of A.H. Zehmer admitted that at the time mentioned W.O. Lucy offered him $50,000 cash for the farm, but that he, Zehmer, considered that the offer was made in jest; that so thinking, and both he and Lucy having had several drinks, he wrote out "the memorandum" quoted above and induced his wife to sign it; that he did not deliver the memorandum to Lucy, but that Lucy picked it up, read it, put it in his pocket, attempted to offer Zehmer $5 to bind the bargain, which Zehmer refused to accept, and realizing for the first time that Lucy was serious, Zehmer assured him that he had no intention of selling the farm and that the whole matter was a joke. Lucy left the premises insisting that he had purchased the farm.

Depositions were taken and the decree appealed from was entered holding that the complainants had failed to establish their right to specific performance, and dismissing their bill. The assignment of error is to this action of the court.

W.O. Lucy, a lumberman and farmer, thus testified in substance: He had known Zehmer for fifteen or twenty years and had been familiar with the Ferguson farm for ten years. Seven or eight years ago he had offered Zehmer $20,000 for the farm which Zehmer had accepted, but the agreement was verbal and Zehmer backed out. On the night of December 20, 1952, around eight o'clock, he took an employee to McKenney, where Zehmer lived and operated a restaurant, filling station and motor court. While there he decided to see Zehmer and again try to buy the Ferguson farm. He entered the restaurant and talked to Mrs. Zehmer until Zehmer came in. He asked Zehmer if he had sold the Ferguson farm. Zehmer replied that he had not. Lucy said, "I bet you wouldn't take $50,000.00 for that place." Zehmer replied, "Yes, I would too; you wouldn't give fifty." Lucy said he would and told Zehmer to write up an agreement to that effect. Zehmer took a restaurant check and wrote on the back of it, "I do hereby agree to sell to W.O. Lucy the Ferguson Farm for $50,000 complete." Lucy told him he had better change it to "We" because Mrs. Zehmer would have to sign it too. Zehmer then tore up what he had written, wrote the agreement quoted above and asked Mrs. Zehmer, who was at the other end of the counter ten or twelve feet away, to sign it. Mrs. Zehmer said she would for $50,000 and signed it. Zehmer brought it back and gave it to Lucy, who offered him $5 which Zehmer refused, saying, "You don't need to give me any money, you got the agreement there signed by both of us."

The discussion leading to the signing of the agreement, said Lucy, lasted thirty or forty minutes, during which Zehmer seemed to doubt that Lucy could raise $50,000. Lucy suggested the provision for having the title examined and Zehmer made the suggestion that he would sell it "complete, everything there," and stated that all he had on the farm was three heifers.

Lucy took a partly filled bottle of whiskey into the restaurant with him for the purpose of giving Zehmer a drink if he wanted it. Zehmer did, and he and Lucy had one or two drinks together. Lucy said that while he felt the drinks he took he was not intoxicated, and from the way Zehmer handled the transaction he did not think he was either.

December 20 was on Saturday. Next day Lucy telephoned to J.C. Lucy and arranged with the latter to take a half interest in the purchase and pay half of the consideration. On Monday he engaged an attorney to examine the title. The attorney reported favorably on December 31 and on January 2 Lucy wrote Zehmer stating that the title was satisfactory, that he was ready to pay the purchase price in cash and asking when Zehmer would be ready to close the deal. Zehmer replied by letter, mailed on January 13, asserting that he had never agreed or intended to sell.

Mr. and Mrs. Zehmer were called by the complainants as adverse witnesses. Zehmer testified in substance as follows:

He bought this farm more than ten years ago for $11,000. He had had twenty-five offers, more or less, to buy it, including several from Lucy, who had never offered any specific sum of money. He had given them all the same answer, that he was not interested in selling it. On this Saturday night before Christmas it looked like everybody and his brother came by there to have a drink. He took a good many drinks during the afternoon and had a pint of his own. When he entered the restaurant around eight-thirty Lucy was there and he could see that he was "pretty high." He said to Lucy, "Boy, you got some good liquor, drinking, ain't you?" Lucy then offered him a drink. "I was already high as a Georgia pine, and didn't have any more better sense than to pour another great big slug out and gulp it down, and he took one too."

After they had talked a while Lucy asked whether he still had the Ferguson farm. He replied that he had not sold it and Lucy said, "I bet you wouldn't take $50,000.00 for it." Zehmer asked him if he would give $50,000 and Lucy said yes. Zehmer replied, "You haven't got $50,000.00 in cash." Lucy said he did and Zehmer replied that he did not believe it. They argued "pro and con for a long time," mainly about "whether he had $50,000 in cash that he could put up right then and buy that farm."

Finally, said Zehmer, Lucy told him if he didn't believe he had $50,000, "you sign that piece of paper here and say you will take $50,000.00 for the farm." He, Zehmer, "just grabbed the back off of a guest check there" and wrote on the back of it. At that point in his testimony Zehmer asked to see what he had written to "see if I recognize my own handwriting." He examined the paper and exclaimed, "Great balls of fire, I got 'Firgerson' for Ferguson. I have got satisfactory spelled wrong. I don't recognize that writing if I would see it, wouldn't know it was mine."

After Zehmer had, as he described it, "scribbled this thing off," Lucy said, "Get your wife to sign it." Zehmer walked over to where she was and she at first refused to sign but did so after he told her that he "was just needling him [Lucy], and didn't mean a thing in the world, that I was not selling the farm." Zehmer then "took it back over there * * * and I was still looking at the dern thing. I had the drink right there by my hand, and I reached over to get a drink, and he said, 'Let me see it.' He reached and picked it up, and when I looked back again he had it in his pocket and he dropped a five dollar bill over there, and he said, 'Here is five dollars payment on it.' * * * I said, 'Hell no, that is beer and liquor talking. I am not going to sell you the farm. I have told you that too many times before.' "

* * *

On examination by her own counsel [Mrs. Zehmer testified] that her husband laid this piece of paper down after it was signed; that Lucy said to let him see it, took it, folded it and put it in his wallet, then said to Zehmer, "Let me give you $5.00," but Zehmer said, "No, this is liquor talking. I don't want to sell the farm, I have told you that I want my son to have it. This is all a joke." Lucy then said at least twice, "Zehmer, you have sold your farm," wheeled around and started for the door. He paused at the door and said, "I will bring you $50,000.00 tomorrow. * * * No, tomorrow is Sunday. I will bring it to you Monday." She said you could tell definitely that he was drinking and she said to her husband, "You should have taken him home," but he said, "Well, I am just about as bad off as he is."

* * *

The defendants insist that the evidence was ample to support their contention that the writing sought to be enforced was prepared as a bluff or dare to force Lucy to admit that he did not have $50,000; that the whole matter was a joke; that the writing was not delivered to Lucy and no binding contract was ever made between the parties.

It is an unusual, if not bizarre, defense. When made to the writing admittedly prepared by one of the defendants and signed by both, clear evidence is required to sustain it.

In his testimony Zehmer claimed that he "was high as a Georgia pine," and that the transaction "was just a bunch of two doggoned drunks bluffing to see who could talk the biggest and say the most." That claim is inconsistent with his attempt to testify in great detail as to what was said and what was done. It is contradicted by other evidence as to the condition of both parties, and rendered of no weight by the testimony of his wife that when Lucy left the restaurant she suggested that Zehmer drive him home. The record is convincing that Zehmer was not intoxicated to the extent of being unable to comprehend the nature and consequences of the instrument he executed, and hence that instrument is not to be invalidated on that ground. * * * It was in fact conceded by defendants' counsel in oral argument that under the evidence Zehmer was not too drunk to make a valid contract.

The evidence is convincing also that Zehmer wrote two agreements, the first one beginning "I hereby agree to sell." Zehmer first said he could not remember about that, then that "I don't think I wrote but one out." Mrs. Zehmer said that what he wrote was "I hereby agree," but that the "I" was changed to "We" after that night. The agreement that was written and signed is in the record and indicates no such change. Neither are the mistakes in spelling that Zehmer sought to point out readily apparent.

The appearance of the contract, the fact that it was under discussion for forty minutes or more before it was signed; Lucy's objection to the first draft because it was written in the singular, and he wanted Mrs. Zehmer to sign it also; the rewriting to meet that objection and the signing by Mrs. Zehmer; the discussion of what was to be included in the sale, the provision for the examination of the title, the completeness of the instrument that was executed, the taking possession of it by Lucy with no request or suggestion by either of the defendants that he give it back, are facts which furnish persuasive evidence that the execution of the contract was a serious business transaction rather than a casual, jesting matter as defendants now contend.

* * *

If it be assumed, contrary to what we think the evidence shows, that Zehmer was jesting about selling his farm to Lucy and that the transaction was intended by him to be a joke, nevertheless the evidence shows that Lucy did not so understand it but considered it to be a serious business transaction and the contract to be binding on the Zehmers as well as on himself. The very next day he arranged with his brother to put up half the money and take a half interest in the land. The day after that he employed an attorney to examine the title. The next night, Tuesday, he was back at Zehmer's place and there Zehmer told him for the first time, Lucy said, that he wasn't going to sell and he told Zehmer, "You know you sold that place fair and square." After receiving the report from his attorney that the title was good he wrote to Zehmer that he was ready to close the deal.

Not only did Lucy actually believe, but the evidence shows he was warranted in believing, that the contract represented a serious business transaction and a good faith sale and purchase of the farm.

In the field of contracts, as generally elsewhere, "We must look to the outward expression of a person as manifesting his intention rather than to his secret and unexpressed intention. 'The law imputes to a person an intention corresponding to the reasonable meaning of his words and acts.' " First Nat.

Exchange Bank of Roanoke v. Roanoke Oil Co., 169 Va. 99, 114, 192 S.E. 764, 770.

At no time prior to the execution of the contract had Zehmer indicated to Lucy by word or act that he was not in earnest about selling the farm. They had argued about it and discussed its terms, as Zehmer admitted, for a long time. Lucy testified that if there was any jesting it was about paying $50,000 that night. The contract and the evidence show that he was not expected to pay the money that night. Zehmer said that after the writing was signed he laid it down on the counter in front of Lucy. Lucy said Zehmer handed it to him. In any event there had been what appeared to be a good faith offer and a good faith acceptance, followed by the execution and apparent delivery of a written contract. Both said that Lucy put the writing in his pocket and then offered Zehmer $5 to seal the bargain. Not until then, even under the defendants' evidence, was anything said or done to indicate that the matter was a joke. Both of the Zehmers testified that when Zehmer asked his wife to sign he whispered that it was a joke so Lucy wouldn't hear and that it was not intended that he should hear.

* * *

An agreement or mutual assent is of course essential to a valid contract but the law imputes to a person an intention corresponding to the reasonable meaning of his words and acts. If his words and acts, judged by a reasonable standard, manifest an intention to agree, it is immaterial what may be the real but unexpressed state of his mind. 17 C.J.S., Contracts, § 32, p. 361; 12 Am.Jur., Contracts, § 19, p. 515.

So a person cannot set up that he was merely jesting when his conduct and words would warrant a reasonable person in believing that he intended a real agreement. * * *

Whether the writing signed by the defendants and now sought to be enforced by the complainants was the result of a serious offer by Lucy and a serious acceptance by the defendants, or was a serious offer by Lucy and an acceptance in secret jest by the defendants, in either event it constituted a binding contract of sale between the parties.

Defendants contend further, however, that even though a contract was made, equity should decline to enforce it under the circumstances. These circumstances have been set forth in detail above. They disclose some drinking by the two parties but not to an extent that they were unable to understand fully what they were doing. There was no fraud, no misrepresentation, no sharp practice and no dealing between unequal parties. The farm had been bought for $11,000 and was assessed for taxation at $6,300. The purchase price was $50,000. Zehmer admitted that it was a good price. There is in fact present in this case none of the grounds usually urged against specific performance.

* * *

The complainants are entitled to have specific performance of the contract sued on. The decree appealed from is therefore reversed and the cause is remanded for the entry of a proper decree requiring the defendants to perform the contract in accordance with the prayer of the bill.

Reversed and remanded.

THANK YOU

We hereby agree to sell to W.O. Lucy the Ferguson farm complete for $50,000.00, Title satisfactory to buyer.

A. H. Zehmer

Ida S. Zehmer

Please pay handwritten total on reverse

---

19 A. LEOPOLD, G. BEYER, & D. PARK, WEST'S LEGAL FORMS

§ 5.3 (2d ed. 1986).

Offer to Purchase and Acceptance Form

1. **Real Property.** The undersigned _____ residing at _____, hereinafter called the Purchaser, hereby offers and agrees to purchase from _____, residing at _____, hereinafter called the Seller, the premises locally known as _____, situated in _____, County of _____ and State of _____, and more particularly described as _____.

Together with and including all buildings and other improvements thereon and all rights of seller in and to any and all streets, roads, highways, alleys, driveways, easements, and rights of way appurtenant thereto.

2. **Personal Property.** All heating, plumbing and lighting fixtures, all flowers, shrubs, trees, linoleum, window shades, venetian blinds, curtain rods, storm windows and storm doors, screens and awnings, whatever and if any, belonging to and now in or on said premises, are included in this sale and shall become the property of the purchaser at closing.

3. **Purchase Price.** The Purchaser shall pay to the Seller for the above described real and personal property the sum of $_____ payable as follows:

On signing this instrument as a deposit .... $_____
On the delivery of the deed as hereinafter provided, in cash or
   certified check, the sum of .... $_____
By assuming and agreeing to pay according to its terms, the principal
   balance of a mortgage in the amount of $_____ which mortgage is
   not a first lien on said premises, bearing interest at the rate of
   _____ per cent per annum and payable _____

By giving Seller a purchase money bond and mortgage in the amount of .... $_____ which bond and mortgage shall be in statutory form and a _____ lien on said premises, and which shall run for a term of _____ years, bearing interest at the rate of _____ per cent per annum and payable as follows: _____.

4. **Title Policy.** The Seller shall deliver to the Purchaser within 30 days a commitment for a policy of title insurance to be issued by the _____ Guaranty Company and to be delivered to the Purchaser at the closing, for an amount not less than the purchase price hereunder, guaranteeing title in the condition required herein.

5. **Defects in Title.** If objection to the title is made, based upon a written opinion of the Purchaser's attorney that the title is not in the condition required hereunder, the Seller shall have 30 days from the date he is notified in writing of the particular defects claimed either (a) to remedy the title, or (b) to refund the deposit, in full termination of this agreement, if he is unable to remedy the title or obtain title insurance. If the Seller remedies the title within the time specified, the Purchaser agrees to complete the sale within 10 days of written notification thereof. If the Seller fails to remedy the title or to give the Purchaser the above written notification within such 10 days, the deposit shall be refunded forthwith in full termination of this agreement.

6. **Mortgage Commitment.** The Purchaser agrees, on acceptance by the Seller, to apply forthwith and in good faith for a _____ year _____ mortgage commitment in the amount of $_____ at _____ per cent. If such mortgage commitment is not obtained by _____, 19__, either party may cancel this contract by giving written notice of such cancellation to the other party, in which event the money paid on account hereof shall be returned to Purchaser and this contract shall become null and void and neither party hereto shall have any claim against the other.

7. **Adjustments at Closing.** Rentals, mortgage interest, taxes computed on a fiscal year basis including all items in the current county tax bill excepting returned school taxes, insurance premiums (fire and extended coverage), water and sewer charges, and all other matters not herein otherwise provided for shall be prorated and adjusted as of date of delivery of deed. The Seller shall assign to purchaser all right, title, and interest in and to any and all reserves held in escrow by the mortgagee for payment of taxes, interest, and other items and the Purchaser shall repay to the Seller the amount of such reserves. The Purchaser will accept title subject to, and will pay all assessments and installments of assessments for local improvements that are not payable as of date of delivery of deed.

8. **Rights of Tenants.** The Seller shall deliver and the Purchaser shall accept possession of such property at the date of closing subject to the rights of tenants, a list of which is hereto attached. All the leases to tenants named therein shall be assigned to the Purchaser and the security rental deposits, if any, shall be transferred to the Purchaser. The Seller shall in addition represent that there are no prepaid rentals other than those disclosed in such leases.

9. **Date of Closing.** If this offer is accepted by the Seller and if title can be conveyed in the condition required hereunder, the Purchaser agrees to complete the sale within 30 days after delivery of the commitment for the policy of title insurance. At least three-days notice of the date of closing shall be given to the Seller by the Purchaser. In the event of default by the Purchaser, the Seller may declare a forfeiture hereunder and retain the deposit as liquidated damages.

10. **Place of Closing.** The closing of the sale shall take place at the office of the _____ Guaranty Company.

11. **Notices.** All notices, deliveries, or tenders given or made in connection herewith shall be deemed completed and legally sufficient if in writing and if mailed or delivered to the respective party for whom the same is intended at his address herein set forth.

12. **Term of Offer.** If acceptance by the Seller is not made in writing on or before _____, 19__, this offer shall be deemed withdrawn, and the deposit shall be returned to the Purchaser.

13. **Representations.** This instrument, on acceptance by the Seller, shall constitute the entire agreement between the parties hereto relating to said sale and purchase and supersedes all prior or other agreements and representations in connection with said sale and purchase.

14. **Binding Effect.** The covenants herein shall bind the heirs, personal representatives, administrators, executors, assigns, and successors of the respective parties.

Dated _____, 19__.

_____   _____
Witness   Purchaser

Receipt

Received from the Purchaser the deposit money above mentioned which will be returned forthwith if the foregoing offer is not accepted within the time above set forth.

_____
Broker

_____
Address

Acceptance

The foregoing offer is hereby accepted and the Seller agrees to sell the property described upon the terms stated. Receipt of the deposit money is acknowledged.

The Seller agrees to pay the broker for services rendered and for value received a commission of _____% of the sale price, which shall be due only if the sale is consummated and shall be payable at the closing of title.

By the execution of this instrument, the Seller acknowledges the receipt of a copy of this agreement.

Dated _____, 19__.

_____   _____
Witness   Seller

Note
Theories of Obligation Revisited

Did the court adopt the wrong theory of obligation in Lucy v. Zehmer? Instead of agreement with consideration, should the court have found that the Zehmers' careless use of language constituted a tort? Consider these views:

WHITTIER, THE RESTATEMENT OF CONTRACTS AND MUTUAL ASSENT

17 Cal.L.Rev. 441, 442–43 (1929).

It would have simplified our law of contracts if actual meeting of the minds mutually communicated had remained essential. The liability for carelessly misleading the other party into the reasonable belief that there was assent might well have been held to be in tort. With such a liability in tort the danger that one could falsely claim that he did not assent and so escape the contract would be rendered insubstantial. In most cases the triers of the fact would not be misled by his false evidence of non-assent. If they concluded that he truly did not assent then there would be liability in tort unless his mistake was also found to have been non-negligent or to have resulted in no damage. Under the present law the non-consenting party is liable on the contract itself if careless. The chief unfortunate result of this state of law is that he is bound to the contract though the other party is notified of the mistake before the latter has changed his position or suffered any damage. To hold one for the merely careless use of language which causes no damage whatever to the party to whom the language is addressed is certainly inconsistent with principles generally applied. If D drives down Michigan Avenue, Chicago, in a careless manner but no one is hurt, can any of those who might have been hurt sue D?

But taking the law as settled that one is liable on the contract where he carelessly misleads the other party to reasonably believe there was assent, is it wise to state the entire law of mutual assent in terms of these admittedly exceptional cases? Why not say that actual assent communicated is the basis of "mutual assent" except where there is careless misleading which induces a reasonable belief in assent? The writer thinks that this approach to the problems involved is more likely to lead one to just conclusions.

Problem 4–5

Assume that Edgar Denny was counsel for Lucy. During the early stages of preparation for trial, the following exchange took place in Denny's office. Consider whether Denny acted contrary to Opinion No. 79 of the Committee on Legal Ethics of the District of Columbia bar, below (which we will assume to be applicable).

Denny: You know, don't you, that you will not win this case unless you understood, and reasonably so, that Zehmer was making a present offer to sell to you when you were together there in the restaurant.

Lucy: Well, it was Saturday night before Christmas, and we was in Zehmer's restaurant a drinkin' together, and it all started out we were a jokin' around * * *.

Denny: What's that?

Lucy: We were a drinkin' and a jokin' around.

Denny: Well, when did you get serious?

Lucy: Oh, not until I got home and started sobering up a bit did I really think how much I wanted that farm, and I got the piece of paper out of my pocket, and those words on there looked real good to me.

Denny: Do you mean you never, for a moment, thought Zehmer was really serious while you were at the restaurant?

Lucy: Oh, well, I guess I did. A little. That's right, when we started writin' everything down. Then I thought maybe it was a little serious.

Denny: Well, now how do you plan to testify?

Lucy: I'll say I was serious midway through and that is the way Zehmer looked to me.

Denny: Only midway?

Lucy: Well maybe even earlier, when we started talkin' figures.

OPINION NO. 79, LEGAL ETHICS COMMITTEE OPINION 169

Committee on Legal Ethics, District of Columbia Bar (1980).

[A] lawyer may not prepare, or assist in preparing, testimony that he or she knows, or ought to know, is false or misleading. So long as this prohibition is not transgressed, a lawyer may properly suggest language as well as the substance of testimony, and may—indeed, should—do whatever is feasible to prepare his or her witnesses for examination.

* * *

It follows, therefore * * * that the fact that the particular words in which testimony, whether written or oral, is cast originated with a lawyer rather than the witness whose testimony it is has no significance so long as the substance of that testimony is not, so far as the lawyer knows or ought to know, false or misleading. If the particular words suggested by the lawyer, even though not literally false, are calculated to convey a misleading impression, this would be equally impermissible from the ethical point of view. Herein, indeed, lies the principal hazard (leaving aside outright subornation of perjury) in a lawyer's suggesting particular forms of language to a witness instead of leaving the witness to articulate his or her thought wholly without prompting: there may be differences in nuance among variant phrasings of the same substantive point, which are so significant as to make one version misleading while another is not. Yet it is obvious that by the same token, choice of words may also improve the clarity and precision of a statement: even subtle changes of shading may as readily improve testimony as impair it. The fact that a lawyer suggests particular language to a witness means only that the lawyer may be affecting the testimony as respects its clarity and accuracy; and not necessarily that the effect is to debase rather than improve the testimony in these respects. It is not, we think, a matter of undue difficulty for a reasonably competent and conscientious lawyer to discern the line of impermissibility, where truth shades into untruth, and to refrain from crossing it.

Problem 4–6

1) Assume Zehmer phoned you prior to the restaurant episode and said that Lucy wanted to buy the Ferguson farm. Zehmer asks you to draft a proposed agreement and you suggest a meeting first in your office. Make a list of the major questions you would want to ask Zehmer at such a meeting. In preparing your list, consider the form at pages 390–393.

2) According to the Associated Press, Jay Arsenault caught Barry Bond's 600th home run. A friend had given Arsenault tickets to the game, the friend alleges, in exchange for Arsenault's promise to split the value of the ball if he caught it. The Associated Press reports that "[u]nder California law, oral promises are contracts under most circumstances * * *. But is there a chitchat exception—an allowance that friends shooting the breeze might not always be serious?" If the reporter had called you to explain whether Arsenault's promise was enforceable (if true),what would you have said?

MORROW v. MORROW

Court of Appeals of Oklahoma, 1980.
612 P.2d 730.

Romang, Judge:

The Plaintiffs–Appellants, Warren and Betty Morrow (husband and wife), brought this action to recover for services rendered to the decedent Maude Morrow, mother of Warren and Defendant–Appellee Woodye Morrow. They also sought to set aside a conveyance of certain mineral interests from Woodye to Defendant–Appellee Dennis M. Morrow, Woodye's son. This conveyance was made without consideration. Woodye had acquired title from Maude by warranty deed.

At trial the District Court, sitting without a jury as chancellor, found the evidence insufficient to support the Plaintiffs' claim for services and ordered the mineral conveyance set aside and the proceeds of the surface sale (less certain expenses) and mineral rights be evenly distributed to 8 surviving children of Maude.

* * *

The Plaintiffs' theory was that after receiving title to Maude's real property, Woodye orally agreed with Plaintiffs that if they would care for Maude that on her death Woodye would sell the property and first pay the Plaintiffs for the care of Maude and divide the remainder equally among her heirs.

* * *

* * * [T]he findings of the trial court, sitting without a jury, are entitled to the weight of a jury's verdict, i. e. they must be affirmed if supported by any probative evidence.

* * *

Whether there was a contract is a matter as to which the party asserting the contract has the burden. * * * As part of the fact finders process, courts are convinced that in our society the vast majority of family arrangements are not expected to be attended with contractual consequences. * * * This expectation may be upset by any facts showing the parties expected to be bound legally an element not normally relevant in agreements between nonfamily members. As Corbin says:

> The following statements may be of assistance in distinguishing between non-enforceable social engagements and contractual agreements: 1. If the subject matter and terms of a transaction are such as customarily have affected legal relations and there is nothing to indicate that the one now asserting their existence had reasons to know that the other party intended not to affect his legal relations, thus the transaction will be operative legally. 2. If the subject matter and terms are not such as customarily have affected legal relations, the transaction is not legally operative unless the expressions of the parties indicate an intention to make it so. (Footnotes omitted.) 1 Corbin on Contracts s 34. See also Restatement of Contracts (Second) s 21B comment c (T.D. 1973).

Nothing in our cases hold that family members may not make their arrangements contractual in nature. * * * Rather the point of our cases and scholarly comment is that there is a norm of societal expectation. The subject matter here involved is care for an invalid mother. Such arrangements are frequently gratuitous, founded in love and affection. But where there are a number of children, it is also frequently the case that one child and spouse will undertake primary care and the others will contribute financially in agreed amounts or as they can. Whether these arrangements are contractual or not depends on the intent of the parties. But in such cases the party asserting the contract has the burden of setting aside our belief that most such arrangements are not contractual.

* * *

In this case the trier of fact was unpersuaded. Based on the record evidence we cannot say as a matter of law he was wrong. Accordingly, we affirm.

AFFIRMED.

Calvin and Hobbes   by Bill Watterson

TILBERT v. EAGLE LOCK CO.

Supreme Court of Errors of Connecticut, 1933.
116 Conn. 357, 165 A. 205.

Action by Annie Tilbert against the Eagle Lock Company to recover upon a "certificate of benefit" issued by the defendant to the husband of the plaintiff brought to the court of common pleas and reserved for the advice of this court.

Judgment in favor of plaintiff.

* * *

HINMAN, JUSTICE.

The crucial question reserved is whether the demurrer to the amended complaint should be sustained; it being stipulated that, if the facts alleged entitle the plaintiff to recover, judgment shall be rendered accordingly. The complaint as amended alleged, in substance, that the plaintiff's husband, Kasimierz Tilbert, entered the employ of the defendant corporation prior to January 1, 1922, and continued therein until his death on August 28, 1931. On or about June 29, 1923, the defendant canceled the group insurance which covered the plaintiff's intestate and issued a so-called "Certificate of Benefit" to him, a copy of which and of a letter attached thereto are annexed to the complaint as schedules A and B. It is alleged that "in accordance with the terms of said certificate the plaintiff's intestate remained in the employ of the defendant more than five years and at the time of his death was employed by said defendant and was not notified of any attempted cancellation of said certificate." By the terms of the certificate the plaintiff as beneficiary is entitled to $1,000, with interest. The plaintiff notified the defendant of the death of her husband and demanded payment, which the defendant refused.

It is further alleged that on or before August 22, 1931, the officers of the defendant corporation decided to withdraw the certificates of benefit and on August 24th the treasurer caused notices to be printed, dated August 28, 1931, stating, "Effective immediately, all certificates of benefit are hereby canceled and the benefit plan discontinued." Notice of a reduction in wages was also included. The treasurer inserted in each printed notice the number of a particular employee, and these were put in the pay envelopes given by the paymaster to the employees on August 28, 1931, which was the regular pay day at the defendant's factory. Among said notices was one bearing the factory number of Tilbert and the amount of the hourly pay which he was thereafter to receive. The plaintiff's intestate had been ill for about four weeks and died about 2 o'clock in the morning of August 28th. Schedule A, above mentioned, reads as follows:

"Certificate of Benefit

"Certificate No. 970

"From Eagle Lock Co., Terryville, Conn.

"Accruing to Kasimierz Tilbert (Hereinafter called the Employee) the sum of Seven Hundred (700) Dollars,

"Payable to Annie Tilbert, wife as Beneficiary so named by above employee should death of said employee occur while in the employ of said Eagle Lock Co.

"The schedule below indicates the rate of increase of this benefit as determined by continuous service. [Schedule of increases yearly, up to $1,000 for term of service of five years and over.]

"This certificate automatically is made void when the holder ceases to be an employee. [Provision for payment of full benefit then effective if any employee holding certificate shall before attaining the age of 60, become wholly and permanently disabled by bodily injuries or disease.]

"Eagle Lock Co.

"O.B. Hough, Treasurer.

"Dated June 29th, 1923."

Schedule B, which was printed on the same sheet as schedule A, reads in part as follows:

"To Our Employees:

"The success of this Company depends in a large degree on the efficiency and loyalty of its Employees and, of course, just as truly does the prosperity of the community and our Employees and their families depend upon the success of the Company.

"Desiring to show our appreciation of the continuing service and the efficiency and loyalty of the Employees, in a substantial manner which will aid each Employee to provide for his dependents in the event of death or permanent disability, we offer the following plan of benefits, grading the amounts according to term of continuous service."

An explanation of the plan and its operation is then given, followed by:

"This benefit plan being voluntary on the part of Eagle Lock Co., it is understood that it constitutes no contract with any Employee or any beneficiary, and confers no legal rights on him or them. It in no way interferes with his freedom to leave our employ whenever he pleases, nor on the other hand, does it take away our right as Employer to dismiss any Employee.

"We fully expect and hope that this benefit plan as outlined above will continue indefinitely and will be appreciated by the Employees to the extent that we feel justified in continuing the plan indefinitely. We must, however, and do reserve to ourselves the right to discontinue these benefits at any time without any liability on our part to any employee or any beneficiary, either or both.

"We trust every Employee will appreciate the value of these benefits to those he leaves behind should death occur, as it does often unexpectedly and very often prematurely, and not sacrifice these benefits to his dependents by hastily making a change of employment, thus making void the certificate.

"Respectfully,

"Eagle Lock Co."

* * *

As to the claimed lack of consideration, it appears clearly enough from schedule B that a prime purpose of the granting of the benefits was to secure the good will, loyalty, and efficiency of the defendant's employees, and especially, through the progressive premium placed on long-continued service, to minimize labor turnover and obtain the advantages of experienced operatives. The attainment of these purposes constituted a benefit or advantage received by the defendant, who must be assumed to have requested, because it desired it and regarded it as beneficial to its interests. Tilbert remained in the employ of the defendant more than seven years after receiving the certificate. By so doing he manifested his acceptance of the promise, forebore his right to terminate the employment and engage elsewhere, and conferred the benefit which the defendant sought. * * *

The declaration in schedule B, above quoted, that the plan constitutes no contract and confers no legal rights, when read, as it must be, with due regard to the other provisions, may and should be construed as preserving the right of the employer to discharge the employee and of the latter to leave the employment at any time, and the right of the employer to discontinue the benefits without liability for such discontinuance or for benefits for death occurring subsequent thereto. To construe it as meaning, further, that, notwithstanding acceptance by an employee and compliance therewith, no obligation whatever was imposed upon the defendant, and that, without exercise of the reserved right of discontinuance or other action terminating the agreement, it might refuse to perform it, would ascribe to the defendant an intention to mislead its employees, to its advantage, by an inducement which was known and intended by it to be entirely nugatory, and which this record does not require us to attribute to it. Surely Exhibits A and B constitute more than an offer or promise made with an understood intention that, even if accepted and acted on, it was not to be legally binding at any time but only expressive of a present intention, and therefore not a contract. Wellington v. Apthorp, 145 Mass. 69, 74, 13 N.E. 10; Page, Contracts, § 77. It is by no means analogous to the illustrations cited by the defendant—an intention announced by a corporation to open a social center for its workmen, or an announcement by an individual of a purpose to give a Christmas present to a friend. Nor is the situation of the employee comparable with that of a person who voluntarily renders occasional services merely in the expectation of receiving gratuities therefor. Gibbs v. Downs, 94 Conn. 487, 490, 109 A. 170. It amounted to and constituted a promise, unless and until it was withdrawn, to employees who accepted and acted upon it, and the beneficiaries of those who died while it was in effect.

It is clear that the defendant reserved the right to discontinue the benefit system at any time, without the consent of the employees or any notice to them expressly provided for. Its action, as alleged in the complaint, in withdrawing the certificates of benefit, was in line with this reservation and authorized by it. The only inference to be drawn from the facts alleged is that, on or before August 22, 1931, it was decided to do so, the withdrawal to take effect when the next pay envelopes were distributed, which would be on the 28th. The allegations as to the preparations made and the sending of the notice so indicate. The plaintiff's decedent died on that date, but long before the commencement of the working day, and therefore before the notice could be or was intended to be distributed and the withdrawal put into effect. The general rule that the law knows no fractions of a day is not allowed to operate against right and justice, and these fractions will be taken into account when, as here, from the nature of the case, justice requires that it be done or when necessary to save a vested right. * * * Also, under the general rule, the entire day upon which a contract expires is open for compliance with it. * * * As the termination of the agreement was not complete until the end of the day of August 28th, Tilbert's death at any time on that date entitled his beneficiary to the designated benefit.

Our answers to the questions reserved are that the demurrer should be overruled, and that, on the facts stated in the amended complaint, judgment should be rendered for the plaintiff. No costs will be taxed in this court.

In this opinion the other Judges concurred, except MALTBIE, C.J., who dissented.

1 CORBIN ON CONTRACTS
§ 34 at 138 (1963).

It should be noted that when the subject matter of an agreement is of a kind that is customarily dealt with in enforceable contracts, and the parties have in fact acted under the agreement, a court is likely to look with some distaste at provisions that seem to exclude all sanction and remedy.

Problem 4–7

If Eagle Lock Co. had asked you to draft its "Certificate of Benefit" and had told you it did not want to be bound under any circumstances, what would you have told the company? If you represented Mrs. Tilbert and the case arose today, what additional theories of obligation, if any, would you pursue?

CARGILL COMMISSION CO. v. MOWERY, 99 Kan. 389, 161 P. 634 (1916). [Through a series of telegrams, Cargill negotiated with the Hutchinson Grain Company for the purchase of wheat. Seller Hutchinson used the wrong "code word" concerning the number of bushels it was offering to sell so that, while it intended to sell only 3,000 to 3,500 bushels, Cargill reasonably believed Hutchinson had agreed to sell 35,000 bushels. Thinking it had bought 35,000 bushels from Hutchinson, Cargill immediately resold 35,000 bushels of wheat on the market. Cargill later received a letter and telegram from Hutchinson correcting its error. Cargill brought an action against Hutchinson for its refusal to deliver more than 3,500 bushels of wheat.

Cargill appealed from an order denying its motion for judgment on the pleadings, and from an order sustaining a demurrer to its evidence.]

WEST, J.

* * *

The telegrams themselves consist of a bid for 30,000 to 35,000 bushels, a direction to book that amount, and a reply that it had been booked. Had the correspondence ended here no question could arise as to its meaning or obligation. When the additional fact appears that pursuant thereto the plaintiff at once sold 35,000 bushels of wheat in reliance upon this contract, the final and binding character of the deal is accentuated. When the news of the defendant's position and intention reached the plaintiff the sale of the 35,000 bushels had already been made. Had the contract contained in the messages of June 29th been in the form of a written agreement signed by the parties, and the plaintiff relying thereon had acted as it did, the defendant could not then have been heard to say at the expense of the plaintiff that he had made a mistake in the number of bushels he wrote into the contract, and therefore was not bound.

Had the mistake been discovered and made known to the plaintiff before acting on the contract the error could have been corrected, but it was not the plaintiff's mistake nor was it the plaintiff's fault that the defendant used the wrong word in the contract, and did not make this known until the plaintiff had obligated itself to furnish the amount of wheat which the written contract or written evidence of the contract—the telegrams—between the parties called for. * * *

* * *

The order sustaining the demurrer to the evidence of plaintiff is reversed, and the cause is remanded, with directions to render judgment for the plaintiff in accordance herewith. All the Justices concurring.

RAFFLES v. WICHELHAUS

Court of Exchequer, 1864.
2 Hurlstone & Coltman 906.

Declaration. For that it was agreed between the plaintiff and the defendants, to wit, at Liverpool, that the plaintiff should sell to the defendants, and the defendants buy of the plaintiff, certain goods, to wit, 125 bales of Surat cotton, guaranteed middling fair merchant's Dhollorah, to arrive ex "Peerless" from Bombay; and that the cotton should be taken from the quay, and that the defendants would pay the plaintiff for the same at a certain rate, to wit, at the rate of $17\frac{1}{4}$d. per pound, within a certain time then agreed upon after the arrival of the said goods in England.—Averments: that the said goods did arrive by the said ship from Bombay in England, to wit, at Liverpool, and the plaintiff was then and there ready, and willing and offered to deliver the said goods to the defendants, & c. Breach: that the defendants refused to accept the said goods or pay the plaintiff for them.

Plea. That the said ship mentioned in the said agreement was meant and intended by the defendants to be the ship called the "Peerless," which sailed from Bombay, to wit, in October; and that the plaintiff was not ready and willing and did not offer to deliver to the defendants any bales of cotton which arrived by the last mentioned ship, but instead thereof was only ready and willing and offered to deliver to the defendants 125 bales of Surat cotton which arrived by another and different ship, which was also called the "Peerless," and which sailed from Bombay, to wit, in December.

Demurrer, and joinder therein.

Milward, in support of the demurrer.—The contract was for the sale of a number of bales of cotton of a particular description, which the plaintiff was ready to deliver. It is immaterial by what ship the cotton was to arrive, so that it was a ship called the "Peerless." The words "to arrive ex 'Peerless,'"only mean that if the vessel is lost on the voyage, the contract is to be at an end. [POLLOCK, C.B.—It would be a question for the jury whether both parties meant the same ship called the "Peerless."] That would be so if the contract was for the sale of a ship called the "Peerless;" but it is for the sale of cotton on board a ship of that name. [POLLOCK, C.B.—The defendant only bought that cotton which was to arrive by a particular ship. It may as well be said, that if there is a contract for the purchase of certain goods in warehouse A, that is satisfied by the delivery of goods of the same description in warehouse B.] In that case there would be goods in both warehouses; here it does not appear that the plaintiff had any goods on board the other "Peerless."

[MARTIN, B. It is imposing on the defendant a contract different from that which he entered into. POLLOCK, C.B. It is like a contract for the purchase of wine coming from a particular estate in France or Spain, where there are two estates of that name.] The defendant has no right to contradict by parol evidence a written contract good upon the face of it. He does not impute misrepresentation or fraud, but only says that he fancied the ship was a different one. Intention is of no avail, unless stated at the time of the contract. [POLLOCK, C.B.—One vessel sailed in October and the other in December.] The time of sailing is no part of the contract.

Mellish (Cohen with him), in support of the plea.—There is nothing on the face of the contract to shew that any particular ship called the "Peerless" was meant; but the moment it appears that two ships called the "Peerless" were about to sail from Bombay there is a latent ambiguity, and parol evidence may be given for the purpose of shewing that the defendant meant one "Peerless" and the plaintiff another. That being so, there was no consensus ad idem, and therefore no binding contract.—He was then stopped by the Court.

PER CURIAM—There must be judgment for the defendants.

Judgment for the defendants.

RESTATEMENT (SECOND) OF CONTRACTS § 20.

Effect of Misunderstanding

(1) There is no manifestation of mutual assent to an exchange if the parties attach materially different meanings to their manifestations and

(a) neither party knows or has reason to know the meaning attached by the other; or

(b) each party knows or each party has reason to know the meaning attached by the other.

(2) The manifestations of the parties are operative in accordance with the meaning attached to them by one of the parties if

(a) that party does not know of any different meaning attached by the other, and the other knows the meaning attached by the first party; or

(b) that party has no reason to know of any different meaning attached by the other, and the other has reason to know the meaning attached by the first party.

RESTATEMENT (SECOND) OF CONTRACTS § 201.

Illustration

4. "A agrees to sell and B to buy a quantity of eviscerated 'chicken.' A tenders 'stewing chicken' or 'fowl'; B rejects on the ground that the contract calls for 'broilers' or 'fryers.' Each party makes a claim for damages against the other. It is found that each acted in good faith and that neither had reason to know of the difference in meaning. Both claims fail."

A.W.B. SIMPSON, LEADING CASES IN THE COMMON LAW
154 (1995).

Assuming that there had been a genuine misunderstanding when the contract was made, what harm had this done to Wichelhaus and Busch? Surely none. Given the way prices had fallen, whichever ship they took delivery from they had made a losing contract, and if cotton had been delivered to them from *Peerless* (Major), the October ship they said they had in mind, they would have suffered a *larger* loss than they would incur by accepting delivery from *Peerless* (Flavin), the December ship. In common sense they had nothing to complain about. * * *

Had the matter been handled by arbitrators, they might well have decided that the sensible and decent way to handle the problem, the equitable solution, would be to require Wichelhaus and Busch to take delivery from Raffles, and consider themselves lucky not to have lost more. * * * What they would surely never have countenanced would be for them to escape all liability on their losing contract. * * *

DICKEY v. HURD, 33 F.2d 415 (1st Cir.1929). [Dickey in Georgia sent a letter to Hurd in Massachusetts requesting the price of Hurd's land in Georgia. On July 8, 1926, Hurd offered to sell the land at "$15 per acre cash" and stated that he would give Dickey "till July 18, 1926 including that day to accept this offer." Dickey telegraphed an acceptance on July 17 and promised to send a $500 down payment. Although Hurd received the telegram on July 17, he claimed his offer required Dickey to pay the cash price by July 18.]

BINGHAM, C.J.

A * * * difficult question is whether the offer calls for payment of the purchase price, an act of acceptance, on or before July 18; or whether it simply calls for a notice of acceptance. The language of the offer is: "I will sell the same to you for [having named the price] cash and give you till July 18, 1926, including that day to accept this offer." Standing alone and apart from the surrounding circumstances, the words "to accept this offer" are equivocal. They may mean that he would give through July 18 to accept the offer by paying the price fixed; or would give him through that date to accept the offer by giving him notice to that effect. But two letters were put in evidence, written by Mr. Dickey to Mr. Hurd between the 8th and the 17th of July. The first is dated July 12th and the second July 15th. In both of these letters Mr. Dickey clearly discloses that he understood the offer did not require him to pay the purchase price on or before July 18, but to give an answer, notice of acceptance, on or before that day. In the letter of the 12th he says: "Answering your favor of the 8th inst., I thank you for giving me through the 18th of July to give you an *answer* about your property. * * * I expect to give you a *definite answer* about your property before that time," and later on in the same letter he states: "I will give you an *answer* within the time you were kind enough to allow me." And in the letter of July 15th, after explaining difficulties he was having, he stated: "If possible I am going to give you an *answer* within the time you have allowed me." When Mr. Hurd received these communications, he was fully apprised of how Mr. Dickey understood the language of his offer, and, if that was not the meaning which he intended to give to it, it was his duty to have at once informed him that the offer called for payment of the price on or before the 18th of July, and not simply for a notice of acceptance. It was not open to him to lie quietly by until after the time of acceptance had expired and then say my offer called for payment of the price on or before July 18, and you have not met the requirements.

SECTION FIVE: THE OFFER

1 CORBIN ON CONTRACTS

§ 11 at 23 (1963).

An offer is an expression by one party of his assent to certain definite terms, provided that the other party involved in the bargaining transaction will likewise express his assent to the identically same terms.

LEFKOWITZ v. GREAT MINNEAPOLIS SURPLUS STORE, INC.

Supreme Court of Minnesota, 1957.
251 Minn. 188, 86 N.W.2d 689.

MURPHY, JUSTICE.

This is an appeal from an order of the Municipal Court of Minneapolis denying the motion of the defendant for amended findings of fact, or, in the alternative, for a new trial. The order for judgment awarded the plaintiff the sum of $138.50 as damages for breach of contract.

This case grows out of the alleged refusal of the defendant to sell to the plaintiff a certain fur piece which it had offered for sale in a newspaper advertisement. It appears from the record that on April 6, 1956, the defendant published the following advertisement in a Minneapolis newspaper:

"Saturday 9 A.M. Sharp
3 Brand New
Fur
Coats
Worth to $100.00
First Come

> First Served
> $1
> Each"

On April 13, the defendant again published an advertisement in the same newspaper as follows:

> "Saturday 9 A.M.
> 2 Brand New Pastel
> Mink 3–Skin Scarfs
> Selling for $89.50
> Out they go
> Saturday. Each.... $1.00
> 1 Black Lapin Stole
> Beautiful,
> worth $139.50.... $1.00
> First Come
> First Served"

The record supports the findings of the court that on each of the Saturdays following the publication of the above-described ads the plaintiff was the first to present himself at the appropriate counter in the defendant's store and on each occasion demanded the coat and the stole so advertised and indicated his readiness to pay the sale price of $1. On both occasions, the defendant refused to sell the merchandise to the plaintiff, stating on the first occasion that by a "house rule" the offer was intended for women only and sales would not be made to men, and on the second visit that plaintiff knew defendant's house rules.

The trial court properly disallowed plaintiff's claim for the value of the fur coats since the value of these articles was speculative and uncertain. The only evidence of value was the advertisement itself to the effect that the coats were "Worth to $100.00," how much less being speculative especially in view of the price for which they were offered for sale. With reference to the offer of the defendant on April 13, 1956, to sell the "1 Black Lapin Stole * * * worth $139.50 * * * "the trial court held that the value of this article was established and granted judgment in favor of the plaintiff for that amount less the $1 quoted purchase price.

1. The defendant contends that a newspaper advertisement offering items of merchandise for sale at a named price is a "unilateral offer" which may be withdrawn without notice. He relies upon authorities which hold that, where an advertiser publishes in a newspaper that he has a certain quantity or quality of goods which he wants to dispose of at certain prices and on certain terms, such advertisements are not offers which become contracts as soon as any person to whose notice they may come signifies his acceptance by notifying the other that he will take a certain quantity of them. Such advertisements have been construed as an invitation for an offer of sale on the terms stated, which offer, when received, may be accepted or rejected and which therefore does not become a contract of sale until accepted by the seller; and until a contract has been so made, the seller may modify or revoke such prices or terms. * * *.

The defendant relies principally on Craft v. Elder & Johnston Co., 38 N.E.2d 416. In that case, the court discussed the legal effect of an advertisement offering for sale, as a one-day special, an electric sewing machine at a named price. The view was expressed that the advertisement was (38 N.E.2d 417) "not an offer made to any specific person but was made to the public generally. Thereby it would be properly designated as a unilateral offer and not being supported by any consideration could be withdrawn at will and without notice." It is true that such an offer may be withdrawn before acceptance. Since all offers are by their nature unilateral because they are necessarily made by one party or on one side in the negotiation of a contract, the distinction made in that decision between a unilateral offer and a unilateral contract is not clear. On the facts before us we are concerned with whether the advertisement constituted an offer, and, if so, whether the plaintiff's conduct constituted an acceptance.

There are numerous authorities which hold that a particular advertisement in a newspaper or circular letter relating to a sale of articles may be construed by the court as constituting an offer, acceptance of which would complete a contract. * * *

The test of whether a binding obligation may originate in advertisements addressed to the general public is "whether the facts show that some performance was promised in positive terms in return for something requested." 1 Williston, Contracts (Rev. ed.) § 27.

The authorities above cited emphasize that, where the offer is clear, definite, and explicit, and leaves nothing open for negotiation, it constitutes an offer, acceptance of which will complete the contract. The most recent case on the subject is Johnson v. Capital City Ford Co., La.App., 85 So.2d 75, in which the court pointed out that a newspaper advertisement relating to the purchase and sale of automobiles may constitute an offer, acceptance of which will consummate a contract and create an obligation in the offeror to perform according to the terms of the published offer.

Whether in any individual instance a newspaper advertisement is an offer rather than an invitation to make an offer depends on the legal intention of the parties and the surrounding circumstances. Annotation, 157 A.L.R. 744, 751; 77 C.J.S., Sales, § 25b; 17 C.J.S., Contracts, § 389. We are of the view on the facts before us that the offer by the defendant of the sale of the Lapin fur was clear, definite, and explicit, and left nothing open for negotiation. The plaintiff having successfully managed to be the first one to appear at the seller's place of business to be served, as requested by the advertisement, and having offered the stated purchase price of the article, he was entitled to performance on the part of the defendant. We think the trial court was correct in holding that there was in the conduct of the parties a sufficient mutuality of obligation to constitute a contract of sale.

2. The defendant contends that the offer was modified by a "house rule" to the effect that only women were qualified to receive the bargains advertised. The advertisement contained no such restriction. This objection may be disposed of briefly by stating that, while an advertiser has the right at any time before acceptance to modify his offer, he does not have the right, after acceptance, to impose new or arbitrary conditions not contained in the published offer. * * *

Affirmed.

FORD MOTOR CREDIT CO. v. RUSSELL, 519 N.W.2d 460 (Minn.App.1994). [Monticello Ford advertised a 1988 Ford Escort Pony in the *Monticello Shopper* for $7,826. The monthly payments set forth were "$159.29, based on a 60–month loan at 11% A.P.R." The Russells sought to purchase a Ford Escort as advertised but Monticello Ford could not obtain financing for them at 11%. The parties signed a contract at 13.75%. When the Russells defaulted on "numerous payments," Ford Credit Company, Monticello Ford's assignee, repossessed and resold the car. Ford Credit Company then sought to recover a deficiency judgment. The Russells counterclaimed, contending that they had accepted an offer in the *Monticello Shopper* and the failure of Ford to obtain 11% financing was a breach of contract.] Generally, if goods are advertised for sale at a certain price, it is not an offer and no contract is formed; such an advertisement is merely an invitation to bargain rather than an offer. 1 Samuel Williston, *A Treatise on the Law of Contracts* § 4:7 (4th ed. 1990); Restatement (Second) of Contracts § 26 (1981). The test of whether a binding obligation may originate in advertisements addressed to the general public is "whether the facts show that some performance was promised in positive terms in return for something requested." *Lefkowitz v. Great Minneapolis Surplus Store, Inc.,* 251 Minn. 188, 191, 86 N.W.2d 689, 691 (1957) (quoting 1 Samuel Williston, *A Treatise on the Law of Contracts* § 27) (3rd ed. 1957)).

We conclude that the advertisement here did not constitute an offer of sale to the general public. *See id.* (an advertisement may constitute an offer where it is clear, definite, explicit, and leaves nothing open for negotiation). Because not everyone qualifies for financing and Monticello Ford does not have an unlimited number of Ford Escorts to sell, it was unreasonable for appellants to believe that the advertisement was an offer binding the advertiser.

COURTEEN SEED CO. v. ABRAHAM

Supreme Court of Oregon, 1929.
129 Or. 427, 275 P. 684.

BROWN, J. * * * The defendant assigns error of the court in overruling his motion for nonsuit in and by which he asserts that the evidence fails to show that defendant ever made a binding offer to plaintiff to sell clover seed.

Contracts in general are reached by an offer on the one side and acceptance on the other. 1 Page on the Law of Contracts, § 74. So it becomes necessary to determine whether the defendant actually offered to sell the clover seed to the plaintiff corporation, and whether it was defendant's intention that contractual relations should exist between them on plaintiff's acceptance.

The writing upon which the plaintiff relies to show an offer to sell is a telegram sent by defendant to plaintiff on October 8, 1927, which reads: "I am asking 23 cents per pound for the car of red clover seed from which your sample was taken. No 1. seed, practically no plantain whatever. Have an offer 22¾ per pound, f.o.b. Amity."

Plaintiff's acceptance of the alleged offer reads: "Telegram received. We accept your offer. Ship promptly, route care Milwaukee Road at Omaha."

A contract should be construed to effect the intention of the parties thereto, as gathered from the entire writings constituting the contract. It is this intent that constitutes the essence of every contract. * * * Giving due consideration to every word contained in the defendant's telegram to plaintiff, we are not prepared to say that telegram constituted an express offer to sell. It would be poor reasoning to say that the defendant meant to make the plaintiff an offer when he used this language: "I am asking 23 cents per pound for the car of red clover." That does not say, "I offer to you at 23 cents per pound the car of red clover," nor does it say, "I will sell to you the carload of red clover at 23 cents per pound." The writer of the telegram used the word "offer" with reference to some other person when he concluded by saying: "Have an offer 22¾ per pound, f.o.b. Amity." Each of the words "offer" and "asking" has its meaning; and we cannot assume that the writer of the telegram meant to use these words in the same sense, nor can we eliminate the word "asking" from the writing.

Now, going back to September 21, 1927, we find that defendant was then mailing out samples of clover seed to divers persons, each sample being enclosed in an envelope on the face of which appeared the following words:

"Red clover. 50,000 lbs. like sample. I am asking 24 cents per, f.o.b. Amity, Oregon.

> "Amity Seed & Grain Warehouse,
>
> "Amity, Oregon."

It will be noted that on the envelope the defendant used the language, "I am asking." The plaintiff acknowledged receipt of the sample received by it, and advised the sender that it had accumulated quite a stock of clover seed and preferred to wait a while "before operating further." On October 4th following, owing to rainy weather, which brought about conditions not favorable for hulling the clover seed, the defendant, in search of buyers, wrote the plaintiff, and, on October 8th, plaintiff wired defendant as follows: "Special delivery sample received. Your price too high. Wire firm offer, naming absolutely lowest f.o.b." The defendant then wired, in reply, that he was asking 23 cents per pound, and had received an "offer of 22¾." This is the writing upon which the plaintiff rests its case.

* * *

* * * [In] Nebraska Seed Co. v. Harsh, 98 Neb. 89, 152 N.W. 310, L.R.A. 1915F, 824, * * * the defendant wrote the plaintiff company the following:

> "Lowell, Nebraska, 4—24—1912.

"Nebraska Seed Co., Omaha, Neb.—Gentlemen: I have about 1,800 bu. or thereabouts of millet seed of which I am mailing you a sample. This millet is recleaned and was grown on sod and is good seed. I want $2.25 per cwt. for this seed, f.o.b. Lowell.

> "Yours truly,
>
> "H.F. Harsh."

Upon receipt of this letter, the plaintiff wired defendant as follows:

> "4—26—'12.

"H.F. Harsh, Lowell, Nebraska.

"Sample and letter received. Accept your offer Millet like sample $2.25 per cwt. Wire how soon can load.

"The Nebraska Seed Co."

On the same day the plaintiff wrote the defendant a letter confirming the wire, which stated, among other things:

"Have booked purchase of you 1,800 bushels of millet seed to be fully equal to sample you sent us at $2.25 per cwt., your track. Please be so kind as to load this seed at once and ship to us at Omaha. We thank you in advance for prompt attention. * * *

"The Nebraska Seed Company."

The letter was received by defendant at Lowell in due course. After due demand and tender of the purchase price, the defendant refused to deliver the seed. An action followed, in which the alleged contract was set up. Defendant filed a demurrer to the complaint, but his pleading was overruled. On trial plaintiff had verdict. Defendant appealed, and the Supreme Court of Nebraska held that the language, "I want $2.25 per cwt. for this seed, f.o.b. Lowell," did not constitute an offer of sale; that the language was general, and, as such, might be used in an advertisement or circular addressed generally to those engaged in the seed business; and that such language was not an offer by which the defendant was bound, if accepted by any or all of the persons addressed. * * *

* * *

There are many cases of record, the great majority of which seem to follow the doctrine announced in * * * [cases like Nebraska Seed Co.] From a review of the decisions, and of the law governing the question at issue in the instant case, we are of opinion that the motion for a nonsuit should have been sustained.

This cause is reversed and remanded, with directions to enter a nonsuit.

FELDMAN v. GREEN, 138 Mich.App. 360, 364, 360 N.W.2d 881, 884 (1984). "Contractual intent cannot be based exclusively on * * * formalisms."

FAIRMOUNT GLASS WORKS v. GRUNDEN–MARTIN WOODENWARE CO.

Court of Appeals of Kentucky, 1899.
106 Ky. 659, 51 S.W. 196.

Action by the Grunden–Martin Woodenware Company against the Fairmount Glass Works to recover damages for breach of contract. Judgment for plaintiff, and defendant appeals. Affirmed.

* * *

HOBSON, J. On April 20, 1895, appellee wrote appellant the following letter:

"St. Louis, Mo., April 20, 1895. Gentlemen: Please advise us the lowest price you can make us on our order for ten car loads of Mason green jars, complete, with caps, packed one dozen in a case, either delivered here, or f.o.b. cars your place, as you prefer. State terms and cash discount. Very truly, Grunden–Martin W.W. Co."

To this letter appellant answered as follows:

"Fairmount, Ind., April 23, 1895. Grunden–Martin Wooden Ware Co., St. Louis, Mo.—Gentlemen: Replying to your favor of April 20, we quote you Mason fruit jars, complete, in one-dozen boxes, delivered in East St. Louis, Ill.: Pints $4.50, quarts $5.00, half gallons $6.50, per gross, for immediate acceptance, and shipment not later than May 15, 1895; sixty days' acceptance, or 2 off, cash in ten days. Yours, truly, Fairmount Glass Works.

"Please note that we make all quotations and contracts subject to the contingencies of agencies or transportation, delays or accidents beyond our control."

For reply thereto, appellee sent the following telegram on April 24, 1895:

"Fairmount Glass Works, Fairmount, Ind.: Your letter twenty-third received. Enter order ten car loads as per your quotation. Specifications mailed. Grunden–Martin W.W. Co."

In response to this telegram, appellant sent the following:

"Fairmount, Ind., April 24, 1895. Grunden–Martin W.W. Co., St. Louis, Mo.: Impossible to book your order. Output all sold. See letter. Fairmount Glass Works."

Appellee insists that, by its telegram sent in answer to the letter of April 23d, the contract was closed for the purchase of 10 car loads of Mason fruit jars. Appellant insists that the contract was not closed by this telegram, and that it had the right to decline to fill the order at the time it sent its telegram of April 24. This is the chief question in the case. The court below gave judgment in favor of appellee, and appellant has appealed, earnestly insisting that the judgment is erroneous.

We are referred to a number of authorities holding that a quotation of prices is not an offer to sell, in the sense that a completed contract will arise out of the giving of an order for merchandise in accordance with the proposed terms. There are a number of cases holding that the transaction is not completed until the order so made is accepted. * * * But each case must turn largely upon the language there used. In this case we think there was more than a quotation of prices, although appellant's letter uses the word "quote" in stating the prices given. The true meaning of the correspondence must be determined by reading it as a whole. Appellee's letter of April 20th, which began the transaction, did not ask for a quotation of prices. It reads: "Please advise us the lowest price you can make us on our order for ten car loads of Mason green jars. * * * State terms and cash discount." From this appellant could not fail to understand that appellee wanted to know at what price it would sell it ten car loads of these jars; so when, in answer, it wrote: "We quote you Mason fruit jars * * * pints $4.50, quarts $5.00, half gallons $6.50, per gross, for immediate acceptance; * * * 2 off, cash in ten days,"—it must be deemed as intending to give appellee the information it had asked for. We can hardly understand what was meant by the words "for immediate acceptance," unless the latter was intended as a proposition to sell at these prices if accepted immediately. In construing every contract, the aim of the court is to arrive at the intention of the parties. * * * In Fitzhugh v. Jones, 6 Munf. 83, the use of the expression that the buyer should reply as soon as possible, in case he was disposed to accede to the terms offered, was held sufficient to show that there was a definite proposition, which was closed by the buyer's acceptance. The expression in appellant's letter, "for immediate acceptance," taken in connection with appellee's letter, in effect, at what price it would sell it the goods, is, it seems to us, much stronger evidence of a present offer, which, when accepted immediately, closed the contract. Appellee's letter was plainly an inquiry for the price and terms on which appellant would sell it the goods, and appellant's answer to it was not a quotation of prices, but a definite offer to sell on the terms indicated, and could not be withdrawn after the terms had been accepted. It will be observed that the telegram of acceptance refers to the specifications mailed. These specifications were contained in the following letter: "St. Louis, Mo., April 24, 1895. Fairmount Glass–Works Co., Fairmount, Ind.—Gentlemen: We received your letter of 23rd this morning, and telegraphed you in reply as follows: 'Your letter 23rd received. Enter order ten car loads as per your quotation. Specifications mailed,'—which we now confirm. We have accordingly entered this contract on our books for the ten cars Mason green jars, complete, with caps and rubbers, one dozen in case, delivered to us in East St. Louis at $4.50 per gross for pint, $5.00 for quart, $6.50 for one-half gallon. Terms, 60 days' acceptance, or 2 per cent. for cash in ten days, to be shipped not later than May 15, 1895. The jars and caps to be strictly first-quality goods. You may ship the first car to us here assorted: Five gross pint, fifty-five gross quart, forty gross one-half gallon. Specifications for the remaining 9 cars we will send later. Grunden–Martin W.W. Co." It is insisted for appellant that this was not an acceptance of the offer as made; that the stipulation, "The jars and caps to be strictly first-quality goods," was not in their offer; and that, it not having been accepted as made, appellant is not bound. But it will be observed that appellant declined to furnish the goods before it got this letter, and in the correspondence with appellee it nowhere complained of these words as an addition to the contract. Quite a number of other letters passed, in which the refusal to deliver the goods was placed on other grounds, none of which have been sustained by the evidence. Appellee offers proof tending to show that these words, in the trade in which parties were engaged, conveyed the same meaning as the words used in appellant's letter, and were only a different form of expressing the same idea. Appellant's conduct would seem to confirm this evidence.

Appellant also insists that the contract was indefinite, because the quantity of each size of the jars was not fixed, that 10 car loads is too indefinite a specification of the quantity sold, and that appellee had no right to accept the goods to be delivered on different days. The proof shows that "10 car loads" is an expression used in the trade as equivalent to 1,000 gross, 100 gross being regarded a car load. The offer to sell the different sizes at different prices gave the purchaser the right to name the quantity of each size, and, the offer being to ship not later than May 15th, the buyer had the right to fix the time of delivery at any time before that. * * * The petition, if defective, was cured by the judgment, which is fully sustained by the evidence. Judgment affirmed.

Note
More on the Contract—No Contract Dichotomy

The contract-no contract dichotomy, discussed earlier at pages 33–34, 42, suggests to some the lack of interplay between theories of obligation and remedies. Some assume, for example, that the strength or weakness of a theory of obligation in relation to a set of facts is (and ought to be) determined solely by reference to the requirements of the applicable theory without considering the availability of an appropriate remedy. But some courts do weigh the appropriateness of a remedy when deciding the availability of a theory of obligation. The availability of a suitable remedy may cure or offset a weakness (e.g., indefiniteness) in the theory of obligation (and vice versa). Indeed, in the sale of goods field, section 2–204(3) of the Uniform Commercial Code explicitly provides that:

> Even though one or more terms are left open a contract for sale does not fail for indefiniteness if the parties have intended to make a contract and there is a reasonably certain basis for giving an appropriate remedy.

Consider whether the last paragraph of the Fairmount Glass case illustrates the approach in U.C.C. section 2–204(3). U.C.C. section 2–311(1) further reinforces such an approach in the Fairmount Glass context:

> An agreement for sale which is otherwise sufficiently definite (subsection (3) of section 2–204) to be a contract is not made invalid by the fact that it leaves particulars of performance to be specified by one of the parties. Any such specification must be made in good faith and within limits set by commercial reasonableness.

SOUTHWORTH v. OLIVER

Supreme Court of Oregon, 1978.
284 Or. 361, 587 P.2d 994.

Tongue, Justice.

This is a suit in equity for a declaratory judgment that defendants "are obligated to sell" to plaintiff 2,933 acres of ranch lands in Grant County. Defendants appeal from a decree of specific performance in favor of plaintiff. We affirm.

Defendants contend on this appeal that a certain "writing" mailed by them to plaintiff was not an offer to sell such lands. * * *

Defendants are ranchers in Grant County and owned ranches in both the Bear Valley area and also in the John Day valley. In 1976 defendants came to the conclusion that they should "cut the operation down" and sell some of the Bear Valley property. * * * Defendant Joseph Oliver then had "a discussion with Mr. Southworth [the plaintiff] about the possibility of * * * selling this Bear Valley property." Plaintiff Southworth was also a cattle rancher in Bear Valley. The land which defendants had decided to sell was adjacent to land owned by him and was property that he had always wanted.

The initial meeting between the parties on May 20, 1976.

According to plaintiff, defendant Joseph Oliver stopped by his ranch on May 20, 1976, and said that he [Oliver] was interested in "selling the ranch" and asked "would I be interested in buying it, and I said 'yes'." Mr.

Southworth also testified that "he thought I would be interested in the land and that Clyde [Holliday, also a neighbor] would be interested in the permits" and that "I told him that I was very interested in the land * * *."

* * *

Plaintiff also testified that on May 26, 1976, he called Clyde Holliday to ask if he was interested in buying the land and Mr. Holliday said "no," that he was interested only in the permits, but would be interested in trading some other land for some of the land plaintiff was buying from defendants.

* * *

The letters of June 17, June 21, and June 24, 1976.

Several days later plaintiff received from defendants a letter dated June 17, 1976, as follows:

"Enclosed please find the information about the ranch sales that I had discussed with you previously.

"These prices are the market value according to the records of the Grant County Assessor.

"Please contact me if there are any questions."

There were two enclosures with that letter. The first was as follows:

"JOSEPH C. and ARLENE G. OLIVER 200 Ford Road, John Day, OR 97845

"Selling approximately 2933 Acres in Grant County in

T. 16 S., R. 31 E., W. M.

near Seneca, Oregon at the assessed market value of:

LAND	$306,409
IMPROVEMENTS	18,010
Total	$324,419

"Terms available—29% down—balance over 5 years at 8% interest. Negotiate sale date for December 1, 1976 or January 1, 1977.

"Available after hay is harvested and arrangements made for removal of hay, equipment and supplies.

"ALSO: Selling

"Little Bear Creek allotment permit——100 head @ $225

"Big Bear Creek allotment permit——200 head @ $250"

The second enclosure related to "selling approximately 6365 acres" in Grant County near John Day—another ranch owned by the Oliver family.

Defendant Joseph Oliver testified that this letter and enclosures were "drafted" by his wife, defendant Arlene Oliver; that he then read and signed it; that he sent it not only to plaintiff, but also to Clyde Holliday and two other neighbors; that it was sent because "I told them I would send them all this information and we would go from there," that it was not made as an offer, and that it was his intention that the "property" and "permits" be transferred "together."

Upon receiving that letter and enclosures, plaintiff immediately responded by letter addressed to both defendants, dated June 21, 1976, as follows:

"Re the land in Bear Valley near Seneca, Oregon that you have offered to sell; I accept your offer."

Plaintiff testified that on June 23, 1976, Clyde Holliday called and said he needed to acquire a portion of the land "that I had agreed to buy from Joe [Oliver], and I said I have bought the land," and that we would "work out an exchange in accord with what we have previously mentioned," but that "[h]e said he needed more land."

Defendant Joseph Oliver testified that after receiving plaintiff's letter dated June 21, 1976, Clyde Holliday told him that "they [Holliday and plaintiff] were having a little difficulty getting this thing worked out," apparently referring to the "exchange" previously discussed between plaintiff and Holliday, and that he (Oliver) then told plaintiff that:

"* * * [T]here seemed to be some discrepancies between what I was getting the two parties and that I didn't exactly want to be an arbitrator or say you are right or you are wrong with my neighbors. I wished they would straighten the thing out, and if they didn't, I really didn't have to sell it, that I would pull it off the market, because I didn't want to get in trouble. I would have to live with my neighbors."

Finally, on June 24, 1976, defendants mailed the following letter to plaintiff:

"We received your letter of June 21, 1976. You have misconstrued our prior negotiations and written summaries of the lands which we and J.C. wish to sell. That was not made as or intended to be a firm offer of sale, and especially was not an offer of sale of any portion of the lands and permits described to any one person separately from the rest of the lands and permits described.

"The memorandum of ours was for informational purposes only and as a starting point for further negotiation between us and you and the others also interested in the properties.

"It is also impossible to tell from the attachment to our letter of June 17, 1976, as to the legal description of the lands to be sold, and would not in any event constitute an enforceable contract.

"We are open to further negotiation with you and other interested parties, but do not consider that we at this point have any binding enforceable contract with you."

This lawsuit then followed.

Defendants' letter of June 17, 1976, was an "offer to sell" the ranch lands.

Defendants first contend that defendants' letter of June 17, 1976, to plaintiff was "not an offer, both as a matter of law and under the facts of this case." In support of that contention defendants say that their testimony that the letter was not intended as an offer was uncontradicted and that similar writings have been held not to constitute offers.[a] Defendants also say that

a. Citing *Courteen Seed Co. v. Abraham,* 129 Or. 427, 275 P. 684 (1929); *Klimek v.* *Perisich,* 231 Or. 71, 371 P.2d 956 (1962); *Nebraska Seed Co. v. Harsh,* 98 Neb. 89, 152

there is "authority for the proposition that all the evidence of surrounding circumstances may be taken into consideration in making that determination"[b] and that the circumstances in this case were such as to require the conclusion that defendants did not intend the letter as an offer and that plaintiff knew or reasonably should have known that it was not intended as an offer because:

"1.   Defendants obviously did not intend it as an offer.

"2.   The wording of the 'offer' made it clear that this was 'information' that plaintiff had previously expressed an interest in receiving.

"3.   It did not use the term offer, but only formally advised plaintiff that defendants are selling certain lands and permits and set forth generally the terms upon which they would consider selling.

"4.   The plaintiff knew of the custom of transferring permits with land and had no knowledge from the writing or previous talk that defendants were selling any cattle.

"5.   Plaintiff knew and expected this same information to go to others."

Defendants conclude that

"Considering the factors determined important by the authorities cited, these factors preponderate heavily that this was not an offer to sell the land only, or to sell at all, and should not reasonably have been so construed by the plaintiff."

* * *

The difficulty in determining whether an offer has been made is particularly acute in cases involving price quotations, as in this case. It is recognized that although a price quotation, standing alone, is not an offer, there may be circumstances under which a price quotation, when considered together with facts and circumstances, may constitute an offer which, if accepted, will result in a binding contract. It is also recognized that such an offer may be made to more than one person. Thus, the fact that a price quotation is sent to more than one person does not, of itself, require a holding that such a price quotation is not an offer.

* * *

* * * [W]e are of the opinion that defendants' letter to plaintiff dated June 17, 1976, was an offer to sell the ranch lands. We believe that the "surrounding circumstances" under which this letter was prepared by defendants and sent by them to plaintiff were such as to have led a reasonable person to believe that defendants were making an offer to sell to plaintiff the lands described in the letter's enclosure and upon the terms as there stated.

That letter did not come to plaintiff "out of the blue," as in some of the cases involving advertisements or price quotations. Neither was this a price quotation resulting from an inquiry by plaintiff. According to what we believe

N.W. 310 (1915); *Mellen v. Johnson,* 322 Mass. 236, 76 N.E.2d 658 (1948); *Owen v. Tunison,* 131 Me. 42, 158 A. 926 (1932); and *Richards v. Flower,* 193 Cal.App.2d 233, 14 Cal.Rptr. 228 (1961).

b.   Citing *Metropolitan Life Ins. Co. v. Kimball,* 163 Or. 31, 94 P.2d 1101 (1939); *Nebraska Seed Co. v. Harsh,* supra n. 1; *Klimek v. Perisich,* supra n. 1; *Mellen v. Johnson,* supra n. 1; and 1 Restatement of Contracts § 25 (1932).

to be the most credible testimony, defendants decided to sell the lands in question and defendant Joseph Oliver then sought out the plaintiff who owned adjacent lands. Defendant Oliver told plaintiff that defendants were interested in selling that land, inquired whether plaintiff was interested, and was told by plaintiff that he was "very interested in the land," after which they discussed the particular lands to be sold. That conversation was terminated with the understanding that Mr. Oliver would "determine" the value and price of that land, i.e., "what he wanted for the land," and that plaintiff would undertake to arrange financing for the purchase of that land. In addition to that initial conversation, there was a further telephone conversation in which plaintiff called Mr. Oliver "to ask him if his plans for selling * * * continued to be in force" and was told "yes"; that there had been some delay in getting information from the assessor, as needed to establish the value of the land; and that plaintiff then told Mr. Oliver that "everything was in order" and that "he had the money available and everything was ready to go."

Under these facts and circumstances, we agree with the finding and conclusion by the trial court, in its written opinion, that when plaintiff received the letter of June 17th, with enclosures, which stated a price of $324,419 for the 2,933 acres in T 16 S, R 31 E., W.M., as previously identified by the parties with reference to a map, and stating "terms" of 29 percent down—balance over five years at eight percent interest—with a "sale date" of either December 1, 1976, or January 1, 1977, a reasonable person in the position of the plaintiff would have believed that defendants were making an offer to sell those lands to him.

This conclusion is further strengthened by "the definiteness of the proposal," not only with respect to price, but terms, and by the fact that "the addressee was not an indefinite group." * * *

As previously noted, defendants contend that they "obviously did not intend [the letter] as an offer." While it may be proper to consider evidence of defendants' subjective intent under the "objective test" to which this court is committed, it is the manifestation of a previous intention that is controlling, rather than a "person's actual intent." We do not agree with defendants' contention that it was "obvious" to a reasonable person, under the facts and circumstances of this case that the letter of January 17th was not intended to be an offer to sell the ranch lands to plaintiff.

We recognize, as contended by defendants, that the failure to use the word "offer," the fact that the letter included the "information" previously discussed between the parties, and the fact that plaintiff knew that the same information was to be sent to others, were important facts to be considered in deciding whether plaintiff, as a reasonable person, would have been led to believe that this letter was an "offer." * * * We disagree, however, with defendants' contention that these and other factors relied upon by defendants "preponderate" so as to require a holding that the letter of January 17th was not an offer.

The failure to add the word "offer" and the use of the word "information" are also not controlling, and, as previously noted, an offer may be made to more than one person. The question is whether, under all of the facts and circumstances existing at the time that this letter was received, a reasonable person in the position of the plaintiff would have understood the letter to be an offer by defendants to sell the land to him.

[Affirmed.]

Problem 4–8

Suppose Joseph Oliver consulted you before sending his letter of June 17, 1976, with enclosures. What would you have advised?

Problem 4–9

People sometimes make unusual offers. But sometimes people try to take advantage of others by claiming to "accept" what they know or should know are not offers. For an example of the latter, in Leonard v. Pepsico, Inc., 210 F.3d 88 (2d Cir. 2000), the court described the so-called offer and then rendered its brief decision:

> In 1995, defendant-appellee Pepsico, Inc. conducted a promotion in which it offered merchandise in exchange for "points" earned by purchasing Pepsi Cola. A television commercial aired by Pepsico depicted a teenager gloating over various items of merchandise earned by Pepsi points, and culminated in the teenager arriving at high school in a Harrier Jet, a fighter aircraft of the United States Marine Corps. For each item of merchandise sported by the teenager (a T shirt, a jacket, sunglasses), the ad noted the number of Pepsi points needed to get it. When the teenager is shown in the jet, the ad prices it as 7 million points.

> Plaintiff-appellant John D.R. Leonard alleges that the ad was an offer, that he accepted the offer by tendering the equivalent of 7 million points, and that Pepsico has breached its contract to deliver the Harrier jet. Pepsico characterizes the use of the Harrier jet in the ad as a hyperbolic joke ("zany humor"), cites the ad's reference to offering details contained in the promotional catalog (which contains no Harrier fighter plane), and argues that no objective person would construe the ad as an offer for the Harrier jet.

> The United States District Court for the Southern District of New York (Wood, J.) agreed with Pepsico and granted its motion for summary judgment on the grounds (1) that the commercial did not amount to an offer of goods; (2) that no objective person could reasonably have concluded that the commercial actually offered consumers a Harrier Jet; and (3) that the alleged contract could not satisfy the New York statute of frauds.

> We affirm for substantially the reasons stated in Judge Wood's opinion. See 88 F.Supp.2d 116 (S.D.N.Y.1999).

Here are some true additional examples of possible offers. In which cases, if any, do you think the "offeror" should be held to the "offer?"

(1) Radio disk jockey Ben Stone announced that anyone who got a permanent "93 Rock" tattoo on his or her forehead would receive $30,000 per year for five years. Two men have sued Stone and his station for failing to pay after they received the tattoos. They also seek consequential damages because they have been unable to get jobs with the tattoos on their foreheads.

(2) During the height of the Monica Lewinsky scandal, on his television program, Geraldo Rivera promised to pay $10,000 to anyone who could find a case in which someone was criminally prosecuted for lying about a sexual matter. The

National Law Journal reported on November 9, 1998 that Marc Bogatin, a criminal defense lawyer, claimed payment for finding several such cases. On February 22, 1999, the same newspaper reported that NBC Television agreed to pay Bogatin (and two other lawyers who also submitted examples), although NBC "continues to believe that none of the claims have satisfied the challenge."

(3) Nationwide Mutual Insurance Company offered "his-and-her" Mercedes to the person who wrote the best slogan for its 1994 regional convention. David Mears' eight-word slogan won the contest, but Nationwide claimed the promotion was "just a joke."

(4) In an advertisement in USA Today in December 1995, Haley Barbour, Republican National Chairman, promised $1 million "to the first American who can prove the following statement is false: 'In November 1995, the U.S. House and Senate passed a balanced budget bill. It increases total federal spending on Medicare by more than 50% from 1995 to 2002, pursuant to Congressional Budget Office standards.' "Eighteen people claimed to have proven the assertion false. The RNC claimed that the advertisement was not a "bona fide offer."

(5) In 2005, a Florida lawyer offered to give $10,000 to charity if any videogame company manufactured a game according to the lawyer's plot line, which involved extremely violent murders of videogame company officers. The lawyer was angered that such officers had claimed that the violence in their games did not cause violence among young game users.

SECTION SIX: THE ACCEPTANCE

CORBIN, OFFER AND ACCEPTANCE, AND SOME OF THE RESULTING LEGAL RELATIONS

26 Yale L.J. 169, 199–200 (1917).

An acceptance is a voluntary act of the offeree whereby he exercises the power conferred upon him by the offer, and thereby creates the set of legal relations called a contract. What acts are sufficient to serve this purpose? We must look first to the terms in which the offer was expressed, either by words or by other conduct. The offeror is the creator of the power and at the time of its creation he has full control over both the fact of its existence and its terms. The offeror has, in the beginning, full power to determine the acts that are to constitute acceptance. After he has once created the power, he may lose his control over it, and may become disabled to change or to revoke it; but the fact that, in the beginning, the offeror has full control of the immediately succeeding relation called a power, is the characteristic that distinguishes contractual relations from non-contractual ones. After the offeror has created the power, the legal consequences thereof are out of his hands, and he may be brought into numerous consequential relations of which he did not dream, and to which he might not have consented. These later relations are nevertheless called contractual.

ARDENTE v. HORAN

Supreme Court of Rhode Island, 1976.
117 R.I. 254, 366 A.2d 162.

DORIS, JUSTICE.

Ernest P. Ardente, the plaintiff, brought this civil action in Superior Court to specifically enforce an agreement between himself and William A.

and Katherine L. Horan, the defendants, to sell certain real property. The defendants filed an answer together with a motion for summary judgment * * *. [J]udgment was entered by a Superior Court justice for the defendants. The plaintiff now appeals.

In August 1975, certain residential property in the city of Newport was offered for sale by defendants. The plaintiff made a bid of $250,000 for the property which was communicated to defendants by their attorney. After defendants' attorney advised plaintiff that the bid was acceptable to defendants, he prepared a purchase and sale agreement at the direction of defendants and forwarded it to plaintiff's attorney for plaintiff's signature. After investigating certain title conditions, plaintiff executed the agreement. Thereafter plaintiff's attorney returned the document to defendants along with a check in the amount of $20,000 and a letter dated September 8, 1975, which read in relevant part as follows:

> "My clients are concerned that the following items remain with the real estate: a) dining room set and tapestry wall covering in dining room; b) fireplace fixtures throughout; c) the sun parlor furniture. I would appreciate your confirming that these items are a part of the transaction, as they would be difficult to replace."

The defendants refused to agree to sell the enumerated items and did not sign the purchase and sale agreement. They directed their attorney to return the agreement and the deposit check to plaintiff and subsequently refused to sell the property to plaintiff. This action for specific performance followed.

In Superior Court, defendants moved for summary judgment on the ground that the facts were not in dispute and no contract had been formed as a matter of law.[a] The trial justice ruled that the letter quoted above constituted a conditional acceptance of defendants' offer to sell the property and consequently must be construed as a counteroffer. Since defendants never accepted the counteroffer, it followed that no contract was formed, and summary judgment was granted.

* * *

The trial justice proceeded on the theory that the delivery of the purchase and sale agreement to plaintiff constituted an offer by defendants to sell the property. Because we must view the evidence in the light most favorable to the party against whom summary judgment was entered, in this case plaintiff, we assume as the trial justice did that the delivery of the agreement was in fact an offer.[b]

---

a. Although the contract would appear to be within the statute of frauds, defendants did not raise this defense in the trial court, nor do they raise it here. Where a party makes no claim to the benefit of the statute, the court sua sponte will not interpose it for him. *Conti v. Fisher,* 48 R.I. 33, 36, 134 A. 849, 850 (1926).

b. The conclusion that the delivery of the agreement was an offer is not unassailable in view of the fact that defendants did not sign the agreement before sending it to plaintiff, and the fact that plaintiff told defendants' attorney *after* the agreement was received that he would have to investigate certain conditions of title before signing the agreement. If it was not an offer, plaintiff's execution of the agreement could itself be no more than an offer, which defendants never accepted.

The question we must answer next is whether there was an acceptance of that offer. The general rule is that where, as here, there is an offer to form a bilateral contract, the offeree must communicate his acceptance to the offeror before any contractual obligation can come into being. A mere mental intent to accept the offer, no matter how carefully formed, is not sufficient. The acceptance must be transmitted to the offeror in some overt manner. * * * A review of the record shows that the only expression of acceptance which was communicated to defendants was the delivery of the executed purchase and sale agreement accompanied by the letter of September 8. Therefore it is solely on the basis of the language used in these two documents that we must determine whether there was a valid acceptance. Whatever plaintiff's unexpressed intention may have been in sending the documents is irrelevant. We must be concerned only with the language actually used, not the language plaintiff thought he was using or intended to use.

There is no doubt that the execution and delivery of the purchase and sale agreement by plaintiff, without more, would have operated as an acceptance. The terms of the accompanying letter, however, apparently conditioned the acceptance upon the inclusion of various items of personalty. In assessing the effect of the terms of that letter we must keep in mind certain generally accepted rules. To be effective, an acceptance must be definite and unequivocal. "An offeror is entitled to know in clear terms whether the offeree accepts his proposal. It is not enough that the words of a reply justify a probable inference of assent." 1 Restatement *Contracts* § 58, comment *a* (1932). The acceptance may not impose additional conditions on the offer, nor may it add limitations. "An acceptance which is equivocal or upon condition or with a limitation is a counteroffer and requires acceptance by the original offeror before a contractual relationship can exist." * * *

However, an acceptance may be valid despite conditional language if the acceptance is clearly independent of the condition. Many cases have so held. Williston states the rule as follows:

"Frequently an offeree, while making a positive acceptance of the offer, also makes a request or suggestion that some addition or modification be made. So long as it is clear that the meaning of the acceptance is positively and unequivocally to accept the offer whether such request is granted or not, a contract is formed." 1 Williston, *Contracts* § 79 at 261–62 (3d ed. 1957).

Corbin is in agreement with the above view. 1 Corbin, * * * § 84 at 363–65. Thus our task is to decide whether plaintiff's letter is more reasonably interpreted as a qualified acceptance or as an absolute acceptance together with a mere inquiry concerning a collateral matter.

In making our decision we recognize that, as one text states, "The question whether a communication by an offeree is a conditional acceptance or counter-offer is not always easy to answer. It must be determined by the same common-sense process of interpretation that must be applied in so many other cases." 1 Corbin, *supra* § 82 at 353. In our opinion the language used in plaintiff's letter of September 8 is not consistent with an absolute acceptance accompanied by a request for a gratuitous benefit. We interpret the letter to impose a condition on plaintiff's acceptance of defendants' offer. The letter does not unequivocally state that even without the enumerated items plaintiff is willing to complete the contract. In fact, the letter seeks "confirmation" that the listed items "are a part of the transaction". Thus, far from being an independent, collateral request, the sale of the items in question is explicitly referred to as a part of the real estate transaction. Moreover, the letter goes on to stress the difficulty of finding replacements for these items. This is a further indication that plaintiff did not view the inclusion of the listed items as merely collateral or incidental to the real estate transaction.

A review of the relevant case law discloses that those cases in which an acceptance was found valid despite an accompanying conditional term generally involved a more definite expression of acceptance than the one in the case at bar. * * *

Accordingly, we hold that since the plaintiff's letter of acceptance dated September 8 was conditional, it operated as a rejection of the defendants' offer and no contractual obligation was created.

The plaintiff's appeal is denied and dismissed, the judgment appealed from is affirmed and the case is remanded to the Superior Court.

Problem 4–10

Howard Wade executed an offer to purchase certain real estate. The offer contained a provision in which the seller agreed that it had no verbal agreements with others to give them a right of first refusal on the particular land. This language was added to the offer because Wade knew that the present tenant on the land had requested from the seller a right of first refusal. The seller signed the purchase offer after adding the following provision: "It is understood and agreed that the present tenant, Robert Tank, has first right of refusal on this offer." (1) Is a contract formed? (2) If the seller wants Tank to have a right of first refusal, but does not want to lose the possible sale to Wade, what advice would you give the seller? (3) Is there a contract if Wade's offer did not contain the provision concerning the right of first refusal?

ELIASON v. HENSHAW

Supreme Court of the United States, 1819.
17 U.S. (4 Wheat.) 225, 4 L.Ed. 556.

WASHINGTON, J., delivered the opinion of the court: This is an action, brought by the seller, to recover damages for the non-performance of an agreement, alleged to have been entered into by the buyers, for the purchase of a quantity of flour at a stipulated price. The evidence of this contract given in the court below is stated in a bill of exceptions, and is to the following effect: A letter from the buyers to the seller, dated the 10th of February, 1813, in which they say: "Capt. Conn informs us that you have a quantity of flour to dispose of. We are in the practice of purchasing flour at all times, in Georgetown, and will be glad to serve you, either in receiving your flour in store, when the markets are dull, and disposing of it when the markets will answer to advantage, or we will purchase at market price when delivered; if you are disposed to engage two or three hundred barrels at present, we will give you $9.50 per barrel, deliverable the first water in Georgetown, or any service we can. If you should want an advance, please write us by mail, and will send you part of the money in advance." In a postscript they add: "Please write by return of wagon whether you accept our offer." This letter was sent from the house at which the writer then was, about two miles from Harper's Ferry, to the seller at his mill, at Mill Creek, distance about 20 miles from Harper's Ferry, by a wagoner then employed by the seller to haul flour from his mill to Harper's Ferry, and then about to return home with his wagon. He delivered the letter to the seller on the 14th of the same month, to which an answer, dated the succeeding day was written by the seller, addressed to the buyers at Georgetown, and despatched by a mail which left Mill Creek on the 19th, being the first regular mail from that place to Georgetown. In this letter the writer says: "Your favor of the 10th inst. was handed me by Mr. Chenoweth last evening. I take the earliest opportunity to answer it by post. Your proposal to engage 300 barrels of flour, delivered in Georgetown, by the first water, at $9.50 per barrel, I accept, and shall send on the flour by the first boats that pass down from where my flour is stored on the river; as to any advance, will be unnecessary—payment on delivery is all that is required."

On the 25th of the same month, the buyers addressed to the seller an answer to the above, dated at Georgetown, in which they acknowledge the receipt of it, and add, "Not having heard from you before, had quite given over the expectation of getting your flour, more particularly as we requested an answer by return of wagon the next day, and as we did not get it, had bought all we wanted."

The wagoner, by whom the buyers' first letter was sent, informed them, when he received it, that he should not probably return to Harper's Ferry, and he did not in fact return in the seller's employ. The flour was sent down to Georgetown some time in March, and the delivery of it to the buyers was regularly tendered and refused.

Upon this evidence, the buyers, moved that court to instruct the jury, that, if they believed the said evidence to be true, as stated, the seller was not entitled to recover the amount of the price of the 300 barrels of flour, at the rate of $9.50 per barrel. The court being divided in opinion, the instruction prayed for was not given.

The question is, whether the court below ought to have given the instruction to the jury, as the same was prayed for? If they ought, the judgment, which was in favor of the seller in that court, must be reversed.

It is an undeniable principle of the law of contracts, that an offer of a bargain by one person to another, imposes no obligation upon the former, until it is accepted by the latter, according to the terms in which the offer was made. Any qualification of, or departure from, those terms, invalidates the offer, unless the same be agreed to by the person who made it. Until the terms of the agreement have received the assent of both parties, the negotiation is open, and imposes no obligation upon either.

In this case, the buyers offered to purchase from the seller two or three hundred barrels of flour, to be delivered at Georgetown, by the first water, and to pay for the same $9.50 per barrel. To the letter containing this offer, they required an answer by the return of the wagon, by which the letter was despatched. This wagon was, at that time, in the service of the seller, and employed by him in hauling flour from his mill to Harper's Ferry, near to which place the buyers then were. The meaning of the writers was obvious. They could easily calculate by the usual length of time which was employed by this wagon, in traveling from Harper's Ferry to Mill Creek, and back again with a load of flour, about what time they should receive the desired answer, and, therefore, it was entirely unimportant whether it was sent by that or another wagon, or in any other manner, provided it was sent to Harper's Ferry, and was not delayed beyond the time which was ordinarily employed by wagons engaged in hauling flour from the seller's mill to Harper's Ferry. Whatever uncertainty there might have been as to the time when the answer would be received, there was none as to the place to which it was to be sent; this was distinctly indicated by the mode pointed out for the conveyance of the answer. The place, therefore, to which the answer was to be sent, constituted an essential part of the buyers' offer.

It appears, however, from the bill of exceptions, that no answer to this letter was at any time sent to the buyers, at Harper's Ferry. Their offer, it is true, was accepted by the terms of a letter addressed Georgetown, and received by the buyers at that place; but an acceptance communicated at a place different from that pointed out by the buyers, and forming a part of their proposal, imposed no obligation binding upon them, unless they had acquiesced in it, which they declined doing.

It is no argument that an answer was received at Georgetown; the buyers had a right to dictate the terms upon which they would purchase the flour, and, unless they were complied with, they were not bound by them. All their arrangements may have been made with a view to the circumstances of place, and they were the only judges of its importance. There was therefore no contract concluded between these parties, and the court ought, therefore, to have given the instructions to the jury, which was asked for.

Judgment reversed. Cause remanded, with directions to award a venire facias de novo.

UNIFORM COMMERCIAL CODE § 2–206(1)(a).

(1) Unless otherwise unambiguously indicated by the language or circumstances

(a) an offer to make a contract shall be construed as inviting acceptance in any manner and by any medium reasonable in the circumstances.

ALLIED STEEL AND CONVEYORS, INC. v. FORD MOTOR CO.

United States Court of Appeals, Sixth Circuit, 1960.
277 F.2d 907.

WILLIAM E. MILLER, DISTRICT JUDGE.

The question presented on this appeal is whether a provision in certain written agreements between appellant and appellee purporting to indemnify appellee against damages resulting from its own acts of negligence was binding upon the parties at the time the damages were sustained.[a]

a. Appellant, Allied Steel & Conveyors, Inc., and appellee, Ford Motor Company, will be referred to herein as "Allied" and "Ford."

On August 19, 1955, Ford ordered from Allied numerous items of machinery and equipment. The consideration to be paid was $71,325.00. Under the terms of the order, Allied was to install the machinery and equipment on Ford's premises for an additional consideration of $6,900.00, with a provision that should Ford elect to install the machinery with its own labor, Allied would furnish a supervisor to direct the installation on a per diem basis. The order further provided that "the signing and returning to Buyer by Seller of the Acknowledgment Copy shall constitute acceptance by Seller of this Purchase Order and of all of its terms and conditions." The order was submitted on printed forms regularly used by Ford, and was designated "Purchase Order No. 15145." Item 15 of the printed form provided that if Allied was required to perform work on Ford's premises, Allied would be responsible for all damages or injuries occurring as a result of the fault or negligence of its own employees, including any damages or injuries to Ford's employees and property. Attached to the Purchase Order and made a part thereof was a printed form designated Form 3618, which included an indemnity provision broader in scope than Item 15 of the purchase order, requiring the Seller to assume full responsibility not only for the fault or negligence of its own employees but also for the fault or negligence of Ford's employees, arising out of or in connection with Allied's work. This provision in Form 3618, however, was marked "VOID." On December 16, 1955, Ford submitted to Allied its Amendment No. 1 to the purchase order, deleting the item of $6,900.00 for the cost of installation by Allied and providing that the installation would be done by Ford. The original Purchase Order and Amendment No. 1 were both duly accepted by Allied and the agreements were performed.

Subsequently, on July 26, 1956, Ford submitted to Allied Amendment No. 2 to Purchase Order 15145, and it is this Amendment which is the focal point of the present controversy. By the amendment Ford proposed to purchase additional machinery to be installed on Ford's premises by Allied, at a total cost of $173,700.00. Amendment No. 2, as did Amendment No. 1, provided:

> "This purchase order agreement is not binding until accepted. Acceptance should be executed on acknowledgment copy which should be returned to buyer."

The copy of Ford's Form 3618 attached to Amendment No. 2 was identical to the printed Form 3618 which was attached to the original Purchase Order, but the broad indemnity provision in Form 3618, making Allied liable for the negligent acts of both its own and Ford's employees, was not marked "VOID." The record makes it clear that the reason for not voiding the broad indemnity provision of Form 3618 attached to Amendment No. 2 was that the installation work on Ford's premises was to be performed by Allied's employees, whereas under the original purchase order as amended by Amendment No. 1 the installation work was to be done by Ford's own employees. Another pertinent provision of Form 3618 was:

> "Such of the terms and conditions of Seller's Purchase Order as are inconsistent with the provisions hereinabove set forth are hereby superseded."

The acknowledgment copy of Amendment No. 2 was duly executed by Allied on or about November 10, 1956, and was received by Ford on November 12, 1956. At that time Allied had already begun installation of the machinery on the Ford premises, although the exact date upon which the installation was commenced is not shown in the record. On September 5, 1956, in the course of the installation, one Hankins, an employee of Allied, sustained personal injuries as a result of the negligence of Ford's employees. Hankins later filed an action against Ford in the District Court for the Eastern District of Michigan, Southern Division. After the complaint was filed, Ford added Allied, Hankins' employer, as a third-party defendant, relying upon the indemnity provisions of Form 3618, and demanding judgment against Allied " * * * for all sums that may be adjudged against the defendant, Ford Motor Company, in favor of plaintiff, John T. Hankins." The trial before a jury resulted in verdicts for $12,500.00 in favor of Hankins and against Ford, and in favor of Ford and against Allied for the same amount. This appeal by Allied followed denial by the District Court of its motion for judgment notwithstanding the verdict of the jury and entry of judgment against it in favor of Ford upon the third-party complaint.

* * *

Allied first says that the contractual provisions evidenced by Amendment No. 2 were not in effect at the time of the Hankins injury because it had not been accepted at that time by Allied in the formal manner expressly required by the amendment itself. It argues that a binding acceptance of the amendment could be effected only by Allied's execution of the acknowledgment copy of the amendment and its return to Ford.

With this argument we cannot agree. It is true that an offeror may prescribe the manner in which acceptance of his offer shall be indicated by the offeree, and an acceptance of the offer in the manner prescribed will bind the offeror. And it has been held that if the offeror prescribes an exclusive manner of acceptance, an attempt on the part of the offeree to accept the offer in a different manner does not bind the offeror *in the absence of a meeting of the minds on the altered type of acceptance.* * * * On the other hand, if an offeror merely suggests a permitted method of acceptance, other methods of acceptance are not precluded. Restatement, Contracts, Sec. 61; Williston on Contracts, Third Ed. Secs. 70, 76. Moreover, it is equally well settled that if the offer requests a return promise and the offeree without making the promise actually does or tenders what he was requested to promise to do, there is a contract if such performance is completed or tendered within the time allowable for accepting by making a promise. In such a case a tender operates as a promise to render complete performance. Restatement, Contracts, Sec. 63; Williston on Contracts, Third Ed. Sec. 75.

Applying these principles to the case at bar, we reach the conclusion, first, that execution and return of the acknowledgment copy of Amendment No. 2 was merely a suggested method of acceptance and did not preclude acceptance by some other method; and, second, that the offer was accepted and a binding contract effected when Allied, with Ford's knowledge, consent and acquiescence, undertook performance of the work called for by the amendment. The only significant provision, as we view the amendment, was that it would not be binding until it was accepted by Allied. This provision was obviously for the protection of Ford * * * and its import was that Ford would not be bound by the amendment unless Allied agreed to all of the conditions specified therein. The provision for execution and return of the acknowledgment copy, as we construe the language used, was not to set forth an exclusive method of acceptance but was merely to provide a simple and convenient method by which the assent of Allied to the contractual provisions of the amendment could be indicated. The primary object of Ford was to have the work performed by Allied upon the terms prescribed in the amendment, and the mere signing and return of an acknowledgment copy of the amendment before actually undertaking the work itself cannot be regarded as an essential condition to completion of a binding contract.

It is well settled that acceptance of an offer by part performance in accordance with the terms of the offer is sufficient to complete the contract. * * * Other authorities are to the effect that the acceptance of a contract may be implied from acts of the parties * * * and may be shown by proving acts done on the faith of the order, including shipment of the goods ordered. * * * It would seem necessarily to follow that an offeree who has unjustifiably led the offerer to believe that he had acquired a contractual right, should not be allowed to assert an actual intent at variance with the meaning of his acts.

It has been argued on behalf of Allied, by way of analogy, that Ford could have revoked the order when Allied began installing the machinery without first having executed its written acceptance. If this point should be conceded * * * it would avail Allied nothing. For, after Allied began performance by installing the machinery called for, and Ford acquiesced in the acts of Allied and accepted the benefits of the performance, Ford was estopped to object and could not thereafter be heard to complain that there was no contract. * * *

* * *

The judgment of the District Court is Affirmed.

RESTATEMENT (SECOND) OF CONTRACTS § 32.
Invitation of Promise or Performance

In case of doubt an offer is interpreted as inviting the offeree to accept either by promising to perform what the offer requests or by rendering the performance, as the offeree chooses.

WHITE v. CORLIES
New York Court of Appeals, 1871.
46 N.Y. 467.

Appeal from judgment of the General Term of the first judicial district, affirming a judgment entered upon a verdict for plaintiff.

The action was for an alleged breach of contract.

The plaintiff was a builder, with his place of business in Fortieth street, New York city.

The defendants were merchants at 32 Dey street.

In September, 1865, the defendants furnished the plaintiff with specifications, for fitting up a suit of offices at 57 Broadway, and requested him to make an estimate of the cost of doing the work.

On September twenty-eighth the plaintiff left his estimate with the defendants, and they were to consider upon it, and inform the plaintiff of their conclusions.

On the same day the defendants made a change in their specifications and sent a copy of the same, so changed, to the plaintiff for his assent under his estimate, which he assented to by signing the same and returning it to the defendants.

On the day following the defendants' book-keeper wrote the plaintiff the following note:

"New York, *September* 29*th.*

"*Upon an agreement* to finish the fitting up of offices 57 Broadway in two weeks from date, you can begin at once.

"The writer will call again, probably between five and six this P.M.

"W.H.R.,

"For J.W. Corlies & Co.,

"32 Dey street."

No reply to this note was ever made by the plaintiff; and on the next day the same was countermanded by a second note from the defendants.

Immediately on receipt of the note of September twenty-ninth, and before the countermand was forwarded, the plaintiff commenced a performance by the purchase of lumber and beginning work thereon.

And after receiving the countermand, the plaintiff brought this action for damages for a breach of contract.

The court charged the jury as follows: "From the contents of this note which the plaintiff received, was it his duty to go down to Dey street (meaning to give notice of assent), before commencing the work?"

"In my opinion it was not. He had a right to act upon this note and commence the job, *and that was a binding contract between the parties.*"

To this defendants excepted.

* * *

FOLGER, J. We do not think that the jury found, or that the testimony shows, that there was any agreement between the parties, before the written communication of the defendants of September thirtieth was received by the plaintiff. This note did not make an agreement. It was a proposition, and must have been accepted by the plaintiff before either party was bound, in contract, to the other. The only overt action which is claimed by the plaintiff as indicating on his part an acceptance of the offer, was the purchase of the stuff necessary for the work, and commencing work, as we understand the testimony, upon that stuff.

We understand the rule to be, that where an offer is made by one party to another when they are not together, the acceptance of it by that other must be manifested by some appropriate act. It does not need that the acceptance shall come to the knowledge of the one making the offer before he shall be bound. But though the manifestation need not be brought to his knowledge before he becomes bound, he is not bound, if that manifestation is not put in a proper way to be in the usual course of events, in some reasonable time communicated to him. Thus a letter received by mail containing a proposal, may be answered by letter by mail, containing the acceptance. And in general, as soon as the answering letter is mailed, the contract is concluded. Though one party does not know of the acceptance, the manifestation thereof is put in the proper way of reaching him.

In the case in hand, the plaintiff determined to accept. But a mental determination not indicated by speech, or put in course of indication by act to the other party, is not an acceptance which will bind the other. Nor does an act, which, in itself, is no indication of an acceptance, become such, because accompanied by an unevinced mental determination. Where the act uninterpreted by concurrent evidence of the mental purpose accompanying it, is as well referable to one state of facts as another, it is no indication to the other party of an acceptance, and does not operate to hold him to his offer.

Conceding that the testimony shows, that the plaintiff did resolve to accept this offer, he did no act which indicated an acceptance of it to the defendants. He, a carpenter and builder, purchased stuff for the work. But it was stuff as fit for any other like work. He began work upon the stuff, but as he would have done for any other like work. There was nothing in his thought formed but not uttered, or in his acts that indicated or set in motion an indication to the defendants of his acceptance of their offer, or which could necessarily result therein.

But the charge of the learned judge was fairly to be understood by the jury as laying down the rule to them, that the plaintiff need not indicate to the defendants his acceptance of their offer; and that the purchase of stuff and working on it after receiving the note, made a binding contract between the parties. In this we think the learned judge fell into error.

* * *

Judgment reversed, and new trial ordered.

DUCOMMUN v. JOHNSON, 252 Iowa 1192, 1197, 110 N.W.2d 271, 274 (1961). [A real estate agent's right to a fee depended on whether one of the sellers had accepted the terms of the sale. The contract of sale was mailed to the seller for her approval, but nothing was heard from her for over thirty days, when the sale fell through. The agent claimed that the seller accepted by failing to object to the terms of the sale.] "We cannot approve this theory. [Seller] was not obligated to say one way or the other whether she approved. Passage of time would be more inclined to express disapproval than approval. Myers v. Smith, 197 Iowa 195, 196 N.W. 989; see 12 Am.Jur.P. 533, Sec. 40, where it is stated: 'It is a general rule of law that silence and inaction do not amount to an acceptance of an offer. Thus, generally speaking, mere silence or failure to reject an offer when it is made does not constitute an acceptance.'"

Problem 4–11

On April 1, Edgar receives a Mozart album in the mail, sent by Nifty Records, with an attached cover letter stating: "We hereby offer you these records at the bargain price of $21. Please remit payment by the end of the month to our business office noted above.'' Edgar opens the package and letter and plays one piece, Mozart's 21st piano concerto (Rubinstein). Thereafter Edgar, dissatisfied with the rendition, puts the record to one side and forgets about it. What are Nifty Records' rights, if any, under the Restatement (Second) and U.S. Code sections set forth below? What if the album had arrived by United Parcel Service?

RESTATEMENT (SECOND) OF CONTRACTS § 69.

Acceptance by Silence or Exercise of Dominion

(1) Where an offeree fails to reply to an offer, his silence and inaction operate as an acceptance in the following cases only:

(a) Where an offeree takes the benefit of offered services with reasonable opportunity to reject them and reason to know that they were offered with the expectation of compensation.

(b) Where the offeror has stated or given the offeree reason to understand that assent may be manifested by silence or inaction, and the offeree in remaining silent and inactive intends to accept the offer.

(c) Where because of previous dealings or otherwise, it is reasonable that the offeree should notify the offeror if he does not intend to accept.

(2) An offeree who does any act inconsistent with the offeror's ownership of offered property is bound in accordance with the offered terms unless they are manifestly unreasonable. But if the act is wrongful as against the offeror it is an acceptance only if ratified by him.

39 U.S.C. § 3009 (1994).

Mailing of Unordered Merchandise

(a) Except for (1) free samples clearly and conspicuously marked as such, and (2) merchandise mailed by a charitable organization soliciting contributions, the mailing of unordered merchandise * * * constitutes an unfair method of competition and an unfair trade practice * * *.

(b) Any merchandise mailed in violation of subsection (a) of this section, or within the exceptions contained therein, may be treated as a gift by the recipient, who shall have the right to retain, use, discard, or dispose of it in any manner he sees fit without any obligation whatsoever to the sender. All such merchandise shall have attached to it a clear and conspicuous statement informing the recipient that he may treat the merchandise as a gift to him and has the right to retain, use, discard, or dispose of it in any manner he sees fit without any obligation whatsoever to the sender.

(c) No mailer of any merchandise mailed in violation of subsection (a) of this section, or within the exceptions contained therein, shall mail to any recipient of such merchandise a bill for such merchandise or any dunning communications.

(d) For the purposes of this section, ''unordered merchandise'' means merchandise mailed without the prior expressed request or consent of the recipient.

Note
Independent Significance of Agreement and Consideration

What is the relation between agreement and consideration? Reflect on the remarks of Professor Patterson:

> Wherein does the requirement of "agreement" by the promisee differ from the requirement of "consideration"? * * * It does seem that the promisee's manifested assent to accept a gift from the promisor does not constitute an "agreement" in Anglo–American law, and probably not in some other legal systems. At all events it does not constitute a "consideration." Aside from this case it is hard to think of a case in which the promisee has "agreed" to anything unless he has given consideration. Possibly such a case is the one in which a father promised to discharge his son's obligation on a promissory note in return for the son's agreeing not to importune his father any more. However, an English court held the father's promise unenforceable on the ground that the father and son did not at the time intend to create a legal obligation. While the decision seems questionable, it may be taken to mean that there was no agreement, or no *exchange* of promise for promise. It has recently been argued that the English doctrine of consideration is merely another aspect of the requirement of offer and acceptance. * * * (Patterson, An Apology for Consideration, 58 Colum.L.Rev. 929, 944 (1958).)

SECTION SEVEN: DURATION OF OFFERS

RESTATEMENT (SECOND) OF CONTRACTS § 36.

Methods of Termination of the Power of Acceptance

(1) An offeree's power of acceptance may be terminated by

(a) rejection or counter-offer by the offeree, or

(b) lapse of time, or

(c) revocation by the offeror, or

(d) death or incapacity of the offeror or offeree.

(2) In addition, an offeree's power of acceptance is terminated by the non-occurrence of any condition of acceptance under the terms of the offer.

AKERS v. J.B. SEDBERRY, INC.

Court of Appeals of Tennessee, 1955.
39 Tenn.App. 633, 286 S.W.2d 617.

FELTS, JUDGE.

These two consolidated causes are before us upon a writ of error sued out by J.B. Sedberry, Inc., and Mrs. M.B. Sedberry, defendants below, to review a decree of the Chancery Court, awarding a recovery against them in favor of each of the complainants, Charles William Akers and William Gambill Whitsitt, for damages for breach of a contract of employment.

The principal question presented is whether complainants resigned their employment, or were wrongfully discharged by defendants; and if there was a breach of contract for which complainants are entitled to recover, there are some further questions as to the measure or extent of the recovery.

J.B. Sedberry, Inc., was a Tennessee corporation with its principal place of business at Franklin, Tennessee. Mrs. M.B. Sedberry owned practically all of its stock and was its president and in active charge of its affairs. It was engaged in the business of distributing "Jay Bee" hammer mills, which were manufactured for it under contract by Jay Bee Manufacturing Company, a Texas corporation, whose plant was in Tyler, Texas, and whose capital stock was owned principally by L.M. Glasgow and B.G. Byars.

On July 1, 1947, J.B. Sedberry, Inc., by written contract, employed complainant Akers as Chief Engineer for a term of five years at a salary of $12,000 per year, payable $1,000 per month, plus 1% of its net profits for the first year, 2% the second, 3% the third, 4% the fourth, and 5% the fifth year. His duties were to carry on research for his employer, and to see that the Jay Bee Manufacturing Company, Tyler, Texas, manufactured the mills and parts according to proper specifications. Mrs. M.B. Sedberry guaranteed the employer's performance of this contract.

On August 1, 1947, J.B. Sedberry, Inc., by written contract, employed complainant Whitsitt as Assistant Chief Engineer for a term of five years at a salary of $7,200 per year, payable $600 per month, plus 1% of the corporation's net profits for the first year, 2% for the second, 3% for the third, 4% for the fourth, and 5% for the fifth year. His duties were to assist in the work done by the Chief Engineer. Mrs. M.B. Sedberry guaranteed the employer's performance of this contract.

Under Mrs. Sedberry's instructions, Akers and Whitsitt moved to Tyler, Texas, began performing their contract duties in the plant of the Jay Bee Manufacturing Company, continued working there, and were paid under the contracts until October 1, 1950, when they ceased work, under circumstances hereafter stated.

In 1947, when these employment contracts were made, Mrs. Sedberry owned no stock in the Jay Bee Manufacturing Company. In 1948 she purchased the shares of stock in this company which were owned by the Glasgow interests, and in 1949 she purchased the 750 shares owned by her brother, B.G. Byars, and gave him her note therefor in the sum of $157,333.93, pledging the 750 shares with him as collateral to her note.

Glasgow had been general manager of the Jay Bee Manufacturing Company, but when he sold his stock, he was succeeded by A.M. Sorenson as manager. There soon developed considerable friction between Sorenson and complainants Akers and Whitsitt. The Jay Bee Manufacturing Company owed large sums to the Tyler State Bank & Trust Co.; and the bank's officers, fearing the company might fail under Sorenson's management, began talking to Akers and Whitsitt about the company's financial difficulties.

One of the bank's vice-presidents, J. Harold Stringer, made a trip to Franklin to see Mrs. Sedberry about the company's indebtedness to the bank. He told her that they could not get along with Sorenson and did not agree with the way he was managing the company's affairs. Mrs. Sedberry asked Stringer as soon as he got back to Tyler to see Akers and Whitsitt and discuss with them plans for the refinancing and the operation of the company; and thereafter the bank's officers had a number of conferences with Akers and Whitsitt about these matters.

While these matters were pending, Akers and Whitsitt flew to Nashville and went to Franklin to talk with Mrs. Sedberry about them. They had a conference with her at her office on Friday, September 29, 1950, lasting from 9:30 a.m. until 4:30 p.m. As they had come unannounced, and unknown to Sorenson, they felt Mrs. Sedberry might mistrust them; and at the outset, to show their good faith, they offered to resign, but she did not accept their offer. Instead, she proceeded with them in discussing the operation and refinancing of the business.

Testifying about this conference, Akers said that, at the very beginning, to show their good faith, he told Mrs. Sedberry that they would offer their resignations on a ninety-day notice, provided they were paid according to the contract for that period; that she pushed the offers aside—"would not accept them", but went into a full discussion of the business; that nothing was thereafter said about the offers to resign; and that they spent the whole day discussing the business. Akers making notes of things she instructed him to do when he got back to Texas.

Whitsitt testified that at the beginning of the meeting Akers stated the position for both of them, and told Mrs. Sedberry, as evidence of their good faith, "we would resign with ninety-days notice if she paid us the monies that she owed us to that date, and on the other hand, if she did not accept that resignation, we would carry forth the rest of our business." He said that she did not accept the offer, but proceeded with the business, and nothing further was said about resigning.

Mrs. Sedberry testified that Akers and Whitsitt came in and "offered their resignations"; that they said they could not work with Sorenson and did not believe the bank would go along with him; and that "they said if it would be of any help to the organization they would be glad to tender their resignation and pay them what was due them." She further said that she "did not accept the resignation", that she "felt it necessary to contact Mr. Sorenson and give consideration to the resignation offer." But she said nothing to complainants about taking the offer under consideration.

On cross-examination she said that in the offer to resign "no mention was made of any ninety-day notice". Asked what response she made to the offer she said, "I treated it rather casually because I had to give it some thought and had to contact Mr. Sorenson." She further said she excused herself from the conference with complainants, went to another room, tried to telephone Sorenson in Tyler, Texas, but was unable to locate him.

She then resumed the conference, nothing further was said about the offers to resign, nothing was said by her to indicate that she thought the offers were left open or held under consideration by her. But the discussion proceeded as if the offers had not been made. She discussed with complainants future plans for refinancing and operating the business, giving them instructions, and Akers making notes of them.

Following the conference, complainants, upon Mrs. Sedberry's request, flew back to Texas to proceed to carry out her instructions. * * *

On Monday, October 2, 1950, Mrs. Sedberry sent to complainants similar telegrams, signed by "J.B. Sedberry, Inc., by M.B. Sedberry, President", stating that their resignations were accepted, effective immediately. We quote the telegram to Akers, omitting the formal parts:

> "Account present unsettled conditions which you so fully are aware we accept your kind offer of resignation effective immediately. Please discontinue as of today with everyone employed in Sedberry, Inc., Engineering Department, discontinuing all expenses in this department writing."

While this said she was "writing", she did not write. * * *

* * * Akers (then wrote) that he was amazed to get her telegram, and called her attention to the fact that no offer to resign by him was open or outstanding when she sent the telegram; that while he had made a conditional offer to resign at their conference on September 29, she had immediately rejected the offer, and had discussed plans for the business and had instructed him and Whitsitt as to things she wanted them to do in the business on their return to Tyler.

This letter further stated that Akers was expecting to be paid according to the terms of his contract until he could find other employment that would pay him as much income as that provided in his contract, and that if he had to accept a position with less income, he would expect to be paid the difference, or whatever losses he suffered by her breach of the contract. Whitsitt's letter contained a similar statement of his position.

On November 10, 1950, Mrs. Sedberry wrote a letter addressed to both Akers and Whitsitt in which she said that "no one deplored the action taken more than the writer", but she did not recede from her position as expressed in the telegram. She stated her contention that the offers to resign had been without condition; and though she also said she would like to make an amicable settlement, no settlement was made.

As it takes two to make a contract, it takes two to unmake it. It cannot be changed or ended by one alone, but only by mutual assent of both parties. A contract of employment for a fixed period may be terminated by the employee's offer to resign, provided such offer is duly accepted by the employer. * * *

An employee's tender of his resignation, being a mere offer is, of course, not binding until it has been accepted by the employer. Such offer must be accepted according to its terms and within the time fixed. The matter is governed by the same rules as govern the formation of contracts. * * *

An offer may be terminated in a number of ways, as, for example, where it is rejected by the offeree, or where it is not accepted by him within the time fixed, or, if no time is fixed, within a reasonable time. An offer terminated in either of these ways ceases to exist and cannot thereafter be accepted. * * *

The question what is a reasonable time, where no time is fixed, is a question of fact, depending on the nature of the contract proposed, the usages of business and other circumstances of the case. Ordinarily, an offer made by one to another in a face to face conversation is deemed to continue only to the close of their conversation, and cannot be accepted thereafter.

The rule is illustrated by Restatement of Contracts, section 40, Illustration 2, as follows:

"2. While A and B are engaged in conversation, A makes B an offer to which B then makes no reply, but a few hours later meeting A again, B states that he accepts the offer. There is no contract unless the offer or the surrounding circumstances indicate that the offer is intended to continue beyond the immediate conversation."

* * *

Professor Corbin says:

"When two negotiating parties are in each other's presence, and one makes an offer to the other without indicating any time for acceptance, the inference that will ordinarily be drawn by the other party is that an answer is expected at once. * * * If, when the first reply is not an acceptance, the offeror turns away in silence, the proper inference is that the offer is no longer open to acceptance." 1 Corbin on Contracts (1950), section 36, p. 111.

The only offer by Akers and Whitsitt to resign was the offer made by them in their conversation with Mrs. Sedberry. They made that offer at the outset, and on the evidence it seems clear that they expected an answer at once. Certainly, there is nothing in the evidence to show that they intended the offer to continue beyond that conversation; and on the above authorities, we think the offer did not continue beyond that meeting.

Indeed, it did not last that long, in our opinion, but was terminated by Mrs. Sedberry's rejection of it very early in that meeting. While she did not expressly reject it, and while she may have intended, as she says, to take the offer under consideration, she did not disclose such an intent to complainants; but, by her conduct, led them to believe she rejected the offer, brushed it aside, and proceeded with the discussion as if it had not been made.

"An offer is rejected when the offeror is justified in inferring from the words or conduct of the offeree that the offeree intends not to accept the offer or to take it under further advisement (Rest. Contracts sec. 36)." 1 Williston on Contracts, section 51.

So, we agree with the Trial Judge that when defendants sent the telegrams, undertaking to accept offers of complainants to resign, there was no such offer in existence; and that this attempt of defendants to terminate their contract was unlawful and constituted a breach for which they are liable to complainants. * * *

* * *

Finally, defendants contend that if complainants are entitled to any recovery at all, such recovery should have been limited to the ninety-day period from and after October 2, 1950, because complainants themselves admitted that they had offered to resign upon ninety days notice with pay for that period.

The answer to this contention is that their offer to resign on ninety days notice was not accepted, but had terminated, and there was no offer in existence when Mrs. Sedberry undertook to accept their offers of resignation. Such attempt by defendants to terminate their contract was unlawful and was a breach for which they become liable for the measure of recovery as above stated.

* * *

All of the assignments of error are overruled and the decree of the Chancellor is affirmed. * * * The causes are remanded to the Chancery Court for further proceedings not inconsistent with this opinion.

E. FARNSWORTH, CONTRACTS

165–66 (3d ed. 1999).

Rejection by the offeree terminates the power of acceptance. If a seller offers to deliver goods to a buyer for $10,000, and the buyer replies, "I don't want your goods," the buyer's power of acceptance is terminated—the buyer cannot later accept. (If the buyer tried to, the purported acceptance might itself be an offer to the seller.) The rationale is that the offeror may rely on the rejection, by action (such as selling the goods elsewhere) or by inaction (such as failing to prepare to deliver them) or by merely failing to revoke the offer. The possibility of reliance is enough and no actual reliance is required. Rejection has this effect even though the offerer has fixed a longer time after which the offer lapses.

VASKIE v. WEST AMERICAN INSURANCE CO.

Superior Court of Pennsylvania, 1989.
383 Pa.Super. 76, 556 A.2d 436.

BECK, JUDGE:

This is an appeal from a grant of summary judgment in favor of plaintiff-appellee Anne Marie Vaskie in her breach of contract action against defendant-appellant West American Insurance Company.

On January 1, 1985, Ms. Vaskie was involved in an automobile accident with a vehicle owned and operated by persons who were insured by West American. Ms. Vaskie retained Harold Murnane, Esquire, to represent her in connection with obtaining recovery for the personal injuries she sustained as a result of this accident. At some point prior to December 1986 Mr. Murnane and West American began negotiations aimed at settling Ms. Vaskie's claim. The parties' correspondence reveals that as of November 1986, West American had offered $25,000. Apparently after continuing negotiations by telephone, on December 1, 1986 West American addressed a letter to Mr. Murnane which concluded by stating that West American had carefully reviewed Ms. Vaskie's claim and that West American's "offer will remain $25,000." This letter did not specify a date on which the offer would terminate. On January 9, 1987, Mr. Murnane sent a mailgram to West American in which he, on behalf of Ms. Vaskie, unconditionally accepted West American's $25,000 offer.

West American refused to pay, arguing that there was no contract between the parties because the statute of limitations on Ms. Vaskie's personal injury claim had run on January 1, 1987, eight days before she accepted West American's offer.

Ms. Vaskie then instituted this suit for breach of the alleged settlement agreement. Both parties filed motions for summary judgment. The trial court granted Ms. Vaskie's motion, awarding her $25,000, and denied West American's motion.

West American appealed, arguing alternatively that either judgment should have been entered in its favor or that at a minimum factual disputes requiring resolution by a jury should have prevented the entry of summary judgment for Ms. Vaskie. Ms. Vaskie cross-appealed solely on the ground that the trial court erred in failing to award her pre-judgment interest and costs.

On review of a grant of summary judgment, we must remain mindful that summary judgment is appropriate only where, viewing all the facts in the light most favorable to the non-moving party and resolving all doubts as to the existence of issues of material fact against the moving party, the moving party is nevertheless entitled to judgment as a matter of law. *Mariscotti v. Tinari,* 335 Pa.Super. 599, 485 A.2d 56 (1984).

The central question to be decided is whether the parties entered into an enforceable contract for the payment of $25,000 to Ms. Vaskie in exchange for her relinquishment of her claim for damages for personal injuries. On their face, the facts reveal just such an agreement. West American made a written unconditional offer to pay $25,000 to settle Ms. Vaskie's claim and Ms. Vaskie responded with a written unconditional acceptance, thereby indicating her willingness to accept $25,000 in exchange for her surrender of her claim and forbearance from suing thereon.

However, West American offers several possible impediments to enforcing this apparent agreement. First, West American argues that no agreement was formed by Ms. Vaskie's acceptance because the offer had lapsed as a matter of law when the statute of limitations on personal injury claims, i.e. two years, had expired. As a variation on this theme, West American argues that there is at least a factual issue as to whether the offer had lapsed by the time of Ms. Vaskie's acceptance. Since the offer itself did not specify an expiration date, West American argues that the offer is legally deemed to expire within a reasonable time and what is a reasonable time is a factual question. * * *

There is no doubt on this record that West American made an offer of $25,000 to settle Ms. Vaskie's claim in a letter dated December 1, 1986. There is also no doubt that this offer did not contain any express expiration date. Moreover, there were no further oral or written communications between the parties in which any expiration date was set, nor was the offer ever withdrawn. Under such circumstances, i.e. where an offer does not specify an expiration date or otherwise limit the allowable time for acceptance, it is both hornbook law and well established in Pennsylvania that the offer is deemed to be outstanding for a reasonable period of time. * * * What is a reasonable time is ordinarily a question of fact to be decided by the jury and is dependent upon the numerous circumstances surrounding the transaction. * * * Such circumstances as the nature of the contract, the relationship or situation of the parties and their course of dealing, and usages of the particular business are all relevant. * * *

However, there are situations where the question of what is a reasonable time for acceptance may be decided by the court as a matter of law. As stated in *Boyd* [*v. Merchants and Farmers Peanut Co.,* 25 Pa.Super. 199 (1904)]:

What is a reasonable time for acceptance is a question of law for the court in such commercial transactions as happen in the same way, day after day, and present the question upon the same data in continually recurring instances; and where the time taken is so clearly reasonable or unreasonable that there can be no question of doubt as to the proper answer to the question. Where the answer to the question is one dependent on many different circumstances, which do not continually recur in other cases of like character, and with respect to which no certain rule of law could be laid down, the question is one of fact for the jury.

Boyd, 25 Pa.Super. at 205.

The trial court in the instant matter decided that this was a case where the issue of reasonableness could be decided as a matter of law and found that Ms. Vaskie's acceptance on January 9, 198[7] was tendered within a reasonable time.

We reject West American's contention that its offer of December 1, 1986 lapsed as a matter of law two years after Ms. Vaskie suffered her injuries. However, we do agree with West American insofar as it argues that the trial court erred in deciding as a matter of law that Ms. Vaskie's acceptance was tendered within a reasonable time. We find that under the circumstances of this case, the question of reasonableness is a disputed material issue of fact that should not have been resolved as a matter of law on summary judgment.

There is no merit in the argument that offers of settlement of personal injury claims automatically terminate two years after the injuries were sustained. West American has offered no precedent that so holds, we have located none and the reasons for the dearth of authority supporting such an argument are clear. First, the argument is based on the incorrect assumption that in every personal injury case the statute of limitations will run precisely two years from the date of the accident. In fact, the statute may be tolled due to the inability of the plaintiff to discover his or her injuries or their cause, *Pocono International Raceway, Inc. v. Pocono Produce, Inc.,* 503 Pa. 80, 86, 468 A.2d 468, 471 (1983), or due to fraud or concealment of material information by the defendant. *Molineux v. Reed,* 516 Pa. 398, 532 A.2d 792, 794 (1987). Thus, in each particular case the date on which the statute would be deemed to have run may vary. Given this variation, we cannot fashion a rule that creates an implied-in-law termination date, fixed on the expiration of the statute of limitations, in all settlement offers. To do so would leave the plaintiff-offeree in the untenable position of having to predict and, for purposes of settlement negotiations, accept the defendant-offeror's view of when the statute should be deemed to have run.

Moreover, to hold that every such offer contains an implied-in-law termination date would be to dictate a term of such offers which the parties themselves can and should decide upon. If an offering defendant wishes to limit the duration of his offer to a certain time, whether a date two years from the accident or otherwise, he need only so state in the offer itself. He is the master of his offer. There is no need for us to provide such a term where, as here, the defendant has not done so.

This is not to say, however, that the passing of the statute of limitations is irrelevant to a determination of whether an offer of settlement of a personal injury claim has been accepted within a reasonable time. The reasonableness of the time an offeree takes to accept an offer is measured from the perspective of the offeree. As the explanatory comment to the pertinent section of the Restatement (Second) of Contracts states:

> In general, the question is what time would be thought satisfactory to the offeror by a reasonable man in the position of the offeree. * * *

Restatement (Second) of Contracts, § 41 comment b (1981).

The fact that the statute of limitations may already have run by the time Ms. Vaskie accepted is unquestionably relevant to a determination of the reasonableness of her conduct in waiting until January 9, 1987 to accept. Further, this is only one of many circumstances surrounding the parties' negotiations and the status of Ms. Vaskie's claim that may be relevant to a determination of reasonableness. This is certainly not a case such as that described above in *Boyd* where the reasonableness question can be decided as a matter of law. It is not a commercial transaction continually occurring in like manner day after day. The course and nature of settlement negotiations varies greatly from case to case. This is very unlike the situation of a merchant who offers goods for sale on a daily basis at a price that changes daily, where it is clear beyond cavil that an offer made at one day's price is not intended to continue to the next day. In settlement negotiations the reasonable duration of an offer is not fixed at a particular time because of clear and uniform courses of dealing and usages of the trade that invariably arise from the very nature of the transaction.

Thus, we conclude that the trial court erred in holding that Ms. Vaskie's January 9th acceptance was tendered within a time that was reasonable as a matter of law. Therefore, the entry of summary judgment in Ms. Vaskie's favor was in error on this ground.

* * *

The judgment is reversed. Jurisdiction is relinquished.

BRIEF OF WEST AMERICAN INSURANCE CO. IN THE SUPERIOR COURT OF PENNSYLVANIA

It was completely unreasonable for the Court below to implicitly require the Defendant to hold open its settlement offer after the Statute of Limitations had expired for the commencement of a personal injury action against its insured. In other words, although the Defendant's settlement offer did not specify a time for acceptance, the nature of the proposed settlement agreement, the purposes of the parties thereto, and the relevant usages of trade all dictate that Plaintiff's counsel could not have reasonably expected that the settlement offer would be held open after the expiration of the Statute of Limitations, unless a timely action for Plaintiff's personal injuries had been commenced.

DEPOSITION OF PLAINTIFF'S LAWYER BY WEST AMERICAN INSURANCE CO.

Q. You further indicated that your understanding at all times relevant to your representation of Anne Marie Vaskie that you were aware that an action against the Krenitskys would have to be brought within two years after the date of the accident?

A. Under ordinary circumstances.

Q. So, therefore, wasn't it, in fact, the case that an action—

A. Let me just interrupt you. You're not, I don't believe, cross-examining me. You're starting your question by telling me, was it not a fact. Why don't you ask me a question instead of stating facts unless these are additional premises in the question that you're going to ask me.

Q. Let me ask the question, and maybe you can answer it.

Isn't it, then, a fact under what you've just said, under ordinary circumstances, that any lawsuit to be brought on behalf of Anne Marie Vaskie against the Krenitskys should have been brought on or before January 1 of '87?

THE WITNESS: I don't think that's an appropriate question. I think the question is objectionable. You know, I think, as I said before, if you want to make that conclusion, the Superior Court of the State of Pennsylvania does not agree with you; and they've already ruled so in this case.

So I'm certainly not going to answer a question that they've already made a decision on that requires a legal conclusion, that they're the ones that are charged with making that conclusion * * *.

* * *

Q. I'm asking you what was your belief, as her counsel, as to what actions, if any, you should have taken to conclude the acceptance on or before January 1 of '87?

A. It was my belief that there was an offer of $25,000 that would remain. And, as a matter of fact, there was a discussion—and I don't know precisely when that discussion took place—at some time between Mr. Hudak and myself in the Fall of 1986. And I believe it was before the end of November of 1986 as to when the statute of limitations would run.

He specifically asked me, when does the statute run in this case, in one of those conversations. And there was no indication from Mr. Hudak in any conversation that we had or in any letter that was sent to me that the offer of $25,000 would not remain open for some period of time after January 1st of 1987.

So it was my belief that since my client wanted to accept the $25,000, that the offer should be accepted within a reasonable period of time, which it was.

Note
Still Further Aspects of
Vaskie v. West American Insurance Co.

In a letter to the editors, West American's lawyer wrote:

Please be advised that this case was settled towards the end of 1989 for the sum of $15,000, in compromise of the full claim of $25,000. I believe that [plaintiff's lawyer] made up the remaining $10,000 to his client, Anne Marie Vaskie, who was also his cousin.

* * * We have since advised West American and a number of our other insurance company clients that they should set a definite date when their

settle-offers would expire, rather than leaving them open-ended, as was the case in the instant matter.

CALDWELL v. CLINE

Supreme Court of Appeals of West Virginia, 1930.
109 W.Va. 553, 156 S.E. 55.

LIVELY, P.

In this chancery suit for the specific performance for a contract for the sale and exchange of real estate, the chancellor sustained a demurrer to plaintiff's bill of complaint and dismissed the bill. Plaintiff appeals.

According to the allegations contained in the bill, W.D. Cline, residing at Valls Creek, McDowell county, W. Va., owner of a tract of land on Indian creek, McDowell county, addressed a letter, dated January 29, 1929, to W.H. Caldwell, at Peterstown, Monroe county, W. Va., in which Cline proposed to pay to Caldwell the sum of $6,000 cash and to deed to Caldwell his land on Indian creek in exchange for Caldwell's land known as the McKinsey farm. The letter further provided that Cline "will give you (Caldwell) eight days in which" to accept or reject the offer. Caldwell received the letter at Peterstown on February 2, 1929. On February 8, 1929, the offeree wired Cline as follows: "Land deal is made. Prepare deed to me. See letter." The telegram reached Cline on February 9, 1929. Upon Cline's refusal to carry out the terms of the alleged agreement, plaintiff instituted this suit for specific performance; the titles to the farms remaining unchanged.

* * *

Defendant's main contention is that the offer was not accepted within the time limit specified in the offer, and counsel for defendant, in his brief, states the law to be as "the time for acceptance runs from the date of the offer and not from the date of its delivery." * * * [C]ourts and text-writers have recognized the rule that, where a person uses the post to make an offer, the offer is not made when it is posted, but when it is received. * * * The reason for such a rule is clear. When contracting parties are present, words spoken by one party must strike the ear of the other before there can be mutual assent. So inter absentes, letters, which perform the office of words, must come to the knowledge of the party to whom they are addressed before they are accorded legal existence. "The distinction between contracts inter presentes and those inter absentes has no metaphysical existence, for even inter presentes some appreciable time must elapse between the offer on the one hand and the acceptance on the other. As the parties withdraw from each other this time increases, and when they are so far apart that they are obliged to resort to writing to communicate their thoughts to each other, it is none the less true of the communications made by this medium, than of those made by means of spoken words, that in law they are allowed no existence until they reach the intelligence of the person to whom they are addressed." 7 Amer.Law Rev. 434, 456.

* * *

The letter, proposing that Cline "will give you eight days" to accept or reject the offer, is, without more, conclusive of the offeror's intention; and, the unconditional acceptance having been received by Cline within the specified time limit, the result was a concurrence of the minds of the contracting parties upon the subject-matter of their negotiations; in other words, a consummated contract * * *.

* * *

Decree reversed; bill reinstated; cause remanded.

RESTATEMENT (SECOND) OF CONTRACTS § 39(2).

An offeree's power of acceptance is terminated by his making of a counter-offer, unless the offeror has manifested a contrary intention or unless the counter-offer manifests a contrary intention of the offeree.

Note
Counter-Offers

Recall Ardente v. Horan (page 418). The court found that the purchaser's response to the sellers' offer of real estate was a counter-offer and not an acceptance because, according to the court, the purchaser indicated that he would not go through with the sale if he did not receive the dining room set and other items with the real estate. But the court noted that it is possible to accept and yet include a "request" dealing with additional matters. Consider also the following illustrative case, drawn from a rather special context:

COLLINS v. THOMPSON, 679 F.2d 168 (9th Cir.1982). [The State of Washington proposed a consent decree to end litigation with inmates of the Washington State Reformatory over the appropriate population of the prison. The consent decree included the wrong date for initial reduction of the population (March 1, 1981) and the state therefore submitted on February 13, 1981, an amended decree including the correct date (April 1, 1981). The inmates moved for approval of the decree with the March 1, 1981 date, or alternatively, for a notice to the class of inmates reflecting the modification to the April 1 date. The magistrate denied both requests and found no contract in light of the absence of "a meeting of the minds" on the date for initial reduction. The inmates' appeal was denied. On May 15, 1981, the inmates filed a notice of acceptance of the offer of settlement with the April 1, 1981 date for initial reduction. Both the magistrate and the district court on appeal held that the inmates had not rejected the state's settlement offer with the April 1, 1981 date and the state had not revoked the offer. They therefore approved the consent decree. The state appealed.]

SKOPIL, C.J.

General contract principles apply to questions of interpretation of consent decrees. *United States v. ITT Continental Baking Co.,* 420 U.S. 223, 236–37, 95 S.Ct. 926, 934–35, 43 L.Ed.2d 148 (1975). * * * Questions regarding formation of consent decrees likewise are to be resolved by general contract principles. A consent decree is essentially an agreement of the parties to resolve their dispute, and the facets of agreement are analyzed by applying contract principles.

* * *

The state argues that the prisoners' actions in strenuously pursuing the enforcement of the proposed consent decree with the March 1, 1981 date constituted a rejection of the February 13, 1981 offer.

Generally, a rejection or counteroffer ordinarily terminates the power to accept the previously-made offer. 1 Jaeger, *Williston on Contracts* § 51 (3d ed. 1957); 1 Corbin, *Contracts* § 90 (1963 & Supp.1980). However,

"The offeree [has] the power to prevent his counteroffer (or even a rejection) from terminating his power of acceptance. Suppose he should say: 'I am still considering your offer; but meantime I am now willing to buy the property you offer if you will reduce your price by $500.' There is no reason why this should lead the offeror into a change of position, or why it should operate to terminate the power of accepting the original offer still under consideration."

1 Corbin, *Contracts* § 92. The *Restatement* also agrees with the above contract principle:

"A manifestation of intention not to accept an offer is a rejection *unless the offeree manifests an intention to take it under further advisement.*"

Restatement (Second) of Contracts § 38 (1981) (emphasis added).

On February 26, 1981 the prisoners moved for either (1) approval of the consent decree with the March 1, 1981 date, or, in the alternative (2) a notice to the class to reflect the change in the decree to April 1, 1981.

The district court found that

"The plaintiff's alternative motion on February 26, 1981 for a new notice to the class clearly indicated that the plaintiffs were not rejecting the entire settlement and that they fully intended settlement even if the date were the April 1st date."

There is sufficient evidence such that this finding cannot be held clearly erroneous. As stated above, the objective test is used to determine questions of contract formation. The February 26th motion would not clearly indicate to a reasonable person that the prisoners were rejecting the proposed settlement offer with the April 1st date. In point of fact, the prisoners in this motion specifically indicated they were still considering the April 1st date.

* * *

Affirmed.

DICKINSON v. DODDS, 2 Ch. Div. 463 (1876). [Dodds gave Dickinson a signed memo on Wednesday, June 10, 1874, offering to sell certain real estate "to Mr. George Dickinson." The memo included a postscript that read: "This offer to be left over until Friday, 9 o'clock a.m. J.D. (the twelfth), 12th June, 1874." The bill alleged that the plaintiff, Dickinson, decided to accept the offer on the morning of Thursday, the 11th of June, but did not at once signify his acceptance to Dodds, thinking he could do so until 9 a.m. on Friday. But later that Thursday afternoon, a Mr. Berry told Dickinson that Dodds "had been offering or agreeing to sell the property to Thomas Allen." Thereafter Dickinson immediately attempted to communicate his acceptance to Dodds, who took the position that his offer had been revoked. Held, for

Dodds.] "[I]t is said that the only mode in which Dodds could assert * * * [the power to revoke] was by actually and distinctly saying to Dickinson, 'Now I withdraw my offer.' It appears to me that there is neither principle nor authority [for that assertion] * * *. [I]n this case, beyond all question, the plaintiff knew that Dodds was no longer minded to sell the property to him."

J. DAWSON, GIFTS AND PROMISES
212–13 (1980).

[Dickinson v. Dodds] concluded with great confidence that a time limit fixed by the offeror could not prevent revocation before the time limit had expired, for in the absence of consideration any restriction on the power to revoke was simply *nodum pactum*. American decisions have dutifully followed this line ever since and thereby made the consideration test a still more prominent target of public ridicule * * *.

Note
The Offeror's Power to Revoke

The approach of Dickinson v. Dodds is still generally followed today. See Restatement (Second) of Contracts § 42 ("An offeree's power of acceptance is terminated when the offeree receives from the offeror a manifestation of an intention not to enter into the proposed contract."). One explanation for this result is that a representation that an offer will remain open is a bare promise, unsupported by consideration, and therefore unenforceable. Another explanation, plausible at the time of decision, was that:

> An offer is merely one of the elements of a contract; and it is indispensable to the making of a contract that the wills of the contracting parties do, in legal contemplation, concur at the moment of making it. An offer, therefore, which the party making it has no power to revoke, is a legal impossibility.

Langdell, A Summary of the Law of Contracts, § 178 at 240 (2d ed. 1880).

We have seen in our study of the nature of mutual assent that contract law no longer adheres to Langdell's subjective will theory. In fact, in the following materials we will see a variety of devices utilized by courts to bar revocation of offers. You should consider why contract law has moved in this direction.

Note that the general rule, according to Restatement (Second) section 42, is that a revocation must be *received* before the offeree's power of acceptance is terminated. One exception to this rule is found in Shuey v. United States, 92 U.S. (2 Otto) 73 (1875). There, the U.S. War Department had published an offer of a reward of $25,000 for the apprehension of a criminal, but then revoked the offer through a similar publication. The claimant saw the reward offer but not the revocation. Five months after the revocation, the claimant, unaware of the withdrawal, gave information that led to the arrest of the criminal. The court held, *inter alia,* that the claimant was not entitled to recover because the revocation was effective. It had been given the same notoriety as the offer and "the offer of the reward not having been made to [the claimant] directly, but by means of a publicized proclamation, he should have known that it could be revoked in the manner in which it was made."

MARSH v. LOTT

Court of Appeal, California, 1908.
8 Cal.App. 384, 97 P. 163.

SHAW, J. Action for specific performance of a contract, whereby plaintiff asserts that in consideration of 25 cents he was given an option to purchase, for the sum of $100,000, certain real estate owned by defendant. Judgment was rendered for defendant. Plaintiff appeals from the judgment, and from an order denying his motion for a new trial.

The contract, specific performance of which is sought, is as follows: "For and in consideration of the sum of twenty-five cents to me in hand paid, I hereby give Robt. Marsh & Co. an option to purchase, at any time up to and including June 1st, 1905, with privilege of 30 days extension, from date hereof, the following described property, to wit: South ½ of lot 9 & all of lot 8, block 101, Bellevue Terrace tract, and all of the property owned by myself in above block, for the sum of one hundred thousand dollars, payable thirty thousand cash, balance on or before 4 years, 4½% net. I agree to furnish an unlimited certificate of title showing said property to be free from all incumbrance, and to convey the same in such condition by deed of grant, bargain and sale, & pay regular commission. M.A. Lott. [Seal.] Date: Feby. 25th, 1905. Property: 90 _ 165. Building: 6 flats—2 cottages. Rents: $260.00." On June 1, 1905, plaintiff notified defendant in writing that he exercised the right accorded by said contract regarding the extension of time therein specified, and elected to extend the same for a period of 30 days. On June 2, 1905, defendant, by a written instrument served upon plaintiff, revoked said option, and notified him that she withdrew said property from sale. On June 29, 1905, within the extended time, plaintiff left at the residence of defendant an instrument, of which the following is a copy: "June 29, 1905. Mrs. M.A. Lott, 507 South Olive street, City. Dear Madame: Referring to your agreement with me dated February 25, 1905, by which you gave me the privilege of purchasing the south half of lot nine and the whole of lot eight, in block one hundred and one, Bellevue Terrace tract, in this city, I again tender you in gold coin of the United States the sum of $30,000 as provided in said agreement, and demand of you performance on your part as in said agreement provided. This tender will also be made to your attorney, J. Wiseman MacDonald, Esq., as per request this morning when I tendered you $30,000 in gold coin at your residence on said property. Yours truly, Robert Marsh & Company." The contention of appellant is that certain findings are not supported by the evidence. The findings material to a consideration of the case are as follows: The court found that the sum of 25 cents paid for the option was an inadequate and insufficient consideration for the same, and that the said option contract was not just and reasonable to defendant and no adequate consideration was paid to her for it. * * *

If there was no sufficient consideration for the option, then it was a mere nudum pactum, and defendant's revocation thereof, notwithstanding her promise to the contrary, was effectual in terminating any right of plaintiff to consummate the purchase. * * * If, on the other hand, the offer was to remain open a fixed time and was made upon a valuable consideration, equity will ignore the attempted revocation, and treat a subsequent acceptance, made within the time defined in the option, exactly as if no attempted revocation had been made. * * * Subdivision 1 of section 3391, of the Civil Code makes an adequate consideration for the contract one of the conditions for the specific enforcement thereof. The provision, however, has reference to the consideration to be paid for the property, the right to purchase which at a stipulated price within a given time is the subject of the option. It has no application to the sufficiency of the consideration paid for the executed contract, whereby defendant transferred to plaintiff the right to elect to purchase at the stipulated price. It is not the option which it is sought to enforce, but that which, by plaintiff's acceptance of defendant's offer, has ripened into an executory contract, whereby, for an adequate consideration, the one agrees to buy and the other agrees to sell. "The sale of an option is an executed contract; that is to say, the lands are not sold, the contract is not executed as to them, but the option is as completely sold and transferred in praesenti as a piece of personal property instantly delivered on payment of the price." Ide v. Leiser, 10 Mont. 5, 24 Pac. 695, 24 Am.St.Rep. 17. From the very nature of the case no standard exists whereby to determine the adequate value of an option to purchase specific real estate. The land has a market value susceptible of ascertainment, but the value of an option upon a piece of real estate might, and oftentimes does, depend upon proposed or possible improvements in the particular vicinity. To illustrate: I A., having information that the erection of a gigantic department store is contemplated in a certain locality, wishes an option for a specified time to purchase property owned by B. in the vicinity of such proposed improvement, and takes the option on B.'s property at the full market price at the time, must he pay a greater sum therefor because of his knowledge and the fact of B.'s ignorance of the proposed improvement? It is not possible that B., upon learning of the proposed improvement, can, in the absence of facts constituting fraud, etc., revoke or rescind the option upon the claim that he sold and transferred the right specified therein for an inadequate consideration. In our judgment any money consideration, however small, paid and received for an option to purchase property at its adequate value is binding upon the seller thereof for the time specified therein, and is irrevocable for want of its adequacy.

The provisions of section 3391, Civ.Code, are but a codification of equitable principles that have existed from time immemorial, and the sufficiency of the price paid for an option has never been measured by its adequacy. In Warvelle on Vendors (2d Ed.) § 125, it is said: "If the option is given for a valuable consideration, whether adequate or not, it cannot be withdrawn or revoked within the time fixed, and it will be binding and obligatory upon the owner, or his assigns with notice, until it expires by its own limitation." In Mathews Slate Co. v. New Empire Slate Co. (C.C.) 122 Fed. 972, it is said: "This court is of the opinion that if two persons enter into a contract in writing under seal, by which the one party, in consideration of $1, the payment of which is acknowledged, agrees to sell and convey to the other party within a specified time certain lands and premises, on payment by the other party of a specified consideration, such contract is valid and binding, and ought to be and may be specifically enforced. The seller has the right to fix his price, and covenant and agree that, on receiving that price within a certain time, he will convey the premises, and, if within that time the purchaser of the option tenders the money and demands a conveyance, he is entitled to it. To hold otherwise is to destroy the efficacy of such contracts and agreements." Mr. Freeman in his note to the case of Mueller v. Nortmann, 96 Am.St.Rep. 997, says: "An option given by the owner of land for a valuable consideration, whether adequate or not, agreeing to sell it to another at a fixed price if accepted within a specified time, is binding upon the owner and all his successors in interest with knowledge thereof." * * * It therefore follows that the purported revocation made by defendant on June 2, 1905, was ineffectual for the purpose of terminating plaintiff's right to exercise the privilege of electing to accept the offer prior to the time designated therein for its expiration.

[The judgment and order were nonetheless affirmed on other grounds].

RESTATEMENT (SECOND) OF CONTRACTS § 87(1).

Option Contract

An offer is binding as an option contract if it

(a) is in writing and signed by the offeror, recites a purported consideration for the making of the offer, and proposes an exchange on fair terms within a reasonable time; or

(b) is made irrevocable by statute.

Comment:

a. Consideration and form. The traditional common-law devices for making a firm offer or option contract are the giving of consideration and the affixing of a seal. * * * But the firm offer serves a useful purpose even though no preliminary bargain is made: it is often a necessary step in the making of the main bargain proposed, and it partakes of the natural formalities inherent in business transactions. The erosion of the formality of the seal has made it less and less satisfactory as a universal formality. As literacy has spread, the personal signature has become the natural formality and the seal has become more and more anachronistic. The rules stated in this section reflect the judicial and legislative response to this situation.

b. Nominal consideration. Offers made in consideration of one dollar paid or promised are often irrevocable under Subsection (1)(a). The irrevocability of an offer may be worth much or little to the offeree, and the courts do not ordinarily inquire into the adequacy of the consideration bargained for. * * * Hence a comparatively small payment may furnish consideration for the irrevocability of an offer proposing a transaction involving much larger sums. But gross disproportion between the payment and the value of the option commonly indicates that the payment was not in fact bargained for but was a mere formality or pretense. In such a case there is no consideration. * * *

Nevertheless, such a nominal consideration is regularly held sufficient to support a short-time option proposing an exchange on fair terms. The fact that the option is an appropriate preliminary step in the conclusion of a socially useful transaction provides a sufficient substantive basis for enforcement, and a signed writing taking a form appropriate to a bargain satisfies the desiderata of form. In the absence of statute, however, the bargaining form is essential: a payment of one dollar by each party to the other is so obviously not a bargaining transaction that it does not provide even the form of an exchange.

UNIFORM COMMERCIAL CODE § 2–205.

Firm Offers.

An offer by a merchant to buy or sell goods in a signed writing which by its terms gives assurance that it will be held open is not revocable, for lack of consideration, during the time stated or if no time is stated for a reasonable time, but in no event may such period of irrevocability exceed three months; but any such term of assurance on a form supplied by the offeree must be separately signed by the offeror.

DAVIS v. JACOBY

Supreme Court of California, 1934.
1 Cal.2d 370, 34 P.2d 1026.

Act for a promise? or promise for a promise.

PER CURIAM.

Plaintiffs appeal from a judgment refusing to grant specific performance of an alleged contract to make a will. The facts are not in dispute and are as follows:

The plaintiff Caro M. Davis was the niece of Blanche Whitehead, who was married to Rupert Whitehead. Prior to her marriage in 1913 to her coplaintiff Frank M. Davis, Caro lived for a considerable time at the home of the Whiteheads, in Piedmont, Cal. The Whiteheads were childless and extremely fond of Caro. The record is replete with uncontradicted testimony of the close and loving relationship that existed between Caro and her aunt and uncle. During the period that Caro lived with the Whiteheads, she was treated as and often referred to by the Whiteheads as their daughter. In 1913, when Caro was married to Frank Davis, the marriage was arranged at the Whitehead home and a reception held there. After the marriage Mr. and Mrs. Davis went to Mr. Davis' home in Canada, where they have resided ever since. During the period 1913 to 1931 Caro made many visits to the Whiteheads, several of them being of long duration. The Whiteheads visited Mr. and Mrs. Davis in Canada on several occasions. After the marriage and continuing down to 1931 the closest and most friendly relationship at all times existed between these two families. They corresponded frequently, the record being replete with letters showing the loving relationship.

By the year 1930 Mrs. Whitehead had become seriously ill. She had suffered several strokes and her mind was failing. Early in 1931 Mr. Whitehead had her removed to a private hospital. The doctors in attendance had informed him that she might die at any time or she might linger for many months. Mr. Whitehead had suffered severe financial reverses. He had had several sieges of sickness and was in poor health. The record shows that during the early part of 1931 he was desperately in need of assistance with his wife, and in his business affairs, and that he did not trust his friends in Piedmont. On March 18, 1931, he wrote to Mrs. Davis telling her of Mrs. Whitehead's condition and added that Mrs. Whitehead was very wistful. "Today I endeavored to find out what she wanted. I finally asked her if she wanted to see you. She burst out crying and we had great difficulty in getting her to stop. Evidently, that is what is on her mind. It is a very difficult matter to decide. If you come it will mean that you will have to leave again, and then things may be serious. I am going to see the doctor, and get his candid opinion and will then write you again. * * * Since writing the above, I have seen the doctor, and he thinks it will help considerably if you come." Shortly thereafter, Mr. Whitehead wrote to Caro Davis further explaining the physical condition of Mrs. Whitehead and himself. On March 24, 1931, Mr. Davis, at the request of his wife, telegraphed to Mr. Whitehead as follows: "Your letter received. Sorry to hear Blanche not so well. Hope you are feeling better yourself. If you wish Caro to go to you can arrange for her to leave in about two weeks. Please wire me if you think it advisable for her to go." On March 30, 1931, Mr. Whitehead wrote a long letter to Mr. Davis, in which he explained in detail the condition of Mrs. Whitehead's health and also referred to his own health. He pointed out that he had lost a considerable portion of his cash assets but still owned considerable realty, that he needed some one to help him with his wife and some friend he could trust to help him with his business affairs and suggested that perhaps Mr. Davis might come to California. He then pointed out that all his property was community property; that under his will all the property was to go to Mrs. Whitehead; that he believed that under Mrs. Whitehead's will practically everything was to go to Caro. Mr. Whitehead again wrote to Mr. Davis under date of April 9, 1931, pointing out how badly he needed some one he could trust to assist him, and giving it as his belief that if properly handled he could still save about $150,000. He then stated: "Having you [Mr. Davis] here to depend on and to help me regain my mind and courage would be a big thing." Three days later, on April 12, 1931, Mr. Whitehead again wrote, addressing his letter to "Dear Frank and Caro," and in this letter made the definite offer, which offer it is claimed was accepted and is the basis of this action. In this letter he first pointed out that Blanche, his wife, was in a private hospital and that "she cannot last much longer * * * my affairs are not as bad as I supposed at first. Cutting everything down I figure 150,000 can be saved from the wreck." He then enumerated the values placed upon his various properties and then continued:

"My trouble was caused by my friends taking advantage of my illness and my position to skin me.

"Now if Frank could come out here and be with me, and look after my affairs, we could easily save the balance I mention, provided I don't get into another panic and do some more foolish things.

"The next attack will be my end, I am 65 and my health has been bad for years, so, the Drs. dont give me much longer to live. So if you can come, Caro will inherit everything and you will make our lives happier and see Blanche is provided for to the end.

"My eyesight has gone back on me, I cant read only for a few lines at a time. I am at the house alone with Stanley [the chauffeur] who does everything for me and is a fine fellow. Now, what I want is some one who will take charge of my affairs and see I dont lose any more. Frank can do it, if he will and cut out the booze.

"Will you let me hear from you as soon as possible, I know it will be a sacrifice but times are still bad and likely to be, so by settling down you can help me and Blanche and gain in the end. If I had you here my mind would get better and my courage return, and we could work things out."

This letter was received by Mr. Davis at his office in Windsor, Canada, about 9:30 a.m. April 14, 1931. After reading the letter to Mrs. Davis over the telephone, and after getting her belief that they must go to California, Mr. Davis immediately wrote Mr. Whitehead a letter, which, after reading it to his wife, he sent by air mail. This letter was lost, but there is no doubt that it was sent by Davis and received by Whitehead; in fact, the trial court expressly so found. Mr. Davis testified in substance as to the contents of this letter. After acknowledging receipt of the letter of April 12, 1931, Mr. Davis unequivocally stated that he and Mrs. Davis accepted the proposition of Mr. Whitehead and both would leave Windsor to go to him on April 25. This letter of acceptance also contained the information that the reason they could not leave prior to April 25 was that Mr. Davis had to appear in court on April 22 as one of the executors of his mother's estate. The testimony is uncontradicted and ample to support the trial court's finding that this letter was sent by Davis and received by Whitehead. In fact, under date of April 15, 1931, Mr. Whitehead again wrote to Mr. Davis and stated:

"Your letter by air mail received this a.m. Now, I am wondering if I have put you to unnecessary trouble and expense, if you are making any money dont leave it, as things are bad here. * * * You know your business and I dont and I am half crazy in the bargain, but I dont want to hurt you or Caro.

"Then on the other hand if I could get some one to trust and keep me straight I can save a good deal, about what I told you in my former letter."

This letter was received by Mr. Davis on April 17, 1931, and the same day Mr. Davis telegraphed to Mr. Whitehead: "Cheer up—we will soon be there, we will wire you from the train."

Between April 14, 1931, the date the letter of acceptance was sent by Mr. Davis, and April 22, Mr. Davis was engaged in closing out his business affairs, and Mrs. Davis in closing up their home and in making other arrangements to leave. On April 22, 1931, Mr. Whitehead committed suicide. Mr. and Mrs. Davis were immediately notified and they at once came to California. From almost the moment of her arrival Mrs. Davis devoted herself to the care and comfort of her aunt, and gave her aunt constant attention and care until Mrs. Whitehead's death on May 30, 1931. * * *

* * * In fact the record shows that after their arrival in California Mr. and Mrs. Davis fully performed their side of the agreement.

After the death of Mrs. Whitehead, for the first time it was discovered that the information contained in Mr. Whitehead's letter of March 30, 1931, in reference to the contents of his and Mrs. Whitehead's wills was incorrect. By a duly witnessed will dated February 28, 1931, Mr. Whitehead, after making several specific bequests, had bequeathed all of the balance of his estate to his wife for life, and upon her death to respondents Geoff Doubble and Rupert Ross Whitehead, his nephews. Neither appellant was mentioned in his will. It was also discovered that Mrs. Whitehead by a will dated December 17, 1927, had devised all of her estate to her husband. The evidence is clear and uncontradicted that the relationship existing between Whitehead and his two nephews, respondents herein, was not nearly as close and confidential as that existing between Whitehead and appellants.

After the discovery of the manner in which the property had been devised was made, this action was commenced upon the theory that Rupert Whitehead had assumed a contractual obligation to make a will whereby "Caro

Davis would inherit everything''; that he had failed to do so; that plaintiffs had fully performed their part of the contract; that damages being insufficient, quasi specific performance should be granted in order to remedy the alleged wrong, upon the equitable principle that equity regards that done which ought to have been done. The requested relief is that the beneficiaries under the will of Rupert Whitehead, respondents herein, be declared to be involuntary trustees for plaintiffs of Whitehead's estate.

It should also be added that the evidence shows that as a result of Frank Davis leaving his business in Canada he forfeited not only all insurance business he might have written if he had remained, but also forfeited all renewal commissions earned on past business. According to his testimony this loss was over $8,000.

* * *

The theory of the trial court and of respondents on this appeal is that the letter of April 12 was an offer to contract, but that such offer could only be accepted by performance and could not be accepted by a promise to perform, and that said offer was revoked by the death of Mr. Whitehead before performance. In other words, it is contended that the offer was an offer to enter into a unilateral contract, and that the purported acceptance of April 14 was of no legal effect.

The distinction between unilateral and bilateral contracts is well settled in the law. It is well stated in section 12 of the American Institute's Restatement of the Law of Contracts as follows: "A unilateral contract is one in which no promisor receives a promise as consideration for his promise. A bilateral contract is one in which there are mutual promises between two parties to the contract; each party being both a promisor and a promisee." This definition is in accord with the law of California. * * *

* * *

Although the legal distinction between unilateral and bilateral contracts is thus well settled, the difficulty in any particular case is to determine whether the particular offer is one to enter into a bilateral or unilateral contract. Some cases are quite clear cut. Thus an offer to sell which is accepted is clearly a bilateral contract, while an offer of a reward is a clear-cut offer of a unilateral contract which cannot be accepted by a promise to perform, but only by performance. * * * Between these two extremes is a vague field where the particular contract may be unilateral or bilateral depending upon the intent of the offer and the facts and circumstances of each case. The offer to contract involved in this case falls within this category. By the provisions of the Restatement of the Law of Contracts it is expressly provided that there is a *presumption* that the offer is to enter into a bilateral contract. Section 31 provides: "In case of doubt it is presumed that an offer invites the formation of a bilateral contract by an acceptance amounting in effect to a promise by the offeree to perform what the offer requests, rather than the formation of one or more unilateral contracts by actual performance on the part of the offeree."

Professor Williston, in his Treatise on Contracts, volume 1, § 60, also takes the position that a presumption in favor of bilateral contracts exists.

In the comment following section 31 of the Restatement the reason for such presumption is stated as follows: "It is not always easy to determine whether an offerer requests an act or a promise to do the act. As a bilateral contract immediately and fully protects both parties, the interpretation is favored that a bilateral contract is proposed."

* * *

Keeping these principles in mind, we are of the opinion that the offer of April 12 was an offer to enter into a bilateral as distinguished from a unilateral contract. Respondents argue that Mr. Whitehead had the right as offerer to designate his offer as either unilateral or bilateral. That is undoubtedly the law. It is then argued that from all the facts and circumstances it must be implied that what Whitehead wanted was performance and not a mere promise to perform. We think this is a non sequitur, in fact the surrounding circumstances lead to just the opposite conclusion. These parties were not dealing at arm's length. Not only were they related, but a very close and intimate friendship existed between them. The record indisputably demonstrates that Mr. Whitehead had confidence in Mr. and Mrs. Davis, in fact that he had lost all confidence in every one else. The record amply shows that by an accumulation of occurrences Mr. Whitehead had become desperate, and that what he wanted was the promise of appellants that he could look to them for assistance. He knew from his past relationship with appellants that if they gave their promise to perform he could rely upon them. The correspondence between them indicates how desperately he desired this assurance. Under these circumstances he wrote his offer of April 12, above quoted, in which he stated, after disclosing his desperate mental and physical condition, and after setting forth the terms of his offer: "*Will you let me hear from you as soon as possible*—I know it will be a sacrifice but times are still bad and likely to be, so by settling down you can help me and Blanche and gain in the end." By thus specifically requesting an immediate reply Whitehead expressly indicated the nature of the acceptance desired by him, namely, appellants' promise that they would come to California and do the things requested by him. This promise was immediately sent by appellants upon receipt of the offer, and was received by Whitehead. It is elementary that when an offer has indicated the mode and means of acceptance, an acceptance in accordance with that mode or means is binding on the offerer.

Another factor which indicates that Whitehead must have contemplated a bilateral rather than an unilateral contract, is that the contract required Mr. and Mrs. Davis to perform services until the death of both Mr. and Mrs. Whitehead. It is obvious that if Mr. Whitehead died first some of these services were to be performed after his death, so that he would have to rely on the promise of appellants to perform these services. It is also of some evidentiary force that Whitehead received the letter of acceptance and acquiesced in that means of acceptance.

* * *

For the foregoing reasons we are of the opinion that the offer of April 12, 1931, was an offer to enter into a bilateral contract which was accepted by the letter of April 14, 1931. Subsequently appellants fully performed their part of the contract. Under such circumstances it is well settled that damages are insufficient and specific performance will be granted. * * *

* * *

For the foregoing reasons the judgment appealed from is reversed.

WORMSER, THE TRUE CONCEPTION OF UNILATERAL CONTRACTS

26 Yale L.J. 136, 136–38 (1916).

Suppose A says to B, "I will give you $100 if you walk across the Brooklyn Bridge," and B walks—is there a contract? It is clear that A is not asking B for B's *promise* to walk across the Brooklyn Bridge. What A wants from B is the *act* of walking across the bridge. When B has walked across the bridge there is a contract, and A is then bound to pay to B $100. At that moment there arises a unilateral contract. A has bartered away his volition for B's act of walking across the Brooklyn Bridge.

When an act is thus wanted in return for a promise, a unilateral contract is created when the act is done. It is clear that only one party is bound. B is not bound to walk across the Brooklyn Bridge, but A is bound to pay B $100 if B does so. Thus, in unilateral contracts, on one side we find merely an act, on the other side a promise. On the other hand, in bilateral contracts, A barters away his volition in return for another promise; that is to say, there is an exchange of promises or assurances. In the case of the bilateral contract both parties, A and B, are bound from the moment that their promises are exchanged. Thus, if A says to B, "I will give you $100 if you will promise to walk across the Brooklyn Bridge," and B then promises to walk across the bridge, a bilateral contract is created at the moment when B promises, and both parties are thereafter bound. * * *

It is plain that in the Brooklyn Bridge case as first put, what A wants from B is the act of walking across the Brooklyn Bridge. A does not ask for B's promise to walk across the bridge and B has never given it. B has never bound himself to walk across the bridge. A, however, has bound himself to pay $100 to B, if B does so. Let us suppose that B starts to walk across the Brooklyn Bridge and has gone about one-half of the way across. At that moment A overtakes B and says to him, "I withdraw my offer." Has B then any rights against A? Again, let us suppose that after A has said "I withdraw my offer," B continues to walk across the Brooklyn Bridge and completes the act of crossing. Under these circumstances, has B any rights against A?

In the first of the cases just suggested, A withdrew his offer before B had walked across the bridge. What A wanted from B, what A asked for, was the act of walking across the bridge. Until that was done, B had not given to A what A had requested. The acceptance by B of A's offer could be nothing but the act on B's part of crossing the bridge. It is elementary that an offeror may withdraw his offer until it has been accepted. It follows logically that A is perfectly within his rights in withdrawing his offer before B has accepted it by walking across the bridge—the act contemplated by the offerer and the offeree as the acceptance of the offer. A did not want B to walk half-way across or three-quarters of the way across the bridge. What A wanted from B, and what

electronic records and signatures. [UETA] is NOT a general contracting statute–
the substantive rules of contracts remain unaffected by UETA." UETA, Prefatory
Note. For more on these and other laws, see the Winn and Pullen article. The
Electronic Signatures in Global and National Commerce Act, 15 U.S.C. § 7001 (as
amended 2006), enforces electronic signatures, but is limited in scope. For more
on this act, see, e.g., Carl, Ciocchetti, Barton & Christensen, Are Online Business
Transactions Executed by Electronic Signatures Legally Binding? 2001 Duke L. &
Tech. Rev. 5.

SECTION NINE: AGREEMENTS TO AGREE AND RELATED MATTERS

After some negotiations, contracting parties often decide to draft a
preliminary writing of some kind. They may want to clarify their respective
bargaining positions or to record points on which they have reached agreement. The writing thus facilitates further negotiation of the ultimate agreement. Sometimes the parties may even intend to be bound by their preliminary agreement, leaving for future negotiation an issue on which they cannot
presently agree or a term dependent on some future development, such as a
change in market rates of interest. The challenge of the law is to determine
when agreements preliminary in some sense should be enforced and, when
enforced, to determine the appropriate remedy for breach.

ARNOLD PALMER GOLF CO. v. FUQUA INDUSTRIES, INC.

United States Court of Appeals, Sixth Circuit, 1976.
541 F.2d 584.

McCree, Circuit Judge.

This is an appeal from the district court's grant of summary judgment in
favor of defendant Fuqua Industries, Inc. (Fuqua) in an action for breach of
contract. The district court determined that a document captioned "Memorandum of Intent" and signed by both parties was not a contract because it
evidenced the intent of the parties not to be contractually bound. We reverse
and remand for trial.

Arnold Palmer Golf Company (Palmer) was incorporated under Ohio law
in 1961, and has been primarily engaged in designing and marketing various
lines of golf clubs, balls, bags, gloves, and other golf accessories. Palmer did
none of its own manufacturing, but engaged other companies to produce its
products. In the late 1960's, Palmer's management concluded that it was
essential for future growth and profitability to acquire manufacturing facilities.

To that end, in January, 1969, Mark McCormack, Palmer's Executive
Vice–President, and E.D. Kenna, Fuqua's President, met in New York City to
consider a possible business relationship between the two corporations. The
parties' interest in establishing a business relationship continued and they
held several more meetings and discussions where the general outline of the
proposed relationship was defined. In November 1969, Fuqua, with Palmer's
assistance and approval, acquired Fernquest and Johnson, a California manu-

facturer of golf clubs. The minutes of the Fuqua Board of Directors meeting on November 3, 1969, reveal that Fuqua:

> proposed that this Corporation participate in the golf equipment industry in association with Arnold Palmer Golf Co. and Arnold Palmer Enterprises, Inc. The business would be conducted in two parts. One part would be composed of a corporation engaged in the manufacture and sale of golf clubs and equipment directly related to the playing of the game of golf. This Corporation would be owned to the extent of 25% by Fuqua and 75% by the Arnold Palmer interests. Fuqua would transfer the Fernquest & Johnson business to the new corporation as Fuqua's contribution.

In November and December of 1969 further discussions and negotiations occurred and revised drafts of a memorandum of intent were distributed.

The culmination of the discussions was a six page document denominated as a Memorandum of Intent. It provided in the first paragraph that:

> This memorandum will serve to confirm the general understanding which has been reached regarding the acquisition of 25% of the stock of Arnold Palmer Golf Company ("Palmer") by Fuqua Industries, Inc. ("Fuqua") in exchange for all of the outstanding stock of Fernquest and Johnson Golf Company, Inc. ("F & J"), a wholly-owned California subsidiary of Fuqua, and money in the amount of $700,000; and for the rendition of management services by Fuqua.

The Memorandum of Intent contained detailed statements concerning, *inter alia,* the form of the combination, the manner in which the business would be conducted, the loans that Fuqua agreed to make to Palmer, and the warranties and covenants to be contained in the definitive agreement.

Paragraph 10 of the Memorandum of Intent stated:

> (10) *Preparation of Definitive Agreement.* Counsel for Palmer and counsel for Fuqua will proceed as promptly as possible to prepare an agreement acceptable to Palmer and Fuqua for the proposed combination of businesses. Such agreement will contain the representations, warranties, covenants and conditions, as generally outlined in the example submitted by Fuqua to Palmer * * *.

In the last paragraph of the Memorandum of Intent, the parties indicated that:

> (11) *Conditions.* The obligations of Palmer and Fuqua shall be subject to fulfillment of the following conditions:
>
> > (i) preparation of the definitive agreement for the proposed combination in form and content satisfactory to both parties and their respective counsel;
> >
> > (ii) approval of such definitive agreement by the Board of Directors of Fuqua; * * *.

The Memorandum of Intent was signed by Palmer and by the President of Fuqua. Fuqua had earlier released a statement to the press upon Palmer's signing that "Fuqua Industries, Inc., and The Arnold Palmer Golf Co. have agreed to cooperate in an enterprise that will serve the golfing industry, from the golfer to the greens keeper."

In February, 1970, the Chairman of Fuqua's Board of Directors, J.B. Fuqua, told Douglas Kenna, Fuqua's President, that he did not want to go through with the Palmer deal. Shortly thereafter Kenna informed one of Palmer's corporate officers that the transaction was terminated.

Palmer filed the complaint in this case on July 24, 1970. Nearly three and one-half years later, on January 14, 1974, the defendant filed a motion for summary judgment. More than one year after the briefs had been filed by the parties, on May 30, 1975, the district court granted defendant's motion.

The district court determined that:

> The parties were not to be subject to any obligations until a definitive agreement satisfactory to the parties and their counsel had been prepared. The fact that this agreement had to be "satisfactory" implies necessarily that such an agreement might be unsatisfactory. * * * The parties by the terms they used elected not to be bound by this memorandum and the Court finds that they were not bound.

The primary issue in this case is whether the parties intended to enter into a binding agreement when they signed the Memorandum of Intent, and the primary issue in this appeal is whether the district court erred in determining this question on a motion for summary judgment. The substantive law of Ohio applies.

We agree with the district court that both parties must have a clear understanding of the terms of an agreement and an intention to be bound by its terms before an enforceable contract is created. As Professor Corbin has observed:

> The courts are quite agreed upon general principles. The parties have power to contract as they please. They can bind themselves orally or by informal letters or telegrams if they like. On the other hand, they can maintain complete immunity from all obligation, even though they have expressed agreement orally or informally upon every detail of a complex transaction. The matter is merely one of expressed intention. If their expressions convince the court that they intended to be bound without a formal document, their contract is consummated, and the expected formal document will be nothing more than a memorial of that contract. 1 Corbin on Contracts, § 30 (1963). [Footnote omitted.]

The decision whether the parties intended to enter a contract must be based upon an evaluation of the circumstances surrounding the parties' discussions. The introduction of extrinsic evidence does not violate the parol evidence rule because that rule applies only after an integrated or a partially integrated agreement has been found. *Itek Corp. v. Chicago Aerial*, 248 A.2d 625 (Del.1968) * * *.

At bottom, the question whether the parties intended a contract is a factual one, not a legal one, and, except in the clearest cases, the question is for the finder of fact to resolve. * * *

* * *

The Delaware Supreme Court considered a case similar to this one in *Itek Corp. v. Chicago Aerial, supra.* Like the district court here, the trial court in *Itek* granted defendants' motion for summary judgment in a breach of contract action based upon a letter of intent. The letter of intent provided that the parties:

> [S]hall make every reasonable effort to agree upon and have prepared as quickly as possible a contract providing for the foregoing purchase by Itek and sale by CAI, subject to the approval of CAI stockholders, embodying the above terms and such other terms and conditions as the parties shall agree upon. If the parties fail to agree upon and execute such a contract they shall be under no further obligations to one another. 248 A.2d at 627.

The trial judge decided in favor of the defendants because of the last sentence quoted above. The Delaware Supreme Court, considering the entire document and other evidence submitted by the plaintiff, reversed, determining that:

> there is evidence which, if accepted by the trier of fact, would support the conclusion that * * * Itek and CAI intended to be bound * * *. There is also evidence which, if accepted by the trier of fact, would support the conclusion that subsequently, * * * CAI willfully failed to negotiate in good faith and to make "every reasonable effort" to agree upon a formal contract, as it was required to do. 248 A.2d at 629.

In a Third Circuit opinion, *Melo-Sonics Corp. v. Cropp*, 342 F.2d 856 (1965), the court reversed a district court's judgment in favor of defendants on a motion to dismiss a complaint. The plaintiffs contended that they had a contract with defendants which the latter had breached. Plaintiffs relied on a telegram they sent to defendants, and defendants' subsequent acceptance, as constituting a contractual agreement. The telegram provided in pertinent part:

> My three clients are willing to sell their capital stock in said corporations for the total price of one million five hundred thousand ($1,500,000) dollars subject to formalizing a preliminary agreement along lines previously discussed. Will be in your office at 10:00 A.M. on February 15, 1960 with my clients for purpose of formalizing such an agreement. 342 F.2d at 858.

The defendants eventually notified plaintiffs that they would not sign the agreement, whereupon plaintiffs filed suit.

The reviewing court pointed out that it would be permissible for the district court to make a finding of fact that no contract existed after it had conducted a full hearing, but that where no trial had been conducted and no findings of fact had been made it was improper to grant the defendants' motion to dismiss because plaintiffs' claim, if proved, entitled them to recovery.

Considering this appeal in the light of these authorities, we determine that our proper course is to remand this case to the district court for trial because we believe that the issue of the parties' intention to be bound is a proper one for resolution by the trier of fact. Upon first blush it may appear that the Memorandum of Intent is no more than preliminary negotiation between the parties. A cursory reading of the conditions contained in paragraph 11, by themselves, may suggest that the parties did not intend to be bound by the Memorandum of Intent.

Nevertheless, the memorandum recited that a "general understanding [had] been reached." And, as the *Itek* court noted, the entire document and relevant circumstances surrounding its adoption must be considered in making a determination of the parties' intention.[1] In this case we find an extensive document that appears to reflect all essential terms concerning the transfer of Arnold Palmer stock to Fuqua in exchange for all outstanding stock in Fernquest and Johnson. The form of combination, the location of the principal office of Palmer, the license rights, employment contracts of Palmer personnel and the financial obligations of Fuqua are a few of the many areas covered in the Memorandum of Intent, and they are all described in unqualified terms. The Memorandum states, for instance, that "Fuqua *will* transfer all of the * * * stock," that the "principal office of Palmer *will* be moved to Atlanta," that "Palmer * * * *shall* possess an exclusive license," and that "Fuqua *agrees* to advance to Palmer up to an aggregate of $700,000 * * *." [Emphasis added.]

Paragraph 10 of the Memorandum states, also in unqualified language, that counsel for the parties "will proceed as promptly as possible to prepare an agreement acceptable to [the parties] * * *." We believe that this paragraph may be read merely to impose an obligation upon the parties to memorialize their agreement. We do not mean to suggest that this is the correct interpretation. The provision is also susceptible to an interpretation that the parties did not intend to be bound.

As we have indicated above, it is permissible to refer to extrinsic evidence to determine whether the parties intended to be bound by the Memorandum of Intent. In this regard, we observe that Fuqua circulated a press release in January 1970 that would tend to sustain Palmer's claim that the two parties intended to be bound by the Memorandum of Intent. Fuqua's statement said that the two companies "have agreed to cooperate in an enterprise that will serve the golfing industry."

Upon a review of the evidence submitted in connection with the motion for summary judgment, we believe that there is presented a factual issue whether the parties contractually obligated themselves to prepare a definitive agreement in accordance with the understanding of the parties contained in the Memorandum of Intent. * * * Because the facts and the inferences from the facts in this case indicate that the parties may have intended to be bound by the Memorandum of Intent, we hold that the district court erred in determining that no contract existed as a matter of law.

We reject appellee's argument that summary judgment was appropriate because the obligations of the parties were subject to an express condition that was not met. We believe a question of fact is presented whether the parties intended the conditions in paragraph 11 to operate only if the definitive agreement was not in conformity with the general understanding contained in the Memorandum of Intent. * * * The parties may well have intended that there should be no binding obligation until the definitive

---

1. Parties may orally or by informal memoranda, or by both, agree upon all essential terms of the contract and effectively bind themselves, if that is their intention, even though they contemplate the execution, at a later time, of a formal document to memorialize their undertaking. *Comerata v. Chaumont, Inc.,* 52 N.J.Super. 299, 145 A.2d 471 (1958).

agreement was signed, but we regard this question as one for the fact finder to determine after a consideration of the relevant evidence.

* * *

Accordingly, the judgment of the district court is reversed and the case is remanded for proceedings not inconsistent with this opinion.

Drawing by Dana Fradon; © 1987 The New Yorker Magazine, Inc.

RESTATEMENT (SECOND) OF CONTRACTS § 27.

Existence of Contract Where Written Memorial is Contemplated

Manifestations of assent that are in themselves sufficient to conclude a contract will not be prevented from so operating by the fact that the parties also manifest an intention to prepare and adopt a written memorial thereof; but the circumstances may show that the agreements are preliminary negotiations.

Comment:

a. Parties who plan to make a final written instrument as the expression of their contract necessarily discuss the proposed terms of the contract before they enter into it and often, before the final writing is made, agree upon all the terms which they plan to incorporate therein. This they may do orally or by exchange of several writings. It is possible thus to make a contract the terms of which include an obligation to execute subsequently a final writing which shall contain certain provisions. If parties have definitely agreed that they will do so, and that the final writing shall contain these provisions and no others, they have then concluded the contract.

b. On the other hand, if either party knows or has reason to know that the other party regards the agreement as incomplete and intends that no obligation shall exist until other terms are assented to or until the whole has been reduced to another written form, the preliminary negotiations and agreements do not constitute a contract.

    c. Among the circumstances which may be helpful in determining whether a contract has been concluded are the following: the extent to which express agreement has been reached on all the terms to be included, whether the contract is of a type usually put in writing, whether it needs a formal writing for its full expression, whether it has few or many details, whether the amount involved is large or small, whether it is a common or unusual contract, whether a standard form of contract is widely used in similar transactions, and whether either party takes any action in preparation for performance during the negotiations. Such circumstances may be shown by oral testimony or by correspondence or other preliminary or partially complete writings.

    d. Even though a binding contract is made before a contemplated written memorial is prepared and adopted, the subsequent written document may make a binding modification of the terms previously agreed to.

EMPRO MANUFACTURING CO., INC. v. BALL–CO MANUFACTURING, INC.

United States Court of Appeals, Seventh Circuit, 1989.
870 F.2d 423.

Easterbrook, Circuit Judge.

    We have a pattern common in commercial life. Two firms reach concord on the general terms of their transaction. They sign a document, captioned "agreement in principle" or "letter of intent", memorializing these terms but anticipating further negotiations and decisions—an appraisal of the assets, the clearing of a title, the list is endless. One of these terms proves divisive, and the deal collapses. The party that perceives itself the loser then claims that the preliminary document has legal force independent of the definitive contract. Ours is such a dispute.

    Ball–Co Manufacturing, a maker of specialty valve components, floated its assets on the market. Empro Manufacturing showed interest. After some preliminary negotiations, Empro sent Ball–Co a three-page "letter of intent" to purchase the assets of Ball–Co and S.B. Leasing, a partnership holding title to the land under Ball–Co's plant. Empro proposed a price of $2.4 million, with $650,000 to be paid on closing and a 10–year promissory note for the remainder, the note to be secured by the "inventory and equipment of Ball–Co." The letter stated "[t]he general terms and conditions of such proposal (which will be subject to and incorporated in a formal, definitive Asset Purchase Agreement signed by both parties)". Just in case Ball–Co might suppose that Empro had committed itself to buy the assets, paragraph four of the letter stated that "Empro's purchase shall be subject to the satisfaction of certain conditions precedent to closing including, but not limited to" the definitive Asset Purchase Agreement and, among five other conditions, "[t]he approval of the shareholders and board of directors of Empro".

    Although Empro left itself escape hatches, as things turned out Ball–Co was the one who balked. The parties signed the letter of intent in November

1987 and negotiated through March 1988 about many terms. Security for the note proved to be the sticking point. Ball–Co wanted a security interest in the land under the plant; Empro refused to yield.

When Empro learned that Ball–Co was negotiating with someone else, it filed this diversity suit. Contending that the letter of intent obliges Ball–Co to sell only to it, Empro asked for a temporary restraining order. The district judge set the case for a prompt hearing and, after getting a look at the letter of intent, dismissed the complaint under Fed.R.Civ.P. 12(b)(6) for failure to state a claim on which relief may be granted. Relying on Interway, Inc. v. Alagna, 85 Ill.App.3d 1094, 41 Ill.Dec. 117, 407 N.E.2d 615 (1st Dist.1980), the district judge concluded that the statement, appearing twice in the letter, that the agreement is "subject to" the execution of a definitive contract meant that the letter has no independent force.

Empro insists on appeal that the binding effect of a document depends on the parties' intent, which means that the case may not be dismissed—for Empro says that the parties intended to be bound, a factual issue. Empro treats "intent to be bound" as a matter of the parties' states of mind, but if intent were wholly subjective there would be no parol evidence rule, no contract case could be decided without a jury trial, and no one could know the effect of a commercial transaction until years after the documents were inked. That would be a devastating blow to business. Contract law gives effect to the parties' wishes, but they must express these openly. Put differently, "intent" in contract law is objective rather than subjective—a point Interway makes by holding that as a matter of law parties who make their pact "subject to" a later definitive agreement have manifested an (objective) intent not to be bound, which under the parol evidence rule becomes the definitive intent even if one party later says that the true intent was different. As the Supreme Court of Illinois said in Schek v. Chicago Transit Authority, 42 Ill.2d 362, 364, 247 N.E.2d 886, 888 (1969), "intent must be determined solely from the language used when no ambiguity in its terms exists". See also Feldman v. Allegheny International, Inc., 850 F.2d 1217 (7th Cir.1988) (Illinois law); Skycom Corp. v. Telstar Corp., 813 F.2d 810, 814–17 (7th Cir.1987) (New York and Wisconsin law). Parties may decide for themselves whether the results of preliminary negotiations bind them, Chicago Investment Corp. v. Dolins, 107 Ill.2d 120, 89 Ill.Dec. 869, 871, 481 N.E.2d 712, 715 (1985), but they do this through their words.

Because letters of intent are written without the care that will be lavished on the definitive agreement, it may be a bit much to put dispositive weight on "subject to" in every case, and we do not read Interway as giving these the status of magic words. They might have been used carelessly, and if the full agreement showed that the formal contract was to be nothing but a memorial of an agreement already reached, the letter of intent would be enforceable. Borg–Warner Corp. v. Anchor Coupling Co., 16 Ill.2d 234, 156 N.E.2d 513 (1958). Conversely, Empro cannot claim comfort from the fact that the letter of intent does not contain a flat disclaimer, such as the one in Feldman pronouncing that the letter creates no obligations at all. The text and structure of the letter—the objective manifestations of intent—might show that the parties agreed to bind themselves to some extent immediately. Borg–Warner is such a case. One party issued an option, which called itself "firm and binding"; the other party accepted; the court found this a binding contract even though some terms remained open. After all, an option to purchase is nothing if not binding in advance of the definitive contract. The parties to Borg–Warner conceded that the option and acceptance usually would bind; the only argument in the case concerned whether the open terms were so important that a contract could not arise even if the parties wished to be bound, a subject that divided the court. See 156 N.E.2d at 930–36 (Schaefer, J., dissenting).

A canvass of the terms of the letter Empro sent does not assist it, however. "Subject to" a definitive agreement appears twice. The letter also recites, twice, that it contains the "general terms and conditions", implying that each side retained the right to make (and stand on) additional demands. Empro insulated itself from binding effect by listing, among the conditions to which the deal was "subject", the "approval of the shareholders and board of directors of Empro". The board could veto a deal negotiated by the firm's agents for a reason such as the belief that Ball–Co had been offered too much (otherwise the officers, not the board, would be the firm's final decisionmakers, yet state law vests major decisions in the board). The shareholders could decline to give their assent for any reason (such as distrust of new business ventures) and could not even be required to look at the documents, let alone consider the merits of the deal. See Earl Sneed, The Shareholder May Vote As He Pleases: Theory and Fact, 22 U.Pittsburgh L.Rev. 23, 31–36, 40–42 (1960) (collecting cases). Empro even took care to require the return of its $5,000 in earnest money "without set off, in the event this transaction is not closed", although the seller usually gets to keep the earnest money if the buyer changes its mind. So Empro made clear that it was free to walk.

Neither the text nor the structure of the letter suggests that it was to be a one-sided commitment, an option in Empro's favor binding only Ball–Co. From the beginning Ball–Co assumed that it could negotiate terms in addition to, or different from, those in the letter of intent. The cover letter from Ball–Co's lawyer returning the signed letter of intent to Empro stated that the "terms and conditions are generally acceptable" but that "some clarifications are needed in Paragraph 3(c) (last sentence)", the provision concerning Ball–Co's security interest. "Some clarifications are needed" is an ominous noise in a negotiation, foreboding many a stalemate. Although we do not know what "clarifications" counsel had in mind, the specifics are not important. It is enough that even on signing the letter of intent Ball–Co proposed to change the bargain, conduct consistent with the purport of the letter's text and structure.

The shoals that wrecked this deal are common hazards in business negotiations. Letters of intent and agreements in principle often, and here, do no more than set the stage for negotiations on details. Sometimes the details can be ironed out; sometimes they can't. Illinois, as Chicago Investment, Interway, and Feldman show, allows parties to approach agreement in stages, without fear that by reaching a preliminary understanding they have bargained away their privilege to disagree on the specifics. Approaching agreement by stages is a valuable method of doing business. So long as Illinois preserves the availability of this device, a federal court in a diversity case must send the disappointed party home empty-handed. Empro claims that it is entitled at least to recover its "reliance expenditures", but the only expenditures it has identified are those normally associated with pre-contractual efforts: its complaint mentions the expenses "in negotiating with defendants, in investigating and reviewing defendants' business, and in preparing to acquire defendants' business." Outlays of this sort cannot bind the other side any more than paying an expert to tell you whether the painting at the auction is a genuine Rembrandt compels the auctioneer to accept your bid.

AFFIRMED.

LLEWELLYN, ON WARRANTY OF QUALITY, AND SOCIETY

37 Colum.L.Rev. 341, 375, 379 (1937).

Our contract-law has yet built no tools to really cope with this vexing and puzzling situation of fact. The standing relation is not only real in business fact, it is also vibrant with legal implication. The trouble is that the legal implication is still—legally—inarticulate. It is felt—no question about that. It is felt—but it is not felt with any clarity. * * *

* * *

The problem, though wholly unsolved, is there, and is in ferment. It is not a theorist's creation; it is a fact, at work in the courts, warping the older, inadequate theory of the single deal. * * * The job is to give direction to the fermentation.

WHITFORD, IAN MACNEIL'S CONTRIBUTION TO CONTRACTS SCHOLARSHIP

1985 Wis.L.Rev. 545, 546–48.

Briefly, relational contracts emerge in the context of ongoing relationships. They are to be contrasted with what Macneil calls discrete contracts. Although all contracts have relational elements, contracts occurring between parties who have little interaction other than the contract itself tend to fall on the discrete end of the relational-discrete continuum. Macneil gives as an example of a mostly discrete transaction the purchase of gasoline at a service station along a superhighway.

The more generally accepted of Macneil's messages is that relational contracts differ from discrete contracts in that typically there is no single moment at which the parties confirm a meeting of the minds respecting the important terms of the contract. Rather, to quote Macneil:

> The exercise of choice [about contract content] is * * * an incremental process in which parties gather increasing information and gradually agree to more and more as they proceed. Indeed, the very process of exercising choice in such circumstances, such as through engineering studies, may entail major parts of the total costs of the whole project as finally agreed.

Both economists and lawyers have come to acknowledge this behavioral reality. There is a growing body of economics literature explaining that in relational contracting it is commonly more in the parties' perceived self-interest to reach agreement gradually rather than all at one time, allowing much performance to occur while important terms remain to be negotiated.

This economics literature speculates about what kinds of contracting strategies might be expected in these circumstances. * * *

Lawyers have had a more difficult task than the economists. Both lawyers and economists need to develop new perceptions about how people behave in relational contract situations. In addition, lawyers must develop a new normative structure to accommodate and regulate that behavior. Classical contract law of the type refined so superbly by Williston presupposed a single moment at which the parties reached agreement on all important terms. Before this grand meeting of minds, there was no contractual liability. And after this point, all important decisions—particularly the determination of the terms governing the relationship and the measurement of expectation damages—could be reached only by referring to that all encompassing agreement. Classical contract law can be coherently applied to situations in which there is no grand meeting of the minds, even though the parties act as though there is a contract only by denying that a contract exists at all. Courts sometimes reach that result, but it often seems harsh because it fails to protect obvious reliance on what the parties believe to be a valid contract. Partly for this reason, this approach is not generally favored today.

If relational contracts lacking a grand meeting of the minds are to be enforced, there is no way to explain the results reached within the structure of classical contract law because that body of law provides only the parties' agreement as a reference point for determining contractual content. If the results of cases purporting to enforce such contracts are not to appear unpredictable and ad hoc, some basis outside the framework of classical contract law must be established for determining when liability begins, defining the terms of relationship, and setting the remedy upon breach.

JOSEPH MARTIN, JR., DELICATESSEN, INC. v. SCHUMACHER

Court of Appeals of New York, 1981.
52 N.Y.2d 105, 436 N.Y.S.2d 247, 417 N.E.2d 541.

FUCHSBERG, JUDGE.

This case raises an issue fundamental to the law of contracts. It calls upon us to review a decision of the Appellate Division, 70 A.D.2d 1, 419 N.Y.S.2d 558 which held that a realty lease's provision that the rent for a renewal period was "to be agreed upon" may be enforceable.

The pertinent factual and procedural contexts in which the case reaches this court are uncomplicated. In 1973, the appellant, as landlord, leased a retail store to the respondent for a five-year term at a rent graduated upwards from $500 per month for the first year to $650 for the fifth. The renewal clause stated that "[t]he Tenant may renew this lease for an additional period of five years at annual rentals to be agreed upon; Tenant shall give Landlord thirty (30) days written notice, to be mailed certified mail, return receipt requested, of the intention to exercise such right". It is not disputed that the tenant gave timely notice of its desire to renew or that, once the landlord made it clear that he would do so only at a rental starting at $900 a month, the tenant engaged an appraiser who opined that a fair market rental value would be $545.41.

The tenant thereupon commenced an action for specific performance in Supreme Court, Suffolk County, to compel the landlord to extend the lease for the additional term at the appraiser's figure or such other sum as the court would decide was reasonable. For his part, the landlord in due course brought a holdover proceeding in the local District Court to evict the tenant. On the landlord's motion for summary judgment, the Supreme Court, holding that a bald agreement to agree on a future rental was unenforceable for uncertainty as a matter of law, dismissed the tenant's complaint. Concordantly, it denied as moot the tenant's motion to remove the District Court case to the Supreme Court and to consolidate the two suits.

It was on appeal by the tenant from these orders that the Appellate Division, expressly overruling an established line of cases in the process, reinstated the tenant's complaint and granted consolidation. In so doing, it reasoned that "a renewal clause in a lease providing for future agreement on the rent to be paid during the renewal term is enforceable if it is established that the parties' intent was not to terminate in the event of a failure to agree". It went on to provide that, if the tenant met that burden, the trial court could proceed to set a "reasonable rent". One of the Justices, concurring, would have eliminated the first step and required the trial court to proceed directly to the fixation of the rent. Each party now appeals by leave of the Appellate Division pursuant to CPLR 5602 (subd. [b], par. 1). The tenant seeks only a modification adopting the concurrer's position. The question formally certified to us by the Appellate Division is simply whether its order was properly made. Since we conclude that the disposition at the Supreme Court was the correct one, our answer must be in the negative.

We begin our analysis with the basic observation that, unless otherwise mandated by law (e.g., residential emergency rent control statutes), a contract is a private "ordering" in which a party binds himself to do, or not to do, a particular thing (*Fletcher v. Peck,* 6 Cranch [10 U.S.] 87, 136; 3 L.Ed. 162. Hart and Sachs, Legal Process, 147–148 [1958]). This liberty is no right at all if it is not accompanied by freedom not to contract. The corollary is that, before one may secure redress in our courts because another has failed to honor a promise, it must appear that the promisee assented to the obligation in question.

It also follows that, before the power of law can be invoked to enforce a promise, it must be sufficiently certain and specific so that what was promised can be ascertained. Otherwise, a court, in intervening, would be imposing its own conception of what the parties should or might have undertaken, rather than confining itself to the implementation of a bargain to which they have mutually committed themselves. Thus, definiteness as to material matters is of the very essence in contract law. Impenetrable vagueness and uncertainty will not do (1 Corbin, Contracts, § 95, p. 394 * * *).

Dictated by these principles, it is rightfully well settled in the common law of contracts in this State that a mere agreement to agree, in which a material term is left for future negotiations, is unenforceable. * * * This is especially true of the amount to be paid for the sale or lease of real property. * * * The rule applies all the more, and not the less, when, as here, the extraordinary remedy of specific performance is sought (11 Williston, Contracts [Jaeger 3d ed.], § 1424; Pomeroy, Equity Jurisprudence, § 1405).

This is not to say that the requirement for definiteness in the case before us now could only have been met by explicit expression of the rent to be paid. The concern is with substance, not form. It certainly would have sufficed, for instance, if a methodology for determining the rent was to be found within the four corners of the lease, for a rent so arrived at would have been the end product of agreement between the parties themselves. Nor would the agreement have failed for indefiniteness because it invited recourse to an objective extrinsic event, condition or standard on which the amount was made to depend. All of these, *inter alia,* would have come within the embrace of the maxim that what can be made certain is certain. * * *

But the renewal clause here in fact contains no such ingredients. Its unrevealing, unamplified language speaks to no more than "annual rentals to be agreed upon". Its simple words leave no room for legal construction or resolution of ambiguity. Neither tenant nor landlord is bound to any formula. There is not so much as a hint at a commitment to be bound by the "fair market rental value" which the tenant's expert reported or the "reasonable rent" the Appellate Division would impose, much less any definition of either. Nowhere is there an inkling that either of the parties directly or indirectly assented, upon accepting the clause, to subordinate the figure on which it ultimately would insist, to one fixed judicially, as the Appellate Division decreed be done, or, for that matter, by an arbitrator or other third party.

Finally, in this context, we note that the tenant's reliance on *May Metropolitan Corp. v. May Oil Burner Corp.,* 290 N.Y. 260, 49 N.E.2d 13 is misplaced. There the parties had executed a franchise agreement for the sale of oil burners. The contract provided for annual renewal, at which time each year's sales quota was "to be mutually agreed upon". In holding that the defendant's motion for summary judgment should have been denied, the court indicated that the plaintiff should be given an opportunity to establish that a series of annual renewals had ripened into a course of dealing from which it might be possible to give meaning to an otherwise uncertain term. * * *

For all these reasons, the order of the Appellate Division should be reversed, with costs, and the orders of the Supreme Court, Suffolk County, reinstated. The certified question, therefore, should be answered in the negative. * * *

* * *

JASEN, JUDGE (dissenting in part).

While I recognize that the traditional rule is that a provision for renewal of a lease must be "certain" in order to render it binding and enforceable, in my view the better rule would be that if the tenant can establish its entitlement to renewal under the lease, the mere presence of a provision calling for renewal at "rentals to be agreed upon" should not prevent judicial intervention to fix rent at a reasonable rate in order to avoid a forfeiture. Therefore, I would affirm the order of the Appellate Division for the reasons stated in the opinion * * * at the Appellate Division.

E. FARNSWORTH, CONTRACTS

113 (1982).

The requirement of definiteness plainly poses serious problems if highly relational exchanges are to be forced into the mold of traditional contracts analysis.

UNIFORM COMMERCIAL CODE § 2–204(3).

Even though one or more terms are left open a contract for sale does not fail for indefiniteness if the parties have intended to make a contract and there is a reasonably certain basis for giving an appropriate remedy.

KLEINSCHMIDT DIVISION OF SCM CORP. v. FUTURONICS CORP., 41 N.Y.2d 972, 973, 395 N.Y.S.2d 151, 152, 363 N.E.2d 701, 702 (1977). "The basic philosophy of the sales article of the Uniform Commercial Code is simple. Practical business people cannot be expected to govern their actions with respect to nice legal formalisms. Thus, when there is basic agreement, however manifested and whether or not the precise moment of agreement may be determined, failure to articulate that agreement in the precise language of a lawyer, with every difficulty and contingency considered and resolved, will not prevent formation of a contract."

SECTION TEN: LIMITS ON THE SCOPE OF TRADITIONAL OFFER–ACCEPTANCE ANALYSIS—A SUMMARY

Some important limits on the applicability of traditional offer-acceptance analysis have been implicit and (in some instances) explicit in the materials so far studied. The excerpt that follows, written by Professor Rudolf Schlesinger, a distinguished professor at Cornell Law School for much of his career, summarizes a number of these limits. We return to this theme again in Section Twelve on contract formation in the form-contract setting.

SCHLESINGER, MANIFESTATION OF ASSENT WITHOUT IDENTIFIABLE SEQUENCE IN OFFER AND ACCEPTANCE

II Formation of Contracts 1583–1587, 1591–92 (R. Schlesinger ed., 1968).

There seems to be no doubt in American law that a contract can be formed without an identifiable sequence of offer and acceptance * * *.

* * *

(a) *Manifestation of assent exchanged simultaneously*

* * *

Speaking on the basis of experience in legal practice, this Reporter can assure the reader that contracts formed without identifiable sequence of offer and acceptance are of far greater frequency and importance today than seems to be realized by any of the authors of textbooks. Especially when large deals are concluded among corporations and individuals of substance, the usual sequence of events is not that of offer and acceptance; on the contrary, the businessmen who originally conduct the negotiations, often will consciously refrain from ever making a binding offer, realizing as they do that a large deal tends to be complex and that its terms have to be formulated by lawyers before it can be permitted to become a legally enforceable transaction. Thus the original negotiators will merely attempt to ascertain whether they see eye to eye concerning those aspects of the deal which seem to be most important from a business point of view. Once they do, or think they do, the negotiation is then turned over to the lawyers, usually with instructions to produce a document which all participants will be willing to sign. * * * When the lawyers take over, again there is no sequence of offer and acceptance, but rather a sequence of successive drafts. These drafts usually will not be regarded as offers, for the reason, among others, that the lawyers acting as draftsmen have no authority to make offers on behalf of their clients. After a number of drafts have been exchanged and discussed, the lawyers may finally come up with a draft which meets the approval of all of them, and of their clients. It is only then that the parties will proceed to the actual formation of the contract, and often this will be done by way of a formal "closing" * * * or in any event by simultaneous execution or delivery, in the course of a more or less ceremonial meeting, of the document or documents prepared by the lawyers.

In the usual negotiation of a large-scale transaction there is thus no room for offer and acceptance (except where options are involved). If the writers on contract law nevertheless continue to analyze the formation of contracts almost exclusively in terms of offer and acceptance, they may be right insofar as they speak of the majority of personal and business transactions of modest or medium size; but in the world of truly large-scale dealings, the traditional analysis is no longer in tune with present-day practice.

* * *

* * * [Another] situation * * * (simultaneous assent by the parties, *inter praesentes,* to a proposal made by a third person), Corbin indicates * * * is a theoretically valid example of a contract without identifiable offer and acceptance; but he adds that "no instance of a contract made in this manner has ever come under the observation of the present writer * * *."

In reality, however, such situations are not at all uncommon in the field of labor relations. Whenever (formal or informal) mediation produces an "acceptable formula" for resolving a contract dispute, there is no party who can be described as offeror or offeree. If the parties do not simultaneously agree on the proposal, of course it is possible to argue that the first acceptor adopts the proposal as his own offer; often, however, such an interpretation would contradict the attitudes and intentions of the parties. And frequently neither party will express unconditional and binding approval of the outside proposal until it is apparent that the other party is ready to do likewise; then both sides assent simultaneously to "save face" against any charge of yielding too easily.

(b) *Long negotiations making identification of offer and acceptance impossible*

* * * There are countless cases where the details of—perhaps protracted—negotiations can no longer be proved, but the existence of a contract is evidenced by the subsequent conduct of the parties. In such cases one may perhaps theoretically assume that one or the other party must have made the last offer or counter-offer the acceptance of which marked the conclusion of the contract. But this theoretical assumption is not helpful if as a practical matter it is impossible to show who was the final offeror and who the final acceptor. For practical purposes, these cases must be treated as situations in which a valid contract comes about without an ascertainable sequence of offer and acceptance. * * *

(c) *Assent manifested gradually*

Situations of this kind are frequent. They are perhaps best exemplified in the many cases in which the courts are asked to find the existence of a partnership despite the absence of any formal partnership agreement. In such cases it is clear that when the other legal requisites are present, the lack of offer and acceptance will not prevent the finding of a valid contract. Thus, where a young woman, contributing her furniture and modest capital, devoted 20 years to the active management of her aunt's lodging houses (begun at the niece's suggestion), the court found a partnership although all activities had been conducted, and all funds were kept, in the aunt's name; the court held the niece to be entitled to half the assets on her aunt's death.

* * *

* * * [I]t is difficult to generalize concerning the nature and effect of contracts formed without an identifiable sequence of offer and acceptance, because until now American legal analysts have neglected this area of contract law. The excuse usually given for this neglect has been that such contracts are rare. Now that the excuse has been exploded, perhaps more attention will be paid to the subject. An interesting beginning, at least, is made in the *Restatement (Second)* [section 22, comment b], where the functions of the two kinds of contract formation are compared as follows:

> Problems of offer and acceptance are important primarily in cases where advance commitment serves to shift a risk from one party to the other, as in sales of goods that are subject to rapid price fluctuations, in sales of land, and in insurance contracts. Controversies as to whether and when the commitment is made are less likely to be important even in such cases once performance is well under way. Offer and acceptance become still less important after there have been repeated occasions for performance by one party where the other knows the nature of the performance and has an opportunity for objection to it. * * *

One might add that there are many other situations—especially in connection with important, large-scale transactions—where the parties consciously refrain from creating any one-sided power of acceptance, and see to it that their mutual rights and obligations arise from a simultaneous exchange of promises or performances. Normally, they will embody such an exchange in one or several documents; their preliminary agreement to reduce the contract to such documentary form may give rise to additional problems * * *.

BUXBAUM, RUDOLF B. SCHLESINGER—A TRIBUTE
43 Am. J. Comp. L. 317, 317 (1995).

To speak of Comparative Law in the United States in the second half of this century is to speak of Rudolf Schlesinger. What Prosser did to establish Torts as a subject Schlesinger did for our field.

SECTION ELEVEN: INTRODUCTION TO CONTRACT FORMATION IN THE FORM CONTRACT SETTING

Much of what you have learned about the formation of contracts pursuant to the general theory of obligation "agreement with consideration" does not apply in any direct way to modern "form-pad" transactions. For one thing, the terminology you have learned is not the terminology employed by merchants employing modern forms. Instead of talk about offer, acceptance, revocation, and rejection, the purchasing manager of a company usually speaks of purchase orders, acknowledgments, and invoices. Furthermore, today's merchants often do not bargain and reach agreement in the relatively logical and orderly fashion portrayed in some of the materials in this chapter. Instead, a seller or buyer sends a form to the other; the other typically does not read the form, but instead, sends a second form back to the first party. The second form may differ substantially from the first. During or after the exchange of forms that neither party reads, the seller frequently ships the goods and the buyer accepts and uses them. Is there a contract between these parties? What are its terms?

The drafters of Article 2 of the Uniform Commercial Code sought to recognize the foregoing complexities in form-pad transactions. Accordingly, they modified the common law of offer and acceptance in the sale of goods context.

UNIFORM COMMERCIAL CODE § 2–204(2).

An agreement sufficient to constitute a contract for sale may be found even though the moment of its making is undetermined.

UNIFORM COMMERCIAL CODE § 2–207.

Additional Terms in Acceptance or Confirmation

(1) A definite and seasonable expression of acceptance or a written confirmation which is sent within a reasonable time operates as an acceptance even though it states terms additional to or different from those offered or agreed upon, unless acceptance is expressly made conditional on assent to the additional or different terms.

(2) The additional terms are to be construed as proposals for addition to the contract. Between merchants such terms become part of the contract unless:

(a) the offer expressly limits acceptance to the terms of the offer;

(b) they materially alter it; or

(c) notification of objection to them has already been given or is given within a reasonable time after notice of them is received.

(3) Conduct by both parties which recognizes the existence of a contract is sufficient to establish a contract for sale although the writings of the parties do not otherwise establish a contract. In such case the terms of the particular contract consist of those terms on which the writings of the parties agree, together with any supplementary terms incorporated under any other provisions of this Act.

Official Comment

1. This section is intended to deal with two typical situations. The one is the written confirmation, where an agreement has been reached either orally or by informal correspondence between the parties and is followed by one or both of the parties sending formal memoranda embodying the terms so far as agreed upon and adding terms not discussed. The other situation is offer and acceptance, in which a wire or letter expressed and intended as an acceptance or the closing of an agreement adds further minor suggestions or proposals such as "ship by Tuesday," "rush," "ship draft against bill of lading inspection allowed," or the like. A frequent example of the second situation is the exchange of printed purchase order and acceptance (sometimes called "acknowledgment") forms. Because the forms are oriented to the thinking of the respective drafting parties, the terms contained in them often do not correspond. Often the seller's form contains terms different from or additional to those set forth in the buyer's form. Nevertheless, the parties proceed with the transaction. [Comment 1 was amended in 1966.]

2. Under this Article a proposed deal which in commercial understanding has in fact been closed is recognized as a contract. Therefore, any additional matter contained in the confirmation or in the acceptance falls within subsection (2) and must be regarded as a proposal for an added term unless the acceptance is made conditional on the acceptance of the additional or different terms. [Comment 2 was amended in 1966.]

3. Whether or not additional or different terms will become part of the agreement depends upon the provisions of subsection (2). If they are such as materially to alter the original bargain, they will not be included unless expressly agreed to by the other party. If, however, they are terms which would not so change the bargain they will be incorporated unless notice of objection to them has already been given or is given within a reasonable time.

4. Examples of typical clauses which would normally "materially alter" the contract and so result in surprise or hardship if incorporated without express awareness by the other party are: a clause negating such standard warranties as that of merchantability or fitness for a particular purpose in circumstances in which either warranty normally attaches; a clause requiring a guaranty of 90% or 100% deliveries in a case such as a contract by cannery, where the usage of the trade allows greater quantity leeways; a clause reserving to the seller the power to cancel upon the buyer's failure to meet any invoice when due; a clause requiring that complaints be made in a time materially shorter than customary or reasonable.

5. Examples of clauses which involve no element of unreasonable surprise and which therefore are to be incorporated in the contract unless notice of objection is seasonably given are: a clause setting forth and perhaps enlarging slightly upon the seller's exemption due to supervening causes beyond his control,

similar to those covered by the provision of this Article on merchant's excuse by failure of presupposed conditions or a clause fixing in advance any reasonable formula of proration under such circumstances; a clause fixing a reasonable time for complaints within customary limits, or in the case of a purchase for sub-sale, providing for inspection by the sub-purchaser; a clause providing for interest on overdue invoices or fixing the seller's standard credit terms where they are within the range of trade practice and do not limit any credit bargained for; a clause limiting the right of rejection for defects which fall within the customary trade tolerances for acceptance "with adjustment" or otherwise limiting remedy in a reasonable manner (see Sections 2–718 and 2–719).

6. If no answer is received within a reasonable time after additional terms are proposed, it is both fair and commercially sound to assume that their inclusion has been assented to. Where clauses on confirming forms sent by both parties conflict each party must be assumed to object to a clause of the other conflicting with one on the confirmation sent by himself. As a result the requirement that there be notice of objection which is found in subsection (2) is satisfied and the conflicting terms do not become a part of the contract. The contract then consists of the terms originally expressly agreed to, terms on which the confirmations agree, and terms supplied by this Act, including subsection (2). The written confirmation is also subject to Section 2–201. Under that section a failure to respond permits enforcement of a prior oral agreement; under this section a failure to respond permits additional terms to become part of the agreement.
* * *

Note
Basic Routes to Contract Formation Under Section 2–207

Section 2–207 contemplates contract formation by at least four routes. Route A consists of that part of subsection 1 up to the comma, closing a contract via a "definite and seasonable expression of acceptance." Route A1 consists of that part of subsection 1 up to the comma, recognizing a contract via "a written confirmation" of terms "agreed upon." Route B consists of that part of subsection 1 after the comma. Route C consists of subsection 3. Be prepared to explain how the terms of the resulting contract may differ depending on which route controls contract formation.

J. WHITE & R. SUMMERS, THE UNIFORM COMMERCIAL CODE
32–36 (5th ed. 2000).

Assume that buyer sends a purchase order which provides that any dispute will be governed by arbitration. Seller responds with an acknowledgement which provides that any dispute will not be resolved by arbitration. At least if the *bargained* terms on the purchase order and acknowledgement agree, we would find that the seller's document is a definite and seasonable expression of acceptance under 2–207 and that a contract has been formed by the exchange of the documents. We would thus bind any party who seeks to get out of the contract before either performs.

Assume that the seller ships the goods, the buyer receives and pays for them, and the parties fall into dispute about their quality. Does the contract call for arbitration or does it not? Buyer will argue that buyer's document was the offer (and it appears to us that buyer's document was the offer since it was sent first)[1] and the seller's document operated as an acceptance of all of the terms on buyer's form. Furthermore, buyer will correctly point out that seller's term (no arbitration) was not an additional term which could come into their contract under 2–207(2) but was a "different" term and therefore could not become part of the contract under 2–207(2).[2] Section 2–207(1) applies to an *acceptance* that "states terms additional to or different from those offered." But the text of 2–207(2) only refers to "additional" terms, and the drafters could easily have inserted "or different" if they had so intended.[3] Yet it would be more than a little difficult to view a different term in an acceptance as a proposal for addition to the contract where the offer already includes a contrary term. It is not possible to have different terms on the same subject as "a part" of the same contract.[4]

First, the seller offeree might respond that his "no arbitration" document differed from the buyer's ("arbitration") so substantially that it did not constitute an "acceptance" under 2–207(1). But in our view, it is clear that a document may be an acceptance under 2–207(1) and yet differ substantially from the offer. The wording of 2–207(2)(b) supports this, too, for it presupposes that a contract can be formed under 2–207(1) even though the acceptance includes an additional term that "materially alters" the offer.

But how much can an acceptance differ? Certainly there is some limit. We think that in the usual purchase order-acknowledgement context the forms do not approach this limit at least if the forms do not diverge as to price, quality, quantity, or delivery terms, but only as to the usual unbargained terms on the reverse side concerning remedies, arbitration, and the like. Here we would reject the seller offeree's argument. A case that goes to the very edge in finding a document to be an acceptance is Southern Idaho Pipe & Steel Co. v. Cal–Cut Pipe & Supply, Inc.[5] There, the Idaho Supreme Court held that an acceptance occurred even though the buyer's "accepting" form was the same form sent by the seller, the buyer having stricken the seller's delivery date,

---

1. Of course, whoever sends the first form is generally the offeror. See, e.g., Reaction Molding Technologies, Inc. v. General Electric Co., 585 F.Supp. 1097, 38 UCC 1518 (E.D.Pa. 1984), opinion amended, 588 F.Supp. 1280, 38 UCC 1537 (E.D.Pa.1984) (seller's form held to be an offer); Technographics, Inc. v. Mercer Corp., 777 F.Supp. 1214, 16 UCC2d 1035 (M.D.Pa.1991), aff'd, 26 F.3d 123 (3d Cir.1994) (seller's price quotation not an offer because of home office acceptance clause).

2. See cases on 2–207(2) cited *infra* in this section.

3. Accord, American Parts Co. v. American Arbitration Ass'n, 8 Mich.App. 156, 154 N.W.2d 5, 6 UCC 119 (1967). Most courts hold that 2–207(2) does not apply to "different" terms. See, e.g., Reaction Molding Technologies, Inc. v. General Electric Co., 588 F.Supp. 1280, 38 UCC 1537, 1546 (E.D.Pa.1984). See also, Murray, The Chaos of the Battle of the Forms, 39 Vand.L.Rev. 1307, 1356 n. 182 (1986). But see Steiner v. Mobil Oil Corp., 20 Cal.3d 90, 141 Cal.Rptr. 157, 569 P.2d 751, 22 UCC 865, 876 n. 6 (1977).

4. Comment 3 to 2–207, which says that 2–207(2) determines whether "additional or different terms will become part of the agreement," goes beyond the text except insofar as it applies to confirmations of a prior agreement. Accord, American Parts Co. v. American Arbitration Ass'n, 8 Mich.App. 156, 154 N.W.2d 5, 6 UCC 119 (1967). § 2–207(2)(c) can be read to confirm that the drafters did not envision the possibility that a contract could include "different" terms on the same matter. § 2–207(2)(c) would automatically eject the different term in the acceptance, since "notification of objection" would already have been given when the offeror included the contrary term initially. Cases supporting this analysis include, Reaction Molding Technologies, Inc. v. General Electric Co., 588 F.Supp. 1280, 38 UCC 1537, 1546 (E.D.Pa.1984).

5. 98 Idaho 495, 567 P.2d 1246, 22 UCC 25 (1977), appeal dism'd, cert. denied, 434 U.S. 1056, 98 S.Ct. 1225, 55 L.Ed.2d 757 (1978).

inserted his own and returned the form. There the parties may still have been bargaining over the delivery date, a fact not present in our hypothetical case.

Second, in our hypothetical case, the seller might contend that its document (seller's acceptance) was "expressly made conditional on assent to the additional or different terms" under 2–207(1). This argument finds some support in the well-known case, Roto–Lith, Ltd. v. F.P. Bartlett & Co.,[6] where the First Circuit held that any responding document "which states a condition materially altering the obligation solely to the disadvantage of the offeror"—here, a disclaimer—was expressly conditional and thus did not operate as an acceptance. We would reject that argument also, for it is inconsistent with our interpretation of the word "acceptance" in 2–207(1) and contrary to the drafter's policy stated above to whittle down the counteroffer rule. Further, Comment 4 to 2–207 refers to disclaimers as "material" alterations under 2–207(2)(b), a reference that would be redundant if disclaimers always made an offer expressly conditional under 2–207(1).

Third, the seller may argue that seller's acceptance is only an acceptance of the terms on which the two documents agree, and they did not agree on arbitration, nor do Code gap fillers provide for arbitration. This argument finds no explicit support in 2–207, but one of us (White) thinks part of Comment 6 supports it:

> If no answer is received within a reasonable time after additional terms are proposed, it is both fair and commercially sound to assume that their inclusion has been assented to. Where clauses on confirming forms sent by both parties conflict each party must be assumed to object to a clause of the other conflicting with one on the confirmation sent by himself. As a result the requirement that there be notice of objection which is found in subsection (2) is satisfied and the conflicting terms do not become a part of the contract. The contract then consists of the terms originally expressly agreed to, terms on which the confirmations agree, and terms supplied by this Act, including subsection (2). The written confirmation is also subject to Section 2–201. Under that section a failure to respond permits enforcement of a prior oral agreement; under this section a failure to respond permits additional terms to become part of the agreement.

In the end, how would our hypothetical case come out under the Code? One of us (White) would turn to the foregoing comment and find that the two terms cancel one another.[7] On this view the seller's form was only an acceptance of terms in the offer which did not conflict with any terms in the acceptance. Thus, the ultimate deal would not include an arbitration clause. The Code does not expressly authorize this result, but White believes it does not bar it either.[8]

6. 297 F.2d 497, 500, 1 UCC 73, 76 (1st Cir.1962).

7. See Lea Tai Textile Co., Ltd. v. Manning Fabrics, Inc., 411 F.Supp. 1404, 19 UCC 1080 (S.D.N.Y.1975) (conflicting terms regarding rules to be used for arbitration cancel each other); Daitom, Inc. v. Pennwalt Corp., 741 F.2d 1569, 39 UCC 1203 (10th Cir.1984) (White's knock-out rule only solution to con-flicting terms which avoids giving undue advantage to party based on fortuity of timing of his form; forms are rarely read in practice.).

8. Many cases involve arbitration clauses. See Marlene Indus. Corp. v. Carnac Textiles, Inc., 45 N.Y.2d 327, 408 N.Y.S.2d 410, 380 N.E.2d 239, 24 UCC 257 (1978) (in New York, a clause for arbitration is never "minor" under 2–207(2)!).

Summers believes that Comment 6 is not applicable. In his view Comment 6 applies only to variant terms on confirming forms, not to variant terms on forms one of which is an offer and the other an acceptance under 2–207(1) (a distinction itself drawn in Comment 1). Thus, in our hypothetical case, the buyer offeror's arbitration clause controls, for the seller's no-arbitration clause, as a different term embodied in the accepting form, simply falls out; 2–207(2) cannot rescue it since that provision applies only to additional terms.[9] White answers that, among other things, this reading gives the sender of the first form (the buyer here) an unearned advantage. Summers does not agree that the "advantage" is entirely unearned. The recipient of the first form at least had an opportunity to object to its contents. Moreover, Summers believes that White's approach is relatively more unfair to the offeror than Summers' approach is to the offeree. According to Summers, offerors have more (even if only a little more) reason to expect that their clauses will control than offerees have to expect that their clauses will. After all, when the offerees send their forms they will have already received a form from the offerors, and offerees know full well that forms of different parties rarely coincide. But even if the offeror's advantage is to some extent unearned, the text of 2–207, according to Summers, appears plainly to authorize it. Section 2–207(1) presupposes an outstanding offer and explicitly applies only to an acceptance (or confirmation). Thus we are to begin the analysis with the offer the terms of which control exclusively except insofar as 2–207 provides otherwise. Section 2–207 does not provide otherwise as to different terms. As to additional terms, the section provides otherwise only insofar as these survive 2–207(2). Summers adds that if the drafters intended the White approach, they could have easily drafted the section accordingly.

Most of the decisions agree with White. For example, the Tenth Circuit canvassed the cases on our dispute in *Daitom, Inc. v. Pennwalt Corp.* The court purported to side with White and remarked that Summers' position "misses the fundamental purpose of the UCC in general and 2–207 in particular, which is to preserve a contract and fill in any gaps if the parties intended to make a contract and there is a reasonable basis for giving an appropriate remedy." With respect, Summers considers this to be a question-begging characterization, and he awaits the court's answer to his specific textual and other arguments.

Consider this further problem. Assume for example that the offer contains an otherwise valid disclaimer of warranties and that the acceptance contains a conflicting express warranty. According to White, neither become part of the contract under 2–207(1) despite the fact that a contract is formed. Likewise neither enters the contract through 2–207(2) because the term in the acceptance is a different, not an additional term. Moreover by its terms 2–207(3) does not apply to this case but applies only to the case where "the writings of the parties do not otherwise establish a contract." Is it possible, nonetheless, that an *implied* warranty enters the contract directly as a gap filler without reference to 2–207(3)? White believes that it does and that indeed most of the gap fillers do not depend upon 2–207 to enter the contract. He says there are many contracts adequately formed by an offer and an

---

9. See, e.g., Reaction Molding Technologies,   38 UCC 1537 (E.D.Pa.1984).
Inc. v. General Electric Co., 588 F.Supp. 1280,

acceptance which a gap filler dealing with price or warranty or terms of delivery would enter without any reference to 2–207. On White's view, that seems the proper result. He thinks that the court in Bosway Tube & Steel Corp. v. McKay Machine Co. reached just this result by applying both 2–207(1) and 2–207(3). It seems to him that the court's result is correct (but that it is technically incorrect in finding that 2–207(3) can apply to a case in which the court has already found a 2–207(1) contract). On White's analysis the foregoing outcome favors neither party. The Code may provide a term substantially identical to one of those rejected. So be it. At least a term so supplied has the merit of being a term that the drafters of the UCC considered fair.

Summers believes White misreads 2–207, both in text and in spirit. Summers would, in the foregoing further hypothetical case, uphold the offeror's otherwise valid disclaimer as to both express and implied warranties. The offeree's term is a different term and falls out.

think about different v additional

DAITOM, INC. v. PENNWALT CORP. *Sided w/ White*

United States Court of Appeals, Tenth Circuit, 1984.
741 F.2d 1569.

WILLIAM E. DOYLE, CIRCUIT JUDGE.

I. STATEMENT OF THE CASE

This is an appeal from the grant of summary judgment against Daitom, Inc. (Daitom), the plaintiff below. The result was dismissal by the United States District Court for the District of Kansas of all three counts of Daitom's complaint.

Daitom had brought this diversity action in federal court on March 7, 1980 against Pennwalt Corporation and its Stokes Vacuum Equipment Division (Pennwalt). Counts I and II of Daitom's complaint alleged breach of various express and implied warranties and Count III alleged negligent design and manufacture by Pennwalt of certain rotary vacuum drying machines sold to and used commercially by Daitom in the production of a vitamin known properly as dextro calcium pantothenate and commonly as Vitamin B–5.

Daitom is a Delaware chartered corporation having its principal place of business in Kansas. It was formed to implement a joint venture between Thompson–Hayward Chemical Company, Inc. of Kansas City, Kansas and Daiichi–Seiyakii Co., Ltd., of Tokyo, Japan. Pennwalt is a Pennsylvania chartered corporation with its principal place of business in Pennsylvania.

Daitom requests a reversal of the district court's grant of summary judgment against Daitom on all counts of its complaint and seeks a remand for a trial on the merits.

We have concluded that there should be a reversal with respect to Counts I and II, together with a remand to the district court for a trial on the merits of those claims. On the other hand, we have concluded that there should be an affirmance of the summary judgment against Daitom on Count III of its complaint.

II. Facts

The essential facts so far as they pertain to the issues presented in this appeal are as follows.

For the purpose of implementing its joint venture, Daitom planned to construct and operate a manufacturing plant to commercially produce dextro calcium pantothenate. The design of the plant was undertaken and handled on behalf of Daitom by Kintech Services, Inc. (which company will be referred to as Kintech), an engineering design firm located in Cincinnati, Ohio. Kintech had the responsibility not only for designing the plant; it also was responsible for investigating various means of drying the product during the production process, and for negotiating the purchase of certain equipment to be used in the plant. Included in the equipment was automated drying equipment to be used in removing methanol and water from the processed vitamin as part of the purification process.

There were numerous tests made and conducted at Kintech's request by equipment manufacturers. Kintech formulated specifications for the automated drying equipment. (This is referred to as Kintech Specification 342, Record, Volume I, at 59–65). On behalf of Daitom, Kintech invited various vendors to bid on the needed equipment.

Proposal by Pennwalt

Pennwalt, on September 7, 1976, submitted a proposal for the sale of two rotary vacuum dryers with dust filters and heating systems to dry dextro calcium pantothenate. The typewritten proposal specified the equipment to be sold, the f.o.b. price, and delivery and payment terms. A pre-printed conditions of sale form was also attached to the proposal and explicitly made an integral part of the proposal by the typewritten sheet.

purchase order

Kintech recommended to Daitom that Pennwalt's proposal be accepted and on October 5, 1976, well within the thirty-day acceptance period specified in the proposal, Daitom issued a purchase order for the Pennwalt equipment. The purchase order consisted of a pre-printed form with the identification of the specific equipment and associated prices typewritten in the appropriate blank spaces on the front together with seventeen lengthy "boilerplate" or "standard" terms and conditions of sale on the back. In addition, on the front of the purchase order in the column marked for a description of the items purchased, Daitom typed the following:

descrip. typed by Daitom

> Rotary vacuum dryers in accordance with Kintech Services, Inc. specification 342 dated August 20, 1976, and in accordance with Stokes proposal dated September 7, 1976.

The two rotary vacuum dryers and the equipment that went along with them were manufactured by Pennwalt and delivered to Daitom's plant in early May 1977. For the reason that there had been no construction of Daitom's plant, the crated equipment was not immediately installed. Instead, it was stored outside in crates. On June 15, 1978, the dryers were finally installed and first operated by Daitom. Daitom notified Pennwalt of serious problems with the operation of the dryers on June 17, 1978.

Daitom's contention was that the dryers suffered from two severe defects: 1) they were delivered with misaligned agitator blades causing a scraping and damaging of the dryer interiors and an uneven distribution of the products being dried; and 2) they were undersized necessitating an overloading of the dryers and a "lumping up" of the product rendering it unsuitable for further use. Pennwalt's repair personnel visited the Daitom plant to investigate the alleged operating difficulties, but Daitom contends the dryers were not repaired and have never performed as required under the specifications and as represented by Pennwalt. This was the basis for the lawsuit.

This suit was brought in federal court on March 7, 1980, after Pennwalt's alleged failure to correct the difficulties with the dryers. On Pennwalt's motion, the district court granted summary judgment against Daitom on all three counts of its complaint. The court dismissed Counts I and II after applying section 2–207 of the Uniform Commercial Code (U.C.C.) and finding that Daitom's breach of warranties claims were barred by the one-year period of limitations specified in Pennwalt's proposal. The court further concluded that alleged damages in Count III for the negligent design and manufacture of the dryers were not available in tort; the sole remedy being in an action for breach of warranties which here was barred by the period of limitations. Consequently, summary judgment was granted against Daitom. Daitom's subsequent motion for reconsideration was denied by the district court on June 3, 1982, and following that, this appeal took place.

III.   Discussion

A.   The Issues

It is to be noted that the district court granted summary judgment against Daitom on Counts I and II of the complaint, finding the breach of warranties claim barred by the one-year period of limitations which was set forth in Pennwalt's proposal. In ruling against Daitom the court followed a three step analysis. First, it concluded that pursuant to U.C.C. § 2–207(1), a written contract for the sale of the rotary dryers was formed by Pennwalt's September 7, 1976 proposal and Daitom's October 5, 1976 purchase order accepting that proposal. Second, the court found that the one-year period of limitations specified in Pennwalt's proposal and shortening the typical four-year period of limitations available under the U.C.C. became part of the contract of sale and governed the claims for breach of warranties. Thus, the court accepted the proposal that was contained in the documents that had been submitted by the defendant-appellee. Third, the court concluded that the one-year period of limitations was not tolled by any conduct of Pennwalt's, so that consequently, Daitom's claims were barred because they were brought after the expiration of the one-year limitations period. The view we have of the submission and response is that the approval was initial and general and contemplated further discussion and improvement.

The circumstances surrounding the delivery of this equipment and what occurred thereafter is of high importance. The equipment was delivered in crates and boxes, and at that time Daitom had no plant. Instead of seeking to protect the equipment in some way, Pennwalt simply delivered the boxes and left. The documents which were part of the delivery provided for this one-year period of limitations specified in the Pennwalt proposal. Seemingly, this conduct on the part of Pennwalt in making a quick delivery and quick departure took hold in connection with the motion for summary judgment, the court ruling that more than one year had passed before they were able to try out the machinery and discover the defects. [No] suggestion is made as to how this machinery could have been utilized or contested because of the conditions that were present. Why, then should the one-year limitations period, created by Pennwalt, be allowed to take effect?

Daitom has challenged the district court's findings as to the terms which became a part of the contract. Daitom argues that its October 5, 1976 purchase order did not constitute an acceptance of Pennwalt's September 7, 1976 proposal. Instead, Daitom claims that its purchase order explicitly made acceptance conditional on Pennwalt's assent to the additional or different terms in the purchase order. As a consequence, Daitom argues, pursuant to U.C.C. § 2–207(1),[1] the exchanged writings of the parties did *not* form a contract, because Pennwalt failed to assent to the additional or different terms in the purchase order. The most relevant additional or different terms Daitom alleges were in *its* purchase order were the terms reserving all warranties and remedies available in law, despite Pennwalt's limitation of warranties and remedies in its proposal. In a sense Pennwalt argues it enjoyed an exclusive right to set the conditions.

Daitom argues that on their face the writings failed to create a contract, and, instead, that a contract was to be formed by *the conduct* of both parties, pursuant to § 2–207(3), and the resulting contract consisted of the terms on which the writings agreed, together with "any supplementary terms incorporated under any other provision of [the UCC]." Therefore, Daitom concludes, the resulting contract governing the sale of the rotary dryers incorporated the U.C.C. provisions for express warranties (§ 2–313), implied warranties (§§ 2–314, 2–315), and a four-year period of limitations.

As an alternative argument, Daitom contends that even if its October 5, 1976 purchase order did constitute an acceptance of Pennwalt's September 7, 1976 proposal and did form a contract, all conflicting terms between the two writings were "knocked out" and did not become part of the resulting contract, because of their being at odds one with the other. Therefore, Daitom concludes once again that the resulting contract consisted of only those terms in which the writings agreed and any supplementary or "gap-filler" terms incorporated under the provisions of the U.C.C.; specifically §§ 2–313, 2–314, 2–315, 2–725.

Daitom makes a further argument which has some appeal and that is that even if the one-year period of limitations specified in Pennwalt's proposal became a part of the sales contract, it was tolled by Pennwalt's wrongful conduct, which included fraudulent concealment of the equipment's defects and failure of the essential purpose of the limited remedies. Since this court's decision does not rely on the question of the tolling of the limitations period, we will not devote detailed argument to this.

* * *

B. *The Applicable Law*

The district court found the dispute between Daitom and Pennwalt involved a "transaction in goods," between persons who are "merchants"

---

1. The parties, throughout this litigation and through their briefs, agree that the law of Pennsylvania governs their warranty claims. The parties further agree that Pennsylvania has adopted the provisions of the Uniform Commercial Code and that for the purpose of this action the Pennsylvania statute does not modify the U.C.C. provisions. See 13 Pa.C.S.A. § 2207 (Purdon's 1984). Therefore, throughout this memorandum the relevant code sections will be referred to only by the U.C.C. numeral designation.

and, therefore, was governed by Article 2 of the U.C.C. U.C.C. §§ 2–102, 2–104. The district court also stated that the dispute is a classic example of the "battle of the forms."

As previously noted, there has been agreement that the law of Pennsylvania governs these claims for breach of warranty and Pennsylvania has adopted the provisions of the U.C.C. Section 2–207 of the U.C.C. was specifically drafted to deal with the battle of the forms and related problems. U.C.C. § 2–207, Comment 1.

Section 2–207 has been commented on in one case as a "murky bit of prose," (*Southwest Engineering Co., Inc. v. Martin Tractor Co., Inc.,* 205 Kan. 684, 473 P.2d 18, 25 (1970)), and as "one of the most important, subtle, and difficult in the entire code, and well it may be said that the product as it finally reads is not altogether satisfactory." (Duesenberg & King, 3 *Sales and Bulk Transfer Under the Uniform Commercial Code,* § 3.03 at 3–12 (1984)). The Pennsylvania Supreme Court has not addressed the issues presented by this case. In the absence, therefore, of an authoritative pronouncement from the state's highest court, our task is to regard ourselves as sitting in diversity and predicting how the state's highest court would rule. * * * This court must also follow any intermediate state court decision unless other authority convinces us that the state supreme court would decide otherwise. * * * Also, the policies underlying the applicable legal doctrines, the doctrinal trends indicated by these policies, and the decisions of other courts may also inform this court's analysis. * * * With these standards in mind, we proceed to consider and analyze the case.

C. *The Writings and the Contract*

The trial court concluded that the parties' exchanged writings formed a contract. Thus, there was not a formal single document. Pennwalt's September 7, 1976 proposal constituted the offer and Daitom's October 5, 1976 purchase order constituted the acceptance.

It is essentially uncontested that Pennwalt's proposal constituted an offer. The proposal set forth in some detail the equipment to be sold to Daitom, the price, the terms of shipment, and specifically stated that the attached terms and conditions were an integral part of the proposal. One of those attached terms and conditions of sale limited the warranties to repair and replacement of defective parts and limited the period of one year from the date of delivery for any action for breach of warranty.[3]

---

3. Paragraph 5 of the terms and conditions of sale stated in full (emphasis added):

6. WARRANTIES:

a. Seller warrants that at the time of delivery of the property to the carrier, it will be, unless otherwise specified, new, free and clear of all lawful liens and security interests or other encumbrances unknown to Buyer. If, within a period of one year from the date of *such delivery* any parts of the property (except property specified to be used property or normal wear parts) fail because of material or workmanship which was defec-

tive at the time of such delivery, Seller will repair such parts, or furnish parts to replace them f.o.b. Seller's or its supplier's plant, provided such failure is due solely to such defective material or workmanship and is not contributed to by any other cause, such as improper care or unreasonable use, and provided such defects are brought to Seller's attention for verification when first discovered, and the parts alleged to be so defective are returned, if requested, to Seller's or its supplier's plant. *No action for breach of war-*

The proposal was sent to Kintech and forwarded to Daitom with a recommendation to accept the proposal. Daitom sent the October 5, 1976 purchase order to Pennwalt. This purchase order constituted an acceptance of Pennwalt's offer and formed a binding contract for the sale only pursuant to 2–207(1), despite the statement of terms additional to or different from those in the offer.[4] But these terms were not without meaning or consequence. However, the acceptance was not expressly conditioned on Pennwalt accepting these additional or different terms.

There is a provision which Daitom contends made the acceptance expressly conditional on Pennwalt's accepting the additional or different terms which appeared in the pre-printed, standard "boilerplate" provisions on the back of the purchase order. It stated:

> Acceptance. Immediate acceptance is required unless otherwise provided herein. It is understood and agreed that the written acceptance by Seller of this purchase order or the commencement of any work [or] performance of any services hereunder by the Seller, (including the commencement of any work or the performance of any service with respect to samples), shall constitute acceptance by Seller of this purchase order and of all the terms and conditions of such acceptance [and] is *expressly limited to such terms and conditions, unless each deviation is mutually recognized therefore in writing.* (Emphasis added.)

This language does not preclude the formation of a contract by the exchanged writings pursuant to § 2–207(1). Nor does it dictate the adoption of a conclusion holding that as a result the acceptance provided the applicable terms of the resulting contract. First, it is well established that a contract for the sale of goods may be made in any manner to show agreement, requiring merely that there be some objective manifestation of mutual assent, but that there must be. There is not a contract until it takes place. See U.C.C. § 2–204; *Ore & Chemical Corporation v. Howard Butcher Trading Corp.,* 455 F.Supp. 1150, 1152 (E.D.Pa.1978). Here there is such an objective manifestation of agreement on essential terms of equipment specifications, price, and the terms of shipment and payment, all of which took place before the machinery was put to any test. The purchase order explicitly referred to and incorporated on its front Kintech's equipment specifications and Pennwalt's proposal. But we are unwilling to hold such a typewritten reference and incorporation by Daitom brings the matter to a close. The acceptance and warranty terms as provided for by the above excerpted acceptance clause, does

---

ranty shall be brought more than one year after the cause of action has accrued SELLER MAKES NO OTHER WARRANTY OF ANY KIND, EXPRESS OR IMPLIED, INCLUDING ANY WARRANTY OF FITNESS OF THE PROPERTY FOR ANY PARTICULAR PURPOSE EVEN IF THAT PURPOSE IS KNOWN TO SELLER. *In no event shall Seller be liable for consequential damage.*

b. Because of varied interpretations of standards at the local level, Seller cannot warrant that the property meets the requirements of the Occupational Safety and Health Act.

4. The principal additional or different terms referred to the reservation of warranties. Specifically:

(8) WARRANTY. The Seller warrants that the supplies covered by this purchase order will conform to the specifications, drawings, samples, or other descriptions furnished or specified by buyer, and will be fit and sufficient for the purpose intended, merchantable, of good material and workmanship, and free from defect. The warranties and remedies provided for in this paragraph * * * shall be in addition to those implied by or available at law * * *.

manifest a willingness on all essential terms to accept the offer and form a contract. *Cf., Daitom v. Henry Vogt Machine Co.,* No. 80–2081 (D.Kan., unpublished 2/22/82) (In that case the court held that under identical factual circumstances and involving the identical purchase order form language, such typewritten reference and incorporation of the offer constituted a written modification of the purchase order's boilerplate acceptance terms to conform to those in the offer.) This was, of course, before an attempt was made to use the equipment.

Second, the boilerplate provision does not directly address the instant case. The purchase order is drafted principally as an *offer* inviting acceptance. Although this court recognizes that the form may serve a dual condition depending on the circumstances, the imprecision of language that permits such service detracts from Daitom's argument of conditional acceptance.

Third, the courts are split on the application of § 2–207(1) and the meaning of "expressly made conditional on assent to the additional or different terms." *See Boese–Hilburn Co. v. Dean Machinery,* 616 S.W.2d 520 (Mo.App.1981). *Roto–Lith Ltd. v. F.P. Bartlett & Co., Inc.,* 297 F.2d 497 (1st Cir.1962) represents one extreme of the spectrum, that the offeree's response stating a term materially altering the contractual obligations solely to the disadvantage of the offeror constitutes a conditional acceptance. The other extreme of the spectrum is represented by *Dorton v. Collins & Aikman Corporation,* 453 F.2d 1161 (6th Cir.1972), in which case the court held that the conditional nature of the acceptance should be so clearly expressed in a manner sufficient to notify the offeror that the offeree is unwilling to proceed with the transaction unless the additional or different terms are included in the contract. The middle of the spectrum providing that a response merely "predicating" acceptance on clarification, addition or modification is a conditional acceptance is represented by *Construction Aggregates Corp. v. Hewitt–Robins, Inc.,* 404 F.2d 505 (7th Cir.1968), *cert. denied,* 395 U.S. 921, 89 S.Ct. 1774, 23 L.Ed.2d 238 (1969).

The facts of this case, Daitom asserts, are not of a character that would suggest that there had been an unequivocal acceptance. The defendant-appellee was aware that the machinery had not even been tried. Once it was tried, it broke down in a very short time. It is hard to see a justifiable acceptance, Daitom asserts, when the buyer does not even know whether it works, and, in fact, learns after the fact, that it does not work. This fact alone renders the "contract" to be questionable.

The better view as to the meaning and application of "conditional acceptance," and the view most likely to be adopted by Pennsylvania, is the view in *Dorton* that the offeree must explicitly communicate his or her unwillingness to proceed with the transaction unless the additional or different terms in its response are accepted by the offeror. * * *

Having found an offer and an acceptance which was not made expressly conditional on assent to additional or different terms, we must now decide the effect of those additional or different terms on the resulting contract and what terms became part of it. The district court simply resolved this dispute by focusing solely on the period of limitations specified in Pennwalt's offer of September 7, 1976. Thus, the court held that while the offer explicitly specified a one-year period of limitations in accordance with § 2–725(1) allowing such a reduction, Daitom's acceptance of October 5, 1976 was silent as to the limitations period. Consequently, the court held that § 2–207(2) was inapplicable and the one-year limitations period controlled, effectively barring Daitom's action for breach of warranties.

While the district court's analysis undertook to resolve the issue without considering the question of the application of § 2–207(2) to additional or different terms, we cannot accept its approach or its conclusion. We are unable to ignore the plain implication of Daitom's reservation in its boiler-plate warranties provision of all its rights and remedies available at law. Such an explicit reservation impliedly reserves the statutory period of limitations; without such a reservation, all other reservations of actions and remedies are without effect.

The statutory period of limitations under the U.C.C. is four years after the cause of action has accrued. U.C.C. § 2–725(1). Were we to determine that this four-year period became a part of the contract rather than the shorter one-year period, Daitom's actions on breach of warranties were timely brought and summary judgment against Daitom was error.[5]

We realize that our conclusion requires an inference to be drawn from a construction of Daitom's terms; however, such an inference and construction are consistent with the judicial reluctance to grant summary judgment where there is some reasonable doubt over the existence of a genuine material fact. *See Williams v. Borden, Inc.,* 637 F.2d 731, 738 (10th Cir.1980). When taking into account the circumstances surrounding the application of the one-year limitations period, we have little hesitation in adopting the U.C.C.'s four-year limitations reservation, the application of which permits a trial on the merits. Thus, this court must recognize that certain terms in Daitom's acceptance differed from terms in Pennwalt's offer and decide which become part of the contract. The district court certainly erred in refusing to recognize such a conflict.[6]

The difficulty in determining the effect of different terms in the acceptance is the imprecision of drafting evident in § 2–207. The language of the provision is silent on how different terms in the acceptance are to be treated once a contract is formed pursuant to § 2–207(1). That section provides that a contract may be formed by exchanged writings despite the existence of additional or different terms in the acceptance. Therefore, an offeree's response is treated as an acceptance while it may differ substantially from the offer. This section of the provision, then, reformed the mirror-image rule; that common law legal formality that prohibited the formation of a contract if the exchanged writings of offer and acceptance differed in any term.

5. Daitom filed its complaint on March 7, 1980. While the parties dispute when the cause of action accrued and the period of limitations began to run, resolution of the dispute is unnecessary if this court concludes the four-year limitations period controls. Even if it is found the action accrued in May 1977 on delivery of the dryers to Daitom's plant, the four-year period of limitations had not expired on March 7, 1980 when the complaint was filed.

6. There is some indication in its memorandum and order that had the district court considered the effect of the conflicting terms, it would have applied § 2–207(2)(b) and concluded that the terms in Pennwalt's offer controlled because Daitom's conflicting terms would have materially altered the content. Memorandum and Order at 11. Because we hold, *infra,* that conflicting terms should not be analyzed pursuant to § 2–207(2), this conclusion of the district court is also in error.

Once a contract is recognized pursuant to § 2–207(1), § 2–207(2) provides the standard for determining if the additional terms stated in the acceptance become a part of the contract. Between merchants, such *additional* terms become part of the resulting contract *unless* 1) the offer expressly limited acceptance to its terms, 2) the additional terms materially alter the contract obligations, or 3) the offeror gives notice of his or her objection to the additional terms within a reasonable time. Should any one of these three possibilities occur, the *additional* terms are treated merely as proposals for incorporation in the contract and absent assent by the offeror the terms of the offer control. In any event, the existence of the additional terms does not prevent a contract from being formed.

Section 2–207(2) is silent on the treatment of terms stated in the acceptance that are *different*, rather than merely additional, from those stated in the offer. It is unclear whether "different" terms in the acceptance are intended to be included under the aegis of "additional" terms in § 2–207(2) and, therefore, fail to become part of the agreement if they materially alter the contract. Comment 3 suggests just such an inclusion.[7] However, Comment 6 suggests that different terms in exchanged writings must be assumed to constitute mutual objections by each party to the other's conflicting terms and result in a mutual "knockout" of both parties' conflicting terms; the missing terms to be supplied by the U.C.C.'s "gap-filler" provisions.[8] At least one commentator, in support of this view, has suggested that the drafting history of the provision indicates that the word "different" was intentionally deleted from the final draft of § 2–207(2) to preclude its treatment under that subsection.[9] The plain language, comments, and drafting history of the provision, therefore, provide little helpful guidance in resolving the disagreement over the treatment of different terms pursuant to § 2–207.

Despite all this, the cases and commentators have suggested three possible approaches. The first of these is to treat "different" terms as included under the aegis of "additional" terms in § 2–207(2). Consequently, different terms in the acceptance would never become part of the contract, because, by definition, they would materially alter the contract (i.e., the offeror's terms). Several courts have adopted this approach. *E.g., Mead Corporation v. McNally–Pittsburg Manufacturing Corporation,* 654 F.2d 1197 (6th Cir.1981) (applying Ohio law); *Steiner v. Mobil Oil Corporation,* 20 Cal.3d 90, 141 Cal.Rptr. 157, 569 P.2d 751 (1977); *Lockheed Electronics Company, Inc. v. Keronix, Inc.,* 114 Cal.App.3d 304, 170 Cal.Rptr. 591 (1981).

---

7. Comment 3 states (emphasis added):

Whether or not *additional* or *different* terms will become part of the agreement depends upon the provision of subsection (2).

It must be remembered that even official comments to enacted statutory text do not have the force of law and are only guidance in the interpretation of that text. *In re Bristol Associates, Inc.,* 505 F.2d 1056 (3d Cir.1974) (while the comments to the Pennsylvania U.C.C. are not binding, the Pennsylvania Supreme Court gives substantial weight to the comments as evidencing application of the Code).

8. Comment 6 states, in part:

Where clauses on confirming forms sent by both parties conflict each party must be assumed to object to a clause of the other conflicting with one on the confirmation sent by himself * * *. The contract then consists of the terms expressly agreed to, terms on which the confirmations agree, and terms supplied by the Act, including subsection (2).

9. See D.G. Baird & R. Weisberg, *Rules, Standards, and the Battle of the Forms: A Reassessment of § 2–207,* 68 Va.L.R. 1217, 1240, n. 61.

The second approach, which leads to the same result as the first, is that the offeror's terms control because the offeree's different terms merely fall out; § 2–207(2) cannot rescue the different terms since that subsection applies only to *additional* terms. Under this approach, Comment 6 (apparently supporting a mutual rather than a single term knockout) is not applicable because it refers only to conflicting terms in confirmation forms following *oral* agreement, not conflicting terms in the *writings* that form the agreement. This approach is supported by Professor Summers. J.J. White & R.S. Summers, *Uniform Commercial Code*, § 1–2, at 29 (2d ed. 1980).

The third, and preferable approach, which is commonly called the "knock-out" rule, is that the conflicting terms cancel one another. Under this view the offeree's form is treated only as an acceptance of the terms in the offeror's form which did not conflict. The ultimate contract, then, includes those non-conflicting terms and any other terms supplied by the U.C.C., including terms incorporated by course of performance (§ 2–208), course of dealing (§ 1–205), usage of trade (§ 1–205), and other "gap fillers" or "off-the-rack" terms (e.g., implied warranty of fitness for particular purpose, § 2–315). As stated previously, this approach finds some support in Comment 6. Professor White supports this approach as the most fair and consistent with the purposes of § 2–207. *White & Summers, supra,* at 29. Further, several courts have adopted or recognized the approach. *E.g., Idaho Power Company v. Westinghouse Electric Corporation,* 596 F.2d 924 (9th Cir.1979) (applying Idaho law, although incorrectly, applying § 2–207(3) after finding a contract under § 2–207(1)); *Owens–Corning Fiberglass Corporation v. Sonic Development Corporation,* 546 F.Supp. 533 (D.Kan.1982) (Judge Saffels applying Kansas law); *Lea Tai Textile Co., Ltd. v. Manning Fabrics, Inc.,* 411 F.Supp. 1404 (S.D.N.Y.1975); *Hartwig Farms, Inc. v. Pacific Gamble Robinson Company,* 28 Wash.App. 539, 625 P.2d 171 (1981); *S.C. Gray, Inc. v. Ford Motor Company,* 92 Mich.App. 789, 286 N.W.2d 34 (1979).

We are of the opinion that this is the more reasonable approach, particularly when dealing with a case such as this where from the beginning the offeror's specified period of limitations would expire before the equipment was even installed. The approaches other than the "knock-out" approach would be inequitable and unjust because they invited the very kind of treatment which the defendant attempted to provide.

Thus, we are of the conclusion that if faced with this issue the Pennsylvania Supreme Court would adopt the "knock-out" rule and hold here that the conflicting terms in Pennwalt's offer and Daitom's acceptance regarding the period of limitations and applicable warranties cancel one another out. Consequently, the other provisions of the U.C.C. must be used to provide the missing terms.

This particular approach and result are supported persuasively by the underlying rationale and purpose behind the adoption of § 2–207. As stated previously, that provision was drafted to reform the infamous common law mirror-image rule and associated last-shot doctrine that enshrined the fortuitous positions of senders of forms and accorded undue advantages based on such fortuitous positions. *White & Summers, supra,* at 25. To refuse to adopt the "knock-out" rule and instead adopt one of the remaining two approaches would serve to re-enshrine the undue advantages derived solely from the fortuitous positions of when a party sent a form. Cf., 3 Duesenberg & King at 93 (1983 Supp.). This is because either approach other than the "knock-out" rule for different terms results in the offeror and his or her terms always prevailing solely because he or she sent the first form. Professor Summers argues that this advantage is not wholly unearned, because the offeree has an opportunity to review the offer, identify the conflicting terms and make his or her acceptance conditional. But this joinder misses the fundamental purpose of the U.C.C. in general and § 2–207 in particular, which is to preserve a contract and fill in any gaps if the parties intended to make a contract and there is a reasonable basis for giving an appropriate remedy. U.C.C. § 2–204(3); § 2–207(1); § 2–207(3). Thus, this approach gives the offeree some protection. While it is laudible for business persons to read the fine print and boilerplate provisions in exchanged forms, there is nothing in § 2–207 mandating such careful consideration. The provision seems drafted with a recognition of the reality that merchants seldom review exchanged forms with the scrutiny of lawyers. The "knock-out" rule is therefore the best approach. Even if a term eliminated by operation of the "knock-out" rule is reintroduced by operation of the U.C.C.'s gap-filler provisions, such a result does not indicate a weakness of the approach. On the contrary, at least the reintroduced term has the merit of being a term that the U.C.C. draftpersons regarded as fair.

We now address the question of reverse and remand regarding Counts I and II. The result of this court's holding is that the district court erred in granting summary judgment against Daitom on Counts I and II of its complaint. Operation of the "knock-out" rule to conflicting terms results in the instant case in the conflicting terms in the offer and acceptance regarding the period of limitations and applicable warranties cancelling. In the absence of any evidence of course of performance, course of dealing, or usage of trade providing the missing terms, §§ 2–725(1), 2–313, 2–314, 2–315 may operate to supply a four-year period of limitations, an express warranty,[10] an implied warranty of merchantability, and an implied warranty of fitness for a particular purpose, respectively. The ruling of the district court on Counts I and II does not invite this kind of a broad inquiry, and thus, we must recognize the superiority in terms of justice of the "knock-out" rule. Consequently, the ruling of the district court on Counts I and II must be reversed and the matter remanded for trial consistent with this court's ruling.

* * *

[The court held that there was no cause of action in tort where an allegedly defective product caused only economic loss.]

Accordingly, the district court correctly concluded that Daitom's requested damages are not recoverable in tort. The court's summary judgment ruling against Daitom on Count III, therefore, should be affirmed. As explained above, we reverse the trial court with respect to Counts I and II. The cause is remanded for further proceedings consistent with this opinion.

10. Daitom alleges that several letters from Pennwalt expressly warrantied the performance of the rotary dryers. *E.g.,* Pretrial Order, Record Volume II at 59, para. 12, 13, 14, 15.

BARRETT, CIRCUIT JUDGE, dissenting:

I respectfully dissent. Insofar as the issue of contract formation is concerned in this case, we are confronted with a "battle of the forms" case involving the interpretation and application of U.C.C. § 2–207. I would affirm.

Pennwalt's proposal of September 7, 1976, was an "offer." It was submitted to Daitom in response to solicitations initiated by Daitom and it contained specific terms relating to price, delivery dates, etc., and its terms were held "open" for Daitom's acceptance within 30 days. In my view, Daitom accepted the offer with its purchase order. That order repeated the quantity, model number, and price for the items as those terms appeared in the Pennwalt proposal and, by reference, it incorporated four pages of specifications attached to Pennwalt's proposal or "offer." The purchase order did contain some different and additional language from that contained in Pennwalt's proposal. However, the Code has rejected the old mirror image rule. Thus, I agree with the district court's finding/ruling that a contract was formed in the circumstances described.

I also agree with the district court's conclusion that the terms of Pennwalt's proposal constituted the "terms of the contract." I do not agree, as Daitom argues, that its "acceptance" was made "conditional" upon Pennwalt's assent to the additional/different terms set forth in Daitom's purchase order. The court correctly found no such *express* condition in Daitom's acceptance.

The "knock-out" rule should not, in my view, be reached in this case. It can be applied only if, as Daitom argues and the majority agrees, the "conflicting terms" cancel each other out. The "knock-out" rule does have substantial support in the law, but I do not believe it is relevant in this case because the *only* conflicting terms relate to the *scope* of the warranty. In this case, it is not an important consideration because, pursuant to the express time limitations contained in Pennwalt's "offer," Daitom lost its right to assert any warranty claim. There was no term in Daitom's purchase order in conflict with the express one-year limitation within which to bring warranty actions. I agree with the district court's reasoning in rejecting Daitom's contentions that the one-year limitation period should not apply because (1) the term failed of "its essential purpose" of providing Daitom with a limited remedy under U.C.C. § 2–719(2) and (2) the time-limit was tolled due to Pennwalt's alleged fraudulent concealment of the defect. I concur with the trial court's finding that Daitom made no showing that the one-year limitation period was unreasonable because of some act of Pennwalt. As to the fraudulent concealment allegation, the court properly observed that Daitom did not plead this claim with the particularity required and, further, that the alleged fraudulent acts were not independent of the alleged breaches proper.

Note
Terms on or in Containers

Suppose a buyer orders goods from a seller and the seller agrees to deliver them. Suppose, further, that the seller includes additional or different terms *on or in the packaging of the goods* and the buyer accepts the goods. Do the new terms become part of the contract? Does section 2–207 apply to this problem? The following two cases shed light on these questions.

HILL v. GATEWAY 2000

United States Court of Appeals, Seventh Circuit, 1997.
105 F.3d 1147.

EASTERBROOK, CIRCUIT JUDGE.

A customer picks up the phone, orders a computer, and gives a credit card number. Presently a box arrives, containing the computer and a list of terms, said to govern unless the customer returns the computer within 30 days. Are these terms effective as the parties' contract, or is the contract term-free because the order-taker did not read any terms over the phone and elicit the customer's assent?

One of the terms in the box containing a Gateway 2000 system was an arbitration clause. Rich and Enza Hill, the customers, kept the computer more than 30 days before complaining about its components and performance. They filed suit in federal court arguing, among other things, that the product's shortcomings make Gateway a racketeer (mail and wire fraud are said to be the predicate offenses), leading to treble damages under RICO for the Hills and a class of all other purchasers. Gateway asked the district court to enforce the arbitration clause; the judge refused, writing that "[t]he present record is insufficient to support a finding of a valid arbitration agreement between the parties or that the plaintiffs were given adequate notice of the arbitration clause." Gateway took an immediate appeal, as is its right. 9 U.S.C. § 16(a)(1)(A).

The Hills say that the arbitration clause did not stand out: they concede noticing the statement of terms but deny reading it closely enough to discover the agreement to arbitrate, and they ask us to conclude that they therefore may go to court. Yet an agreement to arbitrate must be enforced "save upon such grounds as exist at law or in equity for the revocation of any contract." 9 U.S.C. § 2. Doctor's Associates, Inc. v. Casarotto, 116 S.Ct. 1652, 134 L.Ed.2d 902 (1996), holds that this provision of the Federal Arbitration Act is inconsistent with any requirement that an arbitration clause be prominent. A contract need not be read to be effective; people who accept take the risk that the unread terms may in retrospect prove unwelcome. * * * Terms inside Gateway's box stand or fall together. If they constitute the parties' contract because the Hills had an opportunity to return the computer after reading them, then all must be enforced.

ProCD, Inc. v. Zeidenberg, 86 F.3d 1447 (7th Cir.1996), holds that terms inside a box of software bind consumers who use the software after an opportunity to read the terms and to reject them by returning the product. Likewise, Carnival Cruise Lines, Inc. v. Shute, 499 U.S. 585, 111 S.Ct. 1522, 113 L.Ed.2d 622 (1991), enforces a forum-selection clause that was included among three pages of terms attached to a cruise ship ticket. ProCD and Carnival Cruise Lines exemplify the many commercial transactions in which people pay for products with terms to follow; ProCD discusses others. 86 F.3d at 1451–52. The district court concluded in ProCD that the contract is formed when the consumer pays for the software; as a result, the court held, only terms known to the consumer at that moment are part of the contract, and provisos inside the box do not count. Although this is one way a contract could be formed, it is not the only way: "A vendor, as master of the offer, may invite acceptance by conduct, and may propose limitations on the kind of conduct that constitutes acceptance. A buyer may accept by performing the acts the vendor proposes to treat as acceptance." Id. at 1452. Gateway shipped computers with the same sort of accept-or-return offer ProCD made to users of its software. ProCD relied on the Uniform Commercial Code rather than any peculiarities of Wisconsin law; both Illinois and South Dakota, the two states whose law might govern relations between Gateway and the Hills, have adopted the UCC; neither side has pointed us to any atypical doctrines in those states that might be pertinent; ProCD therefore applies to this dispute.

Plaintiffs ask us to limit ProCD to software, but where's the sense in that? ProCD is about the law of contract, not the law of software. Payment preceding the revelation of full terms is common for air transportation, insurance, and many other endeavors. Practical considerations support allowing vendors to enclose the full legal terms with their products. Cashiers cannot be expected to read legal documents to customers before ringing up sales. If the staff at the other end of the phone for direct-sales operations such as Gateway's had to read the four-page statement of terms before taking the buyer's credit card number, the droning voice would anesthetize rather than enlighten many potential buyers. Others would hang up in a rage over the waste of their time. And oral recitation would not avoid customers' assertions (whether true or feigned) that the clerk did not read term X to them, or that they did not remember or understand it. Writing provides benefits for both sides of commercial transactions. Customers as a group are better off when vendors skip costly and ineffectual steps such as telephonic recitation, and use instead a simple approve-or-return device. Competent adults are bound by such documents, read or unread. For what little it is worth, we add that the box from Gateway was crammed with software. The computer came with an operating system, without which it was useful only as a boat anchor. See Digital Equipment Corp. v. Uniq Digital Technologies, Inc., 73 F.3d 756, 761 (7th Cir.1996). Gateway also included many application programs. So the Hills' effort to limit ProCD to software would not avail them factually, even if it were sound legally—which it is not.

For their second sally, the Hills contend that ProCD should be limited to executory contracts (to licenses in particular), and therefore does not apply because both parties' performance of this contract was complete when the box arrived at their home. This is legally and factually wrong: legally because the question at hand concerns the formation of the contract rather than its performance, and factually because both contracts were incompletely performed. ProCD did not depend on the fact that the seller characterized the transaction as a license rather than as a contract; we treated it as a contract for the sale of goods and reserved the question whether for other purposes a "license" characterization might be preferable. 86 F.3d at 1450. All debates about characterization to one side, the transaction in ProCD was no more executory than the one here: Zeidenberg paid for the software and walked out of the store with a box under his arm, so if arrival of the box with the product ends the time for revelation of contractual terms, then the time ended in ProCD before Zeidenberg opened the box. But of course ProCD had not completed performance with delivery of the box, and neither had Gateway. One element of the transaction was the warranty, which obliges sellers to fix defects in their products. The Hills have invoked Gateway's warranty and are not satisfied with its response, so they are not well positioned to say that Gateway's obligations were fulfilled when the motor carrier unloaded the box. What is more, both ProCD and Gateway promised to help customers to use their products. Long-term service and information obligations are common in the computer business, on both hardware and software sides. Gateway offers "lifetime service" and has a round-the-clock telephone hotline to fulfil this promise. Some vendors spend more money helping customers use their products than on developing and manufacturing them. The document in Gateway's box includes promises of future performance that some consumers value highly; these promises bind Gateway just as the arbitration clause binds the Hills.

Next the Hills insist that ProCD is irrelevant because Zeidenberg was a "merchant" and they are not. Section 2–207(2) of the UCC, the infamous battle-of-the-forms section, states that "additional terms [following acceptance of an offer] are to be construed as proposals for addition to a contract. Between merchants such terms become part of the contract unless ...". Plaintiffs tell us that ProCD came out as it did only because Zeidenberg was a "merchant" and the terms inside ProCD's box were not excluded by the "unless" clause. This argument pays scant attention to the opinion in ProCD, which concluded that, when there is only one form, "sec. 2–207 is irrelevant." 86 F.3d at 1452. The question in ProCD was not whether terms were added to a contract after its formation, but how and when the contract was formed—in particular, whether a vendor may propose that a contract of sale be formed, not in the store (or over the phone) with the payment of money or a general "send me the product," but after the customer has had a chance to inspect both the item and the terms. ProCD answers "yes," for merchants and consumers alike. * * *

At oral argument the Hills propounded still another distinction: the box containing ProCD's software displayed a notice that additional terms were within, while the box containing Gateway's computer did not. The difference is functional, not legal. Consumers browsing the aisles of a store can look at the box, and if they are unwilling to deal with the prospect of additional terms can leave the box alone, avoiding the transactions costs of returning the package after reviewing its contents. Gateway's box, by contrast, is just a shipping carton; it is not on display anywhere. Its function is to protect the product during transit, and the information on its sides is for the use of handlers rather than would-be purchasers.

Perhaps the Hills would have had a better argument if they were first alerted to the bundling of hardware and legal-ware after opening the box and wanted to return the computer in order to avoid disagreeable terms, but were dissuaded by the expense of shipping. What the remedy would be in such a case—could it exceed the shipping charges?—is an interesting question, but one that need not detain us because the Hills knew before they ordered the computer that the carton would include some important terms, and they did not seek to discover these in advance. Gateway's ads state that their products come with limited warranties and lifetime support. How limited was the warranty—30 days, with service contingent on shipping the computer back, or five years, with free onsite service? What sort of support was offered? Shoppers have three principal ways to discover these things. First, they can ask the vendor to send a copy before deciding whether to buy. The Magnuson–Moss Warranty Act requires firms to distribute their warranty terms on request, 15 U.S.C. § 2302(b)(1)(A); the Hills do not contend that Gateway would have refused to enclose the remaining terms too. Concealment would be bad for business, scaring some customers away and leading to excess returns from others. Second, shoppers can consult public sources (computer magazines, the Web sites of vendors) that may contain this information. Third, they may inspect the documents after the product's delivery. Like Zeidenberg, the Hills took the third option. By keeping the computer beyond 30 days, the Hills accepted Gateway's offer, including the arbitration clause.

* * * The decision of the district court is vacated, and this case is remanded with instructions to compel the Hills to submit their dispute to arbitration.

STEP–SAVER DATA SYSTEMS, INC. v. WYSE TECHNOLOGY, INC., 939 F.2d 91 (3d Cir. 1991). [Step–Saver purchased computer software from The Software Link, Inc. (TSL). Step–Saver brought an action against TSL for breach of warranty when the software developed problems. One issue was whether the disclaimer of warranties and limitation of remedies clauses *printed on the package containing the software* constituted a term of the parties' agreement.]

WISDOM, Circuit Judge:

* * *

Step–Saver would typically purchase copies of the program in the following manner. First, Step–Saver would telephone TSL and place an order. (Step–Saver would typically order twenty copies of the program at a time.) TSL would accept the order and promise, while on the telephone, to ship the goods promptly. After the telephone order, Step–Saver would send a purchase order, detailing the items to be purchased, their price, and shipping and payment terms. TSL would ship the order promptly, along with an invoice. The invoice would contain terms essentially identical with those on Step–Saver's purchase order: price, quantity, and shipping and payment terms. No reference was made during the telephone calls, or on either the purchase orders or the invoices with regard to a disclaimer of any warranties.

Printed on the package of each copy of the program, however, would be a copy of the box-top license. The box-top license contains five terms relevant to this action:

(1) The box-top license provides that the customer has not purchased the software itself, but has merely obtained a personal, non-transferable license to use the program.

(2) The box-top license, in detail and at some length, disclaims all express and implied warranties except for a warranty that the disks contained in the box are free from defects.

(3) The box-top license provides that the sole remedy available to a purchaser of the program is to return a defective disk for replacement; the license excludes any liability for damages, direct or consequential, caused by the use of the program.

(4) The box-top license contains an integration clause, which provides that the box-top license is the final and complete expression of the terms of the parties's agreement.

(5) The box-top license states: "Opening this package indicates your acceptance of these terms and conditions. If you do not agree with them, you should promptly return the package unopened to the person from whom you purchased it within fifteen days from date of purchase and your money will be refunded to you by that person."

acceptance portion of boxtop

The district court, without much discussion, held, as a matter of law, that the box-top license was the final and complete expression of the terms of the parties's agreement. Because the district court decided the questions of contract formation and interpretation as issues of law, we review the district court's resolution of these questions de novo.

Step–Saver contends that the contract for each copy of the program was formed when TSL agreed, on the telephone, to ship the copy at the agreed price. The box-top license, argues Step–Saver, was a material alteration to the parties's contract which did not become a part of the contract under UCC § 2–207. * * *

TSL argues that the contract between TSL and Step–Saver did not come into existence until Step–Saver received the program, saw the terms of the license, and opened the program packaging. TSL contends that too many material terms were omitted from the telephone discussion for that discussion to establish a contract for the software. Second, TSL contends that its acceptance of Step–Saver's telephone offer was conditioned on Step–Saver's acceptance of the terms of the box-top license. Therefore, TSL argues, it did not accept Step–Saver's telephone offer. * * *

* * * Finding that UCC § 2–207 best governs our resolution of the effect of the box-top license, we then consider whether, under UCC § 2–207, the terms of the box-top license were incorporated into the parties's agreement.

A.   Does UCC § 2–207 Govern the Analysis?

As a basic principle, we agree with Step–Saver that UCC § 2–207 governs our analysis. We see no need to parse the parties's various actions to decide exactly when the parties formed a contract. TSL has shipped the product, and Step–Saver has accepted and paid for each copy of the program. The parties' performance demonstrates the existence of a contract. The dispute is, therefore, not over the existence of a contract, but the nature of its terms. When the parties's conduct establishes a contract, but the parties have failed to adopt expressly a particular writing as the terms of their agreement, and the writings exchanged by the parties do not agree, UCC § 2–207 determines the terms of the contract.

* * * It is undisputed that Step–Saver never expressly agreed to the terms of the box-top license, either as a final expression of, or a modification to, the parties's agreement. In fact, Barry Greebel, the President of Step–Saver, testified without dispute that he objected to the terms of the box-top license as applied to Step–Saver. In the absence of evidence demonstrating an express intent to adopt a writing as a final expression of, or a modification to, an earlier agreement, we find UCC § 2–207 to provide the appropriate legal rules for determining whether such an intent can be inferred from continuing

with the contract after receiving a writing containing additional or different terms.

* * *

The reasons that led to * * * the adoption of section 2–207, apply fully in this case. TSL never mentioned during the parties's negotiations leading to the purchase of the programs, nor did it, at any time, obtain Step–Saver's express assent to, the terms of the box-top license. Instead, TSL contented itself with attaching the terms to the packaging of the software, even though those terms differed substantially from those previously discussed by the parties. Thus, the box-top license, in this case, is best seen as one more form in a battle of forms, and the question of whether Step–Saver has agreed to be bound by the terms of the box-top license is best resolved by applying the legal principles detailed in section 2–207.

[The court went on to find that the contract was sufficiently definite without the terms provided by the box-top license and that term 5 in the box-top license ("opening this product indicates your acceptance of these terms") did not constitute a "conditional acceptance" under section 2–207(1) because the clause did not "clearly express [TSL's] unwillingness to proceed with the transactions unless its additional terms were incorporated into the parties' agreement." The court therefore held that "the box-top license should have been treated as a written confirmation containing additional terms. Because the warranty disclaimer and limitation of remedies terms would materially alter the parties' agreement, these terms did not become a part of the parties' agreement."]

Note
The Battle of the Forms Under Amended Article 2

Section 2–207 of the 2000 Amendments to the Uniform Commercial Code attempted to eliminate ambiguities and resolve issues. Did the drafters succeed? (At the time of publication of this book, no state had enacted the 2000 amendments.)

Section 2–207. Terms of Contract; Effect of Confirmation

* * * [I]f (i) conduct by both parties recognizes the existence of a contract although their records do not otherwise establish a contract, (ii) a contract is formed by an offer and acceptance, or (iii) a contract formed in any manner is confirmed by a record which contains terms additional to or different from those in the contract being confirmed, the terms of the contract are:

(a) terms that appear in the records of both parties;

(b) terms, whether in a record or not, to which both parties agree; and

(c) terms supplied or incorporated under any provision of this Act.

CONVENTION ON CONTRACTS FOR THE INTERNATIONAL SALE OF GOODS.
Article 19

(1) A reply to an offer which purports to be an acceptance but contains additions, limitations or other modifications is a rejection of the offer and constitutes a counter-offer.

(2) However, a reply to an offer which purports to be an acceptance but contains additional or different terms which do not materially alter the terms of the offer constitutes an acceptance, unless the offeror, without undue delay, objects orally to the discrepancy or dispatches a notice to that effect. If he does not so object, the terms of the contract are the terms of the offer with the modifications contained in the acceptance.

(3) Additional or different terms relating, among other things, to the price, payment, quality and quantity of the goods, place and time of delivery, extent of one party's liability to the other or the settlement of disputes are considered to alter the terms of the offer materially.

*

Chapter Five

POLICING AGREEMENTS
AND PROMISES

*The most striking feature of
nineteenth century contract theory is
its narrow scope of social duty. In
our own century, we have witnessed
a socialization of contract.*

GILMORE

*A legal order can indeed be
characterized by the agreements
which it does or does not enforce.*

WEBER

SECTION ONE: POLICING DOCTRINES
AND THE ROLE OF LAWYERS

When the parties satisfy the requirements of a theory of obligation, prima facie duties arise. But a party with such a duty may have one or more defenses, and thus ultimately owe no duty at all (or only a lesser duty). Such defenses may be grouped into two broad categories: (1) those arising pursuant to "policing doctrines"—defenses involving either grossly unfair terms or overreaching by one party at the bargaining or promising stage (or both), and (2) other full or partial defenses such as those based on changed circumstances after making an agreement or promise.

In this chapter, we study only those defenses arising pursuant to policing doctrines. (We study other defenses in Chapters Seven through Nine). We focus mainly on policing doctrines that generate defenses to prima facie duties arising under an agreement with consideration, because courts most often apply these doctrines in this context.

Policing doctrines fall into two basic categories: those addressed to the existence and quality of assent, and those concerned with the content of the agreement or promise. Assent oriented defenses such as duress, misrepresentation, and nondisclosure, if successful, show the lack of a valid agreement or promise. A buyer of a briefcase, for example, can invoke the defense of misrepresentation if the buyer can show that the seller claimed the briefcase was genuine leather when it was actually imitation. Although the buyer did not agree to purchase an imitation leather case, contract law commonly treats the buyer as having incurred a prima facie duty to pay, a duty the buyer can defeat by showing a misrepresentation. As Professor H.L.A. Hart once observed:

When the student has learnt that * * * there are positive conditions required for the existence of a valid contract, i.e. at least two *parties,* an *offer* by one, *acceptance* by the other, a *memorandum* in writing in some cases and *consideration,* his understanding of the legal concept of a contract is still incomplete, and remains so even if he has learnt the lawyers' technique for the interpretation of the technical but still vague terms, "offer," "acceptance," "memorandum," "consideration." For these conditions, although necessary, are not always sufficient and he has still to learn what can *defeat* a claim that there is a valid contract, even though all these conditions are satisfied. That is the student has still to learn what can follow on the word "unless," which should accompany the statement of these conditions.[a]

Other policing defenses focus on the substantive content of an agreement or promise rather than on the quality of assent. For an extreme example, consider a builder who agrees that the owner can cut off the builder's toes if he does not finish construction of a house by a certain date. Obviously the courts will refuse to enforce this term. Doctrines such as inequality of the exchange, public policy, mutuality of obligation and substantive unconscionability all focus on the substantive terms of the exchange.

Today, in addition to case law, numerous statutes set forth policing doctrines. For example, section 2–302 of the Uniform Commercial Code authorizes courts to police for unconscionability agreements for the sale of goods. The Code also includes other provisions designed to protect parties from overreaching, which provisions are not variable by agreement. For example, section 2–316(2) provides that a disclaimer of the warranty of merchantability must include the term merchantability. Professor Rudolf Schlesinger once wrote of the Code drafting project in these terms:

> The core * * * task is to determine the relatively few rules which are *not* subject to change by agreement, the rules which are designed to stake out the necessary minimum area of protection for parties whose bargaining power is inferior.[b]

Policing doctrines sometimes generate affirmative claims for damages, as well as serve as defenses. For example, a misrepresentation may not only provide a defense to a breach of contract claim, but may also generate a cause of action for damages in tort.

We explore various themes in this chapter. First, the lawyer must understand the relationship between policing doctrines and the principle of freedom of contract. Professor Friedrich Kessler discussed freedom of contract in these terms:

> With the development of a free enterprise system based on an unheard of division of labor, capitalistic society needed a highly elastic legal institution to safeguard the exchange of goods and services on the market. Common law lawyers, responding to this social need, transformed "contract" from the clumsy institution that it was in the sixteenth century into a tool of almost unlimited usefulness and pliability. Contract

a. H.L.A. Hart, The Ascription of Responsibility and Rights, in Logic and Language 148 (A. Flew ed. 1951).

b. Schlesinger, The Uniform Commercial Code in the Light of Comparative Law, 1 Inter–Am.L.Rev. 11, 33 (1959).

thus became the indispensable instrument of the enterpriser, enabling him to go about his affairs in a rational way. Rational behavior within the context of our culture is only possible if agreements will be respected. * * *

Under a free enterprise system rationality of the law of contracts has still another aspect. To keep pace with the constant widening of the market the legal system has to place at the disposal of the members of the community an ever increasing number of typical business transactions and regulate their consequences. But the law cannot possibly anticipate the content of an infinite number of atypical transactions into which members of the community may need to enter. Society, therefore, has to give the parties freedom of contract; to accommodate the business community the ceremony necessary to vouch for the deliberate nature of a transaction has to be reduced to the absolute minimum. Furthermore, the rules of the common law of contract have to remain *Jus dispositivum*—to use the phrase of the Romans; that is, their application has to depend on the intention of the parties or on their neglect to rule otherwise. (If parties to a contract have failed to regulate its consequences in their own way, they will be supposed to have intended the consequences envisaged by the common law.) Beyond that the law cannot go. It has to delegate legislation to the contracting parties. As far as they are concerned, the law of contract has to be of their own making.

Thus freedom of contract does not commend itself for moral reasons only; it is also an eminently practical principle. It is the inevitable counterpart of a free enterprise system. As a result, our legal lore of contracts reflects a proud spirit of individualism and of *laissez faire*. This is particularly true for the axioms and rules dealing with the formation and interpretation of contracts, the genuineness and reality of consent. Contract—the language of the cases tells us—is a private affair and not a social institution. The judicial system, therefore, provides only for their interpretation, but the courts cannot make contracts for the parties. There is no contract without assent, but once the objective manifestations of assent are present, their author is bound. * * * Either party is supposed to look out for his own interests and his own protection. Oppressive bargains can be avoided by careful shopping around. Everyone has complete freedom of choice with regard to his partner in contract, and the privity-of-contract principle respects the exclusiveness of this choice. Since a contract is the result of the free bargaining of parties who are brought together by the play of the market and who meet each other on a footing of social and approximate economic equality, there is no danger that freedom of contract will be a threat to the social order as a whole. Influenced by this optimistic creed, courts are extremely hesitant to declare contracts void as against public policy "because if there is one thing which more than another public policy requires it is that men of full age and competent understanding shall have the utmost liberty of contracting, and that their contracts when entered into freely and voluntarily shall be held sacred and shall be enforced by Courts of justice."[c]

c. Kessler, Contracts of Adhesion—Some Thoughts About Freedom of Contract, 43 Co- lum.L.Rev. 629, 629–31 (1943).

Policing doctrines define the boundaries of freedom of contract. If the parties in our earlier example actually agreed to cut off the builder's toes for late performance, why should a court refuse to enforce this agreement? After all, freedom of contract includes freedom not to contract, and the builder did not have to agree to such a term. Of course, such an agreement is abhorrent, and the courts will not enforce it. To consider a less extreme example, what if the penalty for late performance were only a sum of money out of proportion to the harm caused? Should *this* penalty be enforced? We saw in Chapter Three that courts will not enforce penalty claims either. Yet vast scope remains for the exercise of contractual freedom, and one challenge for the lawyer is to draw the often fine line between what is permissible and what is not.

Another theme of this chapter is that courts are mindful of the interplay between factors that may diminish the quality of assent on the one hand and the possibly objectionable character of the *content* of the agreement on the other. May a court bar enforcement of a contract solely on the basis of bargaining improprieties, or must the exchange itself be substantively objectionable as well? Conversely, in the absence of bargaining unfairness, may a court refuse to enforce terms based on substantive objections alone? We have already suggested that some policing doctrines focus primarily on the quality of assent and others primarily on the resulting terms, but the two problems are often closely related. If an agreement really calls for toe amputation in the event performance is delayed, it is likely that something was wrong with the bargaining process as well!

A further theme for study relates to the objective theory of "mutual assent" studied in Chapter Four. Except in the field of insurance contracts and in relation to certain form-pad transactions, most courts today generally adhere to the common law doctrine that a party who signs a contract, understandable to a reasonable person, is bound by its terms regardless of whether he or she read or understood those terms. By signing the agreement, a party manifests assent to the agreement. This so-called "duty to read" rule has been explained in the following way:

> If A sends an offer to B who, without opening it and without suspecting that it is an offer, decides to confuse A by sending a letter which states "I accept," there is a contract because A reasonably believed that B assented to the deal. It is not important to decide whether B has acted intentionally or negligently, because under the objective theory of contracts a party is bound by the impression he reasonably creates. The same principle supplies the basic rule relating to questions of duty to read: a party who signs an instrument manifests assent to it and may not later complain that he did not read the instrument or that he did not understand its contents. A leading case has stated that "one having the capacity to understand a written document who reads it, or, without reading it or having it read to him, signs it, is bound by his signature." The feeling is that no one could rely on a signed document if the other party could avoid the transaction by saying that he had not read or did not understand the writing.

> The same rule applies even without a signature if the acceptance of a document which purports to be a contract implies assent to its terms.

Thus, for example, the acceptance of documents such as bills of lading, passenger tickets, insurance policies, bank books and warehouse receipts may give rise to contracts based upon the provisions contained therein.[d]

Of course, if a party was the victim of fraud, or was unfairly induced to sign an agreement, or if certain terms of the agreement were not truly understandable, courts usually have no difficulty finding an exception to the "duty to read." But the line between cases falling under the duty and those qualifying for exceptional treatment may be difficult to draw. Is a poor consumer with limited education bound to a complex clause the consumer has not read that disclaims or excludes all warranties concerning the quality of the goods? How does a court differentiate between lawful market pressure and unfair coercion? When is a written agreement understandable and when not?

A final theme for study is that courts apply policing doctrines in light of the nature of the transaction involved. For example, the problem of policing fully-negotiated agreements is very different from policing standardized form contracts. And policing a transaction between a merchant and a consumer is very different from policing between two business entities. Courts also apply policing doctrines in light of the remedy sought by the aggrieved party. For example, we will see that a court's policing response may differ dramatically depending on whether a party seeks the return of money, or damages, or the equitable remedy of specific performance, etc.

Policing doctrines are important to the lawyer as planner, drafter, counselor, negotiator and litigator. As we will see, by careful planning and drafting the lawyer can greatly reduce the risk that policing doctrines will be invoked adversely. For example, by determining prior to contracting whether a particular remedy for breach is enforceable, lawyers can help contracting parties avoid litigation over the issue later. In fulfilling this planning role, the lawyer often must identify and apply various standards of fairness generally accepted in the community. Typically, the lawyer must study court decisions dealing with the scope and requirements of relevant policing doctrines. Often the lawyer must engage in careful fact finding about the nature of business practices. The lawyer must draw on similar sources of information to counsel clients who request information on the validity of proposed agreements, or on whether they can avoid agreements already made.

The lawyer must also utilize negotiating skills in dealing with policing problems. For example, a client may ask the lawyer to renegotiate the terms of an agreement in light of perceived problems with the original agreement. In Section Nine of this chapter, we briefly consider some of the special negotiating tactics required of the lawyer.

SECTION TWO: DURESS

STANDARD BOX CO. v. MUTUAL BISCUIT CO.

Court of Appeal, Third District, 1909.
10 Cal.App. 746, 103 P. 938.

[Defendant, Mutual Biscuit Co., had purchased a number of boxes pursuant to a 1905 contract with plaintiff, Standard Box Co. On September 1,

d. Calamari, Duty to Read—A Changing Concept, 43 Fordham L.Rev. 341, 341–42 (1974).

1905, plaintiff offered defendant an option, beginning on July 25, 1906, to buy boxes for one year at the 1905 price. Before defendant exercised the option, San Francisco suffered a serious earthquake on April 18, 1906, which resulted in a very short supply of boxes. On July 25, 1906, defendant sought to exercise the option. Plaintiff refused to sell further boxes to defendant at the 1905 price promised in the option, but was willing to sell at market value. Plaintiff knew that defendant sold bakery products, needed boxes to pack its goods, and would go out of business without the boxes, and that it was "practically impossible" for defendant to get boxes elsewhere. After objecting to plaintiff's refusal to sell at the 1905 price, defendant accepted some boxes on plaintiff's terms in October and November, 1906, but then refused to pay for some of them. Plaintiff brought an action for the price of those boxes. Defendant counterclaimed in part to recover the excess paid for some boxes and in part for damages for plaintiff's refusal to deliver additional boxes at the 1905 price. Defendant appealed a jury verdict in favor of plaintiff.

The court first held that the defendant had not accepted the offered option within a reasonable time, so that by July 25, 1906, it had expired.]

Chipman, P.J.

* * *

As there were no contract relations between plaintiff and defendant by which defendant had any right to demand the merchandise, all considerations of contract obligations on the part of plaintiff must be eliminated from the case. When, therefore, defendant solicited the goods, it stood to plaintiff as a stranger seeking to make purchases. It was told the prices it must pay, and the evidence was, and it is not alleged otherwise, that these prices were the market rates charged to other customers. However pressing defendant's need and whatever consequences to its trade should it fail to get the articles, plaintiff had a clear right to make its own prices and having made them, and defendant having accepted the goods under the agreement then made, its action, it seems to us, was voluntary as was its subsequent payment for the goods. Defendant, in fact, when its averments are reduced to their last analysis, alleged no more than that plaintiff refused to recognize the existence of any contract, demanded the current market prices, and that in order to secure the much needed articles defendant paid to plaintiff the higher price demanded. We fail to discover in the transaction the elements of duress.

* * *

* * * As was said in Phelan v. San Francisco, 120 Cal. 1, 52 P. 38: "There must be some compulsion or coercion which controls the conduct of the party making the payment, * * * some threatened exercise of power or authority over his person or property which can be avoided only by making the payment." In Huddleston v. Washington, the court said: "A payment is not to be regarded as compulsory unless made to emancipate the person or property from an actual and existing duress imposed upon it by the party to whom the money is paid." A threat to refuse performance of a contract cannot be made the predicate of legal duress. * * * In Cable v. Foley, 45 Minn. 421,

Cable v Folly

47 N.W. 1135, certain contracts were sought to be avoided as having been executed under duress. The evidence offered for that purpose, said the court, "amounted to no more than that, the plaintiff being without means to pay his men, the defendants refused to pay what was then due him, unless he executed the contracts. The mere threat to withhold from a party a legal right, which he has an adequate remedy to enforce, is not, in the eyes of the law, duress; certainly not such as will avoid the execution of a contract." Defendant's duty here was to seek aid of the courts to enforce his rights under the contract. He could not receive the goods under the terms upon which they were delivered, afterwards pay for them, and then claim that the payment was compulsory, and recover the difference between the price thus paid and the prices mentioned in the contract. The payment must be regarded as voluntary. Regan v. Baldwin, 126 Mass. 485, 30 Am.Rep. 689.

Appellant says that it seeks relief "on the line of the complaint" in Rowland v. Watson, 4 Cal.App. 476, 88 Pac. 495. The circumstances there were very different from the facts here, and that case furnishes no guide for us here. Burke v. Gould, 105 Cal. 277, 38 Pac. 733, is cited. Without stating the facts in that case, suffice it to quote from the opinion: "The unvarying principle of them all [the cited cases] is that by the performance or threat to perform some unlawful act whereby plaintiff will suffer loss the defendant has induced the plaintiff, under circumstances sufficient to control the action of a reasonable man, to pay money which he otherwise would not have paid." The court then proceeds to show that all that defendant threatened was to foreclose the mortgage which plaintiff had executed, and that this was not an unlawful act; that it was the exercise of a right which the law conferred upon him, and was neither in law nor in morals reprehensible. We fail to see how this case can avail defendant. Here there were no contractual relations, as we have held, and plaintiff did no more than to require defendant to pay for the merchandise its market value. Refusing to sell more goods unless defendant would pay for what it had bought was but an act of common business prudence. There was absolutely nothing unlawful in plaintiff's action in the matter. * * * Conceding that the courts recognize what may be termed moral duress under some circumstances, there is always some element of illegality in the demand complained of, some denial of a right, some unfounded claim, some extortion, as was said by Justice Cooley in Hackley v. Headley, 45 Mich. 569, 8 N.W. 511, "as a condition to the exercise by the party of a legal right." Here defendant had no legal right to demand the goods at his own prices or at all for that matter. On the contrary, plaintiff had the legal right to fix the price upon his own goods. It was no concern of plaintiff that defendant could not get the goods elsewhere. Plaintiff was under no obligation to see that defendant's business was safeguarded. It is not pretended that defendant was treated differently from other customers of plaintiff's or that more than market rates were charged for the goods or that those rates were excessive or burdensome.

* * *

The order is affirmed.

MACHINERY HAULING, INC. v. STEEL OF WEST VIRGINIA, 181 W.Va. 694, 384 S.E.2d 139 (1989). [Plaintiff, Machinery Hauling, a freight transport-

[handwritten top margin: Machine Hauling transported Steel's Steel to 3rd party → 3rd party refused directive.]

er, contracted to transport defendant Steel's steel product to a third party, who rightfully rejected it for defects. Steel instructed Machinery Hauling to pay Steel $31,000, the price of the undelivered product, "or else [Steel] would cease to do business with the plaintiff." Machinery Hauling refused.]

MILLER, JUSTICE: *[handwritten: NO DURESS]*

While we recognize the concept of business or economic duress, we do not find it exists in this case. There was no continuing contract between the plaintiff and the defendants. Thus, the demand by the defendants that the plaintiff pay $31,000 for the defective steel was not coupled with a threat to terminate an existing contract. Furthermore, the plaintiff did not accede to the defendants' demand and pay over the money.

The plaintiff's claim, stripped to its essentials, is that it has been deprived of its future prospects of doing business with the defendants. However, this future expectancy is not a legal right on which the plaintiff can anchor a claim of economic duress. * * *

Finally, there appears to be general acknowledgement that duress is not shown because one party to the contract has driven a hard bargain or that market or other conditions now make the contract more difficult to perform by one of the parties or that financial circumstances may have caused one party to make concessions. * * *

The questions certified to us by the Cabell County Circuit Court are, therefore, answered, and this case is dismissed from the docket.

DALZELL, DURESS BY ECONOMIC PRESSURE I

20 N.C.L.Rev. 237, 237 (1942).

Some economic pressures have for centuries been treated in our courts as requiring restraint, but for the most part our habitual Anglo–Saxon individualism has been in control of the common law, so as to make any such curb exceptional. We have been proud of our "freedom of contract," confident that the maximum of social progress will result from encouragement of each man's initiative and ambition by giving him the right to use his economic powers to the full. One of the most frequently and emphatically declared axioms of contract law is that our courts are not concerned with the equivalence of the consideration given for a promise. But doubts are growing of late years.

* * *

We are not yet ready to allow the idea of individual initiative to be completely swallowed up in the "wave of the future," as has been done in some recently organized societies, but some limitation on economic duress seems inevitable.

S.P. DUNHAM & COMPANY v. KUDRA

Superior Court of New Jersey, Appellate Division, 1957.
44 N.J.Super. 565, 131 A.2d 306.

CLAPP, S.J.A.D.

Plaintiff, S.P. Dunham & Company, sued defendants for the restitution of $3,232.55 paid them allegedly under business compulsion. The trial court,

[handwritten right margin: no continuing contracting; no threat to terminate existing; did not accede]

sitting without a jury, gave judgment for the plaintiff in the amount stated. Defendants appeal.

Plaintiff has for over a century operated a department store in Trenton. For some three years it had leased its fur department to a concessionaire, Elmer A. Hurwitz & Co., but the business of the department was so conducted as to appear to customers to have been a part of plaintiff's operations. During these three years fur coats, left by customers with Hurwitz for storage and cleaning were turned over by him to the defendants Kudra who stored and cleaned them pursuant to an agreement with Hurwitz. Plaintiff knew something of Hurwitz' arrangement with Kudra.

In November 1955 Hurwitz went bankrupt and Dunham thereupon cancelled his concession. However, winter was coming on, and Dunham's customers wanted their coats. On November 23, 1955 Kudra had possession of 412 garments, on which Hurwitz owed Kudra $622.50. This sum plaintiff offered to pay Kudra in return for the garments. But Hurwitz owed Kudra an additional $3,232.55 with respect to other garments that had been delivered back to customers during the preceding two years; and on November 23, Kudra announced that the 412 coats would not be turned over unless plaintiff paid the total sum of $3,855.05. One of the owners of Dunham, much upset, asked Kudra for a few days to think the matter over and consult with counsel. Apparently at about that time, the temperature had dropped to 15°; many substantial customers of the store demanded their coats. When both owners of Dunham then sought to negotiate further, Kudra came up with the proposition that it would deliver the garments directly to plaintiff's customers without charge to the plaintiff, if plaintiff would turn over their names; not only would plaintiff thus place the names of customers in the hands of a competitor in the fur business, but Kudra apparently purposed to bill them directly for Hurwitz' total charges on the coats, which totalled some $4,000. Plaintiff flatly rejected this proposition and on November 29 yielded to Kudra's original demand, paying the $3,855.05. Allegedly, three days later it sought the return of $3,232.55 and on December 15 commenced this action.

Plaintiff seeks the restitution of the $3,232.55 on the ground that the money was paid to defendants, not voluntarily, but under a species of duress, sometimes known as "business compulsion." It claims that defendants, taking advantage of its plight, sought to squeeze it between their own improper demands and the complaints of its customers. Indeed, the predicament in which it was placed was so embarrassing a matter that one of the owners of the store, apprehensive of a serious impairment in its good will, himself spent hours in the fur department talking to customers. There is little doubt but that the pressure which defendants brought to bear upon the plaintiff was an inducing (Restatement, Contracts, § 492f), indeed the sole cause of its payment of the $3,232.55.

A slight examination of the subject will demonstrate that the law of duress is in the process of development. * * * Thus in New Jersey, after some conflicting decisions on the point, our courts have finally rejected the objective test, namely, that duress is irremediable unless it is of such severity as to overcome the will of a person of ordinary firmness; the test now is simply this—has the person complaining been constrained to do what he otherwise would not have done? * * *

Apropos of this, attention may be directed to a point brought up by the respondent. It has repeatedly been held in our cases that a person cannot claim to have made a payment under duress if, before he made the payment, there was available to him an immediate and adequate remedy in the courts to test or resist it. * * * This harsh rule has been rejected by the Restatement, Contracts, § 493, Illustrations 8, 9, and also by Williston. Williston points out that

> "the only reason which could be given for such a rule is that a threat of this sort should not terrify a person of" ordinary firmness. "But, though such statements are still repeated, the rule is artificial and, so far as it would require a person threatened with injury necessarily to endure the injury because the law provides a remedy for it, cannot be accepted." § 1620, at p. 4529.

* * * Now that New Jersey has definitely repudiated the standard of "ordinary firmness," there may be little reason to retain the other rule; the criterion perhaps should be solely whether the will of the victim was really overborne. An attempt has been made to justify the rule stated, upon the ground that the person exerting the duress has relied on the payment made to him by the victim, and having relied, he should be protected. * * * But why should the law have such a tender regard for a wrongdoer? Relief by way of restitution puts no undue burden upon him; he is not subjected to damages for his wrong, but merely called upon to give back that which he forced from his victim. The court granting restitution should have an easy conscience in the matter.

However, we need not pass upon this more fundamental question. If we accept the rule as stated in our cases, we must still ask ourselves whether the plaintiff had a "complete and adequate remedy" * * * enabling it to recover the coats for its customers and avoid the payment of the $3,232.55. * * * [W]e come to plaintiff's third contention, namely, that there was no adequate remedy here through any form of litigation. Plaintiff, faced with the clamoring demands of its customers, plainly did not want it brought home to each of them at that juncture that its competitors, the defendants, were in fact attending to the storing and cleaning of her coat. We think a public suit at that time did not constitute adequate relief.

We turn now to defendants' principal argument, which seems to be that they should not be chargeable by plaintiff with "the duress * * * it itself had long ago prepared." They rely on the fact that plaintiff for three years during the summer months had lent Hurwitz money "in the neighborhood of $2,000, $1,500"; and they claim that, though these amounts were paid back in September each year, plaintiff should have known of Hurwitz' financial difficulties. The argument seems to be that plaintiff itself caused defendants to exert the duress. The point is without the slightest substance.

Next, defendants seem to argue, referring to the early common-law doctrine of "duress of goods," that under our present concepts of "business compulsion" redress could be had by the plaintiff here only if it had been compelled to pay out money in order to recover its own property. There is nothing to this point either. The law today does not take such a narrow view of the matter, if indeed it ever did.

[handwritten margin note: Δ's argument #3]

Further, defendants contend that the plaintiff cannot have been under duress since, for six days, it had an opportunity to deliberate and consult with its own counsel. These are matters which should be taken into account in determining whether in fact the plaintiff made the payment voluntarily and whether the pressure of defendants' demands still subsisted after deliberation and consultation; but they do not of themselves preclude relief. Restatement, Contracts, § 492, comment c.

Again it is urged that one person (Dunham) cannot claim to have been placed under duress if he pays money to the defendants for the relief of another person (i.e., its customers). We need not refer to the law on the subject, cf. Williston, supra, § 1621, because it is apparent that Dunham paid the $3,232.55 for the relief of itself from an injury to its own good will.

* * *

* * * [W]e might refer to the trial court's concluding remarks below: "it [defendant's conduct] is one of the things I prefer not to * * * have to live with in the community. I couldn't justify it."

* * *

Affirmed.

DALZELL, DURESS BY ECONOMIC PRESSURE I
20 N.C.L.Rev. 237, 238 (1942).

We have talked of contracts signed under duress as lacking "real consent." This seems to be a manner of speech rather than a reasoned conclusion. When I feel that I must choose between having a bullet lodged in my head and signing a contract, my desire to escape the bullet would hardly be described as unreal or merely apparent; and the signing of the contract is simply the expression of that fear of death. To call such a consent "unreal" is to characterize the normal human desire to continue alive as mere pretense. The father who pays a ransom to his daughter's kidnappers does so because he fears he will lose his daughter. Of the only two developments which he then foresees with assurance, his choice is for payment; and, *on the assumption on which he acts,* that he must choose between payment and tragedy, his choice is certainly an expression of the most genuine, heartfelt consent—and often a very happy consent indeed.

What we meant by calling such consent unreal, was that it would not have been given except for the unpleasant alternative.

RESTATEMENT (SECOND) OF CONTRACTS § 176.
When a Threat Is Improper

(1) A threat is improper if

(a) what is threatened is a crime or a tort, or the threat itself would be a crime or a tort if it resulted in obtaining property,

(b) what is threatened is a criminal prosecution,

(c) what is threatened is the use of civil process and the threat is made in bad faith, or

(d) the threat is a breach of the duty of good faith and fair dealing under a contract with the recipient.

(2) A threat is improper if the resulting exchange is not on fair terms, and

(a) the threatened act would harm the recipient and would not significantly benefit the party making the threat,

(b) the effectiveness of the threat in inducing the manifestation of assent is significantly increased by prior unfair dealing by the party making the threat, or

(c) what is threatened is otherwise a use of power for illegitimate ends.

DAWSON, ECONOMIC DURESS AND THE FAIR EXCHANGE IN FRENCH AND GERMAN LAW

11 Tul.L.Rev. 345, 345 (1937).

The system of "free" contract described by nineteenth century theory is now coming to be recognized as a world of fantasy, too orderly, too neatly contrived, and too harmonious to correspond with reality. As welcome fiction is slowly displaced by sober fact, the regime of "freedom" can be visualized as merely another system, more elaborate and more highly organized, for the exercise of economic pressure. With new vision has come a more conscious and sustained effort to select the forms of permissible pressure and to control the manner of its exercise. In law, as in politics, the control of economic power has emerged as the central problem of modern times.

M. TREBILCOCK, THE LIMITS OF FREEDOM OF CONTRACT

242–43 (1993).

Difficult questions arise as to when a transaction can be regarded as voluntary or, conversely, coerced. It has proven difficult to construct an autonomy-based theory of coercion without first constructing a moral baseline (or set of rights) for the party choosing to accept a proposal under constrained circumstances, against which the proposal can be evaluated. Similarly, difficulties arise in determining when a contracting party has sufficient information about the contract subject matter or future course of events affecting the value of the contract subject matter for a conclusion to be sustained that the choices in question were autonomous. Although contracting choices made with false information or in the absence of highly material information may, at one level, be regarded as non-autonomous, at another level the decision to forgo opportunities to acquire further information may itself be an autonomous choice. * * *

* * *

[I]t can be argued that a rich conception of individual autonomy entails not only a negative theory of liberty—that is, freedom from external constraint on the individual right of self-determination—but also a positive theory of liberty, which holds that an autonomous ability to choose one's own conception of the good life entails access to economic opportunities and resources that makes non-demeaning, self-fulfilling life choices a realistic possibility. * * * For example with respect to the question of coercion, it might be argued that deliberate exploitation by one party of another party's lack of choices to exact returns that exceed those normally realizable in a more competitive environment should be viewed as suspect.

Problem 5–1

In which of the following factual situations, if any, would you advise the party subject to the "pressure" that he or she could make out a case of duress?

A. The vendors at Yankee Stadium, realizing that they have a captive audience, mark up the cost of refreshments 200%. *No*

B. Vendors sell water in the middle of the desert for $50 per glass to persons literally "dying" of thirst. *Yes*

C. Gasoline stations during an oil supply shortage mark up the price of gasoline 200%. *No*

D. A supplier of construction materials, with knowledge that X has entered into a contract with Y to build a warehouse and that X cannot get supplies in time from anyone but the supplier, marks up the price 200%. *No*

similar to Standard box?

Note
Undue Influence

A policing doctrine related to duress is undue influence. Undue influence has been defined as "undue susceptibility" of one party and "excessive pressure" placed on that party by another. Olam v. Congress Mortg. Co., 68 F. Supp.2d 1110 (N.D. Cal. 1999). The pressure must be exerted by a person enjoying a special relationship with the victim that makes the victim especially susceptible to the pressure. For example, if a lawyer convinces an aged and infirm client to sign over his stocks to the lawyer, the "agreement" may be voidable by the client. Or, if a maternity home persuades an emotionally distraught mother of an illegitimate child to give up the child, the mother's agreement may be voidable. Methodist Mission Home v. NAB, 451 S.W.2d 539 (Tex.Civ.App.1970).

SECTION THREE: MISREPRESENTATION, CONCEALMENT, AND THE DUTY TO DISCLOSE

One contracting party has a duty not to mislead the other. But what are the parameters of that duty? Obviously one may not lie. But how do we differentiate "seller's talk," sometimes called "puffing" ("this is an A–1 Used Car") from misrepresentation ("this is genuine leather"). In addition, in what circumstances (if any) will remaining silent about known defects constitute an actionable wrong or a basis for rescission? When, in other words, does a duty to disclose arise?

BATES v. CASHMAN

Supreme Judicial Court of Massachusetts, 1918.
230 Mass. 167, 119 N.E. 663.

RUGG, C.J. This is a suit to recover for the breach of a written contract to buy the stocks and bonds of the Newburyport Cordage Company. The securities were the means by which to convey control of land with a factory and machinery. There is no controversy that the contract was made. The defendant contends that he was induced to sign it by such false representations by the plaintiff as release him from obligation to perform. This case was referred to a master. It is reserved upon his report with exceptions thereto and the pleadings. There is no report of evidence.

It has been found that during the negotiations preceding the contract the plaintiff represented that a right of way, which was a substantial factor of value in the real estate, was owned by the Newburyport Cordage Company and could not be interfered with. This representation was untrue. The plaintiff did not know that it was untrue. The defendant relied upon it and would not have signed the contract if he had known that it was false. A person seasonably may rescind a contract to which he has been induced to become a party in reliance upon false though innocent misrepresentations respecting a cognizable material fact made as of his own knowledge by the other party to the contract * * *.

* * *

Bill dismissed with costs.

RESTATEMENT (SECOND) OF TORTS § 552C.

Misrepresentation in Sale, Rental or Exchange Transaction

(1) One who, in a sale, rental or exchange transaction with another, makes a misrepresentation of a material fact for the purpose of inducing the other to act or to refrain from acting in reliance upon it, is subject to liability to the other for pecuniary loss caused to him by his justifiable reliance upon the misrepresentation, even though it is not made fraudulently or negligently.

(2) Damages recoverable under the rule stated in this section are limited to the difference between the value of what the other has parted with and the value of what he has received in the transaction.

GIBB v. CITICORP MORTGAGE, INC.

Supreme Court of Nebraska, 1994.
246 Neb. 355, 518 N.W.2d 910.

CAPORALE, J.

I. STATEMENT OF CASE

Through his operative petition, the plaintiff-appellant, Patrick B. Gibb, seeks, under a variety of theories, to recover damages resulting from the termite infestation of the house he purchased through an agent acting for the seller, the defendant-appellee, Citicorp Mortgage, Inc. After Citicorp successfully demurred, Gibb elected to stand on his pleading; the district court thereupon dismissed his action. Gibb then appealed to the Nebraska Court of Appeals, assigning the dismissal as error, claiming in effect that the district court erred in concluding he had failed to state a cause of action. We, on our own motion, removed the matter to this court in order to regulate the caseloads of the two appellate tribunals. We now reverse and remand for further proceedings.

* * *

III.   Factual Allegations

According to the operative petition, Citicorp acquired the house through the foreclosure of a mortgage when the mortgagee abandoned the property because of extensive termite infestation and damage and defaulted on his mortgage obligation. Citicorp's selling agent had been informed through a report of a termite service that the property in question was infested with termites and appeared to have extensive damage. The service recommended that a qualified building inspector assess the damage. However, Citicorp chose to ignore the recommendation and instead hired the service to treat the termites and "[shore] up" the visible damage to the house.

Prior to the purchase, Citicorp's selling agent showed Gibb a single area where termite damage had occurred and assured Gibb that this was the only termite-damaged area and that all necessary repairs and treatments had been made to eliminate the termite problem.

Although neither the agent nor Citicorp made any effort to determine the full extent of the damage, the agent knew that the nonvisible termite damage had not been repaired and that it was much greater than the visible evidence indicated; nonetheless, the agent represented that the damage had been repaired and the termite problem alleviated. Citicorp knew the agent's representations to be false but failed to repudiate them; rather, Citicorp and the agent concealed and suppressed all evidence of termite damage, failed to disclose that the termite damage extended beyond those areas said to be repaired, and concealed and suppressed the fact that the additional " 'wood destroying insect inspection' "required by the purchase agreement to be made at Gibb's cost had not in fact been obtained. In point of fact, at the closing of the transaction, Citicorp provided Gibb with a copy of a 5–month–old report prepared by the termite service after it had submitted its recommendation that the damage be assessed, which indicated that visible evidence of infestation was noted and proper control measures were performed.

The purchase agreement recited that the transaction was "based upon [Gibb's] personal inspection or investigation of the Property and not upon any representation or warranties of condition by [Citicorp] or [its] agent." The agreement further provided that the property was "sold strictly in 'AS IS' condition. [Citicorp] does not make any warranties regarding the condition of the property at the time of sale and thereafter."

Nonetheless, Gibb claims to have relied on the misrepresentations made to him and asserts he has suffered damage as a consequence.

IV.   Analysis

Gibb seeks recovery under any one of two fraud theories, a negligence theory, or a contract theory.

1. Fraud Theories

Gibb first avers he was deceived by the fraudulent misrepresentations and fraudulent concealment made by Citicorp through its agent.

(a) Fraudulent Misrepresentation

In order to maintain an action for fraudulent misrepresentation, the plaintiff must allege and prove the following elements: (1) that a representation was made; (2) that the representation was false; (3) that when made, the representation was known to be false or made recklessly without knowledge of its truth and as a positive assertion; (4) that it was made with the intention that the plaintiff should rely upon it; (5) that the plaintiff reasonably did so rely; and (6) that he or she suffered damage as a result. *Nielsen v. Adams,* 223 Neb. 262, 388 N.W.2d 840 (1986).

Gibb has pled all the essential elements for recovery based on fraudulent misrepresentation. He has claimed that Citicorp's selling agent represented that the only termite damage was the visible damage and further represented that all the necessary repairs and treatments had been made. Therefore, a representation was alleged. In addition, Gibb avers that the representation was false because the report from the termite service reveals extensive damage and recommends that a qualified building inspector assess the damage.

Moreover, it can reasonably be inferred that the representation was made with the intention that Gibb rely on it because it relates to a material fact, and Gibb asserts he did in fact rely on the misrepresentations and that he suffered damage as a consequence.

(b) Fraudulent Concealment

In order to maintain an action based on fraudulent concealment, the plaintiff must allege and prove the following elements: (1) that the defendant concealed or suppressed a material fact; (2) that the defendant had knowledge of this material fact; (3) that this material fact was not within the reasonably diligent attention, observation, and judgment of the plaintiff; (4) that the defendant suppressed or concealed this fact with the intention that the plaintiff be misled as to the true condition of the property; (5) that the plaintiff was reasonably so misled; and (6) that the plaintiff suffered damage as a result. *Nelson v. Cheney,* 224 Neb. 756, 401 N.W.2d 472 (1987).

Gibb's operative petition states sufficient facts to allege all the elements for recovery based on fraudulent concealment. He avers that Citicorp concealed or suppressed the fact that the termite damage was more extensive than the visible damage. In addition, by asserting that Citicorp's agent informed it of the termite service's initial report and recommendations, Gibb claims that Citicorp knew the extent of the damage.

Furthermore, Gibb alleges that the material facts regarding the termite damage were not within his diligent attention or observation because he was misled as to the true condition of the house.

Gibb also charges that Citicorp concealed the extent of the termite damage to intentionally mislead him as to the true condition of the house. In addition, the petition states that Gibb was misled and suffered damage as a result.

(c) Citicorp's Contentions

Notwithstanding that Gibb has pled all of the elements of those two bases of recovery, Citicorp asserts that where an agreement for the sale of real estate contains a disclaimer and an "as is" clause such as those present here, the seller should not be held liable for the fraudulent misrepresentations or concealments of its agent. Citicorp further urges that Gibb had as much access to the relevant information as did Citicorp.

(i) Effect of "As Is" and Disclaimer Clauses

In so arguing, Citicorp acknowledges that under our law, a principal may be liable for the fraudulent actions of its agent, *Corman v. Musselman,* 232 Neb. 159, 439 N.W.2d 781 (1989), but urges that we adopt the position of New York's highest court in *Danann Realty Corp. v. Harris,* 5 N.Y.2d 317, 157 N.E.2d 597, 184 N.Y.S.2d 599 (1959). Therein, the New York Court of Appeals held that a purchaser had no cause of action against a seller for false representation when the contract for the purchase of a lease contained disclaimer, "as is," and merger clauses as follows:

> "The Purchaser has examined the premises agreed to be sold and is familiar with the physical condition thereof. The Seller has not made and does not make any representations as to the physical condition, rents, leases, *expenses, operation* or any other matter or thing affecting or related to the aforesaid premises, except as herein specifically set forth, and the Purchaser hereby *expressly acknowledges that no such representations have been made, and the Purchaser further acknowledges that it has inspected the premises and agrees to take the premises 'as is'* * * * It is understood and agreed that all understandings and agreements heretofore had between the parties hereto are merged in this contract, which alone fully and completely expresses their agreement, *and that the same is entered into after full investigation, neither party relying upon any statement or representation,* not embodied in this contract. . . ."

(Emphasis in original.) *Danann Realty Corp.,* 5 N.Y.2d at 320, 157 N.E.2d at 598, 184 N.Y.S.2d at 601.

The *Danann Realty Corp.* purchaser nonetheless claimed that he had been induced to enter into a contract for the purchase of a lease by the sellers' false oral representations regarding the building's operating expenses. The purchaser sought to affirm the contract and recover damages for fraud.

The *Danann Realty Corp.* majority concluded that the specific disclaimer clause, in conjunction with the merger clause, declared that the parties did not rely on representations not embodied in the contract and thus prevented the purchaser from adducing parol evidence to establish otherwise, thereby destroying the purchaser's allegations of reliance.

However, on several occasions we have addressed whether a disclaimer clause within a contract will bar a purchaser's fraud-based claim. * * *

* * * In *Flakus v. Schug,* 213 Neb. 491, 494–95, 329 N.W.2d 859, 863 (1983), *overruled on other grounds, Nielsen v. Adams,* 223 Neb. 262, 388 N.W.2d 840 (1986), we emphasized:

> It is true that in discussing the elements of fraud we said a disclaimer clause is relevant in determining whether a claimant relied on a false

representation disclaimed in the clause. We also said, however, that the disclaimer is ineffective to preclude the trier of fact from considering whether fraud induced formation of the bargain.

We have also concluded that an "as is" clause does not necessarily bar a purchaser's fraud-based claim, writing in *Wolford v. Freeman*, 150 Neb. 537, 547, 35 N.W.2d 98, 103 (1948), that " '[a] provision that the buyer takes the article in the condition in which it is, or in other words, "as is," does not prevent fraudulent representations relied on by the buyer from constituting fraud....' " *[holding in wolford]*

Claiming fraud, the *Wolford* plaintiff sought to rescind a contract for the purchase of a house, which recited that he had " 'been advised as to settling of structure and is buying same as is.' "150 Neb. at 546, 35 N.W.2d at 101. He asserted that the vendor's agent represented that the cracks in the foundation of the house had been repaired and that the damage had been corrected, so that the purchaser should have no fear of further cracking.

After the purchaser took possession, the cracks in the foundation became progressively worse and eventually appeared in the outer walls and the foundation. The purchaser learned that the house had been built on filled ground, in violation of the city building code, and asserted the vendor knew the house had been built on filled ground, rendering the foundation faulty, yet had concealed those facts.

We determined that the purchaser was entitled to prevail unless the vendor was relieved by the "as is" clause. We then reasoned that while the clause disclosed the purchaser's knowledge of the cracking, it did not disclose or suggest the cause of that condition. We accordingly ruled that the clause did not bind the purchaser to buying a house with the undisclosed or concealed condition which caused the visible cracking. Thus, a clause that an article is taken in the condition in which it is, or in other words, "as is," is relevant in determining whether a claimant relied on a false representation concerning the condition of the article, but is not controlling. *[Rule from wolfad]*

In like fashion here, Gibb agreed to purchase a house with visible termite damage, which Citicorp's agent misrepresented as being the extent of the termite destruction. Like the purchaser in *Wolford*, Gibb was aware of the repair to the visible damage to the structure, but, according to his allegations, was unaware of the extent of the damage. Thus, just as the disclaimer does not necessarily prevent Gibb from stating causes of action for fraudulent misrepresentation or fraudulent concealment, neither does the "as is" clause, nor do the two clauses together prevent him from doing so. Under these circumstances, the question as to whether Gibb acted reasonably is one of fact.

(ii) Principal's Responsibility for Agent

[The court rejected Citicorp's argument that because the house was sold with a disclaimer and an "as is" clause, Gibb necessarily knew that Citicorp's agent had no authority to make any representations. Instead, the court held that such contract terms do not limit the scope of an agent's "ostensible authority."]

* * *

2. *Negligence Theory*

Gibb next asserts that Citicorp negligently misrepresented the situation, declaring that Citicorp, through its agent, failed to use reasonable care when he represented that the property was free of termites. Furthermore, Gibb charges that the representations by Citicorp's agent were false, that he relied upon the representations, and that as a result he suffered damage. And it can be inferred from the setting in which the transaction allegedly arose that both the agent and Citicorp had a pecuniary interest in it.

* * * [W]e, in St. Paul Fire & Marine Ins. Co. v. Touche Ross & Co., 244 Neb. 408, 507 N.W.2d 275 (1993), noted the position of Restatement (Second) of Torts § 552 (1977) regarding negligent misrepresentation as a basis of liability. Thereunder, liability for negligent misrepresentation is based upon the failure of the actor to exercise reasonable care or competence in supplying correct information. Id., § 552, comment a. Section 552 specifies at 126–27:

(1) One who, in the course of his business, profession or employment, or in any other transaction in which he has a pecuniary interest, supplies false information for the guidance of others in their business transactions, is subject to liability for pecuniary loss caused to them by their justifiable reliance upon the information, if he fails to exercise reasonable care or competence in obtaining or communicating the information.

* * * The Restatement further observes that the liability for negligent misrepresentation is more restricted than for fraudulent misrepresentation, explaining that the reason for the narrower scope of liability fixed for negligent misrepresentation is the difference between the obligations of honesty and of care.

Honesty requires only that the maker of a representation speak in good faith and without consciousness of a lack of any basis for belief in the truth or accuracy of what he says. * * * Any user of commercial information may reasonably expect the observance of this standard by a supplier of information to whom his use is reasonably foreseeable.

On the other hand, it does not follow that every user of commercial information may hold every maker to a duty of care. Unlike the duty of honesty, the duty of care to be observed in supplying information for use in commercial transactions implies an undertaking to observe a relative standard, which may be defined only in terms of the use to which the information will be put, weighed against the magnitude and probability of loss that might attend that use if the information proves to be incorrect.

§ 552, comment a. at 128. Therefore, the difference between fraudulent misrepresentation and negligent misrepresentation is the duty required in each claim. In fraudulent misrepresentation, one becomes liable for breaching the general duty of good faith or honesty. However, in a claim of negligent misrepresentation, one may become liable even though acting honestly and in good faith if one fails to exercise the level of care required under the circumstances.

* * *

We * * * specifically adopt the definition of the negligent misrepresentation cause of action found in § 552, supra.

As we have established * * * that a principal may be liable for the representations of its agent, it follows that Gibb's negligence theory does not fail merely because he alleges that Citicorp's liability arises from its agent's negligent misrepresentations.

The rule that a principal is liable for the contracts of its agent applies even though the agent, in contracting, acts in his or her own interests and adversely to the principal, where the party with whom the agent contracts has no knowledge of the agent's dereliction and is not cognizant of any fact charging him or her with knowledge thereof. The principal, having selected its representative and vested him or her with apparent authority, should be the loser in such case, and not the innocent party who relied thereon. Draemel v. Rufenacht, Bromagen & Hertz, Inc., 223 Neb. 645, 392 N.W.2d 759 (1986).

Other jurisdictions have recognized a purchaser's claim against a vendor based on the negligent misrepresentations of the vendor's agent. * * *

* * *

Thus, as was the case with respect to Gibb's fraud theories, the reasonableness of Gibb's reliance on the agent's misrepresentations under these circumstances is a factual question. *he does have a claim*

* * *

[The court also sustained Gibb's contract theory.]

V. JUDGMENT

For the foregoing reasons, the judgment of the district court is reversed and the cause remanded for further proceedings.

REVERSED AND REMANDED FOR FURTHER PROCEEDINGS.

Note
Damages for Fraudulent and Negligent Misrepresentation

According to sections 549 (damages for fraudulent misrepresentation) and 552B (damages for negligent misrepresentation) of the Restatement (Second) of Torts, the aggrieved party may recover the "difference between the value of what he has received" and the purchase price or other value given. In addition, the injured party can recover consequential damages due to detrimental reliance. Victims of fraudulent misrepresentations "in business transactions" (but not victims of negligent misrepresentations) can also recover the benefit of the bargain.

HOLCOMB v. HOFFSCHNEIDER

Supreme Court of Iowa, 1980.
297 N.W.2d 210.

UHLENHOPP, JUSTICE.

This appeal involves a claim [in tort for] fraudulent misrepresentations by a realtor regarding the number of acres in irregularly shaped real estate it sold * * *. A jury awarded the purchasers $6000 actual damages. The realtor appealed * * *.

The realtor contends in this appeal that the purchasers did not rely on any representations as to the size of the property and that because the purchasers knew the actual boundaries of the property they bought, they did not sustain damages.

* * *

We view the evidence in the light most favorable to the purchasers who prevailed before the jury. * * *

I. *Reliance.* Dorothea A. and John Hoffschneider listed their house and lots for sale with defendant C.B. Property Sales. The price was $65,000 and the size of the lots, numbers 6 and 7, was stated as 6.8 acres. Dean Olson, a salesman for C.B. Property, placed advertisements in two local newspapers on several days in May through July 1975. The ads stated the property contained six acres.

The purchasers, plaintiffs James R. and Jacquelyn Holcomb, first saw the property in July 1975. They attended an open house of the property hosted by Olson. Subsequently Olson walked the boundaries of the property with them. He also showed them the listing before they made their offer to buy, and stated at various times prior to the sale that he would guarantee the property contained at least 6.6 acres. Actually it contained 4.6 acres.

The parties dispute whether the Holcombs saw the newspaper ads before they offered to buy. Without question the Holcombs saw the listing contract prior to their offer. James R. Holcomb testified on direct examination:

Q. Was the question of acreage of property that was for sale ever brought up? A. Yes, before we made an offer to buy the property we stopped at Dean's office and he gave us like a listing agreement and it showed the amount of acres. It showed 6.8 and this was on his original copy and before he Xeroxed it he says, I don't know, Jim, I guarantee at least 6.6 acres of ground here. So I put a check by the 6.8 acres and put a question mark and wrote 6.6.

He run a Xerox copy and we took it home and that's what we made the offer to buy off of; that sheet of paper.

Q. How many times prior to the closing of the transaction—how many times did the question of acreage come up? A. Probably 10, 15 times at least.

Q. Was it brought up by you or how? A. By me because it just didn't appear to me that there was that much ground there and he says we sell 90% of the acreages out here and Mr. Herzberg used to live in this house and there is a plat on our wall down in the office and I know that there is that much ground there. So, I took his word for it.

Q. Did he make an explanation? A. He said because it was pie shaped and that hills is deceiving because it is along from the one point to the top of the hill is a long ways. It does look, you know, the distance is deceiving of just how far it is.

Q. What was the terrain like? A. Well, the road comes around like this and it goes, the property goes down like this and goes up like this, you know, it's like that (indicating).

Q. So behind your house there is first a valley and then a hill; is that what you are saying? A. Yeah.

Holcomb reasserted on cross-examination that Olson represented the property contained 6.6 acres and that the Holcombs relied on those statements:

Q. And every time you asked Dean Olson he said about six acres. A. No, he said, I guarantee at least 6.6.

Q. And you asked him the same question 15 to 20 times and every time he said, I guarantee the size to be 6.8 acres. A. He said Mr. Herzberg lived in here. There is a plat of this on our wall. And he said, no, if there was any difference they would catch it.

Q. Why did you ask him 15 to 20 times? A. Because it didn't look like there was that much property there.

Q. Why didn't you check a little further on it? [Objection, overruled.] A. Because Dean guaranteed me there was that much ground there.

Q. Did you walk the boundaries of the land you were talking about? A. Yes.

Q. You went out and looked at it? A. Yes.

Herzberg was president of C.B. Property and also the general contractor who constructed the house in question. He lived in the house prior to its sale to Hoffschneiders.

The Holcombs eventually offered $54,000 for the house and lots, and purchased the property for that price.

As to C.B. Property's contention that the Holcombs did not rely on the misrepresentations, the evidence does show that the Holcombs examined the property. This court has said, however, that a buyer cannot generally be held to be able to judge the contents of a parcel of land by the eye. *Boddy v. Henry*, 126 Iowa 31, 42, 101 N.W. 447, 451 (1904). Even though a buyer examines land before purchasing, he may normally rely upon the representations of the seller as to measurement. *Id.* at 42, 101 N.W. at 450–51.

C.B. Property argues that if the Holcombs really wanted to know the exact acreage, they should have obtained a survey. On cross-examination Holcomb had this to say on that subject:

Q. Do you know what a survey is? A. Yes.

Q. Would you tell the jury what a survey is? A. Well, that's when you have a surveyor come out and tell you how much ground is in there.

Q. And a surveyor would also tell you how many acres you are buying. A. Correct.

Q. And you knew what a survey was at that time you were purchasing this property. A. Yes, but I didn't feel it was necessary to have it surveyed since C.B. Property was engaged in the whole transaction out there in the Rolling Hill Addition.

Q. So you didn't ask for a survey because of that, is that correct? A. Correct.

This court stated in *McGibbons v. Wilder,* 78 Iowa 531, 535, 43 N.W. 520, 522 (1889):

> This court has repeatedly held, in effect, that a party may rely upon representations as to the ownership of property, its location, and the like; and that, to entitle him to recover for fraudulent representations, he is not bound to show that he instituted inquiry by consulting records or plats, or employing a surveyor, or the like. * * *

Under the testimony and these pronouncements, we hold the Holcombs generated a jury issue on reliance. The jury could say that although the Holcombs doubted the representations as to acreage were right, after Olson's repeated assurances they took his word.

II. Damages. Iowa follows the benefit-of-the-bargain rule, that is, a defrauded purchaser is entitled to the difference between the value the property would have had as represented and the value of the property he actually received. * * *

* * *

The gist of C.B. Property's argument on damages is that the Holcombs saw the property they bought, from visual inspection they knew its actual size, and they bid and bought that exact tract for $54,000—they were willing to pay that amount for what they saw. C.B. Property urges that the Holcombs got what they paid for and they therefore sustained no damage.

Involved in an issue of this kind are two kinds of cases: those in which a purchaser intends to purchase a tract, not a quantity in acres or by dimensions, * * * as distinguished from those in which the purchaser intends to purchase a number of acres or by dimensions. In the latter situation the purchaser is damaged if the seller fraudulently misrepresents the acreage or dimensions. * * * The jury could reasonably find on the evidence that this case was of the latter sort. C.B. Property makes a cogent jury argument that the case was of the former kind, but the decision was ultimately for the jury. We do not find merit in this claim of error.

[Although the jury found the misrepresentations to be fraudulent, the trial court refused to submit the issue of punitive damages to the jury and the Supreme Court affirmed, holding that Holcomb's case involved at best "ordinary" or "simple fraud." The court relied on 37 Am.Jur.2d Fraud and Deceit section 347, at 466 (1968), which states in part:

> Generally speaking, a recovery of exemplary or punitive damages in an action based on a fraudulent sale will be allowed only where the fraud is an aggravated one, as where it is malicious, deliberate, gross, or wanton.]

AFFIRMED.

PORRECO v. PORRECO, 571 Pa. 61, 811 A.2d 566 (2002). [Before their marriage, Louis Porreco gave Susan Porreco an engagement ring. At least in part because Louis had showered Susan with other valuable presents prior to giving her the ring, including expensive jewelry, Susan believed the ring was a diamond. Susan later found out the ring was a fake, but not before signing an unfavorable prenuptial agreement granting her only $3500 per month upon a divorce. Louis' net worth was over $3 million. The prenuptial agreement included a personal financial statement, prepared by Louis, that listed the ring as an engagement ring, without further identification, with a value of $21,000. Apparently, it was worth far less. At the divorce proceeding in which Susan sought to avoid the prenuptial agreement, she testified that "she would not have signed the prenuptial agreement if she knew that Louis had given her a fake ring and lied about it and 'would not have married the man.' "]

MADAME JUSTICE NEWMAN

[W]e cannot agree that Susan's alleged reliance on Louis' misrepresentation of the value of the ring on the schedule of her assets was justifiable. Susan had possession of the ring and was not impeded from doing what she ultimately did when the parties separated: obtain an appraisal of the ring. She had sufficient opportunity to inform herself fully of the nature and extent of her own assets, rather than rely on Louis' statements concerning the valuation of her holdings. We find her failure to do this simple investigation to be unreasonable. Although we do not excuse Louis' actions we will not sanction the avoidance of an entire prenuptial agreement—the consequences of which Susan admittedly understood—on the basis of fraud in these circumstances.

"There's no justice in the world, Kirkby, but I'm not convinced that this is an entirely bad thing."

Drawing by Handelsman; © 1986 The New Yorker Magazine, Inc.

WEINTRAUB v. KROBATSCH

Supreme Court of New Jersey, 1974.
64 N.J. 445, 317 A.2d 68.

JACOBS, J.

The [summary judgment] * * * directed that the appellants Donald P. Krobatsch and Estella Krobatsch, his wife, pay the sum of $4,250 to the plaintiff Natalie Weintraub and the sum of $2,550 to the defendant The Serafin Agency, Inc. We granted certification on the application of the appellants. * * *

* * * [W]e must resolve doubts in favor of the appellants and must accept their factual allegations, along with the inferences most favorable to them. * * *

Mrs. Weintraub owned and occupied a six-year-old Englishtown home which she placed in the hands of a real estate broker (The Serafin Agency, Inc.) for sale. The Krobatsches were interested in purchasing the home, examined it while it was illuminated and found it suitable. On June 30, 1971 Mrs. Weintraub, as seller, and the Krobatsches, as purchasers, entered into a contract for the sale of the property for $42,500. The contract provided that the purchasers had inspected the property and were fully satisfied with its physical condition, that no representations had been made and that no responsibility was assumed by the seller as to the present or future condition of the premises. A deposit of $4,250 was sent by the purchasers to the broker to be held in escrow pending the closing of the transaction. The purchasers requested that the seller have the house fumigated and that was done. A fire after the signing of the contract caused damage but the purchasers indicated readiness that there be adjustment at closing.

During the evening of August 25, 1971, prior to closing, the purchasers entered the house, then unoccupied, and as they turned the lights on they were, as described in their petition for certification, "astonished to see roaches literally running in all directions, up the walls, drapes, etc." On the following day their attorney wrote a letter to Mrs. Weintraub, care of her New York law firm, advising that on the previous day "it was discovered that the house is infested with vermin despite the fact that an exterminator has only recently serviced the house" and asserting that "the presence of vermin in such great quantities, particularly after the exterminator was done, rendered the house as unfit for human habitation at this time and therefore, the contract is rescinded." On September 2, 1971 an exterminator wrote to Mr. Krobatsch advising that he had examined the premises and that "cockroaches were found to have infested the entire house." He said he could eliminate them for a relatively modest charge by two treatments with a twenty-one day interval but that it would be necessary to remove the carpeting "to properly treat all the infested areas."

Mrs. Weintraub rejected the rescission by the purchasers and filed an action in the Law Division joining them and the broker as defendants. Though she originally sought specific performance she later confined her claim to damages in the sum of $4,250, representing the deposit held in escrow by the broker. The broker filed an answer and counterclaim seeking payment of its commission in the sum of $2,550. There were opposing motions for summary judgment by the purchasers and Mrs. Weintraub, along with a motion for summary judgment by the broker for its commission. At the argument on the motions it was evident that the purchasers were claiming fraudulent concealment or nondisclosure by the seller as the basis for their rescission. Thus at one point their attorney said: "Your honor, I would point out, and it is in my clients' affidavit, every time that they inspected this house prior to this time every light in the place was illuminated. Now, these insects are nocturnal by nature and that is not a point I think I have to prove through someone. I think Webster's dictionary is sufficient. By keeping the lights on it keeps them out of sight. These sellers had to know they had this problem. You could not live in a house this infested without knowing about it."

The Law Division denied the motion by the purchasers for summary judgment but granted Mrs. Weintraub's motion and directed that the purchasers pay her the sum of $4,250. It further directed that the deposit monies held in escrow by the broker be paid to Mrs. Weintraub in satisfaction of her judgment against the purchasers. * * * It denied the broker's summary judgment motion for its commission but held that matter for trial. On appeal, the Appellate Division sustained the summary judgment in Mrs. Weintraub's favor but disagreed with the Law Division's holding that the broker's claim must await trial. It considered that since the purchasers were summarily held to have been in default in rescinding rather than in proceeding with the closing, they were responsible for the commission. Accordingly, it modified the Law Division's judgment to the end that the purchasers were directed to pay not only the sum of $4,250 to Mrs. Weintraub but also the sum of $2,550 to the broker.

Before us the purchasers contend that they were entitled to a trial on the issue of whether there was fraudulent concealment or nondisclosure entitling them to rescind; if there was, then clearly they were under no liability to either the seller or the broker and would be entitled to the return of their deposit held by the broker in escrow. See Keen v. James, 39 N.J.Eq. 527, 540 (E. & A. 1885) where Justice Dixon, speaking for the then Court of last resort, pointed out that "silence may be fraudulent" and that relief may be granted to one contractual party where the other suppresses facts which he, " 'under the circumstances, is bound in conscience and duty to disclose to the other party, and in respect to which he cannot, innocently, be silent.' " * * *

Mrs. Weintraub asserts that she was unaware of the infestation and the Krobatsches acknowledge that, if that was so, then there was no fraudulent concealment or nondisclosure on her part and their claim must fall. But the purchasers allege that she was in fact aware of the infestation and at this stage of the proceedings we must assume that to be true. She contends, however, that even if she were fully aware she would have been under no duty to speak and that consequently no complaint by the purchasers may legally be grounded on her silence. She relies primarily on cases such as Swinton v. Whitinsville Sav. Bank, 311 Mass. 677, 42 N.E.2d 808, 141 A.L.R. 965 (1942) * * *. *Swinton* is pertinent but, as Dean Prosser has noted [Prosser, Torts 695, 696 (4th ed. 1971)], it is one of a line of "singularly unappetizing cases" which are surely out of tune with our times.

In *Swinton* the plaintiff purchased a house from the defendant and after he occupied it he found it to be infested with termites. The defendant had made no verbal or written representations but the plaintiff, asserting that the defendant knew of the termites and was under a duty to speak, filed a complaint for damages grounded on fraudulent concealment. The Supreme Judicial Court of Massachusetts sustained a demurrer to the complaint and entered judgment for the defendant. In the course of its opinion the court acknowledged that "the plaintiff possesses a certain appeal to the moral sense" but concluded that the law has not "reached the point of imposing upon the frailties of human nature a standard so idealistic as this." 42 N.E.2d at 808–809. That was written several decades ago and we are far from certain that it represents views held by the current members of the Massachusetts court. * * * In any event we are certain that it does not represent our sense of justice or fair dealing and it has understandably been rejected in persuasive opinions elsewhere. * * *

In Obde v. Schlemeyer, 56 Wash.2d 449, 353 P.2d 672, [1960] the defendants sold an apartment house to the plaintiff. The house was termite infested but that fact was not disclosed by the sellers to the purchasers who later sued for damages alleging fraudulent concealment. The sellers contended that they were under no obligation whatever to speak out and they relied heavily on the decision of the Massachusetts court in *Swinton* * * * The Supreme Court of Washington flatly rejected their contention, holding that though the parties had dealt at arms length the sellers were under "a duty to inform the plaintiffs of the termite condition" of which they were fully aware. 353 P.2d at 674. * * * In the course of its opinion the court quoted approvingly from Dean Keeton's article [Keeton, Fraud–Concealment and Nondisclosure, 15 Tex. 1 (1855)]. There the author first expressed his thought that when Lord Cairns suggested in Peek v. Gurney, L.R. 6 H.L. 377 (1873), that there was no duty to disclose facts, no matter how "morally censurable" (at 403), he was expressing nineteenth century law as shaped by an individualistic philosophy based on freedom of contracts and unconcerned with morals. He then made the following comments which fairly embody a currently acceptable principle on which the holding in *Obde* may be said to be grounded:

> In the present stage of the law, the decisions show a drawing away from this idea, and there can be seen an attempt by many courts to reach a just result in so far as possible, but yet maintaining the degree of certainty which the law must have. The statement may often be found that if either party to a contract of sale conceals or suppresses a material fact which he is in good faith bound to disclose then his silence is fraudulent.

> The attitude of the courts toward nondisclosure is undergoing a change and contrary to Lord Cairns' famous remark it would seem that the object of the law in these cases should be to impose on parties to the transaction a duty to speak whenever justice, equity, and fair dealing demand it. This statement is made only with reference to instances where the party to be charged is an actor in the transaction. This duty to speak does not result from an implied representation by silence, but exists because a refusal to speak constitutes unfair conduct. 15 Tex.L.Rev. at 31.

* * *

In Simmons v. Evans, [185 Tenn. 282, 206 S.W.2d 295 (1947)] the defendants owned a home which was serviced by a local water company. The company supplied water during the daytime but not at night. The defendants sold their home to the plaintiffs but made no mention of the limitation on the water service. The plaintiffs filed an action to rescind their purchase but the lower court dismissed it on the ground that the defendants had not made any written or verbal representations and the plaintiffs had "inspected the property, knew the source of the water supply, and could have made specific inquiry of these defendants or ascertained from other sources the true situation and, therefore, are estopped." 206 S.W.2d at 296. The dismissal was reversed on appeal in an opinion which took note of the general rule that " 'one may be guilty of fraud by his silence, as where it is expressly incumbent upon him to speak concerning material matters that are entirely within his own knowledge.' " 206 S.W.2d at 296. With respect to the plaintiffs' failure to ascertain the water situation before their purchase the court stated that the plaintiffs were surely not required "to make a night inspection in order to ascertain whether the water situation with reference to this residence was different from what it was during the day." 206 S.W.2d at 297.

* * *

* * * The purchasers here were entitled to withstand the seller's motion for summary judgment. They should have been permitted to proceed with their efforts to establish by testimony that they were equitably entitled to rescind because the house was extensively infested in the manner described by them, the seller was well aware of the infestation, and the seller deliberately concealed or failed to disclose the condition because of the likelihood that it would defeat the transaction. The seller may of course defend factually as well as legally and since the matter is primarily equitable in nature the factual as well as legal disputes will be for the trial judge alone.

If the trial judge finds such deliberate concealment or nondisclosure of the latent infestation not observable by the purchasers on their inspection, he will still be called upon to determine whether, in the light of the full presentation before him, the concealment or nondisclosure was of such significant nature as to justify rescission. Minor conditions which ordinary sellers and purchasers would reasonably disregard as of little or no materiality in the transaction would clearly not call for judicial intervention. While the described condition may not have been quite as major as in the termite cases which were concerned with structural impairments, to the purchasers here it apparently was of such magnitude and was so repulsive as to cause them to rescind immediately though they had earlier indicated readiness that there be adjustment at closing for damage resulting from a fire which occurred after the contract was signed. We are not prepared at this time to say that on their showing they acted either unreasonably or without equitable justification.

* * *

Reversed and Remanded.

KRONMAN, MISTAKE, DISCLOSURE, INFORMATION AND THE LAW OF CONTRACTS
7 J. of Legal Studies 1, 13, 18 (1978).

As it is used here, the term "deliberately acquired information" means information whose acquisition entails costs which would not have been incurred but for the likelihood, however great, that the information in question would actually be produced. These costs may include, of course, not only direct search costs (the cost of examining the corporation's annual statement) but the costs of developing an initial expertise as well (for example, the cost of attending business school). If the costs incurred in acquiring the information * * * would have been incurred in any case—that is, whether or not the information was forthcoming—the information may be said to have been casually acquired.

* * *

The distinction between deliberately and casually acquired information helps us to understand the pattern exhibited by the cases in which a duty to disclose is asserted by one party or the other. By and large, the cases requiring disclosure involve information which is likely to have been casually acquired (in the sense defined above). The cases permitting nondisclosure, on the other hand, involve information which, on the whole, is likely to have been deliberately produced. Taken as a group, the disclosure cases give at least the appearance of promoting allocative efficiency by limiting the assignment of property rights to those types of information which are likely to be the fruit of a deliberate investment (either in the development of expertise or in actual searching).

C. FRIED CONTRACT AS PROMISE
79, 83 (1981).

An oil company has made extensive geological surveys seeking to identify possible oil and gas reserves. These surveys are extremely expensive. Having identified one promising site, the oil company (acting through a broker) buys a large tract of land from its prosperous farmer owner, revealing nothing about its survey, its purposes, or even its identity. The price paid is the going price for farmland of that quality in that region.

* * *

Anthony Kronman has recently written that [the] arguments in terms of encouraging investment in information show that the results in such cases do and should just depend on a policy of efficiency and redistribution. The decisions favor the oil company because even the sellers will be better off in the long run under a rule that encourages such investments in knowledge. And in general, argues Kronman, what contracts are enforced is (or should be) always just a function of what will make the least advantaged party to the particular kind of transaction better off. But this misconceives the argument. The oil company wins not because we want to encourage its future investments but because it would be unfair to defeat its past reasonable expectations. To be sure, our determination to be fair even in the face of sentimental

pressures to favor a weaker party (the farmer) will encourage investment—
that is, rational planning for the future. But Kronman gets the arguments
exactly the wrong way around. Indeed, if we played fair with the oil company
only because (and only so far as) this led to greater economic productivity or
improved the situation of the least advantaged party, then our playing fair on
a particular occasion would not create confidence and so would not even
procure these supposed general benefits. In general we can get the social,
collective benefits of trust only if we are faithful for the sake of trust itself,
not just for the sake of the resulting benefits.

Problem 5–2

The Stambovskys, residents of New York City, call you because they want to
recover their $32,500 down-payment on the purchase of the Ackleys' home in
Nyack, New York. The Stambovskys tell you that the Ackleys did not disclose
their belief that the house is haunted by ghosts. Ms. Ackley had shared her view
with the public by publishing articles about the house in the Reader's Digest and
in local newspapers. In fact, two months after signing the contract, a local
newspaper described the house as a "riverfront Victorian (with ghosts)." Assume
that the market value of the house and its resale potential are materially affected
by its reputation. Please advise the Stambovskys.

Note
Duty to Disclose the Legal Effect of an Agreement

Some courts have required a party to disclose, not only factual circumstances
surrounding a transaction, such as in Weintraub v. Krobatsch, but also information about the legal effect of contract terms. The duty arises when the contract
contains fine print or otherwise hidden terms, but it also arises in the absence of
these infirmities when one party enjoys superior knowledge or a superior position.
Such superior knowledge or position may be based on a discernible weakness of
the other party, such as lack of education, or it may be based on the type of
transaction, such as a form contract offered on a take-it-or-leave-it basis.

WEAVER v. AMERICAN OIL CO., 257 Ind. 458, 276 N.E.2d 144 (1971). [A
lease between American Oil and station-owner Weaver exculpated American
Oil from liability for its own negligence and required Weaver to indemnify
American Oil for any liability for American Oil's negligence. The litigation
arose when American Oil's employee sprayed gasoline over Weaver and his
assistant, causing them to be burned and American Oil sought a declaratory
judgment determining the extent of *Weaver's* liability. The court first high-
lighted Weaver's lack of education (he had left high school) and his failure to
read the lease (each year a salesman from American Oil brought the lease for
Weaver to sign and he did so without reading it or without a warning from
the salesman about the indemnification clause).]

"When a party can show that the contract, which is sought to be
enforced, was in fact an unconscionable one, due to a prodigious amount of
bargaining power on behalf of the stronger party, which is used to the
stronger party's advantage and is unknown to the lesser party, causing a
great hardship and risk on the lesser party, the contract provision, or the

What must happen for it to be enforced

contract as a whole, if the provision is not separable, should not be enforceable on the grounds that the provision is contrary to public policy. The party seeking to enforce such a contract has the burden of showing that the provisions were explained to the other party and *came to his knowledge* and there was in fact *a real and voluntary meeting of the minds and not merely an objective meeting*.

* * *

"We do not mean to say or infer that parties may not make contracts exculpating one of his negligence and providing for indemnification, but it must be done *knowingly* and *willingly* as in insurance contracts made for that very purpose."

[A dissenting judge took a different view:]

"The facts as found, are that although the defendant never read the lease, he had ample opportunity to do so and to obtain counsel. A general rule in effect not only in Indiana but elsewhere, is that a person who signs a contract, without bothering to read the same, will be bound by its terms. * * *"

P. SIVIGLIA, WRITING CONTRACTS
51 (1996).

Too often lawyers—or, perhaps, just too many lawyers—believe that when they draft an agreement, they must prepare the document to reflect only the interests of their client. They pay little, if any, attention to the legitimate concerns of the other party.

* * *

Highhanded drafting * * * is not only offensive, antagonizing the other party and his or her lawyer, but it needlessly prolongs the negotiating and drafting process, thereby adding to the legal costs of both parties and to the mounting deficit in respect that clients and the general public have for lawyers.

Note
A Comparative View

According to Section 138(2) of the German Civil Code, a transaction is void, "when a person * * * [exploits] the distressed situation, inexperience, lack of judgmental ability, or grave weakness of will of another to obtain the grant, or promise of pecuniary advantages for himself or a third party which are obviously disproportionate to the performance given in return." § 138(2) BGB, translated in A. von Mehren & J. Gordley, The Civil Law System 1188 (2d ed.1977). Is this formulation an improvement over American law?

SECTION FOUR: PUBLIC POLICY

PRINTING AND NUMERICAL REGISTERING CO. v. SAMPSON, 19 L.R.–Eq. 462, 465 (1875). "It must not be forgotten that you are not to extend arbitrarily those rules which say that a given contract is void as being against public policy, because if there is one thing which more than another public policy requires it is that men of full age and competent understanding shall have the utmost liberty of contracting, and that their contracts when entered into freely and voluntarily shall be held sacred and shall be enforced by Courts of justice. Therefore, you have this paramount public policy to consider—that you are not lightly to interfere with this freedom of contract."

McCUTCHEON v. UNITED HOMES CORP.

Washington Supreme Court, 1971.
79 Wn.2d 443, 486 P.2d 1093.

STAFFORD, ASSOCIATE JUSTICE.

The two cases involved herein were considered separately by the trial court. Since the issues presented are identical, they have been consolidated on appeal.

Plaintiff Norma McCutcheon, a tenant of defendant United Homes Corporation, was injured one evening when she fell down an unlighted flight of stairs leading from her apartment. She [sued in tort and] alleged the defendant was negligent because the lights at the top and bottom of the stairwell were not operative.

Plaintiff Douglas R. Fuller, also defendant's tenant, was injured as he descended the outside stairs of his apartment on his way to work. A step pulled loose causing him to fall. He, too, alleged negligence on the part of defendant.

Defendant's answer alleged each plaintiff had executed a form "Month to Month Rental Agreement" which contained the following exculpatory clause:

neither the Lessor, nor his Agent, shall be liable for any injury to Lessee, his family, guests or employees or any other person entering the premises or the building of which the demised premises are a part.

In each case the trial court granted a summary judgment of dismissal.

The question is one of first impression. The issue is whether the lessor of a residential unit within a multi-family dwelling complex may exculpate itself from liability for personal injuries sustained by a tenant, which injuries result from the lessor's own negligence in maintenance of the approaches, common passageways, stairways and other areas under the lessor's dominion and control, but available for the tenants' use. (Hereinafter called the "common areas".)

Basic to the entire discussion is the common law rule that one who leases a portion of his premises but retains control over the approaches, common passageways, stairways and other areas to be used in common by the owner and tenants, has a duty to use reasonable care to keep them in safe condition for use of the tenant in his enjoyment of the demised premises. * * * The landlord is required to do more than passively refrain from negligent acts. He has a duty of affirmative conduct, an affirmative obligation to exercise reasonable care to inspect and repair the previously mentioned portions of the premises for protection of the lessee. * * *

It is readily apparent that the exculpatory clause was inserted in defendant's form "Month to Month Rental Agreement" to bar its tenants from asserting actions for personal injuries sustained through the landlord's own negligence. It was adopted to negative the result of the lessor's failure to comply with its affirmative duty to the tenants.

The defendant asserts that a lessor may contract, in a rental agreement, to exculpate itself from liability to its lessee, for personal injuries caused by lessor's own negligence. 49 Am.Jur.2d Landlord and Tenant § 869, p. 837 (1970). It contends such exculpatory clauses are not contrary to public policy because the landlord-tenant relationship *is not a matter of public interest, but relates exclusively to the private affairs of the parties concerned and that the two parties stand upon equal terms. Thus, there should be full freedom to contract.* * * *

* * *

The importance of "freedom of contract" is clear enough. However, the use of such an argument for avoiding the affirmative duty of a landlord to its residential tenant is no longer compelling in light of today's multi-family dwelling complex wherein a tenant merely rents some space with appurtenant rights to make it more usable or livable. Under modern circumstances the tenant is almost wholly dependent upon the landlord to provide reasonably for his safe use of the "common areas" beyond the four walls demised to him. Quinn and Phillips, The Law of Landlord–Tenant, 38 Fordham L.Rev. 225, 231 (1969).

As early as 1938 Williston recognized that while such exculpatory clauses were recognized as "legal", many courts had shown a reluctance to enforce them. Even then, courts were disposed to interpret them strictly so they would not be effective to discharge liability for the consequences of negligence in making or failing to make repairs. 6 Williston, A Treatise on the Law of Contracts § 1751C p. 4968 (Rev. ed. 1938). * * *

The key to our problem is found in Restatement of Contracts § 574, p. 1079 (1932) which reads:

A bargain for exemption from liability for the consequences of negligence *not falling greatly below the standard established by law* for the protection of others against unreasonable risk of harm, is legal * * *

(Italics ours.) In other words, such an exculpatory clause may be legal, when considered in the abstract. However, when applied to a specific situation, one may be exempt from liability for his own negligence *only when the consequences thereof do not fall greatly below the standard established by law.*

In the landlord-tenant relationship it is extremely meaningful to require that a landlord's attempt to exculpate itself, from liability for the result of its own negligence, *not fall greatly below the standard of negligence set by law.* As indicated earlier, a residential tenant who lives in a modern multi-family dwelling complex is almost wholly dependent upon the landlord for the reasonably safe condition of the "common areas". However, a clause which exculpates the lessor from liability to its lessee, for personal injuries caused by lessor's own acts of negligence, not only lowers the standard imposed by the common law, it effectively *destroys* the landlord's affirmative obligation or duty to keep or maintain the "common areas" in a reasonably safe condition for the tenant's use.

When a lessor is no longer liable for the failure to observe standards of affirmative conduct, or for *any* conduct amounting to negligence, by virtue of an exculpatory clause in a lease, *the standard ceases to exist*. In short, such a clause *destroys* the concept of negligence in the landlord-tenant relationship. Neither the standard nor negligence can exist in abstraction.

It is no answer to argue that the rental agreement relates exclusively to the "personal and private affairs of two parties on equal footing" and thus is "not a matter of public interest." Such a concept had its origin in contracts entered into between *indemnitors* and *indemnitees*. * * * In Cannon v. Bresch, 307 Pa. 31, 35, 160 A. 595 (1932), the court first used the language now relied on by defendant, applying it to an exculpatory clause concerned with *property damage* arising out of a lease for business purposes:

> It is a contract between persons conducting a strictly private business, and relates entirely to their personal and private affairs, and so cannot be opposed to public policy. It would seem to be a matter of no interest to the public or the state.

The foregoing case and its progeny actually forms the basis for the so-called "majority rule" cited in 49 Am.Jur.2d Landlord and Tenant § 870 p. 839 (1970) and Annot., 175 A.L.R. 8, 83–92 (1948). It is safe to say, however, that there is no true majority rule. There are only numerous conflicting decisions, decisions concerned with contracts of indemnity, cases relating to property damage under business leases, and a disposition of the courts to emasculate such exculpatory clauses by means of strict construction. * * * From this, one can reasonably infer that even though such clauses are recognized by some courts, a great number have regarded them with disfavor. * * *

It is inaccurate to characterize the foregoing as a "majority rule". Furthermore, one must ignore present day realities to say that such an exculpatory clause, which relieves a lessor of liability for personal injuries caused by its own negligence, is purely a "personal and private affair" and "not a matter of public interest."

We no longer live in an era of the occasional rental of rooms in a private home or over the corner grocery. In the relatively short span of 30 years the public's use of rental units in this state has expanded dramatically. In the past 10 years alone, in the state of Washington, there has been an increase of over 77,000 rental units. It takes no imagination to see that a business which once had a minor impact upon the living habits of the citizenry has developed into a major commercial enterprise directly touching the lives of hundreds of thousands of people who depend upon it for shelter.

Thus, we are not faced merely with the theoretical duty of construing a provision in an isolated contract specifically bargained for by *one landlord and one tenant* as a "purely private affair". Considered realistically, we are asked to construe an exculpatory clause, the generalized use of which may have an impact upon thousands of potential tenants.

Under these circumstances it cannot be said that such exculpatory clauses are "purely a private affair" or that they are "not a matter of public interest." The real question is whether we should sanction a technique of immunizing lessors of residential units within a multi-family dwelling complex, from liability for personal injuries sustained by a tenant, which injuries result from the lessor's own negligence in maintaining the "common areas"; particularly when the technique employed destroys the concept of negligence and the standard of affirmative duty imposed upon the landlord for protection of the tenant.

An exculpatory clause of the type here involved contravenes long established common law rules of tort liability that exist in the landlord-tenant relationship. As so employed, it offends the public policy of the state and will not be enforced by the courts. It makes little sense for us to insist, on the one hand, that a workman have a safe place in which to work, but, on the other hand, to deny him a reasonably safe place in which to live.

The trial court is reversed and the cause is remanded for trial.

KALISCH–JARCHO, INC. v. NEW YORK CITY, 58 N.Y.2d 377, 461 N.Y.S.2d 746, 448 N.E.2d 413 (1983). [Kalisch–Jarcho, the successful bidder for the heating, ventilating, and air-conditioning work on the construction of the new New York City police headquarters, sought over $3 million in contract damages from New York City, alleging that "the progress of its work was subjected to drastic and costly delays" attributable to the city's countless revisions of plans and failure to coordinate the activities of the contractors "which stretched out the time for the job's completion, originally fixed at 1,000 consecutive calendar days, for an additional 28 months." An exculpatory clause stated:

> "The Contractor agrees to make no claim for damages for delay in the performance of this contract occasioned by any act or omission to act of the City or any of its representatives, and agrees that any such claim shall be fully compensated for by an extension of time to complete performance of the work as provided herein."

The court instructed the jury that Kalisch–Jarcho could recover notwithstanding the exculpatory clause if "the delay was caused by conduct constituting active interference." The jury rendered a verdict in favor of Kalisch–Jarcho for $806,382 for the delay. The city appealed. The Appellate Division affirmed. The Court of Appeals, in an opinion by Judge Fuchsberg, reversed and granted a new trial. The court reasoned that the court's active interference charge was in error because whether conduct is "active" or "passive" does not determine intentional wrongdoing, which was necessary for Kalisch–Jarcho to recover. "[T]he city, at the very least was entitled to the amplifying instruction that unless Kalisch–Jarcho proved that 'the City acted in bad faith and with deliberate intent delayed the plaintiff in the performance of its obligation,' the plaintiff could not recover." Judge Wachtler dissented, asserting that the court's holding "altered the settled meaning of a standard clause in a municipal contract."]

Note
Interplay Between Process and Substance

In Weaver v. American Oil Co. (page 551), the court invalidated the exculpatory clause in part because American Oil failed to explain it to Weaver, an unsophisticated contracting party. But in Kalisch–Jarcho, we saw that an exculpatory clause may be unenforceable even when the contract was entered "at arm's length by sophisticated contracting parties" and no duty of explanation arose. A decision overturning contract terms because of their content tests the limits of freedom of contract and, if carried too far, threatens the sanctity of contract. A decision based not only on objectionable content but also on insufficiency of assent is therefore generally more acceptable. While the following materials in this section and the next focus primarily on the possibly objectionable content of the exchange, you should also attempt to isolate any bargaining infirmities that may be involved and should consider whether the decision would be the same without those infirmities. You should also consider whether a clear line can be drawn between those terms that should be enforceable and those that are simply too objectionable to enforce even when there is "full assent."

Court enforces term on Lottotickets

MOLINA v. GAMES MANAGEMENT SERVICES, 58 N.Y.2d 523, 462 N.Y.S.2d 615, 449 N.E.2d 395 (1983). [Plaintiff claimed she held a winning Lotto ticket worth $166,950, and presented it for payment. Payment was refused because there was no record of the purchase at "Lotto Control" as required by New York rules and the terms of the contract printed on the ticket. Plaintiff brought this action in tort against defendant, the independent contractor operating the Lotto game for the state. She claimed defendant negligently lost the ticket. She submitted an affidavit of an employee of the Donut Shoppe where she had purchased the ticket that supported her claim that she bought and had validated the ticket. Summary judgment in favor of defendant affirmed. Defendant's possible negligence was irrelevant in light of, among other reasons, a term on the ticket exculpating defendant from liability for "neglect or omission." Because the rules were "clear and unequivocal," said the court, they should be enforced. There was no issue of fact concerning gross negligence, the court added.]

Court holding

Problem 5–3

Garretson, an experienced ski jumper and a college student, read the following entry blank necessary to compete in an amateur ski-jumping tournament:

ENTRY BLANK

Please fill out this entry blank properly and return immediately.

NAME _____　　ADDRESS _____

CITY _____　　STATE _____

CLUB & CARD NO. _____

ACCIDENT INSURANCE CO. _____

JUMPING CLASS:

　　Choose one.

( ) Junior Novice　　　　　　　　　　　　( ) B Class
( ) Junior Expert　　　　　　　　　　　　( ) Veteran
　　　　　　　( ) Cross country (if any)

In consideration of the acceptance of my application, I hereby release the Leavenworth Winter Sports Club, U.S. Ski Association, Ski Patrol, U.S. Forest Service, their members or agents and any person officially connected with this competition from all liability for any injuries or damages whatsoever arising from participation in or presence at this competition.

SIGNED _____

APPROVED _____

(parent or guardian)

Mail to: Ralph E. Steele Box 158 Leavenworth, Wash.

Garretson had signed similar entry blanks with releases in other "competitions." He added "A" to the jumping classifications, checked it and signed the form. Garretson was seriously injured in attempting his jump. He sued all the organizations listed in the exculpatory clause on the theory that they were negligent in failing to warn him of unsafe conditions for jumping. What result? If the Leavenworth Winter Sports Club asked you to revise the entry blank, what changes would you make, if any?

LLEWELLYN, BOOK REVIEW: O. PRAUSNITZ, THE STANDARDIZATION OF COMMERCIAL CONTRACTS IN ENGLISH AND CONTINENTAL LAW

52 Harv.L.Rev. 700, 702–703 (1939).

Our courts are loath indeed to throw out a contract clause under the plain justification that it is contrary to public policy, that it is such a clause as "private" parties *cannot* make legally effective in the circumstance. Once we admit that it *is* a contract clause, and admit that it does mean what it says, we tend to regret, but to let the clause stand. And it may be that the English go even further in this than we; certainly some of the cases Prausnitz collects teach justice to shiver and shake. But lacking ready recourse to *gute Sitten* or that near-equivalent in contract law, *l'ordre public* plus the *bonnes moeurs,* we have developed a whole series of semi-covert techniques for somewhat balancing these bargains. A court can "construe" language into patently not meaning what the language is patently trying to say. It can find inconsistencies between clauses and throw out the troublesome one. It can even reject a clause as counter to the whole purpose of the transaction. It can reject enforcement by one side for want of "mutuality," though allowing enforcement by the weaker side because "consideration" in some other sense is present. Indeed, the law of agreeing can be subjected to divers modes of employment, to make the whole bargain or a particular clause stick or not stick according to the status of the party claiming under it: as when, in the interest of the lesser party, the whole contract is conditioned on some presupposition which is held to have failed. The difficulty with these techniques of ours is threefold. First, since they all rest on the admission that the clauses in question are permissible in purpose and content, they invite the draftsman to recur to the attack. Give him time, and he will make the grade. Second, since they do not face the issue, they fail to accumulate either experience or authority in the needed direction: that of marking out for any given type of transaction what the *minimum decencies* are which a court will insist upon as essential to an enforceable bargain of a given type, or as being inherent in a bargain of that type. Third, since they purport to construe, and do not really construe, nor are intended to, but are instead tools of intentional and creative misconstruction, they seriously embarrass later efforts at true

construction, later efforts to get at the true meaning of those wholly legitimate contracts and clauses which call for their meaning to be got at instead of
avoided. The net effect is unnecessary confusion and unpredictability, together with inadequate remedy, and evil persisting that calls for remedy. Covert
tools are never reliable tools.

KARL N. LLEWELLYN

DWYER v. JUNG

Superior Court of New Jersey, 1975.
133 N.J.Super. 343, 336 A.2d 498, aff'd per curiam, 137 N.J.Super. 135, 348 A.2d 208.

KIMMELMAN, J.S.C.

In this action following the termination of a law partnership the court is
called upon to determine the enforceability of a restrictive covenant con-

tained in the partnership agreement which parcels out named clients to specific partners upon dissolution and prevents one partner from intruding upon another's clients for a period of five years.

Effective January 1, 1973 the parties entered into a partnership agreement for the practice of law (primarily defense of negligence actions) under the name of "Jung, Dwyer and Lisbona." Their agreement provided that each partner would contribute a stated amount for capital, cooperate in the business of the partnership and share in the partnership net profits in a stated manner. Upon dissolution each partner would be entitled to a repayment of capital and a distributive share of remaining profits and net assets.

The agreement also contained the following provision:

> Should the partnership terminate, all clients listed in exhibit "A" shall be designated to certain individual partners. Upon termination, and by virtue of this Agreement, all partners shall be restricted from doing business with a client designated as that of another partner for a period of 5 (five) years.

Exhibit A, annexed thereto, contained a list of insurance carriers; 154 were designated to defendant Jung as his clients, 5 were designated to plaintiff Dwyer as his clients, and none was ascribed to plaintiff Lisbona.

On June 7, 1974 defendant notified plaintiffs that the partnership was dissolved as of June 1, 1974. The business of the partnership continued in *de facto* fashion until September 1, 1974 when the former partners went their separate ways. Plaintiffs now practice under the name of "Dwyer and Lisbona." Defendant practices under the name of "Jung and Howard."

In this action brought for an accounting defendant, by way of counterclaim, contends that plaintiffs have violated the restrictive covenant contained in the partnership agreement which designates or assigns certain clients to partners in the event of dissolution. Specifically, plaintiffs are charged with attempting to pirate defendant's clients and undermining his relationship with certain named insurance carriers. These charges are denied.

Plaintiffs argue that the quoted provision is void as against public policy. They claim that they entered into the agreement at the insistence of defendant although all parties regarded the provision as unenforceable.

Initially, it must be recognized that lawyer restrictive covenants are to be distinguished from noncompetitive covenants incident to the sale of a business where the covenants are designed to protect the good will of the business for the benefit of the buyer. Solari Industries, Inc. v. Malady, 55 N.J. 571, 576, 264 A.2d 53 (1970); Whitmyer Bros. Inc. v. Doyle, 58 N.J. 25, 32, 274 A.2d 577 (1971). A lawyer's clients are neither chattels nor merchandise, and his practice and good will may not be offered for sale. Drinker, Legal Ethics, at 161, 189 (1965). In this regard Abraham Lincoln's sage observation (slightly paraphrased) is particularly appropriate: A lawyer's time and advice are his stock in trade.

Nor may lawyer restrictive covenants, whether contained in a partnership agreement or an agreement of employment, be classified within the general category of agreements restricting post-employment competition. The usual employee restrictive covenant is a legitimate business device to protect the business and good will of an employer against various forms of unfair competition. Although not freely as enforceable as a seller's noncompetitive agreement, such restrictive covenant will nevertheless be given effect if it is reasonable under all of the circumstances. "It will generally be found to be reasonable where it simply protects the legitimate interests of the employer, imposes no undue hardship on the employee, and is not injurious to the public." *Solari, supra,* 55 N.J. at 576, 264 A.2d at 56; *Whitmyer, supra,* 58 N.J. at 32, 274 A.2d 577.

Commercial standards may not be used to evaluate the reasonableness of lawyer restrictive covenants. Strong public policy considerations preclude their applicability. In that sense lawyer restrictions are injurious to the public interest. A client is always entitled to be represented by counsel of his own choosing.[1] See Marshall v. Romano, 10 N.J.Misc. 113, 114, 158 A. 751, 752 (C.P.1932). The attorney-client relationship is consensual, highly fiduciary on the part of counsel, and he may do nothing which restricts the right of the client to repose confidence in any counsel of his choice. *Drinker, supra* at 89 et seq. No concept of the practice of law is more deeply rooted. The lawyer's function is to serve, but serve he must with fidelity, devotion and erudition in the highest traditions of his noble profession.

These principles underlie DR 2–108(A) of the Disciplinary Rules of the Code of Professional Responsibility of the American Bar Association which provide:

> A lawyer shall not be a party to or participate in a partnership or employment agreement with another lawyer that restricts the right of a lawyer to practice law after the termination of a relationship created by the agreement except as may be provided in a bona fide retirement plan and then only to the extent reasonably necessary to protect the plan.

Opinion No. 147 of the Supreme Court's Advisory Committee on Professional Ethics, 92 N.J.L.J. 177 (March 20, 1969), applied these precepts in dealing with a restrictive covenant in a law partnership agreement. The agreement provided that a withdrawing partner shall not open an office or associate with or be employed by any attorney engaged in the practice of law in the county for a period of five years from the date of withdrawal.

In deciding that the provision was unethical, the committee said:

> We recognize in the legal profession the existence of a "client market" which is divided among lawyers within a particular locality. But the division of that "market" can be ethically achieved only through individual performance and the "establishment of a well-merited reputation for professional capacity and fidelity to trust." (Original Canon 27, August 27, 1908 (33 A.B.A. Reports 85)) It cannot be achieved by active competition and solicitation of professional employment. The insertion of a restrictive covenant in a law partnership agreement is an attempt to control and divide the "client market" by means other than individual performance. Therefore, it is the opinion of this Committee that the instant restrictive covenant is improper, unworthy of the legal profession, and unethical. See Disciplinary Rule 2–108(A) of the Preliminary Draft of

---

1. Except, perhaps, in cases of indigency.

the Code of Professional Responsibility of the American Bar Association Committee on Evaluation of Ethical Standards, dated January 15, 1969.

Question No. 621 (73–9) posed to the New York County Lawyers' Association Committee on Professional Ethics and reported at 97 N.J.L.J. 199 (March 21, 1974) involved the following issue:

> Is it proper for a lawyer to agree that upon his withdrawal from membership in a partnership he will not for a period of two years thereafter accept professional employment from any person who was a client of the partnership at the time he ceased being a member?

The committee concluded as follows:

> It is not proper for a lawyer to enter into what is in effect a restrictive covenant. DR 2–108(A) provides in substance that a lawyer shall not be a party to or participate in a partnership agreement with another lawyer that restricts the right of a lawyer to practice law after the termination of the partnership, except as a condition to payment of retirement benefits.

> In this connection EC 2–26 provides in substance that in furtherance of the objective of the bar to make legal services fully available, a lawyer should not lightly decline proffered employment; and EC 2–31 provides in substance that full availability of legal counsel requires both that persons be able to obtain counsel and that lawyers who undertake representation, complete the work involved.

> Reading these provisions together leads to the conclusions that a covenant restricting a lawyer after leaving a partnership from accepting employment by persons who were theretofore clients of the partnership, or from otherwise fully practicing his profession, is an unwarranted restriction on the right of the lawyer to choose his clients in the event they seek his services, and an unwarranted restriction on the right of the client to choose the lawyer he wishes to represent him. [N.Y. State 129 (1970)]

Reported cases in this area are almost nonexistent. Only one warrants mention. Hicklin v. O'Brien, 11 Ill.App.2d 541, 138 N.E.2d 47 (App.Ct.1956), upheld a noncompetitive covenant incidental to the sale of a law practice limiting the geographical area in which the selling attorney could practice. While not binding upon this court, it is not at all persuasive. That case, in this court's opinion, incorrectly proceeded upon the theory that the restrictive covenant imposed no undue burden upon the attorney and completely ignored the effect the covenant might have upon potential clients. The court there viewed the matter as a business proposition and failed to respect the underlying ethical considerations affecting the practice of law.

Holding

In view of the foregoing it is apparent that an agreement dividing the client market and prohibiting attorneys from representing certain insurance carriers in the defense of negligence cases has the effect of restricting those carriers in their unlimited choice of counsel. Accordingly, the restrictive covenant contained in the partnership agreement of the former law firm of "Jung, Dwyer and Lisbona" is declared to be void as against public policy. All counts of the pleadings relating thereto will be stricken and the case will continue solely for the purpose of effecting a proper accounting amongst the parties.

KARPINSKI v. INGRASCI

Court of Appeals of New York, 1971.
28 N.Y.2d 45, 320 N.Y.S.2d 1, 268 N.E.2d 751.

FULD, CHIEF JUDGE.

This appeal requires us to determine whether a covenant by a professional man not to compete with his employer is enforceable and, if it is, to what extent.

The plaintiff, Dr. Karpinski, an oral surgeon, had been carrying on his practice alone in Auburn—in Cayuga County—for many years. In 1953, he decided to expand and, since nearly all of an oral surgeon's business stems from referrals, he embarked upon a plan to "cultivate connections" among dentists in the four nearby Counties of Tompkins, Seneca, Cortland and Ontario. The plan was successful, and by 1962 twenty per cent of his practice consisted of treating patients referred to him by dentists located in those counties. In that year, after a number of those dentists had told him that some of their patients found it difficult to travel from their homes to Auburn, the plaintiff decided to open a second office in centrally-located Ithaca.[e] He began looking for an assistant and, in the course of his search, met the defendant, Dr. Ingrasci, who was just completing his training in oral surgery at the Buffalo General Hospital and was desirous of entering private practice. Dr. Ingrasci manifested an interest in becoming associated with Dr. Karpinski and, after a number of discussions, they reached an understanding; the defendant was to live in Ithaca, a locale with which he had no prior familiarity, and there work as an employee of the plaintiff.

A contract, reflecting the agreement, was signed by the defendant in June, 1962. It was for three years and, shortly after its execution, the defendant started working in the office which the plaintiff rented and fully equipped at his own expense. The provision of the contract with which we are concerned is a covenant by the defendant not to compete with the plaintiff. More particularly, it recited that the defendant

"promises and covenants that while this agreement is in effect and forever thereafter, he will never practice dentistry and/or Oral Surgery in Cayuga, Cortland, Seneca, Tompkins or Ontario counties except: (a) In association with the [plaintiff] or (b) If the [plaintiff] terminates the agreement and employs another oral surgeon".

In addition, the defendant agreed, "in consideration of the * * * terms of employment, and of the experience gained while working with" the plaintiff, to execute a $40,000 promissory note to the plaintiff, to become payable if the defendant left the plaintiff and practiced "dentistry and/or Oral Surgery" in the five enumerated counties.[1]

When the contract expired, the two men engaged in extended discussions as to the nature of their continued association—as employer and employee or

---

e. Located on scenic Cayuga Lake in beautiful central New York, Ithaca is one of the world's centers of learning. It is the home of Cornell University, with over 600 students at a great law school.

1. Either party was privileged to terminate the agreement on 60 days' notice within the three-year period and, if the plaintiff were to do so, the contract recited, the defendant was released from the restrictive covenant and the note.

as partners. Unable to reach an accord, the defendant, in February, 1968, left the plaintiff's employ and opened his own office for the practice of oral surgery in Ithaca a week later. The dentists in the area thereupon began referring their patients to the defendant rather than to the plaintiff, and in two months the latter's practice from the Ithaca area dwindled to almost nothing and he closed the office in that city. In point of fact, the record discloses that about 90% of the defendant's present practice comes from referrals from dentists in the counties specified in the restrictive covenant, the very same dentists who had been referring patients to the plaintiff's Ithaca office when the defendant was working there.[2]

The plaintiff, alleging a breach of the restrictive covenant, seeks not only an injunction to enforce it but also a judgment of $40,000 on the note. The Supreme Court, after a nonjury trial, decided in favor of the plaintiff and granted him both an injunction and damages as requested. On appeal, however, the Appellate Division reversed the resulting judgment and dismissed the complaint; it was that court's view that the covenant was void and unenforceable on the ground that its restriction against the practice of both dentistry and oral surgery was impermissibly broad.

There can be no doubt that the defendant violated the terms of the covenant when he opened his own office in Ithaca. But the mere fact of breach does not, in and of itself, resolve the case. Since there are "powerful considerations of public policy which militate against sanctioning the loss of a man's livelihood," the courts will subject a covenant by an employee not to compete with his former employer to an "overriding limitation of 'reasonableness'". (Purchasing Assoc. v. Weitz, 13 N.Y.2d 267, 272, 246 N.Y.S.2d 600, 603, 196 N.E.2d 245 * * *.) Such covenants by physicians are, if reasonable in scope, generally given effect. * * * "It is a firmly established doctrine", it has been noted, "that a member of one of the learned professions, upon becoming assistant to another member thereof, may, upon a sufficient consideration, bind himself not to engage in the practice of his profession upon the termination of his contract of employment, within a reasonable territorial extent, as such an agreement is not in restraint of trade or against public policy" (Ann., Restriction on Practice of Physician, 58 A.L.R. 156, 162).

Each case must, of course, depend, to a great extent, upon its own facts. It may well be that, in some instances, a restriction not to conduct a profession or a business in two counties or even in one, may exceed permissible limits. But, in the case before us, having in mind the character and size of the counties involved, the area restriction imposed is manifestly reasonable. The five small rural counties which it encompasses comprise the very area from which the plaintiff obtained his patients and in which the defendant would be in direct competition with him. Thus, the covenant's coverage coincides precisely with "the territory over which the practice extends", and this is proper and permissible. (6A Corbin, Contracts [1962], § 1393, p. 87 * * *.) In brief, the plaintiff made no attempt to extend his influence beyond

---

2. There are two other oral surgeons, in addition to the plaintiff and the defendant, serving the Ithaca area.

the area from which he drew his patients, the defendant being perfectly free to practice as he chooses outside the five specified counties.

Nor may the covenant be declared invalid because it is unlimited as to time, forever restricting the defendant from competing with the plaintiff. It is settled that such a covenant will not be stricken merely because it "contains no time limit or is expressly made unlimited as to time". (37 N.Y.Jur., Master and Servant § 179, p. 60 * * *). * * * In the present case, the defendant opened an office in Ithaca, in competition with the plaintiff, just one week after his employment had come to an end. Under the circumstances presented, we thoroughly agree with the trial judge that it is clear that nearly all of the defendant's practice was, and would be, directly attributable to his association with his former employer.

This brings us to the most troublesome part of the restriction imposed upon the defendant. By the terms of the contract, he agreed not to practice "dentistry and/or Oral Surgery" in competition with the plaintiff. Since the plaintiff practices only "oral surgery," and it was for the practice of that limited type of "dentistry" that he had employed the defendant, the Appellate Division concluded that the plaintiff went beyond permissible limits when he obtained from the defendant the covenant that he would not engage in any "dentistry" whatsoever. The restriction, *as formulated,* is, as the Appellate Division concluded, too broad; it is not reasonable for a man to be excluded from a profession for which he has been trained when he does not compete with his former employer by practicing it.

The plaintiff seeks to justify the breadth of the covenant by urging that, if it had restricted only the defendant's practice of oral surgery and permitted him to practice "dentistry"—that is, to hold himself out as a dentist generally—the defendant would have been permitted, under the Education Law (§ 6601, subd. 3), to do all the work which an oral surgeon could. We have no sympathy with this argument; the plaintiff was not privileged to prevent the defendant from working in an area of dentistry in which he would not be in competition with him. The plaintiff would have all the protection he needs if the restriction were to be limited to the practice of oral surgery, and this poses the question as to the court's power to "sever" the impermissible from the valid and uphold the covenant to the extent that it is reasonable.

Although we have found no decision in New York directly in point, cases in this court support the existence of such a power. * * * Moreover, a number of out-of-state decisions, and they are supported by authoritative texts and commentators, explicitly recognize the court's power of severance and divisibility in order to sustain the covenant insofar as it is reasonable. As Professor Blake put it (73 Harv.L.Rev., at pp. 674–675), "If in balancing the equities the court decides that his [the employee's] activity would fit within the scope of a reasonable prohibition, it is apt to make use of the tool of severance, paring an unreasonable restraint down to appropriate size and enforcing it." In short, to cull from the Washington Supreme Court's opinion in Wood v. May, 73 Wash.2d 307, 314, 438 P.2d 587, 591, "we find it just and equitable to protect appellant [employer] by injunction to the extent necessary to accomplish the basic purpose of the contract insofar as such contract is reasonable." Accordingly, since his practice is solely as an oral surgeon, the plaintiff gains all the injunctive protection to which he is entitled if effect be given only to that part of the covenant which prohibits the defendant from practicing oral surgery.

The question arises, however, whether injunctive relief is precluded by the fact that the defendant's promissory note for $40,000 was to become payable if he breached the agreement not to compete. We believe not. The mere inclusion in a covenant of a liquidated damages provision does not automatically bar the grant of an injunction. (See Rubinstein v. Rubinstein, 23 N.Y.2d 293, 298, 296 N.Y.S.2d 354, 358, 244 N.E.2d 49, 51; Wirth & Hamid Fair Booking v. Wirth, 265 N.Y. 214, 224, 192 N.E. 297, 301; * * *.) The covenant under consideration in this case may not reasonably be read to render "the liquidated damages provision * * * the sole remedy." (Rubinstein v. Rubinstein, 23 N.Y.2d 293, 298, 296 N.Y.S.2d 354, 358, 244 N.E.2d 49, 51, *supra*.) On the other hand, it would be grossly unfair to grant the plaintiff, in addition to an injunction, the full amount of damages ($40,000) which the parties apparently contemplated for a total breach of the covenant, since the injunction will halt any further violation. The proper approach is that taken in *Wirth* (265 N.Y. 214, 192 N.E. 297, *supra*). The court, there faced with a similar situation, granted the injunction sought and, instead of awarding the amount of liquidated damages specified, remitted the matter for determination of the *actual* damages suffered during the period of the breach.

The hardship necessarily imposed on the defendant must be borne by him in view of the plaintiff's rightful interest in protecting the valuable practice of oral surgery which he built up over the course of many years. The defendant is, of course, privileged to practice "dentistry" generally in Ithaca or continue to practice "oral surgery" anywhere in the United States outside of the five small rural counties enumerated. The covenant, part of a contract carefully negotiated with no indication of fraud or overbearing on either side, must be enforced, insofar as it reasonably and validly may, according to its terms. In sum, then, the plaintiff is entitled to an injunction barring the defendant from practicing oral surgery in the five specified counties and to damages actually suffered by him in the period during which the defendant conducted such a practice in Ithaca after leaving the plaintiff's employ.

The order appealed from should be reversed, with costs, and the case remitted to Supreme Court, Cayuga County, for further proceedings in accordance with this opinion.

QUANDT'S WHOLESALE DISTRIBUTORS, INC. v. GIARDINO, 87 A.D.2d 684, 448 N.Y.S.2d 809 (1982). [Plaintiff, a wholesale distributor of institutional and restaurant food and supplies, hired defendant to service accounts in a three-county area. The employment contract contained a restrictive covenant providing that, for a period of six months immediately following termination of his employment, defendant would not compete with plaintiff in the area to which he had been assigned. After about nine months, defendant resigned and went to work for plaintiff's competitor. Plaintiff sued immediately to enforce the restrictive covenant and sought a preliminary injunction enjoining defendant for six months from competing in the three counties involved. On appeal from the trial court's grant of the preliminary injunction, held for defendant.] "Such covenants will be enforced only if reasonably limited temporally and geographically * * * and then only to the extent necessary to protect the employer from the employee's use or disclosure of trade secrets or confidential customer lists. * * * Plaintiff alleges no trade secrets or confidential customer lists. Certainly the names of plaintiff's institutional and restaurant customers are readily available from directories."

Note
Game Show Covenant Not to Compete

Jeopardy's contract with contestants contains the following clause:

"I agree not to participate in any manner on any other game show or reality show until six (6) months after the initial broadcast of each and any of my appearances on the program. * * * I recognize that a breach by me of any part of this paragraph would cause Producer irreparable injury and damage that cannot be reasonably or adequately compensated by damages in an action at law and, therefore, I hereby expressly agree that Producer shall be entitled to injunctive and other equitable relief to prevent and/or cure any breach or threatened breach of this paragraph by me."

Is the clause enforceable? By injunctive relief?

Problem 5–4

Faces Boutique, a facial spa on Hilton Head Island, offered skin care and face lifts to its customers. Faces hired Deborah Ann Gibbs as an "esthetician," to give facials to customers. Under South Carolina law, an esthetician is "any person who is licensed to practice skin care, make up or similar work. Skin care shall be limited to moisturizing, cleansing, or facial or neck massage for the sole purpose of beautifying the skin." The parties' contract included a covenant not to compete:

> For a period of three (3) years after the termination of this agreement, the Employee will not, WITHIN THE TOWN OF HILTON HEAD ISLAND, SC, directly or indirectly, own, manage, operate, control, be employed by, participate in, or be connected in any manner with the ownership, management, operation, advertisement or control of any business in direct competition with the type of business conducted by [Faces]. It is understood and agreed that this prohibition applies to FACIALS, SELLING OF COSMETICS, AND ALL COSMETIC APPLICATION OR FACIAL SPA RELATED SERVICES. (emphasis in original).

After a maternity leave, Gibbs returned to work as a manicurist at Tara's, a Hilton Head beauty salon. South Carolina law defines a manicurist as "any person who is licensed to practice manicuring or pedicuring the nails or similar work." Faces sought to enforce the covenant not to compete on the theory that Tara's also offered facials. At trial, the owner of Faces argued that Gibbs violated the covenant by taking employment at a competitor even though Gibbs was not giving facials. The owner also testified that "she would not attempt to enforce the clause in a manner which would exceed the 'spirit' of the agreement." Please decide the case.

SECTION FIVE: INEQUALITY OF THE EXCHANGE

1 J. STORY, COMMENTARIES ON EQUITY JURISPRUDENCE AS ADMINISTERED IN ENGLAND AND AMERICA

337 (14th ed. 1918).

[E]very person who is not from his peculiar condition or circumstances under disability is entitled to dispose of his property in such a manner and upon such terms as he chooses; and whether his bargains are wise and discreet or profitable or unprofitable or otherwise, are considerations not for courts of justice but for the party himself to deliberate upon.

BLACK INDUSTRIES, INC. v. BUSH

United States District Court, District of New Jersey, 1953.
110 F.Supp. 801.

FORMAN, CHIEF JUDGE.

The plaintiff, Black Industries, Inc., a citizen of Ohio, is suing the defendant, George F. Bush, a citizen of New Jersey doing business as G.F. Bush Associates, for breach of a contract. The defendant has moved for a summary judgment in its favor.

The complaint alleges as a first cause of action that the plaintiff, a manufacturer of drills, machine parts and components thereof and a purchaser of subcontract work from other suppliers, obtained an invitation to bid upon certain contracts with The Hoover Company upon three parts known as anvils, holder primers and plunger supports. The plaintiff assumed the task of obtaining a supplier of these parts and on about March 22, 1951, the defendant reached an agreement with the plaintiff to manufacture 1,300,000 anvils at a price of $4.40 per thousand; 750,000 holder primers at $11.50 per thousand and 700,000 plunger supports at a price of $12 per thousand, all of which were to be made in accordance with government specifications and in conformity with certain drawings. The plaintiff agreed to "service the contract", be responsible for all dealings with The Hoover Company and would be entitled to the difference between the defendant's quotations and the ultimate price. The Hoover Company agreed to purchase the parts from the plaintiff at a rate of $8.10 per thousand anvils, $16 per thousand holder primers and $21.20 per thousand plunger supports.

The complaint further alleges that after undertaking performance of this contract, the defendant failed to complete the order, which caused a loss of $14,625 to the plaintiff, for which sum, together with interest, the plaintiff demands judgment.

* * *

The defendant now moves for a summary judgment in his favor asserting that the agreements alleged in * * * the first * * * cause of action are void as being against public policy. The alleged contract covering production for The Hoover Company was set forth in a "memorial document" consisting of a letter dated April 13, 1951, signed by Mr. Franklin G. Gepfert of Black Industries and signed and agreed to by the defendant.

"G.F. Bush and Associates
Box 175
Princeton, New Jersey.
"Gentlemen:

"Re: The Hoover Co. contract

"In order clearly to outline the agreement as to the manner in which the contract of The Hoover Co. of North Canton, Ohio, is to be received, manufactured, shipped, billed and paid for, I am taking the liberty of reducing the understanding to writing.

"I have spent considerable time, effort and money in developing the contract and bringing it to the point of issuance of a purchase order by The Hoover Co.

"Your company has agreed to manufacture and ship the contract covered by the purchase order at a fixed price, in accordance with certain communications between yourselves and me, under dates of March 22nd and April 1st, 1951.

"The price to be paid by The Hoover Co. shall be that which is set out in the purchase order from The Hoover Co.

"Compensation to which I shall be entitled for my services, shall be the difference between the firm, fixed price contained in your communications to me under dates of March 22nd and April 1st, 1951; and the ultimate price to be paid by The Hoover Co., upon the basis set out in the purchase order.

"The purchase order, when received, will run directly to G.F. Bush and Associates of Princeton, New Jersey, but will be forwarded to me and then remitted to your company.

"It is understood that I am to service the contract and follow through with certain duties which I have undertaken in connection therewith.

"Your company is to manufacture the order and ship the material directly to The Hoover Co. in accordance with the specifications which are part of the purchase order. Your company, however, is not to bill The Hoover Co. All shipping invoices, documents of transfer and title are to be forwarded to me, and I shall have the exclusive right to bill, upon G.F. Bush and Associates' billing forms and receive payment therefor in your behalf.

"In order to effect this arrangement, it will be necessary for you to forward G.F. Bush and Associates' invoices, shipment and billing forms, together with documents of shipment to me, with instructions to The Hoover Co. that all payments to your company are to be forwarded by The Hoover Co. directly to G.F. Bush and Associates, Box 3037, Euclid 17, Ohio.

"It is understood that I shall have the right to receive payment, cash checks made payable to your company under The Hoover Co. contract; and to remit to you the amounts payable to G.F. Bush and Associates under the agreement contained in the communications of March 22nd and April 1st. I shall be entitled to retain the balance as compensation due me.

"It will be necessary for me to open an agency account at Cleveland, Ohio to deposit payments made by The Hoover Co. and make payments therefrom of sums due you, and to withdraw therefrom the balance as compensation due me.

"I believe that the foregoing sets out the entire understanding between us with reference to The Hoover Co. order. Your acknowledgment of this communication will indicate your approval of the agreement as set out above.

"Sincerely yours,
/s/ Franklin G. Gepfert
Franklin Gepfert

FGG/mdl
"Approved and Agreed to by
G.F. Bush and Associates
/s/ George F. Bush April 19, 1951."
Owner

The defendant points out that the products to be purchased by The Hoover Company * * * were to be used * * * to fulfill government contracts in aid of the defense effort. He notes that on The Hoover Company contract, Black Industries for its relatively minor role, was to receive a profit of 84.09% on the anvils, 39.13% on the holder primers and 68.33% on the plunger supports. * * * The defendant asserts that provisions in the contract as to the manner of ordering the goods, shipping them, billing and paying for them were designed to conceal these large profits from both The Hoover Company and the defendant.

In support of its contention that these alleged contracts are void as against public policy the defendant maintains that the profits accruing to Black Industries would have been passed on to the government and the public in the form of increased prices. As evidence of the policy of Congress to avoid excessive expenditures the defendant [cited a federal statute designed to bar excessive profits on war contracts and "related subcontracts" made with the United States.]

* * *

The contract in the present case * * * does not fall in any [category enabling the Court to find it void as against public policy.] It is not a contract by the defendant to pay the plaintiff for inducing a public official to act in a certain manner; it is not a contract to do an illegal act; and it is not a contract which contemplates collusive bidding on a public contract. It should be noted that the first and third categories of cases, upon which the defendant relies most heavily, involve agreements which directly impinge upon government activities. In the case at hand, the contract's only effect on the government was that ultimately the government was to buy the product of which defendant's goods were to be a component. Neither the defendant nor the plaintiff had any dealings with the United States on account of this contract, and therefore the profit accruing to the plaintiff was not to have been earned as a result of either inducing government action or interfering with the system of competitive bidding. This contract cannot, therefore, be declared void as against public policy on the basis of the precedents cited by the defendant.

It is quite possible that the plaintiff was to have received a very high profit on the sale of the parts, either because The Hoover Company agreed to pay too high a price or because the defendant quoted too low a price. Further proof would be required to establish this as a fact. Even if it were proved that the plaintiff was to have received a far greater profit than the defendants for a much smaller contribution, the defendant would nevertheless be bound by his agreement by the familiar rule that relative values of the consideration in a contract between business men dealing at arm's length without fraud will not affect the validity of the contract. * * *

The fact that the government is the ultimate purchaser of the product in which defendant's parts are used is cited by the defendant as a reason to hold that this contract is void as against public policy. To so hold would necessitate either ruling that all contracts are void if they provide for compensation for middlemen, such as Black Industries, between producer and purchaser of goods which ultimately are incorporated in products sold to the government, a result which is not supported by precedent and which would defy the realities of our economic life, or deciding in every case involving such a contract whether the compensation paid a middleman such as the plaintiff here who locates purchasers and assists the producer in other ways, is reasonable. This latter course would, in effect, impose price regulatory functions on the court. There are other and more effective methods of insuring that the government does not pay an unreasonable price for its supplies. The manufacturer selling directly to the United States must conform to procedures such as bidding designed to protect the government, and which should, in conjunction with the ordinary considerations of profits and loss, insure that prime contractors do not pay outlandish prices for the products they buy in order to fulfill a government contract. The contract may be subject to renegotiation. 50 U.S.C.A.Appendix, § 1211 et seq. I do not believe that it is the function of the court to interfere by determining the validity of a contract between ordinary business men on the basis of its beliefs as to the adequacy of the consideration. Consequently, I hold that, assuming the facts to be as stated by the defendant, the contract sued on in this case is not void as against public policy and the defendant's motion for a summary judgment will, therefore, be denied.

Let an order be submitted in accordance with this opinion.

JACKSON v. SEYMOUR

Supreme Court of Appeals of Virginia, 1952.
193 Va. 735, 71 S.E.2d 181.

[Lucy Jackson brought this action for rescission of a deed by which she conveyed to her brother, Benjamin Seymour, a tract of land for $275. She also sought an accounting. She alleged that she was induced to sell the land as the result of the representations of her brother, in whom she had "complete confidence" concerning the management of her property, that the land was of "no value except for a pasture," and that she later discovered the land contained merchantable timber worth $3,200 to $5,000. Jackson further alleged that certain statements of her brother were "false" and "fraudulent."]

EGGLESTON, JUSTICE.

* * *

Since 1931 Mrs. Jackson had been the owner of a farm of 166 acres in Brunswick county which adjoined lands owned by her brother, Benjamin J. Seymour, the defendant. After the death of her husband (the date of which is not shown in the record) Mrs. Jackson sought and obtained the assistance of her brother, who is a successful farmer and business man, in renting the farm for her. He rented the tillable portions of the farm, collected the rents, and made settlements with her which she never questioned. Up to the time of the transaction with which we are concerned they were devoted to each other and she had, as she says, "the utmost confidence in him."

In 1946 Tazewell Wilkins approached Seymour about the purchase of a tract of Seymour's land containing 30.46 acres for a pasture. He also wanted to buy the adjoining tract of 31 acres, which was a part of the land owned by Mrs. Jackson. Seymour told Wilkins that while he was willing to take $275 for his (Seymour's) land, he did not own the 31–acre tract and suggested that Wilkins see Mrs. Jackson about buying it. While Seymour also conveyed this information to Mrs. Jackson the record discloses no negotiations between Wilkins and Mrs. Jackson for the purchase of her land.

In February, 1947, Mrs. Jackson approached her brother, saying that she was in need of funds and was anxious to sell the 31–acre tract in which Wilkins had shown interest. Seymour did not want to buy the property, but because of his sister's need for money he agreed to purchase it at $275, which was the price which had been mentioned in his negotiations with Wilkins. The brother was then unaware that there was valuable timber on the land and contemplated using it for a pasture. Seymour gave his sister a check for $275 and she signed a receipt therefor. On the next day Mrs. Jackson executed and delivered a deed conveying the property to her brother. The deed was prepared by a local attorney at Seymour's request and expense.

A short while after Seymour had acquired the property it came to his attention that some trees had been cut from the tract. Upon investigation he discovered for the first time that there was valuable timber on the land.

The evidence does not disclose the exact quantity and value of this timber. It shows that in 1948 Seymour cut from the land which he had purchased from his sister and from adjoining lands owned by him, 148,055 feet of lumber and that the greater portion of this came from the Jackson tract. This timber had a stumpage value of approximately $20 per 1,000 feet.

The land in controversy is located in an isolated section and it is undisputed that Mrs. Jackson had never been on it and knew nothing of its character. While Seymour had hunted in the vicinity and been within sight of the property he had never actually been on the land. To use his own words, "I was positive that it was just naked land" and worth $8 or $9 an acre. Thus, neither vendor nor vendee knew that there was valuable timber growing on the land.

On cross-examination Seymour admitted that the presence of timber on the land "was not within the contemplation" of him and his sister at the time the sale was consummated. He testified that if he had known of this timber he would not have bought the property from her for $275.

After Mrs. Jackson discovered that her brother had cut and marketed valuable timber from the land she demanded an accounting from him of the profits derived therefrom. When this demand was refused the present litigation followed.

Upon the conclusion of the evidence the lower court dictated from the bench an opinion holding that the plaintiff's allegations of *actual* fraud had not been sustained by the evidence and that consequently she was not entitled to rescission of the deed on that ground. It took under advisement whether under the allegations of the bill the plaintiff was entitled to relief on the ground of *constructive* fraud because of the "confidential relationship" of the parties and the "gross inadequacy in price."

[While the constructive fraud allegation was under advisement, Jackson attempted to "amend her bill" to include a count based on her "honest and material" mistake of fact, which would make enforcement of the deed a "fraud" upon her rights. The lower court rejected the amendment because it was "tendered too late." Since Jackson's case was based on actual fraud, the lower court denied Jackson any relief. She appealed.]

* * *

* * * We are of opinion that under the evidence, viewed in the light of the trial court's determination of the issues of fact favorable to the defendant, the plaintiff is entitled to equitable relief on the ground of constructive fraud, and that such relief is within the scope of the allegations of the original bill of complaint.

The undisputed evidence shows that shortly after the defendant had acquired this tract of land from his sister for the sum of $275, he cut and marketed therefrom timber valued at approximately ten times what he had paid for the property. A mere statement of the matter shows the gross and shocking inadequacy of the price paid.

This is not the ordinary case in which the parties dealt at arm's length and the shrewd trader was entitled to the fruits of his bargain. The parties were brother and sister. He was a successful business man and she a widow in need of money and forced by circumstances, according to the defendant's own testimony, to sell a part of the lands which she had inherited. Because of their friendly and intimate relations she entrusted to him and he assumed the management and renting of a portion of this very land. He engaged tenants for such of the land as could be cultivated and collected the rents. She accepted his settlements without question.

Moreover, it is undisputed that neither of the parties knew of the timber on the land and we have from the defendant's own lips the admission that as it turned out "afterwards" he had paid a grossly inadequate price for the property and that he would not have bought it from her for the small amount paid if he had then known of the true situation.

To hold that under these circumstances the plaintiff is without remedy would be a reproach to the law. Nor do we think that a court of equity is so impotent.

The controlling principles were thus stated in Planters Nat. Bank v. Heflin Co., 166 Va. 166, 173, 174, 184 S.E. 216, 219:

"* * * Mere failure of consideration or want of consideration will not ordinarily invalidate an executed contract. The owner of the historic estate of 'Blackacre' can give it away, and he can sell it for a peppercorn. Courts, though they have long arms, cannot relieve one of the consequences of a contract merely because it was unwise. They are not guardians in general to the people at large, but where inadequacy of price is such as to shock their conscience equity is alert to seize upon the slightest circumstance indicative of fraud, either actual or constructive." * * *

In Texas Co. v. Northrup, [154 Va. 428, 153 S.E. 659] we quoted with approval this definition by Lord Thurlow of the gross inadequacy of consideration as indicating constructive fraud: " 'An inequality so strong, gross and manifest that it must be impossible to state it to a man of common sense without producing an exclamation at the inequality of it.' * * * Gwynne v. Heaton, 1 Bro.Ch. 1, 9; 28 Rep. 949." 154 Va., at page 443, 153 S.E., at page 663.

Clearly the inadequacy of consideration here meets that definition.

In addition to the gross inadequacy of consideration we have the confidential relation of the parties, the pecuniary distress of the vendor, and the mutual mistake of the parties as to the subject matter of the contract. Unquestionably, we think, to permit the transaction to stand would result in constructive fraud upon the rights of the plaintiff. Hence, she is entitled to relief in equity.

To grant a rescission of the deed, under the circumstances here, does no violence to the principle that the relief granted must conform to the case made out in the bill of complaint. While the bill alleges actual fraud, it also contains allegations of these constituent elements of constructive fraud: The confidential relation of the parties; the reliance by the plaintiff upon the advice and judgment of the defendant in her business affairs; the gross inadequacy of the price paid; her offer to restore the purchase price and rescind the transaction, and his rejection of the offer.

In Moore v. Gregory, 146 Va. 504, 131 S.E. 692, we quoted with approval this definition of constructive fraud as written in 26 C.J., Fraud, § 4, p. 1061, now found in 37 C.J.S., Fraud, § 2–c, pp. 211, 212: " 'Constructive fraud is a breach of legal or equitable duty, which irrespective of the moral guilt of the fraud feasor, the law declares fraudulent, because of its tendency to deceive others, to violate public or private confidence, or to injure public interests. Neither actual dishonesty of purpose nor intent to deceive is an essential element of constructive fraud. An intent to deceive is an essential element of actual fraud. The presence or absence of such an intent distinguishes actual fraud from constructive fraud.' " 146 Va., at page 523, 131 S.E., at page 697.

In the same case we said: "Constructive fraud may be inferred from the intrinsic nature and subject of the bargain itself." 146 Va., at page 527, 131 S.E., at page 698.

It is true that there is no specific allegation in the bill here that the circumstances under which the defendant acquired the property amounted to constructive fraud, but such allegation would have been merely the conclusion of the pleader which necessarily flows from the facts alleged. * * *

* * *

We are, therefore, of opinion that the lower court should have entered a decree granting the plaintiff's prayer for a rescission of the conveyance and restoring the parties to the *status quo* in so far as practicable. By way of incidental relief the plaintiff is entitled to recover of the defendant the fair stumpage value of the timber removed by the latter from the land, with interest from the date of such removal, and the fair rental value of the property during the time the defendant was in possession. The defendant is entitled to a return of the purchase price paid by him, with interest from the date that the plaintiff offered to rescind the transaction, and taxes paid by him on the land since the date of the conveyance, with interest.

The decree appealed from is reversed and the cause remanded for further proceedings in conformity with the views here expressed.

Reversed and remanded.

ATIYAH, BOOK REVIEW: C. FRIED, CONTRACT AS PROMISE

95 Harv.L.Rev. 509, 527 (1981).

The proposition that a person is always the best judge of his own interests is a good starting point for laws and institutional arrangements, but as an infallible empirical proposition it is an outrage to human experience. The parallel moral argument, that to prevent a person, even in his own interests, from binding himself is to show disrespect for his moral autonomy, can ring very hollow when used to defend a grossly unfair contract secured at the expense of a person of little bargaining skill. If a smart operator makes a highly advantageous deal with a person of low intelligence or skill, does the former really show "respect" for the latter's moral autonomy by exploiting his advantage in this way?

* * * Promises ought to be treated as prima facie binding rather than absolutely and conclusively binding. Exchanges of benefits are likely to be in the interests of those who make them, and there is therefore a strong prima facie case for upholding them. Promises are likely to be relied upon and those who rely would suffer loss from breach; these too are prima facie good reasons for upholding the binding nature of a promise.

On the other hand, to say that such results are likely to follow is not to say that they are certain to follow; the presumption must be rebuttable.

SECTION SIX: UNCONSCIONABILITY

A. ORIGINS

In the Middle Ages, the English Chancery Court introduced equitable rules and remedies partly in response to the inflexibility of English courts of law. Eventually the Chancellors began to follow their own precedents, and principles such as mistake, misrepresentation, estoppel, unclean hands, and unconscionability emerged. These principles reflected the general allegiance of equity courts to various ideas of fairness. Equity courts in the United States came to recognize most of the same general principles.

Unconscionability was frequently invoked in equity as a defense to specific performance of contracts for the sale of land, and conflicting authority developed on the precise elements necessary for a finding of unconscionability. Some decisions required not only bargaining improprieties, such as concealment of facts or trickery, but substantive unfairness of terms as well. Other decisions required only one or the other.

Today, the Uniform Commercial Code in section 2–302 incorporates the unconscionability doctrine and makes it available as a defense in all sale of goods cases, not just those in which an equitable remedy such as specific performance is sought. Moreover, many courts today apply the unconscionability doctrine in non-sales cases as well. A detailed history of the drafting of U.C.C. § 2–302 is found in Leff, Unconscionability and the Code—The Emperor's New Clause, 115 U.Pa.L.Rev. 485 (1967).

RYAN v. WEINER

Court of Chancery of Delaware, 1992.
610 A.2d 1377.

ALLEN, CHANCELLOR.

In this action Robert Ryan seeks, *inter alia,* an order canceling a deed to his house that he gave to Norman Weiner in May 1984. Ryan asserts that in making that transfer he was deceived by Weiner and only recently came to understand that the deed in question was not simply a security interest. Mr. Weiner denies all aspects of the complaint. The case has been through a brief trial.

While I do not reach the question whether Weiner in fact deceived Ryan by making false statements to him upon which Ryan relied, I do conclude that the transfer in question represents a shocking and oppressive transaction; that Mr. Weiner took the grossest advantage of Mr. Ryan, who found himself in weakened and distressed circumstances, and that Weiner manipulated their dealings to accomplish that result. In short, for the reasons set forth below, I conclude, that this represents that unusual case in which a court of equity cannot let stand an executed contract but is obligated to grant the remedy of rescission.

I.

Mr. Ryan is a 69 year old man with a ninth grade education. He retired about ten years ago from his work as a laborer and subsists on a small pension and social security benefits. In 1971, Ryan and his now deceased wife purchased a modest house located at 928 Pine Street in Wilmington, Delaware to live in. The price was $8,600. Most of that was borrowed and repayment was secured by a first mortgage.

After about 12 years of mortgage payments, Mr. Ryan (who had become a widower in the interim) fell badly behind in his mortgage payments. The monthly payment was $98 per month at that time. By April 1984, he owed in excess of $1,000 in arrearages.

It is agreed that Ryan's house had a fair market value at that time of $19,800. (Stip. Facts ¶ 18). The balance of the loan secured by the mortgage was less than $8,000. In March 1984, the mortgage lender instituted foreclosure proceedings. Mr. Ryan did not answer the complaint and, on April 16,

1984, a default judgment in the amount of $7,843.26 was entered. A sheriff's sale was scheduled for June 12, 1984.

Ryan testified that throughout this period he was an active alcoholic.

Defendant, Norman Weiner, was (and is) a licensed real estate broker who engages in the business, *inter alia,* of buying and leasing inner-city houses. On Sunday, May 13, 1984, Weiner arrived at Ryan's home unannounced and informed Ryan that he could help him keep his house. The parties had not met prior to that. They disagree about what was said at that meeting. Ryan reports that he understood that Weiner offered to lend him the money to make up the back payments and to take a deed to secure repayment. Weiner reports that he offered to buy the house and to let Ryan continue to live in it as a tenant. They agree, however, that Weiner did not offer to make a cash payment to Ryan.

Weiner showed Ryan no papers but told him he would pick him up the following morning to complete the transaction. When Weiner left that afternoon, he took Ryan's original deed to the property which he said he would hold in his safe deposit box.

At 8:00 a.m. the following day, Weiner picked Ryan up at his house and drove him to the office of Harold Green, a Delaware lawyer, who represented Weiner in real estate transactions and is also a close personal friend and relative. At Green's office, Ryan was asked to sign several documents which Weiner explained were necessary. Green did not explain any of the documents to Ryan, nor did he speak to him during their ten-minute meeting. Neither Weiner nor Green advised Ryan of his right to seek independent legal advice concerning the transaction. (Tr. 26–27, 182). At trial, Green testified that he had no specific recollection of his meeting with Ryan and was unable to confirm any of the alleged conversations or events that took place between the parties. Ryan says that he signed the documents without reading them because he trusted the defendant's statements that the papers were loan documents. (Tr. 19, 28).

In fact, Ryan did not sign loan documents on May 14, 1984, but signed a deed transferring the Pine Street property to Weiner. (Pl.'s Exh. 1). According to Ryan, he did not see the front page of the deed containing the property description when he signed the back of the deed and neither Weiner nor Green told him that he was signing a deed. (Tr. 20, 82). He also claims that he did not understand a one-sentence document that he signed in Green's office, assigning all money held in escrow to Weiner. (Pl.'s Exh. 9). Ryan also signed a document which he later learned was a settlement sheet. He testified that when he signed the document on May 14, 1984, it contained no figures and only had about two inches of writing on it. The document now bears the date May 15, 1984 and contains many figures. (Pl.'s Exh. 2 & Tr. 23). Ryan was not given any copies of documents that he had signed. (Tr. 26, 234).

Before Weiner had gone to Ryan's house, Mr. Green had requested and received from the mortgagee two documents: a "Sale Subject to Mortgage" document (now dated May 14, 1984) and an "Insurance Information and Assignment of Escrow." The assignment form required Ryan's signature and required that Seller's address be set forth. (Pl.'s Exhs. 8 & 16). But, Weiner, not Ryan, signed the Assignment of Escrow form, completing the section which requested the seller's forwarding address with Weiner's own P.O. box number. The forms were then sent back to the mortgage company as an enclosure with a letter from Green of May 15, 1984. (Pl.'s Exh. 14). Ryan never saw the Sale Subject to Mortgage Statement or Insurance Information and Assignment of Escrow form.

The May 14, 1984 deed signed by Ryan recites that $7,000 in consideration was paid to him. He did not, however, receive any cash, nor did Mr. Weiner ever pay off the balance of the outstanding mortgage on the property or satisfy the default judgment entered against Ryan. Weiner did thereafter pay the mortgage company $1,898.30 in order to bring the loan current. But Weiner did not sign any documents assuming the legal obligations of the mortgage. (Tr. 113–115).

The result of the transaction was that Ryan transferred ownership of his property to Weiner without receiving any part of the financial value of the then equity in the property of approximately $12,000. Ryan has remained personally liable for paying off the mortgage balance under the mortgage bond and note.

* * *

Following the May 13 and 14 meetings with Weiner, Ryan continued to live in the house. A lease was executed with an effective date of May 14, 1984. (Pl.'s Exh. 3). Weiner steadily increased Ryan's monthly payments over intervening seven years from $100 a month to $310 per month. (Stip. Facts ¶¶ 20–25). During the same period the mortgage payment also increased, but only from $93 in 1984 to $120 in 1991. (Stip. Facts ¶¶ 13 & 14). Over the course of this arrangement Ryan paid Weiner the following amounts:

Time Period	Number of Monthly Payments	Amount	Total
July 1984	1	$100	$ 100
Aug. 1984—June 1985	11	160	1,760
July 1985—Oct. 1985	4	260	1,040
Nov. 1985—Dec. 1988	38	270	10,260
Jan. 1989—June 1990	18	290	5,220
July 1990—Apr. 1991	10	310	3,100
	Total:		$21,480

Over the years, while Ryan paid him a total of $21,480, Mr. Weiner expended $12,149.27 on the mortgage, insurance, taxes, sewer and water charges, including the amount paid to bring the mortgage up to date in 1984.[1]

* * *

Before his May, 1991 payment was due, Ryan concluded that he had paid Weiner a total amount in excess of the amount of the mortgage on the property and the amount of Weiner's "loan." He refused to make any more

---

1. Ryan asked Weiner to make repairs to the property since it was in a deteriorated condition. Weiner apparently purchased material for repairs to the property but left the repair work to be completed by Ryan or his friends. (Tr. 41–42).

monthly payments to Weiner in May, 1991. Weiner promptly commenced a summary action in the justice of peace court to evict Ryan. On Ryan's motion, this court stayed that proceeding, concluding that issues of the quality of Weiner's title itself and Ryan's alleged right to have Weiner's deed canceled were remedies not available in the justice of peace court.

II.

The right of competent persons to make contracts and thus privately to acquire rights and obligations is a basic part of our general liberty. This ability to enter and enforce contracts is universally thought not only to reflect and promote liberty, but as well to promote the production of wealth. Thus, the right to make and enforce contracts is elemental in our legal order. But not every writing purporting to contain a promise or every document purporting to make a transfer will be given legal effect. A large body of law defines when valid contracts are formed and when and how they can be enforced.

Contracts or transfers induced by fraudulent misrepresentations, for example, can be avoided. Similarly, a lack of legal capacity or the existence of duress can lead a court to declare a promise unenforceable or a transfer voidable. *See, e.g.,* A. Farnsworth, *Contracts* §§ 4.1–4.20 (1982). Ordinarily, an evaluation of relative values of the bargain to the parties will not provide a basis for such judicial action.

It is general rule, recited by courts for well over a century, that the adequacy or fairness of the consideration that adduces a promise or a transfer is not alone grounds for a court to refuse to enforce a promise or to give effect to a transfer. *See, e.g.,* 1 A. Corbin, *Corbin on Contracts* § 127 (1963 & Supp.1991) (adequacy of consideration); 3 J. Pomeroy, *A Treatise on Equity Jurisprudence* § 926 n. 7 (citing numerous federal and state cases). This rule, present in 17th and 18th century cases, achieved its greatest dignity in the jurisprudence of 19th century classical liberalism. *See, e.g.,* P. Atiyah, *The Rise and Fall of Freedom of Contract* 146–152 & 169–180 (Clarendon Press Oxford 1979). Thus, the classical liberal's premise concerning the subjectivity (and thus non-reviewability) of value[2] has plainly been a dominant view in our contract law for a very long time. Countless cases from the 19th and 20th centuries could be cited for the proposition that "mere inadequacy of price" will not invalidate a contract or a transfer. But as standard as that generalization is, it has not precluded courts, on occasion, from striking down contracts or transfers in which inadequacy of price is coupled with some circumstance that amounts to inequitable or oppressive conduct. That is, the "rule" that courts will not weigh consideration or assess the wisdom of bargains, has not fully excluded the opposite proposition, that at some point courts will do so even in the absence of actual fraud, duress or incapacity. *See* 2 Devlin, *Real Property and Deeds* § 814 (1911); Story, *Commentaries on Equity Jurisprudence,* (Cambridge Press 1835), (Arno Press Reprint 1972) §§ 238, 244–247.

The notion that a court can and will review contracts for fairness is apt for good reason to strike us as dangerous, subjecting negotiated bargains to

2. An early statement of this view of the subjective and relative nature of value is Hobbes', in *The Leviathan:*

The value of all things contracted for is measured by the Appetites of the Contractors;

and therefore just value, is that which they be content to give.

The Leviathan (Pelican edition) Part I, Chp. 15, at 208 (Harmondsworth 1974).

the loosely constrained review of the judicial process. Perhaps for this reason, courts have evoked this doctrine with extreme reluctance and then only when all of the facts suggest a level of unfairness that is unconscionable.

The applicable principle is ancient. It was old when Justice Story summarized it in 1835:

> Of a kindred nature, to the cases already considered, are cases of bargains of such an unconscionable nature, and of such gross inequality, as naturally lead to the presumption of fraud, imposition, or undue influence. This is the sort of fraud, to which Lord Hardwicke alluded in the passage already cited, when he said, that they were such bargains, as no man in his senses and not under delusion would make on the one hand, and as no honest and fair man would accept on the other, being inequitable and unconscientious bargains. Mere inadequacy of price, or any other inequality in the bargain, is not, however, to be understood as constituting *per se* a ground to avoid a bargain in Equity....

> * * *

Story, *Commentaries on Equity Jurisprudence, supra,* §§ 244–246 (footnotes omitted).

> * * *

[Real estate] cases give a flavor for the application of this judicial nullification of contract. *Lampley v. Pertuit,* Miss.Supr., 199 So.2d 452 (1967), for example, involved an alleged sale of a house, valued in excess of $1600, for $400. While plaintiffs had given a deed absolute, they testified that they had intended a loan not a sale and had intended the deed as security. In canceling the deed, the court concluded that the parties must have entered a loan transaction, reasoning that, a $400 purchase price would represent "grossly inadequate" consideration for the plaintiffs' house. The court gave weight to the trial court's finding that the defendant had a far superior education and understanding of the intricacies of real estate transactions than the plaintiffs. *Id.* at 454.

> * * *

Statutory developments over the last thirty years reflect an explicit legislative endorsement of this ancient equitable doctrine. The most important example of this mid-twentieth century codification is the unconscionability provision contained in Section 2–302 of the Uniform Commercial Code. That provision has, of course, been adopted in almost all of the states and applies to sale of all goods. Section 2–302 provides, in part:

> (1) If the court as a matter of law finds the contract or any clause ... to have been unconscionable [when] ... made the court may refuse to enforce the contract....

6 *Del.C.* § 2–302 (Michie 1975). The drafters' comments note that "the basic test is whether, in light of the general commercial background and the commercial needs of the particular trade or case, the clauses involved are so one-sided as to be unconscionable under the circumstances existing at the time of the making of the contract." *Id.*

While the UCC does not, of course, apply to sales of land, there is good reason to assume that the legislature's solicitude for parties who are disadvantaged by bargains that are unconscionably oppressive should not be entirely ignored where sales of land are concerned. Such transactions are obviously enormously more significant than a purchase of goods to the average person. They will occur rarely in the typical life and will often involve a person's largest single asset. *See* Leff, *Unconscionability and the Code—The Emperor's New Clause,* 115 U.Pa.L.Rev. 485, 537 (1967).[3]

* * *

[The court found the contract to be unconscionable:]

(a) *The substance:* the financial aspects of the sale are shocking. Mr. Ryan had lived for more than 13 years in this modest house and had until relatively shortly before the sale regularly made his mortgage payment. The house had a fair market value of $19,800 and a mortgage of about $7,800.00. Thus, at the time it represented some $12,000 of equity which, one can safely assume, represented all of the assets that Ryan had acquired over a long life as an employed laborer.

In exchange for the conveyance of this asset, Ryan received no cash, and no release of liability. He received only a promise to be able to occupy the same house at a market-rate rent. That rent was, at first, modestly in excess of the mortgage payment ($100) but within 15 months it had been raised twice, first to $160 (60% increase) then to $260 per month (additional 62% increase). *See* * * * (table) above.

What, on the other hand, did Mr. Weiner get from the transaction and what did he give? He received, of course, the value of the property net of the mortgage. He paid out some cash (about $1,900) but that amount, in large measure, reduced the amount of the mortgage lien on the property and thus immediately accrued to the financial interest, not of Ryan, but of the new equity owner—Weiner himself. Therefore if the transaction is valid all that Weiner extended as consideration to Ryan was the right to be a tenant in his house at a fair market rate in excess of the mortgage amortization cost.

From a financial perspective this transaction is as close to a gift as one is likely to encounter.

(b) *The process:* the process that lead to this one-sided bargain, in part, appears to explain and account for it. Ryan was, of course, vulnerable, and unsophisticated, but those facts do not prevent him from making valid contracts. But Ryan's circumstances—his age, his obvious lack of sophistication, his poverty, his distress and his fear of being dispossessed—are factors that one who initiates a transaction concerning transfer of the other's home should take into account, in order to offer some assurance that whatever deal may be made is made knowingly and with due consideration. But instead of offering Ryan sufficient time to consider his proposal (and to perhaps consult with others), Mr. Weiner moved with urgent speed. He did not give Ryan time to consider the matter, perhaps to seek advice from a Legal Aid lawyer or to

3. " . . . real property is likely to be the only thing that relatively unsophisticated people have which is worth tricking them out of . . . the equity cases are replete with factual patterns involving the old being bilked and farmers sweet-talked into ruinous trades." 115 U.Pa.L.Rev. at 536.

consider alternatives. Weiner rushed Ryan. He picked him up at his home early the next day and took Ryan to Weiner's lawyer to sign papers. I am convinced that Ryan did not understand the nature and effect of the papers he signed.

* * *

[The Court also considered Ryan's fault in agreeing to the transaction:] It is hard to say that Ryan exercised ordinary care of a prudent man in entering this transaction. He did not understand the transaction and appears to have naively placed himself entirely into Mr. Weiner's hands. But while Ryan appears as a financial innocent upon whom Mr. Weiner could practice his skills, Weiner appears a manipulative and skillful predator. When one with substantially greater knowledge, experience, and resources himself seeks out the powerless to deal with them directly on matters of vital importance, he assumes some responsibility to assure, to the extent circumstances permit, that they do understand the nature of the transaction proposed. If he does not do this and if the transaction he initiates is oppressive and shockingly one-sided, he cannot retain the bargain. Even if Weiner did not affirmatively deceive Mr. Ryan (as to which I make no finding), he did not assure that the party from whom he attempted to extract so much understood the nature of this transaction. It was this fact more than Ryan's lack of care that accounts for Mr. Ryan's unilateral mistake of thinking he was signing a secured loan.

It is possible to restore the status quo. On one level, the transaction was entirely financial. Ryan never moved out of his house. The mortgage was not paid off by Mr. Weiner; rather he made monthly payments from the payments that Ryan made to him. Thus it is not difficult to return the parties to the status quo as of May, 1984. All that is required is for Mr. Weiner to establish what he paid on account of the house: mortgage, taxes, insurance, heat, utilities and maintenance. These amounts, including the expenditures necessary to bring the mortgage up to date in May 1984 appear to total $12,149.27. They will be credited to him. On the other hand the $21,480.00 paid by Mr. Ryan to Mr. Weiner should be credited to him. After this operation is gone through (and tax adjusted) a net amount will be owing to Mr. Ryan. Interest is a matter upon which the parties should be heard, if they cannot resolve it. Surely Mr. Weiner is entitled to a fair rate of interest on any amounts of credit that he had extended, for so long as he was a net lender into the transaction. It is, however, not clear in the record how long a time passed before all net expenditures were fully recovered from "rental" payments in excess of mortgage payments. Counsel can work out those details. The significant point is that there is no factor that would preclude the entry of an order that will return defendant, financially speaking, to the position he occupied when he went to Mr. Ryan's home to induce a transaction.

* * *

Thus I conclude that this transaction is one that, under principles applied for more than two hundred years, cannot in equity be allowed to stand.[5] I

5. I accept the evidence that Ryan has only recently realized that he sold his house absolutely to Norman Weiner in 1984 and that he has proceeded promptly thereafter to adjudi-cate his rights. More importantly I cannot conclude that any delay in asserting this claim has substantially prejudiced Mr. Weiner. He has made no such claim with respect to his defense

conclude that it involves shockingly unconscionable financial terms, coupled with innocent failure to understand the transaction on one side and sharp and predatory practices on the other. I am satisfied that these facts clearly are the equivalent of cases in which courts have set aside land transfers as fraudulent or constructively fraudulent.

The plaintiff may submit a form of order consistent with the foregoing, on notice.

UNIFORM COMMERCIAL CODE § 2–302.

Unconscionable Contract or Clause

(1) If the court as a matter of law finds the contract or any clause of the contract to have been unconscionable at the time it was made the court may refuse to enforce the contract, or it may enforce the remainder of the contract without the unconscionable clause, or it may so limit the application of any unconscionable clause as to avoid any unconscionable result.

(2) When it is claimed or appears to the court that the contract or any clause thereof may be unconscionable the parties shall be afforded a reasonable opportunity to present evidence as to its commercial setting, purpose and effect to aid the court in making the determination.

B. PROCEDURAL AND SUBSTANTIVE UNCONSCIONABILITY

INDUSTRALEASE AUTOMATED & SCIENTIFIC EQUIPMENT CORP. v. R.M.E. ENTERPRISES, INC.

New York Supreme Court, Appellate Division, 1977.
58 A.D.2d 482, 396 N.Y.S.2d 427.

Hopkins, Justice Presiding.

The primary issue before us is whether disclaimers of express and implied warranties in a lease of industrial equipment are unconscionable under the circumstances where the equipment never operated (see Uniform Commercial Code [UCC], §§ 2–302, 2–316). * * *

* * *

The defendant R.M.E. Enterprises, Inc. (Enterprises) owned a 40–acre picnic grove in Warren, New Jersey. The operation of the grove necessarily generated considerable refuse during the season, which begins in May. Prior to the events involved in this litigation, the trash was piled in 40–foot open-top steel containers and disposed of by a rubbish collector. Enterprises was wholly owned by the defendant Max Evans who, with his wife, the defendant Irene Evans, managed the picnic grove.

Max Evans became interested in disposing of the rubbish through nonpollutant burning on the premises. He visited Farmingdale, New York, at the invitation of Clean Air Controls, Inc. (Clean Air) to inspect equipment in operation which, Clean Air informed him, would meet the requirements of

of this lawsuit and with respect to his financial position, the rescission to be afforded to plaintiff contemplates that defendant will be re-stored to the May 1984 status quo financially. Thus, I find no detriment to defendant from the passage of time.

Enterprises. Impressed with what he saw, he told Clean Air that he would take two units, one to be in reserve if the other broke down. Eventually, on February 24, 1971, a lease between Clean Air and Enterprises was executed, providing for 60 monthly payments of $322.58 in return for the use of the two units. The lease also contained a clause generally disclaiming any warranties, except that it preserved the warranties if the lessor were the manufacturer of the equipment.[1] As Clean Air was the manufacturer of the leased equipment, under the language of the lease the usual warranties were thus in force for the benefit of Enterprises.

Thereafter, acting under instructions, Evans installed a concrete slab, underground wiring and a fuel tank. Evans testified that on May 13, 1971 (and this is not contested by the plaintiff) he was visited by a representative of Clean Air and a representative of the plaintiff who presented him with a set of new papers which "were like the other papers I signed but with a different company's name on the top", that he was told that the lease he had signed before was "no good", and that the new papers had to be signed "so we can get our money so you can get your incinerator." Evans testified that he signed the new papers, which were a lease between Enterprises and the plaintiff for the same equipment, providing for 60 monthly rental payments of $319.70, plus sales tax, and a guaranty by Max and Irene Evans of the lease. That lease contained an unqualified disclaimer of express and implied warranties.[2] It also contained an option which granted the right to Enterprises to acquire the equipment at the end of the lease by a payment to the plaintiff in the sum of $1,390.

On May 14, 1971, the next day, the incinerators were delivered and installed. Evans testified (and his testimony was not contested by the plaintiff) that they did not then or thereafter work, although he complained to both Clean Air and to the plaintiff, which tried in vain to make the equipment operative. Enterprises during this period made four rental payments to the plaintiff. By letters dated September 16, 1971 and December 30, 1971, Enterprises demanded the removal of the incinerators from its premises, but the plaintiff did not accede and required the continuance of the monthly payments.

This litigation then ensued.

The plaintiff's complaint sought $17,936.76, representing the balance of the payments due under the lease, together with the sum of $2,500 for legal

---

1. The lease provided, in bold print:

"9. Lessor makes no warranties with respect to the fitness or suitability of the Leased Property for any purpose or use or with respect to its durability. Lessee acknowledges that the Leased Property is of a size, design and capacity selected by Lessee as suitable for its purposes. Lessor makes no warranties, expressed or implied, with respect to the Leased Property other than that, if new, the standard manufacturer's warranty of new equipment is in effect and Lessor will exercise its rights thereunder for the mutual benefit of Lessor and Lessee (or if Lessor be the manufacturer, it will comply with the terms and conditions of its warranty)."

2. The lease provided, in bold print:

"2.C. (12) Representations. And Lessee does hereby agree that each unit is of a size, design, capacity, and material selected by Lessee, and that Lessee is satisfied that each such unit is suitable for Lessee's purposes, and sufficiently durable under the conditions of usage thereof by Lessee, and that Lessor has made no representations or warranties with respect to the suitability or durability of any unit for the purposes or uses of Lessee, or with respect to the permissible load thereof, or any other representation or warranty, express or implied, with respect thereto."

expenses. The defendants denied liability, claiming that the plaintiff had breached its warranty that the equipment was properly constructed, free of operational defects, and capable of meeting the need of disposing of the rubbish accumulated as the result of its business: and the defendants counter-claimed in addition for the sum of $5,000, alleged to have been incurred as expenses by them in installing the equipment and attempting to make it function properly.

At the trial the court held that the disclaimer of warranties contained in the lease was not unconscionable as a matter of law. The court left to the jury the determination of the issue whether the plaintiff had made express warranties concerning the capacity of the incinerators to function properly, instructing the jury that if in fact the warranties had been made, and the incinerators had not worked properly, the plaintiff had breached its contract.

The jury returned a verdict on the complaint in favor of the defendants and awarded the defendants $1,342.76 on their counterclaim.

[The court first concluded that the U.C.C. applied to the lease because the lease "assumed the true model of a sale."]

* * *

The UCC plainly recognizes the validity of disclaimers of warranties in sales agreements under certain circumstances (UCC, § 2–316). Here, pursuant to the statute, the exclusion of warranties was accomplished by conspicuous and bold print and thus complied with the statute in that respect. The question whether in this case the disclaimer is unconscionable remains.

The defendants had raised the issue of unconscionability at the trial. Trial Term held that the disclaimer was not unconscionable, but submitted to the jury the issues whether the plaintiff had made express warranties concerning the capacity and operating ability of the incinerators and whether the warranties had been breached by the plaintiff. The submission of these issues was, however, in direct conflict with the language of the disclaimer, which excluded reliance by the defendant on any such warranties. Hence, a reversal of the judgment must be directed, unless, on examination of the facts and the language of the disclaimer, we conclude that the disclaimer is unenforceable because of its unconscionability, in which event the issues of the making of express warranties and their breach would survive and hence were properly submitted to the jury. We turn, accordingly, to the question whether under the circumstances of this case the disclaimer is unconscionable.

Section 2–302 of the UCC provides that the court may refuse to enforce a contract clause once it finds the clause to have been unconscionable at the time it was made. The determination of unconscionability is a matter of law for the court to decide * * * and thus subject to our review. The Official Comment to section 2–302 states that it "is intended to allow the court to pass directly on the unconscionability of the contract or particular clause therein and to make a conclusion of law as to its unconscionability", and that "[t]he basic test is whether, in the light of the general commercial background and the commercial needs of the particular trade or case, the clauses involved are so one-sided as to be unconscionable under the circumstances existing at the time of the making of the contract". * * * The term "unconscionable" is thus flexible, to be applied within the framework of the transaction under scrutiny, and considered in the light of the commercial climate then existing and the common law.

Though unconscionability, as an element in the enforcement of contracts, is equitable in origin, there is evidence to sustain the conclusion that the common-law courts as well were moved by the doctrine to invalidate contracts under certain circumstances (1 Corbin on Contracts, § 128, p. 551). The original concept was broad: An unconscionable contract was one "such as no man in his senses and not under delusion would make on the one hand, and as no honest and fair man would accept on the other" (*Earl of Chesterfield v. Janssen*, 2 Ves.Sen. 125, 155, 28 Eng.Reprint 82, 100; cf. *Hume v. United States*, 132 U.S. 406, 411, 10 S.Ct. 134, 33 L.Ed. 393). The test has been more sharply defined "to include an absence of meaningful choice on the part of one of the parties together with contract terms which are unreasonably favorable to the other party", and characterized "by a gross inequality of bargaining power" (*Williams v. Walker–Thomas Furniture Co.*, 121 U.S.App.D.C. 315, 350 F.2d 445, 449). In dealing with the doctrine, commentators have differentiated between procedural and substantive unconscionability. * * *[3] We need not treat that distinction here, for we think that components of both aspects are present. Moreover, in considering the question, we have put aside the cases holding disclaimers of warranties invalid as against public policy in which damages arising from personal injuries were sought to be recovered * * * for we think different considerations are there present. * * *

We must begin the examination of the facts underlying the contract with the awareness that "[p]arties to a contract are given broad latitude within which to fashion their own remedies for breach of contract" * * * and that under the UCC "the obligations of good faith, diligence, reasonableness and care prescribed by this Act may not be disclaimed" (UCC. § 1–102, subd. [3] * * *). Here the evidence is that shortly before the incinerators were to be delivered, the defendants were told that the contract in existence between themselves and Clean Air could not be performed for not clearly communicated reasons, and that a new contract had to be executed to insure delivery of the equipment. The new contract eliminated the warranties which the Clean Air contract had preserved, since Clean Air was the manufacturer of the equipment. The atmosphere of haste and pressure on the defendants is clearly pervasive. In addition, at this point of the bargaining, with the beginning of the season for the defendants' operations at hand, the defendants were clearly at a disadvantage to bargain further and, indeed, did not profess to understand the size and mechanism of the equipment which would satisfy their needs.

Thus, the defendants did not pretend to have equal expertise in the field; they had dealt with Clean Air as purchasers seeking a means to meet a necessity arising in the business, and Clean Air undertook to design and build equipment to achieve the desired result. The interposition of the plaintiff in

---

3. Procedural unconscionability in general is involved with the contract formation process, and focuses on high pressures exerted on the parties, fine print of the contract, misrepresentation, or unequal bargaining position. Substantive unconscionability, on the other hand, is involved with the content of the terms of the contract per se, such as inflated prices, unfair disclaimers or termination clauses (see *Nu Dimensions Figure Salons v. Becerra*, 73 Misc.2d 140, 143, 340 N.Y.S.2d 268, 272).

the transaction served only the purpose of Clean Air and not of the defendants.

Although the statute prescribes that we are to determine unconscionability as of the time of the making of the contract (UCC, § 2–302), we cannot divorce entirely the events which occur later. In this case, the evidence plainly establishes that the equipment did not work at all, that it achieved none of the purposes of the parties. This is a result so "one-sided", in the words of the authors of the Official Comment to the UCC, that the disclaimer in good conscience should not be enforced. In effect, the equipment was worthless. * * *

We therefore hold that the disclaimer of warranties is unconscionable under the circumstances and may not be enforced.

We thus conclude that as the jury found that the plaintiff had made express warranties to the defendants concerning the incinerators and that the warranties had been breached, the judgment should be affirmed.

Note
Procedural and Substantive Unconscionability

In his leading article on unconscionability,[f] Professor Arthur Leff suggested a framework that many courts have followed. He wrote that the paradigm case for finding unconscionability involves both "bargaining naughtiness," which he characterized as procedural unconscionability, and grossly unfair terms, which he called substantive unconscionability. One can see Professor Leff's analysis at work in the Industralease case.

Because of remaining ambiguities about the proper "mix" of procedural and substantive unconscionability required for a finding of unconscionability and because of the widespread view that the "best" case for finding unconscionability will include a healthy sprinkling of both, courts may go to some lengths to find both. Can an argument be made that Industralease really did *not* involve substantive unconscionability? Consider first sections 2–313 and 2–314 of the Uniform Commercial Code (involving the creation of warranties) and section 2–316 (involving exclusion or modification of warranties), all of which also applied to the case. (You should also review Section 8 of Chapter 2.) Compare, too, the Dillman case, which follows the UCC provisions:

UNIFORM COMMERCIAL CODE § 2–313.

Express Warranties by Affirmation, Promise, Description, Sample

(1) Express warranties by the seller are created as follows:

(a) Any affirmation of fact or promise made by the seller to the buyer which relates to the goods and becomes part of the basis of the bargain creates an express warranty that the goods shall conform to the affirmation or promise.

(b) Any description of the goods which is made part of the basis of the bargain creates an express warranty that the goods shall conform to the description.

f. Leff, Unconscionability and the Code—
The Emperor's New Clause, 115 U.Pa.L.Rev.
485 (1967).

(c) Any sample or model which is made part of the basis of the bargain creates an express warranty that the whole of the goods shall conform to the sample or model.

(2) It is not necessary to the creation of an express warranty that the seller use formal words such as "warrant" or "guarantee" or that he have a specific intention to make a warranty, but an affirmation merely of the value of the goods or a statement purporting to be merely the seller's opinion or commendation of the goods does not create a warranty.

UNIFORM COMMERCIAL CODE § 2–314.

Implied Warranty: Merchantability; Usage of Trade

(1) Unless excluded or modified (Section 2–316), a warranty that the goods shall be merchantable is implied in a contract for their sale if the seller is a merchant with respect to goods of that kind. * * *

(2) Goods to be merchantable must be at least such as

* * *

(c) are fit for the ordinary purposes for which such goods are used * * *

UNIFORM COMMERCIAL CODE § 2–316.

Exclusion or Modification of Warranties

(1) Words or conduct relevant to the creation of an express warranty and words or conduct tending to negate or limit warranty shall be construed wherever reasonable as consistent with each other; but * * * negation or limitation is inoperative to the extent that such construction is unreasonable.

(2) Subject to subsection (3), to exclude or modify the implied warranty or merchantability or any part of it the language must mention merchantability and in case of a writing must be conspicuous, and to exclude or modify any implied warranty of fitness the exclusion must be by a writing and conspicuous. Language to exclude all implied warranties of fitness is sufficient if it states, for example, that "There are no warranties which extend beyond the description on the face hereof."

(3) Notwithstanding subsection (2)

(a) unless the circumstances indicate otherwise, all implied warranties are excluded by expressions like "as is", "with all faults" or other language which in common understanding calls the buyer's attention to the exclusion of warranties and makes plain that there is no implied warranty; and

(b) when the buyer before entering into the contract has examined the goods or the sample or model as fully as he desired or has refused to examine the goods there is no implied warranty with regard to defects which an examination ought in the circumstances to have revealed to him; and

(c) an implied warranty can also be excluded or modified by course of dealing or course of performance or usage of trade.

DILLMAN & ASSOCIATES, INC. v. CAPITOL LEASING CO., 110 Ill.App.3d 335, 66 Ill.Dec. 39, 442 N.E.2d 311 (1982). [In an equipment lease, the lessor disclaimed all responsibility for the performance of the leased equipment. Plaintiff, in the income tax return preparation business, complained that a copying machine it had leased from defendant was defective and that the defendant's disclaimer of all warranties on the preprinted lease was unconscionable. The disclaimer included the following language:

"THERE ARE NO WARRANTIES, EXPRESSED OR IMPLIED OF MERCHANTABILITY, FITNESS, OR OTHERWISE WHICH EXTEND BEYOND THE ABOVE DESCRIPTION OF THE EQUIPMENT. LESSOR ASSUMES NO RESPONSIBILITY FOR PERFORMANCE OR MAINTENANCE. EQUIPMENT WILL BE INSURED BY LESSEE."

" * * * Lessee acknowledges and agrees (1) that each unit is of a size, design, capacity and manufacture selected by Lessee, (2) that Lessee is satisfied that the same is suitable for its purpose, (3) that LESSOR IS NOT A MANUFACTURER THEREOF NOR A DEALER IN PROPERTY OF SUCH KIND, and (4) that LESSOR HAS NOT MADE, AND DOES NOT HEREBY MAKE, ANY REPRESENTATION OR WARRANTY OR COVENANT WITH RESPECT TO THE MERCHANTABILITY, CONDITION, QUALITY, DURABILITY OR SUITABILITY OF ANY SUCH UNIT IN ANY RESPECT OR IN CONNECTION WITH OR FOR THE PURPOSES AND USES OF LESSEE, OR ANY OTHER REPRESENTATION OR WARRANTY OR COVENANT OF ANY KIND OF CHARACTER, EXPRESS OR IMPLIED, WITH RESPECT THERETO.

* * * AS BETWEEN LESSOR AND LESSEE, THE EQUIPMENT SHALL BE ACCEPTED AND LEASED BY LESSEE 'AS IS' AND IF ANY FAULTS PREVAIL LESSEE AGREES TO SETTLE ALL SUCH CLAIMS DIRECTLY WITH THE SUPPLIER AND WILL NOT ASSERT ANY SUCH CLAIMS AGAINST LESSOR OR LESSOR'S ASSIGNEE."

"NO REPRESENTATION REGARDING THE EQUIPMENT HEREIN LEASED HAS BEEN MADE BY CAPITOL LEASING COMPANY. LESSEE HAS SELECTED THE PROPERTY TO BE LEASED AND IT IS ORDERED BY CAPITOL LEASING COMPANY FOR THIS LESSEE AND AT LESSEE'S ENTIRE DIRECTION AND RISK."

The court stated:]

"The lease before us, was * * * entered into by businessmen of equal sophistication. This is not the case of an experienced businessman taking unfair advantage of a poorly educated consumer. Although plaintiff was under no compulsion to lease the equipment and could presumably have purchased it either outright or through the use of conventional financing, it chose to obtain a new copying machine by leasing one for reasons which do not appear in the record. After deciding to lease a new copier, the plaintiff was free to select the machine which would best suit its needs and circumstances. Upon making its selection, the plaintiff signed a lease which contained conspicuous, and thus legally binding * * * disclaimers of warranty in not one, but in three locations. The defendant fulfilled its contractual obligations by purchasing and delivering to plaintiff the machine which plaintiff chose. Apparently, the copier which plaintiff received was either defectively manufactured or was inadequate to handle plaintiff's volume of copying. Plaintiff now asks us to declare the lease unconscionable because it is unable to assert against the lessor claims as to the equipment's inadequacy, for which the lessor bears no responsibility whatsoever. We cannot accede to this request. Courts should not assume an overly paternalistic attitude toward the parties to a contract by relieving one or another of them of the consequences of what is at worst a bad bargain * * *, and in declaring the lease in issue here unconscionable, we would be doing exactly that."

DAVIS v. KOLB, 263 Ark. 158, 563 S.W.2d 438 (1978).

BYRD, JUSTICE.

Appellant Ronnie Davis obtained a timber deed to a 294 acre tract from the appellees, Joseph E. Kolb, et al. The consideration recited in the timber deed was: "First $10,500 to [appellees]; next $2,000 to [appellant], all remaining to be divided fifty/fifty after payment of costs of removal of timber." The chancellor set aside the timber deed on the basis that appellant had misrepresented his experience and knowledge as a timber buyer to the appellees and that since appellant was not an experienced timber buyer, the deed was not supported by consideration. For reversal appellant contends:

I. The chancellor's finding of no consideration is clearly against the preponderance of the evidence.

II. The particular misrepresentation found was not a sufficient ground for cancellation of the timber deed because it was not material to the execution of the deed.

The record shows that during the negotiations, appellant led the appellees to believe that appellant was knowledgeable about the value of timber and that appellant was going to cut and remove the timber. Appellant does not deny that he told appellees during the negotiations that the timber was worth $18,000 to $20,000. After obtaining the contract, appellant started trying to sell his contract to someone else and readily admits that he was shocked to find out that the timber had a value in excess of $50,000.

While we do not disagree with the reasoning of the chancellor, and without intending to indicate that his findings are not sufficient to affirm the setting aside of the deed, we affirm upon the basis of Ark.Stat.Ann. § 85–2–302 (Add.1961), which provides: [the Court set forth U.C.C. § 2–302].

The Uniform Commercial Code is made applicable to timber sales by Ark.Stat.Ann. § 85–2–107 (Add.1961).

When we add to the undisputed facts the further fact that appellant had no capital invested and no risk, it would be unconscionable for any court to enforce the contract. See Annotation 18 A.L.R.3d 1305.

Affirmed.

HILLMAN, DEBUNKING SOME MYTHS ABOUT UNCONSCIONABILITY: A NEW FRAMEWORK FOR U.C.C. SECTION 2–302

67 Cornell L.Rev. 1, 19 (1982).

Simply stated, the application of unconscionability to cases involving bargaining problems without reference to the common law [policing] doctrines causes confusion by increasing the level of abstraction in judicial reasoning. For example, instead of determining whether the specific elements of fraud or duress exist, a court using the current unconscionability approach may merely list the many factors influencing its decision—*e.g.*, age, status, intelligence, business sophistication, bargaining power, explanation (or the lack thereof) of terms, firmness of the seller's position (the take-it-or-leave-it approach), and availability of alternative sources of supply—and then simply conclude that the contract is or is not unconscionable. The court need not make any effort to show which factors are essential, which are sufficient, and which are superfluous. Consequently, factors previously subsumed under appropriate common law categories simply may be lumped together without consideration of their weight and effect.

JONES v. STAR CREDIT CORP.

Supreme Court of New York, Special Term, Nassau County, 1969.
59 Misc.2d 189, 298 N.Y.S.2d 264.

SOL M. WACHTLER, JUSTICE.

On August 31, 1965 the plaintiffs, who are welfare recipients, agreed to purchase a home freezer unit for $900 as the result of a visit from a salesman representing Your Shop At Home Service, Inc. With the addition of the time credit charges, credit life insurance, credit property insurance, and sales tax, the purchase price totalled $1,234.80. Thus far the plaintiffs have paid $619.88 toward their purchase. The defendant claims that with various added credit charges paid for an extension of time there is a balance of $819.81 still due from the plaintiffs. The uncontroverted proof at the trial established that the freezer unit, when purchased, had a maximum retail value of approximately $300. The question is whether this transaction and the resulting contract could be considered unconscionable within the meaning of Section 2–302 of the Uniform Commercial Code * * *.   *buy beware?*

There was a time when the shield of "caveat emptor" would protect the most unscrupulous in the marketplace—a time when the law, in granting parties unbridled latitude to make their own contracts, allowed exploitive and callous practices which shocked the conscience of both legislative bodies and the courts.

The effort to eliminate these practices has continued to pose a difficult problem. On the one hand it is necessary to recognize the importance of preserving the integrity of agreements and the fundamental right of parties to deal, trade, bargain, and contract. On the other hand there is the concern for the uneducated and often illiterate individual who is the victim of gross inequality of bargaining power, usually the poorest members of the community.

Concern for the protection of these consumers against overreaching by the small but hardy breed of merchants who would prey on them is not novel. The dangers of inequality of bargaining power were vaguely recognized in the early English common law when Lord Hardwicke wrote of a fraud, which "may be apparent from the intrinsic nature and subject of the bargain itself; such as no man in his senses and not under delusion would make." The English authorities on this subject were discussed in Hume v. United States, 132 U.S. 406, 411, 10 S.Ct. 134, 136, 33 L.Ed. 393 (1889) where the United States Supreme Court characterized (p. 413, 10 S.Ct. p. 137) these as "cases in which one party took advantage of the other's ignorance of arithmetic to impose upon him, and the fraud was apparent from the face of the contracts."

The law is beginning to fight back against those who once took advantage of the poor and illiterate without risk of either exposure or interference. From the common law doctrine of intrinsic fraud we have, over the years, developed common and statutory law which tells not only the buyer but also the seller to beware. This body of laws recognizes the importance of a free enterprise system but at the same time will provide the legal armor to protect and safeguard the prospective victim from the harshness of an unconscionable contract.

Section 2–302 of the Uniform Commercial Code enacts the moral sense of the community into the law of commercial transactions. It authorizes the court to find, as a matter of law, that a contract or a clause of a contract was "unconscionable at the time it was made", and upon so finding the court may refuse to enforce the contract, excise the objectionable clause or limit the application of the clause to avoid an unconscionable result. "The principle", states the Official Comment to this section, "is one of the prevention of oppression and unfair surprise". It permits a court to accomplish directly what heretofore was often accomplished by construction of language, manipulations of fluid rules of contract law and determinations based upon a presumed public policy.

There is no reason to doubt, moreover, that this section is intended to encompass the price term of an agreement. In addition to the fact that it has already been so applied (State by Lefkowitz v. ITM, Inc., 52 Misc.2d 39, 275 N.Y.S.2d 303; Frostifresh Corp. v. Reynoso, 52 Misc.2d 26, 274 N.Y.S.2d 757, revd. 54 Misc.2d 119, 281 N.Y.S.2d 964; American Home Improvement, Inc. v. MacIver, 105 N.H. 435, 201 A.2d 886, 14 A.L.R.3d 324), the statutory language itself makes it clear that not only a clause of the contract, but the contract in toto, may be found unconscionable as a matter of law. Indeed, no other provision of an agreement more intimately touches upon the question of unconscionability than does the term regarding price.

Fraud, in the instant case, is not present; nor is it necessary under the statute. The question which presents itself is whether or not, under the circumstances of this case, the sale of a freezer unit having a retail value of $300 for $900 ($1,439.69 including credit charges and $18 sales tax) is unconscionable as a matter of law. The court believes it is.

Concededly, deciding the issue is substantially easier than explaining it. No doubt, the mathematical disparity between $300, which presumably includes a reasonable profit margin, and $900, which is exorbitant on its face, carries the greatest weight. Credit charges alone exceed by more than $100 the retail value of the freezer. These alone, may be sufficient to sustain the decision. Yet, a caveat is warranted lest we reduce the import of Section 2–302 solely to a mathematical ratio formula. It may, at times, be that; yet it may also be much more. The very limited financial resources of the purchaser, known to the sellers at the time of the sale, is entitled to weight in the balance. Indeed, the value disparity itself leads inevitably to the felt conclusion that knowing advantage was taken of the plaintiffs. In addition, the meaningfulness of choice essential to the making of a contract, can be negated by a gross inequality of bargaining power. (Williams v. Walker–Thomas Furniture Co., 121 U.S.App.D.C. 315, 350 F.2d 445.)

There is no question about the necessity and even the desirability of instalment sales and the extension of credit. Indeed, there are many, including welfare recipients, who would be deprived of even the most basic conveniences without the use of these devices. Similarly, the retail merchant selling on instalment or extending credit is expected to establish a pricing factor which will afford a degree of protection commensurate with the risk of selling to those who might be default prone. However, neither of these accepted premises can clothe the sale of this freezer with respectability.

Support for the court's conclusion will be found in a number of other cases already decided. In American Home Improvement, Inc. v. MacIver, supra, the Supreme Court of New Hampshire held that a contract to install windows, a door and paint, for the price of $2,568.60, of which $809.60 constituted interest and carrying charges and $800. was a salesman's commission was unconscionable as a matter of law. In State by Lefkowitz v. ITM, Inc., supra, a deceptive and fraudulent scheme was involved, but standing alone, the court held that the sale of a vacuum cleaner, among other things, costing the defendant $140 and sold by it for $749 cash or $920.52 on time purchase was unconscionable as a matter of law. Finally, in Frostifresh Corp. v. Reynoso, supra, the sale of a refrigerator costing the seller $348 for $900 plus credit charges of $245.88 was unconscionable as a matter of law.

* * *

Having already paid more than $600 toward the purchase of this $300 freezer unit, it is apparent that the defendant has already been amply compensated. In accordance with the statute, the application of the payment provision should be limited to amounts already paid by the plaintiffs and the contract be reformed and amended by changing the payments called for therein to equal the amount of payment actually so paid by plaintiffs.

NEHF, WRITING CONTRACTS IN THE CLIENT'S INTEREST
51 S.C.L. Rev. 153, 169–70 (1999).

The drafting lawyer is put in a difficult position if the client insists on including a provision that is likely to be unenforceable * * *. The better course will usually be to explain to the client the legal principles involved and the potential ramifications for both lawyer and client if an unenforceable provision is included. Explanation of the exposure risks often persuades the client that the provision is not in her best interest.

IN RE LISA FAY ALLEN, 174 B.R. 293 (Bkrtcy.Or.1994). [Lisa Allen leased a washer and dryer from Affordable Rent-to-Own. One week later, Allen filed a voluntary petition for Chapter 13 bankruptcy relief. One issue before the court was whether the lease was unconscionable. The court found neither procedural nor substantive unconscionability. First, Affordable did not engage in "oppressive bargaining practices." After having been denied credit to purchase a washer and dryer at two stores, Allen saw Affordable's television advertisements and contacted it about leasing the equipment. Affordable approved her application on the telephone. Two delivery people from Affordable then delivered the equipment and gave her the lease to sign, which was "written in understandable terms." The lease disclosed the weekly payments, Allen's right to terminate, and her right to purchase for half the total weekly payments. Allen also "had the opportunity to read the lease before signing it."

Second, the terms of the lease were also not unreasonably favorable to Affordable. Affordable guaranteed that the equipment would work for the duration of the lease. Allen agreed to lease for a minimum of three months with the right to terminate thereafter. Although the lease payments for the duration of the lease would have been $1558.96 and Affordable had purchased the equipment for $523, Allen had the right to purchase it at any time for $779.48 (half of the total rental obligation). The court termed the purchase price as "not a shocking price."]

POUND, DISCRETION, DISPENSATION AND MITIGATION: THE PROBLEM OF THE INDIVIDUAL SPECIAL CASE
35 N.Y.U.L.Rev. 925, 926–28, 929 (1960).

Discretion is an authority conferred by law to act in certain conditions or situations in accordance with an official's or an official agency's own considered judgment and conscience. It is an idea of morals, belonging to the twilight zone between law and morals. It is objected to strenuously by those who urge the definition of law as a body of rules admitting only of genuine interpretation and application within their expressed terms. In the fore part of the last century it was usual to quote Lord Camden, who is reported to have said:

> The Discretion Of A Judge Is The Law Of Tyrants; It Is Always Unknown; It is Different In Different Men; It is Casual And Depends Upon Constitution, Temper, And Passion. In The Best It is Oftentimes Caprice; In The Worst It Is Every Vice, Folly And Passion To Which Human Nature Is Liable.

* * *

Rule is an instrumentality of the first stage of historical legal development, the stage of the strict law. It is a needed instrumentality in the law of today for criminal law, for the law of property in land, and for those features of commercial law in which exact mathematical certainty is imperative.

But the life of today is too complex and its circumstances are too varied and too variable to make possible, in practice, reduction to rules of everything with which the regime of justice according to law must deal. The maturity of law relies habitually upon principles—authoritatively declared and established starting points for reasoning—as its everyday instrument. A rule of law is a precept attaching a precisely defined fixed consequence to a definite detailed fact or state of facts. There is no scope given for application to circumstances. The cases are fitted to the straitjacket of the rule, not the rule shaped in its application to the circumstances of fact of the case.

Analytical jurists have laid out the legal order to the pattern of a body of rules as commands of the sovereign involving, as a necessary element of command, exactly defined and thoroughly organized sanctions rigorously applied.

* * *

All legal systems which have endured have had to develop, by experience, principles of exercise of discretion. It has been necessary to recognize that, because there is no rule in the strict sense, it does not follow that a tribunal on the one hand has no power to do justice, when appealed to therefor, or on the other hand has unlimited power of doing what it chooses on any grounds or on no grounds. It is to reach a reasoned decision in the light of principles. If we are on the confines or even within the domain of ethics, yet ethics as well as jurisprudence is regarded today as a science and has developed principles to which legal principles may be shaped by experience and reason.

* * *

Both elements, the technical and the discretionary, are to be found in all administration of justice. In no legal system is justice administered wholly by rule. Authoritative ideals, giving form to principles as starting points for reasoning, are part of the everyday apparatus of justice. Kelsen has pointed out that when a legal precept leaves something to the discretion of the court, even if the ground of decision is outside the body of authoritative grounds of decision, it is not outside of the legal order.

FRIEDMAN, LEGAL RULES AND THE PROCESS OF SOCIAL CHANGE
19 Stan.L.Rev. 786, 791–92 (1967).

Some of the substantive content of the legal system consists of rules which are dormant—that is, there is no attempt at conscious, consistent enforcement. Other parts raise classic problems of uncertainty. These are the unsettled, but living, problems of law—such as the question of what constitutes due process of law. A third—and vital—part of the legal system consists of rules which are well settled in the special sense that they are acted upon by many persons in a particular manner and their applicability to given situations is not challenged. "Well settled" may mean, then, not that a dubious situation cannot be imagined or that the application of a rule is inherently free of doubt, but that it is *actually* free of doubt as a matter of ordinary, patterned human behavior. If most of the operating (as opposed to the dormant) rules of the legal system were not well settled in this sense, many of the normal processes and activities of life that people carry on with reference to legal rules would be profoundly altered. In a complex social and economic system, a legal system on the model of * * * appellate cases [selected for law school instruction] would be insupportable. There are strong needs to know what is lawful and unlawful in our common, everyday actions. We need to know, for example, whether we are validly married if we go through certain forms (valid in the sense that our claim to validity will be either unchallenged or highly likely to survive any possible challenge). We need to know the permissible ranges of speed. Moreover, in business affairs, we need to know that a deed in a certain form executed in a standard manner truly passes title to a piece of land. If every such transaction had to be channeled through a discretionary agency, the economic system could not survive in its present form. A market economy and a free society both impose upon the legal system a high demand for operational certainty in parts of the law which regulate important aspects of the conduct of everyday life and everyday business.

The legal system must therefore limit operating rules which do not govern—that is, which do not in themselves provide a clear-cut guide to action on the part of those persons to whom the rule is addressed. Some rules do provide the possibility of a clear-cut mandate; others do not. There is a significant difference between a rule which provides that no will is valid unless it is signed by two witnesses and a rule which provides that wills need or do not need witnesses, depending upon the circumstances and the demands of equity and good faith. Rules of the latter sort (discretionary rules) are tolerable as operational realities only in those areas of law where the social order or the economy can afford the luxury of slow, individuated justice. If there is a social interest in mass handling of transactions, a clear-cut framework of nondiscretionary rules is vital.

Note
Unconscionability and Remedy Limitations

Section 2–719 of the Uniform Commercial Code deals with remedy limitations. It provides:

(1) Subject to the provisions of subsections (2) and (3) of this section and of the preceding section on liquidation and limitation of damages,

(a) the agreement may provide for remedies in addition to or in substitution for those provided in this Article and may limit or alter the measure of damages recoverable under this Article, as by limiting the buyer's remedies to return of the goods and repayment of the price or to repair and replacement of non-conforming goods or parts; and

(b) resort to a remedy as provided is optional unless the remedy is expressly agreed to be exclusive, in which case it is the sole remedy.

(2) Where circumstances cause an exclusive or limited remedy to fail of its essential purpose, remedy may be had as provided in this Act.

(3) Consequential damages may be limited or excluded unless the limitation or exclusion is unconscionable. Limitation of consequential damages for injury to the person in the case of consumer goods is prima facie unconscionable but limitation of damages where the loss is commercial is not.

This section, which permits parties to "shape" their own remedies, reflects the principle of freedom of contract. Nevertheless, because merchant sellers often can dictate terms to consumers, these sellers can often severely limit the remedies of the buyers. For example, although section 2–719(1)(b) states that an agreed remedy is presumed to be optional, sellers need only state that a remedy is exclusive to rebut the presumption.

In two respects, section 2–719 provides some protection for a buyer, however. First, we briefly encountered section 2–719(3), which tests the exclusion of consequential damages against the standard of unconscionability. Courts also often invoke the procedural-substantive analysis in this regard. An example is A & M Produce Co. v. FMC Corp., 135 Cal.App.3d 473, 186 Cal.Rptr. 114 (1982). In that case, certain machinery purchased by the buyer to harvest a tomato crop proved unsatisfactory. The buyer sought consequential damages despite an exclusion of such damages in the agreement. The court found the exclusion unconscionable because it was buried on the back page of a long form contract and not disclosed. In addition, consequential damages were "explicitly obvious" if the machinery was defective and the seller was the only party reasonably able to prevent the loss.

The second measure of protection for the buyer is the "failure of essential purpose" test of section 2–719(2). An agreed remedy may fail of its essential purpose for many reasons. For example, when the exclusive remedy calls for the seller to repair or replace defective parts, the remedy may fail of its essential purpose when the product causes damages to the buyer before it could be repaired or the parts replaced. The remedy also may fail of its essential purpose when the repairs or parts are unsatisfactory. See, e.g., Liberty Truck Sales, Inc. v. Kimbrel, 548 So.2d 1379 (Ala.1989); Riley v. Ford Motor Co., 442 F.2d 670 (5th Cir.1971).

The close connection between the failure of essential purpose test and the unconscionability standard should be obvious. In fact, in some cases, the court invokes both tests to invalidate a clause limiting the remedy to repair or replacement. For example, in Bosway Tube & Steel Corp. v. McKay Machine Co., 65 Mich.App. 426, 237 N.W.2d 488 (1975), the buyer purchased a machine for manufacturing both round and square metal tubing but the machine did not satisfactorily produce square tubing, which was the buyer's primary purpose in purchasing the machine. After some attempts at repair, the seller gave up. The remedy was limited to repair or replacement (although there was some question as to whether the limitation was part of the contract). The court stated, "[t]here is no question that the machine on delivery was grossly defective. Not only does the limitation of remedies provision fail of its essential purpose, but its application in this case would be unconscionable." Id. at 430, 237 N.W.2d at 490.

You should be careful not to confuse the concept of warranty disclaimer with the concept of remedy limitation. The former deals with a seller's attempts to limit its *liability* for defects, while the latter involves a seller's efforts to limit the *remedies* available to a buyer, assuming liability is established. This distinction is important for various reasons. For example, the requirements for a valid remedy limitation are not identical with the requirements for a valid disclaimer. Compare section 2–316, at page 588, with section 2–719, set forth above.

SECTION SEVEN: POLICING THE STANDARD FORM CONTRACT

KESSLER, CONTRACTS OF ADHESION—SOME THOUGHTS ABOUT FREEDOM OF CONTRACT

43 Colum.L.Rev. 629, 631–33, 640–41 (1943).

The development of large scale enterprise with its mass production and mass distribution made a new type of contract inevitable—the standardized mass contract. A standardized contract, once its contents have been formulated by a business firm, is used in every bargain dealing with the same product or service. The individuality of the parties which so frequently gave color to the old type contract has disappeared. The stereotyped contract of today reflects the impersonality of the market. It has reached its greatest perfection in the different types of contracts used on the various exchanges. Once the usefulness of these contracts was discovered and perfected in the transportation, insurance, and banking business, their use spread into all other fields of large scale enterprise, into international as well as national trade, and into labor relations. It is to be noted that uniformity of terms of contracts typically recurring in a business enterprise is an important factor in the exact calculation of risks. Risks which are difficult to calculate can be excluded altogether. Unforeseeable contingencies affecting performance, such as strikes, fire, and transportation difficulties can be taken care of. The standard clauses in insurance policies are the most striking illustrations of successful attempts on the part of business enterprises to select and control risks assumed under a contract. The insurance business probably deserves credit also for having first realized the full importance of the so-called "juridical risk", the danger that a court or jury may be swayed by "irrational factors" to decide against a powerful defendant. Ingenious clauses have been the result. Once their practical utility was proven, they were made use of in other lines of business. * * * Standardized contracts have thus become an important means of excluding or controlling the "irrational factor" in litigation. In this respect they are a true reflection of the spirit of our time with its hostility to irrational factors in the judicial process, and they belong in the same category as codifications and restatements.

In so far as the reduction of costs of production and distribution thus achieved is reflected in reduced prices, society as a whole ultimately benefits from the use of standard contracts. And there can be no doubt that this has been the case to a considerable extent. The use of standard contracts has, however, another aspect which has become increasingly important. Standard contracts are typically used by enterprises with strong bargaining power. The weaker party, in need of the goods or services, is frequently not in a position to shop around for better terms, either because the author of the standard contract has a monopoly (natural or artificial) or because all competitors use the same clauses. His contractual intention is but a subjection more or less voluntary to terms dictated by the stronger party, terms whose consequences are often understood only in a vague way, if at all. Thus, standardized contracts are frequently contracts of adhesion; they are *à prendre ou laisser*.[a]
* * *

---

a. The word "contract of adhesion" was introduced into the legal vocabulary by Patter-son, *The Delivery of a Life Insurance Policy* (1919) 33 Harv.L.Rev. 198, 222.

And yet the tremendous economic importance of contracts of adhesion is hardly reflected in the great texts on contracts or in the Restatement. As a matter of fact, the term "contract of adhesion" or a similar symbol has not even found general recognition in our legal vocabulary. This will not do any harm if we remain fully aware that the use of the word "contract" does not commit us to an indiscriminate extension of the ordinary contract rules to all contracts. But apparently the realization of the deepgoing antinomies in the structure of our system of contracts is too painful an experience to be permitted to rise to the full level of our consciousness. Consequently, courts have made great efforts to protect the weaker contracting party and still keep "the elementary rules" of the law of contracts intact. As a result, our common law of standardized contracts is highly contradictory and confusing, and the potentialities inherent in the common law system for coping with contracts of adhesion have not been fully developed. The law of insurance contracts furnishes excellent illustrations. Handicapped by the axiom that courts can only interpret but cannot make contracts for the parties, courts had to rely heavily on their prerogative of interpretation to protect a policy holder. To be sure many courts have shown a remarkable skill in reaching "just" decisions by construing ambiguous clauses against their author even in cases where there was no ambiguity. * * *

* * *

With the decline of the free enterprise system due to the innate trend of competitive capitalism towards monopoly, the meaning of contract has changed radically. Society, when granting freedom of contract, does not guarantee that all members of the community will be able to make use of it to the same extent. On the contrary, the law, by protecting the unequal distribution of property, does nothing to prevent freedom of contract from becoming a one-sided privilege. Society, by proclaiming freedom of contract, guarantees that it will not interfere with the exercise of power by contract. Freedom of contract enables enterprisers to legislate by contract and, what is even more important, to legislate in a substantially authoritarian manner without using the appearance of authoritarian forms. Standard contracts in particular could thus become effective instruments in the hands of powerful industrial and commercial overlords enabling them to impose a new feudal order of their own making upon a vast host of vassals. This spectacle is all the more fascinating since not more than a hundred years ago contract ideology had been successfully used to break down the last vestiges of a patriarchal and benevolent feudal order in the field of master and servant (*Priestley v. Fowler*). Thus the return back from contract to status which we experience today was greatly facilitated by the fact that the belief in freedom of contract has remained one of the firmest axioms in the whole fabric of the social philosophy of our culture.

FAIRFIELD LEASING CORPORATION v. TECHNI–GRAPHICS, INC.

Superior Court of New Jersey, 1992.
256 N.J.Super. 538, 607 A.2d 703.

DONALD S. COBURN, J.S.C.

In this civil action for breach of contract, the primary issue posed today is whether the court should enforce a waiver of the constitutional right of trial

standardized Mass contract = contract of adhesion

by jury contained in a standardized mass contract, commonly referred to as a contract of adhesion.

On January 30, 1991, defendant Techni–Graphics, Inc., a New Jersey corporation (TGI) signed a 39–month lease for a coffee machine at a rental of $209.50 per month with third-party defendant U–Vend, Inc., a New York corporation (U–Vend). Defendant Robin Umstead guaranteed performance of the lease for TGI. U–Vend assigned the lease to plaintiff, Fairfield Leasing Corporation, a New Jersey corporation (FLC). Under the contract only U–Vend is responsible to TGI for failures with respect to the leased equipment, and payment to the assignee of the monthly rent must continue despite any breach of contract by U–Vend.

TGI alleged that the machine was defective and infested with cockroach larvae. Because U–Vend refused to take corrective action, TGI stopped making the rental payments to FLC in March, 1991. FLC instituted suit and TGI brought in U–Vend by way of a third-party complaint based on breach of contract. TGI demanded a trial by jury on all issues.

This matter is now before the court on the joint motion of plaintiff FLC and third-party defendant U–Vend to strike the jury demand based on the following provision contained in the lease and in the guarantee:

> The undersigned does further waive trials by jury in any action or proceeding brought by the leasing Company, or its assignee, against the undersigned on any matters whatsoever arising out of, under or by virtue of the terms of the Agreement or of this Guarantee.

The agreement is a standardized form contract containing 23 paragraphs. U–Vend prepared it. The jury waiver provision is contained in the last part of the twenty-second paragraph, which also contains a merger clause and a no-modification clause. The guarantee, which is part of the agreement, contains the jury waiver clause on lines 21 to 23 of a 25–line paragraph. The letters of the single-spaced contract and guarantee are $\frac{1}{10}$ of a centimeter in height, or approximately one-half the size of the letters produced by the typical typewriter. It is a classic example of a document which has been prepared with the intent that it neither be negotiated nor read.

Two New Jersey cases have directly considered the question of waiver of trial by jury in civil cases based upon a provision of the contract in litigation: *Sexton v. Newark Dist. Telegraph Co.*, 84 *N.J.L.* 85, 101, 86 *A.* 451 (Sup.Ct. 1913) and *Franklin Discount Co. v. Ford*, 27 *N.J.* 473, 492–493, 143 *A.*2d 161 (1958). Although both cases accept that such a waiver can be made, neither case involved a contract of adhesion.

In *Henningsen v. Bloomfield Motors, Inc.*, 32 *N.J.* 358, 161 *A.*2d 69 (1960), the Supreme Court identified the problem with commercial adhesion contracts in these words:

> The traditional contract is the result of free bargaining of parties who are brought together by the play of the market, and who meet each other on a footing of approximate economic equality. In such a society

there is no danger that freedom of contract will be a threat to the social order as a whole. But in present-day commercial life the standardized mass contract has appeared. It is used primarily by enterprises with strong bargaining power and position. "The weaker party, in need of the goods or services, is frequently not in a position to shop around for better terms, either because the author of the standard contract has a monopoly (natural or artificial) or because all competitors use the same clauses. His contractual intention is but a subjection more or less voluntary to terms dictated by the stronger party, terms whose consequences are often understood in a vague way, if at all." Such standardized contracts have been described as those in which one predominant party will dictate its law to an undetermined multiple rather than to an individual. They are said to resemble a law rather than a meeting of the minds. (at 389–390, 161 A.2d 69) (Citations omitted).

Since *Henningsen,* our courts have invalidated unconscionable or unfair terms of such contracts in a variety of contexts. * * *

The federal courts have been appropriately sensitive to the dangers posed to the public by jury waiver provisions in contracts of adhesion. * * * For example, in *National Equipment Rental, Ltd. v. Hendrix,* 565 F.2d 255 (2d Cir.1977), the court was concerned with an equipment leasing arrangement similar to the one involved in this case. The waiver of jury trial was "literally buried in the eleventh paragraph of a fine-print sixteen clause agreement." *Id.* at 258. The court said:

> It is elementary that the Seventh Amendment right to a jury is fundamental and that its protection can only be relinquished knowingly and intentionally. * * * Indeed, a presumption exists against its waiver. *Aetna Insurance Co. v. Kennedy,* 301 U.S. 389, 393, 57 S.Ct. 809 [811], 81 L.Ed. 1177 (1937). There is little doubt that the provision relied on by NER fails to overcome this presumption. The waiver clause was set deeply and inconspicuously in the contract, and Justice Black, dissenting in *National Equipment Rental, Ltd. v. Szukhent,* 375 U.S. 311, 332–3, 84 S.Ct. 411, 423, 11 L.Ed.2d 354 (1964) aptly characterized the nature of NER's form agreements:
>
>> this printed form provision buried in a multitude of words is too weak an imitation of a genuine agreement to be treated as a waiver of so important a constitutional safeguard ... it exhausts credulity to think that they or any other layman reading these legalistic words would have known or even suspected that they amounted to [such] an agreement ... (*Id.*)

In *Dreiling v. Peugeot Motors of America, Inc.,* 539 F.Supp. 402, 403 (D.Col.1982), the court, in refusing to enforce a contractual jury waiver, observed:

> Jury trial may be waived if done knowingly and intentionally, but courts will indulge every reasonable presumption against waiver. *Aetna Insurance Co. v. Kennedy,* 301 U.S. 389, 393, 57 S.Ct. 809, 811, 81 L.Ed. 1177 (1937); *Rodenbur v. Kaufmann,* 320 F.2d 679, 683 (D.C.Cir.1963). In view of this strong presumption the defendants have a very heavy burden of proving that the plaintiffs knowingly, voluntarily and intentionally agreed upon the jury waiver provision in the 1978 Agreement. A constitu-

tional guarantee so fundamental as the right to jury trial cannot be waived unknowingly by mere insertion of a waiver provision on the twentieth page of a twenty-two page standardized form contract.

Defendants have presented no evidence that the waiver provision was a bargained for term of the contract, was mentioned during negotiations, or was even brought to the plaintiffs' attention. In fact, the defendants have failed to show that the plaintiffs had any choice other than to accept the contract as written. The 1978 Agreement appears to be Peugeot's standardized printed dealer contract, drafted by Peugeot. Obviously, the plaintiffs had little, if any, opportunity to negotiate the provisions. Absent proof to the contrary, such an inequality in relative bargaining positions suggests that the asserted waiver was neither knowing nor intentional.

By contrast, where the parties have been represented by counsel or there was evidence of negotiation without substantial inequality in bargaining positions, or the waiver provision was conspicuous, the tendency has been to enforce the waiver. * * *

Since this case comes within the province of the Uniform Commercial Code, *N.J.S.A.* 12A:1 *et seq.*, analysis is further aided by reference to *Herbstman v. Eastman Kodak Co.*, 131 *N.J.Super.* 439, 330 A.2d 384 (App.Div.1974), where the court applied the Code's requirement of conspicuousness for warranty disclaimers under *N.J.S.A.* 12A:2–316 to the limitations of remedy provision found in *N.J.S.A.* 12A:2–719, even though the latter section did not expressly require conspicuousness for such disclaimers. Significantly, the Code defines conspicuousness in these terms:

> "Conspicuous": A term or clause is conspicuous when it is so written that a reasonable person against whom it is to operate ought to have noticed it. A printed heading in capitals (as: NON–NEGOTIABLE BILL OF LADING) is conspicuous. Language in the body of a form is "conspicuous" if it is in larger or other contrasting type or color. But in a telegram any stated term is "conspicuous." Whether a term or clause is "conspicuous" or not is for decision by the court. *N.J.S.A.* 12A:1–201(10).

By that definition, and any other, the jury waiver in the instant case is utterly inconspicuous.

Since the inestimable right to civil jury trial is preserved in Article 1, paragraph 9, of the New Jersey Constitution, it is fit that the courts protect that right as a matter of public policy at least to the extent that the Uniform Commercial Code protects against waivers of warranties and limitations of remedy. Therefore, where, as here, a non-negotiated jury waiver clause appears inconspicuously in a standardized form contract entered into without assistance of counsel, the waiver should not be enforced.

* * *

In accordance with the law of New Jersey, the motion to strike the jury demand is denied.

STEINER v. MOBIL OIL CORP., 20 Cal.3d 90, 100, 141 Cal.Rptr. 157, 164, 569 P.2d 751, 758 (1977). "[A]dhesion contract analysis teaches us not to enforce contracts until we look behind the facade of the formalistic standardized agreement in order to determine whether any inequality of bargaining power between the parties renders contractual terms unconscionable, or causes the contract to be interpreted against the more powerful party."

C & J FERTILIZER, INC. v. ALLIED MUTUAL INSURANCE CO.

Supreme Court of Iowa, 1975.
227 N.W.2d 169.

[C & J Fertilizer, a fertilizer manufacturer, negotiated with an agent of Allied for the purchase of burglary insurance. The agent told an officer of C & J that visible evidence of burglary was required to recover under the burglary policy. When the policy arrived, the president of C & J, a 37–year-old farmer with a high school education, did not read the definition of burglary, which required visible marks of entry on the *exterior* of the building. C & J suffered a loss of chemicals in an interior room of its warehouse, but Allied asserted that it was not liable because of the absence of exterior signs of forced entry. The trial court, noting the definition of burglary in the policy, found for Allied and C & J appealed.]

REYNOLDSON, JUSTICE.

* * *

Revolution in formation of contractual relationships.

Many of our principles for resolving conflicts relating to written contracts were formulated at an early time when parties of equal strength negotiated in the historical sequence of offer, acceptance, and reduction to writing. The concept that both parties assented to the resulting document had solid footing in fact.

Only recently has the sweeping change in the inception of the document received widespread recognition:

> "Standard form contracts probably account for more than ninety-nine percent of all contracts now made. Most persons have difficulty remembering the last time they contracted other than by standard form; except for casual oral agreements, they probably never have. But if they are active, they contract by standard form several times a day. Parking lot and theater tickets, package receipts, department store charge slips, and gas station credit card purchase slips are all standard form contracts.
> " * * *
>
> " * * * The contracting still imagined by courts and law teachers as typical, in which both parties participate in choosing the language of their entire agreement, is no longer of much more than historical importance."

—W. Slawson, Standard Form Contracts and Democratic Control of Lawmaking Power, 84 Harv.L.Rev. 529 (1971). * * *

It is generally recognized the insured will not read the detailed, cross-referenced, standardized, mass-produced insurance form, nor understand it if he does. 7 Williston on Contracts § 906B, p. 300 ("But where the document thus delivered to him is a contract of insurance the majority rule is that the insured is not bound to know its contents"); 3 Corbin on Contracts § 559, pp.

265–66 ("One who applies for an insurance policy * * * may not even read the policy, the number of its terms and the fineness of its print being such as to discourage him"); Note, Unconscionable Contracts: The Uniform Commercial Code, 45 Iowa L.Rev. 843, 844 (1960) ("It is probably a safe assertion that most involved standardized form contracts are never read by the party who 'adheres' to them. In such situations, the proponent of the form is free to dictate terms most advantageous to himself") * * *.

* * *

REASONABLE EXPECTATIONS.

This court adopted the doctrine of reasonable expectations in Rodman v. State Farm Mutual Ins. Co., 208 N.W.2d 903, 905–908 (Iowa 1973). The Rodman court approved the following articulation of that concept:

> " 'The objectively reasonable expectations of applicants and intended beneficiaries regarding the terms of insurance contracts will be honored even though painstaking study of the policy provisions would have negated those expectations.' "

—208 N.W.2d at 906. * * *

* * *

Nor can it be asserted the above doctrine does not apply here because plaintiff knew the policy contained the provision now complained of and cannot be heard to say it reasonably expected what it knew was not there. A search of the record discloses no such knowledge.

The evidence does show, as above noted, a "dicker" for burglary insurance coverage on chemicals and equipment. The negotiation was for what was actually expressed in the policies' "Insuring Agreements": the insurer's promise "To pay for loss by burglary or by robbery of a watchman, while the premises are not open for business, of merchandise, furniture, fixtures and equipment within the premises * * *."

In addition, the conversation included statements from which the plaintiff should have understood defendant's obligation to pay would not arise where the burglary was an "inside job." Thus the following exclusion should have been reasonably anticipated:

"Exclusions

"This policy does not apply:

" * * *

"(b) to loss due to any fraudulent, dishonest or criminal act by any Insured, a partner therein, or an officer, employee, director, trustee or authorized representative thereof * * *."

But there was nothing relating to the negotiations with defendant's agent which would have led plaintiff to reasonably anticipate defendant would bury within the definition of "burglary" another exclusion denying coverage when, no matter how extensive the proof of a third-party burglary, no marks were left on the exterior of the premises. This escape clause, here triggered by the burglar's talent (an investigating law officer, apparently acquainted with the current modus operandi, gained access to the steel building without leaving *reasonable expectations*

any marks by leaning on the overhead plexiglas door while simultaneously turning the locked handle), was never read to or by plaintiff's personnel, nor was the substance explained by defendant's agent.

Moreover, the burglary "definition" which crept into this policy comports neither with the concept a layman might have of that crime, nor with a legal interpretation. See State v. Murray, 222 Iowa 925, 931, 270 N.W. 355, 358 (1936) ("We have held that even though the door was partially open, by opening it farther, in order to enter the building, this is a sufficient breaking to comply with the demands of the statute"); State v. Ferguson, 149 Iowa 476, 478–479, 128 N.W. 840, 841–842 (1910) ("It need not appear that this office was an independent building, for it is well known that it is burglary for one to break and enter an inner door or window, although the culprit entered through an open outer door * * * "); see State v. Hougland, 197 N.W.2d 364, 365 (Iowa 1972).

The most plaintiff might have reasonably anticipated was a policy requirement of visual evidence (abundant here) indicating the burglary was an "outside" not an "inside" job. The exclusion in issue, masking as a definition, makes insurer's obligation to pay turn on the skill of the burglar, not on the event the parties bargained for: a bona-fide third party burglary resulting in loss of plaintiff's chemicals and equipment.

what I could reasonably expect

The "reasonable expectations" attention to the basic agreement, to the concept of substance over form, was appropriately applied by this court for the insurer's benefit in Central Bearings Co. v. Wolverine Insurance Company, 179 N.W.2d 443 (Iowa 1970), a case antedating Rodman. We there reversed a judgment for the insured which trial court apparently grounded on a claimed ambiguity in the policy. In denying coverage on what was essentially a products liability claim where the insured purchased only a "Premises–Operations" policy (without any misrepresentation, misunderstanding or overreaching) we said at page 449 of 179 N.W.2d:

> "In summation we think the insured as a reasonable person would understand the policy coverage purchased meant the insured was not covered for loss if the 'accident' with concomitant damage to a victim occurred away from the premises and after the operation or sale was complete."

The same rationale of reasonable expectations should be applied when it would operate to the advantage of the insured. Appropriately applied to this case, the doctrine demands reversal and judgment for plaintiff.

* * *

UNCONSCIONABILITY.

Plaintiff is also entitled to a reversal because the liability-avoiding provision in the definition of the burglary is, in the circumstances of this case, unconscionable.

We have already noted the policies were not even before the negotiating persons when the protection was purchased. The fair inference to be drawn from the testimony is that the understanding contemplated only visual evidence of bona-fide burglary to eliminate the risk of an "inside job."

The policies in question contain a classic example of that proverbial fine print (six point type as compared with the twenty-four point type appearing on the face of the policies: "BROAD FORM STOREKEEPERS POLICY" and "MERCANTILE BURGLARY AND ROBBERY POLICY") which "becomes visible only after the event." Such print is additionally suspect when, instead of appearing logically in the "exclusions" of the policies, it poses as a part of an esoteric definition of burglary. * * *

The situation before us plainly justifies application of the unconscionability doctrine:

> "Standardized contracts such as insurance policies, drafted by powerful commercial units and put before individuals on the 'accept this or get nothing' basis, are carefully scrutinized by the courts for the purpose of avoiding enforcement of 'unconscionable' clauses."

—6A Corbin on Contracts § 1376, p. 21.

The rule of selective elimination of unconscionable provisions is articulated in the tentative draft of the Restatement (Second) of Contracts, supra § 234, p. 528:

> "§ 234. Unconscionable Contract or Term [ed. note: now § 208]
>
> "If a contract or term thereof is unconscionable at the time the contract is made a court may refuse to enforce the contract, or may enforce the remainder of the contract without the unconscionable term, or may so limit the application of any unconscionable term as to avoid any unconscionable result."

The following statement appears in comment "*a. Scope:*

> "Particularly in the case of standardized agreements, the rule of this Section permits the court to pass directly on the unconscionability of the contract or clause rather than to avoid unconscionable results by interpretation."

Comment "*d. Weakness in the bargaining process*" incorporates the following observation,

> "[G]ross inequality of bargaining power, together with terms unreasonably favorable to the stronger party, may confirm indications that the transaction involved elements of deception or compulsion, or may show that the weaker party had no meaningful choice, no real alternative, or did not in fact assent or appear to assent to the unfair terms."

* * *

Commentators suggest a court considering a claim of unconscionability should examine the factors of assent, unfair surprise, notice, disparity of bargaining power and substantive unfairness. W. Slawson, supra at 564, and citations, n. 79. We have already touched on those considerations in the factual discussions, above. In addition, it would seem appropriate, in every trial when the unconscionability of a contractual provision is a viable issue, to permit either party the right granted by § 554.2302(2), The Code:

> "When it is claimed or appears to the court that the contract or any clause thereof may be unconscionable the parties shall be afforded a

reasonable opportunity to present evidence as to its commercial setting, purpose and effect to aid the court in making the determination."

In the case *sub judice,* plaintiff's evidence demonstrated the definitional provision was unconscionable. Defendant never offered any evidence, let alone evidence which might support a conclusion the provision in issue, considered in its commercial setting, was either a reasonable limitation on the protection it offered or should have been reasonably anticipated by plaintiff.

[handwritten margin note: never offered evidence that]

Trial court's decision must be reversed because the above provision is unconscionable in view of all the circumstances, including the initial negotiations of these parties.

We reverse and remand for judgment in conformance herewith.

Reversed and remanded.

LeGrand, Justice (dissenting).

* * *

While it may be very well to talk in grand terms about "mass advertising" by insurance companies and "incessant" assurances as to coverage which mislead the "unwary," particularly about "fine-print" provisions, such discussion should somehow be related to the case under review. Our primary duty, after all, is to resolve *this* dispute for *these* litigants under *this* record.

There is total silence in this case concerning any of the practices the majority finds offensive; nor is there any claim plaintiff was beguiled by such conduct into believing it had more protection than it actually did.

The record is even stronger against the majority's fine-print argument, the stereotype accusation which serves as a coup de grace in all insurance cases. Except for larger type on the face sheet and black (but not larger) print to designate divisions and sub-headings, the entire policies are of one size and style of print. To compare the *face* sheet with the body of the policy is like comparing a book's jacket cover with the narrative content; and the use of black type or other means of emphasis to separate one part of an instrument from another is an approved editorial expedient which serves to *assist,* not *hinder,* readability. In fact many of our opinions, including that of the majority in the instant case, resort to that device.

Tested by any objective standard, the size and style of type used cannot be fairly described as "fine print." The majority's description, right or wrong, of the plight of consumers generally should not be the basis for resolving the case now before us.

Like all other appeals, this one should be decided on what the record discloses—a fact which the majority concedes but promptly disregards.

Crucial to a correct determination of this appeal is the disputed provision of each policy defining burglary as "the felonious abstraction of insured property * * * by a person making felonious entry * * * by actual force and violence, of which force and violence there are visible marks made by tools, explosives, electricity or chemicals upon, or physical damage to, the exterior of the premises at the place of such entry * * *." The starting point of any consideration of that definition is a determination whether it is ambiguous. Yet the majority does not even mention ambiguity.

The purpose of such a provision, of course, is to omit from coverage "inside jobs" or those resulting from fraud or complicity by the assured. The overwhelming weight of authority upholds such provisions as legitimate in purpose and unambiguous in application. * * *

Once this indisputable fact is recognized, plaintiff's arguments virtually collapse. We may not—at least we *should* not—by any accepted standard of construction meddle with contracts which clearly and plainly state their meaning simply because we dislike that meaning, even in the case of insurance policies. * * *

Nor can the doctrine of reasonable expectations be applied here. We adopted that rule in Rodman v. State Farm Mutual Automobile Insurance Company, 208 N.W.2d 903, 906, 907 (Iowa 1973). We refused, however to apply it in that case, where we said:

"The real question here is whether the principle of reasonable expectations should be extended to cases where an ordinary layman would not misunderstand his coverage from a reading of the policy and where there are no circumstances attributable to the insurer which foster coverage expectations. Plaintiff does not contend he misunderstood the policy. He did not read it. He now asserts in retrospect that if he had read it he would not have understood it. He does not say he was misled by conduct or representations of the insurer. He simply asked trial court to rewrite the policy to cover his loss because if he had purchased his automobile insurance from another company the loss would have been covered, he did not know it was not covered, and if he had known it was not covered he would have purchased a different policy. Trial court declined to do so. We believe trial court correctly refused in these circumstances to extend the principle of reasonable expectations to impose liability."

Yet here the majority would extend the doctrine far beyond the point of refusal in *Rodman*. Here we have affirmative and unequivocal testimony from an officer and director of the plaintiff corporation that he knew the disputed provision was in the policies because "it was just like the insurance policy I have on my farm."

I cannot agree plaintiff may now assert it reasonably expected from these policies something it knew was not there.

* * *

The remaining ground upon which the majority invalidates the policies—unconscionability—has also been disavowed by the great majority of courts which have decided the question, usually in connection with public policy considerations. See Scanlon v. Western Fire Insurance Company, 4 Mich.App. 234, 144 N.W.2d 677, 679 (1966); * * *.

For these several reasons—the principal one being that the findings of the trial court have substantial evidentiary support—I would affirm the judgment.

MOORE, C.J., and REES and UHLENHOPP, JJ., join this dissent.

MARKLINE CO., INC. v. TRAVELERS INSURANCE CO., 384 Mass. 139, 424 N.E.2d 464 (1981). [Markline purchased a store-owners policy covering "burglary" from defendant. Burglary was defined to require "visible marks." Because of the lack of such marks, defendant refused to indemnify Markline for the loss of inventory, even though a burglar alarm had gone off and the fact of loss was undisputed. The court held, *inter alia,* that the doctrine of reasonable expectations did not apply in Massachusetts, but if it did Markline did not have reasonable expectations of coverage for the loss. According to the court, Markline's president's testimony that it was his understanding that "coverage was complete fire, theft, and liability insurance" "fell fatally short" of sufficient evidence to satisfy the reasonable expectations standard.]

NOLAN, JUSTICE.

* * *

* * * In the Restatement (Second) of Contracts, § 237, Comment f * * * the following description of "reasonable expectation" appears: "Although customers typically adhere to standardized agreements and are bound by them without even appearing to know the standard terms in detail, they are not bound to unknown terms which are beyond the range of reasonable expectation. A debtor who delivers a check to his creditor with the amount blank does not authorize the insertion of an infinite figure. Similarly, a party who adheres to the other party's standard terms does not assent to a term if the other party has reason to believe that the adhering party would not have accepted the agreement if he had known that the agreement contained the particular term. Such a belief or assumption may be shown by the prior negotiations or inferred from the circumstances. Reason to believe may be inferred from the fact that the term is bizarre or oppressive, from the fact that it eviscerates the nonstandard terms explicitly agreed to, or from the fact that it eliminates the dominant purpose of the transaction. The inference is reinforced if the adhering party never had an opportunity to read the term, or if it is illegible or otherwise hidden from view. This rule is closely related to the policy against unconscionable terms and the rule of interpretation against the draftsman." There is nothing in the record before us to bring this case within the sweep of this language.

* * *

LIACOS, JUSTICE (dissenting).

* * *

* * * I feel that the court pays short shrift to the claim of reasonable expectations and the notions of unconscionability inherent therein. * * *

It is patently inconsistent for this court to acknowledge on the one hand that the doctrine lacks precedent in our case law and at the same time to declare that the evidence on record falls short of a reasonable expectation standard. The majority, quoting § 237 of the Restatement (Second) of Contracts, chooses to ignore the clear parallel between this case and the Restatement: "Similarly, a party who adheres to the other party's standard terms does not assent to a term if the other party has reason to believe that the adhering party would not have accepted the agreement if he had known that the agreement contained the particular term. Such a belief or assumption may be shown by the prior negotiations or inferred from the circumstances." Also, "[r]eason to believe may be inferred from the fact that the term * * *

eliminates the dominant purpose of the transaction." *Supra* at 466. Restatement (Second) of Contracts, comment f at 541 (Tent. Draft Nos. 1–7, 1973). The evidence here was that the plaintiff expected "comprehensive coverage," having been assured of such coverage by the insurer's agent. The interpretation of the circumstances of the plaintiff's entering the contract are highly material under the general principle that the intent and reasonable expectations of the parties govern the construction of insurance contracts. *Ayres v. Prudential Ins. Co. of America,* 602 F.2d 1309 (9th Cir.1979); see 12 Couch, Insurance § 45:5 at 107 (2d ed. 1964) (basic guide to insurance contract construction is that "parties apparently intended there should be effective coverage with respect to a particular kind or kinds of risk").

The Restatement informs us that "courts in construing and applying a standardized contract seek to effectuate the reasonable expectations of the average member of the public who accepts it." Restatement (Second) of Contracts § 237, comment e at 540 (Tent. Draft Nos. 1–7 1973). Cf. *Ayres, supra* at 1313 ("the exclusion fails only if the insured can reasonably believe [burglary] is not excluded in light of what is publicly known of such exclusions"). Here, the judge found the plaintiff complied with the insurer's requirement that he install a burglar alarm. As soon as he received notice of the alarm's activation he notified the insurer. These facts, along with the agent's precontract assurances, bespeak the plaintiff's reasonable expectation that if the alarm was activated and a loss of inventory occurred, which was otherwise unexplainable, the loss was covered by the burglary provisions of his policy. The issue of reasonable expectation and the unconscionability of defeating those expectations by obscure exclusionary language was adequately raised in the plaintiff's trial brief requesting findings and rulings, and by the evidence at trial. If the judge did utilize these theories in reaching his conclusion, then the question of the plaintiff's reasonable expectation has been placed squarely before us. Rather than put our own gloss on the unclear rulings of the judge, I would remand for a more specific statement of the reasons underlying the judgment. I dissent.

RESTATEMENT (SECOND) OF CONTRACTS § 211.

Standardized Agreements

(1) Except as stated in Subsection (3), where a party to an agreement signs or otherwise manifests assent to a writing and has reason to believe that like writings are regularly used to embody terms of agreements of the same type, he adopts the writing as an integrated agreement with respect to the terms included in the writing.

(2) Such a writing is interpreted wherever reasonable as treating alike all those similarly situated, without regard to their knowledge or understanding of the standard terms of the writing.

(3) Where the other party has reason to believe that the party manifesting such assent would not do so if he knew that the writing contained a particular term, the term is not part of the agreement.

WHITE, FORM CONTRACTS UNDER REVISED ARTICLE 2
75 Wash.U. Law Q. 315, 346–47 (1997).

* * * [A]ppellate courts in Arizona have not been rigorous in following the letter of section 211(3) * * *. In most cases, the Arizona Supreme Court has interpreted section 211(3) as though it does not require a look at the "drafter's" intent, and the court has paid little heed to the requirement that a signer be freed of a term only if he would not have signed had he known of the term. The court has made mincemeat out of [the] requirement that a signer "take the good with the bad." Generally, the court has looked directly at the state of mind of the "party manifesting assent," not at the belief of the drafter about what a hypothetical signer might think. Indeed, the Arizona courts often describe this approach as the doctrine of "reasonable expectations"—meaning the reasonable expectations of the signer, not of the drafter. The Arizona Supreme Court itself has paid only lip service to the notion that one must show that he, or a hypothetical signer, could not have been expected to sign a form containing the offending term.

Problem 5–5

Sally Williams comes to your law office and tells you that during the last five years she purchased over $1,800 worth of household items from Thomas Appliances for which payments were to be made in installments. Williams' balance at Thomas Appliance was now only $164, but she was in default, and could not pay. Thomas Appliances has just told Williams that it is going to take back *all* of the items she has purchased from the store, not just the most recently purchased one which cost more than $164. The terms of each purchase were contained in a printed form contract. Each form contained the following clause:

> [T]he amount of each periodical installment payment to be made by purchaser to the Company under this present agreement shall be inclusive of and not in addition to the amount of each installment payment to be made by purchaser under such prior agreements or accounts; and all payments now and hereafter made by purchaser shall be credited pro rata on all outstanding agreements and accounts due to the Company by purchaser at the time each such payment is made.

Ms. Williams was not well-educated; she had completed only the eighth grade. Before checking your state's consumer protection legislation, are there any common law approaches to Ms. Williams' problem? Do *you* understand the above provision?

GLADDEN v. CADILLAC MOTOR CAR DIVISION, GENERAL MOTORS CORP., 83 N.J. 320, 416 A.2d 394 (1980). [The Court concluded that the term of a tire manufacturer's guarantee that limited the buyer's remedy to replacement or purchase price refund was unenforceable because the guarantee was a "linguistic maze" of contradictory provisions inducing the purchaser into believing "that he was obtaining a guarantee of performance."]

NEW YORK GENERAL OBLIGATIONS LAW § 5–702.

a. Every written agreement entered into after November first, nineteen hundred seventy-eight, for the lease of space to be occupied for residential purposes, for the lease of personal property to be used primarily for personal, family or household purposes, or to which a consumer is a party and the money, property or service which is the subject of the transaction is primarily for personal, family or household purposes must be:

1.   Written in a clear and coherent manner using words with common and every day meanings;

2.   Appropriately divided and captioned by its various sections.

Any creditor, seller or lessor who fails to comply with this subdivision shall be liable to a consumer who is a party to a written agreement governed by this subdivision in an amount equal to any actual damages sustained plus a penalty of fifty dollars. The total class action penalty against any such creditor, seller or lessor shall not exceed ten thousand dollars in any class action or series of class actions arising out of the use by a creditor, seller or lessor of an agreement which fails to comply with this subdivision. No action under this subdivision may be brought after both parties to the agreement have fully performed their obligation under such agreement, nor shall any creditor, seller or lessor who attempts in good faith to comply with this subdivision be liable for such penalties. This subdivision shall not apply to agreements involving amounts in excess of fifty thousand dollars nor prohibit the use of words or phrases or forms of agreement required by state or federal law, rule or regulation or by a governmental instrumentality.

b.   A violation of the provisions of subdivision a of this section shall not render any such agreement void or voidable nor shall it constitute:

1.   A defense to any action or proceeding to enforce such agreement; or

2.   A defense to any action or proceeding for breach of such agreement.

CASPI v. THE MICROSOFT NETWORK

Superior Court of New Jersey, 1999.
323 N.J.Super. 118, 732 A.2d 528.

Kestin, J.A.D.

We are here called upon to determine the validity and enforceability of a forum selection clause contained in an on-line subscriber agreement of the Microsoft Network (MSN), an on-line computer service. The trial court granted defendants' motion to dismiss the complaint on the ground that the forum selection clause in the parties' contracts called for plaintiffs' claims to be litigated in the State of Washington. Plaintiffs appeal. We affirm.

The amended class action complaint in eighteen counts sought diverse relief against two related corporate entities, The Microsoft Network, L.L.C. and Microsoft Corporation (collectively, Microsoft). Plaintiffs asserted various theories including breach of contract, common law fraud, and consumer fraud in the way Microsoft had "rolled over" MSN membership into more expensive plans. Among the claims was an accusation that Microsoft had engaged in "unilateral negative option billing," a practice condemned by the attorneys general of twenty-one states, including New Jersey's, with regard to a Microsoft competitor, America Online, Inc. Under the practice as alleged, Microsoft, without notice to or permission from MSN members, unilaterally charged them increased membership fees attributable to a change in service plans.

The four named plaintiffs are members of MSN. Two reside in New Jersey; the others in Ohio and New York. Purporting to represent a nation-wide class of 1.5 million similarly aggrieved MSN members, plaintiffs, in May 1997, moved for multi-state class action certification. See R. 4:32.

Shortly thereafter, defendants moved to dismiss the amended complaint for lack of jurisdiction and improper venue by reason of the forum selection clause which, defendants contended, was in every MSN membership agreement and bound all the named plaintiffs and all members of the class they purported to represent. That clause, paragraph 15.1 of the MSN membership agreement, provided:

> This agreement is governed by the laws of the State of Washington, USA, and you consent to the exclusive jurisdiction and venue of courts in King County, Washington in all disputes arising out of or relating to your use of MSN or your MSN membership.

* * *

On November 13, 1997, Judge Fitzpatrick, in a written opinion, expressed his reasons for dismissing the complaint based upon the forum selection clause. Given that conclusion * * * plaintiffs' motion to certify the class was denied as moot. Conforming orders were entered on the same date. * * *

The background of the matter was depicted in the * * * opinion:

Before becoming an MSN member, a prospective subscriber is prompted by MSN software to view multiple computer screens of information, including a membership agreement which contains the above clause. MSN's membership agreement appears on the computer screen in a scrollable window next to blocks providing the choices "I Agree" and "I Don't Agree." Prospective members assent to the terms of the agreement by clicking on "I Agree" using a computer mouse. Prospective members have the option to click "I Agree" or "I Don't Agree" at any point while scrolling through the agreement. Registration may proceed only after the potential subscriber has had the opportunity to view and has assented to the membership agreement, including MSN's forum selection clause. No charges are incurred until after the membership agreement review is completed and a subscriber has clicked on "I Agree."

* * *

Judge Fitzpatrick correctly discerned that New Jersey follows the logic of the United States Supreme Court decision in Carnival Cruise Lines v. Shute, 499 U.S. 585, 111 S.Ct. 1522, 113 L.Ed.2d 622 (1991). * * * In Carnival, cruise ship passengers were held to a forum selection clause which appeared in their travel contract. The clause enforced in Carnival was very similar in nature to the clause in question here, the primary difference being that the Carnival clause was placed in small print in a travel contract while the clause in the case sub judice was placed on-line on scrolled computer screens.

* * *

[Judge Fitzpatrick held that] plaintiffs and the class which they purport to represent were given ample opportunity to affirmatively assent to the forum selection clause. Like Carnival, plaintiffs here "retained the option of rejecting the contract with impunity." 499 U.S. 585, 111 S.Ct. 1522, 113 L.Ed.2d 622. * * *

* * *

After reviewing the record in the light of the arguments advanced by the parties, we are in substantial agreement with the reasons for decision articulated by Judge Fitzpatrick. * * * New Jersey's interest in assuring consumer fraud protection will not be frustrated by requiring plaintiffs to proceed with a lawsuit in Washington as prescribed by the plain language of the forum selection clause. * * * If a forum selection clause is clear in its purport and has been presented to the party to be bound in a fair and forthright fashion, no consumer fraud policies or principles have been violated. * * *

The only viable issues that remain bear upon the argument that plaintiffs did not receive adequate notice of the forum selection clause, and therefore that the clause never became part of the membership contract which bound them. A related, alternative argument is that the question of notice is a factual matter that should be submitted to a jury. Defendants respond by arguing that 1) in the absence of fraud, a contracting party is bound by the provisions of a form contract even if he or she never reads them; 2) this clause met all reasonable standards of conspicuousness; and 3) the sign-up process gave plaintiffs ample opportunity to review and reject the agreement. Defendants also contend that notice is a question of law, decidable by a court, not a jury.

The holding in Carnival Cruise Lines v. Shute, 499 U.S. 585, 111 S.Ct. 1522, 113 L.Ed.2d 622 (1991), does not dispose of the notice question because the plaintiffs there had "essentially ... conceded that they had notice of the forum-selection provision[,]" by stating that they " '[did] not contest ... that the forum selection clause was reasonably communicated to [them], as much as three pages of fine print can be communicated.' " Id. at 590, 111 S.Ct. at 1525, 113 L.Ed.2d at 630. The dissenting justices described the format in which the forum selection clause had been presented as "in the fine print on the back of the [cruise] ticket." Id. at 597, 111 S.Ct. at 1529, 113 L.Ed.2d at 634 (Stevens, J., dissenting).

The scenario presented here is different because of the medium used, electronic versus printed; but, in any sense that matters, there is no significant distinction. The plaintiffs in Carnival could have perused all the fine-print provisions of their travel contract if they wished before accepting the terms by purchasing their cruise ticket. The plaintiffs in this case were free to scroll through the various computer screens that presented the terms of their contracts before clicking their agreement.

Also, it seems clear that there was nothing extraordinary about the size or placement of the forum selection clause text. By every indication we have, the clause was presented in exactly the same format as most other provisions of the contract. It was the first item in the last paragraph of the electronic document. We note that a few paragraphs in the contract were presented in upper case typeface, presumably for emphasis, but most provisions, including the forum selection clause, were presented in lower case typeface. We discern nothing about the style or mode of presentation, or the placement of the provision, that can be taken as a basis for concluding that the forum selection clause was proffered unfairly, or with a design to conceal or de-emphasize its provisions. To conclude that plaintiffs are not bound by that clause would be equivalent to holding that they were bound by no other clause either, since all provisions were identically presented. Plaintiffs must be taken to have known that they were entering into a contract; and no good purpose, consonant with the dictates of reasonable reliability in commerce, would be served by permitting them to disavow particular provisions or the contracts as a whole. See Rudbart v. North Jersey Dist. Water Supply Comm'n, 127 N.J. 344, 351–53, 605 A.2d 681 (referring to the principle that a contracting party may be bound by the terms of a form contract even if he or she has never read them), cert. denied, 506 U.S. 871, 113 S.Ct. 203, 121 L.Ed.2d 145 (1992).

The issue of reasonable notice regarding a forum selection clause is a question of law for the court to determine. * * * We agree with the trial court that, in the absence of a better showing than has been made, plaintiffs must be seen to have had adequate notice of the forum selection clause. The resolution of this notice issue, at this stage of the litigation between plaintiffs and defendants must, of course, be seen to be without prejudice to any showing either party may have the opportunity to make in another jurisdiction in a plenary proceeding on the contract regarding issues apart from the validity and enforceability of the forum selection clause.

Affirmed.

SPECHT v. NETSCAPE COMMUNICATIONS CORP.

United States Court of Appeals, Second Circuit, 2002.
306 F.3d 17.

SOTOMAYOR, CIRCUIT JUDGE.

This is an appeal from a judgment of the Southern District of New York denying a motion by defendants-appellants Netscape Communications Corporation and its corporate parent, America Online, Inc. (collectively, "defendants" or "Netscape"), to compel arbitration and to stay court proceedings. In order to resolve the central question of arbitrability presented here, we must address issues of contract formation in cyberspace. Principally, we are asked to determine whether plaintiffs-appellees ("plaintiffs"), by acting upon defendants' invitation to download free software made available on defendants' webpage, agreed to be bound by the software's license terms (which included the arbitration clause at issue), even though plaintiffs could not have learned of the existence of those terms unless, prior to executing the download, they had scrolled down the webpage to a screen located below the download button. We agree with the district court that a reasonably prudent Internet user in circumstances such as these would not have known or learned of the existence of the license terms before responding to defendants' invitation to download the free software, and that defendants therefore did not provide reasonable notice of the license terms. In consequence, plaintiffs' bare act of downloading the software did not unambiguously manifest assent to the arbitration provision contained in the license terms.

We also agree with the district court that plaintiffs' claims relating to the software at issue—a "plug-in" program entitled SmartDownload ("Smart-Download" or "the plug-in program"), offered by Netscape to enhance the functioning of the separate browser program called Netscape Communicator ("Communicator" or "the browser program")—are not subject to an arbitration agreement contained in the license terms governing the use of Communicator. * * *

We therefore affirm the district court's denial of defendants' motion to compel arbitration and to stay court proceedings.

BACKGROUND

I. FACTS

In three related putative class actions, plaintiffs alleged that, unknown to them, their use of SmartDownload transmitted to defendants private information about plaintiffs' downloading of files from the Internet, thereby effecting an electronic surveillance of their online activities in violation of two federal statutes, the Electronic Communications Privacy Act, 18 U.S.C. §§ 2510 *et seq.,* and the Computer Fraud and Abuse Act, 18 U.S.C. § 1030. [The Court of Appeals consolidated the appeals.]

Specifically, plaintiffs alleged that when they first used Netscape's Communicator—a software program that permits Internet browsing—the program created and stored on each of their computer hard drives a small text file known as a "cookie" that functioned "as a kind of electronic identification tag for future communications" between their computers and Netscape. Plaintiffs further alleged that when they installed SmartDownload—a separate software "plug-in"[1] that served to enhance Communicator's browsing capabilities— SmartDownload created and stored on their computer hard drives another string of characters, known as a "Key," which similarly functioned as an identification tag in future communications with Netscape. According to the complaints in this case, each time a computer user employed Communicator to download a file from the Internet, SmartDownload "assume[d] from Communicator the task of downloading" the file and transmitted to Netscape the address of the file being downloaded together with the cookie created by Communicator and the Key created by SmartDownload. These processes, plaintiffs claim, constituted unlawful "eavesdropping" on users of Netscape's software products as well as on Internet websites from which users employing SmartDownload downloaded files.

In the time period relevant to this litigation, Netscape offered on its website various software programs, including Communicator and SmartDownload, which visitors to the site were invited to obtain free of charge. It is undisputed that five of the six named plaintiffs * * * downloaded Communicator from the Netscape website. These plaintiffs acknowledge that when they proceeded to initiate installation[2] of Communicator, they were automatically

---

1. Netscape's website defines "plug-ins" as "software programs that extend the capabilities of the Netscape Browser in a specific way—giving you, for example, the ability to play audio samples or view video movies from within your browser." (http://wp.netscape.com/plugins/) SmartDownload purportedly made it easier for users of browser programs like Communicator to download files from the Internet without losing their progress when they paused to engage in some other task, or if

their Internet connection was severed. *See Specht,* 150 F.Supp.2d at 587.

2. There is a difference between downloading and installing a software program. When a user downloads a program from the Internet to his or her computer, the program file is stored on the user's hard drive but typically is not operable until the user installs or executes it, usually by double-clicking on the file and causing the program to run.

shown a scrollable text of that program's license agreement and were not permitted to complete the installation until they had clicked on a "Yes" button to indicate that they accepted all the license terms.[3] If a user attempted to install Communicator without clicking "Yes," the installation would be aborted. All five named user plaintiffs expressly agreed to Communicator's license terms by clicking "Yes." The Communicator license agreement that these plaintiffs saw made no mention of SmartDownload or other plug-in programs, and stated that "[t]hese terms apply to Netscape Communicator and Netscape Navigator" and that "all disputes relating to this Agreement (excepting any dispute relating to intellectual property rights)" are subject to "binding arbitration in Santa Clara County, California."

Although Communicator could be obtained independently of SmartDownload, all the named user plaintiffs, except [one], downloaded and installed Communicator in connection with downloading SmartDownload. Each of these plaintiffs allegedly arrived at a Netscape webpage[4] captioned "SmartDownload Communicator" that urged them to "Download With Confidence Using SmartDownload!" At or near the bottom of the screen facing plaintiffs was the prompt "Start Download" and a tinted button labeled "Download." By clicking on the button, plaintiffs initiated the download of SmartDownload. Once that process was complete, SmartDownload, as its first plug-in task, permitted plaintiffs to proceed with downloading and installing Communicator, an operation that was accompanied by the clickwrap display of Communicator's license terms described above.

The signal difference between downloading Communicator and downloading SmartDownload was that no clickwrap presentation accompanied the latter operation. Instead, once plaintiffs had clicked on the "Download" button located at or near the bottom of their screen, and the downloading of SmartDownload was complete, these plaintiffs encountered no further information about the plug-in program or the existence of license terms governing its use. The sole reference to SmartDownload's license terms on the "SmartDownload Communicator" webpage was located in text that would have become visible to plaintiffs only if they had scrolled down to the next screen.

Had plaintiffs scrolled down instead of acting on defendants' invitation to click on the "Download" button, they would have encountered the following invitation: "Please review and agree to the terms of the *Netscape SmartDownload software license agreement* before downloading and using the software."

3. This kind of online software license agreement has come to be known as "clickwrap" (by analogy to "shrinkwrap," used in the licensing of tangible forms of software sold in packages) because it "presents the user with a message on his or her computer screen, requiring that the user manifest his or her assent to the terms of the license agreement by clicking on an icon. The product cannot be obtained or used unless and until the icon is clicked." *Specht,* 150 F.Supp.2d at 593–94 (footnote omitted). Just as breaking the shrinkwrap seal and using the enclosed computer program after encountering notice of the existence of governing license terms has been deemed by some courts to constitute assent to those terms in the context of tangible software, *see, e.g., ProCD, Inc. v. Zeidenberg,* 86 F.3d 1447, 1451 (7th Cir.1996), so clicking on a webpage's clickwrap button after receiving notice of the existence of license terms has been held by some courts to manifest an Internet user's assent to terms governing the use of downloadable intangible software, *see, e.g., Hotmail Corp. v. Van$Money Pie Inc.,* 47 U.S.P.Q.2d 1020, 1025 (N.D.Cal.1998).

4. For purposes of this opinion, the term "webpage" or "page" is used to designate a document that resides, usually with other webpages, on a single Internet website and that contains information that is viewed on a computer monitor by scrolling through the document. To view a webpage in its entirety, a user typically must scroll through multiple screens.

Plaintiffs * * * averred in their affidavits that they never saw this reference to the SmartDownload license agreement when they clicked on the "Download" button. * * *

In sum, plaintiffs allege that the process of obtaining SmartDownload contrasted sharply with that of obtaining Communicator. Having selected SmartDownload, they were required neither to express unambiguous assent to that program's license agreement nor even to view the license terms or become aware of their existence before proceeding with the invited download of the free plug-in program. Moreover, once these plaintiffs had initiated the download, the existence of SmartDownload's license terms was not mentioned while the software was running or at any later point in plaintiffs' experience of the product.

Even for a user who, unlike plaintiffs, did happen to scroll down past the download button, SmartDownload's license terms would not have been immediately displayed in the manner of Communicator's clickwrapped terms. Instead, if such a user had seen the notice of SmartDownload's terms and then clicked on the underlined invitation to review and agree to the terms, a hypertext link would have taken the user to a separate webpage entitled "License & Support Agreements." The first paragraph on this page read, in pertinent part:

The use of each Netscape software product is governed by a license agreement. You must read and agree to the license agreement terms BEFORE acquiring a product. Please click on the appropriate link below to review the current license agreement for the product of interest to you before acquisition. For products available for download, you must read and agree to the license agreement terms BEFORE you install the software. If you do not agree to the license terms, do not download, install or use the software.

Below this paragraph appeared a list of license agreements, the first of which was "*License Agreement for Netscape Navigator and Netscape Communicator Product Family* (Netscape Navigator, Netscape Communicator and Netscape SmartDownload)." If the user clicked on that link, he or she would be taken to yet another webpage that contained the full text of a license agreement that was identical in every respect to the Communicator license agreement except that it stated that its "terms apply to Netscape Communicator, Netscape Navigator, and Netscape SmartDownload." The license agreement granted the user a nonexclusive license to use and reproduce the software, subject to certain terms:

BY CLICKING THE ACCEPTANCE BUTTON OR INSTALLING OR USING NETSCAPE COMMUNICATOR, NETSCAPE NAVIGATOR, OR NETSCAPE SMARTDOWNLOAD SOFTWARE (THE "PRODUCT"), THE INDIVIDUAL OR ENTITY LICENSING THE PRODUCT ("LICENSEE") IS CONSENTING TO BE BOUND BY AND IS BECOMING A PARTY TO THIS AGREEMENT. IF LICENSEE DOES NOT AGREE TO ALL OF THE TERMS OF THIS AGREEMENT, THE BUTTON INDICATING NON–ACCEPTANCE MUST BE SELECTED, AND LICENSEE MUST NOT INSTALL OR USE THE SOFTWARE.

Among the license terms was a provision requiring virtually all disputes relating to the agreement to be submitted to arbitration:

Unless otherwise agreed in writing, all disputes relating to this Agreement (excepting any dispute relating to intellectual property rights) shall be subject to final and binding arbitration in Santa Clara County, California, under the auspices of JAMS/EndDispute, with the losing party paying all costs of arbitration.

[The court's discussion of additional plaintiffs is omitted.]

II. PROCEEDINGS BELOW

In the district court, defendants moved to compel arbitration and to stay court proceedings pursuant to the Federal Arbitration Act ("FAA"), 9 U.S.C. § 4, arguing that the disputes reflected in the complaints, like any other dispute relating to the SmartDownload license agreement, are subject to the arbitration clause contained in that agreement. Finding that Netscape's webpage, unlike typical examples of clickwrap, neither adequately alerted users to the existence of SmartDownload's license terms nor required users unambiguously to manifest assent to those terms as a condition of downloading the product, the court held that the user plaintiffs had not entered into the SmartDownload license agreement. *Specht,* 150 F.Supp.2d at 595–96.

The district court also ruled that the separate license agreement governing use of Communicator, even though the user plaintiffs had assented to its terms, involved an independent transaction that made no mention of SmartDownload and so did not bind plaintiffs to arbitrate their claims relating to SmartDownload. *Id.* at 596. * * *

     * * *

DISCUSSION

I. STANDARD OF REVIEW AND APPLICABLE LAW

A district court's denial of a motion to compel arbitration is reviewed de novo. * * * The determination of whether parties have contractually bound themselves to arbitrate a dispute—a determination involving interpretation of state law—is a legal conclusion also subject to *de novo* review. * * *

If a court finds that the parties agreed to arbitrate, it should then consider whether the dispute falls within the scope of the arbitration agreement. * * * A district court's determination of the scope of an arbitration agreement is reviewed *de novo.* * * *

The FAA provides that a "written provision in any ... contract evidencing a transaction involving commerce to settle by arbitration a controversy thereafter arising out of such contract or transaction ... shall be valid, irrevocable, and enforceable, save upon such grounds as exist at law or in equity for the revocation of any contract." 9 U.S.C. § 2. It is well settled that a court may not compel arbitration until it has resolved "the question of the very existence" of the contract embodying the arbitration clause. *Interocean Shipping Co. v. Nat'l Shipping & Trading Corp.,* 462 F.2d 673, 676 (2d Cir.1972). "[A]rbitration is a matter of contract and a party cannot be required to submit to arbitration any dispute which he has not agreed so to submit." *AT & T Techs., Inc. v. Communications Workers of Am.,* 475 U.S. 643, 648, 106 S.Ct. 1415, 89 L.Ed.2d 648 (1986) (quotation marks omitted). Unless the parties clearly provide otherwise, "the question of arbitrability—

whether a[n] ... agreement creates a duty for the parties to arbitrate the particular grievance—is undeniably an issue for judicial determination." *Id.* at 649, 106 S.Ct. 1415.

The district court properly concluded that in deciding whether parties agreed to arbitrate a certain matter, a court should generally apply state-law principles to the issue of contract formation. * * * Therefore, state law governs the question of whether the parties in the present case entered into an agreement to arbitrate disputes relating to the SmartDownload license agreement. The district court further held that California law governs the question of contract formation here; the parties do not appeal that determination.

II. WHETHER THIS COURT SHOULD REMAND FOR A TRIAL ON CONTRACT FORMATION

* * *

[W]e conclude that the district court properly decided the question of reasonable notice and objective manifestation of assent as a matter of law on the record before it, and we decline defendants' request to remand for a full trial on that question.

III. WHETHER THE USER PLAINTIFFS HAD REASONABLE NOTICE OF AND MANIFESTED ASSENT TO THE SMARTDOWNLOAD LICENSE AGREEMENT

Whether governed by the common law or by Article 2 of the Uniform Commercial Code ("UCC"), a transaction, in order to be a contract, requires a manifestation of agreement between the parties. * * * Mutual manifestation of assent, whether by written or spoken word or by conduct, is the touchstone of contract. * * * Although an onlooker observing the disputed transactions in this case would have seen each of the user plaintiffs click on the Smart-Download "Download" button, * * * a consumer's clicking on a download button does not communicate assent to contractual terms if the offer did not make clear to the consumer that clicking on the download button would signify assent to those terms, *see Windsor Mills,* 25 Cal.App.3d at 992, 101 Cal.Rptr. at 351 ("[W]hen the offeree does not know that a proposal has been made to him this objective standard does not apply."). California's common law is clear that "an offeree, regardless of apparent manifestation of his consent, is not bound by inconspicuous contractual provisions of which he is unaware, contained in a document whose contractual nature is not obvious." *Id.* * * *

* * *

A. The Reasonably Prudent Offeree of Downloadable Software

Defendants argue that plaintiffs must be held to a standard of reasonable prudence and that, because notice of the existence of SmartDownload license terms was on the next scrollable screen, plaintiffs were on "inquiry notice" of those terms. We disagree with the proposition that a reasonably prudent offeree in plaintiffs' position would necessarily have known or learned of the existence of the SmartDownload license agreement prior to acting, so that plaintiffs may be held to have assented to that agreement with constructive notice of its terms. *See* Cal. Civ.Code § 1589 ("A voluntary acceptance of the benefit of a transaction is equivalent to a consent to all the obligations arising from it, so far as the facts are known, or ought to be known, to the person accepting."). It is true that "[a] party cannot avoid the terms of a contract on the ground that he or she failed to read it before signing." *Marin Storage & Trucking,* 89 Cal.App.4th at 1049, 107 Cal.Rptr.2d at 651. But courts are quick to add: "An exception to this general rule exists when the writing does not appear to be a contract and the terms are not called to the attention of the recipient. In such a case, no contract is formed with respect to the undisclosed term." Id. * * *

Most of the cases cited by defendants in support of their inquiry-notice argument are drawn from the world of paper contracting. *See, e.g., Taussig v. Bode & Haslett,* 134 Cal. 260, 66 P. 259 (1901) (where party had opportunity to read leakage disclaimer printed on warehouse receipt, he had duty to do so); *In re First Capital Life Ins. Co.,* 34 Cal.App.4th 1283, 1288, 40 Cal. Rptr.2d 816, 820 (1995) (purchase of insurance policy after opportunity to read and understand policy terms creates binding agreement) * * *.

As the foregoing cases suggest, receipt of a physical document containing contract terms or notice thereof is frequently deemed, in the world of paper transactions, a sufficient circumstance to place the offeree on inquiry notice of those terms. "Every person who has actual notice of circumstances sufficient to put a prudent man upon inquiry as to a particular fact, has constructive notice of the fact itself in all cases in which, by prosecuting such inquiry, he might have learned such fact." Cal. Civ.Code § 19. These principles apply equally to the emergent world of online product delivery, pop-up screens, hyperlinked pages, clickwrap licensing, scrollable documents, and urgent admonitions to "Download Now!". What plaintiffs saw when they were being invited by defendants to download this fast, free plug-in called SmartDownload was a screen containing praise for the product and, at the very bottom of the screen, a "Download" button. Defendants argue that under the principles set forth in the cases cited above, a "fair and prudent person using ordinary care" would have been on inquiry notice of SmartDownload's license terms.

We are not persuaded that a reasonably prudent offeree in these circumstances would have known of the existence of license terms. Plaintiffs were responding to an offer that did not carry an immediately visible notice of the existence of license terms or require unambiguous manifestation of assent to those terms. Thus, plaintiffs' "apparent manifestation of ... consent" was to terms "contained in a document whose contractual nature [was] not obvious." *Windsor Mills,* 25 Cal.App.3d at 992, 101 Cal.Rptr. at 351. Moreover, the fact that, given the position of the scroll bar on their computer screens, plaintiffs may have been aware that an unexplored portion of the Netscape webpage remained below the download button does not mean that they reasonably should have concluded that this portion contained a notice of license terms. In their deposition testimony, plaintiffs variously stated that they used the scroll bar "[o]nly if there is something that I feel I need to see that is on—that is off the page," or that the elevated position of the scroll bar suggested the presence of "mere[ ] formalities, standard lower banner links" or "that the page is bigger than what I can see." Plaintiffs testified, and defendants did not refute, that plaintiffs were in fact unaware that defendants intended to attach license terms to the use of SmartDownload.

We conclude that in circumstances such as these, where consumers are urged to download free software at the immediate click of a button, a reference to the existence of license terms on a submerged screen is not sufficient to place consumers on inquiry or constructive notice of those terms. The SmartDownload webpage screen was "printed in such a manner that it tended to conceal the fact that it was an express acceptance of [Netscape's] rules and regulations." *Larrus,* 266 P.2d at 147. Internet users may have, as defendants put it, "as much time as they need[ ]" to scroll through multiple screens on a webpage, but there is no reason to assume that viewers will scroll down to subsequent screens simply because screens are there. When products are "free" and users are invited to download them in the absence of reasonably conspicuous notice that they are about to bind themselves to contract terms, the transactional circumstances cannot be fully analogized to those in the paper world of arm's-length bargaining. In the next two sections, we discuss case law and other legal authorities that have addressed the circumstances of computer sales, software licensing, and online transacting. Those authorities tend strongly to support our conclusion that plaintiffs did not manifest assent to SmartDownload's license terms.

B.   Shrinkwrap Licensing and Related Practices

Defendants cite certain well-known cases involving shrinkwrap licensing and related commercial practices in support of their contention that plaintiffs became bound by the SmartDownload license terms by virtue of inquiry notice. For example, in *Hill v. Gateway 2000, Inc.,* 105 F.3d 1147 (7th Cir.1997), the Seventh Circuit held that where a purchaser had ordered a computer over the telephone, received the order in a shipped box containing the computer along with printed contract terms, and did not return the computer within the thirty days required by the terms, the purchaser was bound by the contract. *Id.* at 1148–49. In *ProCD, Inc. v. Zeidenberg,* the same court held that where an individual purchased software in a box containing license terms which were displayed on the computer screen every time the user executed the software program, the user had sufficient opportunity to review the terms and to return the software, and so was contractually bound after retaining the product. *ProCD,* 86 F.3d at 1452 * * *.

These cases do not help defendants. To the extent that they hold that the purchaser of a computer or tangible software is contractually bound after failing to object to printed license terms provided with the product, *Hill* [does] not differ markedly from the cases involving traditional paper contracting discussed in the previous section. Insofar as the purchaser in *ProCD* was confronted with conspicuous, mandatory license terms every time he ran the software on his computer, that case actually undermines defendants' contention that downloading in the absence of conspicuous terms is an act that binds plaintiffs to those terms. * * *

C.   Online Transactions

Cases in which courts have found contracts arising from Internet use do not assist defendants, because in those circumstances there was much clearer notice than in the present case that a user's act would manifest assent to contract terms.[5] See, e.g., * * * *Caspi v. Microsoft Network, L.L.C.,* 323

---

5. Defendants place great importance on *Register.com, Inc. v. Verio, Inc.,* 126 F.Supp.2d 238 (S.D.N.Y.2000), which held that a user of the Internet domain-name database, Regis-

ter.com, had "manifested its assent to be bound" by the database's terms of use when it electronically submitted queries to the database. *Id.* at 248. But *Verio* is not helpful to

N.J.Super. 118, 732 A.2d 528, 530, 532–33 (N.J.Super.Ct.App.Div.1999) (upholding forum selection clause where subscribers to online software were required to review license terms in scrollable window and to click "I Agree" or "I Don't Agree"); *Barnett v. Network Solutions, Inc.*, 38 S.W.3d 200, 203–04 (Tex.App.2001) (upholding forum selection clause in online contract for registering Internet domain names that required users to scroll through terms before accepting or rejecting them) * * *.

After reviewing the California common law and other relevant legal authority, we conclude that under the circumstances here, plaintiffs' downloading of SmartDownload did not constitute acceptance of defendants' license terms. Reasonably conspicuous notice of the existence of contract terms and unambiguous manifestation of assent to those terms by consumers are essential if electronic bargaining is to have integrity and credibility. We hold that a reasonably prudent offeree in plaintiffs' position would not have known or learned, prior to acting on the invitation to download, of the reference to SmartDownload's license terms hidden below the "Download" button on the next screen. We affirm the district court's conclusion that the user plaintiffs * * * are not bound by the arbitration clause contained in those terms.

* * *

Conclusion

For the foregoing reasons, we affirm the district court's denial of defendants' motion to compel arbitration and to stay court proceedings.

HILLMAN, ONLINE BOILERPLATE: WOULD MANDATORY WEBSITE DISCLOSURE OF E–STANDARD TERMS BACKFIRE?

104 Mich. L. Rev. 837, 837–840, 854–856 (2006).

A law backfires when it produces results opposite from those its drafters intended. Lots of laws may have backfired. For example, people opposed to hate crimes legislation think that the laws "inflame prejudice rather than eradicate it." The Endangered Species Act, according to some analysts, has helped destroy rather than preserve the creatures listed by the Act. Even consumer protection laws, some believe, increase prices and confuse consumers instead of protecting them.

This Article analyzes whether mandatory website disclosure of e-standard terms, advocated by some as a potential solution to market failures when consumers contract over the Internet, is another potential legal backfire. By mandatory website disclosure, I do not mean a "clickwrap" presentation of terms, in which a consumer must click "I agree" or the like on a screen presenting the terms prior to the completion of a transaction in progress. Mandatory website disclosure would require a business to maintain an Internet presence and to post its terms prior to any particular transaction so that a consumer could read and compare terms without making a purchase at all.

defendants. There, the plaintiff's terms of use of its information were well known to the defendant, which took the information daily with full awareness that it was using the information in a manner prohibited by the terms of the plaintiff's offer. The case is not closely analogous to ours.

The problem is not that mandatory website disclosure would increase the cost of doing business, which would be passed on to consumers in the form of higher prices. Businesses have been unable to demonstrate that displaying their terms on their websites would be costly. Nor should drafting rules that implement the law be too difficult. Businesses could be required to display their terms on their homepage or on another page reachable directly through a clearly identified hyperlink. Further, businesses could be required to prove the availability of their terms by furnishing relatively inexpensive archival records of their websites. Mandatory website disclosure may backfire, however, because it may not increase reading or shopping for terms or motivate businesses to draft reasonable ones, but instead, may make heretofore suspect terms more likely enforceable.

* * *

* * * My preliminary empirical work on e-consumer reading of standard forms, as well as studies of e-shopping behavior suggests that advance disclosure of terms likely will fail to increase reading or shopping for terms. This should be no surprise. Despite the opportunity to read, most e-consumers may still have ample rational reasons for not reading and cognitive processes that deter reading and processing terms. In addition, e-consumers, drawn to the speed and novelty of the Internet, are unlikely to have the patience or discipline to compare terms regardless of when the terms become available. Further, watchdog groups may not positively motivate businesses because they may lack influence and because businesses may conclude that the benefits of particular terms outweigh any potential costs in adverse publicity.

In light of the potential failure of mandatory website disclosure to increase reading and to discipline businesses, the only effects of the proposal may be to insulate businesses from claims of procedural unconscionability and to create a safe harbor for businesses to draft suspect terms. My goal is not to claim that mandatory website disclosure will certainly backfire so that the proposal should be taken off the table. In fact, I conclude that mandatory website disclosure ultimately may be the most viable alternative. I simply want to elaborate on the reasons that the possibility of backfire should be taken seriously before moving in the direction of mandatory website disclosure.

* * *

If courts rarely strike a contract or term based solely on one or the other kind of unconscionability, but use a sliding scale of procedural and substantive unconscionability, what will be the outcome of mandatory website disclosure? Perhaps marginal terms, insufficiently outlandish to motivate a court to strike them on substantive unconscionability grounds alone, will be enforceable because of their early disclosure on the website. For example, consider the term * * * allowing a software vendor to "collect[] certain non-personally identifiable information about [a consumer's] Web surfing and computer usage." If such authorization to "follow around" the consumer is fully disclosed on the vendor's webpage, I doubt that a court would strike it on substantive unconscionability grounds alone. The result of mandatory website disclosure would constitute a legal backfire.

* * *

CONCLUSION

Despite all that has been said, mandatory website disclosure may still be the best strategy for dealing with the problem of e-standard forms. As mentioned, other solutions present significant problems of their own. Further, mandatory website disclosure is cheap, substantiates the claim of consumer assent, and constitutes a symbolic victory for those advocating greater fairness in e-standard-form contracting.

Of course, mandatory website disclosure is attractive for these reasons only if my fear of a legal backfire proves exaggerated because the benefits of disclosure outweigh the costs of the enforcement of some questionable terms. And perhaps I am being unduly pessimistic about the possibility that disclosure will backfire. After all, if disclosure were a good strategy for businesses to avoid unconscionability claims and of little concern because consumers do not read their standard forms, one would expect to see lots of precontract disclosure of e-standard forms already. Businesses tempted to draft unfair terms must therefore believe that disclosure benefits consumers. But I am not convinced by this argument. Business decisionmakers may themselves fail to make rational decisions for much the same reasons as consumers. For example, businesses may be unduly risk averse concerning the outcome of disclosure and therefore prefer to hide their marginal terms, even though disclosing them actually would work to their advantage.

Ultimately, optimism about disclosure may depend on one's time frame for measuring the law's effects. Even if disclosure backfires in the short term, perhaps eventually the word will get out about a business's unsavory terms. Consider the experience of cigarette manufacturers who, in response to legislation, put warning labels on their packages. For a considerable period of time, these labels helped manufacturers " 'fend[] off smokers' suits' " based on smokers' assumption of the risk. As a result, "[w]hat was intended as a burden on tobacco became a shield instead." In the long run, however, the package warnings, along with the many revelations about cigarette manufacturers' attempts to hide other adverse facts about their products, led to a massive change in public opinion and, ultimately, to serious legal sanctions against the cigarette companies. Perhaps mandatory website disclosure will also have a long-term beneficial effect.

SECTION EIGHT: SOME ADDITIONAL POLICING DOCTRINES

Certain additional policing doctrines should be identified. The doctrine of mutuality of obligation studied in Chapter Two is also sometimes employed to police agreements. For example, in Oscar Schlegel Manufacturing Co. v. Peter Cooper's Glue Factory, 231 N.Y. 459, 132 N.E. 148 (1921), the seller agreed to sell to the buyer all buyer's "requirements" of special glue" for 9 cents per pound. The buyer was a jobber selling glue to such customers as it might find. In an action by the buyer, after the seller refused to make deliveries, the court held the agreement invalid for lack of consideration. The opinion contained this telling passage:

> The price of glue having risen during the year 1916 from 9 to 24 cents per pound, it is quite obvious why orders for glue increased

correspondingly. Had the price dropped below 9 cents, it may fairly be inferred such orders would not have been given. In that case * * * plaintiff would not have been liable to the defendant for damages for a breach, since he had not agreed to sell any glue.

According to the court, the buyer had no obligation to buy any glue from the seller, and, thus, the agreement was technically unenforceable under the mutuality doctrine. But what appears to have been the true concern of the court in finding lack of mutuality? See Uniform Commercial Code section 2–306(1)(page 371) for a different approach.

We have also studied how courts invalidate certain agreed damages provisions as penalties. This too is a policing response. Would it be fair to say that courts seem more willing to strike such provisions as penalties, even without evidence of bargaining improprieties, than to strike provisions such as exculpatory clauses? What do you suppose accounts for this?

As Problem 5–5 illustrates, contract interpretation can serve a policing function. Recall Professor Llewellyn's criticism of this policing approach.

In addition to these doctrines that you have seen before, you should also be acquainted with doctrines addressed to problems of mental illness and infancy. Not all forms of mental illness invalidate assent. The Restatement (Second) of Contracts in section 15 posits the following rule:

Mental Illness or Defect

(1) A person incurs only voidable contract duties by entering into a transaction if by reason of mental illness or defect

(a) he is unable to understand in a reasonable manner the nature and consequences of the transaction, or

(b) he is unable to act in a reasonable manner in relation to the transaction and the other party has reason to know of his condition.

(2) Where the contract is made on fair terms and the other party is without knowledge of the mental illness or defect, the power of avoidance under Subsection (1) terminates to the extent that the contract has been so performed in whole or in part or the circumstances have so changed that avoidance would be unjust. In such a case a court may grant relief as justice requires.

Contract law imposes an absolute rule with respect to persons who have not reached the age of majority: those under a certain age (varying from state to state) may disaffirm their contracts. E. Farnsworth, Contracts 228–30 (3d ed. 1999). But as you may have already observed in other contexts, absolute rules tend to generate exceptions. One prime candidate for an exception involves the purchase of "necessaries" by "infants." Contract law typically takes the position that infants should be presumed capable of contracting with respect to some necessaries so that people will be willing to sell such items to them. For example, would you want to sell a car to an infant if the infant could disaffirm the deal? But what if the infant needs a car for work? To ensure that infants can contract for necessaries the law excepts such contracts from the disaffirmance rule. But what is a necessary? What if the infant could take a bus to work? As you can see, exceptions to rules, carved out for policing or other reasons in particular cases, may "cloud" doctrine and cause confusion.

Finally, courts frequently invoke the general obligation of good faith as a policing tool. In Section Five of Chapter Six we will see that good faith is highly fertile in this regard. No lawyer concerned with a policing problem should fail to consider it.

SECTION NINE: POLICING CONTRACT MODIFICATIONS

Contracting parties often desire to modify their agreements because they change their mind or the circumstances change. Suppose, for example, the Benkowskis decided soon after signing their agreement with the Whites that they had not received a fair price for their water service. The Whites might be willing to agree to a price increase for many reasons. They might concede that the deal was too favorable to them. Or they might be willing to pay more to keep their relationship with the Benkowskis harmonious. After all, the Whites may desire to modify the agreement in their own favor sometime in the future.

Because people are relatively free to enter contracts, and to shape the terms of contracts, they should be free to modify their agreements as well. Rules precluding free adjustment, in fact, might even deter some parties from entering contracts (at least long-term ones). Enforcing freely made modifications thus supports the principle of contractual freedom and facilitates economic exchange.

Although freedom to modify should be encouraged, parties must also be able to rely on their agreements so they can plan for the future. They must have some confidence that if they choose to insist on performance as originally agreed, the law will support them. Parties who have made plans in reliance on their contracts may be vulnerable to coercion, however. Planning tends to limit future choices and thus to increase the possibility that the planner will be forced to agree to an unwelcome modification if faced with a threat of nonperformance. The primary rationale for policing contract modifications, then, is to deny enforcement of modifications whereby one party takes undue advantage of the other.

ALASKA PACKERS' ASSOCIATION v. DOMENICO

United States Court of Appeals, Ninth Circuit, 1902.
117 Fed. 99.

Ross, Circuit Judge. The libel in this case was based upon a contract alleged to have been entered into between the libelants and the appellant corporation on the 22d day of May, 1900, at Pyramid Harbor, Alaska, by which it is claimed the appellant promised to pay each of the libelants, among other things, the sum of $100 for services rendered and to be rendered. In its answer the respondent denied the execution, on its part, of the contract sued upon, averred that it was without consideration, and for a third defense alleged that the work performed by the libelants for it was performed under other and different contracts than that sued on, and that, prior to the filing of the libel, each of the libelants was paid by the respondent the full amount due him thereunder, in consideration of which each of them executed a full release of all his claims and demands against the respondent.

The evidence shows without conflict that on March 26, 1900, at the city and county of San Francisco, the libelants entered into a written contract with the appellant, whereby they agreed to go from San Francisco to Pyramid Harbor, Alaska, and return, on board such vessel as might be designated by the appellant, and to work for the appellant during the fishing season of 1900, at Pyramid Harbor, as sailors and fishermen, agreeing to do "regular ship's duty, both up and down, discharging and loading; and to do any other work whatsoever when requested to do so by the captain or agent of the Alaska Packers' Association." By the terms of this agreement, the appellant was to pay each of the libelants $50 for the season, and two cents for each red salmon in the catching of which he took part.

On the 15th day of April, 1900, 21 of the libelants signed shipping articles by which they shipped as seamen on the Two Brothers, a vessel chartered by the appellant for the voyage between San Francisco and Pyramid Harbor, and also bound themselves to perform the same work for the appellant provided for by the previous contract of March 26th; the appellant agreeing to pay them therefor the sum of $60 for the season, and two cents each for each red salmon in the catching of which they should respectively take part. Under these contracts, the libelants sailed on board the Two Brothers for Pyramid Harbor, where the appellant had about $150,000 invested in a salmon cannery. The libelants arrived there early in April of the year mentioned, and began to unload the vessel and fit up the cannery. A few days thereafter, to wit, May 19th, they stopped work in a body, and demanded of the company's superintendent there in charge $100 for services in operating the vessel to and from Pyramid Harbor, instead of the sums stipulated for in and by the contracts; stating that unless they were paid this additional wage they would stop work entirely, and return to San Francisco. The evidence showed, and the court below found, that it was impossible for the appellant to get other men to take the places of the libelants, the place being remote, the season short and just opening; so that, after endeavoring for several days without success to induce the libelants to proceed with their work in accordance with their contracts, the company's superintendent, on the 22d day of May, so far yielded to their demands as to instruct his clerk to copy the contracts executed in San Francisco, including the words "Alaska Packers' Association" at the end, substituting, for the $50 and $60 payments, respectively, of those contracts, the sum of $100, which document, so prepared, was signed by the libelants before a shipping commissioner whom they had requested to be brought from Northeast Point; the superintendent, however, testifying that he at the time told the libelants that he was without authority to enter into any such contract, or to in any way alter the contracts made between them and the company in San Francisco. Upon the return of the libelants to San Francisco at the close of the fishing season, they demanded pay in accordance with the terms of the alleged contract of May 22d, when the company denied its validity, and refused to pay other than as provided for by the contracts of March 26th and April 5th, respectively. Some of the libelants, at least, consulted counsel, and, after receiving his advice, those of them who had signed the shipping articles before the shipping commissioner at San Francisco went before that officer, and received the amount due them thereunder, executing in consideration thereof a release in full, and the others being paid at the office of the company, also receipting in full for their demands.

On the trial in the court below, the libelants undertook to show that the fishing nets provided by the respondent were defective, and that it was on that account that they demanded increased wages. On that point, the evidence was substantially conflicting, and the finding of the court was against the libelants. * * *

The evidence being sharply conflicting in respect to these facts, the conclusions of the court, who heard and saw the witnesses, will not be disturbed. * * *

The real questions in the case as brought here are questions of law, and, in the view that we take of the case, it will be necessary to consider but one of those. Assuming that the appellant's superintendent at Pyramid Harbor was authorized to make the alleged contract of May 22d, and that he executed it on behalf of the appellant, was it supported by a sufficient consideration? From the foregoing statement of the case, it will have been seen that the libelants agreed in writing, for certain stated compensation, to render their services to the appellant in remote waters where the season for conducting fishing operations is extremely short, and in which enterprise the appellant had a large amount of money invested; and, after having entered upon the discharge of their contract, and at a time when it was impossible for the appellant to secure other men in their places, the libelants, without any valid cause, absolutely refused to continue the services they were under contract to perform unless the appellant would consent to pay them more money. Consent to such a demand, under such circumstances, if given, was, in our opinion, without consideration, for the reason that it was based solely upon the libelants' agreement to render the exact services, and none other, that they were already under contract to render. The case shows that they willfully and arbitrarily broke that obligation. As a matter of course, they were liable to the appellant in damages, and it is quite probable, as suggested by the court below in its opinion, that they may have been unable to respond in damages. But we are unable to agree with the conclusions there drawn, from these facts, in these words:

> "Under such circumstances, it would be strange, indeed, if the law would not permit the defendant to waive the damages caused by the libelants' breach, and enter into the contract sued upon,—a contract mutually beneficial to all the parties thereto, in that it gave to the libelants reasonable compensation for their labor, and enabled the defendant to employ to advantage the large capital it had invested in its canning and fishing plant."

Certainly, it cannot be justly held, upon the record in this case, that there was any voluntary waiver on the part of the appellant of the breach of the original contract. The company itself knew nothing of such breach until the expedition returned to San Francisco, and the testimony is uncontradicted that its superintendent at Pyramid Harbor, who, it is claimed, made on its behalf the contract sued on, distinctly informed the libelants that he had no power to alter the original or to make a new contract; and it would, of course, follow that, if he had no power to change the original, he would have no authority to waive any rights thereunder. The circumstances of the present case bring it, we think, directly within the sound and just observations of the supreme court of Minnesota in the case of King v. Railway Co., 61 Minn. 482, 63 N.W. 1105:

> "No astute reasoning can change the plain fact that the party who refuses to perform, and thereby coerces a promise from the other party to the contract to pay him an increased compensation for doing that which he is legally bound to do, takes an unjustifiable advantage of the necessities of the other party. Surely it would be a travesty on justice to hold that the party so making the promise for extra pay was estopped from asserting that the promise was without consideration. A party cannot lay the foundation of an estoppel by his own wrong, where the promise is simply a repetition of a subsisting legal promise. There can be no consideration for the promise of the other party, and there is no warrant for inferring that the parties have voluntarily rescinded or modified their contract. The promise cannot be legally enforced, although the other party has completed his contract in reliance upon it."

[Judgment reversed.]

SCHWARTZREICH v. BAUMAN–BASCH, INC.

Court of Appeals of New York, 1921.
231 N.Y. 196, 131 N.E. 887.

CRANE, J. On the 31st day of August, 1917, the plaintiff entered into the following employment agreement with the defendant:

> "Bauman–Basch, Inc.
> "Coats & Wraps
> "31–33 East 32d Street
> "New York

"Agreement entered into this 31st day of August, 1917, by and between Bauman–Basch, Inc., a domestic corporation, party of the first part, and Louis Schwartzreich, of the borough of Bronx, city of New York, party of the second part, witnesseth:

"The party of the first part does hereby employ the party of the second part, and the party of the second part agrees to enter the services of the party of the first part as a designer of coats and wraps.

"The employment herein shall commence on the 22d day of November, 1917, and shall continue for twelve months thereafter. The party of the second part shall receive a salary of ninety ($90.00) per week, payable weekly.

"The party of the second part shall devote his entire time and attention to the business of the party of the first part, and shall use his best energies and endeavors in the furtherance of its business.

"In witness whereof, the party of the first part has caused its seal to be affixed hereto and these presents to be signed, and the party of the second part has hereunto set his hand and seal the day and year first above written.

"Bauman–Basch, Inc.,

"S. Bauman.

"Louis Schwartzreich.

"In the presence of."

In October the plaintiff was offered more money by another concern. Mr. Bauman, an officer of the Bauman–Basch, Inc., says that in that month he heard that the plaintiff was going to leave and thereupon had with him the following conversation:

"A. I called him in the office, and I asked him, 'Is that true that you want to leave us?' and he said 'Yes,' and I said, 'Mr. Schwartzreich, how can you do that; you are under contract with us?' He said, 'Somebody offered me more money.' * * * I said, 'How much do they offer you?' He said, 'They offered him $115 a week.' * * * I said, 'I cannot get a designer now, and, in view of the fact that I have to send my sample line out on the road, I will give you a hundred dollars a week rather than to let you go.' He said, 'If you will give me $100, I will stay.' "

Thereupon Mr. Bauman dictated to his stenographer a new contract, dated October 17, 1917, in the exact words of the first contract and running for the same period, the salary being $100 a week, which contract was duly executed by the parties and witnessed. Duplicate originals were kept by the plaintiff and defendant.

Simultaneously with the signing of this new contract the plaintiff's copy of the old contract was either given to or left with Mr. Bauman. He testifies that the plaintiff gave him the paper but that he did not take it from him. The signatures to the old contract plaintiff tore off at the time according to Mr. Bauman.

The plaintiff's version as to the execution of the new contract is as follows:

"A. I told Mr. Bauman that I have an offer from Scheer & Mayer of $110 a week, and I said to him: 'Do you advise me as a friendly matter— will you advise me as a friendly matter what to do; you see I have a contract with you, and I should not accept the offer of $110 a week, and I ask you, as a matter of friendship, do you advise me to take it or not.' At the minute he did not say anything, but the day afterwards he came to me in and he said, 'I will give you $100 a week, and I want you to stay with me.' I said: 'All right, I will accept it; it is very nice of you that you do that, and I appreciate it very much.' "

The plaintiff says that on the 17th of October, when the new contract was signed, he gave his copy of the old contract back to Mr. Bauman, who said: "You do not want this contract any more because the new one takes its place."

The plaintiff remained in the defendant's employ until the following December, when he was discharged. He brought this action under the contract of October 17th for his damages.

The defense, insisted upon through all the courts, is that there was no consideration for the new contract as the plaintiff was already bound under his agreement of August 31, 1917, to do the same work for the same period at $90 a week.

The trial justice submitted to the jury the question whether there was a cancellation of the old contract and charged as follows:

> "If you find that the $90 contract was prior to or at the time of the execution of the $100 contract canceled and revoked by the parties by their mutual consent, then it is your duty to find that there was a consideration for the making of the contract in suit, viz., the $100 contract, and, in that event, the plaintiff would be entitled to your verdict for such damages as you may find resulted proximately, naturally, and necessarily in consequence of the plaintiff's discharge prior to the termination of the contract period of which I shall speak later on."

Defendant's counsel thereupon excepted to that portion of the charge in which the court permitted the jury to find that the prior contract may have been canceled simultaneously with the execution of the other agreement. Again the court said:

> "The test question is whether by word or by act, either prior to or at the time of the signing of the $100 contract, these parties mutually agreed that the old contract from that instant should be null and void."

The jury having rendered a verdict for the plaintiff, the trial justice set it aside and dismissed the complaint on the ground that there was not sufficient evidence that the first contract was canceled to warrant the jury's findings.

The above quotations from the record show that a question of fact was presented and that the evidence most favorable for the plaintiff would sustain a finding that the first contract was destroyed, canceled, or abrogated by the consent of both parties.

The Appellate Term was right in reversing this ruling. Instead of granting a new trial, however, it reinstated the verdict of the jury and the judgment for the plaintiff. [The Appellate Division affirmed the decision of the Appellate Term.] The question remains, therefore, whether the charge of the court, as above given, was a correct statement of the law or whether on all the evidence in the plaintiff's favor a cause of action was made out.

Can a contract of employment be set aside or terminated by the parties to it and a new one made or substituted in its place? If so, is it competent to end the one and make the other at the same time?

It has been repeatedly held that a promise made to induce a party to do that which he is already bound by contract to perform is without consideration. But the cases in this state, while enforcing this rule, also recognize that a contract may be canceled by mutual consent and a new one made. * * *

* * *

Any change in an existing contract, such as a modification of the rate of compensation, or a supplemental agreement, must have a new consideration to support it. In such a case the contract is continued, not ended. Where, however, an existing contract is terminated by consent of both parties and a new one executed in its place and stead, we have a different situation and the mutual promises are again a consideration. Very little difference may appear in a mere change of compensation in an existing and continuing contract and a termination of one contract and the making of a new one for the same time and work, but at an increased compensation. There is, however, a marked difference in principle. Where the new contract gives any new privilege or advantage to the promisee, a consideration has been recognized, though in the main it is the same contract. Triangle Waist Co., Inc. v. Todd, 223 N.Y. 27, 119 N.E. 85.

If this which we are now holding were not the rule, parties having once made a contract would be prevented from changing it no matter how willing and desirous they might be to do so, unless the terms conferred an additional benefit to the promisee.

All concede that an agreement may be rescinded by mutual consent and a new agreement made thereafter on any terms to which the parties may assent. Prof. Williston, in his work on Contracts, says (volume 1, § 130a):

> "A rescission followed shortly afterwards by a new agreement in regard to the same subject-matter would create the legal obligations provided in the subsequent agreement."

The same effect follows in our judgment from a new contract entered into at the same time the old one is destroyed and rescinded by mutual consent. The determining factor is the rescission by consent. Provided this is the expressed and acted upon intention, the time of the rescission, whether a moment before or at the same time as the making of the new contract, is unimportant.

* * *

As before stated, in this case we have an express rescission and a new contract.

There is no reason that we can see why the parties to a contract may not come together and agree to cancel and rescind an existing contract, making a new one in its place. We are also of the opinion that reason and authority support the conclusion that both transactions can take place at the same time.

For the reasons here stated, the charge of the trial court was correct, and the judgments of the Appellate Division and the Appellate Term should be affirmed, with costs.

* * *

Judgments affirmed.

CHASE, J., dissents.

Problem 5–6

Suppose Schwartzreich came to your law office after receiving the offer of additional compensation elsewhere, and asked you to represent him in negotiations with Bauman–Basch. Prepare a short outline of the strategy you would propose for conducting those negotiations. Are the divergent views of the parties as to what happened in the actual negotiations surprising?

Note
The Preexisting Duty Rule Today

As in Schwartzreich v. Bauman–Basch, Inc., the language of many court opinions is still today concerned with whether modifications were supported by new consideration and with the intricacies of mutual rescission theory and the like, rather than with whether the modification was voluntarily and fairly made. For example, in the case of Recker v. Gustafson, 279 N.W.2d 744 (Iowa 1979), the Reckers and Gustafsons had agreed that the Reckers would pay $290,000 for a tract of land. Subsequent to the agreement, the Reckers, without legal representation, were told by the Gustafsons' attorney that the Gustafsons were "willing to go to court to get out of their agreement and that litigation was expensive," but that the Gustafsons would agree to perform if the Reckers would pay an additional $10,000. The Reckers, in their early twenties, agreed to the price increase.

Was the Reckers' agreement enforceable? Instead of focusing frontally on the issues of voluntariness and fairness, the Iowa court found that there was no consideration in support of the Reckers' promise of an extra $10,000. The court even stated that if the parties had mutually rescinded the original agreement first, the second agreement would have been enforceable, but found no evidence of a rescission.

If parties freely and fairly enter a modification agreement, should it matter whether they formally rescinded their prior agreement first? By the same token, if the modification agreement was not freely and fairly entered, should the presence of formal consideration make the agreement enforceable? For example, suppose the Gustafsons were clearly guilty of coercion but to make their modification enforceable they agreed to convey one day earlier. Should the agreement be enforced?

UNIFORM COMMERCIAL CODE § 2–209.

Modification, Rescission and Waiver

(1) An agreement modifying a contract within this Article needs no consideration to be binding.

* * *

Official Comment

1. This section seeks to protect and make effective all necessary and desirable modifications of sales contracts without regard to the technicalities which at present hamper such adjustments.

2. Subsection (1) provides that an agreement modifying a sale contract needs no consideration to be binding.

However, modifications made thereunder must meet the test of good faith imposed by this Act. The effective use of bad faith to escape performance on the original contract terms is barred, and the extortion of a "modification" without legitimate commercial reason is ineffective as a violation of the duty of good faith. Nor can a mere technical consideration support a modification made in bad faith.

The test of "good faith" between merchants or as against merchants includes "observance of reasonable commercial standards of fair dealing in the trade" (Section 2–103), and may in some situations require an objectively demonstrable reason for seeking a modification. But such matters as a market shift which makes performance come to involve a loss may provide such a reason even though there is no such unforeseen difficulty as would make out a legal excuse from performance under Sections 2–615 and 2–616.

UNITED STATES v. STUMP HOME SPECIALTIES MFG., INC., 905 F.2d 1117 (7th Cir.1990).

POSNER, CIRCUIT JUDGE.

* * * The cautionary, evidential, and other policies behind the requirement of consideration do not apply, or apply only with much attenuated strength, in the context of written modification. By hypothesis the parties already have a contract, so that the danger of mistaking casual promissory language for an intention to be legally bound is slight; moreover, we deal here with a written, not an oral, modification, so fabrication of a promise is harder.

The requirement of consideration has, however, a distinct function in the modification setting—although one it does not perform well—and that is to prevent coercive modifications. Since one of the main purposes of contracts and of contract law is to facilitate long-term commitments, there is often an interval in the life of a contract during which one party is at the mercy of the other. A may have ordered a machine from B that A wants to place in operation on a given date, specified in their contract; and in expectation of B's complying with the contract, A may have made commitments to his customers that it would be costly to renege on. As the date of scheduled delivery approaches, B may be tempted to demand that A agree to renegotiate the contract price, knowing that A will incur heavy expenses if B fails to deliver on time. A can always refuse to renegotiate, relying instead on his right to sue B for breach of contract if B fails to make delivery by the agreed date. But legal remedies are costly and uncertain, thereby opening the way to duress. Considerations of commercial reputation will deter taking advantage of an opportunity to exert duress on a contract partner in many cases, but not in all: For examples of duress in the contract-modification setting, see *Austin Instrument, Inc. v. Loral Corp.*, 29 N.Y.2d 124, 324 N.Y.S.2d 22, 272 N.E.2d 533 (1971), and *Alaska Packers' Ass'n v. Domenico,* 117 F. 99 (9th Cir.1902); and for general discussion see *Selmer Co. v. Blakeslee–Midwest Co.*, 704 F.2d 924 (7th Cir.1983); *Richards Construction Co. v. Air Conditioning Co. of Hawaii*, 318 F.2d 410, 413–14 (9th Cir.1963) * * *.

The rule that modifications are unenforceable unless supported by consideration strengthens A's position by reducing B's incentive to seek a modification. But it strengthens it feebly, as we pointed out in *Wisconsin Knife Works v. National Metal Crafters, supra,* 781 F.2d at 1285. The law does not require that consideration be adequate—that it be commensurate with what the party accepting it is giving up. Slight consideration, therefore, will suffice to make a contract or a contract modification enforceable. * * * And slight consideration is consistent with coercion. To surrender one's contractual rights in exchange for a peppercorn is not functionally different from surrendering them for nothing.

The sensible course would be to enforce contract modifications (at least if written) regardless of consideration and rely on the defense of duress to prevent abuse. *Wisconsin Knife Works v. National Metal Crafters, supra,* 781 F.2d at 1286; UCC § 2–209, official comment 2; Hillman, *Contract Modification Under the Restatement (Second) of Contracts,* 67 Cornell L.Rev. 680 (1982). All coercive modifications would then be unenforceable, and there would be no need to worry about consideration, an inadequate safeguard against duress.

ANGEL v. MURRAY

Supreme Court of Rhode Island, 1974.
113 R.I. 482, 322 A.2d 630.

[The city of Newport agreed to pay its refuse collector, Maher, an additional $10,000 per year over and above the amount previously agreed upon. Maher had requested the additional money because of a substantial increase in the cost of collection due to an unexpected increase in the number of dwelling units. Angel brought an action claiming that the city had illegally paid $20,000 to Maher for two years service and requested that the collector be ordered to repay it. The lower court ordered the repayment and the city and Maher appealed.]

ROBERTS, C.J.

* * *

The primary purpose of the preexisting duty rule is to prevent what has been referred to as the "hold-up game." * * *

[An] example of the "hold-up game" is found in the area of construction contracts. Frequently, a contractor will refuse to complete work under an unprofitable contract unless he is awarded additional compensation. The courts have generally held that a subsequent agreement to award additional compensation is unenforceable if the contractor is only performing work which would have been required of him under the original contract. *See, e.g.,* Lingenfelder v. Wainwright Brewing Co., 103 Mo. 578, 15 S.W. 844 (1891), which is a leading case in this area. * * *

[This example] clearly illustrate[s] that the courts will not enforce an agreement that has been procured by coercion or duress and will hold the parties to their original contract regardless of whether it is profitable or unprofitable. However, the courts have been reluctant to apply the preexisting duty rule when a party to a contract encounters unanticipated difficulties and the other party, not influenced by coercion or duress, voluntarily agrees to pay additional compensation for work already required to be performed under the contract. For example, the courts have found that the original contract was rescinded, Linz v. Schuck, 106 Md. 220, 67 A. 286 (1907); abandoned, Connelly v. Devoe, 37 Conn. 570 (1871), or waived, Michaud v. McGregor, 61 Minn. 198, 63 N.W. 479 (1895).

Although the preexisting duty rule has served a useful purpose insofar as it deters parties from using coercion and duress to obtain additional compensation, it has been widely criticized as a general rule of law. * * *

The modern trend appears to recognize the necessity that courts should enforce agreements modifying contracts when unexpected or unanticipated difficulties arise during the course of the performance of a contract, even though there is no consideration for the modification, as long as the parties agree voluntarily.

Under the Uniform Commercial Code, § 2–209(1), which has been adopted by 49 states, "[a]n agreement modifying a contract [for the sale of goods] needs no consideration to be binding." *See* G.L.1956 (1969 Reenactment) § 6A–2–209(1). Although at first blush this section appears to validate modifications obtained by coercion and duress, the comments to this section indicate that a modification under this section must meet the test of good faith imposed by the Code, and a modification obtained by extortion without a legitimate commercial reason is unenforceable.

The modern trend away from a rigid application of the preexisting duty rule is reflected by § 89D(a) of the American Law Institute's Restatement Second of the Law of Contracts, [now section 89(a)] which provides: "A promise modifying a duty under a contract not fully performed on either side is binding (a) if the modification is fair and equitable in view of circumstances not anticipated by the parties when the contract was made * * *."

We believe that § 89D(a) is the proper rule of law and find it applicable to the facts of this case. It not only prohibits modifications obtained by coercion, duress, or extortion but also fulfills society's expectation that agreements entered into voluntarily will be enforced by the courts. *See generally* Horwitz, The Historical Foundations of Modern Contract Law, 87 Harv.L.Rev. 917 (1974). Section 89D(a), of course, does not compel a modification of an unprofitable or unfair contract; it only enforces a modification if the parties voluntarily agree and if (1) the promise modifying the original contract was made before the contract was fully performed on either side, (2) the underlying circumstances which prompted the modification were unanticipated by the parties, and (3) the modification is fair and equitable.

The evidence, which is uncontradicted, reveals that in June of 1968 Maher requested the city council to pay him an additional $10,000 for the year beginning on July 1, 1968, and ending on June 30, 1969. This request was made at a public meeting of the city council, where Maher explained in detail his reasons for making the request. Thereafter, the city council voted to authorize the Mayor to sign an amendment to the 1964 contract which provided that Maher would receive an additional $10,000 per year for the duration of the contract. Under such circumstances we have no doubt that the city voluntarily agreed to modify the 1964 contract.

Having determined the voluntariness of this agreement, we turn our attention to the three criteria delineated above. First, the modification was made in June of 1968 at a time when the five-year contract which was made in 1964 had not been fully performed by either party. Second, although the 1964 contract provided that Maher collect all refuse generated within the city, it appears this contract was premised on Maher's past experience that the number of refuse-generating units would increase at a rate of 20 to 25 per year. Furthermore, the evidence is uncontradicted that the 1967–1968 increase of 400 units "went beyond any previous expectation." Clearly, the circumstances which prompted the city council to modify the 1964 contract were unanticipated. Third, although the evidence does not indicate what proportion of the total this increase comprised, the evidence does indicate that it was a "substantial" increase. In light of this, we cannot say that the council's agreement to pay Maher the $10,000 increase was not fair and equitable in the circumstances.

The judgment appealed from is reversed, and the cause is remanded to the Superior Court for entry of judgment for the defendants.

HILLMAN, CONTRACT MODIFICATION UNDER THE RESTATEMENT (SECOND) OF CONTRACTS

67 Cornell L.Rev. 680, 699–700 (1982).

The Inadequacy of Section 89(a)

Perhaps the greatest shortcoming of section 89(a) is not its ambiguity but its underinclusiveness. As an exception to the preexisting-duty rule of section 73, section 89(a) simply may not extend to many situations in which modifications, because they are voluntary, should be enforced. As noted earlier, despite the presence of the "unanticipated circumstances" test, the real thrust of section 89(a) may involve an application of the "fair and equitable" requirement to determine whether a modification was voluntarily made. Nevertheless, the "in view of" connective phrase between "fair and equitable" and "unanticipated circumstances" indicates that some "unanticipated circumstance" must be found before the court can proceed to the voluntariness issue. A host of reasons exist, however, for voluntarily agreeing to a modification in the absence of any unanticipated event. For example, in Illustration 3 to section 89(a), loosely based on *Schwartzreich v. Bauman–Basch, Inc.,* a promise to increase an employee's salary is enforceable when a third party has made the employee a better offer. In *Schwartzreich,* the court did not rest its decision to enforce the modification on the basis of "unanticipated circumstances"; perhaps it did not believe that the third-party offer constituted "unanticipated circumstances." Instead, it found that a rescission-replacement had occurred. Nevertheless, the court's enforcement of the modification does suggest a belief that the modification was "fair and equitable" under the circumstances.

Requiring either additional consideration or an "unanticipated" event to validate modifications presupposes that contracting parties always act with economic rationality in relation to a particular transaction. This assumption simply is not accurate because a particular contract may be only one part of a much more extensive relationship between the parties. When such a complex relationship exists, there may be excellent reasons for one party to give up something in the short term with the expectation of a return in the future. The party actually may be acting with perfect economic rationality, but only a much broader examination of the overall relationship of the parties will make such a conclusion possible.

MACNEIL, ECONOMIC ANALYSIS OF CONTRACTUAL RELATIONS: ITS SHORTFALLS AND THE NEED FOR A "RICH CLASSIFICATORY APPARATUS"

75 N.W.U.L.Rev. 1018, 1048 (1981).

If there is anything plain in the real economic world it is that seldom do participants in contractual relations go for the jugular when trouble arises. The high transaction costs of fighting are undoubtedly one explanation, but even discounting for that factor, a huge residue of nonassertiveness remains explainable only by the willingness to sacrifice immediate exchange-gains to increase relational security.

FLOWERS v. DIAMOND SHAMROCK CORP.

United States Court of Appeals, Fifth Circuit, 1982.
693 F.2d 1146.

TATE, CIRCUIT JUDGE:

In this Texas diversity suit, the plaintiffs (the Flowers), lessors of the mineral rights of Texas oil and gas fields, seek additional royalties under a market value royalty provision contained in their leases with the defendant, Diamond Shamrock Corporation (Shamrock). The Flowers contend that Shamrock did not base royalty payments on the "market value" of subsequent sales of the gas from the leased properties, but rather only on the lower amount of the actual proceeds from Shamrock's long-term sales contract with an intrastate distributor. The plaintiffs Flowers' cause of action is founded upon the Texas jurisprudential holdings that a landowner-lessor is entitled to royalty payment for gas sold off his premises based upon the market value at the time of sale after production, not upon the price established between the producer and the distributor under an earlier long term contract. *Texas Oil & Gas Corporation v. Vela,* 429 S.W.2d 866, 870–71 (Tex.1968).

The district court set aside parts of favorable jury determinations that justified an award to the Flowers of increased royalties. In so doing, the court held * * * that the endorsement of royalty checks as a matter of law constituted an accord and satisfaction as to some of the earlier royalty payments * * *.

* * * [W]e hold * * * that the jury could properly find on the evidence before it that, when the Flowers endorsed the royalty checks, there was no bona fide dispute as to the amount thereof (an essential prerequisite under Texas law to an accord and satisfaction), so that the district court therefore erred in granting judgment notwithstanding the jury verdict. We remand for the determination of additional royalties therefore due * * *.

THE FACTS

The plaintiffs Flowers have royalty interests under an oil and gas lease on lands in Ochiltree County, Texas. The defendant Shamrock, as lessee, agreed to pay the plaintiffs royalties based on the "market value" of the natural gas produced from a well it drilled on the property.[1] Gas was discovered on the

---

1. The gas royalty clause of the lease provides that:

The royalties to be paid by lessee are: * * * on gas, including casinghead gas or other gas-property in 1963 and since that date has been sold and used solely within the state of Texas.

Shamrock pipes the natural gas from the well to its refinery, where the liquid contents of the gas are stripped, and the residue is sold at the plant "tailgate" to a distributor. Although it commingles the gas from many wells at the refinery, Shamrock measures at each well the volume (by thousand cubic feet, or MCF) and the heating value (by British Thermal Unit, or BTU) of the gas. In 1965 Shamrock committed the gas from the Flowers' well, in addition to that produced from other leased properties, to a twenty-year sales contract with the Southwestern Public Service Company (Southwestern), setting a beginning price at 19.5 cents per thousand cubic feet of gas containing 1000 BTU per cubic foot, escalating over the life of the contract to 22.5 cents. Shamrock has paid the Flowers a royalty based on this contract price, or at times a slightly higher price.

Shamrock tendered to the plaintiffs monthly checks for royalty payments calculated upon the contract price, and the plaintiffs endorsed and cashed these checks. A stub was attached to each check which showed lease numbers, a number that presumably showed the volume of production, the amount of severance tax deducted, and an amount labelled "Your Part," which was the amount of the check. The following small print appeared on the back of the check itself:

Endorsements

This check is issued in full settlement of the account stated and the payee accepts it as such by his endorsement. If not correct, return without alteration and state difference.

On February 15, 1974, Shamrock sent a form letter to its royalty owners, including the Flowers, offering to pay higher royalties if the lessor executed a contract agreeing to accept royalties directly based on the sales contract proceeds from the lessee-distributor sales contracts rather than on the market value method of computation set forth in the original leases. On July 29, 1974, Marvin Flowers, for the Flowers, replied that there was no reason to execute an agreement to obtain a rate increase to which the lessors were entitled, and requested payment of "deficit funds" from February.[2] Shamrock

---

eous substances, produced from said land and sold or used off the premises or for the extraction of gasoline or other product therefrom, the market value at the well of one-eighth of the gas so sold or used. * * *

Shamrock is the corporate successor to Shamrock Oil and Gas Corporation, the lessee by assignment of the mineral interests in the Flowers' properties. For convenience, use of the Shamrock name includes the predecessor in title or corporate entity.

2. The July 29, 1974 letter by Marvin Flowers stated:

I have your letter of February 15, 1974, written to me stating that you wished to offer an immediate and substantial increase in my royalty rate pending the signing of an enclosed royalty agreement. The June 1974 gas payment reflected this rate increase.

I am not aware of any previous agreement with you which makes it a requirement for me to sign any document prior to receiving a rate increase on natural gas production from the aforesaid leases.

With this understanding, I am requesting that you pay deficit funds due for the months of February, March, April, and May.

Marvin Flowers testified that he wasn't "sure what the implications" of the communication received by him from Shamrock were, that "he was dissatisfied with what I was getting for my gas," that he thought from Shamrock's letter that he "was due more money going back to February, 1974," but that he was

acknowledged receipt of that letter in a response attached to the plaintiffs' original pleading, but not introduced into evidence, informing the Flowers that it would continue to pay the royalty in accordance with the lease provisions.

The plaintiffs did not express further dissatisfaction with the amount of royalties received, but stopped endorsing and cashing the checks in February, 1977, and eventually brought this lawsuit.

The plaintiff-lessors sued for the difference in the royalties due them under *Vela* since December, 1973. Trial was to a jury, which found the market values for the applicable months and failed to find for the defendant on its affirmative defense of accord and satisfaction. The trial court granted Shamrock's motion for judgment notwithstanding the verdict. * * * [T]he court held that the defendant had established its accord and satisfaction defense as a matter of law as to those months from 1973 to 1977 when royalty checks were cashed by the plaintiffs. No recovery was therefore awarded for those months. * * *

* * *

I. ACCORD AND SATISFACTION

The district court held that the evidence adduced in trial showed, as a matter of law, that the royalty checks cashed by the plaintiffs were accepted in satisfaction of an unliquidated claim. Any dispute over the market value of the gas on which the Flowers' royalties were based was therefore conclusively resolved in an accord and satisfaction with Shamrock that foreclosed recovery of additional amounts.

The plaintiffs Flowers point out that judgment notwithstanding a jury verdict should not be granted by the trial court unless "the facts and inferences point so strongly and overwhelmingly in favor of one party that * * * reasonable men could not arrive at a contrary verdict." *Boeing v. Shipman,* 411 F.2d 365, 374 (5th Cir.1969) (en banc). In ruling upon such a motion, the court must consider all the evidence "in the light and with all reasonable inferences most favorable to the party opposed to the motion." *Id.* Tested by this standard, we agree with the plaintiffs Flowers' contention that the evidence before the jury reasonably permitted a determination, as a factual matter, that at the time the Flowers perfunctorily endorsed their royalty checks, they were not aware of any bona fide dispute between themselves and Shamrock as to the amount of gas royalties due to them under the lease. The jury could thus find under the evidence that, by their endorsements, the Flowers could not have intended to relinquish their rights under *Vela* to additional gas royalties based upon the market value of the gas at the time of production and sale (rather than upon the much lower price received

"not technically sharp enough to know what he was getting for my gas." The evidence reveals that the Flowers did not at that time consult a lawyer and that they were completely unaware of their right under *Vela* to receive royalties at all times after the initial production in 1965 that were based on the actual market value of the gas rather than upon the price received by Shamrock from its sales under the contract with the distributor. The purport of Marvin Flowers' testimony, rather, is that he suspected for reason unknown, but probably related to the measurement of the gas or to the price actually received by Shamrock from the distributor, that since February 1974 the gas royalties paid to the Flowers were insufficient—otherwise Shamrock would not have offered the new contract in February 1974.

by Shamrock as a result of its long-term contract entered into years earlier with the intrastate distributor).

Shamrock argues that the Flowers' endorsement of the checks conclusively indicates that they relinquished claims to a greater amount. Shamrock contends that this amount was disputed by the Flowers at least as early as July, 1974, the date of the plaintiffs' letter to Shamrock indicating their belief that there may have been a deficit in royalty amounts paid. *See* note 2 *supra*.

The Supreme Court of Texas set out the requirements of an accord and satisfaction in *Jenkins v. Henry C. Beck Co.,* 449 S.W.2d 454, 455 (Tex.1969):

> This defense rests upon a new contract, express or implied, in which the parties agree to the discharge of the existing obligation by means of the lesser payment tendered and accepted. * * * The minds must meet and where resting in implication the facts proved must irresistibly point to such conclusion. * * * There must be an unmistakable communication to the creditor that tender of the lesser sum is upon the condition that acceptance will constitute satisfaction of the underlying obligation. It has been said that the conditions must be made plain, definite and certain * * *; that the statement accompanying the tender of a sum less than the contract price must be so clear, full and explicit that it is not susceptible of any other interpretation * * *; that the offer must be accompanied with acts and declarations which the creditor is "bound to understand".
> * * *

* * *

The consideration for the new contract establishing a discharge of the prior obligation is the settlement of a bona fide dispute between the parties.[3] *See Roylex, Inc. v. S & B Engineers, Inc.,* 592 S.W.2d 59, 60 (Tex.Civ.App. 1979) (*see also* " 'The condition that the tender is in full settlement must be brought home to the creditor' ", *id.*) * * *. In the absence of a bona fide dispute as to the obligation owed by the debtor, the acceptance and endorsement of a check marked, "This check is in full settlement of account as shown hereon. Acceptance by endorsement constitutes receipt in full," does not prevent the creditor from collecting the balance of the obligation. *See Ortiz Oil Co. v. Geyer,* 159 S.W.2d 494, 497 (Tex.1942). The requirement of a bona fide dispute presupposes both parties' knowledge that there exists a particular issue as to a greater liability that is settled by the accord. *See Firestone Tire & Rubber Co. v. White,* 274 S.W.2d 452, 455 (Tex.Civ.App.1954), where, even though there was a dispute between the parties as to the debt owed on the purchase of certain merchandise, a judgment for the debtor was reversed because it had not been shown that the money paid was with full knowledge that it was intended to be in full settlement of all matters, including purchases of merchandise the creditor overlooked in preparing the bill.

Mutual assent of the parties to settlement of a dispute is a requirement for an accord and satisfaction, and the creditor must fully understand that the

---

3. Although Texas law continues to distinguish between accord and satisfaction of liquidated claims for a set amount, and of unliquidated claims (where the amount or extent of the obligation is disputed), sufficient consideration for an accord arises out of the settlement of a dispute as to the existence or amount of liability. *See Burgamy v. Davis,* 313 S.W.2d 365, 367 (Tex.Civ.App.1958); *Firestone Tire & Rubber Co. v. White,* 274 S.W.2d 452, 455 (Tex. Civ.App.1954). A bona fide dispute is a prerequisite to an accord of either type of claim. *Id.*

amount tendered is conditioned as full disposition of the underlying obligation. "[I]f the creditor is to be held to have surrendered his claim against the debtor, it must be shown that he understood or should have understood that he was doing so when he received the consideration claimed therefor." *Call of Houston, Inc. v. Mulvey,* 343 S.W.2d 522, 524 (Tex.Civ.App.1961). In *Call of Houston,* an employee with a 90-day notice of termination clause in his employment contract was not aware at the time he received payment covering thirty days of the notice period with a check marked "Account in Full" that there was a dispute with his employer as to the necessity of providing ninety days notice or that he accepted the check in settlement of the employer's breach of contract. Because of lack of knowledge and mutual assent, there was no accord and satisfaction.

The parties may refer to past duties or future liabilities between them to prove or disprove the existence of an accord and satisfaction. Such factual issues are to be determined by the jury. *See Call of Houston, supra,* 343 S.W.2d at 525. The Texas cases reiterate the requirement that the minds of creditor and debtor must be found to have met in the making of the new contract "in which the parties agree to the discharge of the existing obligation by means of the lesser payment tendered and accepted." *Industrial Life Insurance Co. v. Finley,* 382 S.W.2d 100, 104 (Tex.1964).

In the present instance, no evidence whatsoever shows that the Flowers had or should have had any knowledge, at the time, that negotiation of these checks would affect or settle a disagreement as to the market value of the gas on which royalties were based. Shamrock's position at all times was that plaintiffs were being paid in accordance with the lease, and there is no evidence in the record that any of the plaintiffs were aware of the incorrectness of that position under *Vela.* The endorsement says that the "account stated" is fully paid and, indeed, the "your part" amount shown on the stub was paid by each check. No issue or dispute relative to value is suggested on the check or stub, and the statement above the place for the endorsement is far from the unequivocal notice to plaintiffs that the checks were conditionally tendered in full and final satisfaction of a disputed obligation, which Texas law requires for there to be an accord and satisfaction. The Flowers' endorsement of the royalty checks signified to them nothing more than acceptance of their part of the gas measured and the account computed at the rate being paid by Shamrock. There is no unequivocal statement here that the endorsement compromises and settles a disputed rate issue; it just as plainly, if not only, purports to make the endorsement an acceptance of Shamrock's arithmetic.[4]

Nor is there evidence that the trial jury was conclusively required to accept to the effect that the Flowers knew that there was a dispute as to the

---

4. No evidence shows that any of the plaintiffs knew of the holding of *Texas Oil & Gas Corp. v. Vela,* 429 S.W.2d 866 (Tex.1968), and what it meant to their rights in the settlement of the gas royalty. There, as noted, the Texas Supreme Court held that market value should be determined as of the time of delivery of the gas to the purchaser, rather than as of the time of the making of the contract between the lessee and purchaser, and Shamrock undoubt- edly knew four years later of the effect of that holding upon its obligation to these plaintiffs. No other logical reason appears for its attempt to get the plaintiffs to amend the lease in this respect. No explanation was made to the plaintiffs of their *Vela* claim under the existing lease, or of the nature of Shamrock's breach of contract in the payment of royalties on the basis of the 1965 contract.

amount of gas royalties due to them, let alone knew that they were indisputably entitled under *Vela* to receive the market value price at the time of sale after production, as opposed to the below-market-value price determined by the contract between Shamrock and *its* purchasor. It is true that in 1974 the Flowers wrote a letter requesting payment of any deficit royalties, but the letter seems to be a response to Shamrock's offer to amend the contract, not acknowledgement of a dispute concerning calculation of market value. At most, any inferences to be drawn from the letter concerning the Flowers' knowledge of a dispute and of the Flowers' intent to reach an accord and satisfaction, were factual issues to be determined by the jury. Under this record, it cannot be said as a matter of law that with the endorsement of these royalty checks the minds of the royalty owners and Shamrock met to change the market value basis for royalty payment to that of the lesser rate which Shamrock had chosen.

The district court therefore erred in granting summary judgment to Shamrock in contradiction of the jury verdict in favor of the Flowers. The evidence before the jury permitted it to find that there was no factual basis upon which to base an accord and satisfaction between the Flowers and Shamrock, as allegedly resulting from their endorsement of gas royalty payment checks between December 197[3] and March 1977. Accordingly, we reverse that part of the district court's order that denied the Flowers' recovery of additional royalties for this period, and we remand for further calculation of the award due for such royalties. The award is to be based on the jury's month-to-month determination of market value for gas production until March, 1977.

FOAKES v. BEER, 9 App.Cas. 605 (House of Lords 1884). [Foakes owed Beer over £2,000 on a judgment. The parties agreed, according to the Court of Appeal, that if Foakes would pay Beer £500 at once and the rest over a certain period in installments, then Beer would give up the right to interest on the debt. Nevertheless, Beer then sued for the interest. Held for Beer because the agreement lacked consideration. One of the judges, however, pointed out that "all men of business, whether merchants or tradesmen, do every day recognise and act on the ground that prompt payment of a part of their demand may be more beneficial to them than it would be to insist on their rights and enforce payment of the whole."]

CONSOLIDATED EDISON CO. OF NEW YORK, INC. v. ARROLL

Civil Court of the City of New York, 1971.
66 Misc.2d 816, 322 N.Y.S.2d 420.

MILTON SANDERS, JUDGE.

This is an action by Consolidated Edison Company of New York, Inc., ("Con Edison,") to recover a balance alleged to be due from defendant on five electric bills for the summer periods of 1968, 1969, and 1970. Defendant disputed the amounts of these bills on the basis that they exceeded past bills for comparable periods, including the summer of 1967, by too great an amount to have any validity. He questioned the accuracy of the meter and/or the readings taken, as well as Con Edison's statements as to the amount of electricity consumed. After a considerable amount of correspondence had taken place between the parties, defendant sent a letter on December 6, 1969 to the attention of the president of Con Edison, with carbon copies to the company at their local office and to the post office box designated for the payment of bills. The letter stated again defendant's disagreement with the amounts of the first three bills, and advised that he had arbitrarily picked the sum of $35.00 as the proper amount due on each bill, as that sum reflected his past experience, and stated further that he was sending three checks for $35.00 each to the office designated for collection. Each check would bear the legend:

> "This check is in full payment and satisfaction of the bill of Consolidated Edison Company of New York, Inc., to Mark Arroll, Account Number 26–2726–0191–002 for the period of _____ to _____ and negotiation of this check constitutes release of any bills or claims of Consolidated Edison Company of New York, Inc., sometimes known as Con Edison, against Mark Arroll."

The letter went on to state that it is the law that the cashing or mere retention of the checks beyond a reasonable length of time constitutes an accord and satisfaction. On September 25, 1970, defendant took the same action with respect to the remaining two bills in dispute, sending a similar letter to the president of the company, and carbon copies to the same offices. Con Edison subsequently replied to defendant's letters, but it merely re-stated in its replies that the meter and the readings thereof had been found to be accurate, and that the electricity billed for had actually been consumed. The letters made no mention of and completely ignored the paragraphs advising about the checks. Five checks in the amount of $35.00 each were mailed by defendant to the address designated by Con Edison for the payment of bills. Each check bore the legend previously stated on the back thereof. On the face of each check the words "paid in full" were written, together with an identification of the bill to which it related, the defendant's account number, and a reference to the letter of either December 6, 1969 or September 25, 1970. All five checks were received and deposited and Con Edison has retained the proceeds thereof. Con Edison now seeks the difference between the payments received and the full amounts of the bills rendered. The customer's defense is accord and satisfaction.

After considering all of the competent and credible evidence presented, I am satisfied that the meter and the readings taken thereof by Con Edison were accurate, and that the electricity billed for was actually consumed, since defendant failed to submit any evidence to the contrary. I find, therefore, that the disputed bills reflected the proper charges for defendant's use of electricity. We are concerned, however, with whether or not the defense of accord and satisfaction has been established in the light of the facts and circumstances described.

The law is well settled that where an amount due is in dispute, and the debtor sends a check for less than the amount claimed, and clearly expresses his intention that the check has been sent as payment in full, and not on account or in part payment, the cashing or retention of the check by the creditor is deemed an acceptance by the creditor of the conditions stated, and operates as an accord and satisfaction of the claim. * * * Con Edison's contention that there was no *bona fide* dispute as to the amount due has no merit. As the Court stated in Schuttinger v. Woodruff, 259 N.Y.2d 212, 181 N.E. 361, in order for the rule to apply, "the debtor must honestly hold the opinion either that he owes nothing or that he is bound only to the extent of paying less than his adversary seeks to exact. * * * The dispute need not rest upon factors arising from sound reasons. The debtor may be wrong in his contention. That he honestly believes in the correctness of his position is enough." (See also Simons v. Supreme Council American Legion of Honor, 178 N.Y. 263, 70 N.E. 776). It is evident, and I so find, from the testimony and the documents and correspondence offered in evidence, that the defendant honestly and in good faith believed that he owed less than the amount Con Edison claimed. Under the circumstances it cannot be said that a *bona fide* dispute did not exist.

* * *

This brings us to the question as to whether the retention of the proceeds of the checks by Con Edison bound the company to an accord and satisfaction. Evidence was presented by Con Edison that the address designated for mailing payment of bills was a post office box from which all payments were picked up directly by employees of the bank in which the company maintained its account. The company argues that the nature and volume of its operations does not allow for an examination by bank employees of each and every check it receives for language written thereon which could bind it to an accord and satisfaction. What Con Edison is really saying is that because it conducts such a large operation, it should be exempted from the application of well settled principles of law which would bind individuals and all smaller business organizations. I cannot accept this conclusion. To permit Con Edison to follow one set of rules while everyone else is following another would cast an intolerable burden on the orderly functioning of the community. The fact remains that Con Edison accepted the benefits of defendant's checks. Con Edison cannot, by arranging for someone else to accept payment of bills for its own convenience, avoid the consequences of the law.

It should be noted that even if Con Edison had written to defendant and expressly rejected the condition that the checks were to be accepted as full payment, the depositing and retention of the proceeds of the checks would nevertheless operate as an accord and satisfaction. As the court stated in Carlton Credit Corp. v. Atlantic Refining Co., [12 A.D.2d 613, 208 N.Y.S.2d 622, *aff'd* 10 N.Y.2d 723, 219 N.Y.S.2d 269, 176 N.E.2d 837] "The plaintiff could not accept the payment and reject the condition (citations omitted). It was fully aware of the attempt to satisfy the amount claimed with a lesser payment but despite that it accepted the check with the condition imposed. True, it is stated that there was no intention to accept the check in full satisfaction and protest was registered. However, such protest is unavailing." (See also Rosenblatt v. Birnbaum, 16 N.Y.2d 212, 264 N.Y.S.2d 521, 212 N.E.2d 37). It is not the creditor's intent that controls. "What is said is overridden by what is done, and assent is imputed as an inference of law" (CARDOZO, Ch. J., in Hudson v. Yonkers Fruit Co., 258 N.Y. 168, 179 N.E. 373).

There is no question that Con Edison was given sufficient notification that the checks were to be considered as payment in full. Defendant's letters to Con Edison's president clearly indicated defendant's intent. In Carlton Credit Corp. v. Atlantic Refining Co., [supra] a case quite similar to this one, it was said that: "The acceptance and negotiation by the plaintiff of the defendant's check constituted an accord and satisfaction. The covering letter to which the check was annexed, itemizing in detail the deductions claimed, makes it clear that the payment made was conditioned upon its acceptance as payment in full for the larger amount claimed by the plaintiff to be due it from the defendant."

The affirmative defense of accord and satisfaction is sustained. Judgment for defendant.

Problem 5–7

James Geis, a physicist, and his associate, Cofek, were attempting to develop a laser scanning inspection system (LSIS). They formed a corporation, Geisco, Inc., which contracted with Honeywell Radiation Center through a series of "purchase orders" for Geisco to supply services to design and develop the LSIS. The original purchase order provided that the parties' agreement terminated on June 11, 1974; although no clear duration was set forth, supplemental purchase orders suggested that the parties regarded the original contract as extending beyond June 11, 1974.

On August 29, 1974, James Geis received the following letter from Sheldon Busansky, general manager of Honeywell:

"James D. Geis, President
GEISCO
128 Pleasant Drive
Cheshire, Conn. 07410

Dear Jim:

In light of the corporate decision not to proceed with the LSIS Project, this is your notification of termination of all agreements between Honeywell and GEISCO effective 31 August 1974. We will, of course, honor the terms of the nondisclosure of information agreements. As recognition of our original intent to participate in a long term relationship we are offering you the 60 day termination notice which was in the licensing agreement you signed earlier. The termination compensation will be in the form of a lump sum payment of $9,300 covering yourself and Henry Cofek for the 60 day period.

No expenses beyond 31 August will be paid by Honeywell.

Sincerely yours,

Sheldon Busansky"

A few days later Geis received a check made out to Geisco, Inc. for the sum of $9,300. At this time, Geis and Cofek believed that Honeywell had wrongfully terminated Geisco, that Honeywell had failed to use "best efforts" under the agreement to market the LSIS, and that Honeywell had fraudulently induced Geisco to enter the agreements.

Geis has come to your law office and has asked for advice. Can he cash the check without surrendering his rights against Honeywell? If so, must he endorse the check in any special way or send Honeywell any notice? If not, why not?

Note
Executory Accord, Accord and Satisfaction, and Substituted Contract, Under the Restatement (Second) of Contracts

Section 281(1) defines an accord as "a contract under which an obligee promises to accept a stated performance in satisfaction of the obligor's existing duty." Suppose a creditor and a debtor reasonably disagree as to the amount owed. Suppose further that in a settlement, devoid of foul play, made on July 1, the parties agree that on August 1 the debtor will pay 80% of the amount claimed by the creditor. This is called an executory accord. If the debtor pays the 80% on August 1 the executory accord ripens into an "accord and satisfaction." Can the creditor later change his or her mind and recover on the original obligation? No. The accord and satisfaction is a defense to such a claim.

Now suppose the debtor repudiates the July 1 agreement on July 10 so that the executory accord is never performed by the debtor and thus does not become an "accord and satisfaction." In these circumstances, the creditor can pursue the claim for the full amount, not just the 80%.

Section 279 of the Restatement (Second) defines a "substituted contract" as "one that is itself accepted by the obligee in satisfaction of the original duty and thereby discharges it." According to Comment a, "[i]f the parties intend the new contract to replace all of the provisions of the earlier contract, the contract is a substituted contract." Thus, in our example, if the parties intended their July 1 agreement to be a substitute for the original agreement out of which the creditor's claim arose, then the debtor's duty to pay such a claim is discharged even though the debtor repudiates on July 10. That is, despite the repudiation, the creditor can sue only for breach of the July 1 settlement agreement, not for breach of the original agreement. Of course, the intentions of the parties will frequently be unclear as to whether the new agreement is merely an accord or is a substituted contract. Section 281 of the Restatement (Second) presumes that a new agreement is merely an accord unless the parties make clear that it is a substituted contract. Why? Would a reasonable creditor agree to accept a mere promise to pay 80% of a debt in substitution for a duty to pay 100%? Comment c to section 279 suggests not.

UNIFORM COMMERCIAL CODE § 1–207.

Performance or Acceptance Under Reservation of Rights

(1) A party who with explicit reservation of rights performs or promises performance or assents to performance in a manner demanded or offered by the other party does not thereby prejudice the rights reserved. Such words as "without prejudice," "under protest" or the like are sufficient.

(2) Subsection (1) does not apply to an accord and satisfaction.

Official Comment

* * *

(3) Judicial authority was divided on the issue of whether former Section 1–207 (present subsection (1)) applied to an accord and satisfaction. Typically the cases involved attempts to reach an accord and satisfaction by use of a check tendered in full satisfaction of a claim. Subsection (2) of revised Section

1–207 resolves this conflict by stating that Section 1–207 does not apply to an accord and satisfaction. * * *

Problem 5–8

On February 20, Sayles, a manufacturer and seller of appliances, and Borden enter a written agreement for the sale to Borden of a freezer to be delivered on March 20. On February 25, however, Sayles notifies Borden in writing that it cannot deliver the freezer until April 15 because of delays in the receipt of materials from its suppliers. Borden responds in writing on February 26 that the delay in delivery will cause Borden substantial losses because it will result in a slowdown of its production of ice cream. Borden accepts the freezers on April 15 and pays the contract price. Borden later brings an action against Sayles for lost profits due to the delay in delivery.

A) What is the legal effect of Borden's letter of February 26? If you were consulted by Borden prior to the letter, how would you have drafted it?

B) What is the legal effect of the acceptance of the goods on April 15? If you had been consulted by Borden prior to the acceptance, what advice would you have given?

Note
Legal and Non-legal Factors in Negotiating Settlements

Most disputes arising during the performance of a contract are settled long before they reach the courtroom. Legal as well as non-legal factors are considered when settling these disputes. The lawyer's role is to evaluate all of these factors in developing the proper strategy for the negotiations.

Legal factors include the strength of each party's claim based on the "law" of the agreement and the general law of contract. Recall, for example, that the Whites were entitled to a supply of water under their agreement with the Benkowskis and that the remedies available to the Whites for breach were supplied by the court under general contract principles because the agreement did not address the remedies issue.

Non-legal factors include whether the parties desire to deal with each other in the future, the costs and delays of litigation or of alternative dispute resolution, the financial or other outside pressures on the parties to settle the problem, the psychological pressure to take something now rather than wait for an uncertain future, and the emotional strain of litigation. Such non-legal factors often outweigh the legal factors.

*

Part Three

THE PERFORMANCE PROCESS

Chapter Six

SUBSTANTIVE CONTENT OF THE
DUTY TO PERFORM

Chapter Seven

CONDITIONAL NATURE OF THE DUTY TO
PERFORM, AND PERMISSIBLE RESPONSES
TO FAILURE OF CONDITION AND
BREACH OF DUTY

Chapter Six

SUBSTANTIVE CONTENT OF THE DUTY TO PERFORM

In a civilized society people must be able to assume that those with whom they deal will act in good faith, and will carry out their undertakings according to the expectations which the moral sentiment of the community attaches thereto.

POUND

SECTION ONE: THE PERFORMANCE STAGE AND THE ROLE OF LAWYERS

In accord with the primary theory of obligation operative in contract and related fields, parties may create their own governing law by entering into an agreement with consideration. In this way, the parties' agreement (not general law) specifies the content of their duties. In the usual case, privately created law of this kind serves its purposes well. When the performance stage arrives, the parties perform their duties without dispute.

Sometimes, however, questions arise about the content of a valid agreement or promise, and these questions may even generate a serious dispute. A lawyer may be consulted to advise on a course of action, to negotiate a settlement, or even to litigate. To do these things well, the lawyer must understand how courts resolve disputes involving the content and meaning of agreements and promises. This is the subject of the present chapter and the next. These chapters are relevant to the lawyer not only at the performance stage, but at earlier stages as well. As you study the material, consider how a lawyer could have done a better job of planning and drafting to avoid the problem that arose.

Assuming that, for better or worse, the contract has already been drafted, one of the lawyer's roles at the performance stage may be to counsel the client. For example, consider again the plight of the Whites and the Benkowskis. Their agreement imposed a duty of performance calling for the Benkowskis to supply "water." Assume Ruth Benkowski phoned a lawyer after the agreement had been drafted, but before it became effective, and asked whether they must supply potable water. To answer this, the lawyer would have to interpret the agreement.

The lawyer as counselor is also often called on to render advice after the other party's non-performance or even after performance. This, too, usually requires close study of the agreement. For example, suppose the Benkowskis supplied water that was discolored at least once a day for an average of from one to two hours. Would this be a breach?

The lawyer may have to interpret not only the law of the agreement, but communications sent between the parties as well. Suppose the Benkowskis received a letter from the Whites on June 10, indicating that they could not pay on time in July. The Benkowskis might ask their lawyer whether they could cut off the water supply at any time, whether they could cut it off only as of July 1, or whether they could cut it off at all.

The lawyer may have other roles at the performance stage in addition to that of counselor. The lawyer might be asked to negotiate a contract modification to resolve a dispute caused by unforeseen circumstances or by a gap in the parties' agreement. For example, the Whites and the Benkowskis might decide to specify whether the Benkowskis must supply potable water. In such negotiations, the lawyer can seldom ignore the original agreement because it may give bargaining leverage to one party or the other.

When a dispute arises at the performance stage and informal dispute resolution fails, the lawyer may be asked to litigate the "law of the contract" in court.

SECTION TWO: CONTRACT TERMS AND PAROL EVIDENCE RULES

In every jurisdiction, a "parol evidence" rule governs the extent to which a party may introduce in court evidence of a claimed prior or contemporaneous agreement, understanding, or negotiation to explain, supplement, or vary a written agreement. The rule favors written agreements largely on the theory that writings are more reliable than oral agreements. According to *one* version of the parol evidence rule,

> [w]hen two parties have made a contract and have expressed it in a writing to which they have both assented as to the complete and accurate integration of that contract, evidence, whether parol or otherwise, of antecedent understandings and negotiations will not be admitted for the purpose of varying or contradicting the writing.[a]

Observe that we refer to parol evidence *rules* in the title to this section. This is not a typographical error! Scholars, judges, legislatures, and Restatement drafters have recommended or adopted a number of different parol evidence rules. Indeed, one may even find more than one parol evidence rule applicable to the same kind of contract. But all variations have this in common: they seek some middle position between blind adherence to the language of a written agreement and total willingness to give binding effect to all extrinsic evidence of antecedent agreements, understandings, or negotiations that may affect the writing.

---

a. 3 Corbin on Contracts § 573 at 357 (1960). Prior or contemporaneous terms are "integrated" in a writing, according to Professor Corbin, to the extent that the writing embodies them. A writing is "complete" if it integrates all such terms. A "partial" integration only incorporates some of the terms.

Observe also that no matter what version of the parol evidence rule that applies, the rule does not govern post-contract statements or conduct. As one court has put it, "[b]y its express ... language, the rule does not apply to conduct and statements taking place *after* a contract has been executed. Thus, evidence of negotiations occurring after a written agreement will not be excluded by the parol evidence rule.... Indeed, contractual rights and remedies may be modified or waived by subsequent conduct." Hofeldt v. Mehling, 658 N.W.2d 783, 787 (S.D. Sup. Ct. 2003).

MITCHILL v. LATH

Court of Appeals of New York, 1928.
247 N.Y. 377, 160 N.E. 646.

Appeal from Supreme Court, Appellate Division, Second Department.

Action by Catherine C. Mitchill against Charles Lath and another. Judgment of Special Term in plaintiff's favor, directing specific performance of an agreement to remove an icehouse, was affirmed by the Appellate Division (220 App.Div. 776, 221 N.Y.S. 864), and defendants appeal. Judgments of Appellate Division and Trial Term reversed, and complaint dismissed.

ANDREWS, J. In the fall of 1923 the Laths owned a farm. This they wished to sell. Across the road, on land belonging to Lieutenant Governor Lunn, they had an icehouse which they might remove. Mrs. Mitchill looked over the land with a view to its purchase. She found the icehouse objectionable. Thereupon "the defendants orally promised and agreed, for and in consideration of the purchase of their farm by the plaintiff, to remove the said icehouse in the spring of 1924." Relying upon this promise, she made a written contract to buy the property for $8,400, for cash and a mortgage and containing various provisions usual in such papers. Later receiving a deed, she entered into possession, and has spent considerable sums in improving the property for use as a summer residence. The defendants have not fulfilled their promise as to the icehouse, and do not intend to do so. We are not dealing, however, with their moral delinquencies. The question before us is whether their oral agreement may be enforced in a court of equity.

This requires a discussion of the parol evidence rule—a rule of law which defines the limits of the contract to be construed. Glackin v. Bennett, 226 Mass. 316, 115 N.E. 490. It is more than a rule of evidence, and oral testimony, even if admitted, will not control the written contract (O'Malley v. Grady, 222 Mass. 202, 109 N.E. 829), unless admitted without objection (Brady v. Nally, 151 N.Y. 258, 45 N.E. 547). It applies, however, to attempts to modify such a contract by parol. It does not affect a parol collateral contract distinct from and independent of the written agreement. It is, at times, troublesome to draw the line. Williston, in his work on Contracts (section 637) points out the difficulty. "Two entirely distinct contracts," he says, "each for a separate consideration, may be made at the same time, and will be distinct legally. Where, however, one agreement is entered into wholly or partly in consideration of the simultaneous agreement to enter into another, the transactions are necessarily bound together. * * * Then if one of the agreements is oral and the other in writing, the problem arises whether the bond is sufficiently close to prevent proof of the oral agreement." That is the situation here. It is claimed that the defendants are called upon to do

you sat beside me and I became myself.

more than is required by their written contract in connection with the sale as to which it deals.

The principle may be clear, but it can be given effect by no mechanical rule. As so often happens, it is a matter of degree, for, as Prof. Williston also says, where a contract contains several promises on each side it is not difficult to put any one of them in the form of a collateral agreement. If this were enough, written contracts might always be modified by parol. Not form, but substance, is the test.

In applying this test, the policy of our courts is to be considered. We have believed that the purpose behind the rule was a wise one, not easily to be abandoned. Notwithstanding injustice here and there, on the whole it works for good. Old precedents and principles are not to be lightly cast aside, unless it is certain that they are an obstruction under present conditions. New York has been less open to arguments that would modify this particular rule, than some jurisdictions elsewhere. Thus in Eighmie v. Taylor, 98 N.Y. 288, it was held that a parol warranty might not be shown, although no warranties were contained in the writing.

Under our decisions before such an oral agreement as the present is received to vary the written contract, at least three conditions must exist: (1) The agreement must in form be a collateral one; (2) it must not contradict express or implied provisions of the written contract; (3) it must be one that parties would not ordinarily be expected to embody in the writing, or, put in another way, an inspection of the written contract, read in the light of surrounding circumstances, must not indicate that the writing appears "to contain the engagements of the parties, and to define the object and measure the extent of such engagement." Or, again, it must not be so clearly connected with the principal transaction as to be part and parcel of it.

The respondent does not satisfy the third of these requirements. It may be, not the second. We have a written contract for the purchase and sale of land. The buyer is to pay $8,400 in the way described. She is also to pay her portion of any rents, interest on mortgages, insurance premiums, and water meter charges. She may have a survey made of the premises. On their part, the sellers are to give a full covenant deed of the premises as described, or as they may be described by the surveyor, if the survey is had, executed, and acknowledged at their own expense; they sell the personal property on the farm and represent they own it; they agree that all amounts paid them on the contract and the expense of examining the title shall be a lien on the property; they assume the risk of loss or damage by fire until the deed is delivered; and they agree to pay the broker his commissions. Are they to do more? Or is such a claim inconsistent with these precise provisions? It could not be shown that the plaintiff was to pay $500 additional. Is it also implied that the defendants are not to do anything unexpressed in the writing?

That we need not decide. At least, however, an inspection of this contract shows a full and complete agreement, setting forth in detail the obligations of each party. On reading it, one would conclude that the reciprocal obligations of the parties were fully detailed. Nor would his opinion alter if he knew the surrounding circumstances. The presence of the icehouse, even the knowledge that Mrs. Mitchill thought it objectionable, would not lead to the belief that a separate agreement existed with regard to it. Were such an agreement made it would seem most natural that the inquirer should find it in the contract. Collateral in form it is found to be, but it is closely related to the subject dealt with in the written agreement—so closely that we hold it may not be proved.

Where the line between the competent and the incompetent is narrow the citation of authorities is of slight use. Each represents the judgment of the court on the precise facts before it. How closely bound to the contract is the supposed collateral agreement is the decisive factor in each case. * * *

We do not ignore the fact that authorities may be found that would seem to support the contention of the appellant. * * * A line of cases in Massachusetts, of which Durkin v. Cobleigh, 156 Mass. 108, 30 N.E. 474, 17 L.R.A. 270, 32 Am.St.Rep. 436, is an example, have to do with collateral contracts made before a deed is given. But the fixed form of a deed makes it inappropriate to insert collateral agreements, however closely connected with the sale. This may be cause for an exception. Here we deal with the contract on the basis of which the deed to Mrs. Mitchill was given subsequently, and we confine ourselves to the question whether its terms may be modified.

* * *

Our conclusion is that the judgment of the Appellate Division and that of the Special Term should be reversed and the complaint dismissed, with costs in all courts.

LEHMAN, J. (dissenting). I accept the general rule as formulated by Judge ANDREWS. I differ with him only as to its application to the facts shown in the record. The plaintiff contracted to purchase land from the defendants for an agreed price. A formal written agreement was made between the sellers and the plaintiff's husband. It is on its face a complete contract for the conveyance of the land. It describes the property to be conveyed. It sets forth the purchase price to be paid. All the conditions and terms of the conveyance to be made are clearly stated. I concede at the outset that parol evidence to show additional conditions and terms of the conveyance would be inadmissible. There is a conclusive presumption that the parties intended to integrate in that written contract every agreement relating to the nature or extent of the property to be conveyed, the contents of the deed to be delivered, the consideration to be paid as a conditions precedent to the delivery of the deeds, and indeed all the rights of the parties in connection with the land. The conveyance of that land was the subject-matter of the written contract, and the contract completely covers that subject.

The parol agreement which the court below found the parties had made was collateral to, yet connected with, the agreement of purchase and sale. It has been found that the defendants induced the plaintiff to agree to purchase the land by a promise to remove an icehouse from land not covered by the agreement of purchase and sale. No independent consideration passed to the defendants for the parol promise. To that extent the written contract and the alleged oral contract are bound together. The same bond usually exists wherever attempt is made to prove a parol agreement which is collateral to a written agreement. Hence "the problem arises whether the bond is sufficiently close to prevent proof of the oral agreement." See Judge ANDREWS' citation from Williston on Contracts, § 637.

Judge ANDREWS has formulated a standard to measure the closeness of the bond. Three conditions, at least, must exist before an oral agreement may be proven to increase the obligation imposed by the written agreement. I think we agree that the first condition that the agreement "must in form be a collateral one" is met by the evidence. I concede that this condition is met in most cases where the courts have nevertheless excluded evidence of the collateral oral agreement. The difficulty here, as in most cases, arises in connection with the two other conditions.

The second condition is that the "parol agreement must not contradict express or implied provisions of the written contract." Judge ANDREWS voices doubt whether this condition is satisfied. The written contract has been carried out. * * * By the oral agreement the plaintiff seeks to hold the defendants to other obligations to be performed by them thereafter upon land which was not conveyed to the plaintiff. The assertion of such further obligation is not inconsistent with the written contract, unless the written contract contains a provision, express or implied, that the defendants are not to do anything not expressed in the writing. Concededly there is no such express provision in the contract, and such a provision may be implied, if at all, only if the asserted additional obligation is "so clearly connected with the principal transaction as to be part and parcel of it," and is not "one that the parties would not ordinarily be expected to embody in the writing." * * * In this case, therefore, the problem reduces itself to the one question whether or not the oral agreement meets the third condition.

I have conceded that upon inspection the contract is complete. * * * That engagement was on the one side to convey land; on the other to pay the price. The plaintiff asserts further agreement based on the same consideration to be performed by the defendants after the conveyance was complete, and directly affecting only other land. It is true, as Judge ANDREWS points out, that "the presence of the icehouse, even the knowledge that Mrs. Mitchill thought it objectionable, would not lead to the belief that a separate agreement existed with regard to it"; but the question we must decide is whether or not, *assuming* an agreement was made for the removal of an unsightly icehouse from one parcel of land as an inducement for the purchase of another parcel, the parties would ordinarily or naturally be expected to embody the agreement for the removal of the icehouse from one parcel in the written agreement to convey the other parcel. Exclusion of proof of the oral agreement on the ground that it varies the contract embodied in the writing may be based only upon a finding or presumption that the written contract was intended to cover the oral negotiations for the removal of the icehouse which lead up to the contract of purchase and sale. To determine what the writing was intended to cover, "the document alone will not suffice. What it was intended to cover cannot be known till we know what there was to cover. The question being whether certain subjects of negotiation were intended to be covered, we must compare the writing and the negotiations before we can determine whether they were in fact covered." Wigmore on Evidence (2d Ed.) § 2430.

The subject-matter of the written contract was the conveyance of land. The contract was so complete on its face that the conclusion is inevitable that the parties intended to embody in the writing all the negotiations covering at least the conveyance. The promise by the defendants to remove the icehouse from other land was not connected with their obligation to convey except that one agreement would not have been made unless the other was also made. The plaintiff's assertion of a parol agreement by the defendants to remove the icehouse was completely established by the great weight of evidence. It must prevail unless that agreement was part of the agreement to convey and the entire agreement was embodied in the writing.

The fact that in this case the parol agreement is established by the overwhelming weight of evidence is, of course, not a factor which may be considered in determining the competency or legal effect of the evidence. Hardship in the particular case would not justify the court in disregarding or emasculating the general rule. It merely accentuates the outlines of our problem. The assumption that the parol agreement was made is no longer obscured by any doubts. The problem, then, is clearly whether the parties are presumed to have intended to render that parol agreement legally ineffective and nonexistent by failure to embody it in the writing. Though we are driven to say that nothing in the written contract which fixed the terms and conditions of the stipulated conveyance suggests the existence of any further parol agreement, an inspection of the contract, though it is complete on its face in regard to the subject of the conveyance, does not, I think, show that it was intended to embody negotiations or agreements, if any, in regard to a matter so loosely bound to the conveyance as the removal of an icehouse from land not conveyed.

The rule of integration undoubtedly frequently prevents the assertion of fraudulent claims. Parties who take the precaution of embodying their oral agreements in a writing should be protected against the assertion that other terms of the same agreement were not integrated in the writing. The limits of the integration are determined by the writing, read in the light of the surrounding circumstances. A written contract, however complete, yet covers only a limited field. I do not think that in the written contract for the conveyance of land here under consideration we can find an intention to cover a field so broad as to include prior agreements, if any such were made, to do other acts on other property after the stipulated conveyance was made.

In each case where such a problem is presented, varying factors enter into its solution. Citation of authority in this or other jurisdictions is useless, at least without minute analysis of the facts. The analysis I have made of the decisions in this state leads me to the view that the decision of the courts below is in accordance with our own authorities and should be affirmed.

CARDOZO, C.J., and POUND, KELLOGG and O'BRIEN, JJ., concur with ANDREWS, J.

LEHMAN, J., dissents in opinion in which CRANE, J., concurs.

Judgment accordingly.

MASTERSON v. SINE

Supreme Court of California, 1968.
68 Cal.2d 222, 65 Cal.Rptr. 545, 436 P.2d 561.

TRAYNOR, CHIEF JUSTICE.

Dallas Masterson and his wife Rebecca owned a ranch as tenants in common. On February 25, 1958, they conveyed it to Medora and Lu Sine by a grant deed "Reserving unto the Grantors herein an option to purchase the above described property on or before February 25, 1968" for the "same consideration as being paid heretofore plus their depreciation value of any improvements Grantees may add to the property from and after two and a half years from this date." Medora is Dallas' sister and Lu's wife. Since the conveyance Dallas has been adjudged bankrupt. His trustee in bankruptcy and Rebecca brought this declaratory relief action to establish their right to enforce the option.

The case was tried without a jury. Over defendants' objection the trial court admitted extrinsic evidence that by "the same consideration as being paid heretofore" both the grantors and the grantees meant the sum of $50,000 and by "depreciation value of any improvements" they meant the depreciation value of improvements to be computed by deducting from the total amount of any capital expenditures made by defendants grantees the amount of depreciation allowable to them under United States income tax regulations as of the time of the exercise of the option.

The court also determined that the parol evidence rule precluded admission of extrinsic evidence offered by defendants to show that the parties wanted the property kept in the Masterson family and that the option was therefore personal to the grantors and could not be exercised by the trustee in bankruptcy.

The court entered judgment for plaintiffs, declaring their right to exercise the option, specifying in some detail how it could be exercised, and reserving jurisdiction to supervise the manner of its exercise and to determine the amount that plaintiffs will be required to pay defendants for their capital expenditures if plaintiffs decide to exercise the option.

Defendants appeal. They contend that the option provision is too uncertain to be enforced and that extrinsic evidence as to its meaning should not have been admitted. The trial court properly refused to frustrate the obviously declared intention of the grantors to reserve an option to repurchase by an overly meticulous insistence on completeness and clarity of written expression. * * * It properly admitted extrinsic evidence to explain the language of the deed * * * to the end that the consideration for the option would appear with sufficient certainty to permit specific enforcement * * *. The trial court erred, however, in excluding the extrinsic evidence that the option was personal to the grantors and therefore nonassignable.

When the parties to a written contract have agreed to it as an "integration"—a complete and final embodiment of the terms of an agreement—parol evidence cannot be used to add to or vary its terms. * * * When only part of the agreement is integrated, the same rule applies to that part, but parol evidence may be used to prove elements of the agreement not reduced to writing. * * *

The crucial issue in determining whether there has been an integration is whether the parties intended their writing to serve as the exclusive embodiment of their agreement. The instrument itself may help to resolve that issue. It may state, for example, that "there are no previous understandings or agreements not contained in the writing," and thus express the parties' "intention to nullify antecedent understandings or agreements." (See 3 Corbin, Contracts (1960) § 578, p. 411.) Any such collateral agreement itself must be examined, however, to determine whether the parties intended the subjects of negotiation it deals with to be included in, excluded from, or otherwise affected by the writing. Circumstances at the time of the writing may also aid in the determination of such integration. * * *

California cases have stated that whether there was an integration is to be determined solely from the face of the instrument * * * and that the question for the court is whether it "appears to be a complete * * * agreement * * *." * * * Neither of these strict formulations of the rule, however, has been consistently applied. The requirement that the writing must appear incomplete on its face has been repudiated in many cases where parol evidence was admitted "to prove the existence of a separate oral agreement as to any matter on which the document is silent and which is not inconsistent with its terms"—even though the instrument appeared to state a complete agreement. * * * Even under the rule that the writing alone is to be consulted, it was found necessary to examine the alleged collateral agreement before concluding that proof of it was precluded by the writing alone. (See 3 Corbin, Contracts (1960) § 582, pp. 444–446.) It is therefore evident that "The conception of a writing as wholly and intrinsically self-determinative of the parties' intent to make it a sole memorial of one or seven or twenty-seven subjects of negotiation is an impossible one." (9 Wigmore, Evidence (3d ed. 1940) § 2431, p. 103.) For example, a promissory note given by a debtor to his creditor may integrate all their present contractual rights and obligations, or it may be only a minor part of an underlying executory contract that would never be discovered by examining the face of the note.

ex.

In formulating the rule governing parol evidence, several policies must be accommodated. One policy is based on the assumption that written evidence is more accurate than human memory. (Germain Fruit Co. v. J.K. Armsby Co. (1908) 153 Cal. 585, 595, 96 P. 319.) This policy, however, can be adequately served by excluding parol evidence of agreements that directly contradict the writing. Another policy is based on the fear that fraud or unintentional invention by witnesses interested in the outcome of the litigation will mislead the finder of facts. (Germain Fruit Co. v. J.K. Armsby Co., supra, 153 Cal. 585, 596, 96 P. 319; Mitchill v. Lath (1928) 247 N.Y. 377, 388, 160 N.E. 646, 68 A.L.R. 239 [dissenting opinion by Lehman, J.] * * *). McCormick has suggested that the party urging the spoken as against the written word is most often the economic underdog, threatened by severe hardship if the writing is enforced. In his view the parol evidence rule arose to allow the court to control the tendency of the jury to find through sympathy and without a dispassionate assessment of the probability of fraud or faulty memory that the parties made an oral agreement collateral to the written contract, or that preliminary tentative agreements were not abandoned when omitted from the writing. (See McCormick, Evidence (1954) § 210.) He recognizes, however, that if this theory were adopted in disregard of all other considerations, it would lead to the exclusion of testimony concerning oral agreements whenever there is a writing and thereby often defeat the true intent of the parties. (See McCormick, op. cit. supra, § 216, p. 441.)

Evidence of oral collateral agreements should be excluded only when the fact finder is likely to be misled. The rule must therefore be based on the credibility of the evidence. One such standard, adopted by section 240(1) (b) of the Restatement of Contracts, permits proof of a collateral agreement if it "is such an agreement as might *naturally* be made as a separate agreement by parties situated as were the parties to the written contract." (Italics added; see McCormick, Evidence (1954) § 216, p. 441; see also 3 Corbin, Contracts (1960) § 583, p. 475, § 594, pp. 568–569; 4 Williston, Contracts (3d ed. 1961) § 638, pp. 1039–1045.) The draftsmen of the Uniform Commercial Code would exclude the evidence in still fewer instances: "If the additional terms are such that, if agreed upon, they would *certainly* have been included in the document in the view of the court, then evidence of their alleged making must be kept from the trier of fact." (Com. 3, § 2–202, italics added.)[1]

The option clause in the deed in the present case does not explicitly provide that it contains the complete agreement, and the deed is silent on the question of assignability. Moreover, the difficulty of accommodating the formalized structure of a deed to the insertion of collateral agreements makes it less likely that all the terms of such an agreement were included. * * * The statement of the reservation of the option might well have been placed in the recorded deed solely to preserve the grantors' rights against any possible future purchasers and this function could well be served without any mention of the parties' agreement that the option was personal. There is nothing in the record to indicate that the parties to this family transaction, through experience in land transactions or otherwise, had any warning of the disadvantages of failing to put the whole agreement in the deed. This case is one, therefore, in which it can be said that a collateral agreement such as that alleged "might naturally be made as a separate agreement." *A fortiori,* the case is not one in which the parties "would certainly" have included the collateral agreement in the deed.

It is contended, however, that an option agreement is ordinarily presumed to be assignable if it contains no provisions forbidding its transfer or indicating that its performance involves elements personal to the parties. * * * The fact that there is a written memorandum, however, does not necessarily preclude parol evidence rebutting a term that the law would otherwise presume. * * *

In the present case defendants offered evidence that the parties agreed that the option was not assignable in order to keep the property in the Masterson family. The trial court erred in excluding that evidence.

The judgment is reversed.

Peters, Tobriner, Mosk, and Sullivan, JJ., concur.

Dissenting Opinion

Burke, Justice.

I dissent. The majority opinion:

(1) Undermines the parol evidence rule as we have known it in this state since at least 1872 by declaring that parol evidence should have been admitted

---

1. Corbin suggests that, even in situations where the court concludes that it would not have been natural for the parties to make the alleged collateral oral agreement, parol evidence of such an agreement should nevertheless be permitted if the court is convinced that the unnatural actually happened in the case being adjudicated. (3 Corbin, Contracts, § 485, pp. 478, 480; cf. Murray, The Parol Evidence Rule: A Clarification (1966) 4 Duquesne L.Rev. 337, 341–342.) This suggestion may be based on a belief that judges are not likely to be misled by their sympathies. If the court believes that the parties intended a collateral agreement to be effective, there is no reason to keep the evidence from the jury.

by the trial court to show that a written option, absolute and unrestricted in form, was intended to be limited and nonassignable;

(2) Renders suspect instruments of conveyance absolute on their face;

(3) Materially lessens the reliance which may be placed upon written instruments affecting the title to real estate; and

(4) Opens the door, albeit unintentionally to a new technique for the defrauding of creditors.

The opinion permits defendants to establish by parol testimony that their grant to their brother (and brother-in-law) of a written option, absolute in terms, was nevertheless agreed to be nonassignable by the grantee (now a bankrupt), and that therefore the right to exercise it did not pass, by operation of the bankruptcy laws, to the trustee for the benefit of the grantee's creditors.

And how was this to be shown? By the proffered testimony of the bankrupt optionee himself! Thereby one of his assets (the option to purchase defendants' California ranch) would be withheld from the trustee in bankruptcy and from the bankrupt's creditors. Understandably the trial court, as required by the parol evidence rule, did not allow the bankrupt by parol to so contradict the unqualified language of the written option.

The court properly admitted parol evidence to explain the intended meaning of the "same consideration" and "depreciation value" phrases of the written option to purchase defendants' land, as the intended meaning of those phrases was not clear. However, there was nothing ambiguous about the *granting* language of the option and not the slightest suggestion in the document that the option was to be nonassignable. Thus, to permit such words of limitation to be added by parol is to *contradict* the absolute nature of the grant, and to directly violate the parol evidence rule.

Just as it is unnecessary to state in a deed to "lot X" that the house located thereon goes with the land, it is likewise unnecessary to add to "I grant an option to Jones" the words *"and his assigns"* for the option to be assignable. As hereinafter emphasized in more detail, California statutes expressly declare that it *is* assignable, and only if I add language in writing showing my intent to withhold or restrict the right of assignment may the grant be so limited. Thus, to seek to restrict the grant by parol is to *contradict* the written document in violation of the parol evidence rule.

The majority opinion arrives at its holding via a series of false premises which are not supported either in the record of this case or in such California authorities as are offered.

* * *

At the outset the majority in the present case reiterate that the rule against contradicting or varying the terms of a writing remains applicable when only part of the agreement is contained in the writing, and parol evidence is used to prove elements of the agreement not reduced to writing. But having restated this established rule, the majority opinion inexplicably proceeds to subvert it.

* * *

Options are property, and are widely used in the sale and purchase of real and personal property. One of the basic incidents of property ownership is the right of the owner to sell or transfer it. * * * These rights of the owner of property to transfer it, confirmed by the cited code sections, are elementary rules of substantive law and not the mere disputable presumptions which the majority opinion in the present case would make of them. Moreover, the right of transferability applies to an option to purchase, unless there are words of limitation in the option forbidding its assignment or showing that it was given because of a peculiar trust or confidence reposed in the optionee. * * *

The right of an optionee to transfer his option to purchase property is accordingly one of the basic rights which accompanies the option unless limited under the language of the option itself. To allow an optionor to resort to parol evidence to support his assertion that the written option is not transferable is to authorize him to limit the option by attempting to restrict and reclaim rights with which he has already parted. A clearer violation of two substantive and basic rules of law—the parol evidence rule and the right of free transferability of property—would be difficult to conceive.

* * *

* * * [D]espite the law which until the advent of the present majority opinion has been firmly and clearly established in California and relied upon by attorneys and courts alike, that parol evidence may *not* be employed to vary or contradict the terms of a written instrument, the majority now announce * * * that such evidence "should be excluded only when the fact finder is *likely to be misled*," and that "The rule must therefore be based on the *credibility of the evidence*." (Italics added.) But was it not, inter alia, to avoid misleading the fact finder, and to further the introduction of only the evidence which is most likely to *be* credible (the written document), that the Legislature adopted the parol evidence rule as a part of the substantive law of this state?

Next, in an effort to implement this newly promulgated "credibility" test, the majority opinion offers a choice of two "standards": one, a "certainty" standard, quoted from the Uniform Commercial Code * * * and the other a "natural" standard found in the Restatement of Contracts * * * and concludes * * * that at least for purposes of the present case the "natural" viewpoint should prevail.

This new rule, not hitherto recognized in California, provides that proof of a claimed collateral oral agreement is admissible if it is such an agreement as might *naturally* have been made a separate agreement by the parties under the particular circumstances. I submit that this approach opens the door to uncertainty and confusion. Who can know what its limits are? Certainly I do not. For example, in its application to this case who could be expected to divine as "natural" a separate oral agreement between the parties that the assignment, absolute and unrestricted on its face, was intended by the parties to be limited to the Masterson family?

Or, assume that one gives to his relative a promissory note and that the payee of the note goes bankrupt. By operation of law the note becomes an asset of the bankruptcy. The trustee attempts to enforce it. Would the relatives be permitted to testify that by a separate oral agreement made at the time of the execution of the note it was understood that should the payee fail in his business the maker would be excused from payment of the note, or that, as here, it was intended that the benefits of the note would be *personal* to the payee? I doubt that trial judges should be burdened with the task of conjuring whether it would have been "natural" under those circumstances for such a separate agreement to have been made by the parties. Yet, under the application of the proposed rule, this is the task the trial judge would have, and in essence the situation presented in the instant case is no different.

Under the application of the codes and the present case law, proof of the existence of such an agreement would not be permitted, "natural" or "unnatural." But conceivably, as loose as the new rule is, one judge might deem it natural and another judge unnatural. And in each instance the ultimate decision would have to be made ("naturally") on a case-by-case basis by the appellate courts.

In an effort to provide justification for applying the newly pronounced "natural" rule to the circumstances of the present case, the majority opinion next * * * attempts to account for the silence of the writing in this case concerning assignability of the option, by asserting that "the difficulty of accommodating the formalized structure of a deed to the insertion of collateral agreements makes it less likely that all the terms of such an agreement were included." What difficulty would have been involved here, to add the words "this option is nonassignable"? The asserted "formalized structure of a deed" is no formidable barrier. * * *

* * *

Comment hardly seems necessary on the convenience to a bankrupt of such a device to defeat his creditors. He need only produce parol testimony that any options (or other property, for that matter) which he holds are subject to an oral "collateral agreement" with family members (or with friends) that the property is nontransferable "in order to keep the property in the family" or in the friendly group. In the present case the value of the ranch which the bankrupt and his wife held an option to purchase has doubtless increased substantially during the years since they acquired the option. The initiation of this litigation by the trustee in bankruptcy to establish his right to enforce the option indicates his belief that there is substantial value to be gained for the creditors from this asset of the bankrupt. Yet the majority opinion permits defeat of the trustee and of the creditors through the device of an asserted collateral oral agreement that the option was "personal" to the bankrupt and nonassignable "in order to keep the property in the family"!

* * *

I would hold that the trial court ruled correctly on the proffered parol evidence, and would affirm the judgment.

McComb, J., concurs.

N.Y. REAL PROP. LAW § 258
Sched. A (McKinney 1989 & Supp. 2000).

Deed With Full Covenants.

Statutory Form A.

(Individual)

This indenture, made the _____ day of _____ nineteen hundred and _____, between _____ (insert residence) party of the first part, and _____ (insert residence) party of the second part,

Witnesseth, that the party of the first part, in consideration of _____ dollars, lawful money of the United States, paid by the party of the second part, does hereby grant and release unto the party of the second part, _____ and assigns forever, all _____ (description), together with the appurtenances and all the estate and rights of the party of the first part in and to said premises,

To have and to hold the premises herein granted unto the party of the second part _____ and assigns forever. And said _____ covenants as follows:

First. That said _____ is seized of said premises in fee simple, and has good right to convey the same;

Second. That the party of the second part shall quietly enjoy the said premises;

Third. That the said premises are free from incumbrances;

Fourth. That the party of the first part will execute or procure any further necessary assurance of the title to said premises;

Fifth. That said _____ will forever warrant the title to said premises.

In witness whereof, the party of the first part has hereunto set his hand and seal the day and year first above written.

In presence of:

BAKER v. BAILEY
Supreme Court of Montana, 1989.
240 Mont. 139, 782 P.2d 1286.

McDonough, Justice.

Grant and Norma Baker (Bakers) appeal from a judgment of the District Court of the Fourth Judicial District, Missoula County. The District Court, sitting without a jury, found the Bakers liable for breach of the covenant of good faith and fair dealing and further found their claims for damages arising out of breach of contract should not be fully granted. We reverse in part and affirm in part.

The issue on appeal [is]:

Whether the District Court erred when it found the Bakers in breach of contract and the implied covenant of good faith and fair dealing.

* * *

In June of 1976, Arthur and Elma Bailey moved a mobile home onto property owned by their daughter and son-in-law. With their permission, the Baileys hooked onto the water line which serviced their daughter's home and installed a pipeline which would provide water for their trailer.

Approximately six years later, in the spring of 1982, the Baileys' daughter and son-in-law made the decision to sell their residence and the surrounding property. Because they were concerned about taking care of their parents, however, they transferred one acre of the property to the Baileys. This one acre surrounded the mobile home. The remaining property, consisting of forty-five acres, was sold to the Bakers.

In order to insure that the Baileys continued to have access to water, a Water Well Use Agreement was prepared. Mrs. Baker was concerned about future ownership of the one-acre plot. In particular, she was worried that "a bunch of hippies" would move in next to her and consequently she wanted some control over the type of person who may, in the future, buy the Bailey's land. In order to address this concern, the well agreement specifically provided that the right to use water would only extend to the Baileys. In the event the Baileys conveyed the property, the Bakers were under no obligation to provide the new owners with water.

Despite the plain language used in the agreement, the Baileys believed that although not specifically set forth, the Bakers would transfer the right to use the water well to a subsequent "reasonable purchaser" of the Bailey property. The language of the agreement, according to testimony of both the Baileys and the Bakers, was included for the purpose of addressing Mrs. Baker's concern over potentially undesirable neighbors. This purpose was not, however, articulated within the contract.

In addition to the water well use agreement, the Bakers, at the time of purchase, asked for and received a right of first refusal in the event the Baileys received an offer to purchase their property. If an offer was received, the Baileys were to notify the Bakers of the offer in writing. The Bakers would then have the opportunity to exercise their "right of first refusal" within fifteen days of the offer.

Following sale of the land, the Bakers and Baileys lived next to one another and in fact became friends. The Baileys, however, decided to move to Butte, Montana, in the spring of 1984. On June 30, 1984, they executed a standard form listing contract with a local realty company. Under the terms of the listing, the Baileys represented that the property would be sold with "shared well water." Based upon the realtor's valuation of the property with water, it was listed for $47,500.00.

Shortly after the decision was made to sell the property, the water system developed several problems. As a result of these problems pressure in the line was reduced and the Baileys were unable to obtain sufficient water to meet their needs. As a result, they found it necessary to bring water to their residence in plastic jugs. [Editors' note: In the words of Yogi Berra, are you experiencing "deja vu all over again?"]

The Bakers were not as significantly affected by the problems. The Bakers always had sufficient water. In fact, during the entire period the Baileys were deprived of water, the Bakers had enough water to irrigate their lawn. Despite the fact this use adversely affected the Baileys' water supply, the Bakers refused to reduce their consumption. This problem persisted until August when the water system was finally repaired.

After the problems with the water well surfaced, the Bakers informed the Baileys that they would not share the water supply with any new purchaser. Consequently, the property would have to be sold without access to water from the well.

The Baileys searched for alternative sources of water, but unfortunately none was available. They approached the Bakers and offered to purchase joint use of the well. This offer was refused.

Recognizing that they would not be able to provide water for the property, the Baileys realized that the property was virtually without value. They, therefore, agreed to sell it for $8,000.00, which was the fair market value of the trailer and other improvements on the land.

After the Baileys made the decision to accept the $8,000.00 offer, they gave the Bakers notice of its terms in compliance with the right of first refusal provisions in the contract. On August 20, 1984, the Bakers exercised their option and purchased the property for $8,000.00. The transaction was closed on September 10, 1984. At that time, the Bakers acquired the Baileys' one-acre parcel which, if supplied with water, allegedly could be marketed for $40,000.00–$47,500.00.

The Bakers then filed a lawsuit to recover for the value of a refrigerator and certain unpaid expenses which they felt were owed by the Baileys. The Baileys, on the other hand, counterclaimed and sought damages for breach of the Water Well Use Agreement. The District Court found the Bakers in breach of contract and in breach of the implied covenant of good faith and fair dealing. It also found the Baileys liable for less than one-half of the electrical expenses of the well. Following this judgment, the Bakers appealed the lower court's findings in regard to their liability for breach of contract and the Baileys' limited liability for expenses incurred on the water well.

The facts of this case present a classic parol evidence problem. The parol evidence rule, briefly stated, requires that in the absence of fraud, duress, or mutual mistake, all extrinsic evidence must be excluded if the parties have reduced their agreement to an integrated writing. Under this rule, all prior and contemporaneous negotiations or understandings of the contract are merged, once that contract is reduced to writing. Williston on Contracts, Third Edition § 631.

As this case illustrates, application of the rule can work to create harsh results. However, the policies behind the rule compel its consistent, uniform application. Commercial stability requires that parties to a contract may rely upon its express terms without worrying that the law will allow the other party to change the terms of the agreement at a later date.

The Baileys maintain that all of the parties to the Water Well Use Agreement shared a common understanding that the Bakers would continue to share the well water with subsequent purchasers provided that the purchasers were acceptable to the Bakers. This contention may be true; however it is not found within the terms of the contract.

The Water Well Use Agreement is very explicit concerning the rights and obligations of the parties. Its terms provide: "it being specifically understood that this Agreement is solely for the benefit of [the Baileys] and shall terminate in the event [the Baileys] no longer occupy [the land]." It further provides that "it is the intent of the parties to fully set forth their understanding concerning the utilization of the domestic water supplies for the respective tracts * * *." There are no terms within the contract which state that the Bakers will provide water to subsequent "reasonable" purchasers.

Therefore, the fact there may have been further oral understandings between the parties is not admissible. The language of the Water Well Use Agreement is clear. Where the language of a written contract is clear and unambiguous, there is nothing for the court to construe. Rather, the duty of the court is simply to apply the language as written to the facts of the case and decide the case accordingly. The lower court's reliance upon evidence of the parties' oral negotiations was therefore in error, and there was no breach of contract.

In order to prove that a party acted unreasonably in violation of the implied covenant of good faith and fair dealing, one must show as an element there was a breach of the express terms of the contract. *Nordlund v. School District* (1987), 44 St.Rep. 1183, 227 Mont. 402, 738 P.2d 1299. We have concluded that the Bakers did not breach the terms of the Water Well Use Agreement and accordingly, there was no violation of the covenant of good faith and fair dealing even if all other elements of the violation were met.

* * *

[The court affirmed the District Court's findings with respect to the amount of the Baileys' liability for electrical expenses of the well.] The judgment of the lower court is * * * reversed and remanded for proceedings consistent with this opinion.

TURNAGE, C.J., and SHEEHY, HARRISON, BARZ, WEBER and HUNT, JJ., concur.

BAKER v. BAILEY

DEFENDANTS' AMENDED FINDINGS OF FACT AND CONCLUSIONS OF LAW

MONTANA FOURTH JUDICIAL DISTRICT COURT

* * *

* * * The Bakers wanted more control in the event the Baileys were to sell the property to a third person. Specifically, the Bakers represented that they did not want "hippie type" individuals moving on the property. They would, however, be willing to transfer the use of the water well to a "reasonable" purchaser. While not set forth in the Water Well Use Agreement, each of the parties (both Bakers and both Baileys) testified that this was an essential term of their Agreement. Further, the parties had the reasonable expectation that the Bakers would be willing to transfer the use of the well to a "reasonable" third party purchaser. * * *

4 S. WILLISTON AND W. JAEGER, A TREATISE ON THE LAW OF CONTRACTS

§ 633 at 1014–16 (3d ed. 1957).

Since it is only the intention of the parties to adopt a writing as a memorial which makes that writing an integration of the contract, and makes the parol evidence rule applicable, any expression of their intention in the writing in regard to the matter will be given effect. If they provide in terms that the writing shall be a complete integration of their agreement or that it shall be but a partial integration, or no integration at all, the expressed intention will be effectuated.

The parties, however, rarely express their intention upon this point in the writing, and if the court may seek this intention from extrinsic circumstances, the very fact that the parties made a contemporaneous oral agreement will of itself prove that they did not intend the writing to be a complete memorial. The only question open would be whether such a contemporaneous oral agreement was in fact made.

Even if the oral agreement is repugnant to the writing, what was orally agreed would be of equal importance with what was written, since its existence would prove that there was no complete integration of the contract in regard to the matter to which it related. The parol evidence rule would then be of importance only as establishing a presumption that prior and contemporaneous oral agreements and negotiations were merged in the writing, but the practical value of the rule would be much impaired if either party to a writing were allowed to rebut the presumption by proof of any contemporaneous oral agreement. Certainly the law does not permit this. The question arises chiefly where it is asserted not that there is no integration at all, but only a partial integration. It is generally held that the contract must appear on its face to be incomplete in order to permit parol evidence of additional terms.

Frequently, it is not a necessary inference from the writing itself either that it is a statement of the whole agreement, or that it is not. In such a case it has been held that parol evidence is admissible to show which is the fact. The difficulty with such a principle lies in its application. No written contract which does not in terms state that it contains the whole agreement (and few do so provide though it would be generally a wise provision) precludes the possible supposition of additional parol clauses, not inconsistent with the writing.

3 CORBIN ON CONTRACTS

§ 581 at 441–42 (1960).

How is it to be determined whether or not a specific writing is an "integration" or a mere "partial integration"? The "parol evidence rule" does not itself purport to establish the fact of "integration"; and until that fact is established the "rule" does not purport to have any legal operation. Section 228 of the Restatement tells us that "an agreement is integrated where the parties thereto adopt a writing or writings as the final and complete expression of the agreement." But the writing can in no case prove its own

writing must be clearly integrated before parol evidence comes into play.

"adoption" as such, and in proving the extrinsic expressions of adoption, those expressions are subject to no "parol evidence rule." The alleged "adoption" may be shown to be no adoption at all, or to be a qualified and limited adoption.

From this it appears that it can never be determined by mere interpretation of the words of a writing whether it is an "integration" of anything, whether it is "the final and complete expression of the agreement" or is a mere partial expression of "the agreement." * * * Since the "parol evidence rule" is applicable exclusively to "integrations" and a writing can be shown to be an "integration" only by evidence of adoption and assent, the admissibility of this evidence can not be determined by the "parol evidence rule." Also, the question whether a writing is a complete or a partial integration of "the agreement" can not be determined by mere interpretation of the words of the writing; and relevant evidence in the process of that interpretation can not be excluded by the "parol evidence rule."

CALAMARI & PERILLO, A PLEA FOR A UNIFORM PAROL EVIDENCE RULE AND PRINCIPLES OF CONTRACT INTERPRETATION

42 Ind.L.J. 333, 341 (1967).

The debate [between Williston and Corbin] involves the question: is the public better served by giving effect to the parties' entire agreement written and oral, even at the risk of injustice caused by the possibility of perjury and the possibility that superseded documents [or oral promises] will be treated as operative, or does the security of transactions require that, despite occasional injustices, persons adopting a formal writing be required, on the penalty of voidness of their oral and written side agreements, to put their entire agreement in the formal writing?

Problem 6–1

The Matsons agreed to sell their farm to the Greens for $185,000. The parties entered into a comprehensive contract of sale prepared largely by the Matsons' attorney. On the date of the closing, after inspection of the farm, the Greens refused to tender payment. They claimed that the Matsons had withdrawn all of the furniture from the farmhouse despite the parties' oral agreement (prior to signing the written purchase agreement) that the price included all of the furniture. The contract was silent on the issue. After being sued by the Matsons for breach of contract, the Greens have retained you to defend them at trial. Will you attempt to introduce evidence of the claimed oral agreement, assuming, of course, that you do not think your clients are lying? On what grounds? Whom will you cite in your argument, Williston or Corbin? Why? How would the New York Court of Appeals have resolved the issue in 1929? The California Supreme Court in 1969?

UNIFORM COMMERCIAL CODE § 2–202.

Final Written Expression: Parol or Extrinsic Evidence

Terms with respect to which the confirmatory memoranda of the parties agree or which are otherwise set forth in a writing intended by the parties as a final expression of their agreement with respect to such terms as are included therein may not be contradicted by evidence of any prior agreement or of a contemporaneous oral agreement but may be explained or supplemented

(a) by course of dealing or usage of trade (Section 1–205) or by course of performance (Section 2–208); and

(b) by evidence of consistent additional terms unless the court finds the writing to have been intended also as a complete and exclusive statement of the terms of the agreement.

J. WHITE AND R. SUMMERS, UNIFORM COMMERCIAL CODE

90–91 (5th ed. 2000).

As the late Professor McCormick taught, however, the division of functions between judge and jury in administering the rule can "give preference" to written evidence over oral evidence of contract terms. So, too, can allocations of burden of proof. Section 2–202 does not state very clearly what the division of functions is supposed to be. But the way the rule is worded, the trial is certainly not to be a free-wheeling affair in which the parties may introduce before the jury all evidence of terms, including the writing, with the jury then to decide on terms. Rather, it is plain from the rule and from prior history of similar rules that some of the evidence is to be heard initially only by the judge and that the judge may invoke the rule to keep this evidence from the jury. The evidence that is in this way subject to exclusion will usually be oral evidence. Indeed, before a judge can invoke a parol evidence rule at all, the judge must first admit a writing into evidence before the jury. If the judge thereafter excludes oral evidence of terms on the basis of the parol evidence rule, the judge gives preference to the writing already in evidence by prohibiting the jury from considering the oral evidence.

But when can the judge invoke 2–202 to exclude oral evidence of terms? First, the judge may exclude the evidence on finding that the parties intended the writing to be a *complete and exclusive* statement of the terms of the agreement (unless it be evidence of course of dealing, usage of trade, or course of performance introduced only to explain or supplement the writing). Code and comments both state that the question of completeness and exclusivity is for the judge. Second, the judge may exclude evidence extrinsic to terms set forth in the writing if he or she decides that the writing is a final written expression as to these terms and that the other evidence contradicts these terms. The Code does not say that this question is for the judge, but if "completeness and exclusivity" is for the judge, then whether a writing is a final written expression as to the terms it does include would be for the judge, for the greater ordinarily includes the lesser. The issue of contradictoriness is also generally for the judge. Third, in passing on any parol evidence rule objection, the judge may decide that the proffered evidence of terms extrinsic to the writing is not credible, and he or she may exclude it on that ground alone. Section 2–202 is silent on this, but Professor McCormick thought that the "real service" of the parol evidence rule was here.

The foregoing division of functions between judge and jury in the administration of 2–202 inevitably operates to favor written evidence of terms. Yet there is no necessary identity between a writing and the actual deal. Some commentators and at least a few courts conclude that 2–202 abolishes any presumption that a writing apparently complete on its face is complete and exclusive. We are uncertain. One of us (White) would be quite quick to find completeness from elaborate writings and quite comfortable in stilling the tongues of parties claiming other terms or innovative interpretations. The other (Summers) trusts the jury more and is more suspicious of the drafter.

Note
The Ambiguity Exception to the Parol Evidence Rule

To determine whether evidence of prior understandings and negotiations contradicts or varies a writing, we must first know what the writing means. If the writing is ambiguous, courts admit evidence to ascertain its meaning. Accordingly, apart from whether a writing is fully or partially integrated, much parol evidence rule litigation involves whether or not a writing is ambiguous. The next few cases involve different approaches to the ambiguity exception to the parol evidence rule.

GOLD KIST, INC. v. CARR

Court of Appeals of Texas, 1994.
886 S.W.2d 425.

McCLOUD, CHIEF JUSTICE.

Edward C. Carr, Jr., entered into a written agreement with Gold Kist, Inc. to purchase trucks and peanut hauling equipment from Gold Kist. Carr later sued Gold Kist for damages alleging breach of contract * * *. The central issue in Carr's suit was whether or not Carr had "exclusive hauling rights." Trial was to the jury who found that:

(1) Gold Kist agreed that Carr would have exclusive hauling of Gold Kist' peanut commodities in the State of Texas during the term of the promissory note.

(2) Carr was able to perform in accordance with that agreement.

* * *

[The trial court entered a judgment for Carr pursuant to the jury's finding of damages.]

Gold Kist appeals challenging the judgment * * *. Gold Kist contends that Carr's breach of contract claim is barred by the parol evidence rule * * *. We sustain [this challenge.]

BACKGROUND FACTS

The record reflects that, in August of 1986, Walter Dan Holland was the manager of Gold Kist' peanut shelling plant in Comyn, Texas. Peanuts were transported to the Comyn plant from statewide "buying points" where farmers sold their peanuts. Some of the buying points were owned by Gold Kist; and others, known as "commissioned buying points," were independently owned. Holland contacted Carr and offered to sell Carr Gold Kist' trucks and hauling equipment at the Comyn plant. Holland and Carr began to negotiate the terms of the sale, and both men were aware that any agreement they reached would have to be approved by Gold Kist' corporate headquarters in Atlanta, Georgia.

They first agreed that Carr would purchase the trucks and equipment and that Carr would have the exclusive right to haul peanuts for Gold Kist in Texas. This agreement was submitted to Michael Stimpert, a vice-president for Gold Kist at the Atlanta corporate headquarters. Some of the commissioned buying points wanted to use their own trucks and equipment to haul the peanuts. Gold Kist did not want to risk losing business from these buying points. Stimpert objected to granting Carr exclusive hauling rights and requested that the final contract be drafted so as to exclude any hauling rights. Holland told Carr that Gold Kist would not grant him the exclusive right to haul all of Gold Kist' peanuts.

A contract was drafted under which Carr would purchase Gold Kist' trucks and hauling equipment for $60,000.00 paying $20,000.00 in cash and executing a five-year promissory note for the remaining $40,000.00. The contract stated: "Gold Kist, from time to time, may, but shall be under no obligation to, engage you to haul commodities on its behalf." Stimpert signed the contract as Gold Kist' "Group Vice President–Agricommodities." On September 24, 1986, Carr signed the contract.

Exclusive Hauling Rights

The central issue in Carr's suit is whether or not Gold Kist granted him the exclusive right to haul its peanuts. Carr testified that, after the original agreement was rejected by Gold Kist' corporate headquarters, he renegotiated the agreement with Holland. Under this second agreement, Carr testified that he was to have exclusive hauling rights with the exception that, during the first year of operation, he would not haul peanuts from the buying points that had protested. After the first year, those buying points would be "educated and straightened out"; and Carr would then have the exclusive right to haul from those buying points as well. Because Carr's hauling during the first year would be reduced under the new agreement, the purchase price of the trucks and equipment was reduced from $100,000.00 to $60,000.00.

When he received the written contract signed by Stimpert, Carr questioned the sentence that stated that Gold Kist had no obligation to use Carr because the sentence did not conform with what he thought was the agreement. Carr asked Holland what it meant. Holland called Ron Clark, the Atlanta-based manager of Gold Kist' peanut division, who told Holland that he thought Gold Kist did not have to use Carr if his performance did not meet Gold Kist' expectations. Holland relayed this information to Carr who signed the agreement.

Parol Evidence Rule

The parol evidence rule precludes consideration of extrinsic evidence to contradict, vary, or add to the terms of an unambiguous written agreement absent fraud, accident, or mistake. * * * Whether a contract is ambiguous is "a question of law for the court to decide by looking at the contract as a whole in light of the circumstances present when the contract was entered." *Coker v. Coker*, 650 S.W.2d 391, 393–94 (Tex.1983). A contract is ambiguous when its meaning is genuinely uncertain and doubtful or when it is reasonably susceptible to more than one meaning. *Coker v. Coker, supra.* If a contract can be given a certain or definite legal meaning or interpretation, it is not ambiguous; and the court will construe the contract as a matter of law.

The Gold Kist–Carr contract provided that "Gold Kist, from time to time, may, but shall be under no obligation to, engage you to haul commodities on its behalf." Considering this sentence in light of the contract as a whole and in light of the surrounding circumstances, we conclude that the contract is not ambiguous. The meaning is not genuinely uncertain and doubtful. The contract clearly states that Gold Kist has "no obligation" to use Carr's hauling services. This provision in the contract is not reasonably susceptible to the interpretation suggested by Carr: that Carr would have exclusive hauling rights for the term of the promissory note. Carr's interpretation contradicts the express language of the contract. The mere fact that Gold Kist and Carr take conflicting views of the agreement or that they differ in their expectations is not sufficient to render the contract ambiguous. *Forbau v. Aetna Life Insurance Company,* 876 S.W.2d 132, 134 (Tex.1994).

Because the contract is unambiguous, we must give effect to the objective intention of the parties as expressed or as is apparent in the written agreement. * * * Under the plain language of the contract, Gold Kist had no obligation to engage Carr's services for the hauling of peanuts.

* * *

Carr also contends that Gold Kist' alleged promise to give Carr exclusive hauling rights is enforceable because the promise was an independent, collateral agreement. * * * We disagree.

The contract clearly contemplated the subject matter of hauling and specifically excluded any obligation to use Carr. Any prior or contemporaneous agreement giving Carr exclusive hauling rights would not be an independent or collateral agreement. Rather, such an agreement would have been inconsistent with and would have contradicted the express terms of the written agreement.

* * *

The judgment of the trial court is reversed, and judgment is rendered that Carr take nothing against Gold Kist. * * *

GREENFIELD v. PHILLES RECORDS, INC.

98 N.Y.2d 562, 780 N.E.2d 166, 750 N.Y.S.2d 565 (2002).

GRAFFEO, J.

In this contract dispute between a singing group and their record producer, we must determine whether the artists' transfer of full ownership rights to the master recordings of musical performances carried with it the unconditional right of the producer to redistribute those performances in any technological format. In the absence of an explicit contractual reservation of rights by the artists, we conclude that it did.

In the early 1960s, Veronica Bennett (now known as Ronnie Greenfield), her sister Estelle Bennett and their cousin Nedra Talley, formed a singing group known as "The Ronettes." They met defendant Phil Spector, a music producer and composer, in 1963 and signed a five-year "personal services" music recording contract (the Ronettes agreement) with Spector's production company, defendant Philles Records, Inc. The plaintiffs agreed to perform exclusively for Philles Records and in exchange, Philles Records acquired an ownership right to the recordings of the Ronettes' musical performances. The agreement also set forth a royalty schedule to compensate plaintiffs for their services. After signing with Philles Records, plaintiffs received a single collective cash advance of approximately $15,000.

The Ronettes recorded several dozen songs for Philles Records, including "Be My Baby," which sold over a million copies and topped the music charts. Despite their popularity, the group disbanded in 1967 and Philles Records eventually went out of business. Other than their initial advance, plaintiffs received no royalty payments from Philles Records.

* * *

Defendants subsequently began to capitalize on a resurgence of public interest in 1960s music by making use of new recording technologies and licensing master recordings of the Ronettes' vocal performances for use in movie and television productions, a process known in entertainment industry parlance as "synchronization." The most notable example was defendants' licensing of "Be My Baby" in 1987 for use in the motion picture "Dirty Dancing." Defendants also licensed master recordings to third parties for production and distribution in the United States (referred to as domestic redistribution), and sold compilation albums containing performances by the Ronettes. While defendants earned considerable compensation from such licensing and sales, no royalties were paid to any of the plaintiffs.

As a result, plaintiffs commenced this breach of contract action in 1987, alleging that the 1963 agreement did not provide Philles Records with the right to license the master recordings for synchronization and domestic redistribution, and demanded royalties from the sales of compilation albums. * * * Defendants * * * argued that the agreement granted them absolute ownership rights to the master recordings and permitted the use of the recordings in any format, subject only to royalty rights. * * *

[The trial court awarded plaintiffs more than $3 million and the Appellate Division affirmed "because the contract did not specifically transfer the right to issue synchronization and third-party domestic distribution licenses."]

We are asked on this appeal to determine whether defendants, as the owners of the master recordings of plaintiffs' vocal performances, acquired the contractual right to issue licenses to third parties to use the recordings in connection with television, movies and domestic audio distribution. [Defendants' use of Ronettes' performances on compilation albums was not raised on appeal.] The agreement between the parties consists of a two-page document, which apparently was widely used in the 1960s by music producers signing new artists. Plaintiffs executed the contract without the benefit of counsel. The parties' immediate objective was to record and market the Ronettes' vocal performances and "mak[e] therefrom phonograph records and/or tape recordings and other similar devices * * *. The ownership rights provision of the contract provides:

"All recordings made hereunder and all records and reproductions made therefrom together with the performances embodied therein, shall be entirely [Philles'] property, free of any claims whatsoever by you or any person deriving any rights of interest from you. Without limitation of the foregoing, [Philles] shall have the right to make phonograph records, tape recordings or other reproductions of the performances embodied in such recordings by any method now or hereafter known, and to sell and deal in the same under any trade mark or trade names or labels designated by us, or we may at our election refrain therefrom."

Plaintiffs concede that the contract unambiguously gives defendants unconditional ownership rights to the master recordings, but contend that the agreement does not bestow the right to exploit those recordings in new markets or mediums since the document is silent on those topics. Defendants counter that the absence of specific references to synchronization and domestic licensing is irrelevant. They argue that where a contract grants full ownership rights to a musical performance or composition, the only restrictions upon the owner's right to use that property are those explicitly enumerated by the grantor/artist.

Despite the technological innovations that continue to revolutionize the recording industry, long-settled common-law contract rules still govern the interpretation of agreements between artists and their record producers. The fundamental, neutral precept of contract interpretation is that agreements are construed in accord with the parties' intent. "The best evidence of what parties to a written agreement intend is what they say in their writing" (see Slatt v. Slatt, 64 N.Y.2d 966, 967, 488 N.Y.S. 645, 477 N.E.2d 1099 (1985)). Thus, a written agreement that is complete, clear and unambiguous on its face must be enforced according to the plain meaning of its terms.

Extrinsic evidence of the parties' intent may be considered only if the agreement is ambiguous, which is an issue of law for the courts to decide. A contract is unambiguous if the language it uses has "a definite and precise meaning, unattended by danger of misconception in the purport of the [agreement] itself, and concerning which there is no reasonable basis for a difference of opinion." Thus, if the agreement on its face is reasonably susceptible of only one meaning, a court is not free to alter the contract to reflect its personal notions of fairness and equity.

The pivotal issue in this case is whether defendants are prohibited from using the master recordings for synchronization, and whatever future formats evolve from new technologies, in the absence of explicit contract language authorizing such uses. Stated another way, does the contract's silence on synchronization and domestic licensing create an ambiguity which opens the door to the admissibility of extrinsic evidence to determine the intent of the parties? We conclude that it does not and, because there is no ambiguity in the terms of the Ronettes agreement, defendants are entitled to exercise complete ownership rights, subject to payment of applicable royalties due plaintiffs.

* * *

We agree with [the] prevalent rules of contract construction—the unconditional transfer of ownership rights to a work of art includes the right to use the work in any manner * * * unless those rights are specifically limited by the terms of the contract. However, if a contract grants less than full ownership or specifies only certain rights to use the property, then other, unenumerated rights may be retained by the grantor.

In this case, plaintiffs concede that defendants own the master recordings. Notably, the agreement explicitly refers to defendants' "right to make phonograph records, tape recordings or *other reproductions* of the performances embodied in such recordings by *any method now or hereafter known,* and to sell and deal in the same" (emphasis added). Plaintiffs contend that the breadth of the ownership provision is limited by the agreement's introductory paragraph, which states that defendants' purpose for purchasing plaintiffs' performances was to make "phonograph records and/or tape recordings and other similar devices." However, when read in conjunction with the ownership provision, a reasonable meaning emerges—the phrase "other similar devices" refers to defendants' right to reproduce the performances by any current or future technological methods. * * * We therefore hold that the Ronettes agreement, "read as a whole to determine its purpose and intent" *W.W.W. Assoc. v. Giancontieri,* 77 N.Y.2d at 162, 565 N.Y.S.2d 440, 566 N.E.2d 639), is susceptible to only one reasonable interpretation—defendants are authorized to license the performances for use in visual media, such as movies and television commercials or broadcasts, and for domestic release by third parties in audio formats.

* * *

We realize that our conclusion here effectively prevents plaintiffs from sharing in the profits that defendants have received from synchronization licensing. However sympathetic plaintiffs' plight, we cannot resolve the case on that ground under the guise of contract construction. Our guiding principle must be to neutrally apply the rules of contract interpretation because only in this way can we ensure stability in the law and provide guidance to parties weighing the risks and advantages of entering a binding agreement.

Defendants acknowledge that the royalty schedule for domestic sales encompasses the sale of records, compact discs and other audio reproductions by entities holding domestic third-party distribution licenses from Philles Records. In light of that concession, we remit this case to Supreme Court to recalculate plaintiffs' damages for royalties due on all such sales. Damages should be determined pursuant to the applicable schedule incorporated in the agreement rather than based on industry standards.

* * *

Accordingly, the order of the Appellate Division should be modified, without costs, and the case remitted to Supreme Court for further proceedings in accordance with this opinion and, as so modified, affirmed.

PACIFIC GAS AND ELECTRIC CO. v. G.W. THOMAS DRAYAGE & RIGGING CO.

Supreme Court of California, 1968.
69 Cal.2d 33, 69 Cal.Rptr. 561, 442 P.2d 641.

TRAYNOR, CHIEF JUSTICE.

Defendant appeals from a judgment for plaintiff in an action for damages for injury to property under an indemnity clause of a contract.

In 1960 defendant entered into a contract with plaintiff to furnish the labor and equipment necessary to remove and replace the upper metal cover of plaintiff's steam turbine. Defendant agreed to perform the work "at [its] own risk and expense" and to "indemnify" plaintiff "against all loss, damage, expense and liability resulting from * * * injury to property, arising out of or in any way connected with the performance of this contract." Defendant also agreed to procure not less than $50,000 insurance to cover liability for injury to property. Plaintiff was to be an additional named insured, but the policy was to contain a cross-liability clause extending the coverage to plaintiff's property.

During the work the cover fell and injured the exposed rotor of the turbine. Plaintiff brought this action to recover $25,144.51, the amount it subsequently spent on repairs. During the trial it dismissed a count based on negligence and thereafter secured judgment on the theory that the indemnity provision covered injury to all property regardless of ownership.

Defendant offered to prove by admissions of plaintiff's agents, by defendant's conduct under similar contracts entered into with plaintiff, and by other proof that in the indemnity clause the parties meant to cover injury to property of third parties only and not to plaintiff's property. Although the trial court observed that the language used was "the classic language for a third party indemnity provision" and that "one could very easily conclude that * * * its whole intendment is to indemnify third parties," it nevertheless held that the "plain language" of the agreement also required defendant to indemnify plaintiff for injuries to plaintiff's property. Having determined that the contract had a plain meaning, the court refused to admit any extrinsic evidence that would contradict its interpretation.

When a court interprets a contract on this basis, it determines the meaning of the instrument in accordance with the " * * * extrinsic evidence of the judge's own linguistic education and experience." (3 Corbin on Contracts (1960 ed.) [1964 Supp. § 579, p. 225, fn. 56].) The exclusion of testimony that might contradict the linguistic background of the judge reflects a judicial belief in the possibility of perfect verbal expression. (9 Wigmore on Evidence (3d ed. 1940) § 2461, p. 187.) This belief is a remnant of a primitive faith in the inherent potency[1] and inherent meaning of words.[2]

---

1. E.g., "The elaborate system of taboo and verbal prohibitions in primitive groups; the ancient Egyptian myth of Khern, the apotheosis of the word, and of Thoth, the Scribe of Truth, the Giver of Words and Script, the Master of Incantations; the avoidance of the name of God in Brahmanism, Judaism and Islam; totemistic and protective names in mediaeval Turkish and Finno–Ugrian languages; the misplaced verbal scruples of the 'Précieuses'; the Swedish peasant custom of curing sick cattle smitten by witchcraft, by making them

test as this ct defines it.

Judges should not be the determiners of whether a k is clear + unambig.

The test of admissibility of extrinsic evidence to explain the meaning of a written instrument is not whether it appears to the court to be plain and unambiguous on its face, but whether the offered evidence is relevant to prove a meaning to which the language of the instrument is reasonably susceptible. * * *

A rule that would limit the determination of the meaning of a written instrument to its four-corners merely because it seems to the court to be clear and unambiguous, would either deny the relevance of the intention of the parties or presuppose a degree of verbal precision and stability our language has not attained.

1 view

Some courts have expressed the opinion that contractual obligations are created by the mere use of certain words, whether or not there was any intention to incur such obligations.[3] Under this view, contractual obligations flow, not from the intention of the parties but from the fact that they used certain magic words. Evidence of the parties' intention therefore becomes irrelevant.

In this state, however, the intention of the parties as expressed in the contract is the source of contractual rights and duties.[4] A court must ascertain and give effect to this intention by determining what the parties meant by the words they used. Accordingly, the exclusion of relevant, extrinsic evidence to explain the meaning of a written instrument could be justified only if it were feasible to determine the meaning the parties gave to the words from the instrument alone.

If words had absolute and constant referents, it might be possible to discover contractual intention in the words themselves and in the manner in which they were arranged. Words, however, do not have absolute and constant referents. "A word is a symbol of thought but has no arbitrary and fixed meaning like a symbol of algebra or chemistry, * * *." (Pearson v. State Social Welfare Board (1960) 54 Cal.2d 184, 195, 5 Cal.Rptr. 553, 559, 353 P.2d 33, 39.) The meaning of particular words or groups of words varies with the " * * * verbal context and surrounding circumstances and purposes in view of the linguistic education and experience of their users and their hearers or readers (not excluding judges). * * * A word has no meaning apart from these factors; much less does it have an objective meaning, one true meaning." (Corbin, The Interpretation of Words and the Parol Evidence Rule (1965) 50 Cornell L.Q. 161, 187.) Accordingly, the meaning of a writing " * * * can only be found by interpretation in the light of all the circumstances that reveal the

swallow a page torn out of the psalter and put in dough. * * *" from Ullman, The Principles of Semantics (1963 ed.) 43. (See also Ogden and Richards, The Meaning of Meaning (rev. ed.1956) pp. 24–47.)

2. " 'Rerum enim vocabula immutabilia sunt, homines mutabilia,' " (Words are unchangeable, men changeable) from Dig. XXXI-II, 10, 7, § 2, de sup. leg. as quoted in 9 Wigmore on Evidence, op. cit. supra, § 2461, p. 187.

3. "A contract has, strictly speaking, nothing to do with the personal, or individual, intent of the parties. A contract is an obligation attached by the mere force of law to

certain acts of the parties, usually words, which ordinarily accompany and represent a known intent." (Hotchkiss v. National City Bank of New York (S.D.N.Y.1911) 200 F. 287, 293. * * *

4. "A contract must be so interpreted as to give effect to the mutual intention of the parties as it existed at the time of contracting, so far as the same is ascertainable and lawful." (Civ.Code, § 1636; see also Code Civ.Proc. § 1859; Universal Sales Corp. v. Cal. Press Mfg. Co. (1942) 20 Cal.2d 751, 760, 128 P.2d 665; Lemm v. Stillwater Land & Cattle Co. (1933) 217 Cal. 474, 480, 19 P.2d 785.)

sense in which the writer used the words. The exclusion of parol evidence regarding such circumstances merely because the words do not appear ambiguous to the reader can easily lead to the attribution to a written instrument of a meaning that was never intended. * * * " Universal Sales Corp. v. Cal. Press Mfg. Co., supra, 20 Cal.2d 751, 776, 128 P.2d 665, 679 (concurring opinion) * * *.

Although extrinsic evidence is not admissible to add to, detract from, or vary the terms of a written contract, these terms must first be determined before it can be decided whether or not extrinsic evidence is being offered for a prohibited purpose. The fact that the terms of an instrument appear clear to a judge does not preclude the possibility that the parties chose the language of the instrument to express different terms. That possibility is not limited to contracts whose terms have acquired a particular meaning by trade usage,[5] but exists whenever the parties' understanding of the words used may have differed from the judge's understanding.

Accordingly, rational interpretation requires at least a preliminary consideration of all credible evidence offered to prove the intention of the parties.[6] (Civ.Code, § 1647; Code Civ.Proc. § 1860; see also 9 Wigmore on Evidence, op. cit. supra, § 2470, fn. 11, p. 227.) Such evidence includes testimony as to the "circumstances surrounding the making of the agreement * * * including the object, nature and subject matter of the writing * * * " so that the court can "place itself in the same situation in which the parties found themselves at the time of contracting." (Universal Sales Corp. v. Cal. Press Mfg. Co., supra, 20 Cal.2d 751, 761, 128 P.2d 665, 671 * * *). If the court decides, after considering this evidence, that the language of a contract, in the light of all the circumstances, is "fairly susceptible of either one of the two interpretations contended for * * * ", extrinsic evidence relevant to prove either of such meanings is admissible.[7]

In the present case the court erroneously refused to consider extrinsic evidence offered to show that the indemnity clause in the contract was not

5. Extrinsic evidence of trade usage or custom has been admitted to show that the term "United Kingdom" in a motion picture distribution contract included Ireland (Ermolieff v. R.K.O. Radio Pictures (1942) 19 Cal.2d 543, 549–552, 122 P.2d 3); that the word "ton" in a lease meant a long ton or 2,240 pounds and not the statutory ton of 2,000 pounds (Higgins v. Cal. Petroleum, etc., Co. (1898) 120 Cal. 629, 630–632, 52 P. 1080); that the word "stubble" in a lease included not only stumps left in the ground but everything "left on the ground after the harvest time" (Callahan v. Stanley (1881) 57 Cal. 476, 477–479); that the term "north" in a contract dividing mining claims indicated a boundary line running along the "magnetic and not the true meridian" (Jenny Lind Co. v. Bower & Co. (1858) 11 Cal. 194, 197–199) and that a form contract for purchase and sale was actually an agency contract (Body–Steffner Co. v. Flotill Products (1944) 63 Cal.App.2d 555, 558–562, 147 P.2d 84).

6. When objection is made to any particular item of evidence offered to prove the intention of the parties, the trial court may not yet be in a position to determine whether in the light of all of the offered evidence, the item objected to will turn out to be admissible as tending to prove a meaning of which the language of the instrument is reasonably susceptible or inadmissible as tending to prove a meaning of which the language is not reasonably susceptible. In such case the court may admit the evidence conditionally by either reserving its ruling on the objection or by admitting the evidence subject to a motion to strike. (See Evid.Code, § 403.)

7. Extrinsic evidence has often been admitted in such cases on the stated ground that the contract was ambiguous (e.g., Universal Sales Corp. v. Cal. Press Mfg. Co., supra, 20 Cal.2d 751, 761, 128 P.2d 665). This statement of the rule is harmless if it is kept in mind that the ambiguity may be exposed by extrinsic evidence that reveals more than one possible meaning.

intended to cover injuries to plaintiff's property. Although that evidence was not necessary to show that the indemnity clause was reasonably susceptible of the meaning contended for by defendant, it was nevertheless relevant and admissible on that issue. Moreover, since that clause was reasonably susceptible of that meaning, the offered evidence was also admissible to prove that the clause had that meaning and did not cover injuries to plaintiff's property.[8] Accordingly, the judgment must be reversed.

PETERS, MOSK, BURKE, SULLIVAN and PEEK, JJ., concur. McCOMB, J., dissents. [no opinion]

TRIDENT CENTER v. CONNECTICUT GENERAL LIFE INS. CO., 847 F.2d 564 (9th Cir.1988).

KOZINSKI, CIRCUIT JUDGE:

* * * Two decades ago the California Supreme Court in *Pacific Gas & Electric Co. v. G.W. Thomas Drayage & Rigging Co.,* 69 Cal.2d 33, 442 P.2d 641, 69 Cal.Rptr. 561 (1968), turned its back on the notion that a contract can ever have a plain meaning discernible by a court without resort to extrinsic evidence. The court reasoned that contractual obligations flow not from the words of the contract, but from the intention of the parties. * * *

Under *Pacific Gas,* it matters not how clearly a contract is written, nor how completely it is integrated, nor how carefully it is negotiated, nor how squarely it addresses the issue before the court: the contract cannot be rendered impervious to attack by parol evidence. If one side is willing to claim that the parties intended one thing but the agreement provides for another,

---

8. The court's exclusion of extrinsic evidence in this case would be error even under a rule that excluded such evidence when the instrument appeared to the court to be clear and unambiguous on its face. The controversy centers on the meaning of the word "indemnify" and the phrase "all loss, damage, expense and liability." The trial court's recognition of the language as typical of a third party indemnity clause and the double sense in which the word "indemnify" is used in statutes and defined in dictionaries demonstrate the existence of an ambiguity. (Compare Civ.Code, § 2772, "Indemnity is a contract by which one engages to save another from a legal consequence of the conduct of one of the parties, or of some other person," with Civ.Code, § 2527, "Insurance is a contract whereby one undertakes to indemnify another against loss, damage, or liability, arising from an unknown or contingent event." Black's Law Dictionary (4th ed. 1951) defines "indemnity" as "A collateral contract or assurance, by which one person engages to secure another against an anticipated loss or to prevent him from being damnified by the legal consequences of an act or forbearance on the part of one of the parties or of some third person." Stroud's Judicial Dictionary (2d ed. 1903) defines it as a "Contract * * * to indemnify against a liability. * * * "One of the definitions given to "indemnify" by Webster's

Third New Internat. Dict. (1961 ed.) is "to exempt from incurred penalties or liabilities.")

Plaintiff's assertion that the use of the word "all" to modify "loss, damage, expense and liability" dictates an all inclusive interpretation is not persuasive. If the word "indemnify" encompasses only third-party claims, the word "all" simply refers to all such claims. The use of the words "loss," "damage," and "expense" in addition to the word "liability" is likewise inconclusive. These words do not imply an agreement to reimburse for injury to an indemnitee's property since they are commonly inserted in third-party indemnity clauses, to enable an indemnitee who settles a claim to recover from his indemnitor without proving his liability. * * *

The provision that defendant perform the work "at his own risk and expense" and the provisions relating to insurance are equally inconclusive. By agreeing to work at its own risk defendant may have released plaintiff from liability for any injuries to defendant's property arising out of the contract's performance, but this provision did not necessarily make defendant an insurer against injuries to plaintiff's property. Defendant's agreement to procure liability insurance to cover damages to plaintiff's property does not indicate whether the insurance was to cover all injuries or only injuries caused by defendant's negligence.

the court must consider extrinsic evidence of possible ambiguity. If that evidence raises the specter of ambiguity where there was none before, the contract language is displaced and the intention of the parties must be divined from self-serving testimony offered by partisan witnesses whose recollection is hazy from passage of time and colored by their conflicting interests. *See Delta Dynamics, Inc. v. Arioto,* 69 Cal.2d 525, 532, 446 P.2d 785, 72 Cal.Rptr. 785 (1968) (Mosk, J., dissenting). We question whether this approach is more likely to divulge the original intention of the parties than reliance on the seemingly clear words they agreed upon at the time. *See generally Morta v. Korea Ins. Co.,* 840 F.2d 1452, 1460 (9th Cir.1988).

Pacific Gas casts a long shadow of uncertainty over all transactions negotiated and executed under the law of California. As this case illustrates, even when the transaction is very sizeable, even if it involves only sophisticated parties, even if it was negotiated with the aid of counsel, even if it results in contract language that is devoid of ambiguity, costly and protracted litigation cannot be avoided if one party has a strong enough motive for challenging the contract. While this rule creates much business for lawyers and an occasional windfall to some clients, it leads only to frustration and delay for most litigants and clogs already overburdened courts.

It also chips away at the foundation of our legal system. By giving credence to the idea that words are inadequate to express concepts, *Pacific Gas* undermines the basic principle that language provides a meaningful constraint on public and private conduct. If we are unwilling to say that parties, dealing face to face, can come up with language that binds them, how can we send anyone to jail for violating statutes consisting of mere words lacking "absolute and constant referents"? How can courts ever enforce decrees, not written in language understandable to all, but encoded in a dialect reflecting only the "linguistic background of the judge"? Can lower courts ever be faulted for failing to carry out the mandate of higher courts when "perfect verbal expression" is impossible? Are all attempts to develop the law in a reasoned and principled fashion doomed to failure as "remnant[s] of a primitive faith in the inherent potency and inherent meaning of words"?

* * * It may not be a wise rule we are applying, but it is a rule that binds us. *Erie R.R. Co. v. Tompkins,* 304 U.S. 64, 78, 58 S.Ct. 817, 822, 82 L.Ed. 1188 (1938).

ESKIMO PIE CORP. v. WHITELAWN DAIRIES, INC.

United States District Court, Southern District of New York, 1968.
284 F.Supp. 987.

MANSFIELD, DISTRICT JUDGE.

* * *

The [consolidated] actions arise out of written contracts between Eskimo Pie Corporation ("Eskimo" herein), Whitelawn Dairies, Inc.[1] ("Whitelawn" herein) and Supermarket Advisory Sales, Inc. ("SAS" herein) (Whitelawn and

1. Whitelawn and SAS are subsidiaries of Allstate Dairies, Inc. ("Allstate" herein), also named as a party in these proceedings.

SAS are collectively referred to herein as "Whitelawn–SAS") entered into on or about December 30, 1960, and modified in various respects in 1961 and 1962. These contracts are referred to by the parties as the "Package Deal." All parties agree that the Package Deal is an integrated agreement setting forth in several writings all of the essential terms agreed upon by Eskimo and Whitelawn–SAS. Under the terms of the Package Deal Eskimo granted to Whitelawn, an ice cream manufacturer, the right to manufacture certain ice cream products bearing "Eskimo" wrappers and labels and to SAS the right to purchase such Eskimo-branded products from Eskimo or an Eskimo-authorized manufacturer for sale in the New York City Metropolitan Area as follows:

> "During the term of this Agreement [SAS] shall have the *non-exclusive* right to purchase the Eskimo stock and stickless products listed in Exhibit A hereto, which may be amended from time to time by addition or deletion, from Eskimo or from a manufacturer authorized by Eskimo to manufacture such products within the New York City metropolitan area * * *." (emphasis supplied).

The present lawsuits were instituted after Eskimo, beginning sometime in 1962 and 1963, sold its Eskimo-branded products to others in the New York City Metropolitan Area, and entered into agreements with M.H. Renken Dairy Co. ("Renken" herein) to manufacture, and with Food Enterprises, Inc. ("Food Enterprises" herein) to sell, such products, and assisted Harry L. Darnstaedt and Imperial Ice Cream Novelties, Inc. ("Imperial" herein) in selling such products in the New York City Metropolitan Area. This led to a deterioration in the relationship between the parties to the Package Deal; a purported termination by Whitelawn and SAS of purchases and sales thereunder; and mutual claims of breach of contract, since Whitelawn and SAS appear to have refused to accept and pay for certain products.

* * *

A threshold question, which appears to be central to the entire dispute between the parties, arises out of the meaning of the word "non-exclusive" as used in the above quotation from the Package Deal, and the proposal of Whitelawn–SAS to offer parol evidence with respect to its meaning. Whitelawn and SAS contend that the word "non-exclusive" as used in the Package Deal meant that Eskimo would have the right to continue existing licenses granted by it to others in the New York City Metropolitan Area and to grant new licenses to national companies (such as the Borden Company, National Dairy Products Corporation), but not to grant licenses to so-called "independent" companies unless required to do so by order of a court or governmental agency, and that Eskimo itself was not to compete with Whitelawn and SAS in the sale of Eskimo-branded ice cream products. Eskimo denies such contentions as to the meaning of the word "non-exclusive" and asserts that it plainly meant that Eskimo was granting a bare non-exclusive right to Whitelawn and SAS to manufacture and sell Eskimo products, while retaining the unfettered right to license others as it saw fit to manufacture and sell Eskimo-branded ice cream products.

Whitelawn–SAS proposes, upon the jury trial of the issues of liability raised by the two lawsuits, to introduce not only the written agreements constituting the Package Deal, but also parol and extrinsic evidence as to

What SAS wanted introduced into evidence

what the parties understood and intended the term "non-exclusive" to mean, including earlier drafts of the Package Deal, correspondence and conversations between the parties leading up to its execution, and subsequent conduct of the parties, including a letter written by Darnstaedt on February 12, 1963 stating that the parties "had a gentlemen's agreement that Eskimo would not solicit any stick franchises in New York City except any of the national companies that Eskimo is serving around the country." More specifically, Whitelawn–SAS would offer testimony of its lawyers and others who negotiated the Package Deal on its behalf to the effect that earlier drafts, including one submitted by an Eskimo official named Gunn (now deceased) contained a clause which would have obligated Eskimo not to license or franchise the Eskimo mark, or sell Eskimo-branded ice cream products, to anyone in the New York City Metropolitan Area other than existing licensees or national dairy organizations, unless Eskimo should be required to do so by court or governmental order; that thereafter Eskimo refused to sign an agreement containing the express clause because of a fear expressed by Eskimo's counsel that the proposed clause might violate the federal antitrust laws; and that accordingly, after a series of conferences, the proposed clause was deleted on the understanding that its meaning would be deemed incorporated into the word "non-exclusive" used in the above-quoted license to Whitelawn–SAS.

Although Eskimo, if such parol evidence were admitted at the trial, would offer testimony of its officials contradicting that of the Whitelawn–SAS negotiators, it argues that such evidence is barred by the parol evidence rule, and seeks preliminary rulings before trial is commenced.

* * *

The question of whether parol evidence should be admitted at trial is one of law to be determined and ruled upon by the Court. * * * Normally such rulings are made when the evidence is offered during trial, with the party offering the evidence, should objection be sustained, preserving his rights through an offer of proof out of the jury's presence. In this case, however, Eskimo asserts that since the parol evidence to be offered is extensive (both parties agreeing that if the evidence is admitted several witnesses will be required to testify for at least a few days), Eskimo would be forced to engage in multiple and continuous objections to, and/or motions to strike, testimony as to each of the numerous conversations between the negotiators, and proof of each item of correspondence, drafts, etc., with the result that even if the evidence should ultimately be excluded, Eskimo would be unduly prejudiced before the jury. This argument has much merit and is supported by those who follow the practice in such cases of holding a preliminary hearing for the purpose of ruling on the admissibility of such evidence. Wigmore on Evidence § 1808 at 275–76 (3d ed.). Whitelawn–SAS contends, however, that since the parol evidence should be admitted at trial, a preliminary hearing would result in needless waste and expense occasioned by duplication in testimony and proof. In view of these opposing contentions, consideration by the Court at this time of the applicable evidentiary principles seems appropriate.

* * *

Whitelawn–SAS argues that parol evidence should be admitted on the ground that the term "non-exclusive" is ambiguous, and that even if it in fact lacks ambiguity such evidence may be received to show that the parties gave the term special or particular meaning not to be gathered from the language by a reasonably intelligent person having knowledge of the custom, usage and surrounding circumstances. In support of their position, Whitelawn–SAS relies principally on § 2–202 of the Uniform Commercial Code ("UCC" herein). * * *

* * *

Since the Package Deal predated the effective date of the UCC, and since the UCC was not intended to have retroactive effect, § 2–202 does not apply and the Court must look to prior law. * * *

In any event even if § 2–202 of the UCC were applicable to the written contract here at issue, much of the proof which Whitelawn–SAS would offer to show what the parties intended the word "non-exclusive" to mean would not be admissible. Section 2–202 limits the parties, in explaining the meaning of language in a written integrated contract, to proof of a "course of dealing," "usage of the trade," and a "course of performance." None of these terms encompass testimony or other proof as to the subjective intent of the parties. The term "course of dealing" as defined in § 1–205(1) refers to "previous conduct between the parties" indicating a common basis for interpreting expressions used by them. In short, proof of such conduct is limited to objective facts as distinguished from oral statements of agreement. Likewise the term "usage of trade" is defined in § 1–205(2) as:

> "any practice or method of dealing having such regularity of observance in a place, vocation or trade as to justify an expectation that it will be observed with respect to the transaction in question. The existence and scope of such a usage are to be proved as facts. If it is established that such a usage is embodied in a written trade code or similar writing the interpretation of the writing is for the court."

The comments of the drafters as well as those of independent commentators make it clear that "usage of the trade" refers to evidence of generalized industry practice or similar recognized custom, as distinguished from particular conversations or correspondence between the parties with respect to the terms of the agreement. UCC § 1–205, Official Comment 5. * * * The same general conclusions must be reached with respect to proof of a "course of performance."

* * *

* * * The courts of New York have never subscribed to the view that, in the absence of ambiguity, evidence as to the subjective intent of the parties may be substituted for the plain meaning that would otherwise be ascribed to the language of a written agreement by a reasonably intelligent person having knowledge of the surrounding circumstances, customs and usages. On the contrary, prior New York law adhered to time-honored objective standards to determine the meaning of language found in writings which represent as did the Package Deal here the final and complete integrated agreement reached by the parties. * * * The cardinal principles forming the cornerstone of those standards are (1) that the meaning to be attributed to the language of such an instrument is that which a reasonably intelligent person acquainted with general usage, custom and the surrounding circumstances would attribute to

it; and (2) that in the absence of ambiguity parol evidence will not be admitted to determine the meaning that is to be attributed to such language. * * *

Thus the oral statements of the parties as to what they intended unambiguous language in an integrated document to mean are excluded by the parol evidence rule, because the very purpose and essence of the rule is to avoid fraud that might be perpetrated if testimony as to subjective intent could be substituted for the plain meaning, objectively interpreted in the light of surrounding circumstances, customs and usage. The effect of admitting such testimony in the absence of some showing of ambiguity would be to permit a party to substitute his view of his obligations for those clearly stated. Where—as in the present case—some of the negotiators of the written agreement have died or are unavailable, the door could be opened to fraud. Accordingly, the view of the New York courts has been that an objective standard is essential to maintain confidence in the written integrated agreement as the medium for conducting commercial relations.

The first question to be determined in the present case, therefore, is whether the term "non-exclusive" as used in the Package Deal is ambiguous, which must be decided by the Court. * * * An "ambiguous" word or phrase is one capable of more than one meaning when viewed objectively by a reasonably intelligent person who has examined the context of the entire integrated agreement and who is cognizant of the customs, practices, usages and terminology as generally understood in the particular trade or business. * * * In the absence of proof that the term "non-exclusive" could possibly have the meaning, among others, attributed to it by Whitelawn–SAS, parol evidence must be excluded.

Applying the foregoing principles, the word "non-exclusive" when used— as was the case here—in an integrated license agreement drafted by legal counsel, has an established legal meaning that is usually accepted in the absence of a qualifying context, custom, usage or similar surrounding circumstance. The term has repeatedly been defined as meaning that the licensee is granted a bare right to use the trademark or patent being licensed without any right to exclude others, including other licensees taking from the grantor, from utilizing the mark or invention involved. * * *

Despite the meaning thus usually ascribed by the law to the term "non-exclusive" Whitelawn–SAS urge that here the legal draftsmen intended it to have a contrary meaning, i.e., that subject to certain detailed and specific exceptions (The Borden Company, National Dairy Products Corporation, existing licensees and existing written commitments to others), and except to the extent that Eskimo might be required to deviate therefrom by court or governmental order, the term meant "exclusive." In a business world not noted for its economy of language (the Package Deal covers 70 typewritten pages, including amendments) no business reason, custom or usage is advanced for attaching such an elaborate and paradoxical meaning to the term "non-exclusive," when legal counsel negotiating for both sides could easily have spelled out such specifics in comprehensible terms. Whitelawn–SAS's assertion that the term was used to conceal a detailed secret "gentlemen's agreement" that was feared by Eskimo to violate the antitrust laws hardly comports with the word's having a secondary meaning as a matter of generalized trade usage or custom. On the contrary, such evidence would indicate that the term, despite the definite and plain meaning usually attributed to it, was being used to express a particular, subjective meaning initially conceived by the parties solely for the purpose at hand, and not because the term would be recognized by others as having such a special meaning. Unless the language is meaningless on its face (e.g. "abracadabra") or ambiguous, however, the test for admission of parol evidence is not a secret code meaning given to it by the parties but whether it might objectively be recognized by a reasonably intelligent person acquainted with applicable customs, usages and the surrounding circumstances as having such a special meaning. For instance, would an executive in the ice cream business, who was not privy to the secret oral "gentlemen's agreement," recognize the term "non-exclusive" in this context and setting as granting an "exclusive" right, subject to certain exceptions or as having a meaning other than that usually attributed to it? If so, parol evidence would be admissible. If the law were otherwise, not only the term "non-exclusive" but every apparently clear term in a written agreement, such as a specific purchase price (e.g., "$10,000") could be changed by secret oral agreement to mean something different (e.g., "$25,000").

Nevertheless, although the term "non-exclusive" as used in the Package Deal does not on its face appear to be ambiguous, Whitelawn–SAS will be afforded the opportunity to offer proof showing that the term is ambiguous, and Eskimo the opportunity to rebut such proof. In accordance with the principles hereinabove outlined, proof on the issue of ambiguity may encompass the terms of the Package Deal itself, the surrounding circumstances, common usage and custom as to the meaning attributed to it, and subsequent conduct of the parties under the Package Deal, but evidence of the subjective understanding of the parties as to the meaning attributed by them to the term "non-exclusive" will not be received.

Since the issue of ambiguity must be determined by the Court before ruling on the admission of parol evidence and since Eskimo might suffer prejudice if such rulings were made in the jury's presence, the proof with respect to ambiguity will be received at a preliminary hearing by the Court. Upon conclusion of the preliminary hearing, the Court will rule upon the issue of ambiguity, and the admissibility of the evidence at trial will be governed accordingly. Thereupon, pursuant to Rule 42(b), F.R.C.P., the Court will hold a separate jury trial of the issue of liability, to be followed by trial before the same jury of the damage issues. * * *

So ordered.

JOY v. HAY GROUP, INC., 403 F.3d 875 (7th Cir. 2005).

POSNER, CIRCUIT JUDGE:

[E]ven if a contract is clear "on its face"–which is to say, even if someone who knew nothing of the contract's background or commercial context would think its meaning clear–extrinsic evidence, which is to say evidence besides just the written contract itself, is admissible to demonstrate that the contract may not mean what it says, provided the evidence used to show this is "objective" in the sense of not being merely self-serving, unverifiable testimony. * * *

When * * * the written contract is unclear, *any* evidence admissible under the rules of evidence is usable to establish the contract's meaning.

HARRISON v. FRED S. JAMES, P.A., INC.

United States District Court, Eastern District of Pennsylvania, 1983.
558 F.Supp. 438.

BECHTLE, DISTRICT JUDGE.

This is a diversity action for wrongful discharge and breach of an oral contract for two years' employment. Presently before the Court is the motion of defendants Fred S. James, P.A., Inc. ("James") and Richard Peterson ("Peterson") for summary judgment. For the reasons that follow, the motion will be granted.

I. FACTS

Plaintiff is a former employee of defendant James, an insurance brokerage agency and consulting firm. Defendant Peterson is the executive vice-president of defendant James in charge of the Philadelphia office where plaintiff worked. The cause of action dates back to events occurring in 1980. At that time, plaintiff was employed as a manager in the marketing department of Alexander and Alexander, another insurance brokerage firm. In or about January or February, 1980, plaintiff was contacted by an insurance search firm used by defendant James. Plaintiff was advised that James was looking for a marketing man and was extremely interested in him. Plaintiff agreed to meet with defendant Peterson of the James office. The meeting took place sometime in late February, early March, 1980. After a discussion of goals, objectives, and philosophies, Peterson asked plaintiff whether he was interested in a position with James. Plaintiff indicated that he was not interested in the positions offered. The meeting ended with Peterson stating that he would get back to plaintiff.

About a week later, the first of two luncheon meetings between plaintiff and Peterson took place. During these meetings, Peterson outlined a job as head of the marketing department at James. The job specifically included the responsibility of reorganizing the department. Plaintiff concedes that Peterson never promised him a definite term of employment at this or any other time. Nonetheless, plaintiff contends that "[h]e (Peterson) led me to believe I would be employed at least two years via this discussion." Harrison Dep. at 110. Plaintiff's belief was based on the following exchange. In response to plaintiff's inquiries into the time period he would be allowed to complete a departmental restructure and then "work out the bugs," Peterson replied that a year would be appropriate. Plaintiff then stated to Peterson that he would first need six months to become familiar with the department prior to attempting a reorganization. Peterson indicated that this time frame "seemed sensible."

The actual offer of employment was not made at the luncheon meetings. It was made over the telephone by the search firm. No mention was made on either side of a specific term of employment. A few days later, plaintiff met with Peterson. A salary of $52,500.00 was agreed upon as was a date, April 7, 1980, for plaintiff to begin working for James.

Although plaintiff testified that he did not recall the details of April 7, 1980, his first day at James, he believed he met with James' personnel manager, Mrs. Ward. At this time plaintiff executed various documents including a Memorandum of Agreement. This agreement covered compensation, confidentiality, non-competition, and termination. The document plainly states that it is "intended to set forth the terms and conditions of the employment relationship between James and its Employee." Harrison Dep. at 144–145; Exhibit D–6. Paragraph 11 is a termination clause which states that employment "may be terminated by either party upon fifteen (15) days prior written notice." *Id.* at Exhibit D–6 ¶ 11. Paragraph 10 stipulates that "this Agreement sets forth the entire agreement" between the parties, and "supercedes any and all prior agreements and understandings with respect of such employment."

That plaintiff reviewed the agreement prior to signing it is revealed by his questioning Mrs. Ward as to the document's necessity. Upon Mrs. Ward's confirmation of necessity, plaintiff executed the agreement without further objection or discussion.

During plaintiff's employment with James, by his own account his relationships with subordinates, account executives, and Peterson were good to very good. Plaintiff's termination during a meeting with Peterson on November 25, 1980, some seven months after he joined James, appears to have resulted from nebulous office "politics" and a loss of confidence in plaintiff by "other people." Harrison Dep. at 188–189. Plaintiff and Peterson discussed the details of the firing and it was agreed that plaintiff would be relieved of his responsibilities immediately, but would remain on the company payroll with full salary and benefits, including the use of company car, office space, and phone privileges, through March, 1981. This was to allow plaintiff time to find another job. Plaintiff voiced some concern over the announcement of his firing, but Peterson stated that "in the interests of the James organization," he had no choice but to immediately let others know that plaintiff had "resigned." *Id.* at 192.

Immediately after this meeting plaintiff returned to his office. There he found a message to call Harold O'Hanlon, a friend of plaintiff's who worked in the insurance industry in New York. When plaintiff returned the call, O'Hanlon reported that he had heard plaintiff was fired. Plaintiff claims this call indicates that other people in the insurance industry outside of James had advance notice of his firing.

As agreed, plaintiff continued to receive full salary and benefits until March 31, 1981. Plaintiff spent this time looking for another job, and did no work for James. Upon the completion of his severance from James, plaintiff received an additional five days' vacation pay and a profit sharing plan refund. At no time on or after November 25, 1980, the date of his firing, did plaintiff communicate to anyone at James that his termination breached his employment agreement.

II. DISCUSSION

A. Breach of an Express Oral Contract

Count I of plaintiff's complaint avers that defendant James, by firing plaintiff, breached an express oral contract for two years' employment.

Plaintiff's claim is based exclusively upon his pre-employment lunch discussions with defendant Peterson. According to plaintiff, these discussions resulted in an oral contract between himself and James under which plaintiff was to be employed by James for at least two years.

In the face of the unambiguous terms of the subsequent written employment contract between the parties, signed by plaintiff April 7, 1980, plaintiff's claim is without legal force. Paragraph 11 of this agreement expressly indicates that the employment relationship between the parties is at-will, and "may be terminated by either party upon fifteen (15) days prior written notice. * * *" Harrison Dep., Exhibit D–6. Further, paragraph 10 of the agreement specifically states that the written agreement is an integrated one which "sets forth the entire agreement between the employee and James, and supercedes any and all prior agreements and understandings with respect of such employment." *Id.* In Pennsylvania the law is clear that when a written contract sets forth in plain and unambiguous terms the entire agreement between the parties, parol evidence of prior inconsistent negotiations, terms, or agreements may not be considered. "Unless fraud, accident or mistake [is] averred, the writing constitutes the agreement between the parties, and its terms cannot be added to nor subtracted from by parol evidence." *Scott v. Bryn Mawr Arms,* 454 Pa. 304, 307, 312 A.2d 592, 594 (1973) (citations omitted). Further, when a writing contains an integration clause which expressly provides that the written instrument contains the entire agreement of the parties, it is conclusively presumed to do so, absent a showing that this clause was procured through fraud, accident, or mistake. *United States Gypsum Co. v. Schiavo Bros., Inc.,* 450 F.Supp. 1291, 1302 (E.D.Pa.1978).

Plaintiff makes several arguments in his brief in opposition in an effort to show fraudulent inducement, duress or mistake, and thereby avoid the parol evidence rule and cast doubt on the applicability of the written contract. These arguments, however, are without merit.

Plaintiff first contends that Ward, defendant James' personnel employee, led him to believe that he was signing a non-competition agreement only, as a mere first day of employment formality. Plaintiff in effect is claiming deceit or fraud. Under Pennsylvania law fraud is shown by clear and convincing evidence of all of the following: (1) a misrepresentation; (2) a fraudulent utterance thereof; (3) an intention that another person will thereby be induced to act, or to refrain from acting; (4) justifiable reliance by the recipient; and (5) damage to the recipient. *United States Gypsum Co. v. Schiavo Bros., Inc.,* 450 F.Supp. 1291 (E.D.Pa.1978). The facts as adduced from plaintiff's own deposition indicate that a viable defense to the contract based on fraud does not exist.

There is nothing to suggest that Ward said or did anything even remotely approaching what could be called misrepresentation. Without a misrepresentation, the first element of a fraud, plaintiff's claim of fraud collapses. Moreover, even assuming the existence of the first three elements of a fraud claim, there is no evidence whatsoever upon which the Court could find the requisite justifiable reliance. In fact, the available evidence points the other way. Plaintiff, a college graduate, testified that he had over 10 years' experience in the insurance industry. Plaintiff further testified that he read the employment agreement, understood its binding nature, and asked whether it was necessary that he sign it. Harrison Dep. at 144–148. It is difficult to see how, under these facts, plaintiff can argue that he didn't understand either that which the agreement clearly set forth or its binding nature. * * *

Plaintiff next argues that he signed the agreement because, having terminated his prior employment, he was not in a position to refuse. In effect, plaintiff's position is that he executed the contract under duress and therefore it is unenforceable against him. However, even viewing the circumstances in a light most favorable to plaintiff, the Court concludes as a matter of law that there has been no showing of duress. *See* Restatement (Second) of Contracts § 175 When Duress by Threat Makes a Contract Voidable (1979). It is not even suggested that there was any threat made to plaintiff by anyone associated with James. Then too, merely because one enters into an agreement which he would not enter if his financial circumstances were more secure, does not mean that a claim for duress exists as will void the contract. * * * Aside from plaintiff's bare allegation, there is nothing in the present record which would support a finding that the employment contract was executed under duress. Plaintiff thus cannot avoid the written employment contract by such a claim.

Plaintiff also asserts that inclusion of the termination clause in the agreement was a mistake. There is no proof of such a mistake, however, except plaintiff's own contention that his intention was contrary to that expressed in the written contract. Plaintiff seeks to introduce parol evidence of the prior negotiations to buttress his claim of mistake. Unfortunately for plaintiff, the parol evidence rule prohibits the Court from considering evidence of prior negotiations. Under the rule, any oral representations made during the negotiation stage are merged in and superceded by the written agreement. *Scott v. Bryn Mawr Arms, supra.* In order for evidence of the prior negotiations to be admissible, plaintiff must *first* prove mistake. *Kattelman v. Sabol,* 425 Pa. 197, 228 A.2d 379 (1967). Plaintiff cannot use evidence barred by the parol evidence rule to prove the mistake necessary to allow admission of that evidence.

Plaintiff next claims that the employment agreement is unenforceable because there was no meeting of the minds on the terms of the written agreement. This argument is similar to plaintiff's mistake argument and is similarly unpersuasive. Again, the same parol evidence rule which plaintiff is seeking to avoid through his allegation of lack of intent to contract under the terms of the written agreement, bars consideration of testimony regarding the parties' intent prior to the time when the contract was executed. * * * Plaintiff is thus bound by the objective manifestation of his intent as plainly expressed in the written contract he executed.

Plaintiff's final argument, that the written agreement is unenforceable because it modified the parties' oral agreement without consideration, must be rejected. Since plaintiff has not proved the existence of a prior oral agreement, the written agreement cannot be deemed a modification. The lunch discussions upon which plaintiff bases his claim of an oral contract cannot be used to support plaintiff's position because of the parol evidence rule.

In sum, plaintiff cannot avoid the written employment agreement that he executed. There is no basis on the undisputed facts in the record upon which the Court could find fraud, duress, or mistake. The parol evidence rule thus preempts consideration of the negotiations plaintiff claims constitute an express oral contract. As discussed above, plaintiff's lack of consideration theory is without merit. Summary judgment on Count I shall therefore be entered in defendants' favor.

[The court also concluded that public policy was not violated by Harrison's discharge because he could not show a "specific intent to harm" him by the discharge.]

Problem 6–2

Consider the "merger" ("full integration") clause of Paragraph 10 of Harrison's Memorandum of Agreement with Fred S. James, P.A. Inc. What was the purpose of this clause?

    (a) to indicate unmistakably that the parties intended their written agreement to be a complete and exclusive embodiment of all *terms* of the agreement?

    (b) to foreclose issues of interpretation as to the meaning of the agreement?

    (c) to put persons such as Harrison on notice that an agent of Fred S. James has only limited authority as to the terms on which Fred S. James may contract?

    (d) other?

Did the clause serve its purpose?

Note
The Parol Evidence Rule and Other
Theories of Obligation

In Harrison v. Fred S. James, P.A., Inc., could Harrison have recovered on a reliance theory of obligation (promissory estoppel)? Assume Fred S. James, Inc. had promised to employ Harrison for two years and Harrison offered evidence of this promise in order to make out a case of promissory estoppel. Does the parol evidence rule bar admissibility of the evidence? Should it?

Please evaluate the following arguments: (1) The parol evidence rule only bars evidence offered to vary or contradict written *contracts,* i.e. agreements with consideration, and therefore does not apply to the proof of a different theory of obligation. (2) Admitting evidence of an oral promise to prove promissory estoppel does not frustrate the policies behind the parol evidence rule because the promissory estoppel remedy differs from the breach of contract remedy. (3) The parol evidence rule deters fraudulent assertion of the existence of agreements. Proof of reliance on a promise, such as Harrison's reliance on the promise of employment, tends to show that a promise was made; therefore the parol evidence rule should not apply. (4) The problem of the relationship between the parol evidence rule and promissory estoppel is very similar to the problem of the relationship between the statute of frauds and promissory estoppel (see pages 195–200), and should be handled in the same way. For a case holding that the parol evidence rule bars evidence of promissory estoppel, see Kinn v. Coast Catamaran Corp., 582 F.Supp. 682 (E.D.Wis.1984).

HIELD v. THYBERG

Supreme Court of Minnesota, 1984.
347 N.W.2d 503.

SIMONETT, JUSTICE.

Although the trial court properly allowed plaintiff to use parol evidence to explain the purpose and vary the term of a written contract, we conclude, on the facts of this case, that plaintiff should have been required to prove his case by clear and convincing evidence. We reverse for a new trial.

On June 10, 1977, plaintiff-respondent Willard R. Hield sold his half interest in a corporation, Beauticians Supply, Inc., to defendant-appellant Edwin R. Thyberg, owner of the other half interest. The sale was accomplished by a written document entitled "Assignment," signed by Hield, which provided in part:

> For and in consideration of *Fifteen Thousand* Dollars (*$15,000.00*), Willard R. Hield, of Minneapolis, Minnesota, does hereby assign, order and transfer to Edwin R. Thyberg, of Sioux Falls, South Dakota, all of my right, title and interest in Beauticians Supply, Inc., a corporation, including but not limited to any and all advances made by me to the said corporation and all of my common shares of capital stock * * *.

> * * *

> The undersigned assignor hereby acknowledges that the assignee assumes no other personal liability toward assignor * * *.

The $15,000 was paid at the time the assignment was signed by Hield. Sometime thereafter, Hield transferred his stock certificates to Thyberg.

In January 1979, plaintiff Hield sued defendant Thyberg, alleging in his complaint that he had sold his corporate shares "for a total consideration of $50,000, $15,000 cash at closing and $35,000 in a promissory note." Plaintiff further alleged that Thyberg, by agreeing to pay $50,000 and then refusing to perform, had committed fraud. The case was tried to a jury. Over defendant's objections, plaintiff was permitted to testify that defendant, indeed, had agreed to pay an additional $35,000 for the corporate stock. Defendant denied any such agreement. The trial court dismissed the fraud allegations, but submitted the contract issue to the jury. The jury resolved the fact issues in favor of plaintiff and, pursuant to the verdict, judgment was entered in favor of plaintiff and against defendant for $35,000 plus 6% interest from June 10, 1977. Defendant Thyberg appeals from the judgment.

The issue is whether the parol evidence rule applies. If it does, plaintiff is bound by the $15,000 agreed consideration set out in the written document and can collect no more. If the parol evidence rule does not apply, there is evidence to sustain the jury's verdict that the true consideration was $50,000, not $15,000. We conclude that parol evidence may be used here but under a higher burden of proof.

When the case was called for trial, the trial court denied defendant's motion to exclude parol evidence and allowed plaintiff's evidence to be received.[1] At the close of all the testimony, defendant's motion for a directed verdict was denied, the trial court observing, "I have grave reservations about this particular lawsuit and I have no hesitancy about stating it."

[Negotiations between the parties began in the spring of 1977. At that time a bank was threatening to foreclose a mortgage on the corporation. Hield had personally guaranteed the loan. On April 18, 1977, Thyberg said he would purchase Hield's stock for ten or fifteen thousand dollars plus an additional sum paid over five years, not to exceed $72,000.]

The key date is June 10, 1977. On that day defendant Thyberg came to Minneapolis to close the deal with plaintiff Hield. Thyberg brought with him the typed "Assignment" paper previously mentioned, which had been drafted by his attorney in Sioux Falls with a blank space provided for insertion of the amount of consideration. Thyberg and Hield held three meetings on that day—at 8 a.m., then about 11 a.m., and finally again at 5 p.m. Hield testified that Thyberg agreed to pay $50,000, $15,000 down and the balance by a demand note which Thyberg would send as soon as he got back to Sioux Falls. Hield testified that Thyberg was intending to get an SBA loan and consequently did not want the $35,000 to show on his balance sheet. With this understanding, Hield says he had his secretary type in the blank space a $15,000 consideration, plus an indemnity provision at the bottom of the paper. He then signed the assignment and accepted Thyberg's check for $15,000. Thyberg testified that at the 8 a.m. meeting, he did, indeed, say that payment of a sum in addition to $15,000 "might be a possibility," and that "[i]f there was any other way I could raise any more money, I would,"—but that this depended on whether the business would be profitable and would be able to use the tax loss carryover. It was Thyberg's position that after these preliminaries, however, he offered to pay only $15,000 plus agreeing to save Hield harmless on his personal guarantee of the bank mortgage. Thyberg said he would have elected to liquidate the company if these terms had not been agreeable to Hield.

[Another witness, Flaten, an attorney for Beauticians Supply, Inc., testified that his notes of two conversations with Hield on June 10 indicated that Hield thought the company if liquidated might net $70,000 to $90,000 subject to a $20,000 advance owed Thyberg, that Flaten suggested that Hield should negotiate for more money to be paid on an installment basis, and that the parties were concerned that any additional consideration over $15,000 might prejudice the SBA loan and that it might be better to defer this aspect of their deal. Flaten also told Hield that "camouflaging" additional consideration might be fraudulent and that the "proper procedure" would be a note subordinated to the SBA loan.]

* * * Flaten testified that he explained to Hield that the assignment document "purported to be a complete sale of his entire interest both debt and equity in the corporation *for whatever sum was to be inserted in the*

---

1. "The evidence that the rule seems to exclude must sometimes be heard and weighed before it can be excluded by the rule." 3 Corbin, Contracts § 582 at 450 (1960). Much is left to the trial court's discretion in the particular case. Rather than say that the parol evidence rule prohibits "admission" or "allowance" of certain evidence, it may be better to say that the rule, if it applies, prevents the "use" of parol evidence.

contract if it was executed and I told him that the contract would be effective for that purpose." (Emphasis added.)

We have, then, a classic fact dispute. Thyberg and Hield were alone together when they concluded their agreement, and each has a different version of the purchase price finally agreed upon. Both parties were vague in their recollections in important respects and uncertain what the business was really worth. Did Hield and Thyberg, notwithstanding the attorney's warning, agree to another $35,000 undocumented consideration? Or did Thyberg, knowing Hield's need for cash, simply drive a hard bargain, and Hield, not willing to risk a corporate liquidation, accept $15,000 as payment in full?

The parol evidence rule encourages parties to put their agreements in writing so that there may be fewer, not more, lawsuits. Thus the rule, as generally stated, is that evidence outside a written document is not to be used to vary or contradict the plain terms of the document. The sometimes harsh effect of this rule is, however, ameliorated by a host of exceptions. This is not, however, a case of subsequent modification of the written contract. Nor is it a case of ambiguity in the terms of the written agreement itself. Nor is it a case of the written contract itself being incomplete or silent on a term to which the written contract might not normally be expected to speak. Nor is this a case of no enforceable contract ever being made. If there is an exception to the rule, we must look elsewhere.

Plaintiff Hield argues that while he assented to the written assignment he did not assent to it as a document setting out the complete understanding of the parties. In other words, Hield contends that the written document did not "integrate" the parties' complete understanding and so the jury should be free to use parol evidence to determine the true, entire agreement. This seems to be an attempt to show a written contract is incomplete by introducing through parol evidence a term flatly contradictory to the written contract. Hield seems to imply that he would never have signed the written document if Thyberg had not promised to pay an additional $35,000. The trial court, however, held as a matter of law, there was no fraud in the inducement. Rather, it appears that Hield is claiming that the written assignment is, in part, illusory; that the written assignment containing the $15,000 stated consideration was executed for the purpose of showing it to the Small Business Administration so that an SBA loan could be obtained—a loan, incidentally, which would be used to pay off the bank mortgage which Hield had personally guaranteed; and that the separate oral agreement for Thyberg to give Hield a $35,000 demand note was, together with the note itself, to be kept secret from the SBA.

Hield wants to show that he intended the consideration to be $50,000 even though he himself wrote in the figure $15,000. In other words, he really wants to show the *purpose* of the written contract is other than as stated in the writing. * * *

This case has a curious twist to it. Hield denies any deceit on his part and stops short of claiming that Thyberg intended to use the written contract to deceive. Hield says only that he assumed Thyberg would tell SBA about the undocumented $35,000 debt.[2] The record indicates that Thyberg got his SBA

---

2. On direct examination, Hield testified: Q. Well, were you involved in some scheme to defraud the Small Business Administration?

loan. Presumably he did not disclose to SBA any $35,000 debt to Hield or Hield would surely have put such an admission in evidence. In other words, the net impact of Hield's claim is that Thyberg defrauded the SBA with the written assignment. * * *

We hold, * * * that where the parties have entered into a written contract, complete and unambiguous on the consideration to be paid, but it is claimed that the consideration was not as stated so that the contract might be used to mislead or deceive a third party, parol evidence is usable; but the party seeking to vary the terms of the written contract in this situation has the burden of establishing his claim by clear and convincing evidence.

Here the jury was not instructed on the clear and convincing evidence standard. While defendant Thyberg did not request the instruction, he did strenuously throughout the trial claim the benefit of the parol evidence rule. We believe the case should be retried with the appropriate burden of proof instruction.

Reversed and remanded for a new trial.

A.B.A. MODEL CODE OF PROFESSIONAL RESPONSIBILITY
DR 7–102(A)(7) (Rev'd 1984 ed.).

(A) In his representation of a client, a lawyer shall not:

* * *

(7) Counsel or assist his client in conduct that the lawyer knows to be illegal or fraudulent.

Problem 6–3

A letter to the editors from counsel for Thyberg, dated April 30, 1985, states:

As a result of this case, we have concluded that virtually no written contract is safe from attack regardless of the clarity of its wording. It appears that anyone wishing to escape the consequences of a written contract can get to the jury with an argument that there was a parol agreement for something which is directly at variance with the terms of the written contract since it does not seem difficult to be able to show some latent ambiguity or lack of integration.

Do you agree with counsel?

Note
The "Condition Precedent" Exception to the
Parol Evidence Rule

Courts sometimes hold that parol evidence is admissible to prove a condition precedent to the legal enforcement of a written agreement. For example, where

A. No, sir.

Q. Well, if you weren't going to show this in a written form so that would not affect his balance sheet, why isn't that doing something improper?

A. Well, at this point he—whether he was the president of the company he, in effect, then became the owner. I guess this was up to him at that point.

After absolving himself of any responsibility for whatever use the $15,000 written assignment would be put to, Hield went on to testify that he assumed Thyberg would arrange for the $35,000 debt to be subordinated to the SBA loan.

the parties to a written agreement merging their two corporations orally agreed that the merger was conditioned on the prior accumulation of $672,500 "equity expansion funds," evidence of this oral agreement and of failure of the condition was held admissible to prove a defense of the party resisting the merger. Hicks v. Bush, 10 N.Y.2d 488, 225 N.Y.S.2d 34, 180 N.E.2d 425 (1962). The court stated that evidence of an oral condition precedent is admissible where the evidence does not "directly" or "explicitly" contradict the writing. In MCM Partners v. Andrews–Bartlett & Assoc., 161 F.3d 443, 447 (7th Cir.1998), on the other hand, the court held that the parol evidence rule barred evidence of a condition precedent because the contract was clear and the evidence would "alter unilaterally the terms of the agreement."

This discussion suggests the similarities between the condition precedent exception and the issue of whether an agreement is integrated. For example, some courts applying the condition precedent exception have inquired whether the written contract was detailed and contained an integration clause. See, e.g., Whirlpool Corp. v. Regis Leasing Corp., 29 A.D.2d 395, 288 N.Y.S.2d 337 (1st Dept.1968).

3 CORBIN ON CONTRACTS

§ 575 at 380–81 (1960).

The statute of frauds and the "parol evidence rule" are sometimes both applied in a single case. To promote clear thinking and correct decision, they should be compared and contrasted. They appear to have a similar purpose, at least when we regard the latter rule as in truth a rule of admissibility; that purpose is the prevention of successful fraud and perjury. In each case, this purpose is only haltingly attained; and if attained at all it is at the expense and to the injury of many honest contractors. Both the statute and the rule may have caused more litigation than they have prevented. Both may have done more harm than good. Both have been convenient hooks on which a judge can support a decision actually reached on other grounds. Both are attempts to determine justice and the truth by a mechanistic device, alike evidencing a distrust of the capacity of courts and juries to weigh human credibility. And both alike have forced the courts, in the effort to prevent them from doing gross injustice to honest men, to make numerous exceptions and fine distinctions, with such resulting complexity and inconsistency that a reasoned statement of their operations requires volumes instead of pages and the case must be rare in which a plausible argument can not be made for deciding either way.

So much for the apparent similarities of the statute and the rule, these similarities being found in their social aims and practical effects. In the means that they employ and in their juristic effects, they are very different.

The statute makes certain oral contracts unenforceable by action, if not evidenced by a signed memorandum; the "parol evidence rule" protects a completely integrated writing from being varied and contradicted by parol.

The statute does not exclude any parol evidence, such evidence always being admissible to show that the writing does not correctly represent the agreement actually made; the "parol evidence rule," as commonly stated, purports to exclude such evidence.

The statute does not require that the written memorandum shall be an "integration" of the agreement, although such an integration satisfies its requirements; the "parol evidence rule" does not purport to have any operation at all unless such an integration exists.

When the statute is applied because its requirements are not satisfied, an agreement that may actually have been made is not enforced; when the "parol evidence rule" is applied, the court finds that there is a complete integration in writing and enforces the contract thus evidenced.

The statute, when strictly applied, may prevent the enforcement of a contract that the parties in fact made; the application of the "parol evidence rule" results in the enforcement of a contract that the parties did not make, if in fact the written document was not agreed upon as a final and complete integration of terms.

The statute makes a requirement for enforceability that the party to be charged can at any time supply, without knowledge or consent of the other party, recognizes the oral agreement as operative for many purposes, and is in no respect a rule as to discharge of contract; the "parol evidence rule," in its only true operation, is a rule of discharge, a discharge of previous understandings by mutual agreement, a discharge the nullification of which requires the assent of both parties.

SECTION THREE: GENERAL PRINCIPLES OF INTERPRETATION

We have already studied some important aspects of the interpretation of written contracts in the preceding section on parol evidence. For example, in Pacific Gas and Electric Co. v. G.W. Thomas Drayage and Rigging Co., Inc., we saw how a court may disregard the "plain meaning" rule and admit extrinsic evidence to interpret an agreement. In Eskimo Pie Corp. v. Whitelawn Dairies, Inc., we saw how a court may resort to extrinsic evidence of a course of dealing, course of performance, or trade custom when interpreting an agreement. But you should not assume that the problem of the admissibility of parol evidence is the same as the problem of interpretation. Parol evidence of an alleged extrinsic term may be clearly admissible although the evidence may pose a problem of interpretation. Conversely, a problem of the admissibility of parol evidence may arise although the parties do not dispute the meaning of the alleged extrinsic term. Even when both problems arise together, the parol evidence rule operates to identify the admissible evidence of an agreement to which the court may then apply the principles of interpretation.

Before considering the following materials, you should review Sections Two and Three of Chapter Four on planning and drafting. Those sections help explain why the interpretation process is often fraught with difficulties for lawyers and courts.

prob. admissability of parol evidence ≠ prob. of interpretation (handwritten annotation)

PATTERSON, THE INTERPRETATION AND CONSTRUCTION OF CONTRACTS

64 Colum.L.Rev. 833, 833–34 (1964).

What is interpretation? It is the process of endeavoring to ascertain the meaning or meanings of symbolic expressions used by the parties to a contract, or of their expressions in the formative stage of arriving at the creation of one or more legally obligatory promises. Since most contracts are temporary in their effects, the process of interpretation often consists merely of the direct application of the symbols used to the factual situation that gives rise to controversy.

BERKE MOORE CO. v. PHOENIX BRIDGE CO.

Supreme Court of New Hampshire, 1953.
98 N.H. 261, 98 A.2d 150.

[The defendant, Phoenix Bridge Company, a general contractor, entered a contract with New Hampshire to build a bridge with concrete surfaces. According to the contract, Phoenix Bridge was to receive $12.60 per square yard of "concrete surface included in the bridge deck." The state's printed estimate of the quantity of concrete necessary was "3,933 S.Y." (3,933 square yards). Phoenix Bridge entered a subcontract with the plaintiff, Berke Moore, in which Phoenix Bridge agreed to pay Berke Moore $12.00 per square yard of "concrete surface included in the bridge deck." Berke Moore was aware at the time of contracting of the general contract's printed estimate of 3,933 square yards.

Berke Moore performed the concrete work and ultimately claimed that, according to the above contract language and estimate, it should be paid for the amount of concrete it placed on all of the deck's outer surfaces, including the top, bottom and sides. This totaled 8100 square yards, which at $12.00 per square yard came to $97,200. Phoenix Bridge responded that the contract obligated it to pay at a rate measured only by the amount of concrete in the upper surface area, i.e. 4184 square yards at $12.00 per square yard, or $50,208.

The trial court found that the words "concrete surface included in the bridge deck" were "not so plain and clear that reasonable men could not differ as to their meaning." The Supreme Court of New Hampshire upheld this ruling, although noting that in light of the specifications, which indicated that several surfaces of the deck were of concern to the state, "a strong argument (could) be made" that the parties meant more than "the upper surface alone."

The Supreme Court also affirmed the trial court's finding that both Phoenix Bridge and Berke Moore believed at the time of the execution of the contract that Berke Moore was to be paid only at a rate measured by the top surface, and that this view "was opposed to (Berke Moore's) understanding at the time of trial." The Supreme Court's decision was based both on Berke Moore's knowledge of the general contract quantity estimate and unit price and on the parties' subsequent negotiations to modify a portion of the

Since there was doubt the line understand (handwritten annotation in right margin)

subcontract. The court was not persuaded by Berke Moore's insistence that the quantity estimate was inconsequential "since payment was to be made for 'actual quantities.'"]

DUNCAN, JUSTICE.

* * * The rule which precludes the use of the understanding of one party alone is designed to prevent imposition of his private understanding upon the other party to a bilateral transaction. * * * But when it appears that the understanding of one is the understanding of both, no violation of the rule results from determination of the mutual understanding according to that of one alone.

Where the understanding is mutual, it ceases to be the "private" understanding of one. Having thus determined the mutual understanding of the parties, the Court properly interpreted the contract accordingly.

RESTATEMENT (SECOND) OF CONTRACTS § 201.

Whose Meaning Prevails

(1) Where the parties have attached the same meaning to a promise or agreement or a term thereof, it is interpreted in accordance with that meaning.

(2) Where the parties have attached different meanings to a promise or agreement or a term thereof, it is interpreted in accordance with the meaning attached by one of them if at the time the agreement was made

(a) that party did not know of any different meaning attached by the other, and the other knew the meaning attached by the first party; or

(b) that party had no reason to know of any different meaning attached by the other, and the other had reason to know the meaning attached by the first party.

(3) Except as stated in this Section, neither party is bound by the meaning attached by the other, even though the result may be a failure of mutual assent.

Berkes knowledge of the general K price. →

Problem 6–4

Charles Leslie agreed to manufacture 7500 humidifiers for Pennco, Inc. The purchase order drafted by Pennco included the following provision:

PLEASE NOTE THE ABOVE RELEASE SCHEDULE TO BE REVIEWED QUARTERLY

The order specified certain dates for production and delivery. After 3946 humidifiers were delivered to Pennco, it refused to accept further delivery. Pennco claimed that the release schedule provision permitted it to cancel at quarterly intervals. Evaluate the following examination of witnesses at the trial of Leslie v. Pennco, Inc. by Leslie's lawyer.

DIRECT EXAMINATION OF CHARLES LESLIE

Q. Now, in capital letters down at the bottom of the page [of the purchase order] would you read to the Court and the jury what it says?

A. "Please note the above release schedule to be reviewed quarterly."

Q. What is the, quotes, above release schedule? What is that?

A. Release schedule is up above here. There's—in capital letters it says, "Released as follows." This is following the amount of humidifiers that were ordered within the designated amount of time, and this was merely the rate at which we would—we are asked to produce and deliver the humidifiers.

Q. Now, was that acceptable to you to permit the review of the release schedule as you went along?

A. Yes, sir, it was.

Q. And what was the background discussion that led to the insertion of that phraseology?

A. It was posed to me that this was the start and that they would—they anticipated wanting a greater number or wanted them faster than seven-hundred-and-fifty a month as the sales program took off.

Q. When you say "they," would you identify the person with whom you discussed this matter?

A. Tom Fadale.

Q. And at any time did you and Mr. Fadale talk about the contingency of reducing that monthly release schedule?

A. No, sir.

Q. Was there ever any hint or indication at any time that at a given quarter the whole deal could be canceled?

A. No, sir.

CROSS EXAMINATION OF THOMAS FADALE OF PENNCO, INC.

Q. My question is this: Did you and Mr. Haas at any time discuss the idea that you could terminate this contract and not buy seventy-five-hundred units?

A. [by Fadale]: No, sir.

Q. Then you agree with me that what was contemplated here was that [Leslie] would supply seventy-five-hundred in the—in the monthly projections and you would ultimately buy seventy-five hundred.

A. No, sir, I don't agree with you on that.

Q. You don't agree?

A. No.

Q. Well, I thought a moment ago you said that you were obligated to buy the seventy-five-hundred. Did you talk about buying fewer than that and terminating?

A. We did not discuss buying fewer, but on the bottom of the purchase order we did put the statement that we could review quarterly, which meant that we could increase our production—or his production or decrease his production.

Q. Mr. Fadale, I'm going to ask you the question again because obviously I didn't make it clear. I'm going to make it very simple. Recognizing you could increase or decrease by a quarterly review the monthly deliveries, recognizing that, did you ever with Mr. Haas discuss the idea that you could walk in and say stop, we are not going to buy the full seventy-five-hundred?

A. No.

Q. Now, when that matter—When it came time for a purchase order to be given to L & W, this matter never even came up, did it?

A. No, sir.

Q. It was never even discussed between you and Mr. Leslie.

A. No.

Q. The only discussions of rescheduling were with Mr. Haas at Iroquois and neither with Mr. Haas nor indeed with Mr. Leslie was there any suggestion that you could buy fewer than seventy-five-hundred units. Do you agree with me?

A. Yes.

---

1. Was Pennco right that it could cancel?

2. Is the interpretation question here a question of law for the court or fact for the jury? Consider Restatement (Second) of Contracts § 212(2):

> A question of interpretation of an integrated agreement is to be determined by the trier of fact if it depends on the credibility of extrinsic evidence or on a choice among reasonable inferences to be drawn from extrinsic evidence. Otherwise a question of interpretation of an integrated agreement is to be determined as a question of law.

TURNER HOLDINGS, INC. v. HOWARD MILLER CLOCK CO.

United States District Court, Western District of Michigan, 1987.
657 F.Supp. 1370.

OPINION

HILLMAN, CHIEF JUDGE.

Plaintiff, Turner Holdings, Inc. ("THI"), a New York investment banking company, entered into a "letter" agreement with defendant Howard Miller Clock Company ("HMCC"), a Michigan furniture manufacturing company, whereby THI agreed that it would "endeavor to locate appropriate candidates for acquisition and to advise you as to the best way to proceed towards one or more completed transactions." * * *

Plaintiff now seeks to recover $177,000, which it alleges is due as a success fee under the contract as a result of defendant's acquisition of Hekman Furniture Company, a company which plaintiff claims was "under consideration" during the term of the contract. Plaintiff also seeks $968.44 to cover reimbursable expenses which it incurred during the term of the contract.

* * *

Two issues are in dispute. The first is whether the suit is barred by the operation of the Michigan Real Estate Brokers Act, M.C.L. § 339.2501, et seq., (hereinafter "The Act"). The second involves the interpretation of a portion of the contract which provides that HMCC "will continue to be obligated to THI for 'success fees' for a period of two years beyond the termination date [of the contract] for any company which has been under consideration." The controversy centers around the meaning of the term "under consideration," and whether Hekman Furniture Company, a company which HMCC purchased within two years of the termination of the contract, was "under consideration" during the term of the contract. * * *

* * *

Webb Turner, Jack Miller, and Philip Miller, Jack Miller's brother and vice-president of marketing for HMCC, first met in High Point, North Carolina on April 12, 1981. They met again on August 27, 1981 in Zeeland, Michigan. During these meetings and in several intervening telephone conversations, the Millers and Turner discussed the types of acquisitions which HMCC was interested in making and Turner's qualifications for assisting them in attaining their goals.

On August 31, 1981, Turner sent Miller a draft letter which embodied the terms of engagement discussed during the prior meetings and telephone conversations. The contract was executed by HMCC on November 3, 1981. Apparently, the contract was never reviewed by counsel for HMCC. Nor did the parties have any specific discussion about when a company was to be deemed "under consideration."

The contract provided, in relevant part, that HMCC would retain THI in connection with HMCC's "acquisition program" as its "exclusive agent" to "locate appropriate candidates for acquisition and to advise [HMCC] as to the best way to proceed." In consideration for its services, HMCC agreed to pay THI its expenses and a "success fee" "upon the consummation of any acquisition or investment in the furniture manufacturing field." The fee was to be calculated using the "Lehman Formula": five percent of the first million dollars of the purchase price, plus four percent of the second million, three percent of the third million, two percent of the fourth million, and one percent of the remainder of the purchase price. This fee arrangement is customary in the investment banking industry. This fee was to be the sole compensation received by THI for its work under the contract and was not to be paid if HMCC did not acquire a company which had been "under consideration" during the pendency of the contract. The contract expressly stated that "no distinction would be made, in determining THI's right to its fee, between companies introduced by HMCC and those introduced by THI."

The contract further provided that THI's duties would include "identify[ing] all public companies, divisions of public companies, as well as all private companies which * * * meet [HMCC's] acquisition criteria" and "contacting these companies with a view towards obtaining the requisite financial and operating information for comparative analysis." It went on to discuss THI's role in the later phases of HMCC's broad based acquisition program. Over an engagement period of several years, HMCC hoped that THI would "develop appropriate strategy for the follow up on acquisitions."

The contract included a tentative time frame for the completion of HMCC's first acquisition. Within three months of execution the parties hoped to select four to ten prime targets and, "with reasonable fortune" and "assuming" the issue of price was successfully dealt with, a first closing was envisioned two to three months thereafter.

HMCC's retention of THI was subject to cancellation at any time upon thirty day written notice by either party. HMCC remained obligated to pay THI a fee for a period of two years beyond the termination day. Such post-termination clauses are standard for contracts of this type and are necessary to protect a party in the position of THI, where its sole compensation was contingent and the client had the right to terminate at will. HMCC's post-termination obligation applied only to the acquisition of those companies which had been "under consideration" during the term of the contract.

Following the execution of the contract, the parties arranged a meeting to "zero in on target companies."

[Eventually, Turner made various studies and contacts, including ones focusing on Hekman Furniture Company in Grand Rapids, Michigan. Turner was told Hekman was not presently for sale. By December 1, 1982 no acquisition or contract therefor had been made.]

* * *

As they anticipated no acquisitions in the immediate future, the contract between THI and HMCC was terminated, by mutual assent, on December 1, 1982. It is clear that Jack Miller was frustrated by the lack of progress in acquiring a company. The parties, of course, knew a commission would be due Turner on any HMCC acquisition during the next two years if it had been "under consideration" while the contract was in force. In the letter of termination from Jack Miller to Turner, in an apparent effort to avoid any misunderstanding, two companies were listed as being "under consideration": Jasper Cabinet Company and Kittinger Company. Jack Miller testified that he listed Jasper because it was for sale; HMCC had received four years of financial data on it; he had visited the plant and had worked out a purchase price for it. Kittinger was listed because it was for sale by General Mills; there had been talk of joining forces with Turner to buy it; and, there was an understanding that Turner would continue to "work on it." In the December 1 letter HMCC also requested a bill for THI's out-of-pocket expenses.

Turner did not respond immediately to Miller's letter. He did, however, continue to work on Kittinger and several other companies for HMCC. Among them was Hekman. HMCC also began to cultivate contacts at Hekman. In February of 1983, Beatrice announced that it intended to sell Hekman. In early July, Salomon Brothers, a New York investment banking firm hired by Beatrice to handle the sale, forwarded information on Beatrice to companies and persons who might be interested in bidding on Hekman. On July 14, Turner forwarded the information he received to HMCC. On the previous day, however, HMCC received the same information directly from Salomon Brothers, and on July 22, returned the information which had been forwarded by THI.

In a letter to Jack Miller dated May 5, 1983, Turner listed Hekman among 84 other companies which he believed were "under consideration" during the pendency of the THI–HMCC contract. He also included the list of his outstanding expenses requested in HMCC's December 1, 1982 letter. On

July 27 Turner sent another letter stating his belief that THI would be entitled to a "success fee" if HMCC were to acquire Hekman. Jack Miller responded to Turner's July 27 letter on August 3. He sent a copy of a letter dated May 20, which THI claims it never received. The May 20 letter contained a revised listing of eight companies which Miller was willing to accept as being "under consideration." Hekman was not on the list. Both Turner and HMCC eventually bid on Hekman. HMCC was successful and, in the fall of 1983, purchased Hekman for $7.7 million. No "success fee" was ever paid to Turner.

At trial, Turner testified that he was "flabbergasted" by Jack Miller's suggestion on December 1 that only two companies were "under consideration" during the term of the contract. He also testified that he did not immediately express his anger because he and Miller were still working together on HMCC's acquisition program. Turner also testified that he bid on Hekman in order to "protect his investment."

* * *

What remains is for the court to decide whether HMCC owes THI a "success fee" because Hekman was "under consideration" during the term of their contract. The first task is to ascertain the meaning of the phrase "under consideration" within the context of the THI–HMCC contract. As a general proposition language in a contract is interpreted according to its ordinary meaning. * * * Where the meaning of the language of the contract is plain and unambiguous the terms of the contract and the intent of the parties will be interpreted as being consistent with that language. * * *

However, "[t]he cardinal rule in the interpretation of contracts is to ascertain the intention of the parties. To this rule all others are subordinate." *McIntosh v. Groomes,* 227 Mich. 215, 218, 198 N.W. 954, 955 (1924). "Courts are governed by what the parties said and did, and not merely by their unexpressed subjective intent." *Fletcher v. Board of Education,* 323 Mich. 343, 348, 35 N.W.2d 177, 180 (1948). Although subordinate, it is still important that "a contract be construed as a whole; that all its parts are * * * harmonized so far as reasonably possible." *Associated Truck Lines v. Baer,* 346 Mich. 106, 110, 77 N.W.2d 384, 386 (1956) (citation omitted).

Defendant argues that the term "under consideration," as used in its contract with THI, is ambiguous. The term "ambiguous" is itself ambiguous in that Michigan law recognizes two types of ambiguity: patent and latent.

A patent ambiguity is one apparent upon the face of the instrument, arising by reason of inconsistency, obscurity or an inherent uncertainty of the language adopted, such that the effect of the words in the connection used is either to convey no definite meaning or a double one.

Zilwaukee Township v. Saginaw Bay City Railway Co., 213 Mich. 61, 69, 181 N.W. 37, 39–40 (1921). A latent ambiguity exists "where the language employed is clear and intelligible and suggests but a single meaning, but some extrinsic fact or extraneous evidence creates a necessity for interpretation or a choice among two or more possible meanings." *McCarty v. Mercury Metalcraft Co.,* 372 Mich. 567, 575, 127 N.W.2d 340, 344 (1964), *cert den sub nom Mercury Metalcraft Co. v. McCarty,* 380 U.S. 952, 85 S.Ct. 1085, 13 L.Ed.2d 969 (1965).

there may be latent ambiguity

Clearly no patent ambiguity exists in the phrase "under consideration" as it is used in the THI–HMCC contract. There may, however, be a latent ambiguity. At trial plaintiff objected to the defendant's attempt to elicit information from Jack Miller on the purpose of the termination clause in the contract, and implicitly on the meaning of the phrase "under consideration." To determine the existence of a latent ambiguity the court must first examine extrinsic evidence to determine if in fact such evidence supports the contention that the language of the contract, under the particular circumstances of its formation, is susceptible to more than one interpretation. * * * If a latent ambiguity is detected, the court must again examine the extrinsic evidence to ascertain the meaning of the language contained in the contract. * * *

Miller testified that, in his mind, four conditions had to be met for him to believe that a company was "under consideration" and to trigger HMCC's obligation to compensate THI for its services. They were that:

4 conditions Miller thought had to be present for "UC"

1. the company must have been for sale during the term of the contract;

2. financial information must have been available about the company;

3. contact must have been established with officials of the target company; and

4. the target company must have been the subject of negotiation or reflection in terms of an appropriate purchase price.

This definition of "under consideration" is clearly narrower than the commonly understood meaning. Defendant also claimed that when the parties entered into the contract it was their intent that the purchase of another corporation was to occur "rapidly." The engagement letter from THI to HMCC does, in fact, mention some time periods within which it was "hoped" that an acquisition could be completed, but the contract does not contain anything which resembles a "time is of the essence" provision.

From this evidence, and based on several Michigan cases finding various words and phrases ambiguous * * * defendant asks this court to find that in this contract the phrase "under consideration" has a meaning different than its usual and ordinary meaning. Defendant also argues that the phrase could not possibly have had its ordinary meaning in light of the purpose of the contract, which defendant claims was a rapid acquisition of a furniture company. *∆S thoughts on what the purpose of the K was.*

As noted above, the role of the court is to ascertain, and effectuate the intent of the parties at the time of contract formation. It is the expressed, and not secret intent which is operative. Where the language of the contract is clear on its face, the court looks to it to ascertain the parties' intent. Where, as here, a party claims that an ambiguity exists in the language the court then looks to see if there is extrinsic evidence which supports this contention. However, one party's uncommunicated understanding concerning the specialized meaning of contract language is not binding on the other party. *Fletcher,* 323 Mich. at 348, 35 N.W.2d at 180. Therefore, Jack Miller's undisclosed and uncommunicated belief about what the words "under consideration" meant in the contract is not sufficient to establish the existence of a latent ambiguity.

what Ct needs to do.

Holding

No latent ambiguity

Ct says   phrase is not ambiguous

Ch. 6 SUBSTANTIVE CONTENT 707

Nor am I convinced by the evidence that the parties intended to narrow the definition of "under consideration" because of HMCC's sense of urgency. I therefore find that the phrase is not ambiguous. As used in the contract between HMCC and THI the phrase "under consideration" has its ordinary meaning. *The Random House Dictionary of the English Language* (1967) defines consideration as "the act of considering; careful thought; meditation; deliberation." *Webster's Third New International Dictionary* (1966) defines consideration as meaning "observation, contemplation." *Roget's International Thesaurus* lists, as synonymous with the phrase "under consideration": "in question," "at issue," "on the agenda," "under investigation".

The evidence presented at trial clearly supports a finding that Hekman was "under consideration" during the term of the contract. According to their contract, THI's role in this relationship was to "locate appropriate candidates for acquisition, and to advise [HMCC] as to the best way to proceed towards one or more acquisitions." As the facts set forth above reflect, the acquisition of Hekman was the subject of much thought and deliberation by Miller and Turner. At HMCC's request, THI expended time, energy and expense ascertaining if Hekman was a desirable acquisition; whether it could be bought or "shaken loose" and whether it would come up for sale in the not too distant future. Hekman was at or near the top of HMCC's list of desirable acquisitions during the entire term of the contract. Its availability was frequently discussed and Turner was urged to pursue it. Hekman's name appeared frequently on memos and notes immediately following conferences between Miller and Turner. Hekman was clearly "under consideration" in the common, ordinary usage and understanding of these words. If Miller wanted to say something different, or give these words some technical, special meaning he could easily have so provided in the contract. Having failed to do so, he can not now ask the court to rewrite the contract for HMCC. Consequently, I find THI's efforts on behalf of HMCC sufficient to trigger HMCC's obligation under the termination clause of the contract to pay THI's fee.

Judgment shall be entered in favor of Turner Holdings, Inc. and against defendant Howard Miller Clock Company in the amount of $177,000, plus $968.44, representing uncontested expenses, plus interest from November 18, 1983. Costs to be taxed.

SUTTER INSURANCE CO. v. APPLIED SYSTEMS, INC., 393 F.3d 722 (7th Cir. 2004) "Commercial reasonableness is a useful guide to the interpretation of an ambiguous contract. * * * 'Generally the contract price is roughly equivalent to the value of the contractual performance * * *. An enormous disparity between price and value is a clue that something may be amiss.' *PMC, Inc. v. Sherwin–Williams Co.,* 151 F.3d 610, 615 (7th Cir.1998) * * *. Or as the Illinois Appellate Court put it in the *NutraSweet* case, 'where a contract is susceptible to one of two constructions, one of which makes it fair, customary, and such as prudent men would naturally execute, while the other makes it inequitable, unusual, or such as reasonable men would not be likely to enter into, the interpretation which makes a rational and probable agreement must be preferred.' 635 N.E.2d at 445."

UNIFORM COMMERCIAL CODE § 1–203.

"Agreement" means the bargain of the parties in fact as found in their language or by implication from other circumstances including course of dealing or usage of trade or course of performance * * *.

UNIFORM COMMERCIAL CODE § 2–208.
Course of Performance or Practical Construction

(1) Where the contract for sale involves repeated occasions for performance by either party with knowledge of the nature of the performance and opportunity for objection to it by the other, any course of performance accepted or acquiesced in without objection shall be relevant to determine the meaning of the agreement.

(2) The express terms of the agreement and any such course of performance, as well as any course of dealing and usage of trade, shall be construed whenever reasonable as consistent with each other; but when such construction is unreasonable, express terms shall control course of performance and course of performance shall control both course of dealing and usage of trade (Section 1–205).

(3) Subject to the provisions of the next section on modification and waiver, such course of performance shall be relevant to show a waiver or modification of any term inconsistent with such course of performance.

UNIFORM COMMERCIAL CODE § 1–205.
Course of Dealing and Usage of Trade

(1) A course of dealing is a sequence of previous conduct between the parties to a particular transaction which is fairly to be regarded as establishing a common basis of understanding for interpreting their expressions and other conduct.

(2) A usage of trade is any practice or method of dealing having such regularity of observance in a place, vocation or trade as to justify an expectation that it will be observed with respect to the transaction in question. The existence and scope of such a usage are to be proved as facts. If it is established that such a usage is embodied in a written trade code or similar writing the interpretation of the writing is for the court.

(3) A course of dealing between parties and any usage of trade in the vocation or trade in which they are engaged or of which they are or should be aware give particular meaning to and supplement or qualify terms of an agreement.

(4) The express terms of an agreement and an applicable course of dealing or usage of trade shall be construed wherever reasonable as consistent with each other; but when such construction is unreasonable express terms control both course of dealing and usage of trade and course of dealing controls usage of trade.

(5) An applicable usage of trade in the place where any part of performance is to occur shall be used in interpreting the agreement as to that part of the performance.

NANAKULI PAVING AND ROCK
CO. v. SHELL OIL CO., INC.

United States Court of Appeals, Ninth Circuit, 1981.
664 F.2d 772.

HOFFMAN, DISTRICT JUDGE:

Appellant Nanakuli Paving and Rock Company (Nanakuli) initially filed this breach of contract action against appellee Shell Oil Company (Shell) in Hawaiian State Court in February, 1976.[1] Nanakuli, the second largest asphaltic paving contractor in Hawaii, had bought all its asphalt requirements from 1963 to 1974 from Shell under two long-term supply contracts; its suit charged Shell with breach of the later 1969 contract. The jury returned a verdict of $220,800 for Nanakuli on its first claim, which is that Shell breached the 1969 contract in January, 1974, by failing to price protect Nanakuli on 7200 tons of asphalt at the time Shell raised the price for asphalt from $44 to $76. Nanakuli's theory is that price-protection, as a usage of the asphaltic paving trade in Hawaii, was incorporated into the 1969 agreement between the parties, as demonstrated by the routine use of price protection by suppliers to that trade, and reinforced by the way in which Shell actually performed the 1969 contract up until 1974. Price protection, appellant claims, required that Shell hold the price on the tonnage Nanakuli had already committed because Nanakuli had incorporated that price into bids put out to or contracts awarded by general contractors and government agencies. The District Judge set aside the verdict and granted Shell's motion for judgment n.o.v., which decision we vacate. We reinstate the jury verdict because we find that, viewing the evidence as a whole, there was substantial evidence to support a finding by reasonable jurors that Shell breached its contract by failing to provide protection for Nanakuli in 1974. * * *

Nanakuli * * * argues [that] all material suppliers to the asphaltic paving trade in Hawaii followed the trade usage of price protection and thus it should be assumed, under the U.C.C., that the parties intended to incorporate price protection into their 1969 agreement. This is so, Nanakuli continues, even though the written contract provided for price to be "Shell's Posted Price at time of delivery," F.O.B. Honolulu. Its proof of a usage that was incorporated into the contract is reinforced by evidence of the commercial context, which under the U.C.C. should form the background for viewing a particular contract. The full agreement must be examined in light of the close, almost symbiotic relations between Shell and Nanakuli on the island of Oahu, whereby the expansion of Shell on the island was intimately connected to the business growth of Nanakuli. The U.C.C. looks to the actual performance of a contract as the best indication of what the parties intended those terms to mean. Nanakuli points out that Shell had price protected it on the two occasions of price increases under the 1969 contract other than the 1974 increase. In 1970 and 1971 Shell extended the old price for four and three months, respectively, after an announced increase. This was done, in the

---

1. Shell removed the suit to United States   March 2 of that year.
District Court for the District of Hawaii on

words of Shell's agent in Hawaii, in order to permit Nanakuli's to "chew up" tonnage already committed at Shell's old price.[2]

* * *

Shell presents three arguments for upholding the judgment n.o.v. or, on cross appeal, urging that the District Judge erred in admitting certain evidence. First, it says, the District Court should not have denied Shell's motion *in limine* to define trade, for purposes of trade usage evidence, as the sale and purchase of asphalt in Hawaii, rather than expanding the definition of trade to include other suppliers of materials to the asphaltic paving trade. Asphalt, its argument runs, was the subject matter of the disputed contract and the only product Shell supplied to the asphaltic paving trade. Shell protests that the judge, by expanding the definition of trade to include the other major suppliers to the asphaltic paving trade, allowed the admission of highly prejudicial evidence of routine price protection by all suppliers of aggregate. Asphaltic concrete paving is formed by mixing paving asphalt with crushed rock, or aggregate, in a "hot-mix" plant and then pouring the mixture onto the surface to be paved. Shell's second complaint is that the two prior occasions on which it price protected Nanakuli, although representing the only other instances of price increases under the 1969 contract, constituted mere waivers of the contract's price term, not a course of performance of the contract. A course of performance of the contract, in contrast to a waiver, demonstrates how the parties understand the terms of their agreement. Shell cites two U.C.C. Comments in support of that argument: (1) that, when the meaning of acts is ambiguous, the preference is for the waiver interpretation, and (2) that one act alone does not constitute a relevant course of performance. Shell's final argument is that, even assuming its prior price protection constituted a course of performance and that the broad trade definition was correct and evidence of trade usages by aggregate suppliers was admissible, price protection could not be construed as reasonably consistent with the express price term in the contract, in which case the Code provides that the express term controls.

We hold that the judge did not abuse his discretion in defining the applicable trade, for purposes of trade usages, as the asphaltic paving trade in Hawaii, rather than the purchase and sale of asphalt alone. * * * Additionally, we hold that, under the facts of this case, a jury could reasonably have found that Shell's acts on two occasions to price protect Nanakuli were not ambiguous and therefore indicated Shell's understanding of the terms of the agreement with Nanakuli rather than being a waiver by Shell of those terms.

Lastly we hold that, although the express price terms of Shell's posted price of delivery may seem, at first glance, inconsistent with a trade usage of price protection at time of increases in price, a closer reading shows that the jury could have reasonably construed price protection as consistent with the express term. * * *

[The court first discussed the negotiations prior to the 1969 contract, and, specifically, testimony of Nanakuli's president and vice president that they

2. Price protection was practiced in the asphaltic paving trade by either extending the old price for a period of time after a new one went into effect or charging the old price for a specified tonnage, which represented work committed at the old price. In addition, several months' advance notice was given of price increases.

"understood" they would receive price protection despite the absence of a written provision to that effect. This testimony was not "flatly contradicted" by Shell.]

TRADE USAGE BEFORE AND AFTER 1969

The key to price protection being so prevalent in 1969 that both parties would intend to incorporate it into their contract is found in one reality of the Oahu asphaltic paving market: the largest paving contracts were let by government agencies and none of the three levels of government—local, state, or federal—allowed escalation clauses for paving materials. If a paver bid at one price and another went into effect before the award was made, the paving company would lose a great deal of money, since it could not pass on increases to any government agency or to most general contractors. Extensive evidence was presented that, as a consequence, aggregate suppliers routinely price protected paving contractors in the 1960's and 1970's, as did the largest asphaltic supplier in Oahu, Chevron. Nanakuli presented documentary evidence of routine price protection by aggregate suppliers as well as two witnesses: Grosjean, Vice–President for Marketing of Ameron H.C. & D., and Nihei, Division Manager of Lone Star Industries for Pacific Cement and Aggregate (P.C. & A.). Both testified that price protection to their knowledge had always been practiced: at H.C. & D. for many years prior to Grosjean's arrival in 1962 and at P.C. & A. routinely since Nihei's arrival in 1960. Such protection consisted of advance notices of increases, coupled with charging the old price for work committed at that price or for enough time to order the tonnage committed. The smallness of the Oahu market led to complete trust among suppliers and pavers. H.C. & D. did not demand that Nanakuli or other pavers issue purchase orders or sign contracts for aggregate before incorporating its aggregate prices into bids. Nanakuli would merely give H.C. & D. a list of projects it had bid at the time H.C. & D. raised its prices, without documentation. "Their word and letter is good enough for us," Grosjean testified. Nihei said P.C. & A. at the time of price increases would get a list of either particular projects bid by a paver or simply total tonnage bid at the old price. "We take either one. We take their word for it." None of the aggregate companies had a contract with Nanakuli expressly stating price protection would be given; Nanakuli's contract with P.C. & A. merely set out that P.C. & A. would not charge Nanakuli more than it charged its other customers.

* * *

SHELL'S COURSE OF PERFORMANCE OF THE 1969 CONTRACT

The Code considers actual performance of a contract as the most relevant evidence of how the parties interpreted the terms of that contract. In 1970 and 1971, the only points at which Shell raised prices between 1969 and 1974, it price protected Nanakuli by holding its old price for four and three months, respectively, after announcing a price increase. In the late summer of 1970, Shell had announced a price increase from $35 to $40 a ton effective September 1, 1970. When Nanakuli protested to Bohner [Shell's Hawaiian representative] that it should be price protected on work already committed, Blee [a "top Shell asphalt official"] wrote Bohner an in-house memo that, if Bohner could not "convince" Nanakuli to go along with the price increase on

September 1, he should try to "bargain" to get Nanakuli to accept the price raise by at least the first of the year, which was what was finally agreed upon. During that four-month period, Nanakuli bought 3,300 tons. Shell announced a second increase in October, 1970, from $40 to $42 effective December 31st. Before that increase went into effect, on November 25 Shell increased the raise to $4, making the price $44 as of the first of the year. Shell again agreed to price protect Nanakuli by holding the price at $40, which had been the official price since September 1, for three months from January to March, 1971. Shell did not actually raise prices again until January, 1974, but at several points it believed that increases would be necessary and gave several months' advance notice of those possible increases. Those actions were in accord with Shell's own policy, as professed by Bohner, and that of other asphalt and aggregate suppliers: to give at least several months' advance notice of price increases. On January 14, 1971, Shell wrote its asphalt customers that the maximum 1971 increase would be to $46. On July 9, 1971, another letter promised the price would not go over $50 in 1972. In addition, Bohner volunteered on direct the information that Shell price protected Nanakuli on the only two occasions of price increases after 1974 by giving 6 months' advance notice in 1977 and 3 or 4 months' advance notice in 1978, a practice he described as "in effect carryover pricing," his term for price protection. By its actions, Bohner testified, Shell allowed Nanakuli time to make arrangements to buy up tonnage committed at the old price, that is, to "chew up" tonnage bid or contracted. Shell apparently offered this testimony to impress the jury with its subsequent good faith toward Nanakuli. In fact, it also may have reinforced the impression of the universality of price protection in the asphaltic paving trade on Oahu and, by showing Shell's adherence to that practice on every relevant occasion except 1974, have highlighted for the jury what was the commercially reasonable standard of fair dealing in effect on Oahu in 1974.

[The court next referred to "structural changes" at Shell in 1973, which left Shell with no one with knowledge about the "peculiarities of the Hawaiian market or about Shell's long-time relations with Nanakuli or its 1969 agreement, beyond the printed contract."]

We conclude that the decision to deny Nanakuli price protection was made by new Houston management without a full understanding of Shell's 1969 agreement with Nanakuli or any knowledge of its past pricing practices toward Nanakuli. If Shell did commit itself in 1969 to price protect Nanakuli, the Shell officials who made the decisions affecting Nanakuli in 1974 knew nothing about that commitment. Nor did they make any effective effort to find out. They acted instead solely in reliance on the 1969 contract's express price term, devoid of the commercial context that the Code says is necessary to an understanding of the meaning of the written word. Whatever the legal enforceability of Nanakuli's right, Nanakuli officials seem to have acted in good faith reliance on its right, as they understood it, to price protection and rightfully felt betrayed by Shell's failure to act with any understanding of its past practices toward Nanakuli.

SCOPE OF TRADE USAGE

The validity of the jury verdict in this case depends on four legal questions. First, how broad was the trade to whose usages Shell was bound under its 1969 agreement with Nanakuli: did it extend to the Hawaiian asphaltic paving trade or was it limited merely to the purchase and sale of asphalt, which would only include evidence of practices by Shell and Chevron? Second, were the two instances of price protection of Nanakuli by Shell in 1970 and 1971 waivers of the 1969 contract as a matter of law or was the jury entitled to find that they constituted a course of performance of the contract? Third, could the jury have construed an express contract term of Shell's posted price at delivery as reasonably consistent with a trade usage and Shell's course of performance of the 1969 contract of price protection, which consisted of charging the old price at times of price increases, either for a period of time or for specific tonnage committed at a fixed price in non-escalating contracts? [The fourth issue involving commercial reasonableness is omitted.]

* * *

The Code defines usage of trade as "any practice or method of dealing having such regularity of observance in a *place, vocation or trade* as to justify an expectation that it will be observed with respect to the transaction in question." *Id.* [U.C.C. §] 1–205(2) (emphasis supplied). We understand the use of the word "or" to mean that parties can be bound by a usage common to the *place* they are in business, even if it is not the usage of their particular vocation or trade. That reading is borne out by the repetition of the disjunctive "or" in subsection 3, which provides that usages "in the vocation or trade in which they are engaged *or* of which they are or should be aware give particular meaning to and supplement or qualify terms of an agreement." *Id.* [U.C.C. §] 1–205(3). The drafters' Comments say that trade usage is to be used to reach the " * * * commercial meaning of the agreement * * * " by interpreting the language "as meaning what it may fairly be expected to mean to parties involved in the particular transaction *in a given locality or* in a given *vocation or trade.*" *Id.,* Comment 4 (emphasis supplied). The inference of the two subsections and the Comment, read together, is that a usage need not necessarily be one practiced by members of the party's own trade or vocation to be binding if it is so commonly practiced in a locality that a party should be aware of it. Subsection 5 also shows the importance of the place where the usage is practiced: "An applicable usage of trade in the place where any part of performance is to occur shall be used in interpreting the agreement as to that part of the performance." The validity of this interpretation is additionally demonstrated by the Comment of the drafters: "Subsection (3), giving the prescribed effect to usages of which the parties 'are or should be aware', reinforces the provision of subsection (2) requiring not universality but only the described 'regularity of observance' of the practice or method. This subsection also reinforces the point of subsection (2) that such usages may be either *general to trade or particular to a special branch of trade.*" *Id.,* Comment 7 (emphasis supplied). This language indicates that Shell would be bound not only by usages of sellers of asphalt but by more general usages on Oahu, as long as those usages were so regular in their observance that Shell should have been aware of them. This reading of the Code, in our opinion, achieves an equitable result. A party is always held to conduct generally observed by members of his chosen trade because the other party is justified in so assuming unless he indicates otherwise. He is held to more general business practices to the extent of his actual knowledge of those practices or to the degree his ignorance of those practices is not excusable: they were so generally practiced he should have been aware of them.

No U.C.C. cases have been found on this point, but the court's reading of the Code language is similar to that of two of the best-known commentators on the U.C.C.:

> Under pre-Code law, a trade usage was not operative against a party who *was not a member of the trade unless* he actually knew of it or *the other party* could reasonably believe he knew of it.

J. White & R. Summers, *Uniform Commercial Code,* § 12–6 at 371 (1972) (emphasis supplied) (citing 3 A. Corbin, *Corbin on Contracts* § 557 at 248 (1960)). * * * White and Summers add (emphasis supplied):

> This view has been carried forward by 1–205(3). * * * [U]sage of the trade is only binding on *members of the trade* involved *or persons* who know or *should know about it.* Persons who should be aware of the trade usage doubtless *include those who regularly deal with members of the relevant trade,* and also members of a second trade that commonly deals with members of a relevant trade (for example, farmers should know something of seed selling).

White & Summers, *supra,* § 12–6 at 371. Using that analogy, even if Shell did not "regularly deal" with aggregate supplies, it did deal constantly and almost exclusively on Oahu with one asphalt paver. It therefore should have been aware of the usage of Nanakuli and other asphaltic pavers to bid at fixed prices and therefore receive price protection from their materials suppliers due to the refusal by government agencies to accept escalation clauses. Therefore, we do not find the lower court abused its discretion or misread the Code as applied to the peculiar facts of this case in ruling that the applicable trade was the asphaltic paving trade in Hawaii. An asphalt seller should be held to the usages of trade in general as well as those of asphalt sellers and common usages of those to whom they sell. Certainly, under the unusual facts of this case it was not unreasonable for the judge to extend trade usages to include practices of other material suppliers toward Shell's primary and perhaps only customer on Oahu. He did exclude, on Shell's motion *in limine,* evidence of cement suppliers. He only held Shell to routine practices in Hawaii by the suppliers of the two major ingredients of asphaltic paving, that is, asphalt and aggregate. Those usages were only practiced towards two major pavers. It was not unreasonable to expect Shell to be knowledgeable about so small a market. In so ruling, the judge undoubtedly took into account Shell's half-million dollar investment in Oahu strictly because of a long-term commitment by Nanakuli, its actions as partner in promoting Nanakuli's expansion on Oahu, and the fact that its sales on Oahu were almost exclusively to Nanakuli for use in asphaltic paving. The wisdom of the pre-trial ruling was demonstrated by evidence at trial that Shell's agent in Hawaii stayed in close contact with Nanakuli and was knowledgeable about both the asphaltic paving market in general and Nanakuli's bidding procedures and economics in particular.

Shell argued not only that the definition of trade was too broad, but also that the practice itself was not sufficiently regular to reach the level of a usage and that Nanakuli failed to show with enough precision how the usage was carried out in order for a jury to calculate damages. The extent of a usage is ultimately a jury question. The Code provides, "The existence and scope of such a usage are to be proved as facts." [U.C.C. §] 1–205(2). The practice must have "such regularity of observance . . . as to justify an expectation that it will be observed. . . ." *Id.* The Comment explains:

> The ancient English tests for "custom" are abandoned in this connection. Therefore, it is not required that a usage of trade be "ancient or immemorial," "universal" or the like. * * * [F]ull recognition is thus available for new usages and for usages currently observed by the great majority of decent dealers, even though dissidents ready to cut corners do not agree.

Id., Comment 5. The Comment's demand that "not universality but only the described 'regularity of observance' " is required reinforces the provision only giving "effect to usages of which the parties 'are or should be aware'. * * * " *Id.*, Comment 7. A "regularly observed" practice of protection, of which Shell "should have been aware," was enough to constitute a usage that Nanakuli had reason to believe was incorporated into the agreement.

Nanakuli went beyond proof of a regular observance. It proved and offered to prove that price protection was probably a universal practice by suppliers to the asphaltic paving trade in 1969. It had been practiced by H.C. & D. since at least 1962, by P.C. & A. since well before 1960, and by Chevron routinely for years, with the last specific instance before the contract being March, 1969, as shown by documentary evidence. The only usage evidence missing was the behavior by Shell, the only other asphalt supplier in Hawaii, prior to 1969. That was because its only major customer was Nanakuli and the judge ruled prior course of dealings between Shell and Nanakuli inadmissible. Shell did not point in rebuttal to one instance of failure to price protect by any supplier to an asphalt paver in Hawaii before its own 1974 refusal to price protect Nanakuli. Thus, there clearly was enough proof for a jury to find that the practice of price protection in the asphaltic paving trade existed in Hawaii in 1969 and was regular enough in its observance to rise to the level of a usage that would be binding on Nanakuli and Shell.

* * *

[The court also upheld the jury's decision that Shell's two instances of price protection of Nanakuli in 1970 and 1971 were a "course of performance" under U.C.C. Section 2–208. Further, the court concluded that the jury's finding in favor of Nanakuli was consistent with U.C.C. Section 1–205(4), which provides that express terms "control" usage of trade. In the court's view, the price protection trade usage did not completely negate the express term "Shell's Posted Price at time of delivery," but formed an exception to it that the jury could find was "incorporated into the 1969 agreement."]

* * * [W]e reverse the judgment of the District Court and reinstate the jury verdict for Nanakuli in the amount of $220,800, plus interest according to law.

REVERSED AND REMANDED WITH DIRECTIONS TO ENTER FINAL JUDGMENT.

KENNEDY, CIRCUIT JUDGE, concurring specially:

The case involves specific pricing practices, not an allegation of unfair dealing generally. Our opinion should not be interpreted to permit juries to import price protection or a similarly specific contract term from a concept of good faith that is not based on well-established custom and usage or other objective standards of which the parties had clear notice. Here, evidence of custom and usage regarding price protection in the asphaltic paving trade was not contradicted in major respects, and the jury could find that the parties knew or should have known of the practice at the time of making the contract. In my view, these are necessary predicates for either theory of the case, namely, interpretation of the contract based on the course of its performance or a finding that good faith required the seller to hold the price. With these observations, I concur.

HURST v. W.J. LAKE & CO., 141 Or. 306, 16 P.2d 627 (1932). "The flexibility of or multiplicity in the meaning of words is the principal source of difficulty in the interpretation of language. Words are the conduits by which thoughts are communicated, yet scarcely any of them have such a fixed and single meaning that they are incapable of denoting more than one thought. In addition to the multiplicity in meaning of words set forth in the dictionaries, there are the meanings imparted to them by trade customs, local uses, dialects, telegraphic codes, etc. One meaning crowds a word full of significance, while another almost empties the utterance of any import. The various groups above indicated are constantly amplifying our language; in fact, they are developing what may be called languages of their own. Thus one is justified in saying that the language of the dictionaries is not the only language spoken in America. For instance, the word "thousand" as commonly used has a very specific meaning; it denotes ten hundreds or fifty scores, but the language of the various trades and localities has assigned to it meanings quite different from that just mentioned. Thus in the bricklaying trade a contract which fixes the bricklayer's compensation at "$5.25 a thousand" does not contemplate that he need lay actually 1,000 bricks in order to earn $5.25, but that he should build a wall of a certain size. Brunold v. Glasser, 25 Misc. 285, 53 N.Y.S. 1021; Walker v. Syms, 118 Mich. 183, 76 N.W. 320. In the lumber industry a contract requiring the delivery of 4,000 shingles will be fulfilled by the delivery of only 2,500 when it appears that by trade custom two packs of a certain size are regarded as 1,000 shingles, and that hence the delivery of eight packs fulfills the contract, even though they contain only 2,500 shingles by actual count. Soutier v. Kellerman, 18 Mo. 509. * * * Numerous other instances could readily be cited showing the manner in which the meaning of words has been contracted, expanded, or otherwise altered by local usage, trade custom, dialect influence, code agreement, etc. In fact, it is no novelty to find legislative enactments preceded by glossaries or brief dictionaries defining the meaning of the words employed in the act. Technical treatises dealing with aeronautics, the radio, engineering, etc., generally contain similar glossaries defining the meaning of many of the words employed by the craft. A glance at these glossaries readily shows that the different sciences and trades, in addition to coining words of their own, appropriate common words and assign to them new meanings. Thus it must be evident that one cannot understand accurately the language of such sciences and trades without knowing the peculiar meaning attached to the words which they use. It is said that a court in construing the language of the parties must put itself into the shoes of the parties. That alone would not suffice; it must also adopt their vernacular."

GEWIRTZ, COMMENTARY ON KARL N. LLEWELLYN, WHAT PRICE CONTRACT?—AN ESSAY IN PERSPECTIVE

100 Yale L.J. 1508, 1508–10 (1991).

Sixty years after publication, Llewellyn's article still amazes with the richness of its ideas, the scale of its ambition, and the craggy grandeur of its execution.

What Price Contract?[1] is an interpretive essay about the relationship between contract law and society, investigating contract's features as a social institution rather than dissecting legal doctrine. With Llewellyn widely regarded today as the most important "legal realist," this article's protean quality continues to make it influential.

Several themes stand out, and they retain much of their radical edge:

(1) *Social Practices.* First, and most importantly, Llewellyn exhorts us to "awake to people and their doings," to the life of commercial customs and other social practices that exist "apart from law." Llewellyn's goal is partly descriptive: pointing to the diversity of bargaining relations that other scholars ignore, describing how contracting practices have adjusted to an evolving economic system. But his normative claim is central: the truest bases for sound judicial decisions are "understandings in the world of dealings" and "pressure from the facts."

(2) *System, Rule and Form.* Insisting on the primacy of social practices has other consequences. Unlike other legal realists, Llewellyn was not contemptuous of legal rules, formality, or the scholar's impulse to systematize. But he thought all systems, rules, and forms tend to become rigid, to insulate us from the rich particularity in fact situations and the ongoing changes in social practices—indispensable ingredients for rightly resolving cases. He thus underscores a perpetual tension: inescapably, life in its urgent particularity strains against and modifies ever-ossifying generalizations and forms.

(3) *Law's Place.* Emphasizing social practices also brings Llewellyn to insist that contract law plays a more marginal role than commonly assumed. In most commercial relations (for example, long-term contractual relationships), nonlegal sanctions shape behavior more than legal sanctions do. Parties continually make informal adjustments with little attention to the contract terms, and typically resolve disputes without resort to law. Law reporters, therefore, contain the rare "hospital case," not the typical commercial transaction. Thus, Llewellyn sees contract law as a backdrop to the world of bargaining and dealing, providing rarely-invoked sanctions and, perhaps more importantly, quietly strengthening an "ideology of duty" that encourages adherence to promises.

---

1. * * * The first part of the title apparently alludes to a well known anti-war play of the 1920's, *What Price Glory?,* by Maxwell Anderson and Laurence Stallings.

R. SCOTT, IS ARTICLE 2 THE BEST WE CAN DO?
52 Hastings L. J. 677, 686–688 (2001).

* * *. For me, the value of predictability suggests, quite counter-intuitively, that there are good reasons to favor acontextual modes of interpretation. In other words, true or substantive uniformity argues for a return to textualist, formal rules of interpretation. * * * Depending on your normative perspective, clear, predictable rules can as often be used as swords for consumer interests as well as shields to protect commercial interests.

One who argues for a return to acontextual modes of interpretation has to concede, and I do, that there are real costs to a return to the common law approach. Common law plain meaning interpretation ignores the commercial context except where the parties have expressly written relevant customs and usages into their contracts. Writing contracts in a formalist world becomes very much more laborious and error prone. Moreover, textualist interpretation imposes a social cost on future contracting parties because formal modes of interpretation reduce the stock of tried and true understandings, customs and usages that can be incorporated from the context and thereafter announced by courts as useful defaults for other contacting parties. Llewellyn's fundamental insight was to recognize the benefits that could potentially flow from this incorporation process. * * * [T]he theoretical possibility of those benefits should be acknowledged straightforwardly. But if we are going to evaluate Article 2 on its own terms, we must look to what courts do rather than to what Llewellyn wanted them to do. And on its own terms the incorporation process simply has not occurred. Courts don't do it.

There are several plausible reasons why that might be so. I have come to agree with David Charny's view. In his view, the incorporation process has failed because it is grounded in the belief in a mythical pre-modern age "a nostalgia for intimate local communities of shared value and custom enforced by knowledge, reputation, and ties of affectional loyalty."

Problem 6–5

On February 7, 1984, Evelyn Faquar sold the Faquar Photographic Studio of Grant County, Hampshire to Bart W. Savage III for $55,000. Grant County contains five sizeable towns: Oldham, Bestwick, Ontario, Westin, and Weiser. The studio's only source of income was photographic work for four public high schools and twelve elementary and junior high schools. Weiser, the smallest of the towns, had no public schools; Weiser children were bused to nearby Westin. However, Marion College, a two-year junior college, was located on the outer edge of Weiser.

The Faquar–Savage contract drafted by Savage's lawyer, Ed Harmore, included the following provisions:

* * *

(2) Evelyn Faquar hereby sells and conveys to Bart Weatherford Savage III her business known as Photographic Studio of Grant Co., Hampshire, together with all equipment (list appended), supplies (list appended), and goodwill.

(3) Faquar hereby leases to Savage all four rooms in the Westwood building in Oldham now occupied by said business for a term of five years at a

rental of $500 a month, Savage to have an option on a fifth (adjoining room) in said premises in case he decides to expand the business.

* * *

(5) Savage to pay $25,000 down at date of closing and $10,000 a year on July 1 (beginning this year) for three years until the total sale price of $55,000 is paid.

(6) Faquar hereby agrees not to compete with Savage for school photography work in Oldham, Bestwick, Ontario, Westin and Weiser for a period of ten years. * * *

On February 14, 1986, Evelyn Faquar photographed Marion College students for their yearbook. Savage wants to "stop this," and he wants damages as well. He retains you to represent him in this matter. You learn that Hampshire photography businesses rarely deal both with public schools and institutions of higher learning. Savage will testify that the parties intended that "schools" included colleges. The Hampshire general education act defines schools in section 1:

> The word "school" is a generic term, denoting an institution or place for instruction or education, or the collective body of instructors and pupils in any such place or institution. In its ordinary meaning, a school is a place where instruction is imparted to the young. It is an institution of a lower grade, below a college or a university; a place of primary instruction.

You also find nine definitions of "school," some of which include college, in Webster's New Collegiate Dictionary.

What further investigations, if any, would you make? What evidence would you introduce at any trial to lay a foundation for interpreting the word school and related words? What specific interpretational arguments would you make? Do you think you would prevail?

Note
The Importance of Clear Drafting

The following contract language illustrates the importance of clear drafting. It led the parties into litigation instead of performance. Do you see why? Could you have drafted more clearly?

> "In consideration of the performance by the said contractor of all of the covenants and conditions contained in this agreement and contained in the plans and specifications the owners agree to pay to the contractor an amount equal to the amount of all material furnished by the contractor and the labor furnished by the contractor together with payroll taxes and Insurance, also together with the sum total of the net amount due the subcontractors performing work or furnishing work for said construction. *The Owners also agree to pay to the contractor, in addition to the amount specified hereinabove, a fee equal to 10% of the actual cost of the said residence, said fee to be paid after completion of said residence and acceptance thereof by the Owners. It is specifically agreed by and between the parties that notwithstanding the agreement hereinabove by the owners shall not be required, under the terms of this agreement, to pay to the contractor any amount in excess of the sum of Thirty-Four Thousand, Five Hundred Dollars ($34,500.00) which is the estimated cost of construction, plus the fee provided for herein.*" (Emphasis added).

The court in Lewis v. Carnaggio, 257 S.C. 54, 183 S.E.2d 899 (1971), stated in regard to this matter:

Plaintiff contends that the foregoing language establishes the contract price as the cost of construction plus ten percent, with the cost of construction not to exceed $34,500.00. Defendant, on the other hand, construes the above provision as providing that the total cost of the building, including the ten percent fee, could not under any circumstances exceed the sum of $34,500.00.

* * *

* * * In the first sentence of the emphasized portion of paragraph 3 the parties agree that the contract price would be the cost of construction plus ten percent. The following sentence provides that, notwithstanding the previous agreement, the owners (defendants) were not required "to pay to the contractor (plaintiff) any amount in excess of the sum of thirty-four thousand, five hundred dollars ($34,500.00) which is the estimated cost of construction, plus the fee (10%) provided herein." The clause reading "which is the estimated cost of construction" clearly modifies the antecedent figure of $34,500.00 and restricts its meaning. The phrase "plus the fee provided for herein" is separated from the preceding clause by a comma, showing that it was not included in the preceding clause but was in addition thereto. The fee was therefore recognized as being in addition to the cost of construction. This is the plain grammatical effect of the use of the comma to separate the above phrase from the preceding clause.

When read as punctuated, the present contract is not ambiguous and its meaning is clear. The provisions in question placed a limit of $34,500.00 on the cost of construction of the building and required the defendants to pay, in addition, the contractor's fee of ten percent.

A dissenting judge pointed out:

* * * I am of the opinion that there is an ambiguity, and accordingly, parol testimony should be considered to determine the true intent of the parties. The evidence shows that the home owner sought fixed-figure bids for the construction of the house involved. He testified that among the fixed-figure bids he received was one submitted by the plaintiff for $34,500. The contract actually signed came about through discussions growing out of the $34,500 fixed-figure bid. It indicated an effort on the part of the home owner to possibly end up paying less than $34,500, and a willingness on the part of the contractor to give the home owner an advantage.

* * * The punctuation mark relied upon * * * should not be used to defeat what I conceive to be the true intent of the parties.

Actually, the contractor testified that he copied the paragraph in dispute (No. 3) out of a form book. There is nothing in the record to indicate that any of the parties attached significance to the controversial comma until after the dispute arose. Nor is there evidence that either party at the time the contract was signed, had any understanding of the impact of the comma.

SECTION FOUR: GAP FILLERS

A contract may simply fail to deal with some matter—it may have a gap. Recall, for example, the Whites' and the Benkowskis' failure to deal with the issue of the quality of the water to be supplied. Did it have to be potable? Recall also the materials on planning and the limits of planning in Chapter

Four. When a gap exists, a court may turn to a variety of sources and methods to fill it. We study these matters in this section.

A sharp line between gap filling and interpretation of contracts cannot be drawn. First, a court may fill an apparent gap by interpreting written contract language in light of extrinsic evidence and the circumstances. The court may correctly conclude that the parties intended a particular approach to the apparent gap so that there really is no gap at all. Second, a court may purport to ascertain the intentions of the parties even though the parties clearly had no intentions concerning the matter. For example, a court may fill a gap as to the time for performance by finding that the parties "intended" performance in a reasonable time, although the parties did not in fact address the issue. Here the court is actually filling a gap, not interpreting the contract in light of the parties' intentions. See also Greenfield v. Philles Records, Inc. (page 674). Even when a court does acknowledge that it must fill a gap, the court may seek to determine what the parties probably would have intended had they addressed the contingency. Why do courts strive so hard to find the "intentions of the parties"?

COHEN, THE BASIS OF CONTRACT
46 Harv.L.Rev. 553, 584 (1933).

Just as the process of interpreting a statute is really a process of subsidiary legislation, so is the interpretation of a contract really a method of supplementing the original agreement by such provisions as are necessary to determine the point at issue.

HAINES v. CITY OF NEW YORK
Court of Appeals of New York, 1977.
41 N.Y.2d 769, 396 N.Y.S.2d 155, 364 N.E.2d 820.

GABRIELLI, JUDGE.

In the early 1920's, respondent City of New York and intervenors Town of Hunter and Village of Tannersville embarked upon negotiations for the construction of a sewage system to serve the village and a portion of the town. These negotiations were prompted by the city's need and desire to prevent the discharge of untreated sewage by residents of the area into Gooseberry Creek, a stream which fed a reservoir of the city's water supply system in the Schoharie watershed.

In 1923, the Legislature enacted enabling legislation authorizing the city to enter into contracts with municipalities in the watershed area "for the purpose of providing, maintaining [and] operating systems and plants for the collection and disposal of sewage" (L.1923, ch. 630, § 1). The statute further provided that any such contracts would be subject to the approval of the New York City Board of Estimate and Apportionment.

The negotiations culminated in an agreement in 1924 between the city and intervenors. By this agreement, the city assumed the obligation of constructing a sewage system consisting of a sewage disposal plant and sewer mains and laterals, and agreed that "all costs of construction and subsequent operation, maintenance and repair of said sewerage system with the house connections thereof and said disposal works shall be at the expense" of the city. The agreement also required the city to extend the sewer lines when "necessitated by future growth and building constructions of the respective communities". The village and town were obligated to and did obtain the necessary easements for the construction of the system and sewage lines.

The Board of Estimate, on December 9, 1926, approved the agreement and authorized the issuance of $500,000 of "corporate stock" of the City of New York for construction of the system by appropriate resolution. It is interesting to here note that a modification of the original agreement occurred in 1925 wherein the village agreed to reimburse the city for a specified amount representing the expense of changing the location of certain sewer lines. The plant was completed and commenced operation in 1928. The city has continued to maintain the plant through the ensuing years and in 1958 expended $193,000 to rehabilitate and expand the treatment plant and facilities.

Presently, the average flow of the plant has increased from an initial figure of 118,000 gallons per day to over 600,000 gallons daily and the trial court found that the plant "was operating substantially in excess of design capacity". The city asserts, and it is not disputed by any of the parties in this action, that the system cannot bear any significant additional "loadings" because this would result in inadequate treatment of all the sewage and consequently harm the city's water supply. The instant controversy arose when plaintiff, who is the owner of a tract of unimproved land which he seeks to develop into 50 residential lots, applied to the city for permission to connect houses, which he intends to construct on the lots, to existing sewer lines. The city refused permission on the ground that it had no obligation to further expand the plant, which is presently operating at full capacity, to accommodate this new construction.

Plaintiff then commenced this action for declaratory and injunctive relief, in which intervenors town and village joined as plaintiffs, maintaining that the 1924 agreement is perpetual in duration and obligates the city to expend additional capital funds to enlarge the existing plant or build a new one to accommodate the present and future needs of the municipalities. Both the trial court and the Appellate Division, by a divided court, held in favor of plaintiff and intervenors concluding, that, while the contract did not call for perpetual performance, the city was bound to construct additional facilities to meet increased demand until such time as the village or town is legally obligated to maintain a sewage disposal system. Two members of the court dissented in part stating that the agreement should not be construed as requiring the city to construct new or additional facilities.

We conclude that the city is presently obligated to maintain the existing plant but is not required to expand that plant or construct any new facilities to accommodate plaintiff's substantial, or any other, increased demands on the sewage system. The initial problem encountered in ascertaining the nature and extent of the city's obligation pursuant to the 1924 agreement, is its duration. We reject, as did the courts below, the plaintiff's contention that the city is perpetually bound under the agreement. The contract did not expressly provide for perpetual performance and both the trial court and the Appellate Division found that the parties did not so intend. Under these circumstances, the law will not imply that a contract calling for continuing performance is perpetual in duration. * * *

On the other hand, the city's contention that the contract is terminable at will because it provides for no express duration should also be rejected. In the absence of an express term fixing the duration of a contract, the courts may inquire into the intent of the parties and supply the missing term if a duration may be fairly and reasonably fixed by the surrounding circumstances and the parties' intent * * *. It is generally agreed that where a duration may be fairly and reasonably supplied by implication, a contract is not terminable at will * * *.

While we have not previously had occasion to apply it, the weight of authority supports the related rule that where the parties have not clearly expressed the duration of a contract, the courts will imply that they intended performance to continue for a reasonable time * * *. For compelling policy reasons, this rule has not been, and should not be, applied to contracts of employment or exclusive agency, distributorship, or requirements contracts which have been analogized to employment contracts * * *. The considerations relevant to such contracts do not obtain here. Thus, we hold that it is reasonable to infer from the circumstances of the 1924 agreement that the parties intended the city to maintain the sewage disposal facility until such time as the city no longer needed or desired the water, the purity of which the plant was designed to insure. The city argues that it is no longer obligated to maintain the plant because State law now prohibits persons from discharging raw sewage into streams such as Gooseberry Creek. However, the parties did not contemplate the passage of environmental control laws which would prohibit individuals or municipalities from discharging raw, untreated sewage into certain streams. Thus, the city agreed to assume the obligation of assuring that its water supply remained unpolluted and it may not now avoid that obligation for reasons not contemplated by the parties when the agreement was executed, and not within the purview of their intent, expressed or implied.

Having determined the duration of the city's obligation, the scope of its duty remains to be defined. By the agreement, the city obligated itself to build a specifically described disposal facility and to extend the lines of that facility to meet future increased demand. At the present time, the extension of those lines would result in the overloading of the system. Plaintiff claims that the city is required to build a new plant or expand the existing facility to overcome the problem. We disagree. The city should not be required to extend the lines to plaintiffs' property if to do so would overload the system and result in its inability to properly treat sewage. In providing for the extension of sewer lines, the contract does not obligate the city to provide sewage disposal services for properties in areas of the municipalities not presently served or even to new properties in areas which are presently served where to do so could reasonably be expected to significantly increase the demand on present plant facilities.

Thus, those paragraphs of the judgment which provide that the city is obligated to construct any additional facilities required to meet increased demand and that plaintiff is entitled to full use of the sewer lines should be stricken.

* * *

Order modified. * * *

FARNSWORTH, DISPUTES OVER OMISSION IN CONTRACTS

68 Colum.L.Rev. 860, 891 (1968).

The traditional approach to disputes over omission in contracts has disguised the role played by the courts. It has referred to a fictional "intention" of the parties which is in turn supposed to take the form of fictional "terms" of the contract. The result has been to create an extensive framework of implied terms to deal with omissions. It has been suggested here that it is more realistic to assume that the parties form their expectations in connection with a limited number of significant situations, selected from a much larger number of foreseeable ones. As to those situations that are excluded by this process of selection, there is an absence of expectation. When they reduce their expectations to contract language, a second process of selection takes place, and they use their language only in connection with a limited number of the significant situations with respect to which they formed their expectations. As to the rest, there is an understatement of expectation.

A situation that does not survive these two processes of selection is a *casus omissus*. The process of determining whether there is a *casus omissus* is that of interpretation. The process of resolving the *casus omissus* is * * * based either on actual expectations or on general principles of fairness and justice. So where a dispute over omission concerns the qualification of a duty that has been expressed without qualification, a court must first determine by the process of interpretation whether the case at hand was one of the significant situations with respect to which the language was used. If it was not, then it is a *casus omissus* and the court should recognize that it is within its power to extend the duty by analogy to the case at hand, to refuse to extend it, or to reach an adjustment that lies between these extremes. In making these kinds of judgments it is sometimes helpful to view a dispute over omission in terms of the burden of expression.

KEPPY v. LILIENTHAL, 524 N.W.2d 436 (Iowa App.1994). [Keppy and the Lilienthals orally agreed that Keppy would "revitalize [the Lilienthals'] pig herd which had been ravaged by pseudo-rabies." The Lilienthals agreed to lease sows and boars to Keppy, who would breed, feed, and otherwise care for them until their sale. Keppy agreed to lease the Turkle farm and farrowing facility to carry out the operation. The parties were to divide the proceeds from the sale of the offspring. After a disagreement over who should supply the feed, the Lilienthals terminated the agreement. Keppy sought an injunction barring the Lilienthals from removing the hogs. The Lilienthals counterclaimed, seeking the return of the hogs. They claimed the agreement was terminable at will, since it was silent as to duration.]

The law in Iowa is not well developed regarding the duration of contracts where the parties fail to specify a duration. A contract granting a sole distributorship for an indefinite period was found to continue for a reasonable time and could be terminated without cause only upon reasonable notice. Des Moines Blue Ribbon Distrib. v. Drewrys Ltd., 256 Iowa 899, 129 N.W.2d 731 (1964). When the duration of employment contracts is indefinite, the contract can be terminated at will by either party. Blackhawk Bldg. Sys. v. Law Firm, 428 N.W.2d 288 (Iowa 1988).

> If a period of duration can be fairly implied from the nature of the contract, its subject matter and relationship of the parties, the contract is not terminable at the pleasure of either party and the court will give effect to the manifest intent of the parties. It has also been held that a contract will be held terminable within a reasonable time or revocable at will, depending on the circumstances, where no termination date was within the contemplation of the parties, or where their intention in regard thereto could not be ascertained.

17A C.J.S. Contracts § 398, at 480 (1963).

Evidence was presented which fairly implied the duration of the contract given the nature of the contract and the surrounding circumstances. Lilienthals entered the agreement in order to revitalize their herd and earn money. There was also testimony that Keppy made it known to Lilienthals that she intended to have her own farrowing operation within three years. Keppy testified she told Lilienthals she leased Turkle's farm and farrowing facility for three years. Turkle's testimony supported Keppy's assertion that the duration of the contract with Lilienthals was to be about three years. We find there was substantial evidence to support the district court's conclusion the contract was not terminable at will.

HASLUND v. SIMON PROPERTY GROUP, INC.

United States Court of Appeals, Seventh Circuit, 2004.
378 F.3d 653.

POSNER, CIRCUIT JUDGE.

In a diversity suit for breach of contract governed by Illinois law, the district judge after a bench trial awarded Shannon Haslund $537,634.41 in damages, plus prejudgment interest, against Simon Property Group (SPG). 284 F.Supp.2d 1102 (N.D.Ill.2003). SPG's appeal argues that the provision of the contract that it was found to have violated was too indefinite to be enforceable, that no injury was proved, and that in any event no prejudgment interest should have been awarded.

During the dot-com boom of the late 1990s, SPG, a real estate company that operates hundreds of shopping malls, decided to form a subsidiary, "clixnmortar.com," to create Internet-related services ancillary to its mall business. It appointed its chief information officer, Melanie Alshab, to be the president of the new subsidiary. She approached Haslund, a management consultant who had done work for SPG in the past and was employed by Ernst & Young, to be clixnmortar's vice president for operations. Haslund was interested, but told Alshab that she wanted not only a substantial raise (from $125,000, her salary at Ernst & Young, to $175,000), but also equity in clixnmortar. She was taking a chance by leaving an established firm for a startup, and so she wanted upside potential. She made clear that unless she was given equity she wouldn't sign on with the new company. Alshab got authorization from her superiors to offer Haslund not only the salary increase that she requested but also one percent of clixnmortar's equity. The deal was confirmed in a letter to Haslund from SPG's director of human resources that under the caption "Annual Salary" recited "$175,000 plus 1% equity in clixnmortar.com, structure to be determined."

Haslund started her new job at the end of 1999 shortly after receiving this letter. No stock was issued to her, however, either then or later. She kept badgering SPG for the stock to no avail, and 10 months after starting work she was fired, having denounced SPG's boss in an email to a firm that was in the process of acquiring an interest in clixnmortar. The startup never turned a profit—in fact never had any significant income—and was soon moribund, though it wasn't dissolved until last year.

The fact that a contract is incomplete, presents interpretive questions, bristles with unresolved contingencies, and in short has as many holes as a Swiss cheese does not make it unenforceable for indefiniteness. Otherwise there would be few enforceable contracts. Complete contingent contracts are impossible. The future, over which contractual performance evolves, is too uncertain. We once decided a case in which the contract exceeded 2000 pages yet the dispute that gave rise to the suit had not been anticipated (or, if anticipated, provided for). S.A. *Healy Co. v. Milwaukee Metropolitan Sewerage District*, 50 F.3d 476 (7th Cir.1995). If contracting parties had to provide for every contingency that might arise, contract negotiations would be interminable. Contracts can be shorter and simpler and cheaper when courts stand ready to fill gaps and resolve ambiguities in the minority of contracts that get drawn into litigation.

But that is in general and not in every case. A contract is rightly deemed unenforceable for indefiniteness when it leaves out (1) a crucial term that (2) a court cannot reasonably be asked to supply in the name of interpretation * * *. An example is the contract price. * * * Not only is price central, so that if the choice of price could be delegated to a court it would be the court and not the parties that was the contract maker, but there is no interpretive path that leads from the terms the parties agreed on to the price they would have agreed on. In the division of functions between parties and the judiciary in the joint enterprise of fixing contractual meaning, the selection of the contract price falls clearly on the parties' side. What is more, the omission of crucial terms is powerful evidence that no contract was intended.

So if the employment agreement had said that Haslund would receive equity but hadn't indicated how much, a court could not supply the missing percentage.* * * No interpretive technique would enable the court to build a bridge between what the parties had agreed to and the percentage of the equity in the new firm that she would receive. But the contract did specify the percentage. What it omitted was a number of details, such as the form of the equity—would it be voting stock or nonvoting stock?—and whether there would be restrictions on vesting: could Haslund show up for work on December 27, 1999, and the next day announce she was quitting and demand her shares? Important details, to be sure; but their absence did not necessarily

4.1 Apple Computer shall have the exclusive worldwide right, as between the parties, to use and authorize others to use the Apple Computer Marks on or in connection with goods and services within the Apple Computer Field of Use.

4.2 Apple Corps. shall have the exclusive worldwide right, as between the parties, to use and authorize others to sue the Apple Corps. Marks on or in connection with goods and services within the Apple Corps. Field of Use.

Note
Gap Fillers Under the Uniform Commercial Code

The Uniform Commercial Code provides in section 2–204(3) that "[e]ven though one or more terms are left open a contract for sale does not fail for indefiniteness if the parties have intended to make a contract and there is a reasonably certain basis for giving an appropriate remedy." Under the Code, therefore, even if important terms, such as those dealing with duration, quantity, delivery, or price are omitted, the agreement can be enforced if the parties intended to contract and an appropriate remedy can be supplied.

How are gaps filled under the Code? The Code provides a series of sections to guide courts in filling such gaps. We now sample one court's approach to gap filling under the Code.

SOUTHWEST ENGINEERING CO.
v. MARTIN TRACTOR CO.

Supreme Court of Kansas, 1970.
205 Kan. 684, 473 P.2d 18.

FONTRON, JUSTICE.

This is an action to recover damages for breach of contract. Trial was had to the court which entered judgment in favor of the plaintiff. The defendant has appealed.

Southwest Engineering Company, Inc., the plaintiff, is a Missouri corporation engaged in general contracting work, while the defendant, Martin Tractor Company, Inc., is a Kansas corporation. The two parties will be referred to hereafter either as plaintiff, or Southwest, on the one hand and defendant, or Martin, on the other.

We glean from the record that in April, 1966, the plaintiff was interested in submitting a bid to the United States Corps of Engineers for the construction of certain runway lighting facilities at McConnell Air Force Base at Wichita. However, before submitting a bid, and on April 11, 1966, the plaintiff's construction superintendent, Mr. R.E. Cloepfil, called the manager of Martin's engine department, Mr. Ken Hurt, who at the time was at Colby, asking for a price on a standby generator and accessory equipment. Mr. Hurt replied that he would phone him back from Topeka, which he did the next day, quoting a price of $18,500. This quotation was re-confirmed by Hurt over the phone on April 13.

Southwest submitted its bid on April 14, 1966, using Hurt's figure of $18,500 for the generator equipment, and its bid was accepted. On April 20, Southwest notified Martin that its bid had been accepted. Hurt and Cloepfil thereafter agreed over the phone to meet in Springfield on April 28. On that date Hurt flew to Springfield, where the two men conferred at the airfield restaurant for about an hour. Hurt took to the meeting a copy of the job specifications which the government had supplied Martin prior to the letting.

At the Springfield meeting it developed that Martin had upped its price for the generator and accessory equipment from $18,500 to $21,500. Despite this change of position by Martin, concerning which Cloepfil was understandably amazed, the two men continued their conversation and, according to Cloepfil, they arrived at an agreement for the sale of a D353 generator and accessories for the sum of $21,500. In addition it was agreed that if the Corps of Engineers would accept a less expensive generator, a D343, the aggregate price to Southwest would be $15,000. The possibility of providing alternative equipment, the D343, was suggested by Mr. Hurt, apparently in an attempt to mollify Mr. Cloepfil when the latter learned that Martin had reneged on its price quotation of April 12. It later developed that the Corps of Engineers would not approve the cheaper generator and that Southwest eventually had to supply the more expensive D353 generator.

At the conference, Mr. Hurt separately listed the component parts of each of the two generators on the top half of a sheet of paper and set out the price after each item. The prices were then totaled. On the bottom half of the sheet Hurt set down the accessories common to both generators and their cost. This handwritten memorandum, as it was referred to during the trial, noted a 10 per cent discount on the aggregate cost of each generator, while the accessories were listed at Martin's cost. The price of the D353 was rounded off at $21,500 and D343 at $15,000. The memorandum was handed to Cloepfil while the two men were still at the airport. We will refer to this memorandum further during the course of this opinion.

On May 2, 1966, Cloepfil addressed a letter to the Martin Tractor Company, directing Martin to proceed with shop drawings and submittal documents for the McConnell lighting job and calling attention to the fact that applicable government regulations were required to be followed. Further reference to this communication will be made when necessary.

Some three weeks thereafter, on May 24, 1966, Hurt wrote Cloepfil the following letter:

Hurt/Martin backs out

"MARTIN TRACTOR
COMPANY, INC.

Topeka Chanute Concordia Colby

CATERPILLAR*

"P.O. Box 1698
Topeka, Kansas
May 24, 1966

Mr. R.E. Cloepfil
Southwest Engineering Co., Inc.
P.O. Box 3314, Glenstone Station
Springfield, Missouri 65804

Dear Sir:

Due to restrictions placed on Caterpillar products, accessory suppliers, and other stipulations by the district governing agency, we cannot accept your letter to proceed dated May 2, 1966, and hereby withdraw all verbal quotations.

> Regretfully,
>
> /s/ Ken Hurt
> Ken Hurt, Manager
> Engine Division"

On receipt of this unwelcome missive, Cloepfil telephoned Mr. Hurt who stated they had some work underway for the Corps of Engineers in both the Kansas City and Tulsa districts and did not want to take on any other work for the Corps at that time. Hurt assured Cloepfil he could buy the equipment from anybody at the price Martin could sell it for. Later investigation showed, however, that such was not the case.

In August of 1966, Mr. Cloepfil and Mr. Anderson, the president of Southwest, traveled to Topeka in an effort to persuade Martin to fulfill its contract. Hurt met them at the company office where harsh words were bandied about. Tempers eventually cooled off and at the conclusion of the verbal melee, hands were shaken all around and Hurt went so far as to say that if Southwest still wanted to buy the equipment from them to submit another order and he would get it handled. On this promising note the protagonists parted.

After returning to Springfield, Mr. Cloepfil, on September 6, wrote Mr. Hurt placing an order for a D353 generator (the expensive one) and asking that the order be given prompt attention, as their completion date was in early December. This communication was returned unopened.

A final effort to communicate with Martin was attempted by Mr. Anderson when the unopened letter was returned. A phone call was placed for Mr. Martin, himself, and Mr. Anderson was informed by the girl on the switchboard that Martin was in Colorado Springs on a vacation. Anderson then placed a call to the motel where he was told Mr. Martin could be reached. Martin refused to talk on the call, on learning the caller's name, and Anderson was told he would have to contact his office.

Mr. Anderson then replaced his call to Topeka and reached either the company comptroller or the company treasurer who responded by cussing him and saying "Who in the hell do you think you are? We don't have to sell you a damn thing."

Southwest eventually secured the generator equipment from Foley Tractor Co. of Wichita, a company which Mr. Hurt had one time suggested, at a price of $27,541. The present action was then filed, seeking damages of $6,041 for breach of the contract and $9,000 for loss resulting from the delay caused by the breach. The trial court awarded damages of $6,041 for the breach but rejected damages allegedly due to delay. The defendant, only, has appealed; there is no cross-appeal by plaintiff.

[The court first found that Hurt's handwritten memo satisfied U.C.C. § 2–201.]

Hurt * * * testified that in his opinion the thing which stood in the way of a firm deal was Martin's terms of payment—that had Southwest agreed with those terms of payment, so far as he was concerned, he would have considered a firm deal was made. Mr. Hurt acknowledged while on the stand that he penned the memorandum and that as disclosed therein a 10 per cent discount was given Southwest on the price of either of the generators listed (depending on which was approved by the Corps of Engineers), and that the accessories common to both generators were to be net—that is, sold without profit.

It is quite true, as the trial court found, that terms of payment were not agreed upon at the Springfield meeting. Hurt testified that as the memorandum was being made out, he said they wanted 10 per cent with the order, 50 per cent on delivery and the balance on acceptance, but he did not recall Cloepfil's response. Cloepfil's version was somewhat different. He stated that after the two had shaken hands in the lobby preparing to leave, Hurt said their terms usually were 20 per cent down and the balance on delivery; while he (Cloepfil) said the way they generally paid was 90 per cent on the tenth of the month following delivery and the balance on final acceptance. It is obvious the parties reached no agreement on this point.

However, a failure on the part of Messrs. Hurt and Cloepfil to agree on terms of payment would not, of itself, defeat an otherwise valid agreement reached by them. K.S.A. 84–2–204(3) reads:

> "Even though one or more terms are left open a contract for sale does not fail for indefiniteness if the parties have intended to make a contract and there is a reasonably certain basis for giving an appropriate remedy."

The official U.C.C. Comment is enlightening:

> "Subsection (3) states the principle as to 'open terms' underlying later sections of the Article. If the parties intend to enter into a binding agreement, this subsection recognizes that agreement as valid in law, despite missing terms, if there is any reasonably certain basis for granting a remedy. The test is not certainty as to what the parties were to do nor as to the exact amount of damages due the plaintiff. Nor is the fact that one or more terms are left to be agreed upon enough of itself to defeat an otherwise adequate agreement. Rather, commercial standards on the point of 'indefiniteness' are intended to be applied, this Act making provision elsewhere for missing terms needed for performance, open price, remedies and the like.

> "The more terms the parties leave open, the less likely it is that they have intended to conclude a binding agreement, but their actions may be frequently conclusive on the matter despite the omissions."

* * *

So far as the present case is concerned, K.S.A. 84–2–310 supplies the omitted term. This statute provides in pertinent part:

> "Unless otherwise agreed

"(a) payment is due at the time and place at which the buyer is to receive the goods even though the place of shipment is the place of delivery;"

In our view, the language of the two Code provisions is clear and positive. Considered together, we take the two sections to mean that where parties have reached an enforceable agreement for the sale of goods, but omit therefrom the terms of payment, the law will imply, as part of the agreement, that payment is to be made at time of delivery. In this respect the law does not greatly differ from the rule this court laid down years ago.

* * *

We do not mean to infer that terms of payment are not of importance under many circumstances or that parties may not condition an agreement on their being included. However, the facts before us hardly indicate that Hurt and Cloepfil considered the terms of payment to be significant, or of more than passing interest. Hurt testified that while he stated his terms he did not recall Cloepfil's response, while Cloepfil stated that as the two were on the point of leaving, each stated their usual terms and that was as far as it went. The trial court found that only a brief and casual conversation ensued as to payment, and we think that is a valid summation of what took place.

Moreover, it is worthy of note that Martin first mentioned the omission of the terms of payment, as justifying its breach, in a letter written by counsel on September 15, 1966, more than four months after the memorandum was prepared by Hurt. On prior occasions Martin attributed its cancellation of the Springfield understanding to other causes. In its May 24 letter, Martin ascribed its withdrawal of "all verbal quotations" to "restrictions placed on Caterpillar products, accessory suppliers, and other stipulations by the district governing agency." In explaining the meaning of the letter to Cloepfil, Hurt said that Martin was doing work for the Corps of Engineers in the Kansas City and Tulsa districts and did not want to take on additional work with them at this time.

The entire circumstances may well give rise to a suspicion that Martin's present insistence that future negotiations were contemplated concerning terms of payment, is primarily an afterthought, for use as an escape hatch. Doubtless the trial court so considered the excuse in arriving at its findings.

We are aware of Martin's argument that Southwest's letter of May 2, 1966, referring to the sale is evidence that no firm contract had been concluded. Granted that some of the language employed might be subject to that interpretation, the trial court found, on what we deem to be substantial, competent evidence, that an agreement of sale *was* concluded at Springfield.
* * *

The defendant points particularly to the following portion of the May 2 letter, as interjecting a new and unacceptable term in the agreement made at Springfield.

" * * * We are not prepared to make a partial payment at the time of placing of this order. However, we will be able to include 100% of the engine-generator price in our first payment estimate after it is delivered, and only 10% will have to be withheld pending acceptance. Ordinarily this means that suppliers can expect payment of 90% within about thirty days after delivery."

It must be conceded that the terms of payment proposed in Southwest's letter had not been agreed to by Martin. However, we view the proposal as irrelevant. Although terms of payment had not been mutually agreed upon, K.S.A. 84-2-310 supplied the missing terms, *i.e.*, payment on delivery, which thus became part of the agreement already concluded. In legal effect the proposal was no more than one to change the terms of payment implied by law. Since Martin did not accept the change, the proposal had no effect, either as altering or terminating the agreement reached at Springfield. * * *

* * *

We find no error in this case and the judgment of the trial court is affirmed.

SECTION FIVE: GOOD FAITH

We have already encountered the doctrine of good faith on several occasions. For example, we saw in Section Two of Chapter Two how it may impose an obligation on one party so that there is no want of mutuality of obligation; in Section Three of Chapter Three how it may serve as one factor influencing a court's choice between measures of damages; in Section Nine of Chapter Four how it helps define the scope of any legal obligation in an agreement to agree; and in Section One of Chapter Five how it can function as a policing doctrine. Moreover, we will see that good faith is relevant in the remaining chapters of this book. In this section, we see its special role in shaping the content of the duty to perform. We also take this occasion to identify the general authoritative sources of good faith doctrine, and to explore the nature of good faith concepts.

Many common law courts have held that in every contract "there exists an implied covenant of good faith and fair dealing." A leading example is Kirke La Shelle Co. v. Paul Armstrong Co., 263 N.Y. 79, 87, 188 N.E. 163, 167 (1933). A rapidly increasing number of judicial decisions recognizes the covenant of good faith and fair dealing in a wide variety of contexts. Section 1–203 of the Uniform Commercial Code also provides: "Every contract or duty within this Act imposes a duty of good faith in its performance or enforcement." A number of additional statutes also impose duties of good faith in various settings. See, for example, the Automobile Dealer's Day in Court Act, 15 U.S.C. §§ 1221–1225 (1994).

FORTUNE v. NATIONAL CASH REGISTER CO.

Supreme Judicial Court of Massachusetts, 1977.
373 Mass. 96, 364 N.E.2d 1251.

ABRAMS, JUSTICE.

Orville E. Fortune (Fortune), a former salesman of The National Cash Register Company (NCR), brought a suit to recover certain commissions allegedly due as a result of a sale of cash registers to First National Stores Inc. (First National) in 1968. Counts 1 and 2 of Fortune's amended declaration claimed bonus payments under the parties' written contract of employment. The third count sought recovery in quantum meruit for the reasonable value of Fortune's services relating to the same sales transaction. Judgment on a jury verdict for Fortune was reversed by the Appeals Court * * * and this court granted leave to obtain further appellate review. We affirm the judgment of the Superior Court. We hold, for the reasons stated herein, there was no error in submitting the issue of "bad faith" termination of an employment at will contract to the jury.

The issues before the court are raised by NCR's motion for directed verdicts. Accordingly, we summarize the evidence most favorable to the plaintiff. * * *

Fortune was employed by NCR under a written "salesman's contract" which was terminable at will, without cause, by either party on written notice. The contract provided that Fortune would receive a weekly salary in a fixed amount plus a bonus for sales made within the "territory" (i.e., customer accounts or stores) assigned to him for "coverage or supervision," whether the sale was made by him or someone else. The amount of the bonus was determined on the basis of "bonus credits," which were computed as a percentage of the price of products sold. Fortune would be paid a percentage of the applicable bonus credit as follows: (1) 75% if the territory was assigned to him at the date of the order, (2) 25% if the territory was assigned to him at the date of delivery and installation, or (3) 100% if the territory was assigned to him at both times. The contract further provided that the "bonus interest" would terminate if shipment of the order was not made within eighteen months from the date of the order unless (1) the territory was assigned to him for coverage at the date of delivery and installation, or (2) special engineering was required to fulfil the contract. In addition, NCR reserved the right to sell products in the salesman's territory without paying a bonus. However, this right could be exercised only on written notice.

In 1968, Fortune's territory included First National. This account had been part of his territory for the preceding six years; he had been successful in obtaining several orders from First National, including a million dollar order in 1963. Sometime in late 1967, or early 1968, NCR introduced a new model cash register, Class 5. Fortune corresponded with First National in an effort to sell the machine. He also helped to arrange for a demonstration of the Class 5 to executives of First National on October 4, 1968. NCR had a team of men also working on this sale.

On November 27, 1968, NCR's manager of chain and department stores, and the Boston branch manager, both part of NCR's team, wrote to First National regarding the Class 5. The letter covered a number of subjects, including price protection, trade-ins, and trade-in protection against obsolescence. While NCR normally offered price protection for only an eighteen-month term, apparently the size of the proposed order from First National caused NCR to extend its price protection terms for either a two-year or four-year period. On November 29, 1968, First National signed an order for 2,008 Class 5 machines to be delivered over a four-year period at a purchase price of approximately $5,000,000. Although Fortune did not participate in the negotiation of the terms of the order,[1] his name appeared on the order form in the

---

1. Fortune was not authorized to offer the price protection terms which appeared in the November 27 letter, as special covenant A, par. 3 of his contract prohibited him from varying the prices of items.

space entitled "salesman credited." The amount of the bonus credit as shown on the order was $92,079.99.

On January 6, 1969, the first working day of the new year, Fortune found an envelope on his desk at work. It contained a termination notice addressed to his home dated December 2, 1968. Shortly after receiving the notice, Fortune spoke to the Boston branch manager with whom he was friendly. The manager told him, "You are through," but, after considering some of the details necessary for the smooth operation of the First National order, told him to "stay on," and to "[k]eep on doing what you are doing right now." Fortune remained with the company in a position entitled "sales support." In this capacity, he coordinated and expedited delivery of the machines to First National under the November 29 order as well as servicing other accounts.

Commencing in May or June, Fortune began to receive some bonus commissions on the First National order. Having received only 75% of the applicable bonus due on the machines which had been delivered and installed, Fortune spoke with his manager about receiving the full amount of the commission. Fortune was told "to forget about it." Sixty-one years old at that time, and with a son in college, Fortune concluded that it "was a good idea to forget it for the time being."

NCR did pay a systems and installations person the remaining 25% of the bonus commissions due from the First National order although contrary to its usual policy of paying *only* salesmen a bonus. NCR, by its letter of November 27, 1968, had promised the services of a systems and installations person; the letter had claimed that the services of this person, Bernie Martin (Martin), would have a forecasted cost to NCR of over $45,000. As promised, NCR did transfer Martin to the First National account shortly after the order was placed.

Approximately eighteen months after receiving the termination notice, Fortune, who had worked for NCR for almost twenty-five years, was asked to retire. When he refused, he was fired in June of 1970. Fortune did not receive any bonus payments on machines which were delivered to First National after this date.

At the close of the plaintiff's case, the defendant moved for a directed verdict, arguing that there was no evidence of any breach of contract, and adding that the existence of a contract barred recovery under the quantum meruit count. Ruling that Fortune could recover if the termination and firing were in bad faith, the trial judge, without specifying on which count, submitted this issue to the jury. NCR then rested and, by agreement of counsel, the case was sent to the jury for special verdicts on two questions:[2]

"1. Did the Defendant act in bad faith * * * when it decided to terminate the Plaintiff's contract as a salesman by letter dated December 2, 1968, delivered on January 6, 1969?

"2. Did the Defendant act in bad faith * * * when the Defendant let the Plaintiff go on June 5, 1970?"

2. The defendant reserved the right to argue on appeal that the judge should have directed verdicts, and that bad faith was not a proper issue in the case.

The jury answered both questions affirmatively, and judgment entered in the sum of $45,649.62.[3]

The central issue on appeal is whether this "bad faith" termination constituted a breach of the employment at will contract. Traditionally, an employment contract which is "at will" may be terminated by either side without reason. * * * Although the employment at will rule has been almost uniformly criticised * * * it has been widely followed.

The contract at issue is a classic terminable at will employment contract. It is clear that the contract itself reserved to the parties an explicit power to terminate the contract without cause on written notice. It is also clear that under the express terms of the contract Fortune has received all the bonus commissions to which he is entitled. Thus, NCR claims that it did not breach the contract, and that it has no further liability to Fortune.[4] According to a literal reading of the contract, NCR is correct.

However, Fortune argues that, in spite of the literal wording of the contract, he is entitled to a jury determination on NCR's motives in terminating his services under the contract and in finally discharging him. We agree. We hold that NCR's written contract contains an implied covenant of good faith and fair dealing, and a termination not made in good faith constitutes a breach of the contract.

We do not question the general principles that an employer is entitled to be motivated by and to serve its own legitimate business interests; that an employer must have wide latitude in deciding whom it will employ in the face of the uncertainties of the business world; and that an employer needs flexibility in the face of changing circumstances. We recognize the employer's need for a large amount of control over its work force. However, we believe that where, as here, commissions are to be paid for work performed by the employee, the employer's decision to terminate its at will employee should be made in good faith. NCR's right to make decisions in its own interest is not, in our view, unduly hampered by a requirement of adherence to this standard.

On occasion some courts have avoided the rigidity of the "at will" rule by fashioning a remedy in tort.[5] We believe, however, that in this case there is

---

3. The amount apparently represented 25% of the commission due during the eighteen months the machines were delivered to First National, and which was paid to Martin, and 100% of the commissions on the machines delivered after Fortune was fired.

4. Damages were, by stipulation of the parties, set equal to the unpaid bonus amounts. Thus we need not consider whether other measures of damages might be justified in cases of bad faith termination. * * *

Although the order called for purchase of 2,008 Class 5 machines for a total sale of $5,040,080, at trial the parties stipulated that "1,503 machines were actually delivered and installed" under the First National order. The stipulated damages in the instant case were based on the number of registers actually delivered and installed.

5. This theory has generally been utilized in order to protect public policy. See, e.g.,

Montalvo v. Zamora, 7 Cal.App.3d 69, 86 Cal. Rptr. 401 (1970) (employee terminated after hiring an attorney to negotiate a claim that the employer had violated the minimum wage law); *Petermann v. International Broth. of Teamsters, Local 396,* 174 Cal.App.2d 184, 344 P.2d 25 (1959) (employee discharged for refusing to commit perjury before government commission); *Frampton v. Central Ind. Gas Co.,* 260 Ind. 249, 297 N.E.2d 425 (1973) (employee fired for filing a workman's compensation claim); *Nees v. Hocks,* 272 Or. 210, 536 P.2d 512 (1975) (employee fired for performing jury duty in violation of company policy). Cf. *Geary v. United States Steel Corp.,* 456 Pa. 171, 319 A.2d 174 (1974) (tort remedy not available where employee fired for not following corporate hierarchy procedure in protesting company policy as to safety of a product).

remedy on the express contract.[6] In so holding we are merely recognizing the general requirement in this Commonwealth that parties to contracts and commercial transactions must act in good faith toward one another. Good faith and fair dealing between parties are pervasive requirements in our law; it can be said fairly, that parties to contracts or commercial transactions are bound by this standard. See G.L. c. 106, § 1–203 (good faith in contracts under Uniform Commercial Code); G.L. c. 93B, § 4(3)(c) (good faith in motor vehicle franchise termination).

A requirement of good faith has been assumed or implied in a variety of contract cases. *Druker v. Roland Wm. Jutras Assocs.*, 348 N.E.2d 763 (1976). *Kerrigan v. Boston,* 361 Mass. 24, 33, 278 N.E.2d 387 (1972) (collective bargaining contract). *Murach v. Massachusetts Bonding & Ins. Co.,* 339 Mass. 184, 187, 158 N.E.2d 338 (1959) (insurance contract—insurer must exercise discretionary power to settle claims in good faith). *Krauss v. Kuechler,* 300 Mass. 346, 15 N.E.2d 207 (1938). *Clark v. State St. Trust Co.,* 270 Mass. 140, 153, 169 N.E. 897 (1930) (secondary agreement to a stock option agreement). *Elliott v. Kazajian,* 255 Mass. 459, 462, 152 N.E. 351 (1926) (broker's commission). *Chandler, Gardner & Williams, Inc. v. Reynolds,* 250 Mass. 309, 314, 145 N.E.476 (1924) (contracts to be performed to the satisfaction of the other party).

* * *

Recent decisions in other jurisdictions lend support to the proposition that good faith is implied in contracts terminable at will. In a recent employment at will case, *Monge v. Beebe Rubber Co.,* 114 N.H. 130, 133, 316 A.2d 549, 552 (1974), the plaintiff alleged that her oral contract of employment had been terminated because she refused to date her foreman. The New Hampshire Supreme Court held that "[i]n all employment contracts, whether at will or for a definite term, the employer's interest in running his business as he sees fit must be balanced against the interest of the employee in maintaining his employment, and the public's interest in maintaining a proper balance between the two. * * * We hold that a termination by the employer of a contract of employment at will which is motivated by bad faith or malice * * * constitutes a breach of the employment contract. * * * Such a rule affords the employee a certain stability of employment and does not interfere with the employer's normal exercise of his right to discharge, which is necessary to permit him to operate his business efficiently and profitably."

We believe that the holding in the *Monge* case merely extends to employment contracts the rule that " 'in *every* contract there is an implied covenant that neither party shall do anything which will have the effect of destroying or injuring the right of the other party to receive the fruits of the contract, which means that in *every* contract there exists an implied covenant of good faith and fair dealing' [emphasis supplied]. *Uproar Co. v. National Broadcasting Co.,* 81 F.2d 373, 377 (1st Cir.), cert. denied, 298 U.S. 670, 56 S.Ct. 835, 80 L.Ed. 1393 (1936), quoting from *Kirke LaShelle Co. v. Paul Armstrong Co.,* 263 N.Y. 79, 87, 188 N.E. 163 (1933)." * * *

In the instant case, we need not pronounce our adherence to so broad a policy nor need we speculate as to whether the good faith requirement is

---

6. Thus, we do not reach the issues raised by count 3 for quantum meruit recovery.

implicit in every contract for employment at will. It is clear, however, that, on the facts before us, a finding is warranted that a breach of the contract occurred. Where the principal seeks to deprive the agent of all compensation by terminating the contractual relationship when the agent is on the brink of successfully completing the sale, the principal has acted in bad faith and the ensuing transaction between the principal and the buyer is to be regarded as having been accomplished by the agent. Restatement (Second) of Agency § 454, and Comment a (1958). The same result obtains where the principal attempts to deprive the agent of any portion of a commission due the agent. Courts have often applied this rule to prevent overreaching by employers and the forfeiture by employees of benefits almost earned by the rendering of substantial services. * * * In our view, the Appeals Court erroneously focused only on literal compliance with payment provisions of the contract and failed to consider the issue of bad faith termination. Restatement (Second) of Agency § 454, and Comment a (1958).

NCR argues that there was no evidence of bad faith in this case; therefore, the trial judge was required to direct a verdict in any event. We think that the evidence and the reasonable inferences to be drawn therefrom support a jury verdict that the termination of Fortune's twenty-five years of employment as a salesman with NCR the next business day after NCR obtained a $5,000,000 order from First National was motivated by a desire to pay Fortune as little of the bonus credit as it could. The fact that Fortune was willing to work under these circumstances does not constitute a waiver or estoppel; it only shows that NCR had him "at their mercy." *Commonwealth v. DeCotis,* 366 Mass. 234, 243, 316 N.E.2d 748 (1974).

NCR also contends that Fortune cannot complain of his firing in June, 1970, as his employment contract clearly indicated that bonus credits would be paid only for an eighteen-month period following the date of the order. As we have said, the jury could have found that Fortune was stripped of his "salesman" designation in order to disqualify him for the remaining 25% of the commissions due on cash registers delivered prior to the date of his first termination. Similarly, the jury could have found that Fortune was fired (or not assigned to the First National account) so that NCR could avoid paying him *any* commissions on cash registers delivered after June, 1970.

Conversely, the jury could have found that Fortune was assigned by NCR to the First National account; that all he did in this case was arrange for a demonstration of the product; that he neither participated in obtaining the order nor did he assist NCR in closing the order; and that nevertheless NCR credited him with the sale. This, however, did not obligate the trial judge to direct a verdict. Where evidence is conflicting, the rule is clear: "If upon any reasonable view of the evidence there is found any combination of circumstances from which a rational inference may be drawn in favor of the plaintiff, then there was no error in the denial of the motion, even if there may be other and different circumstances disclosed in the evidence which, if accepted as true by the jury, would support a conclusion adverse to the plaintiff." *Howes v. Kelman,* 326 Mass. 696, 696–697, 96 N.E.2d 394, 395 (1951).

We think that NCR's conduct in June, 1970 permitted the jury to find bad faith.

* * *

Judgment of the Superior Court affirmed.

"My leaving Wilkins & Jennings was perfectly amicable. They felt that I should be fired, and I agreed."

Drawing by Handelsman; © 1986 The New Yorker Magazine, Inc.

TYMSHARE, INC. v. COVELL, 727 F.2d 1145 (D.C.Cir.1984). [Covell's employment contract with Tymshare granted Covell commissions on sales above a particular quota. The contract also expressly permitted Tymshare to increase the quota retroactively, which would have the effect of decreasing Covell's compensation: "(M)anagement reserves the right to change the quota plan and individual quota * * * payments at any time during the quota year within their sole discretion." Covell sued Tymshare, claiming that Tymshare exercised the clause in bad faith to deprive him of compensation. Tymshare appealed a grant of summary judgment in favor of Covell.]

SCALIA, CIRCUIT JUDGE:

* * *

Whether pursued under the rubric of "good faith" or the more traditional rubric (for most contracts) of "implied limitation," the object of our inquiry is whether it was reasonably understood by the parties to this contract that there were at least certain purposes for which the expressly conferred power to adjust quotas could not be employed. If not, then appellant is correct that no action in this regard could constitute "bad faith"—or, as we would put it, there is no implicit contractual restriction.

In conducting this inquiry we must reject at the outset the proposition which appellant seeks to extract from certain cases to the effect that "[a]s to acts and conduct authorized by the express provisions of the contract, no covenant of good faith and fair dealing can be implied which forbids such acts and conduct," *VTR, Inc. v. Goodyear Tire & Rubber Co.,* 303 F.Supp. 773, 778 (S.D.N.Y.1969). * * * We have no doubt that proposition is correct (assuming that the provisions of the contract are not void as unconscionable * * *) as an elaboration of the fundamental principle, set forth in another case cited by appellant, that "[w]hat the intent of the parties was in making the contract must control; it is possible to so draw a contract as to leave decisions absolutely to the uncontrolled discretion of one of the parties and in such a case the issue of good faith is irrelevant." *MacDougald Construction Co. v. State Highway Department,* 125 Ga.App. 591, 594, 188 S.E.2d 405, 407 (1972). But the trick is to tell *when* a contract has been so drawn—and surely the mere recitation of an express power is not always the test. Sometimes it may suffice, depending upon the nature of the expressed power. We cannot imagine, for example, entertaining a claim that a demand for payment of a demand note has been made "in bad faith." In the understood nature of human arrangements, a loan of money in exchange for a promise to repay on demand does not import an obligation to make the demand only if the money is really needed, or only without the purpose and effect of inconveniencing the obligor. But to say that every expressly conferred contractual power is of this nature is virtually to read the doctrine of good faith (or of implied contractual obligations and limitations) out of existence. Many cases, for example, place "good faith" limitations upon the reasons for which an express power to terminate a contract "at will" can be exercised, *see, e.g., Fortune v. National Cash Register Co.,* 373 Mass. 96, 364 N.E.2d 1251 (1977). (One application of this principle has been embodied in the RESTATEMENT (SECOND) OF AGENCY § 454 (1958).) And in much earlier times, before the "good faith" terminology was generally applied, the same principle was employed to find that an unqualified option to terminate if a specified event occurs "clearly implied" that the option had to be exercised within a reasonable time after the happening of the event. *Davidson Hardware Co. v. Delker Bros. Buggy Co.,* 170 N.C. 298, 300, 86 S.E. 958, 959 (1915); *see generally* Annot., 164 A.L.R. 1014, 1024–26 (1946).

Here, however, appellant does not rely solely upon the express conferral of a power to alter quotas, but also upon the expansive fashion in which that power is contractually described. The Compensation Plan states and reiterates that Tymshare may change the quota plan "within [its] sole discretion," Sections I A, V, *supra.* But as the administrative law concept of "abuse of discretion" suggests, *see* 5 U.S.C. § 706(2)(A) (1982), this phrase is not necessarily the equivalent of "for any reason whatsoever, no matter how arbitrary or unreasonable." As applied to some contractual powers, it may indeed connote the sort of unfettered authority appellant would wish. But just as, as discussed above, certain express powers, even without an expansive modifier, are implicitly absolute (the power to call a demand note) while others are not (the power to terminate certain continuing contractual arrangements); so also, the reasonably understood effect of an expansive modifier varies from case to case depending upon the nature of the power at issue. Where what is at issue is the retroactive reduction or elimination of a central compensatory element of the contract—a large part of the *quid pro quo* that induced one party's assent—it is simply not likely that the parties had in mind a power quite as absolute as appellant suggests. In the present case, agreeing to such a provision would require a degree of folly on the part of these sales representatives we are not inclined to posit where another plausible interpretation of the language is available. It seems to us that the "sole discretion" intended was discretion to determine the existence or nonexistence of the various factors that would reasonably justify alteration of the sales quota. Those factors would include (as the company's practice under the provisions bears out) an unanticipated volume of business from a particular customer unconnected with the extra sales efforts of the employee assigned to that account; and they may perhaps include other eventualities, such as a poor overall sales year for the company, leaving less gross income to be expended on commissions. The company's genuine determination that one or another of these factors exists can presumably not be questioned. But the language need not (and therefore can not reasonably) be read to confer discretion to reduce the quota for any reason whatever—including what Covell has alleged here, a simple desire to deprive an employee of the fairly agreed benefit of his labors.

[The court reversed the summary judgment in favor of Covell and remanded for a factual determination of Tymshare's motive.]

CITY OF MIDLAND v. O'BRYANT, 18 S.W.3d 209 (Sup.Ct.Tex.2000). [Plaintiffs were police officers who had previously brought claims against the city alleging violations of the Americans with Disabilities Act and the Texas Commission on Human Rights Act. After the plaintiffs voluntarily dismissed those lawsuits, the city reclassified their positions. Plaintiffs claimed in this lawsuit that the new positions were inferior and that the city reclassified them to retaliate for the previous lawsuits. One of the plaintiffs' theories was that the city's retaliation breached the duty of good faith and fair dealing.]

JUSTICE OWEN delivered the opinion of the court.

* * *

This Court has held that not every contractual relationship creates a duty of good faith and fair dealing. * * * We have "specifically rejected the implication of a general duty of good faith and fair dealing in all contracts." * * * But see Restatement (Second) of Contracts § 205 (1979) (providing that "[e]very contract imposes upon each party a duty of good faith and fair dealing in its performance and its enforcement"). * * *

As the plaintiffs recognize, this Court has imposed an actionable duty of good faith and fair dealing only when there is a special relationship, such as that between an insured and his or her insurance carrier. See Arnold v. National County Mut. Fire Ins. Co., 725 S.W.2d 165, 167 (Tex.1987). We have held that a special relationship exists in the insurance context because of "the parties' unequal bargaining power and the nature of insurance contracts which would allow unscrupulous insurers to take advantage of their insureds' misfortunes in bargaining for settlement or resolution of claims." Id. The Court concluded in Arnold that without a cause of action for breach of a duty of good faith and fair dealing, "insurers can arbitrarily deny coverage and delay payment of a claim" and that an insurer has "exclusive control over the evaluation, processing, and denial of claims." Id.

But the elements which make the relationship between an insurer and an insured a special one are absent in the relationship between an employer and its employees. First, in Texas, the employment relationship is generally at-will unless the parties enter into an express agreement that provides otherwise. Second, insurance contracts are typically much more restrictive than employment agreements. If an insured suffers a loss, he cannot simply contract with another insurance company to cover that loss. By contrast, an employee who has been demoted, transferred, or discharged may seek alternative employment. See, e.g., Foley v. Interactive Data Corp., 47 Cal.3d 654, 254 Cal.Rptr. 211, 765 P.2d 373, 390 (Cal.1988).

Moreover, this Court has thus far recognized only one limited common-law exception to the at-will employment doctrine. We held in Sabine Pilot Service, Inc. v. Hauck, 687 S.W.2d 733 (Tex.1985), that an employer may not discharge an employee for the sole reason that the employee refused to perform an illegal act that carried criminal penalties. Id. at 735. We have not, however, recognized other common-law exceptions to the employment at-will doctrine. We declined to recognize a common-law whistleblower cause of action * * *. We did so primarily on the basis that the Legislature has been active in crafting whistleblower statutes that often vary from one another in material respects.

The adoption of a general common-law whistleblower cause of action would have undercut the many distinctions drawn by the Legislature among the various statutory whistleblower causes of action. Similarly, we decline to impose a duty of good faith and fair dealing on employers in light of the variety of statutes that the Legislature has already enacted to regulate employment relationships. Recognizing a new common-law cause of action based on the duty plaintiffs advocate would tend to subvert those statutory schemes by allowing employees to make an end-run around the procedural requirements and specific remedies the existing statutes establish.

Here, for instance, plaintiffs have alleged claims for discrimination and retaliation under sections 21.051 and 21.055 of the Texas Labor Code. * * * But the court of appeals determined that plaintiffs had failed to exhaust their administrative remedies as required by the Labor Code, and that therefore the trial court did not have jurisdiction over those claims. * * * Plaintiffs do not contest this determination. Rather, they ask us to excuse them from the Labor Code's administrative requirements by creating a common-law cause of action for the same actions of the City on which they based their suit under the Labor Code. We decline to do so.

In holding that there is no duty of good faith and fair dealing in the employment context, we perceive no distinction between government and private employers, inasmuch as both types of employers are subject to applicable laws, regulations, and contractual agreements. Nor do we see any meaningful basis to distinguish between employment at-will and employment governed by an express agreement. A court-created duty of good faith and fair dealing would completely alter the nature of the at-will employment relationship, which generally can be terminated by either party for any reason or no reason at all, and we accordingly decline to change the at-will nature of employment in Texas. If, as plaintiffs argue, they could only be terminated or transferred for reasons of "merit," that fact militates against imposing a common-law duty of good faith and fair dealing because such a contractual limitation would afford more rights to the plaintiffs than at-will employees possess. Moreover, such a duty would be unnecessary when there are express contractual limits on an employer's right to terminate.

Accordingly, we hold that the City of Midland was entitled to summary judgment on the plaintiffs' claims that the defendants breached a duty of good faith and fair dealing.* * *

SUMMERS, "GOOD FAITH" IN GENERAL CONTRACT LAW AND THE SALES PROVISIONS OF THE UNIFORM COMMERCIAL CODE

54 Va.L.Rev. 195, 199–202 (1968).

What is the best way to determine a judge's meaning when he uses the phrase "good faith"? In the case law taken as a whole, does the term have a single general meaning of its own, or perhaps several such meanings? (The answers to these questions are closely linked.) Sometimes what a judge means by good faith will be instantly obvious, but frequently it will not be. When not, it may be that he is using the phrase loosely. But even if he is using it with care, there may still be unclarity. He might indicate only that, in a given context, parties are to act in good faith or that a party did or did not act in good faith, without elaborating at all. Or he might elaborate without communicating in any specific way—for example, by laying down some very general definition of good faith, such as acting "honestly" or "being faithful to one's duty or obligation." The analyst of such an opinion is likely to inquire: What is the meaning of good faith itself? He seems to assume that the phrase has some general meaning or meanings, one of which the judge presumably intends.

One of the principal theses of this Article is that in cases of doubt, a lawyer will determine more accurately what the judge means by using the phrase "good faith" if he does not ask what good faith itself means, but rather asks: What in the actual or hypothetical situation, does the judge intend to rule out by his use of this phrase? Once the relevant form of bad faith is thus identified, the lawyer can, if he wishes, assign a specific meaning to good faith by formulating an "opposite" for the species of bad faith being ruled out. For example, a judge may say: "A public authority must act in good faith in letting bids." And from the facts or the language of the opinion it may appear that the judge is, in effect, saying: "The defendant acted in bad faith because he let bids only as a pretense to conceal his purpose to award the contract to a favored bidder." It can then be said that "acting in good faith" here simply means: letting bids without a preconceived design to award the contract to a favored bidder.

If good faith had a general meaning or meanings of its own—that is, if it were either univocal or ambiguous—there would seldom be occasion to derive a meaning for it from an opposite; its specific uses would almost always be readily and immediately understood. But good faith is not that kind of doctrine. In contract law, taken as a whole, good faith is an "excluder." It is a phrase without general meaning (or meanings) of its own and serves to exclude a wide range of heterogeneous forms of bad faith. In a particular context the phrase takes on specific meaning, but usually this is only by way of contrast with the specific form of bad faith actually or hypothetically ruled out. Aristotle was one of the first to recognize that the function of some words and phrases is not to convey general, "extractable" meanings of their own, but rather is to exclude one or more of a variety of things. He thought "voluntary" was such a word. And the late Professor J.L. Austin of Oxford made much of "excluders."

RESTATEMENT (SECOND) OF CONTRACTS § 205.

Duty of Good Faith and Fair Dealing

Every contract imposes upon each party a duty of good faith and fair dealing in its performance and its enforcement.

Comment:

a. *Meanings of "Good Faith."* * * * The phrase "good faith" is used in a variety of contexts, and its meaning varies somewhat with the context. Good faith performance or enforcement of a contract emphasizes faithfulness to an agreed common purpose and consistency with the justified expectations of the other party; it excludes a variety of types of conduct characterized as involving "bad faith" because they violate community standards of decency, fairness or reasonableness. The appropriate remedy for a breach of the duty of good faith also varies with the circumstances.

* * *

d. *Good faith performance.* Subterfuges and evasions violate the obligation of good faith in performance even though the actor believes his conduct to be justified. But the obligation goes further: bad faith may be overt or may consist of inaction, and fair dealing may require more than honesty. A complete catalogue of types of bad faith is impossible, but the following types are among those which have been recognized in judicial decisions: evasion of the spirit of the bargain, lack of diligence and slacking off, willful rendering of imperfect performance, abuse of a power to specify terms, and interference with or failure to cooperate in the other party's performance.

1970 PROCEEDINGS OF THE AMERICAN LAW INSTITUTE
47 A.L.I.Proc. 489–91 (1970).

R. Braucher[b] * * *

I should call attention to a limitation on this. The black letter is limited, as is the section of the Commercial Code, to good faith in performance and enforcement, and is not a requirement, as stated here, of good faith in bargaining, good faith in offer and acceptance.

Now, there are some obligations of good faith and fair dealing in the making of a contract, as distinguished from performance and enforcement. I

b. Robert Braucher was the Reporter of the Restatement (Second) of Contracts from 1960 to 1971. From 1946 to 1971, he was a member of the Harvard Law School faculty. In 1971, he was appointed Associate Justice of the Massachusetts Supreme Judicial Court, a position he held until his death in 1981.

don't think you can find a case in the whole history of the common law in which a court says that good faith is not required in the performance of a contract or in enforcement of a contract.

Now, the trouble with this section, of course, is that it's very general, very abstract, and it needs specification the worst way, and specification is not to be had. * * *

* * *

Anyway, the principle is to be found in judicial opinions. I haven't invented it. It's also to be found in the Commercial Code. I think there are more judicial opinions along this line in the New York Court of Appeals and the Supreme Court of California than there are in most of the other courts. * * *

Anyway, there it is. [There was no comment]

SUMMERS, THE GENERAL DUTY OF GOOD FAITH— ITS RECOGNITION AND CONCEPTUALIZATION

67 Cornell L.Rev. 810, 823–824 (1982).

In my view, a judge in a novel case posing an issue of good faith under section 205 with its excluder conceptualization is far from lacking meaningful guidance of the kind legitimately to be demanded in the name of the rule of law. He should start with the language of the section. Second, he should turn to the purposes of section 205 as set forth mainly in Comment a. These purposive rationales will infuse the excluder analysis with meaning in all the ways that purposive interpretation is known generally to provide guidance to judges (as in the case of statutes). Third, after completing this, he should seek guidance by the time-honored common-law method of reasoning by analogy, not only from past cases, but from the various illustrations set forth in the Comments to section 205. Such reasoning, particularly that which is done with an eye to the *reasons* given by prior judges, can provide substantial insight into how novel cases should be decided. Fourth, also in light of the purposes of section 205 and any general analogies, he can analyze the relevant facts—alleged or proven—to see what specific reasons these facts, and the values they implicate, generate for and against characterizing the action or inaction in question as bad-faith behavior. Fifth, because of the very nature of the problem, the excluder analysis is not only faithful to the reality involved, but it is itself a distinctive source of illumination. It does not focus on some presumed positive and unitary element or cluster of elements called "good faith"; instead, it focuses on whether the alleged form of bad-faith behavior really is, in the context, ruled out by section 205, when considered in light of its purposes and in relation to the facts of the case. The foregoing factors do not exhaust all the forms of guidance that section 205 provides, but they are more than sufficient to rebut the charge that a section in which good faith is conceptualized as an excluder leaves the judges at sea and the "law" merely whatever the judges say it is.

FELD v. HENRY S. LEVY & SONS, INC.

Court of Appeals of New York, 1975.
37 N.Y.2d 466, 373 N.Y.S.2d 102, 335 N.E.2d 320.

COOKE, JUDGE.

Plaintiff operates a business known as the Crushed Toast Company and defendant is engaged in the wholesale bread baking business. They entered into a written contract, as of June 19, 1968, in which defendant agreed to sell and plaintiff to purchase "all bread crumbs produced by the Seller in its factory at 115 Thames Street, Brooklyn, New York, during the period commencing June 19, 1968, and terminating June 18, 1969", the agreement to "be deemed automatically renewed thereafter for successive renewal periods of one year" with the right to either party to cancel by giving not less than six months notice to the other by certified mail. No notice of cancellation was served. Additionally, pursuant to a contract stipulation, a faithful performance bond was delivered by plaintiff at the inception of the contractual relationship, and a bond continuation certificate was later submitted for the yearly term commencing June 19, 1969.

Interestingly, the term "bread crumbs" does not refer to crumbs that may flake off bread; rather, they are a manufactured item, starting with stale or imperfectly appearing loaves and followed by removal of labels, processing through two grinders, the second of which effects a finer granulation, insertion into a drum in an oven for toasting and, finally, bagging of the finished product.

Subsequent to the making of the agreement, a substantial quantity of bread crumbs, said to be over 250 tons, were sold by defendant to plaintiff but defendant stopped crumb production on about May 15, 1969. There was proof by defendant's comptroller that the oven was too large to accommodate the drum, that it was stated that the operation was "very uneconomical", but after said date of cessation no steps were taken to obtain more economical equipment. The toasting oven was intentionally broken down, then partially rebuilt, then completely dismantled in the summer of 1969 and, thereafter, defendant used the space for a computer room. It appears, without dispute, that defendant indicated to plaintiff at different times that the former would resume bread crumb production if the contract price of 6 cents per pound be changed to 7 cents, and also that, after the crumb making machinery was dismantled, defendant sold the raw materials used in making crumbs to animal food manufacturers.

Special Term denied plaintiff's motion for summary judgment on the issue of liability and turned down defendant's counter-request for a summary judgment of dismissal. From the Appellate Division's order of affirmance, by a divided court, both parties appeal.

Defendant contends that the contract did not require defendant to manufacture bread crumbs, but merely to sell those it did, and, since none were produced after the demise of the oven, there was no duty to then deliver and, consequently from then on, no liability on its part. Agreements to sell all the goods or services a party may produce or perform to another party are commonly referred to as "output" contracts and they usually serve a useful commercial purpose in minimizing the burdens of product marketing (see 1 Williston, Contracts [3d ed.], § 104A). The Uniform Commercial Code rejects the ideas that an output contract is lacking in mutuality or that it is unenforceable because of indefiniteness in that a quantity for the term is not specified. * * * Official Comment 2 to section 2–306 * * * states in part: "Under this Article, a contract for output * * * is not too indefinite since it is held to mean the actual good faith output * * * of the particular party. Nor does such a contract lack mutuality of obligation since, under this section, the party who will determine quantity is required to operate his plant or conduct his business in good faith and according to commercial standards of fair dealing in the trade so that his output * * * will proximate a reasonably foreseeable figure." * * *

The real issue in this case is whether the agreement carries with it an implication that defendant was obligated to continue to manufacture bread crumbs for the full term. Section 2–306 of the Uniform Commercial Code, entitled "Output, Requirements and Exclusive Dealings" provides:

> "(1) A term which measures the quantity by the output of the seller or the requirements of the buyer means such actual output or requirements as may occur in good faith, except that no quantity unreasonably disproportionate to any stated estimate or in the absence of a stated estimate to any normal or otherwise comparable prior output or requirements may be tendered or demanded.

> "(2) *A lawful agreement* by either the seller or the buyer *for exclusive dealing* in the kind of goods concerned *imposes* unless otherwise agreed an obligation *by the seller to use best efforts to supply the goods* and by the buyer to use best efforts to promote their sale." (Emphasis supplied.)

The Official Comment thereunder reads in part: "Subsection (2), on exclusive dealing, makes explicit the commercial rule embodied in this Act under which the parties to such contracts are held to have impliedly, even when not expressly, bound themselves to use reasonable diligence as well as good faith in their performance of the contract. * * * An exclusive dealing agreement brings into play all of the good faith aspects of the output and requirement problems of subsection (1). It also raises questions of insecurity and right to adequate assurance under this Article."

Section 2–306 is consistent with prior New York case law. * * * Every contract of this type imposes an obligation of good faith in its performance. (Uniform Commercial Code, § 1–203 * * *). Under the Uniform Commercial Code, the commercial background and intent must be read into the language of any agreement and good faith is demanded in the performance of that agreement * * * and, under the decisions relating to output contracts, it is clearly the general rule that good faith cessation of production terminates any further obligations thereunder and excuses further performance by the party discontinuing production. * * *

This is not a situation where defendant ceased its main operation of bread baking. * * * Rather, defendant contends in a conclusory fashion that it was "uneconomical" or "economically not feasible" for it to continue to make bread crumbs. Although plaintiff observed in his motion papers that defendant claimed it was not economically feasible to make the crumbs, plaintiff did not admit that as a fact. In any event, "economic feasibility", an expression subject to many interpretations, would not be a precise or reliable test.

There are present here intertwined questions of fact, whether defendant performed in good faith and whether it stopped its manufacture of bread crumbs in good faith, neither of which can be resolved properly on this record. The seller's duty to remain in crumb production is a matter calling for a close scrutiny of its motives (1 Hawkland, A Transactional Guide to the Uniform Commercial Code, p. 52, see, also, p. 48), confined here by the papers to financial reasons. It is undisputed that defendant leveled its crumb making machinery only after plaintiff refused to agree to a price higher than that specified in the agreement and that it then sold the raw materials to manufacturers of animal food. There are before us no componential figures indicating the actual cost of the finished bread crumbs to defendant, statements as to the profits derived or the losses sustained, or data specifying the net or gross return realized from the animal food transactions.

The parties by their contract gave the right of cancellation to either by providing for a six months' notice to the other. The apparent purpose of such a stipulation was to provide an opportunity to either the seller or buyer to conclude their dealings in the event that the transactions were not as profitable or advantageous as desired or expected, or for any other reason. Correspondingly, such a notice would also furnish the receiver of it a chance to secure another outlet or source of supply, as the case might be. Short of such a cancellation, defendant was expected to continue to perform in good faith and could cease production of the bread crumbs, a single facet of its operation, only in good faith. Obviously, a bankruptcy or genuine imperiling of the very existence of its entire business caused by the production of the crumbs would warrant cessation of production of that item; the yield of less profit from its sale than expected would not. Since bread crumbs were but a part of defendant's enterprise and since there was a contractual right of cancellation, good faith required continued production until cancellation, even if there be no profit. In circumstances such as these and without more, defendant would be justified, in good faith, in ceasing production of the single item prior to cancellation only if its losses from continuance would be more than trivial, which, overall, is a question of fact.

The order of the Appellate Division should be affirmed, without costs.

Note
Good Faith in the Uniform Commercial Code

As we have seen, Uniform Commercial Code section 1–203 provides that "[e]very contract or duty within this Act imposes an obligation of good faith in its performance or enforcement." In Feld v. Henry S. Levy & Sons, Inc., however, the New York Court of Appeals invoked section 2–306, one of thirteen sections of Article 2 of the Code (on the sale of goods) which explicitly requires good faith. Nineteen sections of Article 2 include comments which also use the phrase.

Article 1 of the U.C.C. ("General Provisions") defines good faith in section 1–201(19) to mean (unless the context otherwise requires) "honesty in fact in the conduct or transaction concerned." However, in Article 2 on sales of goods, section 2–103(1)(b) states that "unless the context otherwise requires * * * '[g]ood faith' in the case of a merchant means honesty in fact and the observance of reasonable commercial standards of fair dealing in the trade." (Revised Article 1 adopts the Article 2 definition for all parties in section 1–201(b)(20).) Certain other articles of the Uniform Commercial Code also incorporate the term "good faith," usually with definitions. In cases in which the Code does not apply, courts often cite by analogy the Code's general provision on good faith, section 1–203.

PILLOIS v. BILLINGSLEY

United States Court of Appeals, Second Circuit, 1950.
179 F.2d 205.

CHASE, CIRCUIT JUDGE:

This appeal is from a judgment in a suit brought under the diversity jurisdiction of the court to recover the reasonable value of the appellee's services, performed at the request of the appellant, in procuring a contract for a corporation of which the appellant was a director.

* * *

* * * [T]he suit was tried by court and it was found on evidence, sufficient though in part conflicting, that the defendant had employed the plaintiff to obtain "from La Societe Le Galion a long term exclusive representation of S.A. Le Galion perfumes in the United States of America and elsewhere in the Western Hemisphere in the name of Cigogne, Inc.," and that the defendant agreed to pay the plaintiff for his services in so doing such sum as the defendant in his sole judgment might decide to be reasonable. It was further found that "the plaintiff went to France and returned with a contract giving Cigogne, Inc., exclusive representation in the United States, Alaska, Puerto Rico, Hawaii, and the Philippine Islands for the Le Galion perfumes for a term of 99 years"; that Cigogne, Inc., accepted the contract and was operating under it; and that the defendant had refused to pay the plaintiff anything for his services in obtaining it and had not given any consideration to determining what would be reasonable compensation for them. It was held that under these circumstances the plaintiff could recover the reasonable value of his services, which the court determined to be $6,000. The judgment entered was for that amount with interest and costs.

* * *

* * * This suit is confined to the alleged breach of the agreement relating to the procurement of the long term contract between the French manufacturer and Cigogne, Inc. That was set forth in a letter which the appellant had his own attorneys prepare and which was addressed to the appellant and signed by the appellee as follows:

"July 9, 1947
"New York City

"Mr. Sherman Billingsley,
"Stork Restaurant Inc.,
"3 East 53rd Street,
"New York, N.Y.
"Dear Sir:

"This will confirm our understanding in connection with the exclusive representation of the S.A. Le Galion trade mark under contracts of March 20,

1946 and July 25, 1946, now being held by Cigogne, Inc., a New York corporation by assignment from Chapman & Keane, as follows:

"You will provide funds for expenses for my trip to France forthwith for the purpose of my obtaining from La Societe Le Galion a long term exclusive representation of S.A. Le Galion perfumes in the United States of America and elsewhere in the western hemisphere in the name of Cigogne, Inc., with the right of Cigogne, Inc. to appoint national or area distributors in its discretion.

"My compensation for such services as I may render in this connection shall be such sum as you, in your sole judgment, may decide is reasonable.

"You have made no other commitment and have no other obligation to me of any kind whatsoever.

"Yours very truly

"Raymond Pillois (s)
"Raymond Pillois

This letter, as the trial judge held, shows an agreement which is not too indefinite to be enforced, the appellee having performed his part of it. It entitled him to have the appellant in good faith determine the reasonable value of his services and to pay him that amount. * * * And when the appellant failed to make any determination whatever as to what such services were reasonably worth the appellee became entitled to recover as on a quantum meruit basis. * * *

We are here dealing with the legal results which flow from the performance by one party to a contract and not with what legal obligations, if any, are created by a wholly executory contract. See 1 Williston on Contracts § 49. It may be acknowledged that the appellant was not satisfied with the terms of the contract procured from the French manufacturer because, among other things, the territory embraced in the former contract was diminished, but the fact remains that Cigogne, Inc., did accept it, as both its answer admits and the evidence clearly shows.

While it is true that many difficulties are encountered in fixing the reasonable worth of the appellee's services in procuring the contract, that did not deprive him of the right to compensation. * * * In this instance the evidence showed that the appellee made a return trip from New York to Paris; that he negotiated for twelve days with the French manufacturer; that it was unusual in this business to enter into such a contract for a term as long as 99 years; and that the appellant was experienced in the perfume business and well and favorably known to M. Vacher who had charge of the negotiations in Paris for the French manufacturer. The appellee testified that his services were worth $100,000 but the trial judge, who has had many years of experience on the bench, evidently considered that greatly exaggerated. There was other evidence that the contract itself was worth from $25,000 to $50,000 to Cigogne, Inc., and that of course was a relevant matter for consideration in determining the value of appellee's services. The weight to be given all this evidence was to be decided by the trial judge. We are concerned only with whether there was substantial support for his determination that $6,000 was the reasonable value, and we think there was.

Judgment affirmed.

CENTRONICS CORP. v. GENICOM CORP., 132 N.H. 133, 562 A.2d 187 (1989).

SOUTER, JUSTICE.

Despite the variety of their fact patterns, [good faith] cases illustrate a common rule: under an agreement that appears by word or silence to invest one party with a degree of discretion in performance sufficient to deprive another party of a substantial proportion of the agreement's value, the parties' intent to be bound by an enforceable contract raises an implied obligation of good faith to observe reasonable limits in exercising that discretion, consistent with the parties' purpose or purposes in contracting. A claim for relief from a violation of the implied covenant of good faith contractual performance therefore potentially raises four questions:

1. Does the agreement ostensibly allow to or confer upon the defendant a degree of discretion in performance tantamount to a power to deprive the plaintiff of a substantial proportion of the agreement's value? Contracts may be broken in a multitude of ways and theories of relief are correspondingly numerous, but the concept of good faith in performance addresses the particular problem raised by a promise subject to such a degree of discretion that its practical benefit could seemingly be withheld.

2. If the ostensible discretion is of that requisite scope, does competent evidence indicate that the parties intended by their agreement to make a legally enforceable contract?

3. Assuming an intent to be bound, has the defendant's exercise of discretion exceeded the limits of reasonableness? The answer to this question depends on identifying the common purpose or purposes of the contract, against which the reasonableness of the complaining party's expectations may be measured, and in furtherance of which community standards of honesty, decency and reasonableness can be applied.

4. Is the cause of the damage complained of the defendant's abuse of discretion, or does it result from events beyond the control of either party, against which the defendant has no obligation to protect the plaintiff? Although this question is cast in the language of causation, it may be seen simply as the other face of question three. Suffice it to say here that its point is to emphasize that the good faith requirement is not a fail-safe device barring a defendant from the fruits of every plaintiff's bad bargain, or empowering courts to rewrite an agreement even when a defendant's discretion is consistent with the agreement's legally contractual character.

Note
Good Faith in German Law

The American legal system has, at a relatively late stage, come to recognize good faith in contract law. Section 242 of the German BGB (Bürgerliches Gesetzbuch) or Civil Code provides: "Der Schuldner ist verpflichtet, die Leistung so zu bewirken, wie Treu und Glauben mit Rücksicht auf die Verkehrssitte es erfordern." This has been translated: "The debtor is bound to effect performance according to the requirements of good faith, common habits being duly taken into consideration." 1 Cohn, Manual of German Law 96–97 (2d ed. 1968). (Note that the term "Schuldner" might be better rendered as obligor, not debtor, in English.) Section 242 dates from the late 19th century and has roots in ancient Roman law. The case law that has accumulated under section 242 vastly exceeds that arising under any other BGB section.

Section 1–203 of the Uniform Commercial Code, imposing a general obligation of good faith, was, as we have noted, drafted by Professor Karl N. Llewellyn. It has often been asserted that he modeled section 1–203 on section 242 of the BGB. Do you find this credible? Consider, again, the wording of Section 1–203: "Every contract or duty within this Act imposes a duty of good faith in its performance or enforcement."

HOLMES, THE PATH OF THE LAW

10 Harv.L.Rev. 457, 459–60, 462 (1897).

The first thing for a business-like understanding of [a] matter is to understand its limits, and therefore I think it desirable at once to point out and dispel a confusion between morality and law, which sometimes rises to the height of conscious theory, and more often and indeed constantly is making trouble in detail without reaching the point of consciousness. * * *

* * *

* * * If you want to know the law and nothing else, you must look at it as a bad man, who cares only for the material consequences which such knowledge enables him to predict, not as a good one, who finds his reasons for conduct, whether inside the law or outside of it, in the vaguer sanctions of conscience. The theoretical importance of the distinction is no less, if you would reason on your subject aright. The law is full of phraseology drawn from morals, and by the mere force of language continually invites us to pass from one domain to the other without perceiving it, as we are sure to do unless we have the boundary constantly before our minds. * * *

* * *

Nowhere is the confusion between legal and moral ideas more manifest than in the law of contract. Among other things, here again the so called primary rights and duties are invested with a mystic significance beyond what can be assigned and explained. The duty to keep a contract at common law means a prediction that you must pay damages if you do not keep it,—and nothing else. If you commit a tort, you are liable to pay a compensatory sum. If you commit a contract, you are liable to pay a compensatory sum unless the promised event comes to pass, and that is all the difference. But such a mode of looking at the matter stinks in the nostrils of those who think it advantageous to get as much ethics into the law as they can.

L. FULLER, THE LAW IN QUEST OF ITSELF
93–95 (1940).

It is a very convincing figure which [Holmes] offers us, and it makes a working kind of positivism seem quite plausible. Yet it is apparent that this bad man of Holmes' is himself an abstraction, in two senses.

In the first place, it will be noted that it is a peculiar sort of bad man who is worried about judicial decrees and is indifferent to extra-legal penalties, who is concerned about a fine of two dollars but apparently not about the possible loss of friends and customers. To define the law in terms of the viewpoint of one with this attitude is to some extent a begging of the question, and amounts almost to saying that the law is that which concerns one who is concerned only with the law.

In the second place, Holmes assumes that his bad man has already reached a conclusion concerning the legal risks of a particular line of conduct, and he neglects to inquire into the process by which this man would actually arrive at such a conclusion. Let us see for ourselves how this bad man, faced with a specific problem of conduct, would have to reason. He wants to know what it is likely to cost him to attain a particular objective. Because of the peculiarly juristic orientation of his fears, he will be deterred only by judicial penalties. He must ask himself, then, "What are the chances that my conduct may lead to a detrimental interference in my affairs by the courts?" To answer that, he must ask, "How will my conduct be viewed by judges?" This question he cannot answer merely by consulting the letter of the law, for he will still not know in what direction the letter will be strained in cases of doubt. Nor will it be enough for him "to know his judge." Even if the judge who will decide his case has pronounced and recognizable biases, a bias is, after all, only one factor in a complex equation, and to calculate its effects one must analyze the ethical forces with which it will come in conflict. In the end, our bad man cannot escape having to decide a question of morality. He will have to ask, "How would I myself view my conduct if I were not interested in it? How would it be viewed by a disinterested third party? Would it seem to him to be good or evil?" Only when he has answered this question will he have rounded out the equation on the basis of which he can calculate accurately the chances of judicial intervention in his affairs.

In short, our bad man, if he is effectively to look after his own interests, will have to learn to look at the law through the eyes of a good man.

*

Chapter Seven

CONDITIONAL NATURE OF THE DUTY TO PERFORM, AND PERMISSIBLE RESPONSES TO FAILURE OF CONDITION AND BREACH OF DUTY

Since an express condition depends for its validity on the intentions of the parties, it has the same sanctity as the promise itself.

WILLISTON

The construction of conditions protects a party against impairment of expectation.

PATTERSON

SECTION ONE: CONDITIONS AND THE ROLE OF LAWYERS

Suppose Ben Builder and Oswald Owner negotiate for the construction of a new sidewalk for Owner at a price of about $4,500. A lawyer asked to draft an agreement between Builder and Owner will try to anticipate all important sources of dispute and deal with them in the agreement. Two major sources are the order of performance and the quality of performance. Who must perform first—Builder, by constructing the sidewalk, or Owner, by paying? And of what quality must Builder's completed performance be? Must it be perfect? By what standards? The lawyer should not leave gaps in the agreement with regard to such matters. To fill the first of these gaps, the lawyer can draft what is called an express condition precedent (pronounced preceedent) requiring Builder to perform the work before Owner's duty to pay matures: "Builder's constructing the sidewalk is a condition precedent to Owner's duty to pay." Why the language "condition precedent"? The duty of Owner to pay does not *mature* until the other party, Builder in our example, has first performed. Alternatively, the lawyer might expressly condition Builder's duty to perform on Owner first paying the $4,500. Of course, if a duty to perform does not mature because of the failure of an express condition, there can be no breach of that duty.

The lawyer can also specify the quality of performance required of Builder as part of an express condition precedent, and thus fill the second gap. Suppose the parties agree that Builder must perform first and that the job

755

must be done in accord with specific standards, e.g., that the finished concrete has no cracks in it. The lawyer can then draft an express condition precedent requiring Builder to perform by constructing all sidewalk slabs without any cracking before Owner's duty to pay arises.

In preceding chapters, we saw that contracting parties frequently do not cover all matters in their express agreement (especially when they draft without the aid of lawyers), and we addressed how courts generally fill gaps.[a] In this chapter, we consider not only how the lawyer may plan and draft express conditions to deal with order of performance, quality of performance, and related problems, but also study how courts fill gaps in agreements that are silent on these matters.

Suppose, for example, that the drafter of the Builder–Owner contract fails to specify the order of performance and the quality of performance. Under principles of interpretation and gap-filling law, can Builder require that Oswald Owner pay him the $4,500 *before* Builder starts work? Or suppose that Builder builds the sidewalk, that it consists of 48 slabs, and that a crack emerges across one side of the eleventh slab. Despite this defect, is Builder entitled to the contract price—the $4,500—less any deduction for the cost to Owner of repairing the eleventh slab? Or would Builder have to perform perfectly to mature Owner's duty to pay the contract price?

When confronted with such gaps, courts turn to resources studied in the preceding chapter. Typically they first attempt to ascertain the intentions of the parties by examining contractual language and the overall circumstances. In some cases this evidence is sufficiently clear for a court to conclude that the parties intended a particular approach to a problem. For example, a course of dealing between the parties in which Builder always performed first may be enough to justify a finding that the parties actually intended Builder to perform first in this contract. In such a case, Owner's duty to pay is said to be *impliedly-in-fact* conditional on Builder's prior performance. In other cases, less substantial evidence, such as a general trade custom that builders perform before payment, may indicate the probable intentions of the parties as to the order of performance in their contract. Recognizing that such evidence is inconclusive, a court may present its findings simply as the reasonable expectations of the parties. In still other cases, there may be no evidence of the actual or probable intentions of Builder and Owner with respect to the order of performance. In such cases, judges must fill the gap by devising a general *rule of law* such as: "in case of a gap in the contract as to the order of performance, builders must perform first." Here, Owner's duty to pay is said to be *impliedly-in-law* conditional on Builder's performance, and the gap-filling rule invoked is justified not on the basis of the probable intentions of the parties but on general policies and principles. Courts have traditionally called the term supplied by such a gap-filler rule either an implied-in-law condition precedent, or a constructive condition precedent. Again, if such a condition does not occur, the duty to perform does not mature and there can be no breach.

a. See Chapter One, Sections Two and Three of Chapter Four, and Section Four of Chapter Six.

Sometimes it will be difficult to tell whether a court's decision is based on evidence of intentions, on some rule of law, or on a combination of both. In this chapter we will, with some refinement, use the terminology of "implied conditions" (and occasionally, "constructive conditions") to refer to these forms of gap-filling. As we will see, the courts have developed a variety of gap-filler rules.

We now introduce some alternative terminology that was prominent in the older cases and still creeps into some modern opinions in which courts fill gaps with respect to the order of performance and the quality of performance. When a court holds that the performance of a promise is an implied condition precedent to the other party's duty to perform—for example, suppose a court holds that Builder's building of the sidewalk is a condition precedent to Owner's duty to pay—the court might also refer to Owner's duty as a "dependent covenant" and Builder's duty as an "independent covenant." The covenant to pay—Owner's promise—is not to be performed in our example unless and until Builder performs. Hence Owner's promise is "dependent" on Builder's prior performance. On the other hand, the duty of Builder to build falls due prior to and thus "independently" of the owner's duty to pay. Builder's covenant is therefore an "independent" covenant. (As we will later see, however, circumstances may arise in which Builder is excused from performing or tendering performance in light of the Owner's circumstances— e.g. insolvency or a threat not to pay—so that Builder's "prior" duty under his promise is not totally "independent" of the owner's prospective performance or nonperformance.)

The leading common law case introducing the doctrine of implied conditions precedent ("dependency of covenants") was the famous House of Lords decision in Kingston v. Preston, 2 Douglas 689 (1773). In that case, Lord .Mansfield, confronted with a gap in an agreement as to the order of performance, chose to fill the gap in light of "the evident sense and meaning of the parties." By this criterion, and if the agreement is otherwise silent, does it follow in our example that Builder is required to build before becoming entitled to payment from Owner? What further criteria are relevant here? Do the equities between the parties ever suggest an order of performance the court should adopt? Does custom? Does sound risk allocation? We will return to these questions.

Let us consider further the second basic gap in our agreement between Builder and Owner, the "quality of performance" gap. Assume the agreement simply required the construction of a "48 slab sidewalk." What if Builder satisfactorily constructed 47 of 48 sidewalk slabs, but the eleventh one was cracked? By performing so substantially, would Builder have matured Owner's duty to pay the $4,500 contract price (less costs of repairing the cracked one), or would Builder have to perform *perfectly* in order to mature Owner's duty to pay the contract price? Again, a court will initially look to evidence of the actual or probable intentions of the parties and, if this evidence is sufficient, imply (in fact) the appropriate condition with respect to quality of performance. But here, too, the evidence may not be sufficient. In that event, the court must turn to gap-filler rules of law, i.e. implied-in-law conditions. These rules are not the same for all settings, however. In the construction setting, assuming a gap as to the quality of performance, a builder typically must "substantially perform" in order to satisfy an implied-in-law condition precedent to the owner's duty to pay. Would 47 good slabs and one cracked one constitute substantial performance? We treat this issue in detail later.

We have now introduced the problem of whether a contracting party's duty to perform has *matured* under an agreement. Suppose a duty to perform has not matured—e.g., suppose that Builder's constructing the sidewalk is a condition precedent to Owner's duty to pay and that Builder does not perform—at what point is Owner *discharged* from the agreement? Obviously Owner does not have to wait forever for Builder to perform. But can Owner bar Builder from performing and immediately hire someone else? Contract law's answer is that a party is discharged when it is "too late" for the condition to occur. This time may be stated expressly in the agreement or it may be implied from the circumstances. We consider this problem in detail in Section Nine of the present chapter.

SECTION TWO: SPECIFIC USES OF EXPRESS CONDITIONS AND THEIR OPERATION AND EFFECT

In Section One, we considered how parties, through their lawyers, might incorporate express conditions in their agreement as to order of performance and quality of performance, and thereby fill such gaps. The parties might use express conditions in further related ways, too. Compare the following examples:

(1) Ben Builder promises to construct a sidewalk during the month of October for Oswald Owner in accord with attached plans. Oswald Owner promises to pay $4,500 for the sidewalk on condition that Builder construct the sidewalk.

(2) Ben Builder promises to construct a sidewalk during the month of October for Oswald Owner in accord with attached plans. Oswald Owner promises to pay $4,500 for the sidewalk on condition that Alice Taub, Architect, is satisfied that the sidewalk was built as agreed and has issued a certificate to Builder to that effect.

(3) Ben Builder promises to construct a sidewalk during the month of October for Oswald Owner in accord with attached plans on condition that weather conditions are satisfactory to Builder. Oswald Owner promises to pay $4,500 for the sidewalk.

(4) Oswald Owner promises to pay $4,500 to Builder on condition that Ben Builder constructs a sidewalk during the month of October in accord with attached plans.

In the first example, the subject matter of the express condition (the construction) is also the principal consideration moving to Owner. But in the second example, Owner is not bargaining principally for Builder's securing the certificate from the architect. Rather, Owner is bargaining principally for the construction of a sidewalk. (Of course, the subject matter of the express condition—the architect's approval and issuance of a certificate—is an event that signifies that the constructed sidewalk is of the quality Owner desires.) In the third example, the subject matter of the express condition (satisfactory weather) is again not the performance of a promise constituting one side of an agreed exchange. Rather, the subject matter is a qualification on the duty of one of the promisors to perform—if the weather is bad, Builder's duty to perform does not mature.

The fourth example *is* like the first in the respect that the subject matter of the condition—Builder's construction of the sidewalk—is the principal consideration that the other party, Owner, is to receive. But there is this important difference. In the first example, the event of constructing the sidewalk is made an express condition precedent to the duty of Owner to pay. In addition, Builder promises to bring that event about. Builder makes no such promise in the fourth example. Just because an event is made the subject matter of a condition precedent, it does not also follow that one of the parties promises to bring it about. This can be seen not only in the fourth example, but in the third example as well. There, the builder does not promise good weather. Such *non-promissory or pure conditions* are not uncommon. In the typical insurance contract, for example, the party who buys insurance coverage does not promise to pay the premium, but the contract makes the event of premium payment one of the conditions precedent to the insurer's duty to pay any insured loss that materializes.

It should be obvious why a party may choose to exact a *promise,* as in the first example. After all, such a party typically wants to bind the other party to a legal obligation. But why would a party want to make an event an *express condition* of that party's duty to perform a promise? The Restatement (Second) of Contracts' Introductory Note to Conditions and Similar Events, contains the following two possible explanations: "An obligor may make an event a condition of his duty in order to shift to the obligee the risk of its non-occurrence. * * * An obligor may also make an event a condition of his duty in order to induce the obligee to cause the event to occur." Which of these explanations accounts for the use of the express condition in our insurance example? Which accounts for the use of an express condition in each of the above four examples? Can you think of any other possible explanations for the use of express conditions?

Of course, as in example one, a contracting party such as Owner may choose *both* to make an event a condition of his own duty *and* to have the other party promise to bring the event about. The late Professor Corbin called an event that is both a condition and a promise a *promissory condition.*

It should be evident from what we have said so far that the lawyer must be able to differentiate between (1) an event that is merely promised by a party, (2) an event that is both promised by a party and designated as an express condition to the other party's duty—a promissory condition, and (3) an event that is merely an express condition to one party's duty—a non-promissory or pure condition. Thus, it is essential to understand the differences between a promise and an express condition. Professor Corbin once concisely summarized these differences:

CORBIN, CONDITIONS IN THE LAW OF CONTRACTS
28 Yale L.J. 739, 743, 745–46 (1919).

The word "condition" is used in the law of property as well as in the law of contract and it is used with some variation in meaning. In the law of contract it is sometimes used in a very loose sense as synonymous with "term," "provision," or "clause." In such a sense it performs no useful service. * * * In its proper sense the word *"condition" means some operative fact subsequent to acceptance and prior to discharge,* a fact upon which the rights and duties of the parties depend. Such a fact may be an act of one of the two contracting parties, an act of a third party, or any other fact of our physical world. It may be a performance that has been promised or a fact as to which there is no promise.

* * *

A promise is always made by the act or acts of one of the parties, such acts being words or other conduct expressing intention; a fact can be made to operate as a condition only by the agreement of both parties or by the construction of the law. The purpose of a promise is the creation of a duty or a disability in the promisor; the purpose of constituting some fact as a condition is always the postponement of an instant duty (or other specified legal relation). The fulfilment of a promise discharges a duty; the occurrence of a condition creates a duty. The non-fulfilment of a promise is called a breach of contract, and creates in the other party a * * * right to damages; it is the failure to perform that which was required by a previous duty. The non-occurrence of a condition will prevent the existence of a duty in the other party; but it may not create any [right to recover damages] at all, and it *will* not unless someone has promised that it shall occur.

* * *

It may be observed that both a promise and a condition are means that are used to bring about certain desired action by another person. For example, an insurance company desires the payment of premiums. One means of securing this desired object would be to obtain a promise by the insured to pay premiums; on failure to pay them an action would lie. In fact, however, insurance policies seldom contain such a promise; the payment of the premiums is secured in a more effective way than that. The insurance company makes its own duty to pay the amount of the policy expressly conditional upon the payment of premiums. Here is no express promise of the insured creating a duty to pay premiums, but there is an express condition precedent to his right to recover on the policy. Payment by the insured is obtained not by holding a lawsuit over him *in terrorem* but by hanging before him a purse of money to be reached only by climbing the ladder of premiums. Before bilateral contracts became enforceable this was the only contractual way for a promisor to secure his desired object.

ARTHUR L. CORBIN

MERRITT HILL VINEYARDS INC. v. WINDY HEIGHTS VINEYARD, INC.

Court of Appeals of New York, 1984.
61 N.Y.2d 106, 472 N.Y.S.2d 592, 460 N.E.2d 1077.

KAYE, JUDGE.

In a contract for the sale of a controlling stock interest in a vineyard, the seller's undertaking to produce a title insurance policy and mortgage confirmation at closing constituted a condition and not a promise, the breach of which excused the buyer's performance and entitled it to the return of its deposit, but not to consequential damages. On the buyer's motion for summary judgment seeking recovery of both the deposit and consequential damages, the Appellate Division 94 A.D.2d 947, 463 N.Y.S.2d 960, correctly awarded summary judgment to the buyer for its deposit and to the seller dismissing the cause of action for consequential damages, even though the seller had not sought this relief by cross appeal.

In September, 1981, plaintiff, Merritt Hill Vineyards, entered into a written agreement with defendants, Windy Heights Vineyard and its sole shareholder Leon Taylor, to purchase a majority stock interest in respondents' Yates County vineyard, and tendered a $15,000 deposit. The agreement provides that "[i]f the sale contemplated hereby does not close, Taylor shall retain the deposit as liquidated damages unless Taylor or Windy Heights failed to satisfy the conditions specified in Section 3 thereof." Section 3, in turn, lists several "conditions precedent" to which the obligation of purchaser to pay the purchase price and to complete the purchase is subject. Among the conditions are that, by the time of the closing, Windy Heights shall have obtained a title insurance policy in a form satisfactory to Merritt Hill, and Windy Heights and Merritt Hill shall have received confirmation from the Farmers Home Administration that certain mortgages on the vineyard are in effect and that the proposed sale does not constitute a default.

In April, 1982, at the closing, plaintiff discovered that neither the policy nor the confirmation had been issued. Plaintiff thereupon refused to close and demanded return of its deposit. When defendants did not return the deposit, plaintiff instituted this action, asserting two causes of action, one for return of the deposit, and one for approximately $26,000 in consequential damages allegedly suffered as a result of defendants' failure to perform.

Special Term denied plaintiff's motion for summary judgment on both causes of action. The Appellate Division unanimously reversed Special Term's order, granted plaintiff's motion for summary judgment as to the cause of action for return of the deposit, and upon searching the record pursuant to CPLR 3212 (subd. [b]), granted summary judgment in favor of defendants, dismissing plaintiff's second cause of action for consequential damages. Both plaintiff and defendants appealed from that decision. * * *

* * *

On the merits, plaintiff's right to return of its deposit or to consequential damages depends upon whether the undertaking to produce the policy and mortgage confirmation is a promise or a condition.

A promise is "a manifestation of intention to act or refrain from acting in a specified way, so made as to justify a promisee in understanding that a commitment has been made." (Restatement, Contracts 2d, § 2, subd. [1].) A *condition,* by comparison, is "an event, not certain to occur, which must occur, unless its non-occurrence is excused, before performance under a contract becomes due." (Restatement, Contracts 2d, § 224.) Here, the contract requirements of a title insurance policy and mortgage confirmation are expressed as conditions of plaintiff's performance rather than as promises by defendants. The requirements are contained in a section of the agreement entitled "Conditions Precedent to Purchaser's Obligation to Close," which provides that plaintiff's obligation to pay the purchase price and complete the purchase of the vineyard is "subject to" fulfillment of those requirements. No words of promise are employed. Defendants' agreement to sell the stock of the vineyard, not those conditions, was the promise by defendants for which plaintiff's promise to pay the purchase price was exchanged.

Defendants' failure to fulfill the conditions of section 3 entitles plaintiff to a return of its deposit but not to consequential damages. While a contracting party's failure to fulfill a condition excuses performance by the other party whose performance is so conditioned, it is not, without an independent promise to perform the condition, a breach of contract subjecting the nonfulfilling party to liability for damages (Restatement, Contracts 2d, § 225, subds. [1], [3]; 3A Corbin, Contracts, § 663; 5 Williston, Contracts [Jaeger–3d ed.], § 665). This is in accord with the parties' expressed intent, for section 1 of their agreement provides that if defendants fail to satisfy the conditions of section 3 plaintiff's deposit will be returned. It does not provide for payment of damages.

On the merits of this case the Appellate Division thus correctly determined that plaintiff was entitled to the return of its deposit but not to consequential damages.

Accordingly, the order of the Appellate Division should be affirmed.

JACOB & YOUNGS, INC. v. KENT

Court of Appeals of New York, 1921.
230 N.Y. 239, 129 N.E. 889.

Cardozo, J. The plaintiff built a country residence for the defendant at a cost of upwards of $77,000, and now sues to recover a balance of $3,483.46, remaining unpaid. The work of construction ceased in June, 1914, and the defendant then began to occupy the dwelling. There was no complaint of defective performance until March, 1915. One of the specifications for the plumbing work provides that—

"All wrought-iron pipe must be well galvanized, lap welded pipe of the grade known as 'standard pipe' of Reading manufacture."

The defendant learned in March, 1915, that some of the pipe, instead of being made in Reading, was the product of other factories. The plaintiff was accordingly directed by the architect to do the work anew. The plumbing was then encased within the walls except in a few places where it had to be exposed. Obedience to the order meant more than the substitution of other pipe. It meant the demolition at great expense of substantial parts of the completed structure. The plaintiff left the work untouched, and asked for a certificate that the final payment was due. Refusal of the certificate was followed by this suit.

The evidence sustains a finding that the omission of the prescribed brand of pipe was neither fraudulent nor willful. It was the result of the oversight and inattention of the plaintiff's subcontractor. Reading pipe is distinguished from Cohoes pipe and other brands only by the name of the manufacturer stamped upon it at intervals of between six and seven feet. Even the defendant's architect, though he inspected the pipe upon arrival, failed to notice the discrepancy. The plaintiff tried to show that the brands installed, though made by other manufacturers, were the same in quality, in appearance, in market value, and in cost as the brand stated in the contract—that they were, indeed, the same thing, though manufactured in another place. The evidence was excluded, and a verdict directed for the defendant. The Appellate Division reversed, and granted a new trial.

We think the evidence, if admitted, would have supplied some basis for the inference that the defect was insignificant in its relation to the project. The courts never say that one who makes a contract fills the measure of his duty by less than full performance. They do say, however, that an omission, both trivial and innocent, will sometimes be atoned for by allowance of the resulting damage, and will not always be the breach of a condition to be followed by a forfeiture. * * * The distinction is akin to that between dependent and independent promises, or between promises and conditions. Anson on Contracts (Corbin's Ed.) § 367; 2 Williston on Contracts, § 842. Some promises are so plainly independent that they can never by fair construction be conditions of one another. Rosenthal Paper Co. v. Nat. Folding Box & Paper Co., 226 N.Y. 313, 123 N.E. 766; Bogardus v. N.Y. Life Ins. Co., 101 N.Y. 328, 4 N.E. 522. Others are so plainly dependent that they must always be conditions. Others, though dependent and thus conditions when there is departure in point of substance, will be viewed as independent and collateral when the departure is insignificant. * * * Considerations partly of justice and partly of presumable intention are to tell us whether this or that promise shall be placed in one class or in another. The simple and the uniform will call for different remedies from the multifarious and the intricate. The margin of departure within the range of normal expectation upon a sale of common chattels will vary from the margin to be expected upon a contract for the construction of a mansion or a "skyscraper." There will be harshness sometimes and oppression in the implication of a condition when the thing upon which labor has been expended is incapable of surrender because united to the land, and equity and reason in the implication of a like condition when the subject-matter, if defective, is in shape to be returned. From the conclusion that promises may not be treated as dependent to the extent of their uttermost minutiae without a sacrifice of justice, the progress is a short one to the conclusion that they may not be so treated without a perversion of intention. Intention not otherwise revealed may be presumed to hold in contemplation the reasonable and probable. If something else is in view, it must not be left to implication. There will be no assumption of a purpose to visit venial faults with oppressive retribution.

Those who think more of symmetry and logic in the development of legal rules than of practical adaptation to the attainment of a just result will be troubled by a classification where the lines of division are so wavering and blurred. Something, doubtless, may be said on the score of consistency and certainty in favor of a stricter standard. The courts have balanced such considerations against those of equity and fairness, and found the latter to be the weightier. The decisions in this state commit us to the liberal view, which is making its way, nowadays, in jurisdictions slow to welcome it. Dakin & Co. v. Lee, 1916, 1 K.B. 566, 579. Where the line is to be drawn between the important and the trivial cannot be settled by a formula. "In the nature of the case precise boundaries are impossible." 2 Williston on Contracts, § 841. The same omission may take on one aspect or another according to its setting. Substitution of equivalents may not have the same significance in fields of art on the one side and in those of mere utility on the other. Nowhere will change be tolerated, however, if it is so dominant or pervasive as in any real or substantial measure to frustrate the purpose of the contract. Crouch v. Gutmann, 134 N.Y. 45, 51, 31 N.E. 271, 30 Am.St.Rep. 608. There is no general license to install whatever, in the builder's judgment, may be regarded as "just as good." Easthampton L. & C. Co., Ltd. v. Worthington, 186 N.Y. 407, 412, 79 N.E. 323. The question is one of degree, to be answered, if there is doubt, by the triers of the facts (Crouch v. Gutmann; * * * supra), and, if the inferences are certain, by the judges of the law (Easthampton L. & C. Co., Ltd. v. Worthington, supra). We must weigh the purpose to be served, the desire to be gratified, the excuse for deviation from the letter, the cruelty of enforced adherence. Then only can we tell whether literal fulfillment is to be implied by law as a condition. This is not to say that the parties are not free by apt and certain words to effectuate a purpose that performance of every term shall be a condition of recovery. That question is not here. This is merely to say that the law will be slow to impute the purpose, in the silence of the parties, where the significance of the default is grievously out of proportion to the oppression of the forfeiture. The willful transgressor must accept the penalty of his transgression. Schultze v. Goodstein, 180 N.Y. 248, 251, 73 N.E. 21; Desmond–Dunne Co. v. Friedman–Doscher Co., 162 N.Y. 486, 490, 56 N.E. 995. For him there is no occasion to mitigate the rigor of implied conditions. The transgressor whose default is unintentional and trivial may hope for mercy if he will offer atonement for his wrong. * * *

In the circumstances of this case, we think the measure of the allowance is not the cost of replacement, which would be great, but the difference in value, which would be either nominal or nothing. Some of the exposed sections might perhaps have been replaced at moderate expense. The defendant did not limit his demand to them, but treated the plumbing as a unit to be corrected from cellar to roof. In point of fact, the plaintiff never reached the stage at which evidence of the extent of the allowance became necessary. The trial court had excluded evidence that the defect was unsubstantial, and in view of that ruling there was no occasion for the plaintiff to go farther with an offer of proof. We think, however, that the offer, if it had been made, would not of necessity have been defective because directed to difference in value. It is true that in most cases the cost of replacement is the measure. * * * The owner is entitled to the money which will permit him to complete, unless the cost of completion is grossly and unfairly out of proportion to the good to be attained. When that is true, the measure is the difference in value. Specifications call, let us say, for a foundation built of granite quarried in Vermont. On the completion of the building, the owner learns that through the blunder of a subcontractor part of the foundation has been built of granite of the same quality quarried in New Hampshire. The measure of allowance is not the cost of reconstruction. * * * The rule that gives a remedy in cases of substantial performance with compensation for defects of trivial or inappreciable importance has been developed by the courts as an instrument of justice. The measure of the allowance must be shaped to the same end.

The order should be affirmed, and judgment absolute directed in favor of the plaintiff upon the stipulation, with costs in all courts.

McLaughlin, J. I dissent. The plaintiff did not perform its contract. Its failure to do so was either intentional or due to gross neglect which, under the uncontradicted facts, amounted to the same thing, nor did it make any proof of the cost of compliance, where compliance was possible.

Under its contract it obligated itself to use in the plumbing only pipe (between 2,000 and 2,500 feet) made by the Reading Manufacturing Company. The first pipe delivered was about 1,000 feet and the plaintiff's superintendent then called the attention of the foreman of the subcontractor, who was doing the plumbing, to the fact that the specifications annexed to the contract required all pipe used in the plumbing to be of the Reading Manufacturing Company. They then examined it for the purpose of ascertaining whether this delivery was of that manufacture and found it was. Thereafter, as pipe was required in the progress of the work, the foreman of the subcontractor would leave word at its shop that he wanted a specified number of feet of pipe, without in any way indicating of what manufacture. Pipe would thereafter be delivered and installed in the building, without any examination whatever. Indeed, no examination, so far as appears, was made by the plaintiff, the subcontractor, defendant's architect, or any one else, of any of the pipe except the first delivery, until after the building had been completed. Plaintiff's architect then refused to give the certificate of completion, upon which the final payment depended, because all of the pipe used in the plumbing was not of the kind called for by the contract. After such refusal, the subcontractor removed the covering or insulation from about 900 feet of pipe which was exposed in the basement, cellar, and attic, and all but 70 feet was found to have been manufactured, not by the Reading Company, but by other manufacturers, some by the Cohoes Rolling Mill Company, some by the National Steel Works, some by the South Chester Tubing Company, and some which bore no manufacturer's mark at all. The balance of the pipe had been so installed in the building that an inspection of it could not be had without demolishing, in part at least, the building itself.

I am of the opinion the trial court was right in directing a verdict for the defendant. The plaintiff agreed that all the pipe used should be of the Reading Manufacturing Company. Only about two-fifths of it, so far as appears, was of that kind. If more were used, then the burden of proving that fact was upon the plaintiff, which it could easily have done, since it knew where the pipe was obtained. The question of substantial performance of a contract of the character of the one under consideration depends in no small degree upon the good faith of the contractor. If the plaintiff had intended to, and had, complied with the terms of the contract except as to minor omissions, due to inadvertence, then he might be allowed to recover the contract price, less the amount necessary to fully compensate the defendant for damages caused by such omissions. Woodward v. Fuller, 80 N.Y. 312; Nolan v. Whitney, 88 N.Y. 648. But that is not this case. It installed between 2,000 and 2,500 feet of pipe, of which only 1,000 feet at most complied with the contract. No explanation was given why pipe called for by the contract was not used, nor that any effort made to show what it would cost to remove the pipe of other manufacturers and install that of the Reading Manufacturing Company. The defendant had a right to contract for what he wanted. He had a right before making payment to get what the contract called for. It is no answer to this suggestion to say that the pipe put in was just as good as that made by the Reading Manufacturing Company, or that the difference in value between such pipe and the pipe made by the Reading Manufacturing Company would be either "nominal or nothing." Defendant contracted for pipe made by the Reading Manufacturing Company. What his reason was for requiring this kind of pipe is of no importance. He wanted that and was entitled to it. It may have been a mere whim on his part, but even so, he had a right to this kind of pipe, regardless of whether some other kind, according to the opinion of the contractor or experts, would have been "just as good, better, or done just as well." He agreed to pay only upon condition that the pipe installed were made by that company and he ought not to be compelled to pay unless that condition be performed. * * * The rule, therefore, of substantial performance, with damages for unsubstantial omissions, has no application. * * *

* * *

I am of the opinion the trial court did not err in ruling on the admission of evidence or in directing a verdict for the defendant.

For the foregoing reasons I think the judgment of the Appellate Division should be reversed and the judgment of the Trial Term affirmed.

HISCOCK, C.J., and HOGAN and CRANE, JJ., concur with CARDOZO, J.

POUND and ANDREWS, JJ., concur with MCLAUGHLIN, J.

Order affirmed, etc.[b]

ATIYAH, BOOK REVIEW OF C. FRIED, CONTRACT AS PROMISE

95 Harv.L.Rev. 509, 522–23 (1981).

Consider the * * * case of *Jacob & Youngs v. Kent,* the Reading pipes case. Fried stigmatizes as "absurd" the owner's claim that he could keep the house without paying for it * * *. Even at the height of classical times, some might have agreed with Fried, though there is certainly evidence that others, including Baron Bramwell, would not. Faced with such a case, Bramwell might well have argued that he had no means of knowing whether the house as built was worth its price, or worth anything, to the owner. The defendant has decided what the house is worth with the Reading pipes. The court has no power to force him to pay for a house with different pipes. To do so would be to show disrespect for the defendant's autonomy, his free choice. I do not see anything illogical or absurd about such an argument. If it would seem unreasonable to most people today, that is surely because we no longer have quite the same respect for individual autonomy and free choice. We are prepared to overrule the owner's defense in such a case because we feel that

---

b. According to J. Dawson, W. Harvey, and S. Henderson, Cases and Comment on Contracts 816–17 (4th ed. 1982), the record showed that the contract contained the following provision: "Any work furnished by the Contractor, the material or workmanship of which is defective or which is not fully in accordance with the drawings and specifications, in every respect, will be rejected and is to be immediately torn down, removed and remade or replaced in accordance with the drawings and specifications, whenever discovered." Further, Danzig and Watson report that another provision stated that "[w]here any particular brand of manufactured article is specified, it is to be considered as a standard." According to the provision, the plaintiff contractor had to obtain written approval of the architect before using a substitute. R. Danzig & G. Watson, The Capability Problem in Contract Law 99 (2004).

the loss to the plaintiff would be too great, and we are prepared to judge for ourselves (through our courts) whether the change in pipes has in fact diminished the value of the house.

Problem 7–1

You represent the defendant owner in Jacob & Youngs, Inc. v. Kent at the planning and drafting stage. Draft an express condition precedent that would have precluded the maturation of your client's duty to make the final payment on the contract price if the contractor failed to install Reading pipe.

BROWN–MARX ASSOCIATES, LTD. v. EMIGRANT SAVINGS BANK

United States Court of Appeals, Eleventh Circuit, 1983.
703 F.2d 1361.

GODBOLD, CHIEF JUDGE:

This diversity case concerns a dispute between a prospective borrower and a bank over a $1.1 million loan commitment for financing an office building. Emigrant Savings Bank refused to lend the money, maintaining among other things that Brown–Marx Associates, the would-be borrower, had failed to satisfy the minimum rental requirement of the commitment. Brown–Marx sued the bank alleging breach of contract and various tort theories of recovery. The matter was tried to a jury which found for Brown–Marx on its contract claim [and awarded $543,000 damages]. The district court granted the bank's motion for new trial, primarily on the ground it had erroneously instructed the jury on the applicable law. Later the court granted summary judgment for the bank on all claims. We affirm.

I. BACKGROUND

a. The Initial Dealings

Brown–Marx is an Alabama limited partnership with Gary Smith its sole general partner. Smith formed the partnership to purchase and renovate an office building in Birmingham. In May 1978 Brown–Marx obtained a loan commitment for permanent financing of the building from Emigrant Savings Bank of New York. Brown–Marx paid the bank $22,000 for the commitment, which was to expire May 1, 1979. Later Brown–Marx paid the bank $11,000 to extend the commitment to November 1, 1979.

Under the commitment the bank agreed to lend Brown–Marx $1.1 million, the "ceiling loan," if Brown–Marx provided satisfactory documentation of renovations, signed leases providing for at least $714,447 annual rentals, and a satisfactory appraisal that the building was worth at least $2.4 million. The commitment provided in the alternative for a "floor loan" of $750,000 if the major requirements for the ceiling loan were not met. The provisions for the alternative loans, floor or ceiling, are at the heart of the dispute:

The Bank has agreed to lend the sum of $1,100,000 secured by a permanent mortgage on the * * * [building].

* * *

2.　Loan to close upon the following conditions being satisfactorily complied with:

a.　Exhibition of all required government certificates, permits, licenses, etc.

b.　[Details of renovation to be done "in a workmanlike manner satisfactory to the Bank."]

c.　Exhibition of signed leases for a term of not less than one year covering not more than 140,449 net rentable square feet at a rental of not less than $714,447 per annum and the space rented is rented on a basis so that if the building were 100% rented, the annual rentroll would be at least $840,526. Said rentals to be on an unfurnished basis without any concessions or offsets thereto. Leases to be approved by the Bank and assigned to the Bank.

* * *

It is also understood and agreed that in the event that condition 2.a. is met, but conditions 2.b. and c. are not, the loan shall be in the amount of $750,000 * * *.

The loan, whether ceiling or floor amount, was to be secured by a first mortgage on the building.

On the strength of this commitment Brown–Marx obtained from two Alabama banks $1.1 million interim financing to purchase and renovate the building, to be repaid from the proceeds of the permanent loan from Emigrant. Brown–Marx bought the building, renovated it, and proceeded to lease space in it.

* * *

II.　The ceiling loan: substantial vs. perfect compliance

The loan commitment imposed several conditions on the $1.1 million ceiling loan. Among these was the requirement in paragraph 2.c. for "[e]xhibition of signed leases for a term of not less than one year covering not more than 140,449 net rentable square feet at a rental of not less than $714,447 per annum * * *". The main reason the bank gave for not making the ceiling loan was that Brown–Marx did not meet the $714,447 minimum annual rental requirement.

The trial judge submitted the breach of contract claim to the jury with an instruction that plaintiffs had the burden to prove by a preponderance of the evidence "that they had substantially performed all of the ultimately agreed upon conditions precedent to the ceiling loan." The court granted a new trial, concluding that this instruction was erroneous because substantial compliance was not applicable to the minimum annual rental clause in the commitment and Brown–Marx was, therefore, required to comply fully with the minimum annual rental requirement. Later the court granted the bank's motion for summary judgment with respect to the ceiling loan, finding there was no genuine issue of material fact as to whether Brown–Marx had failed to satisfy the minimum annual rental requirement.

There is no dispute in material facts concerning Brown–Marx's failure to comply fully with the minimum rental requirement, even when the leases brought to New York on closing day are considered. Five of the leases submitted were month-to-month leases rather than for a term of at least a year. Two leases covered space that was not in the building. Another had never been executed, and the supposed tenant had neither paid rent nor occupied the space. The rental amount on one lease was overstated. There was a shortfall in the dollar amount of annual rental. While there was considerable dispute about the size of the deficiency,[1] Brown–Marx does not contend that annual rentals were as much as $714,447, but rather that substantial compliance with the minimum rental provision was adequate. There is a paucity of Alabama case law on this subject. Alabama has applied the substantial performance doctrine in only one situation outside the field of construction contracts and then on facts that it found were analogous to a building contract situation. *See* discussion of *Bruner v. Hines,* 295 Ala. 111, 324 So.2d 265 (Ala.1975), below. We conclude that the Alabama courts would hold that substantial performance does not apply to the minimum required rental provision of the loan commitment.

Courts have usually treated the terms and conditions of a loan commitment as conditions precedent to the lender's obligation to perform. * * * The loan commitment fee is paid for the privilege of later borrowing the money if the conditions are met. The language of the loan commitment here expressly provides that compliance with the minimum annual rentals provisions is a "condition" to receiving the loan. Concerning such an express condition, 5 *Williston on Contracts* (Third Edition), Section 675, states:

> As a general rule, conditions which are either expressed or implied in fact must be exactly fulfilled or no liability can arise on the promise which such conditions qualify.

Id. at 184.

The substantial performance doctrine provides that where a contract is made for an agreed exchange of two performances, one of which is to be rendered first, substantial performance rather than exact, strict or literal performance by the first party of the terms of the contract is adequate to entitle the party to recover on it. The intent of the doctrine is equitable: to prevent unjust enrichment or the inequity of one party's getting the benefit of performance, albeit not strictly in accord with the contract's terms, with no obligation in return. The courts will allow recovery under the contract, less allowance for deviations, where a party in good faith has substantially performed its obligation. *See generally,* 3A *Corbin on Contracts,* Sections 700–701; 6 *Williston on Contracts* (Third Edition), Section 842. The doctrine is widely applied to building contracts, though not always limited to them.

The doctrine is not primarily concerned with substantial performance of a "condition" but rather with substantial performance by one party of his obligations arising out of the agreed exchange under the contract. Its object is to prevent forfeiture of work, labor and materials supplied by the substantially performing party. Its application is illustrated in terms of construction contracts in 3A *Corbin on Contracts,* Section 701:

---

1. Brown–Marx, conceding that some leases were properly excludable from the tally, maintained below that annual rentals were $713,526. The bank calculated them as $700,826; the district court concluded that at most they were $706,176.

[I]t is not with express conditions or interpretation that we are now primarily concerned. We are now dealing with a contract that consists of two exchanged promises requiring the rendition of two promised performances, without making either promise expressly conditional on anything. The builder promises to build and the owner promises to pay.

* * *

It is substantial performance of what the builder promised to do, of the construction work, of the equivalent for which the owner has promised to pay, that is the "condition" of the owner's duty to pay. It is not substantial performance of "a condition" that must be rendered; "substantial performance" *is* the condition—the fact that must exist before payment is due.

Id. at 314.

Under the Restatement of Contracts the loan commitment would be termed an "option contract" with Brown–Marx's performance being "acceptance" of the offer to lend money. Despite equity's dislike of forfeiture, the requirements of an option contract governing the manner of acceptance are strictly applied. *See* 1 *Restatement Second of Contracts* Section 26 and comment d.

* * *

Bruner v. Hines, 295 Ala. 111, 324 So.2d 265 (Ala.1975), is the only Alabama decision we have found that has applied substantial performance outside the field of construction contracts. In *Bruner* a sales contract included a "rough plat" drawn by the buyer describing the land to be sold, in which the road frontage of land was estimated at 366 feet based on a steel tape measurement, and the land was to contain 15 acres. The final survey showed 15.1 acres with 376.5 feet of road frontage. The buyer offered the seller $500 extra for the additional 0.1 acre, but the seller refused to convey, maintaining that the buyer's survey did not comply with the contract. The buyer sued claiming substantial performance. The Alabama Supreme Court held substantial performance applicable. The court reasoned that using a steel tape rather than survey equipment as the basis of the road frontage showed that the plat's acreage was only an estimate and that the seller's promise to convey should not be strictly conditioned on the buyer's furnishing a survey identical to the rough plat. The court emphasized the practical difficulty of surveying land to a numerically exact degree. It noted an analogy between building contracts and the facts before it. The court applied substantial performance but intimated that its application was limited:

> Because both the individual and societal interests are vital coordinates in a private enterprise system, the compromise of full performance should be kept minimal, and compensation should be paid whenever a party's bargained for exchange is not fulfilled.

Id. at 270.

Here the requirement for minimum annual rentals is expressed in paragraph 2.c. of the contract in a definite and precise manner. The contingency of less than perfect performance is specifically dealt with in the provision that if condition 2.a., but not conditions 2.b. and 2.c., is met, then the loan is to be made in the floor amount. In the face of these explicit contractual expressions there is no leeway for substantial performance without frustrating the intent of the parties. Nor is the requirement here inequitable. The minimum rental requirement is a matter of vital interest to the bank because it provides a major part of the loan's security. And, unlike *Bruner,* the requirement not met is possible to achieve as a practical matter.

* * *

We conclude that as a matter of Alabama law the bank was entitled to require total compliance with the minimum annual rental requirement. The district court correctly granted the motion for new trial and later the motion for summary judgment on the ceiling loan claim. * * *

[The court also held that Brown–Marx could not recover for breach of the agreement to make a loan in the floor amount because Brown–Marx did not establish that it wanted to "avail itself" of that loan and that it was ready to close a loan in that amount.]

AFFIRMED.

RESTATEMENT (SECOND) OF CONTRACTS § 237.
Comment d.

Substantial Performance. In an important category of disputes over failure of performance, one party asserts the right to payment on the ground that he has completed his performance, while the other party refuses to pay on the ground that there is an uncured material failure of performance. * * * A typical example is that of the building contractor who claims from the owner payment of the unpaid balance under a construction contract. In such cases it is common to state the issue, not in terms of whether there has been an uncured material failure by the contractor, but in terms of whether there has been substantial performance by him. This manner of stating the issue does not change its substance, however. * * * If there has been substantial although not full performance, the building contractor has a claim for the unpaid balance and the owner has a claim only for damages. If there has not been substantial performance, the building contractor has no claim for the unpaid balance, although he may have a claim in restitution. * * * If, however, the parties have made an event a condition of their agreement, there is no mitigating standard of materiality or substantiality applicable to the non-occurrence of that event. If, therefore, the agreement makes full performance a condition, substantial performance is not sufficient and if relief is to be had under the contract, it must be through excuse of the non-occurrence of the condition to avoid forfeiture.

Note
Special Rules Applicable to Express Conditions

As we have just seen in the Brown–Marx case, courts require strict compliance with express conditions precedent relating to quality of performance. (The same rule also applies to implied-in-fact conditions requiring perfect performance.) You should compare the rule of strict compliance with the very different gap-filling rule concerning quality of performance encountered in Jacob & Youngs v. Kent. When does the Jacob & Youngs rule apply? Why such a major difference? As a contract planner and drafter, you might want to insert an express condition precisely to avoid (or to try to avoid) the doctrine of substantial performance. Review once again Problem 7–1.

In subsequent sections of this chapter and in later chapters of this book, we encounter further special approaches and rules applicable only to express conditions. For example, courts approach the interpretation of claimed express conditions in distinctive ways, and apply special rules to excuse certain failures of express conditions.

SECTION THREE: INTERPRETATION OF CONTRACT LANGUAGE TO DETERMINE IF IT CREATES AN EXPRESS CONDITION

Courts must often consider whether contract language means that (1) a party promises to bring an event about, or (2) the event is only an express condition precedent to a duty of the other party, or (3) the event is both a promise and a condition, or (4) the event is neither. From the cases that immediately follow, you should develop a list of factors that may influence a court's interpretation. In each case, you should also consider how a drafter of the language being interpreted could have made matters clearer.

GLAHOLM v. HAYS

The Court of Common Pleas, 1841.
133 Eng.Rep. 743.

TINDAL, C.J. * * *

The question raised upon this record is, whether the clause contained in the charter-party set out in the declaration, viz.: "the vessel to sail from England on or before the 4th day of February next," is a condition precedent on the part of the ship-owner, upon the non-compliance wherewith on his part, the defendants, the freighters, were at liberty to throw up the charter. The defendants, in their plea, have treated the clause as importing a condition; alleging in such plea that the vessel "did not sail from England on or before the said 4th day of February, but on the contrary remained and continued in England, without the leave and against the will of the defendants, for a long time after; whereupon the defendants refused to perform and fulfil the said charter-party, as they lawfully might;" and the plaintiff, having demurred to this plea, the question on the legal construction of the charter-party is thereby raised.

Whether a particular clause in a charter-party shall be held to be a condition, upon the non-performance of which by the one party, the other is at liberty to abandon the contract, and consider it at an end; or whether it amounts to an agreement only, the breach whereof is to be recompensed by an action for damages, must depend upon the intention of the parties to be collected, in each particular case, from the terms of the agreement itself, and from the subject matter to which it relates. "It cannot depend," as Lord Ellenborough observes, "on any formal arrangement of the words, but (must depend) on the reason and sense of the thing as it is to be collected from the whole contract:" see Ritchie v. Anderson (10 East 295). And looking, in the first place, at the terms of this agreement, we think some distinction must have been intended by the contracting parties, between this particular clause and those which precede and follow it, as to the nature of the obligations thereby respectively created. All the clauses of the charter-party, both prior and subsequent to the clause in dispute, are framed strictly and properly in the language of agreement only. The charter-party states, "it is mutually agreed between the parties that the ship being tight, & c., shall proceed to Trieste, and there load a complete cargo; that the said vessel being so loaded shall therewith proceed to a good and safe port in the United Kingdom; that the cargo shall be sent alongside; that the freight shall be paid in the manner therein stipulated; that forty running days shall be allowed the merchants." And then is interposed the clause now under discussion, viz.: "the vessel to sail from England on or before the 4th day of February next." After which, the charter-party continues in the same frame as before: That the vessel shall be addressed to the charterers' agents, & c. Referring, therefore, in the first place, to the variation between the language of the particular clause, and that of the clauses amongst which it is found, there is reasonable ground for surmising, that some distinction must have been intended between them; and no other distinction can exist, except that the one set of clauses sounds in agreement, and the other clause, in condition.

The very words themselves, "*to sail* on or before a given day," do, by common usage, import the same as the words "*conditioned* to sail," or "*warranted* to sail on or before such a day;" and, undoubtedly, if in the middle of a common bought and sold note, for a cargo of corn, or any other goods, were found the words, "to be delivered on or before such a day," they would be held to amount to a condition; and the purchaser would not be bound to accept the cargo, if not ready for delivery by the day appointed.

And looking at the subject matter of the contract, without regarding the precise words, we think that construing the words as a condition precedent, will carry into effect the intention of the parties, with more certainty, than holding them to be matter of contract only, and merely the ground of an action for damages.

Both parties were aware that the whole success of a mercantile adventure, does, in ordinary cases, depend upon the commencement of the voyage by a given time. The nature of the commodity to be imported, the state of the foreign and home market at the time the contract of charter-party is made, and the various other calculations which enter into commercial speculations, all combine to shew, that dispatch and certainty are of the very first importance to their success; and certainly nothing will so effectually insure both dispatch and certainty, as the knowledge that the obligation of the contract itself shall be made to depend upon the actual performance of the stipulation which relates to them.

The present case appears to us to be distinguishable from those cited on the part of the plaintiff, in both the particulars to which we have adverted; viz. that in this case the form of the stipulation is more nearly in the language of condition than in that of agreement, whilst in the cases cited the stipulation is in the language of covenant only; and again, that in this case the performance of the stipulation goes more to the very root and the whole consideration of the contract. And, indeed, in most or all of those cases, the objection has not been taken until after the voyage had been performed, nor, in many cases, until after the goods had been accepted; so that, it is manifest, the breach of the agreement of which the defendant complained, and which he sought to set up as the non-performance of a condition precedent, could not go *to the whole* of the consideration of the contract.

Such was the case of Constable v. Cloberie (Palmer 397, 81 Eng.Rep. 1141 (X.B. 1626),) where the shipowner covenanted, that his ship should sail with the first fair wind. * * *

Upon the whole, therefore, we think the intention of the parties to this contract sufficiently appears to have been, to insure the ship's sailing at latest by the 4th of February, and that the only mode of effecting this is by holding the clause in question to form a condition precedent; which we consider it to have been.

Judgment for the defendant.

RESTATEMENT (SECOND) OF CONTRACTS § 227(1).

In resolving doubts as to whether an event is made a condition of an obligor's duty, and as to the nature of such an event, an interpretation is preferred that will reduce the obligee's risk of forfeiture, unless the event is within the obligee's control or the circumstances indicate that he has assumed the risk.

HOWARD v. FEDERAL CROP INS. CORP.

United States Court of Appeals, Fourth Circuit, 1976.
540 F.2d 695.

WIDENER, CIRCUIT JUDGE:

Plaintiff-appellants sued to recover for losses to their 1973 tobacco crop due to alleged rain damage. The crops were insured by defendant-appellee, Federal Crop Insurance Corporation (FCIC). * * * The district court granted summary judgment for the defendant. * * * We remand for further proceedings. Since we find for the plaintiffs as to the construction of the policy, we express no opinion on the procedural questions.

Federal Crop Insurance Corporation, an agency of the United States, in 1973, issued three policies to the Howards, insuring their tobacco crops, to be grown on six farms, against weather damage and other hazards.

The Howards (plaintiffs) established production of tobacco on their acreage, and have alleged that their 1973 crop was extensively damaged by heavy rains, resulting in a gross loss to the three plaintiffs in excess of $35,000. The plaintiffs harvested and sold the depleted crop and timely filed notice and proof of loss with FCIC, but, prior to inspection by the adjuster for FCIC, the Howards had either plowed or disked under the tobacco fields in question to prepare the same for sowing a cover crop of rye to preserve the soil. When the FCIC adjuster later inspected the fields, he found the stalks had been largely obscured or obliterated by plowing or disking and denied the claims, apparently on the ground that the plaintiffs had violated a portion of the policy which provides that the stalks on any acreage with respect to which a loss is claimed shall not be destroyed until the corporation makes an inspection.

[margin note: Why DC ruled for Δ →]

The holding of the district court is best capsuled in its own words:

"The inquiry here is whether compliance by the insureds with this provision of the policy was a condition precedent to the recovery. The court concludes that it was and that the failure of the insureds to comply worked a forfeiture of benefits for the alleged loss."[1]

There is no question but that apparently after notice of loss was given to defendant, but before inspection by the adjuster, plaintiffs plowed under the tobacco stalks and sowed some of the land with a cover crop, rye. The question is whether, under paragraph 5(f) of the tobacco endorsement to the policy of insurance, the act of plowing under the tobacco stalks forfeits the coverage of the policy. Paragraph 5 of the tobacco endorsement is entitled *Claims.* Pertinent to this case are subparagraphs 5(b) and 5(f), which are as follows:

"5(b) *It shall be a condition precedent* to the payment of any loss that the insured establish the production of the insured crop on a unit and that such loss has been directly caused by one or more of the hazards insured against during the insurance period for the crop year for which the loss is claimed, and furnish any other information regarding the manner and extent of loss as may be required by the Corporation. (Emphasis added)"

"5(f) The tobacco stalks on any acreage of tobacco of types 11a, 11b, 12, 13, or 14 with respect to which a loss is claimed *shall not be destroyed until the Corporation makes an inspection.* (Emphasis added)"

[margin note: obligation = promise]

The arguments of both parties are predicated upon the same two assumptions. First, if subparagraph 5(f) creates a condition precedent, its violation caused a forfeiture of plaintiffs' coverage. Second, if subparagraph 5(f) creates an obligation (variously called a promise or covenant) upon plaintiffs not to plow under the tobacco stalks, defendant may recover from plaintiffs (either in an original action, or, in this case, by a counterclaim, or as a matter of defense) for whatever damage it sustained because of the elimination of the stalks. However, a violation of subparagraph 5(f) would not, under the second premise, standing alone, cause a forfeiture of the policy.

[margin note: Rules]

Generally accepted law provides us with guidelines here. There is a general legal policy opposed to forfeitures. *United States v. One Ford Coach,* 307 U.S. 219, 226, 59 S.Ct. 861, 83 L.Ed. 1249 (1939); *Baca v. Commissioner of Internal Revenue,* 326 F.2d 189, 191 (5th Cir.1964). Insurance policies are generally construed most strongly against the insurer. *Henderson v. Hartford Accident & Indemnity Co.,* 268 N.C. 129, 150 S.E.2d 17, 19 (1966). When it is doubtful whether words create a promise or a condition precedent, they will be construed as creating a promise. *Harris and Harris Const. Co. v. Crain and Denbo, Inc.,* 256 N.C. 110, 123 S.E.2d 590, 595 (1962). The provisions of a contract will not be construed as conditions precedent in the absence of language plainly requiring such construction. *Harris,* 123 S.E.2d at 596. * * *

---

1. The district court also relied upon language in subparagraph 5(b), infra, which required as a condition precedent to payment that the insured, in addition to establishing his production and loss from an insured case, "furnish any other information regarding the man-ner and extent of loss as may be required by the Corporation." The court construed the preservation of the stalks as such "information." We see no language in the policy or connection in the record to indicate this is the case.

Plaintiffs rely most strongly upon the fact that the term "condition precedent" is included in subparagraph 5(b) but not in subparagraph 5(f). It is true that whether a contract provision is construed as a condition or an obligation does not depend entirely upon whether the word "condition" is expressly used. Appleman, *Insurance Law and Practice* (1972), vol. 6A, § 4144. However, the persuasive force of plaintiffs' argument in this case is found in the use of the term "condition precedent" in subparagraph 5(b) but not in subparagraph 5(f). Thus, it is argued that the ancient maxim to be applied is that the expression of one thing is the exclusion of another.

The defendant places principal reliance upon the decision of this court in *Fidelity-Phenix Fire Insurance Company v. Pilot Freight Carriers,* 193 F.2d 812, 31 A.L.R.2d 839 (4th Cir.1952). Suit there was predicated upon a loss resulting from theft out of a truck covered by defendant's policy protecting plaintiff from such a loss. The insurance company defended upon the grounds that the plaintiff had left the truck unattended without the alarm system being on. The policy contained six paragraphs limiting coverage. Two of those imposed what was called a "condition precedent." They largely related to the installation of specified safety equipment. Several others, including paragraph 5, pertinent in that case, started with the phrase, "It is further warranted." In paragraph 5, the insured warranted that the alarm system would be on whenever the vehicle was left unattended. Paragraph 6 starts with the language: "The assured agrees, by acceptance of this policy, that the foregoing conditions precedent relate to matters material to the acceptance of the risk by the insurer." Plaintiff recovered in the district court, but judgment on its behalf was reversed because of a breach of warranty of paragraph 5, the truck had been left unattended with the alarm off. In that case, plaintiff relied upon the fact that the words "condition precedent" were used in some of the paragraphs but the word "warranted" was used in the paragraph in issue. In rejecting that contention, this court said that "warranty" and "condition precedent" are often used interchangeably to create a condition of the insured's promise, and "[m]anifestly the terms 'condition precedent' and 'warranty' were intended to have the same meaning and effect." 193 F.2d at 816.

holding in Fidelity

Fidelity-Phenix thus does not support defendant's contention here. Although there is some resemblance between the two cases, analysis shows that the issues are actually entirely different. Unlike the case at bar, each paragraph in *Fidelity-Phenix* contained either the term "condition precedent" or the term "warranted." We held that, in that situation, the two terms had the same effect in that they both involved forfeiture. That is well established law. See Appleman, *Insurance Law and Practice* (1972), vol. 6A, § 4144. In the case at bar, the term "warranty" or "warranted" is in no way involved, either in terms or by way of like language, as it was in *Fidelity-Phenix*. The issue upon which this case turns, then, was not involved in *Fidelity-Phenix*.

The *Restatement of the Law of Contracts* states:

"§ 261. INTERPRETATION OF DOUBTFUL WORDS AS PROMISE OR CONDITION.

Where it is doubtful whether words create a promise or an express condition, they are interpreted as creating a promise; but the same words may sometimes mean that one party promises a performance and that the other party's promise is conditional on that performance."

Two illustrations (one involving a promise, the other a condition) are used in the *Restatement*:

"2.   A, an insurance company, issues to B a policy of insurance containing promises by A that are in terms conditional on the happening of certain events. The policy contains this clause: 'provided, in case differences shall arise touching any loss, *the matter shall be submitted to impartial arbitrators,* whose award shall be binding on the parties.' This is a promise to arbitrate and does not make an award a condition precedent of the insurer's duty to pay.

3.   A, an insurance company, issues to B an insurance policy in usual form containing this clause: 'In the event of disagreement as to the amount of loss it shall be ascertained by two appraisers and an umpire. The loss shall *not be payable until 60 days after the award of the appraisers when such an appraisal is required.*' This provision is not merely a promise to arbitrate differences but makes an award a condition of the insurer's duty to pay in case of disagreement." (Emphasis added)

We believe that subparagraph 5(f) in the policy here under consideration fits illustration 2 rather than illustration 3. Illustration 2 specifies something to be done, whereas subparagraph 5(f) specifies something not to be done. Unlike illustration 3, subparagraph 5(f) does not state any conditions under which the insurance shall "not be payable," or use any words of like import. We hold that the district court erroneously held, on the motion for summary judgment, that subparagraph 5(f) established a condition precedent to plaintiffs' recovery which forfeited the coverage.[2]

From our holding that defendant's motion for summary judgment was improperly allowed, it does not follow the plaintiffs' motion for summary judgment should have been granted, for if subparagraph 5(f) be not construed as a condition precedent, there are other questions of fact to be determined. At this point, we merely hold that the district court erred in holding, on the motion for summary judgment, that subparagraph 5(f) constituted a condition precedent with resulting forfeiture.

The explanation defendant makes for including subparagraph 5(f) in the tobacco endorsement is that it is necessary that the stalks remain standing in order for the Corporation to evaluate the extent of loss and to determine whether loss resulted from some cause not covered by the policy. However, was subparagraph 5(f) inserted because without it the Corporation's opportunities for proof would be more difficult, or because they would be impossible? Plaintiffs point out that the Tobacco Endorsement, with subparagraph 5(f), was adopted in 1970, and crop insurance goes back long before that date. Nothing is shown as to the Corporation's prior 1970 practice of evaluating losses. Such a showing might have a bearing upon establishing defendant's intention in including 5(f). Plaintiffs state, and defendant does not deny, that another division of the Department of Agriculture, or the North Carolina Department, urged that tobacco stalks be cut as soon as possible after

2. The district court also referred to sub-paragraph 5(f) as a condition subsequent. The difference in terminology is of no consequence here.

harvesting as a means of pest control. Such an explanation might refute the idea that plaintiffs plowed under the stalks for any fraudulent purpose. Could these conflicting directives affect the reasonableness of plaintiffs' interpretation of defendant's prohibition upon plowing under the stalks prior to adjustment?

We express no opinion on these questions because they were not before the district court and are mentioned to us largely by way of argument rather than from the record. * * * Nothing we say here should preclude FCIC from asserting as a defense that the plowing or disking under of the stalks caused damage to FCIC if, for example, the amount of the loss was thereby made more difficult or impossible to ascertain whether the plowing or disking under was done with bad purpose or innocently. To repeat, our narrow holding is that merely plowing or disking under the stalks does not of itself operate to forfeit coverage under the policy.

The case is remanded for further proceedings not inconsistent with this opinion.

Vacated and Remanded.

Problem 7–2

O & G Engineers rendered engineering services to Taleghani–Dabtary (T–D), a consultant to the Iranian government on the construction of water resource projects. Their letter agreement provided that "T–D agrees to make payments to O & G in the amount of $157,755.19 within fifteen days of the availability of funds." The parties agree that the purpose of the provision was to protect O & G by ensuring prompt payment, while simultaneously providing T–D a grace period in which to pay its obligation to O & G. After Iran failed to pay T–D, T–D claimed that such payment was a condition precedent to its obligation to O & G. Is it? Draft a provision that O & G should have insisted upon in its agreement with T–D, protecting O & G from such a defense.

SECTION FOUR: INTERPRETATION OF THE CONTENT OF EXPRESS CONDITIONS

In the cases in the preceding section, the court focused mainly on issues of interpretation with respect to the possible *existence* of an express condition precedent. Courts must also face important issues of interpretation with respect to the *content* of conditions. In the following cases, you should focus not only on techniques of interpretation but also on how the language in question could have been better drafted.

GIBSON v. CRANAGE
Supreme Court of Michigan, 1878.
39 Mich. 49.

MARSTON, J. Plaintiff in error brought assumpsit to recover the contract price for the making and execution of a portrait of the deceased daughter of defendant. It appeared from the testimony of the plaintiff that he at a certain time called upon the defendant and solicited the privilege of making an enlarged picture of his deceased daughter. He says "I was to make an enlarged picture that he would like, a large one from a small one, and one that he would like and recognize as a good picture of his little girl, and he was to pay me.''

The defendant testified that the plaintiff was to take the small photograph and send it away to be finished, "and when returned if it was not perfectly satisfactory to me in every particular, I need not take it or pay for it. I still objected and he urged me to do so. There was no risk about it; if it was not perfectly satisfactory to me I need not take it or pay for it.''

There was little if any dispute as to what the agreement was. After the picture was finished it was shown to defendant who was dissatisfied with it and refused to accept it. Plaintiff endeavored to ascertain what the objections were, but says he was unable to ascertain clearly, and he then sent the picture away to the artist to have it changed.

On the next day he received a letter from defendant reciting the original agreement, stating that the picture shown him the previous day was not satisfactory and that he declined to take it or any other similar picture, and countermanded the order. A farther correspondence was had, but it was not very material and did not change the aspect of the case. When the picture was afterwards received by the plaintiff from the artist, he went to see defendant and to have him examine it. This defendant declined to do, or to look at it, and did not until during the trial, when he examined and found the same objections still existing.

We do not consider it necessary to examine the charge in detail, as we are satisfied it was as favorable to plaintiff as the agreement would warrant.

The contract (if it can be considered such) was an express one. The plaintiff agreed that the picture when finished should be satisfactory to the defendant, and his own evidence showed that the contract in this important particular had not been performed. It may be that the picture was an excellent one and that the defendant ought to have been satisfied with it and accepted it, but under the agreement the defendant was the only person who had the right to decide this question. Where parties thus deliberately enter into an agreement which violates no rule of public policy, and which is free from all taint of fraud or mistake, there is no hardship whatever in holding them bound by it.

Artists or third parties might consider a portrait an excellent one, and yet it prove very unsatisfactory to the person who had ordered it and who might be unable to point out with clearness or certainty the defects or objections. And if the person giving the order stipulates that the portrait when finished must be satisfactory to him or else he will not accept or pay for it, and this is agreed to, he may insist upon his right as given him by the contract. *McCarren v. McNulty,* 7 Gray 139; *Brown v. Foster,* 113 Mass. 136: 18 Amer., 465.

The judgment must be affirmed with costs.

FORMAN v. BENSON

Appellate Court of Illinois, Second District, 1983.
112 Ill.App.3d 1070, 68 Ill.Dec. 629, 446 N.E.2d 535.

HOPF, JUSTICE:

Defendant, Art Benson, appeals from an order of the circuit court of Lee County granting plaintiff Eric Forman specific performance of an installment contract to purchase commercial real estate owned by defendant. * * *

On March 23, 1981, the plaintiff, a chiropractor, executed an offer to purchase certain real estate in Dixon, Illinois, owned by the defendant, an electrician and a refrigeration and heating repairman. The offer was communicated the same day to the defendant at a conference attended by the defendant and three realtors. One of the realtors was Ken Burnell, with whom the defendant had listed the property. The other realtors attending the conference were Cheryl Blackorby and Bill Blackorby, spouses who are partners in another real estate firm. The plaintiff was a client of the Blackorbys, who had been assisting him for the previous several months in his search for a commercial building suitable for use as a chiropractic clinic.

The conference at which the offer was communicated took place in the office of the realtor, Ken Burnell. The terms of the offer were explained to defendant by Cheryl Blackorby. The offer proposed to purchase the property for $125,000, to be paid over a ten-year period. Payments were to be based upon a 30–year amortization rate at 9% interest. Plaintiff was to take possession of the property on September 1, 1981.

Before signing the agreement, defendant expressed concern over the plaintiff's credit worthiness, stating that he "didn't know him from a load of hay." Plaintiff's credit was of special significance to the defendant, since defendant was essentially "acting as a loan company" for plaintiff's benefit. As an assurance to the defendant, Mrs. Blackorby suggested that the contract be made subject to a favorable credit report. This suggestion eased defendant's feelings about the credit, and Ken Burnell thereafter added the following handwritten statement to the offer:

> "Subject to seller's approving buyer's credit report, oral on March 24, 1981, and written when ready."

The meaning of this statement was not explained in any detail at the time it was inserted by Mr. Burnell. However, it was uncontroverted that the clause was inserted for defendant's benefit. The contract was subsequently signed by defendant, and $1,000 was deposited by the plaintiff as earnest money.

Ken Burnell, defendant's realtor, testified on behalf of plaintiff Forman. Mr. Burnell stated that defendant indicated to him that he would approve the contract if plaintiff had a good credit report. Mrs. Blackorby also indicated that defendant said he would accept the contract if the credit report was favorable. However, it was defendant's understanding and belief that he would be given time to examine the credit documents, evaluate them and make a decision.

The day after the offer and acceptance was executed, Mrs. Blackorby telephoned the defendant and advised him that an excellent oral credit report had been received. She further told defendant that a written report would be ready in a few days. Defendant sounded agreeable to the oral report and stated he would pick up the written report when it arrived. On Friday, March 27, 1981, Mrs. Blackorby received the written credit report, as well as a personal financial statement prepared by the plaintiff and a letter from Dixon National Bank stating it would lend $35,000 to plaintiff. Mrs. Blackorby gave these documents to defendant that day, explaining the credit report in detail. Defendant stated the report "looks real good," and that he would have his attorney review it and begin the title work on the property.

Between Friday, March 27, 1981, and May 14, 1981, the plaintiff and defendant discussed the pending sale on three occasions. Those occasions took place in the latter part of April, at which time additional financial material, including copies of income tax returns, were furnished at the defendant's request. During those conversations the parties also discussed increases in the purchase price and the interest rate on the contract, as well as retention by the seller of certain personal property on the premises. Plaintiff testified that the seller wanted to raise the purchase price and interest rate, while the defendant testified that, prior to his rejection of the contract, he did mention a different price but not in terms of an ultimatum.

On May 14, 1981, the defendant, through the office of Ken Burnell, furnished a written statement rejecting plaintiff's credit and directing the realtor to refund the $1,000 deposit. Plaintiff attempted to discuss the matter further with the defendant, apparently making another offer as an inducement to complete the contract without litigation. Although defendant went to plaintiff's office to discuss another offer, no other offer was accepted by him. In July of 1981 the plaintiff brought this action seeking specific performance of the agreement. On September 1, 1981, plaintiff was ready and able to pay the balance of the down payment, complete the other obligations required by the installment agreement and take possession of the premises. The defendant denied the demand for possession under the terms of the agreement.

The defendant testified that he rejected the credit information because the plaintiff had liabilities of $80,000 and liquid assets of only $24,000. When defendant sought additional information, he was furnished with a corporate tax return showing a $2,000 loss for the tax year. Based on this information, defendant believed the plaintiff was "just breaking even." He had asked for the additional information because he believed the information furnished in the credit bureau report was not very significant. Defendant has had no prior experience as a bank or loan officer.

Thomas Schmidt, loan officer with a local savings and loan association, testified on behalf of the plaintiff. His testimony was uncontroverted to the effect that the plaintiff had an excellent credit rating. Based upon the credit application and credit report of the plaintiff, the savings and loan association would not have hesitated to extend credit to the plaintiff, although not under the terms of this particular contract.

The trial court found that defendant was held to a standard of reasonableness in his rejection of the contract on the basis of plaintiff's credit report, and found that defendant's rejection here was unreasonable. The court also found that defendant attempted to renegotiate the contract prior to his rejection of plaintiff's offer and that this action waived any objection which defendant might reasonably have had to plaintiff's credit worthiness. Finally, waiver was also found in defendant's delay of over 30 days "before giving notice of his intention to rely upon the credit clause in question." The court found in favor of the plaintiff and entered a decree for specific performance. The instant appeal followed.

Δ Appealed

Argu #1

Defendant first argues that approval of the buyer's credit worthiness was intended to be a matter of personal satisfaction on the part of the seller and was not subject to a standard of reasonableness, as the plaintiff claims and the trial court held.

No cases on pt.

We have discovered no case dealing with the interpretation of the specific clause in question. However, there is some Illinois case law regarding the interpretation of "satisfaction" clauses in general. In *Reeves & Co. v. Chandler* (1904), 113 Ill.App. 167, 170, the court found that satisfaction clauses generally fall into one of two classes. In one class, the decision as to whether a party is satisfied is completely reserved to the party for whose benefit the clause is inserted, and the reasons for his decision may not be inquired into and overhauled by either the other party or the courts. Cases falling into this class generally involve matters which are dependent upon the feelings, taste, or judgment of the party making the decision. (*Reeves; The Union League Club v. The Blymyer Ice Machine Co.* (1903), 204 Ill. 117, 68 N.E. 409.) The second class of cases are those in which the party to be satisfied is to base his determination on grounds which are just and reasonable. (*Reeves.*) These cases generally involve matters which are capable of objective evaluation, or which involve considerations of operative fitness or mechanical utility. (*Reeves; The Union League Club.*) Matters of financial concern generally fall into this second category of cases. The adequacy of the grounds of a determination in this class are open to judicial scrutiny and are judged by a reasonable man standard. *Reeves; Wood Machine Co. v. Smith* (1883), 50 Mich. 565, 15 N.W. 906.

Class one

Class two

test for class 2 - Judicial scrutiny - reasonable man standard

✱ However, the *Reeves* case also made it clear that the parties may agree to a reservation in one party of the absolute and unqualified freedom of choice on a matter not involving fancy, taste, or whim. (113 Ill.App. 167, 170.) Quoting from *Wood Machine Co. v. Smith* (1883), 50 Mich. 565, 15 N.W. 906, the court stated:

Another rule of Reeves

> " 'It sometimes happens that the right is fully reserved where it is the chief ground, if not the only one, that the party is determined to reserve an unqualified option, and is not willing to leave his freedom of choice exposed to any contention or subject to any contingency. He will not enter into any bargain except upon the condition of reserving the power to do what others might regard as unreasonable.' " (113 Ill.App. 167, 170–71.)

holding in Reeves →

Applying this reasoning, the court in *Reeves* found that a satisfaction clause regarding certain machinery—a matter which would normally be capable of objective evaluation—was intended to allow the purchaser of the machinery to exercise his judgment in accepting or rejecting the machinery:

> "It is apparent from the grammatical construction and arrangement of the clause in question that the words 'and satisfactory' were added thereto after the preceding portion was written and as a concession to defendant in error. It may be reasonably inferred that he was determined that no opportunity should be given plaintiff in error to force the outfit

upon him if he finally concluded not to take it. The words referred to were undoubtedly added to the clause at his request or suggestion and for the purpose of inducing him to sign the order." (113 Ill.App. 167, 171.)

Thus, it is apparent that under *Reeves* the fact that the clause was added as a concession or inducement to one of the parties is significant in determining whether the reasonableness standard should be applied.

In *Quinn v. Daly* (1921), 300 Ill. 273, 133 N.E. 290, a provision similar to the one here in question was interpreted by the Illinois Supreme Court as providing for a decision based on personal judgment. In that case, the seller in a contract sale for realty stated that she would agree to the terms of the contract "if party is reliable and has other property clear * * *." (133 N.E. 290, 291.) The court held that this statement was intended to reserve in the seller the right to pass on the question of the buyer's reliability and trustworthiness. 133 N.E. 290, 291.

* * *

Although these * * * cases seem to stand for the proposition that personal judgment is involved when the evaluation of a credit rating is at issue, a different conclusion was reached in *Weisz Trucking Co., Inc. v. Emil R. Wohl Construction* (1970), 13 Cal.App.3d 256, 91 Cal.Rptr. 489. In that case a contract between a contractor and a subcontractor provided that "[t]he subcontractor shall furnish, if requested, a corporate surety contract bond * * * written * * * by a company acceptable to the contractor * * *." (13 Cal.App.3d 256, 258, 91 Cal.Rptr. 489, 490.) The subcontractor thereafter submitted a surety bond in the amount of $168,000 which was written by a company with a Treasury rating of only $61,000. The contractor rejected the bond, stating that it wanted a company with a Treasury rating of $500,000. The contractor cancelled the contract and the subcontractors sued for breach. The appellate court held that the sufficiency of the performance bond should be determined by the application of an objective test of reasonableness. In reaching this conclusion, the court relied upon numerous decisions dealing with satisfaction clauses in which it was generally found that "where the contract calls for satisfaction as to commercial value or quality or sufficiency which can be evaluated objectively, the standard of a reasonable person should be used in determining whether or not satisfaction has been received." 13 Cal.App.3d 256, 262, 91 Cal.Rptr. 489, 493.

It seems clear from the foregoing cases that a reasonableness standard is favored by the law when the contract concerns matters capable of objective evaluation. However, where the circumstances are such that it is clear the provision was added as a personal concession to one of the contracting parties, the subjective, rather than the objective standard, should be applied. *Reeves & Co. v. Chandler* (1904), 113 Ill.App. 167.

In the present case, it is uncontroverted that the clause in question was inserted as a concession to the defendant and as an inducement to him to sign the contract, which he subsequently did. Ken Burnell testified that the addition of the provision indeed eased defendant's mind about the plaintiff's credit worthiness. In light of the fact that the relationship between the parties was to endure over a ten-year period of time, we think it is a reasonable construction of the provision that it was intended to allow defendant the

[handwritten margin note: TC erred in applying a reasonableness standard b/c it should have been subjective]

freedom of making a personal and subjective evaluation of plaintiff's credit worthiness. We, therefore, conclude that the trial court erred in applying a reasonableness standard to the instant case.

The personal judgment standard, however, does not allow the defendant to exercise unbridled discretion in rejecting plaintiff's credit, but rather is subject to the requirement of good faith. * * * In the instant case the trial court made no specific finding whether defendant Benson rejected plaintiff's credit in good faith. However, the trial court did find that between the time the contract was executed and the time the offer was rejected, defendant attempted to renegotiate the purchase price of the building as well as the interest rate. Defendant has challenged this finding on appeal, claiming it was against the manifest weight of the evidence. We disagree. Both plaintiff and defendant testified that an increased purchase price was discussed. Thus, the trial court's finding in this regard was supported by the record and was not against the manifest weight of the evidence. Further, we hold that while defendant may have had a basis in his personal judgment for rejecting plaintiff's credit (*i.e.,* outstanding debts and a $2,000 loss reflected in an income tax return), his attempted renegotiation demonstrates that his rejection was based on reasons other than plaintiff's credit rating and was, therefore, in bad faith.

[handwritten margin note: Δ ends up losing b/c of bad faith.]

* * *

For the foregoing reasons, the decree of the circuit court of Lee County granting specific performance to the plaintiff is affirmed.

Affirmed.

Van Deusen, J., concurs.

Lindberg, Justice, dissenting. *[handwritten: there was no contract]*

I am compelled to disagree with the respected trial court and my colleagues in the majority. I believe the parties, the trial court and the majority have proceeded far deeper into the intricacies of contract law than the facts of this cause permit. I do not believe questions of reasonableness or good faith are involved where the issue is whether the seller accepted and assented to the contract.

* * *

The addendum to the contract "Subject to seller approving buyer's credit report, oral on March 24, 1981, written when ready" was indisputably a condition to the seller's acceptance of the buyer's offer. It is an elementary rule of contract law that a condition precedent must be performed before contractual liability arises. (*Godare v. Sterling Steel Casting Co.* (1981), 103 Ill.App.3d 46, 58 Ill.Dec. 588, 430 N.E.2d 620 (and the cases cited therein).) The seller's acceptance of the offer must be unequivocal. (*Milani v. Proesel* (1958), 15 Ill.2d 423, 155 N.E.2d 38.) The seller never approved the buyer's credit report and it is not suggested by the parties or the trial court that the seller performed this necessary act. Nor is it urged that his silence between March 23 and May 14 (except when he was solicited by the buyer two or three times in April and May) constituted an acceptance.

[handwritten margin note: No acceptance b/c clause was a condition precedent therefore CP must be performed before K liability]

* * *

I conclude, * * * that neither the contract nor case law imposed upon the seller a standard of reasonableness in accepting or rejecting the contract. As to an implied agreement in every contract that the parties act in good faith I simply respond that there was no contract. But, also, the majority's conclusion that the seller lacked good faith by renegotiating other terms of the contract is not supported by the evidence. The buyer approached the seller and offered more documents regarding his "financial capabilities". During these meetings initiated by the buyer, seller indicated he might accept the contract at the original asking price of $135,000 and a half to one percent increase in the interest rate. Even if there was a contract, I would not hold that such discussions, where the seller has never indicated satisfaction with the buyer's credit, constitute bad faith.

I would reverse the judgment of the circuit court of Lee County.

Note
Further Aspects of Forman v. Benson

Benson argued in his appellate brief that he had not (as the court ultimately found) acted in bad faith in seeking to renegotiate the price (at page 20):

The obvious innocent interpretation of any discussion of change in price or rates is that the Defendant saw a greater risk than anticipated and wished to have a greater return for that risk. There is no evidence of duplicity on the part of the Defendant, although the inference is attempted to be made by the Plaintiff. In any event it is clear from the facts that the seller sought additional financial information and examined it at length before rejecting the buyer's credit. Discussions regarding additional compensation, if any took place, would not necessarily suggest that the Defendant had approved the credit but wanted more money.

Should the appellate court have paid more attention to this argument? Could the argument have been drafted more persuasively?

The circuit court entered its decree of specific performance on January 5, 1982. On February 2, 1982, Benson's lawyer wrote a letter to him that stated in part:

I received a call from Attorney Gehlbach. He advises me that his client is willing to make another offer in order to avoid the cost and delay of an appeal. He offers an additional $3,000 on the down payment. This would not increase the total amount of the contract, but would result in that additional amount paid "up front". As you know from my earlier conversations and correspondence I recommend that you work out some kind of accord with Dr. Forman. I believe it is in your best interests to avoid the expense of the appeal. Since your chances for success are not substantial, I urge you to either accept this proposal or make a counterproposal that is reasonable enough to induce Dr. Forman to accept. Perhaps a counterproposal for the additional $3,000 advance plus an increase of one-quarter of a per cent on the balance might be of interest to him.

Should Benson's lawyer have tried harder to bring about a settlement? What are the general constraints under which the lawyer operates?

Read this and more carefully

RIZZOLO v. POYSHER, 89 N.J.L. 618, 99 A. 390 (Err. & App. 1916). [Rizzolo, a contractor, sought payment from Stahl, the owner. One of Stahl's defenses was that Rizzolo failed to procure the architect's certificate required as a condition precedent under the contract. Rizzolo claimed that the architect was guilty of "fraud" in refusing to issue the certificate.]

PARKER, J.

* * *

* * * It is inferable from the architect's own testimony that he was ready to issue the certificate, but that the defendants wished to cut down the final payment by several hundred dollars on account of a counterclaim which the architect refused to recognize or support except for a much smaller sum; that he advised the plaintiff to "get after them and get his money"; and that when plaintiff asked for the certificate it was on the day before suit was begun, after plaintiff had retained counsel, and that he then refused it because he "did not want it to appear that he was issuing a certificate for a case." Such a reason was, of course, no reason at all, and led the judge very naturally to inquire of the witness whether he did not think that he had assumed responsibilities not belonging to his duties as architect. If the witness' statement was true, and there was no reason to believe the contrary, his refusal under such circumstances was fraudulent. * * * It is claimed that, to constitute such fraud, the owner must be a participant. If this were the rule, a corrupt architect would be greatly aided in extorting money from the contractor as a condition of awarding a certificate that was fully earned. The injustice of such a situation is obvious.

LUTTINGER v. ROSEN

Supreme Court of Connecticut, 1972.
164 Conn. 45, 316 A.2d 757.

LOISELLE, ASSOCIATE JUSTICE.

The plaintiffs contracted to purchase for $85,000 premises in the city of Stamford owned by the defendants and paid a deposit of $8500. The contract was "subject to and conditional upon the buyers obtaining first mortgage financing on said premises from a bank or other lending institution in an amount of $45,000 for a term of not less than twenty (20) years and at an interest rate which does not exceed 8½ per cent per annum." The plaintiffs agreed to use due diligence in attempting to obtain such financing. The parties further agreed that if the plaintiffs were unsuccessful in obtaining financing as provided in the contract, and notified the seller within a specific time, all sums paid on the contract would be refunded and the contract terminated without further obligation of either party.

In applying for a mortgage which would satisfy the contingency clause in the contract, the plaintiffs relied on their attorney who applied at a New Haven lending institution for a $45,000 loan at 8¼ percent per annum interest over a period of twenty-five years. The plaintiffs' attorney knew that this lending institution was the only one which at that time would lend as much as $45,000 on a mortgage for a single-family dwelling. A mortgage commitment was obtained for $45,000 with "interest at the prevailing rate at the time of closing but not less than 8¾%." Since this commitment failed to meet the

conditioned on these terms

contract requirement, timely notice was given to the defendants and demand was made for the return of the down payment. The defendants' counsel thereafter offered to make up the difference between the interest rate offered by the bank and the 8½ percent rate provided in the contract for the entire twenty-five years by a funding arrangement, the exact terms of which were not defined. The plaintiffs did not accept this offer and on the defendants' refusal to return the deposit an action was brought. From a judgment rendered in favor of the plaintiffs the defendants have appealed.

The defendants claim that the plaintiffs did not use due diligence in seeking a mortgage within the terms specified in the contract. The unattacked findings by the court establish that the plaintiffs' attorney was fully informed as to the conditions and terms of mortgages being granted by various banks and lending institutions in and out of the area and that the application was made to the only bank which might satisfy the mortgage conditions of the contingency clause at that time. These findings adequately support the court's conclusion that due diligence was used in seeking mortgage financing in accordance with the contract provisions. Brauer v. Freccia, 159 Conn. 289, 293, 268 A.2d 645. The defendants assert that notwithstanding the plaintiffs' reliance on their counsel's knowledge of lending practices, applications should have been made to other lending institutions. This claim is not well taken. The law does not require the performance of a futile act. * * *

The remaining assignment of error briefed by the defendants is that the court erred in concluding that the mortgage contingency clause of the contract, a condition precedent, was not met and, therefore, the plaintiffs were entitled to recover their deposit. "A condition precedent is a fact or event which the parties intend must exist or take place before there is a right to performance." Lach v. Cahill, 138 Conn. 418, 421, 85 A.2d 481, 482. If the condition precedent is not fulfilled the contract is not enforceable. Lach v. Cahill, supra; Bialeck v. Hartford, 135 Conn. 551, 556, 66 A.2d 610. In this case the language of the contract is unambiguous and clearly indicates that the parties intended that the purchase of the defendants' premises be conditioned on the obtaining by the plaintiffs of a mortgage as specified in the contract. From the subordinate facts found the court could reasonably conclude that since the plaintiffs were unable to obtain a $45,000 mortgage at no more than 8½ percent per annum interest "from a bank or other lending institution" the condition precedent to performance of the contract was not met and the plaintiffs were entitled to the refund of their deposit. Any additional offer by the defendants to fund the difference in interest payments could be rejected by the plaintiffs. See Lach v. Cahill, supra, 138 Conn. 418, 85 A.2d 481. There was no error in the court's exclusion of testimony relating to the additional offer since the offer was obviously irrelevant.

There is no error.

Problem 7–3

A lawyer should not attempt to draft contract clauses without having some knowledge of how courts tend to interpret such clauses. You have studied the differences between promises and conditions and also how courts interpret language that may purport to create them. Now assume that an agreement being drafted in your office includes the following clause: "In return for Artist's promise to prepare and deliver holiday greeting card designs in accord with attached specifications by November 15, Manufacturer promises to pay $4,000 for those designs." Your senior partner has asked you to draft further alternative clauses for consideration which would make Artist's performance "by November 15": (1) only a duty of Artist; (2) only a condition of Manufacturer's duty; (3) both a duty of Artist and a condition of Manufacturer's duty. Draft the clauses.

SECTION FIVE: EXCUSE AND AVOIDANCE OF EXPRESS CONDITIONS

E.I. DU PONT DE NEMOURS POWDER CO. v. SCHLOTTMAN

United States Court of Appeals, Second Circuit, 1914.
218 Fed. 353.

WARD, CIRCUIT JUDGE. In July, 1908, one Grubb was negotiating with T.C. Du Pont, president of the Du Pont Powder Company, for the sale of the whole capital stock of the Pittsburgh Fuse Company to the Du Pont Company. July 20th Du Pont wrote to Grubb as follows:

> "Mr. Chas. G. Grubb, Building—Dear Sir: Should the deal now under discussion for the Pittsburgh Fuse Mfg. Co. go through, and after we have had the property a year, it is understood that if in my judgment the property has for any reason been worth $175,000 to our company, and we manufactured double tape fuse at $2 per thousand with powder at $3.60 per keg, we are to pay you $25,000 in either bonds, preferred or common stock of our company as we may elect.

> "Yours truly,

> T.C. Du Pont, President."

On July 24th the deal referred to in the letter went through in a formal agreement whereby the Du Pont Company agreed to pay Grubb $75,000 of its preferred and $75,000 of its common stock for the whole capital stock of the Pittsburgh Fuse Company. Grubb delivered the Fuse Company's stock and the Du Pont Company transferred to it its own stock, but, after operating the plant for about six months, sold it to other parties, who dismantled it.

Grubb, the plaintiff's assignor, died before suit brought, and Mr. T.C. Du Pont did not testify to the circumstances attending the writing of the letter of July 20th. At the conclusion of the case each party asked Judge Ray to direct a verdict in his favor, and he did direct a verdict in favor of the plaintiff for $25,000.

The complaint treats the letter and the formal agreement as one contract, alleges that the defendant by selling the plant of the Fuse Company wrongfully prevented the test agreed upon, and claims damages for the difference between the fair and reasonable value of the Fuse Company's capital stock alleged to be $175,000 and the market value of the defendant's stock actually received, alleged to be $120,000.

The defendant contends that the letter of July 20th is a separate contract, and, as it is not to be performed within the year, is void under the statute of frauds, because it does not state any consideration. We think, however, that the two documents are to be considered together. The Du Pont Company was to pay $25,000 more in securities if in the judgment of T.C. Du Pont upon operating for one year, the plant was worth $175,000 to his company and was capable of making double tape fuse at $2 per thousand feet with powder at $3.60 a keg. This was to be additional compensation for additional value, so that the objection of the statute of frauds is unavailing.

The letter does not contain any express promise to operate the plant for one year, and the question is whether such a promise is to be implied. We think the court below rightly held that it was. The seller evidently thought the plant worth $175,000 in the defendant's securities, and the buyer was willing to pay the additional $25,000 if such value was demonstrated in the way provided. The letter implies a promise on the Du Pont Company's part to operate the plant for a year, and that promise must be taken as part of the consideration for which Grubb sold the capital stock. * * *

* * *

The question of damages is the only other question we think needing consideration. If the plaintiff could now perform or secure a performance of the agreed test, he might be obliged to do so as a condition of recovering the contract price. But the defendant has made performance impossible by selling the plant within the period of one year to a purchaser who has dismantled it. No similar test can be substituted. It was personal in its nature, viz., the operation for a year by a wealthy and expert corporation actuated by self-interest to make tape fuse at $2 a thousand feet. Because the defendant has made the performance of this test impossible, the plaintiff should not be remediless. We think he had the right to show, if he could, in other ways, that the value of the plant was greater by $25,000 than the sum paid for it. As Judge Bartlett said in Hopedale Co. v. Electric Storage Battery Co., 184 N.Y. 356, 364, 77 N.E. 394, 397:

> "In other words, the performance of a condition for valuation having been prevented by the act of the vendee, the price of the thing sold was to be fixed by the jury on a quantum valebat."

Though the contract contemplated that the defendant should pay the additional amount in its own securities, having refused to pay at all, the plaintiff has a right to recover money. New York Publishing Co. v. Steamship Co., 148 N.Y. 39, 42 N.E. 514. One witness stated that the plant was worth $175,000, and the Du Pont Company actually sold it for $150,000. The plaintiff's assignor received $122,000, the market value of the defendant's securities, aggregating $150,000. Therefore there was evidence to support the finding of the trial judge that the plant was worth $147,000, which may be implied from his direction of a verdict for $25,000.

Judgment affirmed.

HANNA v. COMMERCIAL TRAVELERS' MUTUAL ACCIDENT ASSOCIATION

Supreme Court of New York, Appellate Division, 1922.
204 App.Div. 258, 197 N.Y.S. 395, aff'd, 236 N.Y. 571, 142 N.E. 288 (1923).

Appeal from Supreme Court, New York County.

Action by William E. Hanna against the Commercial Travelers' Mutual Accident Association of America. From a judgment for plaintiff for $5,978.40, and from an order denying defendant's motion to set aside the verdict and for a new trial, defendant appeals. Judgment and order reversed, and complaint dismissed.

FINCH, J. The action is upon a policy of accident insurance. In 1913 the insured disappeared, and no trace of him was found until 1917, when his automobile was dredged up from the bottom of the Delaware river. When last seen he was driving this automobile upon a stormy, rainy morning in 1913. He had previously expressed an intention to go from Philadelphia to New York, and one of the usual routes existing at that time was down Dyott street, turning left for the ferry. Dyott street terminates in the Delaware river, and the only protection at the foot thereof was some posts extending across the street, two of which were found to be broken. It was the plaintiff's claim that the insured failed to turn off from Dyott street, and suffered death by accidentally driving his car from the street into the river. This claim, as well as a defense set up by the defendant that the alleged injury and death of the insured happened while he was under the influence of intoxicating drink, was determined in plaintiff's favor by the jury. Among other separate defenses pleaded, however, was failure to comply with the following provisions of the policy:

"Notice of every accident for or on account of which a claim may be made shall be given immediately after it happens to the secretary at Utica, N.Y., in writing, with full particulars of the accident and injury, and failure to give such immediate notice shall invalidate all claims under this contract which may be made on account of such accident, and unless affirmative and positive proof of the death or injury and that the same resulted from causes covered by the contract shall be furnished within six months of the happening of such accident, then all claims based thereon shall be forfeited to the association. Notice of death for which a claim may be made shall be given in writing to the secretary of the association within ten days from the date of such death, and failure to give such notice within said ten days shall invalidate any claim for loss by death."

Concededly notice was not given within the time required by the terms of the policy, and, as was found by the trial court, no waiver of such provisions by the defendant was shown. It is the contention of the respondent that such noncompliance was excused by the impossibility of compliance before a discovery of the facts which gave rise to the claim. The weight of authority, however, appears to be that, while as a general rule, where the performance of a duty created by law is prevented by inevitable accident without the fault of a party, the default will be excused, yet when a person by express contract engages absolutely to do an act not impossible or unlawful at the time, neither inevitable accident nor other unforeseen contingency not within his control will excuse him, for the reason that he might have provided against them by his contract. Whiteside v. North American Accident Ins. Co., 200 N.Y. 320, 93 N.E. 948, 35 L.R.A. (N.S.) 696. In the case at bar by the express terms of the contract the provisions as to notice were made conditions precedent to any liability.

Defendant is only liable by reason of its promise and this promise cannot be enlarged by the court, so as to fasten a liability on the defendant, which the latter did not undertake. The insured was at liberty either to accept or reject the offer of the defendant. The defendant was within its rights in undertaking only to be responsible for those accidents which were reported to it in time to permit it to seek witnesses of the occurrence while it was still fresh and the witnesses were still living. As was said by Chief Judge Hiscock in the Whiteside Case:

> "All of these provisions and engagements enter into the substance of the contract which respondent is seeking to enforce, and under such circumstances the courts will not relieve either party under the conditions here presented from fulfillment of the engagement which he has voluntarily undertaken."

The plaintiff relies upon the case of Trippe v. Provident Fund Soc., 140 N.Y. 23, 35 N.E. 316, 22 L.R.A. 432, 37 Am.St.Rep. 529, as an authority for the contention that the time in which to give notice did not begin to run until discovery of the facts constituting the claim. It appears, however, that the decision arrived at in that case was in fact based upon a waiver by the defendant of the provisions of the contract, and therefore the statements of the court, upon which reliance is placed by the plaintiff, must be regarded as dicta, which have not been followed by the later decisions of the same court. Whiteside v. North American Accident Ins. Co., supra.

It follows that the judgment must be reversed, with costs, and the complaint dismissed, with costs.

MERRELL and GREENBAUM, JJ., concur.

CLARKE, P.J. (dissenting). With great respect to the opinion of the Court of Appeals, I do not believe that Whiteside v. North American Accident Insurance Co., 200 N.Y. 320, 93 N.E. 948, 35 L.R.A. (N.S.) 696, controls in the case at bar. In that case the facts were quite different. There the policy contained a provision:

> "That written notice from the insured or his representative, stating the time, place and nature of injury, or death, or commencement of sickness, must be mailed to the secretary of the company at its home office * * * within ten days after the date of such injury, * * * as conditions precedent to recovery."

And the complaint alleged that during the early part of said sickness he was delirious and unable to remember that he had said policy of insurance, and had wholly forgotten that fact until about the 10th day of December, 1904, when he caused notice to be sent to the defendant of such sickness, and the court said:

> "That [the plaintiff] must be held to the terms of the contract which he had voluntarily made, and that, having assented to a provision

requiring notice of sickness within a certain time as a condition to recovery, he cannot be excused from fulfillment for the reasons alleged, and especially that this is true in view of the fact already mentioned that the notice called for by his contract might have been served by another person if he was disabled from personally so doing."

* * *

On April 28, 1913, insured disappeared. On May 24, 1913, the defendant wrote to Lyman, the insured, calling upon him to pay an assessment due under the policy on July 8, 1913. On July 10, 1913, Mrs. Lyman, the beneficiary, sent a check in payment of the assessment. This amount was never returned. On July 12, 1913, the defendant wrote inclosing a receipt and asking whether Lyman had changed his address. On July 17, 1913, a reply was sent stating that Lyman had disappeared on April 28, 1913, and had not been heard from since that date. On July 30th the defendant wrote saying, in view of Mr. Lyman's disappearance, the board of directors had terminated his membership in the association and canceled his certificate of insurance. On December 10, 1917, Mrs. Lyman's attorneys wrote the defendant, giving it notice that Lyman's automobile had been dredged from the Delaware river on December 5th, recalling to defendant the fact of his disappearance and the unsuccessful efforts to discover his whereabouts, and making a claim for the beneficiary for the full amount of the policy. On December 13, 1917, the defendant inclosed the usual proof of loss blanks, although not having been requested to do so by the beneficiary. On December 15, 1917, this letter was acknowledged with the statement, "We will prepare the proof of loss and forward same to you in due course," and on June 1, 1918, less than six months after Lyman's car was dredged from the river, Mrs. Lyman sent her proof of loss to the defendant, accompanied by a letter demanding a check for the amount of the insurance. This proof of loss was retained by the defendant, and after its receipt defendant communicated in no way with the plaintiff or her attorneys until the action was commenced.

The verdict of the jury upon the facts establishes that the insured met his death by accident on the 28th day of April, 1913, by reason of his car plunging from an unguarded street into the Delaware river. Of course it was impossible for him to give the notice required in case of accident by the policy. It was equally impossible for his widow to give such notice because the sole fact apparent at that time was that he had disappeared, and although investigations were immediately instituted, handbills printed, and every possible effort made to discover his whereabouts, it was not until three years later that in a dredging of the Delaware river his automobile was discovered and the cause of his disappearance established. It is obvious that the death occurred by accident and that it was within the terms of the policy. It is also obvious that the attempted cancellation of the policy above alluded to is without effect, because at that time the loss had occurred and the rights of the beneficiary to recover therefor were vested.

The sole question which survives the verdict of the jury is whether the failure under the facts and circumstances of this case to furnish the notice provided for in the policy, which it was impossible for any one to do by reason of the peculiar accident which caused the loss, is a complete defense to the action. * * *

* * *

In Ewing v. Commercial Travelers' Mutual Accident Association of America, 55 App.Div. 241, 66 N.Y.Supp. 1056, affirmed 170 N.Y. 590, 63 N.E. 1116, the insured died on June 23, 1897. The policy provided as a condition precedent to a recovery that immediate notice shall be given in writing of the accident or injury with full particulars. No one knew, until after the report of the chemist who had in charge the stomach and other organs of the deceased for chemical analysis upon an autopsy, the cause of death, which was from the effect of taking morphine accidentally. This report was made on the 8th or 9th of July following, and on July 9th the beneficiary notified the defendant. The court said:

> "The term 'immediate' should be interpreted reasonably. Trippe v. P.F. Society, 140 N.Y. 23. The context in which the word is here found implies that before notice is given the 'full particulars' must be first discovered by the person required to give the notice."

In Melcher v. Ocean Accident & Guarantee Corporation, Limited, 175 App.Div. 77, 161 N.Y.Supp. 586, this court reversed a judgment in favor of the plaintiff entered upon the verdict of a jury in an action on a policy whereby the defendant insured the plaintiff against accident upon and adjacent to his apartment house. One Didier was injured through the alleged negligence of the plaintiff on the premises on the 3d of November, 1913, from which injuries he died on the 22d day of March thereafter. By the terms of the policy it was provided that the assured upon the occurrence of an accident shall give immediate written notice thereof, with the fullest information obtainable at the time. Immediately after the accident, which occurred through the negligent operation of a freight elevator, which struck Didier when he was standing on an I-beam at work, he said he was not hurt and finished his job that afternoon, and the incident was not reported to the insurance company. On February 14, 1914, [more than three] months after the accident, the plaintiff received from an attorney employed by Didier a letter prior to Didier's death notifying him that Didier was seriously injured at the apartment on the 3d of November, 1913, while making certain repairs in an elevator shaft. The first notice that the defendant had of the accident was by the delivery of this letter to it by an insurance broker, employed by the plaintiff on the 17th day of February, 1914. This court reversed the judgment upon the ground of failure to give the notice required. The Court of Appeals reversed, quoting with approval Chapin v. Ocean Accident & Guarantee Corporation, 96 Neb. 213, 147 N.W. 465, 52 L.R.A.(N.S.) 227, which said:

> "If no apparent injury occurred from the mishap, and there was no reasonable ground for believing at the time that bodily injury would result from the accident, there was no duty upon the assured to notify the insurer."

While the majority of the court feel that they are constrained to reverse the judgment appealed from in the case at bar under the Whiteside Case, supra, it seems to me that the facts are so different from those presented in that case that the principle laid down in the cases cited by me ought to be applied, and therefore I vote to affirm the judgment appealed from.

Dowling, J., concurs.

CONNECTICUT FIRE INSURANCE CO. v. FOX

United States Court of Appeals, Tenth Circuit, 1966.
361 F.2d 1.

[Plaintiffs, A.H. Fox and Edith Fox, sole proprietors of the Firebird Motor Hotel, Cheyenne, Wyoming, entered into a contract of fire insurance with Connecticut Fire Insurance Company. The contract was in force when, early in the morning of March 25, 1964, a substantial portion of the motel was either destroyed or damaged by fire. The contract provided that: "The insured shall give immediate notice to this company of any loss * * * and within sixty days after the loss, unless such time is extended in writing by this company, the insured shall render to this company a proof of loss. * * * " A Mr. Foster, an adjuster for General Adjustment Bureau, Inc. (G.A.B.), appeared on the scene the day after the fire and persuaded the Foxes to sign a "non-waiver" agreement (even though the Foxes' attorney apparently advised against it), which essentially provided that no action of the insurer in investigating the loss would waive any conditions of the policy and that no representative of the company had any authority to waive any conditions of the policy unless in writing. Mr. Foster explained to the Foxes the procedures to be followed to recover on the policy without mentioning the proof of loss requirement. On May 5, the parties met again, and according to Mr. Fox's testimony, he presented an inventory of losses.

On June 3, after the sixty day period for filing proof of loss had run, Foster met again with the Foxes and proposed a settlement, which was rejected. At this time, Foster also gave the Foxes a letter stating that although the sixty days had expired, if the proof of loss was filed before July 3, no objection would be made. According to Fox, he then told Foster he would fill out the proof of loss immediately and that he had not been aware that he had to do so because in the past an adjuster had always done such things. The Foxes filled out the proof of loss form and sent the inventories to the insurer on June 6. On June 8, two attorneys for the insurer met with the Foxes and assured them the whole thing would be settled soon. The Foxes heard nothing, and brought suit on July 7th. The insurer rejected the proof of loss thirty days later. The insurer defended on the ground that the Foxes caused the fire and on the ground that the Foxes failed to file a timely proof of loss. The jury found for the Foxes on both issues. On appeal the defendant insurer asserted, among other things, that the proof of loss was not timely as a matter of law.]

Hill, Circuit Judge.

* * *

It is undisputed that the Foxes did not file their proofs of loss within sixty days after the fire as required by the policy. As a general rule, a proof of loss requirement is valid and may be considered as a condition precedent to recovery. However, this technical policy requirement may be waived by the insurer either directly or through the acts of its agents. The question to decide is whether under the facts and circumstances of this case, the insurer is deemed to have waived the proof of loss requirement.

Appellants' main contention is that the non-waiver agreement signed by the insured precludes a waiver by the insurer or its agents of a proof of loss requirement. Although we can find no Wyoming law directly in point, there can be no doubt of the validity of insurance non-waiver agreements, which, despite investigation into a claim by an insurer, nevertheless maintains the status quo of the policy and its conditions precedent to recovery. Had the insurer here through its adjusters done no more than investigate the fire loss, we would be loathe to say in light of the non-waiver agreement that this effectively waived the proof of loss requirement. But more was done than a mere investigation.

Non-waiver agreements are not so sacrosanct that they immunize an insurer from responsibility for any and all actions taken in adjusting a loss. The agreement being solely for the benefit of the insurer must be strictly construed against it under sound contract principles. In this case, the agreement merely allows the insurer to investigate to determine the cause and the amount of loss. The actions of the adjusters however went far beyond a mere investigation and to us cannot be considered protected under the non-waiver agreement. Nor can it be seriously doubted that the adjusters here, and particularly Foster, had the power to waive requirements of the policy like those under consideration.

At the first meeting, Agent Foster explained to the Foxes the conditions of the policy and their responsibility thereunder, but no mention was made of the proofs of loss. Foster did furnish inventory forms to be completed and submitted to the insurer and the accuracy and correctness of the forms thereafter seemed to be a main source of difficulty between the parties. No indication was ever made by Foster that proofs of loss were also required. On May 5th, when the Foxes had prepared these inventory forms, Foster rejected them as unsatisfactory. Fox submitted a bid to Foster at the May 5th meeting to completely rebuild the property but it was rejected for lack of detail. On May 12th, G.A.B. sent Mr. Wyatt of Underwriters Salvage Company to the motel to verify the inventory, which he did with Mr. Fox's assistance. Under the circumstances, Fox had a right to believe that once the inventory forms and bids were satisfactorily completed no further action on his part was necessary to perfect the claim. The cases are legion to the effect that once the insurer or its authorized agents indicate by a course of conduct that proofs of loss are unnecessary, such a requirement is waived. But Foster even went further. In taking complete charge of the loss, he instructed the Foxes to secure the property, to winterize the motel and to have the area cleaned and the remaining undamaged units made available for business, all of which was done. According to Mrs. Fox, Foster told them to keep a file on all these expenses and it would be included in settlement. Clearly by all these acts, Foster went beyond a mere investigation of the fire. It is no surprise in light of his apparent authority that the Foxes relied upon Foster to know what they must do to recover their loss.

One other factor certainly bears mentioning. The insurer actually paid a claim under the policy to a motel guest. Agent McMaster of G.A.B. in fact completed the proof of loss for the guest and the company paid $100. Having prepared a proof of loss and assumed liability for a guest in that instance under the policy, it seems rather astonishing that the insurer should now insist on proof of loss from the motel owner. As the final indication of the insurer's intention to waive the proof of loss requirement, appellee points to the letter of June 3rd, which waived the time for filing the proof of loss. The appellant insurer, while acknowledging this letter, contends that Foster had no authority to do so and, even if he did, the time for filing the proofs had already expired when the letter was given on June 3rd and that a waiver cannot be effectuated after the time for filing proofs of loss had expired. While there is some authority to that effect, we believe the other rule should prevail under the facts here and allow the insurer to waive or extend the requirement even though the original time requirement had expired. The contention that Foster lacked authority to make the waiver is not persuasive particularly in light of the company's reliance on the earlier non-waiver agreement which was also signed by Foster in behalf of the insurer. At any rate, had the insurer been dissatisfied with the waiver or extension for filing the proofs, the time for repudiating it would have been when the proofs were received on June 6th, not two months later after suit had been filed. In answer to an interrogatory, the jury expressly found that the agents of G.A.B., and specifically Foster, did have authority to extend the time for filing the proofs of loss. We are satisfied that finding is supported by substantial evidence and must therefore be affirmed.

3A CORBIN ON CONTRACTS

§ 753 at 484–85 (1960).

Generally, the waiver of a condition by a promisor is followed by a substantial change of position by the promisee. At the very least, he will be induced by the waiver not to perform the condition. * * *

In many cases, however, the waiver takes place after the failure to perform the condition has already occurred, and there is no subsequent change of position by the promisee on which to base an estoppel.

* * *

* * * A condition of a promisor's duty can be eliminated by a mere voluntary expression of his willingness to waive it, if its performance does not constitute a material part of the agreed equivalent of the promise and its non-performance does not materially affect the value received by the promisor.

R. HILLMAN, PRINCIPLES OF CONTRACT LAW

274 (2004).

[W]aivers are, as Johnny Carson used to say, "some crazy stuff," and they represent a significant exception to the rule requiring that promises must be supported by consideration or be relied on to be legally enforceable. One significant limitation on all of this is that courts tend to restrict waivers to non-material relinquishments of a right, such as a waiver of an insured's duty to file proofs of loss within a particular time period. Parties generally cannot waive material terms without consideration. For example, suppose Champ's Sporting Goods promises to pay $2000 to Ron D. Jockefeller, a manufacturer of sports apparel, for 1000 athletic supporters. Contract law would not recognize Champ's waiver if, after paying, it released Jockefeller from its duty to deliver the goods.

Problem 7–4

Your client, Betty Franklin, entered a retail installment contract with Essco Motors to purchase a Ford Thunderbird. The price was $1,352, of which Franklin paid $300, leaving a balance of $1,052. With finance and insurance charges, Franklin's debt to Essco was $1,656. Her contract called for 24 monthly payments of $69 due on the 15th of each month. Franklin paid $69 on February 15, March 15, April 25, May 23, June 24, July 26, August 24, September 27 and October 27. On November 26, Essco repossessed the car for failure of Franklin to pay the November installment. Advise Franklin on her rights based on the following possible additional facts.

(A) Essco accepted the March through October payments without protest and had given no notice in November before repossessing the car.

(B) Essco accepted the March through October payments without protest, but had notified Franklin in writing on November 5 that payment for November and thereafter would have to be on time.

(C) Essco and Franklin had agreed in April that payment would be on the 27th of each month instead of the 15th and Essco had given no notice before repossessing in November.

(D) Essco and Franklin had agreed in April that payment would be made on the 27th of each month, but Essco had notified Franklin in writing on November 5 that payment for November and thereafter would have to be on time, *e.g.* on the 15th of each month.

Q. VANDENBERG & SONS v. SITER, 204 Pa.Super. 392, 204 A.2d 494 (1964). [Seller warranted that flower bulbs were capable of flowering properly. The contract provided, however, that "[a]ll claims hereunder shall be deemed waived unless presented within eight (8) days after receipt of the goods." The trial court struck buyer's evidence that defects in the bulbs, although existing at the time of delivery, were latent, and could not be discovered until long after the eight days. Held, error.] "A limitation which renders the warranties ineffective as regards latent defects, literally covered by the warranty but not discoverable within the limitation period of the contract, is manifestly unreasonable and therefore invalid under § 1–204 of the code."

UNIFORM COMMERCIAL CODE § 1–204.

Time; Reasonable Time; "Seasonably"

(1) Whenever this Act requires any action to be taken within a reasonable time, any time which is not manifestly unreasonable may be fixed by agreement.

(2) What is a reasonable time for taking any action depends on the nature, purpose and circumstances of such action.

(3) An action is taken "seasonably" when it is taken at or within the time agreed or if no time is agreed at or within a reasonable time.

SECTION SIX: THE OVERRIDING OF EXPRESS CONDITIONS TO PREVENT FORFEITURE

J.N.A. REALTY CORP. v. CROSS BAY CHELSEA, INC.

Court of Appeals of New York, 1977.

42 N.Y.2d 392, 397 N.Y.S.2d 958, 366 N.E.2d 1313.

WACHTLER, JUDGE.

J.N.A. Realty Corp., the owner of a building in Howard Beach, commenced this proceeding to recover possession of the premises claiming that the lease has expired. The lease grants the tenant, Cross Bay Chelsea, Inc., an option to renew and although the notice was sent, through negligence or inadvertence, it was not sent within the time prescribed in the lease. The landlord seeks to enforce the letter of the agreement. The tenant asks for equity to relieve it from a forfeiture.

The Civil Court, after a trial, held that the tenant was entitled to equitable relief. The Appellate Term affirmed, without opinion, but the Appellate Division, after granting leave, reversed and granted the petition. The tenant has appealed to this court.

Two primary questions are raised on the appeal. First, will the tenant suffer a forfeiture if the landlord is permitted to enforce the letter of the agreement. Secondly, if there will be a forfeiture, may a court of equity grant the tenant relief when the forfeiture would result from the tenant's own neglect or inadvertence.

At the trial it was shown that J.N.A. Realty Corp. (hereafter JNA) originally leased the premises to Victor Palermo and Sylvester Vascellero for a 10–year term commencing on January 1, 1964. Paragraph 58 of the lease, which was attached as part of 12–page rider, granted the tenants an option to renew for a 10–year term provided "that Tenant shall notify the landlord in writing by registered or certified mail six (6) months prior to the last day of the term of the lease that tenant desires such renewal." The tenants opened a restaurant on the premises. In February, 1964 they formed the Foro Romano Corp. (Foro) and assigned the lease to the corporation.

By December of 1967 the restaurant was operating at a loss and Foro decided to close it down and offer it for sale or lease. In March, 1968 Foro entered into a contract with Cross Bay Chelsea, Inc. (hereafter Chelsea), to sell the restaurant and assign the lease. As a condition of the sale Foro was required to obtain a modification of the option to renew so that Chelsea would have the right to renew the lease for an additional term of 24 years.

The closing took place in June of 1968. First JNA modified the option and consented to the assignment. The modification, which consists of a separate document to be attached to the lease, states: "the Tenant shall have a right to renew this lease for a further period of Twenty–Four (24) years, instead of Ten (10) years, from the expiration of the original term of said lease * * *. All other provisions of Paragraph #58 in said lease, * * * shall remain in full force and effect, except as hereinabove modified." Foro then assigned the lease and sold its interest in the restaurant to Chelsea for $155,000. The bill of sale states that "the value of the fixtures and chattels included in this sale is the sum of $40,000 and that the remainder of the purchase price is the value of the leasehold and possession of the restaurant premises." At that point five and one-half years remained on the original term of the lease.

In the summer of 1968 Chelsea reopened the restaurant. JNA's president, Nicholas Arena, admitted on the stand that throughout the tenancy it regularly informed Chelsea in writing of its obligations under the lease, such as the need to pay taxes and insurance by certain dates. For instance on June 13, 1973 JNA sent a letter to Chelsea informing them that certain taxes were due to be paid. When that letter was sent the option to renew was due to expire in approximately two weeks but JNA made no mention of this. A similar letter was sent to Chelsea in September, 1973.

Arena also admitted that throughout the term of the tenancy he was "most assuredly" aware of the time limitation on the option. In fact there is some indication in the record that JNA had previously used this device in an attempt to evict another tenant. Nevertheless it was not until November 12, 1973 that JNA took any action to inform the tenant that the option had lapsed. Then it sent a letter noting that the date had passed and, the letter states, "not having heard from you as prescribed by paragraph #58 in our lease we must assume you will vacate the premises" at the expiration of the original term, January 1, 1974. By letter dated November 16, 1973 Chelsea, through its attorney, sent written notice of intention to renew the option which, of course, JNA refused to honor.

At the trial Chelsea's principals claimed that they were not aware of the time limitation because they had never received a copy of paragraph 58 of the rider. They had received a copy of the modification but they had assumed that it gave them an absolute right to retain the tenancy for 24 years after the expiration of the original term. However, at the trial and later at the Appellate Division, it was found that Chelsea had knowledge of, or at least was "chargeable with notice" of, the time limitation in the rider and thus was negligent in failing to renew within the time prescribed.

Chelsea's principals also testified that they had spent an additional $15,000 on improvements, at least part of which had been expended after the option had expired. Toward the end of the trial JNA's attorney asked the court whether it would "take evidence from" Arena that he had negotiated with another tenant after the option to renew had lapsed. However, the court held that this testimony would be immaterial.

It is a settled principle of law that a notice exercising an option is ineffective if it is not given within the time specified * * *. Thus the tenant had no legal right to exercise the option when it did, but to say that is simply to pose the issue; it does not resolve it. Of course the tenant would not be asking for equitable relief if it could establish its rights at law.

The major obstacle to obtaining equitable relief in these cases is that default on an option usually does not result in a forfeiture. The reason is that the option itself does not create any interest in the property, and no rights accrue until the condition precedent has been met by giving notice within the time specified. Thus equity will not intervene because the loss of the option does not ordinarily result in the forfeiture of any vested rights. * * *

But when a tenant in possession under an existing lease has neglected to exercise an option to renew, he might suffer a forfeiture if he has made valuable improvements on the property. This of course generally distinguishes the lease option, to renew or purchase, from the stock option or the option to buy goods. This was a distinction which some of the older cases failed to recognize. * * * More recently it has been noted that "although the tenant has no legal interest in the renewal period until the required notice is given, yet an equitable interest is recognized and protected against forfeiture in some cases where the tenant has in good faith made improvements of a substantial character, intending to renew the lease, if the landlord is not harmed by the delay in the giving of the notice and the lessee would sustain substantial loss in case the lease were not renewed" (2 Pomeroy, Equity Jurisprudence [5th ed.], § 453b, p. 296).

* * * In *Jones v. Gianferante,* 305 N.Y. 135, 138, 111 N.E.2d 419, 420, citing [Fountain Co. v. Stein, 97 Conn. 619, 118 A. 47], we held that the tenant was entitled to "the benefit of the rule or practice in equity which relieves against such forfeitures of valuable lease terms when default in notice has not prejudiced the landlord, and has resulted from an honest mistake, or similar excusable fault." The rule was extended in *Sy Jack Realty Co. v. Pergament Syosset Corp.,* 27 N.Y.2d 449, 453, 318 N.Y.S.2d 720, 722, 267 N.E.2d 462, 464, * * * to preserve the tenant's interest in a "long-standing location for a retail business" because this is "an important part of the good

will of that enterprise, [and thus] the tenant stands to lose a substantial and valuable asset."

In neither of those cases were we asked to consider whether the tenant would be entitled to equitable relief from the consequences of his own neglect or "mere forgetfulness" as the court had held in the *Fountain* case, *supra*. In *Gianferante* the default was due to an ambiguous lease, and in *Sy Jack* the notice was mailed but never delivered (but see *Roy's of North Syracuse v. P & C Food Markets,* 51 A.D.2d 641, 377 N.Y.S.2d 1019, mot. for lv. to app. den. 38 N.Y.2d 711, 384 N.Y.S.2d 1026, 348 N.E.2d 927; and the dissenting opn. in *Sy Jack, supra,* 27 N.Y.2d p. 456, n. 1, 318 N.Y.S.2d p. 725, 267 N.E.2d p. 466, where it is noted that the three cases cited in Williston—the principle one being the *Fountain* case—"obviously warranted equitable relief. For not only in those cases was there 'excusable fault', but also in each one the tenant had made substantial improvements"). But the principle involved is well established in this State. A tenant or mortgagor should not be denied equitable relief from the consequences of his own neglect or inadvertence if a forfeiture would result (*Giles v. Austin,* 62 N.Y. 486; *Noyes v. Anderson,* 124 N.Y. 175, 26 N.E. 316; *Roy's of North Syracuse v. P & C Food Markets, supra;* see, also, 2 Pomeroy, Equity Jurisprudence [5th ed.], § 452, p. 287). The rule applies even though the tenant or mortgagor, by his inadvertence, has neglected to perform an affirmative duty and thus breached a covenant in the agreement (*Giles v. Austin, supra; Noyes v. Anderson, supra*).

On occasion the court has cautioned that equitable relief would be denied where there has been a willful or gross neglect (*Noyes v. Anderson, supra,* 124 N.Y. p. 179, 26 N.E. p. 317), but it has been reluctant to employ the sanction when a forfeiture would result. In *Giles v. Austin, supra,* p. 491, for instance, the landlord sought to recover possession of the premises after the tenant had neglected to pay the taxes as required by a covenant in the lease. We held that although the tenant had not paid the taxes since the inception of the lease in 1859, and had only paid them after suit was commenced in 1868, the tenant's default was not "so willful, or his neglect so inexcusable, that a court of equity should have denied him any relief."

There are several cases in which this court has denied a tenant or mortgagor equitable relief because of his own neglect to perform within the time fixed in the lease or mortgage, but only when it has found that there was "no penalty, no forfeiture". * * * Cardozo took a different view. He felt that even though there may be no penalty or forfeiture "in a strict or proper sense" equity should "relieve against it if default has been due to mere venial inattention and if relief can be granted without damage to the lender". Even in those cases he would apply the general equitable principle that "the gravity of the fault must be compared with the gravity of the hardship" (*Graf v. Hope Bldg. Corp.,* * * * 254 N.Y. pp. 9–10, 13, 171 N.E. p. 888 [Cardozo, Ch. J., dissenting]; see, also, 2 Pomeroy, Equity Jurisprudence [5th ed.], § 439, p. 220).

Here, as noted, the tenant has made a considerable investment in improvements on the premises—$40,000 at the time of purchase, and an additional $15,000 during the tenancy. In addition, if the location is lost, the restaurant would undoubtedly lose a considerable amount of its customer good will. The tenant was at fault, but not in a culpable sense. It was, as

Cardozo says, "mere venial inattention." There would be a forfeiture and the gravity of the loss is certainly out of all proportion to the gravity of the fault. Thus, under the circumstances of this case, the tenant would be entitled to equitable relief if there is no prejudice to the landlord.

However, it is not clear from the record whether JNA would be prejudiced if the tenant is relieved of its default. Because of the trial court's ruling, JNA was unable to submit proof that it might be prejudiced if the terms of the agreement were not enforced literally. Its proof of other negotiations was considered immaterial. It may be that after the tenant's default the landlord, relying on the agreement, in good faith, made other commitments for the premises. But if JNA did not rely on the letter of the agreement then, it should not be permitted to rely on it now to exact a substantial forfeiture for the tenant's unwitting default. This, however, must be resolved at a new trial.

Finally we would note, as the dissenters do, that it is possible to imagine a situation in which a tenant holding an option to renew might intentionally delay beyond the time prescribed in order to exploit a fluctuating market. However, as the dissenters also note, there is no evidence to suggest that that is what occurred here. On the contrary there has been an affirmed finding of fact that the tenant's late notice was due to negligence. Of course a tenant who has intentionally delayed should not be relieved of a forfeiture simply because this tenant, who was merely inadvertent, may be granted equitable relief. But, on the other hand, we do not believe that this tenant, or any tenant, guilty only of negligence should be denied equitable relief because some other tenant, in some other case, may be found to have acted in bad faith. By its nature equitable relief must always depend on the facts of the particular case and not on hypotheticals.

Accordingly, the order of the Appellate Division should be reversed and a new trial granted.

BREITEL, CHIEF JUDGE (dissenting).

Relieving the tenant of its negligent failure to exercise its option to renew a lease within the prescribed time upsets established precedent, introduces instability in business transactions, and disregards commercial realities. I therefore dissent.

This case involves an option to renew a lease, not a mortgage foreclosure or an acceleration clause in a lease or mortgage. The categories and applicable precedents are not to be confused.

* * *

Had an honest mistake or similar "excusable fault", as opposed to what is undoubtedly mere carelessness, occasioned the tenant's tardiness, absent prejudice to the landlord, equitable relief would be available * * *. At issue, instead, is the availability of equitable relief where the only excuse for the commercial tenant's dilatory failure to exercise its option to renew is sheer carelessness.

Enough has been said to uncover a common situation. Experienced and even hardened businessmen at cross-purposes over the renewal of a valuable lease term seek on the one hand to stand by the written agreement, and on the other, to loosen the applicable rules to receive ad hoc adjustment of equities and relief from economic detriment. The landlord wants a higher return. The tenant wants to keep the old bargain. Which of the profit-seeking parties in this particular case should prevail as a matter of morals is not within the province of the courts. The well-settled doctrine is that with respect to options, whether they be lease renewal options, options to purchase real or personal property, or stock options, time is of the essence. The exceptions, namely, estoppel, fraud, mistake, accident, or overreaching, are few. Commercial stability and certainty are paramount, and always the dangers of unsolvable issues of fact and speculative manipulation (as with stock options) are to be avoided.

The landlord should be awarded possession of the premises in accordance with the undisputed language and manifested intention of the written lease, its 12–page rider, and modification. It does not suffice that the tenant may suffer an economic detriment in losing the renewal period. Nor does it suffice that the delay in giving notice may have caused the landlord no "prejudice", other than loss of the opportunity to relet the property or renegotiate the terms of a lease on a fresh basis. Once an option to renew a lease has been conditioned upon the tenant's giving timely notice, the commercial lessee should not be heard to complain that through carelessness a valued asset has been lost, anymore than one would allow the landlord to complain of the economic detriment to him in agreeing to an improvident option to renew.

* * *

In this State, as in others, relief has been afforded tenants threatened with loss of an expected renewal period (see, generally, Effect of Lessee's Failure or Delay in Giving Notice Within Specified Time, of Intention to Renew Lease, Ann., 44 A.L.R.2d 1359, esp. 1362–1369). But in New York, as elsewhere, the circumstances conditioning such relief have been carefully limited. It is only where the tenant can show, not mere negligence, but an excuse such as fraud, mistake, or accident, that is, one or more of the categories common and integral to invocation of equity, that courts have, despite the literal agreement and intention of the parties, stepped in to prevent a loss. * * *

* * *

The majority facilely disposes of the tenant's delinquency in exercising its option by relying on cases in which a party, notwithstanding its negligence, was relieved from a forfeiture * * *. But indiscriminate application of principles evolved to deal with mortgage foreclosures or a lessor's right to re-enter upon a tenant's failure to pay taxes and assessments when due does not withstand analysis. Since ever so long, enforcement of a mortgage has rested in equity * * *. It is also significant that as to foreclosure, time is not of the essence (see 10 N.Y.Jur., Contracts, § 270). Even where acceleration clauses are involved and a strong argument can be made for allowing relief, time has been of the essence and negligence has not been excused * * *. It is equally inappropriate to analogize to a lessee's failure to comply with a lease requirement that taxes and assessments be paid as they become due * * *. For the loss of an existing lease term subject to a condition subsequent distinguishes that situation from the loss of a possible option period subject to a condition precedent. An option is a right to purchase or acquire an interest in personal or real property in the future, and, if precise, it carries an invulnerable requirement to comply with all conditions, including that of time which is therefore of the essence in law and equity.

There are cases, not binding on this court, which express the principles discussed. For reasons that are not persuasive they would distinguish, however, between mere neglect or forgetfulness and gross or willful negligence, whatever that might be * * *. This is not a distinction generally accepted and is hardly a pragmatic one to apply in an area where the opportunities for distortion and manipulation are so great. The instability and uncertainty would be dangerous and would allow for ad hoc dispensations in particular cases without reliable rule so essential to commercial enterprise.

To begin with, under the guise of sheer inadvertence, a tenant could gamble with a fluctuating market, at the expense of his landlord, by delaying his decision beyond the time fixed in the agreement. The market having resolved in favor of exercising the option, the landlord, even though the day appointed in the agreement has passed, could be held to the return set out in the option, although if the market had resolved otherwise, the tenant could not be held to the renewal period.

None of this is to say that the tenant in this case was guilty of any manipulation. Hardly so. But what the court is concerned with is a rule for this case which perforce must cover other cases of like kind, where there will be no assurance that the "forgetfulness" is no more than that. The worst of the matter is that the kind of paltry record made in this case is hardly one on which a new rule with potential for mischief should be based. When the option, especially one requiring notice well in advance of the expiration of the lease, permits of economic manipulation, in commercial fairness the parties, especially if represented by counsel, should be held to their bargain, if plainly expressed.

Considering investments in the premises or the renewal term a "forfeiture" as alone warranting equitable relief would undermine if not dissolve the general rule upon which there is agreement. For, it is difficult to imagine a dilatory commercial tenant, particularly one in litigation over a renewal, who would not or could not point, scrupulously or unscrupulously, to some threatened investment in the premises, be it a physical improvement or the fact of good will. As a practical matter, it is not unreasonable to expect the commercial tenant, as compared with his residential counterpart, to protect his business interests with meticulousness, a meticulousness to which he would hold his landlord. All he, or his lawyer, need do is red-flag the date on which he has to act.

Having established no excuse, other than its own carelessness, Chelsea's claim is unfounded. Even if Chelsea honestly thought it enjoyed a 30–year lease, it does not change the result. Nor is it helpful to argue that Chelsea, always represented by a lawyer, was unable to procure a copy of the entire lease agreement. Indeed, it borders on the utterly incredible that experienced, sophisticated businessmen and their lawyers would not have assembled and scrutinized every relevant document affecting a long-term lease covering, with a renewal, a 30–year period.

That adherence to well-settled principles, like a Statute of Limitations or a Statute of Frauds works a hardship on some does not, alone, permit a court to depart from sound doctrine and principles. Even if precedent did not control the same doctrines and principles discussed should be applied.

Accordingly, I dissent and vote that the order of the Appellate Division should be affirmed, and the landlord awarded possession of the premises.

GABRIELLI, FUCHSBERG and COOKE, JJ., concur with WACHTLER, J.

BREITEL, C.J., dissents and votes to affirm in a separate opinion in which JASEN and JONES, JJ., concur.

Order reversed, with costs, and a new trial granted.

KNAPP, JUDGMENT CALL: THEORETICAL APPROACHES TO CONTRACT DECISION–MAKING
1988 Ann.Surv.Am.L. 307, 333, 336.

From the record, it appears that the tenant Chelsea had by 1973 established a profitable restaurant at the Howard Beach location, one which it wished to continue. You may assume that it would at that point have been possible for Chelsea to find comparable space in some other building close enough so that at least some of the "good will" attributable to location would be retained, but that the high costs of moving (including both the costs of physical removal and the loss of profits occasioned by an interruption of business) plus uncertainty about the transferability of its good will made Chelsea strongly prefer to stay at its present location on the JNA premises. This could have been the case even if rental levels in the area had not risen to levels higher than those provided for in its lease-renewal agreement with JNA; since apparently they had, Chelsea's decision to invest resources in an attempt to stay on at its present location is easily seen as the act of one motivated by rational self-interest.

For its part, the landlord JNA appears to have been motivated entirely by a desire to realize from the property a level of rental income higher than that provided by the lease extension agreement. To analyze more completely the economic factors at work, however, it appears relevant to note that landlords in similar cases (i.e., landlords resisting lease renewal) might well be motivated by a variety of concerns, and that these various possibilities should be taken into account in any economic analysis of the case. At least three distinguishable cases may be suggested: (1) The landlord may believe that the property could be sold for an advantageous price if it were unencumbered by this tenancy; (2) the landlord may be willing to continue to rent to a tenant of this type, perhaps even on comparable terms, but may wish to get rid of this particular tenant; (3) the landlord may be willing to continue to rent to this tenant, but only at a higher rental (as was apparently true in JNA's case). * * *

* * *

* * * So far as one can tell from the record or from discussions with the attorneys involved, JNA had no wish to sell the building or to convert it to another use; nor did it have any particular complaints about Chelsea as a tenant. It merely wanted to receive a higher rental than provided for in the lease extension agreement. This is the third situation imagined above. In this variation of the case, a decision in the landlord's favor serves neither to

facilitate some fundamentally different utilization of the property in question nor to save the landlord (and society) the expense of effecting what might well be a deserved termination of the tenancy. Instead, [the] court's decision will merely affect the distribution of wealth as between the landlord and the tenant: the tenant either will be forced to agree to a rent increase, or it won't.

RESTATEMENT (SECOND) OF CONTRACTS § 229.

To the extent that the non-occurrence of a condition would cause disproportionate forfeiture, a court may excuse the non-occurrence of that condition unless its occurrence was a material part of the agreed exchange.

HOLIDAY INNS OF AMERICA, INC. v. KNIGHT

Supreme Court of California, 1969.
70 Cal.2d 327, 74 Cal.Rptr. 722, 450 P.2d 42.

TRAYNOR, CHIEF JUSTICE.

Plaintiffs appeal from a judgment for defendants in an action seeking a declaration that a contract was still effective. The judgment was entered after plaintiffs' motion for summary judgment was denied and defendants' motion for summary judgment was granted.

The pleadings and affidavits of the parties establish the following undisputed facts.

Plaintiffs are the successors in interest to the optionee under a written option contract between the optionee and the owners of the option property, defendant D. Manley Knight and his mother, Mary Knight. Mary Knight is now deceased and D. Manley Knight is the sole owner of the property. Although his wife is also named a defendant herein, she has no interest in the contract or the option property. We will therefore refer to D. Manley Knight as defendant.

The contract, executed on September 30, 1963, granted an option to purchase real property in Orange County for $198,633, the price to be subject, however, to prescribed adjustments for changes in the cost of living. Unless cancelled as provided in the agreement, the option could be exercised by giving written notice thereof no later than April 1, 1968. The contract provided for an initial payment of $10,000 and for four additional payments of $10,000 to be made directly to the optionors on July 1 of each year, commencing in 1964, unless the option was exercised or cancelled before the next such payment became due. These payments were not to be applied to the purchase price. The cancellation provision provided that "it is mutually understood that failure to make payment on or before the prescribed date will automatically cancel this option without further notice." On December 9, 1963, the parties amended the contract by executing escrow instructions that provided that the annual payments were to be deposited in escrow with the Security Title Insurance Company, and that, in "the event you [Security Title] do not receive the $10,000 annual payments [by July 1] and upon receiving notice from Optionors to cancel the option, without further instructions from Optionee you are to terminate the escrow."

The initial payment of $10,000 and the annual installments for 1964 and 1965 were paid. After the execution of the contract, plaintiffs expended "great amounts of money" to develop a major residential and commercial center on the land adjacent to the option property. These expenditures have caused the option property to increase substantially in value since the contract was executed. Plaintiffs' purpose in entering into the contract was to put themselves in a position to secure the advantage of this increase in value resulting from their development efforts.

In 1966 plaintiffs mailed a check for $10,000 to defendant. It was made out to D. Manley Knight and his wife, Lavinia Knight, and dated June 30, 1966. Defendant received the check on July 2, 1966 and returned it to plaintiffs on July 8, stating that the option contract was cancelled. On July 8 plaintiffs tendered another check directly to defendant, and he again refused it. On July 15 plaintiffs deposited a $10,000 check with Security Title payable to defendant. Security Title tendered the check to defendant, but his attorney returned it to plaintiffs on July 27 and advised them that the agreement was terminated pursuant to the cancellation provision.

Plaintiffs contend that payment of the annual installment was timely on the ground that the check became the property of defendant when mailed; that even if the payment was late, the trial court should have relieved them from forfeiture and declared the option in force under section 3275 of the Civil Code; and that, in any event, the trial court erred in excluding extrinsic evidence offered to prove that the escrow instructions modified the contract to permit payment at any time before defendant notified the title company that the option was cancelled. Since the undisputed facts establish that plaintiffs are entitled to relief from forfeiture pursuant to section 3275, it is unnecessary to consider plaintiffs' other contentions.

Section 3275 provides: "Whenever, by the terms of an obligation, a party thereto incurs a forfeiture, or a loss in the nature of a forfeiture, by reason of his failure to comply with its provisions, he may be relieved therefrom, upon making full compensation to the other party, except in case of a grossly negligent, willful, or fraudulent breach of duty." The tumultuous history of this section has been recorded in a lengthy series of major decisions in the area of property and contract law.

Although most of the cases considering section 3275 have involved land sale contracts, its proscriptions against forfeiture apply in any case in which the party seeking relief from default has brought himself within the terms of the section by pleading and proving facts that justify its application. (Barkis v. Scott, 34 Cal.2d [16] at pp. 118, 120, 208 P.2d 367.) In determining whether a given case falls within section 3275, however, it is necessary to consider the nature of the contract and the specific clause in question. Although the contract in the instant case is an option contract, the question is not whether the exercise of the option was timely, but whether the right to exercise the option in the future was forfeited by a failure to pay the consideration for that right precisely on time. Defendant's reliance on Cummings v. Bullock (9th Cir.1966) 367 F.2d 182, and Wilson v. Ward (1957) 155 Cal.App.2d 390, 317 P.2d 1018, is therefore misplaced. Both those cases dealt with the time within which an option must be exercised and correctly held that such time cannot be extended beyond that provided in the contract. To hold otherwise would give the optionee, not the option he bargained for, but a longer and therefore more extensive option. In the present case, however, plaintiffs are not seeking to extend the period during which the option can be exercised but only to secure relief from the provision making time of the essence in tendering the annual payments. * * * In a proper case, relief will be granted under section 3275 from such a provision. (Barkis v. Scott, supra 34 Cal.2d at p. 122, 208 P.2d 367.)

The sole issue in this case is whether the plaintiffs have brought themselves within section 3275; whether there would be a loss in the nature of a forfeiture suffered by plaintiffs if the option contract were terminated. Essentially, the position of defendant is that there is no forfeiture since plaintiffs got precisely what they bargained for, namely, the exclusive right to buy the property for the three years during which they made payments. Cancellation because of the late 1966 payment amounts to nothing more than terminating a contract providing for that exclusive right during 1966. As viewed by defendant, this contract is in effect wholly executory and therefore its termination would not result in a forfeiture to either party. (Martin v. Morgan (1890) 87 Cal. 203, 25 P. 350.)

To sustain defendant's argument, the contract would have to be viewed as a series of independent contracts, each for a one-year option. Only if this were true, could it be said that plaintiffs received their bargained for equivalent of the $30,000 payments. (Sheveland v. Reed (1958) 159 Cal.App.2d 820, 822, 324 P.2d 633.) The economic realities of the transaction, however, do not support this analysis. First, the language of the agreement states that the "Optioners hereby grant to Optionee the exclusive right and option for a five year period * * *." The parties agreed to bind themselves to a period of five years with the price payable in five installments. On the basis of risk allocation, it is clear that each payment of the $10,000 installment was partially for an option to buy the land during that year and partially for a renewal of the option for another year up to a total of five years. With the passage of time, plaintiffs have paid more and more for the right to renew, and it is this right that would be forfeited by requiring payment strictly on time. At the time the forfeiture was declared, plaintiffs had paid a substantial part of the $30,000 for the right to exercise the option during the last two years. Thus, they have not received what they bargained for and they have lost more than the benefit of their bargain. In short, they will suffer a forfeiture of that part of the $30,000 attributable to the right to exercise the option during the last two years.[1]

Plaintiffs have at all times remained willing and able to continue with the performance of the contract and have acted in good faith to accomplish this end. Defendant has not suffered any injury justifying termination of the contract, and none of his reasonable expectations have been defeated. Moreover, he will receive the benefit of his bargain, namely, the full price of the option granted plaintiffs. As we stated in *Barkis,* "when the default has not been serious and the vendee is willing and able to continue with his perform-

---

1. Plaintiffs also allege forfeiture of "great amounts of money" expended for the development of surrounding land. Evidently none of the investment was made in the option property. Since there is nothing to indicate that the development was not highly profitable in its own right or that inclusion of defendant's property was necessary to make the development a success, it would not seem that any part of these expenditures can be considered forfeited by a termination of the contract. * * *

ance of the contract, the vendor suffers no damage by allowing the vendee to do so." (Barkis v. Scott, supra, 34 Cal.2d at p. 122, 208 P.2d at p. 371.)

The judgment is reversed and the trial court is directed to enter a summary judgment for plaintiffs in accord with the views herein expressed.

Problem 7–5

Compare once again Jacob & Youngs, Inc. v. Kent with Brown–Marx Assocs., Ltd. v. Emigrant Savings Bank. (See Section Two of this chapter.) We saw that the latter case affirms the general doctrine that a party must strictly comply with an express condition, while Jacob & Youngs holds that, in the absence of an express condition as to quality of performance, there is an implied condition of substantial performance. In light of the cases on excuse, avoidance, and overriding of express conditions, what remains of the initial sharpness of the foregoing distinction?

Note
Unjust Enrichment as a Theory to Prevent Forfeiture

As we have seen, courts avoid forfeiture resulting from the failure to satisfy a condition precedent under an "agreement with consideration." Courts also avoid forfeiture by invoking the unjust enrichment theory of obligation. In a particular case, of course, that theory may be unavailable because one or more of the requirements for an unjust enrichment recovery may not be met. See Chapter Two. Even when those requirements are met, the recovery may be less than a recovery on the contract. For example, suppose that an express condition precedent to Owner's duty to pay Builder $4500 for construction of a sidewalk is the completion of 48 slabs. Suppose further that Builder is only able to complete 36 slabs. The market value of 36 slabs is $2500 and Owner has not sustained any damages resulting from the breach. Builder may recover $2500 based on unjust enrichment, whereas a ratable portion of the contract price would be $3375.

SECTION SEVEN: EXPRESS CONDITIONS AND THE LAW OF PLEADING AND PROCEDURE

Sometimes a court allocates burdens of pleading and proof depending on whether a condition is cast in the form of a condition precedent or a condition subsequent. Suppose the buyer and the seller of a house agree that the buyer will pay $75,000 for the house on May 1 on condition that the buyer sells his own house by that date. Such a condition is usually denominated a condition precedent because the duty of the buyer to pay has not ripened—the buyer must sell his house first. In the seller's suit for the buyer's failure to pay, some courts allocate to the seller the burdens of pleading and proving that the buyer has sold his house and thus that the buyer's duty to perform has matured. Indeed, some court rules require such an allocation with respect to pleading. Rule 9(c) of the Federal Rules of Civil Procedure provides:

> In pleading the performance or occurrence of conditions precedent, it is sufficient to aver generally that all conditions precedent have been performed or have occurred. A denial of performance or occurrence shall be made specifically and with particularity.

Suppose, however, that the parties' agreement calls for the buyer to purchase the house on May 1, "but if the buyer is unable to sell his own house, the buyer is released from the duty to purchase." This condition is cast in the form of a condition subsequent. Here the buyer's duty to perform has already arisen, but is discharged if the buyer cannot sell the house. Some courts allocate to the buyer the burdens of pleading and proving that he has failed to sell his house and thus that his duty of performance has been discharged.

You can see that the drafters of a contract can draft most conditions in either precedent or subsequent *form* and thus have some control over the allocations of burdens of pleading and proof at a potential trial. But the law may also permit a court to take into account many additional factors in allocating burdens of proof, such as the probability of the truth of an allegation, and which party has better access to the available evidence.

Occasionally a court may view a condition subsequent as more than merely a matter of form. For example, a policy of fire insurance may require notice and proof of loss as conditions precedent to the insurer's duty to pay. The policy may also require that the insured bring any action within a certain time. Technically, the insured's duty to bring the action could be drafted as a condition precedent to the duty of the insurer to pay. But would this make sense? Instead, the insurance company drafts the duty to pay as subject to the condition subsequent that the insured bring the action. Therefore, once the insured files the notice and proof of loss, the insurer's duty to pay matures, but it is subsequently discharged if the insured does not sue within the specified time.

SECTION EIGHT: IMPLIED CONDITIONS FIXING THE ORDER OF PERFORMANCE

In Section One of this chapter, we introduced the problem that arises when the parties leave a gap in their agreement as to the order of performance. We now return to this problem. In subsection A, we consider gap-filler rules that apply when simultaneous exchange is possible. In subsection B, we consider gap-filler rules that apply when one party must perform before the other.

A. SIMULTANEOUS EXCHANGE

Assume that in a signed writing a vendor agrees to sell Blackacre to a vendee on July 2 for $15,000. Assume the agreement does not set forth whether one party is to perform first or whether the two are to perform simultaneously. Nor do the circumstances demonstrate that the parties intended any particular approach. Thus, there are no express or implied-in-fact conditions fixing the order of performance. In the absence of precedent, a court confronted with a dispute over the order of performance would have to decide how to fill the gap. One possibility would be to adopt a rule requiring the vendor to perform first by transferring a deed to the vendee and by allowing the vendee to enter possession before paying the $15,000 price. Another possibility would be to require the vendor to deliver the deed and the vendee to pay the $15,000 at the same time, with the vendee to take

#3 Vendee pay first

possession thereafter. Still another possibility would be to require the vendee to pay before the vendor transfers a deed. What policies are relevant to this choice of gap fillers? As we will see, one policy is that of facilitating the consummation of agreed exchanges. A related policy is that of eliminating, or at least minimizing, the risk that one party will perform without receiving due performance in return. Which of the alternative rules above would best serve these policies?

Suppose that the order of performance gap is filled by a rule of law requiring concurrent performances. Suppose also that the vendor does not perform at all, or does not substantially perform, and the agreement is silent on the consequences. Must the vendee nevertheless perform? A court might choose to fill this further gap by adopting a rule that the non-performing party—here, the vendor—must pay any damages to the vendee for breach of contract, but that the vendee must still perform or be liable for breach as well. Would such an approach make sense? As an alternative to the foregoing rule, a court might provide that the vendee could not only recover damages upon the vendor's breach but could also withhold his own promised performance. Put another way, contract law might make the vendor liable for breach and also regard the breach as a failure of an implied-in-law ("constructive") condition precedent to the vendee's duty to pay, with the result that the vendee's duty does not mature at all. Which of the foregoing basic alternatives would maximize the likelihood that agreed exchanges will take place? Which alternative would minimize the risk that one party will perform without receiving due performance in return?

An additional related problem is this. Let us suppose that the court adopts a rule requiring the parties to perform simultaneously and that the vendor does not show up on July 2 with the deed. What must the aggrieved vendee show in court to establish a right to damages for the vendor's nonperformance? One approach would be to require the vendee only to allege and prove the vendor's nonperformance of the contract. An alternative would be to require not only such allegations and proof but *also* allegations and proof that the vendee duly tendered performance to the vendor (or that for some reason this tender was excused), that the vendee then demanded performance from the vendor, and that all this was unavailing. Which of these rules would reveal who was responsible for the failure of the exchange? Which of these rules would maximize the likelihood that agreed exchanges will occur without a default?

Observe that if the vendee were to sue for specific performance, the court could order a simultaneous exchange, with the vendor to deliver the deed upon the vendee's payment. According to this approach, the exchange would take place under court supervision without risk that one party would perform and the other not. But the court cannot so effectively facilitate the aims of the parties where it has no direct intervening role, such as in a damages action after the time for performance. The court can then only require that the vendee allege and prove that the vendee took those steps (in a timely fashion) that would have been likely, were the vendor willing, to lead to performance by both parties, or at least require that the vendee allege and prove that those steps would have been useless.

3A CORBIN ON CONTRACTS

§ 656 at 144–47 (1960).

When the two full performances reciprocally promised in a bilateral contract are the agreed exchange each for the other, and the contract provides that they are to be rendered * * * at the same moment of time, it has now long been held that the two promises are mutually dependent. The two performances are said to be "concurrent conditions" of the reciprocal duties of the parties. * * *

* * *

In many cases, the parties make a bilateral agreement for the exchange of two such performances as above without specifying any time for the rendition of either one. * * * [T]he parties are now bound to perform at and within a reasonable time. * * * Neither party having agreed to give "credit," the two performances are again required to be simultaneous; the two promises are mutually "dependent" and concurrently "conditional."

In still other cases, the bilateral agreement for such an exchange specifies a definite time for the rendition of one of the performances without specifying a time for the return performance. * * * Again, * * * the return performance must be rendered on the day that is specified for the other performance, the two to be rendered simultaneously. * * *

A fourth kind of provision is found in bilateral agreements such as these. It may be agreed that one or both of the performances shall be rendered within a stated period of time, or "on or before" a specified day. Here, too, there is no "credit" period and performances are to be concurrent.

UNIFORM COMMERCIAL CODE § 2–507(1).

Tender of delivery is a condition to the buyer's duty to accept the goods and, unless otherwise agreed, to his duty to pay for them. Tender entitles the seller to acceptance of the goods and to payment according to the contract.

UNIFORM COMMERCIAL CODE § 2–511(1).

Unless otherwise agreed tender of payment is a condition to the seller's duty to tender and complete any delivery.

RESTATEMENT (SECOND) OF CONTRACTS § 234(1).

Where all or part of the performances to be exchanged under an exchange of promises can be rendered simultaneously, they are to that extent due simultaneously, unless the language or the circumstances indicate the contrary.

3 S. WILLISTON AND G. THOMPSON, A TREATISE ON THE LAW OF CONTRACTS

§ 832 at 2327–28 (rev'd ed. 1936).

It is one of the consequences of concurrent conditions that a situation may arise where no right of action ever arises against either party. Since a conditional tender is necessary to put either party in default, so long as both parties remain inactive, neither is liable and neither has acquired a right of action. Moreover, the possibility of putting either party in default will cease if the delay is too long. It may be supposed by the terms of the contract the concurrent performances were to be rendered on a day fixed, or it may be supposed that no time was stated for the performance. Under the first supposition if time was of the essence of the contract both parties will be discharged unless one or the other takes the initiative and makes a conditional tender at or about the time stated in the contract. Even though time is not of the essence or if no time is mentioned in the contract for its performance the lapse of an unreasonable time must necessarily deprive the parties of the possibility of thereafter making an effective tender.

COHEN v. KRANZ

Court of Appeals of New York, 1963.
12 N.Y.2d 242, 238 N.Y.S.2d 928, 189 N.E.2d 473.

BURKE, JUDGE.

On September 22, 1959 plaintiff contracted to purchase defendants' one-family house in Nassau County for $40,000. Four thousand dollars was paid on the signing of the contract and the balance due upon delivery of the deed was in the form of $24,500 cash and the assumption of an $11,500 first mortgage. Closing was set for November 15. Plaintiff obtained an adjournment of the closing date to December 15 without any indication that title would be rejected. On November 30, plaintiff's attorney sent defendants' attorney a letter stating: "An investigation has disclosed that the present structure of the premises is not legal and thus title is unmarketable. Unless a check to the order of Lester Cohen, as attorney in fact, for Sarah Cohen is received in five days, we shall be obligated to commence proceedings against your client."

Plaintiff's attorney appeared at the office of defendants' attorney on the adjourned law date and demanded return of the $4,000 deposit, which was refused by the latter. Neither party was then able to perform and neither made any tender. Plaintiff thereafter commenced this action for return of the deposit plus the costs of searching title; defendants counterclaimed for damages for breach of contract.

Trial Term, Nassau County, gave judgment for plaintiff. The court found that the premises were subject to protective covenants filed in the Nassau County Clerk's office and that the insurability clause of the contract was not complied with because a swimming pool on the premises, installed under a permit, lacked a certificate of occupancy from the Oyster Bay Architectural Control Committee. Further, a split rail fence projected beyond the front line of the dwelling. The court also found that plaintiff had notified defendants of the claimed defects prior to the December 15 closing date and that defendants had taken no steps to remedy the defects, nor had it been established that the violations were minor. The court held, therefore, that the defective title excused plaintiff from tender of payment and awarded plaintiff judgment in the amount of her deposit.

The Appellate Division, Second Department, unanimously reversed Trial Term on the law and facts and directed judgment on the counterclaim for $1,500. It is from this judgment that plaintiff appeals.

In reversing Trial Term's findings of fact, the Appellate Division expressly found that plaintiff's letter of November 30 rejecting title and demanding return of the deposit failed to specify the claimed illegality, and that specific objections to title were not raised until January 25, 1960. The letter speaks for itself and the Appellate Division is obviously correct. Plaintiff's arguments directed at the Appellate Division's finding of January 25th as the date when specific objections were first communicated to defendants are unavailing inasmuch as the earliest further communication of objections supported by the evidence took place upon the commencement of this action by plaintiff on December 31st, still more than two weeks after the law date. It was also found, contrary to the trial court, that the objections to title were curable upon proper and timely notice and demand. We think the weight of the evidence supports the Appellate Division here too. The swimming pool was constructed with a permit and lacked only a certificate of occupancy (which was in fact obtained before defendants sold the house to a third person). The fence projection likewise could clearly be found to be a readily curable objection. These were the only two objections that possibly violated the "DECLARATION OF PROTECTIVE COVENANTS" recorded in the Nassau County Clerk's office and to which the title insurer excepted.

The Appellate Division also found that defendants had not waived a tender by plaintiff and that plaintiff's rejection of title in advance was a default precluding her from recovery of the deposit. Since it is undisputed that defendants made no tender, the Appellate Division's award of damages for breach of contract necessarily implies that no such tender was required. We agree.

While a vendee can recover his money paid on the contract from a vendor who defaults on law day without a showing of tender or even of willingness and ability to perform where the vendor's title is incurably defective (Greene v. Barrett, Nephews & Co., 238 N.Y. 207, 144 N.E. 503), a tender and demand are required to put the vendor in default where his title could be cleared without difficulty in a reasonable time. * * * Further, the vendor in such a case is entitled to a reasonable time beyond law day to make his title good (Ballen v. Potter, 251 N.Y. 224, 167 N.E. 424). It is, therefore, clear that plaintiff's advance rejection of title and demand for immediate return of the deposit was unjustified and an anticipatory breach of contract. This position, adhered to throughout, prevented defendants' title defects from ever amounting to a default. Consequently, plaintiff is barred from recovering the deposit from a vendor whose title defects were curable and whose performance was never demanded on law day. (Higgins v. Eagleton, supra.) Ansorge v. Belfer, 248 N.Y. 145, 150, 161 N.E. 450, 452, is not to the contrary. It merely holds that a vendee may recover his deposit from a clearly defaulting vendor despite his own unjustified refusal to agree to an adjournment of the law date. It does not deny the doctrine that a vendor whose title defects are curable is not automatically in default but, rather, must be put in default by the vendee's tender of performance and demand for a good title deed. The vendor was there put in default by the vendee's tender. The vendor simply never retrieved his default by curing the defects and tendering a good title (as he could have—Harris v. Shorall, 230 N.Y. 343, 130 N.E. 572). True, defendants here never offered to clear their title and perform; but they were never put in default in the first place by a demand for good title. So Ansorge merely holds with respect to curable title defects what Greene v. Barrett, Nephews & Co., supra, held with respect to incurable defects—namely, that where the vendor is in default the deposit can be recovered even though the vendee himself is in default or breach, e.g., no showing of performance of conditions precedent or excuse for nonperformance (the Greene case); or an unjustified refusal to adjourn the closing date (the Ansorge case). The difference is that a vendor with incurable[1] title defects is automatically in default, whereas a vendor with curable title defects must be placed in default by a tender and demand, which was not done here.

Defendants obtained an affirmative recovery on their counterclaim for breach of contract based on the loss they sustained when they sold the house to a third person for what the courts below found to be its fair market value. This recovery stands on a different footing from their right to retain the deposit. As Judge Andrews pointed out, in speaking of a vendee, in Greene v. Barrett, Nephews & Co., supra, while the vendee's right to recover the deposit from a defaulting vendor can rest solely upon the latter's default, an action for *damages* for breach of contract requires a showing that the plaintiff himself (the vendee in the Greene case) has performed all conditions precedent and concurrent, unless excused. In the case of a purchase of real estate, this would be a showing of tender and demand or, if that be unnecessary, an idle gesture, because of the incurable nature of the title defect, then at least a showing at the trial that the plaintiff vendee was in a position to perform had the vendor been willing and able to perform his part. (Greene v. Barrett, Nephews & Co., supra; Stern v. McKee, 70 App.Div. 142, 75 N.Y.S. 157; Norris v. McMechen, 134 Misc. 866, 236 N.Y.S. 486; Restatement, Contracts, § 306.) Likewise, a vendor such as the defendants here must show a basic ability to perform even if actual tender and demand is unnecessary. However, while it cannot be denied that defendants did not have a title conformable to the contract at law date, an applicable corollary of the above rule excuses even inability to perform conditions precedent or concurrent where such inability is caused by advance notice from the other party that he will not perform his part. (Clarke v. Crandall, 27 Barb. 73; Kotcher v. Edelblute, 250 N.Y. 178, 164 N.E. 897; Restatement, Contracts, §§ 270, 284, 306). Not only did plaintiff's unjustified attempt to cancel the contract and recover her deposit before the adjourned law date render unnecessary and wasteful any attempt by defendants to cure the minor defects before that date, but the failure to specify the objections rendered it impossible. The finding of the Appellate Division, supported by the weight of the evidence, that the defects were curable, means that defendants were basically able to perform and whatever technical inability existed in this regard on the law date was caused by plaintiff and is excused fully as much as the lack of formal tender.

The judgment should be affirmed, without costs.

Judgment affirmed.

1. We use "incurable" to mean not within the vendor's power to remedy within a reasonable time. * * *

B.   SEQUENTIAL PERFORMANCES

E. FARNSWORTH, CONTRACTS

558 (3d ed.1999).

The timing of the parties' performances imposes some limits on the use of constructive conditions. One party's duty to perform can be conditioned or dependent on the other party's rendering a performance that is due at an earlier time. But one party's duty to perform cannot be conditioned or dependent on the other party's rendering a performance that is to come at a later time. If the builder is to build first and the owner is to pay later, the law can afford the owner security by conditioning the duty to pay on the house being built first, but it cannot afford the builder comparable security. If the owner is to make payments as the work progresses, the owner gives up some security with each payment. Thus the order in which parties are to perform under a bilateral contract takes on an enhanced importance because of its relation to constructive conditions of exchange. The security afforded by the concept of constructive conditions cannot easily be extended to protect the party whose duty it is to go first.

[handwritten margin note: You can't just abandon work... you can't demand payment until a substantial amount is computed]

STEWART v. NEWBURY

Court of Appeals of New York, 1917.
220 N.Y. 379, 115 N.E. 984.

CRANE, J. The defendants are partners in the pipe fitting business under the name of Newbury Manufacturing Company. The plaintiff is a contractor and builder residing at Tuxedo, N.Y.

The parties had the following correspondence about the erection for the defendants of a concrete mill building at Monroe, N.Y.:

                       "Alexander Stewart,
                  "Contractor and Builder,

                            "Tuxedo, N.Y., July 18, 1911.

"Newbury Mfg. Company, Monroe, N.Y.—Gentlemen: With reference to the proposed work on the new foundry building I had hoped to be able to get up and see you this afternoon, but find that impossible and am, in consequence, sending you these prices, which I trust you will find satisfactory.

"I will agree to do all excavation work required at sixty-five ($.65) cents per cubic yard.

"I will put in the concrete work, furnishing labor and forms only, at two and 05–100 ($2.05) dollars per cubic yard.

"I will furnish labor to put in reenforcing at four ($4.00) dollars per ton.

"I will furnish labor only to set all window and door frames, window sash and doors, including the setting of hardware for one hundred twelve ($112) dollars. As alternative I would be willing to do any or all of the above work for cost plus 10 per cent., furnishing you with first class mechanics and giving the work considerable of my personal time.

"Hoping to hear favorably from you in this regard, I am.

"Respectfully yours,
"[Signed] Alexander Stewart."

"The Newbury Mfg. Co.,
"Steam Fittings, Grey Iron Castings,
"Skylight Opening Apparatus,
"Monroe, N.Y.

"Telephone Connection.

"Monroe, N.Y., July 22, 1911.

"Alexander Stewart, Tuxedo Park, N.Y.—Dear Sir: Confirming the telephone conversation of this morning we accept your bid of July the 18th to do the concrete work on our new building. We trust that you will be able to get at this the early part of next week.

"Yours truly,

The Newbury Mfg. Co.,

"H.A. Newbury."

Nothing was said in writing about the time or manner of payment. The plaintiff, however, claims that after sending his letter, and before receiving that of the defendant, he had a telephone communication with Mr. Newbury and said: "I will expect my payments in the usual manner," and Newbury said, "All right, we have got the money to pay for the building." This conversation over the telephone was denied by the defendants. The custom, the plaintiff testified, was to pay 85 per cent. every 30 days or at the end of each month, 15 per cent. being retained till the work was completed.

In July the plaintiff commenced work and continued until September 29th, at which time he had progressed with the construction as far as the first floor. He then sent a bill for the work done up to that date for $896.35. The defendants refused to pay the bill and work was discontinued. The plaintiff claims that the defendants refused to permit him to perform the rest of his contract, they insisting that the work already done was not in accordance with the specifications. The defendants claimed upon the trial that the plaintiff voluntarily abandoned the work after their refusal to pay his bill.

On October 5, 1911, the defendants wrote the plaintiff a letter containing the following:

"Notwithstanding you promised to let us know on Monday whether you would complete the job or throw up the contract, you have not up to this time advised us of your intention. * * * Under the circumstances, we are compelled to accept your action as being an abandonment of your contract and of every effort upon your part to complete your work on our building. As you know, the bill which you sent us and which we declined to pay is not correct, either in items or amount, nor is there anything due you under our contract as we understand it until you have completed your work on our building."

To this letter the plaintiff replied the following day. In it he makes no reference to the telephone communication agreeing, as he testified, to make "the usual payments," but does say this:

"There is nothing in our agreement which says that I shall wait until the job is completed before any payment is due, nor can this be reasonably implied. * * * As to having given you positive date as to when I should let you know what I proposed doing, I did not do so; on the contrary, I told you that I would not tell you positively what I would do until I had visited the job, and I promised that I would do this at my earliest convenience and up to the present time I have been unable to get up there."

The defendant Herbert Newbury testified that the plaintiff "ran away and left the whole thing." And the defendant F.A. Newbury testified that he was told by Mr. Stewart's man that Stewart was going to abandon the job; that he thereupon telephoned Mr. Stewart, who replied that he would let him know about it the next day, but did not.

In this action, which is brought to recover the amount of the bill presented, as the agreed price and $95.68 damages for breach of contract, the plaintiff had a verdict for the amount stated in the bill, but not for the other damages claimed, and the judgment entered thereon has been affirmed by the Appellate Division.

The appeal to us is upon exceptions to the judge's charge. The court charged the jury as follows:

"Plaintiff says that he was excused from completely performing the contract by the defendants' unreasonable failure to pay him for the work he had done during the months of August and September. * * * Was it understood that the payments were to be made monthly? If it was not so understood, the defendants only obligation was to make payments at reasonable periods, in view of the character of the work, the amount of work being done, and the value of it. In other words, if there was no agreement between the parties respecting the payments, the defendants' obligation was to make payments at reasonable times. * * * But whether there was such an agreement or not, you may consider whether it was reasonable or unreasonable for him to exact a payment at that time and in that amount."

The court further said, in reply to a request to charge:

"I will say in that connection, if there was no agreement respecting the time of payment, and if there was no custom that was understood by both parties, and with respect to which they made the contract, then the plaintiff was entitled to payments at reasonable times."

The defendants' counsel thereupon made the following request, which was refused:

"I ask your honor to instruct the jury that, if the circumstances existed as your honor stated in your last instruction, then the plaintiff was not entitled to any payment until the contract was completed."

The jury was plainly told that if there were no agreement as to payments, yet the plaintiff would be entitled to part payment at reasonable times as the work progressed, and if such payments were refused he could abandon the work and recover the amount due for the work performed.

This is not the law. Counsel for the plaintiff omits to call our attention to any authority sustaining such a proposition and our search reveals none. In fact, the law is very well settled to the contrary. This was an entire contract. * * * Where a contract is made to perform work and no agreement is made as to payment, the work must be substantially performed before payment can be demanded. * * *

This case was also submitted to the jury upon the ground that there may have been a breach of contract by the defendants in their refusal to permit the plaintiff to continue with his work, claiming that he had departed from the specifications, and there was some evidence justifying this view of the case; but it is impossible to say upon which of these two theories the jury arrived at its conclusion. The above errors, therefore, cannot be considered as harmless and immaterial. * * * As the verdict was for the amount of the bill presented and did not include the damages for a breach of contract, which would be the loss of profits, it may well be presumed that the jury adopted the first ground of recovery charged by the court as above quoted and decided that the plaintiff was justified in abandoning work for nonpayment of the installment.

The judgment should be reversed, and a new trial ordered; costs to abide the event.

PATTERSON, CONSTRUCTIVE CONDITIONS IN CONTRACTS

42 Colum.L.Rev. 903, 919–920 (1942).

[O]ne may ask, why should the party whose promised performance takes time be required to extend credit to the one whose performance does not? The typical case falling under this rule—of which it is a kind of extrapolation—is the contract to do work for money. The usual practice in the community to which the rule was applicable was to pay for the work after it was completed. This "belief as to the practice of a community or a class" is empirically verified, but it does not settle the questions of justice or policy with which the law is concerned. The practice may be ascribed to the influence of employers as a dominant class, and to judicial inertia which allows an outmoded rule to continue unchanged. The dominance of employers as a class is not what it used to be, yet no demand has appeared to require that employees generally be paid their wages or salaries in advance. There may be sufficient reasons for the survival of the rule. Professor Williston suggests two: 1. The normally greater responsibility of the employer; and 2., the fact that the employee cannot be compelled to perform specifically.

The policy of the law, here as in the tendency to construct concurrent conditions, is to minimize credit risks. If employers usually present less credit risks than employees, the rule of construction effectuates this end. That colleges and theatres ordinarily require payment in advance for the services which they furnish merely exemplifies the operation of the principle. A further justification may be found in the belief that a moderate postponement of reward stimulates productivity of social goods; such a belief is operative as a part of the mores of a particular culture. This justification, like the second reason given by Professor Williston, must be limited in scope of application, if it is not to conflict with the prohibition of involuntary servitude; that is, it may become a too-effective means of coercing the employee to work. The rule which makes performance by the employee a condition precedent of the duty of payment by the employer and which thus places the credit risk and the credit strain on the employee, has been mitigated in its severity by statutes requiring that wages be paid at short intervals (weekly or biweekly) to certain classes of employees (in the lower income brackets), by provisions making wage claims preferred in the case of bankruptcy of the employer and by a limited relief for unjust enrichment. The order-of-performance test of credit burdens is thus supplemented by custom and by policy.

Problem 7–6

Buyer contracted with seller to buy five truckloads of chopped wood to be burned in fireplaces in buyer's motel. The price was $1100 for the five truckloads, delivery over a five week period. After seller delivered the first truckload, he demanded $220. Buyer refused to pay until seller delivered in full. Seller comes to your law office. How would this problem be resolved under the Uniform Commercial Code sections set forth below?

§ 2–507.   Effect of Seller's Tender; Delivery on Condition

(1) Tender of delivery is a condition to the buyer's duty to accept the goods and, unless otherwise agreed, to his duty to pay for them. Tender entitles the seller to acceptance of the goods and to payment according to the contract.

§ 2–511.   Tender of Payment by Buyer; Payment by Check

(1) Unless otherwise agreed tender of payment is a condition to the seller's duty to tender and complete any delivery.

§ 2–307.   Delivery in Single Lot or Several Lots

Unless otherwise agreed all goods called for by a contract for sale must be tendered in a single delivery and payment is due only on such tender but where the circumstances give either party the right to make or demand delivery in lots the price if it can be apportioned may be demanded for each lot.

SECTION NINE: IMPLIED CONDITIONS FIXING THE QUALITY OF PERFORMANCE

PLANTE v. JACOBS

Supreme Court of Wisconsin, 1960.
10 Wis.2d 567, 103 N.W.2d 296.

Suit to establish a lien to recover the unpaid balance of the contract price plus extras of building a house for the defendants, Frank M. and Carol H. Jacobs, who in their answer allege no substantial performance and breach of the contract by the plaintiff and counterclaim for damages due to faulty workmanship and incomplete construction. The defendants, Sterling Savings & Loan Association and Marguerite A. Hoenig, claim an interest in the property by virtue of a mortgage; and the defendant, City Bank and Trust

Company, as a judgment lien creditor. After a trial to the court, judgment was entered for the plaintiff in the amount of $4,152.90 plus interest and costs, from which the defendants, Jacobs, appealed and the plaintiff petitioned for a review. The other defendants have not appealed.

The Jacobs, on or about January 6, 1956, entered into a written contract with the plaintiff to furnish the materials and construct a house upon their lot in Brookfield, Waukesha county, in accordance with plans and specifications, for the sum of $26,765. During the course of construction the plaintiff was paid $20,000. Disputes arose between the parties, the defendants refused to continue payment, and the plaintiff did not complete the house. On January 12, 1957, the plaintiff duly filed his lien.

The trial court found the contract was substantially performed and was modified in respect to lengthening the house two feet and the reasonable value of this extra was $960. The court disallowed extras amounting to $1,748.92 claimed by the plaintiff because they were not agreed upon in writing in accordance with the terms of the agreement. In respect to defective workmanship the court allowed the cost of repairing the following items: $1,550 for the patio wall; $100 for the patio floor; $300 for cracks in the ceiling of the living room and kitchen; and $20.15 credit balance for hardware. The court also found the defendants were not damaged by the misplacement of a wall between the kitchen and the living room, and the other items of defective workmanship and incompleteness were not proven. The amount of these credits allowed the defendants was deducted from the gross amount found owing the plaintiff, and the judgment was entered for the difference and made a lien on the premises subject to the mortgage of the Sterling Savings & Loan Association, but prior to the claims of the defendants, Marguerite A. Hoenig and The City Bank and Trust Company.

HALLOWS, JUSTICE.

The defendants argue the plaintiff cannot recover any amount because he has failed to substantially perform the contract. The plaintiff conceded he failed to furnish the kitchen cabinets, gutters and downspouts, sidewalk, closet clothes poles, and entrance seat amounting to $1,601.95. This amount was allowed to the defendants. The defendants claim some 20 other items of incomplete or faulty performance by the plaintiff and no substantial performance because the cost of completing the house in strict compliance with the plans and specifications would amount to 25 or 30 per cent of the contract price. The defendants especially stress the misplacing of the wall between the living room and the kitchen, which narrowed the living room in excess of one foot. The cost of tearing down this wall and rebuilding it would be approximately $4,000. The record is not clear why and when this wall was misplaced, but the wall is completely built and the house decorated and the defendants are living therein. Real estate experts testified that the smaller width of the living room would not affect the market price of the house.

The defendants rely on Manitowoc Steam Boiler Works v. Manitowoc Glue Co., 1903, 120 Wis. 1, 97 N.W. 515, for the proposition there can be no recovery on the contract as distinguished from *quantum meruit* unless there is substantial performance. This is undoubtedly the correct rule at common law. * * * The question here is whether there has been substantial performance. The test of what amounts to substantial performance seems to be whether the performance meets the essential purpose of the contract. In the Manitowoc case the contract called for a boiler having a capacity of 150 per cent of the existing boiler. The court held there was no substantial performance because the boiler furnished had a capacity of only 82 per cent of the old boiler and only approximately one-half of the boiler capacity contemplated by the contract. In Houlahan v. Clark, 1901, 110 Wis. 43, 85 N.W. 676, the contract provided the plaintiff was to drive pilings in the lake and place a boat house thereon parallel and in line with a neighbor's dock. This was not done and the contractor so positioned the boat house that it was practically useless to the owner. Manthey v. Stock, 1907, 133 Wis. 107, 113 N.W. 443, involved a contract to paint a house and to do a good job, including the removal of the old paint where necessary. The plaintiff did not remove the old paint, and blistering and roughness of the new paint resulted. The court held that the plaintiff failed to show substantial performance. The defendants also cite Manning v. School District No. 6, 1905, 124 Wis. 84, 102 N.W. 356. However, this case involved a contract to install a heating and ventilating plant in the school building which would meet certain tests which the heating apparatus failed to do. The heating plant was practically a total failure to accomplish the purposes of the contract. See also Nees v. Weaver, 1936, 222 Wis. 492, 269 N.W. 266, 107 A.L.R. 1405 (roof on a garage).

Substantial performance as applied to construction of a house does not mean that every detail must be in strict compliance with the specifications and the plans. Something less than perfection is the test of * * * performance unless all details are made the essence of the contract. This was not done here. There may be situations in which features or details of construction of special or of great personal importance, which if not performed, would prevent a finding of substantial performance of the contract. In this case the plan was a stock floor plan. No detailed construction of the house was shown on the plan. There were no blueprints. The specifications were standard printed forms with some modifications and additions written in by the parties. Many of the problems that arose during the construction had to be solved on the basis of practical experience. No mathematical rule relating to the percentage of the price, of cost of completion or of completeness can be laid down to determine substantial performance of a building contract. Although the defendants received a house with which they are dissatisfied in many respects, the trial court was not in error in finding the contract was substantially performed.

The next question is what is the amount of recovery when the plaintiff has substantially, but incompletely, performed. For substantial performance the plaintiff should recover the contract price less the damages caused the defendant by the incomplete performance. Both parties agree. Venzke v. Magdanz, 1943, 243 Wis. 155, 9 N.W.2d 604, states the correct rule for damages due to faulty construction amounting to such incomplete performance, which is the difference between the value of the house as it stands with faulty and incomplete construction and the value of the house if it had been constructed in strict accordance with the plans and specifications. This is the diminished-value rule. The cost of replacement or repair is not the measure of such damage, but is an element to take into consideration in arriving at value under some circumstances. The cost of replacement or the cost to make whole the omissions may equal or be less than the difference in value in some cases and, likewise, the cost to rectify a defect may greatly exceed the added value to the structure as corrected. The defendants argue that under the Venzke rule their damages are $10,000. The plaintiff on review argues the defendants' damages are only $650. Both parties agree the trial court applied the wrong rule to the facts.

The trial court applied the cost-of-repair or replacement rule as to several items, relying on Stern v. Schlafer, 1943, 244 Wis. 183, 11 N.W.2d 640, 12 N.W.2d 678, wherein it was stated that when there are a number of small items of defect or omission which can be remedied without the reconstruction of a substantial part of the building or a great sacrifice of work or material already wrought in the building, the reasonable cost of correcting the defect should be allowed. However, in Mohs v. Quarton, 1950, 257 Wis. 544, 44 N.W.2d 580, the court held when the separation of defects would lead to confusion, the rule of diminished value could apply to all defects.

In this case no such confusion arises in separating the defects. The trial court disallowed certain claimed defects because they were not proven. This finding was not against the great weight and clear preponderance of the evidence and will not be disturbed on appeal. Of the remaining defects claimed by the defendants, the court allowed the cost of replacement or repair except as to the misplacement of the living-room wall. Whether a defect should fall under the cost-of-replacement rule or be considered under the diminished-value rule depends upon the nature and magnitude of the defect. This court has not allowed items of such magnitude under the cost-of-repair rule as the trial court did. Viewing the construction of the house as a whole and its cost we cannot say, however, that the trial court was in error in allowing the cost of repairing the plaster cracks in the ceilings, the cost of mud jacking and repairing the patio floor, and the cost of reconstructing the non-weight-bearing and nonstructural patio wall. Such reconstruction did not involve an unreasonable economic waste.

The item of misplacing the living room wall under the facts of this case was clearly under the diminished-value rule. There is no evidence that defendants requested or demanded the replacement of the wall in the place called for by the specifications during the course of construction. To tear down the wall now and rebuild it in its proper place would involve a substantial destruction of the work, if not all of it, which was put into the wall and would cause additional damage to other parts of the house and require replastering and redecorating the walls and ceilings of at least two rooms. Such economic waste is unreasonable and unjustified. The rule of diminished value contemplates the wall is not going to be moved. Expert witnesses for both parties, testifying as to the value of the house, agreed that the misplacement of the wall had no effect on the market price. The trial court properly found that the defendants suffered no legal damage, although the defendants' particular desire for specified room size was not satisfied. For a discussion of these rules of damages for defective or unfinished construction and their application see Restatement, 1 Contracts, pp. 572–573, sec. 346(1)(a) and illustrations.

* * *

Judgment affirmed.

O.W. GRUN ROOFING AND CONSTRUCTION CO. v. COPE

Court of Civil Appeals of Texas, 1975.
529 S.W.2d 258.

[Defendant Grun installed a roof on Cope's home for $648, pursuant to a contract. When Cope refused to pay, claiming defects, Grun filed a mechanic's lien. Cope brought an action to set aside the lien and for damages. Grun filed a cross-claim for foreclosure on the mechanic's lien and for the money allegedly due. After a jury trial, the trial court entered judgment for Cope for $122.60 and set aside the mechanic's lien.]

* * * CADENA, JUSTICE.

The written contract required defendant to install a new roof on plaintiff's home for $648.00. The contract describes the color of the shingles to be used as "russet glow," which defendant defined as a "brown varied color." Defendant acknowledges that it was his obligation to install a roof of uniform color.

After defendant had installed the new roof, plaintiff noticed that it had streaks which she described as yellow, due to a difference in color or shade of some of the shingles. Defendant agreed to remedy the situation and he removed the nonconforming shingles. However, the replacement shingles do not match the remainder, and photographs introduced in evidence clearly show that the roof is not of a uniform color. Plaintiff testified that her roof has the appearance of having been patched, rather than having been completely replaced. According to plaintiff's testimony, the yellow streaks appeared on the northern, eastern and southern sides of the roof, and defendant only replaced the non-matching shingles on the northern and eastern sides, leaving the southern side with the yellow streaks still apparent. The result is that only the western portion of the roof is of uniform color.

When defendant originally installed the complete new roof, it used 24 "squares" of shingles. In an effort to achieve a roof of uniform color, five squares were ripped off and replaced. There is no testimony as to the number of squares which would have to be replaced on the southern, or rear, side of the house in order to eliminate the original yellow streaks. Although there is expert testimony to the effect that the disparity in color would not be noticeable after the shingles have been on the roof for about a year, there is testimony to the effect that, although some nine or ten months have elapsed since defendant attempted to achieve a uniform coloration, the roof is still "streaky" on three sides. One of defendant's experts testified that if the shingles are properly applied the result will be a "blended" roof rather than a streaked roof.

In view of the fact that the disparity in color has not disappeared in nine or ten months, and in view of the fact that there is testimony to the effect that it would be impossible to secure matching shingles to replace the nonconforming ones, it can reasonably be inferred that a roof or uniform coloration can be achieved only by installing a completely new roof.

The evidence is undisputed that the roof is a substantial roof and will give plaintiff protection against the elements.

The principle which allows recovery for part performance in cases involving dependent promises may be expressed by saying that a material breach or a breach which goes to the root of the matter or essence of the contract defeats the promisor's claim despite his part performance, or it may be expressed by saying that a promisor who has substantially performed is entitled to recover, although he has failed in some particular to comply with his agreement. The latter mode of expressing the rule is generally referred to as the doctrine of substantial performance and is especially common in cases involving building contracts, although its application is not restricted to such contracts.

It is difficult to formulate a definitive rule for determining whether the contractor's performance, less than complete, amounts to "substantial performance," since the question is one of fact and of degree, and the answer depends on the particular facts of each case. But, although the decisions furnish no rule of thumb, they are helpful in suggesting guidelines. One of the most obvious factors to be considered is the extent of the nonperformance. The deficiency will not be tolerated if it is so pervasive as to frustrate the purpose of the contract in any real or substantial sense. The doctrine does not bestow on a contractor a license to install whatever is, in his judgment, "just as good." The answer is arrived at by weighing the purpose to be served, the desire to be gratified, the excuse for deviating from the letter of the contract and the cruelty of enforcing strict adherence or of compelling the promisee to receive something less than for which he bargained. Also influential in many cases is the ratio of money value of the tendered performance and of the promised performance. In most cases the contract itself at least is an indication of the value of the promised performance, and courts should have little difficulty in determining the cost of curing the deficiency. But the rule cannot be expressed in terms of a fraction, since complete reliance on a mathematical formula would result in ignoring other important factors, such as the purpose which the promised performance was intended to serve and the extent to which the nonperformance would defeat such purpose, or would defeat it if not corrected. See, generally, 3A Corbin, Contracts Secs. 700–07 (1960).

* * *

* * * It should not come as a shock to anyone to adopt a rule to the effect that a person has, particularly with respect to his home, to choose for himself and to contract for something which exactly satisfies that choice, and not to be compelled to accept something else. In the matter of homes and their decoration, as much as, if not more than, in many other fields, mere taste or preference, almost approaching whimsy, may be controlling with the homeowner, so that variations which might, under other circumstances, be considered trifling, may be inconsistent with that "substantial performance" on which liability to pay must be predicated. Of mere incompleteness or deviations which may be easily supplied or remedied after the contractor has finished his work, and the cost of which to the owner is not excessive and readily ascertainable, present less cause for hesitation in concluding that the performance tendered constitutes substantial performance, since in such cases the owner can obtain complete satisfaction by merely spending some money and deducting the amount of such expenditure from the contract price.

In the case before us there is evidence to support the conclusion that plaintiff can secure a roof of uniform coloring only by installing a completely new roof. We cannot say, as a matter of law, that the evidence establishes that in this case that a roof which so lacks uniformity in color as to give the appearance of a patch job serves essentially the same purpose as a roof of uniform color which has the appearance of being a new roof. We are not prepared to hold that a contractor who tenders a performance so deficient that it can be remedied only by completely redoing the work for which the contract called has established, as a matter of law, that he has substantially performed his contractual obligation.

* * *

Finally, defendant argues that it was entitled to judgment at least on the theory of quantum meruit on its cross claim because the evidence establishes as a matter of law that defendant installed a good weatherproof roof which was guaranteed for 15 years, and that such roof was installed properly in accordance with factory specifications and was of use and benefit to plaintiff.

The evidence does not conclusively establish that the shingles were properly installed. There is evidence to the effect that if shingles of this type are properly installed the result will be a roof which "blends," rather than a roof with clearly discordant streaks. In any event, the evidence does not conclusively establish that plaintiff has received any benefit from defendant's defective performance. As already pointed out, there is evidence that plaintiff will have to install a completely new roof. Because of defendant's deficient performance, plaintiff is not in a position which requires that she pay for a new roof.

Nor does the evidence conclusively establish that plaintiff accepted the claimed benefit. She complained immediately and has expressed dissatisfaction at all times. We cannot infer an acceptance from the fact that plaintiff continued to live in the house. She was living in the house before defendant installed the new roof, and we know of no rule which would require that, in order to avoid a finding of implied acceptance, plaintiff was obligated to move out of her home.

The judgment of the trial court is affirmed.

E. FARNSWORTH, CONTRACTS

594–95 (3d ed. 1999).

For the most part, the rules governing waiver of constructive conditions are similar to those governing express conditions. * * * In contrast to the rule governing express conditions, however, a constructive condition of exchange can be waived, even if it is a material part of the agreed exchange, since the injured party will still be compensated for the breach. Thus an owner can waive the constructive condition of substantial performance under a building contract by promising to pay despite material defects and still retain a claim for damages for partial breach.

Note
Substantial Performance in Land Sale Contracts

A land-sale agreement entitles the buyer to the seller's performance, but must the seller's tender be perfect? Or does substantial performance entitle the seller to the consideration? Some cases hold that substantial performance is enough in the absence of an express condition requiring perfect performance. Thus a mistake as to the quantity of land to be conveyed—seller promised ten acres when there were only nine—might not be so material as to permit the buyer to escape his or her obligations under the contract. For example, when the buyer is more interested in a particular plot of land than the precise amount of acreage, a small acreage deficiency may not permit the buyer to avoid the deal. The buyer, of course, would be entitled to damages for seller's breach of promise as to the number of acres. Conversely, even a very small deficiency in the number of acres promised might be material, thereby permitting the buyer to avoid the deal. Suppose, for example, the buyer wanted waterfront property and the acreage deficiency was land that bordered the water. A useful general treatment appears in D. Dobbs, Remedies 822–24 (1993).

WALKER & CO. v. HARRISON
Supreme Court of Michigan, 1957.
347 Mich. 630, 81 N.W.2d 352.

SMITH, JUSTICE.

This is a suit on a written contract. The defendants are in the dry-cleaning business. Walker & Company, plaintiff, sells, rents, and services advertising signs and billboards. These parties entered into an agreement pertaining to a sign. The agreement is in writing and is termed a "rental agreement." It specifies in part that:

"The lessor agrees to construct and install, at its own cost, one [eighteen feet, nine inches high and eight feet, eight inches] wide pylon type d.f. neon sign with electric clock and flashing lamps * * *. The lessor agrees to and does hereby lease or rent unto the said lessee the said SIGN for the term, use and rental and under the conditions, hereinafter set out, and the lessee agrees to pay said rental * * *.

"(a) The term of this lease shall be 36 months * * *.

"(b) The rental to be paid by lessee shall be $148.50 per month for each and every calendar month during the term of this lease; * * *.

"(d) Maintenance. Lessor at its expense agrees to maintain and service the sign together with such equipment as supplied and installed by the lessor to operate in conjunction with said sign under the terms of this lease; this service is to include cleaning and repainting of sign in original color scheme as often as deemed necessary by lessor to keep sign in first class advertising condition and make all necessary repairs to sign and equipment installed by lessor. * * *."

At the "expiration of this agreement," it was also provided, "title to this sign reverts to lessee." This clause is in addition to the printed form of agreement and was apparently added as a result of defendants' concern over title, they having expressed a desire "to buy for cash" and the salesman, at one time, having "quoted a cash price."

The sign was completed and installed in the latter part of July, 1953. The first billing of the monthly payment of $148.50 was made August 1, 1953, with payment thereof by defendants on September 3, 1953. This first payment was also the last. Shortly after the sign was installed, someone hit it with a tomato. Rust, also, was visible on the chrome, complained defendants, and in its corners were "little spider cobwebs." In addition, there were "some children's sayings written down in here." Defendant Herbert Harrison called Walker for the maintenance he believed himself entitled to under subparagraph (d) above. It was not forthcoming. He called again and again. "I was getting, you might say, sorer and sorer. * * * Occasionally, when I started calling up, I would walk around where the tomato was and get mad again. Then I would call up on the phone again." Finally, on October 8, 1953, plaintiff not having responded to his repeated calls, he telegraphed Walker that:

> "You Have Continually Voided Our Rental Contract By Not Maintaining Signs As Agreed As We No Longer Have A Contract With You Do Not Expect Any Further Remuneration."

Walker's reply was in the form of a letter. After first pointing out that "your telegram does not make any specific allegations as to what the failure of maintenance comprises," and stating that "We certainly would appreciate your furnishing us with such information," the letter makes reference to a prior collateral controversy between the parties, "wondering if this refusal on our part prompted your attempt to void our rental contract," and concludes as follows:

> "We would like to call your attention to paragraph G in our rental contract, which covers procedures in the event of a Breach of Agreement. In the event that you carry out your threat to make no future monthly payments in accordance with the agreement, it is our intention to enforce the conditions outlined under paragraph G[1] through the proper legal

---

1. "(g) Breach of Agreement. Lessee shall be deemed to have breached this agreement by default in payment of any installment of the rental herein provided for; abandonment of the sign or vacating premises where the sign is located; termination or transfer of lessee's interest in the premises by insolvency, appointment of a receiver for lessee's business; filing of a voluntary or involuntary petition in bankruptcy with respect to lessee or the violation of any of the other terms or conditions hereof. In the event of such default, the lessor may, upon notice to the lessee, which notice shall conclusively be deemed sufficient if mailed or delivered to the premises where the sign was or is located, take possession of the sign and declare the balance of the rental herein provided for to be forthwith due and payable, and lessee hereby agrees to pay such balance upon any such contingencies. Lessor may terminate this lease and without notice, remove and repossess said sign and recover from the lessee such amounts as may be unpaid for the remaining unexpired term of this agreement. Time is of the essence of this lease with respect to the payment of rentals herein provided for. Should lessee after lessor has declared the balance of rentals due and payable, pay the full amount of rental herein provided, he shall then be entitled to the use of the sign, under all the terms and provisions hereof, for the balance of the term of this lease. No waiver by either party hereto of the nonperformance of any term, condition or obligation hereof shall be a waiver of any subsequent breach of, or failure to perform the same, or any other term, condition or obligation hereof. It is understood and agreed that the sign is especially constructed for the lessee and for use at the premises now occupied by the lessee for the term herein provided; that it is of no value unless so used and that it is a material consideration to the lessor in entering into this agreement that the lessee shall continue to use the sign for the period of time provided herein and for the payment of the full rental for such term."

channels. We call to your attention that your monthly rental payments are due in advance at our office not later than the 10th day of each current month. You are now approximately 30 days in arrears on your September payment. Unless we receive both the September and October payments by October 25th, this entire matter will be placed in the hands of our attorney for collection in accordance with paragraph G which stipulates that the entire amount is forthwith due and payable."

No additional payments were made and Walker sued in assumpsit for the entire balance due under the contract, $5,197.50, invoking paragraph (g) of the agreement. Defendants filed answer and claim of recoupment, asserting that plaintiff's failure to perform certain maintenance services constituted a prior material breach of the agreement, thus justifying their repudiation of the contract and grounding their claim for damages. The case was tried to the court without a jury and resulted in a judgment for the plaintiff. The case is before us on a general appeal.

Defendants urge upon us again and again, in various forms, the proposition that Walker's failure to service the sign, in response to repeated requests, constituted a material breach of the contract and justified repudiation by them. Their legal proposition is undoubtedly correct. Repudiation is one of the weapons available to an injured party in event the other contractor has committed a material breach. But the injured party's determination that there has been a material breach, justifying his own repudiation, is fraught with peril, for should such determination, as viewed by a later court in the calm of its contemplation, be unwarranted, the repudiator himself will have been guilty of material breach and himself have become the aggressor, not an innocent victim.

What is our criterion for determining whether or not a breach of contract is so fatal to the undertaking of the parties that it is to be classed as "material"? There is no single touchstone. Many factors are involved. They are well stated in section 275 of Restatement of the Law of Contracts in the following terms:

"In determining the materiality of a failure fully to perform a promise the following circumstances are influential:

"(a) The extent to which the injured party will obtain the substantial benefit which he could have reasonably anticipated:

"(b) The extent to which the injured party may be adequately compensated in damages for lack of complete performance;

"(c) The extent to which the party failing to perform has already partly performed or made preparations for performance;

"(d) The greater or less hardship on the party failing to perform in terminating the contract;

"(e) The wilful, negligent or innocent behavior of the party failing to perform;

"(f) The greater or less uncertainty that the party failing to perform will perform the remainder of the contract."

We will not set forth in detail the testimony offered concerning the need for servicing. Granting that Walker's delay (about a week after defendant

Herbert Harrison sent his telegram of repudiation Walker sent out a crew and took care of things) in rendering the service requested was irritating, we are constrained to agree with the trial court that it was not of such materiality as to justify repudiation of the contract, and we are particularly mindful of the lack of preponderant evidence contrary to his determination. Jones v. Eastern Michigan Motorbuses, 287 Mich. 619, 283 N.W. 710. The trial court, on this phase of the case, held as follows:

"Now Mr. Harrison phoned in, so he testified, a number of times. He isn't sure of the dates but he sets the first call at about the 7th of August and he complained then of the tomato and of some rust and some cobwebs. The tomato, according to the testimony was up on the clock; that would be outside of his reach, without a stepladder or something. The cobwebs are within easy reach of Mr. Harrison and so would the rust be. I think that Mr. Bueche's argument that these were not materially a breach would clearly be true as to the cobwebs and I really can't believe in the face of all the testimony that there was a great deal of rust seven days after the installation of this sign. And that really brings it down to the tomato. And, of course, when a tomato has been splashed all over your clock, you don't like it. But he says he kept calling their attention to it, although the rain probably washed some of the tomato off. But the stain remained, and they didn't come. I really can't find that that was such a material breach of the contract as to justify rescission. I really don't think so."

Nor, we conclude, do we. There was no valid ground for defendants' repudiation and their failure thereafter to comply with the terms of the contract was itself a material breach, entitling Walker, upon this record, to judgment.

* * * Judgment was, therefore, rendered for the cash price of the sign, for such services and maintenance as were extended and accepted, and interest upon the amount in default. There was no error.

Affirmed. Costs to appellee.

MACNEIL, A PRIMER OF CONTRACT PLANNING
48 S.Cal.L.Rev. 627, 680 & n. 151 (1975).

A constant risk of contractual relationships is the uncertain-duty-risk—the need to act or refrain from acting in the face of uncertainty concerning the duties of the parties. We associate this risk most often with disputes, but it also exists even in the absence of a present dispute. A party often has to act on his interpretation of performance obligations at the peril of being held wrong in the event of a subsequent dispute. Nevertheless, the uncertain-duty-risk is most likely to be serious where a dispute has arisen or seems likely to arise. In such circumstances parties often find themselves having to act or refrain from acting at considerable risk that their premises for action will subsequently be held erroneous.

It is impossible through planning of contractual relationships to avoid uncertain-duty-risks completely. Nevertheless, such risks can be drastically reduced in many ways through prior planning. * * *

At least one important technique, tender of performance, is available for reducing the uncertain-duty-risk after disputes arise. In many situations the best way to eliminate some or all of the uncertain-duty-risk is to make a tender of performance to the other party. "Tender is an offer to perform a condition or obligation coupled with the present ability of immediate performance, so that were it not for the refusal of cooperation by the party to whom tender is made, the condition or obligation would be immediately satisfied."

Problem 7–7

Suppose Harrison had called you soon after the sign was installed and complained about the tomato and about Walker & Co.'s lack of maintenance. Would you have advised him that Walker & Co. had materially breached and that Harrison could cease paying rent? Suppose the delay in maintenance had been two weeks? Three weeks? Observe that the lawyer called on to advise a client after an allegedly defective performance by the other party must determine whether there has been a breach and, if so, whether the breach is sufficiently egregious to permit cessation of performance by the client. Do the criteria of the Restatement of Contracts § 275 offer sufficient guidance to the lawyer? What are the consequences if the lawyer mistakenly advises that the other party's breach is material?

Now suppose Harrison had called you before he entered the agreement with Walker & Co. What would you have advised him? Draft an express condition that would have protected him.

CONVENTION ON CONTRACTS FOR THE INTERNATIONAL SALE OF GOODS.
Article 25

A breach of contract committed by one of the parties is fundamental if it results in such detriment to the other party as substantially to deprive him of what he is entitled to expect under the contract, unless the party in breach did not foresee, and a reasonable person of the same kind in the same circumstances would not have foreseen, such a result.

Article 49(1)(a)

(1) The buyer may declare the contract avoided:

 (a) If the failure by the seller to perform any of his obligations under the contract or this Convention amounts to a fundamental breach of contract * * *.

Article 64(1)(a)

(1) The seller may declare the contract avoided:

 (a) If the failure by the buyer to perform any of his obligations under the contract or this Convention amounts to a fundamental breach of contract * * *.

JOHN v. UNITED ADVERTISING INC.
Supreme Court of Colorado, 1968.
165 Colo. 193, 439 P.2d 53.

McWILLIAMS, JUSTICE.

This is a contract case. The central issue is whether the contract in question is "entire" or "severable" in nature.

Dwight John, who will hereinafter be referred to as the plaintiff, as the owner and operator of two motels located on South Broadway Street in Englewood, Colorado entered into a written contract with United Advertising, Inc., a corporation which will hereinafter be referred to as the defendant. Under the terms and provisions of this contract the defendant agreed to construct, install and then maintain at its own expense for a period of three years seven outdoor display signs advertising the two motels owned and operated by the plaintiff, in return for which the plaintiff promised to pay the defendant the sum of $95 per month for three years.

In view of the trial court's ultimate disposition of this controversy, two other provisions of the contract between the parties should now be mentioned. The contract "broke down" the aggregate monthly rental of $95 and provided that the rental on one of the seven signs, which was to be 10 [by] 30 in size, would be $35 per month and that the rental on each of the remaining six signs, which were each to be 4 [by] 8 in size, would be $10 per month. As concerns possible termination or modification of the agreement, there was a provision that the termination or modification "of any item of this agreement constitutes that part of the agreement only and does not affect any other item or part of the agreement."

The present writ of error stems from the plaintiff's claim against the defendant for damages for an alleged breach of contract. In his complaint the plaintiff alleged that the defendant failed to erect and maintain the advertising signs as it had agreed to do and averred that as a result thereof plaintiff suffered damages in the total sum of $10,655. Of this amount, according to the plaintiff, $10,000 represented a so-called loss of business profits, and the remaining $655 represented monies paid the defendant under the contract.

By answer the defendant alleged that each of the seven signs had been properly erected and maintained, except for one small sign which will be referred to as sign No. 4. The defendant asserted no counterclaim for the reason that shortly before the institution of the present action, the defendant assigned its claim against the plaintiff for unpaid monthly rentals to a collection agency.

Trial of this matter was to the court, at the conclusion of which the trial court made very detailed findings of fact and conclusions of law. Specifically, the trial court found that five signs which were referred to as signs No. 1, 2, 3, 6 and 7 were erected in substantial compliance with the terms of the contract. However, the trial court found that sign No. 4 was never erected and that sign No. 5 though erected, was not erected in the particular location called for by the contract. In short, then, the trial court found that the defendant had in fact breached the contract in these two particulars.

It was in this particular setting, that the trial court then found that the contract in question was "divisible" and that the failure of the defendant to properly erect and maintain signs No. 4 and 5 constituted only a "severable breach." However, the trial court then went on to find that even though the plaintiff had established two so-called severable breaches, he nonetheless had failed to establish by "satisfactory evidence" that he sustained *any* damage by reason of the failure of the defendant to properly install signs No. 4 and 5.

The trial court accordingly entered judgment dismissing the plaintiff's claim for relief, and by writ of error plaintiff now seeks reversal of the judgment thus entered.

As above indicated, probably the basic issue is whether the contract between the parties is entire or severable. In other words, whether the seven signs in question were, or were not, erected in substantial compliance with the terms and provisions of the contract is basically a question of fact. Our review of the record convinces us that there is evidence to support the trial court's determination that signs No. 1, 2, 3, 6 and 7 were installed substantially in accord with the contract, but that on the contrary the defendant did in fact breach the contract as concerns signs No. 4 and 5. These findings then cannot be disturbed, as there is evidence to support them.

[The court sustained the trial court's determination that John had not proven that he had lost profit as a result of defendant's breach.]

* * * [T]here is one remaining item of damage which must be considered, and that is the money paid by plaintiff to defendant under the contract. The contract itself called for plaintiff to pay the defendant the *last* four months rent on *all* seven signs. This the plaintiff did, paying defendant the total sum of $380 upon the signing of the contract, or within a very short time thereafter. Then, while the defendant was in the process of erecting the various signs, plaintiff also paid defendant additional sums totaling $300. In other words, the evidence showed that the plaintiff paid defendant the *total* sum of $680 under the contract, and this was the eventual finding of the trial court. However, the trial court apparently did not consider this to be an item of damage, and in this particular it did err.

Of the total sum given defendant by the plaintiff, namely $680, our study of the findings made by the trial court indicates that $120 represented money paid for the two signs (signs No. 4 and 5) which defendant failed to properly install. So, if the contract be *severable* or *divisible,* then the plaintiff is *only* entitled to recover those monies paid defendant for signs No. 4 and 5, which sum is $120. But if the contract be deemed entire in nature, the plaintiff would be entitled to recover *all* of the monies paid by him to the defendant, which would be the sum of $680. It is in this setting that it then becomes necessary to determine the correctness of the trial court's determination that the contract is severable, and not entire.

Whether a contract is entire or severable is a matter which cannot be determined with mathematical precision, as it has been said that there is no set formula which furnishes a foolproof method for determining in a given case just which contracts are severable and which are entire. 12 Am.Jur. 870 and 17 C.J.S. Contracts § 98, p. 785. The primary objective is to ascertain the intent of the contracting parties, as such intent is manifested by not only the several terms and provisions of the contract itself, but also as such are viewed in the light of all the surrounding circumstances, including the conduct of the parties before any dispute has arisen. * * * And the singleness or apportionability of the consideration is said to be an important factor to be considered. * * *

It has also been stated that whether a number of promises constitute one contract, or more than one, is to be determined by inquiring "whether the parties assented to all the promises as a single whole, so that there would have been no bargain whatever, if any promise or set of promises were struck out." United States v. Bethlehem Steel Corp., 315 U.S. 289, 62 S.Ct. 581, 86 L.Ed. 855. * * *

Plaintiff's position on this point is that it was intended that this be a "package deal," that at least four of the signs were to be so situated as to "lead" tourists to the very doorstep of his motel, and that he received *no* benefit under the contract unless all seven signs were properly erected and in place. Therefore, it is argued, the contract is entire in nature.

The defendant, on the contrary, urges that it was the intent of the parties that the contract be severable. In support thereof defendant points to the fact that the money due it from the plaintiff was not a lump sum for the seven signs, but was apportioned as so much, per individual sign. Also, the defendant argues that the termination and modification clause, referred to at the outset of this opinion, certainly looks toward severability. Finally, defendant notes that the several billings were on a "so much per sign basis," and each sign is said to be complete within itself, with no one sign by any language printed thereon being "tied in" to any other sign.

The foregoing recital indicates that the testimony bearing on this particular matter is in at least a degree of conflict. Certainly reasonable persons could well differ as to the proper inferences to be drawn from the testimony and documentary evidence which was before the trial court. In such circumstances we are not at liberty to overturn the trial court's determination that the contract in the instant case was a severable one. There being evidence, then, to support this finding of the trial court, its determination must therefore be upheld. Briano, In Behalf of Rubio v. Rubio, 141 Colo. 264, 347 P.2d 497.

Accordingly, the judgment of the trial court dismissing plaintiff's claim is reversed and the cause remanded with direction that judgment be entered in favor of plaintiff and against defendant in the sum of $120, which is the rental paid on signs No. 4 and 5.

PATTERSON, CONSTRUCTIVE CONDITIONS IN CONTRACTS

42 Colum.L.Rev. 903, 927–28 (1942).

[U]njust enrichment is an influential factor in situations where the remedy is, or is conceived to be, contractual, not quasi contractual. * * * The rule that substantial performance of the promise is a sufficient compliance with the constructive condition to permit recovery "on the contract," is apparently limited to cases in which the defendant has received the benefit of the performance. * * * Another example is "severability," which divides and weakens the force of constructive conditions and which is influenced by the principle of avoiding unjust enrichment as well as by the terms of the contract. The doctrine of "waiver," which permits a partial failure of a constructive condition to be excused by loose and sometimes dubious manifestations of consent, is likewise influenced by the principle of unjust enrichment. Finally, the quasi contractual remedy for unjust enrichment has grown up alongside the contractual remedy, and even under the same procedural forms, to mitigate the hardships of constructive conditions.

CARRIG v. GILBERT–VARKER CORP.

Supreme Judicial Court of Massachusetts, 1943.
314 Mass. 351, 50 N.E.2d 59.

* * *

Action by James A. Carrig against Gilbert–Varker Corporation to recover for breach of construction contract, and cross-action by defendant to recover money due thereon. From adverse judgments, both parties appeal.

Judgment in original action affirmed, and judgment in cross-action reversed, and judgment entered for cross-complainant.

* * *

RONAN, JUSTICE.

Carrig, hereinafter referred to as the owner, entered into a contract with Gilbert–Varker Corporation, hereinafter called the contractor, for the construction of * * * thirty-five houses on a lot of land in Watertown. The declaration filed by the owner seeks * * * to recover damages on account of the refusal of the contractor to erect fifteen houses in Watertown, and damages for its failure to erect in accordance with the contract the twenty houses that it actually built. The action of the owner and the second action, brought by the contractor, were referred to an auditor, whose findings of fact were to be final. * * * [The auditor] found that the owner was not entitled to recover damages for breach of contract in the construction of the twenty houses in Watertown, and that the contractor had repudiated its contract in refusing to proceed with the construction of fifteen more houses. He found for the owner for $9,935 together with interest. The judge ordered judgment for this last mentioned amount with interest. The contractor appealed.

The second action is brought by the contractor to recover * * * a balance of $3,143.85 alleged to be due upon the Watertown contract. * * * The auditor found that the contractor had not been paid $2,816.35, after making certain adjustments and allowances for work performed and materials furnished in erecting the twenty Watertown houses, but he found and ruled that the contractor was not entitled to recover this amount, on the ground that he had refused to carry out the Watertown contract by not erecting the fifteen houses. * * * [The contractor appealed.]

The parties on May 2, 1941, entered into a written contract by which the contractor agreed to build thirty-five houses in Watertown in accordance with certain plans and specifications accompanying the contract. The contract set forth four types of construction together with the basic price to be paid for each type. A schedule was included in the contract showing the various prices that were to be allowed the contractor for such alterations or additions as the owner might desire to have made in the construction of any of these houses. The type of the house to be erected on each of the thirty-five lots was designated in the contract together with the basic price for the structure to be erected upon that particular lot. The total basic price for the erection of these thirty-five houses amounted to $132,928. The houses were to be built in groups of not less than ten. The owner agreed to place a temporary construction loan mortgage on each lot upon which a house was to be built and to assign the proceeds of these mortgages to the contractor, who was not required to commence work until such assignment was made. The contractor was to be paid on each house certain percentages of the contract prices when certain stages were reached in its construction, and the final payment was to be made forty days after its completion. After the work began the contractor agreed to release a certain amount from the proceeds of the mortgage on each lot to enable the owner to sell the house, and the latter agreed to reimburse the contractor from the first proceeds of the sale. The bank paid the amounts of the various mortgages to the contractor. The contractor made various releases of funds. As the work progressed it became necessary to keep full accounts so that the financial situation between the owner and the contractor could be determined from time to time.

[The court first affirmed the auditor's finding that the contractor repudiated the contract by failing to build the fifteen houses.] We think the proper measure of damages was the cost in excess of the contract price that would be incurred by the owner in having the houses built, and that there was no error * * * in ordering judgment for this amount, with interest.

The remaining question is the right of the contractor to recover the unpaid balance arising from the construction of the twenty Watertown houses. The auditor has found that this work was done in substantial compliance with the contract and has made allowances to the owner for minor defects and for a small amount of uncompleted work. It is a general rule that one who has breached an entire contract to be performed for an entire price cannot recover * * * on the contract * * * but that where the contract consists of several and distinct items to be furnished or performed by one party, the consideration to be apportioned to each item according to its value and as a separate unit rather than as a part of the whole, then the contract is severable or divisible. * * * Whether a contract is entire or divisible depends upon the intention of the parties as disclosed by the language of the contract, the manner in which it is to be performed, the method of payment, and the circumstances attending its execution and operation. * * * The contract covered the construction of thirty-five houses, the money for which was secured by a separate mortgage placed on each lot and from the sale of each house upon its completion. Payments to the contractor for each house were made in instalments as the construction of that house reached certain stages. Each house was treated as a unit. The sum of $132,928 named in the contract was nothing more than the sum total of the basic prices for the erection of thirty-five different houses according to the basic type of construction designated for each house. A portion of this sum equal to the basic price of each particular house was allocated to the construction of that house, and the final instalment payment became due and payable to the contractor forty days after its completion. The construction of each house and the payment therefor were mutual and dependent provisions of the contract. We think the contract was a divisible one, and that the refusal of the contractor to construct the fifteen houses included in the contract, which were in addition to the twenty houses erected by the contractor, did not bar the contractor from recovering the unpaid balance for work done and materials furnished in constructing the twenty houses. * * *

[Order reversed.]

KIRKLAND v. ARCHBOLD, 113 N.E.2d 496 (Ohio App.1953). [Plaintiff agreed to repair and alter defendant's home. The trial court held that plaintiff was in default under the contract for failing to line the outside walls with rock wool before plastering, as required by the contract, and that defendant properly prevented plaintiff from proceeding with the plastering. The trial court nevertheless gave judgment for plaintiff, reasoning that plaintiff was entitled to be paid on a divisible contract theory for work completed.]

SKEEL, PRESIDING JUDGE.

* * *

Paragraph 20 of the contract provides:

"The Owner agrees to pay the Contractor, as follows: $1,000.00 when satisfactory work has been done for ten days; an additional $1,000.00 when twenty days work has been completed; an additional $1,000.00 when thirty days work has been completed, and $1,000.00 on completion of the contract. $2,000.00 shall be paid within thirty days after the completion of the contract."

The court held that paragraph 20 of the contract provided for progressive payments and that such provisions "are severable from the remainder of the contract and if there has been full or substantial compliance with these provisions, the plaintiff is entitled to recover such progress payment." The court further held that the defendant having paid $800 on the first payment provided for, was an admission that ten days of satisfactory work had been done and therefore rendered judgment for $200, the balance due on the first payment.

* * *

The court committed error prejudicial to the rights of plaintiff in holding that the provisions of the contract were severable. The plaintiff agreed to make certain repairs and improvements on the defendant's property for which he was to be paid $6,000. The total consideration was to be paid for the total work specified in the contract. The fact that a schedule of payments was set up based on the progress of the work does not change the character of the agreement. Newman Lumber Co. v. Purdum, 41 Ohio St. 373.

[The court reversed the judgment and remanded the case for a determination of how much the plaintiff should recover on the basis of unjust enrichment, citing Britton v. Turner (page 132) in support.]

K & G CONST. CO. v. HARRIS

Court of Appeals of Maryland, 1960.
223 Md. 305, 164 A.2d 451.

PRESCOTT, JUDGE.

Feeling aggrieved by the action of the trial judge of the Circuit Court for Prince George's County, sitting without a jury, in finding a judgment against it in favor of a subcontractor, the appellant, the general contractor on a construction project, appealed.

The principal question presented is: Does a contractor, damaged by a subcontractor's failure to perform a portion of his work in a workmanlike manner, have a right, under the circumstances of this case, to withhold, in partial satisfaction of said damages, an installment payment, which, under the terms of the contract, was due the subcontractor, unless the negligent performance of his work excused its payment?

* * *

The statement [of the case according to a Maryland rule] in relevant part, is as follows:

" * * * K & G Construction Company, Inc. (hereinafter called Contractor), plaintiff and counter-defendant in the Circuit Court and appellant herein, was owner and general contractor of a housing subdivision project being constructed (herein called Project). Harris and Brooks (hereinafter called Subcontractor), defendants and counter-plaintiffs in the Circuit Court and appellees herein, entered into a contract with Contractor to do excavating and earth-moving work on the Project. Pertinent parts of the contract are set forth below:

" 'Section 3. The Subcontractor agrees to complete the several portions and the whole of the work herein sublet by the time or times following:

" '(a) Without delay, as called for by the Contractor.

" '(b) It is expressly agreed that time is of the essence of this contract, and that the Contractor will have the right to terminate this contract and employ a substitute to perform the work in the event of delay on the part of Subcontractor, and Subcontractor agrees to indemnify the Contractor for any loss sustained thereby, provided, however, that nothing in this paragraph shall be construed to deprive Contractor of any rights or remedies it would otherwise have as to damage for delay.

" 'Section 4. (b) Progress payments will be made each month during the performance of the work. Subcontractor will submit to Contractor, by the 25th of each month, a requisition for work performed during the preceding month. Contractor will pay these requisitions, less a retainer equal to ten per cent (10%), by the 10th of the months in which such requisitions are received.[1]

" '(c) No payments will be made under this contract until the insurance requirements of Sec. 9 hereof have been complied with.

* * *

" 'Section 8. * * * All work shall be performed in a workmanlike manner, and in accordance with the best practices.

" 'Section 9. Subcontractor agrees to carry, during the progress of the work, * * * liability insurance against * * * property damage, in such amounts and with such companies as may be satisfactory to Contractor and shall provide Contractor with certificates showing the same to be in force.'

---

1. This section is not a model for clarity.

"While in the course of his employment by the Subcontractor on the Project, a bulldozer operator drove his machine too close to Contractor's house while grading the yard, causing the immediate collapse of a wall and other damage to the house. The resulting damage to contractor's house was $3,400.00. Subcontractor had complied with the insurance provision (Sec. 9) of the aforesaid contract. Subcontractor reported said damages to their liability insurance carrier. The Subcontractor and its insurance carrier refused to repair damage or compensate Contractor for damage to the house, claiming that there was no liability on the part of the Subcontractor.

* * *

"Contractor was generally satisfied with Subcontractor's work and progress as required under Sections 3 and 8 of the contract until September 12, 1958, with the exception of the bulldozer accident of August 9, 1958.

"Subcontractor performed work under the contract during July, 1958, for which it submitted a requisition by the 25th of July, as required by the contract, for work done prior to the 25th of July, payable under the terms of the contract by Contractor on or before August 10, 1958. Contractor was current as to payments due under all preceding monthly requisitions from Subcontractor. The aforesaid bulldozer accident damaging Contractor's house occurred on August 9, 1958. Contractor refused to pay Subcontractor's requisition due on August 10, 1958, because the bulldozer damage to Contractor's house had not been repaired or paid for. Subcontractor continued to work on the project until the 12th of September, 1958, at which time they discontinued working on the project because of Contractor's refusal to pay the said work requisition and notified Contractor by registered letters of their position and willingness to return to the job, but only upon payment. At that time, September 12, 1958, the value of the work completed by Subcontractor on the project for which they had not been paid was $1,484.50.

"Contractor later requested Subcontractor to return and complete work on the Project which Subcontractor refused to do because of nonpayment of work requisitions of July 25 and thereafter. Contractor's house was not repaired by Subcontractor nor compensation paid for the damage.

"It was stipulated that Subcontractor had completed work on the Project under the contract for which they had not been paid in the amount of $1,484.50 and that if they had completed the remaining work to be done under the contract, they would have made a profit of $1,340.00 on the remaining uncompleted portion of the contract. It was further stipulated that it cost the Contractor $450.00 above the contract price to have another excavating contractor complete the remaining work required under the contract. It was the opinion of the Court that if judgment were in favor of the Subcontractor, it should be for the total amount of $2,824.50.

" * * * Contractor filed suit against the Subcontractor in two counts: (1), for the aforesaid bulldozer damage to Contractor's house, alleging negligence of the Subcontractor's bulldozer operator, and (2) for the $450.00 costs above the contract price in having another excavating subcontractor complete the uncompleted work in the contract. Subcontractor filed a counter-claim for recovery of work of the value of $1,484.50 for which they had not received payment and for loss of anticipated profits on uncompleted portion of work in the amount of $1,340.00. By agreement of the parties, the first count of Contractor's claim, i.e., for aforesaid bulldozer damage to Contractor's house, was submitted to jury who found in favor of Contractor in the amount of $3,400.00. Following the finding by the jury, the second count of the Contractor's claim and the counter-claims of the Subcontractor, by agreement of the parties, were submitted to the Court for determination, without jury. All of the facts recited herein above were stipulated to by the parties to the Court. Circuit Court Judge Fletcher found for counter-plaintiff Subcontractor in the amount of $2,824.50 from which Contractor has entered this appeal."

The $3,400 judgment has been paid.

It is immediately apparent that our decision turns upon the respective rights and liabilities of the parties under that portion of their contract whereby the subcontractor agreed to do the excavating and earth-moving work in "a workmanlike manner, and in accordance with the best practices," with time being of the essence of the contract, and the contractor agreed to make progress payments therefor on the 10th day of the months following the performance of the work by the subcontractor.[2] The subcontractor contends, of course, that when the contractor failed to make the payment due on August 10, 1958, he breached his contract and thereby released him (the subcontractor) from any further obligation to perform. The contractor, on the other hand, argues that the failure of the subcontractor to perform his work in a workmanlike manner constituted a material breach of the contract, which justified his refusal to make the August 10 payment; and, as there was no breach on his part, the subcontractor had no right to cease performance on September 12, and his refusal to continue work on the project constituted another breach, which rendered him liable to the contractor for damages. The vital question, more tersely stated, remains: Did the contractor have a right, under the circumstances, to refuse to make the progress payment due on August 10, 1958?

The answer involves interesting and important principles of contract law. Promises and counter-promises made by the respective parties to a contract have certain relations to one another, which determine many of the rights and liabilities of the parties. Broadly speaking, they are (1) independent of each other, or (2) mutually dependent, one upon the other. They are independent of each other if the parties intend that *performance* by each of them is in no way conditioned upon *performance* by the other. 5 Page, The Law of Contracts, ¶ 2971. In other words, the parties exchange promises for promises, not the *performance* of promises for the *performance* of promises. 3 Williston, Contracts (Rev.Ed.), ¶ 813, n. 6. A failure to perform an independent promise does not excuse non-performance on the part of the adversary party, but each

---

2. The statement of the case does not show the exact terms concerning the remuneration to be paid the subcontractor. It does not disclose whether he was to be paid a total lump sum, by the cubic yard, by the day, or in some other manner. It does state that the excavation finally cost the contractor $450 more than the "contract price."

is required to perform his promise, and, if one does not perform, he is liable to the adversary party for such non-performance. (Of course, if litigation ensues questions of set-off or recoupment frequently arise.) Promises are mutually dependent if the parties intend *performance* by one to be conditioned upon *performance* by the other, and, if they be mutually dependent, they may be (a) precedent, i.e., a promise that is to be performed before a corresponding promise on the part of the adversary party is to be performed, (b) subsequent, i.e., a corresponding promise that is not to be performed until the other party to the contract has performed a precedent covenant, or (c) concurrent, i.e., promises that are to be performed at the same time by each of the parties, who are respectively bound to perform each. Page, op. cit., ¶ ¶ 2941, 2951, 2961.

Professor Page, op. cit., ¶ 2971, says there are three classes of independent promises left: (1) those in which the acts to be performed by the respective parties are, by the terms of the contract, to be performed at fixed times or on the happening of certain events which do not bear any relation to one another; (2) those in which the covenant in question is independent because it does not form the entire consideration for the covenants on the part of the adversary party, and ordinarily forms but a minor part of such consideration; and (3) those in which the contract shows that the parties intended performance of their respective promises without regard to performance on the part of the adversary, thus relying upon the promises and not the performances (Cf. Brown v. Fraley, 222 Md. 480, 161 A.2d 128).

In the early days, it was settled law that covenants and mutual promises in a contract were *prima facie* independent, and that they were to be so construed in the absence of language in the contract clearly showing that they were intended to be dependent. Williston, op. cit., ¶ 816; Page, op. cit., ¶ ¶ 2944, 2945. In the case of Kingston v. Preston, 2 Doug. 689, decided in 1774, Lord Mansfield, contrary to three centuries of opposing precedents, changed the rule, and decided that performance of one covenant might be dependent on prior performance of another, although the contract contained no express condition to that effect. Page, op. cit., ¶ 2946; Williston, op. cit., ¶ 817. The modern rule, which seems to be of almost universal application, is that there is a presumption that mutual promises in a contract are dependent and are to be so regarded, whenever possible. Page, op. cit., ¶ 2946; Restatement, Contracts, ¶ 266. Cf. Williston, op. cit., ¶ 812.

While the courts assume, in deciding the relation of one or more promises in a contract to one or more counter-promises, that the promises are dependent rather than independent, the intention of the parties, as shown by the entire contract as construed in the light of the circumstances of the case, the nature of the contract, the relation of the parties thereto, and the other evidence which is admissible to assist the court in determining the intention of the parties, is the controlling factor in deciding whether the promises and counter-promises are dependent or independent. * * *

Considering the presumption that promises and counter-promises are dependent and the statement of the case, we have no hesitation in holding that the promise and counter-promise under consideration here were mutually dependent, that is to say, the parties intended performance by one to be conditioned on performance by the other; and the subcontractor's promise was, by the explicit wording of the contract, precedent to the promise of payment, monthly, by the contractor. In Shapiro Engineering Corp. v. Francis O. Day Co., 215 Md. 373, 380, 137 A.2d 695, we stated that it is the general rule that where a total price for work is fixed by a contract, the work is not rendered divisible by progress payments. It would, indeed present an unusual situation if we were to hold that a building contractor, who has obtained someone to do work for him and has agreed to pay each month for the work performed in the previous month, has to continue the monthly payments, irrespective of the degree of skill and care displayed in the performance of work, and his only recourse is by way of suit for ill-performance. If this were the law, it is conceivable, in fact, probable, that many contractors would become insolvent before they were able to complete their contracts. As was stated by the Court in Measures Brothers Ltd. v. Measures, 2 Ch. 248: "Covenants are to be construed as dependent or independent according to the intention of the parties and the good sense of the case."

We hold that when the subcontractor's employee negligently damaged the contractor's wall, this constituted a breach of the subcontractor's promise to perform his work in a "workmanlike manner, and in accordance with the best practices." * * * And there can be little doubt that the breach was material: the damage to the wall amounted to more than double the payment due on August 10. Speed v. Bailey, 153 Md. 655, 661, 662, 139 A. 534. 3A Corbin, Contracts, § 708, says: "The failure of a contractor's [in our case, the subcontractor's] performance to constitute 'substantial' performance may justify the owner [in our case, the contractor] in refusing to make a progress payment * * *. * * * If the refusal to pay an installment is justified on the owner's [contractor's] part, the contractor [subcontractor] is not justified in abandoning work by reason of that refusal. His abandonment of the work will itself be a wrongful repudiation that goes to the essence, even if the defects in performance did not." * * * Professor Corbin, in § 954, states further: "The unexcused failure of a contractor to render a promised performance when it is due is always a breach of contract * * *. Such failure may be of such great importance as to constitute what has been called herein a 'total' breach. * * *. For a failure of performance constituting such a 'total' breach, an action for remedies that are appropriate thereto is at once maintainable. Yet the injured party is not required to bring such action. He has the option of treating the non-performance as a 'partial' breach only * * *."[c] In permitting the subcontractor to proceed with work on the project after August 9, the contractor, obviously, treated the breach by the subcontractor as a partial one. As the promises were mutually dependent and the subcontractor had made a material breach in his performance, this justified the contractor in refusing to make the August 10 payment; hence, as the contractor was not in default, the subcontractor again breached the contract when he, on September 12, discontinued work on the project, which rendered him liable (by the express terms of the contract) to the contractor for his increased cost in having the excavating done—a stipulated amount of $450. Cf. Keystone Engineering Corp. v. Sutter, 196 Md. 620, 628, 78 A.2d 191.

c. The Restatement (Second) of Contracts in section 236(1) defines a claim for "total breach" as a claim for damages "based on all of the injured party's remaining rights to performance." A claim for "partial breach" is "a claim for damages based on only part of the injured party's remaining rights to performance."

The appellees suggest two minor points that may be disposed of rather summarily. They argue that the contractor "gave no written notice to subcontractor for any services rendered or materials furnished by the contractor to the subcontractor," in accordance with the terms of the contract. It is apparent that the contractor's claim against the subcontractor for ill-performance did not involve, in any way, "services rendered or materials furnished" by the contractor; hence, the argument has no substance. They also contend that the contractor had no right to refuse the August 10 payment, because the subcontractor had furnished the insurance against property damage, as called for in the contract. There is little, or no, merit in this suggestion. The subcontractor and his insurance company denied liability. The furnishing of the insurance by him did not constitute a license to perform his work in a careless, negligent, or unworkmanlike manner; and its acceptance by the contractor did not preclude his assertion of a claim for unworkmanlike performance directly against the subcontractor.

Judgment against the appellant reversed; and judgment entered in favor of the appellant against the appellees for $450, the appellees to pay the costs.

UNIFORM COMMERCIAL CODE § 2–717.

Deduction of Damages From the Price

The buyer on notifying the seller of his intention to do so may deduct all or any part of the damages resulting from any breach of the contract from any part of the price still due under the same contract.

Note
The Right Under the Second Restatement Not to Perform and to Cancel After Material Breach

The Restatement (Second) of Contracts sets forth a series of special rules dealing with the aggrieved party's rights in the face of a material breach. Under sections 237, 241 and 242, a material breach does not necessarily entitle the aggrieved party to cancel the deal. According to these sections, the aggrieved party may initially only suspend performance and must continue to stand by to accept cure. How long must this party wait? Until it is too late. How late is too late? Consider the rules below.

§ 237. Effect on Other Party's Duties of a Failure to Render Performance

[I]t is a condition of each party's remaining duties to render performances to be exchanged under an exchange of promises that there be no uncured material failure by the other party to render any such performance due at an earlier time.

§ 241. Circumstances Significant in Determining Whether a Failure Is Material

In determining whether a failure to render or to offer performance is material, the following circumstances are significant:

(a) the extent to which the injured party will be deprived of the benefit which he reasonably expected;

(b) the extent to which the injured party can be adequately compensated for the part of that benefit of which he will be deprived;

(c) the extent to which the party failing to perform or to offer to perform will suffer forfeiture;

(d) the likelihood that the party failing to perform or to offer to perform will cure his failure, taking account of all the circumstances including any reasonable assurances;

(e) the extent to which the behavior of the party failing to perform or to offer to perform comports with standards of good faith and fair dealing.

§ 242. Circumstances Significant in Determining When Remaining Duties are Discharged

In determining the time after which a party's uncured material failure to render or to offer performance discharges the other party's remaining duties to render performance under the rule[] stated in § 237 * * * the following circumstances are significant:

(a) those stated in § 241;

(b) the extent to which it reasonably appears to the injured party that delay may prevent or hinder him in making reasonable substitute arrangements;

(c) the extent to which the agreement provides for performance without delay, but a material failure to perform or to offer to perform on a stated day does not of itself discharge the other party's remaining duties unless the circumstances, including the language of the agreement, indicate that performance or an offer to perform by that day is important.

E. FARNSWORTH, CONTRACTS
579–80 (3d ed. 1999).

Suppose that in breach of a construction contract the owner has delayed making a required progress payment, and the builder, after first refusing to go forward with the work, has finally terminated the contract, leaving the building unfinished. * * * Under the concept of constructive conditions of exchange, the owner's payment of progress payments is an implied condition of the builder's duty to continue to work. Therefore, the owner's breach in failing to make a progress payment may have two effects on the builder's duty. First further performance will not become due, so the builder will be justified in exercising a right to self-help by suspending performance. Second after an appropriate period of time, the builder can choose to treat its remaining duties of performance under the contract as discharged and can exercise a right to self-help by terminating the contract. Two distinct issues are therefore raised. First, was the owner's breach in failing to make the progress payments significant enough to justify the builder's suspending performance? Second, did the owner's breach continue long enough to justify the builder's terminating the contract? If the answer to both questions is yes, the builder was entitled to terminate the contract and claim damages for total breach against the owner. But if the answer to either is no, the builder's action was precipitous and unjustified, itself amounting to a breach that gave the owner a right to terminate and claim damages for total breach against the builder.

This sensible two-step analysis is carefully articulated in the Restatement Second.

ROSETT, CONTRACT PERFORMANCE: PROMISES, CONDITIONS AND THE OBLIGATION TO COMMUNICATE

22 U.C.L.A. L.Rev. 1083, 1086–87, 1096–97, 1100–1101 (1975).

The parties have exchanged promises, committing themselves to future performance. But prior to or during performance one party finds its expectations are not being fulfilled: The promised building is not completed or does not conform to plans; the goods delivered may not be quite what was expected or they are late, etc. The disappointed party will ask two questions: (1) shall I continue to perform my half of the contract or will the deal be terminated, and (2) how will I be compensated for the loss associated with my disappointment?

In answering these questions, traditional theory makes four inquiries. First, it asks whether one or both parties breached a promise; if so, the breaching party is liable to the other for damages. Second, it asks whether one or more of these breaches was material, that is, whether the breach was so serious that it justified the other side in suspending and ultimately terminating his own performance. Since most ruptures involve an interrelated set of failures on both sides, the answer to the last question is likely to require analysis of a third inquiry: the relationship between the promises the parties have exchanged. If it is concluded that the promise of performance of one was given in exchange for the performance of the other, then the failure of one performance affects the obligation to render the return performance. On the other hand, if the promises are deemed independent, any disappointment with performance does not relieve the obligation of counter-performance. The answers to the last two inquiries are likely to provide the resolution of the fourth—the determination of who committed the first material breach. That party is liable, not only for losses associated with the partial breach, but for damages measured by the value of the entire contract.

This brief description is unlikely to explain conventional contract law analysis to anyone not already familiar with it. However, it does make explicit the traditional approach, which is to sort out the conflicting claims that have arisen long after the contractual relationship has gone sour. From the standpoint of the businessman, this four-step analysis is likely to be of little use. It assumes that the crucial need is to advise judges and lawyers how to dispose of litigation. This assumption is misguided, for at the time of litigation courts are engaged in salvage operations at best, seeking to raise the hulk or to apportion blame for the sinking. At worst, courts serve a function analogous to that of the men with brooms who follow the passage of the circus parade.

* * *

Too little weight is given the likelihood that most failures of performance are curable when, or soon after they occur. Breaches and failures become material in part because they are treated that way rather than promptly adjusted. When a party is faced with present or threatened failure of performance, the Restatement II analyzes the issue in terms of whether his behavior is a breach and whether that breach is material. The party who is guilty of the first uncured material breach bears the loss. The Restatement emphasis is on characterizing the performance of the parties, not upon guiding them in determining whether to continue with the contract. Although the Restatement II recognizes the possibility of communication, assurance, and cure, little emphasis is placed on whether the parties have tried to communicate to adjust the difficulties. No duty to communicate candidly is imposed, nor are the parties bound by what they say if they do communicate. Not only are the parties not required to communicate, but there seems to be a real danger that candid communication advising the other side of the circumstances jeopardizing performance and requesting a modification to accommodate the changed circumstances, unless carefully phrased, will be interpreted as a repudiation— a material breach by the communicating party.

This traditional orientation is unrealistic, because most business transactions are part of an ongoing relationship between people who are or can easily be in direct communication. The first thing a contracting party in difficulty should do is contact the other party, explain the situation, and give assurances that the defect will be cured, or if that is not possible, seek to modify the agreement so that it can be performed, or else terminate it altogether. * * *

In summary, when trouble arises during the life of a contract as a result of a present or threatened failure of performance, an insecure party should be justified in suspending his performance long enough to communicate with the other side to seek cure of past failures and to receive assurances of future compliance with the contract. A party who communicates candidly should not be considered to have repudiated unless he unequivocally refuses to perform or to give assurances of future performance. The quality of communications between the parties should be a major factor in the court's evaluation of their competing claims. Failure of a party to seek cure or assurances promptly creates a strong inference that the party did not regard the trouble a threat to the contract relationship. In such a case, the trouble would not condition either party's further performance; that is, it would not be a potential contract terminating event. Of course, the aggrieved party would always be able to press a claim for damages measured by a partial breach.

Problem 7–8

Resolve the following problems under Restatement (Second) of Contracts sections 237, 241 and 242 set forth above at pages 844–845.

(1) Vendor promises to convey land to vendee on July 1, vendee to pay $100,000 on July 1 and the balance of $175,000 one year later. On July 1, vendee learns that vendor has sold the property to Edgar. When can vendee cancel?

(2) Owner contracts with Builder for the construction of a warehouse to be built during the months of July, August, and September, Owner to make a $150,000 progress payment on the 15th of each month. Owner erroneously concludes that the work is being done contrary to specifications and withholds the first progress payment. On July 23, Builder suspends performance. He has fourteen employees on the project, who are paid weekly. Their pay is due July 23, and Builder has to borrow money to meet the payroll. On July 25, Owner tenders the $150,000 due on July 15.

Builder wants to know if he can refuse the tender and cancel. He says he wants to turn to another job he has lined up "free of such difficulties." What would you advise?

HILLMAN, CONTRACT LORE

27 J. Corp. L. 505, 509–510 (2002).

Contracts people show no hesitancy in proclaiming that the reasons for a breach, whether willful, negligent, or unavoidable, have no bearing in determining the rights of the contracting parties. Contract liability is said to be "strict," meaning that the reasons for a breach are irrelevant. The goal is to make the injured party whole, not to punish contract breakers.

But a host of exceptions swallow up the rule, so much so that most theorists, if pressed, understand that the true "rule" is that the breacher's conduct matters a lot. For example, in construction contracts, the degree of willfulness of a contractor's breach helps courts determine whether to grant expectancy damages measured by the cost of repair or the diminution in value caused by the breach, the latter often a smaller measure. Deliberateness also constitutes an express factor in determining the materiality of a promisor's breach and whether the promisee is excused from the contract. Even after being excused from performance, a promisee may have to deal further with a contract breaker to minimize damages, depending on a promisor's motive for the breach. A promisor also may commit a bad-faith breach of contract and therefore trigger rights in favor of the promisee that are not expressly set forth in the contract. Finally, courts have created "independent torts" that arise in the contract setting, including when a party misrepresents facts during negotiations or recklessly performs a contract.

None of these rules should be surprising or even very controversial. Fairness principles such as the "rule of reciprocity" dictate that one should not try to increase one's gains at the expense of the other party. Moreover, on moral grounds, people should keep their promises, and unintentional breaches deserve less moral approbation than intentional ones. Considering the deliberateness of a breach makes sense on instrumental grounds too. Courts should deter a promisor from taking advantage of the promisee's reliance on an expected performance or of changed circumstances that back the promisee into a corner. By deterring such "opportunistic breaches," contract law encourages contracting and thwarts useless wealth transfers from an innocent party to a wrongdoer. Perhaps most obvious, judges and juries are human beings who cannot help but be influenced by the degree of nastiness and inconsiderateness of a breach.

Problem 7–9

If a materially breaching party makes a new offer to perform, is the injured party under a duty to accept such an offer in order to mitigate damages? If so, is the "right" of an injured party to suspend performance after a material breach illusory? For example, suppose a seller, under contract to deliver lumber to a buyer on credit, refuses to perform except for cash (but at a price reduction equal to the amount of interest the buyer would lose by paying earlier). Assume the refusal constitutes a material breach. Must the buyer nevertheless take the lumber and pay cash in order to minimize damages? In Lawrence v. Porter, 63 F. 62, 66 (6th Cir.1894), the court answered affirmatively, stating: "[t]here seems to be no insurmountable objection in * * * permitting a delinquent contractor to minimize his loss." Do you agree?

SECTION TEN: EXPRESS AND IMPLIED CONDITIONS—SOME COMPARISONS

At this point, you should identify and review the major differences between express and implied conditions precedent. Many students have difficulty with at least some of the distinctions. Students who understand the differences should be able to answer the following questions.

1. You should now understand why a contracting party, A, should insist that B expressly promise in the contract to render performance to A (and vice versa). But why might A want to draft a *further* provision making the occurrence of B's promised performance an express condition precedent to A's duties under the contract? After all, even without such an express condition, A still has an action for damages if B breaches. Moreover, if B's breach constitutes an incurable material breach (also called a failure of an implied condition precedent to A's duties), A will be excused from performance. Are these results sufficient to protect A? Review, in particular, the first two sections of this chapter. Make a list of the benefits to A of drafting an express condition precedent to A's duties.

2. Under the Restatement (Second) of Contracts, if a party materially breaches a promise, the injured party may suspend performance. The breaching party's failure to cure within the required time constitutes the non-occurrence of an implied condition precedent to the injured party's duty to perform and discharges the injured party. Does the same analysis apply to the non-occurrence of an express condition precedent? Assume an express condition precedent to a vendee's duty to take and pay for land is vendee "procuring of a mortgage at no more than 8%." The parties do not set a definite date for the closing. Vendee searches, but cannot get a mortgage at less than 8 1/2%. Is the vendee excused? Or must the vendee continue to search for an 8% mortgage rate for an additional period? If the parties set a date for the closing but, after a diligent search, the vendee is unable by that date to obtain a mortgage at less than 8 1/2%, what result?

3. Review the materials in Sections Five (Excuse and Avoidance of Express Conditions) and Nine (Implied Conditions Fixing the Quality of Performance) of this chapter. What are the similarities and differences between the grounds for excusing the non-occurrence of an express condition precedent and the grounds for excusing the non-occurrence of an implied condition precedent? Can you explain the rationales for any differences?

4. Review the materials in Section Six (The Overriding of Express Conditions to Prevent Forfeiture) of this chapter. Does the law provide a comparable doctrine for the overriding of implied-in-law conditions to prevent forfeiture? Explain.

5. In light of your answers to questions 3 and 4, do the cases in Sections 5 and 6 of this chapter *soften* the general distinction between express conditions and implied conditions?

6. Suppose a contract for the carriage of goods expressly states that sailing on or before July 4 is an express condition precedent to the duty of shipper to pay freight at the contract rate. Assume as part of the contract, shipper also exacts an explicit promise from the carrier to sail on or before July 4. Assume the carrier sails on July 5 and arrives late at the destination, a delay that damages the shipper. Is the failure of the carrier to sail on or before July 4 a failure of an express condition precedent that excuses the shipper from the duty to pay the freight at the contract rate, *even though the carrier delivered the goods to their destination*? If so, would the carrier have any theory for recovering any of the cost of carrying the goods? Can the shipper recover damages for the carrier's breach of its promise to sail on or before July 4?

Now assume the absence of an express condition as to the sailing date in the above case. Suppose the carrier substantially performed. What are the rights and remedies of the parties? Suppose the carrier materially breached. What are the rights and remedies of the parties?

7. An immaterial breach does not constitute the failure of an implied condition and the injured party cannot withhold performance or terminate the contract. However, the injured party can claim damages for partial breach. Does the law treat minor failure of an express condition in the same way?

8. Suppose a contracting party erroneously concludes that a condition precedent to its obligation has not occurred. Do the consequences for that party differ depending on whether the condition is express or implied? Which error is easier to make?

SECTION ELEVEN: CONDITIONS AND ARTICLE 2 OF THE UNIFORM COMMERCIAL CODE

UNIFORM COMMERCIAL CODE § 2–601.
Buyer's Rights on Improper Delivery

Subject to the provisions of this Article on breach in installment contracts (Section 2–612) and unless otherwise agreed under the sections on contractual limitations of remedy (Sections 2–718 and 2–719), if the goods or the tender of delivery fail in any respect to conform to the contract, the buyer may

(a) reject the whole; or

(b) accept the whole; or

(c) accept any commercial unit or units and reject the rest.

UNIFORM COMMERCIAL CODE § 2–602(1).

Rejection of goods must be within a reasonable time after their delivery or tender. It is ineffective unless the buyer seasonably notifies the seller.

WILSON v. SCAMPOLI
District of Columbia Court of Appeals, 1967.
228 A.2d 848.

MYERS, ASSOCIATE JUDGE.

This is an appeal from an order of the trial court granting rescission of a sales contract for a color television set and directing the return of the purchase price plus interest and costs.

Appellee purchased the set in question on November 4, 1965, paying the total purchase price in cash. The transaction was evidenced by a sales ticket showing the price paid and guaranteeing ninety days' free service and replacement of any defective tube and parts for a period of one year. Two days after purchase the set was delivered and uncrated, the antennae adjusted and the set plugged into an electrical outlet to "cook out."[1] When the set was turned on however, it did not function properly, the picture having a reddish tinge. Appellant's delivery man advised the buyer's daughter, Mrs. Kolley, that it was not his duty to tune in or adjust the color but that a service representative would shortly call at her house for that purpose. After the departure of the delivery men, Mrs. Kolley unplugged the set and did not use it.[2]

On November 8, 1965, a service representative arrived, and after spending an hour in an effort to eliminate the red cast from the picture advised Mrs. Kolley that he would have to remove the chassis from the cabinet and take it to the shop as he could not determine the cause of the difficulty from his examination at the house. He also made a written memorandum of his service call, noting that the television "Needs Shop Work (Red Screen)." Mrs. Kolley refused to allow the chassis to be removed, asserting she did not want a "repaired" set but another "brand new" set. Later she demanded the return of the purchase price, although retaining the set. Appellant refused to refund the purchase price, but renewed his offer to adjust, repair, or, if the set could not be made to function properly, to replace it. Ultimately, appellee instituted this suit against appellant seeking a refund of the purchase price. After a trial, the court ruled that "under the facts and circumstances the complaint is justified. Under the equity powers of the Court I will order the parties put back in their original status, let the $675 be returned, and the set returned to the defendant."

Appellant does not contest the jurisdiction of the trial court to order rescission in a proper case, but contends the trial judge erred in holding that rescission here was appropriate. He argues that he was always willing to comply with the terms of the sale either by correcting the malfunction by minor repairs or, in the event the set could not be made thereby properly operative, by replacement; that as he was denied the opportunity to try to correct the difficulty, he did not breach the contract of sale or any warranty thereunder, expressed or implied.

D.C.Code § 28:2–508 (Supp. V, 1966) provides:

> (1) Where any tender or delivery by the seller is rejected because non-conforming and the time for performance has not yet expired, the seller may seasonably notify the buyer of his intention to cure and may then within the contract time make a conforming delivery.

---

1. Such a "cook out," usually over several days, allows the set to magnetize itself and to heat up the circuit in order to indicate faulty wiring.

2. Appellee, who made his home with Mrs. Kolley, had been hospitalized shortly before delivery of the set. The remaining negotiations were carried on by Mrs. Kolley, acting on behalf of her father.

(2) Where the buyer rejects a non-conforming tender which the seller had reasonable grounds to believe would be acceptable with or without money allowance the seller may if he seasonably notifies the buyer have a further reasonable time to substitute a conforming tender.

A retail dealer would certainly expect and have reasonable grounds to believe that merchandise like color television sets, new and delivered as crated at the factory, would be acceptable as delivered and that, if defective in some way, he would have the right to substitute a conforming tender. The question then resolves itself to whether the dealer may conform his tender by adjustment or minor repair or whether he must conform by substituting brand new merchandise. The problem seems to be one of first impression in other jurisdictions adopting the Uniform Commercial Code as well as in the District of Columbia.

Although the Official Code Comments do not reach this precise issue, there are cases and comments under other provisions of the Code which indicate that under certain circumstances repairs and adjustments are contemplated as remedies under implied warranties. In L & N Sales Co. v. Little Brown Jug, Inc., 12 Pa.Dist. & Co.R.2d 469 (Phila.County Ct.1957), where the language of a disclaimer was found insufficient to defeat warranties under §§ 2–314 and 2–315, the court noted that the buyer had notified the seller of defects in the merchandise, and as the seller was unable to remedy them and later refused to accept return of the articles, it was held to be a breach of warranty. In Hall v. Everett Motors, Inc., 340 Mass. 430, 165 N.E.2d 107 (1960), decided shortly before the effective date of the Code in Massachusetts, the court reluctantly found that a disclaimer of warranties was sufficient to insulate the seller. Several references were made in the ruling to the seller's unsuccessful attempts at repairs, the court indicating the result would have been different under the Code.

While these cases provide no mandate to require the buyer to accept patchwork goods or substantially repaired articles in lieu of flawless merchandise, they do indicate that minor repairs or reasonable adjustments are frequently the means by which an imperfect tender may be cured. In discussing the analogous question of defective title, it has been stated that:

> The seller, then, should be able to cure [the defect] under subsection 2–508(2) in those cases in which he can do so without subjecting the buyer to any great inconvenience, risk or loss. Hawkland, Curing an Improper Tender of Title to Chattels: Past, Present and Commercial Code, 46 Minn.L.Rev. 697, 724 (1962). * * *

Removal of a television chassis for a short period of time in order to determine the cause of color malfunction and ascertain the extent of adjustment or correction needed to effect full operational efficiency presents no great inconvenience to the buyer. In the instant case, appellant's expert witness testified that this was not infrequently necessary with new televisions. Should the set be defective in workmanship or parts, the loss would be upon the manufacturer who warranted it free from mechanical defect. Here the adamant refusal of Mrs. Kolley, acting on behalf of appellee, to allow inspection essential to the determination of the cause of the excessive red tinge to the picture defeated any effort by the seller to provide timely repair or even replacement of the set if the difficulty could not be corrected. The cause of the defect might have been minor and easily adjusted or it may have been substantial and required replacement by another new set—but the seller was never given an adequate opportunity to make a determination.

We do not hold that appellant has no liability to appellee,[3] but as he was denied access and a reasonable opportunity to repair, appellee has not shown a breach of warranty entitling him either to a brand new set or to rescission. We therefore reverse the judgment of the trial court granting rescission and directing the return of the purchase price of the set.

Reversed.

UNIFORM COMMERCIAL CODE § 2–608.

Revocation of Acceptance in Whole or in Part

(1) The buyer may revoke his acceptance of a lot or commercial unit whose non-conformity substantially impairs its value to him if he has accepted it

(a) on the reasonable assumption that its non-conformity would be cured and it has not been seasonably cured; or

(b) without discovery of such non-conformity if his acceptance was reasonably induced either by the difficulty of discovery before acceptance or by the seller's assurances.

(2) Revocation of acceptance must occur within a reasonable time after the buyer discovers or should have discovered the ground for it and before any substantial change in condition of the goods which is not caused by their own defects. It is not effective until the buyer notifies the seller of it.

(3) A buyer who so revokes has the same rights and duties with regard to the goods involved as if he had rejected them.

HUBBARD v. UTZ QUALITY FOODS, INC.

United States District Court, W.D. New York, 1995.
903 F.Supp. 444.

TRIAL DECISION AND ORDER

LARIMER, DISTRICT JUDGE.

This is a breach-of-contract action brought by Daniel Hubbard ("Hubbard") against UTZ Quality Foods, Inc. ("UTZ"). Hubbard is a Bath, New York potato farmer and UTZ is a Pennsylvania corporation that purchases potatoes for processing into potato chips.

On April 20, 1992, Hubbard executed a written contract to supply UTZ with a quantity of potatoes. The contract, a two-page, form-contract prepared by UTZ, required that the potatoes comply with certain quality standards. Hubbard claims that he was ready and able to deliver the required shipments of potatoes but that UTZ wrongfully and without basis rejected his potatoes.

3. Appellant on appeal has renewed his willingness to remedy any defect in the tender, and thus there is no problem of expiration of his warranties. He should be afforded the right to inspect and correct any malfunction. If appellee refuses to allow appellant an opportunity to do so, then no cause of action can lie for breach of warranty, express or implied, and the loss must be borne by appellee.

Hubbard contends that the sample potatoes provided to UTZ complied with all the quality requirements and, therefore, he complied with all terms of the contract. Hubbard claims that UTZ breached the contract and claims damages for the full contract price, $68,750.

UTZ denies Hubbard's allegations. UTZ contends that the potatoes supplied by Hubbard did not meet the quality requirements of the contract and, therefore, they were properly rejected. UTZ filed a counterclaim against Hubbard contending that he breached the contract by failing to provide the potatoes required by contract.

The case was tried to the Court for 5 days. The Court took testimony from 13 witnesses and received numerous documents and deposition testimony in evidence. This decision constitutes my findings of fact and conclusions of law pursuant to Fed.R.Civ.P. 52.

FACTS

April 20, 1992 Potato Contract.

On April 20, 1992, Hubbard signed the two-page contract prepared by UTZ for farmers who produced potatoes for UTZ. UTZ is a large food processor in Hanover, Pennsylvania whose principal products are potato chips and other snack foods. The contract required Hubbard, beginning "approximately September 5, 1992" to ship 11,000 hundred-weight of Norwis (657) new chipping potatoes. Hubbard was to ship 2,000 to 4,000 hundred-weight per week with schedules to be arranged with UTZ. The price was $6.25 per hundred-weight, F.O.B. New York.

The contract provided that the potatoes must meet certain quality standards. The buyer, UTZ, was entitled to reject the potatoes if they failed to do so. The potatoes had to meet United States Department of Agriculture ("USDA") standards for No. 1 white chipping potatoes. They had to have a minimum size and be free from bruising, rotting and odors which made them inappropriate for use in the processing of potato chips.

The principal standard at issue in this lawsuit is the color standard. UTZ did not want dark potato chips but white or light ones and, therefore, the potatoes had to be the whitest or lightest possible color. The specific paragraph in the contract relating to color reads as follows:

"Color" shall be at least #1 or #2 on the 1978 Snack Food Association "Fry Color Chart."

The Fry Color Chart is a color chart prepared by the Potato Chip/Snack Food Association which has five color designations. Color designation No. 1 is the best or lightest and the chart contains a visual depiction of potato chips with that color. The last color designation, No. 5, is the darkest reading. The contract required that the chips produced from Hubbard's potatoes must at least meet the No. 2 color designation.

Claims of the Parties.

In a nutshell, this lawsuit revolves around the color of the potato chips processed from potatoes submitted by Hubbard to UTZ. UTZ rejected all of the submitted potatoes claiming that they did not meet the required "color" standard. UTZ claims that the samples were too dark and did not meet UTZ' standards for producing white or light chips. Hubbard, on the other hand, contends that UTZ was arbitrary in its refusal to accept his potatoes and that his potatoes substantially complied with the color requirement. Hubbard contends in his pleadings that UTZ' rejection was motivated by concerns about price, not by quality. Hubbard alleges that after rejecting his potatoes, UTZ obtained similar potatoes from other sources at prices below his contract price.

The ultimate factual issue in this case is whether the potato chips made from Hubbard's potatoes failed to meet the color specifications of the contract. In other words, was UTZ' rejection of the installments proper?

In large part, this case turns on matters of law relating to the rights of a buyer, such as UTZ, to reject a seller's goods that are deemed to be non-conforming. The facts and the rights and obligations of the parties must be analyzed pursuant to the New York Uniform Commercial Code ("UCC").

Before discussing the principal issue, whether UTZ wrongfully rejected Hubbard's potatoes, I will deal with several other issues raised by the parties at trial. Some are material, some are not. Based on the evidence and the reasonable inferences from that evidence, I find the following facts.

Rejection of Hubbard's Potatoes.

Hubbard contends that he sent several sample loads of potatoes to UTZ for inspection. On or about September 22, 1992, he sent 1,000 pounds of potatoes from one of his fields to UTZ for testing. These were rejected. Hubbard thought that they looked good when he harvested them but UTZ reported that when they were processed the color was poor. Hubbard discussed this rejection with Richard P. Smith, UTZ' Potato Manager, who told Hubbard to keep sending samples.

Thereafter, on October 1, 1992, Hubbard sent an entire truck load of potatoes to UTZ for processing under the contract. This installment consisted of 425–450 one-hundred-pound bags. Hubbard did not accompany this shipment to Pennsylvania but he was advised by telephone that none of the potatoes would be accepted due to their poor color.

Hubbard requested that UTZ put the reasons for this rejection in writing and Smith did so in a letter dated October 1, 1992 (Ex. 404).

Smith stated in that letter that the load had been rejected because the color (a No. 3 color designation) was unacceptable under the contract. Smith attached a photograph of the potato chips which had been processed and he returned a sample bag of those processed chips.

Smith told Hubbard that he did not intend to cancel the entire contract but told [Hubbard] that more tests should be run on Hubbard's other fields to see if the contract could be filled with crops from those fields.

About a week later, on October 7, Hubbard and his brother prepared a 1,000 pound load of potatoes and drove it to UTZ' facility in Pennsylvania to see if the potatoes would pass muster. Hubbard watched the chips go through UTZ' lines, and he made a video tape of some of the process. On that tape, Hubbard is heard to say that when he saw the chips being processed, they looked "better" than he thought they would. Once again, the chips were rejected, this time by an UTZ employee Kim R. DeGroft. DeGroft had been employed by UTZ for 16 years and in 1991 he was a "lead" person or supervisor in the Potato Department. He recalled that when these chips were processed, Hubbard commented that they should have been sold to Wise, a company that routinely accepted darker chips for processing. DeGroft testified that he had been inspecting potatoes for 5–6 years, and he believed Hubbard's lot was in the No. 3 color range.

expert testimony said #3

Hubbard testified that he became quite upset at this rejection, because he believed that the chips looked good enough to meet the No. 1 and No. 2 color designation. * * *

* * *

Hubbard stopped delivery

After October 7, Hubbard never delivered, or caused to be delivered, any other shipments of potatoes for UTZ pursuant to the contract.

After allegedly conversing with certain government officials, Hubbard advised UTZ by telegram that he intended to sell his potatoes on the open market and charge UTZ for the difference in price.

* * *

Inclement Weather.

I also find as a fact that the weather during the summer of 1992 was very bad for potato farming.

Virtually every witness at trial who was involved in farming or processing potatoes in 1992 testified that it was a cold, rainy growing season which had a negative impact on the potato crop. It appears that the rain produced an ample crop but the cool weather prevented the crop from maturing properly and, therefore, the entire crop that season was immature and very poor. To the extent that there was disagreement on this issue, I accept and find as fact that the poor weather adversely affected the potato crop in New York during the summer of 1992. I find as fact that the entire potato industry suffered that season because of the weather and that other farmers had their potatoes rejected by UTZ for the same reasons that Hubbard's potatoes were rejected.

*Visual Inspection * * *.*

* * *

Concerning testing, the primary issue is whether [UTZ's] rejection based on visual inspection was unreasonable. In other words, was it unreasonable for UTZ to visually inspect Hubbard's potatoes when more sophisticated machinery was allegedly available?

I find as a fact that under all the circumstances that existed in the fall of 1992, it was reasonable for UTZ to rely on visual inspection when it determined whether Hubbard's installments complied with the contract.

As mentioned, the contract did not require [use of machinery for inspection]. Therefore, the contract did not prevent UTZ from using visual inspections. Second, the testimony was uncontradicted that those in the industry consistently used visual inspections when grading potatoes under contracts of this nature. Even at the trial, almost three years after the events at issue, visual inspection is still the norm. Hubbard's expert, Wilbur Gould, testified that in his view the Agtron machine was the preferred method for testing, but he conceded that visual inspection is used in the industry. Some processors did not wish to incur the $20,000 cost of obtaining an Agtron machine and so visual inspections persist.

Furthermore, both Smith, UTZ' Potato Manager, and Jack Corriere, UTZ' General Manager, testified that the first Agtron machine obtained by UTZ was in October 1992, and that it was not properly calibrated and used until late October 1992, well after Hubbard's potatoes had been rejected. Both Smith and Corriere testified that visual inspection of chips was the standard in the industry at the time Hubbard presented his potatoes for inspection. Hubbard presented no evidence to contradict that testimony. Smith testified that he had been potato manager for UTZ for over 30 years and during that time he relied on visual inspection and his expertise to determine whether to accept or reject loads.

I credit the testimony, and I find as a fact, that in September and October 1992, visual inspection of potatoes was the standard used in the industry. I also find that plaintiff understood that his crop would be judged by the visual observations of UTZ' inspectors at the plant, since that was the standard procedure that had been used prior to 1992 when Hubbard and his father had sent potatoes to UTZ for processing.

Motivation of UTZ.

Hubbard has also failed to convince me, by a preponderance of the evidence, that UTZ benefited by its rejection of Hubbard's potatoes. Smith and Corriere testified that they had suffered significant losses in the past when their potatoes had turned bad in storage. In 1992, UTZ took steps to see that such a disaster did not reoccur and so they were careful in their decisions to accept or reject potatoes.

Furthermore, there is no compelling evidence that UTZ purchased potatoes at lower market prices after it rejected Hubbard's crop. On the contrary, the evidence (Ex. 39) suggests that the market price during late 1992 and early 1993 was equal to or higher than Hubbard's contract price. Hubbard has failed to convince me that UTZ' motivation for rejecting his potatoes was to obtain similar potatoes but at a reduced cost. Therefore, I find as a fact, that UTZ' reason and motivation for rejection was its belief that the potatoes failed to meet the quality standards in the contract.

DISCUSSION

UTZ' Rejection of Hubbard's Potatoes.

The primary legal issue in this matter is whether UTZ' rejection of Hubbard's potatoes was proper or wrongful. It is clear that the transaction at issue is a sale of goods governed by the New York Uniform Commercial Code ("UCC") Article 2. Indeed, the parties have stipulated that both Hubbard and UTZ are "merchants" as defined by UCC § 2–104(3).

It is also clear that the contract between the parties is an "installment contract" as that term is defined in UCC § 2–612(1): it contemplates "delivery of goods in separate lots to be separately accepted." That the contract is an installment contract does not appear to have been disputed by the parties. However, it is also evident as a matter of law from terms found throughout the contract.

For instance, in paragraph 1, the contract calls for the sale of "11,000 hundred weight of new chipping potatoes ..." to be shipped in quantities of "2,000 to 4,000 hundred weight per week" starting around September 5, 1992. This language clearly contemplates between 3 and 6 total shipments.

Additionally, paragraphs 3(a) and 3(b) specifically note that standards must be met by "all shipments," which suggests that more than one shipment is contemplated.

Finally, paragraph 4, concerning payment, states that "[b]uyer agrees to pay for all potatoes accepted within 30 days of acceptance...." This language suggests paying per shipment, since each shipment is separately subject to inspection (and acceptance), as indicated by paragraph 3. Clearly this is an "installment" contract as defined in UCC § 2–612(1).

As an installment contract, the question of whether UTZ' rejection was wrongful or proper is governed by UCC § 2–612(2) and (3). UCC § 2–612(2) states that a "buyer may reject any installment which is non-conforming if the non-conformity substantially impairs the value of that installment and cannot be cured...." UCC § 2–612(3) states that "whenever non-conformity or default with respect to one or more installments substantially impairs the value of the whole contract there is a breach of the whole."

The purpose of this "substantial impairment" requirement is "to preclude a party from canceling a contract for trivial defects." *Emanuel Law Outlines, Inc. v. Multi–State Legal Studies*, 1995 WL 519999, *7, No. 93 Civ. 7212 (S.D.N.Y.1995). In this case, UTZ rejected Hubbard's potatoes based upon their failure to satisfy the color standard set forth in paragraph 3(c) of the contract. Thus, the issue for me to decide is whether the failure of Hubbard's potatoes to meet the required #1 or #2 color minimum constitutes a "substantial impairment" of the installments.[1]

Whether goods conform to contract terms is a question of fact. * * * Moreover, in determining whether goods conform to contract terms, a buyer is bound by the "good faith" requirements set forth in N.Y.U.C.C. § 1–203— "Every ... duty within this Act imposes an obligation of good faith in its enforcement or performance." Thus, UTZ' determination that Hubbard's potatoes failed to satisfy the contract terms must have been fairly reached.

The UTZ–Hubbard contract contains many specific requirements regarding the quality of the potatoes. In paragraph 1 the contract states that "only specified varieties as stated in contract will be accepted...." Paragraph 3(a) states that

> All shipments shall meet the United States Standards For Grades of Potatoes for Chipping, USDA, January 1978 ..., in addition to other provisions enumerated in this 'Section 3'. Loads that do not meet these standards may be subject to rejection....

Paragraph 3(b) sets forth specific size requirements (85% or better ... graded to a 1⅞ minimum size); paragraph 3(c) sets forth specific gravity requirements (at least 1.070 in a standard eight pound test); paragraph 3(d) contains the color requirements at issue in this case; and paragraph 3(f) sets forth a

---

1. There is no dispute that UTZ' rejection was timely and effective, as required by UCC § 2–602. I find as a fact that UTZ promptly notified Hubbard of its rejection.

number of other defects or incidents of improper treatment or handling of the potatoes that provide UTZ with the right to reject the potatoes.

Clearly, the quality standards are of great importance to UTZ. They are the most detailed aspect of the contract—far more so than timing or even quantity specifications.

In a contract of this type, where the quality standards are set forth with great specificity, the failure to satisfy one of the specifically enumerated standards is a "substantial impairment." UTZ obviously cares the most about the specific quality specifications, as is evident from the numerous references throughout the contract.

Additionally, I find that UTZ' determination that the potatoes did not meet the required #2 color standard was made in good faith, as required by UCC § 1–203. As noted above, the manner of visual testing utilized by UTZ was reasonable and customary. Further, Smith and DeGroft, the UTZ testers who rejected Hubbard's potatoes, provided credible testimony about their respective experience (Smith—30 years, DeGroft—5–6 years) and method of making such determinations. Accordingly, I find that UTZ fairly and in good faith determined that Hubbard's potatoes were nonconforming.

Thus, I find that Hubbard's failure to meet the proper color standard amounted to a "substantial impairment" of the installments (§ 2–612(2)), substantially impairing the whole contract (§ 2–612(3)). Accordingly, I find that UTZ' rejection of Hubbard's potatoes was proper.[2]

* * *

CONCLUSION

I find that plaintiff has failed to establish the claims set forth in his complaint by a preponderance of the evidence and, therefore, I find in favor of defendant on plaintiff's claims. Plaintiff's complaint is dismissed and judgment shall be entered accordingly in favor of defendant.

Defendant has failed to prove its counterclaims against plaintiff, and they are all dismissed.

IT IS SO ORDERED.

SECTION TWELVE: ANTICIPATORY REPUDIATION AND PROSPECTIVE INABILITY TO PERFORM

HOCHSTER v. DE LA TOUR

Queens Bench, 1853.
2 Ellis & Bl. 678, 118 Eng.Rep. 922.

Action of Assumpsit.

On the trial, before Erle J., at the London sittings in last Easter Term, it appeared that plaintiff was a courier, who, in April, 1852, was engaged by

---

2. This is not a case where UTZ has rejected the potatoes because they were a week (or a month) late or where the quantities were lower than anticipated. Such nonconformity would not constitute "substantial impairment" of this contract because timing and quantity are not its critical components. *See, e.g., Emanuel, supra,* (delay in installment shipment of bar review study aids not significant where shipment was still timely for the purposes of the contract); *Hudson Feather & Down Products, Inc. v. Lancer Clothing Corp.,* 128 A.D.2d 674, 513 N.Y.S.2d 173 (2d Dep't 1987) (delay in installment payment did not substantially impair value of whole contract).

defendant to accompany him on a tour, to commence on 1st June 1852, on the terms mentioned in the declaration. On 11th May 1852, defendant wrote to plaintiff that he had changed his mind, and declined his services. He refused to make him any compensation. The action was commenced on 22d May. The plaintiff, between the commencement of the action and the 1st June, obtained an engagement with Lord Ashburton, on equally good terms, but not commencing till 4th July. The defendant's counsel objected that there could be no breach of the contract before the 1st of June. The learned Judge was of a contrary opinion, but reserved leave to enter a nonsuit on this objection. The other questions were left to the jury, who found for plaintiff.

Hugh Hill, in the same Term, obtained a rule Nisi to enter a nonsuit, or arrest the judgment. * * *

* * *

LORD CAMPBELL C.J. * * *

On this motion in arrest of judgment, the question arises, Whether, if there be an agreement between A. and B., whereby B. engages to employ A. on and from a future day for a given period of time, to travel with him into a foreign country as a courier, and to start with him in that capacity on that day, A. being to receive a monthly salary during the continuance of such service, B. may, before the day, refuse to perform the agreement and break and renounce it, so as to entitle A. before the day to commence an action against B. to recover damages for breach of the agreement; A. having been ready and willing to perform it, till it was broken and renounced by B. The defendant's counsel very powerfully contended that, if the plaintiff was not contented to dissolve the contract, and to abandon all remedy upon it, he was bound to remain ready and willing to perform it till the day when the actual employment as courier in the service of the defendant was to begin; and that there could be no breach of the agreement, before that day, to give a right of action. But it cannot be laid down as a universal rule that, where by agreement an act is to be done on a future day, no action can be brought for a breach of the agreement till the day for doing the act has arrived. If a man promises to marry a woman on a future day, and before that day marries another woman, he is instantly liable to an action for breach of promise of marriage; *Short v. Stone* (8 Q.B. 358). If a man contracts to execute a lease on and from a future day for a certain term, and, before that day, executes a lease to another for the same term, he may be immediately sued for breaking the contract; *Ford v. Tiley* (6 B.C. 325). So, if a man contracts to sell and deliver specific goods on a future day, and before the day he sells and delivers them to another, he is immediately liable to an action at the suit of the person with whom he first contracted to sell and deliver them; *Bowdell v. Parsons* (10 East, 359). One reason alleged in support of such an action is, that the defendant has, before the day, rendered it impossible for him to perform the contract at the day: but this does not necessarily follow; for, prior to the day fixed for doing the act, the first wife may have died, a surrender of the lease executed might be obtained, and the defendant might have repurchased the goods so as to be in a situation to sell and deliver them to the plaintiff. Another reason may be, that, where there is a contract to do an act on a future day, there is a relation constituted between the parties in the meantime by the contract, and that they impliedly promise that in the meantime neither will do any thing to the prejudice of the other inconsistent with that relation. As an example, a man and woman engaged to marry are affianced to one another during the period between the time of the engagement and the celebration of the marriage. In this very case, of traveller and courier, from the day of the hiring till the day when the employment was to begin, they were engaged to each other; and it seems to be a breach of an implied contract if either of them renounces the engagement. * * *.

The declaration in the present case, in alleging a breach, states a great deal more than a passing intention on the part of the defendant which he may repent of, and could only be proved by evidence that he had utterly renounced the contract, or done some act which rendered it impossible for him to perform it. If the plaintiff has no remedy for breach of the contract unless he treats the contract as in force, and acts upon it down to the 1st June 1852, it follows that, till then, he must enter into no employment which will interfere with his promise "to start with the defendant on such travels on the day and year," and that he must then be properly equipped in all respects as a courier for a three months' tour on the continent of Europe. But it is surely much more rational, and more for the benefit of both parties, that, after the renunciation of the agreement by the defendant, the plaintiff should be at liberty to consider himself absolved from any future performance of it, retaining his right to sue for any damage he has suffered from the breach of it. Thus, instead of remaining idle and laying out money in preparations which must be useless, he is at liberty to seek service under another employer, which would go in mitigation of the damages to which he would otherwise be entitled for a breach of contract. It seems strange that the defendant, after renouncing the contract, and absolutely declaring that he will never act under it, should be permitted to object that faith is given to his assertion, and that an opportunity is not left to him of changing his mind. If the plaintiff is barred of any remedy by entering into an engagement inconsistent with starting as a courier with the defendant on the 1st June, he is prejudiced by putting faith in the defendant's assertion: and it would be more consonant with principle, if the defendant were precluded from saying that he had not broken the contract when he declared that he entirely renounced it. Suppose that the defendant, at the time of his renunciation, had embarked on a voyage for Australia, so as to render it physically impossible for him to employ the plaintiff as a courier on the continent of Europe in the months of June, July and August 1852: according to decided cases, the action might have been brought before 1st June; but the renunciation may have been founded on other facts, to be given in evidence, which would equally have rendered the defendant's performance of the contract impossible. The man who wrongfully renounces a contract into which he has deliberately entered cannot justly complain if he is immediately sued for a compensation in damages by the man whom he has injured: and it seems reasonable to allow an option to the injured party, either to sue immediately, or to wait till the time when the act was to be done, still holding it as prospectively binding for the exercise of this option, which may be advantageous to the innocent party, and cannot be prejudicial to the wrongdoer. An argument against the action before the 1st of June is urged from the difficulty of calculating the damages: but this argument is equally strong against an action before the 1st of September, when the three months would expire. In either case, the jury in assessing the damages would be justified in looking to all that had happened, or was likely to happen, to increase or mitigate the loss of the plaintiff down to the day of trial. * * *

Upon the whole, we think that the declaration in this case is sufficient. It gives us great satisfaction to reflect that, the question being on the record, our opinion may be reviewed in a Court of Error. In the meantime we must give judgment for the plaintiff.

Judgment for plaintiff.

ROSETT, PARTIAL, QUALIFIED, AND EQUIVOCAL REPUDIATION OF CONTRACT

81 Colum.L.Rev. 93, 95 (1981).

Many repudiations in the real world are not total, absolute, and unequivocal. The repudiating party, without totally renouncing performance, indicates that his performance will be late; that he may not be able to deliver some items of performance; that unless problems are somehow resolved, he does not see how the contract payments can be made on time. He expresses doubt, temporizes, and equivocates. The repudiator may not intend to terminate the agreement; he may sincerely attempt to perform or may seek to induce an advantageous modification of the agreement by the vulnerable other party. The expression of doubt as to will or ability to perform shades subtly into a statement that the performance will not occur. Although for convenience I refer to these actions as repudiations or renunciations, it is not clear that those are appropriate characterizations for essentially uncertain signals.

RESTATEMENT (SECOND) OF CONTRACTS § 250.

When a Statement or an Act Is a Repudiation

A repudiation is

(a) a statement by the obligor to the obligee indicating that the obligor will commit a breach that would of itself give the obligee a claim for damages for total breach * * * or

(b) a voluntary affirmative act which renders the obligor unable or apparently unable to perform without such a breach.

Comment:

* * *

b. *Nature of statement.* In order to constitute a repudiation, a party's language must be sufficiently positive to be reasonably interpreted to mean that the party will not or cannot perform. Mere expression of a doubt as to his willingness or ability to perform is not enough to constitute a repudiation. * * * [L]anguage that under a fair reading "amounts to a statement of intention not to perform except on conditions which go beyond the contract" constitutes a repudiation. Comment 2 to Uniform Commercial Code § 2–610.

Illustrations:

    1. On April 1, A contracts to sell and B to buy land, delivery of the deed and payment of the price to be on July 30. On May 1, A tells B that he will not perform. A's statement is a repudiation.

    2. A contracts to build a house for B for $50,000, progress payments to be made monthly in an amount equal to 85% of the price of the work performed during the preceding month, the balance to be paid on the architect's certificate of satisfactory completion of the house. Without justification B fails to make a $5,000 progress payment and tells A that because of financial difficulties he will be unable to pay him anything for at least another month. If, after a month, it would be too late for B to cure his material failure of performance by making the delayed payment, B's statement is a repudiation. * * *

    3. The facts being otherwise as stated in Illustration 1, A does not tell B that he will not perform but says, "I am not sure that I can perform, and I do not intend to do so unless I am legally bound to." A's statement is not a repudiation.

* * *

    c. *Nature of Act.* In order to constitute a repudiation, a party's act must be both voluntary and affirmative, and must make it actually or apparently impossible for him to perform. * * *

Illustrations:

    5. The facts being otherwise as stated in Illustration 1, A says nothing to B on May 1, but on that date he contracts to sell the land to C. A's making the contract with C is a repudiation.

    6. The facts being otherwise as stated in Illustration 1, A says nothing to B on May 1, but on that date he mortgages the land to C as security for a $40,000 loan which is not payable until one year later. A's mortgaging the land is a repudiation. * * *

    7. A contracts to employ B, and B to work for A, the employment to last a year beginning in ten days. Three days after making the contract B embarks on a ship for a voyage around the world. B's embarking for the voyage is a repudiation.

UNIFORM COMMERCIAL CODE § 2–610.

Anticipatory Repudiation

When either party repudiates the contract with respect to a performance not yet due the loss of which will substantially impair the value of the contract to the other, the aggrieved party may

    (a) for a commercially reasonable time await performance by the repudiating party; or

    (b) resort to any remedy for breach (Section 2–703 or Section 2–711), even though he has notified the repudiating party that he would await the latter's performance and has urged retraction; and

    (c) in either case suspend his own performance or proceed in accordance with the provisions of this Article on the seller's right to identify goods to the contract notwithstanding breach or to salvage unfinished goods (Section 2–704).

CONVENTION ON CONTRACTS FOR THE INTERNATIONAL SALE OF GOODS.

Article 72

(1) If prior to the date for performance of the contract it is clear that one of the parties will commit a fundamental breach of contract, the other party may declare the contract avoided.

(2) If time allows, the party intending to declare the contract avoided must give reasonable notice to the other party in order to permit him to provide adequate assurance of his performance.

(3) The requirements of the preceding paragraph do not apply if the other party has declared that he will not perform his obligations.

HATHAWAY v. SABIN

Supreme Court of Vermont, 1891.
63 Vt. 527, 22 A. 633.

Munson, J.

* * *

The contract required the defendant to furnish a hall for the concert, and to pay $75 after the entertainment. The plaintiff alleged readiness to perform on his part, and assigned as the breach the defendant's failure to furnish a hall. The court directed a verdict for the plaintiff for $75 and interest. The defendant insists that, inasmuch as the non-payment of the $75 was not assigned as the breach, and as there was no proof of any loss except in the non-payment of the $75, there was no proof of loss from any breach complained of, and that consequently there could be no recovery. We think it cannot be said that the proof of loss in the non-receipt of the $75 did not apply to the breach declared upon. The plaintiff was ready to give the concert, and on giving it would have been entitled to the $75, but he was prevented from giving it by the defendant's failure to furnish a hall. This failure was properly assigned as the breach from which the plaintiff suffered damage. The plaintiff does not sue for the compensation to which he would have been entitled if the contract had been carried out, but for the damages he has sustained in being compelled to leave the contract unperformed. The breach is not the non-payment of the unearned compensation, but the failure to perform the antecedent stipulation which would have enabled the plaintiff to earn it.

The defendant also contends that he was excused from opening and heating the hall by the apparent impossibility of the musicians' reaching the town. During the 36 hours preceding the evening appointed for the concert a snow-storm of unusual violence prevailed in Montpelier and vicinity, which early on the day of the concert rendered the streets of that village and the roads from the surrounding country practically impassable. The quartette by which the concert was to be given was in Barre, having gone there from Montpelier the evening before, and trains on the spur from Montpelier to

Barre were suspended. Late in the afternoon, however, an irregular train went to Barre, and on this the musicians returned to Montpelier, arriving early in the evening, and going to the hall at the time appointed. It is claimed that the defendant's conduct must be tested by the situation as it was at the time when action on his part became necessary, and that he is saved from liability by the doctrine that, when one party ascertains that the other will not be able to perform what he has undertaken, the party ascertaining this is excused from performing the obligations resting upon him. It is doubtless true that, when one party has put it out of his power to perform, the other party can maintain an action without having tendered performance on his part. But a party who becomes involved in difficulties for which he is not responsible, if ultimately able to perform, is not to be deprived of the benefits of his contract because of an assumption by the other party that the difficulties would prove insurmountable. Here the defendant was mistaken in supposing that the plaintiff would not be able to perform, and we know of no rule which permits him to plead reasonable cause to believe so in excuse for the failure on his part. It is apparent, also, that the defendant's course was determined before the time when action on his part became necessary. It was not necessary to commence the heating of the hall until 4 o'clock in the afternoon, but about 10 o'clock in the forenoon the defendant telephoned the manager that, owing to the condition of the streets in Montpelier, it would be impossible to have the entertainment that evening. It is evident from this that the defendant based his action upon his belief that there would be no audience, rather than upon the supposition that the musicians could not reach the place of entertainment. He did not wait until it was necessary to take action about the hall before deciding that there could be no concert. But, at the time when action on his part became necessary, there was nothing in the situation which could relieve him from liability. The contract contains no provision for his protection from such a misfortune, and the loss must fall on him.

The defendant also insists that upon being held liable he was entitled to have the damages assessed by the jury. We think, however, that the plaintiff was entitled to have this verdict directed. Having incurred all the expense necessary to enable him to give the concert, the plaintiff's damages were necessarily the amount to which he would have been entitled for giving it. It is not for the defendant to say that the damages were less than the amount he had agreed to pay, when the plaintiff had done and incurred everything on his part, and was prevented from earning the compensation agreed upon solely by the defendant's failure. The message sent the manager in the forenoon, even if treated as a sufficient notice to stop performance, did not require any different action as regards the damages. It afforded no ground for an application of the doctrine which forbids the making of expense after receiving notice of the repudiation of a contract, for the expense afterwards incurred by the musicians was only such as was required by the situation in which the notice found them. Neither did the case permit an application of the rule which requires a party who is stopped in the performance of a contract for service to do what he can to lessen the damages by seeking like employment elsewhere. Judgment affirmed.

Note
The Uniform Commercial Code, the Restatement, and the
Right to Adequate Assurances of Performance

U.C.C. section 2–609 provides in part:

Right to Adequate Assurance of Performance

(1) A contract for sale imposes an obligation on each party that the other's expectation of receiving due performance will not be impaired. When reasonable grounds for insecurity arise with respect to the performance of either party the other may in writing demand adequate assurance of due performance and until he receives such assurance may if commercially reasonable suspend any performance for which he has not already received the agreed return.

* * *

(4) After receipt of a justified demand failure to provide within a reasonable time not exceeding thirty days such assurance of due performance as is adequate under the circumstances of the particular case is a repudiation of the contract.

The approach of section 2–609, which entitles a promisee to demand assurance that the promisor will perform when the promisee has reasonable grounds to believe the promisor will not perform, has also been adopted by the Restatement (Second) of Contracts in section 251 and the Convention on Contracts for the International Sale of Goods in Article 71. Together the Code, Restatement (Second), and Convention offer contracting parties (and their lawyers who must render advice) a new tool designed to avoid contract breakdown. For example, suppose a seller of goods receives information that reasonably suggests that the buyer is in financial distress. Such facts might include that the buyer had defaulted on other loans and had misrepresented the size of its factory. A seller who has reasonable grounds for insecurity, may demand assurance before proceeding. But what are "reasonable grounds for insecurity" and when are assurances "adequate"? Both "standards" will engender more occasions for lawyers to give advice. Will the approach avoid contract breakdown?

Problem 7–10

Review Illustration 1 to section 250 of the Second Restatement, set forth at page 863. Suppose A told B on May 1 that A was not sure that he could perform on July 30 and that he was looking for a better deal. You represent B. What course of action, if any, do you advise?

MAGNET RESOURCES, INC. v. SUMMIT MRI, INC.

Superior Court of New Jersey, Appellate Division, 1998.
318 N.J.Super. 275, 723 A.2d 976.

Brochin, J.

This appeal arises from a breach of contract action. The * * * legal issue[] of particular importance with which we deal [is]: the right of a contracting party that reasonably deems itself insecure because of the other contracting party's threatened material breach to demand concrete assurances of performance and to suspend its own performance pending their receipt * * *.

Plaintiff Magnet Resources, Inc. ("Magnet Resources") and defendant Summit MRI, Inc. ("Summit") each charged the other with a material breach of contract and sued for damages.* * * The parties' * * * breach of contract claims were tried to a jury. The jury found that both parties had breached, and it awarded $492,320 to Magnet Resources and $18,470 to Summit. Summit has appealed and Magnet Resources has cross-appealed.

Summit did not object to the trial court's jury instructions. However, it argues to us that the instructions were incomplete and misleading because the jury was not told that one party's material breach relieves the other party of its duty to perform. * * *

* * *

Magnetic resonance imagers ("MRIs") are devices used by physicians and hospitals for diagnostic purposes. Magnet Resources sells and services new and used MRIs. Summit operated MRI installations in Jersey City, Paterson and Irvington, New Jersey. Magnet Resources contracted with Summit to provide preventive maintenance and emergency repair services for the MRIs at Summit's Paterson and Irvington installations. Magnet Resources also supplied cryogens for all of Summit's installations, including its Jersey City installation.

The charge for the services to be provided for the Irvington installation was $120,000 for the first year and $150,000 annually for subsequent years of the contract. Payments were to be made monthly in advance beginning with the fourth month of the contract. The testimony of both parties implies that there was a separate service agreement for the Paterson installation with terms similar to those of the Irvington contract, but the Paterson contract was not offered into evidence. However, neither party attaches any significance to this omission. For purposes of the case, both parties treated the service agreements for the two sites as a single contract, and we will do the same.

Summit's monthly payments were habitually late. On May 10, 1994, Magnet Resources faxed a memorandum to Summit complaining that seven of its checks had been dishonored.[1] The memorandum declared that thereafter payments more than ten days late would have to be made by certified check, the provision of the service contracts imposing a surcharge for late payment would be enforced, and neither essential supplies nor emergency service would be provided except under special arrangements if an invoice was late by thirty days or more. On June 7, 1994, Magnet Resources faxed a memorandum to Summit complaining that it had still not received a $13,250 payment due for April.

On December 20, 1994, Summit requested repair service for its Jersey City installation. Magnet Resources had no contract for emergency service or preventive maintenance for that site. It declined to provide the service because Summit then owed it $35,000. Summit promised that if the necessary

---

1. The dishonored checks were paid within a few days after they were returned.

work was done, Magnet Resources would get "most of the money by the end of the week." In reliance on that promise, Magnet Resources installed a necessary piece of equipment from its inventory for a total charge of $8,750.

Neither that charge nor the other unpaid bills had yet been paid when Summit called a Magnet Resources service person at his home on Saturday, December 24, requesting immediate emergency service for its Paterson installation. Under its service contract, however, Summit was entitled to service only from Monday through Friday. Magnet Resource did not make the emergency repair.

On Tuesday, December 27, Summit still had not paid its outstanding bills to Magnet Resources. That day, the person in charge of Summit's Paterson facility telephoned Magnet Resources and urgently requested service for that site. The caller was informed that Magnet Resources would not respond because of Summit's continuing failure to pay overdue bills.

The director of Summit's centers called Ronald Hynes, Magnet Resources' president. The amount due and unpaid was then more than $40,000. Summit offered $10,000 if the emergency service problem was taken care of. Hynes refused; he decided to suspend service until "things were improved, or somebody talked to us [Magnet Resources] and made some arrangements." He faxed a memorandum to Summit which referred to the previous week's payment promise and declared, "[W]e have suspended service to each site where payment is overdue." The suspension was effective December 27.

Some time after the suspension of service, Hynes spoke with Hanafy and complained that Summit had ordered cryogens from Magnet Resources' supplier on Magnet Resources' credit. Summit responded that it had made arrangements to have another company provide service for its sites. Summit changed the locks on its MRI installations to bar access by Magnet Resources' service personnel who previously had been able to enter to service the MRI's after regular business hours.

* * *

1. Failure to ask the jury whose breach was material

It is black letter contract law that a material breach by either party to a bilateral contract excuses the other party from rendering any further contractual performance. * * * Restatement (Second) of Contracts § 237 (1981). Neither Summit nor Magnet Resources asked the trial court to charge that proposition, and neither objected to the omission of that charge. Summit is therefore not entitled to a new trial because of this omission unless it constituted "plain error," * * * capable of producing an unjust result .* * *

"Material breach" has been described as follows:

Where a contract calls for a series of acts over a long term, a material breach may arise upon a single occurrence or consistent recurrences which tend to "defeat the purpose of the contract." [citation omitted] In applying the test of materiality to such contracts a court should evaluate "the ratio quantitatively which the breach bears to the contract as a whole, and secondly the degree of probability or improbability that such a breach will be repeated." [citation omitted] [Medivox Productions, Inc. v.

Hoffmann–LaRoche, Inc., 107 N.J.Super. 47, 59, 256 A.2d 803 (Law Div.1969).]

See Restatement (Second) of Contracts §§ 241 and 242. In the present case, there was evidence of three events or series of events which could arguably have constituted material breaches. In their order of occurrence, these were, first, Summit's continual late payments and, at the end, its failure to pay for either two or three months' service and for emergency service at Jersey City that was not covered by the contracts; second, Magnet Resources' failure and refusal to provide service for the Paterson installation beginning December 24, 1994; and third, Summit's cancellation of the service contracts the following week.

Whether conduct constitutes a breach of contract and, if it does, whether the breach is material are ordinarily jury questions. * * * However, the court's failure to pose those questions to the jury would have been prejudicial to Summit only if the jury could have found that Magnet Resources' refusal to provide service at the Paterson installation was a material breach which justified Summit's canceling the contract.

Magnet Resources has argued to us that its refusal to provide service was not a material breach because Summit's non-compliance with its payment obligations was itself a prior material breach that excused it from any further duty of performance. * * * Summit's non-compliance indisputably breached the contract. But Magnet Resources, by declaring a suspension and not a cancellation of its undertaking to service Summit's facilities, implied its willingness to resume service upon payment and, perhaps, upon adequate assurance of timely future payments. That statement of its implied readiness to continue the contract waived the materiality of the breach; that is, it precluded Magnet Resources from successfully relying on Summit's payment history to excuse its refusal to provide service. * * *

Nonetheless, Magnet Resources had the legal right to do what it said it was doing, suspend its performance pending Summit's cure of its defaults within a reasonable time. Magnet Resources was a relatively small company. It did not contract to extend credit. Just the opposite. Its contract called for payment in advance. After repeatedly failing to make payments when they were due, Summit promised to pay most of what it owed. When Summit failed to keep that promise, perhaps Magnet Resources would have been entitled to treat Summit's failure as a material breach. It did not do so. Instead, in order to avoid extending further credit which had not been bargained for, it withheld further performance of its contractual obligations until it had received either the payment that was due or reasonable assurances that payment would be promptly made. For the following reasons, we conclude that as a matter of law, this suspension of performance—refusing service at Paterson beginning December 24—did not materially breach Magnet Resources' contractual obligations.

Section 251 of the Restatement (Second) of Contracts has been accepted as part of New Jersey law. * * *

Section 251 states:

> (1) Where reasonable grounds arise to believe that the obligor will commit a breach by non-performance that would of itself give the obligee

a claim for damages for total breach * * *, the obligee may demand adequate assurance of due performance and may, if reasonable, suspend any performance for which he has not already received the agreed exchange until he receives such assurance.

(2) The obligee may treat as a repudiation the obligor's failure to provide within a reasonable time such assurance of due performance as is adequate in the circumstances of the particular case.

The Comment to this section explains that an obligee of an executory promise "who believes, for whatever reason, that the obligor will not or cannot perform without a breach, is always free to act on that belief" by withholding his own performance. But if he cannot prove that his belief was correct, his non-performance may itself be a material breach of the contract, making him liable for damages. The Comment continues:

> This Section affords him an opportunity, in appropriate cases, to demand assurance of due performance and thereby avoid the uncertainties that would otherwise inhere in acting on his belief. If it is then reasonable for the obligee to suspend his own performance while he awaits assurance by the obligor, he may do so under Subsection (1).... If the obligee does not, within a reasonable time, obtain adequate assurance of due performance, he may under Subsection (2) treat the obligor's failure to provide such an assurance as a repudiation.

Significantly for the present case, Summit's failure to pay in accordance with its contract or with the promise by which it induced the provision of emergency service for the Jersey City facility did not have to amount to a material breach in order to have entitled Magnet Resources to demand assurances that Summit would comply with its obligations and to suspend performance for a reasonable time until those assurances were forthcoming. * * *

Kunian v. Development Corp. of America, 165 Conn. 300, 334 A.2d 427 (Conn.1973), illustrates the application of § 251 to facts closely analogous to those of the present case. Although Kunian was decided on the basis of § 2–609 of the Uniform Commercial Code, it is an appropriate guide to the decision of the present case because, according to the Comment to Restatement (Second) of Contracts § 251, that section is "a generalization, applicable without regard to the subject matter of the contract, from [the rule stated in] Uniform Commercial Code § 2–609."

The contract in Kunian provided for A. Merowitz and Company, Inc. to sell and deliver plumbing and heating supplies for a total cost of $358,381 to DCA Builders, a general contractor building a low cost housing project. The deliveries were to be made to the job site when and as ordered by the contractor. Materials delivered before the fifteenth of the month were to be paid for on the twenty-fifth; materials delivered between the fifteenth and thirtieth were to be paid for on the tenth day of the following month. The contract also provided that DCA Builders could take a two percent discount if it complied with these payment terms. From approximately March 18, 1969 to October 31, 1969, DCA Builders paid all amounts invoiced for materials received except for $7,502.75. A. Merowitz continued to deliver materials despite the indebtedness and, by November 26, 1969, the contractor owed approximately $38,000. On December 12, 1969, A. Merowitz met with DCA

Builders and insisted on full payment, but received only $5,000. However, DCA Builders promised to make payments during January 1970 to reduce its debt, provided that A. Merowitz continue to deliver materials as ordered. The seller complied, but the contractor did not make any further payments either to reduce its indebtedness or for the new deliveries. In early January 1970, DCA Builders began purchasing plumbing and heating supplies from another source; however, on January 14, 1970, it wrote A. Merowitz demanding delivery of the balance of the supplies due under its contract. DCA Builders had not performed its previous promise to make payments on what it already owed. In response to DCA Builder's January 14 letter, A. Merowitz stated that it would deliver the balance of the required materials but, in view of the large indebtedness outstanding, only if DCA Builders deposited sufficient cash in escrow to pay for the delivered materials. When DCA Builders refused to comply by January 27, 1970, A. Merowitz ceased making deliveries. DCA Builders then owed A. Merowitz approximately $51,000; materials previously delivered totaled approximately $200,000.

Rejecting DCA Builders' contention that A. Merowitz had breached the contract by refusing further deliveries without a guarantee of payment, the Court said:

> [DCA Builders] argues that [A. Merowitz] should have continued making deliveries and its failure to do so after January 27, 1970, was a breach of contract. It is undisputed, however, that at the December 12, 1969, meeting between the parties [A. Merowitz] demanded adequate assurance that [DCA Builders] would pay its outstanding indebtedness before [A. Merowitz] would continue making deliveries. Under the circumstances, this was equivalent to a written demand for adequate assurance. It is further undisputed that [DCA Builders] failed to abide by its promise made at the conference to pay its outstanding indebtedness or even to pay for the subsequent deliveries which it thus had induced [A. Merowitz] to make. [A. Merowitz] then had 'reasonable grounds for insecurity' and justifiably informed [DCA Builders] that it would deliver the balance of the material only if payment of the entire contract was guaranteed by [DCA Builders'] depositing sufficient cash in escrow to pay for the delivered materials. [DCA Builders'] failure, therefore, to provide adequate assurance of due performance within a reasonable time after the request and after the action had been brought was a repudiation of the contract and [A. Merowitz] was excused from further performance under the contract.

These legal principles reflected in Restatement (Second) of Contracts § 251 and illustrated by the cited cases lead us to the conclusion that Magnet Resources was entitled to condition service after December 24, 1994 on payment or an acceptable arrangement for payment of the amount which Summit owed in accordance with its contract. In our view, a properly instructed jury could not reasonably have found otherwise. Consequently, we hold that, as a matter of law, Magnet Resources' suspension of performance was not a breach and, therefore, not a material breach. Summit's repudiation of the contract by arranging to have another firm service its MRI installations was consequently the first material breach, making it liable to Magnet Resources for lost profits. Because, as a matter of law, Magnet Resources' withholding service beginning December 24 was not a material breach,

Summit was not prejudiced by the trial court's failure to instruct the jury that one party's material breach avoids liability by the other party for subsequent non-performance. That omission therefore entitles Summit neither to reversal of the judgment and a new trial nor to a judgment notwithstanding the verdict.

We agree with Summit, however, that the jury's verdict awarding it $18,470 is inconsistent with the verdict awarding Magnet Resources $492,320. But we disagree with Summit about the consequence of this inconsistency. The only basis Summit offered for its claim of damages was Magnet Resources' refusal to provide emergency service for the Paterson installation on and after December 24, 1994. Since Magnet Resources was legally justified in withholding service, its doing so did not constitute a breach and does not make Magnet Resources liable for losses which Summit may have sustained as a consequence. There is therefore no legal basis for the verdict in favor of Summit on its counterclaim.

* * *

The judgment in favor of Magnet Resources is affirmed. The judgment in favor of Summit is vacated and the case is remanded to the Law Division for the entry of a judgment of no cause for action on Summit's counterclaim.

WHITE, EIGHT CASES AND SECTION 251
67 Cornell L.Rev. 841, 853–55 (1982).

Where there is a good-faith dispute between the parties and there are plausible arguments on both sides of the dispute, neither or both of the parties will have reasonable grounds for insecurity. In such cases sections 2–609 and 251 do little to advance one's analysis about which party should be held in default.

* * *

* * * If we assume that each party was sparring with the other in a wary but good-faith effort to get what it wanted out of the contract, we see that section 2–609 does little to resolve matters. If a party has reasonable grounds for insecurity, he may suspend his performance. If he does not have such grounds, his suspension will likely constitute an anticipatory repudiation. Presumably if each party is at all times willing and able to perform the contract, then there are no reasonable grounds for insecurity. * * * Conceivably each party could * * * [ask] for assurances from the other, each could have granted assurances, yet neither's position would have changed. The same is true where the parties have a legitimate disagreement about the meaning of the specifications or other terms in the contract. If each has a plausible and good-faith interpretation that favors his position, how does section 2–609 help to resolve that dispute? The section's impotence in good faith disputes is nicely illustrated by *Cherwell-Ralli, Inc. v. Rytman Grain Co.*[1] There a buyer of grain, Rytman, had become concerned that the seller, Cherwell–Ralli, might not complete performance because the market price of the grain had risen significantly above the contract price. In a telephone

1. 180 Conn. 714, 433 A.2d 984 (1980).

conversation, Cherwell–Ralli's president assured Rytman's president that deliveries would continue if Rytman would pay for the goods already delivered. Thereupon, Rytman sent Cherwell–Ralli a check for $9,824.60 to cover shipments already made. Several days later, Rytman stopped payment when he was told by a truck driver not employed by Cherwell–Ralli that the shipment would be his last load. The trial court, affirmed by the Connecticut Supreme Court, concluded that Rytman, not Cherwell–Ralli, breached the contract. It found that Rytman had no reasonable grounds for insecurity and that Rytman had breached the contract by stopping payment and refusing to pay for goods already delivered.

If, as it seems, Rytman truly believed that Cherwell–Ralli was not going to perform yet Cherwell–Ralli was willing to perform but had an understandable wish to be paid, we have a classic case of capable parties involved in a good-faith dispute. Section 2–609 does nothing to eliminate Rytman's honest but misplaced anxiety. Having demanded assurances and stopped payment, he is left in exactly the same position as if he had merely stopped payment.

This is a body of repudiation cases with tangles that sections 2–609 and 251 will not unsnarl. In these cases the courts will continue to search unassisted to determine whether a given act was a repudiation. Each party will have to bear continued uncertainty about whether the other party's act is sufficiently egregious to allow him to suspend performance. With these cases we are back in the nineteenth-century common law of contract.

GREGUHN v. MUTUAL OF OMAHA INSURANCE CO.

Supreme Court of Utah, 1969.
23 Utah 2d 214, 461 P.2d 285.

[Plaintiff suffered a debilitating injury while working as a brick mason. After making some payments to plaintiff under a health and accident insurance policy, Mutual of Omaha and another defendant asserted that plaintiff's ailment was due to a preexisting illness and refused to make further payments. In plaintiff's action against the insurance company, the jury found that plaintiff was permanently disabled under the terms of the policy and that the disability resulted proximately from the accident. The trial court's judgment awarded not only the damages due plaintiff to the time of trial, but also awarded a lump sum for future benefits based on the plaintiff's life expectancy. Defendants appealed.]

TUCKETT, J.

* * *

This brings us to what we consider the most critical problem in the case. Did the court err in granting an award for future disability under the doctrine of anticipatory breach? This problem is one of first impression in this jurisdiction. * * * The decisions of a number of the states permit an insured to recover a money judgment for the present value of future payments based upon the insured's life expectancy. However, the great majority of decisions permit recovery under a disability policy only of installments accrued and unpaid. The doctrine of anticipatory breach has not ordinarily been extended

(handwritten margin note: "can't get damages on future potential breaches" and "correct thing to do.")

to unilateral contracts. As stated in the Restatement of Contracts:[1] In a unilateral contract for the payment in installments after default of one or more, no repudiation can amount to an anticipatory breach of the rest of the installments not yet due. We are of the opinion that it was error for the trial court to enter judgment for future benefits to become due under the policies.

The verdict and the decision of the trial court amounts to a determination that the plaintiff is entitled to the monthly payments as specified in the insurance policies so long as he is totally and permanently disabled. Defendants are not relieved of the obligation of making the payments unless the plaintiff should recover or die. Should the defendants fail in the future to make payment in accordance with the terms of the policies without just cause or excuse and the plaintiff is compelled to file another action for delinquent installments, the court at that time should be able to fashion such relief as will compel performance.

This matter is remanded to the trial court with directions to modify its judgment so as to eliminate that part of the judgment pertaining to future benefits under the policies. Plaintiff (respondent) is entitled to costs.

CROCKETT, C.J., and CALLISTER and HENROID, JJ., concur.

ELLETT, JUSTICE (dissenting).

I dissent.

The plaintiff claimed that he was totally and permanently disabled under the terms of the policies written by the defendants. After making some periodic payments, the defendants denied any liability to make further payments on the grounds that if the plaintiff had any disability, it was not related to causes covered in the policies.

By rendering its verdict in favor of the plaintiff, the jury found that plaintiff was permanently and totally disabled under the terms of the policies. There was evidence to support the verdict and, therefore, the issue of the permanency and totality of the disability under the policies has been concluded, and the prevailing opinion accepts these facts.

While the majority of cases listed in the digests have held that recovery in actions involving health and accident policies is limited to accrued and past-due installments, there is respectable and, in my opinion, better reasoned authority to the contrary.

In those actions which have been brought to interpret, apply, or enforce the terms of a policy and where no repudiation of further liability is involved, then the recovery is properly limited to accrued and past-due installments. However, where there is a repudiation of all contractual obligations, I think it is the better policy to allow full recovery in one action, as was done in the case now before us.

Some of the cases which limit recovery to past-due installments do so because of a provision in the policy requiring the insured to furnish proof of continued disability as a condition of liability to pay. This should not be

---

1. Restatement of Contracts, Vol. 1, Sec. 318 * * *.

necessary where there has been a determination in court that the disability is *total* and *permanent*.

* * *

There can be no quarrel with the rule that where the contract has become wholly unilateral, as where nothing further is to be done by the plaintiff, the mere failure to pay one or more installments when due would not, in and of itself, be considered a repudiation of the contract as to future payments, since the breach does not go to the essence of the contract. However, where there is a failure to pay one installment, coupled with an announcement by the insurer that no future payments will be made, then damages for the partly anticipatory breach should be allowed. See Corbin on Contracts, Sec. 966.

Since the plaintiff in this case was determined to be totally and permanently disabled, the defendants cannot relitigate those matters. By assuming the defendants would pay according to the contract, the prevailing opinion ignores the fact that the plaintiff sued for damages, not specific performance, and would compel him to abide by terms of the contract when neither party requests such a ruling. The decision grants to the defendants an opportunity to refuse again to pay the installments to plaintiff and says that in such an event the trial court "should be able to fashion such relief as will compel performance." I am unable to know just what relief the decision has in mind. Under the pleadings as framed in this case, the relief to which plaintiff was entitled has already been given him.

If it appears, as in this case, that a party to a contract makes an outright refusal to comply with the terms thereof and so notifies the other party, then I can see no legal reason why the other party may not accept the anticipatory breach of the contract and sue for his damages. What reason is there in law or good conscience to give a locus penitentiae to the party whose wrongful conduct precipitates a lawsuit? Why should an appellate court set the stage for further litigation when the matters have already been fully determined?

By informing the plaintiff herein that no further payments would be made upon the policies, the defendants were guilty of an executory breach of the contracts which entitled the plaintiff to sue for his damages and to put an end to further litigation.

I would affirm the judgment of the trial court. * * *

*

Part Four

THE CESSATION PROCESS

Chapter Eight

GROUNDS OF RIGHTFUL CESSATION

*In the ordinary course, contracts
come to an end with performance.*
                              RICHARDSON

*The best laid schemes o' mice and
men gang aft a-gley.*

                              BURNS

SECTION ONE: CESSATION AND
THE ROLE OF LAWYERS

We use the word "cessation" to refer to the termination of relations.
Cessation may or may not be rightful. Our primary focus in this chapter will
be on the grounds of *rightful* cessation. Although we consider remedial issues
to some extent in the present chapter, that subject also demands the more
systematic and unified treatment provided in the next chapter.

The grounds of rightful cessation are numerous. Most often, the parties
to a valid agreement with consideration terminate their relations simply
because they have fully performed their duties under the agreement. For
example, a builder may complete construction of a building and be paid in full
by the owner. This type of cessation leaves little role for the lawyer. Yet it
may represent the culmination of a well-planned and drafted agreement for
which the lawyer's reward is the client's satisfaction and willingness to retain
the lawyer in the future.

Although full performance is by far the most common ground of rightful
cessation, a party may rightfully refuse to perform or may cease performing
on a variety of other grounds. We have already studied some of these. For
example, a party may claim lack of consideration or unconscionability, and
rightfully refuse to go forward on these grounds. Or a party may show that
the other party materially broke the agreement or that an express condition
precedent failed to occur. At this point, you should review the various grounds
of rightful cessation already studied: lack of consideration and non-compliance
with the statute of frauds in Chapter Two, lack of a valid agreement in
Chapter Four, unconscionability and the like in Chapter Five, and material
breach and failure of condition in Chapter Seven. In the present chapter and
the next, we will concentrate on several new grounds of rightful cessation:
mistake, impossibility of performance, impracticability of performance, and
frustration of purpose. After studying these, you will be in a position to
integrate them into an overall picture of the law of cessation.

The new grounds of cessation on which we now focus are based on either
mistaken views of the facts at the time of contracting or on events that arise

thereafter. For example, an oil supplier may seek an excuse from the duty to supply oil because of an unforeseeable oil boycott that causes huge price increases, even though the contract says nothing about such an excuse. Courts seldom allow such relief. After all, the oil supplier typically promises to supply the oil *without* condition. But did the supplier really agree to supply no matter what the circumstances?

One can see from this oil supply example that the law of conditions studied in Chapter Seven is also relevant here. If the lawyer for the oil supplier had included an *express* condition relieving the supplier from the duty to perform in the event of an oil boycott, the supplier's duty to perform would not mature. But if this is so, then one may ask: should not the supplier also be excused from performance on the basis of an *implied-in-fact* condition?

As we will see, courts do sometimes resolve disputes similar to our oil supply problem by invoking the concept of implied-in-fact conditions. But usually courts permit cessation only when the parties, without fault, were unaware of existing facts at the time of contracting or reasonably did not foresee the supervening circumstances. Generally, a court will find only in such situations that the parties "impliedly" conditioned their duties on the *absence* of such onerous facts or supervening circumstances. Of course, if the parties were unaware of the facts or failed to foresee the supervening circumstances and the court excuses performance, the court is not really enforcing the intentions of the parties when it "finds" an implied condition, for the parties could not have had any intentions. In these instances, it is best to say that the agreement contains an unallocated risk that must be allocated by the court. Put another way, the agreement contains a gap calling for a condition *implied in law*.

As with the law governing duties of performance treated in Chapters Six and Seven, the parties, through their lawyers, can displace much of the cessation law to be studied in Chapters Eight and Nine. The lawyer must plan and draft not only with an eye to the grounds of rightful cessation that the client may wish to claim, but must also consider the various possible grounds on which the other party may wish to terminate. For example, the lawyer for the oil supplier in our example may seek both to assure that the supplier will be excused in the face of onerous events, and to bar escape hatches favoring the buyer. Of course, one cannot hope to foresee all events and even the best lawyer cannot always secure an excuse for the client or protect the client from the other party's claim of excuse.

When an unallocated risk materializes, the parties may want to renegotiate the agreement. Their lawyers will then assume many of the roles previously studied in this book, such as those of counselor, negotiator, and even planner and drafter. Some of these roles may be especially difficult to fulfill at this stage because the lawyers must evaluate the strength of the promisor's claim to cease performance. If, for example, the oil supplier has a strong case for relief, the buyer's lawyer must consider whether to counsel the buyer to agree to a price increase and the supplier's lawyer must consider whether to counsel the supplier to insist on one. The lawyers also must consider the effect on the reputation and good will of their clients of either insisting on performance when the other party is in a difficult position or of seeking an excuse from duties of performance.

When it is not possible to modify the agreement, the lawyer may be called upon, as litigator, to try to persuade the court that the contract expressly or impliedly in fact allocates the risk in favor of the client. Or, if the court believes that the case involves a true gap, the lawyer's task is to persuade the court to fill it favorably to the client. This may require the construction and evaluation of legal, business, and moral arguments.

Rightful cessation may occur immediately after the agreement is consummated. Thus a party may announce that he or she will not perform, claiming, for example, that the agreement is unenforceable because of indefiniteness or because the parties made a mutual mistake. Or a party may make such claims later, on the eve of performance. Or a party may begin performance, and then cease for the foregoing reasons or because of impossibility, impracticability of performance, or frustration of purpose. A party may also cease performance because of failure of a condition or a material breach. In our treatment of cessation in this chapter, we will take up the various grounds of rightful cessation in the order that they most commonly arise during the life of an agreement.

SECTION TWO: INVALIDITY AND RELATED DEFENSES—A BRIEF RETROSPECT

In Chapter Two, Sections Two and Nine, and in Chapter Four, we studied the requirements of the leading theory of obligation in contract and related matters, agreement with consideration. An alleged agreement may fail for lack of consideration, for want of an offer and acceptance, for lack of definiteness, and so on. When an agreement is legally deficient in any one of these ways, either party may justifiably claim a right of cessation. As we have seen, however, usually a lawyer can, through careful planning and drafting, set up an arrangement that will not lack "formational" validity. At this point, you should review the central themes of the relevant sections of Chapters Two and Four.

You may also wish to review the related "policing" defenses studied in Chapter Five: duress, misrepresentation, unconscionability, conflict with public policy, and the like. With regard to each, we saw that the lawyer may have important planning, drafting, negotiating, counseling and litigating roles. To fulfill these well, the lawyer must understand the substantive requirements of each ground of invalidity as well as the various "policing" defenses.

SECTION THREE: MUTUAL MISTAKE

As with invalidity and related defenses, the mutual mistake ground of cessation, arises at the agreement stage. A party who learns that the circumstances at the time of contracting were materially different from what the parties had assumed at that time may claim relief on the ground of "mutual mistake."

SHERWOOD v. WALKER

Supreme Court of Michigan, 1887.
66 Mich. 568, 33 N.W. 919.

MORSE, J. Replevin for a cow. Suit commenced in justice's court; judgment for plaintiff; appealed to circuit court of Wayne county, and verdict and judgment for plaintiff in that court. The defendants bring error, and set out 25 assignments of the same.

The main controversy depends upon the construction of a contract for the sale of the cow. * * * The defendants reside at Detroit, but are in business at Walkerville, Ontario, and have a farm at Greenfield, in Wayne county, upon which were some blooded cattle supposed to be barren as breeders. The Walkers are importers and breeders of polled Angus cattle. The plaintiff is a banker living at Plymouth, in Wayne county. He called upon the defendants at Walkerville for the purchase of some of their stock, but found none there that suited him. Meeting one of the defendants afterwards, he was informed that they had a few head upon their Greenfield farm. He was asked to go out and look at them, with the statement at the time that they were probably barren, and would not breed. May 5, 1886, plaintiff went out to Greenfield, and saw the cattle. A few days thereafter, he called upon one of the defendants with the view of purchasing a cow, known as "Rose 2d of Aberlone." After considerable talk, it was agreed that defendants would telephone Sherwood at his home in Plymouth in reference to the price. The second morning after this talk he was called up by telephone, and the terms of the sale were finally agreed upon. He was to pay five and one-half cents per pound, live weight, fifty pounds shrinkage. He was asked how he intended to take the cow home, and replied that he might ship her from King's cattle-yard. He requested defendants to confirm the sale in writing, which they did by sending him the following letter:

"WALKERVILLE, May 15, 1886.

"*T.C. Sherwood, President, etc.*—DEAR SIR: We confirm sale to you of the cow Rose 2d of Aberlone, lot 56 of our catalogue, at five and a half cents per pound, less fifty pounds shrink. We inclose herewith order on Mr. Graham for the cow. You might leave check with him, or mail to us here, as you prefer.

"Yours, truly,
HIRAM WALKER & SONS."

The order upon Graham inclosed in the letter read as follows:

"WALKERVILLE, May 15, 1886.

"*George Graham:* You will please deliver at King's cattle-yard to Mr. T.C. Sherwood, Plymouth, the cow Rose 2d of Aberlone, lot 56 of our catalogue. Send halter with the cow, and have her weighed.

"Yours truly,
HIRAM WALKER & SONS."

On the twenty-first of the same month the plaintiff went to defendants' farm at Greenfield, and presented the order and letter to Graham, who informed him that the defendants had instructed him not to deliver the cow. Soon after, the plaintiff tendered to Hiram Walker, one of the defendants, $80, and demanded the cow. Walker refused to take the money or deliver the cow. The plaintiff then instituted this suit. After he had secured possession of the cow under the writ of replevin, the plaintiff caused her to be weighed by the constable who served the writ, at a place other than King's cattle-yard. She weighed 1,420 pounds.

When the plaintiff, upon the trial in the circuit court, had submitted his proofs showing the above transaction, defendants moved to strike out and exclude the testimony from the case, for the reason that it was irrelevant and did not tend to show that the title to the cow passed, and that it showed that the contract of sale was merely executory. The court refused the motion, and an exception was taken. The defendants then introduced evidence tending to show that at the time of the alleged sale it was believed by both the plaintiff and themselves that the cow was barren and would not breed; that she cost $850, and if not barren would be worth from $750 to $1,000; that after the date of the letter, and the order to Graham, the defendants were informed by said Graham that in his judgment the cow was with calf, and therefore they instructed him not to deliver her to plaintiff, and on the twentieth of May, 1886, telegraphed plaintiff what Graham thought about the cow being with calf, and that consequently they could not sell her. The cow had a calf in the month of October following. On the nineteenth of May, the plaintiff wrote Graham as follows:

"PLYMOUTH, May 19, 1886.

"*Mr. George Graham, Greenfield*—DEAR SIR: I have bought Rose or Lucy from Mr. Walker, and will be there for her Friday morning, nine or ten o'clock. Do not water her in the morning.

"Yours, etc.,
T.C. SHERWOOD."

Plaintiff explained the mention of the two cows in this letter by testifying that, when he wrote this letter, the order and letter of defendants was at his home, and, writing in a hurry, and being uncertain as to the name of the cow, and not wishing his cow watered, he thought it would do no harm to name them both, as his bill of sale would show which one he had purchased. Plaintiff also testified that he asked defendants to give him a price on the balance of their herd at Greenfield, as a friend thought of buying some, and received a letter dated May 17, 1886, in which they named the price of five cattle, including Lucy, at $90, and Rose 2d at $80. When he received the letter he called defendants up by telephone, and asked them why they put Rose 2d in the list, as he had already purchased her. They replied that they knew he had, but thought it would make no difference if plaintiff and his friend concluded to take the whole herd.

The foregoing is the substance of all the testimony in the case.

* * * The [circuit] court * * * charged the jury that it was immaterial whether the cow was with calf or not. * * *

* * *

It appears from the record that both parties supposed this cow was barren and would not breed, and she was sold by the pound for an insignificant sum as compared with her real value if a breeder. She was evidently sold and purchased on the relation of her value for beef, unless the plaintiff had learned of her true condition, and concealed such knowledge from the defendants. Before the plaintiff secured the possession of the animal, the defendants learned that she was with calf, and therefore of great value, and undertook to rescind the sale by refusing to deliver her. The question arises whether they had a right to do so. The circuit judge ruled that this fact did not avoid the sale and it made no difference whether she was barren or not. I am of the opinion that the court erred in this holding. I know that this is a close question, and the dividing line between the adjudicated cases is not easily discerned. But it must be considered as well settled that a party who has given an apparent consent to a contract of sale may refuse to execute it, or he may avoid it after it has been completed, if the assent was founded, or the contract made, upon the mistake of a material fact,—such as the subject-matter of the sale, the price, or some collateral fact materially inducing the agreement; and this can be done when the mistake is mutual. * * *

If there is a difference or misapprehension as to the substance of the thing bargained for; if the thing actually delivered or received is different in substance from the thing bargained for, and intended to be sold,—then there is no contract; but if it be only a difference in some quality or accident, even though the mistake may have been the actuating motive to the purchaser or seller, or both of them, yet the contract remains binding. "The difficulty in every case is to determine whether the mistake or misapprehension is as to the substance of the whole contract, going, as it were, to the root of the matter, or only to some point, even though a material point, an error as to which does not affect the substance of the whole consideration." *Kennedy v. Panama, etc., Mail Co.*, L.R. 2 Q.B. 580, 587. It has been held, in accordance with the principles above stated, that where a horse is bought under the belief that he is sound, and both vendor and vendee honestly believe him to be sound, the purchaser must stand by his bargain, and pay the full price, unless there was a warranty.

It seems to me, however, in the case made by this record, that the mistake or misapprehension of the parties went to the whole substance of the agreement. If the cow was a breeder, she was worth at least $750; if barren, she was worth not over $80. The parties would not have made the contract of sale except upon the understanding and belief that she was incapable of breeding, and of no use as a cow. It is true she is now the identical animal that they thought her to be when the contract was made; there is no mistake as to the identity of the creature. Yet the mistake was not of the mere quality of the animal, but went to the very nature of the thing. A barren cow is substantially a different creature than a breeding one. There is as much difference between them for all purposes of use as there is between an ox and a cow that is capable of breeding and giving milk. If the mutual mistake had simply related to the fact whether she was with calf or not for one season, then it might have been a good sale, but the mistake affected the character of the animal for all time, and for its present and ultimate use. She was not in fact the animal, or the kind of animal, the defendants intended to sell or the plaintiff to buy. She was not a barren cow, and, if this fact had been known, there would have been no contract. The mistake affected the substance of the whole consideration, and it must be considered that there was no contract to sell or sale of the cow as she actually was. The thing sold and bought had in fact no existence. She was sold as a beef creature would be sold; she is in fact a breeding cow, and a valuable one. The court should have instructed the jury that if they found that the cow was sold, or contracted to be sold, upon the understanding of both parties that she was barren, and useless for the purpose of breeding, and that in fact she was not barren, but capable of breeding, then the defendants had a right to rescind, and to refuse to deliver, and the verdict should be in their favor.

The judgment of the court below must be reversed, and a new trial granted, with costs of this court to defendants.

CAMPBELL, C.J., and CHAMPLIN, J., concurred.

SHERWOOD, J., (*dissenting.*) I do not concur in the opinion given by my brethren in this case. * * * I * * * agree with [my Brother Morse] that the plaintiff was entitled to a delivery of the property to him when the suit was brought, unless there was a mistake made which would invalidate the contract, and I can find no such mistake. * * *

As has already been stated by my brethren, the record shows that the plaintiff is a banker and farmer as well, carrying on a farm, and raising the best breeds of stock, and lived in Plymouth, in the county of Wayne, 23 miles from Detroit; that the defendants lived in Detroit, and were also dealers in stock of the higher grades; that they had a farm at Walkerville, in Canada, and also one in Greenfield in said county of Wayne, and upon these farms the defendants kept their stock. The Greenfield farm was about 15 miles from the plaintiff's. In the spring of 1886 the plaintiff, learning that the defendants had some "polled Angus cattle" for sale, was desirous of purchasing some of that breed, and meeting the defendants, or some of them, at Walkerville, inquired about them, and was informed that they had none at Walkerville, "but had a few head left on their farm in Greenfield, and asked the plaintiff to go and see them, stating that in all probability they were sterile and would not breed." In accordance with said request, the plaintiff, on the fifth day of May, went out and looked at the defendants' cattle at Greenfield, and found one called "Rose, Second," which he wished to purchase, and the terms were finally agreed upon at five and a half cents per pound, live weight, 50 pounds to be deducted for shrinkage. The sale was in writing, and the defendants gave an order to the plaintiff directing the man in charge of the Greenfield farm to deliver the cow to plaintiff. This was done on the fifteenth of May. On the twenty-first of May plaintiff went to get his cow, and the defendants refused to let him have her; claiming at the time that the man in charge at the farm thought the cow was with calf, and, if such was the case, they would not sell her for the price agreed upon. The record further shows that the defendants, when they sold the cow, believed the cow was not with calf, and barren; that from what the plaintiff had been told by defendants (for it does not appear he had any other knowledge or facts from which he could form an opinion) he believed the cow was farrow, but still thought she could be made to breed. The foregoing shows the entire interview and treaty between the parties as to the sterility and qualities of the cow sold to the plaintiff. The cow had a calf in the month of October.

There is no question but that the defendants sold the cow representing her of the breed and quality they believed the cow to be, and that the purchaser so understood it. And the buyer purchased her believing her to be of the breed represented by the sellers, and possessing all the qualities stated, and even more. He believed she would breed. There is no pretense that the plaintiff bought the cow for beef, and there is nothing in the record indicating that he would have bought her at all only that he thought she might be made to breed. Under the foregoing facts,—and these are all that are contained in the record material to the contract,—it is held that because it turned out that the plaintiff was more correct in his judgment as to one quality of the cow than the defendants, and a quality, too, which could not by any possibility be positively known at the time by either party to exist, the contract may be annulled by the defendants at their pleasure. I know of no law, and have not been referred to any, which will justify any such holding, and I think the circuit judge was right in his construction of the contract between the parties.

It is claimed that a mutual mistake of a material fact was made by the parties when the contract of sale was made. There was no warranty in the case of the quality of the animal. When a mistaken fact is relied upon as ground for rescinding, such fact must not only exist at the time the contract is made, but must have been known to one or both of the parties. Where there is no warranty, there can be no mistake of fact when no such fact exists, or, if in existence, neither party knew of it, or could know of it; and that is precisely this case. If the owner of a Hambletonian horse had speeded him, and was only able to make him go a mile in three minutes, and should sell him to another, believing that was his greatest speed, for $300, when the purchaser believed he could go much faster, and made the purchase for that sum, and a few days thereafter, under more favorable circumstances, the horse was driven a mile in 2 min. 16 sec., and was found to be worth $20,000, I hardly think it would be held, either at law or in equity, by any one, that the seller in such case could rescind the contract. The same legal principles apply in each case.

In this case neither party knew the actual quality and condition of this cow at the time of the sale. The defendants say, or rather said, to the plaintiff, "they had a few head left on their farm in Greenfield, and asked plaintiff to go and see them, stating to plaintiff that in all probability they were sterile and would not breed." Plaintiff did go as requested, and found there these cows, including the one purchased, with a bull. The cow had been exposed, but neither knew she was with calf or whether she would breed. The defendants thought she would not, but the plaintiff says that he thought she could be made to breed, but believed she was not with calf. The defendants sold the cow for what they believed her to be, and the plaintiff bought her as he believed she was, after the statements made by the defendants. No conditions whatever were attached to the terms of sale by either party. It was in fact as absolute as it could well be made, and I know of no precedent as authority by which this court can alter the contract thus made by these parties in writing,—interpolate in it a condition by which, if the defendants should be mistaken in their belief that the cow was barren, she could be returned to them and their contract should be annulled. It is not the duty of courts to destroy contracts when called upon to enforce them, after they have been legally made. There was no mistake of any material fact by either of the parties in the case as would license the vendors to rescind. There was no difference between the parties, nor misapprehension, as to the substance of the thing bargained for, which was a cow supposed to be barren by one party, and believed not to be by the other. As to the quality of the animal, subsequently developed, both parties were equally ignorant, and as to this each party took his chances. If this were not the law, there would be no safety in purchasing this kind of stock. * * *

I entirely agree with my brethren that the right to rescind occurs whenever "the thing actually delivered or received is different in substance from the thing bargained for, and intended to be sold; but if it be only a difference in some quality or accident, even though the misapprehension may have been the actuating motive" of the parties in making the contract, yet it will remain binding. In this case the cow sold was the one delivered. What might or might not happen to her after the sale formed no element in the contract. * * *

According to this record, whatever the mistake was, if any, in this case, it was upon the part of the defendants, and while acting upon their own judgment. It is, however, elementary law, and very elementary, too, "that the mistaken party, without any common understanding with the other party in the premises as to the quality of an animal, is remediless if he is injured through his own mistake." Leake, Cont. 338; *Torrance v. Bolton,* L.R. 8 Ch. 118; *Smith v. Hughes,* L.R. 6 Q.B. 597.

* * *

* * * In this case, if either party had superior knowledge as to the qualities of this animal to the other, certainly the defendants had such advantage. I understand the law to be well settled that "there is no breach of any implied confidence that one party will not profit by his superior knowledge as to facts and circumstances" actually within the knowledge of both, because neither party reposes in any such confidence unless it be specially tendered or required, and that a general sale does not imply warranty of any quality, or the absence of any; and if the seller represents to the purchaser what he himself believes as to the qualities of an animal, and the purchaser buys relying upon his own judgment as to such qualities, there is no warranty in the case, and neither has a cause of action against the other if he finds himself to have been mistaken in judgment.

* * * The judgment should be affirmed.

G. PALMER, MISTAKE AND UNJUST ENRICHMENT
95 (1962).

I find it most difficult to accept the statement of the majority of the court that the buyer, Sherwood, shared the mistake. Sherwood was a banker who also had a stock farm on which he raised purebred cattle. The whole sense of the matter suggested that he was not buying the purebred cow, known as Rose 2d of Aberlone, to fatten and sell for beef; rather, as a dissenting judge concluded, he thought there was a chance that Rose 2d would breed. This alone should have been enough to prevent Walker from insisting that Sherwood be held to Walker's mistaken assumption. In addition, if the dissenting judge was right on the facts, there probably was uncertainty as to a vital matter, since two men in the business had different opinions, with nothing in the circumstances to fairly prevent Sherwood from dealing on the basis of his own opinion.

Sherwood's state of mind does become important. If it were true that he shared Walker's erroneous belief, rescission of the sale would be proper. The gain would then be unanticipated, whereas, on the facts as found by the dissenting judge, it was within the range of the buyer's legitimate expectations.

WOOD v. BOYNTON, 64 Wis. 265, 25 N.W. 42 (1885). [Wood sold a small stone she had found, the value of which she did not know, for $1 to Boynton, the proprietor of a jewelry store. Later it was determined that the stone was a rough diamond worth about $700 and Wood sought return of the diamond. Boynton testified that at the time he bought the stone he had never seen an uncut diamond and had no idea the stone was a diamond.]

TAYLOR, J.

* * *

* * * The only question in the case is whether there was anything in the sale which entitled the vendor (the appellant) to rescind the sale and so revest the title in her. The only reasons we know of for rescinding a sale and revesting the title in the vendor so that he may maintain an action at law for the recovery of the possession against his vendee are (1) that the vendee was guilty of some fraud in procuring a sale to be made to him; (2) that there was a mistake made by the vendor in delivering an article which was not the article sold,—a mistake in fact as to the identity of the thing sold with the thing delivered upon the sale. This last is not in reality a rescission of the sale made, as the thing delivered was not the thing sold, and no title ever passed to the vendee by such delivery.

In this case, upon the plaintiff's own evidence, there can be no just ground for alleging that she was induced to make the sale she did by any fraud or unfair dealings on the part of Mr. Boynton. Both were entirely ignorant at the time of the character of the stone and of its intrinsic value. Mr. Boynton was not an expert in uncut diamonds, and had made no examination of the stone, except to take it in his hand and look at it before he made the offer of one dollar, which was refused at the time, and afterwards accepted without any comment or further examination made by Mr. Boynton. The appellant had the stone in her possession for a long time, and it appears from her own statement that she had made some inquiry as to its nature and qualities. If she chose to sell it without further investigation as to its intrinsic value to a person who was guilty of no fraud or unfairness which induced her to sell it for a small sum, she cannot repudiate the sale because it is afterwards ascertained that she made a bad bargain. *Kennedy v. Panama, etc., Mail Co.*, L.R. 2 Q.B. 580. There is no pretense of any mistake as to the identity of the thing sold. It was produced by the plaintiff and exhibited to the vendee before the sale was made, and the thing sold was delivered to the vendee when the purchase price was paid. * * * Suppose the appellant had produced the stone, and said she had been told it was a diamond, and she believed it was, but had no knowledge herself as to its character or value, and Mr. Boynton had given her $500 for it, could he have rescinded the sale if it had turned out to be a topaz or any other stone of very small value? Could Mr. Boynton have rescinded the sale on the ground of mistake? Clearly not, nor could he rescind it on the ground that there had been a breach of warranty, because there was no warranty, nor could he rescind it on the ground of fraud, unless he could show that she falsely declared that she had been told it was a diamond, or, if she had been so told, still she knew it was not a diamond.

* * *

The judgment of the circuit court is affirmed.

Problem 8–1

(1) Suppose Boynton had known that the stone was a diamond. Did Boynton have a duty to disclose that information? Reconsider the materials in Section Three of Chapter Five.

(2) These facts are based on an actual episode at Cornell University. The Cornell Veterinary School sold a Holstein breeder cow, weighing 2300 pounds, for $1.2 million to a farm in upstate New York. Soon after the farm took delivery, the cow died of a genetic disorder. Neither Cornell nor the buyer had reason to know of the disease at the time of the sale. The buyer wants its money back. Please advise Cornell of the likely result under the doctrine of Sherwood v. Walker.

(3) These facts are also true. A New York farmer hired Michael Stone for $65 to clean some pens and wash some cows at the State Fair. While performing the work, Stone became fond of a newborn calf and proposed to take the calf instead of receiving the $65. The farmer told Stone that the calf was not worth $65, but agreed to the proposition. Six years later, the calf, named Jacob, is a top breeder bull whose semen is marketed for $1.2 million per year. At the time of the original deal, no one realized that Jacob's father was himself a superior breeder. Does the farm have any legal rights against Stone?

LENAWEE COUNTY BOARD OF HEALTH v. MESSERLY

Supreme Court of Michigan, 1982.
417 Mich. 17, 331 N.W.2d 203.

RYAN, JUSTICE.

In March of 1977, Carl and Nancy Pickles, appellees, purchased from appellants, William and Martha Messerly, a 600–square-foot tract of land upon which is located a three-unit apartment building. Shortly after the transaction was closed, the Lenawee County Board of Health condemned the property and obtained a permanent injunction which prohibits human habitation on the premises until the defective sewage system is brought into conformance with the Lenawee County sanitation code.

We are required to determine whether appellees should prevail in their attempt to avoid this land contract on the basis of mutual mistake and failure of consideration. We conclude that the parties did entertain a mutual misapprehension of fact, but that the circumstances of this case do not warrant rescission.

I

The facts of the case are not seriously in dispute. In 1971, the Messerlys acquired approximately one acre plus 600 square feet of land. A three-unit apartment building was situated upon the 600–square-foot portion. The trial court found that, prior to this transfer, the Messerlys' predecessor in title, Mr. Bloom, had installed a septic tank on the property without a permit and in violation of the applicable health code. The Messerlys used the building as an income investment property until 1973 when they sold it, upon land contract, to James Barnes who likewise used it primarily as an income-producing investment.[1]

Mr. and Mrs. Barnes, with the permission of the Messerlys, sold approximately one acre of the property in 1976, and the remaining 600 square feet and building were offered for sale soon thereafter when Mr. and Mrs. Barnes defaulted on their land contract. Mr. and Mrs. Pickles evidenced an interest in the property, but were dissatisfied with the terms of the Barnes–Messerly land contract. Consequently, to accommodate the Pickleses' preference to enter into a land contract directly with the Messerlys, Mr. and Mrs. Barnes executed a quitclaim deed which conveyed their interest in the property back to the Messerlys. After inspecting the property, Mr. and Mrs. Pickles executed a new land contract with the Messerlys on March 21, 1977. It provided for a purchase price of $25,500. A clause was added to the end of the land contract form which provides:

> "17. Purchaser has examined this property and agrees to accept same in its present condition. There are no other or additional written or oral understandings."

Five or six days later, when the Pickleses went to introduce themselves to the tenants, they discovered raw sewage seeping out of the ground. Tests conducted by a sanitation expert indicated the inadequacy of the sewage system. The Lenawee County Board of Health subsequently condemned the property and initiated this lawsuit in the Lenawee Circuit Court against the Messerlys as land contract vendors, and the Pickleses, as vendees, to obtain a permanent injunction proscribing human habitation of the premises until the property was brought into conformance with the Lenawee County sanitation code. The injunction was granted, and the Lenawee County Board of Health was permitted to withdraw from the lawsuit by stipulation of the parties.

When no payments were made on the land contract, the Messerlys filed a cross-complaint against the Pickleses seeking foreclosure, sale of the property, and a deficiency judgment. Mr. and Mrs. Pickles then counterclaimed for rescission against the Messerlys, and filed a third-party complaint against the Barneses, which incorporated, by reference, the allegations of the counterclaim against the Messerlys. In count one, Mr. and Mrs. Pickles alleged failure of consideration. Count two charged Mr. and Mrs. Barnes with willful conceal-

---

1. James Barnes was married shortly after he purchased the property. Mr. and Mrs. Barnes lived in one of the apartments on the property for three months and, after they moved, Mrs. Barnes continued to aid in the management of the property.

ment and misrepresentation as a result of their failure to disclose the condition of the sanitation system. Additionally, Mr. and Mrs. Pickles sought to hold the Messerlys liable in equity for the Barneses' alleged misrepresentation. The Pickleses prayed that the land contract be rescinded.

After a bench trial, the court concluded that the Pickleses had no cause of action against either the Messerlys or the Barneses as there was no fraud or misrepresentation. This ruling was predicated on the trial judge's conclusion that none of the parties knew of Mr. Bloom's earlier transgression or of the resultant problem with the septic system until it was discovered by the Pickleses, and that the sanitation problem was not caused by any of the parties. The trial court held that the property was purchased "as is", after inspection and, accordingly, its "negative * * * value cannot be blamed upon an innocent seller". Foreclosure was ordered against the Pickleses, together with a judgment against them in the amount of $25,943.09.[2]

Mr. and Mrs. Pickles appealed from the adverse judgment. The Court of Appeals unanimously affirmed the trial court's ruling with respect to Mr. and Mrs. Barnes but, in a two-to-one decision, reversed the finding of no cause of action on the Pickleses' claims against the Messerlys. *Lenawee County Board of Health v. Messerly,* 98 Mich.App. 478, 295 N.W.2d 903 (1980). It concluded that the mutual mistake[3] between the Messerlys and the Pickleses went to a basic, as opposed to a collateral, element of the contract,[4] and that the parties intended to transfer income-producing rental property but, in actuality, the vendees paid $25,500 for an asset without value.[5]

We granted the Messerlys' application for leave to appeal. 411 Mich. 900 (1981).[6]

II

We must decide initially whether there was a mistaken belief entertained by one or both parties to the contract in dispute and, if so, the resultant legal significance.

A contractual mistake "is a belief that is not in accord with the facts". 1 Restatement Contracts, 2d, § 151, p. 383. The erroneous belief of one or both of the parties must relate to a fact in existence at the time the contract is

2. The parties stipulated that this amount was due on the land contract, assuming that the contract was valid and enforceable.

3. Mr. and Mrs. Pickles did not allege mutual mistake as a ground for rescission in their pleadings. However, the trial court characterized their failure of consideration argument as mutual mistake resulting in failure of consideration. Recognizing a potential difficulty in reversing the trial court on an issue not raised by the pleadings, the Court of Appeals devoted a footnote to an explanation of its decision to consider the mutual mistake argument. * * *

4. Mr. and Mrs. Pickles did not appeal the trial court's finding that there was no fraud or misrepresentation by the Messerlys or Mr. and Mrs. Barnes. Likewise, the propriety of that ruling is not before this Court today.

5. The trial court found that the only way that the property could be put to residential use would be to pump and haul the sewage, a method which is economically unfeasible, as the cost of such a disposal system amounts to double the income generated by the property. There was speculation by the trial court that the adjoining land might be utilized to make the property suitable for residential use, but, in the absence of testimony directed at that point, the court refused to draw any conclusions. The trial court and the Court of Appeals both found that the property was valueless, or had a negative value.

6. The Court of Appeals decision to affirm the trial court's finding of no cause of action against Mr. and Mrs. Barnes has not been appealed to this Court and, accordingly, the propriety of that ruling is not before us today.

executed. *Richardson Lumber Co. v. Hoey,* 219 Mich. 643, 189 N.W. 923 (1922); *Sherwood v. Walker,* 66 Mich. 568, 580, 33 N.W. 919 (1887) (Sherwood, J., dissenting). That is to say, the belief which is found to be in error may not be, in substance, a prediction as to a future occurrence or non-occurrence. *Henry v. Thomas,* 241 Ga. 360, 245 S.E.2d 646 (1978); *Hailpern v. Dryden,* 154 Colo. 231, 389 P.2d 590 (1964). But see *Denton v. Utley,* 350 Mich. 332, 86 N.W.2d 537 (1957).

The Court of Appeals concluded, after a *de novo* review of the record, that the parties were mistaken as to the income-producing capacity of the property in question. 98 Mich.App. 487–488, 295 N.W.2d 903. We agree. The vendors and the vendees each believed that the property transferred could be utilized as income-generating rental property. All of the parties subsequently learned that, in fact, the property was unsuitable for any residential use.

Appellants assert that there was no mistake in the contractual sense because the defect in the sewage system did not arise until after the contract was executed. The appellees respond that the Messerlys are confusing the date of the inception of the defect with the date upon which the defect was discovered.

* * *

An examination of the record reveals that the septic system was defective prior to the date on which the land contract was executed. The Messerlys' grantor installed a nonconforming septic system without a permit prior to the transfer of the property to the Messerlys in 1971. Moreover, virtually undisputed testimony indicates that, assuming ideal soil conditions, 2,500 square feet of property is necessary to support a sewage system adequate to serve a three-family dwelling. Likewise, 750 square feet is mandated for a one-family home. Thus, the division of the parcel and sale of one acre of the property by Mr. and Mrs. Barnes in 1976 made it impossible to remedy the already illegal septic system within the confines of the 600–square-foot parcel.[7]

Appellants do not dispute these underlying facts which give rise to an inference contrary to their contentions.

Having determined that when these parties entered into the land contract they were laboring under a mutual mistake of fact, we now direct our attention to a determination of the legal significance of that finding.

A contract may be rescinded because of a mutual misapprehension of the parties, but this remedy is granted only in the sound discretion of the court. *Harris v. Axline,* 323 Mich. 585, 36 N.W.2d 154 (1949). Appellants argue that the parties' mistake relates only to the quality or value of the real estate transferred, and that such mistakes are collateral to the agreement and do not justify rescission, citing *A & M Land Development Co. v. Miller,* 354 Mich. 681, 94 N.W.2d 197 (1959).

---

7. It is crucial to distinguish between the date on which a belief relating to a particular fact or set of facts becomes erroneous due to a change in the fact, and the date on which the mistaken nature of the belief is discovered. By definition, a mistake cannot be discovered until after the contract is executed. If the parties were aware, prior to the execution of a contract, that they were in error concerning a particular fact, there would be no misapprehension in signing the contract. Thus stated, it becomes obvious that the date on which a mistaken fact manifests itself is irrelevant to the determination whether or not there was a mistake.

In that case, the plaintiff was the purchaser of 91 lots of real property. It sought partial rescission of the land contract when it was frustrated in its attempts to develop 42 of the lots because it could not obtain permits from the county health department to install septic tanks on these lots. This Court refused to allow rescission because the mistake, whether mutual or unilateral, related only to the value of the property.

> "There was here no mistake as to the form or substance of the contract between the parties, or the description of the property constituting the subject matter. * * * In the case at bar plaintiff received the property for which it contracted. The fact that it may be of less value than the purchaser expected at the time of the transaction is not a sufficient basis for the granting of equitable relief, neither fraud nor reliance on misrepresentation of material facts having been established." 354 Mich. 693–694, 94 N.W.2d 197.

Appellees contend, on the other hand, that in this case the parties were mistaken as to the very nature of the character of the consideration and claim that the pervasive and essential quality of this mistake renders rescission appropriate. They cite in support of that view *Sherwood v. Walker,* 66 Mich. 568, 33 N.W. 919 (1887), the famous "barren cow" case. In that case, the parties agreed to the sale and purchase of a cow which was thought to be barren, but which was, in reality, with calf. When the seller discovered the fertile condition of his cow, he refused to deliver her. * * *

As the parties suggest, the foregoing precedent arguably distinguishes mistakes affecting the essence of the consideration from those which go to its quality or value, affording relief on a per se basis for the former but not the latter. See, *e.g., Lenawee County Board of Health v. Messerly,* 98 Mich.App. 478, 492, 295 N.W.2d 903 (1980) (Mackenzie, J., concurring in part).

However, the distinctions which may be drawn from *Sherwood* and *A & M Land Development Co.* do not provide a satisfactory analysis of the nature of a mistake sufficient to invalidate a contract. Often, a mistake relates to an underlying factual assumption which, when discovered, directly affects value, but simultaneously and materially affects the essence of the contractual consideration. It is disingenuous to label such a mistake collateral. *McKay v. Coleman,* 85 Mich. 60, 48 N.W. 203 (1891). Corbin, Contracts (One Vol. ed.), § 605, p. 551.

Appellant and appellee both mistakenly believed that the property which was the subject of their land contract would generate income as rental property. The fact that it could not be used for human habitation deprived the property of its income-earning potential and rendered it less valuable. However, this mistake, while directly and dramatically affecting the property's value, cannot accurately be characterized as collateral because it also affects the very essence of the consideration. "The thing sold and bought [income generating rental property] had in fact no existence". *Sherwood v. Walker,* 66 Mich. 578, 33 N.W. 919.

We find that the inexact and confusing distinction between contractual mistakes running to value and those touching the substance of the consideration serves only as an impediment to a clear and helpful analysis for the equitable resolution of cases in which mistake is alleged and proven. Accordingly, the holdings of *A & M Land Development Co.* and *Sherwood* with respect to the material or collateral nature of a mistake are limited to the facts of those cases.

Instead, we think the better-reasoned approach is a case-by-case analysis whereby rescission is indicated when the mistaken belief relates to a basic assumption of the parties upon which the contract is made, and which materially affects the agreed performances of the parties. *Denton v. Utley,* 350 Mich. 332, 86 N.W.2d 537 (1957); *Farhat v. Rassey,* 295 Mich. 349, 294 N.W. 707 (1940); *Richardson Lumber Co. v. Hoey,* 219 Mich. 643, 189 N.W. 923 (1922). 1 Restatement Contracts, 2d, § 152, p. 385–386. Rescission is not available, however, to relieve a party who has assumed the risk of loss in connection with the mistake. *Denton v. Utley,* 350 Mich. 344–345, 86 N.W.2d 537 * * *.

All of the parties to this contract erroneously assumed that the property transferred by the vendors to the vendees was suitable for human habitation and could be utilized to generate rental income. The fundamental nature of these assumptions is indicated by the fact that their invalidity changed the character of the property transferred, thereby frustrating, indeed precluding, Mr. and Mrs. Pickles' intended use of the real estate. Although the Pickleses are disadvantaged by enforcement of the contract, performance is advantageous to the Messerlys, as the property at issue is less valuable absent its income-earning potential. Nothing short of rescission can remedy the mistake. Thus, the parties' mistake as to a basic assumption materially affects the agreed performances of the parties.

Despite the significance of the mistake made by the parties, we reverse the Court of Appeals because we conclude that equity does not justify the remedy sought by Mr. and Mrs. Pickles.

Rescission is an equitable remedy which is granted only in the sound discretion of the court. *Harris v. Axline,* 323 Mich. 585, 36 N.W.2d 154 (1949); *Hathaway v. Hudson,* 256 Mich. 694, 239 N.W. 859 (1932). A court need not grant rescission in every case in which the mutual mistake relates to a basic assumption and materially affects the agreed performance of the parties.

In cases of mistake by two equally innocent parties, we are required, in the exercise of our equitable powers, to determine which blameless party should assume the loss resulting from the misapprehension they shared.[8] Normally that can only be done by drawing upon our "own notions of what is reasonable and just under all the surrounding circumstances".[9]

Equity suggests that, in this case, the risk should be allocated to the purchasers. We are guided to that conclusion, in part, by the standards announced in § 154 of the Restatement of Contracts 2d, for determining when a party bears the risk of mistake. * * * Section 154(a) suggests that the court should look first to whether the parties have agreed to the allocation of

8. This risk-of-loss analysis is absent in both *A & M Land Development Co.* and *Sherwood,* and this omission helps to explain, in part, the disparate treatment in the two cases. Had such an inquiry been undertaken in *Sherwood,* we believe that the result might have been different. Moreover, a determination as to which party assumed the risk in *A & M Land Development Co.* would have alleviated the need to characterize the mistake as collateral so as to justify the result denying rescission. Despite the absence of any inquiry as to the assumption of risk in those two leading cases, we find that there exists sufficient precedent to warrant such an analysis in future cases of mistake.

9. *Hathaway v. Hudson,* 256 Mich. 702, 239 N.W. 859, quoting 9 C.J., p. 1161.

the risk between themselves. While there is no express assumption in the contract by either party of the risk of the property becoming uninhabitable, there was indeed some agreed allocation of the risk to the vendees by the incorporation of an "as is" clause into the contract which, we repeat, provided:

"Purchaser has examined this property and agrees to accept same in its present condition. There are no other or additional written or oral understandings."

That is a persuasive indication that the parties considered that, as between them, such risk as related to the "present condition" of the property should lie with the purchaser. If the "as is" clause is to have any meaning at all, it must be interpreted to refer to those defects which were unknown at the time that the contract was executed.[10] Thus, the parties themselves assigned the risk of loss to Mr. and Mrs. Pickles.

We conclude that Mr. and Mrs. Pickles are not entitled to the equitable remedy of rescission and, accordingly, reverse the decision the Court of Appeals.

BRIEF OF DEFENDANT–APPELLANTS—PICKLES TO THE COURT OF APPEALS OF MICHIGAN

10–11, 24–27.

The property involved here had been utilized by Defendants Messerlys and Cross–Defendants Barnes as a three-unit apartment house, and prior to the sale to Pickles it was listed and advertised as such and was sold and purchased as an income property. Neither Messerlys, Barnes nor Pickles were aware at the time the land contract was executed that the property in question, the subject matter of the contract, was unfit and uninhabitable for humans.

Mr. and Mrs. Messerly and the Barnes, as evidenced by their listing of the property, thought they were selling a three-unit apartment house. The Pickles, by undisputed testimony, thought they were purchasing an income property. When the parties later learned that the property in question was absolutely devoid of any value, unfit for human habitation, it became apparent that both Buyer and Seller had been mistaken as to the nature and character of the subject matter of the contract.

Michigan courts have consistently held that mutual mistake constitutes a ground for rescission of a contract. * * *

* * *

Paragraph 17 of the Land Contract in question reads:

"Purchaser has examined this property and agrees to accept same in its present condition. There are no other or additional written or oral understandings."

---

10. An "as is" clause waives those implied warranties which accompany the sale of a new home, *Tibbitts v. Openshaw*, 18 Utah 2d 442, 425 P.2d 160 (1967), or the sale of goods. M.C.L. § 440.2316(3)(a); M.S.A. § 19.2316(3)(a). Since implied warranties pro- tect against latent defects, an "as is" clause will impose upon the purchaser the assumption of the risk of latent defects, such as an inadequate sanitation system, even when there are no implied warranties.

At trial, both the Messerlys and Barnes urged that such a provision appearing in the contract estopped the Pickles from relief in the form of rescission. The trial Judge noted in his opinion that the Pickles bought the subject property "as is".

Defendants–Appellants Pickles would respectfully disagree with the Court's conclusion that the sale was on an "as is" basis. A reasonable construction of the plain language utilized in Paragraph 17 reveals only that the Pickles agreed to accept the property in its present condition, premised upon their having inspected the parcel. Thus, it appears that the practical effect of Paragraph 17 is to charge the Purchaser merely with reasonable inspection of the premises.

* * *

The Court in the present case specifically found that the Pickles conducted a physical examination and inspection of the premises and interviewed tenants of the apartment house. It therefore appears that the Pickles satisfied that duty imposed upon them by Paragraph 17 of the contract and agreed to accept the property subject to conditions that would have been revealed by reasonable inspection. As to defects not discoverable through such inspection, there is no estoppel under the terms of Paragraph 17.

* * *

In summary, under the terms of the contract involved here, the Pickles are only estopped from complaining of conditions which would have been revealed by reasonable inspection. The record in this case is clear, the Pickles did conduct a reasonable examination and inspection and the condition complained of here could not have been discovered through such inspection. This is evidenced by the fact that the Barnes and Messerlys had owned and had contact with the tenants for a number of years. The Pickles, it is clear, could not have discovered in one or two inspections a condition which had not come to the attention of the Barnes or Messerlys over a period of years.

Problem 8–2

Turlway, president of Ajax Construction Co., comes to your law office with the following problem. Ajax was the successful bidder for the construction of New City's police headquarters. Ajax began the project on July 18, 1978 and the agreed completion date was August 6, 1980. Ajax actually completed the project on August 5, 1983, at a cost over twice the projected amount. Turlway explains that Ajax's excavation work was delayed because it encountered solid rock that required difficult and time-consuming blasting. The rock covered 45% of the excavation site. Turlway points out that the plans and specifications furnished to prospective bidders by New City contained information on test soil borings performed by the City. These test borings, concededly accurate, showed no rock under the planned construction area because only three such borings were taken and because the borings were not located over the rock area. Most plans and specifications of a project of this size contained at least ten test borings. Turlway believes that the plans and specifications were accurate as to all other points. Before submitting its bid, Ajax took seven additional test borings of its own, which also failed to discover the rock.

The contract between Ajax and New City contains the following pertinent term:

Article 4.16:

The Bidder must ascertain for itself all of the facts concerning conditions to be found at the site of this project including all physical characteristics below the ground surface. The Bidder promises to make all necessary investigations relating to site conditions and the City assumes no responsibility whatsoever with respect to ascertaining for the Bidder such facts concerning physical characteristics at the site of the Project. The Contractor agrees that he will make no claim for additional payment or extension of time for completion of the work because of failure to fully acquaint itself with all conditions relating to the work.

Is Ajax entitled to any additional compensation resulting from the soil conditions?

NOROSKI v. FALLET

Supreme Court of Ohio, 1982.
2 Ohio St.3d 77, 442 N.E.2d 1302.

On September 25, 1975, an auto accident occurred on State Route 19 outside Oak Harbor, involving Frank E. Noroski, plaintiff-appellant and Ervin C. Fallet, defendant-appellee. As a result of the collision, plaintiff experienced back pain, causing him to incur medical expenses and lost wages. On October 10, an adjuster for defendant's insurer, the Celina Mutual Insurance Company, contacted plaintiff by phone to discuss the loss suffered in the accident. Upon determining that plaintiff incurred $429.76 in property damage, the adjuster mailed plaintiff a draft for $454.76, which included an allowance of $25 to cover the anticipated medical expense of x-rays. Along with the check, a release form was sent for plaintiff to sign and return. However, he neither signed the release nor deposited the check.

On December 3, 1975, plaintiff mailed to the insurer copies of medical bills totalling $119.10, and a copy of the uncashed check. On December 31, plaintiff and the adjuster held another telephone conversation, parts of which were taped with plaintiff's consent. As a result of this conversation, the insurer mailed plaintiff a draft for $299.64, all but $100 of which constituted agreed upon property damage and medical expenses. Nothing appeared on the check to indicate that it constituted a complete settlement and release of all claims. Plaintiff then cashed both the first and second checks, which totalled $754.40.

Thereafter, plaintiff incurred substantial additional medical expenses and lost wages, which the insurer refused to pay. A complaint was brought, and defendant raised the affirmative defense of full and complete settlement of the claim. The trial court ordered bifurcation of the issue of the affirmative defense from those of negligence and damages, and conducted a hearing on the matter without benefit of a jury. Testimony concerning the December 31, 1975 conversation was heard, and the tape recording was played for the court. The trial court held that although the insurance adjuster failed to follow the company's prescribed procedure for a telephone release, the recorded telephone conversation constituted a valid and enforceable release of all claims arising from the September 25, 1975 accident, and granted judgment to defendant on the complaint.

The court of appeals affirmed, and the cause is now before this court upon the allowance of a motion to certify the record.

PER CURIAM.

The only evidence of the release at issue here is a tape recording of a telephone conversation between appellant and the adjuster for appellee's insurer. That conversation appears in the record as two exhibits: the first an eight-page transcription regarding the facts surrounding the accident, and the second a one-page transcription, apparently from the same telephone conversation, which purports to be the recorded settlement agreement. That conversation, as transcribed, was as follows:

"This is JEANNE CAMPBELL speaking: I am discussing settlement of a claim with MR. FRANK NOROSKI regarding his collision of September 25, 1975 in Oak Harbor, Ohio. This involved ERVIN FALLET as our insured.

"Q. Mr. Noroski would you please state your full name and address once again?

"A. Frank Edward Noroski, 117 Center Street, Apt. 6, Oak Harbor, Ohio 43449.

"Q. Do you realize I am recording this agreement and do I have your permission to do so?

"A. Yes.

"Q. Do you agree that the draft I will be sending you in the total amount of $754.40 is the full and complete settlement for your bodily injuries as well as the property damage resulting from this accident?

"A. Yes.

"S. [sic] Okay this concludes the recorded settlement with Mr. Frank Noroski."

The issue before the court is whether the recorded telephone conversation relied upon by appellee constitutes a valid and enforceable release. A release, or compromise agreement, is a particular kind of contract, and, like other contracts, requires a definite offer and an acceptance thereof. 15 Ohio Jurisprudence 3d 517, Compromise, Accord, and Release, Section 4. A release must be the result of a meeting of the parties' minds in order to be binding. See 30 Ohio Jurisprudence 2d 801, Insurance, Section 875. While this court has previously recognized that an oral settlement agreement requires no more formality and not greater particularity than appears in the law for the formation of a binding contract, see *Spercel v. Sterling Industries* (1972), 31 Ohio St.2d 36, 39, 285 N.E.2d 324, neither can less formality and less particularity be countenanced when an oral release is brought before the court for enforcement.

The law is clear that to constitute a valid contract, there must be a meeting of the minds of the parties, and there must be an offer on the one side and an acceptance on the other. * * * Our examination of the record and the facts surrounding the purported release leads us to the conclusion that no meeting of the minds occurred in this case. The conversation which appellee seeks to interpose as an affirmative defense contains no reference to the term "release," speaking instead of "full and complete settlement." Bearing in mind that appellant, a civil engineer, had little familiarity with the legal ramifications of "settlement" or "release," his testimony concerning his understanding of the December 31 telephone conversation is elucidating:

> "A: * * * the next time I believe I talked to her, which was December 31st, there were medical claims and I am not totally naive of what complications can come out of a back injury but at that time I wasn't about to settle under any conditions because there was the possibility of future medical problems and I thought I addressed that to her very clearly.
>
> " * * *
>
> "A: Well again with that conversation in December, I left her, I believe, with the impression that these were bills that I accrued to that date, that I didn't plan on spending any time in the hospital and I hadn't planned on any major surgery and that I had no intentions of racking up hundreds of dollars in bills and sending to her every couple of months. And that I would, in fact, get a hold of her if I felt things were going to get serious and I really had no intention of getting to this point and that I wanted to leave the thing open just in case.
>
> " * * *
>
> "A: Well, my understanding [of the effect of the unsigned written release previously mailed to plaintiff] would be that I would have to sign a release, that is a piece of paper that said release in order that I wouldn't have any recourse in the future and that is what I honestly believed was the understanding at that time."

This testimony indicates that appellant never understood his conversation to constitute a release of present *and all future* claims arising out of the accident. Moreover, the draft sent to appellant as a result of this conversation contained no indication that it constituted a release. Testimony indicated that the insurer's standard operating procedure for all oral releases included stamping release wording on the reverse side of the draft. The failure to stamp such a release on this draft further indicates that no release was intended. Finally, the piecemeal manner in which the recorded statement was made by the adjuster renders unavailable further clarifying statements concerning the meaning of the purported release which may have been made in the conversation.

Given the imprecise language contained in the recorded statement, appellant's testimony concerning his understanding of the conversation and his previous refusal to sign a printed release form, together with the failure of the insurer to take action consistent with a release and the absence of a verified context in which the statements were made, we hold that no meeting of the minds occurred during the telephone conversation of December 31 sufficient to constitute a binding release of claims. Accordingly, the lower courts erred in dismissing the complaint, and the cause is remanded for further proceedings.

Judgment reversed and cause remanded.

CELEBREZZE, C.J. and W. BROWN, C. BROWN and SWEENEY, JJ., concur.

LOCHER, HOLMES and KRUPANSKY, JJ., dissent.

HOLMES, JUSTICE, dissenting.

* * *

It would appear that there was a proper quantum of evidence to show the existence of a contract of release between the parties. * * *

As to the question of mistake in the entering of the release of December 31, 1975, the appellant takes the position that such a release was for the known extent of the injuries and the medical bills and expenses at that time. He states that his injuries turned out to be more serious than he had anticipated, and his resulting costs much greater. However unfortunate the result may appear for the appellant, it still remains a fact that a release had been entered into by the parties, and a later discovery of a mistake of fact by one of the parties will offer no ground for the setting aside of the release.

Accordingly, I would affirm the judgment of the court of appeals.

LOCHER AND KRUPANSKY, JJ., concur in the foregoing dissenting opinion.

Comments and Questions

1. What result in Noroski v. Fallet if the insurance company had followed all proper procedures—i.e., it had prepared a signed release expressly stating that Noroski released all future claims arising out of the accident? Could Noroski claim mutual material mistake?

2. In a letter to the editors, Fallet's lawyer stated:

> What strikes me as being of particular significance in this case, and which is difficult for laymen to comprehend, is that a total of eleven judges reviewed the evidence in this case—one Common Pleas judge, three judges on the Court of Appeals, and the seven justices of the Ohio Supreme Court. Presumably, all are applying the same legal principles to the same set of facts. Yet, seven of the judges felt there was a valid and binding release which terminated the plaintiff's ability to further prosecute a personal injury claim against the defendant. A minority of four of the judges, who unfortunately for my client, comprised the majority of the seven Ohio Supreme Court justices, felt there was no contract whatsoever because there was no meeting of the minds.

> Thus, this case is a good object lesson to clients as to the uncertainties of litigation (as well as perhaps providing comfort to law students who felt that *their* examination answers were also correct).

3. CNN's website reported on April 5, 2006, that Smith (a fictitious name), infected with AIDS and suffering from AIDS related cancer, entered a contract in 1994 with Life Partners. Life Partners bought Smith's $150,000 life insurance policy in return for $90,000 and a promise to pay her life and health insurance premiums if she lived more than two years. At Smith's death, Life Partners would recover the full $150,000 from the policy.

Some twelve years later, Smith is still alive, thanks to new medicines that fight the ravages of AIDS, but which were not yet discovered in 1994. Life Partners has already paid $100,000 in premiums (plus the initial $90,000 to

Smith) and faces premiums of $29,000 per year. Life Partners wants to stop paying. Does it have any legal rights?

RESTATEMENT (SECOND) OF CONTRACTS § 152.

When Mistake of Both Parties Makes a Contract Voidable

(1) Where a mistake of both parties at the time a contract was made as to a basic assumption on which the contract was made has a material effect on the agreed exchange of performances, the contract is voidable by the adversely affected party unless he bears the risk of the mistake under the rule stated in § 154.

(2) In determining whether the mistake has a material effect on the agreed exchange of performances, account is taken of any relief by way of reformation, restitution, or otherwise.

RESTATEMENT (SECOND) OF CONTRACTS § 154.

When A Party Bears The Risk of A Mistake

A party bears the risk of a mistake when

(a) the risk is allocated to him by agreement of the parties, or

(b) he is aware, at the time the contract is made, that he has only limited knowledge with respect to the facts to which the mistake relates but treats his limited knowledge as sufficient, or

(c) the risk is allocated to him by the court on the ground that it is reasonable in the circumstances to do so.

G. PALMER, MISTAKE AND UNJUST ENRICHMENT

36, 37, 38–39 (1962).

When mistake in assumptions occurs, the context that shaped the making of the agreement is seen to be false, and if the discrepancy is radical the policies favoring enforcement of the contract lose much of their force. They may finally be overbalanced by hardship to one party or enrichment of the other. * * *

* * * In most cases permitting rescission for mistake, a serious lack of equivalence appears. The apparent equilibrium of the transaction is upset, and there is enrichment in its most obvious form if the one who is harmed is held to his promise or denied restitution. The mistake may either lessen the value he was to receive or enhance the value he was to give.

* * *

The recognition of unjust enrichment as a principal reason for giving relief for mistake in basic assumptions has come slowly in our law. Even today the problems are often discussed with little or no reference to this factor. This is not to say that unjust enrichment is always essential to relief, for later discussion will disclose occasional instances of rescission without regard to enrichment. Nonetheless, it is the idea that brings most of the cases together. I am using unjust enrichment to mean lack of economic equivalence, attributable to the mistake. * * *

The nature of the mistake interacts with the factor of enrichment in ways that cannot be charted. It is reasonably clear that the extent of enrichment required for relief may vary with the nature of the mistake, the type of transaction, the stage of performance reached, and many other factors. Attempts to put the required discrepancy in reasonably precise quantitative terms are not likely to succeed, except possibly in some well-defined class of cases such as a shortage of acreage in the sale of land. Even there, statements that the shortage must be at least 50 per cent to warrant rescission have not proved reliable. Almost inevitably, one turns to a discussion of the relation of the mistake to the transaction, and especially to its terms—but with a warning that the amount of enrichment remains as an element to be taken into account.

Problem 8–3

The following facts are true. They are taken from Siegel v. National Comics Publications, Supreme Court, Westchester County, 1099–1947 (unreported). In 1933, Jerome Siegel "conceived the idea of a cartoon strip, the feature character of which would be a man of superhuman strength and power who would perform feats of great magnitude for the public good." Together with Joseph Shuster, an artist, Siegel produced the first Superman comic strip.

In 1938, Detective Comics, Inc. sought material for a new publication, "Action Comics." It learned of the Superman strip, still unpublished after rejection by a major newspaper syndicate. Detective Comics had previously purchased other comics from Siegel and Shuster at the rate of $10 per page. Detective Comics and Siegel and Shuster agreed that the latter two would produce a "thirteen page production" of Superman for the first issue of Action Comics.

On March 1, 1938, Detective Comics sent a check to Siegel for $130 for the thirteen page Superman strip. Detective Comics also enclosed the following contract:

Detective Comics, Inc.

480 Lexington Avenue

New York, N.Y.

    I, the undersigned, am an artist or author and have performed work for strip entitled 'Superman'.

    In consideration of $130 agreed to be paid me by you, I hereby sell and transfer such work and strip, all good will attached thereto and exclusive right to the use of the characters and story, continuity and title of strip contained therein, to you and your assigns to have and hold forever and to be your exclusive property and I agree not to employ said characters or said story in any other strips or sell any like strip or story containing the same characters by their names contained therein or under any other names at any time hereafter to any other person, firm or corporation, or permit the use thereof by said other parties, without obtaining your written consent therefor.

    The intent hereof is to give you exclusive right to use and acknowledge that you own said characters or story and the use thereof exclusive. I have received the above sum of money.

Siegel and Shuster signed the contract.

In 1947, after a spectacular growth in popularity of the "man of steel," Siegel and Shuster sought to avoid the above and other contracts in which they had transferred all their rights in Superman. By that time, Detective Comics had substantially increased the rate per page paid to the authors, but insisted that the above contract was enforceable.

Assume you represent Siegel and Shuster. At stake are millions of dollars. What arguments will you make in their behalf? What are the strengths and weaknesses of your clients' case?

SHRUM v. ZELTWANGER

Supreme Court of Wyoming, 1977.
559 P.2d 1384.

RAPER, JUSTICE.

What is a "cow?" This appeal comes here as an ultimate result of a dispute between plaintiffs-appellees contract buyers and defendants-appellants contract sellers of 134 "cows," over the answer to that question. The trial judge granted summary judgment to the plaintiffs for return of $6,700.00 they paid as a deposit on purchase of the cows and by the same summary action denied defendants' counterclaim. We will hold that summary judgment was improvidently granted, reverse and remand for trial of genuine issues of fact.

* * *

One significant fact is not in dispute. The parties entered into a written agreement as follows:

"Aug. 3, 1973

"LIVESTOCK BILL OF SALE AND CONTRACT

"This Certifies, that <u>Howard Shrum</u> of <u>Sheridan</u> has this day bargained and sold to <u>Heinhold Cattle Mkt.</u>, <u>134</u> head of <u>Cows</u> to be delivered F.O.B. cars, on or before <u>17</u> day of <u>Sept.</u>, <u>1973</u> at $<u>450.</u> per head or at $__ per cwt., to be weighed on twelve hours overnight stand and hauled at _____ with _____ cut back. Received as part payment $<u>6,700</u> balance of $<u>53,600</u> to be paid on delivery. I hereby guarantee title thereto, viz:

No Hd.	Description	Brands	Location of Brands	Price Per Head
134	Hereford-Few BB Cows	☐	RH	

"All of above stock to be free from encumbrance, including taxes for year of delivery, and to pass federal and state inspection for interstate shipment. Health and brand certificates to be furnished purchaser, free of charge, on delivery. Above to be free of contagious disease and in merchantable condition.

"(Seal) <u>/s/ Howard A. Shrum, Seller</u>

"Witness <u>/s/ Steve Harris</u>
"<u>/s/ Wm. Zeltwanger, Jr., Purchaser</u>"

Steve Harris, shown as a witness on the document, was the agent-buyer for the plaintiffs as purchasers. He negotiated the contract and was the active participant for the plaintiffs. Defendant Shrum negotiated the sale for the defendants.

From depositions on file, other peripheral circumstances are apparent. Prior to and when time for delivery arrived, defendants' cattle were in two groups, 54 at Story, Wyoming, and 80 at Otter, Montana. About two weeks before the delivery date, Harris went to Story along with a prospective buyer from his principal to look at the animals. Harris, though requested, did not inspect the Story group at the time of signing the contract. Defendant Shrum claims that at the time of the pre-delivery visit Harris said they were better than he expected. Harris claims he saw no yearling heifers. The visit is not in dispute. At the date of delivery, however, at that site, there were six or seven that had not been bred.

Harris made no examination of the cattle at Otter at any time prior to the delivery date, though at the time the contract was signed, Shrum asked Harris to inspect them, as well as those at Story. Harris said he trusted Shrum and thought no inspection necessary. Of all the cattle, at both Story and Otter, Harris refused to accept 72, as being heifers, which he claimed were not "cows" under the contract.

Shrum, when testifying by deposition, claimed that at the time the contract was signed, he told Harris that he "had 134 heifers and some young cows on them"; "I told him they weren't cows, they were heifers and some young cows on them. And he said that took care of the female end of the bovine family. So, I trusted his word and left it go." Harris deposed that Shrum represented all were cows that had lost calves and he assumed he was buying bred cows.

Harris, in his deposition, further testified as follows:

> "Well, it's always been my thought that a cow is a female bovine that's already had a calf. Normally they're not referred to as a cow until after they've weaned their first calf. Even at that time they were often referred to as first-calf heifers."

Harris offered to take what he considered to be cows under the contract but refused the others. Shrum refused, claiming all were cows under their agreement.

The trial judge entered an order granting summary judgment for plaintiffs for the recited reason that: "There was a mutual mistake in the formation of the contract and the Plaintiffs should be entitled to judgment as a matter of law." As we read the depositions and as outlined in the foregoing narration, the district judge apparently decided that since the plaintiffs assert they intended one thing and the defendants assert they intended another, there was mutual mistake. That is not mutual mistake.

As nearly as we can determine, through search of West's Wyoming Digest, this court has not undertaken to define the expression "mutual mistake," though it has recognized that a contract may be cancelled on that ground. *Goodson v. Smith,* 1952, 69 Wyo. 439, 243 P.2d 163, reh. den. 244 P.2d 805. Mutual mistake makes a contract voidable. *Kipp v. Agee,* Wyo.1969, 457 P.2d 673, reh. den. 458 P.2d 728. In this tribunal it has likewise been recognized that an instrument may be reformed on that ground. * * *

"Mutual mistake" is a common utterance in the law of contracts, however, and has come to have a universal meaning. A mutual mistake is one which is reciprocal and common to both parties, each alike laboring under the same misconception in respect to the terms of the written instrument. * * * More briefly stated, it means a situation where both parties share the same misconception. 13 Williston on Contracts, 3d Ed. (Jaeger) § 1550A, p. 168, and, in the same volume § 1543, p. 75, pulling its effect into play, it is said:

"'Where both parties assume the existence of a certain state of facts as the basis on which they enter a transaction, the transaction can be avoided by a party who is harmed, if the assumption is erroneous.'"

Some courts have worded their definitions in different ways and it is probably well to set out some of those because they are clarifying. If the intention of the parties is identical at the time of the transaction, and the written agreement does not express that intention, then a mutual mistake has occurred. *Tenco, Inc. v. Manning,* 1962, 59 Wash.2d 479, 368 P.2d 372. Mutual mistake may be defined as error in reducing the concurring intention of the parties to writing. *Naisbitt v. Hodges,* 1957, 6 Utah 2d 116, 307 P.2d 620. A mutual mistake exists where there has been a meeting of the minds of the parties and an agreement actually entered into but the agreement does not in its written form express what was really intended by the parties. *Sierra Blanca Sales Company, Inc. v. Newco Industries, Inc.,* 1972, 84 N.M. 524, 505 P.2d 867, cert. den. 84 N.M. 512, 505 P.2d 855.

The New Mexico court has used the expression "meeting of the minds." We cite the case for an occasion to update and supersede use of that well-known old contract phrase with the modern expression "mutual assent." In order for there to be a binding contract, there must be mutual assent—a mutual manifestation to the same terms. Calamari & Perillo, Law of Contracts, HB, §§ 11 and 12, pp. 13–14. 13 Williston on Contracts, 3d Ed. (Jaeger), § 1536, p. 33, refers to "meeting of the minds" as a "quaintly archaic expression." When there is mutual mistake, then there can be no mutual assent.

Since there was no mutual mistake the trial judge stated an erroneous ground for granting summary judgment. There remains a genuine dispute as to the meaning of the contract term "cows." One says it means one thing, the other, another. It must be realized that all that is before the court is the subjective expressions of the plaintiffs' buyer agent and the defendants and those expressions are at opposite poles. One or the other may or may not represent what the parties really intended by their transaction. The intent of the parties can only be ascertained by an objective not subjective approach in contract situations. The subjective intent of the parties is ordinarily irrelevant. An objective test is applied. A party's intention will be held to be what a reasonable man in the position of the other party would conclude his manifestations to mean. Calamari & Perillo, Law of Contracts, HB, § 12, p. 14; 13 Williston on Contracts, 3d Ed. (Jaeger), § 1536, p. 11.

The only way to shake out what the parties intended or did not intend is by the adversary process of a trial. There may have been mutual mistake but from what we have examined it seems unlikely, though we would not foreclose that conclusion. The cancellation of a written agreement is a drastic interference with the right of parties to contract. While we have authority to do so, in a proper case, a court should not compel a party to relinquish the fruits of an honestly-made contract and deprive him of its benefits in the absence of clear, convincing and well-founded evidence. The burden of proving mistake is upon the party asserting it. *Goodson v. Smith,* supra.

* * *

Since we decide that there was no mutual mistake as a matter of law, we must now see whether the summary judgment can be sustained on other grounds. * * *

The whole case revolves around what the parties intended by the use of the word "cows" in describing the subject matter of the contract. Taken by itself, it has any number of meanings: Webster's Third New International Dictionary, Unabridged: "Cow: 1 a; * * * the mature female of wild or domestic cattle of the genus *Bos* or of any of the various animals the male of which is called *bull* * * * b: a domestic bovine animal regardless of its sex or age * * *." Black's Law Dictionary, 4th Ed.1951: "Cow. Female of bovine genus of animals. Strictly, one that has calved. Often loosely used to include heifer, or young female that has not calved. [Citing cases.]" Ballantine's Law Dictionary With Pronunciations, 2d Ed., under the word "cow," the volume states: "See * * * heifer." "Heifer. A female calf of the bovine species, from the end of the first year until she has had a calf; a young cow. [Citing case.]" See also West's Words and Phrases, p. 516, under the word "cow." We can conclude that it has within the corral of this case, no plain and ordinary meaning. From the definitions, the positions of either plaintiffs or defendants could be supported. Since the term "cows" is not clear, there must be a trial.[1]

* * *

Reversed and remanded for trial of the issues as we have noted and may otherwise appear.

---

1. The trial court and parties may find something useful in the following examples. Extrinsic evidence may be received to find the intent of parties as to the meaning of "timber" when not clear from the contract. Walter v. Potlatch Forests, Inc., 1972, 94 Idaho 738, 497 P.2d 1039. Whether the word "chickens" in a contract for their sale means young broilers or old stewing hens throws the burden on plaintiff to show use of the word was in the narrow rather than broad sense. Frigaliment Importing Co. v. B.N.S. International Sales Corp., U.S.D.C., S.D.N.Y.1960, 190 F.Supp. 116. Frigaliment and the problem of word interpretation in general, is discussed at length in "The Interpretation of Words and the Parol Evidence Rule" by Professor Corbin, author of Corbin on Contracts in 50 Cornell Law Quarterly 161. The general theme of the work is that extrinsic evidence is a necessary aid in arriving at the intent of contracting parties. This court has held that the Uniform Commercial Code was intended to liberalize the parol evidence rule and limit the presumption that a written contract is a total integration and a court, following trial, can find under § 34–2–202(b), W.S.1957, Cum.Supp., that there are consistent additional terms unless it finds the agreement to be a complete and exclusive statement of its terms. Zwierzycki v. Owens, Wyo.1972, 499 P.2d 996.

Question

Can you articulate the distinction between the mutual material mistake doctrine and the problem of misunderstanding studied in Section Four of Chapter Four? Which doctrine better fits the facts of Shrum v. Zeltwanger?

SECTION FOUR: UNILATERAL MISTAKE

TRIPLE A CONTRACTORS, INC. v. RURAL WATER DISTRICT NO. 4, NEOSHO COUNTY

Supreme Court of Kansas, 1979.
226 Kan. 626, 603 P.2d 184.

PER CURIAM:

This appeal is from a judgment denying equitable relief in the form of cancellation of a public construction bid and the discharge and release of the bid bond.

The only issue before us is whether the successful bidder for a public construction contract will be granted equitable relief by way of cancellation of the construction bid and the discharge and release of its bid bond because of a unilateral error in calculating costs.

On March 4, 1976, Rural Water District No. 4, Neosho County, Kansas, issued a notice to contractors that bids would be received for the construction of a water distribution and storage system. We are concerned here only with the water distribution system. The bids were to be accompanied by a check or bid bond in the amount of 5% of the total bid. The stated purpose of the bid bond was to guarantee that the contractor would enter into a construction contract within ten days of the award of the contract.

The plaintiff company submitted its bid and a bid bond in the amount of $40,637.65. It might be explained here that the plaintiff company is a family corporation consisting of Glen Anderson and his five children. Steve Anderson, the twenty-seven year old son of Glen Anderson, was assistant general manager. The bid submitted by plaintiff was prepared by Steve Anderson.

The bids were opened on March 24, 1976. The plaintiff's bid was $812,753.00. This was $169,079.50 lower than the next lowest bid and $486,154.50 lower than the defendant's consulting engineer's estimate. Because of the wide variation between the low bidder and the second low bidder all parties concerned suspected an error. Glen and Steve Anderson spent two or three days going through the plans and cost estimate sheets looking for an error.

The error was found on March 27, 1976. The chief error had been made in transferring the calculated amount of shot rock from the adding machine tape to the bid project estimate sheets. Only 6,000 lineal feet of the 36,000 lineal feet had been carried over to the estimate sheets. Glen Anderson testified this was the sole purpose for requesting withdrawal of the bid. On March 29, 1976, defendant's consulting engineer talked to Glen Anderson about the bid. Glen Anderson informed the defendant's consulting engineer that an error had been made and he wished to withdraw the bid. No mention was made of the nature of the error.

On March 31, 1976, the plaintiff sent a letter to the defendant requesting withdrawal of the bid on the basis of gross error in cost estimating. Glen Anderson testified that he did not use the term "mathematical error" in the letter because he did not know the type of error was important. The defendant, the Rural Water District Board, voted to accept appellant's bid on April 21, 1976. Glen Anderson met with the board on May 4, 1976, and explained the exact nature of the error. At the meeting the plaintiff rejected the contract.

Plaintiff brought action in the district court, alleging a mistake in the form of a clerical error in the computation of the quantity of rock to be excavated and prayed that the acceptance of the bid be cancelled, its bid be rescinded and cancelled, and its bid bond be cancelled.

The district court in memorandum opinion stated as follows:

"The controlling question is whether a bidder on a construction contract can be relieved from obligation under his bid bond for his unilateral mistake in figuring his bid. No Kansas decision has been turned up and the authorities in other states are divided, probably the majority rule being that he can.

"As simple contract law the Kansas Supreme Court has consistently held that unilateral mistake will not excuse non performance."

The trial court followed the Kansas general rule that a unilateral mistake will not excuse nonperformance of a contract and denied the plaintiff any relief. The plaintiff has appealed.

Before we proceed with a discussion of the law we should be clear on the issue before us. There has been a great deal of confusion in the decisions because of the failure to distinguish between the contract involved in the bid and the construction contract which would result from the bid contract. The appellee is not attempting to hold the plaintiff to a construction contract which because of errors might result in a tremendous loss of an unknown amount. The appellee is holding appellant to his bid contract under which he can forfeit the bid bond in a known amount and be relieved of the obligations of the construction contract.

We have no Kansas case dealing with the effect of an error on a bid contract. However, we see no reason why our cases announcing the rule that in the absence of fraud a unilateral mistake will not excuse the nonperformance of a contract should not apply. * * *

The courts of other states are divided on the question. Appellant calls our attention to the general rule set forth in 52 A.L.R.2d 796, as follows:

"Equity will relieve from the consequences of a bid for a public contract which has been submitted as the result of a remediable unilateral mistake, although a contract has not been consummated, and the principles applied are generally similar to those applied in relieving against completed contracts resulting from unilateral mistake."

This may state the position of those state courts which have granted relief on a unilateral mistake. We are more impressed with a contrary decision in Colella v. Allegheny County, Aplnt., 391 Pa. 103, 107, 137 A.2d 265, 267

(1957), where the court denied relief under facts quite similar to those in the case before us and stated:

> "If a person, firm or corporation submits a sealed bid on public works, the principle contended for by the contractor, namely, that after all the bids are opened he can withdraw his bid under the plea of a clerical mistake, would seriously undermine and make the requirement or system of sealed bids a mockery; it could likewise open wide the door to fraud and collusion between contractors and/or between contractors and the Public Authority. What is the use or purpose of a sealed bid if the bidder does not have to be bound by what he submits under seal? What is the use or purpose of requiring a surety bond as further protection for the public, i.e. the municipality, if a bidder can withdraw his bid under plea of clerical mistake, whenever he sees that his bid is so low that he must have made an error of judgment?"

We see no occasion to make a distinction between a clerical error and an error in judgment. The very purpose of the bid bond was to require the bidder to go forward with the construction contract regardless of his errors in arithmetic or judgment. The ruling does not require plaintiff to perform a contract at a terrific loss. It does require that he pay the penalty contemplated by and inherent in the bidding procedure. Were we to hold otherwise we would materially weaken the purpose of the bidding procedure on public contracts.

We are inclined to agree with the trial court in its conclusions. The bid contract was complete and the bid bond was in effect when the bids were opened. The general rule in Kansas, that in the absence of fraud a unilateral mistake does not excuse the nonperformance of a contract, applies to a bid contract for a public construction project.

The judgment is affirmed.

FROMME, J., not participating.

PRAGER, JUSTICE, dissenting.

I respectfully dissent. The majority has chosen to adopt a minority position in holding that one who makes a unilateral mistake in bidding on a construction contract is precluded in all cases from seeking equitable relief by way of rescission. Jones, The Law of Mistaken Bids, 48 Cin.L.Rev. 43 (1979). The basis of the court's decision is the fear that to hold otherwise would undermine the integrity of the bidding system. The opinion makes it clear that the bid contract, not the construction contract, is what is being enforced.

Most jurisdictions allow relief by rescission from a unilateral mistake in the bid situation when the following criteria are met:

1. The bidder has acted honestly, in good faith, and without gross or willful negligence;

2. The bidder was reasonably prompt in notifying the contracting party of the error;

3. The mistake pertained to a material part of the contract;

4. The mistake was of such magnitude that enforcement or forfeiture would be unconscionable;

5.   Relief would return the parties to the status quo without prejudice to the contracting party; and

6.   Evidence is presented which convincingly establishes the mistake in fact exists.

* * *

Some courts distinguish the bid bond from the performance bond and deny relief when the issue is forfeiture of the bid bond posted as liquidated damages for failure to enter into the awarded contract. See, e.g. Trvlrs. Indm. Co., Aplnt. v. Susqha. Co. Com., 17 Pa.Cmwlth. 209, 331 A.2d 918 (1975); Board v. S–W Co., 22 Ohio St.2d 107, 258 N.E.2d 605 (1970). The vast majority of the jurisdictions, however, allow relief from forfeiture in bid bond cases when the accepting party knew or should have known of the error before acceptance, as when the party has been specifically notified or the price disparity indicates probable error. * * *

In the case before us, the six criteria for rescission of the contract are present. The findings of the district court justify rescission of the bid bond in this case. Defendant was notified of Triple A's error before acceptance, and was able to award the contract to the next lowest bidder without readvertising. Defendant was not prejudiced by the withdrawal of the bid and had no change of position. Plaintiff should not be subjected to a $40,000 loss because a young man made an innocent mistake in transferring the calculated amount of shot rock from the adding machine tape to the bid project estimate sheets. The purpose of rescission is to prevent unjust enrichment. To unjustly enrich defendant by allowing enforcement of the bid bond in this case is unfair, unjust, and grossly inequitable.

Accordingly, I dissent.

MILLER, J., joins the foregoing dissenting opinion.

DONOVAN v. RRL CORPORATION

Supreme Court of California, 2001.
26 Cal.4th 261, 27 P.3d 702, 109 Cal.Rptr.2d 807.

GEORGE, C.J.

Defendant RRL Corporation is an automobile dealer doing business under the name Lexus of Westminster. Because of typographical and proofreading errors made by a local newspaper, defendant's advertisement listed a price for a used automobile that was significantly less than the intended sales price. Plaintiff Brian J. Donovan read the advertisement and, after examining the vehicle, attempted to purchase it by tendering the advertised price. Defendant refused to sell the automobile to plaintiff at that price, and plaintiff brought this action against defendant for breach of contract. The municipal court entered judgment for defendant on the ground that the mistake in the advertisement precluded the existence of a contract. The appellate department of the superior court and the Court of Appeal reversed, relying in part upon Vehicle Code section 11713.1, subdivision (e), which makes it unlawful for an automobile dealer not to sell a motor vehicle at the advertised price while the vehicle remains unsold and before the advertisement expires.

We conclude that a contract satisfying the statute of frauds arose from defendant's advertisement and plaintiff's tender of the advertised price, but that defendant's unilateral mistake of fact provides a basis for rescinding the contract. Although Vehicle Code section 11713.1, subdivision (e), justifies a reasonable expectation on the part of consumers that an automobile dealer intends that such an advertisement constitute an offer, and that the offer can be accepted by paying the advertised price, this statute does not supplant governing common law principles authorizing rescission of a contract on the ground of mistake. As we shall explain, rescission is warranted here because the evidence establishes that defendant's unilateral mistake of fact was made in good faith, defendant did not bear the risk of the mistake, and enforcement of the contract with the erroneous price would be unconscionable. Accordingly, we shall reverse the judgment of the Court of Appeal.

While reading the April 26, 1997, edition of the Costa Mesa Daily Pilot, a local newspaper, plaintiff noticed a full-page advertisement placed by defendant. The advertisement promoted a "PRE–OWNED COUP–A–RAMA SALE!/ 2–DAY PRE–OWNED SALES EVENT" and listed, along with 15 other used automobiles, a 1995 Jaguar XJ6 Vanden Plas. The advertisement described the color of this automobile as sapphire blue, included a vehicle identification number, and stated a price of $25,995. The name Lexus of Westminster was displayed prominently in three separate locations in the advertisement, which included defendant's address along with a small map showing the location of the dealership. The following statements appeared in small print at the bottom of the advertisement: "All cars plus tax, lic., doc., smog & bank fees. On approved credit. Ad expires 4/27/97[.]"

Also on April 26, 1997, plaintiff visited a Jaguar dealership that offered other 1995 Jaguars for sale at $8,000 to $10,000 more than the price specified in defendant's advertisement. The following day, plaintiff and his spouse drove to Lexus of Westminster and observed a blue Jaguar displayed on an elevated ramp. After verifying that the identification number on the sticker was the same as that listed in defendant's April 26 Daily Pilot advertisement, they asked a salesperson whether they could test drive the Jaguar. Plaintiff mentioned that he had seen the advertisement and that the price "looked really good." The salesperson responded that, as a Lexus dealer, defendant might offer better prices for a Jaguar automobile than would a Jaguar dealer. At that point, however, neither plaintiff nor the salesperson mentioned the specific advertised price.

After the test drive, plaintiff and his spouse discussed several negative characteristics of the automobile, including high mileage, an apparent rust problem, and worn tires. In addition, it was not as clean as the other Jaguars they had inspected. Despite these problems, they believed that the advertised price was a very good price and decided to purchase the vehicle. Plaintiff told the salesperson, "Okay. We will take it at your price, $26,000." When the salesperson did not respond, plaintiff showed him the advertisement. The salesperson immediately stated, "That's a mistake."

After plaintiff asked to speak with an individual in charge, defendant's sales manager also told plaintiff that the price listed in the advertisement was a mistake. The sales manager apologized and offered to pay for plaintiff's fuel, time, and effort expended in traveling to the dealership to examine the automobile. Plaintiff declined this offer and expressed his belief that there had been no mistake. Plaintiff stated that he could write a check for the full purchase price as advertised. The sales manager responded that he would not sell the vehicle at the advertised price. Plaintiff then requested the sales price. After performing some calculations, and based upon defendant's $35,000 investment in the automobile, the sales manager stated that he would sell it to plaintiff for $37,016. Plaintiff responded, "No, I want to buy it at your advertised price, and I will write you a check right now." The sales manager again stated that he would not sell the vehicle at the advertised price, and plaintiff and his spouse left the dealership.

Plaintiff subsequently filed this action against defendant for breach of contract, fraud, and negligence. In addition to testimony consistent with the facts set forth above, the following evidence was presented to the municipal court, which acted as the trier of fact.

Defendant's advertising manager compiles information for placement in advertisements in several local newspapers, including the Costa Mesa Daily Pilot. Defendant's advertisement published in the Saturday, April 19, 1997, edition of the Daily Pilot listed a 1995 Jaguar XJ6 Vanden Plas but did not specify a price for that automobile; instead, the word "Save" appeared in the space where a price ordinarily would have appeared. The following Thursday afternoon, defendant's sales manager instructed the advertising manager to delete the 1995 Jaguar from all advertisements and to substitute a 1994 Jaguar XJ6 with a price of $25,995. The advertising manager conveyed the new information to a representative of the Daily Pilot that same afternoon.

Because of typographical and proofreading errors made by employees of the Daily Pilot, however, the newspaper did not replace the description of the 1995 Jaguar with the description of the 1994 Jaguar, but did replace the word "Save" with the price of $25,995. Thus, the Saturday, April 26, edition of the Daily Pilot erroneously advertised the 1995 Jaguar XJ6 Vanden Plas at a price of $25,995. The Daily Pilot acknowledged its error in a letter of retraction sent to defendant on April 28. No employee of defendant reviewed a proof sheet of the revised Daily Pilot advertisement before it was published, and defendant was unaware of the mistake until plaintiff attempted to purchase the automobile.

Except for the 1995 Jaguar XJ6 Vanden Plas, defendant intended to sell each vehicle appearing in the April 26, 1997, Daily Pilot advertisement at the advertised price. Defendant's advertisements in the April 26 editions of several other newspapers correctly listed the *1994* Jaguar XJ6 with a price of $25,995. In May 1997, defendant's advertisements in several newspapers listed the 1995 Jaguar XJ6 Vanden Plas for sale at $37,995. Defendant subsequently sold the automobile for $38,399.

[The Supreme Court first held that the defendant's ad constituted an offer, in part based on Vehicle Code section 11713.1, and in part based on Lefkowitz v. Great Minneapolis Surplus Store, 251 Minn. 188, 86 N.W.2d 689, 691 (1957). As to the former, the court stated: "In sum, because section 11713.1(e) makes it unlawful for a dealer not to sell a particular vehicle at the advertised price while the vehicle remains unsold and before the advertisement expires, plaintiff reasonably could believe that defendant intended the advertisement to be an offer." As to Lefkowitz, the court stated: "Various advertisements involving transactions in goods also have been held to constitute offers where they invite particular action. For example, a merchant's advertisement that listed particular goods at a specific price and included the phrase "First Come First Served" was deemed to be an offer, because it constituted a promise to sell to a customer at that price in exchange for the customer's act of arriving at the store at a particular time."]

* * * [W]e next consider whether defendant can avoid enforcement of the contract on the ground of mistake. [The court concluded that "defendant's error constituted a mistake of fact."]

* * *

mistake of fact

* * * [T]he Restatement Second of Contracts authorizes rescission for a unilateral mistake of fact where "the effect of the mistake is such that enforcement of the contract would be unconscionable." (Rest.2d Contracts, § 153, subd. (a).)[2] The comment following this section recognizes "a growing willingness to allow avoidance where the consequences of the mistake are so grave that enforcement of the contract would be unconscionable." (*Id.*, com. a, p. 394.) * * * Although the most common types of mistakes falling within this category occur in bids on construction contracts, section 153 of the Restatement Second of Contracts is not limited to such cases. (Rest.2d Contracts, § 153, com. b, p. 395.)

RST allows recession where it would be unconscion!

Because the rule in section 153, subdivision (a), of the Restatement Second of Contracts, authorizing rescission for unilateral mistake of fact where enforcement would be unconscionable, is consistent with our previous decisions, we adopt the rule as California law. * * *

k may be rescinded on unilateral mistake of fact →

Having concluded that a contract properly may be rescinded on the ground of unilateral mistake of fact as set forth in section 153, subdivision (a), of the Restatement Second of Contracts, we next consider whether the requirements of that provision, construed in light of our previous decisions, are satisfied in the present case. Where the plaintiff has no reason to know of and does not cause the defendant's unilateral mistake of fact, the defendant must establish the following facts to obtain rescission of the contract: (1) the defendant made a mistake regarding a basic assumption upon which the defendant made the contract; (2) the mistake has a material effect upon the agreed exchange of performances that is adverse to the defendant; (3) the defendant does not bear the risk of the mistake; and (4) the effect of the mistake is such that enforcement of the contract would be unconscionable. We shall consider each of these requirements below.

are the reqs satisfied?

4 req

A significant error in the price term of a contract constitutes a mistake regarding a basic assumption upon which the contract is made, and such a mistake ordinarily has a material effect adverse to the mistaken party. * * * In establishing a material mistake regarding a basic assumption of the contract, the defendant must show that the resulting imbalance in the agreed

(1)

usually bidding cases

---

2. Section 153 of the Restatement Second of Contracts states: "Where a mistake of one party at the time a contract was made as to a basic assumption on which he made the contract has a material effect on the agreed exchange of performances that is adverse to him, the contract is voidable by him if he does not bear the risk of the mistake under the rule stated in § 154, and [¶] (a) the effect of the mistake is such that enforcement of the contract would be unconscionable, or [¶] (b) the other party had reason to know of the mistake or his fault caused the mistake."

exchange is so severe that it would be unfair to require the defendant to perform. (Rest.2d Contracts, § 152, com. c, p. 388.) Ordinarily, a defendant can satisfy this requirement by showing that the exchange not only is less desirable for the defendant, but also is more advantageous to the other party. (*Ibid.*)

Measured against this standard, defendant's mistake in the contract for the sale of the Jaguar automobile constitutes a material mistake regarding a basic assumption upon which it made the contract. Enforcing the contract with the mistaken price of $25,995 would require defendant to sell the vehicle to plaintiff for $12,000 less than the intended advertised price of $37,995—an error amounting to 32 percent of the price defendant intended. The exchange of performances would be substantially less desirable for defendant and more desirable for plaintiff. Plaintiff implicitly concedes that defendant's mistake was material.

The parties * * * vigorously dispute, however, whether defendant should bear the risk of its mistake. Section 154 of the Restatement Second of Contracts states: "A party bears the risk of a mistake when [¶] (a) the risk is allocated to him by agreement of the parties, or [¶] (b) he is aware, at the time the contract is made, that he has only limited knowledge with respect to the facts to which the mistake relates but treats his limited knowledge as sufficient, or [¶] (c) the risk is allocated to him by the court on the ground that it is reasonable in the circumstances to do so." Neither of the first two factors applies here. Thus, we must determine whether it is reasonable under the circumstances to allocate to defendant the risk of the mistake in the advertisement.

Civil Code section 1577, as well as our prior decisions, instructs that the risk of a mistake must be allocated to a party where the mistake results from that party's neglect of a legal duty.* * * It is well established, however, that ordinary negligence does not constitute neglect of a legal duty within the meaning of Civil Code section 1577. * * * For example, we have described a careless but significant mistake in the computation of the contract price as the type of error that sometimes will occur in the conduct of reasonable and cautious businesspersons, and such an error does not necessarily amount to neglect of legal duty that would bar equitable relief. * * *

A concept similar to neglect of a legal duty is described in section 157 of the Restatement Second of Contracts, which addresses situations in which a party's fault precludes relief for mistake. Only where the mistake results from "a failure to act in good faith and in accordance with reasonable standards of fair dealing" is rescission unavailable. (Rest.2d Contracts, § 157.) This section, consistent with the California decisions cited in the preceding paragraph, provides that a mistaken party's failure to exercise due care does not necessarily bar rescission under the rule set forth in section 153.

* * *

Plaintiff contends that section 11713.1(e) imposes a legal duty upon licensed automobile dealers to ensure that their advertisements containing sale prices are accurate. As established above, section 11713.1(e) provides that it is a violation of the Vehicle Code for a dealer to "[f]ail to sell a vehicle to any person at the advertised total price ... while the vehicle remains unsold, unless the advertisement states the advertised total price is good only for a specified time and the time has elapsed." * * *

Even if we were to conclude that the foregoing statutes impose a duty of care upon automobile dealers to ensure that prices in an advertisement are accurate, a violation of such a duty would not necessarily preclude the availability of equitable relief. Our prior decisions instruct that the circumstance that a statute imposes a duty of care does not establish that the violation of such a duty constitutes "the neglect of a legal duty" (Civ.Code, § 1577) that would preclude rescission for a unilateral mistake of fact.

* * *

Section 11713.1(e) does not eliminate mistake as a ground for rescission of the contract, as plaintiff contends. The statute is part of a regulatory scheme that subjects licensed dealers to potential discipline for a violation of the duties set forth therein. * * * [N]othing in section 11713.1(e) or the regulatory scheme reflects a legislative intent completely to remove the contract-making process from the purview of the common law. At most, section 11713.1(e) reflects an intent to *supplement* contract law by establishing a ceiling for the price term of a contract for the sale of an advertised vehicle. Therefore, the common law, including the law governing mistake, remains applicable.

[I]f we were to accept plaintiff's position that section 11713.1(e), by requiring a dealer to sell a vehicle at the advertised price, necessarily precludes relief for mistake, and that the dealer always must be held to the strict terms of a contract arising from an advertisement, we would be holding that the dealer intended to assume the risk of all typographical errors in advertisements, no matter how serious the error and regardless of the circumstances in which the error was made. For example, if an automobile dealer proofread an advertisement but, through carelessness, failed to detect a typographical error listing a $75,000 automobile for sale at $75, the defense of mistake would be unavailable to the dealer.

* * *

Giving such an effect to section 11713.1(e), however, "is contrary to common sense and ordinary business understanding and would result in the loss of heretofore well-established equitable rights to relief from certain types of mistake." (*Kemper,* 37 Cal.2d at p. 704, 235 P.2d 7.) Although this statute obviously reflects an important public policy of protecting consumers from injury caused by unscrupulous dealers who publish deceptive advertisements * * * and establishes that automobile dealers that violate the statute can suffer the suspension or revocation of their licenses, there is no indication in the statutory scheme that the Legislature intended to impose such an absolute *contractual* obligation upon automobile dealers who make an honest mistake. Therefore, absent evidence of bad faith, the violation of any obligation imposed by this statute does not constitute the neglect of a legal duty that precludes rescission for unilateral mistake of fact.

The municipal court made an express finding of fact that "the mistake on the part of [defendant] was made in good faith[;] it was an honest mistake, not intended to deceive the public...." The Court of Appeal correctly recognized that "[w]e must, of course, accept the trial court's finding that there was a 'good faith' mistake that caused the error in the advertisement." The evidence presented at trial compellingly supports this finding.

* * *

No evidence presented at trial suggested that defendant knew of the mistake before plaintiff attempted to purchase the automobile, that defendant intended to mislead customers, or that it had adopted a practice of deliberate indifference regarding errors in advertisements. * * *

Defendant's fault consisted of failing to review a proof sheet reflecting the change made on Thursday, April 24, 1997, and/or the actual advertisement appearing in the April 26 edition of the Daily Pilot—choosing instead to rely upon the Daily Pilot's advertising staff to proofread the revised version. Although, as the Court of Appeal found, such an omission might constitute negligence, it does not involve a breach of defendant's duty of good faith and fair dealing that should preclude equitable relief for mistake. In these circumstances, it would not be reasonable for this court to allocate the risk of the mistake to defendant.

As indicated above, the Restatement Second of Contracts provides that during the negotiation stage of a contract "each party is held to a degree of responsibility appropriate to the justifiable expectations of the other." (Rest.2d Contracts, § 157, com. a, p. 417.) No consumer reasonably can expect 100 percent accuracy in each and every price appearing in countless automobile advertisements listing numerous vehicles for sale. The degree of responsibility plaintiff asks this court to impose upon automobile dealers would amount to strict contract liability for any typographical error in the price of an advertised automobile, no matter how serious the error or how blameless the dealer. We are unaware of any other situation in which an individual or business is held to such a standard under the law of contracts. Defendant's good faith, isolated mistake does not constitute the type of extreme case in which its fault constitutes the neglect of a legal duty that bars equitable relief. Therefore, whether or not defendant's failure to sell the automobile to plaintiff could amount to a violation of section 11713.1(e)—an issue that is not before us—defendant's conduct in the present case does not preclude rescission.

The final factor defendant must establish before obtaining rescission based upon mistake is that enforcement of the contract for the sale of the 1995 Jaguar XJ6 Vanden Plas at $25,995 would be unconscionable.

* * *

In the present case, enforcing the contract with the mistaken price of $25,995 would require defendant to sell the vehicle to plaintiff for $12,000 less than the intended advertised price of $37,995—an error amounting to 32 percent of the price defendant intended. Defendant subsequently sold the automobile for slightly more than the intended advertised price, suggesting that that price reflected its actual market value. Defendant had paid $35,000 for the 1995 Jaguar and incurred costs in advertising, preparing, displaying, and attempting to sell the vehicle. Therefore, defendant would lose more than $9,000 of its original investment in the automobile. Plaintiff, on the other hand, would obtain a $12,000 windfall if the contract were enforced, simply because he traveled to the dealership and stated that he was prepared to pay the advertised price.

[The court next discusses California cases authorizing rescission based on the unconscionability of enforcing the mistaken price.]

* * *

The circumstance that section 11713.1(e) makes it unlawful for a dealer not to sell a vehicle at the advertised price does not preclude a finding that enforcing an automobile sales contract containing a mistaken price would be unconscionable. Just as the statute does not eliminate the defense of mistake, as established above, the statute also does not dictate that enforcing a contract with an erroneous advertised price necessarily must be considered equitable and fair for purposes of deciding whether the dealer is entitled to rescission on the ground of mistake.* * *

* * *

Having determined that defendant satisfied the requirements for rescission of the contract on the ground of unilateral mistake of fact, we conclude that the municipal court correctly entered judgment in defendant's favor.

[Dissenting opinion by WERDEGAR, J. omitted.]

Note
More Mistakes

1. The Ithaca Journal reported that the owner of Ball–Mart Baseball Cards and the thirteen-year-old buyer of a 1968 Nolan Ryan card settled their lawsuit over the ownership of the card. Ball–Mart sold the card, apparently worth $1200, to the buyer for $12. Ball–Mart claimed, however, that "an inexperienced clerk who didn't understand the '1200' marking" mistakenly sold the card to the buyer. Ball–Mart therefore sued for return of the card or money damages measured by the contract-market differential. The parties settled the dispute by agreeing to sell the card at an auction and to donate the proceeds to two charities. The junior-high-school student buyer observed that "people should settle their disputes themselves rather than let other people take them to court and settle them for them." Ithaca Journal, Apr. 24, 1991, § 1, at 6, Col. 3.

Question: Suppose the buyer were not so settlement-oriented. Would he have won the lawsuit?

2. In December, 2005, the Associated Press reported that a trader at one of Japan's largest brokerage firms sought to sell one share of a job-recruiting firm for 610,000 yen ($5,041) but, because of a typing error, actually sold 610,000 shares at 1 yen (less than one cent) per share. This cost the firm, according to the report, more than $225 million if the sale stand.

Question: What are the trader's rights, if any?

RIEGERT, THE WEST GERMAN CIVIL CODE, ITS ORIGIN AND ITS CONTRACT PROVISIONS
45 Tul.L.Rev. 48, 90–93 (1970).

The BGB contains what for Americans are some surprising provisions regarding unilateral mistake. Under section 119 a person may avoid a contract (or any declaration of will) for three different categories of unilateral mistake. As a pre-condition to avoidance the court must find that he would not have made the declaration had he known the correct facts. That the obligor be without negligence is *not* a requirement, and declarations of will can be avoided by the obligor regardless of whether the other party had reason to know of the mistake.

After the obligor learns of the mistake he must immediately make a reasonable effort to give the other party notice. Ordinarily, no special form of notice is required, but the intent to avoid must be clear. If the other party is unavailable, the notice should be forwarded to him where it will reach him the quickest. Such notice is effective when he receives it.

The German system operates successfully with this rule excusing the performance because section 122 requires a party taking advantage of unilateral mistake to reimburse the other party for reliance damages. The other party gets his expenses, so he only loses his profit. Reliance damages cannot exceed the contract price. If the obligee knew of the obligor's mistake or if the obligee caused the mistake, reliance damages are disallowed.

* * *

Numerous mistakes are not excuses for avoiding contracts. A person contracts to buy a car, not realizing he is ineligible to obtain a driver's license; a merchant orders a particular product, forgetting he has an oversupply stored in the back of his warehouse. These mistakes are said to be *mere* mistakes in motive.

* * *

Section 119 cuts a wide swath. Not only contracts which are based upon declarations of will but also all declarations of will can be avoided under section 119. A tenant who has given his landlord notice of his intent to terminate the lease can avoid the notice if he made a section 119 mistake, but he must compensate the landlord for reliance losses. One declaration of will cannot be avoided by a unilateral mistake: the marriage vow. A few provisions, such as those relating to the acceptance or rejection of an inheritance, require a special form for the avoidance.

American jurists, who stress the need for security of transactions, might expect the German courts to have whittled down the rule of section 119. Instead, insofar as attempts to avoid contracts before they are performed, the rule usually is literally enforced.

The ease with which a party can escape an executory contract in Germany tends on the one hand to render contracts less useful, because they are less reliable. On the other hand, the ease of escape has the advantage of making contracts less dangerous, so people are more willing to enter contracts. Finally, by permitting a promisor to avoid an obligation he never intended, the Code makes the contract less an instrument for exploiting the unwary.

SECTION FIVE: IMPOSSIBILITY
OF PERFORMANCE

In mutual mistake cases, the circumstances at the time of contracting are materially different from what the parties reasonably assumed. What if, instead, the circumstances materially change *after* the parties make their agreement? The effect of supervening events is the subject of Sections Five through Seven dealing with impossibility of performance, impracticability, and frustration of purpose. More than one writer has observed, however, that these doctrines are essentially concerned with "mistake as to the future" and are therefore "not basically different from * * * mistake with respect to an existing fact."[a]

We turn first to impossibility. Early contract cases excused performance on this ground only when performance was objectively impossible—when the promisor was literally incapable of performing due to circumstances "unforeseeable" at the time of contracting. But when is a promisor truly unable to perform?

TAYLOR v. CALDWELL

Queens Bench, 1863.
3 B. & S. 826, 122 Eng.Rep. 309.

Blackburn J. In this case the plaintiffs and defendants had, on the 27th May, 1861, entered into a contract by which the defendants agreed to let the plaintiffs have the use of The Surrey Gardens and Music Hall on four days then to come, viz., the 17th June, 15th July, 5th August and 19th August, for the purpose of giving a series of four grand concerts, and day and night fetes at the Gardens and Hall on those days respectively; and the plaintiffs agreed to take the Gardens and Hall on those days, and pay 100*l*. for each day.

The parties inaccurately call this a "letting," and the money to be paid a "rent"; but the whole agreement is such as to shew that the defendants were to retain the possession of the Hall and Gardens so that there was to be no demise of them, and that the contract was merely to give the plaintiffs the use of them on those days. Nothing however, in our opinion, depends on this. The agreement then proceeds to set out various stipulations between the parties as to what each was to supply for these concerts and entertainments, and as to the manner in which they should be carried on. The effect of the whole is to shew that the existence of the Music Hall in the Surrey Gardens in a state fit for a concert was essential for the fulfilment of the contract,—such entertainment as the parties contemplated in their agreement could not be given without it.

After the making of the agreement, and before the first day on which a concert was to be given, the Hall was destroyed by fire. This destruction, we must take it on the evidence, was without the fault of either party, and was so complete that in consequence the concerts could not be given as intended.

---

a. H. Havighurst, The Nature of Private Contract 62 (1961). Of course, not all mistakes are mistakes as to the existing facts.

And the question we have to decide is whether, under these circumstances, the loss which the plaintiffs have sustained [the costs of advertising and preparing for the concerts] is to fall upon the defendants. The parties when framing their agreement evidently had not present to their minds the possibility of such a disaster, and have made no express stipulation with reference to it, so that the answer to the question must depend upon the general rules of law applicable to such a contract.

There seems no doubt that where there is a positive contract to do a thing, not in itself unlawful, the contractor must perform it or pay damages for not doing it, although in consequence of unforeseen accidents, the performance of his contract has become unexpectedly burthensome or even impossible. The law is so laid down in 1 Roll.Abr. 450, Condition (G), and in the note (2) to *Walton v. Waterhouse* (2 Wms. Saund. 421 a. 6th ed.), and is recognised as the general rule by all the Judges in the much discussed case of *Hall v. Wright* (E.B. & E. 746). But this rule is only applicable when the contract is positive and absolute, and not subject to any condition either express or implied: and there are authorities which, as we think, establish the principle that where, from the nature of the contract, it appears that the parties must from the beginning have known that it could not be fulfilled unless when the time for the fulfilment of the contract arrived some particular specified thing continued to exist, so that, when entering into the contract, they must have contemplated such continuing existence as the foundation of what was to be done; there, in the absence of any express or implied warranty that the thing shall exist, the contract is not to be construed as a positive contract, but as subject to an implied condition that the parties shall be excused in case, before breach, performance becomes impossible from the perishing of the thing without default of the contractor.

There seems little doubt that this implication tends to further the great object of making the legal construction such as to fulfil the intention of those who entered into the contract. For in the course of affairs men in making such contracts in general would, if it were brought to their minds, say that there should be such a condition.

Accordingly, in the Civil law, such an exception is implied in every obligation of the class which they call obligatio de certo corpore. * * *

Although the Civil law is not of itself authority in an English Court, it affords great assistance in investigating the principles on which the law is grounded. And it seems to us that the common law authorities establish that in such a contract the same condition of the continued existence of the thing is implied by English law.

There is a class of contracts in which a person binds himself to do something which requires to be performed by him in person; and such promises, e.g. promises to marry, or promises to serve for a certain time, are never in practice qualified by an express exception of the death of the party; and therefore in such cases the contract is in terms broken if the promisor dies before fulfilment. Yet it was very early determined that, if the performance is personal, the executors are not liable; Hyde v. The Dean of Windsor (Cro.Eliz. 552, 553). See 2 Wms.Exors. 1560, 5th ed., where a very apt illustration is given. "Thus," says the learned author, "if an author undertakes to compose a work, and dies before completing it, his executors are discharged from this contract: for the undertaking is merely personal in its nature, and, by the intervention of the contractor's death, has become impossible to be performed." * * *

* * *

These are instances where the implied condition is of the life of a human being, but there are others in which the same implication is made as to the continued existence of a thing. For example, where a contract of sale is made amounting to a bargain and sale, transferring presently the property in specific chattels, which are to be delivered by the vendor at a future day; there, if the chattels, without the fault of the vendor, perish in the interval, the purchaser must pay the price and the vendor is excused from performing his contract to deliver, which has thus become impossible.

* * *

It may, we think, be safely asserted to be now English law, that in all contracts of loan of chattels or bailments if the performance of the promise of the borrower or bailee to return the things lent or bailed, becomes impossible because it has perished, this impossibility (if not arising from the fault of the borrower or bailee from some risk which he has taken upon himself) excuses the borrower or bailee from the performance of his promise to redeliver the chattel.

* * * The principle seems to us to be that, in contracts in which the performance depends on the continued existence of a given person or thing, a condition is implied that the impossibility of performance arising from the perishing of the person or thing shall excuse the performance.

In none of these cases is the promise in words other than positive, nor is there any express stipulation that the destruction of the person or thing shall excuse the performance; but that excuse is by law implied, because from the nature of the contract it is apparent that the parties contracted on the basis of the continued existence of the particular person or chattel. In the present case, looking at the whole contract, we find that the parties contracted on the basis of the continued existence of the Music Hall at the time when the concerts were to be given; that being essential to their performance.

We think, therefore, that the Music Hall having ceased to exist, without fault of either party, both parties are excused, the plaintiffs from taking the gardens and paying the money, the defendants from performing their promise to give the use of the Hall and Gardens and other things. Consequently the rule must be absolute to enter the verdict for the defendants.

Rule absolute.

BELL v. CARVER

Supreme Court of Arkansas, 1968.
245 Ark. 31, 431 S.W.2d 452.

WARD, JUSTICE.

This is an appeal from a decree against a property owner establishing a lien to secure payment of $2,724. A brief summary of the facts out of which this litigation arises is set out below.

Facts. R.B. Bell and his wife (appellants here) are the owners of a lot in the town of Mena on which was a building used as a cafe. On June 14, 1966 they executed a ten year lease to J.H. Cameron and his wife who were to operate the cafe. Under the terms of the lease the Camerons were to make repairs necessary for the operation of a first class restaurant. About three months later J.A. Carver, d/b/a Carver Air Conditioning Co., (appellee herein) began work on installing an air conditioner and a heating unit in the cafe building for an agreed price—whether appellants or lessees were responsible for the "agreed price" was one of the issues raised at the trial.

Before installation of said units was completed the building was practically destroyed by fire on November 1, 1966. Following the fire appellants did not choose to rebuild and the Camerons ceased trying to operate the cafe.

Pleadings. On January 26, 1967 appellee filed a complaint in chancery court, seeking (a) to recover from appellants $1291 expended for labor and $1955 expended for materials being lost as a result of the fire, and (b) to establish a lien on appellants' property to secure payment of the above items. Appellants pleaded a general denial and a cross-complaint against the Camerons alleging they were obligated, under the lease, to pay any amount due appellee. Answering the cross-complaint, the Camerons denied they were liable in any amount to appellee or appellants.

At the close of a hearing on the above issues the trial court made the following findings: appellants contracted with appellee for said installation; appellee is entitled to a judgment, on a quantum meruit basis, against appellants; said judgment is a lien on the premises (subject to a lien in favor of the Union Bank of Nena), and; when appellants satisfy said judgment they will be entitled to a judgment against the Camerons. The trial court retained jurisdiction to make any further necessary orders.

The court entered a judgment in favor of appellee in the amount of $2,727 which was less than was asked for, but appellee does not question the reduction here. Also, the Camerons have not perfected their appeal.

* * *

Appellants' first point is stated as follows:

"The court erred in its findings of fact and conclusion of law that Appellee is entitled to judgment based upon quantum meruit."

As we understand the argument here it is contended [that] * * * quantum meruit was not the proper measure of damages. We find no merit in [this] contention.

* * *

In Williston and Thompson, Revised Edition on Contracts, Section 1975, at page 948, this statement appears:

"One who works upon a building or other property under an indivisible contract with the owner, requiring him to complete a certain task or accomplish a certain result, cannot perform his full undertaking if the building or property in question is destroyed. He is excused from liability for his failure, because the contract required the continued existence of the building. Equally clearly he cannot sue the owner for loss of profit. If the destruction of the building was without fault on the part of the latter, he, as well as the workman, is excused from liability on the contract. But most American decisions allow recovery on a quantum meruit for the value of the work which had been done prior to the destruction."

Here, the record also reflects that part of the heater system was not destroyed and was of some benefit to appellants.

* * *

Finding no reversible error, the decree of the trial court is affirmed, and the cause is remanded for further required proceedings.

FOGLEMAN, JUSTICE [dissents].

3A CORBIN ON CONTRACTS
§ 667   at 193 (1960).

In very numerous cases involving a contract for the sale of land, the question has arisen as to which party shall carry the risks of loss and destruction, of buildings or of the land itself, after the contract has been made but before the formal deed of conveyance has been executed. The facts in these many cases vary in important respects; and there is variation and some conflict in the allocation of risks of loss. The question may be regarded as one of partial impossibility of performance. * * *

STONE, EQUITABLE CONVERSION BY CONTRACT
13 Colum.L.Rev. 369, 385–86 (1913).

There still remains for consideration the case where, pending performance of the contract for the sale of land, a substantial part of the subject matter of the contract, for example, buildings or improvements, are destroyed without the fault of the vendor. By the weight of authority the "burden of loss" is held to fall on the vendee. * * * The explanations [for this result] which do not frankly rest on fiction are based upon the fundamental notion that since in equity the vendee is for some purposes, dealt with as an owner of realty he should be so dealt with for all purposes, and that consequently the loss should fall on him * * * that is to say, in equity the vendee's right is treated as an interest in land.

* * *

* * * [This] theory of equitable ownership of land, subject to a contract of sale, is literally an incident of the right of specific performance, and cannot exist apart from it.

DAVIS v. SKINNER
Court of Civil Appeals of Alabama, 1985.
474 So.2d 1136.

ROBERT M. PARKER, RETIRED CIRCUIT JUDGE.

This is an appeal from the denial of motion for new trial.

The trial court rendered a judgment in favor of Paul and Shirley Skinner in the sum of $2,200 against Jackie Davis and ordered her to convey certain lands in Autauga County to the Skinners. * * *

SKINNER JUDGMENT

The evidence is in conflict but the record reveals that Davis entered into a written agreement to sell a house and acreage to the Skinners for the sum of $50,000. Skinner paid $1,000 down and moved on the property. While the agreement was still in the executory stage, the house burned and was a total loss. Davis carried an insurance policy on the house, which was mentioned in the agreement, and collected $51,200 from the insurer. * * *

The trial court found, in the Skinner case, that the sales price for the house and land was $50,000; that Skinner paid $1,000 down; that Davis received $51,200 from her insurance company; therefore, Davis was overpaid $2,200 for the property and that sum should be paid by Davis to Skinner. This, essentially, is in compliance with the doctrine established in this state by the case of *Alabama Farm Bureau Mutual Insurance Service, Inc. v. Nixon,* 268 Ala. 271, 105 So.2d 643 (1958). In that case the supreme court adopted and quoted the general rule, which applies in this case, from *Bruce v. Jennings,* 190 Ga. 618, 10 S.E.2d 56 (1940):

> "It is the general rule that, where the purchaser goes into possession under a binding executory contract for the sale of improved realty which the seller is able to convey, but where, before the transfer of the legal title is consummated, the improvements are destroyed by fire, without the fault of either party, the loss falls on the purchaser as the owner of the equitable title (citing authority). If in such a case the property was insured by the seller, he holds the insurance money which he may collect on the bargained property as trustee for the purchaser, subject, however, to his own claims for any unpaid purchase money plus the insurance premiums."

In its judgment, the trial court failed to give credit for the premium Davis paid for the insurance, which was $721. One of the grounds of the motion for new trial was that the judgment was excessive. It was error for the trial court not to give Davis credit for the insurance premium paid by her.

* * *

The judgment of *Skinner v. Davis* is due to be reversed for excessiveness. However, if the Skinners file remittitur in the amount of $721 with the trial court within ten days from the date of the judgment of this court, the judgment will stand affirmed.

* * *

AFFIRMED conditionally for Skinners.

All the Judges concur.

UNIFORM VENDOR AND PURCHASER RISK ACT.

§ 1. Risk of Loss

Any contract hereafter made in this State for the purchase and sale of realty shall be interpreted as including an agreement that the parties shall have the following rights and duties, unless the contract expressly provides otherwise:

(a) If, when neither the legal title nor the possession of the subject matter of the contract has been transferred, all or a material part thereof is destroyed without fault of the purchaser or is taken by eminent domain, the vendor cannot enforce the contract, and the purchaser is entitled to recover any portion of the price that he has paid;

(b) If, when either the legal title or the possession of the subject matter of the contract has been transferred, all or any part thereof is destroyed without fault of the vendor or is taken by eminent domain, the purchaser is not thereby relieved from a duty to pay the price, nor is he entitled to recover any portion thereof that he had paid.

[This act has been enacted in less than a quarter of the states, including, however, California and New York.]

NOTE, RISK OF LOSS AND DISTRIBUTION OF INSURANCE PROCEEDS UNDER REAL ESTATE CONTRACTS IN NEW YORK

28 Alb.L.Rev. 253, 257–58 (1964).

To place the risk of loss on the party in possession is basically sound. In so doing, the [Uniform Vendor and Purchaser Risk Act] is giving effect to the probable intention of the parties had they thought to agree on the contingency of a loss. Placing the loss on the party in possession further imposes a duty on him to care for the property at his own peril. If he is negligent or careless in protecting his interest, he should bear the burden of his neglect or carelessness. Furthermore, if there has been change in neither title nor possession, it should be the policy of the law to let the loss remain where it falls rather than shift it upon some fiction to another party. It must be assumed that a vigilant vendor would not cancel his insurance until the closing date since he has a valuable interest to protect. It is, therefore, not too harsh to impose upon the vendor the burden of keeping the premises insured until either transfer of title or possession. Upon transfer of either possession or title, the purchaser should be alerted as to the need for insurance. In placing the risk of loss on the party in possession, the statute applied the same rules as to real property as had been applied to personal property.

UNIFORM COMMERCIAL CODE § 2–509.
Risk of Loss in the Absence of Breach

* * *

(3) In any case not [involving a carrier or a bailee] the risk of loss passes to the buyer on his receipt of the goods if the seller is a merchant; otherwise the risk passes to the buyer on tender of delivery.

(4) The provisions of this section are subject to contrary agreement of the parties * * *.

UNIFORM COMMERCIAL CODE § 2–104(1).

"Merchant" means a person who deals in goods of the kind or otherwise by his occupation holds himself out as having knowledge or skill peculiar to the practices or goods involved in the transaction or to whom such knowledge or skill may be attributed by his employment of an agent or broker or other intermediary who by his occupation holds himself out as having such knowledge or skill.

UNIFORM COMMERCIAL CODE § 2-613.

Casualty to Identified Goods

Where the contract requires for its performance goods identified when the contract is made, and the goods suffer casualty without fault of either party before the risk of loss passes to the buyer, * * * then

(a) if the loss is total the contract is avoided; and

(b) if the loss is partial or the goods have so deteriorated as no longer to conform to the contract the buyer may nevertheless demand inspection and at his option either treat the contract as avoided or accept the goods with due allowance from the contract price for the deterioration or the deficiency in quantity but without further right against the seller.

CANADIAN INDUSTRIAL ALCOHOL CO. v. DUNBAR MOLASSES CO.

Court of Appeals of New York, 1932.
258 N.Y. 194, 179 N.E. 383.

Cardozo, C.J.

A buyer sues a seller for breach of an executory contract of purchase and sale.

The subject-matter of the contract was "approximately 1,500,000 wine gallons Refined Blackstrap [molasses] of the usual run from the National Sugar Refinery, Yonkers, N.Y., to test around 60% sugars."

The order was given and accepted December 27, 1927, but shipments of the molasses were to begin after April 1, 1928, and were to be spread out during the warm weather.

After April 1, 1928, the defendant made delivery from time to time of 344,083 gallons. Upon its failure to deliver more, the plaintiff brought this action for the recovery of damages. The defendant takes the ground that, by an implied term of the contract, the duty to deliver was conditioned upon the production by the National Sugar Refinery at Yonkers of molasses sufficient in quantity to fill the plaintiff's order. The fact is that the output of the refinery, while the contract was in force, was 485,848 gallons, much less than its capacity, of which amount 344,083 gallons were allotted to the defendant and shipped to the defendant's customer. The argument for the defendant is that its own duty to deliver was proportionate to the refinery's willingness to supply, and that the duty was discharged when the output was reduced.

The contract, read in the light of the circumstances existing at its making, or more accurately in the light of any such circumstances apparent from this record, does not keep the defendant's duty within boundaries so narrow. We may assume, in the defendant's favor, that there would have been a discharge of its duty to deliver if the refinery had been destroyed * * * or if the output had been curtailed by the failure of the sugar crop * * * or conceivably in some circumstances by unavoidable strikes * * *. We may even assume that a like result would have followed if the plaintiff had bargained not merely for a quantity of molasses to be supplied from a particular refinery, but for molasses to be supplied in accordance with a particular contract between the defendant and the refiner, and if thereafter such contract had been broken without fault on the defendant's part. Scialli v. Correale, 97 N.J. Law, 165, 117 A. 255; cf., however, Marsh v. Johnston, 125 App.Div. 597, 109 N.Y.S. 1106; Id., 196 N.Y. 511, 89 N.E. 1104. The inquiry is merely this, whether the continuance of a special group of circumstances appears from the terms of the contract, interpreted in the setting of the occasion, to have been a tacit or implied presupposition in the minds of the contracting parties, conditioning their belief in a continued obligation. * * *

Accepting that test, we ask ourselves the question: What special group of circumstances does the defendant lay before us as one of the presuppositions immanent in its bargain with the plaintiff? The defendant asks us to assume that a manufacturer, having made a contract with a middleman for a stock of molasses to be procured from a particular refinery, would expect the contract to lapse whenever the refiner chose to diminish his production, and this in the face of the middleman's omission to do anything to charge the refiner with a duty to continue. Business could not be transacted with security or smoothness if a presumption so unreasonable were at the root of its engagements. There is nothing to show that the defendant would have been unable by a timely contract with the refinery to have assured itself of a supply sufficient for its needs. There is nothing to show that the plaintiff, in giving the order for the molasses, was informed by the defendant that such a contract had not been made, or that performance would be contingent upon obtaining one thereafter. If the plaintiff had been so informed, it would very likely have preferred to deal with the refinery directly, instead of dealing with a middleman. The defendant does not even show that it tried to get a contract from the refinery during the months that intervened between the acceptance of the plaintiff's order and the time when shipments were begun. It has wholly failed to relieve itself of the imputation of contributory fault. 3 Williston on Contracts, § 1959. So far as the record shows, it put its faith in the mere chance that the output of the refinery would be the same from year to year, and finding its faith vain, it tells us that its customer must have expected to take a chance as great. We see no reason for importing into the bargain this aleatory element. The defendant is in no better position than a factor who undertakes in his own name to sell for future delivery a special grade of merchandise to be manufactured by a special mill. The duty will be discharged if the mill is destroyed before delivery is due. The duty will subsist if the output is reduced because times turn out to be hard and labor charges high. * * *

* * *

The judgment should be affirmed, with costs.

Note
Additional Cases Finding Impossibility

The impossibility defense is often raised by a promisor, but is rarely successful. Courts typically find that the particular risk was allocated to the promisor or that performance was not impossible. In a few recent cases the defense has succeeded, however. For example, in UNCC Properties, Inc. v. Greene, 111 N.C.App. 391, 432 S.E.2d 699 (1993), the court excused a landowner from a contract to convey an easement when the county condemned the property for public use. In Oneal v. Colton Consol. School Dist. No. 306, 16 Wn.App. 488, 557 P.2d 11 (1976), the court excused a secondary school teacher on impossibility grounds because of deteriorating eyesight. In Net Realty Holding Trust v. Franconia Properties, Inc., 544 F.Supp. 759 (E.D.Va.1982), the court excused a real estate lessor from leasing space only to a department store under the trade name "Korvettes" when Korvettes went bankrupt.

SECTION SIX: IMPRACTICABILITY
OF PERFORMANCE

Today, courts may permit cessation even when performance is not "objectively" impossible. Some courts recognize the lack of sense in compelling performance (or awarding damages for non-performance) in certain situations where performance has become extremely onerous due to an unanticipated event. Yet the line is fine between those cases where courts excuse performance on impracticability grounds and those where they refuse to do so, with refusal the rule and excuse the exception. Typically, the refusal is on the ground that the parties have expressly or impliedly allocated the risk to the promisor.

MARCOVICH LAND CORP. v. J.J. NEWBERRY CO.

Court of Appeals of Indiana, 1980.
413 N.E.2d 935.

MILLER, JUDGE.

Paul March and Walter March (the latter being the executor of the estate of defendant Michael H. March, deceased), legal successors in interest to defendant-landlord Marcovich Land Corporation, appeal a judgment granting plaintiff-tenant, J.J. Newberry Company, a variety store chain, some $117,000, and denying the Marches the damages they requested in a counterclaim. Newberry, former tenant in a building owned by Marcovich located in East Chicago, Indiana, was awarded lost business profits for a period of three years[1] because Marcovich refused to rebuild the structure occupied by Newberry after it was destroyed by fire. The parties had a written lease which the trial court determined was enforceable and required such reconstruction by Marcovich. The court rejected the Marches' dual contentions in their counterclaim or set off that Newberry had not cooperated in efforts to rebuild and that in any event the covenant requiring rebuilding was impossible to perform. We affirm the trial court's judgment.

---

    1. Although the remaining term of its lease was 7 years, the land had been condemned,   apparently as part of an urban renewal project, some 4 years after the building burned.

On appeal, the legal successors to Marcovich present several questions for our review, which issues may be summarized as follows:

1) that the lease does not anticipate or require rebuilding where there has been a total destruction as occurred under the circumstances of the instant case;

2) that it would be "unconscionable" as well as impossible (or, as the Marches contend, commercially impractical) to require such rebuilding in light of the amount of the insurance proceeds, the time remaining on the lease, the "blighted" condition of the area, and the alleged difficulty in obtaining financing;

3) that the trial court improperly ignored the prohibitive circumstances noted in 2) above, as evidenced by its findings and conclusions;

* * *

Newberry's complaint, filed January 4, 1973, generally alleged the parties entered into their 25–year written lease agreement on September 30, 1953 with respect to real estate and the improvements thereon located in the Indiana Harbor region of the City of East Chicago, and that thereafter, on July 14, 1958, Marcovich assigned its interest in the lease to Paul March and Michael H. March as trustees operating under the name of March Realty. The parties do not dispute these general facts, nor the further assertion that a fire of unknown origin completely destroyed the building in question on December 30, 1971. * * *

Count II of the complaint presents the issue involved in the instant appeal, since specific performance was prevented by the condemnation of the property on June 16, 1976 by the City of East Chicago. Newberry contends it lost net profits as a result of the failure by Marcovich to reconstruct the demised premises, and accordingly, in its complaint requested damages of $210,000. As noted above, the trial court awarded Newberry approximately $117,000, consisting of lost profits of about $122,000 until June 16, 1976 minus $5,000 Newberry owed under the rental obligation imposed by the lease.

Because of its significance to the instant appeal, the so-called "fire clause" relied upon by both parties is quoted herein at the outset. That language in the lease provides as follows:

"In the event the demised premises are damaged or destroyed by fire or other casualty, or damaged by the demolition of any portion of the building necessitated by the enforcement of any law or Ordinance, or declared unsafe by any public authority, the Landlord shall, at own cost [sic] and expense, immediately repair, reconstruct and replace the demised premises, including improvements, extensions, alterations and additions to building made by Landlord or Tenant, all such work to be done in compliance with State Laws and City Ordinances. If the extent or character of such damage, destruction or unsafe condition renders the demised premises unfit for the proper conduct of the business of the Tenant, all rent shall cease and abate during the cessation of business of the Tenant and until the complete restoration of the demised premises ready for occupancy. If, however, the Tenant is able to and does continue its business in said premises pending the restoration or reconstruction of the demised premises, then a fair and just proportion of the rent shall abate until the demised premises are restored and ready for occupancy. Any rent paid in advance beyond the happening of any of the contingencies above mentioned shall be returned by the Landlord to the Tenant."

Before applying such provision in its judgment and conclusions of law, the trial court, which decided this case without intervention of a jury, arrived at the following findings of fact significant to the rights of Newberry and the successors to Marcovich's interest:

"6. That at the time the lease of September 30, 1953 was negotiated between the parties, the defendants, Paul March and Michael March, deceased, principals of the defendant, Marcovich Land Corporation, were experienced and competent real estate brokers and landlords.

7. That the defendant, Paul March, had over 40 years of experience in the real estate field which included purchasing, selling and leasing of real estate including commercial properties.

8. That the defendant, Michael March, had over 60 years of experience in the real estate field which included purchasing, selling and leasing of real estate including commercial properties.

9. That at all times during the negotiation of the lease agreement of September 30, 1953, both the plaintiff and the defendants had equal bargaining power for the purposes of negotiating said lease.

10. That from September 30, 1953 until the time of the fire (December 30, 1971) both parties to the lease had completely performed pursuant to the terms of the lease and that neither of the parties to the lease had in any way breached the lease or its terms and conditions.

11. That on December 30, 1971, the building which was the subject-matter of the lease of September 30, 1953, was complete [sic] destroyed by fire. The building was a total loss and nothing was saved.

* * *

13. That on December 31, 1971 the defendants were advised by J.J. Newberry Company that the plaintiff wanted the building rebuilt pursuant to the lease agreement."

Significantly, the conclusions of law which accompanied the above findings determined that the lease agreement between the parties was in all respects valid, enforceable and conscionable, and that the parties to the lease had equal bargaining power when the agreement was made. Thus, since Marcovich did not rebuild, and according to the trial court was apparently not hindered in such efforts by Newberry, damages were awarded to Newberry under what the court thought to be a reasonable determination.

The ultimate award was based on the profits Newberry would have received from May of 1973 until June of 1976, (the latter being, as noted above, the date the property was condemned), apparently because it would take a year to construct a new building. Thus, the profit calculation did not include the 12 months following Michael March's abandonment of the lease in May of 1972. The findings listed specific predicted lost profits for the years (or parts thereof) 1973, 1974, 1975 and 1976.

We first address what amounts to a threshold question in this case, namely, whether the so-called "fire clause" in the parties' lease agreement applies on its face to a situation where, as here, the leased premises were not merely damaged by fire, but rather (as the trial court found) were completely destroyed with nothing saved. The Marches contend, relying principally on an early Kentucky case, *Davis v. Parker,* (1923) 200 Ky. 847, 255 S.W. 836, the language of the lease does not contemplate rebuilding where there has been such a total destruction.

We disagree. While it is true the Court in *Davis* found the lease there at issue anticipated only the restoration or reconstruction of premises which had merely been partially destroyed, as opposed to the complete rebuilding of a demised structure, it is significant that in the *Davis* case the relevant lease provision stated the landlord must "replace the buildings in the same condition as they now are" whenever they are "destroyed by fire or tempest *in such a manner as to render the same untenantable."* *Id.* at 847, 255 S.W. at 836. (emphasis supplied by the Kentucky Court). The Court observed, "[i]f the word [destroyed] stood alone in the sentence there could be no discussion or question, * * *." *Id.* at 849, 255 S.W. at 836. This latter situation is now before this Court. Thus, even if we were to apply the general reasoning of that case in Indiana, it is evident the instant lease provision is distinguishable in light of the fact the modifying language found in *Davis* is omitted from the unambiguous promise in the case at bar to "repair, reconstruct and replace" the demised premises where they are "damaged *or* destroyed." (Emphasis added.)

Similarly, although the Marches contend in this context that "[p]arties to [a] contract are not always able to provide for all the possibilities of which they are aware," *quoting Transatlantic Financing Corp. v. United States,* (D.C.Cir.1966) 363 F.2d 312, 316 it is evident (in contrast to the position urged by the Marches) both sides in the instant litigation did anticipate and provide for what in fact occurred, namely, a fire which completely destroyed the building, consisting of the original premises plus "improvements, extensions, alterations and additions" made by Newberry. An unambiguous document such as the one at bar neither requires nor permits the extrinsic interpretative evidence offered by the Marches. *New Harmony Realty Corp. v. Superior Oil Co.* (1941) 108 Ind.App. 668, 31 N.E.2d 673. Although it is unnecessary to our interpretation of such lease provision we note, in this regard, that it was perhaps partly in anticipation of the landlord's clear duty to rebuild upon complete destruction of the premises that he was elsewhere in the lease required to insure the building and improvements against fire "to the extent of the reasonable insurable value thereof." We accordingly conclude the trial court did not err in its determination of the parties' intent based on the language of this lease agreement.

* * *

* * * With regard to [the Marches' impossibility] defense, both parties cite and discuss this Court's opinion in *Kruse, Kruse & Miklosko, Inc. v. Beedy,* (1976) 170 Ind.App. 373, 353 N.E.2d 514, where the theory is discussed at some length. By way of background—before considering the particular merits of the Marches' argument in the case at bar—we observe the following language in *Kruse* pertaining generally to the impossibility defense in this State:

> "The law in Indiana in regard to impossibility of performance as a defense to a contract action is well stated in *Krause v. Board, etc.* (1904), 162 Ind. 278, at 283–84, 70 N.E. 264, at 265:
>
> > 'We regard it as thoroughly settled that the words of a mere general covenant will not be construed as an undertaking to answer for a subsequent event, happening without the fault of the covenantor, which renders performance of the covenant itself *not merely difficult or relatively impossible, but absolutely impossible,* owing to the act of God, the act of the law, or the loss or destruction of the subject-matter of the contract. Where performance is thus rendered impossible, the inquiry naturally arises as to whether there was a purpose to covenant against such an extraordinary and therefore presumably unapprehended event, the happening of which it was not within the power of the covenantor to prevent.' "

Id. 394, 353 N.E.2d at 528. (emphasis supplied in *Kruse.*)

Significantly (in light of this language in *Kruse*), it does not appear the Marches argue it was absolutely impossible to rebuild the structure rented by Newberry at the time of the fire, since they suggest in their brief "[p]erformance is possible, but the value (benefit) (investment) has been destroyed by an unforeseen event, a totally and completely destroyed building, * * *." Indeed, the only evidence presented at trial which was arguably intended to show such absolute impossibility of performance concerned the purported inability of the Marcovich representatives to obtain financing for a new building under the existing lease terms with Newberry. In this regard, however, we must note not only that there was no showing such financing was essential to permit rebuilding,[2] but also that the depositions of defendant-appellant Paul March and Michael March, deceased (for whom defendant-appellant Walter March acts as executor), suggest the family in fact never tried to obtain financing based on the remaining lease term. Paul March, for example, stated as follows:

> "Q.　* * * Did you ever try to obtain financing from any bank or lending institution to rebuild the building?
>
> A.　I didn't, no.
>
> Q.　Did anyone that you know of try to do that?
>
> A.　It wasn't necessary yet. We hadn't gotten anywhere.
>
> Q.　As far as you know, nobody from March Realty ever tried to obtain financing or ever approached a bank concerning financing, is that correct?
>
> A.　Not as yet."

Similarly, Michael March asserted "I didn't have to try. I know [it was impossible]." These statements, which in essence amount to admissions by the parties they were unaware of any efforts to obtain such financing based

---

2.　It is significant with respect to this question that the Marches acknowledge receiving $200,000 in insurance proceeds which could be applied toward rebuilding, along with whatever other assets the family may have had available.

on the original lease, were controverted (if at all) only by the unelaborated suggestion by Martin March, who was not a party either to the lease or this lawsuit, that the Marches were not able to get financing to rebuild under the remaining term of the lease. He did not explain the basis for such assertion. In this context, we also observe that the possible inability to obtain financing is not generally an unforeseeable circumstance which the parties do not consider in commercial leases or contracts. *See Kruse, Kruse & Miklosko v. Beedy, supra* at 394–95, 353 N.E.2d at 529, where the Court noted "the possibility that Small could not obtain financing not only should have been foreseen by the parties, but was provided for in their agreement."

The Marches maintain, however, that apart from any issue of "absolute" impossibility, the essential question raised by this appeal is whether in Indiana impossibility of performance should include the defense that performance is "impractical" where it involves "excessive and unreasonable cost." They concede such issue is unanswered in any Indiana precedent, but contend their position should be adopted in light of the practice in other jurisdictions, *citing Transatlantic Financing Corp. v. United States,* [363 F.2d 312 (D.C.Cir. 1966)], a case in which Judge Wright acknowledged such a defense but concluded it was not "commercially impractical" under a contract to require a ship carrying wheat to travel 3,000 additional miles on an original 10,000–mile trip, at an alleged cost of almost $44,000, because of the closing of the Suez Canal. *See also Aluminum Co. of America v. Essex Group, Inc.,* 499 F.Supp. 53 (U.S.D.C., W.D.Pa.1980), a case purporting to apply Indiana law.

In response to such argument, we conclude, even assuming *arguendo* the affirmative defense in Indiana extends beyond "absolute" impossibility to encompass the doctrine urged by the Marches, that the trial court could properly have determined there was no evidence before it of the kind of commercially senseless expense contended by the Marches, but rather that the parties had *anticipated* and *allocated between them* the unextraordinary risk which in fact occurred.

* * *

Turning to the evidence relied on by the Marches in support of their theory we note the uncontroverted (though challenged by objection) testimony of the Marches' expert, Richard J. Kestle, that it would cost at least $452,000 in 1972 to construct a building on the site in accordance with certain rough plans prepared by Newberry. Additionally, the Marches presented evidence they received only $200,000 in insurance proceeds, such lesser figure presumably being attributable to the fact the Marches chose not to insure the structure for its replacement cost.[3] The Marches also presented evidence in this regard, however, in the form of testimony from a real estate appraiser using the $452,000 reconstruction figure and a six-year lease, that rebuilding would not be economically or commercially "feasible," a conclusion which he explained in an offer to prove took into account what return a prudent investor would want for his money invested in a new building in 1972,

---

3. We are cognizant the trial court implicitly found the building had been insured for its "reasonable insurable value" when it concluded neither party had breached the lease, but we do not find such determination to be inconsistent with the Marches' right, if they chose, to protect themselves against their ultimate liability for rebuilding by insuring for the replacement cost.

assuming such an investor "would want at least 8% on his money and we said that the recapture or depreciation rate would be 2½% or a total capitalization rate of 10½%." The same expert observed the property in question was in an "urban renewal" area in 1974 or 1975 (though not in 1972), and concluded, "I would advise my client that this is a very poor deal to get into."

In viewing such evidence we are cognizant that even under the standard advocated by the Marches, the test is not simply whether a particular performance would be a bad business risk or even a "very poor deal" for a prudent investor, but rather whether there was "*extreme* ... difficulty, expense, injury, or loss" which goes well beyond the normal range of what might have been expected, Comment d to the proposed Restatement (Second) of Contracts, [§ 281] and whether the parties failed to allocate such risk. *Transatlantic Financing Corp. v. United States, supra.* We believe the trial court could properly have concluded the evidence in the instant case, involving regrettable but unextraordinary rebuilding considerations, did not rise to such a level, but that the risk was anticipated by the parties, and thus not [un]expected and that such risk was, moreover, intended to be allocated between them by the "fire clause" itself.

* * *

[Affirmed.]

MINERAL PARK LAND CO. v. HOWARD

Supreme Court of California, 1916.
172 Cal. 289, 156 P. 458.

SLOSS, J. The defendants appeal from a judgment in favor of plaintiff for $3,650. The appeal is on the judgment roll alone.

The plaintiff was the owner of certain land in the ravine or wash known as the Arroyo Seco, in South Pasadena, Los Angeles county. The defendants had made a contract with the public authorities for the construction of a concrete bridge across the Arroyo Seco. In August, 1911, the parties to this action entered into a written agreement whereby the plaintiff granted to the defendants the right to haul gravel and earth from plaintiff's land, the defendants agreeing to take therefrom all of the gravel and earth necessary in the construction of the fill and cement work on the proposed bridge, the required amount being estimated at approximately 114,000 cubic yards. Defendants agreed to pay 5 cents per cubic yard for the first 80,000 yards, the next 10,000 yards were to be given free of charge, and the balance was to be paid for at the rate of 5 cents per cubic yard.

The complaint was in two counts. The first alleged that the defendants had taken 50,131 cubic yards of earth and gravel, thereby becoming indebted to plaintiff in the sum of $2,506.55, of which only $900 had been paid, leaving a balance of $1,606.55 due. The findings support plaintiff's claim in this regard, and there is no question of the propriety of so much of the judgment as responds to the first count. The second count sought to recover damages for the defendants' failure to take from plaintiff's land any more than the 50,131 yards.

It alleged that the total amount of earth and gravel used by defendants was 101,000 cubic yards, of which they procured 50,869 cubic yards from some place other than plaintiff's premises. The amount due the plaintiff for this amount of earth and gravel would, under the terms of the contract, have been $2,043.45. The count charged that plaintiff's land contained enough earth and gravel to enable the defendants to take therefrom the entire amount required, and that the 50,869 yards not taken had no value to the plaintiff. Accordingly the plaintiff sought, under this head, to recover damages in the sum of $2,043.45.

The answer denied that the plaintiff's land contained any amount of earth and gravel in excess of the 50,131 cubic yards actually taken, and alleged that the defendants took from the said land all of the earth and gravel available for the work mentioned in the contract.

The court found that the plaintiff's land contained earth and gravel far in excess of 101,000 cubic yards of earth and gravel, but that only 50,131 cubic yards, the amount actually taken by the defendants, was above the water level. No greater quantity could have been taken "by ordinary means," or except by the use, at great expense, of a steam dredger, and the earth and gravel so taken could not have been used without first having been dried at great expense and delay. On the issue raised by the plea of defendants that they took all the earth and gravel that was available the court qualified its findings in this way: It found that the defendants did take all of the available earth and gravel from plaintiff's premises, in this, that they took and removed "all that could have been taken advantageously to defendants, or all that was practical to take and remove from a financial standpoint"; that any greater amount could have been taken only at a prohibitive cost, that is, at an expense of 10 or 12 times as much as the usual cost per yard. It is also declared that the word "available" is used in the findings to mean capable of being taken and used advantageously. It was not "advantageous or practical" to have taken more material from plaintiff's land, but it was not impossible. There is a finding that the parties were not under any mutual misunderstanding regarding the amount of available gravel, but that the contract was entered into without any calculation on the part of either of the parties with reference to the amount of available earth and gravel on the premises.

The single question is whether the facts thus found justified the defendants in their failure to take from the plaintiff's land all of the earth and gravel required. This question was answered in the negative by the court below. The case was apparently thought to be governed by the principle—established by a multitude of authorities—that where a party has agreed, without qualification, to perform an act which is not in its nature impossible of performance, he is not excused by difficulty of performance, or by the fact that he becomes unable to perform. * * *

It is, however, equally well settled that, where performance depends upon the existence of a given thing, and such existence was assumed as the basis of the agreement, performance is excused to the extent that the thing ceases to exist or turns out to be nonexistent. 1 Beach, Contr. § 217; 9 Cyc. 631. Thus, where the defendants had agreed to pasture not less than 3,000 cattle on plaintiff's land, paying therefor $1 for each and every head so pastured, and it developed that the land did not furnish feed for more than 717 head, the number actually put on the land by defendant, it was held that plaintiff could not recover the stipulated sum for the difference between the cattle pastured and the minimum of 3,000 agreed to be pastured. Williams v. Miller, 68 Cal. 291, 9 Pac. 166 * * *.

We think the findings of fact make a case falling within the rule of these decisions. The parties were contracting for the right to take earth and gravel to be used in the construction of the bridge. When they stipulated that all of the earth and gravel needed for this purpose should be taken from plaintiff's land, they contemplated and assumed that the land contained the requisite quantity, available for use. The defendants were not binding themselves to take what was not there. And, in determining whether the earth and gravel were "available," we must view the conditions in a practical and reasonable way. Although there was gravel on the land, it was so situated that the defendants could not take it by ordinary means, nor except at a prohibitive cost. To all fair intents then, it was impossible for defendants to take it.

"A thing is impossible in legal contemplation when it is not practicable; and a thing is impracticable when it can only be done at an excessive and unreasonable cost." 1 Beach on Contr. § 216. We do not mean to intimate that the defendants could excuse themselves by showing the existence of conditions which would make the performance of their obligation more expensive than they had anticipated, or which would entail a loss upon them. But, where the difference in cost is so great as here, and has the effect, as found, of making performance impracticable, the situation is not different from that of a total absence of earth and gravel.

On the facts found, there should have been no recovery on the second count.

The judgment is modified by deducting therefrom the sum of $2,043.45, and, as so modified, it stands affirmed.

TRANSATLANTIC FINANCING CORP. v. UNITED STATES

United States Court of Appeals, District of Columbia Circuit, 1966.
363 F.2d 312.

J. Skelly Wright, Circuit Judge:

This appeal involves a voyage charter between Transatlantic Financing Corporation, operator of the SS CHRISTOS, and the United States covering carriage of a full cargo of wheat from a United States Gulf port to a safe port in Iran. The District Court dismissed a libel filed by Transatlantic against the United States for costs attributable to the ship's diversion from the normal sea route caused by the closing of the Suez Canal. We affirm.

On July 26, 1956, the Government of Egypt nationalized the Suez Canal Company and took over operation of the Canal. On October 2, 1956, during the international crisis which resulted from the seizure, the voyage charter in suit was executed between representatives of Transatlantic and the United States. The charter indicated the termini of the voyage but not the route. On October 27, 1956, the SS CHRISTOS sailed from Galveston for Bandar Shapur, Iran, on a course which would have taken her through Gibraltar and the Suez Canal. On October 29, 1956, Israel invaded Egypt. On October 31, 1956, Great Britain and France invaded the Suez Canal Zone. On November

2, 1956, the Egyptian Government obstructed the Suez Canal with sunken vessels and closed it to traffic.

On or about November 7, 1956, Beckmann, representing Transatlantic, contacted Potosky, an employee of the United States Department of Agriculture, who appellant concedes was unauthorized to bind the Government, requesting instructions concerning disposition of the cargo and seeking an agreement for payment of additional compensation for a voyage around the Cape of Good Hope. Potosky advised Beckmann that Transatlantic was expected to perform the charter according to its terms, that he did not believe Transatlantic was entitled to additional compensation for a voyage around the Cape, but that Transatlantic was free to file such a claim. Following this discussion, the CHRISTOS changed course for the Cape of Good Hope and eventually arrived in Bandar Shapur on December 30, 1956.

Transatlantic's claim is based on the following train of argument. The charter was a contract for a voyage from a Gulf port to Iran. Admiralty principles and practices, especially stemming from the doctrine of deviation, require us to imply into the contract the term that the voyage was to be performed by the "usual and customary" route. The usual and customary route from Texas to Iran was, at the time of contract, via Suez, so the contract was for a voyage from Texas to Iran via Suez. When Suez was closed this contract became impossible to perform. Consequently, appellant's argument continues, when Transatlantic delivered the cargo by going around the Cape of Good Hope, in compliance with the Government's demand under claim of right, it conferred a benefit upon the United States for which it should be paid in *quantum meruit*.

The doctrine of impossibility of performance has gradually been freed from the earlier fictional and unrealistic strictures of such tests as the "implied term" and the parties' "contemplation." Page, *The Development of the Doctrine of Impossibility of Performance,* 18 Mich.L.Rev. 589, 596 (1920). See generally 6 Corbin, Contracts §§ 1320–1372 (rev. ed. 1962); 6 Williston, Contracts §§ 1931–1979 (rev.ed.1938). It is now recognized that " 'A thing is impossible in legal contemplation when it is not practicable; and a thing is impracticable when it can only be done at an excessive and unreasonable cost.' " Mineral Park Land Co. v. Howard, 172 Cal. 289, 293, 156 P. 458, 460, L.R.A. 1916E, 1 (1916). *Accord,* Whelan v. Griffith Consumers Company, D.C.Mun.App., 170 A.2d 229 (1961); Restatement, Contracts § 454 (1932); Uniform Commercial Code (U.L.A.) § 2–615, comment 3. The doctrine ultimately represents the ever-shifting line, drawn by courts hopefully responsive to commercial practices and mores, at which the community's interest in having contracts enforced according to their terms is outweighed by the commercial senselessness of requiring performance.[1] When the issue is raised, the court is asked to construct a condition of performance[2] based on the changed circumstances, a process which involves at least three reasonably

---

1. While the impossibility issue rarely arises, as it has here, in a suit to recover the cost of an alternative method of performance, compare Annot. 84 A.L.R.2d 12, 19 (1962), there is nothing necessarily inconsistent in claiming commercial impracticability for the method of performance actually adopted; the concept of impracticability assumes perform-ance was physically possible. Moreover, a rule making nonperformance a condition precedent to recovery would unjustifiably encourage disappointment of expectations.

2. Patterson, *Constructive Conditions in Contracts,* 42 Colum.L.Rev. 903, 943–954 (1942).

definable steps. First, a contingency—something unexpected—must have occurred. Second, the risk of the unexpected occurrence must not have been allocated either by agreement or by custom. Finally, occurrence of the contingency must have rendered performance commercially impracticable. Unless the court finds these three requirements satisfied, the plea of impossibility must fail.

The first requirement was met here. It seems reasonable, where no route is mentioned in a contract, to assume the parties expected performance by the usual and customary route at the time of contract. Since the usual and customary route from Texas to Iran at the time of contract was through Suez, closure of the Canal made impossible the expected method of performance. But this unexpected development raises rather than resolves the impossibility issue, which turns additionally on whether the risk of the contingency's occurrence had been allocated and, if not, whether performance by alternative routes was rendered impracticable.

Proof that the risk of a contingency's occurrence has been allocated may be expressed in or implied from the agreement. Such proof may also be found in the surrounding circumstances, including custom and usages of the trade. See 6 CORBIN, *supra,* § 1339, at 394–397; 6 WILLISTON, *supra,* § 1948, at 5457–5458. The contract in this case does not expressly condition performance upon availability of the Suez route. Nor does it specify "via Suez" or, on the other hand, "via Suez or Cape of Good Hope."[3] Nor are there provisions in the contract from which we may properly imply that the continued availability of Suez was a condition of performance.[4] Nor is there anything in custom or

---

3. In Glidden Company v. Hellenic Lines, Limited, 2 Cir., 275 F.2d 253 (1960), the charter was for transportation of materials from India to America "via Suez Canal or Cape of Good Hope, or Panama Canal," and the court held performance was not "frustrated." In his discussion of this case, Professor Corbin states: "Except for the provision for an alternative route, the defendant would have been discharged, for the reason that the parties contemplated an open Suez Canal as a specific condition or means of performance." 6 CORBIN, *supra,* § 1339, at 399 n. 57. Appellant claims this supports its argument, since the Suez route was contemplated as usual and customary. But there is obviously a difference, in deciding whether a contract allocates the risk of a contingency's occurrence, between a contract specifying no route and a contract specifying Suez. We think that when Professor Corbin said, "Except for the provision for an alternative route," he was referring, not to the entire *provision*—"via Suez Canal or Cape of Good Hope" etc.—but to the fact that *an alternative route* had been provided for. Moreover, in determining what Corbin meant when he said "the parties contemplated an open Suez Canal as a specific condition or means of performance," consideration must be given to the fact, recited by Corbin, that in *Glidden* the parties were specifically aware when the contract was made the Canal might be closed, and the promisee had refused to include a

clause excusing performance in the event of closure. Corbin's statement, therefore, is most accurately read as referring to cases in which a route is specified after negotiations reflecting the parties' awareness that the usual and customary route might become unavailable. Compare Held v. Goldsmith, 153 La. 598, 96 So. 272 (1919).

4. The charter provides that the vessel is "in every way fitted for *the voyage*" (emphasis added), and the "P. & I. Bunker Deviation Clause" refers to "the contract voyage" and the "direct and/or customary route." Appellant argues that these provisions require implication of a voyage by the direct and customary route. Actually they prove only what we are willing to accept—that the parties expected the usual and customary route would be used. The provisions in no way condition performance upon nonoccurrence of this contingency.

There are two clauses which allegedly demonstrate that time is of importance in this contract. One clause computes the remuneration "in steaming time" for diversions to other countries ordered by the charterer in emergencies. This proves only that the United States wished to reserve power to send the goods to another country. It does not imply in any way that there was a rush about the matter. The other clause concerns demurrage and despatch. The charterer agreed to pay Transatlantic demurrage of $1,200 per day for all time in

trade usage, or in the surrounding circumstances generally, which would support our constructing a condition of performance. The numerous cases requiring performance around the Cape when Suez was closed, see *e.g.,* Ocean Tramp Tankers Corp. v. V/O Sovfracht (The Eugenia), [1964] 2 Q.B. 226, and cases cited therein, indicate that the Cape route is generally regarded as an alternative means of performance. So the implied expectation that the route would be via Suez is hardly adequate proof of an allocation to the promisee of the risk of closure. In some cases, even an express expectation may not amount to a condition of performance.[5] The doctrine of deviation supports our assumption that parties normally expect performance by the usual and customary route, but it adds nothing beyond this that is probative of an allocation of the risk.[6]

If anything, the circumstances surrounding this contract indicate that the risk of the Canal's closure may be deemed to have been allocated to Transatlantic. We know or may safely assume that the parties were aware, as were most commercial men with interests affected by the Suez situation, see The Eugenia, *supra,* that the Canal might become a dangerous area. No doubt the tension affected freight rates, and it is arguable that the risk of closure became part of the dickered terms. UNIFORM COMMERCIAL CODE § 2–615, comment 8. We do not deem the risk of closure so allocated, however. Foreseeability or even recognition of a risk does not necessarily prove its allocation.[7] Compare UNIFORM COMMERCIAL CODE § 2–615, Comment 1; RESTATE-

excess of the period agreed upon for loading and unloading, and Transatlantic was to pay despatch of $600 per day for any saving in time. Of course this provision shows the parties were concerned about time, see GILMORE & BLACK, THE LAW OF ADMIRALTY § 4–8 (1957), but the fact that they arranged so minutely the consequences of any delay or speedup of loading and unloading operates against the argument that they were similarly allocating the risk of delay or speed-up of the voyage.

5. UNIFORM COMMERCIAL CODE § 2–614(1) provides: "Where without fault of either party * * * the *agreed* manner of delivery * * * becomes commercially impracticable but a commercially reasonable substitute is available, such substitute performance must be tendered and accepted." (Emphasis added.) Compare Mr. Justice Holmes' observation: "You can give any conclusion a logical form. You always can imply a condition in a contract. But why do you imply it? It is because of some belief as to the practice of the community or of a class, or because of some opinion as to policy * * *." Holmes, *The Path of the Law,* 10 HARV.L.REV. 457, 466 (1897).

6. The deviation doctrine, drawn principally from admiralty insurance practice, implies into all relevant commercial instruments naming the termini of voyages the usual and customary route between those points. 1 ARNOULD, MARINE INSURANCE AND AVERAGE § 376, at 522 (10th ed. 1921). Insurance is cancelled when a ship unreasonably "deviates" from this course, for example by extending a voyage or by putting in at an irregular port, and the shipowner

forfeits the protection of clauses of exception which might otherwise have protected him from his common law insurer's liability to cargo. See GILMORE & BLACK, *supra* Note 8, § 2–6, at 59–60. This practice, properly qualified, see *id.* § 3–41, makes good sense, since insurance rates are computed on the basis of the implied course, and deviations in the course increasing the anticipated risk make the insurer's calculations meaningless. ARNOULD, *supra,* § 14, at 26. Thus the route, so far as insurance contracts are concerned, is crucial, whether express or implied. But even here, the implied term is not inflexible. Reasonable deviations do not result in loss of insurance, at least so long as established practice is followed. See Carriage of Goods by Sea Act § 4(4), 49 STAT. 1210, 46 U.S.C. § 1304(4); and discussion of "held covered" clauses in GILMORE & BLACK, *supra,* § 3–41, at 161. Some "deviations" are required. *E.g.,* Hirsch Lumber Co. v. Weyerhaeuser Steamship Co., 2 Cir., 233 F.2d 791, *cert. denied,* 352 U.S. 880, 77 S.Ct. 102, 1 L.Ed.2d 80 (1956). The doctrine's only relevance, therefore, is that it provides additional support for the assumption we willingly make that merchants agreeing to a voyage between two points expect that the usual and customary route between those points will be used. The doctrine provides no evidence of an allocation of the risk of the route's unavailability.

7. See Note, *The Fetish of Impossibility in the Law of Contracts,* 53 COLUM.L.REV. 94, 98 n. 23 (1953), suggesting that foreseeability is properly used "as a *factor* probative of assump-

MENT, CONTRACTS § 457 (1932). Parties to a contract are not always able to provide for all the possibilities of which they are aware, sometimes because they cannot agree, often simply because they are too busy. Moreover, that some abnormal risk was contemplated is probative but does not necessarily establish an allocation of the risk of the contingency which actually occurs. In this case, for example, nationalization by Egypt of the Canal Corporation and formation of the Suez Users Group did not necessarily indicate that the Canal would be blocked even if a confrontation resulted.[8] The surrounding circumstances do indicate, however, a willingness by Transatlantic to assume abnormal risks, and this fact should legitimately cause us to judge the impracticability of performance by an alternative route in stricter terms than we would were the contingency unforeseen.

We turn then to the question whether occurrence of the contingency rendered performance commercially impracticable under the circumstances of this case. The goods shipped were not subject to harm from the longer, less temperate Southern route. The vessel and crew were fit to proceed around the Cape.[9] Transatlantic was no less able than the United States to purchase insurance to cover the contingency's occurrence. If anything, it is more reasonable to expect owner-operators of vessels to insure against the hazards of war. They are in the best position to calculate the cost of performance by alternative routes (and therefore to estimate the amount of insurance required), and are undoubtedly sensitive to international troubles which uniquely affect the demand for and cost of their services. The only factor operating here in appellant's favor is the added expense, allegedly $43,972.00 above and beyond the contract price of $305,842.92, of extending a 10,000 mile voyage by approximately 3,000 miles. While it may be an overstatement to say that increased cost and difficulty of performance never constitute impracticability, to justify relief there must be more of a variation between expected cost and the cost of performing by an available alternative than is present in this case, where the promisor can legitimately be presumed to have accepted some degree of abnormal risk, and where impracticability is urged on the basis of added expense alone.

We conclude, therefore, as have most other courts considering related issues arising out of the Suez closure, that performance of this contract was not rendered legally impossible. Even if we agreed with appellant, its theory of relief seems untenable. When performance of a contract is deemed impossible it is a nullity. In the case of a charter party involving carriage of goods, the

---

tion of the risk of impossibility." (Emphasis added.)

8. Sources cited in the briefs indicate formation of the Suez Canal Users Association on October 1, 1956, was viewed in some quarters as an implied threat of force. See N.Y. Times, Oct. 2, 1956, p. 1, col. 1, noting, on the day the charter in this case was executed, that "Britain has declared her freedom to use force as a last resort if peaceful methods fail to achieve a satisfactory settlement." Secretary of State Dulles was able, however, to view the statement as evidence of the canal users' "dedication to a just and peaceful solution." THE SUEZ PROBLEM 369–370 (Department of State Pub. 1956).

9. The issue of impracticability should no doubt be "an objective determination of whether the promise can reasonably be performed rather than a subjective inquiry into the promisor's capability of performing as agreed." Symposium, *The Uniform Commercial Code and Contract Law: Some Selected Problems,* 105 U.PA.L.REV. 836, 880, 887 (1957). Dealers should not be excused because of less than normal capabilities. But if both parties are aware of a dealer's limited capabilities, no objective determination would be complete without taking into account this fact.

carrier may return to an appropriate port and unload its cargo, The Malcolm Baxter, Jr., 277 U.S. 323, 48 S.Ct. 516, 72 L.Ed. 901 (1928), subject of course to required steps to minimize damages. If the performance rendered has value, recovery in *quantum meruit* for the entire performance is proper. But here Transatlantic has collected its contract price, and now seeks *quantum meruit* relief for the additional expense of the trip around the Cape. If the contract is a nullity, Transatlantic's theory of relief should have been *quantum meruit* for the entire trip, rather than only for the extra expense. Transatlantic attempts to take its profit on the contract, and then force the Government to absorb the cost of the additional voyage.[10] When impracticability without fault occurs, the law seeks an equitable solution, see 6 CORBIN, *supra*, § 1321, and *quantum meruit* is one of its potent devices to achieve this end. There is no interest in casting the entire burden of commercial disaster on one party in order to preserve the other's profit. Apparently the contract price in this case was advantageous enough to deter appellant from taking a stance on damages consistent with its theory of liability. In any event, there is no basis for relief.

Affirmed.

POSNER AND ROSENFIELD, IMPOSSIBILITY AND RELATED DOCTRINES IN CONTRACT LAW: AN ECONOMIC ANALYSIS

6 J.Leg.Stud. 83, 89–91 (1977).

The typical case in which impossibility or some related doctrine is invoked is one where, by reason of an unforeseen or at least unprovided-for event, performance by one of the parties of his obligations under the contract has become so much more costly than he foresaw at the time the contract was made as to be uneconomical (that is, the costs of performance would be greater than the benefits). The performance promised may have been delivery of a particular cargo by a specified delivery date—but the ship is trapped in the Suez Canal because of a war between Israel and Egypt. Or it may have been a piano recital by Gina Bachauer—and she dies between the signing of the contract and the date of the recital. The law could in each case treat the failure to perform as a breach of contract, thereby in effect assigning to the promisor the risk that war, or death, would prevent performance (or render it uneconomical). Alternatively, invoking impossibility or some related notion, the law could treat the failure to perform as excusable and discharge the contract, thereby in effect assigning the risk to the promisee.

From the standpoint of economics—and disregarding, but only momentarily, administrative costs—discharge should be allowed where the promisee is the superior risk bearer; if the promisor is the superior risk bearer, nonperformance should be treated as a breach of contract. "Superior risk bearer" is to be understood here as the party that is the more efficient bearer

---

10. The argument that the UNIFORM COM-MERCIAL CODE requires the buyer to pay the additional cost of performance by a commercially reasonable substitute was advanced and rejected in Symposium, *supra* Note, [11] 105 U.PA.L.REV. at 884 n. 205. In Dillon v. United States, 156 F.Supp. 719, 140 Ct.Cl. 508 (1957), relief was afforded for some of the cost of delivering hay from a commercially unreasonable distance, but the suit was one in which the plaintiff had suffered losses far in excess of the relief given.

of the particular risk in question, in the particular circumstances of the transaction. Of course, if the parties have expressly assigned the risk to one of them, there is no occasion to inquire which is the superior risk bearer. The inquiry is merely an aid to interpretation.

A party can be a superior risk bearer for one of two reasons. First, he may be in a better position to prevent the risk from materializing. This resembles the economic criterion for assigning liability in tort cases. * * * Discharge would be inefficient in any case where the promisor could prevent the risk from materializing at a lower cost than the expected cost of the risky event. In such a case efficiency would require that the promisor bear the loss resulting from the occurrence of the event, and hence that occurrence should be treated as precipitating a breach of contract.

But the converse is not necessarily true. It does not necessarily follow from the fact that the promisor could not at any reasonable cost have prevented the risk from materializing that he should be discharged from his contractual obligations. Prevention is only one way of dealing with risk; the other is insurance. The promisor may be the superior insurer. If so, his inability to prevent the risk from materializing should not operate to discharge him from the contract, any more than an insurance company's inability to prevent a fire on the premises of the insured should excuse it from its liability to make good the damage caused by the fire.

Problem 8–4

Transatlantic has asked you to draft a clause protecting it in the future from the necessity of undertaking diversions from its "usual and customary" sea routes. Please draft the clause.

UNIFORM COMMERCIAL CODE § 2–615.
Excuse by Failure of Presupposed Conditions

Except so far as a seller may have assumed a greater obligation and subject to the preceding section on substituted performance:

(a) Delay in delivery or non-delivery in whole or in part by a seller who complies with paragraphs (b) and (c) is not a breach of his duty under a contract of sale if performance as agreed has been made impracticable by the occurrence of a contingency the non-occurrence of which was a basic assumption on which the contract was made or by compliance in good faith with any applicable foreign or domestic governmental regulation or order whether or not it later proves to be invalid.

(b) Where the causes mentioned in paragraph (a) affect only a part of the seller's capacity to perform, he must allocate production and deliveries among his customers but may at his option include regular customers not then under contract as well as his own requirements for further manufacture. He may so allocate in any manner which is fair and reasonable.

(c) The seller must notify the buyer seasonably that there will be delay or non-delivery and, when allocation is required under paragraph (b), of the estimated quota thus made available for the buyer.

CONVENTION ON CONTRACTS FOR THE INTERNATIONAL SALE OF GOODS.

Article 79(1)

(1) A party is not liable for a failure to perform any of his obligations if he proves that the failure was due to an impediment beyond his control and that he could not reasonably be expected to have taken the impediment into account at the time of the conclusion of the contract or to have avoided or overcome it or its consequences.

MISHARA CONSTRUCTION CO. v. TRANSIT–MIXED CONCRETE CORP.

Supreme Judicial Court of Massachusetts, 1974.
365 Mass. 122, 310 N.E.2d 363.

REARDON, JUSTICE.

In this action of contract a verdict was returned for the defendant. The case is here on the plaintiff's exceptions.

The plaintiff Mishara Construction Company, Inc. (Mishara) was the general contractor under contract with the Pittsfield Housing Authority for the construction of Rose Manor, a housing project for the elderly. In September, 1966, the plaintiff negotiated with the defendant Transit–Mixed Concrete Corp. (Transit) for the supplying of ready-mixed concrete to be used on the project. An agreement was reached that Transit would supply all the concrete needed on the project at a price of $13.25 a cubic yard, with deliveries to be made at the times and in the amounts as ordered by Mishara. This agreement was evidenced by a purchase order signed by the parties on September 21, 1966. That purchase order identified the Rose Manor project and indicated that delivery was to be made "[a]s required by Mishara Construction Company." Performance under this contract was satisfactory to both parties until April, 1967. In that month a labor dispute disrupted work on the job site. Although work resumed on June 15, 1967, a picket line was maintained on the site until the completion of the project in 1969. Throughout this period, with very few exceptions, no deliveries of concrete were made by Transit notwithstanding frequent requests by Mishara. After notifying Transit of its intention, Mishara purchased the balance of its concrete requirements elsewhere. Mishara sought in damages the additional cost of concrete incurred by virtue of the higher price of the replacement product, as well as the expenses of locating an alternate source.

The plaintiff's exceptions relate to the introduction of certain evidence and the failure of the trial judge to give certain requested instructions. * * *

* * *

[There was no] error in the refusal to give request 13, that on the evidence the jury "must find that [the] defendant breached its contract with [the] plaintiff by failing to deliver" Mishara's concrete requirements. The principal issue in the case was the defendant's claimed excuse of impossibility of performance. The determination of that issue depended on facts and circumstances which were for the jury to decide. While we suppose one could develop a nice technical argument that impossibility does not nullify a breach but rather provides an excuse for it, to give the instruction requested would surely have misled the jury on the ultimate question of liability. Moreover, the failure to give it was of no detriment to the plaintiff of which it can complain. See Howes v. Grush, 131 Mass. 207 (1881). * * *

The remainder of the plaintiff's exceptions relate to the proffered defense of the impossibility of performance. Objection was made to the introduction of all evidence regarding the existence of a picket line at the job site and the difficulty which Transit did encounter or might have encountered in attempting to make deliveries through that picket line. Furthermore, Mishara requested an instruction that Transit "was required to comply with the contract regardless of picket lines, strikes or labor difficulties."[1] As a result Mishara would have completely withdrawn the question of impossibility resulting from the picket line from the jury. We are asked to decide as matter of law and without reference to individual facts and circumstances that "picket lines, strikes or labor difficulties" provide no excuse for nonperformance by way of impossibility. This is too sweeping a statement of the law and we decline to adopt it.

The excuse of impossibility in contracts for the sale of goods is controlled by the appropriate section of the Uniform Commercial Code, G.L. c. 106, § 2–615. That section sets up two requirements before performance may be excused. First, the performance must have become "impracticable." Second, the impracticability must have been caused "by the occurrence of a contingency the non-occurrence of which was a basic assumption on which the contract was made." This section of the Uniform Commercial Code has not yet been interpreted by this court. Therefore it is appropriate to discuss briefly the significance of these two criteria.

With respect to the requirement that performance must have been impracticable, the official Code comment to the section stresses that the reference is to "commercial impracticability" as opposed to strict impossibility. G.L. c. 106, § 2–615, comments 3–4. This is not a radical departure from the common law of contracts as interpreted by this court. Although a strict rule was originally followed denying any excuse for accident or "inevitable necessity," e.g., Adams v. Nichols, 19 Pick. 275 (1837), it has long been assumed that circumstances drastically increasing the difficulty and expense of the contemplated performance may be within the compass of "impossibility." See Rowe v. Peabody, 207 Mass. 226, 233–234, 93 N.E. 604 (1911) (dictum); Fauci v. Denehy, 332 Mass. 691, 696–697, 127 N.E.2d 477 (1955). By adopting the term "impracticability" rather than "impossibility" the drafters of the Code appear to be in accord with Professor Williston who stated that "the essence of the modern defense of impossibility is that the promised performance was at the making of the contract, or thereafter became, impracticable owing to some extreme or unreasonable difficulty, expense, injury, or loss involved, rather than that it is scientifically or actually impossible."

---

1. Requests 16 and 17 essentially asked for instructions that in the absence of clauses in the contract to the contrary, the impossibility of performance provides no excuse. This, in effect, requires a charge that no set of circumstances will ever excuse a supplier from performing. Since we conclude in the text that request 15, to the effect that picket lines and labor disputes provide no excuse, is an incorrect statement of the law, it follows a fortiori that these requests were rightly refused.

Williston, Contracts (Rev. ed.) § 1931 (1938). See Restatement: Contracts, § 454 (1932); Corbin, Contracts, § 1339 (1962).

The second criterion of the excuse, that the intervening circumstance be one which the parties assumed would not occur, is also familiar to the law of Massachusetts. Baetjer v. New England Alcohol Co., 319 Mass. 592, 600, 66 N.E.2d 798 (1946). Boston Plate & Window Glass Co. v. John Bowen Co., Inc., 335 Mass. 697, 699–700, 141 N.E.2d 715 (1957). The rule is essentially aimed at the distribution of certain kinds of risks in the contractual relationship. By directing the inquiry to the time when the contract was first made, we really seek to determine whether the risk of the intervening circumstance was one which the parties may be taken to have assigned between themselves. It is, of course, the very essence of contract that it is directed at the elimination of some risks for each party in exchange for others. Each receives the certainty of price, quantity, and time, and assumes the risk of changing market prices, superior opportunity, or added costs. It is implicit in the doctrine of impossibility (and the companion rule of "frustration of purpose") that certain risks are so unusual and have such severe consequences that they must have been beyond the scope of the assignment of risks inherent in the contract, that is, beyond the agreement made by the parties. To require performance in that case would be to grant the promisee an advantage for which he could not be said to have bargained in making the contract. "The important question is whether an unanticipated circumstance has made performance of the promise vitally different from what should reasonably have been within the contemplation of both parties when they entered into the contract. If so, the risk should not fairly be thrown upon the promisor." Williston, Contracts (Rev. ed.) § 1931 (1938). The emphasis in contracts governed by the Uniform Commercial Code is on the commercial context in which the agreement was made. The question is, given the commercial circumstances in which the parties dealt: Was the contingency which developed one which the parties could reasonably be thought to have foreseen as a real possibility which could affect performance? Was it one of that variety of risks which the parties were tacitly assigning to the promisor by their failure to provide for it explicitly? If it were, performance will be required. If it could not be so considered, performance is excused. The contract cannot be reasonably thought to govern in these circumstances, and the parties are both thrown upon the resources of the open market without the benefit of their contract. See Boston Plate & Window Glass Co. v. John Bowen Co., Inc., *supra,* at 699–700, 141 N.E.2d 715.

With this backdrop, we consider Mishara's contention that a labor dispute which makes performance more difficult never constitutes an excuse for nonperformance. We think it is evident that in some situations a labor dispute would not meet the requirements for impossibility discussed above. A picket line might constitute a mere inconvenience and hardly make performance "impracticable." Likewise, in certain industries with a long record of labor difficulties, the nonoccurrence of strikes and picket lines could not fairly be said to be a basic assumption of the agreement. Certainly, in general, labor disputes cannot be considered extraordinary in the course of modern commerce. See Restatement: Contracts, § 461, illustration 7 (1932). Admitting this, however, we are still far from the proposition implicit in the plaintiff's requests. Much must depend on the facts known to the parties at the time of contracting with respect to the history of and prospects for labor difficulties during the period of performance of the contract, as well as the likely severity of the effect of such disputes on the ability to perform. From these facts it is possible to draw an inference as to whether or not the parties intended performance to be carried out even in the face of the labor difficulty. Where the probability of a labor dispute appears to be practically nil, and where the occurrence of such a dispute provides unusual difficulty, the excuse of impracticability might well be applicable. Thus in discussing the defence of impossibility, then Chief Judge Cardozo noted an excuse would be provided "conceivably in some circumstances by unavoidable strikes." Canadian Industrial Alcohol Co., Ltd. v. Dunbar Molasses Co., 258 N.Y. 194, 198, 179 N.E. 383, 384 (1932). The many variables which may bear on the question in individual cases were canvassed by Professor Williston in Williston, Contracts (Rev. ed.) § 1951A (1938), and he concluded that the trend of the law is toward recognizing strikes as excuses for nonperformance. We agree with the statement of the judge in Badhwar v. Colorado Fuel & Iron Corp., 138 F.Supp. 595, 607 (S.D.N.Y.1955), affd. 245 F.2d 903 (2d Cir.1957), on the same question: "Rather than mechanically apply any fixed rule of law, where the parties themselves have not allocated responsibility, justice is better served by appraising all of the circumstances, the part the various parties played, and thereon determining liability." Since the instructions requested by the plaintiff and the exclusion of the evidence objected to would have precluded such a factual determination, the requests were more properly refused, and the evidence was properly admitted.

Exceptions overruled.

Problem 8–5

Your client, Westinghouse Electric Corp., agreed to build and fuel two Florida Power and Light Company nuclear steam supply systems and to remove the spent fuel. Westinghouse agreed to a contract price fixed for ten years solely by reference to the amount of electricity generated by the systems and independent of its costs. The parties also contemplated that Westinghouse would reprocess the spent fuel, which would permit Westinghouse to recoup between $16 and $19 million over the life of the contract, although the contract expressly required only that Westinghouse remove the spent fuel and "dispose of it as Westinghouse sees fit." After the agreement was reached, a federal government order halted commercial reprocessing, but spent fuel could still be stored in storage racks. Is Westinghouse bound to its agreement with Florida Power?

Consider individually and collectively the import of the following additional facts: (1) At the time of the agreement no commercial reprocessing firm existed, but the government had been encouraging firms to engage in it. (2) Florida Power would be forced to shut down its reactors and would incur potential future costs of $1 million per day for replacement power, if Westinghouse were excused. (3) If forced to perform, Westinghouse would not lose money on the "package deal" of plant and fuel contracts with Florida Power. (4) Westinghouse had insufficient information in computing its costs for the fuel contract. (5) Florida had little knowledge of the nuclear power industry, whereas Westinghouse was knowledgeable. (6) From the outset, Florida sought a fixed-price contract and Westinghouse knew this. What additional information would you elicit?

SECTION SEVEN: FRUSTRATION OF PURPOSE

KRELL v. HENRY

King's Bench, 1903.
2 K.B. 740.

APPEAL from a decision of DARLING J.

The plaintiff, Paul Krell, sued the defendant, C.S. Henry, for 50*l.*, being the balance of a sum of 75*l.*, for which the defendant had agreed to hire a flat at 56A, Pall Mall on the days of June 26 and 27, for the purpose of viewing the processions to be held in connection with the coronation of His Majesty. The defendant denied his liability, and counterclaimed for the return of the sum of 25*l.*, which had been paid as a deposit, on the ground that, the processions not having taken place owing to the serious illness of the King, there had been a total failure of consideration for the contract entered into by him.

The facts, which were not disputed, were as follows. The plaintiff on leaving the country in March, 1902, left instructions with his solicitor to let his suite of chambers at 56A, Pall Mall on such terms and for such period (not exceeding six months) as he thought proper. On June 17, 1902, the defendant noticed an announcement in the windows of the plaintiff's flat to the effect that windows to view the coronation processions were to be let. The defendant interviewed the housekeeper on the subject, when it was pointed out to him what a good view of the processions could be obtained from the premises, and he eventually agreed with the housekeeper to take the suite for the two days in question for a sum of 75*l.*

On June 20 the defendant wrote the following letter to the plaintiff's solicitor:—

"I am in receipt of yours of the 18th instant, inclosing form of agreement for the suite of chambers on the third floor at 56A, Pall Mall, which I have agreed to take for the two days, the 26th and 27th instant, for the sum of 75*l.* For reasons given you I cannot enter into the agreement, but as arranged over the telephone I inclose herewith cheque for 25*l.* as deposit, and will thank you to confirm to me that I shall have the entire use of these rooms during the days (not the nights) of the 26th and 27th instant. You may rely that every care will be taken of the premises and their contents. On the 24th inst. I will pay the balance, viz., 50*l.*, to complete the 75*l.* agreed upon."

On the same day the defendant received the following reply from the plaintiff's solicitor:—

"I am in receipt of your letter of to-day's date inclosing cheque for 25*l.* deposit on your agreeing to take Mr. Krell's chambers on the third floor at 56A, Pall Mall for the two days, the 26th and 27th June, and I confirm the agreement that you are to have the entire use of these rooms during the days (but not the nights), the balance, 50*l.*, to be paid to me on Tuesday next the 24th instant."

The processions not having taken place on the days originally appointed, namely, June 26 and 27, the defendant declined to pay the balance of 50*l.*

alleged to be due from him under the contract in writing of June 20 constituted by the above two letters. Hence the present action.

Darling J., on August 11, 1902, held, upon the authority of *Taylor v. Caldwell* and *The Moorcock,* that there was an implied condition in the contract that the procession should take place, and gave judgment for the defendant on the claim and counter-claim.

The plaintiff appealed.

* * *

Aug. 11. VAUGHAN WILLIAMS L.J. read the following written judgment. * * * The contract is contained in two letters of June 20 which passed between the defendant and the plaintiff's agent, Mr. Cecil Bisgood. These letters do not mention the coronation, but speak merely of the taking of Mr. Krell's chambers, or, rather, of the use of them, in the daytime of June 26 and 27, for the sum of 75*l.*, 25*l.* then paid, balance 50*l.* to be paid on the 24th. But the affidavits, which by agreement between the parties are to be taken as stating the facts of the case, shew that the plaintiff exhibited on his premises, third floor, 56A, Pall Mall, an announcement to the effect that windows to view the Royal coronation procession were to be let, and that the defendant was induced by that announcement to apply to the housekeeper on the premises, who said that the owner was willing to let the suite of rooms for the purpose of seeing the Royal procession for both days, but not nights, of June 26 and 27.

In my judgment the use of the rooms was let and taken for the purpose of seeing the Royal procession. It was not a demise of the rooms, or even an agreement to let and take the rooms. It is a licence to use rooms for a particular purpose and none other. And in my judgment the taking place of those processions on the days proclaimed along the proclaimed route, which passed 56A, Pall Mall, was regarded by both contracting parties as the foundation of the contract; and I think that it cannot reasonably be supposed to have been in the contemplation of the contracting parties, when the contract was made, that the coronation would not be held on the proclaimed days, or the processions not take place on those days along the proclaimed route; and I think that the words imposing on the defendant the obligation to accept and pay for the use of the rooms for the named days, although general and unconditional, were not used with reference to the possibility of the particular contingency which afterwards occurred.

It was suggested in the course of the argument that if the occurrence, on the proclaimed days, of the coronation and the procession in this case were the foundation of the contract, and if the general words are thereby limited or qualified, so that in the event of the non-occurrence of the coronation and procession along the proclaimed route they would discharge both parties from further performance of the contract, it would follow that if a cabman was engaged to take some one to Epsom on Derby Day at a suitable enhanced price for such a journey, say 10*l.*, both parties to the contract would be discharged in the contingency of the race at Epsom for some reason becoming impossible; but I do not think this follows, for I do not think that in the cab case the happening of the race would be the foundation of the contract. No doubt the purpose of the engager would be to go to see the Derby, and the price would be proportionately high; but the cab had no special qualifications for the purpose which led to the selection of the cab for this particular occasion. Any other cab would have done as well. Moreover, I think that, under the cab contract, the hirer, even if the race went off, could have said, "Drive me to Epsom; I will pay you the agreed sum; you have nothing to do with the purpose for which I hired the cab," and that if the cabman refused he would have been guilty of a breach of contract, there being nothing to qualify his promise to drive the hirer to Epsom on a particular day. Whereas in the case of the coronation, there is not merely the purpose of the hirer to see the coronation procession, but it is the coronation procession and the relative position of the rooms which is the basis of the contract as much for the lessor as the hirer; and I think that if the King, before the coronation day and after the contract, had died, the hirer could not have insisted on having the rooms on the days named. It could not in the cab case be reasonably said that seeing the Derby race was the foundation of the contract, as it was of the licence in this case. Whereas in the present case, where the rooms were offered and taken, by reason of their peculiar suitability from the position of the rooms for a view of the coronation procession, surely the view of the coronation procession was the foundation of the contract, which is a very different thing from the purpose of the man who engaged the cab—namely, to see the race—being held to be the foundation of the contract.

Each case must be judged by its own circumstances. In each case one must ask oneself, first, what, having regard to all the circumstances, was the foundation of the contract? Secondly, was the performance of the contract prevented? Thirdly, was the event which prevented the performance of the contract of such a character that it cannot reasonably be said to have been in the contemplation of the parties at the date of the contract? If all these questions are answered in the affirmative (as I think they should be in this case), I think both parties are discharged from further performance of the contract. I think that the coronation procession was the foundation of this contract, and that the non-happening of it prevented the performance of the contract; and, secondly, I think that the non-happening of the procession, to use the words of Sir James Hannen in *Baily v. De Crespigny,* was an event "of such a character that it cannot reasonably be supposed to have been in the contemplation of the contracting parties when the contract was made, and that they are not to be held bound by general words which, though large enough to include, were not used with reference to the possibility of the particular contingency which afterwards happened."

The test seems to be whether the event which causes the impossibility was or might have been anticipated and guarded against. It seems difficult to say, in a case where both parties anticipate the happening of an event, which anticipation is the foundation of the contract, that either party must be taken to have anticipated, and ought to have guarded against, the event which prevented the performance of the contract. * * * I myself am clearly of opinion that in this case, where we have to ask ourselves whether the object of the contract was frustrated by the non-happening of the coronation and its procession on the days proclaimed, parol evidence is admissible to shew that the subject of the contract was rooms to view the coronation procession, and was so to the knowledge of both parties. When once this is established, I see no difficulty whatever in the case. It is not essential to the application of the principle of *Taylor v. Caldwell* that the direct subject of the contract should perish or fail to be in existence at the date of performance of the contract. It is sufficient if a state of things or condition expressed in the contract and essential to its performance perishes or fails to be in existence at that time. In the present case the condition which fails and prevents the achievement of that which was, in the contemplation of both parties, the foundation of the contract, is not expressly mentioned either as a condition of the contract or the purpose of it; but I think for the reasons which I have given that the principle of *Taylor v. Caldwell* ought to be applied.

This disposes of the plaintiff's claim for 50*l.* unpaid balance of the price agreed to be paid for the use of the rooms. The defendant at one time set up a cross-claim for the return of the 25*l.* he paid at the date of the contract. As that claim is now withdrawn it is unnecessary to say anything about it.

I think this appeal ought to be dismissed.

ROMER L.J. With some doubt I have also come to the conclusion that this case is governed by the principle on which *Taylor v. Caldwell* was decided, and accordingly that the appeal must be dismissed. The doubt I have felt was whether the parties to the contract now before us could be said, under the circumstances, not to have had at all in their contemplation the risk that for some reason or other the coronation processions might not take place on the days fixed, or, if the processions took place, might not pass so as to be capable of being viewed from the rooms mentioned in the contract; and whether, under this contract, that risk was not undertaken by the defendant. But on the question of fact as to what was in the contemplation of the parties at the time, I do not think it right to differ from the conclusion arrived at by Vaughan Williams L.J., and (as I gather) also arrived at by my brother Stirling. This being so, I concur in the conclusions arrived at by Vaughan Williams L.J. in his judgment, and I do not desire to add anything to what he has said so fully and completely.

STIRLING L.J. said he had had an opportunity of reading the judgment delivered by Vaughan Williams L.J., with which he entirely agreed. Though the case was one of very great difficulty, he thought it came within the principle of *Taylor v. Caldwell.*

Appeal dismissed.

"Oh Say, Can You See?"

Said Henry to Krell, You can't sue
Though I've rented your room with a view
Now (Oh Damn! Dearie Me!)
There's nothing to see
For they've cancelled the spectacle due.

What you've got (Said Vaughan Williams L.J.)
Is a license to watch, by the day
What you both contemplated
Has now been frustrated
So there'd better be nothing to pay.

GEOFFREY MARSHALL
19 SEPTEMBER 1986

Krell? and Henry?
in front of 56A Pall Mall.

LLOYD v. MURPHY

Supreme Court of California, 1944.
25 Cal.2d 48, 153 P.2d 47.

TRAYNOR, JUSTICE.

On August 4, 1941 plaintiffs leased to defendant for a five-year term beginning September 15, 1941, certain premises located at the corner of

Almont Drive and Wilshire Boulevard in the city of Beverly Hills, Los Angeles county, "for the sole purpose of conducting thereon the business of displaying and selling new automobiles (including the servicing and repairing thereof and of selling the petroleum products of a major oil company) and for no other purpose whatsoever without the written consent of the lessor" except "to make an occasional sale of a used automobile." Defendant agreed not to sublease or assign without plaintiffs' written consent. On January 1, 1942 the federal government ordered that the sale of new automobiles be discontinued. It modified this order on January 8, 1942 to permit sales to those engaged in military activities, and on January 20, 1942, it established a system of priorities restricting sales to persons having preferential ratings of A–1–j or higher. On March 10, 1942, defendant explained the effect of these restrictions on his business to one of the plaintiffs authorized to act for the others, who orally waived the restrictions in the lease as to use and subleasing and offered to reduce the rent if defendant should be unable to operate profitably. Nevertheless defendant vacated the premises on March 15, 1942, giving oral notice of repudiation of the lease to plaintiffs, which was followed by a written notice on March 24, 1942. Plaintiffs affirmed in writing on March 26th their oral waiver and, failing to persuade defendant to perform his obligations, they rented the property to other tenants pursuant to their powers under the lease in order to mitigate damages. On May 11, 1942, plaintiffs brought this action praying for declaratory relief to determine their rights under the lease, and for judgment for unpaid rent. Following a trial on the merits, the court found that the leased premises were located on one of the main traffic arteries of Los Angeles County; that they were equipped with gasoline pumps and in general adapted for the maintenance of an automobile service station; that they contained a one-story storeroom adapted to many commercial purposes; that plaintiffs had waived the restrictions in the lease and granted defendant the right to use the premises for any legitimate purpose and to sublease to any responsible party; that defendant continues to carry on the business of selling and servicing automobiles at two other places. Defendant testified that at one of these locations he sold new automobiles exclusively and when asked if he were aware that many new automobile dealers were continuing in business replied: "Sure. It is just the location that I couldn't make a go, though, of automobiles." Although there was no finding to that effect, defendant estimated in response to inquiry by his counsel, that 90 per cent of his gross volume of business was new car sales and 10 per cent gasoline sales. The trial court held that war conditions had not terminated defendant's obligations under the lease and gave judgment for plaintiffs, declaring the lease as modified by plaintiffs' waiver to be in full force and effect, and ordered defendant to pay the unpaid rent with interest, less amounts received by plaintiffs from re-renting. Defendant brought this appeal, contending that the purpose for which the premises were leased was frustrated by the restrictions placed on the sale of new automobiles by the federal government, thereby terminating his duties under the lease.

Although commercial frustration was first recognized as an excuse for nonperformance of a contractual duty by the courts of England (Krell v. Henry, C.A., 1903, 2 K.B. 740 * * *) its soundness has been questioned by those courts (see Maritime National Fish, Ltd. v. Ocean Trawlers, Ltd., [1935] A.C. 524, 528–29; 56 L.Q.Rev. 324, arguing that Krell v. Henry, supra, was a misapplication of Taylor v. Caldwell, 1863, 3 B. & S. 826, the leading case on impossibility as an excuse for nonperformance), and they have refused to apply the doctrine to leases on the ground that an estate is conveyed to the lessee, which carries with it all risks. Swift v. McBean, 1942, 1 K.B. 275 * * *. Many courts, therefore, in the United States have held that the tenant bears all risks as owner of the estate * * * but the modern cases have recognized that the defense may be available in a proper case, even in a lease. * * *

Although the doctrine of frustration is akin to the doctrine of impossibility of performance, * * * since both have developed from the commercial necessity of excusing performance in cases of extreme hardship, frustration is not a form of impossibility even under the modern definition of that term, which includes not only cases of physical impossibility but also cases of extreme impracticability of performance (see Mineral Park Land Co. v. Howard, 172 Cal. 289, 293, 156 P. 458, L.R.A.1916E, 1 * * *). Performance remains possible but the expected value of performance to the party seeking to be excused has been destroyed by a fortuitous event, which supervenes to cause an actual but not literal failure of consideration. Krell v. Henry, supra * * *.

The question in cases involving frustration is whether the equities of the case, considered in the light of sound public policy, require placing the risk of a disruption or complete destruction of the contract equilibrium on defendant or plaintiff under the circumstances of a given case, * * * and the answer depends on whether an unanticipated circumstance, the risk of which should not be fairly thrown on the promisor, has made performance vitally different from what was reasonably to be expected (6 Williston, op. cit. supra, § 1963, p. 5511; Restatement, Contracts, § 454). The purpose of a contract is to place the risks of performance upon the promisor, and the relation of the parties, terms of the contract, and circumstances surrounding its formation must be examined to determine whether it can be fairly inferred that the risk of the event that has supervened to cause the alleged frustration was not reasonably foreseeable. If it was foreseeable there should have been provision for it in the contract, and the absence of such a provision gives rise to the inference that the risk was assumed.

The doctrine of frustration has been limited to cases of extreme hardship so that businessmen, who must make their arrangements in advance, can rely with certainty on their contracts. Anglo–Northern Trading Co. v. Emlyn Jones and Williams, 2 K.B. 78; 137 A.L.R. 1199, 1216–1221. The courts have required a promisor seeking to excuse himself from performance of his obligations to prove that the risk of the frustrating event was not reasonably foreseeable and that the value of counterperformance is totally or nearly totally destroyed, for frustration is no defense if it was foreseeable or controllable by the promisor, or if counterperformance remains valuable. * * *

Thus laws or other governmental acts that make performance unprofitable or more difficult or expensive do not excuse the duty to perform a contractual obligation. * * * It is settled that if parties have contracted with reference to a state of war or have contemplated the risks arising from it, they may not invoke the doctrine of frustration to escape their obligations. * * *

At the time the lease in the present case was executed the National Defense Act, Public Act No. 671 of the 76th Congress, 54 Stats. 676, § 2(a), 50 U.S.C.A.Appendix § 1152(a), approved June 28, 1940, authorizing the President to allocate materials and mobilize industry for national defense, had been law for more than a year. The automotive industry was in the process of conversion to supply the needs of our growing mechanized army and to meet lend-lease commitments. Iceland and Greenland had been occupied by the army. Automobile sales were soaring because the public anticipated that production would soon be restricted. These facts were commonly known and it cannot be said that the risk of war and its consequences necessitating restriction of the production and sale of automobiles was so remote a contingency that its risk could not be foreseen by defendant, an experienced automobile dealer. Indeed, the conditions prevailing at the time the lease was executed, and the absence of any provision in the lease contracting against the effect of war, gives rise to the inference that the risk was assumed. Defendant has therefore failed to prove that the possibility of war and its consequences on the production and sale of new automobiles was an unanticipated circumstance wholly outside the contemplation of the parties.

Nor has defendant sustained the burden of proving that the value of the lease has been destroyed. The sale of automobiles was not made impossible or illegal but merely restricted and if governmental regulation does not entirely prohibit the business to be carried on in the leased premises but only limits or restricts it, thereby making it less profitable and more difficult to continue, the lease is not terminated or the lessee excused from further performance. * * * Defendant may use the premises for the purpose for which they were leased. New automobiles and gasoline continue to be sold. Indeed, defendant testified that he continued to sell new automobiles exclusively at another location in the same county.

* * *

The consequences of applying the doctrine of frustration to a leasehold involving less than a total or nearly total destruction of the value of the leased premises would be undesirable. Confusion would result from different decisions purporting to define "substantial" frustration. Litigation would be encouraged by the repudiation of leases when lessees found their businesses less profitable because of the regulations attendant upon a national emergency. Many leases have been affected in varying degrees by the widespread governmental regulations necessitated by war conditions.

* * *

The judgment is affirmed.

Problem 8–6

On March 15, 1979, Jenson entered a two-year lease of a tract of 700 acres in Fremont County, Iowa, with lessor Haynes. The parties agreed to semi-annual rent of $22,600. The first installment was paid on March 15, 1979, but in November, when the next installment was due, Jenson refused to pay. He claimed that farming of the land was "frustrated" by "unusual, sudden, violent and extraordinary floods of the East Nishnabotna River." Assume that the river had flooded the farm land for much of the summer of 1979, substantially impairing the prospect of cultivating crops on the leased land. Assume further that crop failures from causes such as excess moisture, drought and insect infestation are quite common in Iowa, but that the lease was silent on these problems. Evaluate Jenson's defense. What further facts do you need? If Jenson sought your advice before entering the lease, what would you have told him?

DOWNING v. STILES, 635 P.2d 808 (Wyo.1981). [Plaintiffs sold their half interest in the "Maverick Recreation Center," a restaurant, to their partner defendant, Stiles. Stiles gave plaintiffs a promissory note for $25,000 to pay for the interest in the restaurant. Much of Maverick's business resulted from patronage by customers of a bar in the same building. Six or seven months after the bar ceased doing business, Stiles stopped making installment payments to the plaintiffs on the purchase price of the restaurant. A month later, the building burned down. The trial court, in a non-jury trial, found in favor of Stiles based on commercial frustration in that Maverick "was dependent on the business with Rustler Bar." Held, reversed.]

ROONEY, JUSTICE.

In this case, Stiles did not contend that the supervening event was the fire. The discontinuance of the Rustler Bar business was the event designated as supervening. The contract was partly executory, the event occurred subsequent to the making of the contract, and appellants had not agreed, expressly or impliedly, to perform in spite of the occurrence of the event. Although subject to considerable dispute, it may even be said that the non-occurrence of the event was a basic assumption on which the contract was made. But the evidence does not establish the continuation of Rustler Bar's business as the principal purpose for which the contract was made, and, therefore, that the frustration was substantial. Certainly, the frustration was not "total or nearly total."

The principal purpose of the purchase was to carry on a restaurant business. The fact is that such restaurant business was continued to be carried on for six or seven months after the Rustler Bar ceased doing business. It was not until just prior to the fire that Stiles refused to make payment under the contract. This fact reflects the recognition that one of the risks assumed by Stiles under the contract was the decrease and discontinuance of Rustler Bar's business. Because of the lease, Stiles could not be evicted. But Stiles had not sought any provision in the agreement whereby Rustler Bar was bound to use Stiles for its food service. If such were the principal purpose of the purchase agreement between Stiles and appellants, assurance of such should have been secured along with the lease. And such assurance should designate the extent of such service. For otherwise, where is the line drawn? Can Stiles be discharged from performance of her contract with appellants when service to Rustler Bar's customers falls off 10%? or 25%? or 90%? In the language of Comment *a* to § 285, Restatement, Contracts 2d, supra:

> * * * It is not enough that the transaction has become less profitable for the affected party or even that he will sustain a loss. The frustration must be so severe that it is not fairly to be regarded as within the risks that he assumed under the contract. * * *

The circumstances of this case are similar to Illustration 7 to [Section 265] of the Restatement [Second]:

7. A leases a gasoline station to B. A change in traffic regulations so reduces B's business that he is unable to operate the station except at a substantial loss. B refuses to make further payments of rent. If B can still operate the station, even though at some loss, his principal purpose of operating a gasoline station is not substantially frustrated. B's duty to pay rent is not discharged, and B is liable to A for breach of contract. The result would be the same if the loss were caused by a governmental regulation rationing gasoline or a termination of the franchise under which B obtained gasoline.

* * *

Accordingly, it was error to apply the doctrine of commercial frustration to the circumstances of this case.

SMITH v. ROBERTS, 54 Ill.App.3d 910, 12 Ill.Dec. 648, 370 N.E.2d 271 (1977).

MILLS, JUSTICE.

We have here a lease.

And with it we have the doctrine of commercial frustration.

The trial judge held that the doctrine applied and that the lease was terminated thereby.

He was right. We affirm.

The Smiths and Roberts Brothers entered into a lease agreement for the rental of the first floor and basement of property located in Springfield at 111–113 North Sixth Street. Roberts Brothers was already operating a men's clothing store next to the leased premises and intended to make an opening through their east wall and Smith's west wall in order to establish a department which would be called the Gas Light Room. Thereafter, the main store building of Roberts Brothers was completely destroyed by fire. Questions concerning the rights and liabilities of the parties under the lease were raised as a result of that conflagration and those questions then ripened into litigation.

After Roberts Brothers failed to reoccupy the leased premises—which suffered only smoke damage—the Smiths filed suit for breach of the lease. * * * The trial court found that the lease had been terminated because the destruction of Roberts Brothers' main store excused performance on its part. * * *

We concur with the trial judge and affirm.

* * *

At issue is the doctrine of *commercial frustration*.

* * *

The doctrine of commercial frustration is not to be applied liberally. (*Greenlee Foundries v. Kussel* (1973), 13 Ill.App.3d 611, 301 N.E.2d 106.)

However, the defense of commercial frustration is a viable doctrine in Illinois and will be applied when the defendant has satisfied two rigorous tests: (1) the frustrating event was not reasonably foreseeable; and (2) the value of counterperformance by the lessee had been totally or nearly totally destroyed by the frustrating cause. *Greenlee, citing Lloyd v. Murphy* (1944), 25 Cal.2d 48, 153 P.2d 47.

The factual circumstances here satisfy these stringent tests. First, although it might be foreseeable that the main Roberts Brothers' store would be destroyed and the leased premises would remain intact, it is a remote contingency to provide for in a lease. The parties were, in fact, diligent enough to put a catastrophe clause in the lease concerning destruction of the *leased* premises. We find that their failure to include such a clause as to Roberts Brothers' main store was not due to a lack of diligence since such a contingency was not reasonably foreseeable.

The second horn of the two-prong test is also satisfied—the value of the Smith counterperformance was totally—or nearly totally—destroyed. Although it would be physically possible to operate the leased premises as a separate entity, testimony revealed that operations would have to be changed drastically in order to make the premises self-sufficient. Furthermore, the record clearly demonstrates that the leased premises were never intended to be autonomous. Therefore, the trial court's finding that the existence of the main store was an implied condition of the contract between the parties and that its destruction frustrated the lease is an accurate interpretation of the lease. The court's finding results in the fairest disposition of the parties' respective interests.

* * *

Affirmed.

Problem 8–7

You represent Alvin Parker, a 37 year-old bachelor, who believed his marriage prospects would improve if he took dancing lessons. He contracted for 2,734 hours of lessons for which he paid over $24,000 in advance. The contract signed by Parker contained the following clause:

> NON–CANCELLABLE * * * CONTRACT * * * I UNDERSTAND THAT NO REFUNDS WILL BE MADE UNDER THE TERMS OF THIS CONTRACT.

A few weeks after signing this agreement Parker was severely injured in an auto accident rendering him incapable of continuing his lessons. Can Parker get his money back? If Parker had asked you to review the agreement before signing, what would you have recommended?

SECTION EIGHT: FAILURE OF CONDITION, MATERIAL BREACH, AND THE LIKE—A BRIEF RETROSPECT

Grounds of rightful cessation include failure of a condition precedent to a party's duty to perform, material breach, anticipatory repudiation, and prospective inability to perform (all studied in Chapter Seven). You should review the specific requirements of each of these grounds of cessation and compare them with those studied in this chapter. The close kinship of these grounds of cessation and the excuse doctrines studied in this chapter should now be apparent.

In light of all the grounds of cessation studied earlier or for the first time in this chapter, several basic questions arise. Which ground or grounds seem most freely available? Which are least available? Which can a party effectively protect against at the planning stage?

*

Chapter Nine

CESSATION, THEORIES OF OBLIGATION, AND REMEDIES

*When we turn from theory to
decisions, we find that every legal
system attempts a compromise
between the conflicting equities of
the parties.*

McKEEG

SECTION ONE: REMEDIAL IMPLICATIONS OF CESSATION AND THE ROLE OF LAWYERS

Most often, the parties perform in full and neither party has occasion to invoke a remedy. As we saw in the preceding chapter, however, grounds of cessation may arise short of full performance or even before performance begins. As we also saw, the grounds of cessation vary greatly, ranging from invalidity and unconscionability to mistake, impossibility, and frustration, and to failure of condition and material breach.

The grounds of justified cessation do not always give rise to the same remedial rights, partly because different theories of obligation may dictate different remedial rights. For example, when impossibility or frustration applies to excuse a party, the other party is not entitled to invoke the theory of "agreement with consideration" and recover lost expectancy damages. Nevertheless, the disappointed party may have conferred a benefit on the excused party and thus may be entitled to recover for unjust enrichment. On the other hand, when one party proves the other party materially breached, the injured party usually can recover expectancy damages (or perhaps even specific performance).

In earlier chapters, we studied the remedies available after such grounds of cessation as invalidity, unconscionability, failure of condition, and material breach. Although in Chapter Eight we considered some remedial implications of cessation based on mistake, impossibility of performance, impracticability, and frustration of purpose, we have reserved the present chapter for the more systematic and unified treatment that this subject demands.

We saw in Chapter Three that lawyers must plan, draft, interpret, counsel, negotiate, and litigate with a firm eye towards the remedies available after a breach. The lawyer must also consider the remedial implications of the grounds of cessation studied in Chapter Eight. For example, the parties entering a contract may desire to set forth their own remedial approach to unanticipated circumstances, such as requiring the favored party to bargain in good faith to achieve an adjustment of terms onerous to the other. The lawyer may be asked to draft such a clause.

SECTION TWO: REMEDIES IN CASES OF INVALIDITY—A BRIEF RETROSPECT

Invalidity may take many forms including lack of offer or acceptance (or both), lack of consideration, indefiniteness, and lack of compliance with the statute of frauds. After cessation on such grounds, we saw that a party may be entitled to recover reliance expenditures or the value of any benefit conferred on the other party. See Chapter Three, Sections Five and Eight.

As we saw in Chapter Five, an agreement also may be invalid or unenforceable because of duress, unconscionability, conflict with public policy, or the like. Here the courts generally rescind the contract and grant restitution of any benefit conferred by either party. Recall, for example, that in Jackson v. Seymour, at page 571, the seller was allowed rescission, restitution of her land, and the value of timber removed from it on the ground of "constructive fraud." At the same time, the purchaser, who had not engaged in any actual deceit or other wrongdoing, was entitled to a return of the purchase price, taxes paid, and interest. If the conduct of the party seeking to enforce the agreement is sufficiently egregious, however, that party may be denied any recovery.

SECTION THREE: REMEDIES IN CASES OF MISTAKE, IMPOSSIBILITY, IMPRACTICABILITY, AND FRUSTRATION—THE APPROACHES IN THE CASES

The remedies available for mistake, impossibility, impracticability, and frustration may include reliance expenditures, restitution, specific performance of some portion of the contract, or some combination of these. In addition, we will see in Section Five that judicial reformation is also a potential remedy. The availability of a reliance recovery or of judicial reformation raises fundamental issues of theory and justification.

COMMENT, APPORTIONING LOSS AFTER DISCHARGE OF A BURDENSOME CONTRACT: A STATUTORY SOLUTION

69 Yale L.J. 1054, 1056–57 (1960).

A court which has discharged full performance of a contract can adopt five general approaches to the treatment of loss. (1) Conditions may be left as they are at the time of discharge, so that a party who has sustained any type of loss must bear it and a party who has gained any benefit may keep it. (2) A party may be required to disgorge benefit accruing to him from reliance expenditures made by the other. Under this "restitutionary" approach, non-recoverable reliance expenses not benefiting another party remain losses to the party incurring the expense. (3) A party may be allowed to set off some or all of the losses he has suffered against the value of any benefit received from the performance of the other party. Losses exceeding the value of any benefit received are sustained by the party who has suffered them. To the extent that losses are less than or equal to the value of benefit received, this approach allows the court equitably to divide losses between the parties. (4) All or some of the losses may be divided between the parties without regard to any benefit either or both may or may not have received. This approach allows the court equitably to apportion loss without the inhibition imposed by a requirement that loss be set off against correlative benefit. (5) The court may adjust contractual obligations of the parties in order to minimize the total loss of both; new obligations would be substituted for the original ones and enforced as if they were the terms of the contract. Loss remaining after performance of the modified obligations could then be apportioned.

Selection of the most appropriate method of treating losses suffered by parties to a discharged contract depends upon the decisionmaker's concepts of fairness and is intimately related to the fact of discharge and the circumstances which give rise to it.

20TH CENTURY LITES, INC. v. GOODMAN

Appellate Department, Superior Court of California, 1944.
64 Cal.App.2d Supp. 938, 149 P.2d 88.

KINCAID, JUDGE.

This appeal arises out of an action commenced by plaintiff to recover certain monthly payments claimed due under a written contract whereby plaintiff leased neon sign installations to defendant in consideration of agreed payments to be made by defendant for the contractual period. The defendant, among other defenses, alleges that by reason of the governmental order of August 5, 1942, prohibiting the illumination of all outside neon or lighting equipment between the hours of sunset and sunrise, he has been prevented, without fault on his part, from using such installations during the nighttime, and that such use was the desired object and effect contemplated by the parties at the time of the execution of the contract.

The lease contract of September 3, 1941 is one wherein plaintiff retains the title to the neon signs and tubing which it installed and maintained on the exterior of defendant's "drive-in" restaurant. The court found from the evidence that the parties had each performed all terms and conditions of the contract to August 4, 1942; that on August 5, 1942 the Government of the United States, as an emergency war measure, ordered a cessation of all outside lighting, including neon illuminated signs, at all hours between sunset and sunrise, covering the district in which defendant's place of business is located; that said proclamation of cessation has, during all the time in question, remained in full force and effect, and that, because of this fact, the defendant has been prevented from illuminating such signs during such hours; that subsequent to August 5, 1942 defendant offered to surrender to plaintiff such contract, to terminate same, and to permit plaintiff to remove such signs, but plaintiff refused to accept the offer and thereafter, beginning September 1, 1942, defendant failed to pay the monthly rental payments in the contract set forth.

The trial court properly concluded and found that, by reason of such governmental proclamation, the desired object or effect that the parties to the contract intended to attain at the time it was entered into, was frustrated without the fault of either party on and after August 5, 1942, and that defendant was harmed thereby. It further found that on and after said date both parties to said contract were excused from any further performance of any one of the terms or conditions thereof, and that said contract thereupon terminated.

* * *

Plaintiff argues that * * * the doctrine of commercial frustration cannot be invoked in this case, because of the fact that it has been put to an expense in manufacturing and installing the signs; that the termination of the contract on such grounds would violate the principles of equity. It relies strongly on the case of San Joaquin L. & P. Corp. v. Costaloupes, 1929, 96 Cal.App. 322, 274 P. 84, in support of this contention. The latter case may be distinguished from the one here under consideration, as the court there held the contract to be one to deliver electrical energy to a certain described piece of land irrespective of its use. Although a fire had destroyed the factory wherein it had been contemplated that the electricity would be used, the court said (page 327 of 96 Cal.App., page 86 of 274 P.): "All that appears here is that by reason of the premises the defendants could not use any more power or light in these particular buildings, but, if at any time, they chose to rebuild or make other use or application of the light and power, they could have enforced their right of delivery of electrical energy." This is a vastly different situation than is presented by the contract and the facts of our case. Here, the plaintiff agreed to furnish an "electrical advertising display" which contemplated its being continuously operatable by electrified illumination at night. Furthermore, the defendant was not in the position of the user of electricity in the cited case, in that he could not relieve his situation by any voluntary act of his own, such as rebuilding his factory or making other use of the hired product. The facts herein are such as to prohibit the application of this exception to the general rule.

* * *

The judgment is affirmed, respondent to recover his costs of appeal.

SIEGEL v. EATON & PRINCE CO., 165 Ill. 550, 557–58, 46 N.E. 449, 451 (1896). "We think the law is, that where a contract is entered into with reference to the existence of a particular thing, and that thing is destroyed before the time for the performance of the contract, without the fault of either party, both parties are excused from performing the contract, but neither is entitled to recover anything for a part performance thereof."

Question

Are 20th Century Lites, Inc. and the language from Siegel consistent with Bell v. Carver, set forth at page 920?

QUAGLIANA v. EXQUISITE HOME BUILDERS, INC.

Supreme Court of Utah, 1975.
538 P.2d 301.

[Plaintiffs, desiring to build a home in Salt Lake City, hired K.M. Design to modify existing plans and specifications owned by plaintiffs. Plaintiffs showed K.M. a prospective building lot and K.M. promised plaintiffs that the plans as modified would provide plaintiffs with a view of the valley desired by plaintiffs. Plaintiffs then purchased the lot and entered a written agreement with Exquisite Home Builders, Inc. to build the house according to the plans and specifications. After completing excavation and pouring the concrete, and after plaintiffs had made progress payments to Exquisite, the parties learned that the plans and specifications violated a city ordinance and restrictive covenants in various respects and that in order to correct these defects, plaintiffs' view of the valley would be obscured. Construction work stopped and, after fruitless discussions, plaintiffs terminated Exquisite, purchased a home elsewhere, and sold the original lot at a profit.

Plaintiffs sued Exquisite and K.M. for breach of contract. Although the report is unclear, both parties apparently counterclaimed. The trial court found (sitting without a jury) that plaintiffs had breached the contract by terminating Exquisite, and granted Exquisite unreimbursed costs. The trial court also found that K.M. was not in breach and was entitled to the balance of its fee. The Supreme Court of Utah reversed. It held that K.M. was in breach and that plaintiffs were entitled to compensation for "those injuries which K.M. had reason to foresee"—damages which the trial court was to determine on remand and offset against the balance of K.M.'s fee. The court also held that plaintiffs were not in breach of their contract with Exquisite because the purpose of the contract was frustrated.]

MAUGHAN, JUSTICE:

* * *

At the time plaintiffs and Exquisite entered into the construction contract, each assumed that the purpose of the contract could be achieved, and that the designed construction could be so placed on the available lot, as to give plaintiffs the house they wanted, and so situated as to provide a view of the valley. This was the purpose of the contract, and was well known to Exquisite and K.M., from the outset. Exquisite promised to locate the house in compliance "with all zoning ordinances and regulations and all building restrictions and protective covenants governing said real property." This it could not do, from the outset.

There is substantial evidence that it was impossible to place the subject residence on the available land in compliance with zoning ordinances, regulations, building restrictions, and protective covenants, and at the same time achieve the purpose of the contract.

* * *

The evidence here is clear that the object desired by plaintiffs was a specifically designed house, in Oak Hills, with a view of the valley. This formed the basis on which both parties bargained, and it was frustrated from the outset because it could not be achieved. Further, there is no evidence showing plaintiffs were at fault in causing the frustration.

* * *

Here Exquisite and the plaintiffs dealt under erroneous assumptions. Further, there is nothing in the agreement, from which an interpretation can be inferred, that it was the intention of either party to assume the risks produced by the erroneous assumptions. The time significant here is that at which plaintiffs and Exquisite engaged the bargain. At the moment of execution, that for which the bargain was made was impossible of production.

* * *

Since the performance for which the parties had bargained—the construction of a house with a view of the valley, in accordance with the plans and specifications and in conformity with all zoning ordinances and restrictive covenants—was impossible from its inception, the sole remedy available to Exquisite for reimbursement was restitution.

The trial court erred in awarding Exquisite unreimbursed costs it had put in the building. It found plaintiffs had breached the contract and awarded these damages in accordance with Section 346(2)(b) and Section 333 of Restatement of Contracts [dealing with damages measured by expenditures in part performance]. Under comment (e) of Section 333, it is explained that the amount of the expenditure as damages in an action under this section is not identical with the remedy of restitution of the value of part performance rendered by the plaintiff. The remedy of restitution requires the return of value received. The remedy of Section 333 covers expenditures without any reference to value received, the outlay of the plaintiff without regard to the result of that outlay, or its benefit to defendant.

Where a loss is caused by impossibility or frustration neither party can be compelled to pay for the other's disappointed expectations, but neither can be allowed to profit from the situation; one must pay for what one has received. If Exquisite had adhered to its duty set forth in the contract, to locate the house in compliance with city ordinances, * * * it would have discovered the impossibility of locating the house on this particular lot prior to expending money for excavation, footings, and pouring the foundation. These expenditures could have been averted; on the other hand, plaintiffs sold the lot with these foundations and excavations intact, which were subsequently utilized to a certain extent in the construction of a home without a direct view of the valley. To the extent that this work enhanced the value of the lot, and was thus a benefit to plaintiffs, Exquisite should be compensated. However, Exquisite had previously received disbursements as the work progressed, the trial court must determine which party is entitled to restitution by ascertaining the value of the benefit to the land, in relation to the expenditures by Exquisite. Each party must bear its own loss, but neither may profit at the expense of the other.

* * *

Reversed and remanded with instructions to determine damages and restitution in accordance with this opinion.

ALBRE MARBLE AND TILE CO. v. JOHN BOWEN CO.

Supreme Judicial Court of Massachusetts, 1959.
338 Mass. 394, 155 N.E.2d 437.

[Plaintiff agreed to supply labor and materials to defendant general contractor of a hospital building in Boston. The general contract with the state of Massachusetts was declared invalid because of irregularities in the contractor's bid and when, in counts 1 and 2 of its complaint, plaintiff brought an action for breach of two subcontracts, the court affirmed an "immediate entry of judgment" in favor of defendant on the grounds of impossibility. The plaintiff also sought in counts 3 and 4 of its complaint, on a quantum meruit theory, recovery for work and labor furnished the defendant. "Immediate judgment" was also in favor of defendant on this theory and plaintiff appealed.]

SPALDING, JUSTICE.

* * *

We turn now to counts 3 and 4 by which the plaintiff seeks a recovery for the fair value of work and labor furnished to the defendant prior to the termination of the general contract. The plaintiff seeks recovery in count 3 for "preparation of samples, shop drawings, tests and affidavits" in connection with the tile work; in count 4 recovery for similar work in connection with the marble contract is sought.

The defendant in its affidavit maintains that the tile and marble work to be furnished by the plaintiff could not have been done until late in the construction process; that no tile or marble was actually installed in the building; and that the expenses incurred by the plaintiff prior to the time the general contract was declared invalid consisted solely of expenditures in preparation for performance. Relying on the decision in Young v. Chicopee, 186 Mass. 518, 72 N.E. 63, the defendant maintains that where a building contract has been rendered impossible of performance a plaintiff may not recover for expenses incurred in preparation for performance, but may recover only for the labor and materials "wrought into" the structure. Therefore, the defendant says, the plaintiff should take nothing here.

The plaintiff places its reliance upon a clause appearing in both contracts which provides in part: "It is agreed you [the plaintiff] will furnish and submit all necessary or required samples, shop drawings, tests, affidavits, etc., for approval, all as ordered or specified * * *." The plaintiff in effect concedes that no labor or materials were actually [wrought] into the structure, but argues that the contract provision quoted above placed its preparatory efforts under the supervision of the defendant, and that this circumstance removes this case from the ambit of those decisions which apply the "wrought-in" principle.

* * *

The problem of allocating losses where a building contract has been rendered impossible of performance by a supervening act not chargeable to either party is a vexed one. In situations where the part performance of one party measurably exceeds that of the other the tendency has been to allow recovery for the fair value for work done in the actual performance of the contract and to deny recovery for expenditures made in reliance upon the contract or in preparing to perform. This principle has sometimes been expressed in terms of "benefit" or "lack of benefit." In other words, recovery may be had only for those expenditures which, but for the supervening act, would have enured to the benefit of the defendant as contemplated by the contract. See, e.g. Young v. Chicopee, 186 Mass. 518, 520, 72 N.E. 63. The "wrought-in" principle applied in building contract cases is merely a variant of this principle. It has long been recognized that this theory is unworkable if the concept of benefit is applied literally. In M. Ahern Co. v. John Bowen Co. Inc., 334 Mass. 36, 41, 133 N.E.2d 484, 487, we quoted with approval the statement of Professor Williston that "It is enough that the defendant has actually received in part performance of the contract something for which when completed he had agreed to pay a price." Williston on Contracts (Rev. ed.) § 1976.

Although the matter of denial of reliance expenditures in impossibility situations seems to have been discussed but little in judicial opinions, it has, however, been the subject of critical comment by scholars. See Fuller and Perdue, The Reliance Interest in Contract Damages, 46 Yale L.J. 52, 373, 379–383. Note, 46 Mich.L.Rev. 401. In England the recent frustrated contracts legislation provides that the court may grant recovery for expenditures in reliance on the contract or in preparation to perform it where it appears *"just to do so having regard to all the circumstances of the case"* (emphasis supplied). 6 & 7 George VI, c. 40.

We are of the opinion that the plaintiff here may recover for those expenditures made pursuant to the specific request of the defendant as set forth in the contract clause quoted above. A combination of factors peculiar to this case justifies such a holding without laying down the broader principle that in every case recovery may be had for payments made or obligations reasonably incurred in preparation for performance of a contract where further performance is rendered impossible without fault by either party. See Boston Plate & Window Glass Co. v. John Bowen Co. Inc., 335 Mass. 697, 702, 141 N.E.2d 715.

The factors which determine the holding here are these: First, this is not a case of mere impossibility by reason of a supervening act. The opinion of this court in M. Ahern Co. v. John Bowen Co. Inc., 334 Mass. 36, 133 N.E.2d 484, points out that the defendant's involvement in creating the impossibility [by submitting a bid that was unlawful] was greater than that of its subcontractors. The facts regarding the defendant's conduct are set forth in that opinion and need not be restated. Although the defendant's conduct was not so culpable as to render it liable for breach of contract (Boston Plate & Window Glass Co. v. John Bowen Co. Inc., 335 Mass. 697, 141 N.E.2d 715), nevertheless, it was a contributing factor to a loss sustained by the plaintiff which as between the plaintiff and the defendant the latter ought to bear to the extent herein permitted.

We attach significance to the clause in the contract, which was prepared by the defendant, specifically requesting the plaintiff to submit samples, shop drawings, tests, affidavits, etc., to the defendant. This is not a case in which all efforts in preparation for performance were solely within the discretion and control of the subcontractor. * * *

Moreover, the acts requested here by their very nature could not be "wrought into" the structure. * * *

* * *

We hold that the damages to be assessed are limited solely to the fair value of those acts done in conformity with the specific request of the defendant as contained in the contract. Expenses incurred prior to the execution of the contract, such as those arising out of preparing the plaintiff's bid, are not to be considered.

The plaintiff's exceptions as to counts 1 and 2 are overruled and are sustained as to counts 3 and 4; as to those counts the case is remanded to the Superior Court for further proceedings in conformity with this opinion. The appeal is dismissed.

So ordered.

SECTION FOUR: REMEDIES IN CASES OF MISTAKE, IMPOSSIBILITY, IMPRACTICABILITY, AND FRUSTRATION—THE APPROACH OF THE RESTATEMENT (SECOND) OF CONTRACTS

RESTATEMENT (SECOND) OF CONTRACTS § 158.

Relief Including Restitution

(1) In any case governed by the rules stated in this Chapter [Mistake], either party may have a claim for relief including restitution * * *.

(2) In any case governed by the rules stated in this Chapter, if those rules together with the rules stated in Chapter 16 [Remedies] will not avoid injustice, the court may grant relief on such terms as justice requires including protection of the parties' reliance interests.

RESTATEMENT (SECOND) OF CONTRACTS § 272.

Relief Including Restitution

(1) In any case governed by the rules stated in this Chapter [Impracticability and Frustration], either party may have a claim for relief including restitution * * *.

(2) In any case governed by the rules stated in the Chapter, if those rules together with the rules stated in Chapter 16 [Remedies] will not avoid injustice, the court may grant relief on such terms as justice requires including protection of the parties' reliance interests.

PERILLO, RESTITUTION IN THE SECOND *RESTATEMENT OF CONTRACTS*

81 Colum.L.Rev. 37, 40 (1981).

Sections 158 and 272 of the *Restatement (Second)* were amended in 1979 to provide that where an obligation has been discharged or a contract avoided for impracticability, frustration, mistake, or the like, the court may grant, instead of or in addition to restitution, "relief on such terms as justice requires including protection of the parties' reliance interests."

Reliance has traditionally been linked to the doctrine of promissory estoppel, which renders binding a promise that induces foreseeable action or forebearance to the promisee's detriment, notwithstanding the absence of consideration or of other requirements for an enforceable promise. In each of the instances in which the *Restatement (Second)* engages promissory estoppel, the promisee's reliance interest is protected by enforcement of an otherwise defective contract against a party in breach. On the other hand, when a contract is discharged or avoided for impracticability, frustration, or mistake, there is no enforceable contract; no party is in breach. Heretofore, absent tortious conduct, the only common law action that was permitted in such circumstances was the quasi-contractual action of restitution—an action for reliance was unavailable. However, under the new formulation of sections 158 and 272, when a contract fails for impracticability, frustration, or mistake, an action for reliance is permitted. Although there is clearly some relationship between this action and the concept of promissory estoppel, the degree of kinship is unclear. If a new kind of action based solely on reliance is to be created, it should be given an analytic and procedural framework.

HUDEC, RESTATING THE "RELIANCE INTEREST"

67 Cornell L.Rev. 704, 715–16 (1982).

In what sense is the remedy of sections 158 and 272 different from contract liability and the more familiar forms of reliance liability (*e.g.,* [section] 90 * * *)? The distinction does not lie in the nature of the conduct that gives rise to liability. Sections 158 and 272 apply to parties who have made contracts, or other promises that are binding due to reliance. The conduct that gives rise to sections 158 and 272 liability is thus the same promise-making that triggers contract and other reliance liability.

The difference is that sections 158 and 272 have recognized additional obligations arising from the same conduct. Both contract liability and the more familiar reliance liability of [section] 90 * * * protect the promisee by imposing an obligation upon the promisor to perform. Breach of the duty of performance is the "wrong," and the harm to be compensated is the loss caused by that wrong. Sections 158 and 272 go beyond this and make promisors liable for some reliance losses that have not been caused by wrongful nonperformance, including some that occur because the promisee is unable to perform. It is difficult to be precise about the basis and the exact dimensions of this added liability. The justification is usually stated in terms of overall equities, and several different and even contradictory theories of justification may be involved.

The most distinctive theory of liability in this area would be a loss sharing theory which asserts that the parties to a contract are participants in a common venture, and so should bear common responsibility for losses caused by unforeseen disasters for which neither party is to blame. If one thinks about the basis of such a theory, it is evident that the *conduct* being relied upon to justify liability (for at least fifty percent, anyway), is no more than the ordinary promise-making behavior that began the contract venture. The liability does not depend on any further duty to do or not do anything. It is simply an insurance-type responsibility for disaster losses, resting on the reliance-inducing promise alone.

THIEME v. WORST

Court of Appeals of Idaho, 1987.
113 Idaho 455, 745 P.2d 1076.

SWANSTROM, JUDGE.

The buyers in a land sale contract, Norris and Katherine Thieme, brought this action for rescission of the contract [and] for damages * * *. They sued the sellers, Richard and Rebecca Worst, * * * alleging misrepresentation of the availability of irrigation water. * * * The district court, finding a mutual mistake of fact regarding the delivery of water to the property, "reformed" the land sale contract by requiring the Worsts to provide a system for delivery of water to the property and granted damages to the Thiemes. * * * The Thiemes have appealed and the Worsts * * * have cross-appealed. We affirm in part, vacate in part and remand for further proceedings.

On appeal, the Thiemes have raised several issues, all relating to whether the trial court erred in: (1) granting the remedy of "reformation" based on mutual mistake rather than granting rescission for the alleged misrepresentations of the sellers and their agents; [and] (2) failing to award damages to the buyers for costs they expended in starting construction of a house on the property * * *. The Worsts raise additional issues on cross-appeal, asserting that the trial court erred in finding that * * * a mutual mistake of fact existed * * *.

The pertinent facts are as follows. In 1977, the Worsts acquired a five-acre parcel of land on the rim of the Snake River Canyon in Twin Falls County, Idaho, intending to build a home there. They later decided not to build on the site. In 1982, they listed the parcel for sale with Irwin Realty and included the property in a multiple listing service. The listing described the land as being five acres, together with seven shares of Twin Falls Canal Company water. Another real estate broker, John Tolk, who worked for Interstate Realty, learned that the Thiemes were looking for a home building site. He contacted the Thiemes and offered to show them several pieces of property. The Thiemes indicated to Tolk that they were interested in property for the purpose of building a home and that they desired irrigation water on the property in order to pasture a few animals and raise a garden.

Tolk twice accompanied Norris Thieme to the Worsts' property. The northern boundary of the property is the high rim of the Snake River Canyon and the southern boundary adjoins a county road. Thieme viewed the property and observed a system of ditches. He also observed a culvert under the county road. The culvert ran from the southeast corner of the property to a neighbor's field on the south side of the county road. The culvert led to an open ditch running along the road in the neighbor's field. Although the Thiemes did not know it at the time, this ditch had been used in the past to convey water from a headgate of the Twin Falls Canal Company to the five-acre parcel. The slope of the land is such that the water delivered to the southeast corner of the parcel could be made to flow through ditches either to the west or north to the rim of the canyon. After viewing the property, the Thiemes assumed that irrigation water could be delivered to the southeast corner of the property. From this point the Thiemes believed that the property could be irrigated simply by gravity flow through existing ditches.

The Thiemes decided to purchase the land in March, 1983, without ever having any direct contact with the Worsts or with Irwin Realty, the listing broker. The Thiemes and the Worsts signed a sale agreement stating that the land was sold "together with 7 shares of Twin Falls Canal Co. water." The Thiemes paid cash for the property, receiving a deed and a certificate for the water shares. After the purchase, the Thiemes planted a garden. They allowed a third party to cultivate the land and to plant wheat. The Thiemes also began construction of a house on the property, completing excavation of the basement and laying a foundation.

In the spring of 1983, the Thiemes discovered that there was a cement barrier in front of the headgate, obstructing the delivery of water into the ditch which had previously conveyed water to the parcel. All parties were unaware of this obstruction at the time of the purchase. The Thiemes made several attempts to obtain delivery of the water to the property. The neighboring farmer told the Thiemes that the ditch across his property had not been used in at least five years and that he considered it abandoned. He allegedly refused to give the Thiemes permission to use the ditch. Evidence presented at trial indicated that the ditch had not been used since 1977. Through their inquiries the Thiemes became aware of some practical and legal difficulties in obtaining irrigation water from alternative sources.

The Thiemes ceased construction on the house and filled in the excavation. On September 22, 1983, the Thiemes sent a letter to the Worsts stating they were rescinding the purchase because of "fraudulent nondisclosure" that the Worsts had abandoned the easement for conveying water to the property. When no response was received, the Thiemes filed this action in November, 1983, seeking a rescission of the sale, together with damages and attorney fees. A trial was held without a jury. The court determined there was no fraud or actionable misrepresentation. The court did find that when the sale took place both parties mistakenly believed the shares of water could be delivered to the southeast corner of the property. The court "reformed" the contract as if the parties had understood and agreed that the water would be deliverable to the southeast corner of the property when requested. The court held that under the parties' agreement, as "reformed," the Worsts had breached their contractual duty to provide the water. Nevertheless, the court refused to grant rescission, the relief the Thiemes had requested. Rather, the court held that the Worsts should be required to specifically perform the "reformed" contract by providing a permanent delivery system that would again conduct the water to the southeast corner of the Thiemes' property. The court awarded damages of $151.53 for expenses the Thiemes had incurred in planting the garden in 1983. The court awarded no damages in connection with the aborted home construction. The Thiemes were not satisfied with the relief granted and they initiated this appeal.

I

We first address whether the evidence supports the trial court's conclusion that a mutual mistake of fact occurred in the formation of the contract. The trial court found that both parties mistakenly thought irrigation water could be delivered to the high corner of the property, when needed, at no additional cost to the Thiemes except for the canal company charges. * * *

* * *

* * * The Worsts testified that when they owned the property they never farmed it or personally used the shares of water. The Worsts also testified that they did not inspect the ditches and had no idea where the water would be delivered to the property or how the property could be irrigated. They were aware that water could be "lost" if not used on the property for some period of time. Accordingly, in 1980, they contacted Robert Blass who owned and farmed the adjacent property to the east. In 1980 and again in 1981, Blass agreed to farm the parcel. Richard Worst testified that Blass "would farm the land, run the water on it, and pay us for it." Worst further testified that he assumed Blass was going to use their water shares. In fact, during both years Blass irrigated the property, he utilized waste water from his own property rather than the seven shares of water from the canal company. Worst testified that he did not have any reason to doubt, when the Thiemes purchased the property, that they could use the water shares to irrigate the property. He said that had he known a cement barrier obstructed the delivery of water he would have informed the Thiemes of the obstruction.

Thus, the evidence shows that the Worsts believed Blass used their water on the property in 1980 and in 1981 when he farmed the tract. The court found that when the Worsts listed the property and sold it to the Thiemes, the Worsts believed the water was deliverable to the parcel through an existing system. The "existing system" previously had delivered the water to the southeastern corner of the property. Substantial evidence supports the court's finding that the Worsts did have a mistaken belief. The finding will not be disturbed on appeal.

Similarly, the Thiemes' view of the property and its ditches, coupled with the knowledge that it was being sold with seven shares of water, led them to believe the water was available through the existing system at the southeastern corner of the tract. Because the Thiemes intended to pasture animals and grow a garden, the ready availability of water was a material consideration. The trial court found that the Thiemes would not have entered into the contract had they been aware of the water difficulties. Also, there was evidence showing that, during negotiations conducted through the brokers, Richard Worst rejected one offer made by the Thiemes and held out for a higher figure, contending that the water shares were worth the difference. Thus, we uphold the district judge's ruling that there was a mutual mistake. Both parties were mistaken "at the time [the] contract was made as to a basic assumption on which the contract was made...." RESTATEMENT (SECOND) OF CONTRACTS § 152 (1979) (hereinafter cited as Restatement).

The Worsts have also argued that if there was a mutual mistake, the Thiemes should bear the risk of the mistake because they acted upon incomplete information derived from their own view of the premises and not from any representations made by the Worsts. However, as the findings of the district judge and the evidence show, the Thiemes' view of the property would logically confirm their belief that seven shares of water were deliverable through an existing irrigation system. We are not persuaded that the Thiemes should bear the risk of the mistake * * *. Accordingly, we must determine whether the trial court was correct in denying the remedy of rescission, in favor of "reformation" of the contract of sale.

II

As noted in § 152 of the Restatement, where the mistake has a material effect on the agreed exchange of performances, the contract is voidable. The availability of water has been held basic to the lease or purchase of real property so that when water is not deliverable, rescission of the transaction is an available remedy. See, e.g., Fowler v. Uezzell, 94 Idaho 951, 500 P.2d 852 (1972) (lease of farm ground); Blythe v. Coney, 228 Ark. 824, 310 S.W.2d 485 (1958) (mutual mistake over availability of water resulted in rescission of contract to purchase home). However, rescission is not the exclusive remedy for mutual mistake; a court may consider other equitable remedies in fashioning a just result. Indeed, the avoidance rule of Restatement § 152 expressly recognizes that the materiality of the parties' mistake may be alleviated by other equitable relief. Correspondingly, § 158(2) of the Restatement acknowledges the power of an equity court to eliminate the effect of mistake by supplying a new term or otherwise modifying the agreement as justice requires, thus protecting the parties' reliance interests.

In devising an equitable remedy for the mistake here, the trial judge stopped short of allowing rescission. The judge ordered "reformation" of the real estate purchase and sale agreement to create a duty on the Worsts to provide a water system for the land as contemplated by the parties at the time of contracting. The judge's use of the term "reformation" was incorrect. Reformation is an equitable remedy available in a limited situation when the parties, having reached an agreement, failed to express it correctly in the writing. Restatement § 155. It is apparent that the judge here actually was reshaping the contract duties to achieve a just result, consistent with the parties' intent.

In our view, the trial judge fashioned the correct remedy. The Worsts, apparently, are willing to perform the duty of providing a permanent water system for the Thiemes. This is not a situation of impossibility or impracticability of performance. Neither party has committed fraud or misrepresentation. They both simply suffer from a common mistake of fact. The duty required of the Worsts is reasonable. Its performance will conform to the intent held by the parties at the time of contracting and will avoid the drastic remedy of rescission. Rescission, or avoidance, by the Thiemes would result in an injustice in this case because the Worsts, apparently, are willing to perform their duty, thus alleviating the effect of the mistake. Furthermore, the result here protects the parties' reliance interests existing at the time the sale agreement was entered into. The Thiemes, however, contend that the Worsts are unable to perform their duty. Therefore, we believe this case should be remanded to allow the trial court to reconsider its remedy in light of any circumstances occurring since its previous order.

We offer the following guidance to the trial court. We uphold the trial court's order requiring the Worsts to provide a permanent water system capable of delivering water to the southeast corner of the land, comparable to the system the parties believed existed at the time the land sale agreement was made. We agree with the trial court that the Worsts must obtain any necessary, permanent easements for the water system; mere licenses will not suffice. We further agree that the Thiemes should not have to await the outcome of any new litigation between the Worsts and third parties over easements for the water system. We direct the trial court to establish specific deadlines for commencing and completing the Worsts' duty. The deadlines should reflect an appropriate regard for the parties' agreement that time is of the essence. Should the Worsts choose not to perform their duty as required, or if they fail to timely meet the trial court's deadlines, rescission is to be promptly ordered. Rescission remains a viable remedy and, if granted, the trial court in its discretion may also grant appropriate restitutionary relief to the parties. As long as the trial court properly exercises its discretion, within permitted bounds, we will defer to that court's discretionary authority to determine the appropriate amount of restitutionary relief as the circumstances and justice require. See, e.g., Lewiston Pre–Mix Concrete, Inc. v. Rohde, 110 Idaho 640, 718 P.2d 551 (Ct.App.1985).

* * *

In summary, we affirm the judgment in part, vacate it in part, and remand the case for further proceedings consistent with this opinion.

WALTERS, C.J., and BURNETT, J., concur.

Problem 9–1

Selco, Inc. agrees to specially manufacture and lease to Buyco, Inc. certain slush freezers for Buyco's production of ice cream, which are unsuitable for use by others. After manufacture but before delivery, Buyco's premises are completely destroyed by fire, thereby rendering the freezers useless to Buyco. Buyco refuses to go through with the lease of the freezers. What are Selco's rights, if any? Assuming that Buyco is excused, must Selco suffer the entire loss?

SECTION FIVE: THE REMEDY OF JUDICIAL REFORMATION—AVAILABILITY AND LIMITS

Judicial reformation of disrupted contracts is not uncommon. For example, a court may excuse only part of a promised performance and enforce the remainder. Professor Dawson set forth the following case: "A public accountant * * * sells for a lump sum ($30,000) his business assets, including accounts receivable, with an undertaking on his part to remain active for two years as an associate in that office. The seller dies not quite two months later. Since he is excused and the parties have 'separately agreed on' a contract price for the assets transferred ($4,682.20), this is the sum the seller's representative can recover."[a] To cite another example, courts also unhesitat-

---

a. Dawson, Judicial Revision of Frustrated Contracts: The United States, 64 B.U.L.Rev. 1, 7 (1984), citing Mullen v. Wafer, 252 Ark. 541, 480 S.W.2d 332 (1972).

ingly reform agreements for the sale of land where the parties err as to the quantity of land sold.

Some forms of court reformation are more controversial. For example, in Aluminum Co. of America v. Essex Group, 499 F.Supp. 53 (W.D.Pa.1980), the parties adopted the Wholesale Price Index–Industrial Commodities (WPI) as a measure for adjusting certain production charges of Alcoa in processing aluminum pursuant to a long-term contract with Essex. The WPI did not reflect unexpected cost increases caused by inflation in oil prices and pollution controls and Alcoa stood to lose more than $75 million under the contract. The court agreed with Alcoa that "the shared objectives of the parties with respect to the use of the WPI had been frustrated." The court therefore reformed the contract according to a formula the court concocted to allow Alcoa a profit of "one cent per pound of Aluminum," subject to an already agreed contractual ceiling.

The first two excerpts that follow illustrate the reception the Alcoa case received in some quarters. The third excerpt supplies empirical evidence concerning business's perspective on adjustment of contracts.

DAWSON, JUDICIAL REVISION OF FRUSTRATED CONTRACTS: THE UNITED STATES

64 B.U.L.Rev. 1, 1, 28, 37–38 (1984).

One of the significant changes in the law of contract in recent decades has been the expansion of unforeseen change of conditions as a ground for discharge of contract obligations. More recently several authors have proposed to go one step further by ordering, instead of discharge, a revision to be accomplished by court order after the court had found that its intervention in some form was needed. The argument usually advanced to explain this result is that discharge, if it were granted, would be on the ground that an event had occurred for which the parties themselves could not have provided, for by hypothesis they had not foreseen it. From this premise the conclusion is drawn that a court should intervene to fill what is thus found to be an unintended gap and do for the parties what they, with good reason, could not do for themselves. If this argument comes to be more widely accepted our judges have the prospect of acquiring some new tasks of considerable difficulty and magnitude, though first they will need to find somewhere a higher source that had conferred these powers on them.

* * *

* * * [The court in Aluminum Co. of America v. Essex Group] flatly rejected "the hoary maxim" that the courts will not make a contract for the parties. So it ordered that the complex scheme for price determination approved by the parties, tied to three price indices, was to be entirely replaced by one invented by the court and shifting completely to a cost-plus basis. Under its scheme the costs of production incurred during each quarter at the Warwick plant were all to be added up after each quarter had ended and Essex was then to pay prices that would ensure to Alcoa for all the aluminum it delivered a profit of one cent a pound.

The judge claimed that in reaching out for this bizarre solution he was inspired by becoming modesty: "the court willingly concedes that the managements of Alcoa and Essex are better able to conduct their business than is the court." But he claimed also that his information, being derived from hindsight, was "far superior" to that of the parties when they had made their contract and that a rule precluding adjustments by courts would have had "the perverse effect" of discouraging the parties from resolving this dispute or future disputes on their own. Only slightly paraphrased, this suggestion seems to mean that when basic provisions are revised by a judge, who knows only what he can learn from presiding at a trial, the result will probably be so unacceptable to both parties that by their own agreement they will reject the dictated terms and reassert the right that they fortunately still retain, to recover control over their own affairs. If that was his object it was soon realized in the *Alcoa* case. The judge's decree was appealed and after argument had been heard in the Court of Appeals for the Third Circuit but before that court could decide, a settlement was reached, Alcoa's action to "reform" was voluntarily dismissed and Alcoa surrendered any rights it had acquired under the trial court decree.[1]

This is, I believe, the only instance in which an American court has claimed power to recast by its own direct order, without some transparent disguise like "reformation," an essential term in an exchange that was still in progress when some unforeseen external event produced major imbalance. This form of "adjustment" to govern the performances not yet rendered is the one recommended by some authors in American law reviews.

* * *

The first reason that I have urged (for me it is a sufficient reason) for judges to abstain from rewriting the contracts of other people is that they are not qualified for such tasks. Nothing in their prior training as lawyers or their experience in directing litigation and giving coherence to its results will qualify them to invent viable new designs for disrupted enterprises, now gone awry, that the persons most concerned had tried to construct but without success. As one able author has contended, judges, trained as judges, are "institutionally incapable" of achieving success in such undertakings.

The second reason, however, is important enough to be stated first for it raises an issue that I regard as a major issue of civil liberty. The question that I have repeatedly raised but have not tried to answer is the question—when an unforeseen event has so drastically altered a contract that the parties to it are fully excused from its further performance, from what source does any court derive the power to impose on them a new contract without the free assent of both? Where rescission is awarded on any of the other standard grounds—fraud, mistake,[2] substantial breach, defective capacity, duress—no

---

1. This I have learned through private communication from counsel for Essex who had requested me to comment on the briefs that were being prepared for the appeal by Essex. I had thus had considerably earlier an opportunity to form a highly adverse opinion of the trial court's decision.

2. If one could imagine, as I cannot, that an unexpected rise in energy costs occurring nine

years after the contract was a mistake of present fact, it would have to be described, as the court itself said, 499 F.Supp. at 64–65, as a mistake in a "basic assumption." For this the standard remedies, if any were to be granted, would all require rescission of the contract. How far-fetched the notion of court-ordered revision would have seemed in such a case can be illustrated by imagining a variation on a

one has even suggested that such a power lay hidden somewhere. For myself, I do not propose to spend time looking for the source of the power. I am convinced that it does not exist.

JOHN P. DAWSON

time-worn relic of our contract law, the sale of the fertile cow. Sherwood v. Walker, 66 Mich. 568, 33 N.W. 919 (1887). The cow was Rose of Aberlone, of distinguished Scottish lineage, who was believed by its owner to be sterile and was sold to a local banker for a price that was calculated to be her value as beef. She was in fact pregnant at the time of the sale and therefore worth about ten times the price agreed. Should the seller be told that he could not keep the cow, as the court allowed him to do in the original case, and that he must deliver her to the buyer, but that he would be given judgment for the value of a well-bred pregnant cow (the two attributes, I assume, being compatible in a cow), an amount that the court would fix with perhaps the help of a jury? If the buyer then protested that he did not want the cow if he had to pay for it a sum possibly ten times as much as he had agreed to pay, there would not be much comfort in the only justification that a judge could give—that being a banker he could afford it.

SPEIDEL, THE NEW SPIRIT OF CONTRACT
2 J.Law & Comm. 193, 206–08 (1982).

[C]an a case be made for imposing a duty on the advantaged party to accept a "fair and equitable" adjustment proposal made by the disadvantaged party? If so, what remedies are appropriate? Keeping the *ALCOA* facts in mind, a tentative case can be made that does not convert the law of contracts into a pervasive duty to be altruistic.

First, the disadvantaged party must propose a modification that would be enforceable if accepted by the advantaged party. Under the Restatement (Second), this occurs if the disrupted contract is not "fully performed on either side" and if the modification is "fair and equitable in view of circumstances not anticipated by the parties when the contract was made."[1] The changed circumstances are similar to but less than those required to discharge a contract for impracticability. This first requirement both neutralizes any opportunism by the disadvantaged party, *e.g.*, duress, and affirms that agreed adjustments are preferred—that contract is available to resolve the dilemma and has been employed by the disadvantaged party.

Second, it must be clear that the disadvantaged party did not assume the risk of the unanticipated event by agreement, or under the test stated in the UCC in section 2–615(a), or otherwise. If the disadvantaged party did assume the risk, then the advantaged party has no duty to accept any proposed modification. The risk assumption question is complicated, and the answer will probably not be clear at the time that the adjustment is proposed. Why should the advantaged party be held to reject at his peril? Because it is in this precise situation—where there are substantial unbargained-for gains and losses caused by unanticipated events—that a case for the duty to rescue can be made. In this setting where the risk of changed circumstances has not been allocated to either party, a refusal to adjust by the advantaged party leaves all of the loss on the disadvantaged party and permits the advantaged party to salt away all of the gains. Short of discharging the contract and leaving the parties to restitution, a duty to adjust is necessary to avoid opportunism.

Thus, imposing the duty here is consistent with emerging notions of good faith performance and ALCOA's second peg in the "new" spirit, loss avoidance. More importantly, it is an imposition with little damage to the requirement of consent in contract law. Since there is a "gap" in the agreement on risk allocation * * * the parties have "some obligation to share unexpected benefits and losses in the case of an accident" in the course of a joint enterprise where they are not strangers to each other.[2] This "sharing principle" is derived from a more general principle of altruism and is similar to what has been called the duty of "easy rescue" in the law of torts.

Last, this conclusion is bolstered by what might be the imperatives of an emerging theory of relational contract law. In *ALCOA*, the parties, at the time

---

1. RESTATEMENT (SECOND) OF CONTRACTS § 89 (1979). *See* U.C.C. § 2–209(1) and comment 2, where it states that a modification "needs no consideration to be binding" but that the "extortion of a 'modification' without legitimate commercial reason is ineffective as a violation of the duty of good faith."

2. C. Fried, Contract As Promise 72–73 (1981).

of contracting, were unable adequately to deal with certain changed circumstances over the duration of a seventeen-year contract. Yet preserving the contract was important to the parties and to third parties dependent upon its performance but not represented in the litigation. Ian Macneil has argued that in situations such as this there are relational norms that the contract should be preserved and conflict harmonized by adjustment. These norms put a high premium upon developing mechanisms for adjustment over time and good faith efforts to adjust in the light of change. Thus, if in an *ALCOA*-type case, the court concludes that the disadvantaged party is entitled to "some relief" but not discharge, and the advantaged party has refused to accept a reasonable adjustment in light of risks that the disadvantaged party did not assume, relational theory also supports a court imposed adjustment to preserve the contract, to adjust the price and to avoid the twin devils of unbargained-for hardship and unjust enrichment.

WEINTRAUB, A SURVEY OF CONTRACT PRACTICE AND POLICY

1992 Wis.L.Rev. 1, 1–2, 14, 18–20, 24–25, 41–43.

In June 1988, I sent a questionnaire to the general counsels of 182 corporations of various sizes in all parts of the United States. The questionnaire sought information on a broad range of contract practices and solicited opinion on how the law should deal with some classic contract problems.

* * *

The respondents were engaged in a wide variety of businesses. The largest percentage of respondents (30.5%) were conglomerates that combined two or more of the other categories listed. Although no respondent marked "publisher," one company that marked "other" described itself as a "media company (magazines, books, video programming, cable TV systems)," and another respondent that checked "other" added the note "communications and information management." No respondent marked "business services other than financial," but one of the "other" companies was "petroleum services." The fourth "other" was a "gasoline and convenience store marketer."

The respondents' annual sales ranged from "10 million but less than 100 million" to "1 billion dollars or more." The largest percentage (75.6%) were in the more-than-a-billion category. The largest percentage of returns (17.1% of the respondents as compared with 10.1% of the sample) were in the "100 million but less than 500 million" annual sales group.

* * *

Questions five and six asked whether the respondent would agree to a change in price, if requested by a supplier or customer after a market shift and, if so, why:

5. If, because of a shift in market prices, one of your suppliers or customers requested a modification of the contracted-for price, would your company always insist on compliance with the contract?

		F	%
	yes → go to question 7	4	4.9
	not always → go to question 6	78	95.1

6. If your company would sometimes agree to a modification of the contracted-for price, which of the following factors would be relevant to the decision? (MORE THAN ONE BOX MAY BE MARKED)

		F	%
[A]	the request was reasonable under trade practice	59	75.6
[B]	if the request is made by a supplier, the additional cost can be passed on to customers	20	25.6
[C]	if the request is made by a buyer, our company will make a reasonable profit even if the request is granted	22	28.2
[D]	relations with the company making the request have been long and satisfactory	62	79.5
[E]	either the company making the request or our company is much larger	6	7.7
[F]	other	18	23.1

The overwhelming majority of respondents (95.1%) indicated that they would sometimes grant a supplier's or customer's request for price modification. The respondents least likely to grant such requests were manufacturers of hard goods, 16.7% of whom answered that they would always insist on compliance.

Custom clearly played a key role in identifying those situations in which relief was appropriate. Indeed, 75.6% of the respondents stated that they gave relief when "the request was reasonable under trade practice." The most common reason (79.5%) for granting modification was "relations with the company making the request have been long and satisfactory." Thus, the survey confirms the distinction between relational and discrete contracts.

Relational contracts involve parties who are presently performing a long-term contract or have dealt with one another many times in the past and are likely to do so in the future. Discrete contracts involve parties who have not dealt with one another before or, if they have, probably will not contract again. Relational contracts are likely to predominate in well-organized markets; discrete contracts will typify sales that take place sporadically, such as sales of real estate. There are important differences between situations in which parties have developed a relationship and those in which the contract is an isolated occurrence. When a dispute arises, parties with a history of mutually beneficial dealings are less likely to resort to litigation than are strangers. Efficiency is one incentive for amicable resolution of a relational dispute. Each party has custom-shaped its operations to meet the other's needs and these transaction costs would be wasted if the relationship ended.

Moreover, in well-organized markets where relational contracts predominate, a reputation for litigiousness is particularly undesirable.

* * *

Question nine asked respondents' views on the need for legal sanctions:

9.   If there were no legal sanctions for breach of contract and compliance depended on nonlegal sanctions (e.g., reputation in the business community, intra-corporate incentives for good performance), what is your estimate of how business operations would be affected?

		F	%
[A]	not much if at all	14	17.7
[B]	substantially and detrimentally	52	65.8
[C]	substantially and beneficially	0	0.0
[D]	substantially with about an even amount of detriment and benefit	13	16.5

No respondent thought that business operations would improve substantially if there were no legal sanctions, and 65.8% thought that there would be a substantial detrimental effect. A respondent who checked A (not much effect) commented, "business objectives are more important than legal sanctions." A communications and information management company with annual sales of $1 billion or more did not mark a box but commented:

> Our conduct would change very little because our reputation is critical on a long term basis. My concern would be that smaller companies and start up operations would be substantially disadvantaged. We would be less inclined to take service or products from them. They have no reputation and [there would be] no legal penalty for non-performance.

Respondents who thought business operations would deteriorate without legal sanctions made the following comments: "I suspect that business in general would tend to the lowest common denominator. Probably would be more uncertainty and sharp practices. Legal sanctions for breach of contract are absolutely essential to business. A contract sets the rules for virtually every transaction." * * *

The gas and electric utilities were almost unanimous in believing that legal sanctions were essential for desirable business operation. Twelve of the thirteen who answered this question (92.3%) marked B (substantial detrimental effect) suggesting, again, the effect of regulation.

* * *

The third and final hypothetical situation in the survey concerned frustration of contract that is so severe performance would result in the promissor's liquidation.

17.   Company A has contracted to sell B a fixed quantity of fuel oil per month at a fixed price for 10 years. An unprecedented OPEC oil embargo causes the cost of the oil to A to far exceed the price that B has agreed to pay. A's loss over the 10 years of the contract would be so large as to require liquidation of A. B can pass on the added cost of oil to its

customers without suffering a competitive disadvantage. A refuses to
deliver the oil at the contract price and B sues A for the difference
between the contract price of the oil and the much higher price that B
must pay to obtain oil from other sources. What result should the court
reach?

		F	%
[A]	B should receive a judgment for the difference between the contract price and the market price	28	35.0
[B]	A should be excused from performance	11	13.7
[C]	The contract price should be adjusted to avoid ruinous loss to A, but give B a significant savings over current market price	37	46.2
[D]	other:	4	5.0

* * *

The overall response to question seventeen, a plurality favoring price
adjustment, contrasts with contract doctrine more than any other survey
result. With *Aluminum Co. of America v. Essex Group, Inc.,* as the sole and
much-maligned exception, American courts have assumed that equitable adjustment is not within their powers; they must either excuse reluctant
promisors or hold their feet to the fire. Of course the court can put pressure
on the parties to settle, and perhaps one way to do this is for the judge to
adjust the terms in a manner that both parties will wish to change.

Note
Remedies and Substance

Few courts have followed ALCOA, largely for the reasons discussed by
Professor Dawson. The substantive grounds for granting relief to parties who
confront unanticipated calamities are not likely to expand as long as courts are
unwilling to be more flexible remedially: "Contract's all-or-nothing remedial
tradition * * * disfavors an enthusiastic move to contract excuse. Excuse's balancing methodology too often underscores significant interests on both sides. Courts
inclined to construct a remedy that reflects these interests would be forced to
come to terms with their aversion to a solution based on sharing losses. A host of
hurdles obstructs fabricating a sharing strategy: Consider the challenge of constructing standards for apportioning the loss and comprehending the contextual
implications of complex deals. It is easier for courts to repress their urges to move
to a sharing approach and simply find for the promisee on the basis of freedom of
contract." Hillman, Contract Excuse and Bankruptcy Discharge, 43 Stan.L.Rev.
99, 109 (1990).

UNIFORM COMMERCIAL CODE § 2–615.
Official Comment

* * *

6. In situations in which neither sense nor justice is served by either
answer when the issue is posed in flat terms of "excuse" or "no excuse,"

adjustment under the various provisions of this Article is necessary, especially the sections on good faith, on insecurity and assurance and on the reading of all provisions in the light of their purposes, and the general policy of this Act to use equitable principles in furtherance of commercial standards and good faith.

LAW REFORM (FRUSTRATED CONTRACTS) ACT, 1943.

6 & 7 Geo. 6, ch. 40.

An Act to amend the law relating to the frustration of contracts.

[5th August 1943.]

Be it enacted by the King's most Excellent Majesty, by and with the advice and consent of the Lords Spiritual and Temporal, and Commons, in this present Parliament assembled, and by the authority of the same, as follows:—

(1) Where a contract governed by English law has become impossible of performance or been otherwise frustrated, and the parties thereto have for that reason been discharged from the further performance of the contract, the following provisions of this section shall, subject to the provisions of section two of this Act, have effect in relation thereto.

(2) All sums paid or payable to any party in pursuance of the contract before the time when the parties were so discharged (in this Act referred to as "the time of discharge") shall, in the case of sums so paid, be recoverable from him as money received by him for the use of the party by whom the sums were paid, and, in the case of sums so payable, cease to be so payable:

Provided that, if the party to whom the sums were so paid or payable incurred expenses before the time of discharge in, or for the purpose of, the performance of the contract, the court may, if it considers it just to do so having regard to all the circumstances of the case, allow him to retain or, as the case may be, recover the whole or any part of the sums so paid or payable, not being an amount in excess of the expenses so incurred.

(3) Where any party to the contract has, by reason of anything done by any other party thereto in, or for the purpose of, the performance of the contract, obtained a valuable benefit (other than a payment of money to which the last foregoing subsection applies) before the time of discharge, there shall be recoverable from him by the said other party such sum (if any), not exceeding the value of the said benefit to the party obtaining it, as the court considers just, having regard to all the circumstances of the case and, in particular,—

(a) the amount of any expenses incurred before the time of discharge by the benefited party in, or for the purpose of, the performance of the contract, including any sums paid or payable by him to any other party in pursuance of the contract and retained or recoverable by that party under the last foregoing subsection, and

(b) the effect, in relation to the said benefit, of the circumstances giving rise to the frustration of the contract.

NATIONAL PRESTO INDUS., INC. v. UNITED STATES, 338 F.2d 99, 112 (Ct.Cl.1964). "[I]t is [sometimes] equitable to reform the contract so that each side bears a share of the unexpected costs, instead of permitting the whole loss to remain with the party on whom it chanced to light. In contract suits courts have generally seemed loath to divide damages, but in this class of case we see no objection other than tradition. Reformation, as the child of equity, can mold its relief to attain any fair result within the broadest perimeter of the charter the parties have established for themselves. Where that arrangement has allocated the risk to neither side, a judicial division is fair and equitable. The division can follow from the special circumstances if there are any; in their absence an equal split would fit the basic postulate that the contract has assigned the risk to neither party."

Note
Economic Hardship Clauses

Contracting parties may desire to set forth their own remedial approach to problems of hardship caused by unanticipated circumstances. Especially in the long-term supply contract setting, drafters frequently include a "gross inequities adjustment provision" or an "economic hardship" clause. We set forth below a sample of the latter kind of clause actually found in some coal supply contracts. What problems do such clauses raise? Review the materials on Agreements to Agree in Section Nine of Chapter Four.

(d) Ninety (90) days prior to the end of the fifth year of this agreement and ninety (90) days prior to the end of each subsequent fifth year, the parties shall jointly consider the effect of economic conditions and market prices in the coal industry to ascertain whether the Adjusted Price should be further adjusted in order to avoid economic hardship for SELLER or for BUYER. If it is thus ascertained that a substantial change has occurred in the economic conditions and/or market prices, then the Adjusted Price shall be further adjusted to compensate for such change and the amount of such adjustment and its effective date shall be mutually agreed upon by SELLER and BUYER.

The intent of this Paragraph (d) is to avoid having SELLER experience a significant loss as a result of changed economic conditions and to insure that BUYER will not pay SELLER a price significantly higher than market prices for steam coal of similar quality, specifications, quantity, and long-term availability.

If the parties are unable to agree with respect to a price adjustment, then either party may upon twelve (12) months written notice, terminate this contract.

Problem 9–2

MBS, a construction contractor, submitted a bid for paving a section of road in Anchorage, Alaska. The specifications provided that MBS would furnish gravel and would obtain the necessary permits for gravel removal:

"If sources of materials are not indicated on the plans * * * [the contractor] shall acquire the necessary right to take materials from the sources and shall pay all costs related to obtaining and developing the source including any which may result from an increase in length of haul. * * * "

" * * * Unless otherwise designated in the contract the Contractor shall make his own arrangements for obtaining borrow [gravel] and shall pay all costs involved."

MBS was the low bidder by over $800,000 because it anticipated lower gravel costs by using a gravel pit near the project site. Prior to submitting its bid, MBS had entered an agreement with the gravel pit owner to remove gravel, but kept it secret to gain a competitive advantage. MBS also had met with zoning officials and received assurances that the gravel pit had "grandfather rights" to operate as a prior non-conforming use under the pertinent Anchorage zoning ordinance. After the bid opening, MBS told the Alaska representative that the bid was based on the availability of the gravel pit and, if there was a problem with that pit's availability, MBS would withdraw its bid.

MBS was awarded the contract, which incorporated the specifications and also provided:

[T]he Contractor * * * hereby covenants and agrees to furnish and deliver all the materials. * * * The Contractor hereby agrees to receive the prices set forth in the proposal as full compensation for furnishing all the materials * * * which may be required in the prosecution and completion of the whole work. * * *

Permits, Licenses and taxes. The Contractor shall procure all permits and licenses * * * necessary and incidental to the due and lawful prosecution of the work.

Prior to beginning work, MBS furnished the state, as requested, letters from the municipality of Anchorage setting out the grandfather rights in the pit. After neighboring property owners complained, however, the Zoning Board of Appeals denied MBS the right to remove gravel from the pit. As a result, MBS will be forced to remove gravel from more remote sources. It therefore wants to obtain additional compensation if it goes ahead with the work.

Please advise MBS as to its rights. Please also draft a clause that would protect MBS if it enters similar contracts in the future.

SECTION SIX: REMEDIES IN CASES OF FAILURE OF CONDITION OR MATERIAL BREACH—A BRIEF RETROSPECT

We learned in Chapters Three and Seven that, after a material breach of an agreement with consideration that is not curable, the injured party is discharged and may be entitled to recover expectancy damages.[b] If, for some reason, the injured party cannot prove a lost expectancy, that party may still recover reliance expenses. Or the injured party may elect to recover on an unjust enrichment theory. See Chapter Three, Sections Three, Five, and Eight.

What are the remedial consequences when a material breach is followed by impossibility or the like? Consider again, the facts of Taylor v. Caldwell, set forth at page 918. Assume that on June 17, the date of the first concert, the

---

b. Recall that after a material breach, an injured party may suspend performance (temporary cessation) and that, when it is too late for the breaching party to cure, the injured party is discharged (total cessation).

defendants refused to permit the plaintiffs to use the hall, a material breach, and also repudiated all other obligations. Thereafter, fire destroyed the Hall on July 10, before the dates scheduled for the other three concerts. The plaintiffs would be entitled to recover lost expectancy damages for the defendants' material breach of the agreement to let the plaintiffs use the hall on June 17, but the defendants would be excused as to the other three dates. As one court phrased the rule, "upon breach of contract by a promisor, supervening impossibility occurring through destruction of the subject matter without the fault of the promisor will limit the damages recoverable to the time before the impossibility has taken place." Model Vending, Inc. v. Stanisci, 74 N.J.Super. 12, 180 A.2d 393 (1962).

*

Part Five

RIGHTS AND DUTIES OF THIRD PARTIES

Chapter Ten

THIRD PARTY BENEFICIARIES

Chapter Eleven

ASSIGNMENT AND DELEGATION

Chapter Ten

THIRD PARTY BENEFICIARIES

*In no department of the law has a
more obstinate and persistent battle
between theory and practice been
waged. Nor is the strife ended.*

WILLISTON

SECTION ONE: THIRD PARTY BENEFICIARIES AND THE ROLE OF LAWYERS

In previous chapters, we considered the rights and duties of immediate parties to agreements. Now we turn to the rights and duties of third parties— parties who are neither promisors nor promisees under an agreement, but who have some right (or owe some duty) under it.

When practicing law involving third parties, the lawyer must utilize virtually all of the skills heretofore explored in this book. For example, if Amy promises Helen to pay Esta $10,000 in return for Helen's promise to forgive Amy's $10,500 debt to Helen, Esta may seek to enforce Amy's promise if Amy reneges. The lawyer representing Esta, as a litigator, must show that contract law supports Esta's claim. The lawyer drafting the Amy–Helen deal must ascertain whether the parties desire to create a cause of action in Esta, and, if so, the lawyer must reflect that intent in the agreement. We will see that the law's approach to whether Esta can recover depends on whether the Amy–Helen agreement reflects such an intent.

SECTION TWO: INTENDED AND INCIDENTAL BENEFICIARIES

LAWRENCE v. FOX

Court of Appeals of New York, 1859.
20 N.Y. 268.

APPEAL from the Superior Court of the city of Buffalo. On the trial before MR. JUSTICE MASTEN, it appeared by the evidence of a bystander, that one Holly, in November, 1857, at the request of the defendant, loaned and advanced to him $300, stating at the time that he owed that sum to the plaintiff for money borrowed of him, and had agreed to pay it to him the then next day; that the defendant in consideration thereof, at the time of receiving the money, promised to pay it to the plaintiff the then next day. Upon this state of facts the defendant moved for a nonsuit, upon [the grounds that], viz.: * * * the agreement by the defendant with Holly to pay the plaintiff was void for want of consideration, and that there was no privity between the plaintiff and defendant. The court overruled the motion, and the counsel for the defendant excepted. The cause was then submitted to the jury, and they found a verdict for the plaintiff for the amount of the loan and interest, $344.66, upon which judgment was entered; from which the defendant appealed to the Superior Court, at general term, where the judgment was affirmed, and the defendant appealed to this court. The cause was submitted on printed arguments.

* * *

H. Gray, J. * * * [I]t is claimed that notwithstanding [defendant's] promise was established by competent evidence, it was void for the want of consideration. It is now more than a quarter of a century since it was settled by the Supreme Court of this State—in an able and pains-taking opinion by the late Chief Justice SAVAGE, in which the authorities were fully examined and carefully analysed—that a promise in all material respects like the one under consideration was valid; and the judgment of that court was unanimously affirmed by the Court for the Correction of Errors. (*Farley v. Cleveland, 4 Cow., 432; same case in error, 9 id., 639.*) In that case one Moon owed Farley and sold to Cleaveland a quantity of hay, in consideration of which Cleaveland promised to pay Moon's debt to Farley; and the decision in favor of Farley's right to recover was placed upon the ground that the hay received by Cleaveland from Moon was a valid consideration for Cleaveland's promise to pay Farley, and that the subsisting liability of Moon to pay Farley was no objection to the recovery. The fact that the money advanced by Holly to the defendant was a loan to him for a day, and that it thereby became the property of the defendant, seemed to impress the defendant's counsel with the idea that because the defendant's promise was not a trust fund placed by the plaintiff in the defendant's hands, out of which he was to realize money as from the sale of a chattel or the collection of a debt, the promise although made for the benefit of the plaintiff could not enure to his benefit. The hay which Cleaveland [received from] Moon was not to be paid to Farley, but the debt incurred by Cleaveland for the purchase of the hay, like the debt incurred by the defendant for money borrowed, was what was to be paid. That case has been often referred to by the courts of this State, and has never been doubted as sound authority for the principle upheld by it. (*Barker v. Buklin, 2 Denio, 45; Hudson Canal Company v. The Westchester Bank, 4 id., 97*) It puts to rest the objection that the defendant's promise was void for want of consideration.

The report of that case shows that the promise was not only made to Moon but to the plaintiff Farley. In this case the promise was made to Holly and not expressly to the plaintiff; and this difference between the two cases presents the question, raised by the defendant's objection, as to the want of privity between the plaintiff and defendant. As early as 1806 it was announced by the Supreme Court of this State, upon what was then regarded as the settled law of England, "That where one person makes a promise to another for the benefit of a third person, that third person may maintain an action upon it." *Schermerhorn v. Vanderheyden* (1 *John R.,* 140), has often been re-asserted by our courts and never departed from. * * * This question was subsequently, and in a case quite recent, again the subject of consideration by the Supreme Court, when it was held, that in declaring upon a promise, made to the debtor by a third party to pay the creditor of the debtor, founded upon a consideration advanced by the debtor, it was unnecessary to aver a promise to the creditor; for the reason that upon proof of a promise made to the debtor to pay the creditor, a promise to the creditor would be implied. * * * But it is urged that because the defendant was not in any sense a trustee of the property of Holly for the benefit of the plaintiff, the law will not imply a promise. I agree that many of the cases where a promise was implied were cases of trusts, created for the benefit of the promiser. The case of *Felton v. Dickinson* (10 *Mass.*, 189, 190), and others that might be cited are of that class; but concede them all to have been cases of trusts, and it proves nothing against the application of the rule to this case. The duty of the trustee to pay the *cestuis que trust,* according to the terms of the trust, implies his promise to the latter to do so. In this case the defendant, upon ample consideration received from Holly, promised Holly to pay his debt to the plaintiff; the consideration received and the promise to Holly made it as plainly his duty to pay the plaintiff as if the money had been remitted to him for that purpose, and as well implied a promise to do so as if he had been made a trustee of property to be converted into cash with which to pay. The fact that a breach of the duty imposed in the one case may be visited, and justly, with more serious consequences than in the other, by no means disproves the payment to be a duty in both. The principle illustrated by the example so frequently quoted (which concisely states the case in hand) "that a promise made to one for the benefit of another, he for whose benefit it is made may bring an action for its breach," has been applied to trust cases, not because it was exclusively applicable to those cases, but because it was a principle of law, and as such applicable to those cases.

It was also insisted that Holly could have discharged the defendant from his promise, though it was intended by both parties for the benefit of the plaintiff, and therefore the plaintiff was not entitled to maintain this suit for the recovery of a demand over which he had no control. It is enough that [Holly] did not release the defendant from his promise, and whether he could or not is a question not now necessarily involved; but if it was, I think it would be found difficult to maintain the right of Holly to discharge a judgment recovered by the plaintiff upon confession or otherwise, for the breach of the defendant's promise; and if he could not, how could he discharge the suit before judgment, or the promise before suit, made as it was for the plaintiff's benefit and in accordance with legal presumption accepted by him (*Berly v. Taylor*, 5 *Hill,* 577–584, *et seq.*), until his dissent was shown. The cases cited, and especially that of *Farley v. Cleveland,* establish the validity of a parol promise; it stands then upon the footing of a written one. Suppose the defendant had given his note in which, for value received of Holly, he had promised to pay the plaintiff and the plaintiff had accepted the promise, retaining Holly's liability. Very clearly Holly could not have discharged that promise, be the right to release the defendant as it may. No one can doubt that he owes the sum of money demanded of him, or that in accordance with his promise it was his duty to have paid it to the plaintiff; nor can it be doubted that whatever may be the diversity of opinion elsewhere, the adjudications in this State, from a very early period, approved by experience, have established the defendant's liability; if, therefore, it could be shown that a more strict and technically accurate application of the rules applied, would lead to a different result (which I by no means concede), the effort should not be made in the face of manifest justice.

The judgment should be affirmed.

JOHNSON, CH. J., DENIO, SELDEN, ALLEN and STRONG, JS., concurred. JOHNSON, CH. J., and DENIO, J., were of opinion that the promise was to be regarded as made to the plaintiff through the medium of his agent, whose action he could ratify when it came to his knowledge, though taken without his being privy thereto.

COMSTOCK, J. (Dissenting.) The plaintiff had nothing to do with the promise on which he brought this action. It was not made to him, nor did the consideration proceed from him. If he can maintain the suit, it is because an anomaly has found its way into the law on this subject. In general, there must be privity of contract. The party who sues upon a promise must be the promisee, or he must have some legal interest in the undertaking. In this case, it is plain that Holly, who loaned the money to the defendant, and to whom the promise in question was made, could at any time have claimed that it should be performed to himself personally. He had lent the money to the defendant, and at the same time directed the latter to pay the sum to the plaintiff. This direction he could countermand, and if he had done so, manifestly the defendant's promise to pay according to the direction would have ceased to exist. The plaintiff would receive a benefit by a complete execution of the arrangement, but the arrangement itself was between other parties, and was under their exclusive control. If the defendant had paid the money to Holly, his debt would have been discharged thereby. So Holly might have released the demand or assigned it to another person, or the parties might have annulled the promise now in question, and designated some other creditor of Holly as the party to whom the money should be paid. It has never been claimed, that in a case thus situated, the right of a third person to sue upon the promise rested on any sound principle of law. We are to inquire whether the rule has been so established by positive authority.

* * *

The cases in which some trust was involved are * * * frequently referred to as authority for the doctrine now in question, but they do not sustain it. If A delivers money or property to B, which the latter accepts upon a trust for the benefit of C, the latter can enforce the trust by an appropriate action for that purpose. (*Berly v. Taylor,* 5 *Hill,* 577.) If the trust be of money, I think the beneficiary may assent to it and bring the action for money had and received to his use. If it be of something else than money, the trustee must account for it according to the terms of the trust, and upon principles of equity. There is some authority even for saying that an express promise founded on the possession of a trust fund may be enforced by an action at law in the name of the beneficiary, although it was made to the creator of the trust. Thus, in *Comyn's Digest* (*Action on the case upon Assumpsit, B.* 15), it is laid down that if a man promise a pig of lead to A, and his executor give lead to make a pig to B, who assumes to deliver it to A, an assumpsit lies by A against him. The case of *The Delaware and Hudson Canal Company v. The Westchester County Bank* (4 *Denio,* 97), involved a trust because the defendants had received from a third party a bill of exchange under an agreement that they would endeavor to collect it, and would pay over the proceeds when collected to the plaintiffs. A fund received under such an agreement does not belong to the person who receives it. He must account for it specifically; and perhaps there is no gross violation of principle in permitting the equitable owner of it to sue upon an express promise to pay it over. Having a specific interest in the thing, the undertaking to account for it may be regarded as in some sense made with him through the author of the trust. But further than this we cannot go without violating plain rules of law. In the case before us there was nothing in the nature of a trust or agency. The defendant borrowed the money of Holly and received it as his own. The plaintiff had no right in the fund, legal or equitable. The promise to repay the money created an obligation in favor of the lender to whom it was made and not in favor of any one else.

* * *

GROVER, J., also dissented.

Judgment affirmed.

SEAVER v. RANSOM

Court of Appeals of New York, 1918.
224 N.Y. 233, 120 N.E. 639.

POUND, J. Judge Beman and his wife were advanced in years. Mrs. Beman was about to die. She had a small estate, consisting of a house and lot in Malone and little else. Judge Beman drew his wife's will according to her instructions. It gave $1,000 to plaintiff, $500 to one sister, plaintiff's mother, and $100 each to another sister and her son, the use of the house to her husband for life, and remainder to the American Society for the Prevention of Cruelty to Animals. She named her husband as residuary legatee and executor. Plaintiff was her niece, 34 years old in ill health sometimes a member of the Beman household. When the will was read to Mrs. Beman, she said that it was not as she wanted it. She wanted to leave the house to plaintiff. She had no other objection to the will, but her strength was waning, and, although the judge offered to write another will for her, she said she was afraid she would not hold out long enough to enable her to sign it. So the judge said, if she would sign the will, he would leave plaintiff enough in his will to make up the difference. He avouched the promise by his uplifted hand with all solemnity and his wife then executed the will. When he came to die, it was found that his will made no provision for the plaintiff.

This action was brought, and plaintiff recovered judgment in the trial court, on the theory that Beman had obtained property from his wife and induced her to execute the will in the form prepared by him by his promise to give plaintiff $6,000, the value of the house, and that thereby equity impressed his property with a trust in favor of plaintiff. Where a legatee promises the testator that he will use property given him by the will for a particular purpose, a trust arises. O'Hara v. Dudley, 95 N.Y. 403, 47 Am.Rep. 53; Trustees of Amherst College v. Ritch, 151 N.Y. 282, 45 N.E. 876, 37 L.R.A. 305; Ahrens v. Jones, 169 N.Y. 555, 62 N.E. 666, 88 Am.St.Rep. 620. Beman received nothing under his wife's will but the use of the house in Malone for life. Equity compels the application of property thus obtained to the purpose of the testator, but equity cannot so impress a trust, except on property obtained by the promise. Beman was bound by his promise, but no property was bound by it; no trust in plaintiff's favor can be spelled out.

An action on the contract for damages, or to make the executors trustees for performance, stands on different ground. Farmers' Loan & Trust Co. v. Mortimer, 219 N.Y. 290, 294, 295, 114 N.E. 389. The Appellate Division properly passed to the consideration of the question whether the judgment could stand upon the promise made to the wife, upon a valid consideration, for the sole benefit of plaintiff. The judgment of the trial court was affirmed by a return to the general doctrine laid down in the great case of Lawrence v. Fox, 20 N.Y. 268, which has since been limited as herein indicated.

Contracts for the benefit of third persons have been the prolific source of judicial and academic discussion. * * * The general rule, both in law and equity * * * was that privity between a plaintiff and a defendant is necessary to the maintenance of an action on the contract. The consideration must be furnished by the party to whom the promise was made. The contract cannot be enforced against the third party, and therefore it cannot be enforced by him. On the other hand, the right of the beneficiary to sue on a contract made expressly for his benefit has been fully recognized in many American jurisdictions, either by judicial decision or by legislation, and is said to be "the prevailing rule in this country." Hendrick v. Lindsay, 93 U.S. 143, 23 L.Ed. 855; Lehow v. Simonton, 3 Colo. 346. It has been said that "the establishment of this doctrine has been gradual, and is a victory of practical utility over theory, of equity over technical subtlety." Brantly on Contracts (2d Ed.) p. 253. The reasons for this view are that it is just and practical to permit the person for whose benefit the contract is made to enforce it against one whose duty it is to pay. Other jurisdictions still adhere to the present English rule (7 Halsbury's Laws of England, 342, 343; Jenks' Digest of English Civil Law, § 229) that a contract cannot be enforced by or against a person who is not a party (Exchange Bank v. Rice, 107 Mass. 37, 9 Am.Rep. 1). * * *

In New York the right of the beneficiary to sue on contracts made for his benefit is not clearly or simply defined. It is at present confined: First. To cases where there is a pecuniary obligation running from the promisee to the beneficiary, "a legal right founded upon some obligation of the promisee in the third party to adopt and claim the promise as made for his benefit." Farley v. Cleveland, 4 Cow. 432, 15 Am.Dec. 387; Lawrence v. Fox * * *. Secondly. To cases where the contract is made for the benefit of the wife (Buchanan v. Tilden, 158 N.Y. 109, 52 N.E. 724, 44 L.R.A. 170, 70 Am.St.Rep. 454 * * *), affianced wife, * * * or child * * * of a party to the contract. The close relationship cases go back to the early King's Bench case (1677), long since repudiated in England, of Dutton v. Poole, 2 Lev. 211 (s. c., 1 Ventris, 318, 332). See Schemerhorn v. Vanderheyden, 1 Johns. 139, 3 Am.Dec. 304. The natural and moral duty of the husband or parent to provide for the future of wife or child sustains the action on the contract made for their benefit. "This is the farthest the cases in this state have gone," says Cullen, J., in the marriage settlement case of Borland v. Welch, 162 N.Y. 104, 110, 56 N.E. 556.

The right of the third party is also upheld in, thirdly, the public contract cases * * * where the municipality seeks to protect its inhabitants by covenants for their benefit; and, fourthly, the cases where, at the request of a party to the contract, the promise runs directly to the beneficiary although he does not furnish the consideration. * * *

It may be safely said that a general rule sustaining recovery at the suit of the third party would include but few classes of cases not included in these groups, either categorically or in principle.

The desire of the childless aunt to make provision for a beloved and favorite niece differs imperceptibly in law or in equity from the moral duty of the parent to make testamentary provision for a child. The contract was made for the plaintiff's benefit. She alone is substantially damaged by its breach. The representatives of the wife's estate have no interest in enforcing it specifically. It is said in Buchanan v. Tilden that the common law imposes moral and legal obligations upon the husband and the parent not measured by the necessaries of life. It was, however, the love and affection or the moral sense of the husband and the parent that imposed such obligations in the cases cited, rather than any common-law duty of husband and parent to wife and child. If plaintiff had been a child of Mrs. Beman, legal obligation would have required no testamentary provision for her, yet the child could have enforced a covenant in her favor identical with the covenant of Judge Beman in this case. * * * The constraining power of conscience is not regulated by the degree of relationship alone. The dependent or faithful niece may have a stronger claim than the affluent or unworthy son. No sensible theory of moral obligation denies arbitrarily to the former what would be conceded to the latter. We might consistently either refuse or allow the claim of both, but I cannot reconcile a decision in favor of the wife in Buchanan v. Tilden, based on the moral obligations arising out of near relationship, with a decision against the niece here on the ground that the relationship is too remote for equity's ken. * * *

The court in [Lawrence v. Fox] attempted to adopt the general doctrine that any third person, for whose direct benefit a contract was intended, could sue on it. [The court here discusses cases interpreting Lawrence v. Fox in this way and cases limiting its holding to where " 'there has been a debt or duty owing by the promisee to the party claiming to sue upon the promise.' "]

* * *

But, on principle, a sound conclusion may be reached. If Mrs. Beman had left her husband the house on condition that he pay the plaintiff $6,000, and he had accepted the devise, he would have become personally liable to pay the legacy, and plaintiff could have recovered in an action at law against him, whatever the value of the house. * * * That would be because the testatrix had in substance bequeathed the promise to plaintiff, and not because close relationship or moral obligation sustained the contract. The distinction between an implied promise to a testator for the benefit of a third party to pay a legacy and an unqualified promise on a valuable consideration to make provision for the third party by will is discernible, but not obvious. The tendency of American authority is to sustain the gift in all such cases and to permit the donee beneficiary to recover on the contract. Matter of Edmundson's Estate (1918, Pa.) 103 Atl. 277, 259 Pa. 429. The equities are with the plaintiff, and they may be enforced in this action, whether it be regarded as an action for damages or an action for specific performance to convert the defendants into trustees for plaintiff's benefit under the agreement.

The judgment should be affirmed, with costs.

HOGAN, CARDOZO and CRANE, JJ., concur. HISCOCK, C.J., and COLLIN and ANDREWS, JJ., dissent.

Judgment affirmed.

RESTATEMENT (FIRST) OF CONTRACTS § 133.

Definition of Donee Beneficiary, Creditor Beneficiary, Incidental Beneficiary

(1) Where performance of a promise in a contract will benefit a person other than the promisee, that person is * * *

(a) a donee beneficiary if it appears from the terms of the promise in view of the accompanying circumstances that the purpose of the promisee in obtaining the promise of all or part of the performance thereof is to make a gift to the beneficiary or to confer upon him a right against the promisor to some performance neither due nor supposed or asserted to be due from the promisee to the beneficiary;

(b) a creditor beneficiary if no purpose to make a gift appears from the terms of the promise in view of the accompanying circumstances and performance of the promise will satisfy an actual or supposed or asserted duty of the promisee to the beneficiary, or a right of the beneficiary against the promisee which has been barred by the Statute of Limitations or by a discharge in bankruptcy, or which is unenforceable because of the Statute of Frauds;

(c) an incidental beneficiary if neither the facts stated in Clause (a) nor those stated in Clause (b) exist.

H.R. MOCH CO. v. RENSSELAER WATER CO.

Court of Appeals of New York, 1928.
247 N.Y. 160, 159 N.E. 896.

Action by the H.R. Moch Company, Inc., against the Rensselaer Water Company. From a judgment of the Appellate Division (219 App.Div. 673, 220 N.Y.S. 557), reversing an order of the Special Term, and granting defendant's motion for judgment dismissing the complaint for failure to state facts sufficient to constitute a cause of action, plaintiff appeals. Affirmed.

* * *

CARDOZO, C.J. The defendant, a waterworks company under the laws of this state, made a contract with the city of Rensselaer for the supply of water during a term of years. Water was to be furnished to the city for sewer flushing and street sprinkling; for service to schools and public buildings; and for service at fire hydrants, the latter service at the rate of $42.50 a year for each hydrant. Water was to be furnished to private takers within the city at their homes and factories and other industries at reasonable rates, not exceeding a stated schedule. While this contract was in force, a building caught fire. The flames, spreading to the plaintiff's warehouse near by, destroyed it and its contents. The defendant, according to the complaint, was promptly notified of the fire, "but omitted and neglected after such notice, to supply or furnish sufficient or adequate quantity of water, with adequate pressure to stay, suppress, or extinguish the fire before it reached the warehouse of the plaintiff, although the pressure and supply which the defendant was equipped to supply and furnish, and had agreed by said contract to supply and furnish, was adequate and sufficient to prevent the spread of the fire to and the destruction of the plaintiff's warehouse and its contents." By reason of the failure of the defendant to "fulfill the provisions of the contract between it and the city of Rensselaer," the plaintiff is said to have suffered damage, for which judgment is demanded. A motion, in the nature of a demurrer, to dismiss the complaint, was denied at Special Term. The Appellate Division reversed by a divided court.

Liability in the plaintiff's argument is placed on one or other of three grounds. The complaint, we are told, is to be viewed as stating: (1) A cause of action for breach of contract within Lawrence v. Fox, 20 N.Y. 268; (2) a cause of action for a common-law tort, within MacPherson v. Buick Motor Co., 217 N.Y. 382, 111 N.E. 1050, L.R.A. 1916F, 696, Am.Ann.Cas. 1916C, 440; or (3) a cause of action for the breach of a statutory duty. These several grounds of liability will be considered in succession.

(1) We think the action is not maintainable as one for breach of contract.

No legal duty rests upon a city to supply its inhabitants with protection against fire. Springfield Fire & Marine Ins. Co. v. Village of Keeseville, 148 N.Y. 46, 42 N.E. 405, 30 L.R.A. 660, 51 Am.St.Rep. 667. That being so, a member of the public may not maintain an action under Lawrence v. Fox against one contracting with the city to furnish water at the hydrants, unless an intention appears that the promisor is to be answerable to individual members of the public as well as to the city for any loss ensuing from the failure to fulfill the promise. No such intention is discernible here. On the contrary, the contract is significantly divided into two branches: One a promise to the city for the benefit of the city in its corporate capacity, in which branch is included the service at the hydrants; and the other a promise to the city for the benefit of private takers, in which branch is included the service at their homes and factories. In a broad sense it is true that every city contract, not improvident or wasteful, is for the benefit of the public. More than this, however, must be shown to give a right of action to a member of the public not formally a party. The benefit, as it is sometimes said, must be one that is not merely incidental and secondary. Cf. Fosmire v. National Surety Co., 229 N.Y. 44, 127 N.E. 472. It must be primary and immediate in such a sense and to such a degree as to bespeak the assumption of a duty to make reparation directly to the individual members of the public if the benefit is lost. The field of obligation would be expanded beyond reasonable limits if less than this were to be demanded as a condition of liability. A promisor undertakes to supply fuel for heating a public building. He is not liable for breach of contract to a visitor who finds the building without fuel, and thus contracts a cold. The list of illustrations can be indefinitely extended. The carrier of the mails under contract with the government is not answerable to the merchant who has lost the benefit of a bargain through negligent delay. The householder is without a remedy against manufacturers of hose and engines, though prompt performance of their contracts would have stayed the ravages of fire. "The law does not spread its protection so far." Robins Dry Dock & Repair Co. v. Flint, 275 U.S. 303, 48 S.Ct. 134, 72 L.Ed. 290.

So with the case at hand. By the vast preponderance of authority, a contract between a city and a water company to furnish water at the city hydrants has in view a benefit to the public that is incidental rather than immediate, an assumption of duty to the city and not to its inhabitants. Such is the ruling of the Supreme Court of the United States. German Alliance Ins. Co. v. Homewater Supply Co., 226 U.S. 220, 33 S.Ct. 32, 57 L.Ed. 195, 42 L.R.A. (N.S.) 1000. Such has been the ruling in this state (Wainwright v. Queens County Water Co., 78 Hun, 146, 28 N.Y.S. 987; Smith v. Great South Bay Water Co., 82 App.Div. 427, 81 N.Y.S. 812), though the question is still open in this court. Such with few exceptions has been the ruling in other jurisdictions. Williston, Contracts, § 373, and cases there cited; Dillon, Municipal Corporations (5th Ed.) § 1340. The diligence of counsel has brought together decisions to that effect from 26 states. * * * Only a few states have held otherwise. Page, Contracts, § 2401. An intention to assume an obligation of indefinite extension to every member of the public is seen to be the more improbable when we recall the crushing burden that the obligation would impose. Cf. Hone v. Presque Isle Water Co., 104 Me. 217, at p. 232, 71 A. 769, 21 L.R.A. (N.S.) 1021. The consequences invited would bear no reasonable proportion to those attached by law to defaults not greatly different. A wrongdoer who by negligence sets fire to a building is liable in damages to the owner where the fire has its origin, but not to other owners who are injured when it spreads. The rule in our state is settled to that effect, whether wisely or unwisely. * * * If the plaintiff is to prevail, one who negligently omits to supply sufficient pressure to extinguish a fire started by another assumes an obligation to pay the ensuing damage, though the whole city is laid low. A promisor will not be deemed to have had in mind the assumption of a risk so overwhelming for any trivial reward.

The cases that have applied the rule of Lawrence v. Fox to contracts made by a city for the benefit of the public are not at war with this conclusion. Through them all there runs as a unifying principle the presence of an intention to compensate the individual members of the public in the event of a default. For example, in Pond v. New Rochelle Water Co., 183 N.Y. 330, 76 N.E. 211, 1 L.R.A. (N.S.) 958, 5 Ann.Cas. 504, the contract with the city fixed a schedule of rates to be supplied, not to public buildings, but to private takers at their homes. In Matter of International R. Co. v. Rann, 224 N.Y. 83, 85, 120 N.E. 153, the contract was by street railroads to carry passengers for a stated fare. In Smyth v. City of New York, 203 N.Y. 106, 96 N.E. 409, and Rigney v. New York Cent. & H.R.R. Co., 217 N.Y. 31, 111 N.E. 226, covenants were made by contractors upon public works, not merely to indemnify the city, but to assume its liabilities. These and like cases come within the third group stated in the comprehensive opinion in Seaver v. Ransom, 224 N.Y. 233, 238, 120 N.E. 639, 2 L.R.A. 1187. The municipality was contracting in behalf of its inhabitants by covenants intended to be enforced by any of them severally as occasion should arise.

(2) We think the action is not maintainable as one for a common-law tort.

"It is ancient learning that one who assumes to act, even though gratuitously, may thereby become subject to the duty of acting carefully, if he acts at all." Glanzer v. Shepard, 233 N.Y. 236, 239, 135 N.E. 275, 276 (23 A.L.R. 1425); Marks v. Nambil Realty Co., 245 N.Y. 256, 258, 157 N.E. 129. The plaintiff would bring its case within the orbit of that principle. The hand once set to a task may not always be withdrawn with impunity though liability would fail if it had never been applied at all. A time-honored formula often phrases the distinction as one between misfeasance and nonfeasance. Incomplete the formula is, and so at times misleading. Given a relation involving in its existence a duty of care irrespective of a contract, a tort may result as well from acts of omission as of commission in the fulfillment of the duty thus recognized by law. Pollock, Torts (12th Ed.) p. 555; Kelly v. Metropolitan Ry. Co., [1895] 1 Q.B. 944. What we need to know is not so much the conduct to be avoided when the relation and its attendant duty are established as existing. What we need to know is the conduct that engenders the relation. It is here that the formula, however incomplete, has its value and significance. If conduct has gone forward to such a stage that inaction would commonly result, not negatively merely in withholding a benefit, but positively or actively in working an injury, there exists a relation out of which arises a duty to go forward. Bohlen, Studies in the Law of Torts, p. 87. So the surgeon who operates without pay is liable, though his negligence is in the omission to sterilize his instruments (cf. Glanzer v. Shepard, supra); the engineer, though his fault is in the failure to shut off steam (Kelly v. Metropolitan Ry. Co., supra; cf. Pittsfield Cottonwear Mfg. Co. v. Pittsfield Shoe Co., 71 N.H. 522, 529, 533, 53 A. 807, 60 L.R.A. 116); the maker of automobiles, at the suit of some one other than the buyer, though his negligence is merely in inadequate inspection (MacPherson v. Buick Motor Co., 217 N.Y. 382, 111 N.E. 1050, L.R.A. 1916F, 696, Am.Ann.Cas. 1916C, 440). The query always is whether the putative wrongdoer has advanced to such a point as to have launched a force or instrument of harm, or has stopped where inaction is at most a refusal to become an instrument for good. Cf. Fowler v. Athens Water–Works Co., 83 Ga. 219, 222, 9 S.E. 673, 20 Am.St.Rep. 313.

The plaintiff would have us hold that the defendant, when once it entered upon the performance of its contract with the city, was brought into such a relation with every one who might potentially be benefited through the supply of water at the hydrants as to give to negligent performance, without reasonable notice of a refusal to continue, the quality of a tort. There is a suggestion of this thought in Guardian Trust & Deposit Co. v. Fisher, 200 U.S. 57, 26 S.Ct. 186, 50 L.Ed. 367; but the dictum was rejected in a later case decided by the same court (German Alliance Ins. Co. v. Homewater Supply Co., 226 U.S. 220, 33 S.Ct. 32, 57 L.Ed. 195, 42 L.R.A. [N.S.] 1000) when an opportunity was at hand to turn it into law. We are satisfied that liability would be unduly and indeed indefinitely extended by this enlargement of the zone of duty. The dealer in coal who is to supply fuel for a shop must then answer to the customers if fuel is lacking. The manufacturer of goods, who enters upon the performance of his contract, must answer, in that view, not only to the buyer, but to those who to his knowledge are looking to the buyer for their own sources of supply. Every one making a promise having the quality of a contract will be under a duty to the promisee by virtue of the promise, but under another duty, apart from contract, to an indefinite number of potential beneficiaries when performance has begun. The assumption of one relation will mean the involuntary assumption of a series of new relations, inescapably hooked together. Again we may say in the words of the Supreme Court of the United States, "The law does not spread its protection so far." Robins Dry Dock & Repair Co. v. Flint, supra * * *. We do not need to determine now what remedy, if any, there might be if the defendant had withheld the water or reduced the pressure with a malicious intent to do injury to the plaintiff or another. We put aside also the problem that would arise if there had been reckless and wanton indifference to consequences measured and foreseen. Difficulties would be present even then, but they need not now perplex us. What we are dealing with at this time is a mere negligent omission, unaccompanied by malice or other aggravating elements. The failure in such circumstances to furnish an adequate supply of water is at most the denial of a benefit. It is not the commission of a wrong.

(3) We think the action is not maintainable as one for the breach of a statutory duty.

The defendant, a public service corporation, is subject to the provisions of the Transportation Corporations Act. The duty imposed upon it by that act is in substance to furnish water, upon demand by the inhabitants, at reasonable rates, through suitable connections at office, factory, or dwelling, and to furnish water at like rates through hydrants or in public buildings upon demand by the city, all according to its capacity. Transportation Corporations Law (Consol.Laws, c. 63) § 81; Staten Island Water Supply Co. v. City of New York, 144 App.Div. 318, 128 N.Y.S. 1028; People ex rel. City of New York v. Queens County Water Co., 232 N.Y. 277, 133 N.E. 889; People ex rel. Arthur v. Huntington Water Works Co., 208 App.Div. 807, 808, 203 N.Y.S. 808. We find nothing in these requirements to enlarge the zone of liability where an inhabitant of the city suffers indirect or incidental damage through deficient pressure at the hydrants. The breach of duty in any case is to the one to whom service is denied at the time and at the place where service to such one is due. The denial, though wrongful, is unavailing without more to give a cause of action to another. We may find a helpful analogy in the law of common carriers. A railroad company is under a duty to supply reasonable facilities for carriage at reasonable rates. It is liable, generally speaking, for breach of a duty imposed by law if it refuses to accept merchandise tendered by a shipper. The fact that its duty is of this character does not make it liable to some one else who may be counting upon the prompt delivery of the merchandise to save him from loss in going forward with his work. If the defendant may not be held for a tort at common law, we find no adequate reason for a holding that it may be held under the statute.

The judgment should be affirmed, with costs.

POUND, CRANE, ANDREWS, LEHMAN, and KELLOGG, JJ., concur.

O'BRIEN, J., not sitting.

RESTATEMENT (SECOND) OF CONTRACTS § 302.

Intended and Incidental Beneficiaries

(1) Unless otherwise agreed between promisor and promisee, a beneficiary of a promise is an intended beneficiary if recognition of a right to performance in the beneficiary is appropriate to effectuate the intention of the parties and either

    (a) the performance of the promise will satisfy an obligation of the promisee to pay money to the beneficiary; or

(b) the circumstances indicate that the promisee intends to give the beneficiary the benefit of the promised performance.

(2) An incidental beneficiary is a beneficiary who is not an intended beneficiary.

WATERS, THE PROPERTY IN THE PROMISE: A STUDY OF THE THIRD PARTY BENEFICIARY RULE
98 Harv.L.Rev. 1109, 1145, 1196–97 (1985).

[In Lawrence v. Fox] Judge Gray's discussion of consideration does not address the question of privity, Fox's remaining ground of appeal. Torrance's [Fox's lawyer's] argument was that Lawrence, unlike Farley, was not a party to the contract and therefore could not enforce Fox's promise. In disposing of this argument, while conceding that Lawrence was not in privity, Judge Gray relied on cases dependent on some kind of trust, real or constructive. Torrance had pointed out that these were proprietary claims that depended on a principle peculiar to the law of trusts, and that Fox was no trustee. But Judge Gray had the last word:

> [C]oncede them all to have been cases of trusts, and it proves nothing against the application of the rule to this case. * * * The principle illustrated * * * has been applied to trust cases, not because it was exclusively applicable to those cases, but because it was a principle of law, and as such applicable to those cases.

In that sweeping statement, Judge Gray threw open a door that had been ever closed, the door that now admitted a stranger into the hallowed chamber of contract enforcement.

This bold response was thought necessary to upholding Lawrence's recovery only because [Holly's] delivery of money to Fox was a loan, the critical fact that had been added by hand to the bill of exceptions. In support of his decision, Judge Gray reached for cases that were decided unambiguously in terms of a trust, a fact that he seemed to concede. That is, he used a proprietary explanation for upholding Lawrence's action on the promise, and so consolidated the merger of property with promise that began when someone took a pen to the bill of exceptions back in 1857. * * * In so doing, Judge Gray introduced a brand new rule into the legal world in order to explain Lawrence's recovery from Fox.

* * *

The doctrinal innovation involved in *Lawrence v. Fox* was the substitution of the promise to pay money for the equitable property in the money itself. The rule of *Lawrence v. Fox* made the defendant a "constructive trustee" of the benefit of the promise, extending the potential of the action considerably. So long as the promise remained a promise to pay money, this legal sleight of hand did not matter very much. But once courts developed a generalized right of "intended beneficiaries" to enforce promises of all kinds, this type of "equitable property" was enlarged enormously.

This analysis of the role now being played by the third party beneficiary rule is supported not only by the history of the rule, but also by the nature of the rights it secures. Rights acquired by third party beneficiaries under contracts that are a part of statutory schemes of distribution and protection have a great deal in common with the kinds of rights the Supreme Court has held to be protected property under the due process clauses. This similarity is especially obvious with respect to intangible, "new property" rights, which are not encompassed by traditional legal concepts of property.

Setting aside for a moment the notion that the third party's right, thus created, is a "contract right," the right may be thought of in terms of its restitutionary, quasi-contractual origins. Quasi-contractual rights were dependent on the fiction of a promise "implied by law" from the facts of the case—facts such as the receipt of money by the defendant for and to the use of the plaintiff. If a federal agency pays a subsidy to a provider of low-income housing to be credited toward the rent of an identified tenant, the tenant could maintain an action for money had and received, were it available, against the recipient of the funds if they were not so applied and could certainly recover as an intended beneficiary of the contract under which funds were paid. Thus, where money earmarked for the plaintiff's use or credit is the object of the claim, the grievance is virtually identical to that involved in *Lawrence v. Fox.*

DRAKE v. DRAKE, 89 A.D.2d 207, 455 N.Y.S.2d 420 (1982). "[B]arring unusual circumstances, children have no standing to enforce the periodic support provisions of their parents' separation agreement, although they may enforce other specific provisions of the agreement clearly made exclusively for their benefit, such as a promise to pay college tuition or to make the child a beneficiary of a life insurance policy. The distinction drawn comports with the rules of law applicable to third party beneficiaries and further is rooted in considerations of public policy designed to promote familial harmony and foster the parent-child relationship. A parent's contractual promise to pay support is made with a view toward his statutory duty of support. * * *

"We have no doubt that circumstances may arise, such as death or disability, or outright refusal of a contracting parent to seek enforcement of periodic support provisions for a child, which would give a child the necessary standing to enforce the agreement."

Problem 10–1

Alice Turlway, an intended beneficiary under the will of the deceased, Leon Faquar, tells you that Faquar's attorney, Walter Wemmick, poorly drafted the will and that she (Alice) would receive nothing. It seems that because of Wemmick's negligence, the bequest to Alice of an interest in a trust was invalid under applicable state law. Alice wants to know whether she can recover from Wemmick for breach of contract because Wemmick promised Faquar to prepare a will in which Alice would be a beneficiary. Please advise.

ALANIZ v. SCHAL ASSOCIATES

Appellate Court of Illinois, Second District, 1988.
175 Ill.App.3d 310, 124 Ill.Dec. 851, 529 N.E.2d 832.

JUSTICE DUNN delivered the opinion of the court:

Plaintiff, Horacio Alaniz, appeals from an order of the circuit court of Lake County which granted the motion of defendant, Thorne–McNulty Corporation, to dismiss count III of plaintiff's second amended complaint and which found no reason to delay appeal or enforcement thereof. Plaintiff contends that the trial court erred in dismissing that count because he was an intended third-party beneficiary of construction contracts entered into by Thorne–McNulty, defendant Schal Associates, and plaintiff's employer, Rite–On Roofing, Inc. We affirm.

Plaintiff's initial complaint alleged that on March 1, 1985, while he was working as a roofer at the construction site of the Bannockburn Green Shopping Center, he sustained personal injuries when an extension ladder he was using collapsed. He alleged that his injuries were caused by violations of the Structural Work Act (Ill.Rev.Stat.1985, ch. 48, par. 60 *et seq.*) by Schal Associates, the construction manager of the project. Thorne–McNulty was not named as a defendant in the original complaint.

On June 23, 1987, plaintiff filed his first amended complaint. Count II of that complaint named Thorne–McNulty as a defendant, alleging that Thorne–McNulty had also violated the Structural Work Act. Thorne–McNulty moved to dismiss that count as barred by the two-year statute of limitations pertaining to actions for damages for personal injury (Ill.Rev.Stat.1985, ch. 110, par. 13–202). The motion to dismiss count II was granted on August 21, 1987, and plaintiff does not challenge the dismissal of count II.

Prior to the dismissal of count II, plaintiff filed a second amended complaint adding count III against Thorne–McNulty. Count III alleged that plaintiff was an intended third-party beneficiary of contracts between Thorne–McNulty and Rite–On Roofing, and between Thorne–McNulty and Schal Associates. The subcontract between Thorne–McNulty and Schal Associates called for Thorne–McNulty to perform certain construction work on the Bannockburn project, and article 12 of the general conditions of the subcontract contained the following provision:

"The subcontractor [Thorne–McNulty] has the responsibility for maintaining the safety and loss prevention programs covering all work performed by it, and its subcontractors."

The contract between Thorne–McNulty and Rite–On Roofing, entitled "Hold Harmless Agreement," provided that Thorne–McNulty consented to Rite–On Roofing's use of certain scaffolding under the conditions that Rite–On Roofing indemnify and hold harmless Thorne–McNulty for any claims arising out of the use by Rite–On or its agents of the scaffolding and that no guarantee or representation was made concerning the safety of the scaffolding. Plaintiff alleged that his injuries were a proximate result of Thorne–McNulty's breach of the aforementioned contracts. Thorne–McNulty moved to dismiss count III pursuant to section 2–615 of the Code of Civil Procedure (Ill.Rev.Stat.1985, ch. 110, par. 2–615), and, as noted above, the motion was granted.

On appeal, plaintiff argues that the contract between Thorne–McNulty and Schal Associates made plaintiff an intended third-party beneficiary due to the sentence which provided that Thorne–McNulty had the responsibility to maintain safety programs covering work by Thorne–McNulty and its subcontractor, Rite–On Roofing. Therefore, plaintiff contends, Thorne–McNulty had a contractual duty to him, as an employee of Rite–On Roofing, to have a safety program which provided safe work conditions, including safe equipment. He concludes that, due to Thorne–McNulty's contractual duty, he may maintain a cause of action against Thorne–McNulty for personal injuries resulting from unsafe work conditions and equipment used on the construction project.

Although apparently no case involving contractual language similar to that found here has been decided in Illinois, the law regarding third-party beneficiaries is well established. A third-party beneficiary may sue for breach of a contract made for his benefit. (*Carson Pirie Scott & Co. v. Parrett* (1931), 346 Ill. 252, 257, 178 N.E. 498.) A third-party may only sue for breach of contract, however, if the contract was entered into for the party's direct benefit; if the third-party's benefit is merely incidental, he has no right of recovery on the contract. * * * Whether a third-party is a direct beneficiary depends on the intention of the parties, which must "be gleaned from a consideration of all of the contract and the circumstances surrounding the parties at the time of its execution." *Parrett,* 346 Ill. at 258.

Our review of the contract here and the circumstances surrounding the parties at the time of its execution reveals that neither Thorne–McNulty nor Schal Associates intended to confer a direct benefit to plaintiff by inclusion of the general language regarding safety and loss prevention programs. It appears, rather, that the contract was intended solely to benefit the contracting parties by setting forth their respective responsibilities during construction. As was stated by the court in *Kohlmeier v. Shelter Insurance Co.* (1988), 170 Ill.App.3d 643, 121 Ill.Dec. 288, 525 N.E.2d 94:

> " 'As people usually stipulate for themselves, and not for third persons, a strong presumption obtains in any given case that such was their intention, and that the implication to overcome that presumption must be so strong as to amount practically to an express declaration.' " * * *

Given the nature of the construction industry and the frequency with which construction injuries occur despite safety precautions, we do not believe the presumption set forth above has been overcome. Although plaintiff argues that the hold harmless agreement between Thorne–McNulty and Rite–On Roofing establishes that Thorne–McNulty was attempting to shift its responsibility towards plaintiff to plaintiff's employer, we construe the agreement as evidence that Thorne–McNulty never intended to directly benefit plaintiff or any other workers by guaranteeing their safety.

The cases cited by plaintiff do not alter our conclusion that the contracting parties did not intend to confer a direct benefit to plaintiff by inclusion of the general safety provision. * * *

In *Baker v. S.A. Healy Co.* (1939), 302 Ill.App. 634, 24 N.E.2d 228, the intent to directly benefit the third-party claimants was clear from the contract sued upon. There, property owners brought suit against a construction firm for damages they sustained as a result of blasting during construction of a sewer. In *Baker,* the contract between the contractor and the sanitary district of Chicago provided that the contractor would, at its own expense, repair any damage to property as well as to persons. (*Baker,* 302 Ill.App. at 655.) Because the language of the contract explicitly evidenced an intent to benefit the injured property owners, they were allowed to pursue their third-party claims.

In contrast to *Baker,* the language of the contract in question here contains no promise directed specifically to third parties.

* * *

It is not enough that an incidental benefit will flow to third parties; only a direct beneficiary has a right under a contract. * * * We believe that more than the general safety provision found in the contract between Thorne–McNulty and Schal Associates is required to evidence an intent to directly benefit plaintiff. While plaintiff would most likely have received some benefit by implementation of safety programs, such benefit is incidental to the direct benefit intended for the contracting parties, and thus is not sufficient to allow him to maintain an action on the contract. Plaintiff's action is better characterized as a tort action. See *Pippin v. Chicago Housing Authority* (1979), 78 Ill.2d 204, 210, 35 Ill.Dec. 530, 399 N.E.2d 596.

The trial court's dismissal of count III of plaintiff's second amended complaint is affirmed.

AFFIRMED.

LINDBERG, P.J., and INGLIS, J., concur.

Note
Further Aspects of Alaniz v. Schal Associates

In a letter to the editors, Alaniz's lawyer explained his strategy:

The case was satisfactorily settled against Schal which was the general contractor. It chose not to third-party any other defendant. As attorney for the plaintiff, I thought it would be helpful to have the subcontractor Thorne–McNulty as a defendant too. I argued the intended third-party beneficiary theory of contract law to make them a direct party defendant. But it was not accepted by either the trial or appellate courts. In any event, in retrospect, I'm not sure it was necessary to have Thorne–McNulty as a defendant. The reason being that Schal was clearly in charge of the work and thus liable to the plaintiff. I was thinking probably that I should have as many defendants as possible. But in the facts of this case, the general contractor required the subcontractors to purchase liability insurance so that there was the same insurance company for everyone or at least an understanding on liability among the insurers involved.

The oral argument of Thorne–McNulty's motion to dismiss count III in the Circuit Court contains the following interesting interchange involving the use of precedent:

THE COURT: Are there any personal injury cases?

MR. DANIAN: [Alaniz's lawyer]: The Baker case involved personal injury, Your Honor.

MR. POWER [Thorne–McNulty's lawyer]: Your Honor, the Baker case involved a sewer explosion. There is a specific contract in the case—There is a specific clause in the contract between two of the contracting parties, the sanitary district and one of the contractors, which says they shall at their own expense repair any damage to buildings or other property. That's one clause.

Then they say it requires replacement by the contractors of lawns, trees, shrubs and plants upon private property and then the clause goes on to say the contract in a case of injury by blasting to any portion of the sewer or other structure or to material supporting same to rebuild the sewer or other structure or to replace the material surrounding or supporting same without extra payment.

These are specific clauses that the party put in the contract which definitely expressed their intention to reimburse people for personal injuries and for property damage. The people are definitely referred to [as] intended beneficiaries. No such comparison can be made in this situation, Your Honor.

* * *

* * * There is no clause in the contract that says * * * that I, one of the contracting parties, promise that I am going to pay for this person if he gets injured. On the contrary, there [are] clauses in the contract which take steps, make plans just in case somebody is injured because they recognize the possibility, Your Honor. They are saying quite to the contrary. We hope that nobody gets injured, but if they do, here is what you are supposed to do. They are not saying we are promising that if you get injured we are going to pay for you, unlike what they did say in Baker.

* * *

MR. DANIAN: It is obvious that safety programs pertain to workers. Safe environment and safe equipment is to be provided for these individuals and obviously it can be reasonably inferred from that, although I think there is still language in the contract which these programs are designed for the safety and safety means personal injury. It doesn't mean anything else. And in that respect it's very analogous to the Baker case with respect to personal injury. So I would only cite that particular case at this time.

* * *

THE COURT: Okay. Thank you. The Court will grant the motion.

MR. POWER: To dismiss?

THE COURT: To dismiss.

MR. POWER: Thank you, Your Honor.

Note
Imaginative use of Third Party Beneficiary Theory: Some Successes and Failures

We illustrate here how some imaginative lawyers have sought to utilize third party beneficiary theory:

(1) Plaintiff landlord was a third party beneficiary of an agreement between a tenant and her assignee that explicitly provided that the assignee "assumed all of the tenant's obligations" under the lease. Gateway Co. v. DiNoia, 232 Conn. 223, 654 A.2d 342 (1995).

(2) The personal representative of the estate of an inmate in a correctional facility who died while receiving treatment in the infirmary stated a good cause of action that the inmate was an intended third party beneficiary of a contract between the sheriff's department and a provider of "total health services for inmates." The contract expressly stated that it was made for the benefit of the inmates as well as for the parties themselves. Cherry v. Crow, 845 F.Supp. 1520 (M.D.Fla.1994).

(3) The owners of land with a creek stated a good cause of action as third party beneficiaries seeking damages resulting from defendant chicken processing and fertilizing plant's discharge of noxious wastes into the upstream sewer system of a municipality. According to the complaint, the contract between the municipality and the defendant provided that the latter would not oversaturate the municipality's sewer treatment facilities with certain refuse. Ratzlaff v. Franz Foods of Arkansas, 250 Ark. 1003, 468 S.W.2d 239 (1971).

(4) Plaintiffs were involved in an auto accident with defendant, who was uninsured. Plaintiffs were not intended beneficiaries of a contract between defendant and his employer, in which the employer provided funds to the defendant to purchase automobile liability insurance. Dudley v. Unisys Corp., 852 S.W.2d 435 (Tenn.App.1992).

(5) Purchaser of a yacht was not an intended beneficiary of a contract between the yacht manufacturer and a supplier of defective paint. Neither the contract nor the parties' course of dealing evidenced an intention to benefit the purchaser directly. Caretta Trucking, Inc. v. Cheoy Lee Shipyards, Ltd., 647 So.2d 1028 (Fla.App.1994).

(6) After a property owner ignored a court order to demolish a building that was a public nuisance, a municipality hired a wrecking company to do the work. When the wrecking company improperly demolished the building by failing to remove walls and foundations one foot below grade and to crush the slab, the property owner claimed to be a third-party beneficiary of the contract made by the wrecking company and the municipality. Held, the property owner was an incidental beneficiary rather than an intended beneficiary under the Restatement (Second) approach. Fourth Ocean Putnam Corp. v. Interstate Wrecking Co., Inc., 66 N.Y.2d 38, 495 N.Y.S.2d 1, 485 N.E.2d 208 (1985).

(7) Plaintiff's decedent was not an intended beneficiary of a contract between the New York State Thruway Authority and Chevron Oil Co., which gave Chevron the exclusive right to render service on the Thruway to disabled vehicles and which required Chevron to service the vehicles within 30 minutes from the time of a call for assistance. Plaintiff's decedent had a heart attack while changing a flat tire some 2½ hours after a call to the service station. Kornblut v. Chevron Oil Co., 48 N.Y.2d 853, 424 N.Y.S.2d 429, 400 N.E.2d 368 (1979).

UNIFORM COMMERCIAL CODE § 2–318.

Third Party Beneficiaries of Warranties Express or Implied

Alternative A

A seller's warranty whether express or implied extends to any natural person who is in the family or household of his buyer or who is a guest in his home if it is reasonable to expect that such person may use, consume or be affected by the goods and who is injured in person by breach of the warranty. A seller may not exclude or limit the operation of this section.

Alternative B

A seller's warranty whether express or implied extends to any natural person who may reasonably be expected to use, consume or be affected by the goods and who is injured in person by breach of the warranty. A seller may not exclude or limit the operation of this section.

Alternative C

A seller's warranty whether express or implied extends to any person who may reasonably be expected to use, consume or be affected by the goods and who is injured by breach of the warranty. A seller may not exclude or limit the operation of this section with respect to injury to the person of an individual to whom the warranty extends.

Note
Obligations of Sellers to Remote Purchasers Under Amended Article 2

The 2003 Amendments to Article 2 of the Uniform Commercial Code (still not adopted in any state as of the date of publication of this book) include two new sections dealing with sellers' liability to remote purchasers for defective new goods. Section 2–313A would apply, for example, when a manufacturer sells packaged goods to a retailer that contain written warranties made for the benefit of a party who purchased (or leased) from the retailer. Section 2–313B would apply, for example, when a manufacturer advertises its product to the general public. The text of Section 2–313A follows:

Section 2–313A. Obligation to Remote Purchaser Created by Record Packaged with or Accompanying Goods.

(a) In this Section:

(1) "Goods" means new goods and goods sold or leased as new goods unless the transaction of purchase does not occur in the normal chain of distribution.

(2) "Immediate buyer" means a buyer that enters into a contract with the seller.

(3) "Remote purchaser" means a person that buys or leases goods from an immediate buyer or other person in the normal chain of distribution.

(b) If a seller makes an affirmation of fact or promise that relates to the goods, or provides a description that relates to the goods, or makes a remedial promise, in a record packaged with or accompanying the goods, and the seller reasonably expects the record to be, and the record is, furnished to the remote purchaser, the seller has an obligation to the remote purchaser that the goods will conform to the affirmation of act, promise or description unless a reasonable person in the position of the remote purchaser would not believe that the affirmation of fact, promise or description created an obligation, and an obligation to the remote purchaser that the seller will perform the remedial promise.

(c) It is not necessary to the creation of an obligation under this section that the seller use formal words such as "warrant" or "guarantee" or that the seller have a specific intention to undertake an obligation, but an affirmation merely of the value of the goods or a statement purporting to be merely the seller's opinion or commendation of the goods does not create an obligation.

(d) The following rules apply to the remedies for breach of an obligation created under this section:

(1) The seller may modify or limit the remedies available to the remote purchaser if the modification or limitation is furnished to the remote purchaser no later than the time of purchase or if the modification or limitation is contained in the record that contains the affirmation of fact, promise or description.

(2) Subject to a modification or limitation of remedy, a seller in breach is liable for incidental or consequential damages under Section 2–715 but the seller is not liable for lost profits.

(3) The remote purchaser may recover as damages for breach of a seller's obligation arising under subsection (b) the loss resulting in the ordinary course of events as determined in any manner which is reasonable.

SECTION THREE: DEFENSES

MORSTAIN v. KIRCHER

Supreme Court of Minnesota, 1933.
190 Minn. 78, 250 N.W. 727.

HILTON, JUSTICE.

Defendant appealed from a judgment of the municipal court of Minneapolis in the sum of $432.07.

Frances V. Brown and Thomas W. Brown, husband and wife, were the owners of certain real estate in Hennepin county. On May 4, 1928, they executed and delivered to plaintiff their promissory note for $400, payable in two years from date. The note was secured by a mortgage on the property. On June 12, 1928, the Browns conveyed the premises by warranty deed to defendant, subject to said mortgage, and, as part of the consideration, defendant assumed and agreed to pay the note and mortgage. Defendant, after the conveyance to him, paid two installments of interest to plaintiff. Later, and on November 1, 1928, defendant reconveyed the premises to the Browns by warranty deed for $15, subject to the mortgage.

Plaintiff commenced this action in April, 1931, to recover the amount due and unpaid on the note. At no time had any proceedings been instituted to foreclose the mortgage, nor any other action to collect on the note. The trial court made findings in which the salient facts were as above set forth. As a conclusion of law the judgment above referred to was ordered and was duly entered on February 24, 1933. The only question involved is as to the correctness of the conclusion of law. Defendant's contention is that because of his reconveyance of the land to the Browns his liability was extinguished.

It is settled law in this state that, where a purchaser of mortgaged property from the mortgagor assumes and agrees to pay the mortgage, he becomes personally liable therefor to the mortgagee, who may enforce it in an appropriate action. The right of the mortgagee is purely a personal one, and may be enforced without a foreclosure of the mortgage. 4 Dunnell, Minn.Dig. (2d Ed.) § 6294, and cases cited. The assumption of the mortgage debt by the grantee (defendant) was primarily for the protection of his grantors (the Browns). Nelson v. Rogers, 47 Minn. 103, 49 N.W. 526. It was also secondarily for the benefit of the mortgagee, and, had there been no reconveyance to the mortgagors, plaintiff could have recovered in this action.

By accepting a reconveyance of the property under the circumstances in this case, the Browns released defendant from any obligation to them. Manifestly they could not successfully maintain an action against defendant on his assumption agreement. Neither can their mortgagee. She paid no consideration for defendant's agreement to pay the mortgage debt, nor had she in reliance on the assumption contract placed herself in a position from which she could not retreat without loss. Plaintiff here was a creditor beneficiary. In American Law Institute, Restatement, Contracts, § 143, it is said: "A discharge of the promisor by the promisee in a contract or a variation thereof by them is effective against a creditor beneficiary if, (a) the creditor beneficiary does not bring suit upon the promise or otherwise materially change his position in reliance thereon before he knows of the discharge or variation. * * * "

This rule, as applied to the facts in this case, is a sound and just one, and is supported by many well-considered cases. See 21 A.L.R. page 462 et seq. See, also, Williston on Contracts, vol. 1, § 397.

Plaintiff now is in no worse position than she was when the note and mortgage were given. The property is again in the ownership of the Browns; the mortgage still remains a subsisting lien thereon; plaintiff may foreclose on the mortgage and also has the right to recover in a suit upon the note against the makers thereof.

Judgment reversed.

AHRENS v. FIRST NAT'L LIFE, HEALTH & ACCIDENT INS. CO., 6 La.App. 661 (Orl.1927). [Pritchard made Ahrens the beneficiary of a life insurance policy. Later Pritchard tried to change the beneficiary from Ahrens to Wiltz by filing an application with the insurance company, but Ahrens refused to surrender the policy as required. When Pritchard died both Ahrens and Wiltz claimed to be the beneficiary of the policy. The policy stated:

"The beneficiary or beneficiaries named herein may at the request of the insured be changed at any time to any person or persons having an insurable interest in the life of the insured, provided this policy is returned to the company at its home office, and the endorsement of the change made upon the policy."

In holding for Wiltz, the court stated:]

"The evidence shows that Mrs. Ahrens refused to surrender the policy when requested to do so by the company and by the assured. In other words, she now seeks to profit by her own acts. She wishes to claim proceeds of policy for failure to comply with a provision, when she herself caused that failure."

RESTATEMENT (SECOND) OF CONTRACTS § 311.

Variation of a Duty to a Beneficiary

(1) Discharge or modification of a duty to an intended beneficiary by conduct of the promisee or by a subsequent agreement between promisor and promisee is ineffective if a term of the promise creating the duty so provides.

(2) In the absence of such a term, the promisor and promisee retain power to discharge or modify the duty by subsequent agreement.

(3) Such a power terminates when the beneficiary, before he receives notification of the discharge or modification, materially changes his position in justifiable reliance on the promise or brings suit on it or manifests assent to it at the request of the promisor or promisee.

(4) If the promisee receives consideration for an attempted discharge or modification of the promisor's duty which is ineffective against the beneficiary, the beneficiary can assert a right to the consideration so received. The promisor's duty is discharged to the extent of the amount received by the beneficiary.

ROUSE v. UNITED STATES

United States Court of Appeals for the District of Columbia Circuit, 1954.
215 F.2d 872.

EDGERTON, CIRCUIT JUDGE.

Bessie Winston gave Associated Contractors, Inc., her promissory note for $1,008.37, payable in monthly installments of $28.01, for a heating plant in her house. The Federal Housing Administration guaranteed the note and the payee endorsed it for value to the lending bank, the Union Trust Company.

Winston sold the house to Rouse. In the contract of sale Rouse agreed to assume debts secured by deeds of trust and also "to assume payment of $850 for heating plant payable $28 per Mo." Nothing was said about the note.

Winston defaulted on her note. The United States paid the bank, took an assignment of the note, demanded payment from Rouse, and sued him for $850 and interest.

Rouse alleged as defenses (1) that Winston fraudulently misrepresented the condition of the heating plant and (2) that Associated Contractors did not install it satisfactorily. The District Court struck these defenses and granted summary judgment for the plaintiff. The defendant Rouse appeals.

Since Rouse did not sign the note he is not liable on it. D.C.Code 1951, § 28–119; N.I.L. Sec. 18. He is not liable to the United States at all unless his contract with Winston makes him so. The contract says the parties to it are not "bound by any terms, conditions, statements, warranties or representations, oral or written" not contained in it. But this means only that the written contract contains the entire agreement. It does not mean that fraud cannot be set up as a defense to a suit on the contract. Rouse's promise to "assume payment of $850 for heating plant" made him liable to Associated Contractors, Inc., only if and so far as it made him liable to Winston; one who promises to make a payment to the promisee's creditor can assert against the creditor any defense that the promisor could assert against the promisee. Accordingly Rouse, if he had been sued by the corporation, would have been entitled to show fraud on the part of Winston. He is equally entitled to do so in this suit by an assignee of the corporation's claim. It follows that the court erred in striking the first defense. We do not consider whether Winston's alleged fraud, if shown, would be a complete or only a partial defense to this suit, since that question has not arisen and may not arise.

We think the court was right in striking the second defense. "If the promisor's agreement is to be interpreted as a promise to discharge whatever liability the promisee is under, the promisor must certainly be allowed to show that the promisee was under no enforceable liability. * * * On the other hand, if the promise means that the promisor agrees to pay a sum of money to A, to whom the promisee says he is indebted, it is immaterial whether the promisee is actually indebted to that amount or at all. * * * Where the promise is to pay a specific debt * * * this interpretation will generally be the true one."

The judgment is reversed and the cause remanded with instructions to reinstate the first defense.

Reversed and remanded.

RESTATEMENT (SECOND) OF CONTRACTS § 309.

Defenses Against the Beneficiary

(1) A promise creates no duty to a beneficiary unless a contract is formed between the promisor and the promisee; and if a contract is voidable or unenforceable at the time of its formation the right of any beneficiary is subject to the infirmity.

(2) If a contract ceases to be binding in whole or in part because of impracticability, public policy, non-occurrence of a condition, or present or prospective failure of performance, the right of any beneficiary is to that extent discharged or modified.

(3) Except as stated in Subsections (1) and (2) and in § 311 or as provided by the contract, the right of any beneficiary against the promisor is not subject to the promisor's claims or defenses against the promisee or to the promisee's claims or defenses against the beneficiary.

(4) A beneficiary's right against the promisor is subject to any claim or defense arising from his own conduct or agreement.

Problem 10–2

Felix and Edgar enter an agreement in which Felix promises to mow Edgar's lawn and Edgar promises Felix to pay David the $25 that Felix owes David. Felix mows only half of Edgar's lawn. What are David's rights? Suppose Felix breaks his leg and cannot mow any of the lawn. What are David's rights, if any?

SECTION FOUR: RETROSPECT ON THIRD–PARTY–BENEFICIARY THEORY

Problem 10–3

The City of San Martin, California is considering entering an agreement with County Resource Recovery Inc. for the latter to build and operate a recycling plant for the city. It is clear such a plant will release pollutants into the environment and many concerned citizens oppose the project. These citizens can be mollified only if limits on emissions are established and they have a private right to enforce these limits against County Resource. (They believe that existing environmental laws are insufficient to protect them, that these laws might change, and that these laws are not self-executing.) County Resource is willing to agree to reasonable limits and to sign an agreement with the private group to that effect. Is such an agreement enforceable? What is the consideration? If it is not enforceable or if there is a question of enforceability, could the agreement between the city and County Resource establish a private right of action on behalf of the private group? Review: If the private group can sue, is it entitled to specific performance? (Damage from emissions would likely be in the form of incremental increases to long term irreversible effects of pollution.)

*

Chapter Eleven

ASSIGNMENT AND DELEGATION

*Who made the discovery which has
most deeply affected the fortunes of
the human race? We think—the
person who first discovered that a
debt is a saleable commodity.*

MacLeod

SECTION ONE: ASSIGNMENT, DELEGATION, AND THE ROLE OF LAWYERS

The law of assignment and delegation governs the transfer to third parties of rights and duties under existing contracts. For example, suppose Tex–Oil wishes to purchase the business of an oil supplier that has previously entered enforceable agreements to supply oil to various utilities. Must Tex–Oil assume existing duties of the supplier? What rights will Tex–Oil acquire under the supplier's existing contracts?

If the transaction between Tex–Oil and the oil supplier is itself an agreement with consideration, the lawyers representing the parties must utilize the planning and drafting skills previously studied in this book. The lawyer for Tex–Oil, for example, must determine the supplier's existing duties and whether Tex–Oil is willing to assume them. The lawyer must then plan, negotiate, and draft accordingly. A lawyer representing an oil purchaser under the original agreement with the oil supplier must also consider whether the oil supplier has the right to "assign" the supply contract to a party such as Tex–Oil.

The lawyer who works on an assignment or delegation problem frequently consults sources of law outside general contract law. For example, the Uniform Commercial Code incorporates a number of important provisions on assignment. See especially sections 2–210, 1–201(37), and various provisions of Article 9 governing secured transactions. We do not focus on these provisions here. Also, state regulatory statutes deal, for example, with assignments of wages.

SECTION TWO: THE POWER TO ASSIGN RIGHTS—NATURE AND LIMITS

For centuries, the common law prohibited the assignment of rights. Various factors explain this, including the fear of an increase in litigation. Of course, one effect of the prohibition was to reduce the present value of a right to a future payment or other performance. With the rise of a market economy and of credit, the prohibition against assignment of rights could not be expected to survive, and by the 18th century most restrictions were gone. Professor Gilmore once described the indirect manner in which this was achieved by the common law:

> Although a person to whom a contract right was owed could not transfer it to one to whom the obligor was not bound in privity, he could appoint an agent or attorney to collect in his place or stead. In time the fictitious agency became irrevocable and the nominal owner, after notice of the assignment to the obligor, lost any power to interfere with the assignee's rights. Thus by the typically muddle-headed process of thinking known as the genius of the common law, assignments of intangibles were made effective in fact while basic theory still proclaimed them to be legal impossibilities.[1]

The general assignability of rights was hailed as a major advance of the law. At the close of this section, we provide an inventory of some of the major uses of assignments in today's world.

An assignment of a right is a legally valid present transfer of that right. Such a transfer manifests an intent on the part of the assignor to extinguish his or her own right to another's performance and to convey that right to the assignee. No special form of words is required. A valid assignment may be either gratuitous or for a consideration. According to section 332 of the second Restatement, a gratuitous assignment is irrevocable if it is (1) in writing signed by the assignor (or under seal) and delivered to the assignee, or (2) accompanied by delivery of a writing of a type customarily accepted as a symbol or as evidence of the right, such as a savings bank book. But the assignor can revoke an oral gratuitous assignment and the assignor's notification thereof or the assignor's death, incapacity, or subsequent assignment terminates the assignee's rights. A revocable gratuitous assignment becomes irrevocable if the assignee obtains payment or a judgment against the obligor, or enters a new contract with the obligor directly, or reasonably relies thereon. An assignment for consideration is irrevocable even though oral unless it falls within an applicable statute of frauds provision.

The legal power to assign a right is not without limitations, however. We now consider several limitations.

CRANE ICE CREAM CO. v. TERMINAL FREEZING & HEATING CO.

Court of Appeals of Maryland, 1925.
147 Md. 588, 128 A. 280.

Action by the Crane Ice Cream Company against the Terminal Freezing & Heating Company. Demurrer to the declaration was sustained, and from the judgment entered thereon against plaintiff, it appeals. Judgment affirmed.

* * *

PARKE, J. The appellee and one W.C. Frederick entered into a contract for the delivery of ice by the appellee to Frederick, and, before the expiration of

---

1. 1 G. Gilmore, Security Interests In Personal Property, § 7.3 at 202 (1965).

the contract, Frederick executed an assignment of the contract to the appellant; and on the refusal of the appellee to deliver ice to the assignee it brought an action on the contract against the appellee to recover damages for the alleged breach. * * *

The demurrer admitted the following material allegations: At the execution of the contract the Terminal Freezing & Heating Company, appellee, was a corporation engaged in the manufacture and sale of ice at wholesale within the state of Maryland, and William C. Frederick made and sold ice cream in Baltimore, where his plant was located. * * *

The contract imposed upon the appellee the liability to sell and deliver to Frederick such quantities of ice as he might use in his business as an ice cream manufacturer to the extent of 250 tons per week, at and for the price of $3.25 a ton of 2,000 pounds on the loading platform of Frederick. The contractual rights of the appellee were (a) to be paid on every Tuesday during the continuation of the contract, for all ice purchased by Frederick during the week ending at midnight upon the next preceding Saturday; (b) to require Frederick not to buy or accept any ice from any other source than the appellee, except in excess of the weekly maximum of 250 tons; (c) to annul the contract upon any violation of the agreement by Frederick; and (d) to sustain no liability for any breach of contract growing out of causes beyond its control. The converse of these rights and liabilities of the appellee were the correlative liabilities and rights of Frederick under the contract.

There was a further provision that the contract in its entirety should continue in force from term to term, unless either party thereto gave to the other party at least 60 days' notice in writing before the expiration of the term of the intention to end the contract. The contract did not expressly permit or inhibit an assignment, but neither did it contain any word, such as assigns, to indicate that the parties contemplated an assignment by either.

Before the first year of the second term of the contract had expired Frederick, without the consent or knowledge of the appellee, executed and delivered to the appellant, for a valuable consideration, a written assignment dated February 15, 1921, of the agreement between him and the appellee. The attempted transfer of the contract was a part of the transaction between Frederick and the appellant whereby the appellant acquired by purchase the plant, equipment, rights, and credits, choses in action, "good will, trade, custom, patronage, rights, contracts," and other assets of Frederick's ice cream business, which had been established and conducted by him in Baltimore. The purchaser took full possession and continued the former business carried on by Frederick. It was then and is now a corporation "engaged in the ice cream business upon a large and extensive scale in the city of Philadelphia, as well as in the city of Baltimore, and state of Maryland," and had a large capitalization, ample resources, and credit to meet any of its obligations "and all and singular the terms and provisions" of the contract; and it was prepared to pay cash for all ice deliverable under the contract.

As soon as the appellee learned of this purported assignment and the absorption of the business of Frederick by the appellant, it notified Frederick that the contract was at an end, and declined to deliver any ice to the appellant. Until the day of the assignment the obligations of both original parties had been fully performed and discharged.

* * *

The basic facts upon which the question for solution depends must be sought in the effect of the attempted assignment of this executory bilateral contract on both the rights and the liabilities of the contracting parties, as every bilateral contract includes both rights and duties on each side while both sides remain executory. I Williston on Contracts, § 407. If the assignment of rights and the assignment of duties by Frederick are separated, they fall into these two divisions: (1) The rights of the assignor were (a) to take no ice, if the assignor used none in his business, but, if he did (b) to require the appellee to deliver, on the loading platform of the assignor, all the ice he might need in his business to the extent of 250 tons a week, and (c) to buy any ice he might need in excess of the weekly 250 tons from any other person; and (2) the liabilities of the assignor were (a) to pay to the appellee on every Tuesday during the continuance of the contract the stipulated price for all ice purchased and weighed by the assignor during the week ending at midnight upon the next preceding Saturday, and (b) not directly or indirectly, during the existence of this agreement, to buy or accept any ice from any other person, firm, or corporation than the said the Terminal Freezing & Heating Company, except such amounts as might be in excess of the weekly limit of 250 tons.

Whether the attempted assignment of these rights, or the attempted delegation of these duties must fail because the rights or duties are of too personal a character, is a question of construction to be resolved from the nature of the contract and the express or presumed intention of the parties. Williston on Contracts, § 431.

The contract was made by a corporation with an individual, William C. Frederick, an ice cream manufacturer, with whom the corporation had dealt for 3 years, before it executed a renewal contract for a second like period. The character, credit, and resources of Frederick had been tried and tested by the appellee before it renewed the contract. Not only had his ability to pay as agreed been established, but his fidelity to his obligation not to buy or accept any ice from any other source up to 250 tons a week had been ascertained. In addition, the appellee had not asked in the beginning, nor on entering into the second period of the contract, for Frederick to undertake to buy a specific quantity of ice or even to take any. Frederick simply engaged himself during a definite term to accept and pay for such quantities of ice as he might use in his business to the extent of 250 tons a week. If he used no ice in his business, he was under no obligation to pay for a pound. In any week, the quantity could vary from zero to 250 tons, and its weekly fluctuation, throughout the life of the contract, could irregularly range between these limits. The weekly payment might be nothing or as much as $812.50; and for every week a credit was extended to the eighth day from the beginning of every week's delivery. From the time of the beginning of every weekly delivery of the ice to the date of the payment therefor the title to the ice was in the purchaser, and the seller had no security for its payment except in the integrity and solvency of Frederick. The performances, therefore, were not concurrent, but the performance of the nonassigning party to the contract was to precede the payments by the assignor.

When it is also considered that the ice was to be supplied and paid for, according to its weight on the loading platform of Frederick, at an unvarying price without any reference either to the quantity used, or to the fluctuations in the cost of production or to market changes in the selling price, throughout 3 years, the conclusion is inevitable that the inducement for the appellee to enter into the original contract and into the renewal lay outside the bare terms of the contract, but was implicit in them, and was the appellee's reliance upon its knowledge of an average quantity of ice consumed, and probably to be needed, in the usual course of Frederick's business, at all times throughout the year, and its confidence in the stability of his enterprise, in his competency in commercial affairs, in his probity, personal judgment, and in his continuing financial responsibility. The contract itself emphasized the personal equation by specifying that the ice was to be bought for "use in his business as an ice cream manufacturer," and was to be paid for according to its weight "on the loading platform of the said W.C. Frederick."

When Frederick went out of business as an ice cream manufacturer, and turned over his plant and everything constituting his business to the appellant, it was no longer his business, or his loading platform, or subject to his care, control, or maintenance, but it was the business of a stranger, whose skill, competency, and requirements of ice were altogether different from those of Frederick. The assignor had his simple plant in Baltimore. The assignee, in its purchase, simply added another unit to its ice cream business which it had been, and is now, carrying on "upon a large and extensive scale in the city of Philadelphia and state of Pennsylvania, as well as in the city of Baltimore and state of Maryland." The appellee knew that Frederick could not carry on his business without ice wherewith to manufacture ice cream at his plant for his trade. It also was familiar with the quantities of ice he would require, from time to time, in his business at his plant in Baltimore, and it consequently could make its other commitments for ice with this knowledge as a basis.

The appellant, on the other hand, might wholly supply its increased trade acquired in the purchase of Frederick's business with its ice cream produced upon a large and extensive scale by its manufactory in Philadelphia, which would result in no ice being bought by the assignee of the appellee, and so the appellee would be deprived of the benefit of its contract by the introduction of a different personal relation or element which was never contemplated by the original contracting parties. Again, should the price of ice be relatively high in Philadelphia in comparison with the stipulated price, the assignee could run its business in Baltimore and furnish its patrons, or a portion of them, in Philadelphia with its product from the weekly maximum consumption of 250 tons of ice throughout the year. There can be no denial that the uniform delivery of the maximum quantity of 250 tons a week would be a consequence not within the normal scope of the contract, and would impose a greater liability on the appellee than was anticipated. 7 Halsbury's Laws of England, § 1015, p. 501.

Moreover, the contract here to supply ice was undefined except as indicated from time to time by the personal requirements of Frederick in his specified business. The quantities of ice to be supplied to Frederick to answer his weekly requirements must be very different from, and would not be the measure of the quantities needed by his assignee, and, manifestly, to impose on the seller the obligation to obey the demands of the substituted assignee is to set up a new measure of ice to be supplied, and so a new term in the agreement that the appellee never bound itself to perform. Up to 250 tons of ice a week Frederick engaged not to buy or accept any ice from any other party than the appellee. After Frederick had sold away his business, this covenant could not bind the assignee of his business, and, even if it continued to bind Frederick, his refraining from not buying ice elsewhere was not a contemplated consideration for selling ice to any one except Frederick himself. Kemp v. Baerselman, [1906] 2 K.B. 604, 608, 609. It was argued that Frederick was entitled to the weekly maximum of 250 tons, and that he might have expanded his business so as to require this weekly limit of ice, and that therefore the burdens of the contract might have been as onerous to the appellee, if Frederick had continued in business, as they could become under the purporting assignment by reason of the increased requirements of the larger business of the assignee. The unsoundness of this argument is that the law accords to every man freedom of choice in the party with whom he deals and the terms of his dealing. He cannot be forced to do a thing which he did not agree to do because it is like and no more burdensome than something which he did contract to do.

Under all the circumstances of the case, it is clear that the rights and duties of the contract under consideration were of so personal a character that the rights of Frederick cannot be assigned nor his duties be delegated without defeating the intention of the parties to the original contract. When Frederick went out of the business of making ice cream, he made it impossible for him to complete his performance of the contract, and his personal action and qualifications upon which the appellee relied were eliminated from a contract which presupposed their continuance. Frederick not only attempted an assignment, but his course is a repudiation of the obligations of the contract. He is not even alleged to be ready to pay for any ice which might be delivered after the date of the purporting assignment, but the allegations of the declaration simply aver that the assignee alone had undertaken to perform the further contractual obligations of the assignor. Frederick, however, cannot be heard to say that he has not repudiated a contract, whose contemplated performance his own act has made it impossible for him to fulfill. Eastern Advertising Co. v. McGaw, 89 Md. 72, 88, 42 A. 923.

While a party to a contract may as a general rule assign all his beneficial rights, except where a personal relation is involved, his liability under the contract is not assignable inter vivos, because any one who is bound to any performance whatever or who owes money cannot by any act of his own, or by any act in agreement with any other person than his creditor or the one to whom his performance is due, cast off his own liability and substitute another's liability. If this were not true, obligors could free themselves of their obligations by the simple expedient of assigning them. A further ground for the rule is that, not only is a party entitled to know to whom he must look for the satisfaction of his rights under the contract, but in the familiar words of Lord Denman in Humble v. Hunter, 12 Q.B. 317, "you have a right to the benefit you contemplate from the character, credit, and substance of the person with whom you contract." For these reasons it has been uniformly held that a man cannot assign his liabilities under a contract, but one who is bound so as to bear an unescapable liability may delegate the performance of his obligation to another, if the liability be of such a nature that its performance by another will be substantially the same thing as performance by the promisor himself. In such circumstances the performance of the third party is the act of the promisor, who remains liable under the contract and answerable in damages if the performance be not in strict fulfillment of the contract. * * *

However, the analysis of the facts on this appeal leaves no room for doubt that the case at bar falls into the category of those assignments where an attempt is made both to transfer the rights and to delegate the duties of the assignor under an executory bilateral contract whose terms and the circumstances make plain that the personal qualification and action of the assignor, with respect to both his benefits and burdens under the contract, were essential inducements in the formation of the contract, and, further, that the assignment was a repudiation of any future liability of the assignor. The attempted assignment before us altered the conditions and obligations of the undertaking. The appellee would here be obliged not only to perform the subsequent stipulations of the contract for the benefit of a stranger and in conformity with his will, but also to accept the performance of the stranger in place of that of the assignor with whom it contracted, and upon whose personal integrity, capacity, and management in the course of a particular business he must be assumed to have relied by reason of the very nature of the provisions of the contract and of the circumstances of the contracting parties. The nature and stipulations of the contract prevent it being implied that the nonassigning party had assented to such an assignment of rights and delegation of liabilities. The authorities are clear, on the facts at bar, that the appellant could not enforce the contract against the appellee.

* * *

Judgment affirmed, with costs to the appellee.

RESTATEMENT (SECOND) OF CONTRACTS § 317.

Assignment of a Right

(1) An assignment of a right is a manifestation of the assignor's intention to transfer it by virtue of which the assignor's right to performance by the obligor is extinguished in whole or in part and the assignee acquires a right to such performance.

(2) A contractual right can be assigned unless

(a) the substitution of a right of the assignee for the right of the assignor would materially change the duty of the obligor, or materially increase the burden or risk imposed on him by his contract, or materially impair his chance of obtaining return performance, or materially reduce its value to him, or

(b) the assignment is forbidden by statute or is otherwise inoperative on grounds of public policy, or

(c) assignment is validly precluded by contract.

UNIFORM COMMERCIAL CODE § 2–210(2).

Unless otherwise agreed all rights of either seller or buyer can be assigned except where the assignment would materially change the duty of the other party, or increase materially the burden or risk imposed on him by his contract, or impair materially his chance of obtaining return performance. A right to damages for breach of the whole contract or a right arising out of the assignor's due performance of his entire obligation can be assigned despite agreement otherwise.

Note
The Power to Assign Rights Under General Contract Law and Article 9 of the Uniform Commercial Code

In addition to limitations on the power to assign rights discussed in Crane Ice Cream Co., and set forth in section 317 of the Second Restatement and in section 2–210(2) of the Uniform Commercial Code, a further limitation is that a right expected to arise under a contract not in existence is not a present assignment, but operates only as a promise to assign. Restatement (Second) of Contracts § 321. For example, A has not made an assignment if A, an unemployed gardener, promises to pay B money that A hopes to earn in the future from C, who is opening a new gardening store. As a result, even if C employs A, C does not have to pay A's salary to B. (C may have other defenses as well, such as a statutory prohibition of assignments of wages.)

Article 9 of the Uniform Commercial Code, dealing with secured transactions, permits the assignment of future accounts as collateral for present loans. You will encounter this subject in an upperclass commercial law course.

Problem 11–1

To make an effective assignment, the assignor must manifest an intention to transfer his right to another person. The issue is one of intention—a court will examine any writing and the circumstances to determine intention in the manner we have studied in Chapter 6. This suggests that appropriate drafting can ensure the effectiveness of an assignment. The language should demonstrate that the assignor intends to extinguish its own right to another's performance and give the assignee the right to that performance. Consider whether any of the following constitutes appropriate language:

(1) A will pay B if A gets the money from C.

(2) B is entitled to the commission for the sale of C's home. (B is an employee of A, a real estate agent, with whom C has contracted.)

(3) I, A, for value received, hereby assign, transfer and set over to B my right, title and interest in the funds due me from C.

E. FARNSWORTH, CONTRACTS
702–04 (3d ed. 1999).

The first situation is that of a prospective donor that wants to make a gift. If the prospective donor (B) wants to give $1,000 to a favorite grandchild (C), the prospective donor might, of course, simply give the child cash.

However, if the prospective donor is short of cash but is owed $1,000 by a debtor (A), the prospective donor may instead assign the right to payment to the grandchild as a gift. As assignee, the grandchild will then own the right that the donor previously had against the debtor and will collect the $1,000 from the debtor.

The second situation is that of a retailer that sells to consumers on credit. If the retailer has sold a $1,000 stereo on credit to a consumer (A), the retailer may need cash to finance the business until the $1,000 has been paid. The retailer (B) may therefore assign the right to payment to a financial institution (C) in return for the immediate payment by it of $1,000, less a discount to compensate the financial institution for the loss of the use of the $1,000 until it can collect the money from the consumer.[1] The financial institution will then own the right that the retailer previously had against the consumer and will collect the $1,000 from the consumer.

The third situation is that of a wholesaler that sells to retailers on credit. If the wholesaler (B) has sold $10,000 worth of carpets on credit to a retailer (A), the wholesaler may need cash to finance the business until the $10,000 has been paid. The wholesaler may therefore assign the right to payment, which is known as an "account receivable," to a financial institution (C). However, in contrast to the situation just described, in which a retailer assigns a consumer debt, the wholesaler engages in what is known as "accounts receivable financing" and assigns accounts in bulk, rather than individually, so that the total of all accounts assigned might be, say, $1,000,000. Furthermore, the wholesaler does not assign them outright but only as security for a loan for, say, $800,000 (somewhat less than the value of the collateral). In what is called "non-notification financing," it is understood that the wholesaler, not the financial institution, will collect from the retailer and that the wholesaler will repay the loan out of the proceeds when the retailer has paid for the goods.[2] The financial institution's compensation is the interest on the secured loan.

The fourth situation is that of a builder that makes construction contracts. If the builder (B) has contracted with an owner (A) to build a building for $10,000,000, payable as the work progresses, the builder may need funds immediately to begin work. The builder may therefore assign the right to payment from the owner to a financial institution (C) in return for a loan to help finance the construction. Here, in contrast to the wholesaler's account receivable in the situation just described, the builder's right to payment has not yet been earned, since it is constructively conditioned on performance of the contract. As the builder performs and the progress payments become due, they are collected and used to repay the loan.[3]

The fifth and most complex situation is that of an owner of a business that furnishes goods or services to other businesses. If the owner (B) wants to

---

1. The financial institution in this situation is usually a bank or finance company. * * *

2. The financial institution in this situation is usually a bank or finance company. In contrast to the situation described in the text, the financial institution often does not require the wholesaler to repay the loan as the proceeds are collected, but relies on the assignment of future accounts to secure the loan in the original amount. * * * There is an alternative to the transaction described in the text in which the financial institution (sometimes called a "factor") purchases the account outright, notifies the obligor, and collects the debt.

3. The financial institution in this situation is usually a bank.

transfer the business as a going concern to a buyer (C) by a sale of the assets of the business, the parties may also plan to transfer long-term contracts with, say, a supplier (A) and a customer (A'). With respect to both the supplier and the customer, such a transfer involves not only assignment but delegation. The seller wants both to assign to the buyer the seller's rights against the supplier and the customer, and also to delegate to the buyer the performances that the seller owes them. There are, therefore, two significant problems not present in the four earlier situations. The first is that, with respect to the supplier, the right that the seller wishes to assign is a right to a performance other than the payment of money. The second is that, with respect to both the supplier and the customer, the seller wishes not only to assign rights but also to delegate performance of duties—the duty of paying the supplier for what is supplied and the duty of furnishing the customer with goods or services. If the seller can overcome these problems and transfer these contracts, the buyer will have both a right to be supplied by the supplier in return for payment and a right to be paid by the customer in return for furnishing goods or services.[4]

SECTION THREE: DEFENSES OF THE OBLIGOR AGAINST THE ASSIGNEE

Article 9 of the Uniform Commercial Code and other legislation figure heavily in this topic. You can investigate it fully in upperclass commercial law courses. Here we just scratch the surface by presenting two sections of the Restatement (Second) of Contracts and an excerpt from a very astute author.

RESTATEMENT (SECOND) OF CONTRACTS § 336.
Defenses Against an Assignee

(1) By an assignment the assignee acquires a right against the obligor only to the extent that the obligor is under a duty to the assignor; and if the right of the assignor would be voidable by the obligor or unenforceable against him if no assignment had been made, the right of the assignee is subject to the infirmity.

(2) The right of an assignee is subject to any defense or claim of the obligor which accrues before the obligor receives notification of the assignment, but not to defenses or claims which accrue thereafter except as stated in this Section or as provided by statute.

(3) Where the right of an assignor is subject to discharge or modification in whole or in part by impracticability, public policy, non-occurrence of a condition, or present or prospective failure of performance by an obligee, the right of the assignee is to that extent subject to discharge or modification even after the obligor receives notification of the assignment.

(4) An assignee's right against the obligor is subject to any defense or claim arising from his conduct or to which he was subject as a party or a prior assignee because he had notice.

4. Ordinarily, the buyer will, pursuant to the buyer's contract with the seller, undertake to perform the seller's duties under the seller's contracts with both the supplier and the customer.

RESTATEMENT (SECOND) OF CONTRACTS § 338.

Discharge of an Obligor After Assignment

(1) Except as stated in this Section, notwithstanding an assignment, the assignor retains his power to discharge or modify the duty of the obligor to the extent that the obligor performs or otherwise gives value until but not after the obligor receives notification that the right has been assigned and that performance is to be rendered to the assignee.

(2) So far as an assigned right is conditional on the performance of a return promise, and notwithstanding notification of the assignment, any modification of or substitution for the contract made by the assignor and obligor in good faith and in accordance with reasonable commercial standards is effective against the assignee. The assignee acquires corresponding rights under the modified or substituted contract.

(3) Notwithstanding a defect in the right of an assignee, he has the same power his assignor had to discharge or modify the duty of the obligor to the extent that the obligor gives value or otherwise changes his position in good faith and without knowledge or reason to know of the defect.

R. HILLMAN, PRINCIPLES OF CONTRACT LAW

336–337 (2004).

You assign to Taylor your right to the money Alice owes you for mowing her lawn. * * * Taylor, as an assignee, has a cause of action against Alice if she does not pay him. But does Alice have any defenses against Taylor's claim? Suppose, for example, that you have done a miserable job mowing Alice's lawn and your performance constitutes a material breach. (Suppose, you cut the lawn too low and Alice's lawn burned out.) If you had not assigned your right to payment, Alice could assert this defense against you. Because an assignee receives only what the assignor has to transfer, Alice can also assert your material breach as a defense against Taylor. Similarly, if the contract between you and Alice is unenforceable because of impracticability (or another excuse doctrine), the failure of a condition, or public policy (or another policing doctrine), Alice can assert the defense against Taylor.

* * *

Suppose after you mow Alice's lawn and after your assignment of the $40 to Taylor, but before Alice pays anything to anyone, you accidentally hit Alice's car while backing out of your driveway. Alice's car sustains $40 of damage. (As you know, this is a highly unrealistic example. Car manufacturers make cars so that the slightest impact causes a minimum of $10,000 of damage.) Alice could have asserted your tort liability as a "set off" (a claim unrelated to the contract) if you had not already assigned your right to payment and you were suing her for your $40. But can she assert the set off against Taylor under the actual facts?

The answer depends on when Taylor notified Alice of the assignment and when her tort claim against you "accrued." If Taylor notified Alice before the tort claim accrued, Alice can not assert the set off against Taylor. Conversely if the tort claim accrued first, Alice can assert the set off against Taylor. You're probably wondering what "accrued" means. Basically, it is the time "when a cause of action comes into being." This can be technical, but here the cause of action accrued when you hit Alice's car. A breach of contract cause of action accrues, not when the parties make a contract, but when a party repudiates or breaches it. The moral of the story, of course, is that an assignee such as Taylor should notify the obligor of an assignment immediately to cut off potential set-off defenses.

There is another reason why an assignee should notify the obligor of the assignment immediately. Taylor's notification cuts off the right of you and Alice to modify your contract, for example, so that Alice must pay you instead of Taylor. Without such a notification, Alice would be discharged from her obligation to Taylor if she pays you the $40.

SECTION FOUR: DELEGATION OF DUTIES

LANGEL v. BETZ

New York Court of Appeals, 1928.
250 N.Y. 159, 164 N.E. 890.

Action by John A. Langel against Isidor Betz. From judgment of the Appellate Division (224 App.Div. 266, 229 N.Y.S. 712), affirming a judgment of the Special Term in favor of plaintiff, defendant appeals. Reversed, and complaint dismissed.

* * *

POUND, J. Plaintiff, on August 1, 1925, made a contract with Irving W. Hurwitz and Samuel Hollander for the sale of certain real property. This contract the vendees assigned to Benedict, who in turn assigned it to Isidor Betz, the defendant herein. The assignment contains no delegation to the assignee of the performance of the assignor's duties. The date for performance of the contract was originally set for October 2, 1925. This was extended to October 15, 1925, at the request of the defendant, the last assignee of the vendees. The ground upon which the adjournment was asked for by defendant was that the title company had not completed its search and report on the title to the property. Upon the adjourned date the defendant refused to perform. The vendor plaintiff was ready, able, and willing to do so, and was present at the place specified with a deed, ready to tender it to the defendant, who did not appear.

The plaintiff as vendor brought this action against the defendant assignee for specific performance of the contract. Upon the foregoing undisputed facts he has had judgment therefor.

The question is: "Can the vendor obtain specific performance of a contract for the sale of real estate against the assignee of the vendee, where the assignee merely requests and obtains an extension of time within which to close title?"

Here we have no novation, no express assumption of the obligations of the assignor in the assignment, and no demand for performance by the assignee.

The mere assignment of a bilateral executory contract may not be interpreted as a promise by the assignee to the assignor to assume the performance of the assignor's duties, so as to have the effect of creating a new liability on the part of the assignee to the other party to the contract assigned. The assignee of the vendee is under no personal engagement to the vendor where there is no privity between them. * * * The assignee may, however, expressly or impliedly, bind himself to perform the assignor's duties. This he may do by contract with the assignor or with the other party to the contract. It has been held (Epstein v. Gluckin, 233 N.Y. 490, 135 N.E. 861) that, where the assignee of the vendee invokes the aid of a court of equity in an action for specific performance, he impliedly binds himself to perform on his part and subjects himself to the conditions of the judgment appropriate thereto. "He who seeks equity must do equity." The converse of the proposition, that the assignee of the vendee would be bound when the vendor began the action, did not follow from the decision in that case. On the contrary, the question was wholly one of remedy rather than right, and it was held that mutuality of remedy is important only so far as its presence is essential to the attainment of the ends of justice. This holding was necessary to sustain the decision. No change was made in the law of contracts nor in the rule for the interpretation of an assignment of a contract.

A judgment requiring the assignee of the vendee to perform at the suit of the vendor would operate as the imposition of a new liability on the assignee which would be an act of oppression and injustice, unless the assignee had, expressly or by implication, entered into a personal and binding contract with the assignor or with the vendor to assume the obligations of the assignor.

It has been urged that the probable intention of the assignee is ordinarily to assume duties as well as rights, and that the contract should be so interpreted in the absence of circumstances showing a contrary intention. The American Law Institute's Restatement of the Law of Contracts (section 164) proposes a change in the rule of interpretation of assigned contracts to give as full effect to the assumed probable intention of the parties as the law permits. The following statement is proposed:

"Section 164. Interpretation of Words Purporting to Assign a Bilateral Contract and Effect of Acceptance of the Assignment by the Assignee.

"(1) Where a party to a bilateral contract which is at the time wholly or partially executory on both sides, purports to assign the whole contract, his action is interpreted, in the absence of circumstances showing a contrary intention, as an assignment of the assignor's rights under the contract and a delegation of the performance of the assignor's duties.

"(2) Acceptance by the assignee of such an assignment is interpreted, in the absence of circumstances showing a contrary intention, as both an assent to become an assignee of the assignor's rights and as a promise *to the assignor to assume the performance of the assignor's duties.*"

This promise to the assignor would then be available to the other party to the contract. Lawrence v. Fox, 20 N.Y. 268; 1 Williston on Contracts, § 412. The proposed change is a complete reversal of our present rule of interpretation as to the probable intention of the parties. It is, perhaps, more in harmony with modern ideas of contractual relations than is "the archaic view of a contract as creating a strictly personal obligation between the creditor and debtor" (Pollock on Contracts [9th Ed.] 232), which prohibited the assignee from suing at law in his own name and which denied a remedy to third party beneficiaries. "The fountains out of which these resolutions issue" have been broken up if not destroyed (Seaver v. Ransom, 224 N.Y. 233, 237, 120 N.E. 639, 2 A.L.R. 1187), but the law remains that no promise of the assignee to assume the assignor's duties is to be inferred from the acceptance of an assignment of a bilateral contract, in the absence of circumstances surrounding the assignment itself which indicate a contrary intention.

With this requirement of the interpretation of the intention of the parties controlling we must turn from the assignment to the dealings between the plaintiff and the defendant to discover whether the defendant entered into relations with the plaintiff whereby he assumed the duty of performance. The assignment did not bring the parties together, and the request for a postponement differs materially from the commencement of an action in a court of equity, whereby the plaintiff submits himself to the jurisdiction of the court or from a contractual assumption of the obligations of the assignor. If the substance of the transaction between the vendor and the assignee of the vendee could be regarded as a request on the part of the latter for a postponement of the closing day and a promise on his part to assume the obligations of the vendee if the request were granted, a contractual relation arising from an expression of mutual assent, based on the exchange of a promise for an act, might be spelled out of it; but the transaction is at least as consistent with a request for time for deliberation as to the course of conduct to be pursued as with an implied promise to assume the assignor's duties if the request were granted. The relation of promisor and promisee was not thereby expressly established, and such relation is not a necessary inference from the nature of the transaction. When we depart from the field of intention and enter the field of contract, we find no contractual liability; no assumption of duties based on a consideration.

Plaintiff contends that the request for an adjournment should be construed (time not being the essence of the contract) as an assertion of a right to such adjournment, and therefore as a binding act of enforcement, whereby defendant accepted the obligations of the assignee. Here again we have an equivocal act. There was no demand for an adjournment as a matter of right. The request may have been made without any intent to assert a right. It cannot be said that by that act alone the assignee assumed the duty of performance.

Furthermore, no controlling authority may be found which holds that a mere demand for performance by the vendee's assignee creates a right in the complaining vendor to enforce the contract against him. * * * That question may be reserved until an answer is necessary.

The judgment of the Appellate Division and that of the Special Term should be reversed and the complaint dismissed, with costs in all courts.

* * *

Judgments reversed, etc.

UNIFORM COMMERCIAL CODE § 2–210(3) and (4).

(3) Unless the circumstances indicate the contrary a prohibition of assignment of "the contract" is to be construed as barring only the delegation to the assignee of the assignor's performance.

(4) An assignment of "the contract" or of "all my rights under the contract" or an assignment in similar general terms is an assignment of rights and unless the language or the circumstances (as in an assignment for security) indicate the contrary, it is a delegation of performance of the duties of the assignor and its acceptance by the assignee constitutes a promise by him to perform those duties. This promise is enforceable by either the assignor or the other party to the original contract.

Problem 11–3

In Hield v. Thyberg (page 693), Hield executed the following document:

ASSIGNMENT

For and in consideration of *Fifteen Thousand* Dollars (*$15,000.00*), Willard R. Hield, of Minneapolis, Minnesota, does hereby assign, order and transfer to Edwin R. Thyberg, of Sioux Falls, South Dakota, all of my right, title and interest in Beauticians Supply, Inc., a corporation, including but not limited to any and all advances made by me to the said corporation and all of my common shares of the capital stock of said Beauticians Supply, Inc., a corporation, in my name on the books of said corporation. This assignment shall operate as an assignment separate from the certificates representing said stock and should said certificates be lost, mislaid or impossible to find, I hereby agree to execute an affidavit of lost certificate indemnifying the corporation from issuing new stock representing my shares to the said Edwin R. Thyberg.

Assignor hereby irrevocably constitutes and appoints the assignee, Edwin R. Thyberg, attorney in fact, to transfer the said stock on the books of the said corporation with full power of substitution in the premises and I further authorize him to, as my attorney in fact, to transfer any such obligations of the corporation hereinbefore owed to me and hereby assigned also with full power of substitution in the premises.

The undersigned assignor hereby acknowledges that the assignee assumes no other personal liability toward assignor nor does he assume any obligations of said assignor caused by his relationship with said corporation.

Dated this *10th* day of June, 1977, in Minneapolis, Minnesota.

Willard R. Hield
Willard R. Hield

Assignee agrees to hold assignor harmless to liability from Transport Leasing Corporation and Northwestern National Bank of Minneapolis note. Assignor agrees to hold assignee harmless to any undisclosed matters pertaining to corporation in which assignor was involved.

State of Minnesota   )
)   ss.
County of Hennepin   )

On the 10th day of June, 1977, before me, *Diana L. Knutson*, the undersigned officer, personally appeared Willard R. Hield, known to me or satisfactorily proven to be the person whose name is subscribed to the within instrument and acknowledged that he executed the same for the purposes therein contained.

In witness whereof I hereunto set my hand and official seal.

Notary Public, Minnesota
(Notary Seal)

———

Thyberg wants to know whether he has any obligation to Janet Denny, who made a loan to Hield, who, in turn, bought equipment with the money for Beautician's Supply, Inc. What would you advise? If you had represented Thyberg, would you have drafted the agreement differently?

BRITISH WAGGON CO. AND THE PARKGATE WAGGON CO. v. LEA & CO.

Queen's Bench Division, 1880.
5 Q.B.D. 149.

COCKBURN, C.J. This was an action brought by the plaintiffs to recover rent for the hire of certain railway waggons, alleged to be payable by the defendants to the plaintiffs, or one of them, under the following circumstances:—

By an agreement in writing of the 10th of February, 1874, the Parkgate Waggon Company let to the defendants, who are coal merchants, fifty railway waggons for a term of seven years, at a yearly rent of 600*l.* a year, payable by equal quarterly payments. By a second agreement of the 13th of June, 1874, the company in like manner let to the defendants fifty other waggons, at a yearly rent of 625*l.*, payable quarterly like the former.

Each of these agreements contained the following clause: "The owners, their executors, or administrators, will at all times during the said term, except as herein provided, keep the said waggons in good and substantial repair and working order, and, on receiving notice from the tenant of any want of repairs, and the number or numbers of the waggons requiring to be repaired, and the place or places where it or they then is or are, will, with all reasonable despatch, cause the same to be repaired and put into good working order."

On the 24th of October, 1874, the Parkgate Company passed a resolution, under the 129th section of the Companies Act, 1862, for the voluntary winding up of the company. Liquidators were appointed, and by an order of the Chancery Division of the High Court of Justice, it was ordered that the winding-up of the company should be continued under the supervision of the Court.

By an indenture of the 1st of April, 1878, the Parkgate Company assigned and transferred, and the liquidators confirmed to the British Company and their assigns, among other things, all sums of money, whether payable by way of rent, hire, interest, penalty, or damage, then due, or thereafter to become due, to the Parkgate Company, by virtue of the two contracts with the defendants, together with the benefit of the two contracts, and all the interest of the Parkgate Company and the said liquidators therein; the British Company, on the other hand covenanting with the Parkgate Company "to observe and perform such of the stipulations, conditions, provisions, and agreements contained in the said contracts as, according to the terms thereof were stipulated to be observed and performed by the Parkgate Company." On the execution of this assignment the British Company took over from the Parkgate Company the repairing stations, which had previously been used by the Parkgate Company for the repair of the waggons let to the defendants, and also the staff of workmen employed by the latter company in executing such repairs. It is expressly found that the British Company have ever since been ready and willing to execute, and have, with all due diligence, executed all necessary repairs to the said waggons. This, however, they had done under a special agreement come to between the parties since the present dispute had arisen, without prejudice to their respective rights.

The defendants asserted their right to treat the contracts as at an end on the ground that the Parkgate Co. had incapacitated themselves from performing the contract, first, by going into voluntary liquidation, secondly, by assigning the contracts and giving up the repairing stations to the British Co., between whom and the defendants there was no privity of contract, and whose services in substitution for those to be performed by the Parkgate Co under the contract they, the defendants, were not bound to accept. The Parkgate Co. agreed that the facts should be stated in a Special Case for the opinion of this court, the use of the waggons by the defendants being in the meanwhile continued at a rate agreed on between the parties without prejudice to either with reference to their respective rights.

The first ground taken by the defendants is, in our opinion, altogether untenable in the present state of things, whatever it may be when the affairs of the company shall have been wound-up, and the company itself shall have been dissolved. * * * Pending the winding-up, the company is * * * kept alive, the liquidator having power to carry on the business "so far as may be necessary for the beneficial winding-up of the company," which the continued letting of these waggons and the receipt of the rent payable in respect of them would, we presume, be. What would be the position of the parties on the dissolution of the company it is unnecessary for the present purpose to consider.

The main contention on the part of the defendants, however, was that, as the Parkgate Company had, by assigning the contracts, and by making over their repairing stations to the British Company, incapacitated themselves to fulfil their obligation to keep the waggons in repair, that company had no right, as between themselves and the defendants, to substitute a third party to do the work they had engaged to perform, nor were the defendants bound to accept the party so substituted as the one to whom they were to look for performance of the contract; the contract was therefore at an end.

The authority principally relied on in support of this contention was the case of *Robson v. Drummond* [2 B. & Ad. 303.] * * * In *Robson v. Drummond* a carriage having been hired by the defendant of one Sharp, a coachmaker, for five years, at a yearly rent, payable in advance each year, the carriage to be kept in repair and painted once a year by the maker—Robson being then a partner in the business but unknown to the defendant—on Sharp retiring from the business after three years had expired, and making over all interest in the business and property in the goods to Robson, it was held, that the defendant could not be sued on the contract—by Lord Tenterden on the ground that "the defendant might have been induced to enter into the contract by reason of the personal confidence which he reposed in Sharp, and therefore might have agreed to pay money in advance, for which reason the defendant had a right to object to its being performed by any other person;" and by Littledale and Parke, JJ., on the additional ground that the defendant had a right to the personal services of Sharp, and to the benefit of his judgment and taste, to the end of the contract.

In like manner, where goods are ordered of a particular manufacturer, another, who has succeeded to his business, cannot execute the order, so as to bind the customer, who has not been made aware of the transfer of the business, to accept the goods. The latter is entitled to refuse to deal with any other than the manufacturer whose goods he intended to buy. For this *Boulton v. Jones* [2 H. & N. 564] is a sufficient authority. The case of *Robson v. Drummond* comes nearer to the present case, but is, we think, distinguishable from it. We entirely concur in the principle on which the decision in *Robson v. Drummond* rests, namely, that where a person contracts with another to do work or perform service, and it can be inferred that the person employed has been selected with reference to his individual skill, competency, or other personal qualification, the inability or unwillingness of the party so employed to execute the work or perform the service is a sufficient answer to any demand by a stranger to the original contract of the performance of it by the other party, and entitles the latter to treat the contract as at an end, notwithstanding that the person tendered to take the place of the contracting party may be equally well qualified to do the service. Personal performance is in such a case of the essence of the contract, which, consequently, cannot in its absence be enforced against an unwilling party. But this principle appears to us inapplicable in the present instance, inasmuch as we cannot suppose that in stipulating for the repair of these waggons by the company—a rough description of work which ordinary workmen conversant with the business would be perfectly able to execute—the defendants attached any importance to whether the repairs were done by the company, or by any one with whom the company might enter into a subsidiary contract to do the work. All that the hirers, the defendants, cared for in this stipulation was that the waggons should be kept in repair; it was indifferent to them by whom the repairs should be done. Thus if, without going into liquidation, or assigning these contracts, the company had entered into a contract with any competent party to do the repairs, and so had procured them to be done, we cannot think that this would have been a departure from the terms of the contract to keep the waggons in repair. While fully acquiescing in the general principle just referred to, we must take care not to push it beyond reasonable limits. And we cannot but think that, in applying the principle, the Court of Queen's Bench in *Robson v. Drummond* went to the utmost length to which it can be carried, as it is difficult to see how in repairing a carriage when necessary, or painting it once a year, preference would be given to one coachmaker over another. Much work is contracted for, which it is known can only be executed by means of subcontracts; much is contracted for as to which it is indifferent to the party for whom it is to be done, whether it is done by the immediate party to the contract, or by someone on his behalf. In all these cases the maxim Qui facit per alium facit per se applies.

In the view we take of the case, therefore, the repair of the waggons, undertaken and done by the British Company under their contract with the Parkgate Company, is a sufficient performance by the latter of their engagement to repair under their contract with the defendants. Consequently, so long as the Parkgate Company continues to exist, and, through the British Company, continues to fulfil its obligation to keep the waggons in repair, the defendants cannot, in our opinion, be heard to say that the former company is not entitled to the performance of the contract by them, on the ground that the company have incapacitated themselves from performing their obligations under it, or that, by transferring the performance thereof to others, they have absolved the defendants from further performance on their part.

That a debt accruing due under a contract can, since the passing of the Judicature Acts, be assigned at law as well as equity, cannot since the decision in *Brice v. Bannister* [3 Q.B.D. 569] be disputed.

We are therefore of opinion that our judgment must be for the plaintiffs for the amount claimed.

UNIFORM COMMERCIAL CODE § 2–210(1).

A party may perform his duty through a delegate unless otherwise agreed or unless the other party has a substantial interest in having his original promisor perform or control the acts required by the contract. No delegation of performance relieves the party delegating of any duty to perform or any liability for breach.

MACKE CO. v. PIZZA OF GAITHERSBURG, INC.

Maryland Court of Appeals, 1970.
259 Md. 479, 270 A.2d 645.

SINGLEY, JUDGE.

The appellees and defendants below, Pizza of Gaithersburg, Inc.; Pizzeria, Inc.; The Pizza Pie Corp., Inc. and Pizza Oven, Inc., four corporations under the common ownership of Sidney Ansell, Thomas S. Sherwood and Eugene Early and the same individuals as partners or proprietors (the Pizza Shops) operated at six locations in Montgomery and Prince George's Counties. The appellees had arranged to have installed in each of their locations cold drink vending machines owned by Virginia Coffee Service, Inc., and on 30 December 1966, this arrangement was formalized at five of the locations, by contracts for terms of one year, automatically renewable for a like term in the absence of 30 days' written notice. A similar contract for the sixth location, operated by Pizza of Gaithersburg, Inc., was entered into on 25 July 1967.

On 30 December 1967, Virginia's assets were purchased by The Macke Company (Macke) and the six contracts were assigned to Macke by Virginia. In January, 1968, the Pizza Shops attempted to terminate the five contracts having the December anniversary date, and in February, the contract which had the July anniversary date.

Macke brought suit in the Circuit Court for Montgomery County against each of the Pizza Shops for damages for breach of contract. From judgments for the defendants, Macke has appealed.

The lower court based the result which it reached on two grounds: first, that the Pizza Shops, when they contracted with Virginia, relied on its skill, judgment and reputation, which made impossible a delegation of Virginia's duties to Macke; and second, that the damages claimed could not be shown with reasonable certainty. These conclusions are challenged by Macke.

In the absence of a contrary provision—and there was none here—rights and duties under an executory bilateral contract may be assigned and delegated, subject to the exception that duties under a contract to provide personal services may never be delegated, nor rights be assigned under a contract where *delectus personae* was an ingredient of the bargain. 4 Corbin on Contracts § 865 (1951) at 434. * * *

The six machines were placed on the appellees' premises under a printed "Agreement–Contract" which identified the "customer," gave its place of business, described the vending machine, and then provided:

"TERMS

"1. The Company will install on the Customer's premises the above listed equipment and will maintain the equipment in good operating order and stocked with merchandise.

"2. The location of this equipment will be such as to permit accessibility to persons desiring use of same. This equipment shall remain the property of the Company and shall not be moved from the location at which installed, except by the Company.

"3. For equipment requiring electricity and water, the Customer is responsible for electrical receptacle and water outlet within ten (10) feet of the equipment location. The Customer is also responsible to supply the Electrical Power and Water needed.

"4. The Customer will exercise every effort to protect this equipment from abuse or damage.

"5. The Company will be responsible for all licenses and taxes on the equipment and sale of products.

"6. This Agreement–Contract is for a term of one (1) year from the date indicated herein and will be automatically renewed for a like period, unless thirty (30) day written notice is given by either party to terminate service.

"7. Commission on monthly sales will be paid by the Company to the Customer at the following rate: * * *."

The rate provided in each of the agreements was "30% of Gross Receipts to $300.00 monthly [,] 35% over [$]300.00," except for the agreement with Pizza of Gaithersburg, Inc., which called for "40% of Gross Receipts."

We cannot regard the agreements as contracts for personal services. They were either a license or concession granted Virginia by the appellees, or a lease of a portion of the appellees' premises, with Virginia agreeing to pay a percentage of gross sales as a license or concession fee or as rent * * * and were assignable by Virginia unless they imposed on Virginia duties of a personal or unique character which could not be delegated, S & L Vending Corp. v. 52 Thompkins Ave. Restaurant, Inc., 26 A.D.2d 935, 274 N.Y.S.2d 697 (1966).

The appellees earnestly argue that they had dealt with Macke before and had chosen Virginia because they preferred the way it conducted its business. Specifically, they say that service was more personalized, since the president of Virginia kept the machines in working order, that commissions were paid in cash, and that Virginia permitted them to keep keys to the machines so that minor adjustments could be made when needed. Even if we assume all this to be true, the agreements with Virginia were silent as to the details of the working arrangements and contained only a provision requiring Virginia to "install * * * the above listed equipment and * * * maintain the equipment in good operating order and stocked with merchandise." We think the Supreme Court of California put the problem of personal service in proper focus a century ago when it upheld the assignment of a contract to grade a San Francisco street:

> "All painters do not paint portraits like Sir Joshua Reynolds, nor landscapes like Claude Lorraine, nor do all writers write dramas like Shakespeare or fiction like Dickens. Rare genius and extraordinary skill are not transferable, and contracts for their employment are therefore personal, and cannot be assigned. But rare genius and extraordinary skill are not indispensable to the workmanlike digging down of a sand hill or the filling up of a depression to a given level, or the construction of brick sewers with manholes and covers, and contracts for such work are not personal, and may be assigned." Taylor v. Palmer, 31 Cal. 240 at 247–248 (1866).

* * * Moreover, the difference between the service the Pizza Shops happened to be getting from Virginia and what they expected to get from Macke did not mount up to such a material change in the performance of obligations under the agreements as would justify the appellees' refusal to recognize the assignment. * * *

* * *

Except for the fact that the result has been roundly criticized, see Corbin, *supra,* at 448–49, the Pizza Shops might have found some solace in the facts found in Boston Ice Co. v. Potter, 123 Mass. 28 (1877). There, Potter, who had dealt with the Boston Ice Company, and found its service unsatisfactory, transferred his business to Citizens' Ice Company. Later, Citizens' sold out to Boston, unbeknown to Potter, and Potter was served by Boston for a full year. When Boston attempted to collect its ice bill, the Massachusetts court sustained Potter's demurrer on the ground that there was no privity of contract, since Potter had a right to choose with whom he would deal and could not have another supplier thrust upon him. Modern authorities do not support this result, and hold that, absent provision to the contrary, a duty may be delegated, as distinguished from a right which can be assigned, and that the promisee cannot rescind, if the quality of the performance remains materially the same.

* * *

As we see it, the delegation of duty by Virginia to Macke was entirely permissible under the terms of the agreements. * * *

* * *

Judgment reversed as to liability. * * *

NEHF, WRITING CONTRACTS IN THE CLIENT'S INTEREST
51 S. C. L. Rev. 153, 179–80 (1999).

A deciding factor [in Macke] was that the contract did not mention these benefits which the non-assigning party now claimed were so important. The lesson for contract drafters is that all important expectations should be spelled out in the contract; otherwise, it may be difficult to contend later that they were material parts of the bargain that would be altered through an assignment.

SECTION FIVE: NOVATION

The general view is that a delegating party remains liable to the obligee even after a valid delegation of duties. Suppose, however, that the obligee agrees (expressly or impliedly) to release the delegating party in exchange for the new duty of the delegate. Contract law calls the new contract a novation. The delegate substitutes for the party delegating, who is discharged.

The Restatement (Second) of Contracts section 329 provides that a novation occurs if the obligee, without reservation of rights against the party delegating, accepts any performance from the delegate with knowledge that the party delegating has repudiated his or her obligation to the obligee.

UTICA MUTUAL INSURANCE COMPANY v. VIGO COAL COMPANY, INC.
United States Court of Appeals, Seventh Circuit, 2004.
393 F.3d 707.

Posner, Circuit Judge.

This diversity suit for breach of a suretyship contract, decided in favor of the defendants after a bench trial, presents questions primarily relating to the contract-law doctrine of "novation," but more broadly to principles of contract interpretation; all the questions are governed by the common law of Indiana.

In 1991 defendant Vigo purchased Buck Creek Coal, which operated a coal mine and was required by both federal and state law to post reclamation bonds as a condition of being permitted to operate the mine. 30 U.S.C. § 1259(a); 30 C.F.R. § 800.20; Ind.Code § 14–34–6–1. In connection with the purchase, Vigo, joined by defendant Atlas and by the owners of Vigo and Atlas (the Koesters and the Piepers, respectively, who are also defendants) and by Buck Creek Coal, signed a "General Indemnity Agreement." In it they agreed to indemnify Utica insurance company for any losses that Utica might incur from issuing reclamation bonds to the Indiana state government on behalf of

Buck Creek. The following year (1992) another "General Indemnity Agreement" was signed, identical to the first, except that the only signers were defendant Schulties, who had not signed the previous agreement, and the Piepers (who, remember, are Atlas's owners). Mr. Pieper signed both individually and as president; and because of his having thus signed in his official capacity, as it were, as an agent apparently authorized to bind his principal, the district judge ruled that Atlas was bound by the second agreement. * * * Atlas has not challenged that ruling, even though it appears from the 1992 agreement that Pieper actually was signing in his capacity as president of Buck Creek, not of Atlas. So Atlas is bound; and to simplify our opinion we shall assume that Atlas and Schulties were the signers of the second agreement and Vigo and Atlas the signers of the first; in other words, we'll ignore not only the district court's unchallenged error but also the companies' owners. With this simplification, the case becomes Utica versus Vigo.

The surety bonds were later "forfeited"; that is, Buck Creek proving unable to fulfill its reclamation obligations, the state required the surety, Utica, to do the reclamation. Utica then brought this suit, against all the signers of either agreement, for reimbursement of the expense—some $400,-000—of the reclamation.

The district court concluded that the signers of the 1991 indemnity agreement were off the hook (except Atlas, since it had signed the second agreement as well) because the second agreement was a "novation," that is, a replacement of the first agreement, which therefore released the obligors in that agreement. * * * But the judge also turned down these defendants' counterclaim, in which they sought to recover the attorneys' fees that they had incurred in defending against Utica's claim.

Unable to recover its entire loss from the signers of the 1992 agreement (Atlas and Schulties—the latter now bankrupt), and seeking therefore to enforce the 1991 agreement against Vigo, Utica challenges the finding that the 1992 agreement was a novation.

The agreement does not describe itself as a novation or a substitute, or purport to release the signers of the first agreement. The only clue in the agreements themselves that the second one might be a novation is that Atlas signed both, and if the only purpose of the second was to add an indemnitor, namely Schulties, why did Atlas sign it, having signed the identical first agreement, unless that wasn't the purpose, and the second agreement replaced rather than supplemented the first? Additional evidence, that is, evidence beyond the two agreements themselves, was presented at the trial, and that evidence, together with the anomaly we've just noted, persuaded the judge that the second agreement was indeed a novation.

That evidence revealed the following. In 1992, Vigo sold the coal mine to Atlas and Schulties and they agreed to use their best efforts to replace the existing reclamation bonds and obtain a release of Vigo's liability under those bonds. They failed to do so, but an insurance agent named Jones submitted a "reclamation bonding application" to Utica, proposing to "transfer these bonds over and have new Indemnity Agreements signed by Chuck Schulties." There was no mention of Vigo. The agent testified that the reason Vigo was left off the second agreement was that it and its owners, who had signed the 1991 agreement, "had no ownership, they had no control, they were not party to running the company." Asked at trial whether Vigo's omission from the agreement was "confirmatory of the conversations that you'd had with

[Utica's Gerald Swarthout, who handled the negotiations leading up to the 1992 agreement] that they would not be indemnitors," the agent replied "of course, they were selling."

Swarthout gave contrary testimony, but the district judge disbelieved it, in part because Schulties had (at the time!) substantial assets. That fact, together with his substantial expertise in coal mining, suggested that an indemnity agreement signed by him as well as by Atlas would provide sufficient security to persuade Utica *or some other insurance company* to issue new reclamation bonds to replace those that Utica had issued. For although the General Indemnity Agreement (whether the 1991 or the 1992 version, since they were identical except for the signers) embraced replacement bonds, it was terminable by an indemnitor on 20 days' notice. And therefore as part of Vigo's sale of the coal mine to Atlas and Schulties, Atlas and Vigo could have withdrawn from the 1991 agreement and Atlas and Schulties, with a net worth between them of $7 million, could have persuaded Utica or some other insurance company to issue new surety bonds that Vigo, having withdrawn from the agreement, would not have been a guarantor of. Utica does not deny that its bonds could have been replaced in this fashion. Ind.Code § 14–34–6–14.6.

The consequence of replacing the bonds would have been to release Vigo. But given Schulties' financial wherewithal and mining expertise, and Vigo's natural reluctance to remain a guarantor of performance over which, as a result of the sale, it would no longer have any control, the judge was on solid ground in finding that Utica would have agreed to an express novation rather than lose to another insurance company a business relationship that yielded it significant premiums ($18,000 a year) in exchange for assuming what seemed at the time a modest risk. Modest because underground coal mines (Buck Creek's mine was an underground mine) tend to require less expense to restore the surface after the mine is exhausted than strip mines and because two substantial-seeming parties, Atlas and Schulties, had agreed to indemnify Utica for any loss.

The judge's reconstruction of the parties' deal—his conclusion that they intended the second agreement to substitute for rather than supplement the first—is not clearly erroneous. On the contrary, it makes commercial, economic, and common sense; and good sense, or such synonyms as commercial reasonableness, provides sound guidance for interpreting ambiguous contracts, in Indiana as elsewhere. * * * As Judge Boudin explained recently, "Agreements, especially commercial arrangements, are designed to make sense. If one reading produces a plausible result for which parties might be expected to bargain, that reading has a strong presumption in its favor as against another reading producing an unlikely result (*e.g.*, windfall gains, conditions that cannot be satisfied, dubious incentives)." *National Tax Institute, Inc. v. Topnotch at Stowe Resort & Spa*, 388 F.3d 15, 19 (1st Cir.2004).

The difficult question is whether the district judge was entitled to take evidence—to mine underground, as it were—rather than to stay on the semantic surface of the two agreements. A finding of novation is dynamite, as this case illustrates. Instead of supplementing a previous contract, it wipes it out. Parties that enter into multiple contracts with one another want protection against a trial that may convert a contract that says nothing about novation or release into a release of the obligors under a previous contract. Were it not for what we're calling the dynamite effect of a novation, there would be no reason to treat a novation any differently from any other contract modification.

One way to give obligees protection would be to have a rule that a novation or release must be explicit; that it can never be implied. Indiana rejects that approach, * * * no jurisdiction, to our knowledge, accepts it. So we can set it to one side. There are three alternatives. One, proposed by the Williston treatise, is to require that a novation be proved by clear and convincing evidence. 30 *Williston on Contracts, supra*, § 76:42. The cases do not support this alternative; *Johnston v. Holiday Inns, Inc.*, 565 F.2d 790, 797 (1st Cir.1977), rejects it outright. What the case law, including Indiana case law, does support is that proof of a novation must be "clear and definite" or "clear and satisfactory" or words to that effect. * * * We take this to be an appropriate reminder of the fell consequences of a finding of novation.

Another alternative, which would treat the determination of novation like other issues of contractual interpretation, is that a novation can be implied only if there is an ambiguity as to whether the agreement claimed to be a novation really is one, rather than merely a supplement to the earlier agreement. This approach also has support in Indiana, as in other states. * * *

Still another alternative * * * appears to allow extrinsic evidence to be introduced in *any* novation case, perhaps on the theory (not articulated in the cases, however) that the agreement claimed to be a novation cannot be interpreted without consideration of the meaning of the contract it is alleged to have replaced. This cannot be quite right; if the second agreement states "this is a novation" or "this is not a novation," that surely is the end of the case; extrinsic evidence will not be allowed.

Probably what we have described as alternative rules come to the same thing, in the following sense; the court can always peek at the earlier contract, and if in light of what that contract says it is uncertain whether the new contract is a novation, then the court can treat the interpretive issue as one of fact, that is, can take evidence on it, but always bearing in mind the need for the proof of a novation to be clear. The earlier contract is a bit of extrinsic evidence that is always already in the case, and if it shows that the new contract is ambiguous (as to whether it is a novation), the door is opened to the presentation of additional extrinsic evidence, which may make clear that the new contract really was intended to take the place of the old.
* * *

[E]xtrinsic ambiguity was adequately demonstrated here. There was no integration clause in the 1992 agreement (or in the prior one, for that matter, for remember that the terms, as distinct from their signatories, are identical). And so Judge Hamilton had to consider extrinsic evidence in order to decide whether the agreement was the complete agreement of the parties. It was not. From the sale of the mine and the other circumstances we've recounted it is apparent that the parties understood the 1992 agreement to replace rather than supplement the previous one.
* * *

So the judge's ruling that there was a novation stands. * * *
* * *

AFFIRMED.

*

Appendix A

JUDICIAL REASONS

The reasons set forth by judges to support their decisions are of great importance. It is not possible to understand a court opinion without a firm grasp of these reasons.

It is useful to distinguish between three basic types of reasons: (1) authoritative reasons, (2) substantive reasons, and (3) institutional reasons. Authoritative reasons appeal to recognized authorities including case law, statutes, administrative regulations, and constitutions. These authorities are legally binding within the jurisdictions where they are applicable. They are also "persuasive" authority, or authority by analogy, in other jurisdictions. Other non-binding authorities that generate authoritative reasons are restatements, treatises, law review articles, and the like. The opinion in White v. Benkowski includes appeals both to binding and non-binding authorities.

The justificatory force of authoritative reasons that appeal to binding authorities derives from at least two sources: (1) the various values served when courts follow antecedent law, whatever its content: certainty, predictability, equality before the law, efficiency, etc. and (2) the various values that may inform the content of the case law, statutes, and other authorities involved. The first class of values might be called "formal rule of law values," the second class, simply "substantive values." The general rule denying punitive damages, invoked as an authoritative reason by the court in White v. Benkowski, reflects not only values of the first type but also substantive values, including the values associated with freedom of contract. That is, parties will contract more freely if they know that damages for breach generally do not include a sum for punishment.

Authoritative reasons do not necessarily incorporate values of both types. Thus a given authoritative reason might serve formal "rule of law" values, but not relevant substantive values. The rule invoked by the court might indeed by the relevant and authoritative rule, but the rule might be substantively unsound.

It is important to develop the ability to construct and evaluate authoritative reasons. One possible criticism of an authoritative reason is that it does not apply. For example, a rule may not apply because the case from which it derives is distinguishable—not "in point." Relatedly, a case-law rule may not apply because the reasons for the adoption of the rule are not applicable to the case at hand. Another possible criticism is that the substantive content of a rule is unsound in some way (e.g., perhaps punitive damages have no effect on a party's willingness to contract).

The terms of valid agreements may be viewed as a special class of authoritative reasons. Do you see why?

Substantive reasons do not involve appeals to authority. These reasons consist of moral, economic, political, and other social considerations. Those unfamiliar with the law may think that judges must decide cases according to antecedent law, and thus can give only authoritative reasons, preferably those of a binding nature. This view is reinforced by crude positivist philosophies of law which implicitly hold that truly legal reasons necessarily appeal to antecedent binding authority. In fact, judges frequently give substantive reasons to support their decisions. A judge may not only give an authoritative reason, but may also offer a substantive reason that supports the same result. Or a judge may be faced with an issue not previously decided in the jurisdiction. In such a case, the judge usually decides by comparing the justificatory force of the substantive reasons on each side of the issue. Or a judge may confront an issue on which the authorities are in conflict, or an issue of whether to overrule a prior case. Here, too, the judge usually decides in accord with the weight of the competing substantive reasons.

As with authoritative reasons, it is important to develop the ability to construct and critically evaluate substantive reasons. In this regard, it is useful to distinguish between two different types of substantive reasons. The first type of substantive reason is a "goal" reason. In Sullivan v. O'Connor (page 35), Justice Kaplan stated that: "If actions for breach of promise can be readily maintained, doctors, so it is said, will be frightened into practising 'defensive medicine.'" A goal reason, then, for not readily permitting such actions might be that this will promote effective health care. You can see that the justificatory force of a goal reason derives from the predicted salutary effects of the decision it supports. Two of the possible grounds for criticizing a goal reason are that the decision would not have effects that serve the goal, and that the goal is not a good one.

A second type of substantive reason may be called a "rightness" reason. In Sullivan v. O'Connor, Justice Kaplan offered a rightness reason when he stated: "We should recall that the fee paid by the patient to the doctor for the alleged promise would usually be quite disproportionate to the putative expectancy recovery." This is essentially a rightness argument that an expectancy recovery would be unfair. Unlike a good goal reason, the justificatory force of a good rightness reason does not depend on the predicted effects of the decision it supports. Rather, the justificatory force of a good rightness reason depends upon the soundness and applicability of the rightness norm in which the reason is grounded. Thus the force of the rightness reason set forth by Justice Kaplan depends on a norm that might in this context be articulated as follows: "In the absence of special circumstances, potential liability of a contracting party should be proportionate to that party's expected gain." A rightness reason is subject to criticism on various grounds, including the possible inapplicability of the norm to the facts, and the possible unsoundness of the norm.

Still another type of reason found in judicial opinions is "institutional" in character. In Sullivan v. O'Connor, Justice Kaplan set forth an institutional reason when he said: "But patients may transform such statements into firm promises in their own minds, especially when they have been disappointed in the event, and testify in that sense to sympathetic juries." Here are some further examples of institutional reasons:

—Because the plaintiff's claim calls for a change in the law that cannot justifiably be made without access to "general social facts" that only a legislature can adequately investigate or evaluate, the court ought not to make the change, but should leave it to the legislature.

—Because the court could not supervise the implementation of its decree without undue expenditure of resources, an order for specific performance of the contract will be denied.

—Because of difficulties of measurement, breach of contract damages should not include pain and suffering.

From these examples, it can be seen that an institutional reason is a special kind of goal reason or rightness reason. Such reasons are often influential, and it is important to develop the ability to construct and evaluate them. This requires, among other things, the acquisition of "institutional" knowledge about the processes, personnel, and roles involved.

We now return to the general question: why is it important to study closely the reasons judges give for their decisions? This is a very large subject which can only be introduced here. By close study of authoritative reasons, we can better understand the meaning and likely consequences of a judge's decision. For example, we can determine whether and to what extent a judge follows prior law. If the judge purports to follow applicable law but does not, then the decision rendered will be "lawless" in that respect. Moreover, it will have less precedential value.

The study of substantive reasons also has a special importance. First, substantive reasons may improve and shape the very content of law (and thus improve and shape future authoritative reasons).

Second, by focusing on the substantive reasons that support a rule (or other form of law), we may determine more reliably the true scope of the rule. This is largely because most judges, at least in regard to case law rules, follow Karl N. Llewellyn's maxim: "the rule follows where its reason leads, where reason stops, there stops the rule."

Third, as we have seen, substantive reasons are largely decisive in cases where there is no antecedent binding law, where case law is in conflict, or where a rule originally unsound or now outmoded should be overruled. And in all such cases, a judge may or may not formulate a general rule. When the judge does not formulate a rule, subsequent judges will very likely look upon the substantive reasons given by the first judge as the germ of a new rule. When a judge does formulate a general rule, later judges will consider accompanying substantive reasons in determining the contours of the announced rule.

Fourth, substantive reasons are necessary constituents of all forms of criticism of law and its operation. Those who are unable to construct and evaluate substantive reasons simply cannot engage in effective criticism. A legal system which lawyers and others do not subject to effective criticism almost certainly would not be of high quality.

It is sometimes said that the serious study of judicial reasons is pointless because judges seldom give their "real" reasons. We believe nearly all judges try to give their "real" reasons when writing opinions. But even if this were not so, the study of the reasons actually given would be far from pointless.

Authoritative reasons are analyzed and discussed further in H.L.A. Hart, Essays on Bentham 242–268 (1982), and also in Summers, Two Types of Substantive Reasons: The Core of a Theory of Common–Law Justification, 63 Cornell L.Rev. 707, 724–5 (1978). The latter article also extensively discusses substantive reasons. A related but somewhat different approach to substantive reasons appears in R. Dworkin, Taking Rights Seriously, ch. 4 (1977). An important critique of Dworkin's views on substantive reasons is Greenawalt, Policy, Rights, and Judicial Decision, 11 Ga.L.Rev. 991 (1977). Dworkin's reply appears in Dworkin, Seven Critics, 11 Ga.L.Rev. 1201, 1203–1241 (1977).

Appendix B

HISTORICAL BACKGROUND OF CONSIDERATION AND RELATED DOCTRINES[a]

From the mid 16th century to the late 19th century, courts and commentators often discussed "consideration" in connection with two separate problems. First, they wanted to ensure that the law went far enough in recognizing consensual liability. Early English law had dramatically under-recognized such liability. (In our terms, the courts failed to adopt sufficiently expansive theories of obligation.) The second problem was to see that such liability did not go too far—that due limits were imposed.

The English common law was, until the 19th century, encased in what were called "forms of action" administered primarily by the "common-law courts": Kings Bench, Common Pleas, and Exchequer. These courts were distinguished from the Court of Chancery which, as we saw in the note at page 83, administered a body of law and a set of special remedies called "equity," until the merger of law and equity in the 19th century.

What then were these forms of action? We offer a general functional account. With few exceptions, a lawyer could start a legal proceeding in one of the common-law courts only by purchasing, from a clerk in the office of Chancery, a "writ" embodying the relevant form of action for the case at hand. The lawyer reviewed the Register of Writs (or a copy of it) to see if it included a writ embodying a form of action which covered the fact pattern his client related to him. The early writs (1) directed the sheriff of the shire where the episode occurred to have the defendant appear in court, and (2) authorized the common law court to take jurisdiction of the case. In general, there was no substantive right to a remedy if there was no available form of action. The form of action also usually prescribed certain procedural requirements, including modes of trial. Over hundreds of years, new writs were added to the Register of Writs, more or less haphazardly. As it grew, so the substantive law grew. Sir Henry Maine in his great work, Dissertations on Early Law and Custom, remarked in 1883 (at 389) that "[s]o great is the ascendency of the Law of Actions in the infancy of Courts of Justice, that substantive law has at first the look of being gradually secreted in the interstices of procedure; and the early lawyer can only see the law through the envelope of its technical forms."

a. The editors wish to thank Professor A.W.B. Simpson for reviewing this historical account.

In the field we now know as contract, the two most important early forms of action were called "covenant" and "debt." In medieval times, covenant was available only to recover for breach of promises under seal. The student should review the modern theories of obligation in Chapter Two and identify the one most analogous today to covenant. How, if at all, might Fuller justify the availability of this form of action? (See the extract, Consideration and Form, at page 50.)

The form of action called debt had several uses. One use was to enforce a broken promise to pay a sum certain in money *in return* for a loan, or goods sold, or services received. The plaintiff (in our parlance) would have to prove (if denied) that the defendant had *actually received* the loan, the goods, the services, etc.—a *quid pro quo,* as it was called. The student should review the modern theories of obligation studied in Chapter Two and identify the one or ones most analogous today to debt (as we have here described it). How, if at all, might Fuller, in the extract at pages 52–53, justify the availability of this form of action? Some scholars trace the emphasis on bargained-for exchange and on "benefit to the promisor" in 19th century consideration theory to the influence of the action of debt. (This emphasis on benefit to the promisor is reflected in at least two of the 19th century American consideration cases studied in this book:) Hardesty v. Smith (page 45) and Hamer v. Sidway (page 56).

By about 1500, there were some extensions of debt beyond the above confines. For example, a seller could sue in debt for the agreed price (a "sum certain") of *undelivered* property.

The mode of trial in debt involved appeal to the supernatural. The defendant could "wage his law" and bring in so called "oath helpers" who would in effect swear that the defendant was not liable. Mode of trial aside, do you see how debt and covenant together were woefully deficient compared to the theories of obligation available today? The biggest gap in promissory liability, of course, was that a plaintiff could not, as a general matter, recover damages for the breach of a bilateral executory agreement not under seal. (Of course, the above noted extension of debt was a limited move in this direction.)

During the 1500's and 1600's major developments occurred in a further form of action called "assumpsit" (the Latin word for "undertook"). This form of action did not require a promise under seal, a sum certain, or trial by wager of law.

Assumpsit grew out of the tort form of action called "trespass on the case," and came very largely to supersede debt. Before 1500, assumpsit had become widely available where there was a consensual arrangement in which the defendant undertook to do something for the plaintiff and then did it poorly, i.e. "misfeasance." Here the loss occurred within a relationship defined by an agreement which shaped the contours of the duty later broken. For example, if D agreed to ferry P's horses, cart, goods, and family across the River Isis and D *negligently* dumped everything in the river, P could recover. The theoretical basis of this form of action at this time was not the failure to perform a promise, but rather the tortious wrong by the defendant, causing a loss to P. Some scholars trace the emphasis in 19th century consideration theory on "detriment" incurred by the promisee in reliance on the promisor

to "misfeasance-assumpsit." You should again review the modern theories of obligation studied in Chapter Two and identify the one most analogous today to this use of assumpsit (as we have so far described it). Has Fuller failed to provide a "contractual" rationale for the recognition of this use of assumpsit as a form of action? Of course, this use of assumpsit did not satisfy the need for a general theory of relief for the broken bilateral *executory* agreement.

What, then, if the defendant in our example was guilty only of "nonfeasance?" For example, what if, after promising to ferry the agreed persons and things across the River Isis, the defendant simply refused to carry out the promise at all, thereby causing a loss? During the 1500's and 1600's, such a broken promise came to be redressable in assumpsit, at least if the plaintiff relied on the promise. A major early landmark case was Pickering v. Thoroughgood, decided in 1533. Spilman J. said in that case:

> And in some books a difference has been taken between nonfeasance and malfeasance; thus on the one an action of covenant lies, and on the other an action on the case lies. This is no distinction in reason, for if a carpenter for £100 covenants with me to make me a house, and does not make it before the day assigned, so that I am deprived of lodging, I shall have an action for this nonfeasance just as well as if he had made it badly.[b]

Even in the absence of reliance, a mere promise given in exchange for another's promise also came to be viewed as a "detriment," a "consideration," enabling courts to enforce purely executory exchanges. This was a major step in the growth of liability.[c] (For this use of "detriment" as consideration, see, for example, Hamer v. Sidway.) When these exchanges were enforced, the form of action was called "special assumpsit" because of the specificity required in the pleading form, which had to set forth how the obligation arose.

Assumpsit eventually also occupied most of the field formerly occupied by debt. In this use, assumpsit was called "indebitatus" or "general" assumpsit. The name general assumpsit arose because of the generality permitted in the pleading form. Unlike special assumpsit, it was not necessary to allege specifically how the obligation arose. It was necessary to allege only that the defendant, indebted to the plaintiff in a certain sum, promised or undertook to pay the debt. General assumpsit also grew to include certain very general stylized pleading forms called the "common counts." See pages 137–138 of this book. (The foregoing matters are treated more fully in A.W.B. Simpson, A History of the Common Law of Contract—The Rise of the Action of Assumpsit 303–07 (1975)).

By the 1600's, the presence of "consideration," even then sometimes sloganized as benefit to the promisor or detriment to the promisee,[d] enabled the plaintiff to maintain an action of assumpsit. Professor A.W.B. Simpson, the leading scholar of this branch of our subject, has said:

> The consideration, or considerations, for a promise meant the factors which the promisor considered when he promised, and which moved or

---

b. As found in A.W.B. Simpson's historical introduction to G. Cheshire & C. Fifoot, Law of Contract 5 (10th ed. M. Furmston, editor 1981).

c. See, e.g., Strangeborough v. Warner, 4 Leon 3 (1589).

d. Stone v. Wythipol, Cro.Eliz. 126, 1 Leon 113, Owen 94 (1588).

motivated his promising. Although not a precise equivalent, "motive" is perhaps about as near as one can get by way of synonym. The essence of the doctrine of consideration, then, is the adoption by the common law of the idea that the legal effect of a promise should depend upon the factor or factors which motivated the promise. To decide whether a promise to do X is binding, you need to know why the promise was made. This basic idea can be elaborated in various ways—for example, one might or might not accept love of charity, or a future marriage, or a past payment, as sufficient in law to impose promissory liability. Whatever decisions are made about such matters as these can be fitted into the basic analysis.

The recognition by the common law that a promise, to give rise to legal liability in assumpsit, must be "supported" by good, sufficient, or adequate consideration, entails the idea that a promise on its own, an unsupported promise, is not sufficient to impose liability. * * * In modern terms one can see the plausibility of the theory—a promise which lacks any adequate motive cannot have been serious, and therefore ought not to be taken seriously. (A.W.B. Simpson, A History of the Common Law of Contract—The Rise of the Action of Assumpsit 321–22 (1975).)

You should consider whether the foregoing concept of consideration is truly unitary and whether it is equivalent to the Restatement concept of consideration as a "bargained-for exchange." See page 48–49 of this book. Again, what does Fuller say (pages 66 and 67) about the *justifiability* of imposing liability merely for a broken promise not under seal that is part of a wholly executory bilateral exchange? Is the presence of "consideration" in the form merely of a return promise ("detriment") enough to justify this?

Thus the *presence* of consideration in the late middle ages helped to bring about full recognition of liability for the wholly unperformed promise as part of an executory exchange, and the *absence* of consideration imposed outer limits on the liability that came to be recognized. There is no inherent reason, however, why consideration must mean exactly the same thing in both of its manifestations. For example, if consideration is defined as requiring a bargain (and courts do not always so define it) the presence of a bargain might be held sufficient for prima facie liability, yet the absence of a bargain might not be held fatal. See Hamer v. Sidway. Yet it should be easy to see how *intellectual* pressure grew for a *unitary* conception of consideration. Both Restatements of contract reflect this pressure, the second even more than the first.

Appendix C

THE RESTATEMENT IDEA— SOME SKEPTICISM

This book contains many sections of the contracts restatements. They are a helpful learning tool. Nevertheless, the skeptical remarks about restatements collected here offer some perspective on the uses and abuses of restatements.

CLARK, THE RESTATEMENT OF THE LAW OF CONTRACTS
42 Yale L.J. 643, 646, 652, 654–56 (1933).

[A] black letter sentence * * * can never * * * state pages of history and policy and honest deliberation * * *.

* * *

The * * * [Restatement] is apparently the final answer that the Word alone counts, and the long and tortuous way by which the Word was ascertained is to be forgotten.

* * *

Simplification as an end in itself is false. Simplification as a clarification and orderly statement of intellectual processes and conclusions is desirable. The idea that there is "the law"—the "common" *non-statutory* law—of our forty eight states, our territories and our federal system, which can be stated, is the former kind of simplification. Actually the resulting statement is the law nowhere and in its unreality only deludes and misleads. It is either a generality so obvious as immediately to be accepted, or so vague as not to offend, or of such antiquity as to be unchallenged as a statement of past history.

* * *

The process of statutory interpretation, though inevitable, is difficult and full of pitfalls. * * * [R]estatement interpretation is an unreality. And without interpretation, or *background* against which meaning can be discovered, the black letter statements are not understandable. The idea that words speak for themselves, without interpretation in the light of the circumstance under which they were composed or arranged, has been too often exploded with reference to wills, contracts and written instruments generally, to be believed again with respect to the restatements.

This fallacy, that words speak for themselves or convey a clear meaning of themselves, is * * * at the bottom of the Institute's insistence on the sanctity of the black letter.

* * *

* * * Moreover the black letter itself is, as must be expected, a compromise to cover various views. With one leg it steps forward; with the other it steps backward. It is caught between stating the law which should be and the law which is and often ends by stating only the law that was. * * * The necessity of agreement on black letter forces each participant to a choice of position which, when stated as a group result, must inevitably tend towards (a) the ancient historical rather than the modern rule or possible future trend, (b) the conventional safe and unoriginal point of view and (c) a compromise which goes only to the point whereon all are agreed.

PATTERSON, THE RESTATEMENT
OF THE LAW OF CONTRACTS
33 Colum.L.Rev. 397, 399–400, 405 (1933).

Obviously some propositions of law must be rejected in favor of others with which they are inconsistent; the "weight of authority" test can be applied. The draftsmen of the Restatement were experts in applying this test. Other propositions of law, seemingly diverse, may be capable of translation into common terms. The translation formula is a product of expert opinion, to quote from the preface of the present work. The assertion (in the preface) that it is "the product of expert opinion" seems to imply that there are no divergent expert opinions. This is contrary to fact. The illusion that "the law" can be found in one and only one set of authoritative propositions is not wholly dispelled.

The meaning of Restatement becomes still more ambiguous when one looks at the diverse theories as to the interpretation of precedents. Can a judicial decision of an appellate court be taken to imply a proposition nowhere stated in the opinion? One knows that courts sometimes distinguish their prior decisions by this method; and there is expert opinion in favor of a more extensive use of this type of analysis. The opinion itself will frequently reveal statements of varying degrees of comprehensiveness or abstractness; add to this range of choice the possibility of others not mentioned in the opinion but seen by the divining eye of the expert, and one has a wide variety of choice as to the proposition for which a given precedent shall be taken to stand. A judicial precedent has, practically, a minimum and a maximum value, and a number of values in between these extremes. The expert has to choose between them.

What are the criteria of his choice? The "weight-of-authority" test furnishes some guidance. Yet this is no mere matter of counting cases; respect for the reasoning of an opinion or for the reputation of the court will be thrown into the scale. On many questions of law there either is no weight of authority, or none established beyond the peradventure of a doubt. In such a case one chooses the law that one thinks ought to be. The proposition thus chosen can be shown to be supported by cases; inconvenient facts become irrelevant detail, and incompatible portions of the opinion are disregarded.

Listen to lawyers arguing a question of case-law, and then read the court's opinion. The Restatement Committee, no more than the judges, can avoid choices, value-judgments.

The re-assertion of this conclusion would be needless repetition were it not for the persistence of the belief that a unique and exclusively valid system of rules of law exists somehow and can be discovered by an inexorable process of deduction or of induction.

* * *

* * * As a rational system of norms the Restatement might be expected to reveal the basic ethical principles upon which it rests; but the ethical basis of the law of contract is scarcely mentioned.

HAVIGHURST, THE RESTATEMENT OF THE LAW OF CONTRACTS
27 Ill.L.Rev. 910, 914–15 (1933).

One of the objects of the Restatement as stated in the Introduction is to meet the difficulties occasioned by the ever growing mass of case material. The thought seems to be that the looking up of law will be greatly facilitated. This would suggest the danger of technological unemployment for young lawyers recently turned out. But it is doubtful if they have cause to worry. The Anglo–American lawyer is too thoroughly steeped in the tradition of using cases in building his arguments ever easily to relinquish his search for precedent before exhausting the field. No matter how perfect and authoritative his general principle, the better lawyer will feel on firmer ground if he has one supporting case with similar facts or furnishing an apt analogy.

* * *

Moreover, in some respects, apart from the expense of keeping up libraries, the increasing number of reports may well be a cause for satisfaction rather than alarm. In the preparation of a case, the study of prior cases dealing with a similar problem serves to call attention to elements and social implications which might otherwise be overlooked. In a sense lawyers and judges must educate themselves anew for each occurring problem. There is no method that is more efficient than the case method; and the more cases the better. This is true both for sound advocacy and for wise decision. The habit of using cases as authority rather than for their educational value is doubtless too firmly ingrained to be overcome. This habit, however, is wholesome in that lawyers who would otherwise be conscious of no need, are constantly re-educating themselves in spite of themselves. This, to my mind, is the great advantage of our Anglo–American system over the civil law system. A few cases sacrificed on the altar of blind precedent are a small price to pay for it. Moreover, it is doubtful if the idea that precedents are binding has an appreciable effect in producing stagnation in the law. There are so many possibilities of distinguishing facts. And courts have show a disposition to feel free to overrule if the precedent seems outworn. We may thus in a sense eat our cake and have it too. The Restatement, if it should succeed in leading us away from the cases and back to first principles, will profit us something in flexibility, but such gain will be offset by the loss of the case method in legal self-education. We need case study; and the more complex becomes the organization of society, the more cases we need covering its manifold phases.

GORDLEY, EUROPEAN CODES AND AMERICAN RESTATEMENTS: SOME DIFFICULTIES

81 Colum.L.Rev. 140, 147–51, 153–54 (1981).

Now, as the *Restatement (Second) of Contracts* makes its official appearance, it may be a good time to ask again, what can a restatement or a code do to clarify the law?

* * * [T]here are benefits * * *. But there is no reason to believe that clarity is among them.

* * *

Although the problem of formulating rules is closely related to that of choosing the better rule, it will be helpful to consider each of these problems by itself. Suppose, then, that the main problem confronting judges and scholars is that they have been unable to formulate a plausible rule. They have in mind, in a general way, what they want this rule to do, the policy considerations to which it should respond, or the particular results that it should explain. But they still do not have a rule. They cannot clearly describe a class or category of cases and assign to it a definite legal result, or if they can, the result seems to be the wrong one for at least some of the cases falling within that class.

If that is the predicament of judges and scholars, it is likely to be the predicament of drafters as well, since they are in no better position to find a clear and plausible rule. They may even be in a worse position than scholars; while a scholar can concentrate on one problem and write a specialized article when he thinks he has it solved, drafters must produce a full set of rules. Consequently, the drafters may have only two alternatives. They may formulate a rule that is cloudy and does not clearly describe which cases should come out which way. Or they might formulate a rule that is clearer but is too broad or too narrow. It sweeps in some cases that call for the opposite result or leaves out some of that call for the same result.

* * *

Cloudy rules, however, are found in many other areas of law, even in areas where the courts have had a great deal of time to gain experience. Clark opined that restatements tend to produce cloudy rules because of compromises on the drafting committee. It would be more accurate to say that cloudy rules are inevitable until someone discovers how to state a clear one. * * *

* * *

* * * [T]he difficulty in formulating a clear rule is not always due to inexperience with a legal problem, as Ellinghaus said of the problem of unconscionability, nor to compromises on the drafting committee, as Clark surmised. The difficulty remains until a way has been found to distinguish the cases that call for one result from those that call for another. Until such a way is found, to speak of "basic assumptions" or of characteristics that are "essential" or "substantial" or of "good faith," "immorality," or "unconscionability" is merely to draw a circle around a problem and leave it for someone else to resolve.

When the drafters propose such a cloudy rule, it is hard to see how they have clarified prior law. The most they will have contributed is a hint about the direction in which to look for a solution. Their formulations, although vague, may be suggestive and so may give some guidance. But if so, it is guidance of a peculiarly dangerous kind. It is always perilous for anyone, a court, a scholar, or a draftsman, to tell others where to look for a solution that he himself has not found, even though it may sometimes be helpful, since he may have an insight into the problem without having a solution. But at least when a court formulates a rule, the formulation is regarded as tentative and subject to correction. At least when a scholar formulates a rule, the formulation has no more authority than his arguments or reputation may give it. When a drafter formulates a rule, there is the added danger that courts will look for a solution in the direction vaguely indicated by the rule even when, left to their own judgment, these courts would not regard that direction as particularly fruitful. * * *

* * *

The trouble with overly broad or overly narrow rules is that their clear formulation is purchased at a price. If the drafters realize that the rule is over-or under-inclusive they have two alternatives. They can qualify the rule so as to give notice that the rule should not be applied as written. Or they can let the rule stand without such a qualification. An example of the former approach is the final clause added by the restaters to section 90: "if injustice can only be avoided by enforcement of the promise." These words warn the judge that the rule is overly broad, and leave it to his discretion to refuse to apply it in particular cases. * * *

The trouble with this approach is that once the disclaimer is added, prior law has not been clarified. A rule is laid down and then courts are told not to follow it when it gives the wrong results. With a cloudy rule, the class or category of cases to which the rule refers is left uncertain. Here, the uncertainty has been relocated: the class or category is more definite but the result to be reached when a case falls into that category is less definite. * * *

* * *

The one type of clarity that might be obtained by an exercise of authority is the third mentioned earlier: clarity about which rule a court will follow. Where there are clear alternatives, and courts have failed to adopt one or the other, then a choice could be made for them. The law will be more certain in the sense that it will be easier to know which rule the courts will follow. But the question is, why might the courts have failed to choose among rules and why should the choice be made by the drafters of a code or restatement?

One possibility is that there are several tolerably clear alternatives but serious disagreement about which one should be chosen. A court may hedge, waiver, or try to postpone the moment of decision. A code could settle the law by choosing a rule, and a restatement could throw its weight behind one rule or the other and thus encourage a court to choose that rule. But for that matter, a court could settle on a rule itself, and then the law would be clarified. If the court does not do so, the reason presumably is that it does not deem the advantages of settling on a rule to outweigh the dangers of settling on the wrong rule. And that ultimately is the calculus that must be made, for whenever there is serious disagreement it would presumably be desirable to wait to see where the debate will go; if one does not wait, the reason must be a compelling need to have the law settled. There is no reason to expect codifiers or drafters of restatements to be in a better position to make that calculus than judges themselves.

A similar calculus is required when the problem is not to decide among several clear rules but to decide between a cloudy rule and a clearer rule that is too broad or too narrow. As mentioned earlier, if a rule resists clear formulation, the only way to have a clear rule will be to lay down one that is of the wrong magnitude. Again, the choice requires a weighing, this time a weighing of the need for certainty against the cost of occasionally reaching the wrong result and the chances that further inquiry will produce a clear rule of the right magnitude. Again, there is no reason why drafters are in a better position to do the weighing than judges.

Actually, the drafters of a code or restatement are likely to be in a worse position. To begin with, while judges are continually deciding cases, codes and restatements are completed at a single point in time and are not rewritten very often. But the practical consequences of uncertainty and the chances that further debate will lead to agreement on a rule or to a clearer rule are matters that change over time. It is better, then, to have judges continually reconsider these matters than to have drafters do all the weighing at once. * * *

There is a final danger, and it is suggested by Williston's remark quoted earlier that a restatement should not "continue the existing practice of citing decisions *pro* and *con* and enter into arguments as to their respective merits," since "it would be more likely to achieve an authority of its own that would to some extent, at least, free the courts from part of the troublesome weighing of cases and arguments if exact rules were clearly stated without argument." The danger is precisely that courts would choose among clear but alternative rules without the "troublesome weighing of cases and arguments." It would be dangerous, not because the judgment of the courts is noticeably worse than that of drafters of restatements, but because the law is restated infrequently, and as a result courts would be depending on judgments made years before and on arguments that may since have been answered and cases that are no longer well-regarded. In the extreme case—more likely to occur with a code than with a restatement—argumentation might dry up and become biased. The authoritative rule might become such a permanent feature of the legal landscape that judges and scholars would lose interest in questioning why it should be there. * * *

OBERER, ON LAW LAWYERING AND LAW PROFESSING: THE GOLDEN SAND

39 J.Legal Educ. 203, 211 (1989).

Why is reading law at large, in codes, a painful waste of time? Because codification entails the effort to capture in black-letter postulation the wisdom of the cases, of the ages. The reader is challenged to comprehend not only a "rule" but qualifications of that rule, and qualifications upon the qualifications. Words and phrases of "art" are of the essence of such distillation; they can be understood only against the backdrop of the cases, the decisions in factual situations that produce the "rule," and neighboring factual situations that qualify it. The factual situations that produce the rule and the qualifications upon the rule are subsumed. The foliage obscures the root, and, as an incident, defies comprehending retention.

Now, let us reverse the procedure; which is to say, let us examine the advantages of the "case method" for learning the law. The case method has been derided as repetitive and wasteful of time. What is its core justification? My answer is that it teaches the law *tentatively,* in a context that both justifies the resolution of the issue presented and confines that resolution to the factual context in which it occurs. Both the justification and the confinement are intimately related to the facts involved. The "rule of law" thus produced is inherently limited by the context of its creation and is understood by the student in a way that transcends, invades, black-letter treatment. The student so introduced to a legal "principle" goes to a code not passively but challengingly, as its master, not its minion.

In this regard, and as a culmination of my preachments, I seek to produce lawyers case-trained to an understanding of the "law" that emancipates them from feeling helpless when they represent clients whose cause they deem, after the caution and scrutiny induced by good-faith skepticism, to be meritorious. Their case has never before been decided; if they do the yin-yang job of relating relevant fact to relevant law and conclude, in that process, what the result *ought* to be, the chances are good that they can produce that result in their case.

*

Index

References are to Pages

I–1

†